A CASEBOO

AUSTRALIA
Law Book Co.
Sydney

CANADA and **USA**
Carswell
Toronto

NEW ZEALAND
Brookers
Wellington

SINGAPORE and **MALAYSIA**
Sweet & Maxwell Asia
Singapore and Kuala Lumpur

A CASEBOOK ON

TORT

TENTH EDITION

by

TONY WEIR

Fellow of Trinity College, Cambridge

LONDON
SWEET & MAXWELL
2004

First Edition 1967
Second Edition 1970
Third Edition 1974
Fourth Edition 1979
Fifth Edition 1983
Sixth Edition 1988
Seventh Edition 1992
International Student Edition 1992
Eighth Edition 1996
Reprinted 1997
Ninth Edition 2000
Tenth Edition 2004

Published in 2004 by
Sweet & Maxwell Limited of
100 Avenue Road, London, NW3 3PF
http://www.sweetandmaxwell.co.uk

Computerset by Interactive Sciences Ltd, Gloucester
Printed in England by TJ International

A CIP catalogue record
for this book is available
from the British Library

ISBN: 0 421 87880 0

ACKNOWLEDGMENTS

The Publishers and Compiler would like to record their grateful thanks to the following for permission to reprint part of the publications indicated.

LexisNexis UK: *All England Reports* and *New Law Journal.*

All material from the *All England Reports* and the *New Law Journal* are reproduced by permission of The Butterworths Division of Reed Elsevier (UK) Limited.

The Estates Gazette Limited: *The Estates Gazette* ([1987] 2 E.G.L.R. 173).

The Incorporated Council of Law Reporting for England and Wales: *Appeals Cases, Industrial Cases Reports, Law Reports* and *Weekly Law Reports.*

The Scottish Council of Law Reporting: *Session Cases* (1954 S.C. 56).

The Times, London: *The Times*, March 13, 1953; *The Times*, October 29, 1960; *The Times*, June 13, 1989; [1996] T.L.R. 731.

© Times Newspapers Limited 1953/60/89/96.

While every care has been taken to establish and acknowledge copyright, and contact the copyright owners, the publishers tender their apologies for any accidental infringement. They would be pleased to come to a suitable arrangement with the rightful owners in each case.

PREFACE

"It is not Wisdom, but Authority that makes a Law". The significance of this remark of Thomas Hobbes has not always been appreciated. It means that despite the authority, for the moment, of unappealed and majority decisions one may criticise them as unwise or unreasonable: after all, an appeal might have been successful and the dissents may be persuasive. Barristers may not prosper by ignoring what is authoritative, but students should be encouraged to question it, and this Casebook contains a lot of tiresome questions and severe criticism. That is doubtless why Morland J. once flatteringly observed that the language I had used in a casenote was "perhaps more appropriate to the journalist than the jurist" (*Derbyshire C.C. v Times Newspapers* [1991] 4 All E.R. 795, reversed [1993] A.C. 534).

Certain things are omitted in this edition, including most references to casenotes in learned journals and to pronouncements of the Law Commission. The former are omitted because students hardly ever go to the trouble of finding them in the library; nor need they do so now, for if they type into their computer the following web address, http://www.booksites.net/mcbrideandbagshaw, they can read and greatly profit from the very perceptive views of Nicholas McBride and Roderick Bagshaw on all recent cases of any importance. The emanations of the Law Commission are omitted because so many of their proposals in this area are daft: the courts' deference to it is perplexing, for after all, it is not as if a professor or solicitor gained in either wisdom or authority by being appointed to a committee staffed by recent graduates, even if it is presided over by a High Court judge, who will be rewarded for his furlough from sensible decision-making by promotion to the Court of Appeal. This statutory body, inaugurated in 1965 in unpropitious circumstances, could well now be abolished as a waste of time and money.

Retained in this edition are the extensive treatment of legislative materials, statutes and statutory instruments, which play so important a role in actual litigation, and the frequent cross-references, needed to indicate that while particular decisions have to be placed somewhere, they could equally well be located elsewhere: the law has to be cut into lengths for purposes of exposition, but it is actually a seamless web, and decisions in one area are of relevance in others and should be seen in relation to them.

It is in the area of causation that the major changes have occurred in very recent years. Yet more changes are surely on the way. Perhaps because more defendants are now being held liable, and held liable for more kinds of harm, the courts have started to make them liable for less, by awarding damages not for the whole harm suffered, but only in proportion to their contribution to it.

The three great events which the twentieth century has seen in the area of tort law are *Donoghue v Stevenson*, *Hedley Byrne v Heller* and finally the Human Rights Act 1998. The really crucial event, however, will prove to be our accession to the European Community, for the transfer of supreme legislative and judicial power to bodies theretofore foreign involves the abandonment of the worldwide unity of the English-speaking common law, of which we were the motherland, an abandonment emphasised by recent changes in our legal language: in Australia and Canada the plaintiff is still the plaintiff, not the claimant.

There will be no more editions of this Casebook: predictable developments might well be too painful to relate . . .

Trinity College,
Cambridge
April 13, 2004

CONTENTS

PART I
NEGLIGENCE

PART IV
LAW BETWEEN NEIGHBOURS

PART V
ANIMALS

PART VI
TORTS TO CHATTELS

PART VII
DEFAMATION

PART VIII
DECEPTION AND OTHER WRONGFUL CONDUCT

CONTENTS

PART IX
DAMAGES

TABLE OF CASES

*[Cases in capitals are excerpted at the page denoted in **bold** type. Only the first of successive page references is given.]*

CHRONOLOGICAL TABLE OF STATUTES

*[Excerpts are given at the page indicated in **bold** type. Of immediately successive page references only the first is given.]*

ALPHABETICAL TABLE OF STATUTES

*[Excerpts are given at the page indicated in **bold** type. Only the first of immediately successive page references is given.]*

TABLE OF STATUTORY INSTRUMENTS

EUROPEAN LEGISLATION

DIRECTIVES

INTRODUCTION

In most cases in this book the plaintiff is asking for money (*damages*). Generally he has been hurt in one way or another and is claiming money as *compensation for harm* suffered (sometimes with a bit extra if the defendant behaved very badly), though occasionally, and increasingly, he is more intent on vindication or explanation rather than compensation. Usually, too, he is claiming that the harm was wrongfully caused. Accordingly, we may say that the prime function of the area of social regulation we call "tort" is to determine when one person must pay another compensation for harm *wrongfully* caused. Other functions will be mentioned later (p. 17 *et seq*).

The normal tort suit, then, is quite different from what is by far the commonest action on a contract, the action of debt, where payment is demanded of the specific sum previously agreed, be it wages, the price of goods, the rent of an apartment or the repayment of a loan: this is not compensation for the claimant's loss but enforcement *in specie* of the debtor's promise. A claim against the insurer of property is admittedly limited to the actual loss suffered by the insured (for otherwise a lot of overinsured old bangers would unaccountably get totalled), but it is still not like a tort claim, since there is no suggestion that the insurer *caused* the loss. Nor is a tort claim like a claim for compensation on expropriation or compulsory purchase, where the loss is not *wrongfully* caused (*e.g. Burmah Oil Co v Lord Advocate* [1965] A.C. 75). But a tort claim has much in common with an action for damages for breach of contract, for there, too, the amount claimed is claimed as compensation for harm which the defendant caused wrongfully, the wrongfulness consisting of his not doing what he promised to, even if he is not really to blame for it.

Just as there are several types of contract (employment, sale, and services as various as carriage of goods or persons by land, sea or air, warehousing, insurance, banking, "consultancy", etc.), so there are numerous torts (negligence, trespass, nuisance, defamation, and so on). But whereas the types of contract simply reflect the different kinds of transaction people actually enter into (differentiated according to what the money is paid for), the different torts, rather like specific crimes, consist of different combinations of components, some factual, some legal. Thus *negligence* consists of (1) unreasonable conduct which (2) causes (3) foreseeable harm (4) in breach of a legal duty to take care to avoid harm of that kind; *trespass* consists of (1) doing an act which (2) directly (3) invades a person's (4) right of physical freedom, corporeal integrity or possession of land or goods; *nuisance* consists essentially of making your neighbour's life a misery, and *defamation* consists of being rude about someone to someone else. This book particularises, illustrates and explains the composition of these major torts, and of one or two others.

But the different torts and different contracts (indeed, the different crimes as well) are all at bottom about how and how far the law protects what makes life in society worth living, the interests of the citizen such as physical well-being, freedom to move about, somewhere to live, things (things to eat, to sit on, to drive, to work and play with), social and family relations, and the wealth that enables people to do what they want. Apart from social security and gifts, contract is the legal form by which people acquire money (the contract of employment in the case of most individuals, of sale and services in the case of companies) as well as the form in which they spend it in order to *improve* their health, property, wealth, enjoyment or even appearance: by enforcing such transactions the law enables individuals to develop, to do what they can afford, to arrange their own lives, to make their choices in a market properly policed. The law of tort, by contrast, protects what a person already has, makes good the harm done by wrongful invasions of his existing interests (which may admittedly include expectations). The law of tort determines how much protection the citizen is entitled to enjoy free of charge; the law of contract lets him develop or protect himself by paying for it.

It will be seen that there is an overlap between contract and tort. The person who promises to make you better implicitly also promises not to injure you, and if he would be liable for injuring you whether he promised not to or not, then there are two grounds for making him liable if he does: both in tort, under the general law, and in contract, because of his dealings with you. The overlap has become very much greater in recent years, since the law of tort started to make negligent people pay even if they didn't wound anyone or damage their property but only caused them purely economic harm, made them poorer; indeed, it sometimes does this by saying that such liability in tort arises from an "assumption of responsibility", which is just what contractors undertake. The overlap of categories or concurrence of claims is an accepted part of our law, of which Lord Goff of Chieveley recently said: " . . . the law of tort is the general law, out of which the parties can, if they wish, contract" (though the extent to which they may do so is quite severely restricted by the Unfair Contract Terms Act, below p.254). He added that " . . . an assumption of responsibility . . . may give rise to a tortious duty of care irrespective of whether there is a contractual relationship between the parties, and in consequence, unless his contract precludes him from doing so, the plaintiff, who has available to him concurrent remedies in contract and tort, may choose that remedy which appears to him to be the most advantageous." *Henderson v Merrett Syndicates* [1994] 3 All E.R. 506 at 532, 534.

In England the law of tort is grounded on the common law—the decisions of judges responding to complaints by individuals in the light of precedents laid down by their superiors and predecessors—but now much of the ground has been cut away and an enormous superstructure erected by legislation, laws enacted by Parliament responding to social problems under pressure from various groups, including law reform bodies. Sometimes Parliament has intervened to modify or reverse specific rules applied by the courts. Thus whereas courts would never entertain any claim when a person was killed (as opposed to being injured), Parliament in 1846 allowed widows and orphans to sue (Fatal Accidents Act, now in its 1976 version, as amended in 1982—below, p.113). Likewise, a claim for personal injury expired at common law if the tortfeasor died (as he often did in the very motor accident in which he injured the plaintiff), so the Law Reform Act of 1934 empowered the living to sue the dead (and—rather needlessly—vice versa). Furthermore, if a victim was even slightly to blame for his injuries the common law barred his claim even if the tortfeasor was much more greatly at fault; this rule was very unfair, since victims are rarely *entirely* free from blame, so it was changed in 1945 and now the victim's damages are simply reduced if he was partly to blame for his injuries (see below, p.245). As a final example, the judges said that the central government (unlike local authorities) could not be sued in tort at all; this immunity was displaced in 1947.

No one in 1947, however, could have imagined that a citizen could sue the state for failure to legislate or for a bad decision in the courts, but once we abandoned our sovereignty, in the sense of the right to make our own laws, rather as Esau sold his birthright, that became possible. The Luxembourg Court decided in (*Francovich v Italy* [1992] I.R.L.R. 84) that the state may be liable if as a result of a failure to implement a Directive properly or at all the citizen does not have the right under domestic law that the Directive required. More recently it has held that the liability of the state is engaged if the supreme court of the country renders a decision which infringes the citizen's Community rights (*Köbler v Austria* (Case C–224/01)). More novelties emerge from Brussels. Mrs Donoghue no longer has to prove that Stevenson was at fault in allowing a snail to enter the ginger-beer bottle: see the Directive, below p.27. And as to traffic accidents, it is thanks to Brussels that motorists must carry insurance against their possible liability for causing property damage (usually other cars) and not just personal injury, despite the fact that it is more sensible for people to insure their own cars than other people's, and that now the victim can sue the driver's insurer directly, whereas before he could not.

As for domestic legislation, our own Parliament has sometimes tried to tidy up an area of the law of tort instead of just changing specific rules. Examples would be the Occupiers' Liability Act 1957 (dealing with injuries suffered on someone else's land: the 1984 Act of the same name covered the case where the person injured was a trespasser who shouldn't have been there), the Animals Act 1971 and the Torts (Interference with Goods) Act 1977. There has, however, been no serious proposal to codify the whole of the law of tort. National codes may well now be a thing of the past, given the unremitting flow of pragmatic and unprincipled mandates from Brussels and the demented proposal of the European Parliament that the entire private law of the member states be unified and codified. That aside, codification makes sense only if the area of law is coherent and its rules sufficiently general, and if there are draftsmen who possess the necessary technique and are ready to use it.

In both respects the present situation in England is unpropitious. As to the first, instead of having just a few general principles, the common law still has a considerable number of different torts (in an article entitled *Torticles* Professor Bernard Rudden was able to identify seventy!). Furthermore, although in certain areas it has seemed possible to discern a move towards principle, or, what comes to the same thing, the abolition of narrow distinctions at the factual level, in others the courts seem to commit themselves to pragmatic and gradual development; recent cases in negligence, one judge has said, "signalled the retreat from high principle and the resurgence of pragmatism." (*White v Jones* [1993] 3 All E.R. 481 at 501, *per* Steyn L.J.) As to the second, it must be said that unless we radically alter the drafting technique displayed in the Animals Act 1971 (the first product of the Law Commission, in purported pursuance of its statutory duty to improve the form as well as the substance of our law), a code of tort alone would be insufferably long.

Continental lawyers are more concise. The law of delict in the French *Code civil* consist of a mere five short articles (and one very long one, thanks to Brussels). The first one reads: "Every act whatever of man which causes damage to another binds the person whose fault it was to repair it" (Art.1382). The German Civil Code (BGB) is less general and therefore more extensive, but even so it deals with the law of unlawful acts in 31 brief sections. The main one reads: "A person who deliberately or carelessly injures another contrary to law in his life, body, health, freedom, property or other right is liable to compensate that other for the resulting damage" (§823 BGB). These legislative provisions have naturally been elucidated or obscured by countless judicial glosses since their enactment (in particular, the German courts have notably included "human dignity" among the "other rights" protected against unreasonable conduct), but despite the vast changes in social structure and physical environment which have taken place since their enactment (in 1804 and 1896 respectively), they have remained literally much as they were. Students might find it instructive to test the results of the

English cases against the words of these continental codes, while bearing in mind that there are very important enactments outside the codes, for example, on liability for traffic accidents.

Civil codes are constructed in blocks, laid out in books or chapters, and Tort figures in the book on Obligations, distinct from the books on Property and Family. Within the Obligations book Tort and Contract are dealt with separately. So they are, of course, in England in lecture-halls and books such as this. But on the continent the division is more important than here, for there the parties specify the articles or paragraphs, and consequently the part of the Code, on which they rely, whereas here there is not, so to speak, a green form for tort and a blue one for contract. The different forms of action (where "form" means simply a form such as you get at the Post Office, taking care not to ask for the wrong one) were abolished a hundred and fifty years ago. Accordingly when one says (as one does) that the plaintiff was "suing in tort", all one means is that his counsel was relying on decisions which appear in books called "Tort". Nevertheless it is true—and very important—that counsel more or less determine the basis on which cases are argued, and it is entirely possible—nay, fairly common—for them to concentrate, for tactical reasons, on certain aspects of the situation rather than others. These tend to be the aspects on which the judgment focuses, since courts answer counsel, yet there may be other matters not alluded to or even noticed which are of equal importance to the development of the law. Later cases may point this out, and indeed one quite frequently finds courts, bound in principle by a prior decision indistinguishable on the facts, saying "But this point was not argued in that case, so the decision is not binding on us". Students should be urged to consider aspects of the situation litigated which are not in the forefront of the argument or judgment, but may help to explain the outcome.

There continue to be plenty of proposals for reform by legislation, principally in the area of personal injury and death. The Pearson Commission in 1978 made 188 such proposals (Cmnd. 7054), very few of which have been implemented, and the Law Commission has recently been very active if, thankfully, not very effective.

The Pearson Commission was principally concerned to resolve the tension between the moral basis of tort law, that only wrongdoers pay for the harm they cause, and the rationale of social security, that help from public funds should be available to all victims of misfortune, regardless of how it occurs. Some observers think it wrong to discriminate between people who suffer similar injuries according to whether it is someone else's fault, or no one's fault or even their own fault, while others want some weight to be given to the view that the principles of individual (as opposed to collective) responsibility require only that everyone should conduct himself decently and with due regard for the well-being of his fellow-citizens, on pain of a monetary sanction if he does not, even if this means that the victim of bad luck gets less than the victim of bad management. In more recent years the debate between the advocates of fault liability and the proponents of automatic compensation has become less intense, but we are beginning to hear of a categorical conflict between the demands of corrective and distributive justice—that it may be objectionable to prefer one group to another, be it shocked policemen over shocked spectators (below, p.105) or those who have a baby they don't want over those who want a baby they don't have (below, p.118).

It is one thing to say that victims are entitled to payment: it is another to see that they receive it. Here the law has several devices. First, it makes employers liable for the harm their employees cause while working for them. Secondly, as every motorist knows, the law often requires those likely to cause accidents to take out insurance which will benefit the victim. Two other important institutions are also designed to procure that those entitled to payment actually receive it. Victims of negligence on the highway can ultimately look to the Motor Insurers' Bureau, which has agreed with the Minister to meet claims against which the tortfeasor should have been insured, but wasn't; and the victims of crimes of violence can look to the Criminal Injuries Compensation Authority, which pays out huge sums according to a detailed tariff, using rules of eligibility and compensation which differ in some respects from those of tort law (see below, p.182).

Mostly, however, a person who cannot look to a tortfeasor must look to his own insurer, especially for property damage. In cases where insured property has been tortiously damaged the courts have resolutely held that the owner's claim against the tortfeasor is unaffected by the fact that the owner has insurance. Of course the owner cannot keep both the insurance proceeds and the tort damages: he must refund the insurance proceeds out of the tort damages or, as most often happens, allow the insurance company to prosecute his claim against the tortfeasor. The unsatisfactoriness of the result is concealed from us by the fact that the insurance company, by "subrogation," sues in the name of the insured owner: we therefore fail to realise that money is being claimed by a company which was paid to take the risk of losing it. Insurance has another role, however, for one of the hazards one can, and should, insure against is having to pay damages in tort. The prevalence of such liability-insurance sometimes induces the judges to impose liability on defendants whom they would be very reluctant to make pay if they had to pay out of their own pockets: as Lord Denning, forthright as ever, said in 1967 "We assume that the defendant in an action of tort is insured unless the contrary appears" (*Post Office v Norwich Union Fire Ins.* [1967] 1 All E.R. 577 at 580). Other judges deny that they are so affected: "At common law the circumstance that a defendant is contractually indemnified by a third party against a particular legal liability can have no relevance whatever to the measure of that liability" (*Hunt v Severs* [1994] 2 All E.R. 385 at 395, *per* Lord Bridge).

The law of tort covers a wide range of factual situations, as one will discover. Every situation, however, can be broken down into just a few structural elements, and it is wise (subject to a qualification to be given in a moment) to keep them distinct in one's mind. They are (obviously enough) (1) what the tortfeasor did, (2) what the victim suffered, (3) the connection between what the tortfeasor did and what the victim suffered, and (4) the relationship between the tortfeasor and the victim. These are considered briefly in the forthcoming pages.

The qualification is this. There is a tendency to think that a tort claim is like a hurdle race, that you have to scramble over a number of points in succession, and that if you fail at any hurdle, then you lose. The judges talk in this way, probably because the barristers address them in that manner, taking issue after issue, and laying it out all rational and orderly. In fact a tort claim is really more of a boxing match than a hurdle race; in the absence of a knock-out for either side (and such contests hardly ever reach the courts) success depends on the number of points you make overall. The plaintiff gets extra points if the harm he has suffered is of a serious nature—especially personal injury—or if he is particularly deserving or especially reliant on the defendant; so too if the defendant's conduct was very reprehensible, or if the contribution his conduct made to the harm was very obvious and direct, or if he was very close to the plaintiff so that he should have been especially concerned for his well-being and interests. In brief, the human nature even of judges trained in the superficial rationality of the law ensures that they are affected by what one might call the merits of the case, and try to see that good guys get more and bad guys pay more. What else could one expect, whatever is said?

1. The Victim's Loss

A judge once said "It is difficult to see why liability as such should depend on the nature of the damage." It is difficult to see his difficulty. Liability "as such" never exists; liability is always liability *for* something, and in tort it is liability to pay for the harm caused. To cause harm means to have an adverse effect on something good. There are several good things in life, such as liberty, bodily integrity, land, possessions, reputation, wealth, privacy, dignity, perhaps even life itself. Lawyers call these goods "interests." These interests are all good, but they are not all *equally* good. This is evident when they come into conflict (one may jettison cargo to save passengers, but not vice versa, and one may detain a thing, but not a person, as security for a debt). Because these interests are not equally good, the protection afforded to them by the law is not equal: the law protects the better interests better: murder and rape are, after all, more serious crimes than theft. Accordingly, the better the interest invaded, the more readily does the law give compensation for the ensuing harm. In other words, whether you get the money you claim depends on what you are claiming it for. It would be surprising if it were otherwise.

The kinds of damage most frequently complained of are personal injury, property damage and financial loss, *i.e.* damage to three of the best things of life, namely, health, property and wealth.

As between health and wealth, the priority would seem to be clear: it is better to be well than wealthy. But people who are poorly soon become poor, because they cannot earn their living and have to buy medicaments: personal injury has economic consequences. Is it *because* of those economic consequences that we protect people's bodies, seen as units of production and consumption rather than as sources of pleasure? If the question appears cynical, one should ponder the recommendation of the Pearson Commission in 1976 that victims of personal injury should receive a full indemnity in tort for their lost earnings and extra expenses, but nothing for their pain and suffering for the first three months.

That people are more important than things has been said often enough. But are things more important than money? The question is topical, because the law of tort has recently started to extend to money interests the protection it has long given to tangible property, and it is serious, for its answer may tell us something about the values of our society.

Things, unlike people, can be bought and sold, that is, they can be exchanged for money. Things are "money's worth." But there are valuables, *e.g.* stocks and shares, which are not things. Things are defined as objects which can be touched: if it is invisible and intangible, it isn't a thing. Thus things appeal not only to economists but also to the human senses, and are therefore more valuable than intangible assets. The car which is merely an asset to the finance house which owns it is a positive pleasure to the hire-purchaser who drives it. With regard to immovable property, the point is even clearer: a house has a human value to the family whose home it is, but to the building society which lent the money to buy it its value is merely economic. A legal system which is concerned with human values (and the law is supposed to reflect the proper values of society) would be right to give greater protection to tangible property than to intangible wealth. Until recently this is what the law did: claims for property damage have been welcomed while claims for mere financial loss have been rejected; and the law has been much readier to grant a claim to the possessor of a chattel—the person who is enjoying it—than to the owner out of possession—the person who only profits from it. Of course there is one class of person, the artificial or legal person, such as a trading company, to which this distinction between a thing and a disembodied asset can have no meaning whatever: that is because artificial persons have no senses. For companies it is immaterial whether there is one item less on the stock book or one item less on the credit side of the ledger. For people without senses, things are merely values, and a society without sensibility would so treat them. Our society is showing signs of doing so.

The differing values of the interests in health, things and wealth may be illustrated by three disasters which struck Britain in 1987–88. On October 15–16, a hurricane destroyed about 15 million trees. On October 23, the stock market collapsed, and the "value" of shares fell by nearly a quarter. The following July, 166 workers on the Piper Alpha oil-rig in the North Sea were killed, almost a third of the normal annual total of industrial deaths. Piper Alpha was a tragedy, matter for mourning in all the homes to which the young father and husband would never return, or return in a crippled condition. The hurricane was a great pity, for trees are beautiful and growing things of which poets write with rapture. But no poet could write with rapture of that licensed gambling-hell the stock-market, and to all right-thinking people the stock-market crash was a matter of relative, if not absolute, indifference. Note that the true importance of these events is in *inverse* proportion to the ratings economists would accord them. This obvious point has to be made because people's thinking is grossly corrupted by Marxists and marketeers alike, for both Communists and Capitalists appear equally to believe that money is the root of all good, and the deference of lawyers to economists, indeed their abdication from their proper role as ministers of justice, is one of the most chilling examples of *trahison des clercs* in the late-twentieth century.

The point is not that the legal system should not protect money values at all: it is that they should be protected less well than more important interests. If you want your wealth preserved, you should pay a stockbroker to look after it, and sue him in contract if he fails. There may be a few other people, unpaid but very close to you, on whom you can properly count to be careful of your pelf. But of others you can demand only that they not be wicked, dishonest, fraudulent or otherwise criminal: you cannot expect that they should behave reasonably just to keep you in funds.

In some systems (*e.g.* Germany) compensation is provided only if the damage results from the invasion of a *right*. This is not the position adopted by the common law. But in the common law there are some rights whose mere invasion is actionable even if it causes no damage. These are the most important rights—liberty, corporeal integrity, and physical property in one's possession—and the tort of trespass protects them against direct invasion by positive interference even where no actual harm ensues. In torts where no damage need be proved, said therefore to be *actionable per se* (libel is another, less happy, example), the function of the law in applying a sanction is clearly not compensation, for compensation makes no sense in the absence of harm. Instead, the law is performing a vindicatory function, dealing with a grievance, affirming respect for rights. So tort has a constitutional function as well as a compensatory one.

Discourse in terms of rights had been growing rapidly in recent years under European influence. The Human Rights Act 1998 is a clear example, and in European Union law the strong tendency is to hold that a claim may be brought only if (but always if) a Community right has been infringed. This has caused some problems of analysis in a system like ours which in tort cases was more used to speaking in terms of the defendant's duties rather than the plaintiff's rights.

2. The Actor's Behaviour

(a) The act

As regards the conduct of the alleged tortfeasor, we can distinguish between acts and omissions, acts and activities, acts and speech and between acts and things.

Positive acts trigger liability in tort more easily than omissions to act. The duty not to cause harm seems stronger than the duty to prevent it happening. The thief and the vandal are always liable; not so those who merely fail to deter the miscreants and forestall the harm. It is worse to set fire to Rome than to fiddle while it burns. Speech is more likely to land you in trouble than silence.

This is reflected in the old saying, still true, that "Not doing is no trespass", but if not doing is no trespass, not doing may well be actionable negligence. This is so if there was a duty to act and the failure to do so was unreasonable. A duty to take positive steps to protect others from harm, or at least to issue a warning, may well arise in particular circumstances: the occupier of land must bestir himself for the safety of his visitors, the garage as *bailee* of your car must lock it up lest it be stolen, the parent (and the nanny) must keep the child from harm—and from harming third parties. Absent special circumstances, however, no such legal duty exists. You need not try to tell the driver of the lorry you overtake that it is about to shed its load, or, to take the stock example, you need not pull a drowning child out of a pond (unless it is your child or your pond). Generally speaking, if you want someone to do something for you, you must pay him and then, if he doesn't do it, sue him for breach of contract. Duties to act are not readily imposed by the common law, though they may arise out of an "assumption of responsibility". Such duties are, however, frequently imposed on public bodies by the legislature, and one of the difficult questions of tort law is how far they may be made liable to those injured by their failure to do what they have been told to do. For example, under the Human Rights Act not only is it unlawful for public bodies positively to invade the Convention rights of the citizen, but they may under certain circumstances be liable for failing to protect the citizen from invasions of their rights by private bodies or individuals not themselves bound by the Convention. We have come a long way from the view that "not doing is no trespass," but it remains true that one is more likely to be liable for creating a danger than for failing to remove one.

Thus we can oppose acts to omissions. We can also oppose acts to activities. A Lord Justice of Appeal once said: " . . . our law of torts is concerned not with activities but with acts" (*Read v Lyons* [1945] 1 K.B. 216 at 228 (Scott L.J.)), and he was apparently right. So if a person is run down in the street, he cannot say to the driver: "When you started driving, you enhanced the risk of people being hurt; I have been hurt, so you must compensate me." The victim must show that the defendant drove badly, that in the activity of driving just before the impact the defendant did some particular act he ought not to have done. But although this is generally true, there are areas of the law where liability is imposed because the defendant was running an activity, and although he himself has acted quite properly. Suppose the careless driver was employed by a firm and was on the firm's business at the time of the collision. The victim can sue the firm if he establishes the fault of the driver. The firm responds for careless conduct in its activity, though the firm itself is otherwise free from fault (p.269). Again, in the law as between neighbours, the notion of "activity", with its inherent notion of duration, is relevant: you may not be able to complain of an isolated bang, but you can enjoin the neighbour who keeps banging away needlessly. In the United States a special liability for actual harm is imposed on persons conducting an "extra-hazardous activity", but though this principle has its origin in an English case, our courts are content that we ourselves have not developed the wider principle and extended liability for things to liability for activities (see below, p.458).

The behaviour of things, as opposed to human beings, is of importance to tort lawyers because most people who are physically hurt are hurt by things—metal things, hot things, falling things. The *Code civil* makes the distinction clear: "A person is responsible not only for the damage caused by his own act, but also for the damage caused by the act ... of the things under his control" (Art.1384). There is no such principle in the law of England, but there are instances in which a thing may involve liability. *Donoghue v Stevenson* itself, the keystone of the tort of negligence, was a case where the plaintiff was injured by a thing—a bad bottle of ginger-beer—but the court concentrated on the manufacturer's conduct, not on the thing he manufactured. Nowadays, in this area, attention has moved from the conduct of the producer to the condition of the product, and Mrs Donoghue would no longer have to allege and prove that the ginger-beer bottler was negligent: if the product is defective and causes physical harm to individuals or their personal property, the producer is liable even if he isn't to blame at all. In other cases the behaviour of the thing may be evidence of negligence on the part of the person in control of it: *res ipsa loquitur* is what we say, the thing itself provides the evidence (below p.171). Again, if a thing escapes from the defendant's land and damages mine, he will usually be liable if he was at fault in letting it escape but may sometimes be liable even if he wasn't (see *Transco*, below p.463). If he keeps a savage beast or a domestic one with known nasty propensities, it need not even escape.

Further, we can oppose acts to words. Lawyers have a tendency to confuse them, calling the words of the legislator "Acts" and the documents of individuals "deeds". Not only lawyers, either, for a Yuppie is said to "make a statement" when he guns his Porsche or a skinhead when he displays his cranium. Nevertheless, although acts and speech can both have harmful effects, we should try to keep the relevant difference between them in mind. First, speaking is an exercise of a specifically guaranteed freedom ("freedom of *speech*") in the way that driving a car or playing one's hi-fi is not: one must therefore be chary of unduly restraining verbal expression by too ready an imposition of liability. Secondly, the falsehood of words can be *proved* whereas the unreasonableness of acts can only be *argued for*, so that there is a tendency to forget that being wrong is not the same as doing wrong. Finally, acts commonly impinge directly on the victim, whereas words operate by indirection, by inducing him to hurt himself or others to hurt him; in other words, the action of things is different from the working of words, which are rarely performative in the physical world but rather operate through the way human beings react to them.

It should be stressed that the contrast between acts, on the one hand, and omissions, activities, words and things on the other, is drawn not to suggest that the former alone should or do attract liability, but to emphasise that one should be conscious of which is involved in a particular case, and that the law was probably right to have developed rather differently with regard to them. Indeed, it was a case of negligent speech which inaugurated the acceptance of liability in tort for carelessly causing merely economic harm (see below, p.57). Since 1963, however, liability for causing such harm no longer depends on speech, but may be incurred by the careless performance of services or even reprehensible failure to perform them. There remain, however, special features, particularly a relational element, cognate with the fact what while you can *act* on your own (as in modern dancing) you don't normally *speak* to yourself (as those with mobile phones often seem to be doing).

(b) Quality of the act

In most cases it is not enough to show simply that the defendant caused the damage. His conduct must be appraised and evaluated before liability follows. The pre-eminent test is whether the defendant acted *reasonably*. By and large, a defendant who has acted reasonably is not going to have to pay damages. But there are exceptions, and it is very important to mark them when they occur. Sometimes the plaintiff's interest is so important that it is protected even against reasonable behaviour which infringes it. Thus a person's land is protected against persons who reasonably but erroneously believe themselves entitled to enter it (p.322); a person's liberty may be protected against officials acting bona fide but in excess of their powers (p.385); a person's stolen chattels are protected against persons who reasonably buy or sell them in the normal channels of commerce (p.485); a person's reputation is protected even against imputations unintended by the writer (p.534). These are also the cases where no damage need be proved—and there is a connection between these facts.

Sometimes a person is not liable for acting unreasonably, even though he meant to cause the harm. This is especially true where the harm is purely financial. After all, though the fat cats of the City are discouraged from playing "Monopoly" they are urged to play "Beggar my Neighbour" and get plaudits for winning. Labour is expected to wrestle with management. When the National Union of Mineworkers deliberately caused a loss of £600,000,000,000 by the year-long strike which ended in March 1985, no one said they saw much wrong with that, though associated mayhem and sabotage (*i.e.* damage to person and property) were sternly discountenanced.

Heretofore certain classes of person, or rather persons engaged in certain types of activity, have been protected from liability even if their conduct was culpable and caused harm. Thus, until recently, barristers could not be sued for forensic incompetence, even if it landed their client in jail; judicial officers are still protected; witnesses and others preparing to give evidence in court remain immune from suits in negligence. Again, governmental officers empowered to make decisions could not be sued for damages just because their decision was arguably or provably unreasonable, since constitutionally it was for them rather than for the courts to make the decision, though the courts could monitor the way the decision was made and send it back for redecision if it was done wrong or *very* unreasonably. In such cases where the courts held that there was no *legal* duty, breach of which could lead to liability, the defendant was not only exempt from liability but also freed from an inquiry into his actual conduct: the claim would be struck out as disclosing no cause of action. This approach is now in difficulty. The crunch came with regard to the police. In *Hill v Chief Constable* [1988] 2 All E.R. 338 the House of Lords held that the police were not suable for negligence in the conduct of criminal investigations, but when the Court of Appeal followed this lead in *Osman v Ferguson* [1993] 4 All E.R. 344 the Court of Human Rights in Strasbourg held that this put the United Kingdom in breach of the plaintiff's Convention right to a fair trial (1999) 5 B.H.R.C. 293. The Court backed off from this reasoning, if not from the result, but the effect has been that our courts are much less ready than before to "strike out" claims on the pleadings, assumed to be true, and now prefer to have a trial and hear all the evidence. *Barrett* below p.100 is a clear case in point.

But in accordance with the principle stated above that "bad people pay more", a defendant who has acted very badly indeed may well be liable even though he would not be liable for causing the same harm by mere incompetence or negligence. Thus deliberate liars are more extensively liable than people who misrepresent the facts through inadvertence, and "malice" may sharpen liability considerably: thus one may prosecute a suspected criminal without fear of liability unless one acts maliciously as well as unreasonably. An official who knowingly makes an unauthorised decision may be guilty of "misfeasance in office", for which mere negligence is insufficient.

3. RELATIONSHIP BETWEEN BEHAVIOUR AND DAMAGE

A person is not in general responsible for damage unless he has both caused it and been to blame for it. "Cause" and "blame" are not synonymous—the latter referring to the defendant's conduct and the former to the link between that conduct and the plaintiff's harm—but it is not too easy to keep the notions distinct: we tend to blame people for causing harm, and find that blameworthy conduct is causally more potent than conduct which is unexceptionable. However, a blameworthy person does not have to pay for damage unless he "caused" it, that is, if it would have happened anyway; furthermore, even a blameworthy person is not liable for all the damage he can be said to have "caused". What is "to cause"? Many words—often quite short, brutal Anglo-Saxon verbs like "kill," "burn," "break" or "stab"—contain causal notions, and designate an act, perhaps of a specific kind, which produces a result, possibly a special one, maybe in some particular manner. But where the effect of conduct is less typical or direct, especially outside the physical sphere, even the English language may have no single word to indicate the composite. Helena drew the distinction: "And though I kill him not, I am the cause His death was so effected" (*All's Well* III.ii). Even when one is just trying to explain what happened, causation is not a simple notion. When one uses it, as lawyers do, not for purposes of exposition but in order to attribute responsibility, it gets harder still.

In human affairs, present, past or fictional, effects result from a concatenation of causes, so one must not look for *the* cause, as if there were only one. One should rather ask "Did the conduct *contribute* to the harm?" Now it might be supposed that a person whose conduct had merely contributed to harm need only contribute to its compensation, that is, pay in proportion to his causal contribution. This was certainly not the law until recently. The causal contributor was liable to pay for the full effects to which his conduct conduced. It is not easy for the student to realise that a gallon of cause may go into the pint-pot of effect. But consider. If two people kill a third, neither has half-killed him: both have killed him. All each can say is that though he killed the deceased, another did so too. But that other may be penniless or elusive, so it can be right to hold each contributor liable in full until the victim is fully paid.

But this classical law has been brought into question in very recent times, and defendants are increasingly being held liable only to the extent of their contribution to the harm in issue. This started in cases of incremental industrial diseases such as deafness, vibration white finger and asbestosis where the claimant was affected in successive employments, each contributing something to his present condition, but the idea has taken off quite remarkably, though it has not yet been approved by the House of Lords. This is discussed below, p.234f.

Plaintiffs have traditionally been required to persuade the judge that it was *more likely than not* that the particular defendant's conduct contributed to the occurrence of the harm in issue. This seems fair enough: if one doesn't have to pay for harm unless one contributed to it, then the plaintiff should have to show that he is suing a person who did contribute to it. If he manages to persuade the judge of that, even by a bare margin, then he should obtain full compensation—after all, the boxer who just wins on points nevertheless gets the whole prize. However, "more likely than not" (or "on the balance of probabilities") has caused problems, even for the Master of the Rolls who once said "As a matter of common sense, it is unjust that there should be no liability for failure to treat a patient, simply because the chances of a successful cure by that treatment were less than 50 per cent. Nor, by the same token, can it be just that, if the chances of a successful cure only marginally exceed 50 per cent, the doctor or his employer should be liable to the same extent as if the treatment could be guaranteed to cure. If this is the law, it is high time it was changed." (Sir John Donaldson M.R. in *Hotson v East Berks. A.H.A.* [1987] 1 All E.R. 210 at 215). Well, it *is* the law, as the House of Lords held in reversing him ([1987] 2 All E.R. 909)), but they have been criticised and the law may possibly change, in the light of a dramatic decision of the House of Lords in 2002 that in certain cases it may not even be necessary to show that the defendant's fault probably contributed to the actual occurrence of the harm if it is clear that it contributed to the risk that the harm might occur, as it has (*Fairchild*, below p.211).

In this case it was held fair to impose liability on the defendant even if he was not shown to have contributed to the occurrence of the harm, but often a defendant whose conduct is clearly causative in the old sense escapes liability on the ground that it would not be fair to hold him liable for the harm that eventuated. It is clear that one does not always have to pay for all the eventual consequences of one's misconduct or there would be no end to it. A legal system might require that the harm be the *direct* result, in the sense that nothing surprising intervened between the conduct and the harm, or that it be the *typical* or the *foreseeable* result of the conduct, or that it be the *proximate* consequence, not too *remote*. All these formulae, and more, have been used, but their use should not conceal the fact that underneath the apparent factuality of causal vocabulary lurk value-judgments. This can be seen from the fact that the more blameworthy the conduct is, the more potent it tends to be in causal terms, whether the conduct be that of the defendant, the plaintiff or some third party whose conduct intervenes between the defendant's conduct and the harm to the claimant. Apparently less objective is the teleological test sometimes applied: was this harm the kind of harm which it was the purpose of the rule infringed to guard against?, a test not easy to apply where the rule is not statutory but one of common law.

4. RELATIONSHIP BETWEEN CLAIMANT AND DEFENDANT

We have seen that liability is always liability *for* something; it is also liability *to* someone. Whether you get the money you are claiming depends on whom you are claiming it from. In other words, the relationship between the plaintiff and the defendant is a material consideration in every tort suit. English law uses the device of "special relationship" either to heighten or to lower the duty which is owed when the relationship is merely spatial and involuntary. But in many where the concept of "special relationship" is not mentioned, the results can only be rationalised on the basis that one exists. If one takes as standard the relationship, miscalled "neighbourhood," which is said to exist merely because the defendant should have been thinking of the plaintiff as a possible victim of his carelessness, then there are some relationships which are very different. Take actual neighbourhood, for example, the relationship between those who live next door to each other, or whose properties are adjacent. No legal system could treat such people as if they were total strangers who collide on the highway. In England, the special regime for real neighbours is called "nuisance".

Relationships differ widely, and the use of general terms should not conceal the fact. For instance, plaintiff and defendant may be parties to a contract, and a contract is a very special relationship indeed—there are whole books about it—because the parties have chosen to do business with each other.

In France, a relevant contract between the parties excludes the law of tort completely: tort applies only between strangers, for contractors make law for themselves. In England contractors remain subject to the law of tort, except insofar as it has been effectively excluded by the terms of the contract itself (effective exclusion now being fairly difficult, see p.254), or because the allocation of risks agreed between the parties involved in the arrangement would be disturbed if the law of tort were applied. Two factors at least distinguish the voluntary from the involuntary relationship. On the one hand, where persons have chosen to associate, they must know that they are exposing themselves to the risk of harm from the other. On the other hand, the chosen relationship may throw on one of them a higher liability because he knows that the other is relying on him, of which the best example is employer and employee.

5. The Claimant's Conduct

A person who "has only himself to blame" for an accident cannot claim from anyone else (except his insurer or social security). It would be monstrous if he could. Sometimes one feels that the claimant has only himself to blame even though the defendant is at fault in some way. One feels this mainly where the claimant's behaviour has been particularly unreasonable in comparison with that of the defendant. In such cases, the claimant's behaviour will be referable either to his relationship with the defendant, or to the relationship between the defendant's behaviour and the damage— one will say either. "The defendant doesn't have to pay *him*" or "The defendant doesn't have to pay him for *that*." These points therefore can be dealt with in terms of duty or causation. If the claimant's behaviour was not very unreasonable, then the loss may be shared (below, p.245f).

While Western systems of law rather flatter themselves on paying no heed to the personal merits or demerits of claimants, it is really undeniable that good guys get more and villains less.

6. The Duty Concept

We have seen that the direct invasion of certain rights by positive act constitutes a trespass, even if no harm results; and it may be that the deliberate and unjustifiable violation of any right, if it causes damage, gives rise to a claim in tort, for which we do not yet have a name. (See the fascinating discussion in relation to a parent's "right" to the company of her children in *F v Wirral B.C.* [1991] 2 All E.R. 648 at 677 *et seq.*). Even so, "rights" have not figured very prominently in the discourse of tort law. The concept of "duty", by contrast (even if trespass has been held authoritatively not to consist of a breach of duty (*Stubbings v Webb* [1993] 1 All E.R. 322)), is all-pervasive, an essential component of the tort of negligence. It therefore deserves some attention, even in an introduction.

"In most situations it is better to be careful than careless, but it is quite another thing to elevate all carelessness into a tort. Liability has to be based on a legal duty not to be careless . . . " (*Moorgate Mercantile Co v Twitchings* [1977] A.C. 890 at 919, *per* Lord Edmund-Davies). In the past the "duty" device was very useful, for it enabled the courts to immunise a person from liability for the damage his unreasonable conduct foreseeably caused simply by holding that he was under no duty to take care at all. By so holding—often as a "preliminary question of law" or when the defendant applied to "strike out" the claim as disclosing no cause of action, they could not only ensure that the defendant need not pay but could preclude an inquiry into his actual conduct, unless he was accused of something worse than mere negligence such as malice or conscious wrongdoing. In this way litigants were prevented from obtaining a judicial appraisal of their advocate's forensic performance, victims of crime could not inquire into the deficiencies of the detective methods of the police, and those preparing evidence for a trial could not be questioned by a separate action. In particular, local authority practices were protected from an inquiry which might have disclosed alarming incompetence.

Nowadays, however, this function is largely in abeyance: litigants do not have the door of the court shut in their face, and their right to have an explanation of the circumstances which resulted in their harm or grievance is much more respected. Nevertheless, the duty concept is ingrained in our legal discourse, and its use is of daily occurrence when counsel are arguing that the defendant should not be liable on the facts or the courts are deciding that he is free from liability. Such a holding could often just as well be made in terms of whether the conduct was unreasonable or not or whether it sufficiently related to the harm, but the old usage lingers on. For example, instead of saying that the harm in question is not causally related to the defendant's conduct, one can say that it was not within the scope of his duty.

It is far from easy to say when the courts will accept or deny that the defendant was under a common law duty to take care of the plaintiff's interests. Lord Atkin made a famous generalisation in 1932, to the effect that you owed a duty to anyone ("your neighbour") who, as you should have realised, was likely to be affected by what you were doing if you did it badly; and 35 years later Lord Wilberforce extended it somewhat (the "two-stage" test). Neither formulation emphasised either the nature of the damage in issue (personal injury, property damage, mere economic loss?) nor the nature of the conduct, apart from its being unreasonable (act or omission, action or speech?). These factors are nevertheless of great importance in the decision as to the existence of duty. The current view is that a duty arises where there is sufficient "proximity" between the parties (an amalgam resulting from the relationship between the parties and the nature of the plaintiff's interest), provided it would be "fair, just and reasonable" to impose a duty (which means "to impose liability in the event of damaging carelessness"). A further strand is the notion of "assumption of responsibility" by the defendant. Thus a solicitor who had contracted with his client to prepare a will was held to have assumed responsibility towards the intended beneficiaries who lost their legacies through his dilatoriness (p. 65). The situation is fluid, to say the least, and the fluidity is increased by equivocation between the duty being, on the one hand, the duty to take care not to cause damage and, on the other, the duty not to cause damage by failure to take care (which is not in all respects the same thing). Furthermore, and very importantly, breach of such duties may well not be sanctioned by damages.

The duty to take care, if one is imposed, may vary in scope and intensity, even if its formulation remains the same. Sometimes it is a duty simply to avoid careless action, sometimes a duty to take proper precautions, sometimes a duty to guard the plaintiff from harm. Sometimes the duty is only to take care to avoid causing physical damage, sometimes it extends to harm which is merely economic; sometimes the duty is broken only by the defendant's own misconduct, sometimes it may be broken by the person to whom he quite reasonably delegated its performance; it is then called a "non-deleg-able" duty. It all depends.

So far we have been considering duties at common law, duties laid down by the judges. Duties are often imposed by statute as well. They are quite different. They may not be general duties *of care* at all, but strict and specific duties to procure or avoid a certain result. The persons on whom such duties are imposed are always specified, as are the conditions under which the duty attaches, but the persons to whom the duty is owed may be left at large. Such duties are narrowly construed by the courts, and never applied by analogy, outside in tort, especially if the statute provides for some other remedy: the courts must be convinced that Parliament must have intended that civil liability ensue.

7. PUBLIC BODIES

One often unconsciously assumes that in the law of tort we are concerned with two individuals suing each other—after all, Mrs Donoghue and Mr Stevenson were real people. On reflection, however, we realise that even in personal injury claims (which can only be brought by persons of flesh and blood) the party that pays is usually an insurance company or a corporate employer, and that in cases of property damage or financial loss the real claimant is also often a legal creature, perhaps an insurance company masquerading as the individual assured. Indeed our very language not only bespeaks but also confirms our assumption that they are actually people—we speak of "his" and "who" rather than "its" and "which" even though we know it's a firm which is in issue. One also tends to assume that the parties, be they human or legal, are in the private sector, whereas in fact it is increasingly public bodies from which damages are sought, and the question of their liability is a matter of current debate and dubiety.

European law has added a new twist to the matter. First, it is only on public bodies that the obligation to respect the rights enunciated by the European Convention on Human Rights is imposed. One might suppose that the requisite respect involved only refraining from invading the rights in question, but in fact the distinction between invasion and omission is occluded in that the obligation clearly extends in certain circumstances to the provision of positive protection against harm, such as child abuse or other criminal conduct. To be noted, however, is that infringement of a Convention right does not necessarily lead to an award of full compensatory damages: our Human Rights Act 1998 (below, p.96) is explicit that an award is to be made only if "necessary to afford just satisfaction" and that the principles applied by the Strasbourg court as regards compensation are to be taken into account. Since no such principles are discernible, the result is uncertain.

By contrast, the Luxembourg court insists on full compensation for breach of Community rights, as Britain discovered when it had imposed monetary limits on damages for discrimination in employment, and when it had to pay impressive sums to Spanish fishermen for not letting them catch British fish. Public bodies are specially vulnerable under Community law for they, unlike private individuals, may be bound by Directives even if they have not been implemented into local law (as we must now call it), and the state may itself be liable for failure to implement them. These are extraordinary innovations in English law.

Until 1947 central government in England (the Crown) could not be sued in tort at all: it was immune from liability. Local government, by contrast, could be held liable in tort, as could other public authorities, this having been laid down in 1866. In 1893, however, public authorities were given special protection by the Public Authorities Protection Act, which required suit to be brought within six months of the conduct impugned and also penalised unsuccessful plaintiffs in costs. This protective enactment, whose existence must have diminished the number of reported claims against public bodies, was repealed in 1954, with virtually no discussion in Parliament.

The reasons for special protection have since become apparent. This is because of the remarkable extension of liability in tort as regards (a) the kind of harm and (b) the kind of conduct complained of: after *Hedley Byrne* in 1963 (an action against a private firm, below, p.57) the harm need no longer be physical and after *Dorset Yacht* (a claim against the Home Office, below, p.84) an omission, it seemed, would suffice. Theretofore, with few exceptions, there had been liability only for positive acts causing physical harm. Now since merely legal entities which cannot commit physical acts (though their employees can do so and perhaps render their employer vicariously liable) are very good at failing to act, the extension of liability for omissions made a great difference to them; and whereas an omission to protect can lead to physical harm, economic harm is the commoner outcome. This meant that, unless there was a finding of "no duty" (ostensibly on grounds of "public policy" or not "fair just and reasonable" or "no assumption of responsibility" or, more dangerously, "immunity"), the law of tort would impose liability for unreasonable failure to prevent the occurrence of merely economic harm. This indeed was the very holding in *Anns v Merton L.B.C.* in 1977.

Anns was famously overruled thirteen years later in *Murphy v Brentwood* (below, p.31), though principally on the ground that the harm was not physical but merely economic, rather than on the ground that the defendant was a public body exercising, or rather failing to exercise, the powers of control accorded to it by legislation. Since then, however, this feature of governmental liability, namely that it is inevitably connected with statute (since it is only by statute that public bodies other than the Crown have any legal existence and any rights and powers) has been the focus of attention: to what extent can there be liability under the common law of tort for breach of statutory duties or misuse of statutory powers? There is the added complexity that while duties must be performed (though there is no reason why the sanction for breach should be damages) powers, though conferred in order to be used, need not be used in a particular case unless the authority so decides, a decision accorded by the legislature to the authority and not, in the first instance, to the courts. The courts have therefore developed the principle that liability should not be imposed at common law if this would unduly inhibit the performance of duties imposed or the relative freedom of choice in the exercise of powers conferred by Parliament, but they are very ready nowadays to inquire into the propriety of the exercise of the discretion unless the matter can exceptionally be described as "non-justiciable".

One characteristic of governmental bodies is that they have manifold functions and resources, human as well as financial which, though extensive, are not unlimited. It is a question whether it is right to reduce their resources by making them pay the victims of mismanagement rather than let them use those resources to improve their management for the future, for example, to pay an injured schoolchild or use the money to replace the pane of glass on which she injured herself (below, p.190). Again, lawsuits call for the deployment of much manpower and time in preparing the defence and appearing, if necessary, in court. Policemen should perhaps be upright on the beat rather than lying in the witness box. Again, though perhaps the point has been overemphasised, just as the expansion of medical liability has led to defensive (and expensive) prophylactic treatment, the fear of liability (blame, waste of time, etc.) may have unfortunate effects on public servants. Put briefly, governmental units have duties towards others than their victims, and it would be wrong to ignore that fact just because they are being sued by a victim (see p.149).

There is, of course, no question of public bodies having a general immunity in tort, such as the Crown used to enjoy. Where the analogue with private persons is very close, that is, where specifically governmental activities or inactivities are in issue, it remains the case that public bodies are liable. Public hospitals, for this purpose are like private doctors. Civil servants driving to a meeting are treated just like honest citizens driving to the theatre. Local authority landlords fall under the general law as regards their tenants, visitors and neighbours; likewise when they make mortgage loans. The police are liable for arresting a person without justification, or for setting a shop on fire and then carelessly letting it burn down, as they once did in Northampton. The specifically governmental activities include social services, fire brigades, prisons, police, education, rescue services, health matters, environmental controls, consumer protection and the justice system.

Decisions on the liability of public bodies are made in terms of the general law of tort—thus the question whether it is "fair just and reasonable" to impose a duty of care (and consequent liability for breach) is applicable to public and private bodies alike. Statutory duties may be imposed on private persons (such as employers) as well as on public bodies, though discretionary powers are less frequently accorded to the commonalty. Thus a decision on whether Shell is liable in damages for breach of duty may be treated as relevant in a case where the defendant is the Bogside District Council. Accordingly decisions in cases involving public authorities are relevant to, though not necessarily decisive of, claims against citizens, and vice versa. That is why those cases are, rather reluctantly, incorporated in the main body of this casebook. In future it may be necessary to have a separate section, though few textbooks on tort do so. Readers should, however, always be aware of the nature of the defendant as public or not, since it clearly makes a difference, even if the difference made is not clear.

8. FUNCTIONS OF THE LAW

We have said that compensation is the principal function of tort law. This does not mean that the function is best performed when most compensation is awarded, but that its function is to determine when compensation is rightly payable. The very concept of compensation entails the notion of harm or damage, since only harm or damage can be compensated. But we have also seen that sometimes damages are awarded even though no harm has been suffered, its absence being concealed by the statement that the plaintiff's rights were infringed. In this context the majority of the House of Lords had recently caused consternation to the minority. After holding that no compensation was payable to the parents of a healthy child whose birth was due to the negligence of the defendant, the majority decided nevertheless to award them £15,000. As the minority said, effectively: "If this is not compensation, what is it?" It is perhaps a token of the court's perception that the parents' rights—to plan their family, to live their life as they choose, to have the doctor respect their instructions?—have been infringed (*Rees v Darlington Memorial Hospital*, below p.118).

That is the other function of the law of tort: to vindicate the rights of the citizen and to sanction their infringement. In this respect the flagship of the fleet is not negligence, but trespass, protecting as it does the rights of freedom of movement, physical integrity, and the land and goods in one's possession. The citizen's right to his reputation and good name is also protected, perhaps unduly, by the law of defamation. Further rights may qualify for protection under continental influence, such as human rights under the Convention, the moral rights of the creative artist and the neither human nor moral rights of the multinational trading corporation.

There has been a certain conflict between the functions of compensation and vindication, which presents itself as a dialectical conflict between the torts of negligence and trespass, and there have been disagreeable signs that vindication has not been the clear winner. We shall see later a case where a person was arrested without a warrant under an invalid bye-law (*Percy v Hall*, below p.354), and another where a person was arrested under a warrant intended to cover someone else (*McGrath v Chief Constable*, below p.383), and in neither case did the claimant obtain damages: though it is obvious that the arrests had no lawful justification, liability was denied just because the police couldn't be blamed.

A third function has been proposed: deterrence. Is it the function of the law of tort to compensate the plaintiff or to deter the defendant? The question has some practical significance, since focussing on the defendant's conduct may draw attention away from other aspects of the case. Thus, for example, a person paid in full by his property insurer needs no compensation, and the insurer which pays him should receive none (because it paid the money pursuant to a risk it was paid to take). But many people still think it right that the defendant should pay, as the law says he must, just to teach him to behave better in future and avoid causing another loss, which after all may not be insured the next time. Again where a doctor has negligently done something which makes death more likely, and death then supervenes, one might make him pay even if the death would probably have supervened anyway, that is, though the causation remains unproven. One might make the local authority pay for allowing a builder to build a dangerous house which might collapse, rather than hold it liable only if the house does actually fall on someone and hurt him. And if the defendant has negligently damaged property in the ownership and possession of X, but Y suffers the loss (because he is the buyer, or the charterer) one might make the defendant pay just as if it were Y's property that was damaged, as it so well might have been.

In the three situations just mentioned, the House of Lords has quite recently denied liability, so one can conclude that in England this deterrence approach has not had the effect of extending liability. Rather the reverse. Sometimes the courts deny liability because to impose it might make the defendant overcautious, indulge in "defensive medicine" or refrain from bold decisions.

PART I

NEGLIGENCE

Chapter 1

DUTY

Section 1.—Products

DONOGHUE v STEVENSON

House of Lords [1932] A.C. 562; 101 L.J.P.C. 119; 147 L.T. 281; 48 T.L.R. 494; 76 S.J. 396; 37 Com.Cas. 350; [1932] All E.R.Rep. 1

Action by consumer against manufacturer in respect of personal injury

According to Mrs Donoghue (*née* McAllister), she went to Minchella's café in Paisley with a friend, who ordered her a "ginger beer float." After taking the cap off the bottle, which was made of opaque stone rather than transparent glass, Minchella poured some of the ginger beer over the ice-cream in the tumbler, and Mrs Donoghue partook thereof. As some ginger beer was still left in the bottle, her friend emptied it into her tumbler. A nauseating foreign body floated out— possibly something that had once been a snail. Mrs Donoghue was taken ill, poisoned by the drink or sickened by the thought of it, or both.

Mrs Donoghue claimed that Stevenson, who had bottled the ginger beer and sold it to Minchella, was under a legal duty of care *to her*: he should have had a system for keeping snails out of the bottles and for inspecting the bottles before they were filled, and his breach of duty in these respects had caused her illness.

Stevenson replied that even if she managed to prove the facts she alleged, he was not liable in law, so there was no point in going to trial, but Lord Moncrieff decided to hear the evidence, and Stevenson appealed. The Inner House (Scotland's Court of Appeal) allowed Stevenson's appeal, and was for dismissing the claim. Mrs Donoghue appealed to the House of Lords, and her appeal was allowed, so that the case could proceed to trial (though in fact it never did).

Lord Atkin: My Lords, the sole question for determination in this case is legal: Do the averments made by the pursuer in her pleading, if true, disclose a cause of action? I need not restate the particular facts. The question is whether the manufacturer of an article of drink sold by him to a distributor, in circumstances which prevent the distributor or the ultimate purchaser or consumer from discovering by inspection any defect, is under any legal duty to the ultimate purchaser or consumer to take reasonable care that the article is free from defect likely to cause injury to health. I do not think a more important problem has occupied your Lordships in your judicial capacity: important both because of its bearing on public health and because of the practical test which it applies to the system under which it arises . . . The law . . . appears to be that in order to support an action for damages for negligence the complainant has to show that he has been injured by the breach of a duty owed to him in the circumstances by the defendant to take reasonable care to avoid such injury. In the present case we are not concerned with the breach of the duty; if a duty exists, that would be a question of fact which is sufficiently averred and for present purposes must be assumed. We are solely concerned with the question whether, as a matter of law in the circumstances alleged, the defender owed any duty to the pursuer to take care.

It is remarkable how difficult it is to find in the English authorities statements of general application defining the relations between parties that give rise to the duty. The Courts are concerned with the particular relations which come before them in actual litigation, and it is sufficient to say whether the duty exists in those circumstances. The result is that the Courts have been engaged upon an elaborate classification of duties as they exist in respect of property, whether real or personal, with further divisions as to ownership, occupation or control, and distinctions based on the particular relations of the one side or the other, whether manufacturer, salesman or landlord, customer, tenant, stranger, and so on. In this way it can be ascertained at any time whether the law recognizes a duty, but only where the case can be referred to some particular species which has been examined and classified. And yet the duty which is common to all the cases where liability is established must logically be based upon some element common to the cases where it is found to exist. To seek a complete logical definition of the general principle is probably to go beyond the function of the judge, for the more general the definition the more likely it is to omit essentials or to introduce non-essentials. The attempt was made by Brett M.R. in *Heaven v Pender* ((1883) 11 Q.B.D. 503 at 509), in a definition to which I will later refer. As framed, it was demonstrably too wide, though it appears to me, if properly limited, to be capable of affording a valuable practical guide.

At present I content myself with pointing out that in English law there must be, and is, some general conception of relations giving rise to a duty of care, of which the particular cases found in the books are but instances. The liability for negligence, whether you style it such or treat it as in other systems as a species of "culpa," is no doubt based upon a general public sentiment of moral wrongdoing for which the offender must pay. But acts or omissions which any moral code would censure cannot in a practical world be treated so as to give a right to every person injured by them to demand relief. In this way rules of law arise which limit the range of complainants and the extent of their remedy. The rule that you are to love your neighbour becomes in law, you must not injure your neighbour; and the lawyer's question, Who is my neighbour? receives a restricted reply. You must take reasonable care to avoid acts or omissions which you can reasonably foresee would be likely to injure your neighbour. Who, then, in law is my neighbour? The answer seems to be—persons who are so closely and directly affected by my act that I ought reasonably to have them in contemplation as being so affected when I am directing my mind to the acts or omissions which are called in question. This appears to me to be the doctrine of *Heaven v Pender*, as laid down by Lord Esher (then Brett M.R.) when it is limited by the notion of proximity introduced by Lord Esher himself and A. L. Smith L.J. in *Le Lievre v Gould* ([1893] 1 Q.B. 491 at 497, 504). Lord Esher says: "That case established that, under certain circumstances, one man may owe a duty to another, even though there is no contract between them. If one man is near to another, or is near to the property of another, a duty lies upon him not to do that which may cause a personal injury to that other, or may injure his property." So A. L. Smith L.J.: "The decision of *Heaven v Pender* was founded upon the principle, that a duty to take due care did arise when the person or property of one was in such proximity to the person or property of another that, if due care was not taken, damage might be done by the one to the other." I think that this sufficiently states the truth if proximity be not confined to mere physical proximity, but be used, as I think it was intended, to extend to such close and direct relations that the act complained of directly affects a person who the person alleged to be bound to take care would know would be directly affected by his careless act. That this is the sense in which nearness or "proximity" was intended by Lord Esher is obvious from his own illustration in *Heaven v Pender* of the application of his doctrine to the sale of goods. There will no doubt arise cases where it will be difficult to determine whether the contemplated relationship is so close that the duty arises. But in the class of case now before the Court I cannot conceive any difficulty to arise. A manufacturer puts up an article of food in a container which he knows will be opened by the actual consumer. There can be no inspection by any purchaser and no reasonable preliminary inspection by the consumer. Negligently, in the course of preparation, he allows the contents to be mixed with poison. It is said that the law of England and Scotland is that the poisoned consumer has no remedy against the negligent manufacturer. If this were the result of the authorities I should consider the result a grave defect in the law, and so contrary to principle that I should hesitate long before following any decision to that effect which had not the authority of this House. I would point out that, in the assumed state of the authorities, not only would the consumer have no remedy against the manufacturer, he would have none against any one else, for in the circumstances alleged there would be no evidence of negligence against any one other than the manufacturer; and, except in the case of a consumer who was also a purchaser, no contract and no warranty of fitness, and in the case of the purchase of a specific article under its patent or trade name, which might well be the case in the purchase of some articles of food or drink, no warranty protecting even the purchaser-consumer. There are other instances than of articles of food and drink where goods are sold intended to be used immediately by the consumer, such as many forms of goods sold for cleaning purposes, where the same liability must exist. The doctrine supported by the decision below would not only deny a remedy to the consumer who was injured by consuming bottled beer or chocolates poisoned by the negligence of the manufacturer, but also to the user of what should be a harmless proprietary medicine, an ointment, a soap, a cleaning fluid or cleaning powder. I confine myself to articles of common household use, where everyone, including the manufacturer, knows that the articles will be used by other persons than the actual ultimate purchaser—namely, by members of his family and his servants, and in some cases his guests. I do not think so ill of our jurisprudence as to suppose that its principles are so remote from the ordinary needs of civilized society and the ordinary claims it makes upon its members as to deny a legal remedy where there is so obviously a social wrong.

It will be found, I think, on examination that there is no case in which the circumstances have been such as I have just suggested where the liability has been negatived. There are numerous cases, where the relations were much more remote, where the duty has been held not to exist

My Lords, if your Lordships accept the view that this pleading discloses a relevant cause of action you will be affirming the proposition that by Scots and English law alike a manufacturer of products, which he sells in such a form as to show that he intends them to reach the ultimate consumer in the form in which they left him with no reasonable possibility of intermediate examination, and with the knowledge that the absence of reasonable care in the preparation or putting up the products will result in an injury to the consumer's life or property, owes a duty to the consumer to take that reasonable care.

It is a proposition which I venture to say no one in Scotland or England who was not a lawyer would for one moment doubt. It will be an advantage to make it clear that the law in this matter, as in most others, is in accordance with sound common sense. I think that this appeal should be allowed.

Lord Macmillan: ... The law takes no cognizance of carelessness in the abstract. It concerns itself with carelessness only where there is a duty to take care and where failure in that duty has caused damage. In such circumstances carelessness assumes the legal quality of negligence and entails the consequences in law of negligence. What, then, are the circumstances which give rise to this duty to take care? In the daily contacts of social and business life human beings are thrown into, or place themselves in, an infinite variety of relations with their fellows; and the law can refer only to the standards of the reasonable man in order to determine whether any particular relation gives rise to a duty to take care as between those who stand in that relation to each other. The grounds of action may be as various and manifold as human errancy; and the conception of legal responsibility may develop in adaptation to altering social conditions and standards. The criterion of judgment must adjust and adapt itself to the changing circumstances of life. The categories of negligence are never closed. The cardinal principle of liability is that the party complained of should owe to the party complaining a duty to take care, and that the party complaining should be able to prove that he has suffered damage in consequence of a breach of that duty. Where there is room for diversity of view, it is in determining what circumstances will establish such a relationship between the parties as to give rise, on the one side, to a duty to take care, and on the other side to a right to have care taken.

To descend from these generalities to the circumstances of the present case, I do not think that any reasonable man or any twelve reasonable men would hesitate to hold that, if the appellant establishes her allegations, the respondent has exhibited carelessness in the conduct of his business. For a manufacturer of aerated water to store his empty bottles in a place where snails can get access to them, and to fill his bottles without taking any adequate precautions by inspection or otherwise to ensure that they contain no deleterious foreign matter, may reasonably be characterized as carelessness without applying too exacting a standard. But, as I have pointed out, it is not enough to prove the respondent to be careless in his process of manufacture. The question is: Does he owe a duty to take care, and to whom does he owe that duty? Now I have no hesitation in affirming that a person who for gain engages in the business of manufacturing articles of food and drink intended for consumption by members of the public in the form in which he issues them is under a duty to take care in the manufacture of these articles. That duty, in my opinion, he owes to those whom he intends to consume his products. He manufactures his commodities for human consumption; he intends and contemplates that they shall be consumed. By reason of that very fact he places himself in a relationship with all the potential consumers of his commodities, and that relationship which he assumes and desires for his own ends imposes upon him a duty to take care to avoid injuring them. He owes them a duty not to convert by his own carelessness an article which he issues to them as wholesome and innocent into an article which is dangerous to life and health. It is sometimes said that liability can only arise where a reasonable man would have foreseen and could have avoided the consequences of his act or omission. In the present case the respondent, when he manufactured his ginger-beer, had directly in contemplation that it would be consumed by members of the public. Can it be said that he could not be expected as a reasonable man to foresee that if he conducted his process of manufacture carelessly he might injure those whom he expected and desired to consume his ginger-beer? The possibility of injury so arising seems to me in no sense so remote as to excuse him from foreseeing it. Suppose that a baker, through carelessness, allows a large quantity of arsenic to be mixed with a batch of his bread, with the result that those who subsequently eat it are poisoned, could he be heard to say that he owed no duty to the consumers of his bread to take care that it was free from poison, and that, as he did not know that any poison had got into it, his only liability was for breach of warranty under his contract of sale to those who actually bought the poisoned bread from him? Observe that I have said "through carelessness," and thus excluded the case of pure accident such as may happen where every care is taken. I cannot believe, and I do not believe, that neither in the law of England nor in the law of Scotland is there redress for such a case. The state of facts I have figured might well give rise to a criminal charge, and the civil consequence of such carelessness can scarcely be less wide than its criminal consequences. Yet the principle of the decision appealed from is that the manufacturer of food products intended by him for human consumption does not owe to the consumers whom he has in view any duty of care, not even the duty to take care that he does not poison them . . .

It must always be a question of circumstances whether the carelessness amounts to negligence, and whether the injury is not too remote from the carelessness. I can readily conceive that where a manufacturer has parted with his product and it has passed into other hands it may well be exposed to vicissitudes which may render it defective or noxious, for which the manufacturer could not in any view be held to be to blame. It may be a good general rule to regard responsibility as ceasing when control ceases. So, also, where between the manufacturer and the user there is interposed a party who has the means and opportunity of examining the manufacturer's product before he re-issues it to the actual user. But where, as in the present case, the article of consumption is so prepared as to be intended to reach the consumer in the condition in which it leaves the manufacturer, and the manufacturer takes steps to ensure this by sealing or otherwise closing the container so that the contents cannot be tampered with, I regard his control as remaining effective until the article reaches the consumer and the container is opened by him. The intervention of any exterior agency is intended to be excluded, and was in fact in the present case excluded . . .

The burden of proof must always be upon the injured party to establish that the defect which caused the injury was present in the article when it left the hands of the party whom he sues, that the defect was occasioned by the carelessness of that party, and that the circumstances are such as to cast upon the defender a duty to take care not to injure the pursuer. There is no presumption of negligence in such a case as the present, nor is there any justification for applying the maxim, *res ipsa loquitur*. Negligence must be both averred and proved . . .

Lord Thankerton: . . . A man cannot be charged with negligence if he has no obligation to exercise diligence . . . Unless the consumer can establish a special relationship with the manufacturer, it is clear, in my opinion, that neither the law of Scotland nor the law of England will hold that the manufacturer has any duty towards the consumer to exercise diligence . . . [But here there was a special relationship because the manufacturer] in placing his manufactured article of drink upon the market, has intentionally so excluded interference with, or examination of, the article by any intermediate handler of the goods between himself and the consumer that he has, of his own accord, brought himself into direct relationship with the consumer, with the result that the consumer is entitled to rely upon the exercise of diligence by the manufacturer to secure that the article shall not be harmful to the consumer . . .

Lord Buckmaster dissented on the ground that there were only two exceptions to the principle that "the breach of the defendant's contract with A to use care and skill in and about the manufacture or repair of an article does not of itself give any cause of action to B when he is injured by reason of the article proving to be defective" (*per* Lord Sumner in *Blacker v Lake & Elliot Ltd* (1912) 106 L.T. 533 at 536), namely, where the article was dangerous in itself or had a defect known to the manufacturer. The majority decision was "simply to misapply to tort doctrine applicable to sale and purchase."

Lord Tomlin also dissented.

Quotation
"There may be in the cup
A spider steep'd, and one may drink, depart,
And yet partake no venom, for his knowledge
It is not infected; but if one present
The abhorr'd ingredient to his eye, make known
How he hath drunk, he cracks his gorge, his sides
With violent hefts. I have drunk, and seen the spider."

Shakespeare, *The Winter's Tale*, II.i.37.

Gossip Column
No one can justly accuse British law of being short in human interest. In the autumn of 1990, on the very site of the Wellmeadow café where Mrs Donoghue was so famously taken ill, Alan Minchella, the great grandson of the Minchella who served Mrs Donoghue at the instance of her friend, served less unwholesome ginger beer and ice-cream to Lord Mackay L.C., head of the British judiciary, and Lord President Hope, head of the judiciary in Scotland (see [1990] New L.J. 1375). Their Lordships sat on a memorial bench presented by the Canadian delegates at the current Conference on the Commonwealth Law of Negligence, papers at which were delivered by Wilson J. of the Supreme Court of Canada and Brennan J. of the High Court of Australia.
The fertile tilth of Mrs Donoghue's background has been richly ploughed by Lord Rodger of Earlsferry in his enchanting article "*Mrs Donoghue and Alfenus Varus*"[!] in (1988) 41 Current Legal Problems 1. Mrs Donoghue, who had only £5 to her name at the time of the law-suit, died in 1958 worth £364, having in 1935 received £200 in settlement from the estate of Stevenson. See also A. McBryde, "*Donoghue v Stevenson*: The Story of the 'Snail in the Bottle' Case", in A.J. Gamble (ed.), *Obligations in Context* (Edinburgh, 1990).

Questions
1. Suppose that Mrs Donoghue bought a bottle of Stevenson's ginger beer for £1 and took it home, that when she opened it she saw a decomposed snail at the top of the bottle, and that she suffered shock at the thought of what she might have drunk. In what way would her claim for (a) shock, (b) £1 differ from the claim she actually brought? Should the result be the same?
2. Suppose that Stevenson got his bottles from Louis, and that Mrs Donoghue had been injured because of a defect in the bottle which Stevenson couldn't have discovered. Would Louis or Stevenson be liable, or both?
3. Suppose that the victim is not a regular consumer like Mrs Donoghue but a shoplifter or a tester for *Which*? Would you make the manufacturer liable? If not, would this be because he owed no duty or for some other reason?

Note:

Donoghue v Stevenson is hardly the Last Word on the tort of negligence, since it is over 70 years old, but it still deserves to come first in the book. Its importance lies not only in what it decided but also in how it was decided: it established, as its *ratio decidendi*, that a careless manufacturer who circulates a dangerously defective product is liable to a consumer to whom it causes personal injury, but more importantly, it laid down in *obiter dicta* a general principle of liability for unintended harm, focusing on the duty of care.

The Manufacturer

Donoghue v Stevenson need no longer be invoked by people complaining of *personal injury* caused by a defective product, for the Consumer Protection Act 1987 now makes the manufacturer liable without proof of fault. (The E.C. Directive underlying this Act is given below, p.27.) To most cases of *property damage*, however, *Donoghue v Stevenson* continues to apply, and where mere *financial harm* is suffered by a distant consumer, the manufacturer is not liable at all, even if he was careless (*Muirhead v Industrial Tank Specialities* [1985] 3 All E.R. 705, CA) (noted [1986] Camb.L.J. 13; (1986) 49 M.L.R. 369). The following paragraphs should be read in the light of this.

Lord Thankerton spoke of the special relationship between manufacturer and consumer, *i.e.* the person whose appetite the manufacturer seeks to stimulate ("Don't be Vague: Ask for Stevenson's Ginger Beer"). Certainly a special relationship does exist between manufacturer and consumer, but in fact the manufacturer owes an equal duty to the innocent bystander with whom he has no such relationship: the pedestrian injured by the defective car can sue just as well as its driver (*Lambert v Lewis* [1982] A.C. 225). So the special relationship is not necessary where the harm is physical and it is insufficient where the harm is merely financial.

Lord Macmillan suggested that it was for the plaintiff to prove that the manufacturer was careless, but of course the victim can hardly know what went on in the factory. In *Grant v Australian Knitting Mills* [1936] A.C. 85, the plaintiff complained of dermatitis resulting from the use of underpants manufactured by the defendant which contained excess sulphites. The defendant led evidence that he had manufactured 4,737,600 pairs of underpants with never a complaint. Yet the plaintiff succeeded. No one can reasonably say that a manufacturer with a failure rate of only one in a million is not a reasonably careful manufacturer; it is, indeed, an astonishing performance which should earn a prize. And one cannot say that he was not reasonably careful with the pants in question, since there was no evidence as to them, save their defect. He was in fact made to pay because the pants were defective when they left his factory. Thus the principal case, though it expresses the duty in terms of taking reasonable care, virtually results in a guarantor's liability. Thus when a used and underinflated car tyre exploded and it was shown that it had a structural defect, the manufacturer was held liable for the injuries: "Negligence is found as a matter of inference from the existence of the defect taken in connection with all the known circumstances." *Carroll v Fearon* [1998] Times L.R. 31, CA. Now that it is only in cases of commercial property damage that it matters whether the manufacturer was negligent or not, it is quite possible that the courts will be less ready to find him negligent.

This is important when one considers that commercial property damage should often be borne by the business that suffers it rather than the business which causes it. Consider, for example, *The Esso Bernicia* [1989] 1 All E.R. 37, HL. Owing to the bad construction of a tug built by the defendants, a tanker towed by the tug collided with the Shetland Islands and caused much damage to (a) the tanker and its contents, (b) the terminal it ran into, and (c) the sheep which swallowed the oil which spilt from out of the tanker which crashed on the island because of the tug which the defendants had built. Thanks to the incompetence of Esso's attorneys, the defendant tug-builders were held not liable for the £4 million which Esso had to pay out for the damage done by their oil, and the result is right, regardless of the technicalities: Esso should surely bear the risk that their tankers, almost literally pregnant with disaster, suffer or cause damage, and it is wrong for the law to throw the loss on the builders of the tug (even one designed for the purpose).

Most things that are made are made to be sold. Indeed, there are many more sellers than makers. Even in this case the snail was sold not only by Stevenson (to Minchella) but also by Minchella (to Friend). Long before 1932 it was clear what the seller's duty was: his duty to the buyer was to provide a good thing, not just to take care not to provide a bad one. The seller's liability was strict (*i.e.* not dependent on his carelessness) and it was triggered by the defect, even if the defect did not render the thing dangerous (*i.e.* apt to cause physical harm). Now Friend bought the ginger beer for Mrs Donoghue ("Please can I have a ginger beer for my lady-friend here?") so that one could say that Mrs Donoghue was the intended beneficiary of the contract of sale between Minchella and Friend. That would not, in 1932, have given Mrs Donoghue any right to sue Minchella on the contract, but now she probably does have such a right under the Contracts (Rights of Third Parties) Act 1999. This action, unlike the claim against the manufacturer, would cover the difference in value between a good and a no-good ginger beer, that is, it covers all defects which render the item unsatisfactory, even if it is not dangerous at all (Sale of Goods Act 1979, s.14(2)).

The Principle

The decision did more than simply add manufacturer/consumer to the list of relationships which involved a duty to take care. It also laid down a principle much wider than the facts of the case required, *viz.* "You must take reasonable care to avoid causing foreseeable injury." It is because this principle acts as a unifying force that *Donoghue v Stevenson* is said to denote the birth of negligence as a tort.

There are two areas in respect of which the principle is wider than the rule required by the facts of the case:

(1) In the actual case, the harm allegedly suffered was physical, indeed internal, injury. The principle did not seem to be so limited. Was the principle extensible to purely psychical harm and to purely financial harm? See *White v Chief Constable* (below, p.105) and *Spartan Steel* (below, p.53).

(2) In the actual case Stevenson added a new danger to life by putting a poisonous bottle of ginger beer on the market. He positively caused the harm, he didn't just let it happen. In other words, Stevenson didn't simply fail to protect Mrs Donoghue from the snail: he actually inflicted it on her. Could the principle be extended to those who do simply let the damage occur, that is, those guilty only of an omission? See *Stovin v Wise* (below, p.89), *Murphy v Brentwood* (below, p.31) and *The Nicholas H* (below, p.45).

COUNCIL OF THE EUROPEAN COMMUNITIES DIRECTIVE of JULY 25, 1985

Art.1 The producer shall be liable for damage caused by a defect in his product.

Art.2 For the purpose of this Directive, "product" means all movables even if incorporated into another movable or into an immovable. "Product" includes electricity.

Art.3 (1) "Producer" means the manufacturer of a finished product, the producer of any raw material or the manufacturer of a component part and any person who, by putting his name, trade mark or other distinguishing feature on the product presents himself as its producer.

(2) Without prejudice to the liability of the producer, any person who imports into the Community a product for sale, hire, leasing or any form of distribution in the course of his business shall be deemed to be a producer within the meaning of his Directive and shall be responsible as a producer.

(3) Where the producer of the product cannot be identified, each supplier of the product shall be treated as its producer unless he informs the injured person, within a reasonable time, of the identity of the producer or of the person who supplied him with the product. The same shall apply, in the case of an imported product, if this product does not indicate the identity of the importer referred to in paragraph (2), even if the name of the producer is indicated.

Art.4 The injured person shall be required to prove the damage, the defect and the causal relationship between defect and damage.

Art.5 Where, as a result of the provisions of this Directive, two or more persons are liable for the same damage, they shall be liable jointly and severally, without prejudice to the provisions of national law concerning the rights of contribution or recourse.

Art.6 (1) A product is defective when it does not provide the safety which a person is entitled to expect, taking all circumstances into account, including:

(a) the presentation of the product;
(b) the use to which it could reasonably be expected that the product would be put;
(c) the time when the product was put into circulation.

(2) A product shall not be considered defective for the sole reason that a better product is subsequently put into circulation.

Art.7 The producer shall not be liable as a result of this Directive if he proves:

(a) that he did not put the product into circulation; or

(b) that, having regard to the circumstances, it is probable that the defect which caused the damage did not exist at the time when the product was put into circulation by him or that this defect came into being afterwards; or

(c) that the product was neither manufactured by him for sale or any form of distribution for economic purpose nor manufactured or distributed by him in the course of his business; or

(d) that the defect is due to compliance of the product with mandatory regulations issued by the public authorities; or

(e) that the state of scientific and technical knowledge at the time when he put the product into circulation was not such as to enable the existence of the defect to be discovered; or

(f) in the case of a manufacturer of a component, that the defect is attributable to the design of the product in which the component has been fitted or to the instructions given by the manufacturer of the product.

Art.8 (1) Without prejudice to the provisions of national law concerning the right of contribution or recourse, the liability of the producer shall not be reduced when the damage is caused both by a defect in product and by the act or omission of a third party.

The liability of the producer may be reduced or disallowed when, having regard to all the circumstances, the damage is caused both by a defect in the product and by the fault of the injured person or any person for whom the injured person is responsible.

Art.9 For the purpose of Article 1, "damage" means:

(a) damage caused by death or by personal injuries;

(b) damage to, or destruction of, any item of property other than the defective product itself, with a lower threshold of 500 ECU, provided that the item of property:
  (i) is of a type ordinarily intended for private use or consumption, and
  (ii) was used by the injured person mainly for his own private use or consumption.

This Article shall be without prejudice to national provisions relating to non-material damage.

Art.10 This Directive shall not affect any rights which an injured person may have according to the rules of the law of contractual or non-contractual liability or a special liability system existing at the moment when this Directive is notified. . . .

Note:
The Directive is rather easier to read than the Consumer Protection Act 1987 which purports to implement it and is to be construed in compliance with it.

(i) Indeed, in *A v National Blood Authority* [2001] 3 All E.R. 289 the judge preferred to refer to the Directive rather than to the Act. In that important case the blood which had been transfused into the claimants was contaminated with the hepatitis C virus. The first question was whether the blood (agreed to be a "product") was "defective". Obviously it was defective in common parlance, but was it defective in terms of the Directive which requires that it lack the "safety which a person is entitled to expect, taking all circumstances into account"? The critical fact was that there was no technical method by which the contamination could be detected, that is, no one could tell whether the blood was pure or not. Were people entitled to expect that the blood be purer than it could be made? The judge so held.

(ii) Another very strong decision on "defect" is *Abouzaid v Mothercare* [2001] T.L.R. 136. "Cosytoes", a blanket designed to keep toddlers warm in their prams, had to be affixed at the back, for which purpose two elastic straps were provided, ending in a metal buckle. The 12-year old claimant was helping to affix the blanket when he let go of one of the straps and the buckle hit him in the eye. It was an accident that no one had or could have foreseen, so there was no negligence, but the Court of Appeal held that the design was defective—it could reasonably have been made safer (Velcro?)—and imposed liability. The decision demonstrates the difference between strict liability and liability for negligence.

(iii) Some first-instance decisions have held that it is for the claimant to show what was wrong with the product, and that it is not enough simply to prove that it went wrong, as when a breast-implant or condom burst. These decisions are unlikely to be followed in cases where there is no other explanation for the problem.

(iv) Strict product liability in tort was created by the American courts in the 1960s. Europe took over this creation, but not the distinction now drawn in the United States between (a) manufacturing defects (where the manufacturer himself would admit that the particular item was not as it should have been, like Mrs Donoghue's ginger beer), (b) design defects (where all examples of the product are criticised for not being as safe as they should be) and (c) failure to warn of an inherent danger, not in itself constituting a defect. It is now thought that only (a) is really a strict liability, for (b) certainly depends on a value judgement—should the producer have produced a safer product? (*Abouzaid*) and (c) clearly depends on a finding of negligence.

(v) The defect, if proved, is presumed to have been present when the product was put in circulation: it is for the producer to prove otherwise (Art.7(b)). Likewise, under another Directive (1999/44/EC) if a product purchased by an individual proves unsatisfactory within six months of its purchase, the business seller is presumptively liable (now Sale of Goods Act 1979, s.48A (5)).

(vi) The "development risks" defence in Art.7(e) has caused much emotional debate; indeed the European Commission, being of opinion that our Act had impermissibly extended its scope, sued the United Kingdom in Luxembourg, though without success (Case C–300/95). Under this defence the producer can avoid liability for what is now known to be a defect by showing that at the time of circulation there was no known means of ascertaining the fact. In the blood case this defence was rejected because the defendants knew that there was a risk of contamination, though there was nothing whatever they could do about it (except stop supplying blood altogether). This again is a strong decision, since at the time no one in the world could tell whether any particular batch of blood was contaminated.

Questions

1. In what cases of damage due to a defect in a product will *Donoghue v Stevenson* still be invoked?

2. Under what circumstances, if any, could a computer programme or a book containing errors involve liability under the Directive?

3. The Z Co acquired a van manufactured by Y incorporating brakes supplied by X. By reason of a latent defect in the brakes, the van comes off the road at a bend and crashes into my house. May I sue X or Y or both?

4. Do you approve of the distinction between consumer property and commercial property, even if it means that if my Peke and a shepherd's Collie are both poisoned by canned dog food, I can sue but the shepherd cannot? Would it not have been easier to provide that only human beings could sue, as is done in Directive 93/13, implemented in the Unfair Terms in Consumer Contracts Regulations 1999 (SI 1999/2083)? Or would that have presented problems in jurisdictions like ours where the possessor, and not just the owner, has title to sue for property damage? What of the company car put wholly at the disposal of the sales manager?

5. Stella Liebeck drove up to a McDonald's in Las Cruces, New Mexico, and ordered a cup of coffee. As she drove away it spilt on to her lap and burnt her badly. The local jury awarded her $200,000 damages by way of compensation plus $2.7 million in punitive damages. The latter was reduced by the judge to $480,000 and Ms Liebeck settled for $600,000 (of which her attorney would get at least 40 per cent). Would coffee served in a paper cup at a temperature of 180–190 degrees be held "defective" under the Directive? Was it negligent of the firm to serve coffee at that temperature if some like it hot? A comparable claim in England was dismissed by Field J. in *Bogle v McDonald's Restaurants* [2002] E.W.H.C. 490.

6. What is the manufacturer's duty to warn (a) of dangers due to foreseeable misuse of the product, (b) of "development risks" manifesting themselves only after the product has been put into circulation? When France finally, under threats, got round to implementing the Directive, ten years late, it included a provision rendering the manufacturer liable for failure to take steps to prevent damage arising from a development risk once it had been ascertained (Art.1386(12) Code civil). The Luxembourg Court held that this constituted a mistransposition of the Directive, which says nothing of the sort (Case C–52/00, *Commission v Republic of France*, E.C.J., April 25, 2002): according to the court, the purpose of the Directive was not (as the title of our Act suggests) to protect consumers, but to provide a level playing field for producers throughout the Community. For the common law on notification of defects subsequently discovered, see *Hobbs (Farms) v Baxenden* [1992] 1 Lloyd's Rep. 54, but note that in *Hamble Fisheries v L Gardner* [1999] 2 Lloyd's Rep. 1 and [1999] Times L.R. 7 it was held that a manufacturer was under no duty to inform remote purchasers of defects whose only effect was to cause business interruption and economic loss, thereby declining to accept the admired Canadian decision in *Rivtow Marine* [1974].

7. Art.9(b) is reproduced in our Act, s.5(4), as follows: "No damages shall be awarded . . . in respect of any . . . damage to any property if the amount which would fall to be so awarded . . . does not exceed £275." Do you think this an accurate transposition?

Section 2.—Premises

Prologue to Murphy v Brentwood D.C.

In the early 1960s Mrs Dutton bought a house on the newish Gossamer Estate in Bognor Regis. This was a bad buy, since the house had been built without sufficient foundations on a rubbish tip. Of course the builder was very much to blame, and he paid Mrs Dutton £625 against her repair costs of £2,240. She sued the local authority for the balance, for it had negligently failed to exercise its statutory power to prevent the house being built in breach of Building Regulations.

Lord Denning wrote later that the case was "one of the most important of modern times," and that "Mrs Dutton was not injured herself. The ceiling did not fall down on her. The damage to her was simply financial damage. . . . Was she entitled to recover that economic loss?" (*The Discipline of Law* (1979) 255, 264.) Earlier, in the Court of Appeal he had held her so entitled, saying:

> "The damage done here was not solely economic loss. It was physical damage to the house. If counsel's submission were right, it would mean that, if the inspector negligently passes the house as properly built and it collapses and injures a person, the council are liable: but, if the owner discovers the defect in time to repair it—and he does repair it—the council are not liable. That is an impossible distinction. They are liable in either case. I would say the same about the manufacturer of an article. If he makes it negligently, with a latent defect (so that it breaks to pieces and injures someone), he is undoubtedly liable. Suppose that the defect is discovered in time to prevent the injury. Surely he is liable for the cost of repair." ([1972] 1 Q.B. 373 at 394)

Six years later the House of Lords, in *Anns v Merton LBC* [1978] A.C. 728, effectively upheld this ingenious but disingenuous decision. Like Lord Atkin's speech in *Donoghue v Stevenson* the speech of Lord Wilberforce in *Anns* contains both a general principle and a specific holding. The general principle, about the circumstances under which it is right to hold that a duty relationship exists, has been disavowed on many subsequent occasions and is now not authoritative. As regards the duty Lord Wilberforce said:

> "Through the trilogy of cases in this House, *Donoghue v Stevenson* [above, p.21], *Hedley Byrne & Co v Heller & Partners* [below, p.57] and *Home Office v Dorset Yacht Co* [below, p.84] the position has been reached that in order to establish that a duty of care arises in a particular situation, it is not necessary to bring the facts of that situation within those of previous situations in which a duty of care has been held to exist. Rather the question has to be approached in two stages. First one has to ask whether, as between the alleged wrongdoer and the person who has suffered damage there is a sufficient relationship of proximity or neighbourhood such that, in the reasonable contemplation of the former, carelessness on his part may be likely to cause damage to the latter, in which case a prima facie duty arises. Secondly, if the first question is answered affirmatively, it is necessary to consider whether there are any considerations which ought to negative, or to reduce or limit the scope of the duty or the class of person to whom it is owed or the damages to which a breach of it may give rise . . . "

As regards the damage in the case of *Anns*, Lord Wilberforce said:

> "If classification is required, the relevant damage is in my opinion material, physical damage and what is recoverable is the amount of expenditure necessary to restore the dwelling to a condition in which it is no longer a danger to the health and safety of persons occupying it."

The specific holding, that if the building were presently or imminently dangerous to health or safety, the local authority which had negligently allowed it to be built in breach of statutory regulations was liable to the occupier at common law for the economic loss involved, was dramatically overruled after 13 years of confusion.

MURPHY v BRENTWOOD D.C.

House of Lords [1991] 1 A.C. 398; [1990] 3 W.L.R. 414; [1990] 2 All E.R. 908; [1990] 2 Lloyd's Rep. 467; 89 L.G.R. 24 (noted [1991] Camb.L.J. 24; (1990) 106 L.Q.R. 525)

Claim by purchaser against local authority for reduced value of badly constructed house

In 1970 the plaintiff bought one of 160 houses built pursuant to plans approved by the defendant local authority on the report of independent consulting engineers who had carelessly failed to note an error in calculation which rendered inadequate the concrete raft foundation necessitated by the sloping nature of the site. In 1981 the plaintiff noticed cracks, and the defect which caused the settlement was discovered. He could not afford the £40,000 needed to repair it, so in 1986 he sold it for £35,000 less than the proper market price to a builder who was still living in it, unrepaired, at the time of suit. Despite the doubts cast on *Anns* by *D & F Estates* [1989] A.C. 177, the Court of Appeal held that the local authority, treated as responsible for the negligence of the engineers to whom they had entrusted the vetting of the plans, must pay the diminution in value, seeing that the house was "imminently dangerous." ([1991] 1 A.C. 398). Six Lords of Appeal and the Lord Chancellor heard the appeal, and unanimously allowed it. *Dutton* and *Anns* were overruled.

Lord Keith: ... It being recognised that the nature of the loss held to be recoverable in *Anns* was pure economic loss, the next point for examination is whether the avoidance of loss of that nature fell within the scope of any duty of care owed to the plaintiffs by the local authority. On the basis of the law as it stood at the time of the decision the answer to that question must be in the negative. The right to recover for pure economic loss, not flowing from physical injury, did not then extend beyond the situation where the loss had been sustained through reliance on negligent misstatements, as in *Hedley Byrne*. There is room for the view that an exception is to be found in *Morrison Steamship Co v Greystoke Castle (cargo owners)* [1947] A.C. 265. That case, which was decided by a narrow majority, may, however, be regarded as turning on specialties of maritime law concerned in the relationship of joint adventurers at sea. Further, though the purposes of the 1936 Act as regards securing compliance with building byelaws covered the avoidance of injury to the safety or health of inhabitants of houses and of members of the public generally, these purposes did not cover the avoidance of pure economic loss to owners of buildings (see *Governors of the Peabody Donation Fund v Sir Lindsay Parkinson & Co Ltd* [1985] A.C. 210 at 241). On analysis, the nature of the duty held by *Anns* to be incumbent on the local authority went very much further than a duty to take reasonable care to prevent injury to safety or health. The duty held to exist may be formulated as one to take reasonable care to avoid putting a future inhabitant owner of a house in a position in which he is threatened, by reason of a defect in the house, with avoidable physical injury to person or health and is obliged, in order to continue to occupy the house without suffering such injury, to expend money for the purpose of rectifying the defect.

The existence of a duty of that nature should not, in my opinion, be affirmed without a careful examination of the implications of such affirmation. To start with, if such a duty is incumbent on the local authority, a similar duty must necessarily be incumbent also on the builder of the house. If the builder of the house is to be so subject, there can be no grounds in logic or in principle for not extending liability on like grounds to the manufacturer of a chattel. That would open up an exceedingly wide field of claims, involving the introduction of something in the nature of a transmissible warranty of quality. The purchaser of an article who discovered that it suffered from a dangerous defect before that defect had caused any damage would be entitled to recover from the manufacturer the cost of rectifying the defect, and, presumably, if the article was not capable of economic repair, the amount of loss sustained through discarding it. Then it would be open to question whether there should not also be a right to recovery where the defect renders the article not dangerous but merely useless. The economic loss in either case would be the same. There would also be a problem where the defect causes the destruction of the article itself, without causing any personal injury or damage to other property. A similar problem could arise, if the *Anns* principle is to be treated as confined to real property, where a building collapses when unoccupied . . .

In my opinion it is clear that *Anns* did not proceed on any basis of established principle, but introduced a new species of liability governed by a principle indeterminate in character but having the potentiality of covering a wide range of situations, involving chattels as well as real property, in which it had never hitherto been thought that the law of negligence had any proper place. . . .

In my opinion there can be no doubt that *Anns* has for long been widely regarded as an unsatisfactory decision. . . . I think it must now be recognised that it did not proceed on any basis of principle at all, but constituted a remarkable example of judicial legislation. It has engendered a vast spate of litigation, and each of the cases in the field which have reached this House has been distinguished. Others have been distinguished in the Court of Appeal. The result has been to keep the effect of the decision within reasonable bounds, but that has been achieved only . . . by refusing to accept the logical implications of the decision itself. These logical implications show that the case properly considered has potentiality for collision with long-established principles regarding liability in the tort of negligence for economic loss. There can be no doubt that to depart from the decision would re-establish a degree of certainty in this field of law which it has done a remarkable amount to upset.

So far as policy considerations are concerned, it is no doubt the case that extending the scope of the tort of negligence may tend to inhibit carelessness and improve standards of manufacture and construction. On the other hand, overkill may present its own disadvantages . . . . There may be room for the view that *Anns*-type liability will tend to encourage owners of buildings found to be dangerous to repair rather than run the risk of injury. The owner may, however, and perhaps quite often does, prefer to sell the building at its diminished value, as happened in the present case.

My Lords, I would hold that *Anns* was wrongly decided as regards the scope of any private law duty of care resting on local authorities in relation to their function of taking steps to secure compliance with building byelaws or regulations and should be departed from.

Lord Bridge: . . . If a manufacturer negligently puts into circulation a chattel containing a latent defect which renders it dangerous to persons or property, the manufacturer, on the well-known principles established by *Donoghue v Stevenson* [above, p.21], will be liable in tort for injury to persons or damage to property which the chattel causes. But if a manufacturer produces and sells a chattel which is merely defective in quality, even to the extent that it is valueless for the purpose for which it is intended, the manufacturer's liability at common law arises only under and by reference to the terms of any contract to which he is a party in relation to the chattel; the common law does not impose on him any liability in tort to persons to whom he owes no duty in contract but who, having acquired the chattel, suffer economic loss because the chattel is defective in quality. If a dangerous defect in a chattel is discovered before it causes any personal injury or damage to property, because the danger is now known and the chattel cannot be safely used unless the defect is repaired, the defect becomes merely a defect in quality. The chattel is either capable of repair at economic cost or it is worthless and must be scrapped. In either case the loss sustained by the owner or hirer of the chattel is purely economic. It is recoverable against any party who owes the loser a relevant contractual duty. But it is not recoverable in tort in the absence of a special relationship of proximity imposing on the tortfeasor a duty of care to safeguard the plaintiff from economic loss. There is no such special relationship between the manufacturer of a chattel and a remote owner or hirer.

I believe that these principles are equally applicable to buildings. . . . The only qualification I would make to this is that, if a building stands so close to the boundary of a building owner's land that after discovery of the dangerous defect it remains a potential source of injury to persons or property on neighbouring land or on the highway, the building owner ought, in principle, to be entitled to recover in tort from the negligent builder the cost of obviating the danger, whether by repair or by demolition, so far as that cost is necessarily incurred in order to protect himself from potential liability to third parties.

Lord Ackner, Lord Oliver and **Lord Jauncey** agreed with **Lord Keith** (with whom **Lord Brandon** also agreed) and **Lord Bridge; Lord Mackay L.C.** concurred in the result.

Notes:

1. Although there is another view this decision is entirely right: to make the builder liable for the economic loss suffered by the consumer was inconsistent with the law relating to the manufacturer of chattels, and to impose liability on the local authority for failure to prevent the builder causing such loss was fundamentally incompatible with the general law of negligence, especially in the absence of any special relationship between the authority and the consumer.

2. Certain dicta in *Murphy*, however, suggest that one may not be able to recover for *physical harm* due to a defect once it has been discovered. This is not so. Where the plaintiff tenant fell down the stairs outside his council house, which he well knew were unguarded and unlit, the defendant was held liable notwithstanding the prior "discovery" of this "defect", as it was part of a building which the defendant itself had designed and built (*Targett v Torfaen B.C.* [1992] 3 All E.R. 27).

3. The "qualification" in the above extract from Lord Bridge's speech may prove puzzling, and Lord Oliver expressly reserved his position on the point. It does indeed seem that there are cases where, though one is not liable merely for causing a person financial loss, one may be liable for exposing him to a legal liability, which it costs him money to meet. In *The Esso Bernicia* [1989] 1 All E.R. 37 (see above, p.26) the owner of a tanker became bound by statute to pay the operator of a terminal for the damage done to it by the tanker in a collision which was attributable to a defect in a tug built by the defendants. The House of Lords held that they were liable in tort to indemnify the plaintiff for that sum. In this connection one may consider *The Greystoke Castle* (referred to by Lord Keith, above, p.31) where the owners of cargo on a ship with which the defendant collided were held able to claim the sums they became bound to pay their carrier under the general law (average) though the cargo itself had suffered no damage.

4. Speaking of *Murphy*, in *Department of the Environment v Thomas Bates & Son*, decided the same day, Lord Keith said:

> "The process of reasoning by which the House reached its conclusion necessarily included close examination of the position of the builder who was primarily responsible, through lack of care in the construction process, for the presence of defects in the building. It was the unanimous view that, while the builder would be liable under the principle of *Donoghue v Stevenson* in the event of the defect, before it had been discovered, causing physical injury to persons or damage to property other than the building itself, there was no sound basis in principle for holding him liable for the pure economic loss suffered by a purchaser who discovered the defect, however such discovery might come about, and who was required to expend money in order to make the building safe and suitable for its intended purpose."
> ([1990] 2 All E.R. 943 at 946).

5. The pipework in a chemical factory was found to be cracked. No cause of action in tort arose on the cracking, since this was the manifestation of a defect not the occurrence of damage. Later the cracked pipework caused damage to surrounding property: that was when the cause of action arose. *Nitrigin Eireann Toerant v Inco Alloys* [1992] 1 All E.R. 854.

6. The undeniable break-up of Anglophone common law is not due merely to local legislative diversity or even the Europeanisation of English Law: Canada and Australia have declined to follow *Murphy*, and New Zealand's similar refusal has been accepted by the Privy Council: *Invercargill City Council v Hamlin* [1996] 1 All E.R. 756.

7. *Murphy* was applied by the Court of Appeal in *Bellefield Computer Services v Turner and Sons* [2000] B.L.R. 97: a builder who constructed a wall, inadequate as a fire-wall, between the storage area and the rest of a dairy was liable for the consequent damage to stock but not to the rest of the building.

It seems that if the builder has issued a certificate of adequacy, recovery might have been complete, such being the effect of *Hedley Byrne*, as extended. Thus in *Payne v John Setchell* [2002] B.L.R. 489 the defendants designed and installed raft foundations for cottages which were being reconstructed. They issued a certificate of satisfactory completion. The claimants were subsequent purchasers of the cottages which began to settle by reason of the inadequacy of the foundations and their claim succeeded, since they had relied on the certificate, as the defendants should have expected. The claim under the Defective Premises Act s.1 was time-barred (ten years from completion); and the claimants could not rely on the Latent Damage Act 1986. This enactment grants to a person acquiring property in which an earlier owner had a cause of action for negligence, but did not know of it, a new cause of action on discovering the material facts; this was inapplicable because the previous owner, having suffered only economic loss had no negligence claim in the light of *Murphy*, and the claim for breach of contract didn't count for this purpose.

8. One might, however, ponder the following decision (*Baxall Securities v Sheard Walshaw Partnership* (Judge Bowsher Q.C., TCC, October 30, 2000): Owing to the fault of the defendant architects a building now occupied by the claimants was badly designed in that (a) there were no overflows on the roof to prevent flooding when rains were heavy, and (b) the internal pipework was inadequate. The defendant architects, who were held to owe a duty not only to their client but also to subsequent occupiers, were not liable for a flood due to (a), since that was a defect which could have been discovered by the claimants and their advisers, but were liable for a second flood to which (b) contributed, this defect being undetectable.

DEFECTIVE PREMISES ACT 1972

1.—(1) A person taking on work for or in connection with the provision of a dwelling (whether the dwelling is provided by the erection or by the conversion or enlargement of a building) owes a duty—

(a) if the dwelling is provided to the order of any person, to that person; and
(b) without prejudice to paragraph (a) above, to every person who acquires an interest (whether legal or equitable) in the dwelling;

to see that the work which he takes on is done in a workmanlike or, as the case case may be, professional manner, with proper materials and so that as regards that work the dwelling will be fit for habitation when completed.

(2) A person who takes on any such work for another on terms that he is to do it in accordance with instructions given by or on behalf of that other shall, to the extent to which he does it properly in accordance with those instructions, be treated for the purposes of this section as discharging the duty imposed on him by subsection (1) above except where he owes a duty to that other to warn him of any defects in the instructions and fails to discharge that duty.

(3) A person shall not be treated for the purposes of subsection (2) above as having given instructions for the doing of work merely because he has agreed to the work being done in a specified manner, with specified materials or to a specified design.

(4) A person who—

(a) in the course of a business which consists of or includes providing or arranging for the provision of dwellings or installations in dwellings; or
(b) in the exercise of a power of making such provision or arrangements conferred by or by virtue of any enactment;

arranges for another to take on work for or in connection with the provision of a dwelling shall be treated for the purposes of this section as included among the persons who have taken on the work.

(5) Any cause of action in respect of a breach of the duty imposed by this section shall be deemed, for the purposes of the Limitation Act [1980], to have accrued at the time when the dwelling was completed, but if after that time a person who has done work for or in connection with the provision of the dwelling does further work to rectify the work he has already done, any such cause of action in respect of that further work shall be deemed for those purposes to have accrued at the time when the further work was finished.

. . .

Questions:

1. Is this a duty *of care*? Is the liability imposed herein as strict as that imposed on the manufacturer of products by the Consumer Protection Act 1987? Do the two Acts apply to the same kinds of damage?

2. Do the factual differences between buildings and chattels justify distinct legislative treatment or permit the application of similar common law principles?

3. Does this section apply where the fault is not in the work done but in not doing more work? Yes, according to *Andrews v Schooling Independent* [1991] Times L.R. 149 (damp penetrated plaintiff's flat because work was not done in the basement, not demised).

4. Consider s.1(2). A builder is instructed by a developer to use a material which in the builder's view is dangerously flammable. He so informs the developer but the developer tells him to proceed regardless and the builder does so. The material catches fire; the building is burnt down and some of its occupants badly injured. The developer is bankrupt. Is the builder liable (a) under the Act, (b) at all?

Note:

This Act is Parliament's solution to the problem of defective housing (jerry-building) which the court in *Anns* was also tackling, though without reference to the Act which was already in force. The House could be forgiven for not having the Act in the forefront of its mind, because for many years s.1 of the Act was not litigated at all. That is because s.1 is ousted by s.2 if an approved insurance policy has been supplied and is in force. For some time a policy was indeed officially approved, but approval was then withdrawn, and the first case to impose liability under section 1 was the judgment of Latham J. in *Mirza v Bhandal*, April 27, 1999.

The defective work has to render the dwelling unfit for habitation (*Thompson v Clive Alexander* (1992) 59 Building L.R. 77), but it is to be noted that the Act does *NOT* impose liability on "a person taking on work for or in connection with a dwelling" but on "a person taking on work for or in connection with *the provision* of a dwelling", which is a very different (and less common) matter.

WHEAT v E LACON & CO

House of Lords [1966] A.C. 552; [1966] 2 W.L.R. 581; 110 S.J. 149; [1966] 1 All E.R. 582 (noted (1966) 82 L.Q.R. 465)

Action against occupier in respect of visitor's death

On the facts stated below, Winn J. held that Lacons, as occupier, owed the deceased a duty to take care, but that their breach did not cause his death. In the Court of Appeal a majority held that Lacons owed the deceased no duty as occupier ([1966] 1 Q.B. 335). The plaintiff's appeal to the House of Lords was dismissed on the grounds that, although Lacons owed an occupier's duty to the deceased, the duty was not broken.

Lord Denning: My Lords, The "Golfers Arms" at Great Yarmouth is owned by the brewery company, E Lacon & Co Ltd The ground floor was run as a public-house by Mr Richardson as manager for the brewery company. The first floor was used by Mr and Mrs Richardson as their private dwelling. In the summer Mrs Richardson took in guests for her private profit. Mr and Mrs Wheat and their family were summer guests of Mrs Richardson. About 9 p.m. one evening, when it was getting dark, Mr Wheat fell down the back staircase in the private portion and was killed. Winn J. held that there were two causes; (i) the handrail was too short because it did not stretch to the foot of the stairs; (ii) someone had taken the bulb out of the light at the top of the stairs.

The case raises this point of law: did the brewery company owe any duty to Mr Wheat to see that the handrail was safe to use or to see that the stairs were properly lighted? That depends on whether the brewery company was "an occupier" of the private portion of the "Golfers Arms," and Mr Wheat its "visitor" within the Occupiers' Liability Act 1957: for, if so, the brewery company owed him the "common duty of care." . . .

In the Occupiers' Liability Act 1957, the word "occupier" is used in the same sense as it was used in the common law cases on occupiers' liability for dangerous premises. It was simply a convenient word to denote a person who had a sufficient degree of control over premises to put him under a duty of care towards those who came lawfully on to the premises . . . This duty is simply a particular instance of the general duty of care which each man owes to his "neighbour." When Lord Esher first essayed a definition of this general duty, he used the occupiers' liability as an instance of it: see *Heaven v Pender* ((1883) 11 Q.B.D. 503 at 508–509); and when Lord Atkin eventually formulated the general duty in acceptable terms, he, too, used occupier's liability as an illustration: see *Donoghue v Stevenson* [above, p.21]. Translating this general principle into its particular application to dangerous premises, it becomes simply this: wherever a person has a sufficient degree of control over premises that he ought to realise that any failure on his part to use care may result in injury to a person coming lawfully there, then he is an "occupier" and the person coming lawfully there is his "visitor": and the "occupier" is under a duty to his "visitor" to use reasonable care. In order to be an "occupier" it is not necessary for a person to have entire control over the premises. He need not have exclusive occupation. Suffice it that he has some degree of control. He may share the control with others. Two or more may be "occupiers." And whenever this happens, each is under a duty to use care towards persons coming lawfully on to the premises, dependent on his degree of control. If each fails in his duty, each is liable to a visitor who is injured in consequence of his failure, but each may have a claim to contribution from the other.

The position is best shown by examining the cases in four groups.

First, where a landlord let premises by demise to a tenant, he was regarded as parting with all control over them. He did not retain any degree of control, even though he had undertaken to repair the structure. Accordingly, he was held to be under no duty to any person coming lawfully on to the premises, save only to the tenant under the agreement to repair. In *Cavalier v Pope* ([1906] A.C. 428) it was argued that the premises were under the control of the landlord because of his agreement to repair; but the House of Lords rejected that argument. That case has now been overruled by s.4 of the [Defective Premises Act 1972, next below] to the extent therein mentioned.

Secondly, where an owner let floors or flats in a building to tenants, but did not demise the common staircase or the roof or some other parts, he was regarded as having retained control of all parts not demised by him. Accordingly, he was held to be under a duty in respect of those retained parts to all persons coming lawfully on to the premises. The extent of the duty is now simply the common duty of care. But the old cases still apply so as to show that the landlord is responsible for all parts not demised by him, on the ground that he is regarded as being sufficiently in control of them to impose on him a duty of care to all persons coming lawfully on to the premises.

Thirdly, where an owner did not let premises to a tenant but only licensed a person to occupy them on terms which did not amount to a demise, the owner still having the right to do repairs, he was regarded as being sufficiently in control of the structure to impose on him a duty towards all persons coming lawfully on to the premises. So he was held liable for a visitor who fell on the defective step to the front door in *Hawkins v Coulsdon and Purley U.D.C.* ([1954] 1 Q.B. 319); and to the occupier's wife for the defective ceiling which fell on her in *Greene v Chelsea B.C.* ([1954] 2 Q.B. 127) . . .

Fourthly, where an owner employed an independent contractor to do work on premises or a structure, the owner was usually still regarded as sufficiently in control of the place as to be under a duty towards all those who might lawfully come here. In some cases he might fulfil that duty by entrusting the work to the independent contractor: see *Haseldine v CA Daw & Son* ([1941] 2 K.B. 343) and s.2(4) of the Act of 1957. In other cases he might only be able to fulfil it by exercising proper supervision himself over the contractor's work, using due diligence himself to prevent damage from unusual danger. But in addition to the owner, the courts regarded the independent contractor as himself being sufficiently in control of the place where he worked as to owe a duty of care towards all persons coming lawfully here. He was then said to be an "occupier" also: see *Hartwell's* case ([1947] K.B. 901); but this is only a particular instance of his general duty of care: see *Billings (AC) & Sons Ltd v Riden* ([1958] A.C. 240), *per* Lord Reid.

In the light of these cases, I ask myself whether the brewery company had a sufficient degree of control over the premises to put them under a duty to a visitor. Obviously they had complete control over the ground floor and were "occupiers" of it. But I think that they had also sufficient control over the private portion. They had not let it out to Mr Richardson by a demise. They had only granted him a licence to occupy it, having a right themselves to do repairs. That left them with a residuary degree of control. They were in my opinion "an occupier" within the Act of 1957. Mr Richardson, who had a licence to occupy, had also a considerable degree of control. So had Mrs Richardson, who catered for summer guests. All three of them were, in my opinion, "occupiers" of the private portion of the "Golfers Arms". There is no difficulty in having more than one occupier at one and the same time, each of whom is under a duty of care to visitors.

What did the common duty of care demand of each of these occupiers towards their visitors? Each was under a duty to take such a care as "in all the circumstances of the case" was reasonable to see that the visitor would be reasonably safe. So far as the respondents were concerned, the circumstances demanded that on the ground floor they should, by their servants, take care not only of the structure of the building, but also the furniture, the state of the floors and lighting, and so forth, at all hours of day or night when the premises were open. In regard to the private portion, however, the circumstances did not demand so much of the respondents. They ought to have seen that the structure was reasonably safe, including the handrail, and that the system of lighting was efficient; but I doubt whether they were bound to see that the lights were properly switched on or the rugs laid safely on the floor. The respondents were entitled to leave those day-to-day matters to Mr and Mrs Richardson. They, too, were occupiers. The circumstances of the case demanded that Mr and Mrs Richardson should take care of those matters in the private portion of the house. And of other matters too. If they had realised that the handrail was dangerous, they should have reported it to the respondents.

We are not concerned here with Mr and Mrs Richardson. The judge has absolved them from any negligence and there is no appeal. We are only concerned with the respondents. They were, in my opinion, occupiers and under a duty of care . . . but . . . I can see no evidence of any breach of duty by the respondents. So far as the handrail was concerned, the evidence was over-whelming that no-one had any reason before this accident to suppose that it was in the least dangerous. So far as the light was concerned, the proper inference was that it was removed by some stranger shortly before Mr Wheat went down the staircase. Neither the respondents nor Mr and Mrs Richardson could be blamed for the act of a stranger.

I would, therefore, dismiss this appeal.

Note:

The manufacturer is responsible at common law for the condition of the ginger beer and the occupier is responsible by statute for the state of the premises: both are under a duty to take reasonable care. This equation is delusive, however, since the duties differ in their basis and in their extent. The manufacturer is responsible because he *does* make the thing dangerous, whereas the occupier is responsible because he *can* make the thing safe; the manufacturer's duty arises from his action, the occupier's from his capacity to act (he must because he can). And the extent of the duties differs. Unlike the manufacturer, the occupier is not just under a duty not to cause harm to people; he must prevent harm to them; he must mend the premises and tend the visitor. For example, he must protect the visitor against other visitors. Those other visitors of course owe a duty to everyone present or probably present, but that duty is only the standard one of not hurting them; they are not responsible save in so far as they make the place dangerous; the occupier must make it reasonably safe for the visitor, and is consequently liable for a culpable omission to do so.

The occupier's duty extends also to goods on his premises with his permission; he must protect them from damage, but he need not, unless he is a hotelier, protect them from theft. The distinction is sensible; thieves are not dangerous. The duty to protect goods from theft comes not from *being* in charge of the place where they are but *taking* charge of the goods themselves, *assuming* control of them; the bailee's duty arises not from his capacity to protect the goods but from his undertaking to do so. Indeed, there may be an assumption of responsibility sufficient to give rise to a duty to take positive steps to protect the goods even if there is no proper bailment or even contract (*The Rigoletto* [2000] 2 Lloyd's Rep. 532, below p.306). Liability for failure to take such positive steps is somewhat easier to exclude than liability for damage caused by positive negligence (*Johnson Matthey v Constantine Terminals* [1976] 2 Lloyd's Rep. 215).

Thus we have at least three different sources of duties in tort; the manufacturer's stems from the act, the occupier's from his power to act and the bailee's from his undertaking to act. They are all (need it be said?)

under a duty to take reasonable care; but that simplistic formula masks the difference between the obligation not to act unreasonably and the obligation to act reasonably.

The positive duty may require a finding that the defendant was occupier. Thus trustees who let out a hall owed no duty to visitors injured by the inappropriate use to which the hirers put it: *Wheeler v St. Mary's Hall, The Times*, October 10, 1989. Members' clubs present problems, since the individual member is probably not an occupier and perhaps also not exactly a visitor. If a committee member takes upon himself a task during which he learns of a danger which may harm fellow members unless he warns them, the committee may be liable if he fails to do so. And in *Melhuish v Clifford* (August 18, 1998) where a member was injured leaving by an unlit exit, the committee was held vicariously liable for the fault of the barman in turning off (or perhaps not turning on) the light. But in *Robertson v Ridley* [1989] 2 All E.R. 474 where there was a simple failure to repair a pothole in the driveway, the Court of Appeal had held that in a members' club no duty to take positive steps to render the premises reasonably safe is owed by any member, even a member of the committee, to any other member. In *Melhuish* this decision was said to be obsolete. One wonders what can have made it so.

Question

Why do we have a special rule for people who are injured on someone else's land? Where else are people apt to suffer injury? In what locations is injury least likely to lead to compensation?

DEFECTIVE PREMISES ACT 1972

4. Landlord's duty of care in virtue of obligation or right to repair premises demised

(1) Where premises are let under a tenancy which puts on the landlord an obligation to the tenant for the maintenance or repair of the premises, the landlord owes to all persons who might reasonably be expected to be affected by defects in the state of the premises a duty to take such care as is reasonable in all the circumstances to see that they are reasonably safe from personal injury or from damage to their property caused by a relevant defect.

(2) The said duty is owed if the landlord knows (whether as a result of being notified by the tenant or otherwise) or if he ought in all the circumstances to have known of the relevant defect.

(3) In this section "relevant defect" means a defect in the state of the premises existing at or after the material time and arising from, or continuing because of, an act or omission by the landlord which constitutes or would if he had had notice of the defect, have constituted a failure by him to carry out his obligation to the tenant for the maintenance or repair of the premises; and for the purposes of the foregoing provision "the material time" means—

(a) where the tenancy commenced before this Act, the commencement of this Act; and
(b) in all other cases, the earliest of the following times, that is to say—
  (i) the time when the tenancy commences;
  (ii) the time when the tenancy agreement is entered into;
  (iii) the time when possession is taken of the premises in contemplation of the letting.

(4) Where premises are let under a tenancy which expressly or impliedly gives the landlord the right to enter the premises to carry out any description of maintenance or repair of the premises, then, as from the time when he first is, or by notice or otherwise can put himself, in a position to exercise the right and so long as he is or can put himself in that position, he shall be treated for the purposes of subsections (1) to (3) above (but for no other purpose) as if he were under an obligation to the tenant for that description of maintenance or repair of the premises; but the landlord shall not owe the tenant any duty by virtue of this subsection in respect of any defect in the state of the premises arising from or continuing because of, a failure to carry out an obligation expressly imposed on the tenant by the tenancy.

(5) For the purposes of this section obligations imposed or rights given by any enactment in virtue of a tenancy shall be treated as imposed or given by the tenancy.

(6) This section applies to a right of occupation given by contract or any enactment and not amounting to a tenancy as if the right were a tenancy, and "tenancy" and cognate expressions shall be construed accordingly.

Notes:

1. Since the very reason one pays rent is in order to occupy the rented premises, it is, as Lord Denning explained in *Wheat v Lacon*, the tenant rather than the landlord who is under the occupier's duty to take steps to see that visitors are reasonably safe. But tenants who pay very low rents probably cannot afford to do repairs, and short-term tenants cannot be expected to do substantial work, so s.8(1) of the Landlord and Tenant Act 1985 requires the landlord of extremely low-rent housing to keep it fit for human habitation and s.11 (below) specifies the matters which the landlord must attend to in leases of up to seven years. These provisions only affect the contract between the landlord and the tenant. It is s.4 of the Defective Premises Act 1972 which imposes on the landlord a duty to save third parties, including the tenant, from physical harm by taking reasonable steps to discover and remedy defects in the premises which are his responsibility rather than that of the tenant-occupier.

2. Note that the landlord is liable only for injuries due to a "relevant defect", that is, one which it is the duty of the landlord, under his contract with the tenant, or within his powers under that contract, to correct. Furthermore, the injuries must be due to a failure on the part of the landlord to use reasonable care to prevent them. The beneficiaries of the landlord's duty include the tenant himself (*Sykes v Harry* [2001] Q.B. 1014) as well as others on the premises and even persons outside the premises (injured, perhaps, by the fall of a badly repaired window-frame or notoriously loose roof-tile). This section has therefore rendered *Mint v Good* (below p.202) otiose.

3. Unlike some other systems, the common law has traditionally drawn a very sharp distinction between chattels and land. The builder and the manufacturer used to be exposed to different liabilities in tort, and to some extent this is still true of landlord and hirer.

Until 1972 the builder was free from liability once he sold the land he built on (see the rather enigmatic s.3 of the Defective Premises Act) whereas, of course, the manufacturer's liability really only started once he sold the product, and contrariwise for a period after *Anns* it seemed that the builder, unlike the manufacturer (*Muirhead v Industrial Tank Specialities* [1985] 3 All E.R. 705), might be liable to the ultimate purchaser/consumer simply because his work was defective even if it did no physical damage. It is now clear thanks to *Murphy* (above, p.31) that at common law the builder's liability is like that of the manufacturer (but only at common law, for though the Consumer Protection Act 1987 covers defective building materials it does not cover defective buildings): both are liable whenever, but only if, they are at fault and their unhandiwork causes foreseeable physical damage.

A distinction remains between hirer and landlord, however. Whereas the person who hires out a chattel which he knows or ought to know to be dangerously defective is liable to anyone foreseeably injured by it, the landlord is not liable to persons injured by defects in the unfurnished property he lets out just because he ought to have known of them (*McNerny v Lambeth L.B.C.* [1989] New L.J. 114; [1989] 1 E.G.L.R. 81, CA). This is because *Donoghue v Stevenson* remains pre-empted at common law by *Cavalier v Pope* [1906] A.C. 428, which still applies unless the case can be brought under s.4 of this Act.

LANDLORD AND TENANT ACT 1985

11.—(1) In a lease to which this section applies (as to which see sections 13 and 14) there is implied a covenant by the lessor—

- (a) to keep in repair the structure and exterior of the dwelling-house (including drains, gutters and external pipes),
- (b) to keep in repair and proper working order the installations in the dwelling-house for the supply of water, gas and electricity and for sanitation (including basins, sinks, baths and sanitary conveniences, but not other fixtures, fittings and appliances for making use of the supply of water, gas or electricity), and
- (c) to keep in repair and proper working order the installations in the dwelling-house for space heating and heating water.

(2) The covenant implied by subsection (1) ("the lessor's repairing covenant") shall not be construed as requiring the lessor—

(a) to carry out works or repairs for which the lessee is liable by virtue of his duty to use the premises in a tenant-like manner, or would be so liable but for an express covenant on his part,
(b) to rebuild or reinstate the premises in the case of destruction or damage by fire, or by tempest, flood or other inevitable accident, or
(c) to keep in repair or maintain anything which the lessee is entitled to remove from the dwelling-house.

(3) In determining the standard of repair required by the lessor's repairing covenant, regard shall be had to the age, character, and prospective life of the dwelling-house and the locality in which it is situated. . . .

13.—(1) Section 11 (repairing obligations) applies to a lease of a dwelling-house granted for a term of less than seven years. . . .

Note:
Section 353A of the Housing Act 1985 now reads:

"(1) It is the duty of the person having control of a house in multiple occupation and of the person managing it, to take such steps as are reasonably practicable to prevent the occurrence of a state of affairs calling for the service of a notice or further notice under s.352 [notice requiring execution of works to render house fit for number of occupants]. (2) A breach of that duty is actionable in damages at the suit of any tenant or other occupant of the premises, or any other person who suffers loss, damage or personal injury in consequence of the breach."

OCCUPIERS' LIABILITY ACT 1984

1.—(1) The rules enacted by this section shall have effect, in place of the rules of the common law, to determine—

(a) whether any duty is owed by a person as occupier of premises to persons other than his visitors in respect of any risk of their suffering injury on the premises by reason of any danger due to the state of the premises or to things done or omitted to be done on them; and
(b) if so, what that duty is.

(2) For the purposes of this section, the persons who are to be treated respectively as an occupier of any premises (which, for those purposes, include any fixed or movable structure) and as his visitors are—

(a) any person who owes in relation to the premises the duty referred to in section 2 of the Occupiers' Liability Act 1957 (the common duty of care), and
(b) those who are his visitors for the purposes of that duty.

(3) An occupier of premises owes a duty to another (not being his visitor) in respect of any such risk as is referred to in subsection (1) above if—

(a) he is aware of the danger or has reasonable grounds to believe that it exists;

(b) he knows or has reasonable grounds to believe that the other is in the vicinity of the danger concerned or that he may come into the vicinity of the danger (in either case, whether the other has lawful authority for being in that vicinity or not); and

(c) the risk is one against which, in all the circumstances of the case, he may reasonably be expected to offer the other some protection.

(4) Where, by virtue of this section, an occupier of premises owes a duty to another in respect of such a risk, the duty is to take such care as is reasonable in all the circumstances of the case to see that he does not suffer injury on the premises by reason of the danger concerned.

(5) Any duty owed by virtue of this section in respect of a risk may, in an appropriate case, be discharged by taking such steps as are reasonable in all the circumstances of the case to give warning of the danger concerned or to discourage persons from incurring the risk.

(6) No duty is owed by virtue of this section to any person in respect of risks willingly accepted as his by that person (the question whether a risk was so accepted to be decided on the same principles as in other cases in which one person owes a duty of care to another).

(6A) At any time when the right conferred by section 2(1) of the Countryside and Rights of Way Act 2000 is exercisable in relation to land which is access land for the purposes of Part I of that Act, an occupier of the land owes (subject to subsection (6C) below) no duty by virtue of this section to any person in respect of—

(a) a risk resulting from the existence of any natural feature of the landscape, or any river, stream, ditch or pond whether or not a natural feature, or

(b) a risk of that person suffering injury when passing over, under or through any wall, fence or gate, except by proper use of the gate or of a stile.

(6B) For the purposes of subsection (6A) above, any plant, shrub or tree, of whatever origin, is to be regarded as a natural feature of the landscape.

(6C) Subsection (6A) does not prevent an occupier from owing a duty by virtue of this section in respect of any risk where the danger concerned is due to anything done by the occupier—

(a) with the intention of creating that risk, or

(b) being reckless as to whether that risk is created.

(7) No duty is owed by virtue of this section to persons using the highway, and this section does not affect any duty owed to such persons.

(8) Where a person owes a duty by virtue of this section, he does not, by reason of any breach of the duty, incur any liability in respect of any loss of or damage to property.

1A.—[In determining whether any, and if so what, duty is owed by virtue of section 1 by an occupier of land at any time when the right conferred by section 2(1) of the Countryside and Rights of Way Act 2000 is exercisable in relation to the land, regard is to be had, in particular, to—

(a) the fact that the existence of that right ought not to place an undue burden (whether financial or otherwise) on the occupier,

(b) the importance of maintaining the character of the countryside, including features of historic, traditional or archaeological interest, and

(c) any relevant guidance given under section 20 of that Act.

Notes:

1. Section 1(1). In a judgment replete with errors of law, Neill L.J. was pleased to hold in *Revill v Newbery* [1996] 1 All E.R. 291 that the opening words of s.1(1) do not mean what they conspicuously say, namely that the Act ousts the common law regarding claims against an occupier for unintended injuries suffered on the premises, a result, quite unnecessary on the facts, which he reached by quoting from the Law Commission, as if that body had any authority regarding the construction of existing enactments, which it does not. This led him to hold that not only was the Act inapplicable to a suit by an intrusive burglar injured by a shot fired by an occupier who was attempting to protect his property (and if shooting is not an act done on the premises, what is?), but that the salient fact that the defendant was the occupier was also irrelevànt. Evans L.J. had the good sense to reserve his position on the question of the applicability of the Act.

Section 1(6). In *Ratcliff v McConnell* [1999] 1 W.L.R. 670 the plaintiff, one of a party of drunk students who decided at 2.30 a.m. to go swimming in a college open air swimming pool, climbed over a locked gate, ignored a warning notice and a notice saying that use of the swimming pool was prohibited after 10 p.m., dived into the pool and broke his neck. Allowing the occupier's appeal, the Court of Appeal held that "The plaintiff was aware of the risk and willingly accepted it. Accordingly, the defendants were under no duty towards him." What is astonishing is that the trial judge ordered the defendant to pay the plaintiff damages, subject to a reduction for contributory negligence. The Court of Appeal held the defendant occupier liable in the very important case of *Tomlinson v Congleton DC* (below p.149) where the claimant injured himself in the defendant's reservoir. In the House of Lords, which unanimously allowed the defendant's appeal, there was much discussion whether the applicable enactment was the 1984 Act, since the prohibition of swimming made the claimant a trespasser when he was in the water, or the 1957 Act, on the basis that even before they entered the water the defendants owed visitors a duty to try to prevent them doing so. The discussion was futile, since the outcome (judgment for the defendant) was the same on both hypotheses.

Section 1(7). Persons using the highway do not fall under the Act, but some non-visitors are neither trespassers nor persons using the highway, namely those using a private or public right of way over undedicated land and those exercising rights under the Countryside and Rights of Way Act 2000, s.2(1). The latter become trespassers (and subject to eviction on notice) if in breach of the scheduled restrictions (vehicles, horses, dogs). In fact, of course, highway authorities, though not occupiers, do owe a duty towards users of the highway under another statute (see below, p.154), a duty unaffected by the question whether or not the victim was a trespasser against the owners of the subsoil. Under the abortive Right to Roam Bill a person exercising rights under the proposed Act was not to be treated as a visitor: his rights would therefore depend on the 1984 Act (*pace* Neill L.J.).

Section 1(8). Note the clear preference for persons over property. Damage intentionally done to a trespasser's property (cars, dogs, etc.) will fall under the law of trespass to goods (below, p.407). The occupier's privilege is merely to disembarrass his premises of the intruding chattels, and the manner of its exercise must be reasonable although the decision to exercise it need not be. On car-clamping see below, p.405.

2. In *Adams v Southern Electricity Board* [1993] Times L.R. 512, CA a 15-year old was electrocuted while yet again playing up a pole-mounted transformer whose anti-climbing device, required by statutory regulations, was in disrepair. Subject to a severe reduction for his contributory negligence, he was held entitled to claim damages *at common law*.[!] (See s.1(1)).

3. Trespassers on construction sites now have special protection, since the regulation which provides that reasonable steps must be taken to keep unauthorised persons out is actionable in damages: Construction (Design and Management) Regulations 1994, No.3140 (ex-Brussels Directive 92/57), regs 16(1) and 21.

4. A trespasser's damages are not reduced simply because he was trespassing, but only if he has unwisely endangered himself by doing so: *Westwood v Post Office* [1974] A.C. 1. This binding authority was ignored by Neill L.J. in *Revill v Newbery*.

Questions

1. The driver of a train brakes with unnecessary ferocity and three passengers fall over and are injured. One of them is travelling normally, but the others are a mother and child. The mother has taken a ticket neither for herself nor for her child and was hoping to escape detection and have a free ride. Is the carrier liable to all three?

2. Bill parked his car on Charlie's land, under a notice saying "Parking Prohibited". Doug, employed by Charlie and going about his master's business in his master's van, rounded a bend on the private drive rather faster than he had intended, lost control of the van and collided with Bill's car. Both car and van were damaged. What is the outcome?

DUNN v BRADFORD MDC

Court of Appeal [2002] EWCA Civ 1137; [2003] H.L.R. 15

Suit by tenants against local authority landlord

Mr and Mrs Dunn claimed damages from their local authority as landlords for loss, inconvenience and impairment of enjoyment arising out of the state of the rented premises at 3 Micklethwaite Lane, claiming that the landlords were in breach of the duty imposed by section 4 of the Defective Premises Act 1972. According to the expert evidence, the condition of the property was prejudicial to health by reason of dampness and mould growth due to inadequate space heating and insulation, uncontrolled ventilation, lack of extractor in the bathroom etc., and the defective installation of the damp proof course.

Chadwick L.J.: The fourth issue is whether the Dunns can rely on any duty arising under section 4 of the Defective Premises Act 1972.

In a recent decision of this Court, *Lee v Leeds City Council* [2002] H.L.R. 367, I sought to explain the effect of section 4(4) of the 1972 Act:

> "Section 4(4) of the Act requires the landlord to be treated, for the purposes of subsections (1) and (3), as if he were under an obligation to the tenant for maintenance or repair of the premises where the tenancy 'expressly or impliedly gives the landlord the right to enter the premises to carry out any description of maintenance or repair of the premises'. In those circumstances the scope and extent of the deemed obligation is commensurate with the scope and extent of the right to enter."

The tenancy agreement granted to Mrs Dunn in 1992 contained a covenant by the tenant to permit the Council's officers, contractors or agents to enter the premises for the purpose of inspection "or for the execution of repairs or improvement works". There is no dispute, therefore, that the premises at 3 Micklethwaite Lane were let under a tenancy which gave the landlord the right to enter the premises to carry out works of repair; nor that section 4(4) of the 1972 Act, in conjunction with subsections (1) and (4) of that section, imposed on the Council, as landlord, the duty to take reasonable care to ensure that persons who might reasonably be expected to be affected by defects in the state of the premises were reasonably safe from personal injury "caused by a relevant defect". But that does not lead to the conclusion that the Council was under a duty in relation to personal injury caused by defects in the design of the premises which could be remedied only by carrying out works of improvement—for the reasons which were set out in *Lee v Leeds City Council*:

> "Parliament, when enacting section 4 of the 1972 Act . . . chose to link the duty of care imposed by section 4(1) to the landlord's failure to carry out an obligation 'for the maintenance or repair' of the premises—*ibid.*, section 4(3). That is the framework within which the statutory hypothesis in section 4(4) must operate. Parliament did not, as it might have done, link the duty of care to a failure to remedy defects in any more general sense. The obligation to 'repair' has a well recognised meaning in the law of landlord and tenant; and as the cases show, it does not arise unless the object in respect of which it is imposed is out of repair. If the defect which has caused the injury in respect of which a claim is made under section 4(1) of the Act is not a defect arising from want of repair, it cannot be a 'relevant defect' for the purposes of that section."

I accept, of course, that there will be circumstances in which the only practical or sensible way (having regard, perhaps, to more modern building techniques) in which premises which are out of repair can be put back into repair will be to carry out works which do constitute improvements. . . . The authorities were reviewed in my judgment in *Lee v Leeds City Council*. . . . In the light of that review I said this:

> "The cases show that, where there is a need to repair damage to the structure, the due performance of the obligation to repair may require the landlord to remedy the design fault which is the cause of the damage. They do not support the proposition that the obligation to repair will require the landlord to remedy a design defect which has not been the cause of damage to the structure; notwithstanding that the defect may make the premises unsuitable for occupation or unfit for human habitation."

In the present case the judge directed himself that the question which he had to decide was whether any (and if so which) of the factors identified in the expert's report could have been remedied or avoided by works of repair. He went on to say this:

> " . . . only one of those factors . . . could fall into the category of lack of repair of a relevant defect. If there were defects in the damp proof course which gave rise to the presence of dampness or mould growth in the house then such would be relevant defects of the purposes of the Defective Premises Act against which the landlords, having reserved to themselves a right of entry, had an obligation to act. All the other factors listed there by Mr Wood require work to be done which I would categorise as improvements to property, that is to say neither maintaining the status quo nor restoring the status quo but going above and beyond the status quo and therefore outwith the concept of maintenance or repair."

He concluded that Mr and Mrs Dunn obtained no assistance from section 4 of the 1972 Act save to the extent that they might be able to establish that there was a defect in the damp proof installation which could and should have been (but was not) remedied by the Council.

It is submitted on behalf of the appellants that the judge placed too narrow a construction on section 4(4) of the 1972 Act. It is said that he ought to have held that a landlord who had a right to enter in order to execute "improvement works" was under a duty "to maintain the premises in a reasonable condition or alternatively (by improvement) to prevent any material deterioration of condition which affects the enjoyment of the premises by the Appellants". By that means the appellants seek to circumvent the limited scope of a duty to "repair" by invoking the statutory hypothesis required by section 4(4) so as to impose on the landlord an enhanced obligation to maintain the premises. . . .

I would accept that the landlord's right to enter extends to entry in order to carry out remedial works. That would be the position even in the absence of an express right of entry—at least in so far as those works were required to remedy defects which were a danger to health . . . I would accept, also, that the landlord's right to enter extends to entry in order to maintain the premises. But that begs the question whether the statutory hypothesis introduced by section 4(4) of the 1972 Act requires that a landlord who has the right to enter in order to carry out remedial works—which may be necessary if the premises are to be maintained in "a good condition" or in "a reasonable condition"—must be treated as if he were under an obligation to put the premises into a better condition than they were at the time when they were first let. Does the statutory hypothesis require the landlord to be treated as if he were under an obligation to remedy design defects? I think not; for the reasons which I gave in *Lee v Leeds City Council*: . . .

> " . . . the first question in this context is whether the works which would be required to remedy the inherent defects in design—which are the cause of the excessive condensation and mould—are within the expression 'any description of maintenance or repair of the premises'. If they are not, the fact that the landlord may be entitled to enter the premises in order to carry out those works does not give rise to a deemed obligation on the tenant 'for that description of maintenance or repair'" . . .

I [then] referred to the observations of Ralph Gibson L.J. in *McAuley v Bristol City Council* [1992] 1 Q.B. 134, 145: "There is, I think, no warrant for a wide construction of the words of section 4. They apply to all landlords, and not merely to local authorities, and can operate so as to impose a substantial burden upon a landlord in respect of premises under the immediate control of the tenant and in respect of which the landlord has assumed no contractual obligation."

I am not persuaded that the right of entry to execute improvement works leads to the conclusion that the landlord was under a duty to maintain the premises in "a reasonable condition" or to prevent (by improvement) any material deterioration of condition which affects the enjoyment of the premises. So to construe s.4(4) of the 1972 Act would require—as it seems to me—reading the phrase "any description of maintenance or repair" as if it extended to works of improvement which went beyond maintenance or repair. I do not think that, in the absence of clear words, Parliament should be held to have intended to impose so substantial a burden on landlords.

It follows that I would decide the fourth issue . . . against the appellants.

Waller and **Hale LJJ** agreed.

Section 3.—Economic Loss

THE NICHOLAS H (MARC RICH & CO v BISHOP ROCK MARINE CO)

House of Lords [1996] 1 A.C. 211; [1995] 3 W.L.R. 227; [1995] 3 All E.R. 307; [1995] 2 Lloyd's Rep. 299 (noted (1996) 112 L.Q.R. 209)

Action against classification society by owners of cargo sunk in vessel certified as fit to sail

Laden with cargo owned by the plaintiff, the *Nicholas H* was on its way to the Black Sea from South America when it sprang a nasty leak. It anchored off San Juan, Puerto Rico where, at the instance of the U.S. Coastguard, the owners had it inspected by Mr Ducat, a surveyor employed by the defendant classification society. He recommended that permanent repairs be effected there and then. This the owners were very reluctant to do, so they had temporary repairs done instead, and Mr Ducat agreed that provided the repairs were thoroughly and promptly checked at its destination the vessel could retain its classification for the rest of its voyage across the Atlantic. The *Nicholas H* accordingly sailed. It sank a few days later, with all cargo on board.

The plaintiffs obtained $500,000 from the shipowners (that being the statutory limit of their liability, given the tonnage of the ship), and now sued the classification society for the balance of $5,700,000.

The preliminary issue to be decided in the Commercial Court was "Whether on the facts pleaded . . . [the defendant] owed a duty of care to [the plaintiff] capable of giving rise to a liability in damages." Hirst J., answered the question in the affirmative, but the Court of Appeal unanimously reversed, and the House of Lords upheld the judgment of the Court of Appeal, Lord Lloyd dissenting strongly.

Lord Steyn: . . . on the assumption that the carelessness of the surveyor caused the loss of the cargo the question is whether in law that carelessness amounted to actionable negligence. In short, the question is simply whether in law the classification society owed a duty of care to the owners of the cargo.

At first instance Hirst J. ([1992] 2 Lloyd's Rep. 481) concluded that on the assumed facts NKK did owe the cargo owners a duty of care capable of giving rise to a liability in damages . . . the closeness of the relationship between the NKK surveyors and the owners of the cargo led him to conclude that a duty of care did arise. The Court of Appeal ([1994] 3 All E.R. 686) reversed the decision of Hirst J. . . . Contrary to the submission on behalf of the cargo owners, each member of the court held that in tort claims for physical damage a plaintiff needs to satisfy the requirements of foreseeability and proximity as well as the requirement that the imposition of tort liability is fair, just and reasonable. . . . Balcombe L.J. added that he doubted whether the words "fair, just and reasonable" impose a test additional to that of "proximity".

Mr Gross QC, who appeared on behalf of the cargo owners . . . submitted that, since the claim involved foreseeable physical damage to the cargo owners' property, the additional requirements of proximity and that it is fair, just and reasonable to impose a duty of care are inapplicable. Secondly, and assuming that those requirements are applicable, he submitted that those requirements are fulfilled. He described his way of putting the case as being squarely based on the principles laid down in *Donoghue v Stevenson* . . . and submitted that in cases of physical damage to property in which the plaintiff has a proprietary or possessory interest the only requirement is proof of reasonable foreseeability. For this proposition he relied on observations of Lord Oliver of Aylmerton in *Caparo Industries plc v Dickman* [1990] 1 All E.R. 568 at 585. Those observations, seen in context, do not support his argument. They merely underline the qualitative difference between cases of direct physical damage and indirect economic loss. The materiality of the distinction is plain. But since the decision in *Home Office v Dorset Yacht Co* [below, p.84] it has been settled law that the elements of foreseeability and proximity as well as considerations of fairness, justice and reasonableness are relevant to all cases whatever the nature of the harm sustained by the plaintiff. Saville L.J. explained ([1994] 3 All E.R. 686 at 692–693:

" . . . whatever the nature of the harm sustained by the plaintiff, it is necessary to consider the matter not only by inquiring about foreseeability but also by considering the nature of the relationship between the parties; and to be satisfied that in all the circumstances it is fair, just and reasonable to impose a duty of care. Of course . . . these three matters overlap with each other and are really facets of the same thing. For example, the relationship between the parties may be such that it is obvious that a lack of care will create a risk of harm and that as a matter of common sense and justice a duty should be imposed . . . Again in most cases of the direct infliction of physical loss or injury through carelessness, it is self-evident that a civilised system of law should hold that a duty of care has been broken, whereas the infliction of financial harm may well pose a more difficult problem. Thus the three so-called requirements for a duty of care are not to be treated as wholly separate and distinct requirements but rather as convenient and helpful approaches to the pragmatic question whether a duty should be imposed in any given case. In the end whether the law does impose a duty in any particular circumstances depends upon those circumstances . . . "

That seems to me a correct summary of the law as it now stands. It follows that I would reject the first argument of counsel for the cargo owners.

In the course of their submissions counsel took your Lordships on a tour of many of the landmark cases on negligence from *Donoghue v Stevenson* to *White v Jones* [below, p.65]. In this area the common law develops incrementally on the basis of consideration of analogous cases where a duty has been recognised or desired. But none of the cases cited provided any realistic analogy to be used as a springboard for a decision one way or the other in this case. The present case can only be decided on the basis of an intense and particular focus on all its distinctive features, and then applying established legal principles to it. No doubt those principles are capable of further development but, for present purposes, the applicable principles can readily be identified and require no re-examination.

Not surprisingly, there are substantial factors pointing in favour and against the recognition of a duty of care . . .

For convenience these factors can be considered under six headings, namely: (a) did the surveyor's carelessness cause direct physical loss; (b) did the cargo owners rely on the surveyor's recommendations; (c) the impact of the contract between the shipowners and the owners of the cargo; (d) the impact of the contract between the classification society and the shipowners; (e) the position and role of NKK and (f) policy factors arguably tending to militate against the recognition of a duty of care.

Only after an examination of these features will it be possible to address directly the element of proximity and the question whether it is fair, just and reasonable to impose a duty of care.

(a) Direct physical loss?

Council for the cargo owners argued that the present case involved the infliction of *direct* physical loss. At first glance the issue of directness may seem a matter of terminology rather than substance. In truth it is a material factor. The law more readily attaches the consequences of actionable negligence to directly inflicted physical loss than to indirectly inflicted physical loss. For example, if the NKK surveyor had carelessly dropped a lighted cigarette into a cargo hold known to contain a combustible cargo, thereby causing an explosion and the loss of the vessel and cargo, the assertion that the classification society was in breach of a duty of care might have been a strong one. That would be a paradigm case of directly inflicted physical loss. Counsel for the cargo owners referred your Lordships to *Clay v AJ Crump & Sons Ltd* [1963] 3 All E.R. 687, by way of support for the proposition that, *in this case*, there was a direct infliction of loss in the relevant sense. In that case an architect assured a demolition contractor that he could safely leave a wall standing. The demolition contractor acted on this advice. The wall collapsed on a workman. The workman sued the architect in tort. It was held that the architect owed a duty of care to the workman. The architect was primarily responsible for leaving the wall in a dangerous condition. In the present case the shipowner was primarily responsible for the vessel sailing in a seaworthy condition. The role of the NKK was a subsidiary one. In my view the carelessness of the NKK surveyor did not involve the direct infliction of physical damage in the relevant sense. That by no means concludes the answer to the general question. But it does introduce the right perspective on one aspect of the case.

(b) Reliance

It is possible to visualise direct exchanges between cargo owners and a classification society, in the context of a survey on behalf of the owners of a vessel laden with cargo, which might give rise to an assumption of responsibility in the sense explained by Lord Goff in *Henderson v Merrett Syndicates* [1994] 3 All E.R. 506 at 517–8, 533–4. In the present case there was no contact whatever between the cargo owners and the classification society. Moreover, as Saville L.J. pointed out in this case it is not even suggested that the cargo owners were aware that NKK had been brought in to survey the vessel. The cargo owners simply relied on the owners of the vessel to keep the vessel seaworthy and to look after the cargo. Saville L.J. and Balcombe L.J. regarded this feature as sufficient to demonstrate that the necessary element of proximity was absent. I would approach the matter differently. In my view this feature is not necessarily decisive but it also contributes to placing the claim in the correct perspective.

(c) The bill of lading contracts

. . . The dealings between shipowners and cargo owners are based on a contractual structure, the Hague Rules, and tonnage limitation, on which the insurance of international trade depends. Underlying it is the system of double or overlapping insurance of cargo. Cargo owners take out direct insurance in respect of the cargo. Shipowners take out liability risks insurance in respect of breaches of their duties of care in respect of the cargo. The insurance system is structured on the basis that the potential liability of shipowners to cargo owners is limited under the Hague Rules and by virtue of tonnage limitation provisions. And insurance premiums payable by owners obviously reflect such limitations on the shipowners' exposure.

If a duty of care by classification societies to cargo owners is recognised in this case, it must have a substantial impact on international trade . . .

The result of a recognition of a duty of care in this case will be to enable cargo owners, or rather their insurers, to disturb the balance created by the Hague Rules and Hague Visby Rules as well as by tonnage limitation provisions, by enabling cargo owners to recover in tort against a peripheral party to the prejudice of the protection of shipowners under the existing system. For these reasons I would hold that the international trade system tends to militate against the recognition of the claim in tort put forward by the cargo owners against the classification society.

(d) The contract between the classification society and shipowners

Mr Aikens QC, who appears for NKK, argued that the contract between the shipowners and the classification society must be a factor against the recognition of the suggested duty of care. He referred to *Pacific Associates v Baxter* [1989] 2 All E.R. 159. That was a case where the Court of Appeal held that the network of contracts between a building owner, the head contractor, subcontractors and even suppliers militated against imposing duties in tort on peripheral parties. In the present case the classification society was not involved in such a web of contracts.

(e) The position and role of NKK

The fact that a defendant acts for the collective welfare is a matter to be taken into consideration when considering whether it is fair, just and reasonable to impose a duty of care: see *Hill v Chief Constable of West Yorkshire* [1988] 2 All E.R. 238, and *Elguzouli-Daf v Comr. of Police of the Metropolis* [1995] 1 All E.R. 833. Even if such a body has no general immunity from liability in tort, the question may arise whether it owes a duty of care to aggrieved persons, and, if so, in what classes of case, *e.g.* only in cases involving the direct infliction of physical harm or on a wider basis.

. . . the question is whether NKK, and other classification societies, would be able to carry out their functions as efficiently if they become the ready alternative target of cargo owners, who already have contractual claims against shipowners. In my judgment there must be some apprehension that the classification societies would adopt, to the detriment of their traditional role, a more defensive position.

(f) Policy factors

Counsel for the cargo owners argued that a decision that a duty of care existed in this case would not involve wide ranging exposure for NKK and other classification societies to claims in tort. That is an unrealistic position. If a duty is recognised in this case there is no reason why it should not extend to annual surveys. docking surveys, intermediate surveys, special surveys, boiler surveys, and so forth. And the scale of NKK's potential liability is shown by the fact that NKK conducted an average of 14,500 surveys per year over the last five years.

At present the system of settling cargo claims against shipowners is a relatively simple one. The claims are settled between the two sets of insurers. If the claims are not settled, they are resolved in arbitration or court proceedings. If a duty is held to exist in this case as between the classification society and cargo owners, classification societies would become potential defendants in many cases. An extra layer of insurance would become involved. The settlement process would inevitably become more complicated and expensive. Arbitration proceedings and court proceedings would often involve an additional party. And often similar issues would have to be canvassed in separate proceedings since the classification societies would not be bound by arbitration clauses in the contracts of carriage. If such a duty is recognised, there is a risk that classification societies might be unwilling from time to time to survey the very vessels which most urgently require independent examination. It will also divert men and resources from the prime function of classification societies, namely to save life and ships at sea. These factors are, by themselves, far from decisive. But in an overall assessment of the case they merit consideration.

Is the imposition of a duty of care fair, just and reasonable?

Like Mann L.J. in the Court of Appeal I am willing to assume (without deciding) that there was a sufficient degree of proximity in this case to fulfil that requirement for the existence of a duty of care. The critical question is therefore whether it would be fair, just and reasonable to impose such a duty. For my part I am satisfied that the factors and arguments advanced on behalf of cargo owners are decisively outweighed by the cumulative effect, if a duty is recognised, of the matters discussed in paras (c), (e) and (f), *i.e.* the outflanking of the bargain between shipowners and cargo owners, the negative effect on the public role of NKK and the other considerations of policy. By way of summary, I look at the matter from the point of view of the three parties concerned. I conclude that the recognition of a duty would be unfair, unjust and unreasonable as against the shipowners who would ultimately have to bear the cost of holding classification societies liable, such consequence being at variance with the bargain between shipowners and cargo owners based on an internationally agreed contractual structure. It would also be unfair, unjust and unreasonable towards classification societies, notably because they act for the collective welfare and unlike shipowners they would not have the benefit of any limitation provisions. Looking at the matter from the point of view of cargo owners, the existing system provides them with the protection of the Hague Rules or Hague Visby Rules. But that protection is limited under such rules and by tonnage limitation provisions. Under the existing system any shortfall is readily insurable. In my judgment the lesser injustice is done by not recognising a duty of care. It follows that I would reject the primary way in which counsel for the cargo owners put his case.

Assumption of responsibility

Given that the cargo owners were not even aware of NKK's examination of the ship, and that the cargo owners simply relied on the undertakings of the shipowners, it is in my view impossible to force the present set of facts into even the most expansive view of the doctrine of voluntary assumption of responsibility.

For the reasons already given I would dismiss the appeal.

Lord Lloyd (dissenting): ... Mr Aikens argued that [various cases in which the plaintiff succeeded] could all be distinguished on the ground that they are cases of *direct* physical or personal injury. But what does this mean? Take the case of ship-repairers. Mr Aikens was at first hesitant to concede that ship-repairers called in by the shipowners to make the ship seaworthy owed any duty of care to the cargo on board. But in the end he accepted that this must be so. If a fitter employed by ship-repairers negligently leaves a tap on, and the cargo is soaked, presumably the damage is direct, and his employers would be liable but if he negligently fails to secure an inspection cover, and a week later sea water enters the hold, and damages the cargo, and the vessel sinks with loss of life, is it to be said that the damage is indirect, and that the ship-repairers escape liability because the "primary" responsibility to make the ship seaworthy is on the shipowners? If a delay of a week means that the damage is indirect, then presumably the injury suffered by the pursuer in *Donoghue v Stevenson* was also indirect, and the defenders should have succeeded. The question in every case must surely be not whether the physical damage is direct or indirect, but whether the negligence of the manufacturer or the stevedores or the ship-repairers caused the damage.

How then does the position of a surveyor, called in by shipowners because the vessel is leaking, differ from that of the ship-repairer? The answer is that it differs not at all. If it is fair, just and reasonable to hold a ship-repairer liable to an unlimited extent for damage to cargo on board caused by his negligence, even though the damage does not occur until after the vessel has sailed, why should it not be fair, just and reasonable in the case of a surveyor? Suppose in the case of the inspection cover, the surveyor negligently tells the fitter that four bolts are sufficient to secure the cover, instead of the usual six, how could it be fair, just and reasonable that the surveyor should not be liable? On what principle would the fitter be liable in such circumstances, when he acts unadvised, but not the surveyor who advises him? No "coherent system of law" should permit such a result.

It follows that I cannot share the view of the Court of Appeal that the existence of a contract of carriage between the cargo owners and the shipowners "militates against" the liability of the surveyor in tort. To my mind the existence of the contract is as irrelevant as is the fact that in this particular case it happened to incorporate the Hague Rules.

I now turn to the second of the two grounds on which Saville L.J. based his decision, namely that the relationship between NKK and the cargo was not sufficiently close to support a duty of care. It is said that the cargo owners were not even aware that Mr Ducat had been called in, and could not therefore have relied on anything which he did or failed to do.

In considering proximity, it is convenient to start with a guidance note prepared by NKK for the use of their surveyors. The opening sentence reads: "NKK was founded in 1899 with the purpose of promoting the safeguard of life and property at sea." One would find a similar statement in the rules of most classification societies. So far as safeguarding life is concerned, it would seem almost self-evident that Mr Ducat owed a duty of care towards the members of the crew. He knew that their lives would be at risk if he allowed the ship to sail in an unseaworthy condition. It is true that he had no legal right to stop the ship sailing. But his de facto control was absolute. If he had maintained his original recommendation, and not changed his mind, it is inconceivable that in practice the vessel would have sailed. Mr Aikens argued that de facto control was not sufficient to found the necessary proximity. I disagree. I find it difficult to imagine a closer, or more direct relationship, than that which existed between Mr Ducat and the crew. It calls to mind the example of the negligent garage mechanic given by Lord Devlin in *Hedley Byrne & Co Ltd v Heller & Partners Ltd* [below, p.57].

"A defendant who is given a car to overhaul and repair if necessary is liable to the injured driver (a) if he overhauls it and repairs it negligently and tells the driver it is safe when it is not; (b) if he overhauls it and negligently finds it not to be in need of repair and tells the driver it is safe when it is not; and (c) if he negligently omits to overhaul it at all and tells the driver that it is safe when it is not. It would be absurd in any of these cases to argue that the proximate cause of the driver's injury was not what the defendant did or failed to do but his negligent statement on the faith of which the driver drove the car and for which he could not recover."

Mr Aikens was inclined to accept that Mr Ducat owed a duty of care to the crew, although he made no formal concession to that effect.

What about the cargo? In some ways the relationship between Mr Ducat and the cargo was even closer. For it is a universal rule of maritime law—certainly it is the law of England—that ship and cargo are regarded as taking part in a joint venture. . . .

When the master called in Mr Ducat, and thereafter incurred expenditure for the common safety, he was acting as much in the interests and on behalf of the cargo as of the ship. It seems almost impossible to say, therefore, that while Mr Ducat owed a duty of care to the ship, he owed no duty of care to the cargo on the ground that the relationship between the parties was insufficiently close. The fact that the cargo owners were unaware that Mr Ducat had been called in is quite beside the point. . . .

To my mind the necessary element of proximity was not only present, but established beyond any peradventure. I would only add at this point that if concern is felt that a decision in favour of the cargo owners would open a wide field of liability, I would reply, "Not so". There is an obvious, sensible and readily defensible line between the surveyor in the present case, where the cargo was on board, and the joint venture was in peril, and a surveyor called in to carry out a periodic survey . . .

The overriding consideration in the present case is that the cargo owners, as we are asked to assume, have suffered physical damage to their cargo, and such damage was caused by Mr Ducat's negligence, for which NKK are responsible on ordinary principles of respondeat superior. Since the celebrated formulation of Lord Wilberforce in *Anns v Merton L.B.* a series of important cases in the Court of Appeal and House of Lords have signalled the "retreat from *Anns*" culminating in the decision of the House in *Murphy v Brentwood D.C.* [above, p.31]. Almost all these decisions have concerned claims to recover damages for economic loss, unassociated with physical damage or personal injury. . . .

The concept of proximity, and the requirement that it should be fair, just and reasonable to impose a duty of care on the defendant in the particular circumstances of the case, have been developed as a means of containing liability for pure economic loss under the principles stated in *Donoghue v Stevenson*. At the same time, and by a parallel movement in the opposite direction, the House has in two recent decisions reaffirmed liability for economic loss based on the principle of assumption of responsibility as expounded by the House in *Hedley Byrne & Co*

Ltd v Heller & Partners Ltd [below, p.57]. None of these difficulties arise in the present case. We are not here asked to extend the law of negligence into a new field. We are not even asked to make an incremental advance. All that is required is a straightforward application of *Donoghue v Stevenson*. . . .

In physical damage cases proximity very often goes without saying. Where the facts cry out for the imposition of a duty of care between the parties, as they do here, it would require an exceptional case to refuse to impose a duty on the ground that it would not be fair, just and reasonable. Otherwise there is a risk that the law of negligence will disintegrate into a series of isolated decisions without any coherent principles at all, and the retreat from *Anns* will turn into a rout. Having given Mr Aikens arguments my best consideration, I can see no good reason why, on the facts of this case, ordinary well-established principles of the law of negligence should not be allowed to take effect. Accordingly, I would for my part allow the appeal, and restore the order of Hirst J.

Lord Keith, Lord Jauncey and **Lord Browne-Wilkinson** agreed with **Lord Steyn.**

Questions

1. If, in the absence of prior relations between plaintiff and defendant, the defendant could be liable only vicariously for the conduct of Mr Ducat, their surveyor, do you think that the preliminary question ("whether the defendant owed a duty of care to the plaintiff?") was appropriately phrased? Consider the preliminary question put in the *Dorset Yacht* case (below, p.84).

2. What arguments could be used to support or rebut a claim by the *shipowner* against the classification society? Was the society in breach of its contract with the shipowner in agreeing at the captain's request that the ship could sail when both of them ought to have realised that this was dangerous? Was the contract one for breach of which (if any) the cargo-owner could sue as a third party beneficiary under the Contracts (Rights of Third Parties) Act 1999?

3. In letting the vessel sail, did the surveyor do more than the local authorities did (or didn't do) in *Murphy* to contribute to the harm? Is there a comparison, and is there a difference?

4. Lord Lloyd said that the shipowner was acting "for" the cargo in consulting the surveyor. Compare *Launchbury v Morgans* (below, p.316) where the House of Lords denied that the negligent driver was acting "for" the plaintiff in agreeing with her husband to return the car (and him) to her?

5. There have been some decisions about the liability of a garage which issues an M.o.T. certificate: where would you go to find them?

6. Suppose a garage certifies the fitness of a motor vehicle by issuing an M.o.T. certificate to the owner of a van, and property being carried on the van is damaged when the van crashes because of a defect which careful examination would have disclosed. Could the property owner sue the garage? Would it matter whether the garage had (a) failed to notice a defect which it should have corrected, or (b) actually caused the defect while correcting another? Could the van-owner who sought and paid for the certificate sue in respect of damage to himself or the van?

7. In *Philcox v Civil Aviation Authority* [1995] Times L.R. 332, a plane for which the defendant had issued a certificate of airworthiness crashed. The owner's suit failed, as the Court of Appeal, following the principal case, held that no duty was owed to the owner, though perhaps a duty was owed to members of the public. (Note that just as the shipowner is liable to the cargo-owner, anyone on the ground injured by a crashing plane or anything falling from it has an automatic action against the owner of the aircraft, who is required to be insured: Civil Aviation Act 1982, s.76). In *Perrett v Collins* [1992] 2 Lloyd's Rep. 255, where a passenger was injured in a plane which X had inspected and for which Y had issued a certificate of fitness, Hobhouse L.J. denied the relevance of *The Nicholas H* whose "reasoning was directed to considerations relevant to economic loss and was not germane to personal injury." Here X and Y were not subsidiary to the owner of the aircraft but had an independent role and owed a duty of care to the passenger.

8. In *The Morning Watch* [1990] 1 Lloyd's Rep. 547 the buyer of a yacht sued a classification society which had issued a certificate indicating that the yacht was better than it was. The claim failed for want of proximity: the certificate was not issued to protect buyers.

9. Given that there are quite different legal regimes for carriage of goods by land (whether by road or rail), sea and air (why?), is there any good reason why the rules of tort regarding liability for roadworthiness, seaworthiness and airworthiness should be the same or similar? Is *The Nicholas H* of general application?

Notes:

1. A shipowner is unquestionably liable for cargo carried in an unseaworthy vessel (even if the unseaworthiness is due to the fault of an independent contractor—see *Riverstone*, below, p.304)—but his liability is limited by statutory contract or statute to a sum calculated in relation to the cargo or the tonnage of the vessel, here to $500,000. Normally when two or more people are liable for the same damage (here the loss of the cargo), the loss is ultimately shared between them in such proportion as is "just and reasonable having regard to the extent of [their] responsibility for the damage in question." (Civil Liability (Contribution) Act 1978, below, p.236). Had there been no limit to the shipowner's liability, how would you apportion liability between the classification society and the shipowner? Given the statutory limit, the classification society, if Lord Lloyd had had his way, would have had to bear the whole balance of $5,700,000 (s.2(3)). Would that have been "fair, just and reasonable"? In the light of this, was Lord Steyn correct to say that "enabling cargo owners to recover in tort against a peripheral party [would be] to the prejudice of the protection of shipowners under the existing system"? He was surely correct to observe that "the shipowners . . . would ultimately have to bear the cost of holding classification societies liable", with a question about "ultimately", for if the shipowners had to pay the classification societies, they would pass on the extra cost to the cargo-owners, who would then charge extra freight to the consignees of the cargo, who would then pass this on to their customers, and the consumer would end up bearing the cost.

2. Lord Lloyd founded on the distinction between property damage and mere financial loss. Let us consider. Cargo is invariably insured against damage, partly because the shipowner's liability, if it attaches at all, is limited in amount, partly because the buyer insists on it. Although this suit was brought in the name of the cargo-owners who had suffered property damage, it was really brought by and for their insurers, whose loss was purely financial: the complaint was really about loss of money and not damage to property at all. In 1877 the House of Lords definitively held that an insurance company which suffers financial loss because the defendant negligently damaged the insured property has no tort claim of its own (after all, it has been paid to bear the loss!), but equity (always interfering with the common law!) allows the insurer to pretend to be the insured and to claim as if the property damage had been suffered by itself. Perhaps the distinction between financial loss and (insured) property damage is a weak one? Note that in both *Murphy* (above, p.31) and *Dorset Yacht* (below, p.84) the true plaintiff was an insurance company rather than poor Murphy or the not-so-poor Dorset Yacht Co

3. In personal injury cases the victim, even if he is insured against accident, may keep both full tort damages and the insurance moneys, so these considerations do not apply at all. Does this justify the suggestion that the classification society might be liable to the crew of the *Nicholas H*, just as the architect in *Clay v Crump* was liable to the injured workmen and their widows?

4. The shipowner's liability to the crew is limited by statute, though in a higher amount than his liability to the cargo. His liability to the cargo is also limited by contract and under the Rules; for example, the shipowner is not liable for faults of navigation (just imagine a carrier by road trying to excuse himself if the goods are damaged by bad driving!). The contract has rather extensive effect: third parties involved in the operation may often invoke the shipowner's protection, and though non-contractors can sue, their claim may well be subject to the contract (see *The Starsin* [2003] 2 All E.R. 785 (HL)). Any common law liability of the carrier of persons by air is wholly excluded by the Warsaw Convention (*Sidhu v British Airways* [1997] 1 All E.R. 193), so that a passenger shocked by being fingered by her neighbour has no claim, since the Convention covers only "material damage" (*Morris v KLM Dutch Airlines* [2002] 2 All E.R. 565), those affected by deep vein thrombosis also had no claim ([2003] 1 All E.R. 935, [2003] 3 W.L.R. 956), and an intending passenger injured in the departure lounge had no claim under the Occupiers' Liability Act (*Phillips v Air New Zealand* [2002] E.W.H.C. 800 (Comm)).

5. *The Nicholas H* is by no means the first case where a defendant has been sued by a plaintiff whose claim against a primary party was restricted by the terms of a contract. In *Norwich City v Harvey* [1989] 1 All E.R. 1180 the defendant sub-contractor's employee misused a blow-torch and burnt down the plaintiff's swimming-pool which was being extended. Under the contract with the main building contractor the plaintiff had agreed that the property be at his sole risk as regards loss or damage by fire, and the main contractor was clearly entitled to invoke this clause. The court held that this allocation of risk formed part of the contractual context in which the sub-contractor had taken on the work, so that neither the sub-contractor nor, consequently, his employee, was under any duty to the plaintiff with regard to fire damage. This decision evinces a new approach to the problem poorly dealt with in *Scruttons v Midland Silicones* [1962] A.C. 446 where a stevedore was held fully liable for carelessly dropping an item which the plaintiff owner had bailed to a carrier under a contract limiting the carrier's liability.

This trend has unfortunately been slowed by the decision of the House of Lords in *British Telecommunications v Thomson & Sons* [1999] 2 All E.R. 241 where Lord Mackay held that since the policy which the client site-owner had to take out specifically covered nominated sub-contractors, it would not be fair to grant protection to sub-contractors not nominated but merely approved, for otherwise the plaintiff's insurer, not overtly a party to the litigation, would be deprived of his "right" of subrogation. (Tail wags dog ...) A more generous construction of the contract and a more reasonable result was reached in *Scottish & Newcastle plc v GD Construction* [2003] E.W.C.A. Civ 16.

The fact that the Contracts (Rights of Third Parties) Act 1999, s.1(6) permits third parties under certain circumstances to avail themselves of contractual exclusion or limitation clauses should not be allowed to preempt the common law doctrine of *Norwich City v Harvey* that the contractual matrix may prevent a recognised duty of care from arising.

Gossip Column:

The ostensible claimant in *The Nicholas H* was the firm of Marc Rich, the fugitive American commodities trader who escaped more than 325 years in jail when he was pardoned by President Clinton in one of his final acts in office as President of the United States. Marc Rich's firm, based like himself in Switzerland, trades in metals and grain, with a turnover of about $6 billion. (*The Times*, January 22, 2001).

SPARTAN STEEL AND ALLOYS LTD v MARTIN & CO (CONTRACTORS) LTD

Court of Appeal [1973] 1 Q.B. 27; [1972] 3 W.L.R. 502; 116 S.J. 648; [1972] 3 All E.R. 557 (noted (1973) 89 L.Q.R. 10; [1973] Camb.L.J. 20)

Action by industrialist against highway contractor in respect of property damage and lost profits

Excavating with a mechanical shovel, the defendant carelessly damaged a cable and interrupted the supply of electricity to the plaintiffs' factory 400 yards away. In order to prevent damage to their furnace the plaintiffs had to damage its contents (on which they would have made a profit of £400) by £368, and they were prevented by the absence of electric current from processing four more "melts" which would have netted them £1,767.

Faulks J. held that the plaintiffs were entitled to all three sums; the Court of Appeal (Edmund Davies L.J. dissenting) held that they were entitled to the first two sums only.

Lord Denning M.R.: ... At bottom I think the question of recovering economic loss is one of policy. Whenever the courts draw a line to mark out the bounds of *duty*, they do it as matter of policy so as to limit the responsibility of the defendant. Whenever the courts set bounds to the *damages* recoverable—saying that they are, or are not, too remote—they do it as matter of policy so as to limit the liability of the defendant.

In many of the cases where economic loss has been held not to be recoverable, it has been put on the ground that the defendant was under no *duty* to the plaintiff. Thus where a person is injured in a road accident by the negligence of another, the negligent driver owes a duty to the injured man himself, but he owes no duty to the servant of the injured man—see *Best v Samuel Fox & Co Ltd* ([1952] A.C. 716 at 731): nor to the master of the injured man—*Inland Revenue Commissioners v Hambrook* ([1956] 2 Q.B. 641 at 660): nor to anyone else who suffers loss because he had a contract with the injured man—see *Simpson & Co v Thomson* ((1887) 3 App.Cas. 279 at 289): nor indeed to anyone who only suffers economic loss on account of the accident: see *Kirkham v Boughey* ([1958] 2 Q.B. 338 at 341). Likewise, when property is damaged by the negligence of another, the negligent tortfeasor owes a duty to the owner or possessor of the chattel, but not to one who suffers loss only because he had a contract entitling him to use the chattel or giving him a right to receive it at some later date: see *Elliot Steam Tug Co Ltd v Shipping Controller* ([1922] 1 K.B. 127 at 139) and *Margarine Union GmbH v Cambay Prince Steamship Co Ltd* ([1969] 1 Q.B. 219 at 251–252).

In other cases, however, the defendant seems clearly to have been under a duty to the plaintiff, but the economic loss has not been recovered because it is *too remote*. Take the illustration given by Blackburn J. in *Cattle v Stockton Waterworks Co* ((1875) L.R. 10 Q.B. 453 at 457), when water escapes from a reservoir and floods a coal mine where many men are working. Those who had their tools or clothes destroyed could recover: but those who only lost their wages could not. Similarly, when the defendants' ship negligently sank a ship which was being towed by a tug, the owner of the tug lost his remuneration, but he could not recover it from the negligent ship: though the same duty (of navigation with reasonable care) was owed to both tug and tow: see *Société Anonyme de Remorquage à Hélice v Bennetts* ([1911] 1 K.B. 243 at 248). In such cases if the plaintiff or his property had been physically injured, he would have recovered: but, as he only suffered economic loss, he is held not entitled to recover. This is, I should think, because the loss is regarded by the law as too remote: . . .

On the other hand, in the cases where economic loss by itself has been held to be recoverable, it is plain that there was a duty to the plaintiff and the loss was not too remote. Such as when one ship negligently runs down another ship, and damages it, with the result that the cargo has to be discharged and reloaded. The negligent ship was already under a duty to the cargo owners: and they can recover the cost of discharging and reloading it, as it is not too remote: see *Morrison Steamship Co Ltd v Greystoke Castle (Cargo Owners)* ([1947] A.C. 265). Likewise, when a banker negligently gives a reference to one who acts on it, the duty is plain and the damage is not too remote: see *Hedley Byrne & Co Ltd v Heller & Partners Ltd* [below, p.57].

The more I think about these cases, the more difficult I find it to put each into its proper pigeon-hole. Sometimes I say "There was no duty." In others I say: "The damage was too remote." So much so that I think the time has come to discard those tests which have proved so elusive. It seems to me better to consider the particular relationship in hand, and see whether or not, as a matter of policy, economic loss should be recoverable. . . .

So I turn to the relationship in the present case. It is of common occurrence. The parties concerned are: the electricity board who are under a statutory duty to maintain supplies of electricity in their district; the inhabitants of the district, including this factory, who are entitled by statute to a continuous supply of electricity for their use; and the contractors who dig up the road. Similar relationships occur with other statutory bodies, such as gas and water undertakings. The cable may be damaged by the negligence of the statutory undertaker, or by the negligence of the contractor, or by accident without any negligence by anyone: and the power may have to be cut off whilst the cable is repaired. Or the power may be cut off owing to a short-circuit in the power house: and so forth. If the cutting off of the supply causes economic loss to the consumers, should it as matter of policy be recoverable? And against whom?

The first consideration is the position of the statutory undertakers. If the board do not keep up the voltage or pressure of electricity, gas or water—or, likewise, if they shut it off for repairs— and thereby cause economic loss to their consumers, they are not liable in damages, not even if the cause of it is due to their own negligence. . . . Such is the result of many cases starting with a water board, going on to a gas board and then to an electricity company. In those cases the courts, looking at the legislative enactments, held that Parliament did not intend to expose the board to liability for damages to the inhabitants en masse: see what Lord Cairns L.C. said in *Atkinson v Newcastle and Gateshead Waterworks Co* (2 Ex.D. 441 at 445). In those cases there was *indirect* damage to the plaintiffs, but it was not recoverable. There is another group of cases which go to show that, if the board, by their negligence in the conduct of their supply, cause direct physical damage or injury to person or property, they are liable: see *Milnes v Huddersfield Corp.* ((1886) 11 App.Cas. 511 at 530) by Lord Blackburn; *Midwood & Co Ltd v Manchester Corp.* ([1905] 2 K.B. 597); *Heard v Brymbo Steel Co Ltd* ([1947] 2 K.B. 692) and *Hartley v Mayoh & Co* ([1954] 1 Q.B. 383). But one thing is clear: the statutory undertakers have never been held liable for economic loss only. If such be the policy of the legislature in regard to electricity boards, it would seem right for the common law to adopt a similar policy in regard to contractors. If the electricity boards are not liable for economic loss due to negligence which results in the cutting off of the supply, nor should a contractor be liable.

The second consideration is the nature of the hazard, namely, the cutting of the supply of electricity. This is a hazard which we all run. It may be due to a short circuit, to a flash of lightning, to a tree falling on the wires, to an accidental cutting of the cable, or even to the negligence of someone or other. And when it does happen, it affects a multitude of persons: not as a rule by way of physical damage to them or their property, but by putting them to inconvenience, and sometimes to economic loss. The supply is usually restored in a few hours, so the economic loss is not very large. Such a hazard is regarded by most people as a thing they must put up with—without seeking compensation from anyone. Some there are who install a stand-by system. Others seek refuge by taking out an insurance policy against breakdown in the supply. But most people are content to take the risk on themselves. When the supply is cut off, they do not go running round to their solicitor. They do not try to find out whether it was anyone's fault. They just put up with it. They try to make up the economic loss by doing more work next day. This is a healthy attitude which the law should encourage.

The third consideration is this: if claims for economic loss were permitted for this particular hazard, there would be no end of claims. Some might be genuine, but many might be inflated, or even false. A machine might not have been in use anyway, but it would be easy to put it down to the cut in supply. It would be well-nigh impossible to check the claims. If there was economic loss on one day, did the claimant do his best to mitigate it by working harder next day? And so forth. Rather than expose claimants to such temptation and defendants to such hard labour—on comparatively small claims—it is better to disallow economic loss altogether, at any rate when it stands alone, independent of any physical damage.

The fourth consideration is that, in such a hazard as this, the risk of economic loss should be suffered by the whole community who suffer the losses—usually many but comparatively small losses—rather than on the one pair of shoulders, that is, on the contractor on whom the total of them, all added together, might be very heavy.

The fifth consideration is that the law provides for deserving cases. If the defendant is guilty of negligence which cuts off the electricity supply and causes actual physical damage to person or property, that physical damage can be recovered . . . and also any economic loss truly consequential on the material damage: see *British Celanese Ltd v AH Hunt (Capacitors) Ltd* ([1969] 1 W.L.R. 959) and *SCM (United Kingdom) Ltd v WJ Whittall & Son Ltd* ([1971] 1 Q.B. 337). Such cases will be comparatively few. They will be readily capable of proof and will be easily checked. They should be and are admitted.

These considerations lead me to the conclusion that the plaintiffs should recover for the physical damage to the one melt (£368), and the loss of profit on that melt consequent thereon (£400): but not for the loss of profit on the four melts (£1,767), because that was economic loss independent of the physical damage. I would, therefore, allow the appeal and reduce the damages to £768.

Lawton L.J. agreed in the result; **Edmund Davies L.J.** dissented.

Questions

1. If a company loses profits, its shareholders may lose dividends and its employees wages or jobs. If the company recovers damages, is it the shareholders or the employees who benefit? Could the shareholders or the employees themselves sue? If not, why not? Is it because they tend to be numerous, or for some other reason? On the shareholder problem, see *Johnson v Gore Wood* [2001] 1 All E.R. 481 (HL), especially at 528 ff. (Lord Millett).

2. An articulated lorry jack-knifes on the motorway. The following car collides with it, and the driver is injured. No one else suffers physical harm, but the motorway is closed for two hours, and many people miss valuable appointments. Do you think it would be reasonable to distinguish between the different types of harm caused by a single incident?

3. What class of litigants will bring an action for lost profits if such an action is allowed? What class of litigants can bring an action for personal injuries?

4. Does a proper sense of social responsibility require one to bear in mind the financial well-being of trading companies with limited liability?

5. Suppose that the defendant had been operating, with the plaintiff's permission, on the plaintiff's land. Would the result be the same?

6. The old idea that the law of tort should be determined by a moral view of the demands of social responsibility has been challenged by the theory that the law of tort should be determined by its function as a loss-distributing device. Might the results of the two views diverge in the present case?

Note:

A person's chances of obtaining the money he is claiming depend on what he is claiming it for and who he is claiming it from: in other words, both the type of injury he has suffered and the nature of his relationship with the defendant are material, perhaps vital, considerations.

Since *Donoghue v Stevenson* people who act dangerously may have to pay even a complete stranger if the harm they cause is physical. So here Spartan Steel recovered for the physical harm they suffered (damage to the ore) but not for the purely financial harm (profits lost on undamaged ore), though both results were equally foreseeable. Plaintiff and defendant were total strangers to each other. In *Muirhead v Industrial Tank Specialities* [1985] 3 All E.R. 705, CA the careless manufacturer of a defective recycling pump had to pay the ultimate purchaser for the damage to his property (dead lobsters) but not the purely financial harm resulting from business interruption. But while in *Spartan Steel* the parties were complete strangers, in *Muirhead* they were not: they were in the relationship of consumer and manufacturer. As *Donoghue v Stevenson* laid down, that is a special relationship, but when it comes to liability for purely economic loss, is not special enough. Nor, as we have seen, is the relationship between builder and eventual occupier (*Murphy*, above p.31).

The economic loss in *Spartan Steel* occurred through the defendant's damaging an electricity cable which belonged to a third party. In cases where property has been damaged by carelessness the courts have long held that only those with a proprietary or possessory interest in that property may bring an action, not those who have merely a financial interest in the well-being of the property, whether that interest be positive, in the sense that they stand to gain if the property remains unimpaired, or negative, in the sense that they will have to pay out if it is damaged or destroyed. There are masses of cases: the courts have rejected claims by the insurer who had to pay out on the policy when the insured property was damaged (*Simpson v Thomson* (1877) 3 App.Cas. 179), the salvor who lost his reward when the tow was sunk (*Société Anonyme de Remorquage à Hélice v Bennetts* [1911] 1 K.B. 243), the buyer who was committed to paying for the goods (*The Aliakmon* [1986] 2 All E.R. 145), the auctioneer who would have sold the property on commission (*Weller & Co v Foot and Mouth Disease Research Institute* [1966] 1 Q.B. 569), and the charterer who was paying for the use of the vessel (*The Mineral Transporter* [1985] 2 All E.R. 935). The law could hardly have taken a clearer position, and it has now been reaffirmed so as to allay intervening doubts stemming from *Junior Books v Veitchi Corp.* [1983] A.C. 520. Quite classical is the decision of Moore-Bick J. in *Jan de Nul (UK) v NV Royale Belge* [2000] 2 Lloyd's Rep. 700: when a contractor's dredging operations in an estuary caused loss to many users of the river, suit in negligence could be brought only by those who could show that property in which they had an interest had been affected.

The position adopted is both right and convenient. It is right to distinguish property damage from financial loss because things, being capable of gratifying the senses, are more significant than wealth, just as people are more significant than things. It would also be inconvenient not to distinguish property damage from financial loss because whereas property damage is always limited in extent (thanks to the physical laws of inertia), the incidence of financial loss knows no bounds, and the courts would have a fearful time trying to set them.

Take the interesting case of *Wimpey Constr. Co (U.K.) Ltd v Martin Black & Co*, 1982 S.L.T. 239. The pursuer was one of a consortium of firms engaged on a huge construction project in the Firth of Forth. The project depended on the availability of a certain crane-barge. This was obtained on hire by another member of the consortium, who procured wire slings from the defender. One day while a concrete pile belonging to the pursuer was being raised, the sling snapped. The pile sank and the crane-barge was so badly damaged that it was out of commission for eight weeks. The pursuer naturally recovered for the loss of its concrete pile, but it also sued for the vast expense involved in the delay to the construction work. The Inner House gave judgment on this point for the defenders. But then the House of Lords decided *Junior Books* [1982] 3 All E.R. 201, which so confused the law that the defenders settled for a huge sum rather than face an appeal to the House of Lords as it was then constituted. Happily it is now clear that such an appeal would be promptly dismissed.

Those with a good deal of time to waste can try reading a decision of the Supreme Court of Canada in *Norsk Pacific Steamship Co v Canadian National Railway* [1992] 1 S.C.R. 1021–1184[!], 91 D.L.R. (4th) 289–391 (excerpted with commentary in Markesinis and Unberath, *The German Law of Torts* (4th ed., 2002) 243–265): a barge towed by the defendant's tug collided with a bridge principally used, but not owned, by the plaintiff, which had to reroute its trains at great expense while the bridge was being repaired. A bare majority allowed the plaintiff to recover, but for no reason which commanded majority support.

There seems to be good reason to have a clear rule on the point even if no other reason could be given for it, though actually it can. We should be grateful to the Court in *Spartan Steel* for giving us it.

For comparative law see Bussani and Palmer, *Pure Economic Loss in Europe* (2003).

HEDLEY BYRNE & CO v HELLER & PARTNERS LTD

House of Lords [1964] A.C. 465; [1963] 3 W.L.R. 101; 107 S.J. 454; [1963] 2 All E.R. 575; [1963] 1 Lloyd's Rep. 485 (noted [1963] Camb. L.J. 216)

Action against gratuitous informant in respect of financial loss

The plaintiffs, advertising agents, had booked space and time on behalf of a customer, Easipower Ltd, under contracts making them personally liable. They then had doubts about Easipower's financial position, and asked their bankers to obtain from the defendants, merchant bankers with whom Easipower Ltd had their account, a statement on Easipower's standing. This was done in the first instance by telephone, when the defendants said: "We believe that the company would not undertake any commitments they were unable to fulfil." Three months later the plaintiffs, through their bankers, asked whether Easipower were trustworthy to the extent of £100,000 per year. The defendants replied, in a letter headed "For your private use and without responsibility on the part of this bank or its officials," that Easipower Ltd were a " . . . respectably constituted company, considered good for its ordinary business engagements" and that "Your figures are larger than we are accustomed to see." In reliance upon their view of what these statements meant the plaintiffs refrained from cancelling the advertising contracts, and when Easipower Ltd went into liquidation lost sums calculated at £17,661 18s 6d.

The plaintiffs abandoned an allegation of fraud, but maintained that the defendants' replies were given in breach of their duty of care. McNair J. held that the defendants were careless but that they owed no duty. The Court of Appeal affirmed judgment for the defendants on the same ground [1962] 1 Q.B. 396. The House of Lords affirmed the judgment on different grounds.

Lord Reid: My Lords, this case raises the important question whether and in what circumstances a person can recover damages for loss suffered by reason of his having relied on an innocent but negligent misrepresentation . . .

Before coming to the main question of law, it may be well to dispose of an argument that there was no sufficiently close relationship between these parties to give rise to any duty. It is said that the respondents did not know the precise purpose of the inquiries and did not even know whether the National Provincial Bank wanted the information for its own use or for the use of a customer: they knew nothing of the appellants. I would reject that argument. They knew that the inquiry was in connection with an advertising contract, and it was at least probable that the information was wanted by the advertising contractors. It seems to me quite immaterial that they did not know who these contractors were: there is no suggestion of any speciality which could have influenced them in deciding whether to give information or in what form to give it. I shall therefore treat this as if it were a case where a negligent misrepresentation is made directly to the person seeking information, opinion or advice, and I shall not attempt to decide what kind or degree of proximity is necessary before there can be a duty owed by the defendant to the plaintiff.

The appellants' first argument was based on *Donoghue v Stevenson* [above, p.21]. That is a very important decision, but I do not think that it has any direct bearing on this case. That decision may encourage us to develop existing lines of authority, but it cannot entitle us to disregard them. Apart altogether from authority, I would think that the law must treat negligent words differently from negligent acts. The law ought so far as possible to reflect the standards of the reasonable man, and that is what *Donoghue v Stevenson* sets out to do. The most obvious difference between negligent words and negligent acts is this. Quite careful people often express definite opinions on social or informal occasions even when they see that others are likely to be influenced by them; and they often do that without taking that care which they would take if asked for their opinion professionally or in a business connection. The appellant agrees that there can be no duty of care on such occasions, and we are referred to American and South African authorities where that is recognised, although their law appears to have gone much further than ours has yet done. But it is at least unusual casually to put into circulation negligently made articles which are dangerous. A man might give a friend a negligently prepared bottle of home-made wine and his friend's guests might drink it with dire results. But it is by no means clear that those guests would have no action against the negligent manufacturer.

Another obvious difference is that a negligently made article will only cause one accident, and so it is not very difficult to find the necessary degree of proximity or neighbourhood between the negligent manufacturer and the person injured. But words can be broadcast with or without the consent or the foresight of the speaker or writer. It would be one thing to say that the speaker owes a duty to a limited class, but it would be going very far to say that he owes a duty to every ultimate "consumer" who acts on those words to his detriment. It would be no use to say that a speaker or writer owes a duty but can disclaim responsibility if he wants to. He, like the manufacturer, could make it part of a contract that he is not to be liable for his negligence: but that contract would not protect him in a question with a third party, at least if the third party was unaware of it.

So it seems to me that there is good sense behind our present law that in general an innocent but negligent misrepresentation gives no cause of action. There must be something more than the mere misstatement. I therefore turn to the authorities to see what more is required. The most natural requirement would be that expressly or by implication from the circumstances the speaker or writer has undertaken some responsibility, and that appears to me not to conflict with any authority which is binding on this House. Where there is a contract there is no difficulty as regards the contracting parties: the question is whether there is a warranty. Then there are cases where a person does not merely make a statement but performs a gratuitous service. I do not intend to examine the cases about that, but at least they show that in some cases that person owes a duty of care apart from any contract, and to that extent they pave the way to holding that there can be a duty of care in making a statement of fact or opinion which is independent of con-tract.

[Lord Reid considered *Derry v Peek* (1889) 14 App.Cas. 337, which had erroneously been supposed to have decided that "To found an action for damages there must be a contract and breach, or fraud" (*per* Lord Bramwell at 347), quoted the view of Lord Haldane in *Nocton v Lord Ashburton* [1914] A.C. 932 at 947, and *Robinson v National Bank of Scotland* 1916 S.C. (HL) 154 at 157 and proceeded:]

This passage makes it clear that Lord Haldane did not think that a duty to take care must be limited to cases of fiduciary relationship in the narrow sense of relationships which had been recognised by the Court of Chancery as being of a fiduciary character. He speaks of other special relationships, and I can see no logical stopping place short of all those relationships where it is plain that the party seeking information or advice was trusting the other to exercise such a degree of care as the circumstances required, where it was reasonable for him to do that, and where the other gave the information or advice when he knew or ought to have known that the inquirer was relying on him. I say "ought to have known" because in questions of negligence we now apply the objective standard of what the reasonable man would have done.

A reasonable man, knowing that he was being trusted or that his skill and judgment were being relied on, would, I think, have three courses open to him. He could keep silent or decline to give the information or advice sought: or he could give an answer with a clear qualification that he accepted no responsibility for it or that it was given without that reflection or inquiry which a careful answer would require: or he could simply answer without any such qualification. If he chooses to adopt the last course he must, I think, be held to have accepted some responsibility for his answer being given carefully, or to have accepted a relationship with the inquirer which requires him to exercise such care as the circumstances require.

If that is right, then it must follow that *Candler v Crane, Christmas & Co* ([1951] 2 K.B. 164) was wrongly decided. There the plaintiff wanted to see the accounts of a company before deciding to invest in it. The defendants were the company's accountants, and they were told by the company to complete the company's accounts as soon as possible because they were to be shown to the plaintiff who was a potential investor in the company. At the company's request the defendants showed the completed accounts to the plaintiff, discussed them with him, and allowed him to take a copy. The accounts had been carelessly prepared and gave a wholly misleading picture. It was obvious to the defendants that the plaintiff was relying on their skill and judgment and on their having exercised that care which by contract they owed to the company, and I think that any reasonable man in the plaintiff's shoes would have relied on that. This seems to me to be a typical case of agreeing to assume a responsibility: they knew why the plaintiff wanted to see the accounts and why their employers, the company, wanted them to be shown to him, and agreed to show them to him without even a suggestion that he should not rely on them . . .

Now I must try to apply these principles to the present case. What the appellants complain of is not negligence in the ordinary sense of carelessness, but rather mis-judgment, in that Mr Heller, while honestly seeking to give a fair assessment, in fact made a statement which gave a false and misleading impression of his customer's credit. It appears that bankers now commonly give references with regard to their customers as part of their business. I do not know how far their customers generally permit them to disclose their affairs, but, even with permission, it cannot always be easy for a banker to reconcile his duty to his customer with his desire to give a fairly balanced reply to an inquiry. And inquirers can hardly expect a full and objective statement of opinion of accurate factual information such as skilled men would be expected to give in reply to other kinds of inquiry. So it seems to me to be unusually difficult to determine just what duty beyond a duty to be honest a banker would be held to have undertaken if he gave a reply without an adequate disclaimer of responsibility or other warning . . .

But here the appellants' bank, who were their agents in making the inquiry, began by saying that "they wanted to know in confidence and without responsibility on our part," that is, on the part of the respondents. So I cannot see how the appellants can now be entitled to disregard that and maintain that the respondents did incur a responsibility to them . . .

I am therefore of opinion that it is clear that the respondents never undertook any duty to exercise care in giving their replies. The appellants cannot succeed unless there was such a duty and therefore in my judgment this appeal must be dismissed.

Lord Morris of Borth-y-Gest: . . . My Lords, I consider that it follows and that it should now be regarded as settled that if someone possessed of a special skill undertakes, quite irrespective of contract, to apply that skill for the assistance of another person who relies upon such skill, a duty of care will arise. The fact that the service is to be given by means of or by the instrumentality of words can make no difference. Furthermore, if in a sphere in which a person is so placed that others could reasonably rely upon his judgment or his skill or upon his ability to make careful inquiry, a person takes it upon himself to give information or advice to, or allows his information or advice to be passed on to, another person who, as he knows or should know, will place reliance upon it, then a duty of care will arise . . .

Lord Devlin: . . . I think, therefore, that there is ample authority to justify your Lordships in saying now that the categories of special relationships which may give rise to a duty to take care in word as well as in deed are not limited to contractual relationships or to relationships of fiduciary duty, but include also relationships which in the words of Lord Shaw in *Nocton v Lord Ashburton* are "equivalent to contract," that is, where there is an assumption of responsibility in circumstances in which, but for the absence of consideration, there would be a contract. Where there is an express undertaking, an express warranty as distinct from mere representation, there can be little difficulty. The difficulty arises in discerning those cases in which the undertaking is to be implied. In this respect the absence of consideration is not irrelevant. Payment for information or advice is very good evidence that it is being relied upon and that the informer or adviser knows that it is. Where there is no consideration, it will be necessary to exercise greater care in distinguishing between social and professional relationships and between those which are of a contractual character and those which are not. It may often be material to consider whether the adviser is acting purely out of good nature or whether he is getting his reward in some indirect form. The service that a bank performs in giving a reference is not done simply out of a desire to assist commerce. It would discourage the customers of the bank if their deals fell through because the bank had refused to testify to their credit when it was good.

I have had the advantage of reading all the opinions prepared by your Lordships and of studying the terms which your Lordships have framed by way of definition of the sort of relationship which gives rise to a responsibility towards those who act upon information or advice and so creates a duty of care towards them. I do not understand any of your Lordships to hold that it is a responsibility imposed by law upon certain types of persons or in certain sorts of situations. It is a responsibility that is voluntarily accepted or undertaken, either generally where a general relationship, such as that of solicitor and client or banker and customer, is created, or specifically in relation to a particular transaction. In the present case the appellants were not, as in *Woods v Martins Bank Ltd* ([1959] 1 Q.B. 55), the customers or potential customers of the bank. Responsibility can attach only to the single act, that is, the giving of the reference, and only if the doing of that act implied a voluntary undertaking to assume responsibility. This is a point of great importance because it is, as I understand it, the foundation for the ground on which in the end the House dismisses the appeal. I do not think it is possible to formulate with exactitude all the conditions under which the law will in a specific case imply a voluntary undertaking any more than it is possible to formulate those in which the law will imply a contract. But in so far as your Lordships describe the circumstances in which an implication will ordinarily be drawn, I am prepared to adopt any one of your Lordships' statements as showing the general rule; and I pay the same respect to the statement by Denning L.J. in his dissenting judgment in *Candler v Crane, Christmas & Co* about the circumstances in which he says a duty to use care in making a statement exists . . .

I shall therefore content myself with the proposition that wherever there is a relationship equivalent to contract, there is a duty of care. Such a relationship may be either general or particular. Examples of a general relationship are those of solicitor and client and of banker and customer. There may well be others yet to be established. Where there is a general relationship of this sort, it is unnecessary to do more than prove its existence and the duty follows. Where, as in the present case, what is relied on is a particular relationship created *ad hoc*, it will be necessary to examine the particular facts to see whether there is an express or implied undertaking of responsibility . . .

I regard this proposition as an application of the general conception of proximity. Cases may arise in the future in which a new and wider proposition, quite independent of any notion of contract, will be needed. There may, for example, be cases in which a statement is not supplied for the use of any particular person, any more than in *Donoghue v Stevenson* the ginger beer was supplied for consumption by any particular person; and it will then be necessary to return to the general conception of proximity and to see whether there can be evolved from it, as was done in *Donoghue v Stevenson*, a specific proposition to fit the case. When that has to be done, the speeches of your Lordships today as well as the judgment of Denning L.J. to which I have referred . . . will afford good guidance as to what ought to be said. I prefer to see what shape such cases take before committing myself to any formulation, for I bear in mind Lord Atkin's warning against unnecessary restrictions on the adaptability of English law. I have, I hope, made it clear that I take quite literally the dictum of Lord Macmillan, so often quoted from the same case, that "the categories of negligence are never closed." English law is wide enough to embrace any new category or proposition that exemplifies the principle of proximity.

Lord Hodson and **Lord Pearce** delivered concurring speeches.

Questions

1. At whose risk does a businessman lay out money on credit in the hope of profit?

2. If you had been so suspicious as to make repeated inquiries about Easipower's financial standing, how would you have understood the statement made by the defendant in this case? In what precise respects was the defendant negligent?

3. Suppose that the plaintiff had in his files, but had forgotten it, information suggesting that the defendant could not have meant what he appeared to be saying; would you allow the plaintiff to recover part of his loss on the ground that both were negligent? For the terms of the Law Reform (Contributory Negligence) Act 1945, see below, p.245, and see Lord Reid at [1971] A.C. 793 at 811.

4. The disclaimer of responsibility apart, do you think the plaintiff should have recovered only what it had had to pay to the media (*i.e.* its out-of-pocket loss) or the whole amount it would have charged to Easipower (*i.e.* its loss of profit)?

5. In these cases the debtor (here Easipower) will probably go into liquidation or bankruptcy, and it may be some time before it is clear what portion of their claims the creditors will receive. At what time may the plaintiff issue proceedings against the defendant?

6. Are you amused that the leading case on misrepresentation should involve an advertising agent—as *plaintiff*?

7. Reflect for a moment on the conduct of Mr Heller in writing the letter complained of. The trial judge unhesitatingly found it negligent, the House of Lords taking no view on the matter. Do *you* think that it was negligent to write such a letter? How would you have understood it? Suppose an employee wrote such a letter and thereby landed his employer with a liability for £17,000. Would it be fair for the employer to dismiss him? Is there a risk that conduct which causes financial harm is more likely to be held negligent than conduct which causes physical harm? Is such conduct more likely to occur? Have you ever copied out a paragraph of text with complete accuracy? Have you ever failed to spot a misprint, or struck out the wrong alternative in a form, or put a tick or cross in the wrong box? If liability is to be dependent on fault in such cases, should liability not be roughly proportional to fault?

8. Was the alleged responsibility of Heller and Partners one which was personal to them or was it merely vicarious, they being answerable for Mr Heller's negligence in expressing himself in the way he did? If the plaintiff had paid for the advice, which would it be?

9. The letter from Heller & Partners was accurate but misleading. The plaintiffs were also misled in *Gold Coin Joailliers SA v United Bank of Kuwait* [1996] Times L.R. 615. A rogue phoned the defendant bank pretending to be their customer X, a person in good standing, and asked them to give a reference which would soon be requested. He then went to the plaintiffs, ostensibly to buy some watches, and suggested that they call the bank for a reference. When the plaintiffs did so, the bank replied that the customer had just called and was quite reliable. The plaintiffs let the rogue have the watches against an instruction from him to the bank, which it naturally refused to honour. Judgment for the plaintiff below was reversed: the bank's representation was not that the rogue was its customer but that its customer was solvent.

10. Judgment for the plaintiff was also reversed in *HIT Finance v Cohen Arnold & Co*, October 14, 1999, CA. An erroneous statement of the net worth of a director of a company to which the plaintiff was to lend money was held not to generate liability: it was explicitly based "on information received". Would the Unfair Contract Terms Act 1977 be applicable in this case, as it was held to be to the disclaimer by the surveyor in *Smith v Eric S Bush* ([1988] 1 All E.R. 691, HL)?

Notes:

1. This is the first great case where a person merely negligent was, in principle, held liable for causing merely pecuniary loss to a non-contractor. There is a very interesting article on its background in (1964) 27 M.L.R. 121 (Robert Stevens).

The decision was thought by some to herald a general liability for causing foreseeable economic loss by negligent conduct, but *Spartan Steel* (above p.53) shows that it has not had that effect. Indeed, it is probable that claims for economic harm due to negligence are possible now only if they are capable of subsumption under *Hedley Byrne* as now understood, *i.e.* that *Hedley Byrne* is the sole authoritative source of such liability.

2. As to the grounds of liability in the area of misrepresentation, only one decision has really sought to limit *Hedley Byrne*. In *Mutual Life v Evatt* [1971] A.C. 793 an investor had asked his insurance company about a subsidiary of theirs to which he was thinking of making unsecured loans at a high rate of interest. He got a positive answer and lost his money. He lost his lawsuit too, because a majority of the Privy Council held that it was not the defendant's business to give such advice and that it was therefore not liable. Quite right, too. Lord Reid and Lord Hodson dissented strongly, on the ground that this was to pervert their own decision in *Hedley Byrne*, but their dissent has no special force: an author has no interpretational privilege. However, the High Court of Australia has rejected this limitation on the "principle" of *Hedley Byrne* (*Shaddock v Parramatta* (1981) 36 A.L.R. 385, noted (1982) 2 Oxf.L.S. 440), and it is doubtful if it will be followed in England, though it would be useful to preserve us from pestilential questioners seeking free, or even inside information. Lord Denning has propounded a more flexible test. *viz.* was it clear that in all the circumstances the inquiry was directed towards obtaining considered advice rather than a quick answer? *Howard Marine v Ogden & Sons* [1978] Q.B. 574 at 591.

3. Since the *Hedley Byrne* case has recently been subjected to stringent scrutiny and detailed analysis in the hope of eliciting its animating principle, we shall defer further discussion until after the next principal case, noting en passant an important passage in Lord Goff's speech for the House of Lords in *Henderson v Merrett Syndicates* [1994] 3 All E.R. 506 at 520-521.

The facts of *Henderson* were that individuals rich enough to provide a certificate of wealth and become "names" at Lloyd's agreed to being placed, either by their own agents or by persons selected by those agents, on syndicates which issued policies rendering the names personally liable to the full extent of their estate should an insured event occur. After several profitable years the names discovered to their dismay that insurance involved risks as well as profits, the risks being due to the exuberant law of tort and the dismal weather in the United States. Reacting after the manner of investors with burnt fingers, they sued both their own agents and the sub-agents whom their agents had retained, and the court accepted that those placing the insurance had been negligent in overexposing the names.

In a long speech holding the sub-agents liable in tort, and the agents liable (a) in tort as well as contract for their own negligence, and (b) in contract for the negligence of the subagents, Lord Goff said this:

"In subsequent cases concerned with liability under the *Hedley Byrne* principle in respect of negligent mis-statements, the question has frequently arisen whether the plaintiff falls within the category of persons to whom the maker of the statement owes a duty of care. In seeking to contain that category of persons within reasonable bounds, there has been some tendency on the part of the courts to criticise the concept of "assumption of responsibility" as being "unlikely to be a helpful or realistic test in most cases" (see *Smith v Eric S Bush* (a firm), *Harris v Wyre Forest D.C.* [1989] 2 All E.R. 514 at, 536, *per* Lord Griffiths; and see also *Caparo Industries plc v Dickman* [1990] 1 All E.R. 568 at 582–583, *per* Lord Roskill). However, at least in cases such as the present, in which the same problem does not arise, there seems to be no reason why recourse should not be had to the concept, which appears after all to have been adopted, in one form or another, by all of their Lordships in *Hedley Byrne & Co Ltd v Heller & Partners Ltd.* Furthermore, especially in a context concerned with a liability which may arise under a contract or in a situation "equivalent to contract", it must be expected that an objective test will be applied when asking the question whether, in a particular case, responsibility should be held to have been assumed by the defendant to the plaintiff . . . In addition, the concept provides its own explanation why there is no problem in cases of this kind about liability for pure economic loss; for if a person assumes responsibility to another in respect of certain services, there is no reason why he should not be liable in damages to that other in respect of economic loss which flows from the negligent performance of those services. It follows that, once the case is identified as falling within the *Hedley Byrne* principle, there should be no need to embark upon any further inquiry whether it is "fair, just and reasonable" to impose liability for economic loss—a point which is, I consider, of some importance in the present case. The concept indicates too that in some circumstances, for example where the undertaking to furnish the relevant service is given on an informal occasion, there may be no assumption of responsibility; and likewise that an assumption of responsibility may be negatived by an appropriate disclaimer. I wish to add in parenthesis that . . . an assumption of responsibility by, for example, a professional man may give rise to liability in respect of negligent omissions as much as negligent acts of commission, as for example when a solicitor assumes responsibility for business on behalf of his client and omits to take a certain step, such as the service of a document, which falls within the responsibility so assumed by him . . . "

Note:

It is very odd that Lord Goff should say that in cases falling under *Hedley Byrne* there is no need to ask whether the imposition of a duty of care is "fair, just and reasonable" when (a) *Hedley Byrne*, as extended, is taken to be the sole source of liability for carelessly causing purely economic loss, and (b) as Lord Lloyd observed in *The Nicholas H* (above, p.45), it was precisely for cases of pure economic loss that the "fair, just and reasonable" qualification was introduced. Do you think Lord Goff had any special reason for saying that the "fair, just and reasonable" test was not relevant in the case before him? And can you see any connection between the views expressed by him in this case, in which all his brethren concurred, and in *White v Jones* (below, p.65), on which argument had already been heard and in which the dissent within a Committee identically composed was such as to delay the publication of the speeches for 11 months?

WILLIAMS v NATURAL LIFE HEALTH FOODS

House of Lords [1998] 1 W.L.R. 830; [1998] 2 All E.R. 577 (noted [1998] Camb. L.J. 456)

Action by franchisee against director of franchising company whose overoptimistic advice had misled it

The plaintiffs were interested in obtaining from the defendant company, formed by its managing director, Mistlin, a franchise for a health food shop. The company's brochure laid claim to the necessary expertise on the basis of Mistlin's experience of running such a shop in Salisbury. The company then sent the plaintiffs certain financial projections, largely produced by Mistlin himself. So encouraged, the plaintiffs entered into a franchise agreement, leased a shop, found the turnover much less than predicted and ceased trading. They sued the company and when the company failed added Mistlin as personal defendant on the basis that he had assumed personal responsibility. The trial judge and the Court of Appeal, by a majority, held Mistlin liable in damages. The House of Lords unanimously reversed.

Lord Steyn: In this case, the identification of the applicable principles is straightforward. It is clear, and accepted by counsel on both sides, that the governing principles are stated in the leading speech of Lord Goff of Chieveley in *Henderson v Merrett Syndicates Ltd* [1994] 3 All E.R. 506. First, in *Henderson*'s case it was settled that the assumption of responsibility principle enunciated in the *Hedley Byrne* case is not confined to statements but may apply to any assumption of responsibility for the provision of services. The extended *Hedley Byrne* principle is the rationalisation or technique adopted by English law to provide a remedy for the recovery of damages in respect of economic loss caused by the negligent performance of services. Secondly, it was established that once a case is identified as falling within the extended *Hedley Byrne* principle, there is no need to embark on any further inquiry whether it is "fair, just and reasonable" to impose liability for economic loss. Thirdly, and applying *Hedley Byrne*, it was made clear that—

> "reliance upon [the assumption of responsibility] by the other party will be necessary to establish a cause of action (because otherwise the negligence will have no causative effect) . . . "

Fourthly, it was held that the existence of a contractual duty of care between the parties does not preclude the concurrence of a tort duty in the same respect.

The issue in this case is not peculiar to companies. Whether the principal is a company or a natural person, someone acting on his behalf may incur personal liability in tort as well as imposing vicarious or attributed liability upon his principal. But in order to establish personal liability under the principle of *Hedley Byrne*, which requires the existence of a special relationship between plaintiff and tortfeasor, it is not sufficient that there should have been a special relationship with the principal. There must have been an assumption of responsibility such as to create a special relationship with the director or employee himself.

Two matters require consideration. First, there is the approach to be adopted as to what may in law amount to an assumption of responsibility. This point was elucidated in *Henderson*'s case [1994] 3 All E.R. 506 at 521, by Lord Goff of Chieveley. He observed:

> " . . . especially in a context concerned with a liability which may arise under a contract or in a situation 'equivalent to contract', it must be expected that an objective test will be applied when asking the question whether, in a particular case, responsibility should be held to have been assumed by the defendant to the plaintiff . . . "

The touchstone of liability is not the state of mind of the defendant. An objective test means that the primary focus must be on things said or done by the defendant or on his behalf in dealings with the plaintiff. Obviously, the impact of what a defendant says or does must be judged in the light of the relevant contextual scene. Subject to this qualification, the primary focus must be on exchanges (in which term I include statements and conduct) which cross the line between the defendant and the plaintiff. Sometimes such an issue arises in a simple bilateral relationship. In the present case a triangular position is under consideration: the prospective franchisees, the franchisor company, and the director. In such a case where the personal liability of the director is in question, the internal arrangements between a director and his company cannot be the foundation of a director's personal liability in tort. The inquiry must be whether the director, or anybody on his behalf, conveyed directly or indirectly to the prospective franchisees that the director assumed personal responsibility towards the prospective franchisees.

That brings me to reliance by the plaintiff upon the assumption of personal responsibility. If reliance is not proved, it is not established that the assumption of personal responsibility had causative effect. . . . The test is not simply reliance in fact. The test is whether the plaintiff could *reasonably* rely on an assumption of personal responsibility by the individual who performed the services on behalf of the company.

Mr Mistlin owned and controlled the company. The company held itself out as having the expertise to provide reliable advice to franchisees. The brochure made clear that this expertise derived from Mr Mistlin's experience in the operation of the Salisbury shop. In my view these circumstances were insufficient to make Mr Mistlin personally liable to the plaintiffs. . . . In the present case there were no personal dealings between Mr Mistlin and the plaintiffs. There were no exchanges or conduct crossing the line which could have conveyed to the plaintiffs that Mr Mistlin was willing to assume personal responsibility to them. Contrary to the submissions of counsel for the plaintiffs, I am also satisfied that there was not even evidence that the plaintiffs believed that Mr Mistlin was undertaking personal responsibility to them. Certainly, there was nothing in the circumstances to show that the plaintiffs could reasonably have looked to Mr Mistlin for indemnification of any loss. For these reasons I would reject the principal argument of counsel for the plaintiffs.

Counsel for the plaintiffs tried to support the judgment of the Court of Appeal on the alternative ground that Mr Mistlin had played a prominent part in the production of the negligent projections and had directed that the projections be supplied to the plaintiffs. Accordingly, he submitted, Mr Mistlin was a joint tortfeasor with the company, the latter being liable to the plaintiffs on the extended *Hedley Byrne* principle. . . . The argument is unsustainable. A moment's reflection will show that, if the argument were to be accepted in the present case, it would expose directors, officers and employees of companies carrying on business as providers of services to a plethora of new tort claims. The fallacy in the argument is clear. In the present case liability of the company is dependent on a special relationship with the plaintiffs giving rise to an assumption of responsibility. Mr Mistlin was a stranger to that particular relationship. He cannot therefore be liable as a joint tortfeasor with the company. If he is to be held liable to the plaintiffs, it could only be on the basis of a special relationship between himself and the plaintiffs. There was none. I would therefore reject this alternative argument.

Another of the same:

A circular sent by a company to its shareholders inviting them to subscribe for further shares was grossly misleading. Included in the text of the circular was a letter written to the company by the defendant accountants. Other advice given by the defendants to the company was also contained in the circular but not attributed to the defendants. For any errors in the letter the defendants were clearly liable, if negligent, but not for the unattributed advice: a plaintiff who is unaware that X's misrepresentations were based on the defendant's advice has no claim against the defendant. *Abbott v Strong* [1998] Times L.R. 421.

Yet another of the same—or not?

In *Merrett v Babb* [2001] 3 W.L.R. 1 the claimants bought a modest house which the defendant surveyor, employed by the firm retained and paid by the lender, had negligently overvalued. The plaintiffs knew that the property must have been given a clean bill of health, but had no idea who had given it. The claimants sued the firm and, when it went bankrupt, added the defendant personally.

On these facts a person who has read *Williams* would unhesitatingly assume that the claim against the personal defendant would fail: there was no basis on which the claimants could reasonably have relied on any assumption of responsibility on his part towards them. Yet the Court of Appeal by a majority gave judgment for the claimants and the House of Lords refused leave to appeal.

Why was this? It was because in *Harris v Wyre Forest District Council* [1990] A.C. 831 the House of Lords had said that the anonymous employee who surveyed a property for his employer, the local authority/mortgagee, owed a duty of care to the purchasers, (the principal purpose of this holding being to render the local authority vicariously liable, whereas it might well have been held personally liable for breach of its own duty to have the property properly surveyed prior to lending).

In the light of this decision, May L.J. said that as between valuer and purchaser

" . . . the law recognises that . . . there is a duty of care without the need to find any direct overt dealings" between them. He sidelined *Williams* as being a case involving the liability of the director of a company and limited to that context, though Lord Steyn had made it clear that this was not so, whereas the dissentient, Aldous L.J., by contrast, founded on *Williams* and noted that in *Williams* Lord Steyn had said that *Harris* was "decided on special facts", to which Wilson J. responded by saying that the facts in *Merrett* were equally special.

We clearly have a crux here. Nick McBride thoroughly approves of *Merrett* as showing that it is not the case that all claims for pure economic loss must be brought under the umbrella of *Hedley Byrne*, however extended, but that there is a different principle, which *Harris v Wyre* exemplifies, that a professional who ought to realise that if he misconducts himself he will very likely cause serious loss to another who can ill afford it owes that other a duty to take proper care in what he does. Those who read the next case will note that this is much in line with what Lord Browne-Wilkinson says and Lord Goff does without saying so.

Question:
Do these decisions help us answer question 8 on p.61 above?

WHITE v JONES

House of Lords [1995] 2 A.C. 207; [1995] 2 W.L.R. 187; [1995] 1 All E.R. 691 (noted (1995) 111 L.Q.R. 357; [1995] Camb.L.J. 238)

Action by intended legatee against testator's solicitor

In March a man quarrelled so badly with his two daughters over his wife's will that he made a will of his own, leaving them nothing. After a reconciliation three months later he decided to alter his will and leave them legacies of £9,000 each. On July 17 he so instructed his solicitors, the defendants, but by September 14, when the man died, they had still done nothing, so his daughters got nothing from the estate.

The daughters sued the solicitors, but Turner J. dismissed their claim on the ground that the defendants had been guilty of mere omission and that the harm complained of was too speculative. The Court of Appeal unanimously reversed.

The House of Lords (taking even longer to decide than the solicitors took to act) eventually held by a bare majority that the defendant's appeal should be dismissed.

Lord Goff of Chieveley: . . . [first considered the reasons which made it a matter of "practical justice" to grant a disappointed legatee a claim against a negligent solicitor, namely that (i) there would be a "lacuna in the law" if legatees who had suffered the loss had no claim, seeing that the testator's estate, which did have a claim, had suffered no loss; (ii) legacies were very important as one of the few ways individuals, especially those of modest means, could increase their capital; (iii) solicitors could not complain of having to pay for the consequences of their negligence, especially as (iv) they play an important role in society.] . . .

The question therefore arises whether it is possible to give effect in law to the strong impulse for practical justice which is the fruit of the foregoing considerations. For this to be achieved, I respectfully agree with Nicholls V.-C. when he said that the court will have to fashion "an effective remedy for the solicitor's breach of his professional duty to his client" in such a way as to repair the injustice to the disappointed beneficiary . . .

In *Ross v Caunters* [1980] Ch. 297 Megarry V.-C. approached the problem as one arising under the ordinary principles of the tort of negligence, and on that basis, relying in particular on *Ministry of Housing and Local Government v Sharp* [1970] 2 Q.B. 223 (which he regarded as conclusive of the point before him), he held that here liability could properly be imposed in negligence for pure economic loss, his preferred basis being by direct application of *Donoghue v Stevenson* itself.

An ordinary action in tortious negligence on the lines proposed by Megarry V.-C. in *Ross v Caunters* must, with the greatest respect, be regarded as inappropriate, because it does not meet any of the conceptual problems which have been raised. Furthermore, the *Hedley Byrne* principle cannot, in the absence of special circumstances, give rise on ordinary principles to an assumption of responsibility by the testator's solicitor towards an intended beneficiary. Even so, it seems to me that it is open to your Lordships' House to fashion a remedy to fill a lacuna in the law and so prevent the injustice which would otherwise occur on the facts of cases such as the present . . . since the nature of the transaction was such that, if the solicitors were negligent and their negligence did not come to light until after the death of the testator, there would be no remedy for the ensuing loss unless the intended beneficiary could claim. In my opinion, therefore, your Lordships' House should in cases such as these extend to the intended beneficiary a remedy under the *Hedley Byrne* principle by holding that the assumption of responsibility by the solicitor towards his client should be held in law to extend to the intended beneficiary who (as the solicitor can reasonably foresee) may, as a result of the solicitor's negligence, be deprived of his intended legacy in circumstances in which neither the testator nor his estate will have a remedy against the solicitor. Such liability will not of course arise in cases in which the defect in the will comes to light before the death of the testator, and the testator either leaves the will as it is or otherwise continues to exclude the previously intended beneficiary from the relevant benefit. I only wish to add that, with the benefit of experience during the 15 years in which *Ross v Caunters* has been regularly applied, we can say with some confidence that a direct remedy by the intended beneficiary against the solicitor appears to create no problems in practice. That is therefore the solution which I would recommend to your Lordships.

Lord Browne-Wilkinson: My Lords, . . . I agree that your Lordships should hold that the defendant solicitors were under a duty of care to the plaintiffs arising from an extension of the principle of assumption of responsibility explored in *Hedley Byrne Co Ltd v Heller & Partners Ltd* In my view, although the present case is not directly covered by the decided cases, it is legitimate to extend the law to the limited extent proposed using the incremental approach by way of analogy advocated in *Caparo Industries plc v Dickman* [below, p.80]. To explain my reasons requires me to attempt an analysis of what is meant by "assumption of responsibility" in the law of negligence. To avoid misunderstanding I must emphasise that I am considering only whether some duty of care exists, not with the extent of that duty which will vary according to the circumstances.

I turn then to consider *Hedley Byrne v Heller*. In that case this House had to consider the circumstances in which there could be liability for negligent misstatement in the absence of either a contract or a fiduciary relationship between the parties. . . . The House was seeking to define a further special relationship in addition to, not in substitution for, fiduciary relationships . . .

. . . since this House was concerned with cases of negligent misstatement or advice, it was inevitable that any test laid down required both that the plaintiff should rely on the statement or advice and that the defendant could reasonably foresee that he would do so. In the case of claims based on negligent statements (as opposed to negligent actions) the plaintiff will have no cause of action at all unless he can show damage and he can only have suffered damage if he has relied on the negligent statement. Nor will a defendant be shown to have satisfied the requirement that he should foresee damage to the plaintiff unless he foresees such reliance by the plaintiff as to give rise to the damage. Therefore, although reliance by the plaintiff is an essential ingredient in a case based on negligent misstatement or advice, it does not follow that in all cases based on negligent action or inaction by the defendant it is necessary in order to demonstrate a special relationship that the plaintiff has in fact relied on the defendant or the defendant has foreseen such reliance. If in such a case careless conduct can be foreseen as likely to cause and does in fact cause damage to the plaintiff that should be sufficient to found liability.

Third, it is clear that the basis on which (apart from the disclaimer) the majority would have held the bank liable for negligently giving the reference was that, were it not for the disclaimer, the bank would have assumed responsibility for such reference. Although there are passages in the speeches which may point the other way, the reasoning of the majority in my judgment points clearly to the fact that the crucial element was that, by choosing to answer the inquiry, the bank had assumed to act, and thereby created the special relationship on which the necessary duty of care was founded. . . .

Let me now seek to bring together these various strands so far as is necessary for the purposes of this case: I am not purporting to give any comprehensive statement of this aspect of the law. The law of England does not impose any general duty of care to avoid negligent misstatements or to avoid causing pure economic loss even if economic damage to the plaintiff was foreseeable. However, such a duty of care will arise if there is a special relationship between the parties. Although the categories of cases in which such a special relationship can be held to exist are not closed, as yet only two categories have been identified, *viz.* (1) where there is a fiduciary relationship and (2) where the defendant has voluntarily answered a question or tenders skilled advice or services in circumstances where he knows or ought to know that an identified plaintiff will rely on his answers or advice. In both these categories the special relationship is created by the defendant voluntarily assuming to act in the matter by involving himself in the plaintiff's affairs or by choosing to speak. If he does so assume to act or speak he is said to have assumed responsibility for carrying through the matter he has entered upon. . . . Such relationship can arise even though the defendant has acted in the plaintiff's affairs pursuant to a contract with a third party.

I turn then to apply those considerations to the case of a solicitor retained by a testator to draw a will in favour of an intended beneficiary.

Has the intended beneficiary a cause of action based on breach of a duty of care owed by the solicitor to the beneficiary? The answer to that question is dependent upon whether there is a special relationship between the solicitor and the intended beneficiary to which the law attaches a duty of care. In my judgment the case does not fall within either of the two categories of special relationships so far recognised. There is no fiduciary duty owed by the solicitor to the intended beneficiary. Although the solicitor has assumed to act in a matter closely touching the economic well-being of the intended beneficiary, the intended beneficiary will often be ignorant of that fact and cannot therefore have relied upon the solicitor.

However, it is clear that the law in this area has not ossified. . . . In *Caparo Industries plc v Dickman* [below, p.80] Lord Bridge recognised that the law will develop novel categories of negligence "incrementally and by analogy with established categories". In my judgment, this is a case where such development should take place since there is a close analogy with existing categories of special relationship giving rise to a duty of care to prevent economic loss.

The solicitor who accepts instructions to draw a will knows that the future economic welfare of the intended beneficiary is dependent upon his careful execution of the task. It is true that the intended beneficiary (being ignorant of the instructions) may not rely on the particular solicitor's actions. But, as I have sought to demonstrate, in the case of a duty of care flowing from a fiduciary relationship liability is not dependent upon actual reliance by the plaintiff on the defendant's actions but on the fact that, as the fiduciary is well aware, the plaintiff's economic well-being is dependent upon the proper discharge by the fiduciary of his duty. Second, the solicitor by accepting the instructions has entered upon, and therefore assumed responsibility for, the task of procuring the execution of a skilfully drawn will knowing that the beneficiary is wholly dependent upon his carefully carrying out his function. That assumption of responsibility for the task is a feature of both the two categories of special relationship so far identified in the authorities. It is not to the point that the solicitor only entered on the task pursuant to a contract with the third party (*i.e.* the testator). There are therefore present many of the features which in the other categories of special relationship have been treated as sufficient to create a special relationship to which the law attaches a duty of care. In my judgment the analogy is close.

Moreover there are more general factors which indicate that it is fair, just and reasonable to impose liability on the solicitor. . . .

In all these circumstances, I would hold that by accepting instructions to draw a will, a solicitor does come into a special relationship with those intended to benefit under it in consequence of which the law imposes a duty to the intended beneficiary to act with due expedition and care in relation to the task on which he has entered. For these and the other reasons given by my noble and learned friend, Lord Goff of Chieveley, I would dismiss the appeal.

Lord Mustill (dissenting): . . . I ask myself this question. If A promises B to perform a service for B which B intends, and A knows, will confer a benefit on C if it is performed, does A owe to C in tort a duty to perform that service? So expressed, this is a new question, and the right way to approach it is, as Lord Devlin explained in *Hedley Byrne & Co Ltd v Heller & Partners Ltd* is to "see how far the authorities have gone, for new categories in the law do not spring into existence overnight".

My Lords, when making this inquiry I do not think it profitable to take *Donoghue v Stevenson* as a point of departure. The decision itself is remote from the present, and although the liberating effect of Lord Atkin's celebrated pronouncement is beyond compare, as a practical guide to the consideration of duties in particular situations it does not lead very far—as Lord Devlin had cause to observe in *Hedley Byrne*, and as numerous judgments in your Lordships' House and elsewhere have more recently demonstrated.

As I understand your Lordships' opinions only one feature of existing law is relied upon as the starting point for a new principle wide enough to yield an affirmative answer to the question just posed: namely *Hedley Byrne* itself. Once again, the facts are too distant for the decision to be applied directly. In *Hedley Byrne* the plaintiffs asked the defendants to do something; the defendants did it, and did so imperfectly. Here, leaving aside the special facts of this appeal, and concentrating on the general case of the disappointed beneficiary, the complaint is that the solicitor did not do something which the beneficiary never asked him to do. It is therefore necessary to determine the ratio which underlies the decision in *Hedley Byrne*. In my judgment it is possible to detect within the speeches four themes, which I will label "mutuality", "special relationship", "reliance" and "undertaking of responsibility". . . .

I begin with mutuality. By this I mean that both plaintiff and the defendant played an active part in the transaction from which the liability arose. The relationship fell short of a contract because in the absence of consideration it involved no positive obligation of performance on the part of the defendant. If he chose, he could have declined to give a reference. But it nevertheless had two participants. In *Hedley Byrne v Heller* the plaintiffs initiated the relationship by the request for a reference; the defendants acted on the request; and the plaintiffs relied on what they had done. The importance of these reciprocal dealings is in my judgment evident from a number of passages in the speeches . . .

Turning last to the concept of an undertaking of responsibility, most of the relevant passages have already been cited. . . .

From this extensive quotation I collect the following picture of *Hedley Byrne*. First, that the case was not seen by the House as being in a direct line from *Donoghue v Stevenson*. The situations were far removed, and the solutions adopted by the House in the two cases were not at all the same. In *Donoghue v Stevenson* the liability was derived by the court from the position in which the parties found themselves. It was imposed externally. In *Hedley Byrne* all the members of the House envisaged, perhaps in slightly different ways, that the liability arose internally from the relationship in which the parties had together chosen to place themselves. The House nevertheless attached great importance to *Donoghue v Stevenson* for a reason most forcefully expressed by Lord Devlin where, after discussing the concept of proximity, he said: "What Lord Atkin did was to use his general conception to open up a category of cases giving rise to a special duty".

Liberated therefore by *Donoghue v Stevenson* from the need to force new situations into old categories the House was free to analyse the special relationship which the parties had created for themselves. I use this description, because I believe that the element of what I have called mutuality was central to the decision. I think it clear from the passage in which Lord Devlin summed up not only his own opinion but also his understanding of those expressed by the other members of the House [above, p.60] that the legal responsibility accepted or undertaken by the person in question was one where the acceptance or undertaking was a reflection of the relationship in question. On the facts of *Hedley Byrne* this relationship was bilateral, being created on the one hand by the acts of the plaintiffs in first asking for a reference in circumstances which showed that the bankers' skill and care would be relied upon and then subsequently relying on it; and on the other hand by the bankers' compliance with the request. What conclusion the House would have reached if the element of mutuality had been absent if, for example, the defendants had for some reason despatched the reference spontaneously, without prior request cannot be ascertained from the speeches, but even if a claim had been upheld the reasoning must, I believe, have been fundamentally different.

Two further aspects of the decision call for mention. First, the use of the word "undertaking". There is a degree of ambiguity about this. In context however I think it clear that the word was not used in the sense of taking on or tackling a job. The passages quoted show that the defendants were held liable because the relationship was such as to show that they took upon themselves a legal duty to give with reasonable care whatever reference they chose to furnish.

Secondly, there was the element of reliance, to which great attention has been directed in the present case. This element was of course crucial to the success of the claim in *Hedley Byrne*; for without reliance there could be no damage, and without damage there could be no cause of action in negligence. But, so far as the duty of care was concerned, the reliance merely consummated the relationship already initiated by the plaintiffs' request and the defendants' response. To my mind therefore *Hedley Byrne* says nothing, one way or the other, about reliance or the anticipation of reliance as either necessary or sufficient for the recognition of a duty of care differently conceived.

. . . I turn now to *Henderson v Merrett Syndicates Ltd* [1994] 3 All E.R. 506. . . . I believe that five features material to the present case may be identified without controversy. First, there was the resolution of a long-standing controversy about the co-existence of liabilities in contract and in tort. Since the House recognised the possibility of concurrent liabilities even as between immediate parties in the transaction it would be impossible now to contend that the mere presence of a contract or contracts linking participants in the transaction is an absolute bar to liability in negligence for pure financial loss. Secondly, at a time when the courts had for some years been wrestling with the problems of the general law of negligence exemplified by the line of cases, which extends from *Anns v Merton L.B. to Caparo Industries plc v Dickman* and beyond, the speeches in *Henderson* brought back to prominence *Hedley Byrne* and *Nocton v Lord Ashburton* and gave them new life as a growing point for the law of negligence. Third, the House took the law one stage further by recognising a new type of situation in which there could be a duty of care to avoid pure financial loss. Fourth, the House acknowledged (perhaps for the first time) the possibility that liability might attach to careless or dilatory omissions as well as to careless acts. Finally, of course, there was the identification of the facts which led the House to conclude that the managing agents owed a duty of care to the indirect names. These were summarised by Lord Goff of Chieveley [1994] 3 All E.R. 506 at 522 as follows:

"The managing agents have accepted the names as members of a syndicate under their management. They obviously hold themselves out as possessing a special expertise to advise the names on the suitability of risks to be underwritten; and on the circumstances in which, and the extent to which, reinsurance should be taken out and claims should be settled. The names, as the managing agents well knew, placed implicit reliance on that expertise, in that they gave authority to the managing agents to bind them to contracts of insurance and reinsurance and to the settlement of claims."

On these facts, once the other theoretical difficulties had been overcome, the case fell squarely within the concept of the undertaking of legal responsibility for careful and diligent performance in the context of a mutual relationship which in my opinion was the essence of the decision in *Hedley Byrne*.

Can the principles thus formulated and applied be sufficient in themselves to yield a duty of care owed to an intended beneficiary? The proposition may conveniently be tested by reference to a will intended to be executed in favour of a charity. It often happens that the charity will not only have no knowledge of the testator's intention, but will never even have heard of the testator and his solicitor. In such a situation I can find no trace of a special relationship such as was contemplated by *Hedley Byrne*, and which actually existed in the two leading cases. The charity does nothing. It neither invites the solicitor to prepare the will, nor determines its conduct on the assumption that it will be skilfully and diligently prepared. There is no mutual relationship. Indeed, I find it hard to see that there is a relationship at all, in any ordinary sense, between parties who are linked only by the fact that if the solicitor does his job, and if the testator executes the will and does not revoke it, the charity will be better off. Nor in my opinion is the claim advanced by looking for an assumption or undertaking of liability. The solicitor does of course undertake the task of preparing the will, in the sense of agreeing to take it on. But this is between himself and his client. By virtue of his response to the testator's instructions the solicitor does assume or undertake a legal liability for doing it properly. But he undertakes nothing towards the charity in the sense of doing something on its behalf. So far as he is concerned the charity is no more than an item in the testator's instructions. My Lords, I am obliged to say that in my opinion the reasoning of *Hedley Byrne* and *Henderson* does not apply to such a case. If a cause of action exists at all it must fall into the first, not the second, of the two categories recognised by Lord Devlin. It is not a responsibility voluntarily accepted or undertaken, but is "imposed by law upon certain types of person in certain situations".

For these reasons therefore I conclude that the judgment in favour of the plaintiffs cannot be sustained by the direct application of the existing authorities. [. . . orderly development and certainty suffer], if duties are simply conjured up as a matter of positive law, to answer the apparent justice of an individual case. Be that as it may, the present case does not as it seems to me concern a unique and limited situation, where a remedy might be granted on an ad hoc basis without causing serious harm to the general structure of the law; for I cannot see anything sufficiently special about the calling of a solicitor to distinguish him from others in a much broader category. If the claim in the present case is sound, for any reasons other than those given by my noble and learned friends, it must be sound in every instance of the general situation which I have already identified, namely: where A promises B for reward to perform a service for B, in circumstances where it is foreseeable that performance of the service with care will cause C to receive a benefit, and that failure to perform it may cause C not to receive that benefit. To hold that a duty exists, even prima facie, in such a situation would be to go far beyond anything so far contemplated by the law of negligence. I must emphasise that the purpose here is not to conjure up the spectre of "opening the floodgates". It is simply that I cannot discern a principled reasoning which could lead to the recognition of such an extensive new area of potential liability.

In these circumstances I cannot see my way to join all those judges and commentators who have acknowledged a general right for disappointed beneficiaries to recover a solatium from an errant solicitor in tort.

Lord Keith of Kinkel dissented on the ground that to grant the plaintiff's claim would be to give them the benefit of a contract to which they were not parties, that a remedy in tort could not be arrived at by analogy with decided cases or by their incremental extension, since *Hedley Byrne* involved a direct relationship between the parties which created proximity between them, whereas here there was no relationship between the defendant and the plaintiffs, and the defendant did nothing upon which the plaintiffs acted to their detriment. Unlike the defendants in *Henderson* "Mr Jones was not engaged in managing any aspect of the plaintiffs' affairs. He was employed only to deal with a particular aspect of the testator's affairs." Lord Keith found "the conceptual difficulties involved in the plaintiffs' claim . . . to be too formidable to be resolved by any process of reasoning compatible with existing principles of law."

Lord Nolan agreed with **Lord Goff** and **Lord Browne-Wilkinson**, and said " . . . *Henderson v Merrett Syndicates Ltd* . . . shows that a contractual duty of care owed by the defendant to A may perfectly well co-exist with an equivalent tortious duty of care to B. Both duties depend on an assumption of responsibility by the defendant. In the former case the responsibility is assumed by the making of the contract and is defined by its terms. In the latter the responsibility is assumed by the defendant embarking on a potentially harmful activity and is defined by the general law. If the defendant drives his car on the highway, he implicitly assumes a responsibility towards other road users, and they in turn implicitly rely on him to discharge that responsibility. By taking his car on to the road, he holds himself out as a reasonably careful driver. In the same way, as it seems to me, a professional man or an artisan who undertakes to exercise his skill in a manner which, to his knowledge, may cause loss to others if carelessly performed, may therefore implicitly assume a legal responsibility towards them. . . . "

Questions:

1. X takes a fine picture to D for restoration, saying that it is to be a Christmas present for his favourite niece, P. D uses the wrong chemicals and the picture is ruined. X dies before hearing of the disaster. Can P sue D? (See *The Aliakmon* [1986] 2 All E.R. 145).

2. Lord Browne-Wilkinson and Lord Nolan respectively drew an analogy between a solicitor charged with drawing up a will and (a) a trustee managing property belonging in equity to the beneficiary, and (b) a person driving a car on the highway.

Can you see in what respects these analogies are flawed?

3. Did you note the respects in which, according to Lord Mustill (above, p.69) *Hedley Byrne* was extended by *Henderson*?

4. Lord Goff speaks exclusively of the legatee who is an individual, while Lord Mustill instances the charity which loses the legacy intended for it. . . . Can you see why? Do you see a connection with the observation that the valuer retained by the mortgagee may be liable to the purchaser only if the dwelling is a modest one? (*Smith v Eric S. Bush* [1990] 1 A.C. 831).

5. In *The Nicholas H* (above, p.45) Lord Steyn said that it was impossible to regard the surveyor as having "assumed responsibility" towards the cargo-owners. What would Lord Browne-Wilkinson have said? And would consistency have compelled him to give judgment for the cargo-owners in that case?

6. As we have seen, Lord Goff in *Henderson* said that once a case fell under *Hedley Byrne* there was no need to consider whether it was "fair just and reasonable" to impose a duty. Can this be squared with *The Nicholas H*?

7. The legal structure of the facts in *White v Jones* was identical to that in *Donoghue v Stevenson*, namely that the defendant's breach of contract with X caused foreseeable harm to the plaintiff (X being the testator and cafe-owner respectively). Can we therefore expect *White v Jones* to do for money what was done for safety by *Donoghue v Stevenson* (also decided by a bare majority)?

Notes:

1. Probably not. Remember that while Lord Goff opted for a pocket of liability, regardless of principle, Lord Browne-Wilkinson produced a principle out of his pocket and Lord Mustill found the pocket irreconcilable with any principle. Understandably, therefore, Lord Steyn has contested the view that "the consequences of this decision will long reverberate through the law of tort. I would argue that the decision was made in a one-off situation and that it tells us little about other problems in the law of tort." ("Does Legal Formalism hold sway in England?" [1996] Current Legal Problems 43 at 53), and in *Williams v Natural Life Health Foods* he described it as "decided on special facts", a view which accords better with the speech of Lord Goff than with that of Lord Browne-Wilkinson. (The views of Lord Browne-Wilkinson were disapproved by the High Court of Australia which by a majority allowed a disappointed legatee to sue the solicitor who allowed her spouse to witness the will: *Hill v van Erp* (1997) 188 C.L.R. 159. Likewise, it has been said—in *Carr-Glyn v Frearsons* [1998] 4 All E.R. 225 at 233—that "the reasoning in Lord Goff's speech—and only that reasoning— . . . can be said to have received the support of the majority in the House of Lords.")

2. In *White v Jones* Lord Goff was much moved by the "extraordinary fact" that (a) the estate would have a claim but no loss and (b) the disappointed legatee would have a . . . loss but no claim.

The courts, and especially Lord Goff, seem to be obsessed with the "black hole" syndrome, where loss is suffered by a person who has no title to sue the negligent party who caused it and the person with title to sue has suffered no loss. This occurs, for example, where Y is in breach of his contract with X but the loss is suffered by Z who has no contract with Y. The Contracts (Rights of Third Parties) Act 1999 Act does confer a title to sue on certain *beneficiaries* of contractual promises made to another, which will doubtless be extended to protect third party *victims* of breaches of contract (such as the legatees?), but if it is inapplicable, the common law as laid down in such cases as *Panatown* [2001] A.C. 518 may be invoked, at any rate where the party with title but no loss is allowed to sue for the loss suffered by the third party.

The black hole argument was raised in *Farah v British Airways* [2000] T.L.R. 45. The claimants were refused a British Airways flight to London after a Home Office liaison officer erroneously informed the airline that the claimants' papers were not in order and that they would be refused admission to Britain, with the result that British Airways would be required to repatriate them. Here there was a possible black hole in that British Airways, the misrepresentee, had suffered no loss and the claimants, who had suffered a loss, were not the misrepresentees. The Court of Appeal was ready to fill the hole by making the Home Office liable to the claimants, referring to *White v Jones* and *Spring v Guardian Assurance* as the only relevant authorities in such a tripartite situation, "an area of developing jurisprudence".

It may be observed that the black hole argument has force only if one is fully committed to the view that a negligent party who causes a loss must invariably, one way or another, be made to pay for it, a proposition to which we have already seen several exceptions.

3. (a) In *Carr-Glyn v Frearsons* (above) the estate did have a loss. The testatrix wished to leave her niece Helen her share in a house, the other half of which was vested in her nephew, Peter. If the testatrix's interest was that of a joint tenant as opposed to a tenant in common her share would go directly to Peter on her death, but a joint tenancy is very easily severable and severance would have ensured that her share passed to the testatrix's estate and thence to Helen, as intended. This severance the solicitor negligently failed to ensure, and thereby diminished the value of the estate. In order to allow Helen to sue, the court had to provide that where there was a chance of loss to the estate, the representatives must be joined in the suit of the disappointed legatee—rather a cumbrous way of doing justice to the legatee without doing injustice to a solicitor by exposing him to a double liability.

Again, in *Worby v Rosser* [1999] Times L.R. 612, CA, loss was caused to both the estate and the legatees. In helping the testator make a second will the solicitor failed to realise that the testator lacked the necessary capacity, and the legatees under the first will incurred expense in establishing the invalidity of the second. Their claim was dismissed: they could obtain their costs from the estate (though that would surely diminish their take!). But does a solicitor really owe the testator a duty to tell him he has no capacity? And if so, would he not be liable to the estate for the costs it had to pay the beneficiaries under the first will for establishing the invalidity of the second?

(b) In *Walker v Geo. H Medlicott* [1999] 1 All E.R. 685, by contrast, the disappointed beneficiary did have another claim: he could claim rectification of the will which in this case (unlike *White v Jones*) had actually been executed though it inaccurately reflected the testator's clear instructions. If so, the court held, the disappointed beneficiary's duty to mitigate his loss required him to claim rectification of the will (which would have the advantage that an unintended person no longer benefited).

4. The solicitor's duty to intended legatees is to see that his client's testamentary intentions are carried out. Thus no duty is owed to a potential residuary legatee when the solicitor is advising the testator about an *inter vivos* transaction: *Clarke v Bruce, Lance* [1988] 1 All E.R. 364. Nor is a duty owed to a claimant who might well have benefited if the solicitor had questioned the testator about his expressed intentions: *Gibbons v Nelsons* [2000] T.L.R. 317.

5. The *White v Jones* duty was extended to a financial adviser in *Gorham v British Telecommunications* [2000] 4 All E.R. 867: G's dependants could sue Standard Life for selling him a pension which did not, as he wished, provide for them in the event he predeceased them; the advice was bad because he should have remained with his occupational pension scheme.

Tort and Contract.

Prior to *Hedley Byrne* tort liability was characteristically imposed on persons who caused *physical* harm by *acting dangerously*, while liability in contract was incurred by those who caused *economic* harm by *not acting as promised*. *Hedley Byrne* introduced liability in tort where the harm was purely economic, at least where the relationship of the parties was "equivalent to contract" and *White* has now confirmed that tort liability may arise when merely economic harm results from doing nothing (here a typical breach of contract). If we further note that this novel liability is based on "assumption of responsibility" just as contractual liability used to be asserted in the form of *assumpsit*, it will be clear that the relationship between tort and contract has to be considered afresh.

Three judicial observations may be helpful here, the first two cited by Sir Donald Nicholls V.-C. in *White v Jones* [1993] 3 All E.R. 481 at 490: (1) "The law of contract and the law of tort are, in a modern context, properly to be seen as but two of a number of imprecise divisions, for the purpose of classification, of a general body of rules constituting one coherent system of law" (*per* Deane J. in *Hawkins v Clayton* (1988) 164 C.L.R. 539 at 584, where a solicitor in possession of a decedent's will was held liable to the executor for failure to notify him of his entitlement for a period during which the estate physically deteriorated); (2) "Just as equity remedied the inadequacies of the common law, so has the law of torts filled gaps left by other causes of action where the interests of justice so required" (*per* Bingham L.J. in *Simaan General Contracting Co v Pilkington Glass* [1988] 1 All E.R. 791 at 804). Note, however, (3) the acerbic observation of Lord Templeman: " ... the tort of negligence has not yet subsumed all torts and does not supplant the principles of equity or contradict contractual promises or complement the remedy of judicial review or supplement statutory rights" (*China & South Sea Bank v Tan* [1989] 3 All E.R. 839 at 841).

The delicacy of the interplay of contract and tort arises from the tension between the law's need to protect citizens from harm (tort) and its desire to respect the arrangements they have entered into (contract).

First, it is clear in English law that the mere fact that the defendant's conduct constituted a breach of his contract with the plaintiff does not prevent the plaintiff recovering "in tort" if the conduct would have been tortious in the absence of the contract, save that substantive defences (as opposed to time-bar, for example) good against a contractual claim will be equally good against the claim in tort. This does not, however, mean that a breach of contract is *ipso facto* a tort, seeing that some contractual duties are strict and may be breached without any negligence (*e.g.* the warranty of the quality of goods sold, s.14 of the Sale of Goods Act 1979; contrast s.13 of the Supply of Goods and Services Act 1982—reasonable care and skill). But whenever the breach is due to unreasonable conduct the tendency will be for consequent harm to be actionable in tort, since contractors normally "assume responsibility" and contract is undeniably a relationship "equivalent to contract".

Secondly, it is clear that contractors are free—though only within certain limits—to contract out of the law of tort, to oust its application explicitly. As Lord Goff said: "the law of tort is the general law, out of which the parties can, if they wish, contract." (*Henderson* [1994] 3 All E.R. 506 at 532). The limits of contracting-out are set by the Unfair Contract Terms Act 1977 (below, p.254), whereby courts can strike down almost any clause which fails to pass the test of "reasonableness". Doubtless the test will be easier to pass when the harm is purely economic, but it is a test which even the disclaimer in *Hedley Byrne* would nowadays have to pass (*Smith v Eric S Bush* [1989] 2 All E.R. 514).

Thirdly, in the absence of an explicit exclusion of tort liability the court may find that to impose liability in tort would be incompatible with the transactional set-up or background, including closely-linked arrangements with third parties. Thus in one case a piling contractor had agreed to use reasonable care and skill as regards the design of the works and the choice of materials. Nothing was said about care in the execution of the works. This contractual silence was held to prevent a duty arising in tort (*Greater Nottingham Co-operative Society v Cementation Piling & Foundations* [1988] 2 All E.R. 971). Recall, too, that in *The Nicholas H* (above, p.45) the surveyor was held to owe no duty in tort to the cargo-owner by reason, in part, of the nature of the cargo-owner's contractual relations with the owner of the ship surveyed.

Fourthly, the courts will not allow the law of tort to increase the duties undertaken by the defendant in his contract with the plaintiff. As Lord Scarman said: "Their Lordships do not believe that there is anything to the advantage of the law's development in searching for a liability in tort where the parties are in a contractual relationship . . . particularly . . . in a commercial relationship." *Tai Hing Cotton Mill v Liu Chong Hing Bank* [1985] 2 All E.R. 947 at 957. That is because it is established contract law that additional duties (or, indeed, qualifications of rights) not expressed will not be implied simply because it would be "fair, just and reasonable" to do so, but only if it is necessary for the operation of the contractual enterprise (and note that terms will be implied more readily in cases of physical damage than of merely financial harm (*The Moorcock* (1889) 14 P.D. 64) and in order to protect health sooner than comfort (*Liverpool C.C. v Irwin* [1977] A.C. 239)); furthermore, the unreasonable exercise of contractual rights to the hurt of the other party does not of itself generate liability (*Chapman v Honig* below, p.184; *Johnstone v Bloomsbury H.A.* [1991] 2 All E.R. 293.

Fifthly, it is worth nothing that just as no contractual liability arises from purely social engagements or "gentlemen's agreements" or agreements "subject to contract", so erroneous responses to informal requests are unlikely to trigger liability in tort.

Pre-Contractual Situations.

Although the damages in a contract suit may cover precontractual expenditure (*Anglia Television v Reed* [1971] 3 All E.R. 690), contractual liability cannot arise until there is a contract. Liability in tort, however, may well be incurred during negotiations, even if they prove abortive. *Hedley Byrne* certainly applies in the pre-contractual stage, unless it is made very clear that reliance is not to be put on what a party says. After all, Samuel Montagu were held liable to pay £172,000,000 (reduced by £30 million on appeal) when late at night after prolonged discussions its managing director said, in reply to a question whether a client could afford to buy one of the plaintiff's companies, "they're good for the money" (*British & Commonwealth v Samuel Montagu*, April 10, 1995).

If no contract results from the negotiations, the misrepresentee has to establish the duty and prove the breach, but once the deal is struck, the burden of proof is reversed and the misrepresentor must exculpate himself (Misrepresentation Act 1967, s.2(1)). There can be no good reason for this: the subsequent fact of a contract can hardly render it more likely that the misrepresentor was a fool to believe what he was saying. Of course there has to be a contract before *rescission* can take place (just as one cannot have a divorce without a prior marriage), and rescission is often sought in order to prevent the misrepresentor taking advantage of the mistake he has caused the misrepresentee to make. But this has nothing to do with the question whether the misrepresentor should be liable in *damages* for consequent loss. It is therefore important to keep rescission and damages cases quite separate, especially where there has been not misrepresentation but non-disclosure, not speech but silence: in a few types of contract a party who failed to share relevant information is refused enforcement of the other party's promise, but he is not for that reason liable in damages. *Levett v Barclays Bank* [1995] 2 All E.R. 615, which appears to equate "non-disclosure" and "implied misrepresentation", is a case of rescission, not damages.

Speech and Conduct.

Henderson extended the *Hedley Byrne* principle from speech to conduct, and *White* confirmed this. Yet in *Hedley Byrne* Lord Reid was sure that the law could not treat speech and conduct in quite the same way. Do differences still remain?

As to speech two points may be noted: (1) speech is *addressed* to someone, perhaps more than one, and (2) communication is made with a purpose in mind. Both of these factors have been used to restrict liability for misrepresentation (remember that "misrepresentation" is simply legal jargon for "misleading statement"), but neither factor applies in quite the same way to conduct. If, like Lord Browne-Wilkinson, one abandons the notion of mutuality, *i.e.* that the duty is owed only to the person at whose instance you acted, or agreed to act, then the only control seems to be "Who would be affected by what you were doing?". Instead of asking "Whom were you speaking *to*?" or even "Whom were you acting *for*?", one must now ask, apparently, "Who was to benefit from what you were doing?" or even, worse still, "Who might be harmed by what you were doing?" This renders the outcome of any case much less predictable, and the notion of "special relationship" fades away, as it did when *Donoghue v Stevenson* was extended from the consumer (aimed at) to the bystander (hit). It seems likely, therefore, that even if conduct falls within the liability-generating principle of *Hedley Byrne*, liability for financial harm due to speech and conduct will develop rather separately, though advocates will doubtless tap both streams as suits their argument.

"Reliance" involves taking action on the basis of belief in the truth of what you are told, *i.e.* something more specific (despite Lord Nolan's false equation (above, p.70)) than acting in the belief that strangers will conduct themselves in a particular manner. Reliance in the proper sense was thought to be an essential component of *liability* under *Hedley Byrne*, a necessary factor in the finding that a duty existed: the defendant must have realised that the plaintiff would so rely on what he said, or he would not be liable. Now it has been demoted to a mere element in *causation*: no harm will be caused by what you negligently say unless the addressee relies on its truth and his consequent action proves detrimental. (Similarly, under *Donoghue v Stevenson*, "probability of intermediate inspection", originally featuring among the conditions of the existence of a duty, is now merely an element in the causal link between breach and harm).

There was no such direct relationship in *Ministry of Housing and Local Government v Sharp* [1970] 2 Q.B. 223, a really odd case involving a rare instance of performative language, for the issuance by the Registrar of a clear certificate to the purchaser of land immediately destroyed the incumbrancer's right to claim its money back, *ipso facto* and without any reliance by anyone. Proximity was not a problem because the Registrar had the very name of the incumbrancer before his eyes, just as the solicitor in *White v Jones* had the names of the intended legatees in front of him.

Speech and Silence.

Another respect in which *Henderson* (*obiter*) and *White* (*ratio*) extended *Hedley Byrne* is in equating omission with action, which in the case of representations means equating silence with speech. Yet the courts have been very chary of imposing liability on people for not speaking, perhaps preferring the observation of Leavis that "The only way to avoid misrepresentation is to say nothing" to Camus's remark "I would say nothing were it not that my silence might be interpreted as meaning something."

"Mere silence or inaction cannot amount to a misrepresentation unless there be a duty to disclose or act." as Lord Scarman said in *Tai Hing Cotton Mill* [1985] 2 All E.R. 947 at 959. Even if Heller and Partners had known that Easipower were totally insolvent, they need not have said a word to Hedley Byrne.

Even where physical harm is in view, silence, the omission to warn, does not of itself give rise to liability: thus you need not tell a complete stranger that he is about to fall over a cliff—unless it is your cliff. If it is your cliff, you as occupier will be in a special relationship with the visitor, which generates liability for unreasonable failure to warn and protect. Thus the doctor who is asked by the patient about the risks of proposed treatment must answer truthfully, and must also tell him if anything goes wrong: "the duty of candid disclosure . . . is but one aspect of the general duty of care, arising out of the patient/medical practitioner or hospital authority relationship and gives rise to rights both in contract and in tort" *per* Sir John Donaldson M.R. in *Naylor v Preston A.H.A.* [1987] 2 All E.R. 353 at 360.

Where only financial interests are at stake, liability is much less readily imposed: the witness of an accident is not bound, short of a *subpoena*, to divulge the name and number of the fatal car (*Ricci v Chow* [1987] 3 All E.R. 534; *Norwich Pharmacal* [1974] A.C. 133). "The law does not impose, by reason merely of the knowledge of the existence of fraudulent conduct, any duty on any person to inform the victim of a current fraud so as to be liable in damages for failure to inform." *Bank of Nova Scotia v Hellenic Mutual (The Good Luck)* [1989] 3 All E.R. 628 at 670, CA.

Even where there is a special relationship the courts have been reluctant to impose liability for silence. Thus an insurer does not have to tell the insured that the insured's agent has been untrustworthy and may be so again (*Banque Financière v Westgate Insurance* [1990] 2 All E.R. 947): a school does not have to tell a pupil's parents that no accident insurance is carried by the school (*van Oppen v Trustees of Bedford College* [1989] 1 All E.R. 273); an employer need not inform employees about their pension rights (*Outram v Academy Plastics*, [2000] I.R.L.R. 499) unless, in an exceptional case, a term to that effect can be implied into the contract (*Scally v Southern Health* [1991] 4 All E.R. 563, HL), and, for want of any such implied terms, an employer sending a prospective employee abroad to a place where drivers do not carry liability insurance need not advise him to take out personal cover (*Reid v Rush & Tompkins* [1989] 3 All E.R. 228, CA).

Some qualifications may be necessary, however, for while "No one has ever suggested that in the ordinary case of principal and surety the creditor owes any duty of care to the surety . . . " to inform him of the risks being undertaken, yet if the creditor fails to see that the surety has independent advice in cases where there is reason to suspect that the primary debtor (often a husband, but any cohabitee will do) may be taking advantage of the surety or misleading her, he may be unable to enforce the security or guarantee (*Royal Bank of Scotland v Etridge (No.2)* [2002] 2 A.C. 773), and if he undertakes to explain the document (as a bank may be bound to do to its customer) he may be liable in damages for failure to do so fully (*Cornish v Midland Bank* [1985] 3 All E.R. 513).

But if it is true that any explanation which is actually given must be adequate, the duty of explanation must not be pitched too high: the duty to give correct information is not the same as the duty to give wise advice. Thus the Privy Council has held, by a bare majority, that a bank which supplied information requested by a customer was not liable for failing to add an explanation that it was an insufficient basis for a decision whether to invest or not: they had not undertaken to advise him (*Royal Bank Trust Co v Pampallone* [1987] 1 Lloyd's Rep. 218).

Duty to Whom?

In *Hedley Byrne* the information was not only given to, but also requested by, the plaintiff. The request identifies the plaintiff: more people hear than ask to hear, and people ask to hear because they have an interest in the reply and may act on it. Information which is volunteered attracts liability much less easily, especially if it is widely published. Thus a municipality which published a development plan which had to be abandoned because it was unfeasible was not liable to developers who had bought property on the strength of it: *San Sebastian Pty v Minister* (1986) 68 A.L.R. 161; 61 A.L.J.R. 41; 162 C.L.R. 340, H.Ct.Aus. Weather forecasting is a very clear example, even if the harm is physical in nature, as it tends to be: doubtless it would now be held that no responsibility was assumed, even though what they did was likely to affect others. A like distinction emerges from two French decisions. In one case the writer of a manual on how to commit suicide was held not liable to the dependants of readers who successfully followed his instructions; in another he was held liable to the estate of a reader, who, puzzled by the instructions, wrote for clarification, which he fatally received.

The person you are speaking *about* is as likely to be affected by what you say as the person you are speaking *to*. Yet it is clear law that the mere fact that the defendant was talking *about* the plaintiff rather than *to* him involves no liability in the absence of defamation or malice: the tort is "malicious falsehood" (see below, p.580) not "negligent falsehood" (or misrepresentation). However, there may be a special relationship between the speaker and the object of his speech as well as between the speaker and his addressee: thus in *Spring v Guardian Assurance* [1994] 3 All E.R. 129 an employer was held liable to an ex-employee for writing to a potential future employer a "kiss-of-death" testimonial although it was not through malice but want of care that it was inaccurate. Lord Goff felt bound to base his opinion on "assumption of responsibility", but Lord Slynn and Lord Woolf were able to give judgment for the plaintiff-appellant notwithstanding that "*Hedley Byrne v Heller & Partners* does not decide the present case" (Lord Slynn at 161), on the basis that the employer stood in a special relationship to his ex-employee, such that, indeed, an implied contractual term with similar content could well have been found. Much easier (because physical harm was involved) was *Harrison v Surrey C.C.* [1994] 4 All E.R. 577, where the defendant erroneously told the plaintiff's mother, in response to a specific request, that there was no reason to doubt that X (who later broke the plaintiff's skull) was suitable as a childminder.

Sometimes, however, no duty is owed even though the defendant is responding directly to a question put by the plaintiff. Thus in *Gran Gelato v Richcliff* the buyer of a lease sued the seller and the seller's solicitors, who had given an erroneous answer to an important question relating to the property. The judge held that the solicitors, who gave the answer, were not liable and owed no duty to the plaintiff because the seller would be answerable for the solicitor's negligence in the exercise of his authority to respond on behalf of the seller. ([1992] 1 All E.R. 865.

In principle, though, a duty is owed to the addressee, of whom there may be several, concurrent or consecutive. The range of persons to whom the duty is owed is not yet clear, but the courts may be expected to be hesitant, lest liability become rampant. For example, in *Shankie-Williams v Heavey* (1986) 279 E.G. 316 the defendant was retained by the seller of a house to inspect the floor timbers of the ground floor flat where dry-rot had previously been discovered. He reported that there was no dry-rot left, but sprayed as a precaution and gave a limited guarantee against recurrence. P1 and P2 bought the ground floor flat and P3 the flat above. Both flats were affected by dry-rot. The Court of Appeal held that no duty was owed to P3, and that while the defendant did owe a duty to P1 and P2, he was not liable to them because neither had in fact relied on his report. *Caparo*, the next following case, demonstrates another method of containing liability, namely by focussing on the purpose of the communication.

Hedley Byrne in Practice.

The decision in *Hedley Byrne* has kept the courts very busy indeed. We are concerned here only with common law claims for mere negligence, *i.e.* with cases where the plaintiff could not establish deliberate wrongdoing or breach of an actionable statutory duty:

Professional decision-makers

Judges, arbitrators, valuers and architects, whose job it is to decide how much people are to pay or be paid, are naturally very apt to cause financial loss by their decisions. Now that they may be sued by either party the question of their liability has become very acute. That judges are immune from liability is well established (*Sirros v Moore* [1975] Q.B. 118; a like immunity is extended to magistrates and their clerks by the Courts and Legal Services Act 1990, s.108; the Arbitration Act 1996, s.29(1) gives immunity to arbitrators unless they are in bad faith; so does the Housing Grants Construction and Regeneration Act 1996, s.108 to adjudicators provisionally resolving a dispute between persons involved in construction work (modifying *Sutcliffe v Thackrah* [1974] A.C. 727).

Insurers

Does an insurer owe a duty to a person of whom he knows, through his participation in the negotiations, that he will take an assignment of the policy? Yes: *Punjab National Bank v de Boinville* [1992] 3 All E.R. 104.

Does an insurer owe a duty to the insured to inform him of the suspicious conduct of the insured's broker? No: *Banque Financière* [1990] 2 All E.R. 947.

Does an insurer owe the mortgagee of an insured vessel a duty to report that the vessel is off cover? No: *Bank of Nova Scotia v Hellenic Mutual (The Good Luck)* [1989] 3 All E.R. 628 (rev'd on another point [1991] 3 All E.R. 1).

Does an insurer's broker owe a duty to the insured regarding the adequacy of the insurer's cover against liability to the insured? No—but it was a close thing: *Duncan Stevenson MacMillan v AW Knott Becker Scott* [1990] 1 Lloyd's Rep. 98 (Evans J.).

Does the insurer of a company owe a duty to its directors? No: *Verderame v Commercial Union* [1992] Times L.R. 164.

Do the underwriters of a company's permanent health scheme owe a duty to the company employee to use care in processing claims? No: *Briscoe v Lubrizol* [2000] I.C.R. 694.

Does a liability insurer owe a duty to the claimant against its insured to make a timeous decision about funding the defence? No: *Bristol & West plc v Bhadresa* (Lightman J.), [1999] 1 Lloyd's Rep. I.R. 138.

Security

Does a mortgagee owe a duty to the mortgagor to react reasonably to a request for consent to the letting of the property? No: *Starling v Lloyd's TSB Bank* [2000] Lloyd's Rep. Bank 8.

D was instructed by a client to arrange a security for the person from whom the client wished to borrow money. It was known that the lender would not consult a lawyer of his own. The security was defective, as the defendants should have known, and their client was penniless. Did the defendant owe a duty to the lender? Usually not, but in this case, yes. This was only an incremental step from *White v Jones* and *Gorham: Dean v Allin & Watts* [2001] E.W.C.A. Civ 758, [2001] Lloyd's Rep. 249.

A firm now in liquidation installed burglar alarms in the claimant's warehouse and paid the defendants to alert the police and the keyholder whenever an alarm went. On one occasion they failed to alert the keyholder and much property was stolen. The defendant was held liable: *Bailey v HSS Alarms*, [2000] T.L.R. 477.

Does a mortgagee owe a duty to a surety to sell the security at the right time so as to protect the surety from liability? No: *China and South Sea Bank v Tan* [1989] 3 All E.R. 839, PC.

Does a mortgagee, when he sells the mortgaged property, owe a duty (a) to the mortgagor, (b) to a surety, to try to obtain a proper price? Yes: (a) *Cuckmere Brick Co v Mutual Finance* [1971] Ch. 949; noted (1971) 87 L.Q.R. 303; (b) *Standard Chartered Bank v Walker* [1982] 3 All E.R. 938; noted (1983) 99 L.Q.R. 3. Is a similar duty owed to a known beneficiary? No (and the duty to the mortgagor arises in equity, not in tort) *Parker-Tweedale v Dunbar Bank* [1990] 2 All E.R. 577, CA.

Does a bank taking a mortgage on joint property owe a duty to the debtor's wife to counsel her to seek independent advice? No: *Barclays Bank v Khaira* [1992] 1 W.L.R. 623 (Thomas Morison QC) and see [1993] 1 Fam.L.R. 343, CA.

Is the mortgagee under any duty to protect the sale value of the business prior to taking possession? No: *AIB Finance v Debtors* [1998] 2 All E.R. 929. But a receiver, if put in possession, owes a duty to run the business properly, and this duty is owed to all those with an interest in the equity of redemption (*i.e.* those who get what is left after the debt is paid off): *Medforth v Blake* [1999] Times L.R. 463.

Does the liquidator of a company owe a duty to its majority shareholders who paid X to have him appointed, the breach being failure to inform them of the risk of time-bar of a claim? Possibly: *A & J Fabrications v Grant Thornton* [1998] 2 B.C.L.C. 227, but not the solicitors who negligently failed to advise him to institute a claim for their benefit ([1999] Times L.R. 588).

Does a mortgagee who has, in conjunction with the mortgagor, appointed a manager of the mortgaged property, owe the mortgagor a duty to check the manager's performance? No: *National Bank of Greece v Pinios Shipping Co (The Maira)* [1989] 1 All E.R. 213, CA.

Lawyers

Does a barrister owe a duty to his client's opponent as regards giving an undertaking and explaining it to his client? No: *Connolly-Martin v Davis* [1999] Times L.R. 431.

Does a solicitor retained by father to buy a flat for daughter owe a duty to the daughter? Yes, but limited in extent: *Woodward v Woolferstans* [1997] Times L.R. 189.

Does a solicitor acting for both lender and borrower on remortgage have a duty to tell the lender of the borrower's past payment record? No: *National Home Loans Corp. v Giffen Couch* [1998] 1 W.L.R. 207.

Does a company solicitor owe a duty to the directors who have guaranteed the company's indebtedness? Yes: *Foster v Crusts* (1985) 129 Sol.Jo. 333.

Does a solicitor owe a duty to a prospective client to inform him of available sources of financial support? Yes: *Crossan v Ward Bracewell* [1988] 1 All E.R. 364.

Does a vendor's solicitor whose misleading answers to the purchaser's inquiries render the vendor liable owe the purchaser an independent duty? No: *Gran Gelato v Richcliff* [1992] 1 All E.R. 865; noted (1992) 109 L.Q.R. 539.

Does a solicitor owe a duty to his client's wife to ascertain her consent to a proposed disposition of the property jointly owned by her and the fraudulent client? Yes, with express reference to the "principles laid down" in *White v Jones: Penn v Bristol & West Building Society* [1995] Times L.R. 348.

Is a solicitor liable for giving a reference for a client without disclosing the client's impending prosecution for dishonesty? Yes: *Edwards v Lee, The Independent*, November 1, 1991 (Brooke J.).

Banking

Does a customer owe his bank a duty to check bank statements and run his business carefully so as to prevent and detect fraud? No: *Tai Hing Cotton Mill v Liu Chong Hing Bank* [1986] A.C. 80.

Does the bank on which a cheque is drawn owe a duty to the payee to take care in honouring their customer's cheque? No: *National Westminster Bank v Barclays Bank* [1975] Q.B. 654.

Does a bank which must tell an account-holder of a forged cheque drawn on that account owe a like duty to the customer's agent who operates the account? Yes: *Weir v National Westminster Bank* [1995] 4 Banking L.R. 249.

Employment

Does an employer owe a duty to his employees to notify them of obscure advantages in the group pension scheme incorporated in the individual contracts of employment? No, unless such a duty could be found as an implied term in the contract, as it was in *Scally v Southern Health & Social Services Board* [1991] 4 All E.R. 563, HL, but not in *University of Nottingham v Eyett (No.2)* [1999] 2 All E.R. 437.

Does an employer owe an ex-employee a duty to take care when writing a reference to a prospective employer? Yes: *Spring v Guardian Assurance* [1994] 3 All E.R. 129, HL, amplified in *Bartholomew v Hackney L.B.C.* [1999] I.R.L.R. 246, CA.

Are shipowners under a duty to advise crew of risks and methods of avoidance where ship operating in war zone? Yes: *Tarrant v Ramage* [1997] Times L.R. 434.

Does an employer owe a duty to an employee being sent abroad to advise him to take out personal insurance against accidental injury? No: *Reid v Rush & Tompkins* [1989] 3 All E.R. 228.

Does an employer owe a duty to employees proposing to change employment to take care that the pension information it gives to the prospective employer is accurate? Yes: *Hagen v ICI Chemicals* [2002] I.R.L.R. 31.

Did the Ministry of Defence owe a duty to an officer to process promptly his application for premature voluntary release? No. *Newell v Ministry of Defence* [2002] E.W.H.C. 1006.

Sales

Does an auctioneer owe the unknown owner of goods tendered for sale a duty to carefully inquire into their provenance? No: *Marcq v Christie Manson & Woods* [2003] 3 All E.R. 561.

Does a pension salesman owe a duty to the relatives of a client to avoid giving him advice which would adversely affect their interests without improving his? Yes: *Gorham v British Telecommunications* [2000] 4 All E.R. 867.

Does Lloyd's Register of Shipping owe a duty to prospective purchasers of registered ships to take care that the details given are accurate? No: *Mariola Marine Co v Lloyd's Register of Shipping (The Morning Watch)* [1990] 1 Lloyd's Rep. 547.

Does the supplier of goods owe a duty to those whose intangible property rights may foreseeably be infringed by the purchaser? No: *CBS Songs v Amstrad Plc* [1988] 2 All E.R. 484 at 497; *Paterson Zochonis & Co v Merfarken Packaging* [1986] 3 All E.R. 522.

In *Circuit Systems v Zuken-Redac* [1996] 3 All E.R. 748 the defendant sold computers to a finance company to be let on hire-purchase terms to a firm which then collapsed by reason of faults in the computers. The plaintiff, its managing director, had to pay out on the guarantee he had given to the finance company. The court refused to strike out the claim as unarguable.

Did issuers of a misleading prospectus owe a duty at common law to persons buying shares in the after-market? Possibly, if this was the apparent intention: *Possfund v Diamond* [1996] 2 All E.R. 774.

Accountants

Does a company auditor preparing its annual report owe a duty to shareholders interested in buying more shares? No: *Caparo* (next case).

Does a district auditor owe a duty to (a) the local council whose accounts he is auditing, and (b) the individual councillors criticised in his report? Yes, and No respectively: *West Wilts. D.C. v Garland* [1995] 2 All E.R. 17.

Is an auditor who fails to qualify a report liable to (a) the company and (b) a lender? (a) No, because no reliance; (b) No, because no duty: *Berg Sons & Co v Adams* [1992] E.C.C. 661.

Do auditors of an investment company whose directors run off with investors' trust funds owe the investors a duty? No: *Anthony v Wright* [1995] 1 B.C.L.C. 236.

Does the accountant of a business which is up for sale owe a duty to the eventual purchaser to take care that the projection of profitability he provides at the instance of the lender bank is reasonably accurate? No: the accountant had no duty to advise the buyer of the true trading position or of the wisdom of the purchase. *Peter Lingham & Co v Lonnkvist* [2000] Lloyd's Rep. P.N. 885.

Does an auditor preparing accounts for a travel agency owe a duty to the insurance company which, on the basis of those accounts, issued the bond required by IATA? Yes: *Independent Advantage Insurance Co v Cook* [2002] E.W.C.A. Civ 1103.

Did the auditors of a firm of solicitors owe a duty to the Law Society which had to pay out huge sums to the defrauded clients of the firm to discover and notify them of the fraud? Yes: *Law Society v KPMG Peat Marwick* [2000] 4 All E.R. 540; but probably not to the Indemnity Fund which operated as an insurer.

Does an accountant providing a statement of a client's net worth owe a duty to a party considering making a loan to the client? Yes, (but no undertaking as to the truth of statement "on the basis of information supplied"). *HIT Finance v Cohen Arnold* (October 14, 1999, CA).

Does the auditor of company A and subsidiary A1 owe a duty to subsidiary A2 where their business affairs were thoroughly intertwined? exceptionally Yes: *BCCI (Overseas) v Price Waterhouse* [1998] Times L.R. 125.

Do auditors of company owe its directors a duty to inform them that a proposed purchase of another company by means of a loan made by that company would be illegal? Arguably: *Coulthard v Neville Russell* [1998] 1 B.C.L.C. 143, CA—"the liability of professional advisers for failure to give correct advice or accurate information was in a state of development and it was preeminently an area where the legal result was highly sensitive to the facts."

Local Government

Does a local authority which advertised advice and solicited enquiries owe a duty to persons inquiring by telephone on planning matters? No: *Tidman v Reading B.C.* [1994] Times L.R. 572.

Does a local authority owe a duty of care to a formal applicant for planning permission? No: *Strable v Dartford B.C.* [1984] J.P.L. 329, CA.

Does a planning authority owe a duty to neighbours when granting planning permission? No: *Chung Tak Lam v Brennan* [1997] P.I.Q.R. P488.

Does a local authority which had fixed the route of a pathway owe a duty to those using it? Yes: *Kane v New Forest DC* [2001] 3 All E.R. 914.

Does an officer of the Department of the Environment owe a duty to an applicant for planning permission who sought advice by telephone? "Although a duty could arise in relation to planning matters, that was only likely to arise in exceptional circumstances" *Haddon v Secretary of State* (CA, October 27, 1999).

[But note! Although the 22-year lease between Mr Stretch and the Dorchester Borough Council not only required him to erect buildings for light industrial use but also entitled him to an extension for a further 21 years, his application for the extension was refused on the ground that the original grant was beyond the council's powers. Proceedings before the English courts were unavailing, but the Court in Strasbourg held unanimously that the council had behaved disproportionately in defeating his legitimate expectations, and for this breach of his rights under Art.1 of Protocol No.1 awarded him €31,000 for his pecuniary loss and €5,000 for non-pecuniary loss (!). (Application No. 44277/98).]

Investigators

Does a police officer investigating an offence owe the suspect a duty to act reasonably? No, even if (especially if?) the suspect is another police officer: *Calveley v Chief Constable* [1989] 1 All E.R. 1025 (HL), but see *Waters v Commissioner of Police* [2000] 4 All E.R. 934 (HL).

Do the police, when investigating an allegation of child abuse, owe a duty to (a) the child, (b) the suspect? (a) Yes, (b) No: *L and P v Reading B.C.* [2001] 1 W.L.R. 1575.

Does Railtrack owe a duty to a railway maintenance worker regarding the withdrawal of his safety certificate, required for certain types of work? Yes: *Cassidy v Railtrack plc* (Manchester County Court, October 17, 2002).

Does a teacher owe a duty to a pupil to check for learning disabilities? Yes: *Phelps v Hillingdon L.B.C.* [2001] 2 A.C. 619.

Does a school owe a duty to a pupil with regard to bullying outside school hours and premises? No: *Bradford-Smart v West Sussex C.C.* [2002] E.W.C.A. Civ 7, [2002] T.L.R. 44.

Does an executor owe a duty to the sole beneficiary of an estate a duty to proceed promptly to probate? No: *Chappell v Somers & Blake* [2003] 3 All E.R. 1076.

Do the Customs and Excise owe a duty to taxpayers regarding the advice they give about liability to VAT? Perhaps: *R v Commissioners of Customs and Excise, Ex p. F & I Services* (*The Times*, April 26, 2000).

Do the police have a duty to warn or counsel a voluntary independent "appropriate adult" whom they request to attend interviews with gruesome serial killer? No (with strong dissent): *Leach v Chief Constable* [1999] 1 All E.R. 215.

Does the Law Society owe a duty to a person complaining of a solicitor's incompetence? Not as far as peace of mind is concerned: *Wood v Law Society* [1995] Times L.R. 133, CA, but see Court and Legal Services Act 1990, s.23(2)(d).

Does the Jockey Club owe a duty of reasonable care when considering whether to cancel a racing licence on medical grounds? No, only a contractual duty to act fairly: *Wright v Jockey Club* [1995] Times L.R. 342.

A forensic medical expert instructed by the police or CPS to examine the victim of an alleged rape owes her no duty to attend the trial so as to facilitate a conviction. *N v Agrawal* [1999] Times L.R. 438.

Does a doctor checking an applicant for promotion owe the candidate a duty of care? Positive answer in *Baker v Kaye* [1997] I.R.L.R. 219 doubted in *Kapfunde v Abbey National Plc* [1999] I.C.R. 1, CA.

Does an officer of the Health and Safety Executive owe a duty to the operator of a bungee-jumping business he reports as unsafe? No: *Harris v Evans* [1998] 3 All E.R. 522, CA.

Does an adjudication officer whose decision is appealable owe a duty to an applicant for social security benefits? No: *Jones v Department of Employment* [1988] 1 All E.R. 725, CA.

Does an insurance investigator owe a duty to the insured, suspected of arson? No: *South Pacific Mfg. v NZ Securities Investigations* [1992] 2 N.Z.L.R. 282.

Do the Charity Commissioners, advising and deciding on the scope and validity of a charitable trust, owe a duty to potential objects of that charity? No: *Mills v Winchester Diocesan Board* [1989] 2 All E.R. 317.

Does a member of the organisation which receives, records and divulges information about hire-purchase contracts affecting members' motor-cars owe a duty to fellow-members to take care to supply relevant information? No (by a bare majority): *Moorgate Mercantile v Twitchings* [1977] A.C. 890.

Other Services

Does a trade union owe a duty of care to a member consulting it about an employment dispute? Yes, until a solicitor is engaged. *Fried v Institution of Professional Managers* [1999] I.R.L.R. 173.

Is an adviser liable to the undisclosed principal of the party for whose use the information is provided? There are conflicting decisions.

Does a sperm-testing agency owe a duty to future girl friend of client? No: *Goodwill v Pregnancy Service* [1996] 2 All E.R. 161.

Does an architect retained to design a garage owe a duty to the future tenant, a company associated with the client? No: *Strathford East Kilbride v Film Design* [1997] Times L.R. 612 (neither under *Junior Books* (in the light of *Murphy*) nor, in the absence of an undertaking of responsibility, under *Hedley Byrne*).

Does a life insurer which has issued a policy to be used as security for the repayment of a loan on a house owe a duty to the insured to send the direct debit forms to the correct branch of his bank? Very possibly: *Weldon v GRE Linked Life Assurance* [2002] 2 All E.R. (Comm) 914.

Note:

It will be clear that many of these holdings are incompatible with the wide formulation by Lord Browne-Wilkinson of the situations in which a duty to take care arises. One should bear in mind the observation of Lord Brandon in *The Aliakmon* [1986] 2 All E.R. 145 at 153, 154 that whereas a novel formulation of principle (in that case the formulation of Lord Wilberforce in *Anns*) may well be helpful in deciding in novel cases whether a duty should be held to exist, it cannot be deployed to alter a previous line of decisions to the effect that no such duty exists.

CAPARO INDUSTRIES Plc v DICKMAN

House of Lords [1990] 2 A.C. 605; [1990] 2 W.L.R. 358; [1990] 1 All E.R. 568

Claim by take-over bidder against target's accountant

When the directors of Fidelity Plc announced unexpectedly poor results in May 1984 shares in that firm fell from 143p to 63p. On June 8 Caparo Plc bought 100,000 shares in Fidelity with a take-over in view. Four days later the accounts and the auditor's report, prepared by the respondent accountants, Touche Ross, were issued to shareholders as provided by statute, and Caparo bought a further 50,000 shares. Finally Caparo bought all the rest at a price of 125p. This proved to be a very bad bargain, since far from making a profit of £1.3 million as indicated by the accounts, Fidelity had made a loss of £400,000.

In addition to claiming (and obtaining) damages in deceit from Fidelity's directors, Caparo sued the auditors for negligence, alleging that it had bought the shares in reliance on the accounts and that they would not have bought them at that price or at all if the accounts had presented, as they said they did, a true and fair view of Fidelity's position.

The preliminary issue was whether the accountants owed Caparo any duty of care (a) as potential investors in Fidelity, or (b) as existing shareholders in Fidelity. The Court of Appeal held (O'Connor L.J. dissenting) that a duty was owed to existing shareholders but not to prospective investors [1989] Q.B. 653. The House of Lords held unanimously that no duty was owed to individuals in either group.

Lord Bridge: . . . In determining the existence and scope of the duty of care which one person may owe to another in the infinitely varied circumstances of human relationships there has for long been a tension between two different approaches. Traditionally the law finds the existence of the duty in different specific situations each exhibiting its own particular characteristics. In this way the law has identified a wide variety of duty situations, all falling within the ambit of the tort of negligence, but sufficiently distinct to require separate definition of the essential ingredients by which the existence of the duty is to be recognised.

[Lord Bridge quoted the famous passages from the speeches of Lord Atkin, Lord Reid and Lord Wilberforce in *Donoghue, Dorset Yacht* and *Anns* as advancing "the more modern approach of seeking a single general principle which may be applied in all circumstances to determine the existence of a duty of care."]

But since *Anns's* case a series of decisions of the Privy Council and of your Lordships' House . . . have emphasised the inability of any single general principle to provide a practical test which can be applied to every situation to determine whether a duty of care is owed and, if so, what is its scope. . . . What emerges is that, in addition to the foreseeability of damage, necessary ingredients in any situation giving rise to a duty of care are that there should exist between the party owing the duty and the party to whom it is owed a relationship characterised by the law as one of "proximity" or "neighbourhood" and that the situation should be one in which the court considers it fair, just and reasonable that the law should impose a duty of a given scope on the one party for the benefit of the other. But it is implicit in the passages referred to that the concepts of proximity and fairness embodied in these additional ingredients are not susceptible of any such precise definition as would be necessary to give them utility as practical tests, but amount in effect to little more than convenient labels to attach to the features of different specific situations which, on a detailed examination of all the circumstances, the law recognises pragmatically as giving rise to a duty of care of a given scope. Whilst recognising, of course, the importance of the underlying general principles common to the whole field of negligence, I think the law has now moved in the direction of attaching greater significance to the more traditional categorisation of distinct and recognisable situations as guides to the existence, the scope and the limits of the varied duties of care which the law imposes.

One of the most important distinctions always to be observed lies in the law's essentially different approach to the different kinds of damage which one party may have suffered in consequence of the acts or omissions of another. It is one thing to owe a duty of care to avoid causing injury to the person or property of others. It is quite another to avoid causing others to suffer purely economic loss. . . . Lord Fraser, delivering the judgment of the Privy Council [in *The Mineral Transporter* [1986] A.C. 1 at 25] said:

> "Their Lordships consider that some limit or control mechanism has to be imposed on the liability of a wrongdoer towards those who have suffered economic damage in consequence of his negligence. The need for such a limit has been repeatedly asserted in the cases . . . and their Lordships are not aware that a view to the contrary has ever been judicially expressed."

The damage which may be caused by the negligently spoken or written word will normally be confined to economic loss sustained by those who rely on the accuracy of the information or advice they receive as a basis for action. The question what, if any, duty is owed by the maker of a statement to exercise due care to ensure its accuracy arises typically in relation to statements made by a person in the exercise of his calling or profession. In advising the client who employs him the professional man owes a duty to exercise that standard of skill and care appropriate to his professional status and will be liable both in contract and in tort for all losses which his client may suffer by reason of any breach of that duty. But the possibility of any duty of care being owed to third parties with whom the professional man was in no contractual relationship was for long denied ... until the decision of this House in *Hedley Byrne & Co Ltd v Heller Partners Ltd* [above, p.57].

Consistently with the traditional approach it is to decisions directly relevant to this relatively narrow corner of the field that we should look to determine the essential characteristics of a situation giving rise, independently of any contractual or fiduciary relationship, to a duty of care owed by one party to another to ensure that the accuracy of any statement which the one party makes and on which the other party may foreseeably rely to his economic detriment. ...

The most recent decision of the House, which is very much in point, is that of the two appeals heard together of *Smith v Eric S Bush* and *Harris v Wyre Forest D.C.* ([1990] 1 A.C. 831). The plaintiffs in both cases were house purchasers who purchased in reliance on valuations of the properties made by surveyors acting for and on the instructions of the mortgagees proposing to advance money to the plaintiffs to enable them to effect their purchases. In both cases the surveyors' fees were paid by the plaintiffs and in both cases it turned out that the inspections and valuations had been negligently carried out and that the property was seriously defective so that the plaintiffs suffered financial loss. In *Smith's* case the mortgagees were a building society, the surveyors who carried out the inspection and valuation were a firm employed by the building society, and their report was shown to the plaintiff. In *Harris's* case the mortgagees were the local authority who employed a member of their own staff to carry out the inspection and valuation. His report was not shown to the plaintiff, but the plaintiff rightly assumed from the local authority's offer of a mortgage loan that the property had been professionally valued as worth at least the amount of the loan. In both cases the terms agreed between the plaintiff and the mortgagee purported to exclude any liability on the part of the mortgagee or the surveyor for the accuracy of the mortgage valuation. The House held that in both cases the surveyor making the inspection and valuation owed a duty of care to the plaintiff house purchaser and that the contractual clauses purporting to exclude liability were struck down by sections 2(2) and 11(3) of the Unfair Contract Terms Act 1977.

The salient feature of all these cases is that the defendant giving advice or information was fully aware of the nature of the transaction which the plaintiff had in contemplation, knew that the advice or information would be communicated to him directly or indirectly and knew that it was very likely that the plaintiff would rely on that advice or information in deciding whether or not to engage in the transaction in contemplation. In these circumstances the defendant could clearly be expected, subject always to the effect of any disclaimer of responsibility, specifically to anticipate that the plaintiff would rely on the advice or information given by the defendant for the very purpose for which he did in the event rely on it. So also the plaintiff, subject again to the effect of any disclaimer, would in that situation reasonably suppose that he was entitled to rely on the advice or information communicated to him for the very purpose for which he required it. The situation is entirely different where a statement is put into more or less general circulation and may foreseeably be relied on by strangers to the maker of the statement for any one of a variety of different purposes which the maker of the statement has no specific reason to anticipate. To hold the maker of the statement to be under a duty of care in respect of the accuracy of the statement to all and sundry for any purpose for which they may choose to rely on it is not only to subject him, in the classic words of Cardozo C.J., to "liability in an indeterminate amount for an indeterminate time to an indeterminate class" (see *Ultramares Corp. v Touche* ((1931) 255 N.Y. 170 at 179)), it is also to confer on the world at large a quite unwarranted entitlement to appropriate for their own purposes the benefit of the expert knowledge or professional expertise attributed to the maker of the statement. Hence, looking only at the circumstances of these decided cases where a duty of care in respect of negligent statements has been held to exist, I should expect to find that the "limit or control mechanism ... imposed on the liability of a wrongdoer towards those who have suffered economic damage in consequence of his negligence" ... rested on the necessity to prove, in this category of the tort of negligence, as an essential ingredient of the "proximity" between the plaintiff and the defendant, that the defendant knew that his statement would be communicated to the plaintiff, either as an individual or as a member of an identifiable class, specifically in connection with a particular transaction or transactions of a particular kind (*e.g.* in a prospectus inviting investment) and that the plaintiff would be very likely to rely on it for the purpose of deciding whether or not to enter on that transaction or on a transaction of that kind. ...

These considerations amply justify the conclusion that auditors of a public company's accounts owe no duty of care to members of the public at large who rely on the accounts in deciding to buy shares in the company. If a duty of care were owed so widely, it is difficult to see any reason why it should not equally extend to all who rely on the accounts in relation to other dealings with a company as lenders or merchants extending credit to the company. A claim that such a duty was owed by auditors to a bank lending to a company was emphatically and convincingly rejected by Millett J. in *Al Saudi Banque v Clark Pixley* [1989] 3 All E.R. 361. . . . In this jurisdiction I have no doubt that the creation of such an unlimited duty would be a legislative step which it would be for Parliament, not the courts, to take.

Lord Oliver and **Lord Jauncey** delivered concurring speeches; **Lord Ackner** and **Lord Roskill** agreed.

Question

Do you agree with this? : "Once proximity is no longer treated as expressing a relationship founded simply on foreseeability of damage, it ceases to have an ascertainable meaning, and it cannot therefore provide a criterion for liability" (*per* Goff L.J. in *The Aliakmon* [1985] 2 All E.R. 44 at 74).

Notes:

1. In *Galoo Ltd v Bright Grahame Murray* [1995] 1 All E.R. 16 at 43, Evans L.J. said this: "If it is right to confine the duty of care, meaning, to restrict the class of persons who can recover damages if the adviser/ representer is negligent, to cases where the defendant is shown not merely to have known that the individual plaintiff would or might rely upon the representation but to have intended that it should be relied upon, by him and for the particular purpose and without intermediate examination, then the resulting analysis comes close to the 'voluntary assumption of responsibility' which has been referred to in many of the authorities. . . . " That case considered the requirement that the reliance be "without intermediate examination", reminiscent of the similar requirement stated in *Donoghue v Stevenson*.

2. The accountancy profession, alarmed at the extent of their exposure to crippling claims for damages for negligence, are seriously considering the curtailment of the rule of "joint and several liability", *i.e.* the rule that everyone who is at all liable for contributing to indivisible harm is liable for all of it, regardless of the greater contribution made by others (except the plaintiff himself). Perhaps financial harm is not indivisible in quite the way a broken leg or death are indivisible harms, but any division is surely bound to be impressionistic, as is shown by the cases where the defendant's liability is reduced by reason of the contributory negligence of the recipient of the information in failing to check it or otherwise acting carelessly in reliance upon it. It may be possible to restrict the defendant's liability for faulty information by reference to the "scope" of his duty (*SAAMCO* [1996] 3 All E.R. 365 (HL), or causation (*Galoo*, above n.1, but see *Sasea Finance v KPMG* [2000] 1 All E.R. 676 (CA)). The "scope of duty" device was used in *Corbett v Bond Pearce* [2001] E.W.C.A. Civ 531, [2001] 3 All E.R. 769: a will drawn up by the defendant solicitors in accordance with the testatrix's intentions was held invalid after expensive litigation because though the testatrix had signed it, she had not dated it. The defendants paid the disappointed beneficiaries what they would have received under the invalid will had there been no litigation, and now the administratrix sued for the loss to the estate, including the costs of litigation. The claim was dismissed: "It was necessary to determine the scope of the duty of care owed by the solicitors to the testatrix by reference to the kind of damage from which they had to take care to keep her harmless"; that damage was not the loss to the beneficiaries under the previous will, whom the testatrix had no intention of benefiting at all, and who had had to bear the cost of the litigation, but the loss to the intended beneficiaries, which had been made good. It might be thought odd that the defendants were not liable to their contractor because they were liable to third parties in tort.

Preliminary.

The next few cases involve claims for damages against public bodies, to which some special considerations apply. Reference could usefully be made to the Introduction (above, p.15f).

Section 4.—Omissions

HOME OFFICE v DORSET YACHT CO

House of Lords [1970] A.C. 1004; [1970] 2 W.L.R. 1140; [1970] 2 All E.R. 294; [1970]
1 Lloyd's Rep. 453; 114 S.J. 375

*Action by owner of yacht against Home Office in respect of damage done
by runaway Borstal boys*

Seven Borstal boys, five of whom had escaped before, were on a training exercise on Brownsea Island in Poole Harbour, and ran away one night when the three officers in charge of them were, contrary to instructions, all in bed. The boys boarded one of the many vessels in the harbour, started it and collided with the plaintiff's yacht, which they then boarded and damaged further.

To the preliminary question of law, whether on the facts as pleaded any duty of care capable of giving rise to a liability in damages was owed to the plaintiff by the defendant, their servants or agents, an affirmative answer was given by Thesiger J., by the Court of Appeal [1969] 2 Q.B. 412, and by the House of Lords (Viscount Dilhorne dissenting).

Lord Diplock: . . . It is alleged and conceded that the appellant, the Home Office, is vicariously responsible for the tortious acts of the three borstal officers and any other persons concerned in the management of borstals. It is not contended that the Home Office is vicariously liable for any tortious acts of the youths undergoing sentences of borstal training. . . .

The only cause of action relied on is the "negligence" of the officers in failing to prevent the youths from escaping from their custody and control. It is implicit in this averment of "negligence" and must be treated as admitted not only that the officers by taking reasonable care could have prevented the youths from escaping, but also that it was reasonably foreseeable by them that if the youths did escape they would be likely to commit damage of the kind which they did commit, to some craft moored in the vicinity of Brownsea Island.

The specific question of law raised in this appeal may therefore be stated as: is any duty of care to prevent the escape of a borstal trainee from custody owed by the Home Office to persons whose property would be likely to be damaged by the tortious acts of the borstal trainee if he escaped? This is the first time that this specific question has been posed at a higher judicial level than that of a county court. Your Lordships in answering it will be performing a judicial function similar to that performed in *Donoghue v Stevenson* and more recently in *Hedley Byrne & Co Ltd v Heller & Partners Ltd*, of deciding whether the English law of civil wrongs should be extended to impose legal liability to make reparation for the loss caused to another by conduct of a kind which has not hitherto been recognised by the courts as entailing any such liability.

This function, which judges hesitate to acknowledge as law-making, plays at most a minor role in the decision of the great majority of cases, and little conscious thought has been given to analysing its methodology. Outstanding exceptions are to be found in the speeches of Lord Atkin in *Donoghue v Stevenson* and of Lord Devlin in *Hedley Byrne & Co Ltd v Heller & Partners Ltd*. It was because the former was the first authoritative attempt at such an analysis that it has had so seminal an effect on the modern development of the law of negligence.

It will be apparent that I agree with Lord Denning M.R. that what we are concerned with in this appeal "is . . . at bottom a matter of public policy which we, as judges, must resolve".

The branch of English law which deals with civil wrongs abounds with instances of acts and, more particularly, of omissions which give rise to no legal liability in the doer or omitter for loss or damage sustained by others as a consequence of the act or omission, however reasonably or probably that loss or damage might have been anticipated. The very parable of the good Samaritan which was evoked by Lord Atkin in *Donoghue v Stevenson* illustrates, in the conduct of the priest and of the Levite who passed by on the other side, an omission which was likely to have as its reasonable and probable consequence damage to the health of the victim of the thieves, but for which the priest and Levite would have incurred no civil liability in English law. Examples could be multiplied. One may cause loss to a tradesman by withdrawing one's custom although the goods which he supplies are entirely satisfactory; one may damage one's neighbour's land by intercepting the flow of percolating water to it even though the interception is of no advantage to oneself; one need not warn him of a risk of physical danger to which he is about to expose himself unless there is some special relationship between one and him such as that of occupier of land and visitor; one may watch one's neighbour's goods being ruined by a thunderstorm although the slightest effort on one's part could protect them from the rain and one may do so with impunity unless there is some special relationship between one and him such as that of bailor and bailee.

In *Hedley Byrne & Co Ltd v Heller & Partners Ltd*, which marked a fresh development in the law of negligence, the conduct in question was careless words not careless deeds. Lord Atkin's aphorism, if it were of universal application, would have sufficed to dispose of this case, apart from the express disclaimer of liability. But your Lordships were unanimous in holding that the difference in the characteristics of the conduct in the two cases prevented the propositions of law in *Donoghue v Stevenson* from being directly applicable. Your Lordships accordingly proceeded to analyse the previous decisions in which the conduct complained of had been careless words, from which you induced a proposition of law about liability for damage caused by careless words which differs from the proposition of law in *Donoghue v Stevenson* about liability for damage caused by careless deeds.

In the present appeal, too, the conduct of the Home Office which is called in question differs from the kind of conduct discussed in *Donoghue v Stevenson* in at least two special characteristics. First, the actual damage sustained by the respondents was the direct consequence of a tortious act done with conscious volition by a third party responsible in law for his own acts and this act was interposed between the act of the Home Office complained of and the sustension of damage by the respondents. Secondly, there are two separate "neighbour relationships" of the Home Office involved, a relationship with the respondents and a relationship with the third party. These are capable of giving rise to conflicting duties of care. This appeal, therefore, also raises the lawyer's question "Am I my brother's keeper"? A question which may also receive a restricted reply . . .

There are two cases in which a plaintiff has recovered against a custodian damages for injuries sustained as a consequence of the subsequent act of a human being whom the custodian has carelessly failed to keep in his custody and control. In neither case was the custody penal custody or the human being who did the act causing the damage one who was regarded in law as responsible for his actions. In *Holgate v Lancashire Mental Hospitals Board* [1937] 4 All E.R. 19, tried with a jury on assize, the human being causing the damage was of unsound mind. It was held that the doctors had been negligent in allowing him to be released on a visit. Only the summing-up of Lewis J. is reported. I reserve my opinion whether this decision was right. The second case which was in your Lordships' House, *Carmarthenshire C.C. v Lewis* [1955] A.C. 549, concerned a child of four who ran out into the road from a school maintained by the defendant and caused an accident on the highway to a driver trying to avoid him. The defendant was held liable for not taking reasonable care to keep the gate shut. The headnote reports the ratio decidendi as based on the duty of an occupier of premises adjacent to a highway and Lord Goddard did found his judgment on this. There seems to me to be a clear and relevant distinction between the responsibility of a custodian for acts which are done after escaping from custody by a human being who is not a reasonable man and so not responsible in law for his own acts, on the one hand, and for acts of conscious volition which are done by a responsible human being on the other hand. Furthermore, in the *Carmarthenshire* case there was no possible conflict between the duty of the defendant council to the child and its duty to users of the adjacent highway.

There are other cases in which parents have been held liable for the acts of older children, but these can, in my view, be classified as depending on the duty of the defendant to exercise due care in the control of things involving special danger. As is so often the case in the law of tort the basis of this liability is helpfully expounded in a judgment of Dixon J. in the High Court of Australia, *Smith v Leurs* (1945) 70 C.L.R. 256 at 262:

"The general rule is that one man is under no duty of controlling another man to prevent his doing damage to a third. There are, however, special relations which are the source of a duty of this nature. . . . "

As any proposition which relates to the duty of controlling another man to prevent his doing damage to a third deals with a category of civil wrongs of which the English courts have hitherto had little experience it would not be consistent with the methodology of the development of the law by judicial decision that any new proposition should be stated in wider terms than are necessary for the determination of the present appeal. . . .

The risk of sustaining damage from the tortious acts of criminals is shared by public at large. It has never been recognised at common law as giving rise to any cause of action against anyone but the criminal himself. It would seem arbitrary and therefore unjust to single out for the special privilege of being able to recover compensation from the authorities responsible for the prevention of crime a person whose property was damaged by the tortious act of a criminal, merely because the damage to him happened to be caused by a criminal who had escaped from custody before completion of his sentence instead of by one who had been lawfully released or who had been put on probation or given a suspended sentence or who had never been previously apprehended at all. To give rise to a duty on the part of the custodian owed to a member of the public to take reasonable care to prevent a borstal trainee from escaping from his custody before completion of the trainee's sentence there should be some relationship between the custodian and the person to whom the duty is owed which exposes that person to a particular risk of damage in consequence of that escape which is different in its incidence from the general risk of damage from criminal acts of others which he shares with all members of the public.

What distinguishes a borstal trainee who has escaped from one who has been duly released from custody, is his liability to recapture, and the distinctive added risk which is a reasonably foreseeable consequence of a failure to exercise due care in preventing him from escaping is the likelihood that in order to elude pursuit immediately on the discovery of his absence the escaping trainee may steal or appropriate and damage property which is situated in the vicinity of the place of detention from which he has escaped.

So long as Parliament is content to leave the general risk of damage from criminal acts to lie where it falls without any remedy except against the criminal himself, the courts would be exceeding their limited function in developing the common law to meet changing conditions if they were to recognise a duty of care to prevent criminals escaping from penal custody owed to a wider category of members of the public than those whose property was exposed to an exceptional added risk by the adoption of a custodial system for young offenders which increased the likelihood of their escape unless due care was taken by those responsible for their custody.

I should therefore hold that any duty of a Borstal officer to use reasonable care to prevent a borstal trainee from escaping from his custody was owed only to persons whom he could reasonably foresee had property situate in the vicinity of the place of detention of the detainee which the detainee was likely to steal or to appropriate and damage in the course of eluding immediate pursuit and recapture. Whether or not any person fell within this category would depend on the facts of the particular case including the previous criminal and escaping record of the individual trainee concerned and the nature of the place from which he escaped. . . .

Lord Reid, Lord Morris of Borth-y-Gest and **Lord Pearson** also delivered judgments dismissing the appeal; **Viscount Dilhorne** dissented.

Questions
    1. What is the difference between the duty to take care that your ginger-beer doesn't hurt anyone and the duty to take care that other people don't?
    2. After having 12 double whiskies in X's pub, A drove to Y's roadhouse and asked for more; Y refused to serve him since he was obviously drunk but made no effort to stop him driving away. Just outside the roadhouse A drove into a pedestrian, B. Can B sue X or Y? Why do you think no case of this kind has come before the courts?

3. Which of the following statements is correct?

(a) The warders were responsible for the Borstal boys.
(b) The warders were responsible for the damage done by the Borstal boys.
(c) The warders were responsible for the damage caused by their letting the Borstal boys escape.

4. In *Ellis* [1953] 2 Q.B. 135 the Home Office was held liable to a prisoner who was predictably beaten up by other inmates of the prison. In what relevant respects do the facts of the *Dorset Yacht* case differ?

5. Jacqueline Hill was the last of the Yorkshire Ripper's 20 victims. Her estate sued the police for incompetently failing to catch him sooner. The claim was dismissed on the ground that "the cause of action contended for . . . does not fall within the principle of the *Dorset Yacht* case." (*Hill v Chief Constable of West Yorkshire* [1987] 1 All E.R. 1173). Do you agree with (a) that decision (b) the reason given for it?

In the *Hill* case the public policy argument was played down in the House of Lords, but in *Hughes v National Union of Mineworkers* [1991] 4 All E.R. 278 May J. made public policy the basis for his dismissal of the plaintiff policeman's claim against the Chief Constable for deploying police officers against 4,000 rioting mineworkers in such a way as to expose him to unnecessary risk of physical injury. Can you see why?

6. In his speech Lord Reid said " . . . the question is really one of remoteness of damage" and Lord Pearson also was happy to start with the question of causation and work back to that of duty. How can the question whether the defendants owed a duty to take care be really one of whether their failure to take care could be said to have caused the damage?

7. If through slackness warders permit a confidence trickster and a burglar to escape from confinement, would a person duped by the former or raped by the latter have a claim?

8. The Criminal Injuries Compensation Authority which distributes public funds to the victims of crimes of violence makes no award to victims of criminal damage to property. Why do you think this is?

9. From Harlow, *Compensation and Government Torts* (1982), pp.154–155, we learn that the Home Office, regardless of whether it is at fault or not, regularly pays for property loss due to miscreants absconding from Borstal and open prisons, outside hospitals, working parties and escorted travel, provided that the property in question was in the "neighbourhood" of the escape and *was not insured*. Do you think that their Lordships were aware of this scheme? Should counsel have informed them? Which counsel would have an interest in doing so? Given the existence of this scheme, who actually benefited from the decision of the House of Lords in the principal case?

10. As between the state and the plaintiff's insurance company (which had been paid a premium to take the risk of damage) "on whom should the risk of negligence fall?" Was it "fair, just and reasonable" to make the taxpayer indemnify the Yacht Co.'s insurance company? Does the privatisation of the prison service affect the issue?

11. Lord Denning in the Court of Appeal said that it was "not negligence to keep an open Borstal." Why not? Is there a sensible difference, so far as the victim is concerned, between releasing a prisoner pursuant to a decision to do so and letting him escape contrary to instructions? Is it for the courts to decide whether the prison system is (a) wisely instituted, (b) properly run? Is an action for damages an appropriate proceeding for the resolution of such questions?

12. In *The Nicholas H* (above, p.45) Lord Steyn said: "Since the decision in *Home Office v Dorset Yacht Co* it has been settled law that the elements of foreseeability and proximity as well as considerations of fairness, justice and reasonableness are relevant to all cases whatever the nature of the harm sustained the plaintiffs." Was his reference to *Dorset Yacht* an apt one?

Notes:

1. This decision was rendered during the expansionist phase of tort law. *Murphy* (above, p.31) appeared to bring that phase to an end. Perhaps, as many would wish, on *recule pour mieux sauter*, but it would still be a bold plaintiff who sought to procure any extension of the holding in *Dorset Yacht*, whose leading characteristic is not so much that a duty was imposed regarding the acts of third parties but that such a duty was imposed in favour of total strangers (as it were the owner of the car parked outside the prison), with whom the Home Office was in no special relationship.

The only connecting links between plaintiff and defendant were physical proximity and the manifest risk of harm. In cases where a special relationship exists between plaintiff and defendant, the latter's duty to try to protect the former may be clear: an employer must protect an employee against bullying by other employees (*Hudson v Ridge Manufacturing Co* [1957] 2 All E.R. 229), the occupier must protect his visitors and their property against damage threatened by other visitors, parents must protect their children, the bailee must guard the bailed chattel even against theft, and one must not unreasonably allow one's land to be used by third parties in such a way as to damage the property next door. In the absence of a special relationship between plaintiff and defendant, liability is imposed only if there is a special relationship between the defendant and the third party, the immediate cause of the harm, a relationship involving a power of control:

the mother whose child makes a mess on the supermarket floor owes a duty to other shoppers, total strangers to her, to minimise the danger to them, by at least alerting the staff. In the principal case the Home Office had ample powers of control over the Borstal boys.

2. In his dissent Viscount Dilhorne stated that the concept of foreseeability, on the basis of which the majority were imposing liability, would not serve sufficiently to limit the liability so imposed. The more recent emphasis on "proximity" recognises and allays this danger. With the idea of "immediate neighbourhood" connect that of "immediate aftermath" in the shock cases (below, p.111).

3. Cases of failure to protect are, of course, instances of omissions on the part of the defendant but it is worth noting that the Home Office brought the boys to the island in the first place, and that liability for letting things escape which you have brought on to your land is not unknown to the common law (see *Rylands v Fletcher*, below, p.453). In *Stovin v Wise* (next case) Lord Hoffmann was to say of *Dorset Yacht*:

> " . . . the House plainly did not regard the case as one in which the alleged breach of duty was merely an omission to use a statutory power. The negligence was caused by something which the Borstal officers did, namely to use their statutory powers to bring the trainees onto the island, where they constituted a foreseeable risk to boat owners, and then take no care to prevent them from escaping in the night . . . their Lordships were concerned only whether the Crown had a defence on the grounds that the alleged breach of duty involved the exercise of a statutory discretion, or whether the fact that the damage was caused by the criminal act of the Borstal trainees negatives the causal link with the Crown's breach of duty. Both these defences were rejected."

Furthermore, there is a shadowy principle that you may come under a duty to defuse a danger you have quite innocently caused: thus if you say something you reasonably believe to be true and later find out that it was false or is no longer true, you will be liable for failing to correct the misapprehension you have caused if you could do so before damage ensues from reliance on it, one instance being the manufacturer who discovers that the information he has given about his product is no longer true (*Hobbs (Farms)* [1992] 1 Lloyd's Rep. 54). Again, if a perfectly blameless driver runs over a pedestrian, he must take steps to save the pedestrian from further injury or aggravation of his condition, whereas the mere passer-by is under no such duty.

4. As to failure to prevent harm, one can only be liable for letting someone cause harm if one has the power to prevent him. While it is true that some private citizens have certain powers of control (occupiers of premises, parents, employers), most of the powers to stop people doing things are vested in the government. It is amazing how many things the government can stop people doing, by refusing or withdrawing a licence, or permit them to do by granting one. Thus local authorities have registers of approved child-minders. It has been held that there is no liability for unreasonable failure to deregister a child-minder known to be possibly violent (though there was liability for telling an inquiring mother that the child-minder was all right—*Harrison v Surrey C.C.* [1994] 4 All E.R. 577). So also in *Yuen Kun Yeu* [1987] 2 All E.R. 705, PC where the official in charge of the register of approved deposit-taking bodies owed depositors no duty as regards the register. That case, unlike *Dorset Yacht*, concerned mere financial loss, which is exactly the kind of harm most apt to ensue from governmental decisions or conduct in office. If, as in *Anns*, where the damage was of an ambiguous nature, really economic but apparently physical, liability is imposed on government, we are immediately caught up in a vast extension of governmental liability in the field of private law. The number of people entitled as of right (for tort claims can be brought as of right) to harass the government, especially local government, vastly increased as a result of *Anns*. The courts then realised what they had let loose and decided that if one is questioning a decision of a governmental body in the area of public law, one must use the special procedure for such matters; see now Civil Procedure Rules, Part 54.

5. The borstal boys were doubtless penniless, not worth suing. Tort claims have increasingly been brought not against the insolvent primary villains, but against solvent parties who permitted the villainy to occur, as in this case. *Caparo v Dickman* may be seen as a case where the defendants had failed to alert shareholders to the fraud of Fidelity's directors; *Anns*, now overruled, was a case where the local authority had failed to stop the builder building a bad house; *Yuen Kun-Yeu* [1987] 2 All E.R. 705 was a case where the bank supervisory body was sued for failure to remove a dodgy bank from the list of authorised deposit-takers. As the last two cases indicate, the secondary defendant is often a public or governmental body. That is because governmental bodies often have power to stop people doing things or license them to do things. The public law aspect of *Dorset Yacht* is not merely accidental.

6. *Dorset Yacht* has been cited in several subsequent cases involving the question whether an occupier of premises is liable to his neighbour (*i.e.* the person next door or underneath) whose premises have been burgled or flooded or burnt owing to the misdoings of trespassers on the defendant's premises. Judgment has very usually been for the defendant. The cases are discussed in *Smith v Littlewoods Organisation* [1987] 1 All E.R. 710, HL, noted below, p.129, where Lord Mackay distinguishes damage by fire from loss by theft. Do you see why?

Trespass may be committed to moveable property as well as to land. In *Topp v London Country Bus Ltd* [1993] 3 All E.R. 448 the defendants left their mini-bus unattended with the ignition key visibly in place for nine hours at a bus-stop outside a pub. At 11.15 p.m. a person unknown drove it away, and five minutes later knocked down and killed Mrs Topp who was cycling home. The trial judge held that there was proximity between Mrs Topp and the defendants but that it would not be fair just and reasonable to impose a duty of care on the defendant. The Court of Appeal upheld his decision, while doubting that there was proximity between the parties. See D. Howarth, "My Brother's Keeper? Liability for Acts of Third Parties" (1994) 14 Legal Studies 88. Note that Mrs Topp's dependants would normally have a claim for full damages against the Motor Insurers' Bureau. But consider the following case: X borrows Y's car and leaves it unlocked, with the ignition key in place, in a rough area whence it is stolen by T who sells and delivers it to Z, a good faith purchaser.

7. If one cannot prevent a person under one's control from causing harm, a warning to potential victims may enable them to escape harm. A controversial decision is *Tarasoff v Regents of the University of California* 17 Cal.3d 358; (1976) 551 P.2d 334, where a psychiatrist whose patient had talked of doing violence to his fiancee was held liable when such violence was done. Would this apply to a doctor who failed to tell a patient's fiancee that the man was HIV-positive? Consider also *Tutton v AD Walter* [1985] 3 All E.R. 757 (farmer spraying crops when dangerous to bees held liable for not warning neighbouring apiarist) and *Al-Kandari v JR Brown & Co* [1988] 1 All E.R. 833 where solicitors failed to inform their client's endangered wife that he had, contrary to their undertaking but without their fault, regained access to his passport, and were held liable when he beat her up and fled the country with the kids. Warnings are easy to give, but only where the potential victims (or someone else able and ready to protect or warn them) can be identified and reached. That was not the case in *Hill* where it was not known where the Yorkshire Ripper might next strike. Nor was it really applicable (in the middle of the night) in *Dorset Yacht*.

8. The ability to warn is a good indication of the existence of proximity. Thus in *Osman v Ferguson* [1993] 4 All E.R. 344—where the decision to strike out the claim caused such ructions in Strasbourg—the police were aware of the identity of the probable (and eventual) victim of the madman they failed to apprehend, whereas in both *Clunis v Camden and Islington H.A.* [1998] 3 All E.R. 180 and *Palmer v Tees H.A.* [1999] T.L.R. 496, upholding [1998] Times L.R. 350 the identity of the eventual victim killed by the madman whom the defendants respectively let out and failed to keep in was quite unascertainable in advance. The Court of *Palmer* held that *Holgate*, referred to by Lord Diplock in *Dorset Yacht*, could not stand with the House of Lords' decision in *Hill*, holding that there was no proximity between the police investigating a series of rapes and the rapist's final victim. Nor was there proximity in *M v Surrey C.C.* [2001] EWCA Civ 691 where the claim was that the local authority had failed to warn the claimants that a 13-year old who lived on council premises close to the claimant's home had been charged and bailed for abusing children. The facts of *K v Secretary of State for Home Office* [2002] E.W.C.A. Civ 775 are alarming. After convictions for buggery and burglary, Rashid Musa was imprisoned and recommended for deportation. Persons awaiting deportation are to be kept in detention "unless the Secretary of State directs otherwise." The Secretary having directed otherwise, Musa was released into the community pending his application for *habeas corpus*, and profited from his liberty by raping the claimant at knifepoint before buggering a boy on a train. The Court of Appeal agreed that it was proper to strike out the claim since the absence of proximity between defendant and claimant was clear, and there was no objection under *Barrett* (which went only to "fair, just and reasonable", not proximity) to such striking out.

The finding of proximity is just a start, of course, for even where there is a special relationship between claimant and defendant the defendant's fault must be proved where the damage is inflicted by a third party: in *Dickinson v Cornwall C.C.* (David Steel J., December 10, 1999) when a schoolgirl on a school trip to Brittany was raped and murdered by an intruder into the room where she was sleeping with four other girls in a hostel, chosen but not run by the school, no fault was attributable to the school.

STOVIN v WISE

House of Lords [1996] A.C. 923; [1996] 3 W.L.R. 388; [1996] 3 All E.R. 801; [1996] R.T.R. 354; 95 L.G.R. 260

Action against highway authority in respect of failure to exercise statutory power to improve visibility at junction

A bank of earth on British Rail property in Wymondham made it difficult for drivers wishing to turn right out of Cemetery Lane into the major Station Road to see if there were any traffic approaching from their right. Accidents had occurred at that spot previously, and there was another one when Mrs Wise, emerging from Cemetery Lane, collided with Mr Stovin, a motor cyclist who was proceeding quite normally along Station Road.

Her insurer, having paid off Mr Stovin, now exercised her claim to contribution from the highway authority as an "other person liable in respect of the same damage" on the basis that, if sued by Mr Stovin, the authority would have been held liable to him for failure to implement its earlier decision to have the bank of earth removed, as it had power to do.

The trial judge's holding that the highway authority was liable as to 30 per cent was upheld by a unanimous Court of Appeal, but the House of Lords, by a majority, allowed the highway authority's appeal.

Lord Hoffmann: . . . The judge made no express mention of the fact that the complaint against the council was not about anything which it had done to make the highway dangerous, but about its omission to make it safer. Omissions, like economic loss, are notoriously a category of conduct in which Lord Atkin's generalisation in *Donoghue v Stevenson* offers limited help. There are sound reasons why omissions require different treatment from positive conduct. It is one thing for the law to say that a person who undertakes some activity shall take reasonable care not to cause damage to others. It is another thing for the law to require that a person who is doing nothing in particular shall take steps to prevent another from suffering harm from the acts of third parties (like Mrs Wise) or natural causes. One can put the matter in political, moral or economic terms. In political terms it is less of an invasion of an individual's freedom for the law to require him to consider the safety of others in his actions than to impose upon him a duty to rescue or protect. A moral version of this point may be called the "Why pick on me?" argument. A duty to prevent harm to others or to render assistance to a person in danger or distress may apply to a large and indeterminate class of people who happen to be able to do something. Why should one be held liable rather than another? In economic terms, the efficient allocation of resources usually requires an activity should bear its own costs. If it benefits from being able to impose some of its costs on other people (what economists call "externalities") the market is distorted because the activity appears cheaper than it really is. So liability to pay compensation for loss caused by negligent conduct acts as a deterrent against increasing the cost of the activity to the community and reduces externalities. But there is no similar justification for requiring a person who is not doing anything to spend money on behalf of someone else. Except in special cases (such as marine salvage) English law does not reward someone who voluntarily confers a benefit on another. So there must be some special reason why he should have to put his hand in his pocket.

There may be a duty to act if one has undertaken to do so or induced a person to rely upon one doing so. Or the ownership or occupation of land may give rise to a duty to take positive steps for the benefit of those who come upon the land and sometimes for the benefit of neighbours. In *Hargrave v Goldman* the High Court of Australia held that the owner and occupier of a 600-acre grazing property in Western Australia had a duty to take reasonable steps to extinguish a fire, which had been started by lightning striking a tree on his land, so as to prevent it from spreading to his neighbour's land. This is a case in which the limited class of persons who owe the duty (neighbours) is easily identified and the political, moral and economic arguments which I have mentioned are countered by the fact that the duties are mutual. One cannot tell where the lightning may strike and it is therefore both fair and efficient to impose upon each landowner a duty to have regard to the interests of his neighbour. In giving the advice of the Privy Council affirming the decision (*Goldman v Hargrave* [1966] 2 All E.R. 989) Lord Wilberforce underlined the exceptional nature of the liability when he pointed out that the question of whether the landowner had acted reasonably should be judged by reference to the resources he actually had at his disposal and not by some general or objective standard. This is quite different from the duty owed by a person who undertakes a positive activity which carries the risk of causing damage to others. If he does not have the resources to take such steps as are objectively reasonable to prevent such damage, he should not undertake that activity at all.

The Court of Appeal did advert to the question of omissions. Kennedy L.J. said that the case was not one of pure omission:

"Here the highway authority did not simply fail to act. It decided positively to proceed by seeking agreement from British Rail, and its failure to pursue that course is not an omission on which it can rely to escape liability, any more than a car driver could escape liability simply because his breach of duty consisted in a failure to apply the brakes."

I do not find this analogy convincing. If I am driving at 50 m.p.h. and fail to apply the brakes, the motorist with whom I collide can plausibly say that the damage was caused by my driving into him at 50 m.p.h. But Mr Stovin's injuries were not caused by the negotiations between the council and British Rail or anything else which the council did. So far as the council was held responsible, it was because it had done nothing to improve the visibility at the junction.

Roch L.J. made a different point. Accepting that the alleged breach of duty was an omission, he drew an analogy between the position of the highway authority and an occupier of premises in relation to visitors coming upon his land. But an occupier can ordinarily limit his liability by deciding whom he will allow to come upon his land. He has a limited duty to trespassers and can take steps to keep them out. An occupier of land over which there is a public right of way cannot stop anyone from using it. So in *McGeown v Northern Ireland Housing Executive* [1994] 3 All E.R. 53 this House decided that an occupier of land over which there is a public right of way owes no duty to take reasonable steps to make it safe for members of the public who use it. Because he has no choice as to whether to allow them upon his land or not, he should not be required to spend money for their benefit.

It therefore seems clear that if Station Road and Cemetery Road had been highways over private land which happened to be owned and occupied by the Norfolk County Council instead of being repairable at the public expense, there would have been no liability. The analogy of an occupier is therefore insufficient for the purpose of imposing liability.

The argument that the council had a positive duty to take action giving rise to a claim for compensation in tort must therefore depend, as the judge and the Court of Appeal recognised, upon the public nature of its powers, duties and funding. The argument is that while it may be unreasonable to expect a private landowner to spend money for the benefit of strangers who have the right to cross his land, the very purpose of the existence of a public authority like the council is to spend its resources on making the roads convenient and safe. For that purpose it has a large battery of powers in the 1980 Act.

It is certainly true that some of the arguments against liability for omissions do not apply to public bodies like a highway authority. There is no "Why pick on me?" argument: as Kennedy L.J. said, the highway authority alone had the financial and physical resources, as well as the legal powers, to eliminate the hazard (see [1994] 3 All E.R. 467). But this does not mean that the distinction between acts and omissions is irrelevant to the duties of a public body or that there are not other arguments, peculiar to public bodies, which may negative the existence of a duty of care.

Since *Mersey Docks and Harbour Board Trustees v Gibbs* (1866) L.R. 1 H.L. 93 it has been clear law that, in the absence of express statutory authority, a public body is in principle liable for torts in the same way as a private person. But its statutory powers or duties may restrict its liability. For example, it may be authorised to do something which necessarily involves committing what would otherwise be a tort. In such a case it will not be liable (see *Allen v Gulf Oil Refining Ltd* [1981] 1 All E.R. 353). Or it may have discretionary powers which enable it to do things to achieve a statutory purpose notwithstanding that they involve a foreseeable risk of damage to others. In such a case, a bona fide exercise of the discretion will not attract liability (see *X and ors (minors) v Bedfordshire C.C.* [1995] 3 All E.R. 353 and *Home Office v Dorset Yacht Co Ltd* [1970] 2 All E.R. 294).

In the case of positive acts, therefore, the liability of a public authority in tort is in principle the same as that of a private person but may be *restricted* by its statutory powers and duties. The argument in the present case, however, is that whereas a private person would have owed no duty of care in respect of an omission to remove the hazard at the junction, the duty of the highway authority is *enlarged* by virtue of its statutory powers. The existence of the statutory powers is said to create a "proximity" between the highway authority and the highway user which would not otherwise exist.

Until the decision of this House in *Anns v Merton L.B.* [1977] 2 All E.R. 492 there was no authority for treating a statutory power as giving rise to a common law duty of care. Two cases in particular were thought to be against it. In *Sheppard v Glossop Corp.* [1921] 3 K.B. 132, the council had power to light the streets of Glossop. But their policy was to turn off the lamps at 9 p.m. The plaintiff was injured when he fell over a retaining wall in the dark after the lamps had been extinguished. He sued the council for negligence. The Court of Appeal said that the council owed him no duty of care. . . .

In *East Suffolk Rivers Catchment Board v Kent* [1940] 4 All E.R. 527 at 543, Lord Romer cited *Sheppard v Glossop Corp.* and stated the principle which he said it laid down:

> "Where a statutory authority is entrusted with a mere power, it cannot be made liable for any damage sustained by a member of the public by reason of a failure to exercise that power."

The equally well-known case of *Home Office v Dorset Yacht Co Ltd* [1970] 2 All E.R. 294, also cast no doubt upon the general principle stated by Lord Romer in the *East Suffolk* case. All members of the House plainly did not regard the case as one in which the alleged breach of duty was merely an omission to use a statutory power. The negligence was caused by something which the Borstal officers did, namely to use their statutory powers of custody to bring the trainees onto the island, where they constituted a foreseeable risk to boat owners, and then take no care to prevent them from escaping in the night. The case was therefore prima facie within *Mersey Docks and Harbour Board Trustees v Gibbs*.

The only tool which *Anns'* case provides for defining these circumstances is the distinction between policy and operations.

There are at least two reasons why the distinction is inadequate. The first is that, as Lord Wilberforce himself pointed out, the distinction is often elusive. This is particularly true of powers to provide public benefits which involve the expenditure of money. Practically every decision about the provision of such benefits, no matter how trivial it may seem, affects the budget of the public authority in either timing or amount. The *East Suffolk* case, about which Lord Wilberforce said in *Anns'* case [1977] 2 All E.R. 492 at 502, that the activities of the board, though "operational", were "well within a discretionary area, so that the plaintiff's task in contending for a duty of care was a difficult one" is a very good example. But another reason is that even if the distinction is clear cut, leaving no element of discretion in the sense that it would be irrational (in the public law meaning of that word) for the public authority not to exercise its power, it does not follow that the law should superimpose a common law duty of care. This can be seen if one looks at cases in which a public authority has been under a statutory or common law *duty* to provide a service or other benefit for the public or a section of the public. In such cases there is no discretion, but the courts have nevertheless not been willing to hold that a member of the public who has suffered loss because the service was not provided to him should necessarily have a cause of action, either for breach of statutory duty or for negligence at common law.

In terms of public finance, this is a perfectly reasonable attitude. It is one thing to provide a service at the public expense. It is another to require the public to pay compensation when a failure to provide the service has resulted in loss. Apart from cases of reliance, the same loss would have been suffered if the service had not been provided in the first place. To require payment of compensation increases the burden on public funds. Before imposing such an additional burden, the courts should be satisfied that this is what Parliament intended.

Whether a statutory duty gives rise to a private cause of action is a question of construction (see *Hague v Deputy Governor of Parkhurst Prison, Weldon v Home Office* [1991] 3 All E.R. 733). It requires an examination of the policy of the statute to decide whether it was intended to confer a right to compensation for breach. Whether it can be relied upon to support the existence of a common law duty of care is not exactly a question of construction, because the cause of action does not arise out of the statute itself. But the policy of the statute is nevertheless a crucial factor in the decision. As Lord Browne-Wilkinson said in *X and ors (minors) v Bedfordshire C.C.* [1995] 3 All E.R. 353 at 371 in relation to the duty of care owed by a public authority performing statutory functions:

" . . . the question whether there is such a common law duty and if so its ambit, must be profoundly influenced by the statutory framework within which the acts complained of were done."

The same is true of omission to perform a statutory duty. If such a duty does not give rise to a private right to sue for breach, it would be unusual if it nevertheless gave rise to a duty of care at common law which made the public authority liable to pay compensation for foreseeable loss caused by the duty not being performed. It will often be foreseeable that loss will result if, for example, a benefit or service is not provided. If the policy of the act is not to create a statutory liability to pay compensation, the same policy should ordinarily exclude the existence of a common law duty of care.

In the case of a mere statutory power, there is the further point that the legislature has chosen to confer a discretion rather than create a duty. I do not say that a statutory 'may' can never give rise to a common law duty of care. I prefer to leave open the question of whether *Anns'* case was wrong to create any exception to Lord Romer's statement of principle in the *East Suffolk* case. But the fact that Parliament has conferred a discretion must be some indication that the policy of the Act conferring the power was not to create a right to compensation. The need to have regard to the policy of the statute therefore means that exceptions will be rare.

In summary, therefore, I think that the minimum pre-conditions for basing a duty of care upon the existence of a statutory power, if it can be done at all, are, first, that it would in the circumstances have been irrational not to have exercised the power, so that there was in effect a public law duty to act, and secondly, that there are exceptional grounds for holding that the policy of the statute requires compensation to be paid to persons who suffer loss because the power was not exercised.

I think that it is important, before extending the duty of care owed by public authorities, to consider the cost to the community of the defensive measures which they are likely to take in order to avoid liability. It would not be surprising if one of the consequences of *Anns'* case and the spate of cases which followed, was that local council inspectors tended to insist upon stronger foundations than were necessary. In a case like this, I do not think that the duty of care can be used as a deterrent against low standards in improving the road layout. Given the fact that the British road network largely antedates the highway authorities themselves, the court is not in a position to say what an appropriate standard of improvement would be. This must be a matter for the discretion of the authority. On the other hand, denial of liability does not leave the road user unprotected. Drivers of vehicles must take the highway network as they find it. Everyone knows that there are hazardous bends, intersections and junctions. It is primarily the duty of drivers of vehicles to take due care. And if, as in the case of Mrs Wise, they do not, there is compulsory insurance to provide compensation to the victims. There is no reason of policy or justice which requires the highway authority to be an additional defendant. I would therefore allow the appeal.

Lord Nicholls of Birkenhead (dissenting): My Lords, this case arises at the interface of public and private law obligations: the liability of a public authority in tort for failure to exercise a statutory power. When may a public authority be liable in damages for an unreasonable failure to act, in breach of its public law obligations?

The starting point is that the council did not create the source of danger. This is not a case of a highway authority carrying out road works carelessly and thereby creating a hazard. In the present case the council cannot be liable unless it was under a duty requiring it to act. If the plaintiff is to succeed the council must have owed him a duty to exercise its powers regarding a danger known to it but not created by it. The distinction between liability for acts and liability for omissions is well known. It is not free from controversy.

Despite the difficulties, the distinction is fundamentally sound in this area of the law. There is no difficulty over categorisation in the present case. The council did not bring about the dangerous configuration and poor visibility at the road junction. The question is whether it was in breach of a common law duty by carelessly failing to remove this source of danger.

Common law obligations to take positive action arise mainly in contract and fiduciary relationships. They may also arise in tort. Familiar instances are parent and child, employer and employee, school and pupil. Perhaps the established category nearest to the present case comprises occupiers of land and their neighbours. An occupier is under a common law duty to take positive action to remove or reduce hazards to his neighbours, even though the hazard is not one the occupier brought about. He must take reasonable steps to this end, for the benefit of his neighbours (see *Goldman v Hargrave* [1966] 2 All E.R. 989).

In this situation a combination of features is present: foreseeability of damage or injury if preventive steps are not taken: control by the occupier of a known source of danger; dependence, or vulnerability, of the neighbour; and the prospect of damage or injury out of all proportion to the preventive steps required.

Even this combination is not enough. The classic example of the absence of a legal duty to take positive action is where a grown person stands by while a young child drowns in a shallow pool. Another instance is where a person watches a nearby pedestrian stroll into the path of an oncoming vehicle. In both instances the callous bystander can foresee serious injury if he does nothing. He does not control the source of the danger, but he has control of the means to avert a dreadful accident. The child or pedestrian is dependent on the bystander: the child is unable to save himself, and the pedestrian is unaware of his danger. The prospective injury is out of all proportion to the burden imposed by having to take preventive steps. All that would be called for is the simplest exertion or a warning shout.

Despite this, the recognised legal position is that the bystander does not owe the drowning child or the heedless pedestrian a duty to take steps to save him. Something more is required than being a bystander. There must be some additional reason why it is fair and reasonable that one person should be regarded as his brother's keeper and have legal obligations in that regard. When this additional reason exists, there is said to be sufficient proximity. That is the customary label. In cases involving the use of land, proximity is found in the fact of occupation. The right to occupy can reasonably be regarded as carrying obligations as well as rights.

Norfolk County Council was more than a bystander. The council had a statutory power to remove this source of danger, although it was not under a statutory duty to do so. Before 1978 the accepted law was that the council could be under no common law liability for failing to act. A simple failure to exercise a statutory power did not give rise to a common law claim for damages (see *East Suffolk Rivers Catchment Board v Kent* [1940] 4 All E.R. 527). The decision in *Anns v Merton L.B.* liberated the law from this unacceptable yoke. This was the great contribution *Anns* made to the development of the common law.

However, as with *Hedley Byrne & Co Ltd v Heller & Partners Ltd* [1963] 2 All E.R. 575 another notable development in the law of negligence, so with *Anns*: a coherent, principled control mechanism has to be found for limiting this new area of potential liability. The powers conferred on public authorities permeate so many fields that a private law duty in all cases, sounding in damages, would be no more acceptable than the opposite extreme. Considerable caution is needed lest a welcome development do more harm that good.

I turn to the crucial question: does a highway authority, aware of a danger, owe to road users a common law duty to act as would a reasonable authority in the circumstances, and hence be potentially liable in damages if it fails to attain this standard?

Built into this question are several features which, in combination, seem to me to point to the conclusion that the existence of such a duty and such a liability would indeed be fair and reasonable. First, the subject matter is physical injury. The existence of a source of danger exposes road users to a risk of serious, even fatal, injury. Road users, especially those unfamiliar with the stretch of road, are vulnerable. They are dependent on highway authorities fulfilling their statutory responsibilities. Second, the authority knows of the danger. When an authority is aware of a danger it has knowledge road users may not have. It is aware of a risk of which road users may be ignorant. Third, in the present case, had the authority complied with its public law obligations the danger would have been removed and the accident would not have happened. In such a case the authority can properly be regarded as responsible for the accident just as much as if its employees had carried out roadworks carelessly and thereby created a danger. There is no sensible distinction between an authority's liability for its workmen in the former instance and its liability if, in breach of its public law obligations, office staff fail to do their jobs properly and an avoidable road accident takes place in consequence. Fourth, this is an area where Parliament has recognised that public authorities should be liable in damages for omissions as well as actions. In 1961 Parliament abrogated the old rule which exempted the inhabitants at large and their successors from liability for non-repair of highways (Highways (Miscellaneous Provisions) Act 1961). A highway authority is liable in damages for failing to take reasonable care to keep the highway safe. But no sound distinction can be drawn between dangers on the highway itself, where the authority has a statutory duty to act, and other dangers, where there is a statutory power but not a statutory duty. The distinction would not correspond to the realities of road safety. On the council's argument a highway authority would be liable if it carelessly failed to remove a dead tree fallen onto the road, but not liable if it carelessly failed to act after learning of a diseased overhanging tree liable to fall at any moment. Such a legalistic distinction does not commend itself. It would be at variance with ordinary persons' expectations and perceptions.

Fifth, the purpose of the statutory powers is to protect road users by enabling highway authorities to remove sources of danger, but public law is unable to give an effective remedy if a road user is injured as a result of an authority's breach of its public law obligations. A concurrent common law duty is needed to fill the gap.

Sixth, a common law duty in the present case would not represent an incursion into a wholly novel field. As already noted, an occupier owes a duty to take positive action to protect his neighbours. Until subsumed in legislation, an occupier also owed common law duties to safeguard those who come onto his property, whether lawfully or unlawfully. Although a highway authority does not occupy the highway, there is a certain resemblance. A highway authority has, and alone has, the capacity to remove what would otherwise be a source of physical danger to users of property.

Seventh, for the reason given earlier, a common law duty would not impose on the authority any more onerous obligation, so far as its behaviour is concerned, than its public law obligations.

Finally, and critically, the consequence of a concurrent common law duty would be that in the event of a breach the loss, so far as measurable in terms of money, would fall on the highway authority or, if insured, on highway authorities generally. Sometimes an injured road user, whether driver or passenger or pedestrian, has a claim against an insured road user. This is so in the present case. Then it may be debatable whether there is anything to be gained, any social utility, in shifting the financial loss from road users to a highway authority. But there can be no room for doubt when the injured road user has no such claim. This may well happen. Then it does seem eminently fair and reasonable that the loss should fall on the highway authority and not the hapless road user. And if the existence of a duty of care in all cases, in the shape of a duty to act as a reasonable authority, has a salutary effect on tightening administrative procedures and avoiding another needless road tragedy, this must be in the public interest.

In my view these factors, taken together, constitute special circumstances of sufficient weight for the crucial question to be answered Yes. There is here sufficient proximity. I reserve my view on what the position would be if an authority did not know, but ought to have known, of the existence of a danger.

Lord Goff and **Lord Jauncey** agreed with **Lord Hoffmann**; **Lord Slynn** agreed with **Lord Nicholls** in dissent.

Note:

In *Kane v New Forest DC* [2001] 3 All E.R. 914 a pedestrian was struck by a motor car as he emerged from a footpath debouching on a dangerous bend in the highway where motorists' sightlines were obscured by vegetation. The site of this footpath has been required by the defendant local authority as a condition of granting planning permission to the developer of the riparian land. The pedestrian's claim was reinstated by the Court of Appeal: *Stovin*, relied on by the trial judge, was distinguished, since here the defendant had actually caused the dangerous situation by a positive act.

In *Carpenter v Pembrokeshire C.C.* [2002] E.W.H.C. 1968 it was not a danger that the highway authority had created, but an inconvenience: the construction of a new highway left the riparian claimant with access to her property which was very difficult for vehicular traffic, and she alleged that this had prevented her extending the property for use as a bed and breakfast business. Her claim failed.

But in *Health and Safety Executive v Thames Trains* [2003] E.W.C.A. Civ 720 the accident was very serious indeed, no less than the Ladbroke Grove train crash which killed 31 and injured 259 people when the driver of a slowish Westbound train passed through a signal at danger and collided with an fast Eastbound train. Railtrack and Thames Trains, both of which were surely liable to the victims, agreed that the latter would process the victims' claims, and Thames Trains now sought contribution from HSE, just as Mrs Wise sought contribution from the highway authority, on the ground that HSE could have been sued by the victims for failing to correct the signal which was known to be difficult to see and misleading. The Court of Appeal upheld the trial judge's refusal to strike out the claim. Waller L.J. did not regard *Stovin* as conclusive, and said as regards *Perrett* [1998] 2 Lloyd's Rep. 255, where it was held that an inspector who provided a certificate of fitness for an airplane which crashed, " ... the principles and reasoning in *Perrett* ... make it more likely that a court with distinguish *Stovin v Wise* than hold *Perrett* to have been wrongly decided."

HUMAN RIGHTS ACT 1998

6.—(1) It is unlawful for a public authority to act in a way which is incompatible with a Convention right.

(2) Subsection (1) does not apply to an act if—

(a) as the result of one or more provisions of primary legislation, the authority could not have acted differently; or

(b) in the case of one or more provisions of, or made under, primary legislation which cannot be read or given effect in a way which is compatible with the Convention rights, the authority was acting so as to give effect to or enforce those provisions.

(3) In this section, "public authority" includes—

(a) a court or tribunal, and

(b) any person certain of whose functions are of a public nature,

but does not include either House of Parliament or a person exercising functions in connection with proceedings in Parliament.

(4) In subsection (3) "Parliament" does not include the House of Lords in its judicial capacity.

(5) In relation to a particular act, a person is not a public authority by virtue only of subsection (3)(b) if the nature of the act is private.

(6) "An act" includes a failure to act but does not include a failure to—

(a) introduce in, or lay before, Parliament a proposal for legislation; or

(b) make any primary legislation or remedial order.

8.—(1) In relation to any act (or proposed act) of a public authority which the court finds is (or would be) unlawful, it may grant such relief or remedy, or make such order, within its powers as it considers just and appropriate. . . .

(3) No award of damages is to be made unless, taking account of all the circumstances of the case, including—

(a) any other relief or remedy granted, or order made, in relation to the act in question (by that or any other court), and

(b) the consequences of any decision (of that or any other court) in respect of that act,

the court is satisfied that the award is necessary to afford just satisfaction to the person in whose favour it is made.

(4) In determining—

(a) whether to award damages, or
(b) the amount of an award,

the court must take into account the principles applied by the European Court of Human Rights in relation to the award of compensation under Article 41 of the Convention.

SCHEDULE 1

THE ARTICLES

Article 2. Right to life.

1. Everyone's right to life shall be protected by law. No one shall be deprived of his life intentionally save in the execution of a sentence of a court following his conviction of a crime for which this penalty is provided by law.
2. Deprivation of life shall not be regarded as inflicted in contravention of this Article when it results from the use of force which is no more than absolutely necessary:

(a) in defence of any person from unlawful violence;
(b) in order to effect a lawful arrest or to prevent the escape of a person lawfully detained;
(c) in action lawfully taken for the purpose of quelling a riot or insurrection.

Article 5. Right to liberty and security.

1. Everyone has the right to liberty and security of person. No one shall be deprived of his liberty save in the following cases and in accordance with a procedure prescribed by law:

(a) the lawful detention of a person after conviction by a competent court;
(b) the lawful arrest or detention of a person for non-compliance with the lawful order of a court or in order to secure the fulfilment of any obligation prescribed by law;
(c) the lawful arrest or detention of a person effected for the purpose of bringing him before the competent legal authority on reasonable suspicion of having committed an offence or when it is reasonably considered necessary to prevent his committing an offence or fleeing after having done so;
(d) the detention of a minor by lawful order for the purpose of educational supervision or his lawful detention for the purpose of bringing him before the competent legal authority.
(e) the lawful detention of persons for the prevention of the spreading of infectious diseases, of persons of unsound mind, alcoholics or drug addicts or vagrants;
(f) the lawful arrest or detention of a person to prevent his effecting an unauthorised entry into the country or of a person against whom action is being taken with a view to deportation or extradition.

2. Everyone who is arrested shall be informed promptly, in a language which he understands, of the reasons for his arrest and of any charge against him.

3. Everyone arrested or detained in accordance with the provisions of paragraph 1(c) of this Article shall be brought promptly before a judge or other officer authorised by law to exercise judicial power and shall be entitled to trial within a reasonable time or to release pending trial. Release may be conditioned by guarantees to appear for trial.

4. Everyone who is deprived of his liberty by arrest or detention shall be entitled to take proceedings by which the lawfulness of his detention shall be decided speedily by a court and his release ordered if the detention is not lawful.

5. Everyone who has been the victim of arrest or detention in contravention of the provisions of this Article shall have an enforceable right to compensation.

Article 6. Right to a fair trial.

1. In the determination of his civil rights and obligations or of any criminal charge against him, everyone is entitled to a fair and public hearing within a reasonable time by an independent and impartial tribunal established by law. . . .

Article 8. Right to respect for private and family life.

1. Everyone has the right to respect for his private and family life, his home and his correspondence.

2. There shall be no interference by a public authority with the exercise of this right except such as is in accordance with the law and is necessary in a democratic society in the interests of national security, public safety or the economic well-being of the country, for the prevention of disorder or crime, for the protection of health or morals, or for the protection of the rights and freedoms of others.

Article 10. Freedom of expression.

1. Everyone has the right to freedom of expression. This right shall include freedom to hold opinions and to receive and impart information and ideas without interference by public authority and regardless of frontiers. This Article shall not prevent States from requiring the licensing of broadcasting, television or cinema enterprises.

2. The exercise of these freedoms, since it carries with it duties and responsibilities, may be subject to such formalities, conditions, restrictions or penalties as are prescribed by law and are necessary in a democratic society, in the interests of national security, territorial integrity or public safety, for the prevention of disorder or crime, for the protection of health or morals, for the protection of the reputation or rights of others, for preventing the disclosure of information received in confidence, or for maintaining the authority and impartiality of the judiciary.

THE FIRST PROTOCOL

Article 1. Protection of property.

Every natural or legal person is entitled to the peaceful enjoyment of his possessions. No one shall be deprived of his possessions except in the public interest and subject to the conditions provided for by law and by the general principles of international law. The preceding provisions shall not, however, in any way impair the right of a State to enforce such laws as it deems necessary to control the use of property in accordance with the general interest or to secure the payment of taxes or other contributions or penalties.

Note:

The Human Rights Act 1998 has fundamentally altered the exposure of public authorities to liability in damages, especially as regards omissions (positive acts of negligence causing physical harm were already actionable under domestic law). According to the Strasbourg Court, which is a good deal less concerned than Lord Hoffmann with the solvency of public bodies and the extent of their discretion, public authorities may well be under a positive duty to protect citizens from invasion of their rights, even by third parties who themselves are not bound by the Act to respect those rights.

Although it is only public authorities in the execution of their public functions on whom it is incumbent to respect the rights conferred, the courts also are public authorities, and since they are enjoined not to act unlawfully, there may well be some impact on litigation between private individuals. The extent to which this is true is a matter for furious debate, but it would certainly be alarming if the courts were thought bound to hold an individual defendant liable for invading the claimant's Convention rights in a manner not contrary to domestic law. One can, however, well see that the courts should refrain from giving judgment against a defendant who was exercising a Convention right for a proper purpose (see Art.17).

For the general tort lawyer the most important articles of the Convention are Two, Three and Eight, plus Article One of the First Protocol; Articles Five and Ten vastly affect liability for false imprisonment (police powers) and defamation (freedom of speech).

Perhaps the greatest effect of our subjection to Strasbourg is on our procedure. It used to be common practice to "strike out" claims which had no chance of success under domestic law. Indeed, if the minority in *Donoghue v Stevenson* had had their way, Mrs Donoghue's claim would have been "struck out" under Scottish procedure as "irrelevant", and many of the cases earlier in this book were "striking out" cases. For that purpose one assumed that all the claimant's pleaded allegations were true, and heard no evidence. In a famous case where a claim against the police was struck out, the Strasbourg Court held that striking out was improper and that the case should go to trial, as if Article Six meant that there must be a trial in order to see whether the claimant had any civil rights, not just that if he had such rights, the trial must be fair. Although the Strasbourg Court backed off this holding (replacing it with Art.13, not enacted in Britain), the reaction of our superior courts was to insist that whenever there was the slightest doubt, a trial must take place, without demur (or demurrer): the existence of a duty (and consequent liability if the duty was broken) depended, rather illogically, on the proven facts; it was hardly a question of law any more. Students may find it rather tiresome that so many reported decisions now tell us what the law may be, not what it is.

It may be useful to give some decisions which show how the Human Rights Act has affected tort cases.

The Court of Appeal has held that the Human Rights Act has invalidated the decision of the House of Lords that a local authority was not liable to a child for failing to take it into care when they had reason to know was being abused at home (*JD v East Berkshire Community Health* [2003] E.W.C.A. Civ 1151 at [83]). Trial judges have held (1) that the Home Office was liable for not promptly processing the claimant's application for refugee status and thereby causing him psychological harm (*R. (N) v Secretary of State for the Home Department*, [2003] T.L.R. 134 (" . . . English law was, subject to limited exceptions, of no binding force in determining a cause of action under the 1998 Act because such a statutory claim arose under a separate and discrete regime based on Convention jurisprudence from the European Court of Human Rights at Strasbourg"); (2) that Thames Water was liable for failing to upgrade a drainage system, adequate when installed, whose overuse caused flooding to the claimant's home (*Marcic v Thames Water* [2002] Q.B. 1003, overruled by the House of Lords in [2003] U.K.H.L. 66) (3) that a local authority must pay damages to a claimant for whose family it had failed to provide suitable accommodation (*Bernard v Enfield L.B.C.* [2002] E.W.H.C. Admin 2282, a claim under the Housing Act by another member of the family having been dismissed in E.W.C.A. Civ 1831); and (4) that the Ministry of Defence must pay the bourgeois owners of a large estate affected by the noise produced by Harrier Jump Jets operating from a nearby airfield damages, including the profit from development thereof, of very nearly a million pounds (*Dennis v Ministry of Defence* [2003] E.W.H.C. 793).

Indeed, the Strasbourg Court had awarded damages to groundlings whose homes were near Heathrow Airport, but on appeal to the Grand Chamber of that Court the decision was reversed, the Court observing that "The national authorities have direct democratic legitimation and are . . . in principle better placed than an international court to evaluate local needs and conditions . . . In matters of general policy, on which opinions within a democratic society may reasonably differ widely, the role of the domestic policy maker should be given special weight . . . " *Hatton v United Kingdom* (Application No.36022/97, July 8, 2003, at [97]).

BARRETT v ENFIELD L.B.C.

House of Lords [2001] 2 A.C. 550; [1999] 3 All E.R. 193; [1999] 3 W.L.R. 79; [1999] 2 F.L.R. 426

Claim against local authority for inadequacy of care

When his claim came to the House of Lords, Keith Barrett was 27 years old and a total mess—addicted, according to his own statements, to self-harm, beset with behavioural problems, unable to maintain a relationship, unemployed and alcoholic. The defendant local authority had taken him into care before he was a year old to prevent his mother beating him up again. It was to their treatment of him during the following sixteen years that he attributed his present lamentable condition, alleging many specific shortcomings, such as failing to arrange adoption, not mediating properly between him and his mother, separating him from his half-sister and, in particular, moving him frequently between foster homes and residential accommodation with constant changes of social worker.

The Court of Appeal upheld the judge's decision to strike out the claim as disclosing no cause of action, but the House of Lords unanimously reversed and sent the case for trial on the facts.

Lord Slynn: . . . In summary *X and ors (minors) v Bedfordshire C.C.* ([1995] 3 All E.R. 353) establishes that decisions by local authorities whether or not to take a child into care with all the difficult aspects that involves and all the disruption which may come about are not ones which the courts will review by way of a claim for damages in negligence, though there may be other remedies by way of judicial review or through extra judicial routes such as the ombudsman.

The question in the present case is different, since the child was taken into care; it is therefore necessary to consider whether any acts or omissions and if so what kind of acts or omissions can ground a claim in negligence. The fact that no completely analogous claim has been accepted by the courts previously points to the need for caution and the need to proceed "incrementally" and "by analogy with decided cases".

It is no doubt right for the courts to restrain within reasonable bounds claims against public authorities exercising statutory powers in this social welfare context. It is equally important to set reasonable bounds to the immunity such public authorities can assert. The position is in some respects clear; in others it is far from clear. Thus it is clear that where a statutory scheme *requires* a public authority to take action in a particular area and injury is caused, the authority taking such action in accordance with the statute will not be liable in damages unless the statute expressly or impliedly so provides. Nor will the authority be liable in damages at common law if its acts fall squarely within the statutory duty. Where a statute *empowers* an authority to take action in its discretion, then if it remains within its powers, the authority will not normally be liable under the statute, unless the statute so provides, or at common law. This, however, is subject to the proviso that if it purports to exercise its discretion to use, or it uses, its power in a wholly unreasonable way, it may be regarded as having gone outside its discretion so that it is not properly exercising its power, when liability in damages at common law may arise. It can no longer rely on the statutory power or discretion as a defence because it has gone outside the power.

Where a statutory power is given to a local authority and damage is caused by what it does pursuant to that power, the ultimate question is whether the particular issue is justiciable or whether the court should accept that it has no role to play. The greater the element of policy involved, the wider the area of discretion accorded, the more likely it is that the matter is not justiciable so that no action in negligence can be brought. A claim of negligence in the taking of a decision to exercise a statutory discretion is likely to be barred, unless it is wholly unreasonable so as not to be a real exercise of the discretion, or if it involves the making of a policy decision involving the balancing of different public interests; acts done pursuant to the lawful exercise of the discretion can, however, in my view be subject to a duty of care, even if some element of discretion is involved. Thus accepting that a decision to take a child into care pursuant to a statutory power is not justiciable, it does not in my view follow that, having taken a child into care, an authority cannot be liable for what it or its employees do in relation to the child without it being shown that they have acted in excess of power. It may amount to an excess of power, but that is not in my opinion the test to be adopted: the test is whether the conditions in *Caparo Industries plc v Dickman* [above, p.80] have been satisfied.

Both in deciding whether particular issues are justiciable and whether if a duty of care is owed, it has been broken, the court must have regard to the statutory context and to the nature of the tasks involved. The mere fact that something has gone wrong or that a mistake has been made, or that someone has been inefficient does not mean that there was a duty to be careful or that such duty has been broken. Much of what has to be done in this area involves the balancing of delicate and difficult factors and courts should not be too ready to find in these situations that there has been negligence by staff who largely are skilled and dedicated.

Yet although in my view the staff are entitled to rely mutatis mutandis on the principle stated in *Bolam v Friern Hospital Management Committee* [1957] 2 All E.R. 118 the jurisdiction to consider whether there is a duty of care in respect of their acts and whether it has been broken is there. I do not see how the interests of the child can be sufficiently protected otherwise.

In the present case, the allegations are largely directed to the way in which the powers of the local authority were *exercised*. It is arguable (and that is all we are concerned with in this case at this stage) that if some of the allegations are made out, a duty of care was owed and was broken. Others involve the exercise of a discretion which the court may consider to be not justiciable—*e.g.* whether it was right to arrange adoption at all, though the question of whether adoption was ever considered and if not, why not, may be a matter for investigation in a claim of negligence. I do not think it right in this case to go through each allegation in detail to assess the chances of it being justiciable. The claim is of an on-going failure of duty and must be seen as a whole. I do not think that it is the right approach to look only at each detailed allegation and to ask whether that in itself could have caused the injury. That must be done but it is appropriate also to consider whether the cumulative effect of the allegations, if true, could have caused the injury.

Nor do I accept that because the court should be slow to hold that a child can sue its parents for negligent decisions in its upbringing that the same should apply necessarily to all acts of a local authority. The latter has to take decisions which parents never or rarely have to take (*e.g.* as to adoption or as to an appropriate foster parent or institution). In any case, in respect of some matters, parents do have an actionable duty of care.

On the basis that *X and ors (minors) v Bedfordshire C.C.* does not conclude the present case in my view it is arguable that at least in respect of some matters alleged both individually and cumulatively a duty of care was owed and was broken.

In the present case each member of the Court of Appeal appears to have taken the view that the plaintiff would not be able to show that operational acts, even if negligently performed, either separately or cumulatively caused the condition of which the appellant complained. But causation is largely a question of fact. . . . I do not consider that it would be right to strike out this claim on the basis that causation could not be established. That is a matter for investigation.

Accordingly, I consider that this claim should not be struck out. This does not mean that I think that the appellant must or will win. He faces considerable difficulties, but I consider that he is entitled to have these matters investigated and not to have them summarily dismissed. I would accordingly allow the appeal.

Lord Hutton: I consider that the decision of this House in *Stovin v Wise* is not an authority which precludes a finding that there was a duty of care in this case, because *Stovin's* case was concerned solely with the omission by a highway authority to perform a statutory power, whereas in the present case the allegation of negligence relates to the manner in which the local authority exercised its statutory duty and powers.

Although I would allow this appeal and would permit the action to proceed to trial. I wish to emphasise that the considerations relied on by the defendant on the issue of justiciability will be of relevance and importance when the trial judge comes to consider the question whether the plaintiff has established a breach of the duty to take reasonable care. The standard of care in negligence must be related to the nature of the duty to be performed and to the circumstances in which the defendant has to carry it out. Therefore the standard of care to be required of the defendant in this case in order to establish negligence at common law will have to be determined against the background that it is given discretions to exercise by statute in a sphere involving difficult decisions in relation to the welfare of children. Accordingly when the decisions taken by a local authority in respect of a child in its care are alleged to constitute negligence at common law, the trial judge, bearing in mind the room for differences of opinion as to the best course to adopt in a difficult field and that the discretion is to be exercised by the authority and its social workers and not by the court, must be satisfied that the conduct complained of went beyond mere errors of judgment in the exercise of a discretion and constituted conduct which can be regarded as negligent.

I would allow the appeal.

Lord Browne-Wilkinson also gave a speech allowing the appeal; **Lord Nolan** and **Lord Steyn** agreed.

Note:

If ever (as Serjeant Arabin might have said) there was a clearer case for striking out than this case, that case was this case. It was surely plain that in the event of a trial Keith Barrett will fail to establish his claim. Likewise the claim which the Court of Appeal had refused to strike out could not be established in *Swinney v Chief Constable* ([1996] 3 All E.R. 449 and [1999] Times L.R. 402). Earlier that court had struck out the claim in *Osman v Ferguson* ([1993] 4 All E.R. 344), but the Osmans went off to Strasbourg, where the Court held that by striking out their claim as contrary to our public policy of not holding the police liable for negligence in investigating crime the Court of Appeal had put the United Kingdom in breach of the Osmans' right to a (fair) trial under Art.6 of the Convention, and awarded damages for the loss of the chance that if they had got to court "on the merits" they might have won (*Osman v UK* (1999) 5 B.H.R.C. 293). It was surely this that led the House of Lords to send *Barrett*'s case for a predictably futile trial. In his concurring speech Lord Browne-Wilkinson expressed puzzlement at the Strasbourg decision which was indeed, followed by condemnation of his own very careful decision in *X v Bedfordshire C.C.* ([1995] 3 All E.R. 353), where claims against local authorities in respect of child abuse were struck out on the ground that it would not be fair just and reasonable to subject the authorities to a common law duty to take care in the execution of their discretionary statutory functions.

Having reversed the decision of the Court of Appeal to strike out the claim in *Barrett* against the *social services* of local authorities, the House of Lords proceeded to do likewise in a case against their *educational services*. Seven judges sat in *Phelps v Hillingdon London B.C.* [2001] 2 A.C. 619 because counsel wished to question the decision in *X v Bedfordshire* that no common law duty was owed by the local authority itself with regard to children with a learning disability. That point was never reached, though the holding was doubted, because it was agreed unanimously that the local authority was vicariously liable for breach by its educational psychologists of their duty towards the children they appraised. It was agreed that failure to diagnose and remedy a congenital defect was damage at law, namely personal injury (thereby giving the courts power to extend the period during which a claim can be brought—Limitation Act 1980, s.33). Lord Nicholls, with whom only Lord Jauncey specifically agreed, was of the view that teachers owed the same duty to all children, not just those with special needs, so we may face claims against teachers for setting the wrong syllabus or making mistakes in what they say.

Local authorities will now have a choice: they can incur increased expenditure of time and manpower in actual trials or increased expenditure of money in settling with claimants, as the authority in Cleveland did before the House of Lords decided in *X* that there was no liability in law. But perhaps Cleveland had the gift of Nostradamus, for when X was taken to Strasbourg by the Official Solicitor and became Z, damages of £350K were awarded in total to the four siblings who had been horribly abused for four or five years, each being granted £32K for physical and psychiatric harm in addition to what they had received from the Criminal Injuries Compensation Board.

CAPITAL AND COUNTIES PLC v HAMPSHIRE C.C.

Court of Appeal, [1997] Q.B. 1004; [1997] 3 W.L.R. 331; [1997] 2 All E.R. 865; [1997] 2 Lloyd's Rep. 161; 95 L.G.R. 831

Actions against fire brigades for property damage done by fires

Claims were brought against fire brigades by the owners of properties burnt down in three distinct events. In the *Hampshire* case the fire officer turned off the sprinkler system, in the *London Fire Brigade* case the firemen left the scene on the erroneous assumption that the fire was out when it was not, and in the *West Yorkshire* case the firemen were unable to fight the fire by reason of the inadequacy of the water supply which it was their statutory responsibility to ensure.

In the first case the trial judge awarded damages, in the other two cases the claim was dismissed on the ground of want of proximity. The Court of Appeal dismissed all the appeals, affirming liability in the *Hampshire* case only.

The judgment of the Court was delivered by

Stuart-Smith L.J.: ... In *Alexandrou v Oxford* [1993] 4 All E.R. 328 the plaintiff's clothing shop was burgled on a Sunday evening. The shop was equipped with a 999-type burglar alarm which rang in the police station on being activated and gave a recorded message as to the site of the burglary. The alarm sounded at 7.23 p.m. and police officers went to investigate. The judge held that, if an inspection had been made at the rear as well as the front, as it should have been, the burglars would have been stopped. It is a case therefore on the facts where the police responded to the 999 call, but through negligent failure to inspect, they failed to prevent the loss to the plaintiff, their intervention being ineffectual. For present purposes *Alexandrou*'s case is clear authority for the proposition that there is no sufficient proximity simply on the basis that an emergency call is sent to the police, even if there is a direct line from the premises to the police station. The decision is binding on us, unless it can be distinguished, and in our view on this aspect it cannot. ...

In our judgment the fire brigade are not under a common law duty to answer the call for help and are not under a duty to take care to do so. If therefore they fail to turn up or fail to turn up in time because they have carelessly misunderstood the message, got lost on the way or run into a tree, they are not liable.

Does the fire brigade owe a duty of care to the owner of property on fire once they have arrived and started to fight the fire?

Counsel for the plaintiffs in the *Hampshire* case submit that there are two approaches in principle which lead to the conclusion of liability in their case.

First it is said that, although the correct method for deciding whether there is a duty of care at common law is to adopt the approach advocated by Lord Bridge in *Caparo Industries plc v Dickman* [1990] 1 All E.R. 568 at 573–574, the direct infliction of foreseeable physical damage is an established category of case where a duty exists. It is argued that Station Officer Mitchell's act of switching off the sprinklers was a positive act of misfeasance which foreseeably caused the fire to get out of control and spread and cause the loss of blocks B and C and part of block A which would not otherwise have been affected. It was on this basis that Judge Havery found in the plaintiffs' favour. By reason of the differing circumstances in each appeal this line of argument is only of direct assistance to the plaintiffs in the *Hampshire* case.

The alternative ground upon which it is said that proximity will arise is where someone possessed of a special skill undertakes, quite irrespective of contract, to apply that skill for the assistance of another person who relies upon such skill, and there is direct and substantial reliance by the plaintiffs on the defendant's skill.

We turn to consider the first of these submissions. The peculiarity of fire brigades, together with other rescue services, such as ambulance or coastal rescue and protective services such as the police, is that they do not as a rule create the danger which causes injury to the plaintiff or loss to his property. For the most part they act in the context of a danger already created and damage already caused, whether by the forces of nature, or the acts of some third party or even of the plaintiff himself, and whether those acts are criminal, negligent or non-culpable.

But where the rescue/protective service itself by negligence creates the danger which caused the plaintiff's injury there is no doubt in our judgment the plaintiff can recover. There are many examples of this. In *Rigby v Chief Constable of Northamptonshire* [1985] 2 All E.R. 985 the plaintiff's gun shop was at risk from a lunatic. The police came to deal with the situation; they fired a CS canister of gas into the shop, though it caused a high risk of fire, without ensuring that the fire engine which had previously been available was there to put out any fire that resulted. In *Knightley v Johns* [1982] 1 All E.R. 851, in the course of traffic control following an accident two police constables were instructed to take a course which involved them riding against the traffic flow round a blind bend causing a collision in which one of them was injured. In *Home Office v Dorset Yacht Co Ltd* [1970] 2 All E.R. 294, the defendant's prison officers had brought the borstal boys who had a known propensity to escape into the locality where the yachts were moored and so had created a potential situation of danger for the owners of those yachts, in which they failed to exercise proper supervision over the boys.

These are all cases, however, where a new or different danger has been created from that which the police were seeking to guard against. A comparable situation would be if, on arrival at the scene of a fire, the fire engine was negligently driven into the owner's car parked in the street. But it seems to us that there is no difference in principle if, by some positive negligent act, the rescuer/protective service substantially increases the risk; he is thereby creating a fresh danger, albeit of the same kind or of the same nature, namely fire. The judge held that at the time the sprinkler systems were turned off, the fire was being contained, but that once they were turned off it rapidly went out of control, spreading to blocks B and C which had been deprived of their own sprinkler protection.

Having negligently turned off the sprinklers which were at that stage containing the fire, the defendants by their positive act exacerbated the fire so that it rapidly spread. The question is thus one of causation and has to be tested with the benefit of hindsight by comparing what would have happened if the sprinklers had been left on with what in fact happened.

We now turn to consider the second submission made on behalf of all the plaintiffs that the requisite proximity exists. It involves the concept of assumption of responsibility by the fire brigade and particular reliance by the owner. As a general rule a sufficient relationship of proximity will exist when someone possessed of special skill undertakes to apply that skill for the assistance of another person who relies upon such skill and there is direct and substantial reliance by the plaintiff on the defendant's skill (see *Hedley Byrne & Co Ltd v Heller & Partners* and *Henderson v Merrett Syndicates Ltd*). There are many instances of this. The plaintiffs submit that that which is most closely analogous is that of doctor and patient or health authority and patient. There is no doubt that once the relationship of doctor and patient or hospital authority and admitted patient exists, the doctor or the hospital owe a duty to take reasonable care to effect a cure, not merely to prevent further harm. The undertaking is to use the special skills which the doctor and hospital authorities have to treat the patient.

In *Barnett v Chelsea and Kensington Hospital Management Committee* [1968] 1 All E.R. 1068, Nield J. drew a distinction between a casualty department of a hospital that closes its doors and says no patients can be received, in which case he would by inference have held there was no duty of care, and the case before him where the three watchmen who had taken poison entered the hospital and were given erroneous advice, where a duty of care arose.

There are a number of cases where the courts have held that the relationship of proximity arises so as to give rise to a duty of care for the plaintiff's physical safety which are based on assumption of responsibility and reliance. In *Kirkham v Chief Constable of the Greater Manchester Police* [1990] 3 All E.R. 246, the plaintiff's husband was taken into custody by the police. The police were told by the plaintiff that her husband was a suicide risk. When the husband was remanded in custody to the prison authorities that information was not passed on to the prison authority. The husband committed suicide and the police were held liable to the plaintiff.

In *Barrett v Ministry of Defence* [1995] 3 All E.R. 87, the deceased, a 30-year-old naval airman, engaged in a bout of heavy drinking; having become unconscious, was placed on a bunk lying in the recovery position, but his condition was not checked and he was later found dead having asphyxiated on his vomit. The defendant officer was not liable for preventing the deceased abusing alcohol or for anything prior to his collapse. Beldam L.J. said:

> "Thereafter, when the appellant assumed responsibility for him, it accepts that the measures taken fell short of the standard reasonably to be expected. It did not summon medical assistance and its supervision of him was inadequate."

These are all examples of where the court has considered on the special facts of the case that there is a sufficiently close relationship of proximity to give rise to a duty of care. But we do not think they are anywhere near the circumstances that arise in these appeals. In our judgment, a fire brigade does not enter into a sufficiently proximate relationship with the owner or occupier of premises to come under a duty of care merely by attending at the fire ground and fighting the fire; this is so, even though the senior officer actually assumes control of the fire-fighting operation.

If we had found a sufficient relationship of proximity in the *London Fire Brigade* and *West Yorkshire* cases, we do not think that we would have found the arguments for excluding a duty of care on the grounds that it would not be just fair and reasonable convincing. The analogy with the police exercising their functions of investigating and suppressing crime is not close. The floodgates argument is not persuasive; nor is that based on insurance. Many of the other arguments are equally applicable to other public services for example the National Health Service. We do not think that the principles which underlie those decisions where immunity has been granted can be sufficiently identified in the case of fire brigades.

Questions:

1. The damages payable in the *Hampshire* case were so large (£18.5 million) that the County Council applied to the central government for funds to help them meet this liability. Do you really think that the ratepayers—or the taxpayers—should provide this subvention to a trading company's insurer? The building in the *Hampshire* case was occupied by Digital Equipment, an American computer company. If liability had been denied and there had been no insurance, who would have ended up footing the bill?

2. In *Kent v Griffiths* [2000] 2 All E.R. 474 an ambulance despatched after the acceptance of a 999 call made by a doctor took 38 minutes to arrive whereas the national standard was 14 minutes and the distance was only $6\frac{1}{2}$ miles, no explanation for the delay being provided. Had it arrived in time the claimant would probably have suffered less, and had the doctor been informed of the delay that was to occur, she would have had the patient driven to the hospital by her husband. In a rambling judgment which fails adequately to distinguish the *Capital and Counties* case Lord Woolf, who gave the judgment of the court, said "The acceptance of the call in this case established the duty of care." Can you see grounds on which the earlier case could properly be distinguished? [The claimant obtained £80,000 at the trial, and she was one of the beneficiaries of *Heil v Rankin* [2001] Q.B. 272 where the Court of Appeal raised awards for pain and suffering and loss of amenity, in her case up to £95,000.]

Section 5.—Psychiatric Harm

FROST or WHITE v CHIEF CONSTABLE OF SOUTH YORKSHIRE POLICE

House of Lords [1999] 2 A.C. 455; [1998] 3 W.L.R. 1509; [1999] 1 All E.R. 1

Claims by policemen for shock suffered on duty while helping victims of a disaster for which their employer was responsible

Ninety-five spectators died in Hillsborough Stadium in Sheffield and hundreds more suffered crush wounds when a senior police officer allowed far too many fans to rush into spectator pens. Three of the numerous lawsuits reached the House of Lords. In *Alcock* [1991] 4 All E.R. 907 claims by eyewitnesses and televiewers shocked by what they saw happening to their relatives were rejected. In *Hicks* [1992] 2 All E.R. 65 claims by the estates of two of those crushed to death were dismissed. The present claims were brought by policemen who suffered psychiatric harm as a result of their involvement in the dreadful melee.

The trial judge dismissed their claims. The Court of Appeal by a majority upheld them. The House of Lords by a majority (Lord Griffiths and Lord Goff dissenting) allowed the Chief Constable's appeal.

Lord Steyn: ... The law divides those who were mentally scarred by the events of Hillsborough in different categories. There are those whose mental suffering was a concomitant of physical injury. This type of mental suffering is routinely recovered as "pain and suffering". Next, there are those who did not suffer any physical injuries but sustained mental suffering. For present purposes this category must be subdivided into two groups. First, there are those who suffered from extreme grief. This category may include cases where the condition of the sufferer is debilitating. Secondly, there are those whose suffering amounts to a recognisable psychiatric illness. Diagnosing a case as falling within the first or second category is often difficult. The symptoms can be substantially similar and equally severe. Yet the law denies redress in the former case: see *Hinz v Berry* [1970] 1 All E.R. 1074 at 1075; but compare the observations of Thorpe L.J. in *Vernon v Bosley (No.1)* [1997] 1 All E.R. 577 at 610, that grief constituting pathological grief disorder is a recognisable psychiatric illness and is recoverable. Only recognisable psychiatric harm ranks for consideration. Where the line is to be drawn is a matter for expert psychiatric evidence. This distinction serves to demonstrate how the law cannot compensate for all emotional suffering even if it is acute and truly debilitating.

The four police officers were actively helping to deal with the human consequences of the tragedy and as a result suffered from post traumatic stress disorder. The police officers put in the forefront of their case that they suffered harm as a result of a tort and that justice demands that they should be compensated. A constant theme of the argument of counsel for the police officers was that there is no justification for regarding physical and psychiatric injury as different kinds of damage, and in so arguing he was repeating an observation of Lord Lloyd of Berwick in *Page v Smith* [1995] 2 All E.R. 736 at 768. It is of some importance to examine this proposition. Courts of law must act on the best medical insight of the day. Nowadays courts accept that there is no rigid distinction between body and mind. Courts accept that a recognisable psychiatric illness results from an impact on the central nervous system. In this sense therefore there is no qualitative difference between physical harm and psychiatric harm. And psychiatric harm may be far more debilitating than physical harm.

It would, however, be an altogether different proposition to say that no distinction is made or ought to be made between principles governing the recovery of damages in tort for physical injury and psychiatric harm. The contours of tort law are profoundly affected by distinctions between different kinds of damage or harm: see *Caparo Industries plc v Dickman* [1990] 1 All E.R. 568 at 574. The analogy of the relatively liberal approach to recovery of compensation for physical damage and the more restrictive approach to the recovery for economic loss springs to mind. Policy considerations encapsulated by Cardozo J.'s spectre of liability for economic loss "in an indeterminate amount for an indeterminate time to an indeterminate class" played a role in the emergence of a judicial scepticism since *Murphy v Brentwood D.C.* [1990] 2 All E.R. 269 about an overarching principle in respect of the recovery of economic loss: see Steele "Scepticism and the Law of Negligence" [1993] C.L.J. 437. The differences between the two kinds of damage have led to the adoption of incremental methods in respect of the boundaries of liability for economic loss.

Policy considerations have undoubtedly played a role in shaping the law governing recovery for pure psychiatric harm. The common law imposes different rules for the recovery of compensation for physical injury and psychiatric harm. ... It seems to me useful to ask why such different rules have been created for the recovery of the two types of damage.

[His Lordship considered various factors which might justify this difference in treatment.]

The leading decision of the House of Lords is *Alcock v Chief Constable of the South Yorkshire Police* [1991] 4 All E.R. 907. Before this case the general rule was that only parents and spouses could recover for psychiatric harm suffered as a result of witnessing a traumatic event. In *Alcock*'s case the group of plaintiffs who sued for psychiatric injury resulting from the events at

Hillsborough included relatives who were in the stadium. The House dismissed all the claims including the claim of a plaintiff who himself witnessed the scenes at the football ground where two of his brothers died. This decision established that a person who suffers reasonably foreseeable psychiatric illness as a result of another person's death or injury cannot recover damages unless he can satisfy three requirements, *viz.*: (i) that he had a close tie of love and affection with the person killed, injured or imperilled; (ii) that he was close to the incident in time and space; (iii) that he directly perceived the incident rather than, for example, hearing about it from a third person.

The decision of the House of Lords in *Page v Smith* [1995] 2 All E.R. 736 was the next important development in this branch of the law. The plaintiff was directly involved in a motor car accident. He was within the range of potential physical injury. As a result of the accident he suffered from chronic fatigue syndrome. In this context Lord Lloyd of Berwick adopted a distinction between primary and secondary victims: Lord Ackner and Lord Browne-Wilkinson agreed. Lord Lloyd said that a plaintiff who had been within the range of foreseeable injury was a primary victim. Mr Page fulfilled this requirement and could in principle recover compensation for psychiatric loss. In my view it follows that all other victims, who suffer pure psychiatric harm, are secondary victims and must satisfy the control mechanisms laid down in *Alcock*'s case. There has been criticism of this classification. . . . But, if the narrow formulation by Lord Lloyd of Berwick of who may be a primary victim is kept in mind, this classification ought not to produce inconsistent results.

[In this case], Waller J. rejected the claims of the police officers. The majority in the Court of Appeal upheld their claims. The first route followed by the majority was to allow some claims because the police officers were on duty in the stadium when they witnessed the gruesome events. The second route was to allow some claims because the police officers were said to be rescuers.

[His Lordship then held that the claimants were in no special position just because the shocking incident was due to the negligence of their employer: unless they were themselves exposed to the risk of physical harm they must overcome the hurdles set in *Alcock*. The same was true of rescuers.]

Lord Hoffmann: . . . For a long time during this century it remained unclear whether the basis of liability for causing a recognised psychiatric illness was simply a question of foreseeability of that type of injury in the same way as in the case of physical injury. The decision of the House of Lords in *Bourhill v Young* [1942] 2 All E.R. 396 appeared to many to combine what was in theory a simple foreseeability test with a robust wartime view of the ability of the ordinary person to suffer horror and bereavement without ill effect. Cases soon afterwards, like *King v Phillips* [1953] 1 All E.R. 617, followed this approach, treating foreseeability as a question of fact but keeping potential liability within narrow bounds by taking a highly restrictive view of the circumstances in which it was foreseeable that psychiatric injury might be caused. But such decisions were criticised as out of touch with reality. Everyone knew that some people did suffer psychiatric illnesses as a result of witnessing distressing accidents in which other people, particularly close relatives, were involved. Some judges, sympathetic to the plaintiff in the particular case, took the opportunity to find as a fact that psychiatric injury had indeed been foreseeable. This made it difficult to explain why plaintiffs in other cases had failed. It seemed that if the foreseeability test was to be taken literally and applied in the same way as the test for liability for physical injury, it would be hard to know where the limits of liability could be drawn. In all but exceptional cases, the only question would be whether on the medical evidence, the psychiatric condition had been caused by the defendant's negligent conduct.

There was a time when it seemed that English law might arrive at this position. It came within a hair's breadth of doing so in *McLoughlin v O'Brian*. But the moment passed and when the question next came before your Lordships' House in *Alcock v Chief Constable of the South Yorkshire Police* [1991] 4 All E.R. 907, judicial attitudes had changed. The view which had for some time been in the ascendancy, that the law of torts should, in principle aspire to provide a comprehensive system of corrective justice, giving legal sanction to a moral obligation on the part of anyone who has caused injury to another without justification to offer restitution or compensation, had been abandoned in favour of a cautious pragmatism. The House decided that liability for psychiatric injury should be restricted by what Lord Lloyd of Berwick (in *Page v Smith* [1995] 2 All E.R. 736 at 759) afterwards called "control mechanisms", that is to say more or less arbitrary conditions which a plaintiff had to satisfy and which were intended to keep liability within what was regarded as acceptable bounds . . .

The control mechanisms were plainly never intended to apply to all cases of psychiatric injury. They contemplate that the injury has been caused in consequence of death or injury suffered (or apprehended to have been suffered or as likely to be suffered) by someone else. In *Page v Smith*, Lord Lloyd of Berwick described such a plaintiff as a "secondary victim" who was "in the position of a spectator or bystander". He described the plaintiff in that case (who had suffered psychiatric injury in consequence of being involved in a minor motor accident) as a "primary victim" who was "directly involved in the accident and well within the range of foreseeable physical injury". The issue in *Page v Smith* was whether it is sufficient that a primary victim who, in consequence of a foreseeable accident, has suffered psychiatric injury, should have been within the range of foreseeable physical injury or whether it must have been foreseeable, in the light of the circumstances of the accident as it actually happened, that he would suffer psychiatric illness. A majority of your Lordships held that foreseeability of physical injury was enough to found a claim for any psychiatric injury which the accident caused.

This question does not arise in the present case, but the classification into primary and secondary victims has been debated at length. The plaintiffs say that they were primary victims because they were not "spectators or bystanders". The defendants say that the plaintiffs were secondary victims because they were not "within the range of foreseeable physical injury". Both arguments have some support from the speeches in *Page v Smith*, which did not have the present question in mind. Essentially, however, as I said at the beginning of this speech, the plaintiffs draw two distinctions between their position and that of spectators or bystanders. The first is that they had a relationship analogous to employment with the chief constable. Although constitutionally a constable holds an office rather than being employed, there is no dispute that his chief constable owes him the same duty of care which he would to an employee. The plaintiffs say that they were therefore owed a special duty which required the chief constable and those for whom he was vicariously liable to take reasonable care not to expose them to unnecessary risk of injury, whether physical or psychiatric. Secondly, the plaintiffs (and in this respect there is no difference between the police and many others in the crowd that day) did more than stand by and look. They actively rendered assistance and should be equated to "rescuers," who, it was said, always qualify as primary victims.

[On the employee argument, Lord Hoffmann said "I do not think it would be fair to give police officers the right to a larger claim merely because the disaster was caused by the negligence of other policemen" and as to the rescuer argument: "There does not seem to me to be any logical reason why the normal treatment of rescuers on the issues of foreseeability and causation should lead to the conclusion that, for the purpose of liability for psychiatric injury, they should be given special treatment as primary victims when they were not within the range of foreseeable physical injury and their psychiatric injury was caused by witnessing or participating in the aftermath of accidents which caused death or injury to others."]

Lord Goff, in a long, complex and concerned speech, asserted that the leading principle of liability for psychiatric injury had been, and should remain, the foreseeability of such harm to a normal person subject only, in the case of secondary victims, to the hurdles of *Alcock*. His Lordship engaged at length with the leading speech in *Page*, which he criticised as (1) dispensing with the requirement of the foreseeability of psychiatric injury in the case of primary victims, by holding that a person physically endangered (without being physically hurt) could recover for unforeseeable psychiatric harm due to his abnormal susceptibility, and (2) giving the (unintended) impression that the only victims who were primary were those who had been exposed to the risk of physical harm, with the consequence relevant to this case that unendangered participants, such as the police, would have to overcome the *Alcock* hurdles. He accordingly dissented from the view of the majority in *White* that although the plaintiffs were participants, they were not, according to *Page* as now read, primary victims and so could not recover. Had they not been participants, his Lordship would not have allowed them to recover as employees.

Lord Griffiths regarded employees as exempt from the *Alcock* restrictions only if they were personally imperilled, but would allow rescuers, even if not themselves in danger, to recover if they suffer psychiatric harm which would have affected a normally stalwart person.

Lord Browne-Wilkinson agreed with **Lord Steyn** and **Lord Hoffmann**

Notes and Questions

1. The degree to which opinions may differ on this topic is indicated by the score of judicial votes in the main cases: the successful defendant in *White* scored 5 out of a possible 9, as did the successful plaintiff in *McLoughlin*, whereas the successful plaintiff in *Page* scored 4 only. It was in *Alcock*, so much berated by critics and deplored by the Law Commission, that the judges were most in agreement: the plaintiffs (some of them) got only one vote altogether.

2. Is the following a correct statement? "(a) *Alcock* laid down that persons not involved in the accident had three hurdles to overcome in order to satisfy the proximity requirement, additional to that of foreseeability. Such persons were described by Lord Oliver as secondary victims as opposed to those who were involved in the event or its aftermath: the latter were primary victims, even if not themselves endangered. (b) *Page* decided that primary victims who were physically endangered need not show that their psychiatric harm was foreseeable. (c) *White* has now decided that only those physically endangered are primary victims and that everyone else must overcome the *Alcock* hurdles."

3. To what extent are the "control mechanisms" in *Alcock* simply factors which help us decide whether the harm in issue was or was not reasonably foreseeable?

4. Cl. 9 of the Criminal Injuries Compensation Scheme (2001) reads as follows:

"For the purposes of this Scheme, personal injury includes physical injury (including fatal injury), mental injury (that is temporary mental anxiety, medically verified, or a disabling mental illness confirmed by psychiatric diagnosis) and disease (that is a medically recognised illness or condition). Mental injury or disease may either result directly from the physical injury or from a sexual offence or may occur without any physical injury. Compensation will not be payable for mental injury or disease without physical injury, or in respect of a sexual offence, unless the applicant:
(a) was put in reasonable fear of immediate physical harm to his own person; or
(b) had a close relationship of love and affection with another person at the time when that person sustained physical and/or mental injury (including fatal injury) directly attributable to conduct within paragraph 8(a), (b) or (c), and
   (i) that relationship still subsists (unless the victim has since died), and
   (ii) the applicant either witnessed and was present on the occasion when the other person sustained the injury, or was closely involved in its immediate aftermath in fact but was deemed in law not to have consented);
or . . .
(d) being a person employed in the business of a railway, either witnessed and was present on the occasion when another person sustained physical (including fatal) injury directly attributable to an offence of trespass on a railway, or was closely involved in its immediate aftermath."

5. Why are medical men always discovering new diseases, afflictions, syndromes, etc.? The concluding Note in the Criminal Injuries Compensation Scheme reads:

8. Mental illness includes conditions attributed to post-traumatic stress disorder, depression and similar generic terms within which there may be:
   (a) such psychological symptoms as anxiety, tension, insomnia, irritability, loss of confidence, agoraphobia and preoccupation with thoughts of guilt or self-harm; and
   (b) related physical symptoms such as alopecia, asthma, eczema, enuresis and psoriasis.
9. "Medically verified" means that the mental anxiety has been diagnosed by a registered medical practitioner.
10. "Psychiatric diagnosis/prognosis" means that the disabling mental illness has been diagnosed or the prognosis made by a psychiatrist or clinical psychologist.

11. A mental illness is disabling if it significantly impairs a person's functioning in some important aspect of her/his life, *e.g.* impaired work or school performance or significant adverse effects on social relationships or sexual dysfunction.

6. In *Page* Lord Lloyd made a great point of equating psychiatric with physical injury. They are both, of course, *personal* injury, as many statutory definitions testify (*e.g.* Consumer Protection Act 1987, s.45(1)), and in *R. v Ireland* [1997] 4 All E.R. 225, H.L., it was decided that the words "bodily harm" in ss.20 and 47 of the Offences Against the Person Act 1861 included recognisable psychiatric illness such as anxiety disorder or clinical depression affecting the central nervous system, but not everyday disagreeable feelings even of fear: the making of silent telephone calls could amount to an "assault" under s.47 if they provoked fear of immediate violence, and the perpetrator could be said thereby to "inflict" bodily harm under s.20. It has even been held that PTSD suffered by a fireman constituted "accidental bodily injury" for the purposes of a personal accident policy: *Connelly v New Hampshire Ins. Co* 1997 S.L.T. 1341.

7. The notion of "foreseeability" is not very transparent. It might help to substitute "normality", since there is a link between the two, especially when one is talking of concatenations of physical rather than mental events. One of Lord Goff's objections to Lord Lloyd's speech in *Page* was that it dropped the foreseeability requirement when a person imperilled but unhurt was suing for psychiatric harm, that is, harm resulting from an abnormal reaction. In this respect certainly *Page* is simply a neurotic's charter, and Lord Goff noted that it was based on a misunderstanding of the "thin-skull" rule which is established in physical injury cases, namely that an injury must be actionable before any exacerbation due to an unsuspected predisposition in the victim becomes compensable. Even in physical injury cases this rule is objectionable: in cases of psychiatric harm it is quite unacceptable, and the sly saying that a thin-skull personality is like a person with a fragile cranium is quite wrong.

8. The judges keep saying that they can always tell whether a claim is honest or not, but they can only tell if they are told. In *Vernon v Bosley* [1997] 1 All E.R. 577 and 614 they were not told, and one judge held that the barrister was under no duty to tell them! Two of the plaintiff's daughters were drowned when their nanny drove into a river. The plaintiff witnessed the aftermath and allegedly suffered very serious psychological consequences, involving the collapse of his business and his marriage. Holding that if the shock contributed to his condition, it was immaterial that grief, not compensable standing alone, also made a contribution, the Court of Appeal nevertheless reduced to £600K the award made by the trial judge of over £1 million. Concurrently with his claim for damages, however, the plaintiff was engaged in family proceedings, defending an application for ouster by his divorced wife and seeking residence of his three other children. The evidence given by his expert witnesses in the two cases was fundamentally different, in the shock case that he was still very ill and the prognosis poor, in the family proceedings that he was now quite well. This was known to the plaintiff's advisers but they did not inform the court, and the truth emerged indirectly. The court decided by a majority that damages must be further reduced [1997] 1 All E.R. 614. The case is significant as indicating the fragile nature of evidence of injuries of this kind.

9. Can you sue the person who shocked you by killing himself? The judge in *Greatorex v Greatorex* [2000] 4 All E.R. 769 held not. The case was one where the claimant, a fire officer, was called to the scene of a crash and found his son badly injured at the wheel of the car he had been driving negligently and without insurance. The judge feared the effect on family relations of deciding otherwise. In another drama Gilbert Kopernik-Steckel killed not only himself but also his mother, in the presence of his sister, aged 21, but her claim was brought against the mental hospital which had negligently let him loose, knowing that he had lethal thoughts about his mother (which perhaps establishes proximity, as certainly does the fact that they telephoned her to warn her: see *Tarasoff*, above p.89, n.7). The defendant finally settled for £500,000 (*The Times*, November 5 and 11, 2000).

10. There have recently been extensions regarding (a) sudden shock and (b) aftermath.

(a) *Sudden shock?* In *Walters v North Glamorgan Trust* [2002] E.W.C.A. Civ 1792 the claimant's son, not a year old, was ill with undiagnosed severe hepatitis, and she awoke in his hospital room to find him having a choking fit. She was told that he was unlikely to have suffered any brain damage—in fact such damage was irreparable—and after a CAT scan she was told that there was no brain damage but that he should be transferred to a London hospital for a liver transplant. She followed the ambulance to London where she was told the truth: he was put on a life support machine but the next day she learnt that he would have no quality of life at all and she consented to the termination of the life support. It was held that her witnessing the last 36 hours of her son's life was a sudden horrifying event, and that as a secondary victim she was entitled to damages for her pathological grief. (Imagine the cost to the National Health Service if it has to pay the parents of young patients who die from misdiagnosis, especially if the £10,000 bereavement damages under the Fatal Accidents Act are not deductible).

Consider also *Froggatt v Chesterfield etc. NHS Trust* (Q.B.D., December 13, 2002). A woman was told she had serious cancer and had a mastectomy. This was all a dreadful mistake. She of course got huge damages, but the judge awarded £5,000 to her husband and £1,000 to her son for "psychiatric illness consequent on an affront to the senses".

Industrial injuries benefit is available to those who suffer psychiatric harm, but only if it results from an "accident" arising both out of and in the course of employment. A fire officer developed PSTD after 27 years in the service as a result, he claimed, of attending a series of fatal accidents. The House of Lords held that the accidents to the victims were not necessarily accidents to the claimant, and that it was not enough to suffer as a result of stressful employment. The question was whether the claimant had suffered illness as the result of an accident to him. *Chief Adjudication Officer v Faulds* (HL, [2000] 1 W.L.R. 1035, reversing Inner House).

(b)   *Aftermath?* In *Atkinson v Seghal* (CA, 21/3/2003) a mother returning home came across a police cordon and was told that her 16-year old daughter had been killed. She was then taken by her husband to the mortuary and had another hysterical attack. The trial judge held that her pathological grief was due to being told of the accident, and would have occurred anyway ([2000] 1 W.L.R. 1035). His decision was reversed: the mortuary visit was part of the aftermath.

11. Psychiatric harm does not fall within the "bodily injury" for which alone the Warsaw Convention provides compensation: there must be actual physical injury: a passenger shocked by being fingered by her neighbour consequently had no claim: *Morris v KLM Dutch Airlines* [2002] 2 A.C. 628. The Convention excludes claims at common law against the carrying airline: *Sidhu v British Airways* [1997] 1 All E.R. 193, but if one's package travel agency fails to include the terms of the air travel, it may be liable: *Akehurst v Thomson Holidays* (May 6, 2003).

12. *White* seems to state that where psychiatric harm results from witnessing a tragedy the defendant's employees are in no better position to claim than strangers. This point was not obviously appreciated by the police force which paid some £330,000 to an officer who more than eleven years after the Leppings Lane disaster suffered a "late onset" of PTSD which led him to resign on medical grounds (with an enhanced pension) (*The Times*, March 2, 2001).

Reference was made in *White* to the fact that those in a profession fraught with risk can sue if the risk is triggered by negligence, and certainly in *Ogwo v Taylor* [1987] 3 All E.R. 961, a case of actual physical injury, the House of Lords had rejected the "firemen's rule" which would have barred claims by members of the emergency services. Less reference was made to the fact that policemen's contracts contain a generous disability pension, and no mention at all was made of the fact that policemen and firemen may collect full damages for lost earnings in addition to such a pension (*Parry v Cleaver*, below p.647). Would it not therefore be right, in the case of psychiatric harm resulting from witnessing disasters to distinguish between those who are paid to deal with them and those who are not?

Certainly it would be a pity to depart from *Dooley v Cammell Laird* [1951] Lloyd's Rep. 271 where the plaintiff craneman recovered damages for the shock he experienced when a faulty chain supplied by his employer snapped and the load he was lifting from a ship fell back into the hold where his mates were working. It is not really satisfactory to decide for him on the basis that he was somehow implicated in the disaster.

13. "The control mechanisms were plainly never intended to apply to all cases of psychiatric injury". So said Lord Hoffmann, quite truly. They were, however, applied in a case where the defendant's airplane crashed to the ground quite close to where the claimants lived. The defendant was strictly liable under the Civil Aviation Act 1982, s.76(2) for "loss or damage", which the judge correctly held included psychiatric harm. But he went on to hold that the claimants could not recover for shock unless they were in a close and loving relationship with the primary victims, presumably those in the plane or under it (*Glen v Korean Airlines* [2003] 3 All E.R. 621). This is surely wrong: the control mechanisms are appropriate when the defendant is being sued for negligent breach of duty at common law, whereas in the statutory torts there is no room for any such notion. Likewise in a claim under the Consumer Protection Act 1987.

14. *W v Essex C.C.* [2000] 2 All E.R. 237 was, however, a claim in negligence. The claimants were shocked to learn that their children had been abused by the youth whom the local authority had sent to them for fostering despite having been told that no one suspected of abusive proclivities would be acceptable. In holding their claim quite arguable the House of Lords spoke of classifying the claimants as primary victims in that they felt responsible for bringing about the harmful situation, though of course they did not witness the actual abuse. But one wonders if the control mechanisms were not altogether inapplicable, given the nature of the latter's negligence and the special relationship between the parents and the local authority.

15. There is no talk of primary victims in claims by employees for damaging stress at work. It started with *Walker v Northumberland C.C.* [1995] 1 All E.R. 737 where an area social services officer who had worked for the defendant for 15 years had a second nervous breakdown attributable to the employer's failure to

provide him with extra help, and received £175,000. Unsurprisingly, the number of such claims increased greatly and in *Hatton v Sutherland* [2002] 2 All E.R. 1 the Court of Appeal tried to stauch the flow of undeserving cases. It allowed three appeals by employers against judgments holding them liable, and laid down clear and sensible rules: the employer would be liable under the normal rules of negligence law (there being no special control devices, though these cases had their own peculiarities) only if he had reason to believe, taking account of what the employee himself said, that damaging stress was imminent and failed to take reasonable steps to avert it.

That the only claimant to appeal from this decision was successful is a matter for grave regret (*Barber v Somerset C.C.* [2004] UKHL 13). In fact the House did not really dissent from what Hale L.J. so clearly and sensibly laid down in the Court of Appeal, save in two respects: it preferred to treat such claims as indistinguishable from claims for personal injury due to the adoption of an unsafe system of work(!) and completely ignored her crucial observation, at [33], that "It is essential, once the risk of harm to health from stresses in the workplace is foreseeable, to consider whether and in what respect the employer has broken that duty. There may be a temptation, having concluded that some harm was foreseeable and that harm of that kind has taken place, to go on to conclude that the employer was in breach of his duty of care in failing to prevent that harm (and that that breach of duty caused the harm). But *in every case it is necessary to consider what the employer not only could but should have done*. [emphasis in original]." Lord Walker of Gestingthorpe, with whom Lord Bingham and Lord Steyn agreed, yielded to this temptation. There was virtually no discussion of what the employer should or could have done: all we hear is that the claimant's line managers were "unsympathetic". This approach is actually inconsistent with the basic principle of negligence law, namely that a person is not liable for harm unless it is shown what it was he could and should have done that would probably have prevented it: you cannot tell whether he is in breach of duty or whether the breach contributed to the harm until you have identified the breach in question. There was a persuasive dissent by Lord Scott and Lord Rodger's concurrence was extremely hesitant. Fortunately, since the decision merely holds that the trial judge was "entitled to come to the conclusion he did and that the Court of Appeal was not entitled to differ from him on the facts, it is not an authority at all, though it will be treated as one: it is nevertheless a signal, in an area where the waving of green flags is a serious mistake.

16. Is this develoment consistent with *White*? In *Harrhy v Thames Trains* (Mackay J., July 30, 2003) the claimant, as manager, had to attend the scene of a terrible crash for which his employer was responsible, and alleged that he had developed PTSD in consequence. The defendant argued that the claim was hopeless, since *Walker* must have been displaced by *White*, but the judge let the claim proceed: the claimant could rely on both the *Alcock* line of cases and the cases on stress in employment. In all these cases it is clear that at common law the claimant must show, in Lord Denning's quaint phrase, that he is now "officially ill".

17. We now turn from the stress of doing one's job to the stress or distress of losing it, and will see that damages may be available for persons who have suffered distress falling far short of recognisable psychiatric disorder.

At common law no damages could be claimed for distress, however severe, at the mode and manner of the wrongful dismissal, however brutal. This was taken to be the effect of *Addis v Gramophone Co.* [1909] A.C. 488. As regards the obligations of the employer during the course of the employment the twentieth century saw great developments in favour of the employee (see *Mahmud v BCCI* [1998] A.C. 20), but as regards dismissal the common law remains subject to *Addis*. This is largely because for over 30 years employees unfairly dismissed have enjoyed a different, purely statutory, remedy: it is not at all like the common law remedy of damages, for the claimant must have been employed for a certain period, there is a cap to the amount of recovery (which may be reduced if his conduct has contributed to the unfair dismissal), and jurisdiction is vested in employment tribunals, not the regular courts.

But if the regular courts could not award damages for distress at a wrongful dismissal, could the employment tribunals award damages for distress occasioned by one which was merely unfair? The controlling statute provided that " . . . the compensatory award shall be such amount as the tribunal considers just and equitable in all the circumstances having regard to the loss sustained by the complainant in consequence of his dismissal . . . " (Employment Rights Act 1996, s.123(1)). This had immediately been held in to cover only financial loss and not to extend to distress or non-pecuniary harm (*Norton Tool Co. v Tewson* [1972] I.C.R. 501) but in *Johnson v Unisys* [2003] 1 A.C. 518 Lord Hoffmann opined (at [55]) that this was "too narrow a construction". The Court of Appeal by a majority agreed with him and, overruling the Employment Appeal Tribunal, held that the tribunals were entitled to award damages for distress (*Dunnachie v Kingston-upon-Hull C.C.* [2004] EWCA Civ 84.) Leave to appeal to the House of Lords was granted, and as Sedley L.J. said: "The last word has not been spoken". Note, however, that the award will still be subject to the statutory cap, as it would not be at common law.

18. Damages for distress and disappointment falling far short of a proved clinical condition have been awarded quite widely in other cases. It started with *Jarvis v Swans Tours* [1973] 1 All E.R. 71 where a holiday-maker was miffed because his Alpine holiday was not quite as promised and represented. This was extended to other types of contract provided that they were designed to give pleasure or to avoid distress, but this limitation was dropped by the House of Lords in *Farley v Skinner* [2002] A.C. 732 where a surveyor

failed to report, as instructed to do, on aircraft noise over a property not far from Gatwick Airport which the claimant was minded to, and did, buy. The actual value of the property was not diminished by the sporadic aircraft noise but the disgruntled purchaser obtained damages of £10,000.

19. Furthermore, in line with the principle that bad people pay more, distress damages can be awarded where the defendant has acted very badly. In *Hunter v Canary Wharf* [1997] 2 All E.R. 426, 452 Lord Hoffmann said: "I see no reason why a tort of intention should be subject to the rule which excludes compensation for mere distress, inconvenience or discomfort in actions of negligence", and confirmed this, with reflections on what constitutes "intention", in *Wainwright* (below p.331)). Though it has been (dubiously) questioned whether distress damages can be awarded for breach of confidence (*W v Egdell* [1989] 1 All E.R. 1089, 1108), aggravated damages can be awarded for malicious falsehood (*Khodoparast v Shad*, below p.582), and distress damages are clearly available under the Protection from Harassment Act 1997, (below p.336).

Section 6.—The Family

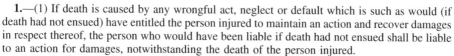

FATAL ACCIDENTS ACT 1976

1.—(1) If death is caused by any wrongful act, neglect or default which is such as would (if death had not ensued) have entitled the person injured to maintain an action and recover damages in respect thereof, the person who would have been liable if death had not ensued shall be liable to an action for damages, notwithstanding the death of the person injured.

(2) Subject to section 1A(2) below, every such action shall be for the benefit of the dependants of the person ("the deceased") whose death has been so caused.

(3) In this Act "dependant" means—

(a) the wife or husband or former wife or husband of the deceased;
(b) any person who—
  (i) was living with the deceased in the same household immediately before the date of the death; and
  (ii) had been living with the deceased in the same household for at least two years before that date; and
  (iii) was living during the whole of that period as the husband or wife of the deceased.
(c) any parent or other ascendant of the deceased;
(d) any person who was treated by the deceased as his parent;
(e) any child or other descendant of the deceased;
(f) any person (not being a child of the deceased) who, in the case of any marriage to which the deceased was at any time a party, was treated by the deceased as a child of the family in relation to that marriage;
(g) any person who is, or is the issue of, a brother, sister, uncle or aunt of the deceased.

(5) In deducing any relationship for the purposes of subsection (3) above—

(a) any relationship by affinity shall be treated as a relationship by consanguinity, any relationship of the half blood as a relationship of the whole blood, and the stepchild of any person as his child, and
(b) an illegitimate person shall be treated as the legitimate child of his mother and reputed father.

1A.—(1) An action under this Act may consist of or include a claim for damages for bereavement.

(2) A claim for damages for bereavement shall only be for the benefit—

(a) of the wife or husband of the deceased; and
(b) where the deceased was a minor who was never married—
    (i) of his parents, if he was legitimate; and
    (ii) of his mother, if he was illegitimate.

(3) Subject to subsection (5) below, the sum to be awarded as damages under this section shall be £10,000.

(4) Where there is a claim for damages under this section for the benefit of both the parents of the deceased, the sum awarded shall be divided equally between them.

(5) The Lord Chancellor may by order made by statutory instrument, subject to annulment in pursuance of a resolution of either House of Parliament, amend this section by varying the sum for the time being specified in subsection (3) above.

2.—(1) The action shall be brought by and in the name of the executor or administrator of the deceased. . . .

3.—(1) In the action such damages, other than damages for bereavement, may be awarded as are proportioned to the injury resulting from the death to the dependants respectively.

(2) After deducting the costs not recovered from the defendant any amount recovered otherwise than as damages for bereavement shall be divided among the dependants in such shares as may be directed.

(3) In an action under this Act where there fall to be assessed damages payable to a widow in respect of the death of her husband there shall not be taken into account the re-marriage of the widow or her prospects of re-marriage.

(4) In an action under this Act where there fall to be assessed damages payable to a person who is a dependant by virtue of section 1(3)(b) above in respect of the death of the person with whom the dependant was living as husband or wife there shall be taken into account (together with any other matter that appears to the court to be relevant to the action) the fact that the dependant had no enforceable right to financial support by the deceased as a result of their living together.

(5) If the dependants have incurred funeral expenses in respect of the deceased, damages may be awarded in respect of those expenses.

(6) Money paid into court in satisfaction of a cause of action under this Act may be in one sum without specifying any person's share.

4. In assessing damages in respect of a person's death in an action under this Act, benefits which have accrued or will or may accrue to any person from his estate or otherwise as a result of his death shall be disregarded.

5. Where any person dies as the result partly of his own fault and partly of the fault of any other person or persons, and accordingly if an action were brought for the benefit of the estate under the Law Reform (Miscellaneous Provisions) Act 1934 the damages recoverable would be reduced under section 1(1) of the Law Reform (Contributory Negligence) Act 1945, any damages recoverable in an action under this Act shall be reduced to a proportionate extent.

Questions
1. Do you think s.3(3) is "constitutional"? What about the claim by a child who has obtained a generous stepfather or the widower who has allowed hope to triumph over experience? In view of s.4 is s.3(3) even necessary?

2. Given that the claim lies in respect of what the claimant would in fact have received from the decedent (and, indeed, what he had even a decent chance of receiving (*Davies v Taylor* [1972] 3 All E.R. 836, HL)), rather than what he was entitled in law to receive, can s.4(4) be attributed to anything other than the pique of a government at the Parliamentary amendment which, contrary to its wish, introduced section 1(3)(b) in favour of cohabitants? But if cohabitants now also have rights on intestacy (Law Reform (Succession) Act 1995) in addition to those under the Inheritance (Provision for Family and Dependants) Act 1975, they have no claim for bereavement damages under the Fatal Accidents Act; they can, however, be awarded £11,000 under the Criminal Injuries Compensation Scheme (paras 38, 39). Unlike the Act, the Scheme also provides for children bereaved of a parent as well as a parent bereaved of an adult or married child, but it is quite like

the Act when there is more than one claimant: the Act provides for the splitting of the award when both parents claim in respect of the death of a child while the Scheme provides that where there is more than one qualified applicant, the sum payable to each is reduced from £11,000 to £5,500.

3. Agatha has a child called Benjamin by a father who has disappeared without trace. For five years now Agatha and Benjamin have been living with Charlie who supports both of them. What is the position under the Act if (a) Charlie is killed, and (b) Agatha and Benjamin are killed? In (a) it was held by Morland J. in *Heap v W E Ford* [1993] C.L.Y.B. § 1396 that Benjamin had no claim.

Notes:

1. We have already seen (above, p.56) how reluctant the common law was to compensate A for financial harm consequent on damage to the property of B. It was equally reluctant to compensate A for harm consequent on personal injury to B, fatal or not. Those affected by a person's *death* had no claim at common law at all, and still have none: they may claim only under the statute. The original Fatal Accidents Act was passed in 1846 when large numbers of people were being killed by the other Stephenson's invention, then just come of age. As amended in 1959, consolidated in 1976 and re-amended in 1982, the Act provides the leading example of liability in tort for negligently causing financial harm to a stranger. It does *not* lay down that any duty is owed by the tortfeasor to the survivors: it simply enables them to sue the tortfeasor if the deceased could have done so at the moment of his death (thus if the deceased had personally settled with the tortfeasor or sued him to judgment or let his claim become time-barred, the survivors have no claim). Remoteness of damage to the survivor (as opposed to the deceased) is equally irrelevant to the statutory claim.

2. Note that although the financial or human harm suffered by the survivors is perfectly foreseeable, they themselves cannot sue on the basis that there was any breach of duty towards them personally. It should be borne in mind when one is making general statements about legal responsibility for the foreseeable consequences of one's unreasonable conduct that you do not owe people any duty not to maim or kill their nearest and dearest, unless you shock them by doing it in their presence. It is true that in 1976 Lord Kilbrandon said "The law now treats the employer as knowing that nearly all the men and many of the women he employs have dependants who are maintained out of the wages he pays and that those dependants will suffer grief as well as patrimonial loss if he, by neglect of his duty of care, occasions his employees physical harm. Those dependants are therefore persons to whom he owes that duty." *Dick v Burgh of Falkirk* 1976 S.L.T. 21 at 25, HL But this "revolutionary" observation was sternly denounced and disavowed by all the members of the House of Lords in *Robertson v Turnbull* 1982 S.L.T. 96.

3. Only the persons specified in the statute, including now the ex-wife and the live-in lover, may sue. Many other people may suffer loss, such as the employer, the partner or the insurance company. None of these may sue.

4. The word "dependants" did not figure in the original Act. It is misleading. One need not be a "dependant" in the normal sense in order to claim (except under s.1(3)(b)). It is enough that anyone defined as a "dependant" in s.1(3) is worse off financially as a result of the death. Thus in *Davies v Whiteways Cyder* [1974] 3 All E.R. 168 a widow and son had had no further expectations of the deceased, *i.e.* they were not "dependent" on him, since he had already made them considerable capital gifts; no duty would have been payable on those gifts had the donor survived for a year or two more, but on his premature death owing to the defendant's negligence they had to pay the duty and he was held liable for this doubtless unforeseeable consequence. In *White v Jones* [1995] 1 All E.R. 691 at 719, Lord Mustill doubted whether a defendant who carelessly killed a person on his way to his solicitors to sign a will which would have given his daughters a legacy would be liable to the daughters for the amount of the legacy lost; his doubt is justified at common law, but the daughters could assuredly sue under the 1976 Act.

Some of the problems in determining the amount of the award for loss of support are discussed below, p.651.

5. The notion of being "dependent" misled counsel in *Cox v Hockenhull* [1999] 3 All E.R. 577, where the plaintiff and his deceased wife lived exclusively off state benefits as the plaintiff continued to do. It was argued that the widower had been dependent not on the wife but on the state, and since he was still so dependent, there was no loss of dependency. The Court of Appeal rightly held that the question was whether there had been any loss consequent on the death. However, the court unfortunately endorsed the erroneous decision of *Burgess v Florence Nightingale Hospital* [1955] 1 Q.B. 349, and held that although the allowance paid to the survivor as carer for his wife had come to an end with her death, this loss was not compensable because it was attributable not to his being her husband but to his being her carer, just as in *Burgess* the widower could not claim for the loss he suffered because his wife's death had robbed him of the dancing partner with whom he used to win prizes in dancing competitions. There is no justification for saying that the loss suffered by a husband owing to his wife's death must be to him in his capacity as husband. The words of the statute are clear: it is enough that he be the husband and that the loss result from the death of his wife.

6. In *Jameson v CEGB* a man contracted a fatal disease as a result of the negligence of both his employer and the occupier of the factory where he worked. Prior to his death his employer agreed to pay him a significant sum "in full and final settlement and satisfaction". This sum was paid to his estate, whence his widow inherited it. She now claimed the full value of her dependency from the occupier (for s.4 of the Fatal Accidents Act stupidly provides that in a widow's claim no account is to be taken of sums received from the deceased's estate), and the occupier claimed contribution from the employer (since the Contribution Act 1978, s.1(3) stupidly provides that a person remains liable to contribute to another tortfeasor even though he has settled with the victim.) The Court of Appeal upheld this outrageous claim, but fortunately the House of Lords was able to dismiss it by holding that in settling with the employer the victim must be taken to have released concurrent tortfeasors, with the result that at the time of the death he no longer had any claim against the occupier and that consequently the widow had none. [1999] 1 All E.R. 193.

7. Until 1982 only financial loss was recoverable under the Act: no damages at all could be awarded for grief. This was particularly hard in the case where a small child, the apple of its parents' eye, was killed, for then there was no financial loss (children being an expense—see *McFarlane* below, p.118) and the appalling human loss went quite unalleviated. But the present provision is odd in some respects. Why did the legislator lay down a fixed sum rather than a ceiling, if it had to set a limit at all? Scottish law is different. Relatives there may claim for the distress and anxiety they endure in contemplation of the suffering of the deceased before his death, and an unlimited sum in respect of grief and sorrow caused by the death. (Damages (Scotland) Act 1993, s.1(1)).

8. But the family may be affected by *non-fatal* injuries to one of its members. Here the very strong tendency is to allow only the primary victim to claim, and to dress up the loss to others as being the primary victim's loss. Thus if the husband is emasculated, the wife will clearly suffer: she cannot sue, however, for he will be paid for the pleasure he can neither receive nor give (*Best v Samuel Fox* [1952] A.C. 716). Again, the wage-earner who will shortly die because of the injury can hardly be said to have lost the wages he will not be on earth to earn; he is, however, treated as having a present interest in providing for his survivors (*Pickett v British Rail Engineering* [1980] A.C. 136). If the mother is incapacitated the family loses her services: she can sue for their value, though she doesn't seem to have lost anything except trouble, and her husband, who has, cannot (*Daly v General Steam Navigation Co* [1980] 3 All E.R. 696: Administration of Justice Act 1982, s.2—and the principle that one can sue for one's inability to perform services within the family has now been generalised: *Lowe v Guise* [2002] Q.B. 1369. If the mother is rendered permanently unconscious, it is only really the family that suffers (pointless visits to the hospital, the near corpse in the upstairs bedroom); they cannot sue, and the immense sum payable to the mother, which she can never use, seems to reflect the fact. (*West v Shephard* (below, p.643)). If a child is injured, the mother may give up her job to nurse him: the child can sue for the value of the free services received, often equal to the wages given up, unless the tortfeasor does the caring himself (*Hunt v Severs* [1994] 2 All E.R. 385, HL; noted [1994] Camb.L.J. 436; (1994) 110 L.Q.R. 524. But though an injured husband can claim from a third party for the caring services of his wife, he cannot claim for her helping out in his business: *Hardwick v Hudson* [1999] 3 All E.R. 425, CA.

9. There is another enactment which also concerns the effect of death on tort liability—the Law Reform (Misc.Prov.) Act 1934. Its role and function are entirely different from those of the Fatal Accidents Act, which, as we have seen, provides survivors with compensation for what *they* have lost. The 1934 Act allows a deceased person (inconveniently called his "estate") to claim for *his* losses prior to his death, *i.e.* lost earnings up to his death, medical expenses and, surprisingly, damages for pain and suffering (the last wisely not covered by the Criminal Injuries Compensation Scheme). This is so whether or not the defendant is responsible for the death, but if he is, funeral expenses may also be claimed—the sole *post mortem* loss which is covered. It is odd that a claim can be brought for the pain and suffering of the deceased, provided that death did not follow very soon on the injury (*Hicks v Chief Constable* [1992] 2 All E.R. 65) but although claims for defamation die with the victim (as well as with the defamer) a claim under the Race Relations Act (though heard by a tribunal, not a proper court) does survive the victim's death, as do claims for unfair dismissal under the Employment Rights Act 1996, s.206. (*Harris v Lewisham and Guy's Mental Health Trust* [2000] 3 All E.R. 769.)

10. It has been suggested that the Fatal Accidents Act is vulnerable to challenge under the Human Rights Act in that it confers no right on the child of a mother who has not yet married the partner, now deceased, who was supporting the "family", although it is clear that the Act does not require a blood relationship and that children of unmarried parents may sue in respect of their loss resulting from the death of either of them. Is this unconstitutionally discriminatory?

11. The text of the Act is good evidence of the nauseating Pharisaism of the government of the day. Not content with depriving unmarried cohabitants of damages for bereavement, the government was opposed to allowing them to sue for economic loss. When Parliament got the amendment carried, the government responded by s.3(4) which tells the judges not to award very much if no marriage licence is produced, on the basis, forsooth and despite the well-known figures for divorce, that marriages are more stable than unlicensed

but durable cohabitation. It is also an ignorant provision, since the widow's claim does not depend, as the provision suggests, on what she was *entitled* to but on what she could *in fact* expect.

12. Strasbourg has its own views on the matter. In *McGlinchey v UK* (72 B.M.L.R. 168 (2003)) a youngish drug-dependent prisoner was not properly looked after in prison and died there. Damages were awarded: €11,500 to her estate, and to her mother and two children, who could have suffered no financial loss, €3,800 each.

13. If a married man is so badly injured by the defendant's negligence that he becomes impossible to live with and his wife sues for divorce, the cost to the husband may well be considerable (especially as, unbelievably, the husband's damages for pain and suffering are available for distribution to the wife!). Nevertheless this cost is not taken into account in the husband's claim against the tortfeasor. *Pritchard v J.H. Cobden* [1987] 1 All E.R. 300. No wonder we need a special section on Tort and the Family!

CONGENITAL DISABILITIES (CIVIL LIABILITY) ACT 1976

1.—(1) If a child is born disabled as the result of such an occurrence before its birth as is mentioned in subsection (2) below, and a person (other than the child's own mother) is under this section answerable to the child in respect of the occurrence, the child's disabilities are to be regarded as damage resulting from the wrongful act of that person and actionable accordingly at the suit of the child.

(2) An occurrence to which this section applies is one which—

(a) affected either parent of the child in his or her ability to have a normal, healthy child; or

(b) affected the mother during her pregnancy, or affected her or the child in the course of its birth, so that the child is born with disabilities which would not otherwise have been present.

(3) Subject to the following subsections, a person (here referred to as "the defendant") is answerable to the child if he was liable in tort to the parent or would, if sued in due time, have been so; and it is no answer that there could not have been such liability because the parent suffered no actionable injury, if there was a breach of legal duty which, accompanied by injury, would have given rise to the liability.

(4) In the case of an occurrence preceding the time of conception, the defendant is not answerable to the child if at the time either or both of the parents knew the risk of their child being born disabled (that is to say, the particular risk created by the occurrence); but should it be the child's father who is the defendant, this subsection does not apply if he knew of the risk and the mother did not.

(5) The defendant is not answerable to the child, for anything he did or omitted to do when responsible in a professional capacity for treating or advising the parent, if he took reasonable care having due regard to then received professional opinion applicable to the particular class of case; but this does not mean that he is answerable only because he departed from received opinion. . . .

(7) If in the child's action under this section it is shown that the parent affected shared the responsibility for the child being born disabled, the damages are to be reduced to such extent as the court thinks just and equitable having regard to the extent of the parent's responsibility.

2. A woman driving a motor vehicle when she knows (or ought reasonably to know) herself to be pregnant is to be regarded as being under the same duty to take care for the safety of her unborn child as the law imposes on her with respect to the safety of other people; and if in consequence of her breach of that duty her child is born with disabilities which would not otherwise have been present, those disabilities are to be regarded as damage resulting from her wrongful act and actionable accordingly at the suit of the child. . . .

4.—(1) . . .

(2) In this Act—

(a) "born" means born alive (the moment of a child's birth being when it first has a life separate from its mother), and "birth" has a corresponding meaning . . .

(5) This Act applies in respect of births after (but not before) its passing, and in respect of any such birth it replaces any law in force before its passing, whereby a person could be liable to a child in respect of disabilities with which it might be born; . . .

Questions:
1. Under s.1(1) why should the mother not be liable if the father is?
2. Under s.1(7) why should the parents' contributory negligence be imputed to the unborn child when it is not imputed to the child once born? (*Oliver v Birmingham & Midland Omnibus Co* [1933] 1 K.B. 35)
3. Under s.2 why should the mother be liable if the foetus is injured by her bad driving but not by her falling downstairs pickled with gin?
4. Can a mother claim bereavement damages under the Fatal Accidents Act for the death of a viable foetus killed by the defendant's fault?
5. A new s.1A was added by the Human Fertilisation and Embryology Act 1990 to cover the case where the child generated is born deformed because of mismanagement of the sperm, ovum or gametes. Why was this thought necessary?

Notes:
1. This Act was passed because it was uncertain whether any duty could be owed to a person not yet born, not yet viable or not yet conceived. This uncertainty, now resolved by *Burton v Islington H.A.*, weakened the case of the Thalidomide victims against the distributors of that drug: see *Att-Gen v Times Newspapers* [1973] 3 All E.R. 54.
2. In *McKay v Essex Area H.A.* [1982] Q.B. 1166 (noted [1982] Camb.L.J. 225) the allegations were that the defendant doctor had negligently failed (a) to diagnose rubella in the pregnant mother, (b) to recommend an abortion, and (c) to take steps which might have reduced the disabilities with which the infant plaintiff was born. The Court of Appeal held that while the mother could sue for the pain and expense of having a disabled child, and while the infant child could sue on the ground that its disabilities were greater than they would have been if the doctor had treated the mother properly, the infant could not claim damages on the ground that the doctor had negligently prevented her being aborted. Stephenson L.J. said " . . . neither defendant was under any duty to the child to give the child's mother an opportunity to terminate the child's life. That duty may be owed to the mother, but it cannot be owed to the child." (at 1180). *McKay* was decided under the common law which was abrogated by the above statute. What would the position be under the statute today?
3. In *McKay* the mother wanted the child, if well, but in many cases she doesn't, and sues the doctor who performed the sterilisation operation negligently. The courts used to allow her to claim for the expense of bringing up the child, even if it is perfectly healthy, as well as the pain and associated expenses of pregnancy and childbirth, with no real setoff, except possibly against the trouble of upbringing, for the joys of reluctant maternity.

REES v DARLINGTON MEMORIAL HOSPITAL NHS TRUST

House of Lords [2003] UKHL 52; [2004] 1 A.C. 309; [2003] 3 W.L.R. 1091; [2004] 1 F.L.R. 234;
[2003] 4 All E.R. 987

Can parents, healthy or disabled, claim the cost of bringing up a child, healthy or disabled, whose birth is due to the negligence of medical advisers?

Lord Bingham of Cornhill: In *McFarlane v Tayside Health Board* [2000] 2 A.C. 59 a husband and wife, themselves healthy and normal, sought to recover as damages the cost of bringing up a healthy and normal child born to the wife, following allegedly negligent advice on the effect of a vasectomy performed on the husband. Differing from the Inner House of the Court of Session (1998 S.L.T. 307), the House unanimously rejected this claim. A factual variant of that case reached the Court of Appeal in *Parkinson v St James and Seacroft University Hospital NHS Trust* [2002] Q.B. 266: the mother, who had undergone a negligently performed sterilisation operation, conceived and bore a child who was born with severe disabilities. Following *McFarlane*, the Court of Appeal held that the mother could not recover the whole cost of bringing up the child; but it held that she could recover the additional costs she would incur so far as they would be attributable to the child's disabilities. There was no appeal from that decision. The present case raises a further factual variant of *McFarlane*. The claimant in these proceedings (Ms Rees) suffers a severe and progressive visual disability, such that she felt unable to discharge the ordinary duties of a mother, and for that reason wished to be sterilised. She made her wishes known to a consultant employed by the appellant NHS Trust, who carried out a sterilisation operation but did so negligently, and the claimant conceived and bore a son. The child is normal and healthy but the claimant's disability remains. She claimed as damages the cost of rearing the child. The Court of Appeal held that she was entitled to recover the additional costs she would incur so far as they would be attributable to her disability: [2003] Q.B. 20. The appellant NHS Trust now challenges that decision as inconsistent with *McFarlane*. The claimant seeks to uphold the decision, but also claims the whole cost of bringing up the child, inviting the House to reconsider its decision in *McFarlane*.

It is convenient to begin by considering *McFarlane*. In that case there were, as it seems to me, broadly three solutions which the House could have adopted to the problem then before it. (1) That full damages against the tortfeasor for the cost of rearing the child may be allowed, subject to the ordinary limitations of reasonable foreseeability and remoteness, with no discount for joys, benefits and support, leaving restrictions upon such recovery to such limitations as may be enacted by a Parliament with authority to do so. (2) That damages may be recovered in full for the reasonable costs of rearing an unplanned child to the age when that child might be expected to be economically self-reliant, whether the child is "healthy" or "disabled" or "impaired" but with a deduction from the amount of such damages for the joy and benefits received, and the potential economic support derived, from the child. (3) That no damages may be recovered where the child is born healthy and without disability or impairment.

An orthodox application of familiar and conventional principles of the law of tort would, I think, have pointed towards acceptance of the first of these solutions. The surgeon whose allegedly negligent advice gave rise to the action was exercising his professional skill for the benefit of the *McFarlanes* who relied on it. The foreseeable result of negligent advice would be the birth of a child, the very thing they wished to avoid. No one can be unaware that bringing up a child has a financial cost. All members of the House accepted that the surgeon owed a duty of care to the *McFarlanes*, and the foreseeable result was that which occurred. Thus the proven violation of a legal right would lead to a compensatory remedy. I do not find it surprising that this solution has been supported by the line of English authority which preceded *McFarlane*, by decisions of the Hoge Raad in the Netherlands and the Bundesverfassungsgericht in Germany and now by a majority of the High Court of Australia. Faithful adherence to the precepts articulated by Lord Scarman in *McLoughlin v O'Brian* [1983] 1 A.C. 410, 429–430 would have pointed towards adoption of this first solution.

The second solution has been adopted in six state courts in the US but did not commend itself to any member of the House in *McFarlane* and the objections to it are in my opinion insuperable. While it would be possible to assess with some show of plausibility the likely discounted cost of rearing a child until the age when the child might reasonably be expected to become self-supporting, any attempt to quantify in money terms the value of the joys and benefits which the parents might receive from the unintended child, or any economic benefit they might derive from it, would, made when the child is no more than an infant, be an exercise in pure speculation to which no court of law should lend itself. I need say no more of this possible solution.

The five members of the House who gave judgment in *McFarlane* adopted different approaches and gave different reasons for adopting the third solution listed in para.(3) above. But it seems to me clear that all of them were moved to adopt it for reasons of policy (legal, not public, policy). This is not a criticism.

The policy considerations underpinning the judgments of the House were, as I read them, an unwillingness to regard a child (even if unwanted) as a financial liability and nothing else, a recognition that the rewards which parenthood (even if involuntary) may or may not bring cannot be quantified and a sense that to award potentially very large sums of damages to the parents of a normal and healthy child against a National Health Service always in need of funds to meet pressing demands would rightly offend the community's sense of how public resources should be allocated. It is indeed hard to think that, if the House had adopted the first solution discussed above, its decision would have long survived the first award to well-to-do parents of the estimated cost of providing private education, presents, clothing and foreign holidays for an unwanted child (even if at no more expensive a level than the parents had provided for earlier, wanted, children) against a National Health Service found to be responsible, by its negligence, for the birth of the child.

In favouring the third solution, holding the damages claimed to be irrecoverable, the House allied itself with the great majority of state courts in the United States. Subject to one gloss, therefore, which I regard as important, I would affirm and adhere to the decision in *McFarlane*.

My concern is this. Even accepting that an unwanted child cannot be regarded as a financial liability and nothing else and that any attempt to weigh the costs of bringing up a child against the intangible rewards of parenthood is unacceptably speculative, the fact remains that the parent of a child born following a negligently performed vasectomy or sterilisation, or negligent advice on the effect of such a procedure, is the victim of a legal wrong. The members of the House who gave judgment in *McFarlane* recognised this by holding, in each case, that some award should be made to Mrs McFarlane. I can accept and support a rule of legal policy which precludes recovery of the full cost of bringing up a child in the situation postulated, but I question the fairness of a rule which denies the victim of a legal wrong any recompense at all beyond an award immediately related to the unwanted pregnancy and birth. The spectre of well-to-do parents plundering the National Health Service should not blind one to other realities: that of the single mother with young children, struggling to make ends meet and counting the days until her children are of an age to enable her to work more hours and so enable the family to live a less straitened existence; the mother whose burning ambition is to put domestic chores so far as possible behind her and embark on a new career or resume an old one. Examples can be multiplied. To speak of losing the freedom to limit the size of one's family is to mask the real loss suffered in a situation of this kind. This is that a parent, particularly (even today) the mother, has been denied, through the negligence of another, the opportunity to live her life in the way that she wished and planned. I do not think that an award immediately relating to the unwanted pregnancy and birth gives adequate recognition of or does justice to that loss. I would accordingly support the suggestion favoured by Lord Millett in *McFarlane* that in all cases such as these there be a conventional award to mark the injury and loss, although I would favour a greater figure than the £5,000 he suggested (I have in mind a conventional figure of £15,000) and I would add this to the award for the pregnancy and birth. This solution is in my opinion consistent with the ruling and rationale of *McFarlane*. The conventional award would not be, and would not be intended to be, compensatory. It would not be the product of calculation. But it would not be a nominal, let alone a derisory, award. It would afford some measure of recognition of the wrong done. And it would afford a more ample measure of justice than the pure *McFarlane* rule.

I would for my part apply this rule also, without differentiation, to cases in which either the child or the parent is (or claims to be) disabled: it is undesirable that parents, in order to recover compensation, should be encouraged to portray either their children or themselves as disabled.

I would accordingly allow the appeal.

Lord Nicholls of Birkenhead: In *McFarlane v Tayside Health Board* [2000] 2 A.C. 59, your Lordships' House held unanimously that a negligent doctor is not required to meet the cost of bringing up a healthy child born in these circumstances. The language, and to some extent the legal reasoning, employed by each of their Lordships differed. But, however expressed, the underlying perception of all their Lordships was that fairness and reasonableness do not require that the damages payable by a negligent doctor should extend so far. The approach usually adopted in measuring recoverable financial loss is not appropriate when the subject of the legal wrong is the birth of an unintended healthy child and the head of claim is the cost of the whole of the child's upbringing.

I have heard nothing in the submissions advanced on the present appeal to persuade me that this decision by the House was wrong and ought to be revisited. On the contrary, that the negligent doctor or, in most cases, the National Health Service should pay all the costs of bringing up the child seems to me a disproportionate response to the doctor's wrong. It would accord ill with the values society attaches to human life and to parenthood. The birth of a child should not be treated as comparable to a parent suffering a personal injury, with the cost of rearing the child being treated as special damages akin to the financially adverse consequences flowing from the onset of a chronic medical condition.

But this is not to say it is fair and reasonable there should be no award at all except in respect of stress and trauma and costs associated with the pregnancy and the birth itself. An award of some amount should be made to recognise that in respect of birth of the child the parent has suffered a legal wrong, a legal wrong having a far-reaching effect on the lives of the parent and any family she may already have. The amount of such an award will inevitably have an arbitrary character. I do not dissent from the sum of £15,000 suggested by my noble and learned friend Lord Bingham of Cornhill in this regard. To this limited extent I agree that your Lordships' House should add a gloss to the decision in *McFarlane*.

Once it is decided that damages do not include the cost of bringing up a healthy child, anomalies become inescapable if an exception is made when either the child or the mother is disabled. The personal circumstances where this problem arises will vary so widely that what is fair and reasonable in one set of family circumstances, including the financial means of the family, may not seem so in another. But awards of damages of this nature cannot sensibly be made by courts on a discretionary or means-tested basis. The preferable approach is an award of a lump sum of modest amount in all circumstances.

For these reasons, and also the reasons given by Lord Bingham of Cornhill, I would allow this appeal, and declare that the claimant is not entitled to recover any of the costs of bringing up the child Anthony, but she is entitled to payment of £15,000.

Lord Steyn: Lord Bingham has explained why he favours a conventional award of £15,000 in the present case. His opinion makes clear that to this extent he would depart from *McFarlane* in the case of a healthy and normal child. He has further observed that he would apply this rule, without differentiation, to cases in which either the child or the parent is (or claims to be) disabled. This involves overruling the majority of the Court of Appeal in the present case. It also involves overruling the Court of Appeal decision in *Parkinson* against which there was no appeal. The other opinions in the present case speak for themselves.

In the present case the idea of a conventional award was not raised at first instance or in the Court of Appeal. For my part it is a great disadvantage for the House to consider such a point without the benefit of the views of the Court of Appeal. And the disadvantage cannot be removed by calling the new rule a "gloss". It is a radical and most important development which should only be embarked on after rigorous examination of competing arguments.

No UK authority is cited for the proposition that judges have the power to create a remedy of awarding a conventional sum in cases such as the present. There is none. It is also noteworthy that in none of the decisions from many foreign jurisdictions, with varying results, is there any support for such a solution. This underlines the heterodox nature of the solution adopted.

Like Lord Hope I regard the idea of a conventional award in the present case as contrary to principle. It is a novel procedure for judges to create such a remedy. There are limits to permissible creativity for judges. In my view the majority have strayed into forbidden territory. It is also a backdoor evasion of the legal policy enunciated in *McFarlane*. If such a rule is to be created it must be done by Parliament. The fact is, however, that it would be a hugely controversial legislative measure. It may well be that the Law Commissions and Parliament ought in any event, to consider the impact of the creation of a power to make a conventional award in the cases under consideration for the coherence of the tort system.

I cannot support the proposal for creating such a new rule.

Lord Hope of Craighead: It has already been held in *Parkinson v St James and Seacroft University Hospital NHS Trust* [2002] Q.B. 266 that the case of a seriously disabled child can be distinguished and that, although the ordinary costs of rearing the child are not recoverable, the decision in *McFarlane* does not preclude recovery of the extra costs which are attributable to the child's disability. This point did not require to be examined in *McFarlane*. The Lord Ordinary, Lord Gill, emphasised at the outset of his opinion that the debate in that case was conducted on the basis that the child was a normal, healthy child: 1997 S.L.T. 211, 212F. The position was unchanged when the case reached your Lordships' House, as can be seen from all the speeches.

I agree with the Court of Appeal that the question whether the extra costs of raising a seriously disabled child are recoverable raises a separate issue. I consider that, as a matter of legal policy, the Court of Appeal were right to hold that in principle these extra costs are recoverable.

Lord Bingham asserts that the conventional award which he favours would not be, and would not be intended to be, compensatory. It would not be the product of calculation nor would it be nominal, but would afford some measure of recognition of the wrong done. This approach seems to me to depart from the principle which has always guided the common law in its approach to the assessment of damages. He does not suggest that the award is intended to be punitive. If it is not, and the case is not one for an award that is purely nominal, what basis can there be for it other than the compensatory principle? Both Lord Millett and Lord Scott use language which suggests that they are seeking to arrive at a figure which would compensate the parents for being deprived of the loss of opportunity or of the benefits which they were entitled to expect. Lord Nicholls does not use the same language, but his brief treatment of the issue leaves me in doubt as to the basis for it. The lack of any consistent or coherent ratio in support of the proposition in the speeches of the majority is disturbing. It underlines Lord Steyn's point that the examination of the issue at the oral hearing was cursory and unaccompanied by research. Like him, I cannot agree with the description of the new rule by Lord Bingham and Lord Nicholls as a "gloss" on the decision in *McFarlane*.

Lord Bingham has given, as one of his reasons for applying the new rule without differentiation to cases whether either the child or the parent is, or claims to be, disabled the acute difficulty of the task of quantifying the additional costs attributable to disability. I agree that care would be needed in sorting out what costs are and are not so attributable. But to describe the task as one of acute difficulty seems to me to be an overstatement.

Lord Hutton: In my opinion the decision of the Court of Appeal in *Parkinson* was right. In *McFarlane* the House confined its considerations to the case of the birth of a healthy child and expressed no opinion in relation to the birth of a child with disabilities. In that case the House considered that it was not fair, just or reasonable to award damages for the costs of bringing up a healthy child. But in my opinion it is fair, just and reasonable to award damages for the extra costs of bringing up a disabled child and I am in agreement with the observation of Robert Walker L.J. in relation to *Parkinson* in his judgment in the present case: "There is not the same intuitive feeling that it would be exorbitant compensation to award damages for financial burdens which are the direct consequence of the disability of a child who was born disabled after a failed sterilisation, and which would not be incurred in consequence of the birth of a normal, healthy child."

Lord Millett: A technical difference of approach is detectable in the speeches [in *McFarlane*]. Lord Clyde and I considered that the question was directed to the admission of a new head of loss. Others considered that the question was whether the loss claimed was within the scope of the duty of care. In my opinion this is merely a difference of exposition. In some cases it is more illuminating to approach the question from one end; in other cases from the other.

In a case of wrongful pregnancy there is no difficulty about causation, whether as a matter of fact or of legal responsibility. The pregnancy and birth of a child are the very things which the defendants are employed to prevent. It is impossible to say that consequential loss falls outside the scope of their duty of care. They are accordingly liable for the normal and foreseeable heads of loss, such as the mother's pain and suffering (and where appropriate loss of earnings) due to the confinement and delivery. The novelty of the claim in *McFarlane* lay in one particular head of damage—the cost of bringing up a healthy child. The House considered it to be morally repugnant to award damages for the birth of a healthy child. It makes for easier exposition to identify the issue by reference to the head of damage rather than the duty of care. It also has the added advantage that identifying the ratio of *McFarlane* in this way may make it simpler to find the answer to the question raised by the present case.

McFarlane decides that the costs of bringing up a normal, healthy child must be taken to be outweighed by the incalculable blessings which such a child brings to his or her parents and do not sound in damages. *Parkinson* decides that the additional costs of bringing up a disabled child are recoverable in damages. It may be that strict logic demands a different answer. A disabled child is not "worth" less than a healthy one. The blessings of his or her birth are no less incalculable. Society must equally "regard the balance as beneficial". But the law does not develop by strict logic; and most people would instinctively feel that there was a difference, even if they had difficulty in articulating it. Told that a friend has given birth to a normal, healthy baby, we would express relief as well as joy. Told that she had given birth to a seriously disabled child, most of us would feel (though not express) sympathy for the parents. Our joy at the birth would not be unalloyed; it would be tinged with sorrow for the child's disability. Speaking for myself, I would not find it morally offensive to reflect this difference in an award of compensation. But it is not necessary for the disposal of the present appeal to reach any conclusion whether *Parkinson* was rightly decided, and I would wish to keep the point open. It would in any case be necessary to limit the compensation to the additional costs attributable to the child's disability; and this may prove difficult to achieve without introducing nice distinctions and unacceptable refinements of a kind which tend to bring the law into disrepute. For the reasons I gave in my speech in *McFarlane* I would not for my part wish to distinguish between the various motives which the parties might have for desiring to avoid a pregnancy.

However that may be, the decision of the Court of Appeal in the present case is not a legitimate extension of *Parkinson*, but an illegitimate gloss on *McFarlane*.

The award of a modest sum would not, of course, go far towards the costs of bringing up a child. It would not reflect the financial consequences of the birth of a normal, healthy child; but it would not be meant to. They are not the proper subject of compensation for the reasons stated in *McFarlane*. A modest award would, however, adequately compensate for the very different injury to the parents' autonomy; moreover it would be available without proof of financial loss, and so would not attract the distaste or moral repugnance which was the decisive factor in *McFarlane*. In that case I suggested that the award should not exceed £5,000 in a straightforward case. On reflection, I am persuaded that the figure should be a purely conventional one which should not be susceptible of increase or decrease by reference to the circumstances of the particular case. I agree with the figure of £15,000 which Lord Bingham has suggested.

Lord Scott of Foscote: The question how the *McFarlane* principle should be applied to a case in which the mother is healthy but the child is born with a disability is not one which needs to be resolved on this appeal. In my opinion, however, a distinction may need to be drawn between a case where the avoidance of the birth of a child with a disability is the very reason why the parent or parents sought the medical treatment or services to avoid conception that, in the event, were negligently provided and a case where the medical treatment or services were sought simply to avoid conception. *Parkinson* was a case in the latter category. In such a case, where the parents have had no particular reason to fear that if a child is born to them it will suffer from a disability, I do not think there is any sufficient basis for treating the expenses occasioned by the disability as falling outside the principles underlying *McFarlane*. It might be otherwise in a case where the very purpose of the sterilisation operation had been to protect against that fear. But on the facts of *Parkinson* I do not think the Court of Appeal's conclusion was consistent with *McFarlane*.

I would allow this appeal. But, like my noble and learned friends Lord Bingham of Cornhill and Lord Millett, I am not sure that the recovery by the respondent of nothing for the frustration of her expectation that her sterilisation operation would safeguard her against conception satisfies justice. She was owed a duty of care in the carrying out of the operation. She was entitled to the benefit of the doctor's contractual obligation to his NHS employers to carry out the operation with due care. It is open to the court to put a monetary value on the expected benefit of which she was, by the doctor's negligence, deprived (compare *Farley v Skinner* [2002] 2 A.C. 732). I would respectfully agree with Lord Bingham's suggestion that she be awarded £15,000. So I, too, while allowing the appeal, would substitute an award of £15,000 as a conventional sum to compensate the respondent for being deprived of the benefit that she was entitled to expect.

Notes:

1. Certain matters are clear:

(i) The healthy parents of a healthy child cannot claim for the cost of bringing it up, but the mother can claim for the pain and suffering of the involuntary pregnancy and parturition plus associated costs (actually this is not so clear, but the layette is not likely to be litigated); the virtually unanimous decision in *McFarlane* to this effect was quite unanimously upheld (7–0) in *Rees*. It is to be hoped that this rule is irrefragably established and beyond cavil.

(ii) The disabled mother of a healthy child cannot claim the extra cost of upbringing due to her disability; this was the 4–3 decision of the House of Lords in *Rees*.

(iii) £15,000 is payable to the disabled mother of a healthy child (that was the actual decision in *Rees*), clearly also to the healthy mother (parents?) of a healthy child, and this is in addition to the pain and suffering mentioned in (1) above.

Other matters are less clear:

(iv) May the healthy mother of a disabled child claim the extra costs of upbringing due to the disability as held by the Court of Appeal in *Parkinson*? Three of the seven Lords of Appeal in *Rees* approved of the decision, three disapproved, and the position of one is ambiguous. The wise money would be on *Parkinson* being followed, and that the holding would not be raised on appeal. Is it relevant why the contraception/termination was sought? Lord Millett and Lord Scott, the only judges who spoke to the issue, differed.

(v) If the mother of a disabled child can claim the extra expense, is this in addition to the £15,000?

2. The excitement about the "conventional" sum is odd. It is simply not true that there was no judicial precedent. In *Benham v Gambling* [1941] A.C. 157 the House of Lords did exactly the same thing, after the damages awarded (by the jury) for "loss of expectation of life" (possible only since the 1934 Act allowed dead people to sue for what they had lost) had got entirely out of hand. Since it had been held that life was good and that therefore it must be damage to be deprived of it, the House of Lords was faced with the unenviable task of deciding just how good life was. Their Lordships hit upon the figure of £200, nothing if not conventional. The decision was prefaced by an absurd discussion of setting off the good things and the bad things of life (premium bond cheque/tax demand?), which at least their successors have been wise enough to avoid in the case of unwanted children. Nor is this fact of purely historical interest: it is unquestionably the predecessor and generator of the statutory award for "bereavement", now £10,000, but starting off at £3,500, which was merely the £200 of 1941 updated for inflation. It is perfectly idle for the Law Commission to insist that the award of "bereavement damages" is compensation for grief: it is nothing of the sort—it is the monetary value put on the life of the departed one. That is why the sum is fixed—all people are equally valuable—and not variable, as grief is.

3. There is more than one way to have too many children. In *Thompson v Sheffield Fertility Clinic* (Hooper J., *The Times*, February 24, 2001) the claimant paid the defendant £1,650 for IVF treatment and got healthy triplets as a result. She sued on the ground that the contract was for two only: she wanted twins. Later she conceived naturally and bore a daughter. After the judge had decided that the defendant was liable, it settled with the claimant for £20,000. In *Rees* Lord Scott said that there was no difference between claims in contract and tort in this matter. Would the Sheffield Fertility Clinic have been held liable had there been no payment?

Chapter 2

BREACH

Preliminary Note:
Judicial decisions involve the application of rules to facts. The distinction between rules and facts is very clear in countries with a code: what is in the code is a rule, and you just have to apply it. Likewise with statutes in our country. Every word that the legislator has chosen to include in the enactment, wisely or not, is law. But at common law the matter is not so easy, for it is what the judges do which is authoritative, not what they say (or even what they say they are doing). In a curious way, therefore, the rules of common law arise out of the facts: the application is not distinct from the rule created.

It has been said often enough that the question whether the defendant and others similarly situated owed a duty of care to the claimant and others similarly situated is a question of law, whereas the question whether the defendant's conduct constituted a breach of that duty is a question of fact. But we have seen that increasingly the courts are saying "we cannot tell whether there was or was not a duty until we have heard all the facts." In some situations, of course, the matter is very clear: it is a rule that the motorised user of the highway owes a duty of care to other users of the highway, that an employer owes a duty of care for not only the safety but also the wellbeing of his personnel, that the bailee must look after the goods and prove, if he cannot return them, that he did so. The occupier's duty will be considered in detail below.

Now the trouble is that students look for rules to learn (though characteristically British students hate statutes and love cases), and consequently tend to think that rules are to be found in cases which are merely illustrations of the application of rules. In this they are abetted by examiners. The reason is that questions in examinations must be short (or candidates will spend their time reading the question when they should be writing an answer to it), whereas the evidence needed for a decision on breach tends to be very copious indeed. Accordingly it is very difficult to set an examination question on breach, so the matter gets left out of lectures. In the contract course a similar situation presents itself: we concentrate on the "rules" as to formation and the consequences of breach, but say very little on the interpretation or construction of contracts, which occupies almost all the time of the courts, and this is true even though the rules in contract law are more important than they are in tort, in that businessmen *use* the contract rules in a way that tortfeasors do not use the rules of negligence.

In the courts the matter is very different: the vast bulk of cases in the court have nothing to do with arguments about whether the defendant was under a duty or not, but turn exclusively on the question of whether his conduct squared with the duty whose existence is not in doubt. To counteract this and to bring study and practice closer together, perhaps a casebook should contain only illustrations of the application of rules stated in propositional form, but considerations of space make this impossible: one needs to know all the circumstances in which the defendant acted before one can determine whether his conduct falls short of what the reasonable person would think right in all those circumstances, and to rehearse all the circumstances would require a novel, not a note.

Section 1.—Specific or General?

QUALCAST (WOLVERHAMPTON) LTD v HAYNES

House of Lords [1959] A.C. 743; [1959] 2 W.L.R. 510; 103 S.J. 310; [1959] 2 All E.R. 38
(noted (1959) 22 M.L.R. 428)

Action by employee against employer in respect of personal injury

The plaintiff was an experienced metal moulder, employed by the defendants; he burnt his left foot when the ladle of molten metal he was holding slipped from his grasp. He was wearing ordinary leather boots at the time. His employers had a stock of protective spats for the asking and of reinforced boots at a price, but they had never urged the plaintiff to wear them. The county court judge felt bound by authority to hold that the employers were under a duty to urge the plaintiff to wear protective clothing, and gave judgment for the plaintiff, subject to 75 per cent contributory negligence. He also said: "I think he knew of all the risks involved and quite voluntarily decided to wear the boots which he was wearing, and I believe that since the accident and since his return to work as a moulder he has not worn any protective clothing."

The Court of Appeal affirmed the judgment for the plaintiff [1958] 1 W.L.R. 225. The defendants appealed to the House of Lords, and their appeal was allowed.

Lord Somervell of Harrow: My Lords, I also would allow the appeal. In the present case the county court judge, after having found the facts, had to decide whether there was, in relation to this plaintiff, a failure by the defendants to take reasonable care for his safety. It is, I think, clear that he would have found for the defendants but for some principle laid down, as he thought, by the authorities, to which he referred.

I hope it may be worth while to make one or two general observations on the effect on the precedent system of the virtual abolition of juries in negligence actions. Whether a duty of reasonable care is owed by A to B is a question of law. In a special relationship such as that of employer to employee the law may go further and define the heads and scope of the duty. There are cases in your Lordships' House which have covered this ground, I would have thought by now, exhaustively (*Wilson's and Clyde Coal Co Ltd v English* ([1938] A.C. 57); *Latimer v AEC Ltd* ([1953] A.C. 643); *General Cleaning Contractors Ltd v Christmas*; and there are, of course, others). There would seem to be little, if anything, that can be added to the law. Its application in borderline cases may, of course, still come before appellate tribunals. When negligence cases were tried with juries the judge would direct them as to the law as above. The question whether on the facts in that particular case there was or was not a failure to take reasonable care was a question for the jury. There was not, and could not be, complete uniformity of standard. One jury would attribute to the reasonable man a greater degree of prescience than would another. The jury's decision did not become part of our law citable as a precedent. In those days it would only be in very exceptional circumstances that a judge's direction would be reported or be citable. So far as the law is concerned they would all be the same. Now that negligence cases are mostly tried without juries, the distinction between the functions of judge and jury is blurred. A judge naturally gives reasons for the conclusion formerly arrived at by a jury without reasons. It may sometimes be difficult to draw the line, but if the reasons given by a judge for arriving at the conclusion previously reached by a jury are to be treated as "law" and citable, the precedent system will die from a surfeit of authorities. In *Woods v Durable Suites Ltd* ([1953] 1 W.L.R. 857) counsel for the plaintiff was seeking to rely on a previous decision in a negligence action. Singleton L.J. said this: "That was a case of the same nature as that which is now under appeal. It is of the greatest importance that it should be borne in mind that though the nature of the illness and the nature of the work are the same, the facts were quite different. Mr Doughty claims that the decision of this court in *Clifford v Charles H Challen & Son Ltd* ([1951] 1 K.B. 495) lays down a standard to be adopted in a case of this nature. In other words, he seeks to treat that decision as deciding a question of law rather than as being a decision on the facts of that particular case."

In the present case, and I am not criticising him, the learned county court judge felt himself bound by certain observations in different cases which were not, I think, probably intended by the learned judges to enunciate any new principles or gloss on the familiar standard of reasonable care. It must be a question on the evidence in each case whether, assuming a duty to provide some safety equipment, there is a duty to advise everyone, whether experienced or inexperienced, as to its use. . . .

I have come to the conclusion that the learned judge's first impulse was the right conclusion on the facts as he found them, and for the reasons which he gives. I will not elaborate these reasons or someone might cite my observations as part of the law of negligence.

Lord Denning: My Lords, in 1944 du Parcq L.J. gave a warning which is worth repeating today: "There is danger, particularly in these days when few cases are tried with juries, of exalting to the status of propositions of law what really are particular applications to special facts of propositions of ordinary good sense"; see *Easson v London & North Eastern Railway Co.* ([1944] K.B. 421 at 426).

In the present case the only proposition of law that was relevant was the well-known proposition—with its threefold sub-division—that it is the duty of a master to take reasonable care for the safety of his workmen. No question arose on that proposition. The question that did arise was this: What did reasonable care demand of the employers in this particular case? That is not a question of law at all but a question of fact. To solve it the tribunal of fact—be it judge or jury—can take into account any proposition of good sense that is relevant in the circumstances, but it must beware not to treat it as a proposition of law. I may perhaps draw an analogy from the Highway Code. It contains many propositions of good sense which may be taken into account in considering whether reasonable care has been taken, but it would be a mistake to elevate them into propositions of law.

Applying this to the present case: You start with the fact that, when a moulder in an iron foundry carries a ladle full of hot molten metal and pours it into the moulding box, there is a danger that the hot metal may splash over onto his feet. In order to safeguard him from injury, the employers ought, I should have thought, to provide protective footwear for him. But in saying so, I speak as a juryman, for it is not a proposition of law at all, but only a proposition of good sense. If the employers fail to provide protective footwear, the tribunal of fact can take it into account in deciding whether the employers took reasonable care for the safety of their men.

But the question here is not whether the employers ought to provide protective footwear for the men—for they clearly did so. The question is whether, having provided spats and boots, they ought to go further and *urge* the men to wear them. Here too I should have thought that the employers ought to advise and encourage the men to wear protective footwear. But again I speak as a juryman and not as a judge: because it is not a proposition of law at all, but a proposition of good sense. And that is the very point where the county court judge fell into error. He treated it as matter of strict law. He thought that, as this man "was never told that they must be worn," he was *bound by authority* to find that the employers were negligent. He treated it almost as on a par with a statutory regulation: whereas it was nothing of the kind. The distinction was taken by Lord Wright 25 years ago: "Whereas at the ordinary law the standard of duty must be fixed by the verdict of a jury, the statutory duty is conclusively fixed by the statute"; see *Lochgelly Iron & Coal Co Ltd v M'Mullan* ([1934] A.C. 1). So here, this being a case governed by the common law and not by any statute or regulation, the standard of care must be fixed by the judge as if he were a jury, without being rigidly bound by authorities. What is "a proper system of work" is a matter for evidence, not for law books. It changes as the conditions of work change. The standard goes up as men become wiser. It does not stand still as the law sometimes does.

I can well see how it came about that the county court judge made this mistake. He was presented with a number of cases in which judges of the High Court had given reasons for coming to their conclusions of fact. And those reasons seemed to him to be so expressed as to be rulings in point of law: whereas they were in truth nothing more than propositions of good sense. This is not the first time this sort of thing has happened. Take accidents on the road. I remember well that in several cases Scrutton L.J. said that "if a person rides in the dark he must ride at such a pace that he can pull up within the limits of his vision". That was treated as a proposition of law until the Court of Appeal firmly ruled that it was not. So also with accidents in factories. I myself once said that an employer must, by his foreman, "do his best to keep [the men] up to the mark". Someone shortly afterwards sought to treat me as having laid down a new proposition of law, but the Court of Appeal, I am glad to say, corrected the error (*Woods v Durable Suites Ltd* ([1953] 1 W.L.R. 857)). Such cases all serve to bear out the warning which has been given in this House before. " . . . we ought to beware of allowing tests or guides which have been suggested by the court in one set of circumstances, or in one class of cases, to be applied to other surroundings," and thus by degrees to turn that which is at bottom a question of fact into a proposition of law. That is what happened in the cases under the Workmen's Compensation Act and it led to a "wagon-load of cases". Let not the same thing happen to the common law, lest we be crushed under the weight of our own reports.

Seeing, then, that the county court judge fell into error, what should the Court of Appeal have done? The answer seems to me this; the Court of Appeal should have done as the judge would have done if he had not felt bound by authority. He would have found that the employers had not been guilty of negligence. . . .   In this case I would not myself be prepared to differ from the judge's view that there was no negligence on the part of the employers in regard to this particular workman. He knew all there was to know, without being told; and he voluntarily decided to wear his own boots, which he had bought for the purpose.

Only one word more. It is on causation. Even if it had been the duty of the employers to urge this workman to wear spats, I do not think their omission should be taken to be one of the causes of the accident. It is often said that a person who omits to do his duty "cannot be heard to say" that it would have made no difference even if he had done it: see *Roberts v Dorman Long & Co Ltd* ([1953] 1 W.L.R. 942 at 946). But this is an overstatement. The judge *may* infer the omission to be a cause, but he is not bound to do so. If, at the end of the day, he thinks that, whether the duty was omitted or fulfilled, the result would have been the same, he is at liberty to say so. So here, this workman, after he recovered from the injury, went back to work and did the same as before. He never wore spats. If the warning given by the accident made no difference, we may safely infer that no advice beforehand would have had any effect.

I would allow the appeal.

Question:

If this case says, as it seems to, that all fact situations are as a matter of law distinguishable, what becomes of the principle of *stare decisis*, if that principle is based on the view that like cases should be treated alike?

Note:

This decision should deter counsel from citing decisions on breach as authority for the case in hand, and dissuade the student faced with a problem from hunting down cases "on all fours," like a housewife seeking a matching thread in a haberdashery. But the student may have to read a good many cases in order to gain vicariously the experience which lies at the root of sound judgment. Despite the best efforts of the higher courts, however, counsel (who are paid by the day) continued to cite enormous numbers of cases (see *Lambert v Lewis* [1982] A.C. 225) and county court judges (who are paid to use their judgment) continue to apply decisions on breach as if they laid down fixed rules ("inching forward into traffic isn't negligence," *Worsfold v Howe* [1980] 1 All ER 1028).

The courts have recently been more assertive. "With a view of limiting the citation of previous authority to cases that are relevant and useful to the court" the Practice Statement of April 9, 2001 ([2001] 1 W.L.R. 1001) lays down a number of rules as to what may be cited. In certain categories "A judgment . . . may not in future be cited before any court unless it clearly indicates that it purports to establish a new principle or to extend the present law" and more generally "Courts will in future pay particular attention . . . to any indication given by the court delivering the judgment that it was seen by that court as only applying decided law to the facts of the particular case; or otherwise as not extending or adding to the existing law."

Many of the cases contained in this book, including almost all the cases in this chapter, will therefore not be citable. In *Jolley v Sutton LBC* [2000] 3 All E.R. 409 Lord Steyn said: " . . . counsel invited your Lordships to compare the facts of the present case with the facts of other decided cases. That is a sterile exercise. Precedent is a valuable stabilising influence in our legal system. But comparing the facts of and outcomes of cases in this branch of the law is a misuse of the only proper use of precedent, namely to identify the relevant rule to apply to the facts of the case." The branch of the law involved was remoteness of damage: was a local authority which had failed to remove an abandoned boat from ground near a housing estate liable to an adolescent who was injured when, in trying with a friend to rehabilitate the boat with a view to using it for piracy, they propped it up and it collapsed on him? Answer: contrary to the holding of the Court of Appeal—Yes.

Qualcast, the principal case, is also useful in emphasising that the proper form of question, when one is dealing with breach of duty, is "Did the defendant take reasonable care?" One must not pick on some feature of the defendant's acts and say: "Was he under a duty not to do that?" (see also *AC Billings & Sons v Riden* [1958] A.C. 240 at 264, *per* Lord Somervell of Harrow). Of course, the plaintiff must normally identify what it was in the defendant's behaviour that he finds objectionable—*e.g.* that he omitted to give a signal before turning right on the highway. But the question remains "Did the defendant drive with reasonable care, considering that he gave no signal?" and does not become "Was the defendant under a duty to give a signal?" Matters of detail are best treated as part of the question of breach, not as raising sub-duties with a specific content.

A different approach is, however, to be found in *Smith v Littlewoods Organisation* [1987] 1 All E.R. 710, HL. In that case some youths entered the defendant's unoccupied and unguarded cinema and started a fire which spread to, and burnt, the plaintiffs' buildings next door. It was agreed, Lord Goff dissenting, that the defendant owed his neighbours a "general duty" to exercise reasonable care to prevent his building becoming a source of danger to theirs. So far, so good. But then, as Lord Brandon put it, "The second question is whether that general duty encompassed a specific duty to exercise reasonable care to prevent young persons obtaining unlawful access to the cinema and, having done so, unlawfully setting it on fire," and Lord Mackay speaks of "the duty to take a particular precaution."

This approach is unsatisfactory for practical as well as aesthetic reasons. For even if it is now accepted that the *foreseeability* of resultant harm is not of itself a sufficient reason for imposing a duty to take care to avoid it, but that in all the circumstances it must be *reasonable* to impose such a duty, nevertheless it is more clearly established that the test of *breach of duty* is not whether the harm was foreseeable or not but whether the defendant's behaviour was reasonable or not (in the light of what might have been foreseen, and how likely it was and how harmful it was likely to be and how much it would have cost to avoid it, etc., etc.).

Lord Goff very appropriately observes that "it would be quite wrong if householders were to be held liable in negligence for acting in a socially acceptable manner," but the reason they are not to be held liable is not that they owe their neighbours no duty to behave in a normally prudent householderly manner but that they have, in fact, so behaved and have not breached the duty incumbent upon them.

In *Smith v Littlewoods Organisation* the real question was whether the defendant should be blamed for not having mounted a 24-hour guard on their premises, which were not especially attractive or inflammable or situated in an area rife with vandalism, seeing that they did not know, and were not at fault in not knowing, that vandals had already tried their hand at arson there. It is the same question as the question in *Bolton v Stone* (below, p.141), namely whether the cricket club, who clearly owed a duty to passersby outside, were to be blamed for continuing to play cricket; or in *Glasgow Corp. v Muir* (below, p.155) whether the manageress of the tea-room was to be blamed for not clearing the premises when a tea-urn was being carried through.

The approach of Lord Griffiths in *Smith* is to be preferred: "I agree that mere foreseeability of damage is certainly not a sufficient basis to found liability. But with this warning I doubt that more can be done than to leave it to the good sense of the judges to apply realistic standards in conformity with generally accepted patterns of behaviour to determine whether in the particular circumstances of a given case there has been a breach of duty sounding in negligence."

So, too, with regard to doctors. The general duty of the doctors treating the plaintiff is, in the words of Lord Diplock, "not subject to dissection into a number of component parts to which different criteria of what satisfy the duty of care apply" (see [1985] A.C. 871 at 893).

NETTLESHIP v WESTON

Court of Appeal [1971] 2 Q.B. 691; [1971] 3 W.L.R. 370; 115 S.J. 624; [1971]
3 All E.R. 581 (noted (1971) 87 L.Q.R. 444)

Action in respect of personal injuries by driving instructor against learner driver

The defendant asked the plaintiff, who was a friend and not a professional driving instructor, to teach her to drive her husband's car. On being assured that there was fully comprehensive insurance cover, he agreed to do so. During the third lesson the defendant stopped at a junction prior to turning left. The plaintiff engaged first gear for her, and she started to turn slowly to the left. Her grip on the steering wheel tightened implacably, and despite the plaintiff's advice and efforts, the car followed a perfect curve, mounted the nearside pavement and struck a lamp post with sufficient impact to fracture the plaintiff's knee.

The trial judge dismissed the plaintiff's claim on the ground that the defendant's only duty to him was to do her best, and this she had done, poor though it was. The Court of Appeal allowed the plaintiff's appeal, subject (Megaw L.J. dissenting) to a reduction of the damages by 50 per cent in respect of his contributory negligence.

Megaw L.J.: ... The important question of principle which arises is whether, because of Mr Nettleship's knowledge that Mrs Weston was not an experienced driver, the standard of care which was owed to him by her was lower than would otherwise have been the case.

In *The Insurance Commissioner v Joyce* ((1948) 77 C.L.R. 39 at 56–60), Dixon J. stated persuasively the view that there is, or may be, a "particular relation" between the driver of a vehicle and his passenger resulting in a variation of the standard of duty owed by the driver. He said (at p.56): "The case of a passenger in a car differs from that of a pedestrian not in the kind or degree of danger which may come from any want of care or skill in driving but in the fact that the former has come into a more particular relation with the driver of the car. It is because that relation may vary that the standard of duty or of care is not necessarily the same in every case ... the gratuitous passenger may expect prima facie the same care and skill on the part of the driver as is ordinarily demanded in the management of a car. Unusual conditions may exist which are apparent to him or of which he may be informed and they may affect the application of the standard of care that is due. If a man accepts a lift from a car driver whom he knows to have lost a limb or an eye or to be deaf, he cannot complain if he does not exhibit the skill and competence of a driver who suffers from no defect." He summarised the same principle in these words (at p.59): "It appears to me that the circumstances in which the defendant accepts the plaintiff as a passenger and in which the plaintiff accepts the accommodation in the conveyance should determine the measure of duty ... " Theoretically, the principle as thus expounded is attractive. But, with very great respect, I venture to think that the theoretical attraction should yield to practical considerations.

As I see it, if this doctrine of varying standards were to be accepted as part of the law on these facts, it could not logically be confined to the duty of care owed by learner drivers. There is no reason in logic why it should not operate in a much wider sphere. The disadvantages of the resulting unpredictability, uncertainty and, indeed, impossibility of arriving at fair and consistent decisions outweigh the advantages. The certainty of a general standard is preferable to the vagaries of a fluctuating standard. ...

I, for my part, with all respect, do not think that our legal process could successfully or satisfactorily cope with the task of fairly assessing or applying to the facts of a particular case such varying standards, depending on such complex and elusive factors, including the assessment by the court, not merely of a particular person's actual skill or experience, but also of another person's knowledge or assessment of that skill or experience at a particular moment of time. ...

In my judgment, in cases such as the present it is preferable that there should be a reasonably certain and reasonably ascertainable standard of care, even if on occasion that may appear to work hardly against an inexperienced driver or his insurers. The standard of care required by the law is the standard of the competent and experienced driver: and this is so, as defining the driver's duty towards a passenger who knows of his inexperience, as much as towards a member of the public outside the car; and as much in civil as in criminal proceedings.

It is not a valid argument against such a principle that it attributes tortious liability to one who may not be morally blameworthy. For tortious liability has in many cases ceased to be based on moral blameworthiness. For example, there is no doubt whatever that if Mrs Weston had knocked down a pedestrian on the pavement when the accident occurred, she would have been liable to the pedestrian. Yet so far as any moral blame is concerned, no different considerations would apply in respect of the pedestrian from those which apply in respect of Mr Nettleship.

In criminal law also, the inexperience of the driver is wholly irrelevant. In the phrase commonly used in directions to juries in charges of causing death by dangerous driving, the driver may be guilty even though the jury think that he was "doing his incompetent best": see *R. v Scammell* ((1967) 51 Cr.App.R. 398). There can be no doubt that in criminal law, further, it is no answer to a charge of driving without due care and attention that the driver was inexperienced or lacking in skill: see *McCrone v Riding* ([1938] 1 All E.R. 157). In the present case, indeed, there was a conviction for that offence.

If the criminal law demands of an inexperienced driver the standard of care and competence of an experienced driver, why should it be wrong or unjust or impolitic for the civil law to require that standard, even *vis-à-vis* an injured passenger who knew of the driver's inexperience?

Lord Denning M.R.: ... The driver owes a duty of care to every passenger in the car, just as he does to every pedestrian on the road; and he must attain the same standard of care in respect of each ...

... Seeing that the law lays down, for all drivers of motor-cars, a standard of care to which all must conform, I think that even a learner-driver, so long as he is the sole driver, must attain the same standard towards all passengers in the car, including an instructor. But the instructor may be debarred ... because he has voluntarily agreed to waive any claim for any injury that may befall him. Otherwise he is not debarred. He may, of course, be guilty of contributory negligence and have his damages reduced on that account ... But apart from contributory negligence, he is not excluded unless it be that he had voluntarily agreed to incur the risk. ...

Salmon L.J.: I agree that a learner driver is responsible and owes a duty in civil law towards persons on or near the highway to drive with the same degree of skill and care as that of the reasonably competent and experienced driver. The duty in civil law springs from the relationship which the driver, by driving on the highway, has created between himself and persons likely to suffer damage by his bad driving. This is not a special relationship. Nor, in my respectful view, is it affected by whether or not the driver is insured. On grounds of public policy, neither this criminal nor civil responsibility is affected by the fact that the driver in question may be a learner, infirm or drunk. The onus, of course, lies on anyone claiming damages to establish a breach of duty and that it has caused the damages which he claims.

Any driver normally owes exactly the same duty to a passenger in his car as he does to the general public, namely, to drive with reasonable care and skill in all the relevant circumstances. As a rule, the driver's personal idiosyncrasy is not a relevant circumstance. In the absence of a special relationship what is reasonable care and skill is measured by the standard of competence usually achieved by the ordinary driver. In my judgment, however, there may be special facts creating a special relationship which displaces this standard or even negatives any duty, although the onus would certainly be upon the driver to establish such facts. With minor reservations I respectfully agree with and adopt the reasoning and conclusions of Sir Owen Dixon in his judgment in *The Insurance Commissioner v Joyce* ((1948) 77 C.L.R. 39). I do not agree that the mere fact that the driver has, to the knowledge of his passenger, lost a limb or an eye or is deaf can affect the duty which he owes the passenger to drive safely. It is well known that many drivers suffering from such disabilities drive with no less skill and competence than the ordinary man. The position, however, is totally different when, to the knowledge of the passenger, the driver is so drunk as to be incapable of driving safely. Quite apart from being negligent, a passenger who accepts a lift in such circumstances clearly cannot expect the driver to drive other than dangerously.

The duty of care springs from relationship. The special relationship which the passenger has created by accepting a lift in the circumstances postulated surely cannot entitle him to expect the driver to discharge a duty of care or skill which *ex hypothesi* the passenger knows the driver is incapable of discharging. Accordingly, in such circumstances, no duty is owed by the driver to the passenger to drive safely, and therefore no question of *volenti non fit injuria* can arise. . . .

There are no authorities which bear directly on the duty owed by a learner driver to his instructor. The instructor is entitled to expect the learner to pay attention to what he is told, perhaps to take exceptional care, and certainly to do his best. The instructor, in most cases such as the present, knows, however, that the learner has practically no driving experience or skill and that, for the lack of this experience and skill the learner will almost certainly make mistakes which may well injure the instructor unless he takes adequate steps to correct them. To my mind, therefore, the relationship is usually such that the beginner does not owe the instructor a duty to drive with the skill and competence to be expected of an experienced driver. The instructor knows that the learner does not possess such skill and competence. The alternative way of putting the case is that the instructor voluntarily agrees to run the risk of injury resulting from the learner's lack of skill and experience. . . .

If, however, the learner, for example, refuses to obey instructions or suddenly accelerates to a high speed or pays no attention to what he is doing and as a result the instructor is injured, then, in my view, the learner is in breach of duty and liable to the instructor in damages. The duty is still the duty to use reasonable care and skill in all the relevant circumstances. What is reasonable depends, however, on the special relationship existing between the learner and his instructor. This relationship, in my view, makes the learner's known lack of skill and experience a highly relevant circumstance.

I do not think that the learner is usually liable to his instructor if an accident occurs as a result of some mistake which any prudent beginner doing his best can be expected to make. I recognise that on this view cases in which a driving instructor is injured while his pupil is driving may raise difficult questions of fact and degree. Equally difficult questions of fact and degree are, however, being assessed and decided in our courts every day. The law lays down principles but not a rule of thumb for deciding issues arising out of any special relationship between the parties. A rule of thumb, if it existed, might no doubt remove difficulties, but could hardly produce justice either in practice or in theory.

It does not appear to me to be incongruous that a learner is responsible for acts or omissions in criminal law and indeed to the public at large in civil law and yet not necessarily responsible for such acts or omissions to his instructor. The learner has no special relationship with the public. The learner is certainly not liable to his instructor if his responsibility is excluded by contract. I can see no reason why, in the absence of contract, the same result should not follow from the special relationship between the parties.

Questions

1. Suppose that the lessons had been given in the plaintiff's car and he sued in respect of damage suffered by it. Same result?

2. Would the result have been the same if the means of harm had been a motorised lawn-mower in the use of which the plaintiff was giving the defendant instruction on the defendant's premises? Suppose Albert was teaching Bella how to play Frisbee in a public park and, owing to her lack of deftness, he is struck in the eye by it.

3. Why must learner drivers carry visible "L" plates on the car?

4. Personal factors, irrelevant to criminal guilt, may be taken into account in sentencing. If personal factors are made irrelevant to liability in private lawsuits, can or should they be taken into account in assessing damages? Consider *Holbeck Hall*, below p.440.

5. What is the duty of a driving *examiner*? And what is the duty of the candidate towards him? The answers are in a case involving a collision between two candidates: *British School of Motoring v Simms* [1971] 1 All E.R. 317.

6. Are you surprised to learn that a teacher may sue his pupil for being inept? Note that symmetry is observed now that the pupil may likewise sue the teacher—see *Phelps*, below p.000. As Shakespeare put it (in the mouth of a villain): "The baby beats the nurse and quite athwart Goes all decorum". (*Measure for Measure* I.iii)

Notes:

1. Lord Denning said that the professional—as opposed to the amateur—instructor might be unable to sue by reason of an implied term to that effect in the contract. Such a term, even if express, would be void by section 149 of the Road Traffic Act 1988 (if the accident took place on the highway). Thus the only way to prevent recovery by the professional instructor is to hold that the pupil is not guilty of negligence at all, simply by reason of his lack of *savoir faire*. The High Court of Australia so held in *Cook v Cook* (1986) 68 A.L.R. 353 and expressly disapproved of the reasoning of Lord Denning and of Megaw L.J. The splendid judgment of Mason, Wilson, Deane & Dawson JJ. contains the following passage: "In relation to other users of the highway, the duty of care of both instructor and pupil will ordinarily fall to be measured by the same objective standard since the relevant relationship will be the ordinary one between a driver and another user of the highway. As between themselves, however, it would be to state a half-truth to say that the relationship was, if the pupil was driving, that of driver and passenger. The special circumstances of such a case remove the relationship into a distinct category or class which, while possessing the requisite degree of proximity, could not rationally be seen as giving rise to a duty to drive with the skill reasonably to be expected of a competent and experienced driver. Indeed, it is the very absence of that skill which lies at the heart of the special relationship between the driving instructor and his pupil. In such a case, the standard of care which arises from the relationship of pupil and instructor is that which is reasonably to be expected of an unqualified and inexperienced driver in the circumstances in which the pupil is placed. The standard of care remains an objective one. It is, however, adjusted to fit the special relationship under which it arises."

2. But driving is not the only activity which can only be learnt by doing it: doctoring is another. The difference is that while no social obloquy attaches to the incompetent driver, a doctor who is held negligent suffers a very serious professional set-back. Thus in *Wilsher v Essex A.H.A.* [1986] 3 All E.R. 810 at 833, the Vice-Chancellor said: "The houseman had to take up his post in order to gain full professional qualification; anyone who . . . wishes to obtain specialist skills has to learn those skills by taking a post in a specialist unit. In my judgment, such doctors cannot in fairness be said to be at fault if, at the start of their time, they lack the skills which they are seeking to acquire." This was countered by Glidewell L.J. at 831: "In my view, the law requires the trainee or learner to be judged by the same standard as his more experienced colleagues. If it did not, inexperience would frequently be urged as a defence to an action for professional negligence." Mustill L.J. took an intermediate line: "In a case such as the present, the standard is not just that of the average competent and well-informed junior houseman (or whatever the position of the doctor) but of such a person who fills a post in a unit offering a highly specialised service. But, even so, it must be recognised that different posts make different demands. If it is borne in mind that the lower rank will be occupied by those of whom it would be wrong to expect too much, the risk of abuse by litigious patients can be mitigated . . . " (*id.* at 813).

3. One's only purpose in asking whether a duty is to do one's best or to do as well as others do (subjective/objective?) is to find out whether what the defendant actually did constituted a breach of his duty, whichever it was.

Take *Roberts v Ramsbottom*, for example ([1980] 1 All E.R. 7. One morning a 73-year-old accountant was about to drive his wife to the office some $2\frac{1}{2}$ miles away when he suffered a quite unheralded stroke which impaired his consciousness considerably. He forgot all about his wife and drove off. He managed to negotiate a few corners but then struck a parked van. He told the van-driver he felt all right and continued his progress. Next he knocked a boy off his bike and finally rammed the plaintiff's stationary car and injured the family by it. He was held liable despite his curious condition because it fell short of automatism and complete loss of consciousness, and because after striking the van he should have realised that he was unfit to continue driving. "An impairment of judgment does not provide a defence."

The first of the reasons in *Roberts* was disapproved by the Court of Appeal in *Mansfield v Weetabix* [1998] 1 W.L.R. 1263 where a 38–ton lorry ploughed into the claimant's shop because the driver, already involved in several incidents earlier in the day, "had an impaired degree of consciousness because of the malfunction in his brain caused by the deficiency in glucose". The trial judge gave judgment for the claimant, relying in part on *Nettleship*, but the Court of Appeal reversed, saying that "There is no reason in principle why a driver should not escape liability where the disabling event is not sudden, but gradual, provided that the driver is unaware of it." See also *Waugh v James K. Allen* (1964) S.L.T. 269 (HL), where the man at the wheel could not be said to be driving at all, as he had suffered a total black-out, and he was not liable for remaining at the wheel since there was no premonition of the heart attack.

Many people believe that one should get damages if one is run into by a driver who has had a heart attack, but is this very different from having a heart attack oneself when at the wheel?

SMOLDON v WHITWORTH

Court of Appeal [1996] Times L.R. 731; [1997] P.I.Q.R. 133

Claim by injured rugby player against referee

Scrums in an under-19 colts rugby match kept collapsing without intervention by the defendant referee. In one such collapse the plaintiff suffered severe spinal injury. His suit against a fellow-player was dismissed but his claim against the referee was upheld by the trial judge and the Court of Appeal.

Lord Bingham C.J. said that although earlier cases had explored the duty owed by one sporting participant to another (see *Condon v Basi* ([1985] 1 W.L.R. 866)) and that owed by a sporting participant to a spectator (for example *Wooldridge v Summer* ([1963] 2 Q.B. 43) and *Wilks v Cheltenham Homeguard Motor Cycle and Light Car Club* ([1971] 1 W.L.R. 668), there appeared to be no previous case in which a rugby football player had sued a referee in negligence.

The present case was of concern to many who feared that the judgment for the plaintiff would emasculate and enmesh in unwelcome legal toils a game which gave pleasure to millions.

His Lordship referred to the context in which the issues arose:

1. That rugby football was a tough, highly physical game, not for the timid or the fragile, in which participants in serious competitive games could expect a fair share of knocks, bruises, strains, abrasions and minor bony injuries.

2. The laws of the game in force during the 1991/1992 season issued by the International Rugby Football Board and their accompanying instructions and notes for the guidance of players and referees, which contained special provisions for under-19s.

His Lordship set out the relevant laws applicable, in particular, to under-19s and relating to protection during scrummages and enforcement of safety measures, which were in place for the 1991–1992 season, specifically to protect young players against the risk of spinal injury caused by collapsed scrums.

He also referred to a further directive issued in March 1991 expressing concern at the continued lack of observance of the phased sequence of engagement within law 20(2) and requiring the strict observance of the engagement sequence, crouch-touch-pause-engage (CTPE).

3. The referee's function was to supervise the playing of the match, endeavouring to apply the rules of the game fairly and judiciously so as to ensure that the flow of play was not unnecessarily interrupted, that points awarded were fairly scored and that foul or dangerous play was discouraged and, where appropriate, penalised or prevented.

His Lordship said that that function had often to be performed in the context of a fast-moving, competitive and vigorous game, calling for split-second judgments and decisions.

The referee could not be in all parts of the field at the same time; he could not hope to see everything that went on; it was a difficult and demanding job, usually, as here, performed out of goodwill by a devotee of the game.

On the question of the duty of care owed to the plaintiff the referee, founding his pleaded defence on observations of Lord Justice Sellers and Lord Justice Diplock in *Wooldridge v*

Sumner ([1963] 2 Q.B. 43 at 57, 67, 68), had argued that while he owed a duty of care and skill, nothing short of reckless disregard of the plaintiff's safety would suffice to establish a breach of that duty.

The judge had adopted the test proposed by the plaintiff in reliance on observations of Sir John Donaldson, M.R., in *Condon v Basi* that the duty owed was to exercise such degree of care as was appropriate in all the circumstances.

In the judgment of the court the judge was correct. The referee accepted that he owed a duty so that there was no issue whether any duty of care arose at all or whether any such duty was owed to the plaintiff.

The issue of policy, or of what was just and reasonable, did not accordingly fall for decision. The only question was what duty was owed. The referee feared that if the plaintiff's test were accepted the threshold of liability would be too low and those in the referee's position would be too vulnerable to suits by injured players.

The court did not accept that fear as well founded. The level of care required was that which was appropriate in all the circumstances and the circumstances were of crucial importance.

Full account had to be taken of the factual context in which he exercised his functions and he could not be properly held liable for errors of judgment, oversight or lapses of which any referee might be guilty in the context of a fast-moving and vigorous contest.

The threshold of liability was a high one. It would not easily be crossed.

There was no inconsistency between that conclusion and that reached by the Court of Appeal in the *Wooldridge* and *Wilks* cases. The position of a referee vis-à-vis the players was not the same as that of a participant in a contest vis-à-vis a spectator.

One of his responsibilities was to safeguard the players' safety. So although the legal duty was the same, the practical content differed according to the quite different circumstances.

The referee had submitted that the injury to the plaintiff had not been caused by him directly, but as the result of acts and omissions on the part of third parties, the other members of the scrum, and that he could not be held liable unless the court found that there was a high level of probability of injury of the kind which the laws were designed to prevent as a result of a scrum collapse.

The court rejected that submission.

If the referee were properly found to be in breach of his duty of care by failing to take appropriate steps to prevent a collapse and if as a result of his failure a scrum did collapse and a player thereby suffered spinal injuries of a kind the rules were designed to prevent, then the referee would be liable in law for that foreseeable result of his breach of duty, despite the fact that, quantified statistically, it was a result which was very unlikely to eventuate.

His Lordship, referring to the judge's findings, said that the judge had been satisfied by the evidence that the scrums were repeatedly coming together in a rushed way and with excessive force; that those impacts were the likely cause of a large majority of scrums collapsing and that the number of impact collapses had been abnormally high.

Referring to the evidence at trial, including that given by four witnesses whom the judge had found impressive and reliable, his Lordship said it had been their clear and unshaken evidence that the referee had not during the match insisted on the CTPE sequence being followed and that it had not been followed.

His Lordship referred to the judge's conclusions that the referee had not enforced the CTPE sequence: that he had, given the extent of collapsed scrums and in the light of his own expert's evidence, fallen below the standard of a reasonably competent referee in refereeing the scrummages in that game.

The judge had emphasised that his judgment in the plaintiff's favour was reached on the very special facts of that case. He had not intended to open the door to a plethora of claims by players against referees and it would be deplorable if that were the result.

In the court's view, that result should not follow provided all concerned appreciated how difficult it was for any plaintiff to establish that a referee failed to exercise such care and skill as was reasonably to be expected in the circumstances of a hotly contested game of rugby football.

The court was caused to wonder whether it would not be beneficial if all players were, as a matter of general practice, to be insured not against negligence but against the risk of catastrophic injury.

That was no doubt a matter to which those responsible for the administration of rugby football had given anxious attention.

Notes

1. Claims for sporting injuries are greatly on the increase. In *Watson v Gray* [1998] Times L.R. 740 a professional footballer was held liable for injuring an opponent by a forceful high challenge: it was a breach to do something which a reasonable professional would have known carried a significant risk of serious injury. In *Condon v Basi* [1985] 2 All E.R. 453 Donaldson M.R. suggested that "a higher degree of care was required in the first division than a local league." Why should this be? Because first division players are better paid or because they are more skilled? His observation was treated with reserve by Drake J. in *Elliott v Saunders* [1994] New L.J. 1094, where the plaintiff from Chelsea lost to Liverpool.

2. In *Evans v Vowles* [2003] EWCA Civ 318, [2003] 1 WLR 1607, Lord Phillips M.R. referred to counsel's suggestion that if the finding below that an amateur referee owed a duty of care to the players under his charge, volunteers would no longer be prepared to serve as referees, and said "We do not believe that this result will, or should, follow. Liability has been established in this case because the injury resulted from a failure to implement a law designed to minimise the risk of just the kind of accident which subsequently occurred. We believe that such a failure is itself likely to be very rare. Much rarer will be the case where there are grounds for alleging that it has caused a serious injury. Serious injuries are happily rare, but they are an inherent risk of the game. That risk is one which those who play rugby believe is worth taking, having regard to the satisfaction that they get from the game. We would not expect the much more remote risk of facing a claim in negligence to discourage those who take their pleasure in the game by acting as referees." What possible basis did Lord Phillips have for this prediction?

3. *Caldwell v Maguire* [2001] EWCA Civ 1054 arose out of thoroughbred racing, described by an Australian judge as "a competitive business, which is played for high stakes. Its participants are large animals ridden by small men at high speed in close proximity. The opportunity for injury is abundant and the choices available to jockeys to avoid or reduce risk are limited." The claimant, a professional jockey, was seriously injured towards the end of a race when, four horses being in contention, the first defendant took the inside lane less than a length in front of two others. The horse of one of them shied at the constriction and caused the claimant's horse to fall. The trial judge found that the defendants were not guilty of negligence in law, despite the relevant but non-determinative decision by the racing authorities to suspend the defendants for careless riding. The Court of Appeal agreed, saying that while recklessness was not required, it was not enough that there had been, as here, momentary carelessness in the circumstances, a mere error of judgment in the heat and commitment of a race.

4. Boxing is perhaps the only sport where the aim is to batter the opponent with one's fist. Hitting below the belt is clearly actionable, but a boxer injured by a fair blow may still be able to sue the boxing authority if it fails to provide or see to the provision of appropriate ringside medical assistance in order to counteract or allay its effect. *Watson v British Boxing Board of Control* [2001] Q.B. 1134 was described as "an extraordinary, if not unique, case whose distinctive features took it outside any established category of duty of care in negligence." The peculiarity here was that the duty was not to avoid personal injury but to care for it if it occurred. That was true also in *Barrett v Ministry of Defence* [1995] 3 All E.R. 87 where the Ministry was not liable for letting an officer drink himself into a stupor, but was (as was conceded) under a duty to look after him when known to be in that parlous condition, but that was a case of employer and employee. What was the source of the duty of the Boxing Board? It was held that it "had assumed the responsibility of determining the nature of the medical facilities and assistance to be provided"; had it simply given general advice there might not be sufficient proximity, but here it laid down the rules.

5. In *Craven v Riches* [2001] EWCA Civ 375 the first defendants organised a "blast round" the second defendant's race-track in Scotland, the motorcyclists being divided into a fast group, a medium group and slow group. The claimant, who had not ridden his motorcycle for a year, was entered in the fast group, and when he came over the brow of a hill he braked to avoid a slow group in front of him, and lost control of his cycle. The trial judge found no one at fault, but the Court of Appeal (including Sedley L.J.) held that it was negligent to allow fast and slow cyclists on the track at the same time, although some participants would obviously always be slower than others. The claimant was contributorily negligent as to two-thirds. Consider this decision in the light of the observations in *Tomlinson*, below p.149.

6. A golfer may be liable for a risky shot which injures another golfer: *Pearson v Lightning* [1998] Times L.R. 270.

7. If you are the victim of violence on the sports field, be sure to tell the police, or the Criminal Injuries Compensation Authority will reject your claim (which must be for over £1,000).

BALAMOAN v HOLDEN & CO

Court of Appeal [1999] New L.J. 898

Claim by client against country solicitor

In 1988 the defendants, a firm of solicitors in Hastings, were instructed by the claimant to pursue a claim for damages for nuisance. The firm's principal was a sole practitioner, and he employed non-qualified staff to handle such claims. By the time a writ was issued in 1990 the claimant, despite raising numerous points, had not seen a qualified lawyer and had only had two 30-minute interviews with members of the firm's staff. Eventually the claimant was advised by counsel in March 1993 that his claim was worth £3,000 at the most, and when he refused to accept that advice, his legal aid certificate was discharged and the defendants' retainer was terminated. In August 1994 the claimant, acting in person, accepted £25,000 and costs in settlement of his claim. He subsequently brought an action against the defendants claiming damages of £1 million which, he asserted, he would have recovered had they handled his claim with reasonable skill and care. He contended, inter alia, that the defendants had failed to gather the necessary evidence to enable him to pursue his action. The circuit judge dismissed the action. The claimant's appeal was allowed.

Brooke L.J. In answering the question whether there was other evidence which reasonably the defendants should have obtained, it was necessary to apply the standard of care reasonably to be expected of a reasonably careful litigation solicitor who held himself out as competent to practise in the field of law in which his client had engaged his services. A one-man firm could not expect a lower standard of care to be applied to it merely because it delegated the conduct of its client's affairs to an unqualified member of its staff, however experienced. If the conduct of that member of staff fell below the standard appropriate for a solicitor, and he failed to seek advice from counsel or from a solicitor in the firm when need arose, then the firm could not complain about a finding of negligence against it. *Richards v Cox* [1942] 2 All E.R. 624, a case involving a solicitor's clerk, was an example of the principle that a solicitor might be acting at his peril if he created unnecessary risks for his client by letting his clerk act in matters beyond his competence by advising on points which ought to have been referred to counsel.

It was a commonplace that if a solicitor acted in accordance with the advice of counsel whom he had properly instructed, then he would usually not be held liable in negligence even if counsel's advice proved to be mistaken or misconceived. The caveat, that it was his duty to reject his counsel's advice if it was obviously or glaringly wrong, had no application on the facts of the instant appeal, since no complaint could reasonably be made of the quality of the advice given by counsel.

In the instant case, the court was concerned with the standard of care reasonably to be required of a solicitor in a small country town who was instructed by a legally aided client to pursue what appeared to be a comparatively small claim. It was of critical importance for the courts not to apply a too rigorous standard in those circumstances, because when pursuing such a claim a solicitor had always to be anxious not to incur costs which he could not, if successful, recover from the other side, because otherwise the Legal Aid Board's charge would reduce his client's compensation. For those reasons the court would necessarily place great weight on the judgment of a local circuit judge as to the standards reasonably to be required of local litigation solicitors.

Having made those allowances, it was clear that the defendants had failed in the duty of care they owed to the claimant to take such steps as were reasonable to ensure either that they took him to see counsel promptly, so that counsel could advise on what evidence should be gathered before the trail went cold, or that they gathered such evidence competently of their own initiative, and that he had suffered as a consequence of that breach of duty. If the defendants had taken the claimant to see counsel in the spring of 1989, he would have advised them of the evidence they needed to gather, at that time and not three or four years later, and would have advised the claimant as to the different heads of claim of damage he was entitled to claim. It was not sufficient to write a letter to a client, whom the solicitor had never met, asking him to make as detailed a written statement as possible of all the matters of which he complained, and then to do nothing when the client's immediate reply posed as many questions as it answered.

For those reasons the appeal would be allowed on the basis that there were acts or omissions which constituted negligence and that their effect was cumulative.

MULLIN v RICHARDS

Court of Appeal [1998] 1 W.L.R. 1304; [1998] 1 All E.R. 920

Claim by one schoolgirl against another

Teresa and Heidi, both aged 15, were fencing with 12-inch plastic rulers in class when Heidi's ruler snapped and a piece of plastic went into Teresa's eye. The trial judge awarded damages to Teresa, subject to a 50 per cent deduction for contributory negligence. In unreserved judgments the Court of Appeal unanimously reversed.

Hutchison L.J.: ... The judge, it seems to me, found negligence without there being material on which he could properly do so. He seems indeed from the language he used to have regarded it as axiomatic that if there was a fight going on, such as he found there was, a play fight, that imported that injury was reasonably foreseeable and from his finding that the ruler broke that there was necessarily dangerous or excessive violence. For my part, I would say that in the absence of evidence one simply does not know why the ruler broke, whether because it was unusually weak, unlike other rulers; whether because it had been damaged in some way; or whether because rulers of this sort are particularly prone to break; one does not know. What certainly one cannot infer, and the judge was, I consider, not entitled to infer, was that there was here excessive violence or inappropriate violence over and above that which was inherent in the play fencing in which these two girls were indulging. This was in truth nothing more than a schoolgirls' game such as on the evidence was commonplace in this school and there was, I would hold, no justification for attributing to the participants the foresight of any significant risk of the likelihood of injury. They had seen it done elsewhere with some frequency. They had not heard it prohibited or received any warning about it. They had not been told of any injuries occasioned by it. They were not in any sense behaving culpably. So far as foresight goes, had they paused to think they might, I suppose, have said: "It is conceivable that some unlucky injury might happen", but if asked if there was any likelihood of it or any real possibility of it, they would, I am sure, have said that they did not foresee any such possibility. Taking the view therefore that the learned judge—who, as I have said, readily and almost without question accepted that on his findings of fact there was negligence on the part of both these young ladies—was wrong in his view and there was no evidence on which he could come to it, I would allow the appeal and direct that judgment be entered for the first defendant. I have to say that I appreciate that this result will be disappointing to the plaintiff for whom one can have nothing but sympathy, because she has suffered a grave injury through no fault of her own. But unfortunately she has failed to establish in my view that anyone was legally responsible for that injury and, accordingly, her claim should have failed.

Butler-Sloss L.J.: Since there has been little earlier authority on the proper approach to the standard of care to be applied to a child, I would like to underline the observations of Hutchison L.J. and rely upon two further passages in the persuasive judgment of Kitto J. in the High Court of Australia in *McHale v Watson* (1966) 115 C.L.R. 199 at 213:

"In regard to the things which pertain to foresight and prudence experience, understanding of causes and effects, balance of judgment, thoughtfulness—it is absurd, indeed it is a misuse of language, to speak of normality in relation to persons of all ages taken together. In those things normality is, for children, something different from what normality is for adults; the very concept of normality is a concept of rising levels until 'years of discretion' are attained. The law does not arbitrarily fix upon any particular age for this purpose, and tribunals of fact may well give effect to different views as to the age at which normal adult foresight and prudence are reasonably to be expected in relation to particular sets of circumstances. But up to that stage the normal capacity to exercise those two qualities necessarily means the capacity which is normal for a child of the relevant age; and it seems to me that it would be contrary to the fundamental principle that a person is liable for harm that he causes by falling short of an objective criterion of 'propriety' in his conduct—propriety, that is to say, as determined by a comparison with the standard of care reasonably to be expected in the circumstances from the normal person to hold that where a child's liability is in question the normal person—to be considered is someone other than a child of corresponding age."

I would respectfully indorse those observations as entirely appropriate to English law and I would like to conclude with another passage of Kitto J. (at 216) particularly relevant to today—

" . . . in the absence of relevant statutory provision, children, like everyone else, must accept as they go about in society the risks from which ordinary care on the part of others will not suffice to save them. One such risk is that boys of twelve may behave as boys of twelve . . . "

—and I would say that girls of 15 playing together may play as somewhat irresponsible girls of 15. I too would allow this appeal.

Questions

Teresa's claim against the school, on the basis that the schoolmistress should have prevented the fencing, was dismissed. Would the liability of the schoolmistress depend simply on the foreseeability of the injury, or would other factors be taken into account? If (like Mrs Alexander in *Muir*, below, p.155) she would not have foreseen the injury, what had Heidi's youth to do with the outcome? Would it have been reasonable for the schoolmistress herself to have been fencing with plastic rulers? Was it unreasonable for the children to be doing so ("normal horseplay"—see *Wilson v Pringle*, below, p.348). Does this suggest whether the proper test for breach of duty is foreseeability of harm or unreasonableness of conduct? What would have been the chances of a successful claim against the manufacturer/importer of the ruler that broke, supposing that the Consumer Protection Act had been in force at the time?

KING v SMITH

Court of Appeal [1995] I.C.R. 339

Action for personal injuries by window-cleaner against employer

The plaintiff was cleaning the windows on the second floor of an office block occupied by Camden Council. Thinking he could neither open the top sash nor, since there was a desk in the way, adopt the "housemaid position" (sitting on the sill with his back to the outside world and his legs inside), he stood on the sill, lost his grip and fell 75 feet to the ground.

The trial judge entered judgment, subject to 30 per cent contributory negligence, against his employer, and the Court of Appeal affirmed his judgment.

Millett L.J.: Rule 3 of the defendant's rule book provides:

"When cleaning the outside of a window above six feet from the ground, then that window must be cleaned as far as possible from the inside or by sitting on the window sill."

The judge was of the opinion that the plaintiff, who was an experienced window cleaner, would not have gone out onto the sill if he had not believed that this was necessary because in his view it was not possible to open the upper sash. The plaintiff was wrong about that, as the judge found. If he had tried harder to open the upper sash he would have succeeded. In my judgment, however, r.3 was inadequate to protect the plaintiff. It failed to protect him from the very misjudgment which he in fact made. I agree with the judge that the rule book ought to have prohibited the men from going out onto the sill where the window was more than six feet from the ground and there was no safe anchorage for harness in any case where the window was so constructed that if working properly it would be capable of being cleaned from the inside.

I have for my part not reached that conclusion without a measure of hesitation. The employer's duty is not to expose his workmen to unnecessary or avoidable risk. He is bound only to employ as safe a system of work as reasonable skill and judgment can make it. Where the work to be performed cannot be made safe or safer by any means within the employer's control, he is not normally obliged to decline the work. On the other hand, some operations are so inherently dangerous that they should not be performed at all. If the work is of that character, an employee should not be required to perform it.

It was argued that in *General Cleaning Contractors Ltd v Christmas* [1953] A.C. 180 the House of Lords laid it down that to clean a window by standing on the sill was not so inherently dangerous that it was an operation which should not be performed at all. But that was not laid down as a rule of law; it was a finding of fact on the evidence in that particular case. In the 40 years that have passed since then more has become known of practices in the industry and it is now well appreciated that this is a dangerous practice and the most frequent cause of serious accidents to window cleaners.

I have come to the conclusion that it would be right now to require an employer to impose an embargo on his employees going out onto the window sill of a window above a certain height, where (1) the customer has not provided anchorage for a safety harness, and (2) the windows are so designed that they should be capable of being cleaned from the inside. If it appears to the employee that it is not possible to open a window from the inside, he should tell the customer that he is not prepared to clean the window from the outside (in the absence of safe anchorage for a safety harness) unless and until the customer has put his window in proper working order.

Accordingly, I have come to the conclusion that the judgment below was correct, and I agree . . . that we should not interfere with the judge's conclusions on liability or contributory negligence.

Notes:

1. The duty to take reasonable care is gratifyingly flexible! Conduct previously acceptable may cease to satisfy its requirements as we become more aware of the existence of hazards and the means of mitigating them. Ever greater precautions may be called for by heightened demands for security as well as by increases in knowledge and technology.

2. Legal proceedings may promote safety not only by sanctioning the neglect of proper precautions but also by stimulating discovery of the causes of accidents (see *Roe*, below, p.166 and the *Cambridge Water Co* case, below, p.461).

3. Sometimes the employer's duty can be pitched too high. A fisherman fell overboard while on watch and was drowned. The trial judge held the employer liable for not providing a particular type of life-jacket and insisting that it be worn, though this was neither common practice on other trawlers nor required by safety regulations. The Court of Appeal reversed: *Gray v Stead* [1999] 1 Lloyd's Rep. 377.

4. In *Pickford v ICI* [1998] 3 All E.R. 462, HL, a secretary now suffering from repetitive strain injury sued her employer on the basis that she, unlike typists in the accounts department, had not been warned to take periodic rests from typing. The trial judge held the employer not liable but the Court of Appeal reversed and

was criticised in the House of Lords for so reversing the burden of proof: the secretary needed no warning to intersperse her typing with other work she had to do.

Section 2.—What is Reasonable?

BOLTON v STONE

House of Lords [1951] A.C. 850; [1951] 1 T.L.R. 977; [1951] 1 All E.R. 1078;
50 L.G.R. 32; 95 S.J. 333

*Action by pedestrian against occupier of land adjoining the highway in
respect of personal injury*

On August 9, 1947, when she was standing on the highway outside her home Miss Bessie Stone was struck by a cricket ball hit by a visiting batsman from the grounds of the Cheetham Cricket Club which adjoined the highway. She sued the committee and members of the Club, though not the batsman in question.

The ground had been used for cricket since 1864, long before the surrounding houses were built. Balls were only rarely hit over the fence during a match, and committee members could not recall an accident. A nearer neighbour said that balls had been hit into his yard. This particular ball had travelled 78 yards before passing over the fence (the top of which was seven feet above the highway and 17 feet above the pitch) and about 25 yards further before striking Miss Stone.

The plaintiff claimed damages on the ground of negligence and nuisance. The particulars of negligence alleged were that the defendants "(a) pitched the cricket pitch too near to the said road; (b) failed to erect a ... fence ... of sufficient height to prevent balls being struck into the said road; (c) failed to ensure that cricket balls would not be hit into the said road."

Oliver J. gave judgment for the defendants [1949] 1 All E.R. 237. The Court of Appeal, by a majority, allowed the plaintiff's appeal, on the grounds that the defendants were guilty of negligence [1950] 1 K.B. 201. The defendants' appeal to the House of Lords was allowed.

Lord Radcliffe: My Lords, I agree that this appeal must be allowed. I agree with regret, because I have much sympathy with the decision that commended itself to the majority of the members of the Court of Appeal. I can see nothing unfair in the appellants being required to compensate the respondent for the serious injury that she has received as a result of the sport that they have organised on their cricket ground at Cheetham Hill. But the law of negligence is concerned less with what is fair than with what is culpable, and I cannot persuade myself that the appellants have been guilty of any culpable act or omission in this case.

I think that the case is in some respects a peculiar one, not easily related to the general rules that govern liability for negligence. If the test whether there has been a breach of duty were to depend merely on the answer to the question whether this accident was a reasonably foreseeable risk, I think that there would have been a breach of duty, for that such an accident might take place some time or other might very reasonably have been present to the minds of the appellants. It was quite foreseeable, and there would have been nothing unreasonable in allowing the imagination to dwell on the possibility of its occurring. But there was only a remote, perhaps I ought to say only a very remote, chance of the accident taking place at any particular time, for, if it was to happen, not only had a ball to carry the fence round the ground but it had also to coincide in its arrival with the presence of some person on what does not look like a crowded thoroughfare and actually to strike that person in some way that would cause sensible injury.

Those being the facts, a breach of duty has taken place if they show the appellants guilty of a failure to take reasonable care to prevent the accident. One may phrase it as "reasonable care" or "ordinary care" or "proper care"—all these phrases are to be found in decisions of authority—but the fact remains that, unless there has been something which a reasonable man would blame as falling beneath the standard of conduct that he would set for himself and require of his neighbour, there has been no breach of legal duty. And here, I think, the respondent's case breaks down. It seems to me that a reasonable man, taking account of the chances against an accident happening, would not have felt himself called upon either to abandon the use of the ground for cricket or to increase the height of his surrounding fences. He would have done what the appellants did: in other words, he would have done nothing. Whether, if the unlikely event of an accident did occur and his play turn to another's hurt, he would have thought it equally proper to offer no more consolation to his victim than the reflection that a social being is not immune from social risks, I do not say, for I do not think that that is a consideration which is relevant to legal liability.

I agree with the others of your Lordships that if the respondent cannot succeed in negligence she cannot succeed on any other head of claim.

Questions
1. Would the defendants be liable if a similar accident occurred today?
2. Would the result have been the same if Miss Stone had been sitting in her garden at the time the ball struck her?
3. Suppose that the ball had been struck during practice at the nets rather than during a match. Same result?
4. Suppose that Miss Stone had been (a) a spectator or (b) the tea-lady in the pavilion. In what terms would one decide her suit against (a) the cricket club and (b) the batsman?
5. How could one reach a sports ground if it were not adjacent to a highway?

Notes:
1. The reason for selecting this speech (rather than Lord Reid's, for example) is that Viscount Radcliffe makes it quite clear that the ultimate and vital question is "Was the conduct unreasonable?" and not "Was the harm foreseeable?" Of course if behaviour is apparently innocuous, *i.e.* such that no one would foresee any harm resulting from it, yet unpredictably causes some freak damage, we would not make the defendant pay. If behaviour is *dangerous*, on the other hand, *i.e.* such that one could foresee physical harm resulting from it, we are tempted to castigate it. But it is not *all* dangerous conduct which renders a person liable, it is only *unreasonably* dangerous conduct, conduct which, in the light (*inter alia*) of the recognisable danger, is *unreasonable*.

Sixteen years later Lord Reid was still in some perplexity over this case. In *The Wagon Mound (No.2)* [1967] 1 A.C. 617, he said this:

"*Bolton v Stone* posed a new problem. There a member of a visiting team drove a cricket ball out of the ground on to an unfrequented adjacent public road and it struck and severely injured a lady who happened to be standing in the road. That it might happen that a ball would be driven on to this road could not have been said to be a fantastic or far-fetched possibility: according to the evidence it had happened about six times in 28 years. Moreover it could not have been said to be a far-fetched or fantastic possibility that such a ball would strike someone in the road: people did pass along the road from time to time. So it could not have been said that, on any ordinary meaning of the words, the fact that a ball might strike a person in the road was not foreseeable or reasonably foreseeable. It was plainly foreseeable; but the chance of its happening in the foreseeable future was infinitesimal. A mathematician given the data could have worked out that it was only likely to happen once in so many thousand years. The House of Lords held that the risk was so small that in the circumstances a reasonable man would have been justified in disregarding it and taking no steps to eliminate it.

It does not follow that, no matter what the circumstances may be, it is justifiable to neglect a risk of such a small magnitude. A reasonable man would only neglect such a risk if he had some valid reason for doing so: *e.g.* that it would involve considerable expense to eliminate the risk. He would weigh the risk against the difficulty of eliminating it. If the activity which caused the injury to Miss Stone had been an unlawful activity there can be little doubt but that *Bolton v Stone* would have been decided differently. In their Lordships' judgment *Bolton v Stone* did not alter the general principle that a person must be regarded as negligent if he does not take steps to eliminate a risk which he knows or ought to know is a real risk and not a mere possibility which would never influence the mind of a reasonable man. What that decision did was to recognise and give effect to the qualification that it is justifiable not to take steps to eliminate a real risk if it is small and if the circumstances are such that a reasonable man, careful of the safety of his neighbour, would think it right to neglect it.

In the present case there was no justification whatever for discharging the oil into Sydney Harbour. Not only was it an offence to do so, but also it involved considerable loss financially. If the ship's engineer had thought about the matter there could have been no question of balancing the advantages and disadvantages. From every point of view it was both his duty and his interest to stop the discharge immediately."

2. Cricket is always giving trouble. In *Miller v Jackson* [1977] Q.B. 966 a couple who had bought a new house on the edge of a small village cricket ground sought to have the cricket stopped and claimed damages. Contrast the views of Lord Denning M.R. and Geoffrey Lane L.J.:

Lord Denning M.R.: "The club were entitled to use this ground for cricket in the accustomed way. It was not a nuisance, nor was it negligence of them so to run it. Nor was the batsman negligent when he hit the ball for six. All were doing simply what they were entitled to do. So if the club had put it to the test, I would have dismissed the claim for damages also."

Geoffrey Lane L.J.: "The evidence . . . makes it clear that the risk of injury to property at least was both foreseeable and foreseen. It is obvious that such injury is going to take place so long as cricket is being played on this field. It is the duty of the cricketers so to conduct their operations as not to harm people they can or ought reasonably to foresee may be affected . . . The risk of injury to persons and property is so great that on each occasion when a ball comes over the fence and causes damage to the plaintiffs, the defendants are guilty of negligence."

Cumming-Bruce L.J. agreed with Geoffrey Lane L.J. in holding the cricket club liable in damages for negligence, but agreed with Lord Denning that the cricket should be allowed to continue: "So on the facts of this case a court of equity must seek to strike a fair balance between the right of the plaintiffs to have quiet enjoyment of their house and garden without exposure to cricket balls occasionally falling like thunderbolts from the heavens, and the opportunity of the inhabitants of the village in which they live to continue to enjoy the manly sport which constitutes a summer recreation for adults and young persons . . . " But can the common law of negligence itself not "seek to strike a fair balance"? Surely the test of what is reasonable in all the circumstances (unlike the question whether harm was foreseeable) is an apt one for the purpose. Safety first equal?

3. So important is it to see that the question here is "was the conduct unreasonable?" rather than "was the harm foreseeable?" that at the risk of labouring the point we cite a glaring example of judicial confusion. *Smith v Blackburn* [1974] R.T.R. 533 involved a head-on collision. Since the plaintiff was driving impeccably and the defendant was driving like a madman, the only question was whether the plaintiff's damages should be reduced on the ground that his failure to wear a seat-belt constituted contributory negligence. The judge said this:

"The accident happened in an unusual place, the Bushey Road Flyover. Here was a one-way road going up to a rise to a crest and along that road Mr Smith was driving his car absolutely normally. He was doing nothing wrong at all, and yet it was really suggested that he should have foreseen that a madman would drive up the flyover in the wrong direction, travelling along a one-way street in the opposite direction to that which he should have been, and at high speed, so that when he did meet somebody minding his own business, they collided head on.

To start with in my judgment the law does not require a person in the position of Mr Smith in the place where he was to foresee that that kind of accident will occur. He may foresee that he may come upon a broken-down vehicle or all sorts of things, but I see no ground for assuming that the law required Mr Smith to foresee that.

If the law does not require him to foresee it, why should the law be said to require him to take precautions against the possible event?"

Even if the accident was unforeseeable by Mr Smith it was unreasonable of him not to be wearing a seat-belt: seat-belts are no trouble to put on and they do in fact reduce the incidence of serious injury, so reasonable people wear them. Whether Mr Smith's injuries would actually have been reduced by a seat-belt is a quite different question, but pointing to the improbability of the collision which took place does not help us to answer it.

Take another case. A man was employed to stamp the initials "CA" on steel tyres. The way everyone does this is to hold the stamp and hit it firmly with a heavy hammer. One day, after many many days of doing this more than 100 times a day, the plaintiff mishit the stamp and broke his thumb. The judge held that the accident was foreseeable (which no one who has used a hammer could deny) and that *therefore* the employer was negligent. The Court of Appeal reversed, because the judge "did not ask the proper and right question." *Pindall v British Steel Corp.* (March 7, 1980). The proper question was whether the employer had acted reasonably, that is, whether the system adopted or endorsed by him exposed the employee to unreasonable risk of harm, and the answer would depend on whether a rubber hammer or a thumb-guard should have been provided, whether there were any avoidable distractions in the workplace, whether the employee was kept at the task too long at a time, and so on, virtually *ad infinitum*.

WATT v HERTFORDSHIRE C. C.

Court of Appeal [1954] 1 W.L.R. 835; 118 J.P. 377; 98 S.J. 372; [1954] 2 All E.R. 368; 52 L.G.R. 383
(noted (1954) 70 L.Q.R. 159)

Action by employee against employer in respect of personal injury

The plaintiff had for 12 years been a fireman at the Watford Fire Station. He was on duty on July 27, 1951, when an emergency call was received; a woman was trapped under a heavy vehicle only 200 or 300 yards away. The sub-officer in charge left the station immediately after giving instructions that the plaintiff's team should follow in a Fordson lorry and bring a large jack for lifting heavy weights. The jack, which stood on four small wheels and weighed two or three hundredweights, was put on the back of the lorry, where the plaintiff with two others steadied it. There was no mechanical means of securing the jack, since the lorry had a smooth floor and there was nothing to which the jack could be lashed. The driver had to brake suddenly. The three men in the back were thrown off balance, and the jack slewed forward, catching the plaintiff's ankle and causing him serious injuries. The fire station normally had a vehicle suitable for carrying the jack safely, but it was not in the station at the time. When that vehicle was not available and the jack was needed, it was the practice to notify another fire station; to follow that practice in this case would have involved a delay of at least 10 minutes.

The plaintiff failed before Barry J. The Court of Appeal, in unreserved judgments, dismissed his appeal.

Singleton L.J.: I am in complete agreement with the judgment of Barry J. but it is right that I should state my reasons for having formed that opinion.

The fire service is a service which must always involve risk for those who are employed in it, and, as Mr Baker on behalf of the plaintiff pointed out, they are entitled to expect that their equipment shall be as good as reasonable care can secure. An emergency arose, as often happens. The sub-officer who had given the order, was asked in re-examination: "From your point of view you thought it was a piece of luck, with this unfortunate woman under the bus, that the Fordson was available and you could use it? (A.) Yes. It is recognised in the service that we use our initiative at all times, and in doing so any reasonable step you take is considered satisfactory if it is a question of saving life. You have to make a sudden decision."

It is not alleged that there was negligence on the part of any particular individual, nor that the driver was negligent in driving too fast, nor that the sub-officer was negligent in giving the order which he did. The case put forward in this court is that as the defendants had a jack, it was their duty to have a vehicle fitted in all respects to carry that jack, from which it follows, I suppose, that it is said that there must be a vehicle kept at the station at all times, or that if there is not one the lifting jack must not be taken out; indeed, Mr Baker claimed that in the case of a happening such as this, if there was not a vehicle fitted to carry the jack the sub-officer ought to have telephoned to the fire station at St. Albans and arranged that they should attend to the emergency. St. Albans is some seven miles away, and it was said that an extra 10 minutes or so would have elapsed if that had been done. I cannot think that that is the right way to approach the matter. There was a real emergency; the woman was under a heavy vehicle; these men in the fire service thought that they ought to go promptly and to take a lifting jack, and they did so. Most unfortunately this accident happened.

What is the duty owed by employers? It has been stated often, and never more clearly than it was by Lord Herschell in *Smith v Baker & Sons* ([1891] A.C. 325 at 362), in these words: "It is quite clear that the contract between employer and employed involves on the part of the former the duty of taking reasonable care to provide proper appliances, and to maintain them in a proper condition, and so to carry on his operations as not to subject those employed by him to unnecessary risk."

The employee in this case was a member of the fire service, who always undertake some risk—but, said Mr Baker, not this risk. Is it to be said that if an emergency call reaches a fire station the one in charge has to ponder on the matter in this way: "Must I send out my men with the lifting jack in these circumstances, or must I telephone to St. Albans, seven miles away, to ask them to undertake the task?" I suppose he must think about his duty; but what would a reasonable man do, faced as he was? Would the reasonably careful head of the station have done anything other than that which the sub-officer did? I think not. Can it be said, then, that there is a duty on the employers here to have a vehicle built and fitted to carry this jack at all times, or if they have not, not to use the jack for a short journey of 200 or 300 yards? I do not think that that will do.

Asquith L.J., in *Daborn v Bath Tramways Motor Co Ltd* said ([1946] 2 All E.R. 333 at 336): "In determining whether a party is negligent, the standard of reasonable care is that which is reasonably to be demanded in the circumstances. A relevant circumstance to take into account may be the importance of the end to be served by behaving in this way or in that. As has often been pointed out, if all the trains in this country were restricted to a speed of five miles an hour, there would be fewer accidents, but our national life would be intolerably slowed down. The purpose to be served, if sufficiently important, justifies the assumption of abnormal risk."

The purpose to be served in this case was the saving of life. The men were prepared to take the risk. They were not, in my view, called on to take any risk other than that which normally might be encountered in this service. I agree with Barry J. that on the whole of the evidence it would not be right to find that the employers were guilty of any failure of the duty which they owed to their workmen. In my opinion the appeal should be dismissed.

Denning L.J.: It is well settled that in measuring due care you must balance the risk against the measures necessary to eliminate the risk. To that proposition there ought to be added this: you must balance the risk against the end to be achieved. If this accident had occurred in a commercial enterprise without any emergency there could be no doubt that the servant would succeed. But the commercial end to make profit is very different from the human end to save life or limb. The saving of life or limb justifies taking considerable risk, and I am glad to say that there have never been wanting in this country men of courage ready to take those risks, notably in the fire service.

In this case the risk involved in sending out the lorry was not so great as to prohibit the attempt to save life. I quite agree that fire engines, ambulances and doctors' cars should not shoot past the traffic lights when they show a red light. That is because the risk is too great to warrant the incurring of the danger. It is always a question of balancing the risk against the end. I agree that this appeal should be dismissed.

Questions

1. Suppose the plaintiff had been a pedestrian run over by the driver in his haste to reach the scene of the emergency. Would his case have been stronger or weaker than that of the present plaintiff?

2. Could Watt recover from the person who carelessly provoked the emergency?

3. Would the answer have been any different if the cause of the injury had been a defective wheel on the jack?

4. Do you think that the pension schemes of local fire services take account of the risks of the calling?

5. The first sentence of the extract from Lord Denning's speech may explain *First National Commercial Bank v Barnet Devanney* [1999] 2 All E.R. (Com.) 233, CA. The plaintiff mortgagee instructed the defendant insurance broker to take out a policy to cover its interest in the mortgaged property. The defendant failed to include a mortgagee protection clause, but as it turned out the policy was just as good as if he had, for the Court of Appeal later held in another case that the mortgagee protection clause was unnecessary. At the time, however, this was uncertain and it was good practice to include such a clause, which did not cost anything. Given the uncertainty at the time, the mortgagee settled with the reluctant insurance company for a moderate sum, and now sues the broker for the balance. It was held that it was negligent of the broker not to include the clause when it cost nothing and could do only good: his duty was not only to protect the insured not only from loss but also from litigation and doubt.

6. An ambulance assistant suffered an injury while helping to carry downstairs a patient who was seriously overweight, the only risk-free way of getting whom into the ambulance would have been to remove the window and call the fire brigade. The employer was held not liable: in the emergency services the duty of the employer to his employees is the same, but must be seen in the light of the concurrent duty to members of the public. *King v Sussex Ambulance NHS Trust* [2002] EWCA Civ 953.

NEGLIGENCE

WARD v HERTFORDSHIRE C.C.

Court of Appeal [1970] 1 W.L.R. 356; 114 S.J. 87; 68 L.G.R. 151; [1970] 1 All E.R. 535

Action for personal injuries by pupil against school

Lord Denning M.R.: On April 29, 1966, Mrs Ward took her two small children to the junior primary school at Sarratt in Hertfordshire. Timothy (the infant plaintiff) was about eight years of age, and Sarah five. She left them at the school at about 8.50 a.m. The school started at about 8.55 a.m. After she left them there, the infant plaintiff played with the other boys in the playground until school was ready. They decided to have a race up and down the playground. As the infant plaintiff was running, he tumbled. He tripped and fell against a wall at one side of the playground.

The wall was of a common type. It was built about 100 years ago. It had brick pillars and in between flints set in mortar. Just an ordinary flint wall. It was quite a low wall, 3 feet to 3 feet 6 inches high. The flints only came up to about 2 feet 3 inches above the ground, and there was a brick coping above. The infant plaintiff fell headlong, almost as it were diving into the wall. His head hit one of the flints. It must have had rather a sharp edge. He was seriously injured. Fortunately, he has made a remarkably good recovery. He had to have a plate put into his head, but he is now nearly normal. He can do most of the things a boy likes to do, except that he must not dive in the swimming bath, and he must not head the ball, and so forth. Naturally, the infant plaintiff's parents were very upset at this accident. They felt that the wall was dangerous; and, further, that there had not been proper supervision. So they brought this action against the local education authority for negligence and breach of duty.

The judge found ([1969] 1 W.L.R. 790 at 794) that the playground "with its flint walls and sharp and jagged flints protruding, was inherently dangerous"; and that the local education authority was wrong in allowing it to be in that condition. He said that it ought to have rendered the wall or put up some railings or netting, or something of that kind, to prevent a child falling against it. Furthermore, he held that one of the teachers ought to have been in the playground supervising from the time when the children came in. The local education authority appeals to this court.

I must say, reviewing all the evidence, that I do not think that this wall was dangerous. One has only to look at the pictures to see that it is a wall of the commonest type. It is an ordinary flint wall. It was built in the days when flints were picked off the ground and used to make walls. One-third of this Hertfordshire village has flint walls like this; 16 of the schools in Hertfordshire have; and goodness knows how many in the country at large. At that time all the church schools were made in this way. These flint walls have, of course, their angles and sharp edges. But that does not mean that they are dangerous. We have lived with them long enough to know.

The judge also held that there should have been supervision over the children in the playground. But I do not think that that was established. The headmaster said that the teachers took charge of the children from the moment they were due to be in school at 8.55 a.m. until the time when they were let out. Before the school began the staff were indoors preparing for the day's work. They cannot be expected to be in the playground, too. He said that even if he had been in the playground, he would not have stopped the children playing. It often happens that children run from one side of the playground to the other. It is impossible so to supervise them that they never fall down and hurt themselves. I cannot think that this accident shows any lack of supervision by the local education authority.

Great as is the respect which I have for the judge, I am afraid on this occasion I cannot go with him. It is a case where a small boy playing at school hurt himself badly, but the local education authority is not liable for it. . . .

Notes:

1. Things have come to a pretty pass when it can solemnly be argued that a local authority should put a fence round a wall, but the trial judge had "no hesitation at all in finding . . . that the defendant was guilty of a breach of its common law duty."

2. Another case in which the trial judge's finding of negligence was reversed is *Wilson v Governors of Sacred Heart Roman Catholic Primary School* [1997] Times L.R. 606. On the way to the school gate at the end of classes young Daniel, aged nine, was confronted by young Adam, waving his coat like a lasso. Struck in the eye by the coat, Daniel sued the school on the ground that an adult should have been supervising egress at the end of the school day and that his presence would have deterred Adam from such boisterous conduct. The trial judge's finding for the plaintiff was reversed: it was one thing—and standard practice—to have an adult supervise the busy playground at lunch, quite another to require supervision of the short period when the kids left school to go home.

3. Schools have been very much in the firing line of late:

(a) In *Kearn-Price v Kent CC* [2002] EWCA Civ 1539 the claimant pupil was struck in the face by a full-sized football in the school playground five minutes before classes started. There were over thirty teachers in the staff room but none in the playground. The use of full-sized footballs had been banned, but the ban had been poorly enforced. The Court of Appeal held that the school owed a duty of care to all those lawfully on the premises, and not just during school hours, and that in failing to enforce the ban it was in breach of that duty.

(b) In *Gough v Upshire Primary School* [2002] E.L.R. 169 an eight-year old pupil, out from class for a toilet trip, climbed on a banister of a stairway and fell twelve feet to the floor. The stairway and banister had been installed in 1939, consistently with building regulations then in force. There was no record of any previous accident, or dangerous propensity in the child or children. Of course it was foreseeable that someone might fall if they climbed on the banister, but no one had considered there to be a risk greater than many which existed on school premises, so the school was not guilty of negligence in failing to take preventative measures prior to the accident. Judgment for the defendant.

(c) A 17-year old on a school skiing trip had been seen skiing off-piste and was reprimanded but not otherwise punished. He was then injured skiing on the red piste. The Court of Appeal reversed the finding that the school should have taken more severe measures, such as withdrawing his ski pass or supervising him the whole time. *Chittock v Woodbridge School* [2002] EWCA Civ 915.

(d) After a picnic with his mother at a sports day the claimant was told to rejoin his teachers but went instead to a playground which was out of bounds, where, claiming to be Superman, he jumped off a swing and broke his arm. The trial judge held the school liable for not locking the swings, but on appeal (after the House of Lords had decided *Tomlinson*, next below!) the decision was reversed. *Simonds v Isle of Wight Council* [2003] EWHC 2303.

OCCUPIERS' LIABILITY ACT 1957

2.—(1) An occupier of premises owes the same duty, the "common duty of care," to all his visitors, except in so far as he is free to and does extend, restrict, modify or exclude his duty to any visitor or visitors by agreement or otherwise.

(2) The common duty of care is a duty to take such care as in all the circumstances of the case is reasonable to see that the visitor will be reasonably safe in using the premises for the purposes for which he is invited or permitted by the occupier to be there.

(3) The circumstances relevant for the present purpose include the degree of care, and of want of care, which would ordinarily be looked for in such a visitor, so that (for example) in proper cases—

(a) an occupier must be prepared for children to be less careful than adults; and

(b) an occupier may expect that a person, in the exercise of his calling, will appreciate and guard against any special risks ordinarily incident to it, so far as the occupier leaves him free to do so.

(4) In determining whether the occupier of premises has discharged the common duty of care to a visitor, regard is to be had to all the circumstances, so that (for example)—

(a) where damage is caused to a visitor by a danger of which he had been warned by the occupier, the warning is not to be treated without more as absolving the occupier from liability, unless in all the circumstances it was enough to enable the visitor to be reasonably safe; and

(b) where damage is caused to a visitor by a danger due to the faulty execution of any work of construction, maintenance or repair by an independent contractor employed by the occupier, the occupier is not to be treated without more as answerable for the danger if in all the circumstances he had acted reasonably in entrusting the work to an independent contractor and had taken such steps (if any) as he reasonably ought in order to satisfy himself that the contractor was competent and that the work had been properly done.

(5) The common duty of care does not impose on an occupier any obligation to a visitor in respect of risks willingly accepted as his by the visitor (the question whether a risk was so accepted to be decided on the same principles as in other cases in which one person owes a duty of care to another).

(6) For the purposes of this section, persons who enter premises for any purpose in the exercise of a right conferred by law are to be treated as permitted by the occupier to be there for that purpose, whether they in fact have his permission or not.

Notes:

1. The Act does not say who is to be treated as occupier or visitor, except that "A person entering any premises in exercise of rights conferred by virtue of (a) s.2(1) of the Countryside and Rights of Way Act 2000, or (b) an access agreement or order under the National Parks and Access to the Countryside Act 1949, is not . . . a visitor of the occupier of the premises." It is left to the common law to determine who is an occupier: see *Wheat v Lacon*, above p.35. The Act does, however, state what the occupier's duty is (s.2), and expressly displaces the common law in this regard (s.1(1)).

2. It cannot be too strongly emphasised that the occupier's duty is one calling for *positive action* on his part to remove and forestall dangers, and not just the (historically subsequent) *Donoghue v Stevenson* duty to refrain from causing harm. Many of the claims by pupils against their schools could have been (or were) brought under the Occupiers' Liability Act, but this is immaterial, since the duty of the school to its pupils, like that of the occupier to its visitors, is a duty to take positive, though reasonable, steps to see to their safety. Likewise the parent, though it is hard to see the child of the family as a "visitor" in the home.

3. It very often happens that a person employed by X is sent to work on premises occupied by Y and is injured there. The victim often has concurrent claims against both his employer (whose duty of care to him is non-delegable) and the occupier (whose duty is not); both may well be subject to statutory safety regulations whose breach leads to liability in damages. At common law the employer must take reasonable steps to see that the premises to which the employee is sent are reasonably safe, but will not be liable for transient dangers (compare the position of the landlord in *Wheat v Lacon* above p.35, and see *Barr v Coventry and Solihull Waste Disposal* [2002] EWCA Civ 863). In *Andrews v Initial Cleaning Services* [1999] Times L.R. 614, for example, an employee of a cleaning firm was injured when the sink in the cleaning cupboard in the customer's building came away from the wall. The room was set aside for the use of the cleaners, but the key was kept by the customer, whose employees could also use the room. A senior employee of the cleaning firm was aware that the sink was loose, but the customer was not. The trial judge apportioned liability as between occupier and employer in the proportion 1:3, but the Court of Appeal altered this to 3:1.

4. A very different position emerged from *Fairchild* in the Court of Appeal where the occupier was held not liable to the employees of a subcontractor who got mesothelioma from the asbestos dust which was floating around the premises as a result of the work going on—a point on which there was no appeal. The decision turns on an extraordinary (mis)interpretation of the 1957 Act. Although the Act says in terms that it replaces (*i.e.* ousts, sidelines, airbrushes) the common law relating to the occupier's duty to a visitor (and makes this clear by laying down that if there is a contract, the term to be implied, contrary to the previous common law, is the common duty of care), the courts insist that common law duties survive. It is true that one of Lord Denning's contributions to the law was to say that a common law duty regarding activities concurred with the occupier's duty as such, but this was prior to the Act and his purpose was to improve the position of the licensee, to whom the occupier's common law duty was weaker than both his duty to the invitee and the duty under *Donoghue v Stevenson*. The discrimination against the licensee was removed by the 1957 Act, but even so the courts seem determined to follow the alleged distinction between the "activity" duty and the "occupancy" duty, contrary to the very clear terms of the statute, which manifestly amalgamates them ("dangers due to the state of the premises or to things done or omitted to be done on them").

The question whether an occupier could be liable to the employee of a subcontractor working on the premises was raised in the confused decision in *Ferguson v Welsh* [1987] 1 W.L.R. 1553 (HL). Lord Goff (alone) gave a remarkable interpretation to s.2(2) of the Act, saying that the contractor's employee could not be said to be "using" the premises and that the duty applies only if the visitor is not reasonably safe "in using the premises for the purposes for which he is invited or permitted to be there." Lord Goff said: " . . . if I ask myself . . . whether it can be said that [the subcontractor's employee] arose from a failure by the [occupier] to take reasonable care to see that persons in his position would be reasonably safe in using the premises for the relevant purposes, the answer must, I think, be no. There is no question, as I see it, of his injury arising from any such failure; for it arose not from his use of the premises but for the manner in which he carried out his work on the premises." Although none of his colleagues in the House adverted to this peculiar reading of the enactment, the Court of Appeal in *Fairchild* could see "nothing in the speeches of the other members of the House which casts any doubt on the correctness of Lord Goff's interpretation of s.2(2)" and proceeded to hold that "The Act does not provide an answer when a question arises whether an occupier, without more, is liable to a visitor for an injury he suffers as a result of an activity conducted by a third party on the premises. For that purpose one has to go to the common law to see if a duty of care exists and, if so, what is its scope . . . " The writer of the biblical *Proverbs* found three or four things too wonderful for him, including the way of an eagle in the air and the way of a man with a maid (*Proverbs* 30.18); we must add the way of the courts with a statute.

But if a main general contractor in occupation of a building site usually owes no duty to the employees of a subcontractor except as regards the safety of the premises, as held in *Makepeace v Evans Bros.* [2001] I.C.R. 241 when a scaffolding tower without inherent defect supplied by the main contractor collapsed and injured a subcontractor's employee working on it, it being the responsibility of the subcontractor to take care that his employees could use it safely, nevertheless the main contractor would be liable for supplying a device which, though not defective, was not suitable for the job: *McGarvey v EVE NCI Ltd* [2002] EWCA Civ 374.

Given that the duty imposed on the occupier is only one to take reasonable care to see that the visitor is reasonably safe, it would do no harm to apply the Act according to its terms, for it may be perfectly reasonable for the occupier to delegate to his contractor the task, already his, of seeing to the safety of this employees. Likewise in *Gwilliam v West Herts. Hospital NHS Trust* [2003] Q.B. 443 the organiser of a summer fun-fair was not liable when a 63-year old participant was injured on a "splat-wall" (throw yourself off a trampoline and hope that Velcro will stick you to the wall!) which an independent entertainment company had set up negligently: the occupier had done enough to check the company's reliability and though it had no insurance cover (which was the claimant's principal complaint) the defendant had fulfilled its duty to check that, too, though according to Sedley L.J. "To construe the duty to ensure that a visitor is reasonably safe from harm at the hands of a third party as embracing a duty to ensure that she is reasonably safe from the consequences of the third party's being uninsured is . . . unprecedented."

5. Any mild surprise that occupier's liability should form a separate sub-chapter of the law of tort may be allayed by considering that as to the *locus in quo* of accidents, there are only three possibilities: the victim is injured either at home, on the highway, or on someone else's premises. We shall see to the liability of the highway authority after considering decisions on the occupier's liability.

TOMLINSON v CONGLETON BOROUGH COUNCIL

House of Lords [2003] UKHL 47; [2004] 1 A.C 46; [2003] 3 W.L.R. 705; [2003] 3 All E.R. 1122

One afternoon on a warm Bank Holiday weekend an 18-year old repaired, as he had done since childhood, to the Brereton Heath Country Park where there was a 14-acre lake bordered by sandy banks. After sitting in the sun for a while he ran, and then plunged prone, into the water. His head struck the sandy bottom rather hard and his neck broke.

The Council as occupier had tried to prevent swimming by prohibition, but this having failed it decided to make it impossible by planting vegetation so as to inhibit access to the water, a decision, still unimplemented, which was taken expressly in order to avoid accidents and possible liability in damages.

Jack J. dismissed the claim; the Court of Appeal, by a majority, reversed; the House of Lords allowed the defendant's appeal and reinstated the judgment of Jack J.

Lord Hoffmann: . . . It is a terrible tragedy to suffer such dreadful injury in consequence of a relatively minor act of carelessness. It came nowhere near the stupidity of Luke Ratcliff, a student who climbed a fence at 2.30 am on a December morning to take a running dive into the shallow end of a swimming pool (see *Ratcliff v McConnell* [1999] 1 W.L.R. 670) or John Donoghue, who dived into Folkestone Harbour from a slipway at midnight on 27 December after an evening in the pub (*Donoghue v Folkestone Properties Ltd* [2003] 2 W.L.R. 1138). John Tomlinson's mind must often recur to that hot day which irretrievably changed his life. He may feel, not unreasonably, that fate has dealt with him unfairly. And so in these proceedings he seeks financial compensation: for the loss of his earning capacity, for the expense of the care he will need, for the loss of the ability to lead an ordinary life. But the law does not provide such compensation simply on the basis that the injury was disproportionately severe in relation to one's own fault or even not one's own fault at all. Perhaps it should, but society might not be able to afford to compensate everyone on that principle, certainly at the level at which such compensation is now paid. The law provides compensation only when the injury was someone else's fault. In order to succeed in his claim, that is what Mr Tomlinson has to prove.

In these proceedings Mr Tomlinson sues the Congleton Borough Council and the Cheshire County Council, claiming that as occupiers of the Park they were in breach of their duties under the Occupiers' Liability Acts 1957 and 1984.

The 1957 Act was passed to amend and codify the common law duties of occupiers to certain persons who came upon their land. The common law had distinguished between invitees, in whose visit the occupier had some material interest, and licensees, who came simply by express or implied permission. Different duties were owed to each class. The Act amalgamated (without redefining) the two common law categories, designated the combined class "visitors" (s.1(2)) and provided that (subject to contrary agreement) all visitors should be owed a "common duty of care". That duty is set out in s.2(2), as refined by subss.2(3) to (5).

At first Mr Tomlinson claimed that the Council was in breach of its common duty of care under s.2(2). His complaint was that the premises were not reasonably safe because diving into the water was dangerous and the Council had not given adequate warning of this fact or taken sufficient steps to prevent or discourage him from doing it. But then a difficulty emerged. The County Council, as manager of the Park, had for many years pursued a policy of prohibiting swimming. Notices had been erected at the entrance and elsewhere saying "Dangerous Water. No Swimming". The Council said that once he entered the lake to swim, he was no longer a "visitor" at all. He became a trespasser, to whom no duty under the 1957 Act is owed. The Council cited a famous *bon mot* of Scrutton L.J. in *The Calgarth* [1927] P. 93, 110: "When you invite a person into your house to use the staircase, you do not invite him to slide down the banisters". Similarly, says the Council, Mr Tomlinson became a trespasser and took himself outside the 1957 Act when he entered the water to swim.

Mr Tomlinson's advisers, having reflected on the matter, decided to concede that he was indeed a trespasser when he went into the water. Although that took him outside the 1957 Act, it did not necessarily mean that the Council owed him no duty. At common law the only duty to trespassers was not to cause them deliberate or reckless injury, but after an inconclusive attempt by the House of Lords to modify this rule in *British Railways Board v Herrington* [1972] A.C. 877, the Law Commission recommended the creation of a statutory duty to trespassers and the recommendation was given effect by the Occupiers' Liability Act 1984. Section 1(1) describes the purpose of the Act: "1. (1) The rules enacted by this section shall have effect, in place of the rules of the common law, to determine—(a) whether any duty is owed by a person as occupier of premises to persons other than his visitors in respect of any risk of their suffering injury on the premises by reason of any danger due to the state of the premises or to things done or omitted to be done on them.

The case has therefore proceeded upon a concession that the relevant duty, if any, is that to a trespasser under s.1(4) of the 1984 Act and not to a lawful visitor under s.2(2) of the 1957 Act.

The duty under the 1984 Act was intended to be a lesser duty, as to both incidence and scope, than the duty to a lawful visitor under the 1957 Act. That was because Parliament recognised that it would often be unduly burdensome to require landowners to take steps to protect the safety of people who came upon their land without invitation or permission. They should not ordinarily be able to force duties upon unwilling hosts. In the application of that principle, I can see no difference between a person who comes upon land without permission and one who, having come with permission, does something which he has not been given permission to do. In both cases, the entrant would be imposing upon the landowner a duty of care which he has not expressly or impliedly accepted. The 1984 Act provides that even in such cases a duty may exist, based simply upon occupation of land and knowledge or foresight that unauthorised persons may come upon the land or authorised persons may use it for unauthorised purposes. But that duty is rarer and different in quality from the duty which arises from express or implied invitation or permission to come upon the land and use it. I shall later return to the question of whether it would have made any difference if swimming had not been prohibited and the 1957 Act had applied.

My Lords, the majority of the Court of Appeal appear to have proceeded on the basis that if there was a foreseeable risk of serious injury, the Council was under a duty to do what was necessary to prevent it. But this in my opinion is an oversimplification. Even in the case of the duty owed to a lawful visitor under s.2(2) of the 1957 Act and even if the risk had been attributable to the state of the premises rather than the acts of Mr Tomlinson, the question of what amounts to "such care as in all the circumstances of the case is reasonable" depends upon assessing, as in the case of common law negligence, not only the likelihood that someone may be injured and the seriousness of the injury which may occur, but also the social value of the activity which gives rise to the risk and the cost of preventative measures. These factors have to be balanced against each other. For example, in *Overseas Tankship (UK) Ltd v Miller Steamship Pty Ltd (The Wagon Mound (No.2))* [1967] 1 A.C. 617, there was no social value or cost saving in the defendant's activity. So the defendants were held liable for damage which was only a very remote possibility. Similarly in *Jolley v Sutton London B.C.* [2000] 1 W.L.R. 1082 there was no social value or cost saving to the Council in creating a risk by leaving a derelict boat lying about. It was something which they ought to have removed whether it created a risk of injury or not. So they were held liable for an injury which, though foreseeable, was not particularly likely. On the other hand, in *Bolton v Stone* [1951] A.C. 850 the House of Lords held that it was not negligent for a cricket club to do nothing about the risk of someone being injured by a cricket ball hit out of the ground. The difference was that the cricket club were carrying on a lawful and socially useful activity and would have had to stop playing cricket at that ground.

This is the kind of balance which has to be struck even in a situation in which it is clearly fair, just and reasonable that there should in principle be a duty of care or in which Parliament, as in the 1957 Act, has decreed that there should be. And it may lead to the conclusion that even though injury is foreseeable, as it was in *Bolton v Stone*, it is still in all the circumstances reasonable to do nothing about it.

In the case of the 1984 Act, there is the additional consideration that unless in all the circumstances it is reasonable to expect the occupier to do something, that is to say, to "offer the other some protection", there is no duty at all. One may ask what difference there is between the case in which the claimant is a lawful visitor and there is in principle a duty under the 1957 Act but on the particular facts no duty to do anything, and the case in which he is a trespasser and there is on the particular facts no duty under the 1984 Act. Of course in such a case the result is the same. But Parliament has made it clear that in the case of a lawful visitor, one starts from the assumption that there is a duty whereas in the case of a trespasser one starts from the assumption that there is none.

My Lords, it will in the circumstances be convenient to consider first the question of what the position would have been if Mr Tomlinson had been a lawful visitor owed a duty under s.2(2) of the 1957 Act. Assume, therefore, that there had been no prohibition on swimming. What was the risk of serious injury? To some extent this depends upon what one regards as the relevant risk. I do not want to put the basis of my decision too narrowly, so I accept that we are concerned with the steps, if any, which should have been taken to prevent any kind of water accident. According to the Royal Society for the Prevention of Accidents, about 450 people drown while swimming in the United Kingdom every year. About 25–35 break their necks diving and no doubt others sustain less serious injuries. So there is obviously some degree of risk in swimming and diving, as there is in climbing, cycling, fell walking and many other such activities.

I turn then to the cost of taking preventative measures. Ward L.J. described it (£5,000) as "not excessive". Perhaps it was not, although the outlay has to be seen in the context of the other items (rated "essential" and "highly desirable") in the Borough Council budget which had taken precedence over the destruction of the beaches for the previous two years.

I do not however regard the financial cost as a significant item in the balancing exercise which the court has to undertake. There are two other related considerations which are far more important. The first is the social value of the activities which would have to be prohibited in order to reduce or eliminate the risk from swimming. And the second is the question of whether the Council should be entitled to allow people of full capacity to decide for themselves whether to take the risk.

The Court of Appeal made no reference at all to the social value of the activities which were to be prohibited. The majority of people who went to the beaches to sunbathe, paddle and play with their children were enjoying themselves in a way which gave them pleasure and caused no risk to themselves or anyone else. This must be something to be taken into account in deciding whether it was reasonable to expect the Council to destroy the beaches.

I have the impression that the Court of Appeal felt able to brush these matters aside because the Council had already decided to do the work. But they were held liable for having failed to do so before Mr Tomlinson's accident and the question is therefore whether they were under a legal duty to do so. Ward L.J. placed much emphasis upon the fact that the Council had decided to destroy the beaches and that its officers thought that this was necessary to avoid being held liable for an accident to a swimmer. But the fact that the Council's safety officers thought that the work was necessary does not show that there was a legal duty to do it. In *Darby v National Trust* [2001] P.I.Q.R. 372 the claimant's husband was tragically drowned while swimming in a pond on the National Trust estate at Hardwick Hall. Miss Rebecca Kirkwood, the Water and Leisure Safety Consultant to the Royal Society for the Prevention of Accidents, gave uncontradicted evidence, which the judge accepted, that the pond was unsuitable for swimming because it was deep in the middle and the edges were uneven. The National Trust should have made it clear that swimming in the pond was not allowed and taken steps to enforce the prohibition. But May L.J. said robustly that it was for the court, not Miss Kirkwood, to decide whether the Trust was under a legal duty to take such steps. There was no duty because the risks from swimming in the pond were perfectly obvious.

The second consideration, namely the question of whether people should accept responsibility for the risks they choose to run, is the point made by Lord Phillips of Worth Matravers M.R. in *Donoghue v Folkestone Properties Ltd* [2003] 2 W.L.R. 1138, 1153 and which I said was central to this appeal. Mr Tomlinson was freely and voluntarily undertaking an activity which inherently involved some risk. By contrast, Miss Bessie Stone, to whom the House of Lords held that no duty was owed, was innocently standing on the pavement outside her garden gate at 10 Beckenham Road, Cheetham when she was struck by a ball hit for 6 out of the Cheetham Cricket Club ground. She was certainly not engaging in any activity which involved an inherent risk of such injury. So compared with *Bolton v Stone*, this is an *a fortiori* case.

I think it will be extremely rare for an occupier of land to be under a duty to prevent people from taking risks which are inherent in the activities they freely choose to undertake upon the land. If people want to climb mountains, go hang gliding or swim or dive in ponds or lakes, that is their affair. Of course the landowner may for his own reasons wish to prohibit such activities. He may be think that they are a danger or inconvenience to himself or others. Or he may take a paternalist view and prefer people not to undertake risky activities on his land. He is entitled to impose such conditions, as the Council did by prohibiting swimming. But the law does not require him to do so.

My Lords, as will be clear from what I have just said, I think that there is an important question of freedom at stake. It is unjust that the harmless recreation of responsible parents and children with buckets and spades on the beaches should be prohibited in order to comply with what is thought to be a legal duty to safeguard irresponsible visitors against dangers which are perfectly obvious. The fact that such people take no notice of warnings cannot create a duty to take other steps to protect them. I find it difficult to express with appropriate moderation my disagreement with the proposition of Sedley L.J. that it is "only where the risk is so obvious that the occupier can safely assume that nobody will take it that there will be no liability". A duty to protect against obvious risks or self-inflicted harm exists only in cases in which there is no genuine and informed choice, as in the case of employees, or some lack of capacity, such as the inability of children to recognise danger (*British Railways Board v Herrington* [1972] A.C. 877) or the despair of prisoners which may lead them to inflict injury on themselves (*Reeves v Commissioner of Police* [2000] 1 A.C. 360).

It is of course understandable that organisations like the Royal Society for the Prevention of Accidents should favour policies which require people to be prevented from taking risks. Their function is to prevent accidents and that is one way of doing so. But they do not have to consider the cost, not only in money but also in deprivation of liberty, which such restrictions entail. The courts will naturally respect the technical expertise of such organisations in drawing attention to what can be done to prevent accidents. But the balance between risk on the one hand and individual autonomy on the other is not a matter of expert opinion. It is a judgment which the courts must make and which in England reflects the individualist values of the common law.

As for the Council officers, they were obviously motivated by the view that it was necessary to take defensive measures to prevent the Council from being held liable to pay compensation. The Borough Leisure Officer said that he regretted the need to destroy the beaches but saw no alternative if the Council was not to be held liable for an accident to a swimmer. So this appeal gives your Lordships the opportunity to say clearly that local authorities and other occupiers of land are ordinarily under no duty to incur such social and financial costs to protect a minority (or even a majority) against obvious dangers. On the other hand, if the decision of the Court of Appeal were left standing, every such occupier would feel obliged to take similar defensive measures. Sedley L.J. was able to say that if the logic of the Court of Appeal's decision was that other public lakes and ponds required similar precautions, "so be it". But I cannot view this prospect with the same equanimity. In my opinion it would damage the quality of many people's lives.

My Lords, for these reasons I consider that even if swimming had not been prohibited and the Council had owed a duty under s.2(2) of the 1957 Act, that duty would not have required them to take any steps to prevent Mr Tomlinson from diving or warning him against dangers which were perfectly obvious. If that is the case, then plainly there can have been no duty under the 1984 Act. The risk was not one against which he was entitled under s.1(3)© to protection. I would therefore allow the appeal and restore the decision of Jack J.

Lord Hobhouse: The fourth point, one to which I know that your Lordships attach importance, is the fact that it is not, and should never be, the policy of the law to require the protection of the foolhardy or reckless few to deprive, or interfere with, the enjoyment by the remainder of society of the liberties and amenities to which they are rightly entitled. Does the law require that all trees be cut down because some youths may climb them and fall? Does the law require the coast line and other beauty spots to be lined with warning notices? Does the law require that attractive water side picnic spots be destroyed because of a few foolhardy individuals who choose to ignore warning notices and indulge in activities dangerous only to themselves? The answer to all these questions is, of course, no. But this is the road down which your Lordships, like other courts before, have been invited to travel and which the Council in the present case found so inviting. In truth, the arguments for the claimant have involved an attack upon the liberties of the citizen which should not be countenanced. They attack the liberty of the individual to engage in dangerous, but otherwise harmless, pastimes at his own risk and the liberty of citizens as a whole fully to enjoy the variety and quality of the landscape of this country. The pursuit of an unrestrained culture of blame and compensation has many evil consequences and one is certainly the interference with the liberty of the citizen.

Lord Scott of Foscote: I have had the advantage of reading in draft the opinion of my noble and learned friend Lord Hoffmann. Subject to one reservation I am in complete agreement with the reasons he gives for allowing this appeal. But I find myself in such fundamental disagreement with the approach to this case by the majority in the Court of Appeal that I want to add, also, a few comments of my own.

My reservation is that the Act which must be applied to the facts of this case in order to decide whether the Council is under any liability to Mr Tomlinson is, in my opinion, the Occupiers' Liability Act 1957, not the 1984 Act.

Mr Tomlinson did not suffer his tragic accident while swimming in the lake. He ran into the water and, when the depth of the water was at mid-thigh level, executed the disastrous "dive" and suffered the accident. At no stage did he swim. It may be that his "dive" was preparatory to swimming. But swimming in water not much above knee level, say 2 feet 6 inches deep, is difficult. In any event, Mr Tomlinson's injury was not caused while he was swimming and cannot be attributed in any way to the dangers of swimming. His complaint against the Council is that the Council did not take reasonable care to discourage him while in the shallows of the lake from executing a "dive". If the "dive" was, which I regard as doubtful for the reasons given, a preliminary to an attempt to swim, the complaint may be regarded as a complaint that the Council failed to prevent him from becoming a trespasser. But this must necessarily, in my view, have been a duty owed to him while he was a visitor.

Lord Nicholls agreed with **Lord Hoffmann**, and **Lord Hutton** gave a concurring speech.

HIGHWAYS ACT 1980

41.—(1) The . . . highway authority for a highway maintainable at public expense are under a duty . . . to maintain the highway.

(1A) In particular, a highway authority are under a duty to ensure, so far as is reasonably practicable, that safe passage along a highway is not endangered by snow or ice.

58.—(1) In an action against a highway authority in respect of damage resulting from their failure to maintain a highway maintainable at the public expense it is a defence (without prejudice to any other defence or the application of the law relating to contributory negligence) to prove that the authority had taken such care as in all the circumstances was reasonably required to secure that the part of the highway to which the action relates was not dangerous for traffic.

(2) For the purposes of a defence under subsection (1) above, the court shall in particular have regard to the following matters:

(a) the character of the highway, and the traffic which was reasonably to be expected to use it;

(b) the standard of maintenance appropriate for a highway of that character and used by such traffic;

(c) the state of repair in which a reasonable person would have expected to find the highway;

(d) whether the highway authority knew, or could reasonably have been expected to know, that the condition of the part of the highway to which the action relates was likely to cause danger to users of the highway;

(e) where the highway authority could not reasonably have been expected to repair that part of the highway before the cause of action arose, what warning notices of its condition had been displayed;

but for the purposes of such a defence it is not relevant to prove that the highway authority had arranged for a competent person to carry out or supervise the maintenance of the part of the highway to which the action relates unless it is also proved that the authority had given him proper instructions with regard to the maintenance of the highway and that he had carried out the instructions.

Notes:
1. Section 41(1A) was added in 2003. Its effect is to reverse the recent House of Lords decision in *Goodes v East Sussex C.C.* [2000] 3 All E.R. 603. That decision had held, following the minority view of Lord Denning in *Haydon v Kent C.C.* [1978] Q.B. 343, that the duty under s.41(1) (which is absolute, subject to the defence of s.58) did not extend to the removal of snow and ice and similar superficial matters not affecting

the physical fabric of the highway: "maintenance" covered fixing but not cleaning or clearing. The statutory amendment appears to introduce a duty which (a) is slightly less than absolute, in that it is a duty to do what is practicable rather than a duty to maintain unless one can show that it was not practicable, and (b) is limited to snow and ice (unless, improbably, the words "in particular" can be treated as coming between "endangered" and "snow or ice"). *Goodes* will accordingly continue to apply where an accident is due to superficial hazards such as pools of water, patches of mud or runnels of slurry. A duty to remove obstructions is certainly imposed by s.150, which mentions accumulations of snow, but this duty is enforceable only through the magistrates and breach of it gives rise to no civil liability.

2. Even as to maintenance, it is not required that the highway be rendered absolutely safe. A person who slips and falls on the pavement must show that that very part of the pavement was dangerous, a conclusion not inferable from the mere fact of the accident (*Meggs v Liverpool Corp.* [1968] 1 All E.R. 1137). "In one sense" said Lloyd L.J. in *James v Preseli Pembrokeshire D.C.* [1993] P.I.Q.R. 114, "it is reasonably foreseeable that any defect in the highway, however slight, may cause an injury. But that is not the test of what is meant by "dangerous" in this context. It must be the sort of danger which an authority may reasonably be expected to guard against. There must . . . be a reasonable balance between private and public interest in these matters." The decision in favour of a plaintiff who had tripped in Market Street, Barnsley, in a hole two inches across and one and a quarter inches deep, was reversed.

3. The duty is to maintain the highway in order to make it safe, not to make it passable: thus a dairy farm which lost business because milk tankers couldn't reach it by road had no claim (*Wentworth v Wilts. C.C.* [1993] 2 All E.R. 256, CA). Furthermore the duty applies only to the highway, not to neighbouring land: *Stovin v Wise* (above, p.89).

4. As we have seen, the highway authority is not liable as occupier, but it may well be subject to other duties. In *Lavis v Kent C.C.* (1992) 90 L.G.R. 416 it was held arguable that the authority might be liable at common law for failure to erect a warning sign at a sudden sharp bend, but at trial ([1994] Times L.R. 600) it was held that this fell within the policy area of decision-making and the injured motorcyclist was denied damages.

5. The highways which the authority is under a duty to maintain are patrolled by the police. The police are not, apparently, under a duty to report dangers they observe (*Ancell v McDermott* [1993] 4 All E.R. 355), but once they take control, responsibility may attach. Thus in *Gibson v Chief Constable* [1999] Times L.R. 357, OH when a bridge collapsed and a policeman took control but later left the scene without putting up cones, barriers or other warning signs, a duty was held to exist. Clearer (because of the creation of the danger) is *Cassin v Bexley L.B.C.* [1999] Times L.R. 113 where, by agreement with the police, the local authority removed "Keep Left" bollards lest they be used as missiles by fans at a forthcoming football match, and the plaintiff motorcyclist collided with one of the plinths. Held that the local authority should have closed the road or put up warning signs. More doubtful is the imposition of liability on the authority in an earlier case where vandals removed warning signs from a road hazard at a time when the council nightwatchman was on his rounds of other sites.

GLASGOW CORP. v MUIR

House of Lords [1943] A.C. 448; 112 L.J.P.C. 1; 169 L.T. 53; 107 J.P. 140; 59 T.L.R. 266; 87 S.J. 182; 41 L.G.R. 173; [1943] 2 All E.R. 44

Action by visitor against occupier in respect of personal injury

One Saturday afternoon in June 1940 a party of 30 to 40 members of the Milton Road Free Church were to have a picnic in the King's Park, Glasgow. It came on to rain, so their leader, McDonald, went to the defender's tearooms and asked the manageress, Mrs Alexander, if they might eat their food there. Mrs Alexander agreed, and charged them 12s. 6d. She then went back to serving a group of children at the sweet counter in the hall. McDonald and a boy of his party accordingly brought the urn of tea down to the building. As they entered the hall, the children at the sweet counter were about five feet away from them, and Mrs Alexander had her back to the scene as she was scooping ice-cream from the freezer. McDonald suddenly lost his grip on the back handle of the urn and six children, including the pursuer, were scalded by its contents.

No one knew why McDonald lost his grip on the urn, since the pursuer did not call him as a witness. The urn itself was a perfectly ordinary metal one with a lid, about 16 inches high, 15 inches in diameter, and weighing, when full, not more than 100 pounds.

After the evidence, the Lord Ordinary dismissed the action; the First Division of the Court of Session (the Lord President dissenting) allowed the pursuer's appeal, 1942 S.C. 126. The Corporation appealed to the House of Lords, who allowed the appeal.

Lord Macmillan: My Lords, the degree of care for the safety of others which the law requires human beings to observe in the conduct of their affairs varies according to the circumstances. There is no absolute standard, but it may be said generally that the degree of care required varies directly with the risk involved. Those who engage in operations inherently dangerous must take precautions which are not required of persons engaged in the ordinary routine of daily life. It is, no doubt, true that in every act which an individual performs there is present a potentiality of injury to others. All things are possible, and, indeed, it has become proverbial that the unexpected always happens, but, while the precept *alterum non laedere* requires us to abstain from intentionally injuring others, it does not impose liability for every injury which our conduct may occasion. In Scotland, at any rate, it has never been a maxim of the law that a man acts at his peril. Legal liability is limited to those consequences of our acts which a reasonable man of ordinary intelligence and experience so acting would have in contemplation. "The duty to take care," as I essayed to formulate it in *Bourhill v Young* ([1943] A.C. 92 at 104), "is the duty to avoid doing or omitting to do anything the doing or omitting to do which may have as its reasonable and probable consequence injury to others, and the duty is owed to those to whom injury may reasonably and probably be anticipated if the duty is not observed." This, in my opinion, expresses the law of Scotland and I apprehend that it is also the law of England. The standard of foresight of the reasonable man is, in one sense, an impersonal test. It eliminates the personal equation and is independent of the idiosyncrasies of the particular person whose conduct is in question. Some persons are by nature unduly timorous and imagine every path beset with lions. Others, of more robust temperament, fail to foresee or nonchalantly disregard even the most obvious dangers. The reasonable man is presumed to be free both from over-apprehension and from over-confidence, but there is a sense in which the standard of care of the reasonable man involves in its application a subjective element. It is still left to the judge to decide what, in the circumstances of the particular case, the reasonable man would have had in contemplation, and what, accordingly, the party sought to be made liable ought to have foreseen. Here there is room for diversity of view, as, indeed, is well illustrated in the present case. What to one judge may seem far-fetched may seem to another both natural and probable.

With these considerations in mind I turn to the facts of the occurrence on which your Lordships have to adjudicate. Up to a point the facts have been sufficiently ascertained ... The question, as I see it, is whether Mrs Alexander, when she was asked to allow a tea urn to be brought into the premises under her charge, ought to have had in mind that it would require to be carried through a narrow passage in which there were a number of children and that there would be a risk of the contents of the urn being spilt and scalding some of the children. If, as a reasonable person, she ought to have had these considerations in mind, was it her duty to require that she should be informed of the arrival of the urn, and, before allowing it to be carried through the narrow passage, to clear all the children out of it in case they might be splashed with scalding water? The urn was an ordinary medium-sized cylindrical vessel of about 15 inches diameter and about 16 inches in height made of light sheet metal with a fitting lid, which was closed. It had a handle at each side. Its capacity was about nine gallons, but it was only a third or a half full. It was not in itself an inherently dangerous thing and could be carried quite safely and easily by two persons exercising ordinary care. A caterer called as a witness on behalf of the pursuers, who had large experience of the use of such urns, said that he had never had a mishap with an urn while it was being carried. The urn was in charge of two responsible persons, McDonald, the church officer, and the lad, Taylor, who carried it between them. When they entered the passage way they called out to the children there congregated to keep out of the way and the children drew back to let them pass. Taylor, who held the front handle, had safely passed the children, when, for some unexplained reason, McDonald loosened hold of the other handle, the urn tilted over, and some of its contents were spilt, scalding several of the children who were standing by. The urn was not upset, but came to the ground on its base.

In my opinion, Mrs Alexander had no reason to anticipate that such an event would happen as a consequence of granting permission for a tea urn to be carried through the passage way where the children were congregated, and, consequently, there was no duty incumbent on her to take precautions against the occurrence of such an event. I think that she was entitled to assume that the urn would be in charge of responsible persons (as it was) who would have regard for the safety of the children in the passage (as they did have regard), and that the urn would be carried with ordinary care, in which case its transit would occasion no danger to bystanders. The pursuers have left quite unexplained the actual cause of the accident. The immediate cause was not the carrying of the urn through the passage, but McDonald's losing grip of his handle. How he came to do so is entirely a matter of speculation. He may have stumbled or he may have suffered a temporary muscular failure. We do not know, and the pursuers have not chosen to enlighten us by calling McDonald as a witness. Yet it is argued that Mrs Alexander ought to have foreseen the possibility, nay, the reasonable probability of an occurrence the nature of which is unascertained. Suppose that McDonald let go his handle through carelessness. Was Mrs Alexander bound to foresee this as reasonably probable and to take precautions against the possible consequences? I do not think so. The only ground on which the view of the majority of the learned judges of the First Division can be justified is that Mrs Alexander ought to have foreseen that some accidental injury might happen to the children in the passage if she allowed an urn containing hot tea to be carried through the passage, and ought, therefore, to have cleared out the children entirely during its transit, which Lord Moncrieff describes as "the only effective step." With all respect, I think that this would impose on Mrs Alexander a degree of care higher than the law exacts. . . .

Lord Wright: . . . It is true that the accident could not have occurred but for the action of Mrs Alexander, the appellants' manageress, in giving permission that the tea urn should be carried through the short but narrow passage in which the children, about a dozen in number, were waiting as customers at the appellants' sweet counter to buy ices or sweets, but, to establish liability, the court has to be satisfied that the appellants owed a duty to the children, that that duty was broken, and that the children were injured in consequence of the breach.

That the appellants owed a duty to the children is not open to question. . . . The question is whether Mrs Alexander knew or ought to have known that what she was permitting involved danger to the children. . . . It is not a question of what Mrs Alexander actually foresaw, but what the hypothetical reasonable person in Mrs Alexander's situation would have foreseen. The test is what she ought to have foreseen. . . .

In the present case, as the permitted operation was intrinsically innocuous, I do not think any obligation rested on Mrs Alexander to attempt to supervise it. As a reasonable person, not having any ground for anticipating harm, she was entitled to go on with her proper work and leave the church party to do what was proper. There might, of course, be circumstances in which, because there was an obvious risk, a duty might rest on the occupier to supervise the actual conducting of the operation if the permission was given. I do not see what Mrs Alexander could have done in that respect unless she had seen that all the children were removed from the passage when the urn was being carried through. That might be her obligation if the operation she permitted had been intrinsically dangerous, but it was not so in the circumstances as I apprehend them. No doubt, some difficult questions of fact may arise in these cases. In the present case, however, as I think that there was no reasonably foreseeable danger to the children from the use of the premises which the appellants permitted to be made, I think the respondents' claim cannot be supported. In my judgment the appeal should be allowed.

Questions:

1. Would the defenders have been liable if the urn had been carried in and dropped by a catering firm under contract with them?

2. Could the defenders have been held liable here without also making liable the inn-keeper whose guest drives his car into the car of another guest in the car-park?

3. Is it significant that Lord Macmillan said that Mrs Alexander was under no duty "to take precautions", whereas Lord Wright said "That the appellants owed a duty to the children is not open to question."?

Note:

McDonald would have been liable, because he could foresee that *if* he was careless the children might well be hurt, and he *was* careless. Mrs Alexander could equally well foresee that *if* McDonald were careless the children might be hurt, but *she* was not careless, since she could not foresee that McDonald would in fact be clumsy, and only such a premonition would require her to put the children out in the rain.

Sometimes, however, one must foresee the carelessness of others. It is not careful to act on the assumption that other people will be careful when it is known that they are not. Drivers do in fact emerge without warning from side-roads. In *London Passenger Transport Board v Upson* [1949] A.C. 155 at 173, Lord Uthwatt said: "A driver is not, of course, bound to anticipate folly in all its forms, but he is not, in my opinion, entitled to put out of consideration the teachings of experience as to the form those follies commonly take." Note that in this case what was alleged was a positive act of misfeasance, namely giving permission for the urn to be brought into the crowded tearoom.

The occupier may well, however, be liable for negligently failing to prevent deliberate injury done by one visitor to another: *Ellis v Home Office* (prison liable for injury done by one prisoner to another) was referred to in *Dorset Yacht* (above p.84). In *Cunningham v Reading FC* [1991] Times L.R. 153 the club was held liable to policemen injured by (mainly Bristol) fans who threw at them pieces of the underfoot concrete which could easily be prised up, as had been shown in the last riot four months previously. (But why did the policemen not claim under the Criminal Injuries Compensation Scheme?)

BELL v DEPARTMENT OF HEALTH AND SOCIAL SECURITY

Queen's Bench, *The Times*, June 13, 1989

Action by employee against employer in respect of personal injury

Drake J. said that the plaintiff was a married lady, aged 56, who had since 1974 been employed by the defendant department in a four-storey office block.

The department did not provide tea or coffee or utensils for their employees there; but they did provide employees with hot water to make their own drinks from a kitchen on the fourth floor.

There were two lifts: a small, automatic one, with a door operated by a push-button, and a larger lift whose doors had to be pulled to and fro by hand.

Some employees used to travel to the kitchen to fetch water which they then carried back to their offices; others carried mugs or cups to the kitchen and having infused their tea or coffee there carried them back, using one or other of the lifts.

On the afternoon of July 30, 1984 the plaintiff, whose office was on the third floor, was passing by the larger of the two lifts when she slipped on a small amount of liquid which, on the balance of probabilities, had been spilt onto the pseudo-marble surface of the passage by someone emerging from that lift while carrying a receptacle containing tea or coffee or hot water. In falling, she had hurt her hand, her chest and her coccyx.

The first question was whether the department's system for checking and dealing with such spillages as occurred had been adequate. On that, *Ward v Tesco Stores Ltd* ([1976] 1 W.L.R. 810) had been cited: but the situation in a supermarket was very different from that in an office, and on the evidence his Lordship was satisfied that in providing for regular inspections of the building by a competent safety officer, a reasonable system had been established.

The second question was whether the department had done all they reasonably could have to prevent spillages occurring and on the principle in *Edwards v National Coal Board* ([1949] 1 K.B. 704) the likelihood of spillages occurring had to be weighed against the cost of the measures necessary to eliminate that risk.

The records had shown that spillages in that block had been common, so that it had been almost inevitable that sooner or later an accident would occur: indeed staff had several times each year, by means of bulletins, been besought to take better care and to put a saucer or tray beneath any cup or mug which they carried from the kitchen.

The first measure, suggested on behalf of the plaintiff, had been the provision of a distribution point for hot water on each of the lower three floors of the building—thus minimising the distance employees would have to travel and obviating any need to use a lift.

His Lordship had not been told what that would have cost, but apparently it had been planned even before the accident and such further points had been installed in 1985.

Next, it was suggested that the department could have supplied appropriate saucers, cups and trays: their answer, that they had not the funds to buy such, his Lordship had not found acceptable.

Third, the risk of slipping could have been eliminated by providing some suitable non-slip surface over the pseudo-marble.

His Lordship had found this a borderline case: but after some hesitation (and indeed a change of mind) he had come to the conclusion that the department could and should have adopted measures to lessen the obvious risks their employees were running in all three of the respects mentioned. There would accordingly be judgment for the plaintiff.

Questions:

1. Do you agree that the employer/occupier should (in the legal sense of being liable for an accident if he didn't) provide cups and saucers, a canteen on each of the four floors and a less attractive but safer floor, simply in order to protect the employees against the carelessness of their colleagues? Do you think that it was probably the fault of another employee that the tea was spilt? Would the employee who spilt the tea be liable for not mopping it up? If so (in either case), why was the claim not based on the vicarious (rather than the personal) liability of the common employer? See below, p.272.

2. As hinted in the principal case, Tesco was once successfully sued by a customer who could not show how long the mess on which she slipped had been on the floor (below, p.171), but the judge held that supermarkets and office blocks were distinguishable. Tesco has also been held liable to an employee who slipped in a puddle of water and did not try to adduce evidence of any system which would have reduced the risk of that happening: *Jacob v Tesco Stores* November 5, 1998, CA. Is the right distinction between supermarkets and office blocks or between visitors and employees? Or should one make both distinctions?

3. *Laverton v Kiapasha (T/A Takeaway Supreme)* [2002] E.W.C.A. Civ 1656 is another slip-and-fall case. In the small hours of Saturday morning, after enjoying ten double Bacardis during a very rainy evening, the claimant, 30 years old, 5′6″ tall, weighing 20 stone and wearing boots with one and a half inch heels, entered the defendant's small shop, where there were already over 20 customers, and slipped on the floor which was wet with rainwater brought in on the feet of the patrons. There was usually, but not on this occasion, a coconut matting doormat just inside the door, the floor was tiled not carpeted, and the mop and bucket which the defendant kept at the back of the shop had not been used, perhaps because of the throng of customers. The trial judge held the defendant liable for the claimant's broken ankle, with no deduction for contributory negligence, but the Court of Appeal reversed, Mance L.J. dissenting as to the defendant's liability. Distinctions were drawn between rainwater, which one could expect, and greasy spillages, which should be wiped up forthwith.

Note:

Students may find this a banal and boring case. So it is. And so are most cases in the courts, for they turn not on matters of high legal policy such as "duty or no duty," but on trivial evaluations of fact, "was it or was it not reasonable of the defendant to do as he did?" This case is illustrative in the sense of being very typical; it is significant only as an instance of the application of a rule, not as an authority for it.

Section 3.—Special Plaintiffs

HALEY v LONDON ELECTRICITY BOARD

House of Lords [1965] A.C. 778; [1964] 3 W.L.R. 479; 129 J.P. 14; 108 S.J. 637; [1964] 3 All E.R. 185
(noted (1964) 80 L.Q.R. 323)

*Action by pedestrian against person working on highway in respect of
personal injury*

The plaintiff, a blind man, was walking carefully with a stick along the pavement in a London suburb when he fell into a trench dug there by the defendants pursuant to statutory powers. He suffered personal injury subsequently evaluated at £7,000. In front of the trench the defendants had put a long-handled hammer, its head resting on the pavement and the handle on some railings two feet high. This was an adequate protection for pedestrians with sight, but it was insufficient for blind people.

Marshall J. gave judgment for the defendants, and the Court of Appeal affirmed this decision [1964] 2 Q.B. 121. The plaintiff's appeal to the House of Lords was allowed.

Lord Reid: . . . The trial judge held that what the respondents' men did gave adequate warning to ordinary people with good sight, and I am not disposed to disagree with that. The excavation was shallow and was to be filled in before nightfall, and the punner (or the pick and shovel) together with the notice boards and the heap of spoil on the pavement beside the trench were, I think, sufficient warning to ordinary people that they should not try to pass along the pavement past the trench. I agree with Somervell L.J. in saying that a person walking along a pavement does not have "to keep his eyes on the ground to see whether or not there is any obstacle in his path" (*Almeroth v WE Chivers & Sons Ltd* [1948] 1 All E.R. 53 at 54). But even allowing for that degree of inadvertence of which most people are often guilty when walking along a pavement, I think that what the respondents' men did was just sufficient to attract the attention of ordinary people with good sight exercising ordinary care.

On the other hand, if it was the duty of the respondents to have in mind the needs of blind or infirm pedestrians I think that what they did was quite insufficient. Indeed, the evidence shows that an obstacle attached to a heavy weight and only nine inches above the ground may well escape detection by a blind man's stick and is for him a trap rather than a warning.

So the question for your Lordships' decision is the nature and extent of the duty owed to pedestrians by persons who carry out operations on a city pavement. The respondents argue that they were only bound to have in mind or to safeguard ordinary able-bodied people and were under no obligation to give particular consideration to the blind or infirm. If that is right, it means that a blind or infirm person who goes out alone goes at his peril. He may meet obstacles which are a danger to him but not to those with good sight because no one is under any obligation to remove or protect them. And if such an obstacle causes him injury he must suffer the damage in silence.

I could understand the respondents' contention if it was based on an argument that it was not reasonably foreseeable that a blind person might pass along that pavement on that day; or that, although foreseeable, the chance of a blind man coming there was so small and the difficulty of affording protection to him so great that it would have been in the circumstances unreasonable to afford that protection. Those are well recognised grounds of defence. But in my judgment neither is open to the respondents in this case.

In deciding what is reasonably foreseeable one must have regard to common knowledge. We are all accustomed to meeting blind people walking alone with their white sticks on city pavements. No doubt there are many places open to the public where for one reason or another one would be surprised to see a blind person walking alone, but a city pavement is not one of them. And a residential street cannot be different from any other. The blind people we meet must live somewhere and most of them probably left their homes unaccompanied. It may seem surprising that blind people can avoid ordinary obstacles so well as they do, but we must take account of the facts. There is evidence in this case about the number of blind people in London and it appears from Government publications that the proportion in the whole country is near one in 500. By no means all are sufficiently skilled or confident to venture out alone, but the number who habitually do so must be very large. I find it quite impossible to say that it is not reasonably foreseeable that a blind person may pass along a particular pavement on a particular day.

No question can arise in this case of any great difficulty in affording adequate protection for the blind. In considering what is adequate protection again one must have regard to common knowledge. One is entitled to expect of a blind person a high degree of skill and care because none but the most foolhardy would venture to go out alone without having that skill and exercising that care. We know that in fact blind people do safely avoid all ordinary obstacles on pavements; there can be no question of padding lamp posts as was suggested in one case. But a moment's reflection shows that a low obstacle in an unusual place is a grave danger: on the other hand, it is clear from the evidence in this case and also, I think, from common knowledge that quite a light fence some two feet high is an adequate warning. There would have been no difficulty in providing such a fence here. The evidence is that the Post Office always provide one, and that the respondents have similar fences which are often used. Indeed the evidence suggests that the only reason there was no fence here was that the accident occurred before the necessary fences had arrived. So if the respondents are to succeed it can only be on the ground that there was no duty to do more than safeguard ordinary able-bodied people. . . .

I can see no justification for laying down any hard-and-fast rule limiting the classes of persons for whom those interfering with a pavement must make provision. It is said that it is impossible to tell what precautions will be adequate to protect all kinds of infirm pedestrians or that taking such precautions would be unreasonably difficult or expensive. I think that such fears are exaggerated, and it is worth recollecting that when the courts sought to lay down specific rules as to the duties of occupiers the law became so unsatisfactory that Parliament had to step in and pass the Occupiers' Liability Act 1957. It appears to me that the ordinary principles of the common law must apply in streets as well as elsewhere, and that fundamentally they depend on what a reasonable man, careful of his neighbour's safety, would do having the knowledge which a reasonable man in the position of the defendant must be deemed to have. I agree with the statement of law at the end of the speech of Lord Sumner in *Glasgow Corp. v Taylor* ([1922] 1 A.C. 44 at 67): "a measure of care appropriate to the inability or disability of those who are immature or feeble in mind or body is due from others, who know of or ought to anticipate the presence of such persons within the scope and hazard of their own operations." I would therefore allow this appeal.

Questions

1. If a sighted person had fallen into the trench, guarded as it was, would that person have recovered (a) nothing, or (b) a sum reduced by reason of his contributory negligence, (i) before this decision, and (ii) after it?

2. Note that it was the defendant's own practice to surround its excavations with a light portable fence, such as is all that the circumstances call for. In other words, the defendant failed to meet its own standards, rather like the manufacturer who circulates a product with a manufacturing defect (such as was involved in *Grant v Australian Knitting Mills* [1936] A.C. 85), as opposed to a design defect (such as was in issue in *Abouzaid* (above, p.28).

Note:
Very often the people to whom accidents happen are those to whom they are particularly likely to happen. The law has some trouble with the susceptible plaintiff. The susceptibility may be physical—the sensitive

housewife who contracts dermatitis from a "safe" detergent (*Board v Thomas Hedley* [1951] 2 All E.R. 432; *Ingham v Emes* [1955] 2 Q.B. 366); or intellectual—the child who takes a bomb for a toy (*Yachuk v Oliver Blais* [1949] A.C. 386); or neurotic—*Page v Smith* ([1995] 2 All E.R. 736, HL).

Since there is nothing unreasonable in being vulnerable, the concept of contributory negligence cannot be used to limit liability to the accident-prone (though if an epileptic takes to working at heights, his recovery may be restricted—*Cork v Kirby Maclean* [1952] 2 All E.R. 402), and its use would conflict with the "thin-skull" rule. Nevertheless one can feel some disquiet at the reaction of the law when a neurotic is totally unhinged by an event which would cause only transitory discomfort in a normal person (*Page v Smith*). But if one's claim for pain and suffering will not be reduced just because others would have suffered much less acutely, one's claim for loss of earnings will be diminished if a pre-existing ailment would in any case have shortened one's earning life. One can sometimes hold that no special duty was owed to the abnormally accident-prone, but if the person to whom one owes a duty of care is particularly susceptible one may be bound to take increased precautions. Thus a one-eyed operative engaged in welding operations was entitled to protection not required for those with two good eyes: *Paris v Stepney BC* [1951] A.C. 367—the risk of an accident may be no greater, but its consequences, should it occur, would be more severe. Likewise in *Tasci v Pekalp of London* [2001] I.C.R. 633 where a Kurdish refugee injured his hand on a circular saw after receiving instructions and supervision which would have been adequate for a relatively experienced machinist. The employer should have realised that the claimant, who understood little English, was likely, in his eagerness to find employment, to have lied about his experience. So the defendant was held liable, subject to 60 per cent contributory negligence.

Children often manage to injure themselves through inexperience or mischievousness or arrant folly (see *Simonds*, above p.147), and the 1957 Act reminds occupiers that children are "less careful than adults" (s.2(4)). One may expect parents to look after their children and see that they are not hurt. Thus when a baby fell off a bed and was burnt on uncased heating pipes, a claim against the landlord under s.4 of the Defective Premises Act 1972 failed, not only because given the slightness of the risk it would have been dispropor-tionate to expect the landlord to lag the pipes but also because the mother should have prevented the accident: *B v Camden LBC* [2001] P.I.Q.R. P9.

Phipps v Rochester Corporation [1955] 1 Q.B. 450 is a good illustration, but it should be borne in mind that it was decided before the Act extended the "common duty of care" to licensees such as the child involved: the plaintiff, a boy of five, and his sister, aged seven, crossed the defendant's land in order to go blackberrying. The defendant knew that people crossed his land and apparently did not mind. The land was being developed as a housing estate and, preparatory to the insertion of a sewer, the defendant had dug a trench about two and a half feet wide, eight or nine feet deep, and about a hundred yards long. The girl negotiated this hazard safely, but the boy fell in and broke his leg. His claim was dismissed.

Devlin J. held that unless the occupier was aware that children came on his premises unaccompanied, he could expect that they would not do so: " ... the responsibility for the safety of little children must rest primarily upon the parents; it is their duty to see that such children are not allowed to wander about by themselves, or at least to satisfy themselves that the places to which they do allow their children to go unaccompanied are safe for them to go to." While it is certainly not the law that the carelessness of parents is imputed to the child injured by another's negligence, the judge's observations still have force.

It is not quite so easy to reach the same conclusion after the 1957 Act, but one could perhaps find that there was no breach of the duty to take reasonable steps to render the child reasonably safe (or perhaps say that he wasn't using the premises at all!). Should the corporation have put a fence round its ditch? Or can one say, as the judge did, that unless unaccompanied children are to be expected, a warning which is adequate for the expected concomitant adult is a good performance of the duty, with the gloss that no warning is needed where the danger, such as an open ditch, is perfectly obvious?

Just as dangers obvious to an adult may not be obvious to a child, so dangers imperceptible to a layman may be obvious to a specialist. That is why the 1957 Act, immediately after referring to children, provides that the occupier may expect visitors who are specialists to appreciate and guard against any special risks ordinarily incident to their calling. Thus in *Roles v Nathan* [1963] 1 W.L.R. Lord Denning applied that provision in dismissing a claim arising out of the death of two chimney-sweeps from the fumes in the defendant's boiler-house; chimney sweeps should know about fumes.

Firemen should know about fires, too. So is the decision of the House of Lords in *Ogwo v Taylor* [1988] 1 A.C. 431 satisfactory? There the claimant fireman was burnt on the defendant's premises where admittedly the defendant had carelessly caused the fire by applying a blowtorch to a fascia board. The claim was allowed at common law, supposedly ousted by the Act, and there was no reference whatsoever to s.2(4).

An alternative reason given by Lord Denning in the case of the chimney-sweeps was that they had been warned of the danger, and the Act provides that the occupier may be able to satisfy his duty by giving a warning which is sufficient to enable the visitor to be reasonably safe. He gives a good example: If there are two footbridges, one rotten and one safe, the occupier could avoid liability by putting up a notice by the rotten one saying "This bridge is dangerous. Do not use it. There is a safe one further upstream".

But if a warning may save you from liability, failure to warn may be a ground of liability. Consider the facts of *Umeh v London Transport Executive* [1984] 134 New L.J. 522. At Neasden Station's platform 4 there was a subway at one end and a footbridge at the other. One morning at rush hour the subway was flooded, and the sole employee on duty had posted a notice saying "Subway flooded—do not cross tracks. Please go round by footbridge." Of course people trooped across the tracks, and the plaintiff was struck by a train. The flooding was not the defendant's fault, and although there was nothing the sole employee could have done physically to stop the people crossing the tracks, the defendants were held liable because he could easily have phoned the next station up the line and stopped the train till the line was clear.

Compare *Scott-Whitehead v National Coal Board* [1987] 53 P. & C.R. 263, where a farmer's crops were ruined one hot dry summer because the water with which he irrigated them was polluted by effluent discharged into the river by the Coal Board. The Coal Board was not liable because the discharge was lawful, but the Water Authority had to pay because although there was nothing they could do about the pollution, they should have told the farmer that the concentration was dangerous for his crops. See also the cases of *Tutton v Walter* and *Al Kandari v Brown*, mentioned above, p.89.

Section 4.—Skilful Defendants

We have seen that the occupier's liability may be affected by the foolishness or skill of the visitor: what about the occupier himself? We saw earlier, also, that the learner driver must meet the standard of the competent qualified driver (*Nettleship v Weston*, above p.130). What of the DIY man, the learner carpenter, electrician etc.?

The question was raised in *Wells v Cooper* [1958] 2 Q.B. 265, where the facts were as follows: the plaintiff went to the defendant's house to deliver fish and was asked to stay for a cup of tea. After drinking it he left by the back door. As he pulled it shut with the force required by a strong wind and the draught-excluded, the door-handle came away in his hand and he fell four feet to the ground from the top of the back steps. The door-handle, which was of the lever type, had been screwed on with three-quarter inch screws by the defendant himself, a "do-it-yourself" man who frequently did such jobs around the house: indeed, it was because he thought the previous door-handle unsafe that he had installed the present one. Stable J. dismissed the claim on the ground that the accident was not one which was reasonably foreseeable (!), and the plaintiff appealed to the Court of Appeal without success.

The answer given by Jenkins L.J. to the question of the standard to be expected of the DIY man is not really very clear:

(1) The work was not so specialised or dangerous that the defendant should have employed a professional rather than doing it himself;
(2) The appropriate standard is "the degree of care and skill to be expected of a reasonably competent carpenter", doubtless lower than that required of a professional carpenter working for pay;
(3) Given the defendant's DIY experience, he was a reasonably competent carpenter;
(4) Accordingly, unless his belief that three-quarter inch screws were adequate was an obvious blunder which no reasonably competent carpenter could reasonably entertain, he had discharged his duty.

The judgment raises the following question: if the defendant had hired a professional carpenter to do the job and that carpenter had done it as the defendant here did, would the carpenter have been liable to the defendant, if it had been the defendant who fell downstairs? Would the carpenter have been liable to the plaintiff who did in fact fall downstairs? And would the defendant also have been liable in that case?

More interesting are the cases where the defendant is indeed a professional. The old cases dealt mainly with medical men, for their negligence caused personal injury; and cases of property damage done by professionals could often be dealt with under the rubric of bailment, but after *Hedley Byrne* introduced liability for merely economic loss due to defective services, the scope of professional liability has expanded enormously, to cover all services, which now bulk so large in our economy. In such cases there is usually a need for expert evidence, for while anyone can tell whether Mrs Alexander acted reasonably in letting the um of tea be carried through the tearoom crowded with boys, it takes another expert to tell what a surgeon or ship's captain or accountant should have done that he didn't or didn't do that he should have done.

BOLITHO v CITY AND HACKNEY H.A.

House of Lords [1998] A.C. 232; [1997] 3 W.L.R. 1151; [1997] 4 All E.R. 771

Claim against hospital for failing to prevent death of child

When a young patient had a breathing crisis and the nurse called a doctor, the doctor failed to come (the battery in her pager being flat!) and the child died. The child would probably have survived if the doctor had come and intubated him, but the doctor said she would not have intubated, and the question was whether her notional failure to do so, had she arrived, would have been negligent.

Lord Browne-Wilkinson: . . . The locus classicus of the test for the standard of care required of a doctor or any other person professing some skill or competence is the direction to the jury given by McNair J. in *Bolam v Friern Hospital Management Committee* [1957] 2 All E.R. 118 at 122:

> "I myself would prefer to put it this way: a doctor is not guilty of negligence if he has acted in accordance with a practice accepted as proper by a responsible body of medical men skilled in that particular art . . . Putting it the other way round, a doctor is not negligent, if he is acting in accordance with such a practice, merely because there is a body of opinion that takes a contrary view."

[Counsel for the plaintiff] submitted that the judge had wrongly treated the *Bolam* test as requiring him to accept the views of one truthful body of expert professional advice, even though he was unpersuaded of its logical force. He submitted that the judge was wrong in law in adopting that approach and that ultimately it was for the court, not for medical opinion, to decide what was the standard of care required of a professional in the circumstances of each particular case.

My Lords, I agree with these submissions to the extent that, in my view, the court is not bound to hold that a defendant doctor escapes liability for negligent treatment or diagnosis just because he leads evidence from a number of medical experts who are genuinely of opinion that the defendant's treatment or diagnosis accorded with sound medical practice. In *Bolam*'s case [1957] 2 All E.R. 118 at 122, McNair J. stated that the defendant had to have acted in accordance with the practice accepted as proper by a "*responsible* body of medical men" (my emphasis). Later he referred to "a standard of practice recognised as proper by a competent *reasonable* body of opinion". Again, in *Maynard*'s case, Lord Scarman refers to a "respectable" body of professional opinion. The use of these adjectives—responsible, reasonable and respectable—all show that the court has to be satisfied that the exponents of the body of opinion relied on can demonstrate that such opinion has a logical basis. In particular, in cases involving, as they so often do, the weighing of risks against benefits, the judge before accepting a body of opinion as being responsible, reasonable or respectable, will need to be satisfied that, in forming their views, the experts have directed their minds to the question of comparative risks and benefits and have reached a defensible conclusion on the matter.

In cases of diagnosis and treatment there are cases where, despite a body of professional opinion sanctioning the defendant's conduct, the defendant can properly be held liable for negligence (I am not here considering questions of disclosure of risk). In my judgment that is because, in some cases, it cannot be demonstrated to the judge's satisfaction that the body of opinion relied on is reasonable or responsible. In the vast majority of cases the fact that distinguished experts in the field are of a particular opinion will demonstrate the reasonableness of that opinion. In particular, where there are questions of assessment of the relative risks and benefits of adopting a particular medical practice, a reasonable view necessarily presupposes that the relative risks and benefits have been weighed by the experts in forming their opinions. But if, in a rare case, it can be demonstrated that the professional opinion is not capable of withstanding logical analysis, the judge is entitled to hold that the body of opinion is not reasonable or responsible.

I emphasise that, in my view, it will very seldom be right for a judge to reach the conclusion that views genuinely held by a competent medical expert are unreasonable. The assessment of medical risks and benefits is a matter of clinical judgment which a judge would not normally be able to make without expert evidence. It would be wrong to allow such assessment to deteriorate into seeking to persuade the judge to prefer one of two views both of which are capable of being logically supported. It is only where a judge can be satisfied that the body of expert opinion cannot be logically supported at all that such opinion will not provide the bench mark by reference to which the defendant's conduct falls to be assessed.

Notes:

1. A court will normally find that the accepted way of doing something is acceptable, but it is always free to decide that there is a better way than the standard way—otherwise there would never be any improvement (consider *King v Smith* above, p.139). Accordingly a deviation from standard practice may be justifiable (but probably has to be justified—see *Brown v Rolls Royce* [1960] 1 All E.R. 577, where an employer decided not to follow the practice of providing barrier cream for employees working with grease, being persuaded that it did more harm than good) and conduct in accordance with standard practice can be held negligent.

In professional matters there may well be different schools of thought at any time (and time is important—see *Roe* below, p.166), that is, no single standard procedure, but several. The *Bolam* test, devised in a case concerning the physical restraint of a patient undergoing electric shock treatment, was taken to mean that a medical procedure supported as proper by any reputable body of medical opinion would not be found negligent. This was much (and unduly) criticised as an abdication of judicial appraisal which gave the medical profession *carte blanche* to determine legality. *Bolitho* makes it clear that the courts do reserve the power to disallow a medical practice even if it is supported by a body of doctors, but it can be expected that the power will rarely be used.

2. The words of McNair J. in *Bolam* were enthusiastically endorsed as "true doctrine" by Lord Edmund-Davies in *Whitehouse v Jordan* [1981] 1 All E.R. 267. That case involved a charge of negligence against a senior registrar in charge of a childbirth in which the child suffered brain damage. The defendant realised that normal birth by contraction was impossible and attempted a trial by forceps in order to see whether delivery by forceps, a better method than Caesarean section, might be possible. The question was whether he pulled too long and too hard. The trial judge found that he had; the Court of Appeal, by a majority, differed; and the House of Lords unanimously upheld the Court of Appeal. Lord Russell said this: "Some passages in the Court of Appeal might suggest that if a doctor makes an error of judgment he cannot be found guilty of negligence. This must be wrong. An error of judgment is not *per se* incompatible with negligence . . . I would accept the phrase 'a mere error of judgment' if the impact of the word 'mere' is to indicate that not all errors of judgment show a lapse from the standard of skill and care required to be exercised to avoid a charge of negligence."

3. Commentators, however, have severely criticised the "English courts' regrettable tendency to apply the *Bolam* test in such a way as automatically to acquit of negligence any practitioner who can find colleagues to condone what he or she did or did not do." (Keown [1995] Camb. L.J. 30 at 31), especially as regards the question of what information about a proposed treatment the doctor must volunteer. On this the English courts have indeed deferred to the judgment of the medical profession (*Sidaway v Royal Bethlem Hospital* [1985] 1 All E.R. 643, HL) whereas in other jurisdictions the test is what a reasonable patient would want to know (thus *Rogers v Whittaker* (1993) 67 A.J.L.R. 47—one in 14,000 chance of losing sight in good eye after proposed operation to improve sight in poor eye).

4. Trial judges, who have seen the victim, tend to apply too strict a test and have to be corrected on appeal. In *Hughes v Waltham Forest H.A.* [1990] Times L.R. 714 the Court of Appeal reversed a judgment for over £220,000 in a case where two medical witnesses had criticised the defendant surgeons' methods: "The question for the judge had been whether the surgeons in reaching their decision displayed such a lack of clinical judgment that no surgeon exercising proper care and skill could have reached the same decision" (*per* Beldam L.J.).

5. Until fairly recently British people displayed a decent distaste for suing those who were trying to cure them. While one can sympathise with the parental grief which turns to grievance and fuels a hopeless vendetta through the courts (*Kay v Ayrshire & Arran H.A.* [1987] 2 All E.R. 471, HL) one can ponder the virtue of claiming damages for a child's blindness from the very doctors whose remarkable devotion and skill kept it alive at all (*Wilsher v Essex A.H.A.* [1987] 1 All E.R. 971, HL).

6. Claims against doctors and hospitals have increased a great deal. Payouts by the NHS rose from £6.3 million in 1974–75 (in 2002 terms) to £446 million in 2001–2002. From March 2001 to March 2002 the

National Audit Office (whose figures are often contested) raised its projected cost to the NHS of all outstanding claims from £4.4 billion to £5.25 billion, in part the result of an increase in the awards for both pain and suffering (*Heil v Rankin* [2001] Q.B. 272) and lost earnings (*Wells v Wells* [1999] 1 A.C. 345—see below p.638). The £15,000 payable under *Rees* (above p.118) to the parents of unwanted children can be seen as a drop in the ocean.

7. Differences of medical opinion are commonly reflected in the view of the experts appointed and instructed by the parties. The Civil Procedure Rules provide, in CPR r.35.7, that "Where two or more parties wish to submit expert evidence on a particular issue, the court may direct that the evidence on that issue is to be given by one expert only . . . Where the instructing parties cannot agree who should be the expert, the court may (a) select the expert from a list prepared or identified by the instructing parties; or (b) direct that the expert be selected in such other manner as the court may direct."

8. " . . . a professional man should command the corpus of knowledge which forms part of the professional equipment of the ordinary member of his profession. He should not lag behind other ordinarily assiduous and intelligent members of his profession in knowledge of new advances, discoveries and developments in his field. He should have such awareness as an ordinarily competent practitioner would have of the deficiencies in his knowledge and the limitations on his skills. He should be alert to the hazards and risks inherent in any profession or task he undertakes to the extent that other ordinarily competent members of the profession would be alert. He must bring to any professional task he undertakes no less expertise, skill and care than other ordinarily competent members of his profession would bring, but need bring no more. The standard is that of the reasonably average. The law does not require of a professional man that he be a paragon, combining the qualities of polymath and prophet." (Lord Bingham in *Eckersley v Binnie & Partners* (1988) 18 Con.L.R. 1).

9. The standard to be expected of a practitioner in alternative medicine was in issue in In *Shakoor v Situ* [2000] 4 All E.R. 181. The defendant, who read no British medical journals but subscribed to the monthly *Register of Chinese Herbal Medicine*, treated his patient's skin disease, for which Western medicine would have prescribed surgery, with a herbal mixture which, owing to a rare and unpredictable idiosyncratic reaction, caused the patient's death.

The judge rejected as inapplicable both the standard of practitioners in Chinese herbal medicine and that of practitioners of orthodox medicine in this country: the right standard was that of a practitioner of alternative medicine in a country where orthodox treatment was normal: he should therefore familiarise himself with orthodox reactions to alternative remedies which had gone wrong.

In the event the defendant was held not liable because he had acted carefully by the standards of traditional Chinese herbal medicine as properly practised in this country.

10. What of hypnotists? In *Gates v McKenna* [1998] Lloyd's Rep. Med. 405 a stage hypnotist was sued by a volunteer who allegedly developed schizophrenia in consequence of the hypnosis. Toulson J. held that the hypnotist must warn his audience that labile personalities should not come forward, must not expose the hypnotised volunteer to physical harm and must take care in the dehypnotising process, since the volunteer may remain suggestible. In this case, however, the judge found that the defendant had not been in breach of duty and that causation was not established. In *Howarth v Green*, by contrast, a stage hypnotist was held liable for suggesting to the volunteer that she was eight years old. She consequently suffered age regression and relived memories of childhood abuse. The hypnotist was held liable since he knew of the risk of age regression and possible psychological damage. See *The Times*, May 26, 2001.

11. It is not only in matters of diagnosis and therapeutics that hospitals may be made liable. In *A v Tameside and Glossop H.A.* [1996] Times L.R. 673, the defendant health authority discovered that over 900 obstetric patients had come into contact with a health worker who was HIV-positive. After ascertaining from each patient's general practitioner which patients should not be informed by simple letter, it sent a letter to the others. Some were shocked at the breakfast table as perhaps they would not have been had they been told face-to-face by their own doctor in the afternoon. The trial judge held that the health authority had been negligent, but the Court of Appeal reversed.

ROE v MINISTER OF HEALTH

Court of Appeal [1954] 2 Q.B. 66; [1954] 2 W.L.R. 915; 98 S.J. 319; [1954] 2 All E.R. 131

Action by patients against hospital and anaesthetist in respect of personal injury

The two plaintiffs in these consolidated actions entered hospital for minor surgery and emerged permanently paralysed from the waist down. The reason was that the ampoules of the anaesthetic, nupercaine, which was injected spinally, had tiny cracks in them, and some phenol, the disinfectant in which they were kept, had percolated through those cracks and had contaminated the anaesthetic.

The action was brought against the Minister of Health, as successor in title to the trustees of the Chesterfield and North Derbyshire Royal Hospital, and the anaesthetist, Dr Graham, who had a private practice but was under an obligation to provide a regular service at the hospital.

The trial judge dismissed the plaintiffs' actions ([1954] 1 W.L.R. 128), and the Court of Appeal dismissed their appeal.

Denning L.J.: No one can be unmoved by the disaster which has befallen these two unfortunate men. They were both working men before they went into the Chesterfield Hospital in October 1947. Both were insured contributors to the hospital, paying a small sum each week, in return for which they were entitled to be admitted for treatment when they were ill. Each of them was operated on in the hospital for a minor trouble, one for something wrong with a cartilage in his knee, the other for a hydrocele. The operations were both on the same day, October 13, 1947. Each of them was given a spinal anaesthetic by a visiting anaesthetist, Dr Graham. Each of them has in consequence been paralysed from the waist down.

The judge has said that those facts do not speak for themselves, but I think that they do. They certainly call for an explanation. Each of these men is entitled to say to the hospital: "While I was in your hands something has been done to me which has wrecked my life. Please explain how it has come to pass." The reason why the judge took a different view was because he thought that the hospital authorities could disclaim responsibility for the anaesthetist, Dr Graham: and, as it might be his fault and not theirs, the hospital authorities were not called upon to give an explanation. I think that that reasoning is wrong. In the first place, I think that the hospital authorities are responsible for the whole of their staff, not only for the nurses and doctors, but also for the anaesthetists and the surgeons. It does not matter whether they are permanent or temporary, resident or visiting, whole-time or part-time. The hospital authorities are responsible for all of them. The reason is because, even if they are not servants, they are the agents of the hospital to give the treatment. The only exception is the case of consultants or anaesthetists selected and employed by the patient himself. I went into the matter with some care in *Cassidy v Ministry of Health* ([1951] 2 K.B. 343) and I adhere to all I there said. In the second place, I do not think that the hospital authorities and Dr Graham can both avoid giving an explanation by the simple expedient of each throwing responsibility on to the other. If an injured person shows that one or other or both of two persons injured him, but cannot say which of them it was, then he is not defeated altogether. He can call on each of them for an explanation: see *Baker v Market Harborough Industrial Co-operative Society* ([1953] 1 W.L.R. 1472).

I approach this case, therefore, on the footing that the hospital authorities and Dr Graham were called on to give an explanation of what has happened. But I think that they have done so. They have spared no trouble or expense to seek out the cause of the disaster. The greatest specialists in the land were called to give evidence. In the result, the judge has found that what happened was this: In October 1947, a spinal anaesthetic was in use at the hospital called nupercaine. It was a liquid supplied by the makers in closed glass ampoules. These were test tubes sealed with glass. When the time came to use it, a nurse filed off the glass top, the anaesthetist inserted his needle and drew off the nupercaine, which he then injected into the spine of the patient. It so happened that in this process there was some risk of the needle becoming infected. The reason was because the outside of the ampoule might become contaminated with a germ of some kind: and the needle might touch it as the anaesthetist was filling it. That this risk was a real one is shown by the fact that quite a number of cases became complicated by some infection or other.

In order to avoid this risk, the senior anaesthetist at the hospital, Dr Pooler, decided to keep the ampoules in a jar of disinfectant called phenol, which was a form of carbolic acid. This disinfectant was made in two strengths. The stronger was tinted light blue and the weaker was tinted pale red. This was so as to distinguish it from water. Following Dr Pooler, the junior anaesthetist, Dr Graham, thought that it was a good thing to disinfect the ampoules in this way and he adopted the same system. By a great misfortune this new system of disinfecting had in it a danger of which Dr Pooler and Dr Graham were quite unaware. The danger was this: the ampoules in the jar might become cracked; the cracks might be so fine or so placed that they could not be detected by ordinary inspection, and the carbolic disinfectant would then seep through the cracks into the nupercaine, and no one would realise that it had taken place. Thus the anaesthetist, who thought he was inserting pure nupercaine into the spine of the patient, was in fact inserting nupercaine mixed with carbolic acid. That is the very thing which happened in the case of these two men. Carbolic acid was inserted into their spines and corroded all the nerves which controlled the lower half of their bodies.

That is the explanation of the disaster, and the question is: were any of the staff negligent? I pause to say that once the accident is explained, no question of *res ipsa loquitur* arises. The only question is whether on the facts as now ascertained anyone was negligent. Mr Elwes said that the staff were negligent in two respects: (1) in not colouring the phenol with a deep dye; (2) in cracking the ampoules. I will take them in order: (1) The deep tinting. If the anaesthetists had foreseen that the ampoules might get cracked with cracks that could not be detected on inspection they would no doubt have dyed the phenol a deep blue; and this would have exposed the contamination. But I do not think that their failure to foresee this was negligence. It is so easy to be wise after the event and to condemn as negligence that which was only a misadventure. We ought always to be on our guard against it, especially in cases against hospitals and doctors. Medical science had conferred great benefits on mankind, but these benefits are attended by considerable risks. Every surgical operation is attended by risks. We cannot take the benefits without taking the risks. Every advance in technique is also attended by risks. Doctors, like the rest of us, have to learn by experience; and experience often teaches in a hard way. Something goes wrong and shows up a weakness, and then it is put right. That is just what happened here. Dr Graham sought to escape the danger of infection by disinfecting the ampoule. In escaping that known danger he unfortunately ran into another danger. He did not know that there could be undetectable cracks, but it was not negligent for him not to know it at that time. We must not look at the 1947 accident with 1954 spectacles. The judge acquitted Dr Graham of negligence and we should uphold his decision.

(2) The cracks. In cracking the ampoules, there must, I fear, have been some carelessness by someone in the hospital. The ampoules were quite strong and the sisters said that they should not get cracked if proper care was used in handling them. They must have been jolted in some way by someone. This raises an interesting point of law. This carelessness was, in a sense, one of the causes of the disaster; but the person who jolted the ampoule cannot possibly have foreseen what dire consequences would follow. There were so many intervening opportunities of inspection that she might reasonably think that if the jolting caused a crack, it would be discovered long before any harm came of it. As Somervell L.J. has pointed out, she herself would probably examine the ampoule for a crack, and seeing none, would return it to the jar. The anaesthetist himself did in fact examine it for cracks, and finding none, used it. The trouble was that nobody realised that there might be a crack which could not be detected on ordinary examination. What, then is the legal position?

The first question in every case is whether there was a duty of care owed to the plaintiff; and the test of duty depends, without doubt, on what you should foresee. There is no duty of care owed to a person when you could not reasonably foresee that he might be injured by your conduct: see *Bourhill v Young* ([1943] A.C. 92).

The second question is whether the neglect of duty was a "cause" of the injury in the proper sense of that term; and causation, as well as duty, often depends on what you should foresee. The chain of causation is broken when there is an intervening action which you could not reasonably be expected to foresee. It is only when those two preliminary questions—duty and causation—are answered in favour of the plaintiff that the third question, remoteness of damage, comes into play.

Even then your ability to foresee the consequences may be vital. It is decisive where there is intervening conduct by other persons: see *Stansbie v Troman* ([1948] 2 K.B. 48); *Lewis v Carmarthenshire C.C.* ([1953] 1 W.L.R. 1439). In all these cases you will find that the three questions, duty, causation and remoteness, run continually into one another. It seems to me that they are simply three different ways of looking at one and the same problem. Starting with the proposition that a negligent person should be liable, within reason, for the consequences of his conduct, the extent of his liability is to be found by asking the one question: Is the consequence fairly to be regarded as within the risk created by the negligence? If so, the negligent person is liable for it: but otherwise not.

Instead of asking three questions, I should have thought that in many cases it would be simpler and better to ask the one question: is the consequence within the risk? And to answer it by applying ordinary plain common sense.

Asking myself, therefore, what was the risk involved in careless handling of the ampoules, I answer by saying that there was such a probability of intervening examination as to limit the risk. The only consequence which could reasonably be anticipated was the loss of a quantity of nupercaine, but not the paralysis of a patient. The hospital authorities are therefore not liable for it.

When you stop to think of what happened in the present case, you will realise that it was a most extraordinary chapter of accidents. In some way the ampoules must have received a jolt, perhaps while a nurse was putting them into the jar or while a trolley was being moved along. The jolt cannot have been very severe. It was not severe enough to break any of the ampoules or even to crack them so far as anyone could see. But it was just enough to produce an invisible crack. The crack was of a kind which no one in any experiment has been able to reproduce again. It was too fine to be seen, but it was enough to let in sufficient phenol to corrode the nerves, whilst still leaving enough nupercaine to anaesthetise the patient. And this very exceptional crack occurred not in one ampoule only, but in two ampoules used on the self-same day in two successive operations; and none of the other ampoules was damaged at all. This has taught the doctors to be on their guard against invisible cracks. Never again, it is to be hoped, will such a thing happen. After this accident a leading textbook was published in 1951 which contains the significant warning: "Never place ampoules of local anaesthetic solution in alcohol or spirit. This common practice is probably responsible for some of the cases of permanent paralysis reported after spinal analgesia." If the hospitals were to continue the practice after this warning, they could not complain if they were found guilty of negligence. But the warning had not been given at the time of this accident. Indeed, it was the extraordinary accident to these two men which first disclosed the danger. Nowadays it would be negligence not to realise the danger, but it was not then.

One final word. These two men have suffered such terrible consequences that there is a natural feeling that they should be compensated. But we should be doing a disservice to the community at large if we were to impose liability on hospitals and doctors for everything that happens to go wrong. Doctors would be led to think more of their own safety than of the good of their patients. Initiative would be stifled and confidence shaken. A proper sense of proportion requires us to have regard to the conditions in which hospitals and doctors have to work. We must insist on due care for the patient at every point, but we must not condemn as negligence that which is only a misadventure. I agree with my Lord that these appeals should be dismissed.

Questions

1. Does the question formulated by Denning L.J. in terms of "risk" invite any other answer than "Yes" or "No"? And would it be better if judges answered it in one word? (See *Qualcast*, above, p.126).

2. Contrast the attitudes of Lord Denning to fire brigades (*Watt*, above, p.144), village cricketers (*Miller*, below, p.445) and hospitals (the principal case). Would the reasons he gives for denying liability in this case apply with equal force to industrial development during the last century? Or now? What about pharmaceutical companies?

3. Would the manufacturer of the ampoules be liable (a) under *Donoghue v Stevenson*? (b) The Consumer Protection Act 1987?

Note:

The requirement of fault clearly entails that a defendant must be judged by the standard prevalent at the time of the conduct being impugned: a person cannot be blamed for not knowing what no one yet knows. Thus a woman who contracted mesothelioma from inhaling asbestos dust from her husband's clothes when she washed them could not recover from his employer, at fault as regards him, since at the relevant date no one knew that the disease could be contracted in this way. (*Gunn v Wallsend Shipping & Eng. Co, The Times,* January 23, 1989). As Lord Denning said, "Every advance in technique is attended by risks." Furthermore, every new technique is followed by complaints when it is not used.

But what if fault is not required? The Directive on Liability for Defective Products (above p.27) contains two relevant rules:

(1) a product is not to be held defective just because a safer product is subsequently produced;

(2) in the case of a product now known to be defective, the producer can escape liability by showing that at the time of circulation there was no possible way of ascertaining that it had a defect at all: see *A v National Blood Authority* (above p.28).

Section 5.—Proof of Breach

In his statement of claim a plaintiff must disclose a cause of action, that is, he must aver facts which, if proved, would entitle him to succeed. If he does not, he may fail right at the outset (*Price v Gregory* [1959] 1 W.L.R. 177; *Fowler v Lanning*, below, p.322). On the whole however, English judges prefer to let the case go to trial; facts involving liability may emerge, and the plaintiff may be allowed to amend his pleadings so as to bring them into line with those facts. On the other hand, if what was proved diverges very widely from what he alleged, he may still fail (*Esso Petroleum Co v Southport Corp.* [1956] A.C. 218 at 241; *Waghorn v George Wimpey & Co* [1970] 1 All E.R. 474).

At the trial itself, the plaintiff must lead some evidence. He will always know what the damage is, and he will be able to show the circumstances in which he was placed when it was suffered. He may not be able to show exactly what caused the damage he complains of, and he may very well not be able to show the other thing that must ultimately be established, namely, that one of its causes was some fault in the behaviour of the defendant. If all the facts come out at the trial, as in *Roe*, then the only question is whether those facts show a breach of duty in the defendant. The question is not whether it was more probable or not that he was negligent, but simply whether he was negligent. As to that, of course, there may be two views; appellate courts are quite ready to substitute their view for that of the judge, unless he is a county court judge and not much money is involved.

But all the facts may not emerge—indeed, they rarely do. The defendant may not want to tell all he knows, though the process of disclosure limits his power of secrecy. The question then is whether the plaintiff has proved enough. If you do not know what the defendant did (a matter of proof), you cannot decide (a matter of judgment) whether what he did was careless or not. It may, however, be possible to say that it is more probable than not that the defendant was careless; this is an elliptical and confusing way of saying that from the facts proved it is possible to *infer* other facts which, if proved, would entitle one to conclude that the defendant had fallen short of the required standard. For example, from the fact that a well-made machine worked badly one may infer that it was not very well maintained; whether that lack of maintenance, if one infers it, amounts to a shortfall in the defendant depends on how expert and frequent the maintenance incumbent on him, as a matter of law, is. But one may not infer bad maintenance at all. The machine may have been badly handled. If the person responsible for maintenance is also responsible for the faults of the operator of the machine, it does not matter which is inferred, and it is enough that it is more likely than not that it must have been one or the other.

When one can infer from the facts proved that the defendant was careless in some respect not specifically shown, then it is said that *res ipsa loquitur*. People have tried to say under what circumstances such an inference is possible or permissible or unavoidable, but it appears from the nature of the matter that there can be no real rules about it. If there are few rules to tell us when a defendant *was* careless, there must be even fewer to tell us when he *must have been* careless. We may, with Megaw L.J. in *Lloyde v West Midlands Gas Board* [1971] 1 W.L.R. 719 at 755, "doubt whether it is right to describe *res ipsa loquitur* as a 'doctrine.'" Judge L.J. was disparaging about the quasi-doctrine in *Carroll v Fearon* [1998] Times L.R. 31, where it was held that there was no need to prove negligence in the manufacturer of a tyre which was shown to have a structural defect: "Negligence is found as a matter of inference from the existence of the defect taken in connection with all the known circumstances." The Supreme Court of Canada has indeed opted for total abandonment of the maxim: *Fontaine v Loewen Estate* (1997) 156 D.L.R. (4th) 181 (1998) 114 L.Q.R. 547.

May L.J. was also disparaging in *Fryer v Pearson* ([2000] T.L.R. 260) where the claimant went to the defendant's home to install a new gas fire, and as he knelt on the carpet beside the cloth which he had laid down, a needle entered his knee. His suit under s.2 of the Occupiers' Liability Act 1957 was dismissed. Although it was found that the needle must have been in the carpet prior to his arrival, this did not show that the private householder had been negligent. It depended on the duty of care under consideration, affected by all the circumstances of the case, including the fact that the needle could not be expected to present any risk of serious injury.

If *res ipsa loquitur*, a matter which need not be specifically pleaded (*Bennett v Chemical Construction (G.B.) Ltd* [1971] 1 W.L.R. 1571), the defendant will lead evidence. His aim is to show that he behaved properly. He may try to prove the physical cause of the accident and that it is not attributable to his fault; but it is enough, even if he cannot do that, to clear himself of fault by showing that he behaved properly throughout. If the facts he proves make it appear less likely than not that there are unproved facts suggesting that he was at fault, then the plaintiff loses.

Take an example. A shopper falls on some spilt yoghourt on the floor of a supermarket. She naturally has no idea how long it has lain there. The supermarket is not responsible just because the yoghourt was dropped (unless by an employee), but only if it has lain there an unreasonable time. So the supermarket is probably not at fault unless the yoghourt is more likely than not to have been there an unreasonable time—and there is no evidence either way on that point. Certainly if the supermarket proves that the floor was swept 10 minutes or so before the accident, the plaintiff will fail, but in a case where the supermarket did not prove when it last swept the floor but only that it normally swept the floor five or six times a day, a divided Court of Appeal upheld the judge's holding for the plaintiff. The same court would not necessarily have reversed a judge's finding for the defendant. (*Ward v Tesco Stores* [1976] 1 All E.R. 219.

Take another example. Suppose that the defendant shows that the physical cause of the accident was a defect in his machine. Proof of that fact excludes the inference that the machine was badly operated. It leaves quite open the inference that the machine was badly maintained (*Colvilles v Devine* [1969] 1 W.L.R. 475, HL.) Suppose that the defendant then proves that his system of maintenance was in accordance with general practice, and that the system was being properly implemented. Then the defendant has very nearly rebutted the inference that there was some respect in which he behaved carelessly. But if he is a specialist, the court may require him to show in addition that he had a system of informing himself of those events which called for more than normal maintenance, and that that system operated properly (*Henderson v Jenkins* [1970] A.C. 282). Or it may not.

Nearer home is this example. The plaintiff stopped his car quite properly at traffic lights, only to be rear-ended by a Sherpa minibus, driven by the first defendant and owned by the second defendant. The judge found that the Sherpa's brakes had suddenly failed without any warning, and that the driver was not to blame. He held the owner liable, however, despite evidence (not subjected to cross-examination) that the minibus had passed its M.O.T. test a month earlier and had had a "full service" a fortnight before that. The Court of Appeal accepted that the crash was evidence of negligence which required rebuttal, but held that while the M.O.T. test did not rebut the inference, the proof of the "full service" did so. The plaintiff accordingly lost his claim. *Worsley v Hollins* [1991] R.T.R. 252.

In *Widdowson v Newgate Meat Corp.* [1997] Times L.R. 622 neither party gave evidence, the plaintiff because he suffered from a serious mental disorder (he had been found lying in the middle of the nearside lane of a dual carriageway) and the defendant because he thought he had no case to answer, having told the police that he had been travelling at about 60 m.p.h. with headlights on high beam and suddenly collided with something, he knew not what, since he had seen nothing. The trial judge refused to apply *res ipsa loquitur* and dismissed the plaintiff's claim. The Court of Appeal said he was wrong, and that though the maxim rarely applied in traffic cases, it was also not usual for there to be no evidence from either party. Here the plaintiff could tellingly have asserted that it was more likely than not that the effective cause of the accident was the failure of the driver, after a long day, to observe and avoid him, and no plausible explanation had been offered to rebut this inference. The Court assessed contributory negligence at 50 per cent, that is, it just split the difference (as it did in *Jenkins v Holt* [1999] Times L.R.

416, CA, a two-car collision where the defendant drove into the plaintiff who was executing a U-turn on a wide straight road, and both parties denied having seen the other).

It may be because of these decisions that in *Hatton v Cooper* [2001] EWCA Civ 623 where there was a head-on collision in the middle of the road with no witnesses and neither driver could remember anything, the defendant admitted that she was negligent but only as to 50 per cent—an utterly dotty pleading. The trial judge held the defendant fully liable since there was no evidence that the claimant had been negligent at all, and it was unlikely that both were suicidal. The Court of Appeal by a majority reversed, and held the parties equally liable, Pill L.J. dissenting.

If Widdowson in the case above had been on the sidewalk at the time, there would clearly have been a prima facie case, and *a fortiori* if he had been on a pedestrian crossing. But if the defendant proves that the driver was dead at the wheel by reason of a cardiac attack, then the inference of facts indicating negligence (the driver can't have been keeping a proper look-out, etc.) vanishes, and the defendant does not then have to go further and show that it was not negligent of the driver to set out when he was about to collapse (*Waugh v James K Allen Ltd*, 1964 S.L.T. 269; [1964] 2 Lloyd's Rep. 1, HL).

The courts are reluctant to hold that traffic accidents take place with no negligence on either side, and incline to find both parties negligent unless there is evidence to the contrary. Sometimes there is such evidence, sufficient to rebut a clear inference of negligence., as where the claimant's car travelling normally in its proper lane is struck head-on by the defendant's oncoming vehicle. When it was proved that the defendant lost control when an XR2, which then disappeared at speed, cut in front of him and clipped his vehicle as he was about to follow a Land Rover overtaking a slower car, the lower court's finding of negligence was reversed. *Luffman v Coshall* (CA, May 23, 2000, Pill L.J. dissenting). On the evidence in that case, the incident was explained. Sometimes it remains a mystery. Such a case was *Carter v Sheath* [1990] R.T.R. 12, CA. A boy of 13 on his way back from a Scout meeting left his two companions on one side of the road and crossed safely to the other, though against the lights. Then he was struck and killed by the defendant's car, neither the defendant nor his wife travelling beside him having seen the boy. It was a mystery how the boy came to be back in the road. The accident being entirely unexplained, the defendant was held not liable).

Difficulties of proof have led other countries to adopt strict liability for traffic accidents: thus under the French law of July 5, 1985 the owner/insurer of a motor vehicle "involved" in an accident on the highway is liable for personal injury or death sustained therein even if he is not at fault at all, and furthermore is liable in full despite the contributory negligence of the claimant unless the claimant himself was driving at the time. Britain is quite exceptional in denying the claims of traffic accident victims who cannot prove that anyone is to blame for their injuries, and it is likely that Brussels will intervene to put an end to an anomaly so unfair to French tourists.

Where the defendant's duty is high (as in the pedestrian crossing instance), it is easier to infer that facts occurred which constituted a breach of it, because there are more sets of such facts. Thus in the tort of public nuisance the burden of proof is said to be reversed. This reversal of the burden of proof may make it practically easier to recover, even if the defendant's duty is stated in terms of reasonable care. There is a positive rule of law that the bailee of a chattel who fails to return it to the bailor must either pay its value or show that he was not at fault in not having it to give back; the plaintiff need prove only the delivery and the fruitless demand (*Houghland v Low*, below, p.504). Yet the duty of the compensated bailee is always said to be the duty to take reasonable care only. In law he bears the risk of carelessness only; in fact he bears the risk of not being able to prove that he was careful.

Note, however, *Blackpool Ladder Centre v BWP Partnership* (CA, Nov 13, 2000): in order to inspect the piers at Blackpool the defendant hired from the claimant firm a Land Rover with hydraulic support legs. After working properly on two piers, the legs on the vehicle refused to rise and it was covered by the incoming tide. It was found as a fact that the operator had not been negligent, so although there was no evidence of any defect in the machine, it must be inferred that it did indeed have an inherent defect, in breach of s.9 Supply of Goods and Services Act 1982, so the bailee was not liable.

BILL v SHORT BROS & HARLAND LTD

House of Lords [1963] N.I. 1

Action by employee against employer in respect of personal injury

The plaintiff was an experienced workman with 14 years' service with the defendants. One day after his lunch-break, he fell over a $1\frac{1}{2}$-inch rubber pipe laid across the floor of the building for the purpose of carrying compressor air. His view of the floor was slightly obstructed by the presence in front of him of a fellow-workman, but he knew that the pipe might be there.

At the trial before Sheil J. and a jury, the plaintiff gave evidence of those facts, said that he knew of two previous accidents caused in a similar way, and that in other factories the air-pipes were laid along a wall or suspended from the roof. Sheil J. withdrew the case from the jury, and dismissed the plaintiff's claim. The Court of Appeal of Northern Ireland dismissed the plaintiff's appeal (Lord MacDermott C.J. dissenting). Curran L.J. said: "This was the case of a man who decided to cross the working floor of a factory and who stumbled on an obstacle which he knew was there." The House of Lords allowed the plaintiff's appeal and ordered a new trial.

Lord Denning: My Lords, it appears to me that the claim at common law depends on three simple propositions. First, it is the duty of the employer to take reasonable care so to carry on his operations as not to subject those employed by him to unnecessary risk. Secondly, if the employer has failed in that duty, then the fact that the employee was fully aware of the risk may go to show that he was guilty of contributory negligence, but it does not by itself disentitle him from recovering. Thirdly, it is for the judge to say where there is any evidence from which the jury *could* infer that there was negligence on the part of the employer or contributory negligence on the part of the employee, but if there is such evidence then it must be left to the jury to say whether it *ought* to be inferred.

There was, in my opinion, evidence on which the jury *could* find that the employers were negligent. I base this particularly on the previous accidents which were drawn to their attention and of the means taken in other workshops to eliminate the risk. There was evidence on which the jury *could* find that the workman was guilty of contributory negligence. I base this particularly on his knowledge of the facts and of the risk. The jury *might* even find that his negligence was so predominant a factor that he was solely responsible for the accident—in short that he was one hundred per cent to blame—but they were not bound so to find. They *could* find him less to blame. And if so, it was for the jury to apportion the responsibility.

I think, therefore, that the common law claim should have been left to the jury . . .

Note:
For "jury" substitute "judge". One still talks of "jury questions", but the civil jury in England is a thing of the past: it exists only in claims for defamation and for false imprisonment.

Question:
Would the claimant now recover under reg.12(3) of the Workplace (Health, Safety and Welfare) Regulations 1992 (below, p.199). What would he have to prove?

Chapter 3

STATUTE, CRIME AND LIABILITY

Introduction

One might think that if *unreasonable* behaviour can give rise to liability for resulting harm, *unlawful* behaviour must certainly do so. Behaviour is constantly being rendered unlawful by statutes and regulations emanating from Parliament or Ministers, telling people to do this or not to do that. When someone has done or not done what such a rule forbids or requires, it is an important question whether he may be sued by a person injured in consequence. It is not, however, an easy question, since statutes and regulations cover a vast range of situations and are drafted in very various terms.

Sometimes the primary purpose of a statute is to change the rules of tort law (*e.g.* Occupiers' Liability Act 1957, Defective Premises Act 1972, Consumer Protection Act 1987). More often an enactment seeks to change human behaviour. It may do this either by empowering people to do what otherwise they could not lawfully do, or by requiring them to do or abstain from doing what they were previously free to do or not to do. It is important to note the distinction. The statute in *Dorset Yacht* did not require, but merely empowered, the defendants to confine the boys: it was the common law which required the defendants to take care how they exercised their statutory powers, not because the powers they were exercising were statutory in origin, but because what they were doing in fact placed them under a duty to do it carefully, according to the rules of the common law. The same question lay at the heart of *Stovin v Wise* (above p.89) and many other recent cases on the liability of public authorities.

Although in principle there is a clear distinction between what one may do and what one must do, between powers and duties, it may not be so clear in practice. This is partly because powers are conferred for a purpose, so that one can argue that there may be a duty to exercise them. But since there may be a discretion how to exercise such powers (which is not the case with a duty), the courts' inquiry into the manner of their exercise may be constrained by a concern not to interfere with a discretion conferred by Parliament on the body in question. Furthermore, if Parliament has said that something must be done, one cannot complain if it is done; Parliament has authorised what might otherwise be a wrong. Nor, if Parliament has said that something may be done, can one complain unless needless damage is caused by the way it is done *and* the conduct is objectionable at common law. It seems clear that the careless exercise of statutory powers is not a tort in itself, and that breach of statutory duties is actionable only if Parliament must have intended that civil liability should ensue.

Most of this chapter is concerned with the latter holding, with claims founded on the unlawfulness, not the unreasonableness, of the defendant's conduct.

An enactment may simply provide that in certain circumstances liability is to exist (Civil Aviation Act 1982, s.76; Data Protection Act 1998, s.13; New Roads and Street Works Act 1991, s.82). It may impose a duty to act in a certain way and then provide that liability is to ensue if the duty is broken (Health and Safety at Work Act 1974, s.47(2) (safety regulations); Building Act 1984, s.38 (building regulations, but not yet in force); Telecommunications Act 1984, s.18; Race Relations Act 1976, s.57; Consumer Credit Act 1974, s.92(3), Privacy and Electronic Communications (EC Directive) Regulations 2003 (SI 2003/2426) reg.30). Sometimes an enactment imposes a duty but provides that there is to be no civil liability for breach (Post Office Act 1969, s.9; Health and Safety at Work Act 1974, s.47(1)(a)). Sometimes conduct is criminalised and civil liability is excluded: thus the Package Travel, Package Holidays and Package Tours Regulations 1992 (SI 1992/3288) reg.27. provides helpfully that " . . . no right of action in civil proceedings in respect of any loss shall arise by reason only of the commission of an offence under regulations 5, 7, 8, 16 or 22 of these Regulations". Quite often an enactment imposes a duty (Mental Health Act 1983, s.117—after care of mental patients: see *Clunis v Camden & Islington H.A.* [1998] 3 All E.R. 180 at 190) or creates an offence (Crossbows Act 1987 [!]) and remains wholly silent about civil liability. In such cases it falls to the judges to determine whether civil liability is to exist or not. Their attitude is distinctly hostile.

Thus it is an offence (now under Environmental Protection Act 1990, s.80(4)) if a person guilty of the statutory nuisance of maintaining premises which are prejudicial to health fails to comply with an abatement notice, and for this offence the Hackney London B.C. was fined £500 and made to pay £1,400 compensation to the tenant. When his children sued for damages, however, the Court of Appeal held that the statute gave rise to no civil liability. *Issa v Hackney L.B.C.* [1997] 1 All E.R. 999.

In the French view, by contrast, it is self-evident that a person who can be punished by the State can be sued by his victim: indeed, they let the victim claim his damages in the criminal prosecution itself. Criminal courts in England can now make limited compensation orders in favour of victims (see below, p.180) but the civil courts, which do not even impose liability on all common law criminals (*Hargreaves v Bretherton* [1959] 1 Q.B. 45 (perjury), *Chapman v Honig* (below, p.184) (contempt of court)), are most reluctant to impose liability on statutory offenders. This is not so unreasonable. It is one thing to make a person pay a small fine and quite another to make him pay for all the consequences of his conduct, especially if the fine is so small that it is exacted even if he is not really to blame at all. Furthermore, since the common law of tort already holds people liable if their unreasonable behaviour causes foreseeable physical harm, the only result of imposing liability on statutory offenders would be to make people pay when they have behaved quite reasonably, or when the harm they have caused is either unforeseeable or merely financial.

Given that "it is not enough for the plaintiff simply to show that she has suffered damage in consequence of a breach of duty imposed by statute" (*Olutu v Home Office* [1997] 1 All E.R. 383 at 395), how is one to determine whether breach of a particular statutory provision leads to civil liability? In Germany the judges ask if the law in question was designed to protect people like the plaintiff from harm of that type. In England that is no more than a factor to be taken into account in answering the principal question, *i.e.* was it the intention of Parliament that there should be civil liability? This is rather an odd question to ask when there is no evidence of the intention it seeks to ascertain, rather like the question in contract cases whether a statute which prohibits an act impliedly prohibits a contract which involves the act (*e.g. St. John Shipping Corp. v Rank* [1957] 1 Q.B. 267 at 285). In both situations it is really the courts which make the decision, and in making the decision they are naturally affected by the same considerations which weigh with them in other cases. They are much more ready to impose liability in tort if the damage is physical, if the relationship is close and if the defendant was at fault—though if liability already exists at common law the judges may always say that statutory liability is unnecessary (*McCall v Abelesz*

[1976] Q.B. 585). In other cases if Parliament wants civil liability to exist, it had better say so in clear terms.

Damage

A water authority is under a duty to maintain a certain pressure in its pipes; it fails to do so and a ratepayer's house is burned down in consequence; the water authority is subject to a fine, but not to liability in damages (*Atkinson v Newcastle Waterworks Co* (1877) 2 Ex.D. 441). The same Act requires the water to be wholesome; it is not, and a ratepayer suffers personal injury from drinking it; the water authority is liable in damages as well as to a fine (*Read v Croydon Corp.* [1938] 4 All E.R. 631). Take education. An education authority is under a duty to provide school accommodation; it fails to do so and a parent is put to the expense of fees at a private school; he cannot recover them (*Watt v Kesteven C.C.* [1955] 1 Q.B. 408). Again, an authority must make particular provision for children with special educational needs, such as those affected by dyslexia: no action in damages lies against it for breach of this duty (*Phelps v Hillingdon LBC* [2001] 2 A.C. 619 (probably). However, the same legislation requires that safety in schools be reasonably assured; a child cuts her hand on a thin pane of glass; she can recover (*Reffell v Surrey C.C.*, below, p.190).

Relationship

The occupier of a factory buys and instals machinery whose dangerous parts are insufficiently fenced; a workman injures himself on it. The victim can recover from the occupier, but not from the vendor, though both are liable to a fine (*Biddle v Truvox Engineering Co* [1952] 1 K.B. 101): the relationship of vendor and consumer (unlike vendor/purchaser and manufacturer/consumer) is rather weak, whereas the relationship of occupier and visitor or employer and employee is extremely strong. Indeed, most of the successful suits for breach of statutory duty are brought by workmen against their employer or the occupier of their place of work. The very many safety regulations issued under the Health and Safety at Work Act 1974 are all actionable, though the hortatory general duties laid down at the beginning of the Act are not. Examples are the Provision and Use of Work Equipment Regulations 1998 [below, p.197] and the Control of Substances Hazardous to Health Regulations 1988 (SI 1988/1657) as amended.

The relationship between common users of the highway, on the other hand, is much less protective and strong. The pedestrian, certainly, can recover from the driver who mows him down on a pedestrian crossing (*London Passenger Transport Board v Upson* [1949] A.C. 155), but those duties breach of which may injure both pedestrians and other motorists, and property as well as person, are not generally so construed as to give a right of action to the person hurt thereby (*Phillips v Britannia Hygienic Laundry Co*, below, p.193). And where the duty is imposed, not on a motorist using the highway, but on a manufacturer, vendor or repairer, the grounds for denying liability seem even stronger.

Fault

German law has an admirable provision: "Liability also attaches to a person who contravenes a statute designed for the protection of another. If the statute may, according to its terms, be contravened even in the absence of fault, liability in damages attaches only where fault is present" (§ 823, German Civil Code). In England, however, liability for breach of an actionable statutory duty is in principle strict. This presumptive liability may well be subject to defences, but they need to be specified, for there is no general defence of lack of fault, though quite often there is a defence if the defendant can prove that it was not "reasonably practicable" to avoid the breach. We have seen a similar defence to breach of the absolute duty of the highway authority to maintain the physical condition of the highway (Highways Act 1980, s.58, above p.154).

Thus if the statutory duty is one which gives rise to liability on breach, there will be liability no matter how the breach arose. Because of this rule, the courts, which dislike imposing liability without fault, are tempted either to deny that a particular statutory duty which can be broken without fault gives rise to liability at all or to construe it in such a manner that unless there is some fault there is no breach.

Subject to all this, the plaintiff who sues for breach of statutory duty has the one great advantage that, depending on its terms, he may not have to persuade the court that the defendant behaved unreasonably: proof that the situation was illicit may suffice without the further proof that it was the defendant's fault. But there are special hurdles, too. The plaintiff must bring both himself and his harm within the ambit of the legislative intention. Thus only the ratepayer and not his family could found on the water company's duty to provide wholesome water (*Read v Croydon Corp.* [1938] 4 All E.R. 631), and where the duty was designed to protect animals from contagion no compensation was payable to the owner of sheep which were drowned as a result of the breach (*Gorris v Scott*, below, p.223).

The Interaction of Statutory and Common Law Duties.

As we have seen, a statute may expressly exclude, oust or replace the rules of common law (*e.g.* Occupiers' Liability Act 1984, s.1(1) (above, p.40); Congenital Disabilities Act 1976, s.4(5)) (above, p.117). If not, duties at common law may well coexist and concur with statutory duties. As Stephenson L.J. said, perhaps a little widely, "In every case where a plaintiff has alleged a breach of statutory duty, he is entitled to allege negligence at common law and to ask the court to answer the question whether he has proved negligence, irrespective of his having proved a breach of statutory duty" (*Bux v Slough Metals* [1974] 1 All E.R. 262 at 273). Common law duties are elastic and extensible by analogy while those imposed by statute are rigid and applicable only within its precise terms. Thus if a statute requires a guardrail beside a drop of two metres or more, it is inapplicable to a lesser drop, however little less, whereas a common law duty may apply wherever danger is perceptible. On the other hand, where there is a common law duty to take reasonable care the courts may hold that the defendant has satisfied it if he has met the statutory requirements in that precise situation. Likewise an alleged defect in a product cannot be a ground of liability if it is due to compliance with statutory requirements (Consumer Protection Act 1987, s.4 (1)(a)). Sometimes, too, where a body is subject to statutory rules, the courts will hesitate to impose more extensive requirements (*Ephraim v Newham L.B.C.* (1993) 91 L.G.R. 412, CA). Furthermore, where the statute confers on a body a discretion to decide how to act, the courts will not impose a common law duty which would interfere with proper freedom in the exercise of that discretion.

Local authorities have statutory duties regarding child care and education. That breaches of these duties were not actionable in damages was held in *X v Bedfordshire CC* [1995] 2 A.C. 633. While it is true that the substantive decision in that case has been held incompatible with the subsequent Human Rights Act (*JD v East Berkshire Community Health* [2003] EWCA Civ 1151), this ruling is still good law; its effect, however, has been sidelined by the decision that the local authority is vicariously liable for the negligence of those they employ to perform their statutory functions (*Phelps v Hillingdon LBC* [2001] 2 A.C. 619).

Common Law Crimes.

So far as the common law is concerned, there appear to be only two cases where the qualification of the defendant's behaviour as criminal is relevant to render him liable to pay damages to a person hurt in consequence of that behaviour. One is conspiracy (see below, p.622) and the other is public nuisance (on whose criminal and civil aspects see J. Spencer, "Public Nuisance—A Critical Examination" [1989] Camb. L.J. 55). The crime of public nuisance (which may be committed in very many ways, as by making obscene telephone calls to enough women (*R. v Johnson* [1996] 2 Cr.App.R. 434)) is of interest to tort lawyers mainly when it takes the form of unreasonably impeding proper use of the Queen's highway (including the Thames), whether by obstruction or danger. If the defendant has been guilty of a public nuisance (by creation or failure to abate) a plaintiff who suffers special damage may sue—special damage being required precisely because the public is affected and one cannot allow the general public to sue. The plaintiff in *Great House at Sonning v Berkshire C.C.* [1996] Times L.R. 181 was certainly going to suffer special damage if the defendant closed the road as it proposed to do, but the injunction issued by the trial judge was vacated by the Court of Appeal: the plaintiff was impugning a governmental decision and must go by way of judicial review. In dissent Saville L.J. said all that the plaintiff need show in order to establish a prima facie common law claim was that the defendant was proposing to obstruct the highway.

Now the public interest in interferences with the highway is primarily in their removal; the Attorney-General seeks an injunction. There is good reason to grant an injunction to abate a proved nuisance even if the defendant was not at fault in causing it; he will be at fault if he doesn't remove it after being put on notice by the action. It is, of course, another question whether he should be amenable to a fine or liable to pay damages if he was not at fault in creating the nuisance. Nevertheless, liability in public nuisance came to be independent of the qualification of the defendant's conduct as reasonable or not; if the obstruction or the danger is unreasonable, it is immaterial how the defendant acted in causing it. On this, however, one must put the gloss that obstructions or dangers which are produced without negligence in the course of reasonable use of the highway do not constitute nuisances; thus a car does not become a nuisance the minute it has unforeseeably broken down.

There are three possible points of divergence between public nuisance and negligence—the fault, the damage, and the factor which links them.

Fault is necessary in negligence, as we have seen. Public nuisance, on the other hand, is based more on causing an unreasonable danger than on causing a danger unreasonably. Accordingly, bearing in mind the gloss mentioned above, we must say that fault in the defendant or his servant is not a necessary element of liability in public nuisance. The faultless instigator of faulty work on the highway and the landlord of dilapidated premises adjoining it are liable. (The first case may be subsumed under the general law of negligence by styling it an instance of liability for the fault of an independent contractor, but the second cannot.) Where, however, an unreasonable danger exists without the fault of anyone at all, the present tendency appears to be to deny liability in public nuisance (*British Road Services v Slater* [1964] 1 W.L.R. 498).

ecently the tort of negligence remedied primarily physical damage. In other ...ligence was about *dangers*. Public nuisance admittedly includes dangers on ...e highway, but it also extends to *obstructions*. An obstruction may be dangerous or it may not. In *Wright v Lodge* (below, p.228) it was said that "there would be no liability, because no relevant danger, if an obstruction was only a danger to a reckless driver . . . ". The typical result of an obstruction on the highway is delay; and time is not blood, but money. "Obstruction damage," therefore, tended to found liability not in negligence but only, if at all, in public nuisance—delay to a traveller (*Anglo-Algerian SS Co v Houlder Line* [1908] 1 K.B. 659), the cutting-off of a valuable view (*Campbell v Paddington B.C.* [1911] 1 K.B. 869), loss of profit through inability to get goods out (*Iveson v Moore* (1699) 1 Ld.Raym. 486; 91 E.R. 1224), or customers or vehicles in (*Wilkes v Hungerford Market Co* (1835) 2 Bing.N.C. 281; 132 E.R. 110; *Tate & Lyle Indus. v G.L.C.* [1983] 1 All E.R. 1159, HL).

What of the link between the conduct and the damage? Negligence remedies primarily foreseeable damage. Suppose that a nuisance by obstruction unpredictably turns out to be a danger and directly causes unforeseeable physical damage. Is this damage compensable? A cogent judgment from New South Wales held that it was, but the Judicial Committee disagreed and said: "It is not sufficient that the injury suffered . . . was the direct result of the nuisance if that injury was in the relevant sense unforeseeable." *The Wagon Mound (No.2)* [1967] 1 A.C. 617 at 640, on appeal from [1963] 1 Lloyd's Rep. 402. In this respect, then, public nuisance has been analogised to negligence, at any rate where physical damage has been caused. Must obstruction damage also be foreseeable? The Judicial Committee said: "the choice is between [foreseeability] being a necessary element in all cases of nuisance or in none," but there will be difficulty in applying this to nuisance by obstruction, at any rate if "necessary" is taken to mean "sufficient"—for how many people foreseeably lose money when a bridge collapses or a level-crossing gate gets stuck or someone floods a road?

Section 1.—Crime and Compensation

POWERS OF CRIMINAL COURTS (SENTENCING) ACT 2000

130.—*Compensation orders against convicted persons*
(1) A court by or before which a person is convicted of an offence, instead of or in addition to dealing with him in any other way, may, on application or otherwise, make an order (in this Act referred to as a "compensation order") requiring him—

(a) to pay compensation for any personal injury, loss or damage resulting from that offence or any other offence which is taken into consideration by the court in determining sentence; or
(b) to make payments for funeral expenses or bereavement in respect of a death resulting from any such offence, other than a death due to an accident arising out of the presence of a motor vehicle on a road;

but this is subject to the following provisions of this section and to section 131 below.
(2) Where the person is convicted of an offence the sentence for which is fixed by law or falls to be imposed under section 109(2), 110(2) or 111(2) above, subsection (1) above shall have effect as if the words "instead of or" were omitted.

(3) A court shall give reasons, on passing sentence, if it does not make a compensation order in a case where this section empowers it to do so.

(4) Compensation under subsection (1) above shall be of such amount as the court considers appropriate, having regard to any evidence and to any representations that are made by or on behalf of the accused or the prosecutor.

(5) In the case of an offence under the Theft Act 1968, where the property in question is recovered, any damage to the property occurring while it was out of the owner's possession shall be treated for the purposes of subsection (1) above as having resulted from the offence, however and by whomever the damage was caused.

(6) A compensation order may only be made in respect of injury, loss or damage (other than loss suffered by a person's dependants in consequence of his death) which was due to an accident arising out of the presence of a motor vehicle on a road, if—

(a) it is in respect of damage which is treated by subsection (5) above as resulting from an offence under the Theft Act 1968; or
(b) it is in respect of injury, loss or damage as respects which—
   (i) the offender is uninsured in relation to the use of the vehicle; and
   (ii) compensation is not payable under any arrangements to which the Secretary of State is a party.

(7) Where a compensation order is made in respect of injury, loss or damage due to an accident arising out of the presence of a motor vehicle on a road, the amount to be paid may include an amount representing the whole or part of any loss of or reduction in preferential rates of insurance attributable to the accident.

(8) A vehicle the use of which is exempted from insurance by section 144 of the Road Traffic Act 1988 is not uninsured for the purposes of subsection (6) above.

(9) A compensation order in respect of funeral expenses may be made for the benefit of anyone who incurred the expenses.

(10) A compensation order in respect of bereavement may be made only for the benefit of a person for whose benefit a claim for damages for bereavement could be made under section 1A of the Fatal Accidents Act 1976; and the amount of compensation in respect of bereavement shall not exceed the amount for the time being specified in section 1A(3) of that Act.

(11) In determining whether to make a compensation order against any person, and in determining the amount to be paid by any person under such an order, the court shall have regard to his means so far as they appear or are known to the court.

(12) Where the court considers—

(a) that it would be appropriate both to impose a fine and to make a compensation order, but
(b) that the offender has insufficient means to pay both an appropriate fine and appropriate compensation,

the court shall give preference to compensation (though it may impose a fine as well).

Notes:

This statute replaces and largely reproduces the Powers of Criminal Courts Act 1973, s.35, under which the cases given below were decided.

1. Despite the clear words of the statute, compensation orders are to be granted by magistrates only in "simple cases"; indeed, the Court of Appeal has on this ground quashed compensation orders granted by the Crown Court: (*R. v Briscoe* (1993) 15 Cr.App.R. (S) 699)). In *Herbert v Lambeth L.B.C.* (1991) 90 L.G.R. 310 Woolf L.J. said that "it would not be an appropriate use of the powers under section 35 of the Act for a magistrates' court to award substantial compensation for matters which can loosely be described as personal injury." The statute requires the magistrates to hear evidence before granting an order; the courts allow them to refuse an order without hearing evidence. Forty-one per cent of those convicted in magistrates courts of violence against the person were ordered to pay compensation in the year 2000.

2. A compensation order is especially useful where there is no civil liability. Thus in *Issa v Hackney L.B.C.* [1997] 1 All E.R. 999 the local authority pleaded guilty to the offence of failure to abate a statutory nuisance and was made to pay the tenant £1,400 compensation; his children had also suffered, but when they claimed it was held that the offence gave rise to no civil liability in damages and no compensation order could be made because the defendant had already been convicted. Magistrates used to adjourn cases in order to allow the local authority to cure the statutory nuisance, but this has been stopped, for then there would be no conviction and no compensation order, whereas "The right to compensation under section 35 of the Act of 1973 following a conviction under section 82(2) of the Act of 1990 is important: it may be the only way a tenant can recover any compensation." *R. v Dudley Magistrates, Ex p. Hollis* [1999] 1 W.L.R. 642.

3. According to the official leaflet "You cannot apply for a compensation order yourself so it is important that you tell the police if you would like to receive compensation." If you provide them with documentary evidence "the police will then pass this information on to the CPS who will make sure that the court knows about it." A sensible system?

4. In the year 2000, some 102,400 offenders were subjected to compensation orders, down 1,700 from 1999. In cases of personal violence the average payment in the magistrates courts was £219, in the Crown Court £530. Note that claims for injuries worth less than £1,000 are rejected by the Criminal Injuries Compensation Authority.

THE CRIMINAL INJURIES COMPENSATION SCHEME (2001)

1. This Scheme is made by the Secretary of State under the Criminal Injuries Compensation Act 1995. Applications received on or after 1 April 2001 for the payment of compensation to, or in respect of, persons who have sustained criminal injury will be considered under this Scheme.

Administration of the Scheme

2. Claims officers in the Criminal Injuries Compensation Authority ("the Authority") will determine claims for compensation in accordance with this Scheme. Appeals against decisions taken on reviews under this Scheme will be determined by adjudicators. Persons appointed as adjudicators are appointed as members of the Criminal Injuries Compensation Appeals Panel ("the Panel"). The Secretary of State will appoint one of the adjudicators as Chairman of the Panel. The Secretary of State will also appoint persons as staff of the Panel to administer the provisions of this Scheme relating to the appeal system.

3. Claims officers will be responsible for deciding, in accordance with this Scheme, what awards (if any) should be made in individual cases, and how they should be paid. Their decisions will be open to review and thereafter to appeal to the Panel, in accordance with this Scheme. No decision, whether by a claims officer or the Panel, will be open to appeal to the Secretary of State.

4. The general working of this Scheme will be kept under review by the Secretary of State. The Accounting Officers for the Authority and the Panel must each submit reports to the Secretary of State and the Scottish Ministers as soon as possible after the end of each financial year, dealing with the operation of this Scheme and the discharge of functions under it. The Accounting Officers must each keep proper accounts and proper records in relation to those accounts, and must each prepare a statement of accounts in each financial year in a form directed by the Secretary of State. These statements of accounts must be submitted to the Secretary of State and the Scottish Ministers as soon as possible after the end of each financial year.

5. The Panel will advise the Secretary of State on matters on which he seeks its advice, as well as on such other matters and at such times as it considers appropriate. Any advice given by the Panel will be referred to by the Accounting Officer for the Panel in his annual report made under the preceding paragraph.

Eligibility to apply for compensation

6. Compensation may be paid in accordance with this Scheme:

(a) to an applicant who has sustained a criminal injury on or after 1 August 1964;

(b) where the victim of a criminal injury sustained on or after 1 August 1964 has since died, to an applicant who is a qualifying claimant for the purposes of paragraph 38 (compensation in fatal cases).

For the purposes of this Scheme, "applicant" means any person for whose benefit an application for compensation is made, even where it is made on his behalf by another person.

7. No compensation will be paid under this Scheme in the following circumstances:

(a) where the applicant has previously lodged any claim for compensation in respect of the same criminal injury under this or any other scheme for the compensation of the victims of violent crime in operation in Great Britain; or

(b) where the criminal injury was sustained before 1 October 1979 and the victim and the assailant were living together at the time as members of the same family.

8. For the purposes of this Scheme, "criminal injury" means one or more personal injuries as described in the following paragraph, being an injury sustained in Great Britain (see *Note 1*) and directly attributable to:

(a) a crime of violence (including arson, fire-raising or an act of poisoning); or

(b) an offence of trespass on a railway; or

(c) the apprehension or attempted apprehension of an offender or a suspected offender, the prevention or attempted prevention of an offence, or the giving of help to any constable who is engaged in any such activity.

13. A claims officer may withhold or reduce an award where he considers that:

(a) the applicant failed to take, without delay, all reasonable steps to inform the police, or other body or person considered by the Authority to be appropriate for the purpose, of the circumstances giving rise to the injury; or

(b) the applicant failed to co-operate with the police or other authority in attempting to bring the assailant to justice; or

(c) the applicant has failed to give all reasonable assistance to the Authority or other body or person in connection with the application; or

(d) the conduct of the applicant before, during or after the incident giving rise to the application makes it inappropriate that a full award or any award at all be made; or

(e) the applicant's character as shown by his criminal convictions (excluding convictions spent under the Rehabilitation of Offenders Act 1974 at the date of application or death) or by evidence available to the claims officer makes it inappropriate that a full award or any award at all be made.

14. In considering the issue of conduct under paragraph 13(d) above, a claims officer may withhold or reduce an award where he considers that excessive consumption of alcohol or use of illicit drugs by the applicant contributed to the circumstances which gave rise to the injury in such a way as to make it inappropriate that a full award, or any award at all, be made.

15. Where the victim has died since sustaining the injury (whether or not in consequence of it), paragraphs 13 and 14 will apply in relation both to the deceased and to any applicant for compensation under paragraphs 37–44 (fatal awards).

16. A claims officer will make an award only where he is satisfied:

(a) that there is no likelihood that an assailant would benefit if an award were made; or

(b) where the applicant is under 18 years of age when the application is determined, that it would not be against his interest for an award to be made.

17. Where a case is not ruled out under paragraph 7(b) (injury sustained before 1 October 1979) but at the time when the injury was sustained, the victim and any assailant (whether or not that assailant actually inflicted the injury) were living in the same household as members of the same family, an award will be withheld unless:

(a) the assailant has been prosecuted in connection with the offence, except where a claims officer considers that there are practical, technical or other good reasons why a prosecution has not been brought; and
(b) in the case of violence between adults in the family, a claims officer is satisfied that the applicant and the assailant stopped living in the same household before the application was made and are unlikely to share the same household again.

For the purposes of this paragraph, a man and woman living together as husband and wife will be treated as members of the same family.

Note:
The Scheme (not made by statutory instrument and therefore not easy to find in a library) contains a list of a vast number of types of injury and fixes a sum payable in respect of each, ranging from £1,000 to a maximum of £250,000. Minor injuries can be aggregated in order to reach the minimum claim, subject to special rules about duration of effect and visits to doctors. Where the crime has merely exacerbated or accelerated a condition, payment is made only for exacerbation or acceleration (para.25).

There are some divergences from the tort rules relating to death claims (above, p.113) and deductions (below, p.652). Thus in fatal cases the two-year partner, even of the same sex, but not a former spouse may claim a standard £11,000, as may a child of any age or status, but if more than one person is qualified, the payment for each is £5,500. The victim's estate gets nothing for pain and suffering (para.37). Pensions payable to the survivor as a result of arrangements with the decedent's employer are deducted as to half, if taxable, otherwise in full (para.47). As to injured applicants, any sums payable by the employer including pensions triggered by the injury as well as social security benefits are deducted from claims for lost earnings, but the proceeds of private pensions are deducted only if they cover the cost of health treatment or residential care for which a claim is made (para.45).

In 2000–2001 the Authority paid out over £200 million, making 39,813 awards. There were about 76,000 applications, of which 37,000 were ineligible, for failure to cooperate with the police (6,512), misconduct before or after the event (4,040), or because the claim was not worth £1,000 or more.

CHAPMAN v HONIG

Court of Appeal [1963] 2 Q.B. 502; [1963] 3 W.L.R. 19; 107 S.J. 374; [1963] 2 All E.R. 513
(noted (1963) 79 L.Q.R. 468; (1972) 88 L.Q.R. 177)

Action of trespass by tenant vindictively evicted by landlord

This was an action of trespass brought by a tenant against his landlord. The plaintiff had given evidence against the defendant in a previous action by another tenant, and the defendant out of pique served a notice to quit on the plaintiff, under such circumstances that the defendant could have been punished for contempt of court. The plaintiff stayed on in the flat after the expiry of the notice to quit, and the defendant entered and padlocked the doors.

The county court judge awarded £50 damages. The defendant appealed, and his appeal was allowed by the Court of Appeal **(Lord Denning M.R. dissenting)**.

Davies L.J.: ... One cannot help but sympathise with the proposition that in general a person injured by a wrongful act should have a remedy in damages against the wrongdoer. But it has to be considered whether, in the first place, that proposition is universally true, and, secondly, whether in the circumstances of this case the defendant's action in serving a notice to quit was, as against the plaintiff, wrongful at all.

It is, no doubt, true that in most cases a person injured by a criminal offence has a right of action against the criminal. That is because most crimes are torts. Acts of criminal violence to person or property would be trespasses; larceny would be conversion; most frauds would give rise to an action of deceit; and so on. But not all crimes give rise to a cause of action. For example, it is well established that perjury does not give rise to a cause of action at the suit of a person injured by the perjury; see the decision of Lord Goddard C.J. in *Hargreaves v Bretherton* ([1959] 1 Q.B. 45), and the authorities there cited. It is true that there may be special features relating to the offence of perjury which might make it difficult to permit of an action based upon it. But this line of authority shows that there is no general rule that all crimes give rise to a cause of action.

Equally relevant to this inquiry is the great body of case law dealing with the question whether the commission of an act forbidden or made punishable by statute gives a cause of action to a person injured by the act. On this question it is notoriously difficult to enunciate any guiding principle. The authorities are discussed in the dissenting *obiter* judgment of Somervell L.J. in *Solomons v R. Gertzenstein Ltd* [1954] 2 Q.B. 243. As examples may be cited the well-known case of *Groves v Lord Wimborne* ([1898] 2 Q.B. 402), the *alma genetrix* of so much litigation under the provisions of the Factories Acts, on the one side of the line, and, on the other, *Phillips v Britannia Hygienic Laundry Co Ltd* [below, p.193]. Perhaps the nearest that one gets to a statement of principle is in the words of Atkin L.J. in the last-cited case, in a passage adopted by Somervell L.J. in *Solomons*'s case: "Therefore the question is," said Atkin L.J., "whether these regulations, viewed in the circumstances in which they were made and to which they relate, were intended to impose a duty which is a public duty only or whether they were intended, in addition to the public duty, to impose a duty enforceable by an individual aggrieved." It is, of course, implicit in this principle that not in every case is an individual who has been injured by a wrongful act entitled to sue, even though the wrongful act is prohibited or made punishable by statute. And the principle can, in my judgment, be applied in the present case by inquiring whether the concept of, and proceedings for, contempt of court are concerned with the preservation of the inviolability of the administration and course of justice and its proper conduct or whether, in addition, they are intended in all cases to give a remedy in damages to an individual injured by the contempt. . . .

Pearson L.J.: . . . I have considered a number of cases in which the court had to decide, in relation to some particular enactment, whether an individual, adversely affected by breach of a statutory duty, had a right of action for damages against the person who had committed the breach. . . . The answer depends on the construction of the particular enactment, *i.e.* on the intention which it manifests. Here there is no enactment which is directly relevant and I can only consider, perhaps in a rather metaphorical way, what intention is to be inferred from the nature and exercise of the jurisdiction. So far as I know, no individual ever has been awarded, or has even claimed, damages or other compensation for contempt of court until the present case. The jurisdiction exists and is exercised *alio intuitu*, for the protection of the administration of justice and not for the protection of individuals. So to speak, the hypothetical enactment should be notionally construed as not conferring on an individual affected by a contempt of court any right of action for damages for the contempt of court as such although of course he may have a right of action for damages on other grounds. . . .

Note:

This case was not cited in *Holleran v Daniel Thwaites* [1989] 2 C.M.L.R. 917, where the judge enjoined a brewery from terminating a publican's lease. The brewery's aim was either to make the publican sign, or to punish him for not signing, a new lease which was arguably in breach of Community law. The judge said: " . . . the court has power to prevent a person from abusing his rights, whether conferred on him by statute or contract, in order to create a breach of Community law."

It would not be too surprising if one of the effects of the Europeanisation of our law were the introduction (alongside "proportionality") of an express doctrine of abuse of rights, such as was so strenuously disavowed by Pearson L.J. in *Chapman* when he said: "Motive is disregarded as irrelevant. A person who has a right under a contract or other instrument is entitled to exercise it and can effectively exercise it for a good reason or a bad reason or no reason at all." This dramatic formula is doubtless a spin-off from the famous (and then recent) decision of the House of Lords in *White & Carter (Councils) v McGregor* [1961] 3 All E.R. 1178 which held that unreasonable performance of an unwanted contractual service did not disentitle the performer from claiming the promised fee, and thereby provoked an embarrassing volte-face in the Court of Appeal on the question whether a hire-purchase company which unreasonably exercised its right to repossess the goods could claim its lost profits as well as the outstanding instalments. *White & Carter (Councils)* has subsequently been trashed and sidelined, and it is unlikely that *Chapman* will long survive.

Note that the European Convention which confers so many rights has a provision which proscribes their abuse (Art.17).

LONRHO LTD v SHELL PETROLEUM CO LTD

House of Lords [1982] A.C. 173; [1981] 3 W.L.R. 33; [1981] 2 All E.R. 456
(noted [1981] Camb.L.J. 230)

Action by pipeline company for trading losses due to illegal conduct by oil companies

The claimants owned a pipeline, leading from the Mozambique coast to Southern Rhodesia, which the respondent oil companies paid to use. After the government of that country had declared itself independent, Orders in Council in the United Kingdom rendered it an offence to supply crude oil to Southern Rhodesia, and oil ceased to flow along the claimants' pipeline to their loss. In arbitration proceedings the claimants claimed over £100m. on the basis that the illegal regime would have collapsed and the profitable use of their pipeline recommenced much sooner had the respondents not supplied the regime with oil in breach of the Orders. It was held by the House of Lords that none of the claimants' allegations stated a cause of action, and the extract printed below gives the opinion of Lord Diplock in answer to question 5, namely " . . . if there were breaches by the Respondents of the 1965 and 1968 Orders [sc. the sanctions orders] (a) Whether breaches of those Orders would give rise to a right of action in the Claimants for damage alleged to have been caused by those breaches . . . "

Lord Diplock: . . . My Lords, it is well settled by authority of this House in *Cutler v Wandsworth Stadium Ltd* ([1949] A.C. 398) that the question whether legislation which makes the doing or omitting to do a particular act a criminal offence renders the person guilty of such offence liable also in a civil action for damages at the suit of any person who thereby suffers loss or damage is a question of construction of the legislation. . . .

[His Lordship considered the provisions of the Southern Rhodesia Act 1965 and the 1965 sanctions order] . . .

The sanctions order thus creates a statutory prohibition on the doing of certain classes of acts and provides the means of enforcing the prohibition by prosecution for a criminal offence which is subject to heavy penalties including imprisonment. So one starts with the presumption laid down originally by Lord Tenterden C.J. in *Doe d. Bishop of Rochester v Bridges* ((1831) 1 B. & Ad. 847 at 859) where he spoke of the "general rule" that "where an Act creates an obligation, and enforces the performance in a specified manner . . . that performance cannot be enforced in any other manner," a statement that has frequently been cited with approval ever since, including on several occasions in speeches in this House. Where the only manner of enforcing performance for which the Act provides is prosecution for the criminal offence of failure to perform the statutory obligation or for contravening the statutory prohibition which the Act creates, there are two classes of exception to this general rule.

The first is where on the true construction of the Act it is apparent that the obligation or prohibition was imposed for the benefit or protection of a particular class of individuals, as in the case of the Factories Acts and similar legislation. . . .

The second exception is where the statute creates a public right (*i.e.* a right to be enjoyed by all those of Her Majesty's subjects who wish to avail themselves of it) and a particular member of the public suffers what Brett J. in *Benjamin v Storr* ((1874) L.R. 9 C.P. 400 at 407) described as "particular, direct and substantial" damage "other and different from that which was common to all the rest of the public." Most of the authorities about this second exception deal not with public rights created by statute but with public rights existing at common law, particularly in respect of use of highways. *Boyce v Paddington B.C.* ([1903] 1 Ch. 109) is one of the comparatively few cases about a right conferred on the general public by statute. . . .

My Lords, it has been the unanimous opinion of the arbitrators with the concurrence of the umpire, of Parker J. and of each of the three members of the Court of Appeal that the sanctions orders made pursuant to the Southern Rhodesia Act 1965 fell within neither of these two exceptions. . . .

In agreement with all those present and former members of the judiciary who have considered the matter I can see no ground on which contraventions by Shell and BP of the sanctions orders, though not amounting to any breach of their contract with Lonrho, nevertheless constituted a tort for which Lonrho could recover in a civil suit any loss caused to them by such contraventions.

Briefly parting from this part of the case, however, I should mention briefly two cases, one in the Court of Appeal of England, *Ex parte Island Records Ltd* ([1978] Ch. 122), and one in the High Court of Australia, *Beaudesert Shire Council v Smith* ((1966) 120 C.L.R. 145), which counsel for Lonrho, as a last resort, relied on as showing that some broader principle has of recent years replaced those long-established principles that I have just stated for determining whether a contravention of a particular statutory prohibition by one private individual makes him liable in tort to another private individual who can prove that he has suffered damage as a result of the contravention.

Ex parte Island Records Ltd was an unopposed application for an Anton Piller order against a defendant who, without the consent of the performers, had made records of musical performances for the purposes of trade. This was an offence, punishable by a relatively small penalty under the Dramatic and Musical Performers' Protection Act 1958. The application for the Anton Piller order was made by performers whose performances had been "bootlegged" by the defendant without their consent and also by record companies with whom the performers had entered into exclusive contracts. So far as the application by performers was concerned, it could have been granted for entirely orthodox reasons. The Act was passed for the protection of a particular class of individuals, dramatic and musical performers; even the short title said so. . . . Lord Denning M.R., however, with whom Waller L.J. agreed (Shaw L.J. dissenting) appears to enunciate a wider general rule, which does not depend on the scope and language of the statute by which a criminal offence is committed, that whenever a lawful business carried on by one individual in fact suffers damage as the consequence of a contravention by another individual of any statutory prohibition the former has a civil right of action against the latter for such damage.

My Lords, with respect, I am unable to accept that this is the law.

Beaudesert Shire Council v Smith is a decision of the High Court of Australia. It appeared to recognise the existence of a novel innominate tort of the nature of an "action for damages upon the case" available to "a person who suffers harm or loss as the inevitable consequence of the unlawful, intentional and positive acts of another." . . . It remains uncertain whether it was intended to include acts done in contravention of a wider range of statutory obligations or prohibitions than those which under the principles that I have discussed above would give rise to a civil action at common law in England if they are contravened. If the tort described in *Beaudesert* was really intended to extend that range, I would invite your Lordships to declare that it forms no part of the law of England. . . .

Notes:

1. *Beaudesert* has now been overruled by a unanimous High Court of Australia: *Northern Territory v Mengel* (1995) 69 A.L.J.R. 527; noted (1995) 111 L.Q.R. 44 at 583. The case involved the unauthorised issuance of a movement restriction order in relation to the plaintiff's stock of cattle.

2. Performers whose performances had been criminally bootlegged were rather doubtfully granted a civil remedy in *Rickless v United Artists Corp.* [1987] 1 All E.R. 679; their rights are now very strongly protected under Part II of the Copyright, Designs and Patents Act 1988.

3. *Richardson v Pitt-Stanley* [1995] 1 All E.R. 460 concerned the Employers' Liability (Compulsory Insurance) Act 1969 which rendered it an offence for an employer to have no insurance against his liability to his employees, and for any officer of a corporate employer to consent to, connive at or facilitate the commission of such an offence. The plaintiff employee, unable to collect on his judgment against the employer because the employer was in liquidation, sued the defendant director for conniving at the absence of the requisite insurance cover. The Court of Appeal held by a majority that the defendant, though guilty of an offence, was not civilly liable, Sir John Megaw dissenting on the ground that the statute was manifestly intended for the protection of employees such as the plaintiff, and therefore fell within the first exception stated by Lord Diplock above. Even given the courts' reluctance to impose civil liability for statutory offences, the majority decision is surprising: admittedly the plaintiff's loss was purely financial, but the employer/employee relationship is a strong one. Likewise, however, in *Scally v Southern Health* [1991] 4 All E.R. 563 at 573, it was held that while an employer could be taken to an industrial tribunal for failure to give an employee particulars of the terms of employment, he could not be sued for damages in a civil court.

4. *Cutler v Wandsworth Stadium* [1949] A.C. 398, cited by everyone, including Lord Diplock, was a hopeless case. The plaintiff was a bookie complaining that he had lost business from punters because the operator of the dog-track had failed to respect the statutory mandate to provide him with space in which to ply his aleatory trade. So great were the odds against the courts' giving the plaintiff what he had been prevented from taking from gamblers that one doubts Cutler's skill at his own business (though he did win at first instance).

5. The surprising decision of the Court of Appeal in *Thornton v Kirklees M.B.C.* [1979] 2 All E.R. 349 that an action for damages lay against a housing authority for failing to provide accommodation to a claimant whom they had accepted as having a priority need, though seemingly endorsed by the House of Lords in *Cocks v Thanet D.C.* [1982] 3 All E.R. 1135, was firmly overruled in *O'Rourke v Camden B.C.* [1997] 3 All E.R. 23, in which Lord Hoffmann quoted with approval the words of Geoffrey Lane L.J. that "a statute . . . which is dealing with the distribution of benefits . . . does not in its very nature give rise to an action by the disappointed . . . person."

CIVIL EVIDENCE ACT 1968

11.—(1) In any civil proceedings the fact that a person has been convicted of an offence by or before any court in the United Kingdom or by a court-martial there or elsewhere shall (subject to subsection (3) below) be admissible in evidence for the purpose of proving, where to do so is relevant to any issue in those proceedings, that he committed that offence, whether he was so convicted upon a plea of guilty or otherwise and whether or not he is a party to the civil proceedings; but no conviction other than a subsisting one shall be admissible in evidence by virtue of this section. . . .

Note:

This section was explained by Lord Diplock in *Hunter v Chief Constable* [1981] 3 All E.R. 727 at 735. Contrary to a view of Lord Denning, evidence introduced under this section can be rebutted by any plausible evidence, and the civil standard of proof applies.

Hunter is objectionable for other reasons. The plaintiffs who alleged that the police had beaten them up were not permitted to sue for assault and battery on the ground that it was an abuse of the process of the court, seeing that when they were prosecuted and convicted, the judge had held that their confessions were voluntary and not exacted by violence. The plaintiffs involved were the Birmingham Six, who were later—very much later—released as wrongly convicted.

More recently a pig farmer who had been convicted wanted to sue his solicitor for failing to lodge an appeal which might well have succeeded. The trial judge struck out his claim as an abuse (!), and it was only after extended discussion that the Court of Appeal allowed the claim to proceed (*Walpole v Partridge Wilson* [1994] 1 All E.R. 385). But *Hunter* still prevents a convict from suing his solicitor for negligently causing him to be convicted: *Smith v Linskills* [1996] 2 All E.R. 353, CA. But a defendant may seek to show that he was innocent of the offence for which he was convicted: so held in a case where the defendant, convicted of rape, was sued by his victim who relied on the convictions as evidence of his guilt: *J v Oyston* [1999] 1 W.L.R. 694.

Section 2.—Statutory Duties

BARNA v HUDES MERCHANDISING CORP.

Court of Appeal (1962) 106 S.J. 194; Crim.L.R. 321

Action by motorist against motorist in respect of property damage

The plaintiff was driving his Citroen along West Heath Avenue to where it ended by forming a T-junction with North End Road, where he planned to turn right. At the junction he stopped. To his left, on the crown of the main road, was a line of cars waiting to turn right into the street from which he was emerging. To his right was a line of parked cars which impeded his vision. He edged slowly forward, and then saw, about 40 yards away, the defendant's car approaching from his right at a speed which the defendant admitted was in excess of the legal limit. The plaintiff stopped, but as there was not enough room between his car and those waiting to turn right, the defendant collided with him, and both vehicles were damaged. The plaintiff claimed the cost of repairs, and the defendant counterclaimed. The county court judge dismissed the claim and allowed the counterclaim. The plaintiff appealed without success to the Court of Appeal.

Ormerod L.J.: There was no doubt that the . . . defendant had exceeded the speed limit and had committed an offence, but that did not make his speed excessive for the purposes of civil liability and did not of itself constitute negligence. The . . . defendant, driving on a fast busy main road, had no reason to anticipate that it would be blocked as it was. In those circumstances the judge's inference, that the speed of the . . . defendant was not excessive and that the plaintiff alone was negligent, was one that could be reasonably drawn from the evidence.

CONSUMER PROTECTION ACT 1987

41. CIVIL PROCEEDINGS

(1) An obligation imposed by safety regulations shall be a duty owed to any person who may be affected by a contravention of the obligation and, subject to any provision to the contrary in the regulations and to the defences and other incidents applying to actions for breach of statutory duty, a contravention of any such obligation shall be actionable accordingly.

(2) This Act shall not be construed as conferring any other right of action in civil proceedings, apart from the right conferred by virtue of Part I of this Act, in respect of any loss or damage suffered in consequence of a contravention of a safety provision or of a provision made by or under Part III of this Act.

Question

Do you understand the distinction between "safety regulations" in subsection (1) and "safety provisions" under subs.(2)? Why are provisions in Part III of the Act not "safety provisions"?

REFFELL v SURREY C.C.

Queen's Bench [1964] 1 W.L.R. 358; 128 J.P. 261; 108 S.J. 119; 62 L.G.R. 186; [1964] 1 All E.R. 743

Action by pupil against education authority in respect of personal injury

The plaintiff, a girl of 12 and a pupil at the defendant's school, hurried down a corridor to the cloakroom. One of its two glazed doors was swinging towards her, so she put out her right hand to stop it. Her hand went through one of the panes of glass which was only one-eighth of an inch thick. It had been installed by a competent architect when the school was built in 1919, and there had never been an accident with that door before. Broken panes were always replaced by toughened glass. The local authority was responsible for over 700 educational establishments, and had about 11 accidents *per* year involving broken glass.

Veale J.: . . . It is in those circumstances that the plaintiff puts her case in two ways. She alleges that the local education authority have been guilty of a breach of their statutory duty. Secondly, she alleges that they are guilty of negligence at common law.

I will deal first with the question of statutory duty. The Education Act 1944 provides by s.10(1): "The Minister shall make regulations prescribing the standards to which the premises of schools maintained by local education authorities are to conform, and such regulations may prescribe different standards for such descriptions of schools as may be specified in the regulations." Section 10(2) provides: "Subject as hereinafter provided, it shall be the duty of a local education authority to secure that the premises of every school maintained by them conform to the standards prescribed for schools of the description to which the school belongs." Be it noted that the duty is a duty to secure conformity with the prescribed standards.

In accordance with the duty laid upon him, the Minister has made regulations. The relevant ones for my consideration are the Standards for School Premises Regulations 1959. Regulation 51, under the heading "Precautions for Health and Safety," reads as follows [His Lordship read regulation 51 and continued:] Omitting irrelevant words, that regulation therefore reads: "In all parts of the buildings of every school . . . the design, the construction . . . and the properties of the materials shall be such that the health and safety of the occupants . . . shall be reasonably assured."

Three points really arise. First, do the statute and reg.51 give a right of action to a pupil at the school? Secondly, if so, what is the nature and extent of the duty? Thirdly, was there any breach of duty which caused this accident?

. . . The question whether or not a private person has a right of action for the breach of a statutory duty is always a very difficult one. Reliance is placed by the plaintiff on cases such as *Groves v Wimborne* ([1898] 2 Q.B. 402) and on the observations of their Lordships in *Cutler v Wandsworth Stadium* ([1949] A.C. 398). It is said that there is a strong presumption that a private right of action can be enforced by a private individual in cases where the statute provides no penalty for the breach. That is the case here, because the Education Act 1944, by section 99, gives powers to the minister to issue directions to an education authority and, if necessary, an application can be made for mandamus.

I think that the best approach to this kind of question is that set out in *Charlesworth on Negligence* (4th ed., 1962), para.963, at p.000: "It has been said: 'No universal rule can be formulated which will answer the question whether in any given case an individual can sue in respect of a breach of statutory duty.' In addition to the general rule set out in the preceding section, however, the most important matters to be taken into consideration appear to be: (a) Is the action brought in respect of the kind of harm which the statute was intended to prevent? (b) Is the person bringing the action one of the class which the statute desired to protect? (c) Is the special remedy provided by the statute adequate for the protection of the person injured? If the first two questions are answered in the affirmative and the third in the negative then, in most cases, the individual can sue."

I do not think that there has been any express decision on s.10 of the Education Act 1944, and reg.51 of the Standards for School Premises Regulations 1959, and I confess that I have had some doubt about the matter; but I have come to the conclusion that the answers in this case to the three questions set out in the paragraph I have just read are "yes" to the first two and "no" to the third. Bearing in mind that no penalty is laid down by the statute for a breach, I think that an action does lie by a pupil or master at a school who can prove a breach of the regulation.

What then is the nature of the duty? Counsel for the plaintiff says that, if in fact there is a breach in the sense that premises are not reasonably safe or that safety is not reasonably assured, this statutory duty is wider than any duty at common law, because—so the argument runs—the test is objective; that is to say, it matters not what this authority or other authorities knew or did not know, did or did not do, or what the past experience was. If safety was not reasonably assured, that, says counsel, is an end of the matter, though he concedes that, at common law, such matters as past experience would indeed be relevant. The local education authority, on the other hand, say that the regulation adds nothing to the common law duty. On the facts as I find them to be in this case I think this argument is largely academic; but it is an important point and I think it right to express my view upon it.

In my judgment, the argument of the plaintiff on this point is right. I think the duty to secure (that is the word in the section) that safety shall be reasonably assured (which are the words of the regulation) is an absolute duty and the test of breach or no is objective. Putting it another way, if safety is not reasonably assured in the premises in fact, then there is a breach.

That leads to the third question. Were the premises on July 15, 1960, with this 1/8 inch glass in the cloakroom door, at a height of four feet, reasonably safe? I have no hesitation in saying that they were not. This 1/8 inch glass in a cloakroom door was, in my view, asking for trouble. True, there had been no previous accident at this door, but there had been accidents of some sort at such doors elsewhere, and there had been an accident at the boys' cloakroom door in 1937, and the boys' cloakroom door was altered because of the danger of unruly boys. Boys are more unruly than girls, or so a witness told me. Boys will be boys; but, equally, I should have thought, girls will be girls. Even if they do not fight like small boys and generally behave with more decorum, they nevertheless have been known to chase each other and to run in corridors. It is easy to visualise one girl following another, the one in front swinging the cloakroom door to and the following girl putting out a hand to arrest it, without any element of horse play at all. I cannot help thinking that the defendants have been lucky that there has been no previous accident at this door.

The distinction between boys and girls has not been drawn by the local education authority since the war. All doors in new schools have toughened glass in doors and all breakages of glass in doors have involved toughened glass as a replacement. One sympathises, of course, with the position of a local education authority with a number of old schools to manage. I have no doubt at all that this local education authority appreciated the risk. But no evidence has been called before me by the local education authority to show that they considered this question; or if they did, to what conclusion they came and why; or that the replacements involved enormous expense which was out of proportion to the risk; or that some form of grille or wooden slat was impracticable. For all I know (and, indeed, the position seems to be this) the local education authority merely waited for either a major adaptation of the buildings, or a breakage to occur, before they did anything at all.

The Middlesex County Council are said now to be gradually changing 1/8 inch glass in school doors. The Essex County Council are said to have issued, only last month, a directive to the same effect to a Mr Jefferson, who takes his orders from the Essex County architect and follows their advice. But I have the evidence of a practical man and a convincing witness whose evidence I accept. This 1/8 inch glass, he said, should have been changed years ago. I am not, I hope, being wise after the event, and I exclude, I hope, the wisdom of hindsight; but, if instead of considering whether there was a breach of reg.51 on an objective basis I were to approach the matter on a common law basis, I should still say, and indeed I find, that the defendants were negligent. This is not the case of an isolated hit for six out of a cricket ground as in *Bolton v Stone*.

It is said for the local education authority that their common law duty *qua* their premises is the common duty of care under the Occupiers' Liability Act 1957 and is a somewhat lower duty than the duty of a school master as a good and prudent father of a family. That is, I think, correct. But it makes very little, if any, difference, on the facts of this case. I am content to take their duty as the common duty of care, which is defined by s.2(2) of the Occupiers' Liability Act 1957 as a duty "to take such care as in all the circumstances of the case is reasonable to see that the visitor will be reasonably safe in using the premises for the purposes for which he is invited or permitted by the occupier to be there." The circumstances here include the circumstance that this was a school and that the door was in constant use by children. I do not accept that the risk was minimal, as was urged upon me by counsel for the local education authority. If it is too much to ask an education authority, confronted with this problem of glass in doors, to change every door with 1/8 inch glass in it, it is not too much to ask them to do something more than merely wait for major adaptations or breakages. Whatever may be the vulnerability of other doors, I should have said that a cloakroom door at the end of a straight corridor was more vulnerable than most. Not only, in my judgment, was the risk of accident a real risk, but it was both a foreseeable risk and was in fact foreseen. If it had not been foreseen there would not have been the policy of replacing broken 1/8 inch glass with toughened glass.

In the result, I find the local education authority liable to the plaintiff both under the statute and regulation and at common law.

Questions

1. Are there any situations in which the plaintiff would have recovered in an action for breach of statutory duty and would have failed to recover at common law?

2. Suppose you want to *make* someone perform his statutory duty, rather than wait for harm and then claim compensation from him. For what remedy should you apply if the duty is (a) public, (b) private? Would the appropriate remedy ever be granted or refused when damages for any harm suffered would not?

3. Suppose that the person injured by the glass was (a) a master, (b) the school janitor, (c) a parent fetching a child, or (d) a burglar. Would recovery be allowed?

Notes:

1. The plaintiff here, who had suffered no financial loss, recovered (tax free) a sum about equal to half her teacher's annual salary, or the cost of a thousand panes of toughened glass.

2. No injunctions will issue to prevent an education authority's setting up a new school in premises which fall short of the standards laid down by Regulations: the only remedy of the parent is to apply to the Secretary of State: *Bradbury v Enfield Borough* [1967] 3 All E.R. 434, CA.

3. "I detect a considerable reluctance on the part of the courts to impose upon local authorities any liability for breach of statutory duty other than that expressly imposed in the statute" said Scott-Baker J. in *T v Surrey C.C.* [1994] 4 All E.R. 577 at 597, after quoting Woolf L.J. in *R. v I.L.E.A., Ex p. Ali* (1990) 2 Admin.L.R. 822 at 830: " . . . it is only in certain exceptional and well-recognised circumstances that someone, even particularly damnified by an authority's non-compliance with a statutory duty, can claim damages for such a breach." In T's case the defendant was held to be under neither a statutory nor a common law liability for failing to remove from the statutory register a childminder suspected of child-abuse, but was held liable for stating to the abused child's mother that the childminder was suitable. The latter liability was said to arise straightforwardly under *Hedley Byrne*, but in fact it is not entirely straightforward.

4. The link between statutory liability and liability at common law also arose in *Ephraim v Newham L.B.C.* (1993) 91 L.G.R. 412. The plaintiff needed accommodation for her family and the defendant advised them to go to a certain bed-and-breakfast place; they went, and were badly burnt because the fire escapes failed to meet the standard laid down by statute for houses in multiple occupation. Reversing the trial judge, the Court of Appeal held that the statute applied only to houses of three or more storeys, and that it would not be just and reasonable to impose on the local authority any further duty regarding fire escapes in premises not controlled by them.

5. In *Todd v Adam* [2002] 2 Lloyd's Rep. 293 it was held that when a trawler sank with all hands neither the Fishing Vessels (Safety Provisions) Rules 1975, nor the Merchant Shipping Act 1995, s.121, gave a claim for damages in respect of the drowned fishermen, but when a marine engineer who was testing lifeboats was injured when the chain on which the lifeboat was being lowered snapped he had a claim under the Merchant Shipping (Life Saving Appliances) Regulations 1980, which absolutely required that the chain be "of adequate strength" (*Ziemniak v ETPM Deep Sea Ltd* [2003] EWCA Civ 636).

PHILLIPS v BRITANNIA HYGIENIC LAUNDRY CO

Court of Appeal [1923] 2 K.B. 832; 93 L.J.K.B. 5; 129 L.T. 777; 39 T.L.R. 530; 68 S.J.
102; 21 L.G.R. 709; [1923] All E.R. Rep. 127

Action between motorists in respect of property damage

Bankes L.J.: This is an appeal from the Divisional Court reversing the county court judge in an action brought by the plaintiff for damage done to his motor van. The axle of the defendants' motor lorry broke and caused the damage. The action in the county court was founded on an alleged breach of a statutory provision contained in the Motor Cars (Use and Construction) Order 1904 and alternatively on the alleged negligence of the defendant. The county court judge absolved the defendant from negligence in relation either to the management of the motor lorry or to the state of its axle, but he found negligence on the part of the repairers to whom the motor lorry had been sent, in not having executed the repairs efficiently, and gave judgment for the plaintiff on the ground that the lorry was not in the condition required by cl.6 of Art.II of the Order. On an appeal by the defendants the Divisional Court reversed this judgment. The plaintiff appeals to this court.

I agree with the conclusion of the Divisional Court. If the judgment of the county court judge were to stand it would have very far-reaching consequences. It is unnecessary to consider what they would be, as in this case there is only one point to be considered, and that has long been governed by well-established rules; and when those rules are applied to the facts of this case, it is clear that the Divisional Court came to the right conclusion.

The only point of substance argued for the appellant was that the Motor Cars (Use and Construction) Order 1904 conferred on him a statutory right of action for breach of its conditions. . . . In the case we are considering the statute creates an obligation and provides a remedy for its non-observance, and the question is whether the scope and language of the statute indicate that the general rule is to prevail so that the remedy provided is the only remedy, or whether an exception to that general rule is to be admitted. The order of the Local Government Board was made under s.6 of the Locomotives on Highways Act 1896, which empowered the Local Government Board to make regulations with respect to the use of light locomotives on highways, their construction, and the conditions under which they may be used. Section 7 of the Act provides that a breach of any regulation made under the Act may be punished by a fine not exceeding £10. The language of the Act includes the expressions the "use of light locomotives" their "construction" and "conditions under which they may be used"; and its scope is the public user of highways, which has been for years subject to rules regulating and controlling it. Thus the Act deals with rights which have always been sufficiently protected by the common law. Under this Act the Local Government order was made. It is divided into sections or articles, five in number. The provision relied on is Art.II: "No person shall cause or permit a motor car to be used on any highway, or shall drive or have charge of a motor car when so used, unless the conditions hereinafter set forth are satisfied." Then follow the conditions on which a motor car may be used on any highway. They are contained in seven clauses. It is clear that some of them are introduced not to protect persons using the highway but to preserve the highway itself; those for instance relating to the width of wheels and the weight of motor cars. If the appellant's contention is to prevail everyone injured by a motor car which does not comply with the regulations has a right of action. There is no reason for differentiating between those who are injured as a legal consequence of a breach from those who are injured in fact irrespective of the breach of the regulations. Take cl.7 for example. That clause provides that a car must have lamps exhibiting a white light in front and a red light in the rear. According to the appellant's contention a foot passenger crossing in front of a motor car would have a right of action if injured without any negligence of the driver, merely because the car had no red light in the rear. That cannot have been the intention of the Legislature. The absence of a red light in the rear may concern the safety of the car itself, or it may be a wise police regulation for other vehicles overtaking it, but it cannot affect the safety of a foot passenger passing in front of the car. This seems to indicate that it is not the intention of the Act to confer a right of action on every person injured by a car which does not conform to the regulations and to confer this right even though the breach of the regulations has no effect on the injury of which he complains. The matter might have been more doubtful if cl.6 had stood alone. It provides that the car and all its fittings "shall be in such a condition as not to cause, or to be likely to cause, danger to any person on the motor car or on any highway." We have not to consider the case of a person injured on the highway. The injury here was done to the appellant's van; and the appellant, a member of the public, claims a right of action as one of a class for whose benefit cl.6 was introduced. He contends that the public using the highway is the class so favoured. I do not agree. In my view the public using the highway is not a class; it is itself the public and not a class of the public. The clause therefore was not passed for the benefit of a class or section of the public. It applies to the public generally, and it is one among many regulations for breach of which it cannot have been intended that a person aggrieved should have a civil remedy by way of action in addition to the more appropriate remedy provided, namely a fine. In my opinion therefore this case is not an exception to the general rule; that rule applies, and the appeal must be dismissed.

Notes:

1. *In Monk v Warbey*, the plaintiff, a bus-driver, was injured by X, who was carelessly driving a car he had borrowed from the defendant. X was not insured against liability to the plaintiff—he had no policy of his own, and he was not an additional insured under the defendant's policy. The defendant had therefore unwittingly committed an offence under the Road Traffic Act 1930, s.35 (now Road Traffic Act 1988, s.143). X had no money with which to pay the plaintiff, so the plaintiff was allowed to recover from the defendant (who had at least the car).

The decision is striking, both because the plaintiff was complaining of financial harm (the defendant's breach of duty did not cause the injuries, but only the plaintiff's failure to get compensation for them—though the applicable time-bar is that for "personal injuries" (*Norman v Ali, The Times*, February 25, 2000)) and because offences under the section in question are so easily committed. Nevertheless, the decision fits very well into the policy of the law that victims of *negligence* on the highway should not only be entitled to compensation, but should actually receive it. The scheme is now completed by the institution of the Motor Insurers' Bureau, which compensates those victims of motor-vehicles who should, by statute, have been able to recover from an insurance company.

But if the policy of the law were to indemnify the victims of traffic *accidents*, then *Phillips* would appear as the anomalous decision. If the offence of putting an *uninsured* vehicle on the roads leads to liability, then why not also the offence of putting a *dangerous* car on the road? The distinction is particularly curious when one considers that, had *Phillips* gone the other way, most of the people caught under it would have the statutory insurance cover against liability to pay those damages, whereas defendants caught under *Monk v Warbey* will normally have to pay out of their own pocket.

Monk v Warbey was distinguished in *Richardson v Pitt-Stanley* (above, p.188) where the Court of Appeal held that breach by employers of their statutory duty to have insurance against liability to their employees (Employers' Liability (Compulsory Insurance) Act 1969) was not actionable. One reason given was that the employer's liability for the injury was already provided for by the common law, whereas Warbey would not be liable in damages at all but for the statutory obligation.

2. *The Motor Insurers Bureau.* The Uninsured Drivers Agreement dated August 13, 1999 between the Secretary of State and the Motor Insurers Bureau provides that, subject to a few exceptions and a great many procedural preconditions, "if a claimant has obtained against any person in a Court in Great Britain a judgment which is an unsatisfied judgment [in respect of a liability in respect of which a contract of insurance must be in force under Part VI of the Road Traffic Act 1988] then MIB will pay the relevant sum to, or to the satisfaction of, the claimant or will cause the same to be so paid." This applies "whether or not the person liable to satisfy the judgment is in fact covered by a contract of insurance and whatever may be the cause of his failure to satisfy the judgment." (para.5).

Excluded are claims (a) by voluntary passengers actually or constructively aware that the vehicle was stolen, uninsured, or being used for criminal purposes or escape from lawful arrest, and (b) for damage to vehicles the use of which was not covered by a mandatory policy, as the claimant knew or should have known. The first £300 of property damage is not recoverable.

Under a separate Untraced Drivers Agreement, where naturally no judgment can have been obtained, the MIB undertakes to pay for personal injury only, not property damage.

The decision to set up the Motor Insurers Bureau by agreement rather than by law gave rise to two difficulties. First, thanks to the doctrine of privity of contract, the victims it was designed to benefit could not sue on it. In *Hardy v Motor Insurers Bureau* [1964] 2 Q.B. 745, 757 Lord Denning was forced to say: "The agreement is as important as any statute . . . No point is taken by the Motor Insurers' Bureau that it is not enforceable by the third person. I trust no such point will ever be taken." Secondly, since it was an agreement and not a law, the House of Lords held, in *White v White* [2001] 2 All E.R. 43, that the *Marleasing* principle—that domestic laws must be interpreted so as to conform with Community law, in this instance the Second Motor Insurance Directive of December 30, 1983 (84/5/EEC)—did not apply to it. The question whether the application of the Untraced Drivers Agreement was consistent with the Directive was referred to Luxembourg.

In *Evans v Motor Insurers Bureau*, Case C–63/01, the Advocate-General (Alber) was of the view that since the victim had no legal right to sue the Bureau or to appeal to a court from its holdings, the British arrangements lacked the requisite legal certainty, a position made "totally unacceptable" by the attitude of the national courts regarding *Marleasing*. He indicated that the U.K. should be liable under the *Francovich* principle for depriving Mr Evans of the rights conferred on him by Community law. His conclusions were not adopted by the Court itself, which held that the British arrangements as actually implemented were compatible with Community law, subject only to this, that whereas the Directive required, though not expressly, that interest be payable on the compensation granted to victims of untraced drivers, the agreement made no provision for this. This was a breach of Community law, but whether it was a breach sufficiently serious to engage the liability of the state was a matter for the national courts.

3. Community law had already required us to extend to property damage the requirement of liability insurance against causing personal injury and death (a very unwise extension, seeing that (a) more property damage is caused on the highway than personal injury, and (b) most of the property damage is caused to cars which their owners should insure and usually do), but now it has generated the European Communities (Rights against Insurers) Regulations 2002 (SI 2002/3061) which provide that "where a party has a cause of action against an insured person in tort and that cause of action arises out of an accident [caused by or arising out of the use of any insured vehicle], the party may issue proceedings against the insurer which issued the policy of insurance relating to the insured vehicle, and that insurer shall be directly liable to the entitled party to the extent that he is liable to the insured person." It is a total novelty in Britain, though not on the Continent, for the victim to be able to sue the tortfeasor's insurer directly. Note that it applies only to motor accidents in public places.

HEALTH AND SAFETY AT WORK ACT 1974

2.—(1) It shall be the duty of every employer to ensure, so far as is reasonably practicable, the health, safety and welfare at work of all his employees.

3.—(1) It shall be the duty of every employer to conduct his undertaking in such a way as to ensure, so far as is reasonably practicable, that persons not in his employment who may be affected thereby are not thereby exposed to risks to their health or safety.

(2) It shall be the duty of every self-employed person to conduct his undertaking in such a way as to ensure, so far as is reasonably practicable, that he and other persons (not being his employees) who may be affected thereby are not thereby exposed to risks to their health or safety. . . .

4.—(1) This section has effect for imposing on persons duties in relation to those who—

(a) are not their employees; but

(b) use non-domestic premises made available to them as a place of work or as a place where they may use plant or substances provided for their use there, and applies to premises so made available and other non-domestic premises used in connection with them.

(2) It shall be the duty of each person who has, to any extent, control of premises to which this section applies or of the means of access thereto or egress therefrom or of any plant or substance in such premises to take such measures as it is reasonable for a person in his position to take to ensure, so far as is reasonably practicable, that the premises, all means of access thereto or egress therefrom available for use by persons using the premises, and any plant or substance in the premises or, as the case may be, provided for use there, is or are safe and without risks to health.

(3) Where a person has, by virtue of any contract or tenancy, an obligation of any extent in relation to

(a) the maintenance or repair of any premises to which this section applies or any means of access thereto or egress therefrom; or

(b) the safety of or the absence of risks to health arising from plant or substances in any such premises;

that person shall be treated, for the purposes of subsection (2) above, as being a person who has control of the matters to which his obligation extends.

(4) Any reference in this section to a person having control of any premises or matter is a reference to a person having control of the premises or matter in connection with the carrying on by him of a trade, business or other undertaking (whether for profit or not).

15.—(2) Without prejudice to the generality of the preceding subsection, health and safety regulations may for any of the general purposes of this Part make provision for any of the purposes mentioned in Schedule 3. . . .

(6) Health and safety regulations—

(a) may specify the persons or classes of persons who, in the event of a contravention of a requirement or prohibition imposed by or under the regulations, are to be guilty of an offence, whether in addition to or to the exclusion of other persons or classes of persons;

(b) may provide for any specified defence to be available in proceedings for any offence under the relevant statutory provisions either generally or in specified circumstances; . . .

47.—(1) Nothing in this Part shall be construed—

(a) as conferring a right of action in any civil proceedings in respect of any failure to comply with any duty imposed by sections 2 to 7 or any contravention of section 8; or

(b) as affecting the extent (if any) to which breach of a duty imposed by any of the existing statutory provisions is actionable; . . .

(2) Breach of a duty imposed by health and safety regulations [. . .] shall, so far as it causes damage, be actionable except in so far as the regulations provide otherwise.

(3) No provision made by virtue of section 15(6)(b) shall afford a defence in any civil proceedings, whether brought by virtue of subsection (2) above or not; but as regards any duty imposed as mentioned in subsection (2) above health and safety regulations [. . .] may provide for any defence specified in the regulations to be available in any action for breach of that duty.

(4) Subsections (1)(a) and (2) above are without prejudice to any right of action which exists apart from the provisions of this Act, and subsection (3) above is without prejudice to any defence which may be available apart from the provisions of the regulations there mentioned.

(5) Any term of an agreement which purports to exclude or restrict the operation of subsection (2) above, or any liability arising by virtue of that subsection, shall be void, except in so far as health and safety regulations [. . .] provide otherwise.

(6) In this section "damage" includes the death of, or injury to, any person (including any disease and any impairment of a person's physical or mental condition).

Note:
    Accidents at work, along with accidents on the highway, form the great bulk of tort suits in Britain today. But whereas breach of statutory duty plays only a very slight role in traffic accidents (see *Phillips v Britannia Hygienic Laundry,* above, p.196), it is very prominent in litigation over accidents at work. Very many claims were brought under the provisions of the Factories Act 1961, the Mines and Quarries Act 1954, the Offices, Shops and Railway Premises Act 1963, and associated regulations. These are now displaced by a myriad of

Regulations made under the Health and Safety at Work Act 1974. The following excerpt from one of these Regulations will indicate their flavour.

PROVISION AND USE OF WORK EQUIPMENT REGULATIONS 1998 (SI 1998/2306)

4.—(1) Every employer shall ensure that work equipment is so constructed or adapted as to be suitable for the purpose for which it is used or provided. . . .

(4) In this regulation "suitable" means suitable in any respect which it is reasonably foreseeable will affect the health or safety of any person.

5.—(1) Every employer shall ensure that work equipment is maintained in an efficient state, in efficient working order and in good repair. . . .

11.—(1) Every employer shall ensure that measures are taken in accordance with paragraph (2) which are effective—

(a) to prevent access to any dangerous part of machinery or to any rotating stock-bar; or

(b) to stop the movement of any dangerous part of machinery or rotating stock-bar before any part of a person enters a danger zone.

(2) The measures required by paragraph (1) shall consist of—

(a) the provision of fixed guards enclosing every dangerous part or rotating stock-bar where and to the extent that it is practicable to do so, but where or to the extent that it is not, then

(b) the provision of other guards or protection devices where and to the extent that it is practicable to do so, but where or to the extent that it is not, then

(c) the provision of jigs, holders, push-sticks or similar protection appliances used in conjunction with the machinery where and to the extent that it is practicable to do so, but where or to the extent that it is not, then

(d) the provision of information, instruction, training and supervision.

(3) All guards and protection devices provided under sub-paragraphs (a) or (b) of paragraph (2) shall—

(a) be suitable for the purpose for which they are provided;

(b) be of good construction, sound material and adequate strength;

(c) be maintained in an efficient state, in efficient working order and in good repair;

(d) not give rise to any increased risk to health or safety;

(e) not be easily bypassed or disabled;

(f) be situated at sufficient distance from the danger zone;

(g) not unduly restrict the view of the operating cycle of the machinery, where such a view is necessary;

(h) be so constructed or adapted that they allow operations necessary to fit or replace parts and for maintenance work, restricting access so that it is allowed only to the area where the work is to be carried out and, if possible, without having to dismantle the guard or protection device.

(4) All protection appliances provided under sub-paragraph (c) of paragraph (2) shall comply with sub-paragraphs (a) to (d) and (g) of paragraph (3).

(5) In this regulation—

"danger zone" means any zone in or around machinery in which a person is exposed to a risk to health or safety from contact with a dangerous part of machinery or a rotating stock-bar; "stock-bar" means any part of a stock-bar which projects beyond the head-stock of a lathe.

12.—(1) Every employer shall take measures to ensure that the exposure of a person using work equipment to any risk to his health or safety from any hazard specified in paragraph (3) is either prevented, or, where that is not reasonably practicable, adequately controlled.

(2) The measures required by paragraph (1) shall—

(a) be measures other than the provision of personal protective equipment or of information, instruction, training and supervision, so far as is reasonably practicable; and

(b) include, where appropriate, measures to minimise the effects of the hazard as well as to reduce the likelihood of the hazard occurring.

(3) The hazards referred to in paragraph (1) are

(a) any article or substance falling or being ejected from work equipment;

(b) rupture or disintegration of parts of work equipment;

(c) work equipment catching fire or overheating;

(d) the unintended or premature discharge of any article or of any gas, dust, liquid, vapour or other substance which, in each case, is produced, used or stored in the work equipment;

(e) the unintended or premature explosion of the work equipment or any article or substance produced, used or stored in it.

(4) For the purposes of this regulation "adequate" means adequate having regard only to the nature of the hazard and the nature and degree of exposure to the risk, and "adequately" shall be construed accordingly.

(5) This regulation shall not apply where any of the following Regulations apply in respect of any risk to a person's health or safety for which such Regulations require measures to be taken to prevent or control such risk, namely—

(a) the Ionising Radiation Regulations 1985;

(b) the Control of Asbestos at Work Regulations 1987;

(c) the Control of Substances Hazardous to Health Regulations 1994;

(d) the Noise at Work Regulations 1989;

(e) the Construction (Head Protection) Regulations 1989;

(f) the Control of Lead at Work Regulations 1998.

24.—(1) Every employer shall ensure that work equipment incorporates any warnings or warning devices which are appropriate for reasons of health and safety.

(2) Without prejudice to the generality of paragraph (1), warnings given by warning devices on work equipment shall not be appropriate unless they are unambiguous, easily perceived and easily understood.

Notes:

1. Other paragraphs of these Regulations deal with Specific Risks, Information and Instructions, Training, Conformity with Community Requirements, High or Very Low Temperatures, Starting Controls, Stop Controls, Emergency Stop Controls, Controls, Control Systems, Isolation from Sources of Energy, Stability, Lighting, Maintenance Operations, and Markings. A Schedule lists as relevant no fewer than 35 EC Directives.

2. Regulation 5 above (actually its predecessor) was involved In *Stark v Post Office* [2001] I.C.R. 1013. A postman delivering mail on his bicycle was badly injured when without warning his front wheel locked and he was propelled over the handlebars. The accident was caused by the fact that the stirrup, part of the

front brake, broke in two, and one part lodged in the front wheel. The judge found that the "defect would not and could not have been discoverable on any routine inspection" and that "a perfectly rigorous examination would not have revealed this defect", so there was no negligence at common law. The Court of Appeal however held that there was a breach of the Regulation. Very strict!

3. Falling off a bicycle is perhaps what one would expect if it is defective. It was otherwise in *Fytche v Wincanton Logistics* [2003] EWCA Civ 874 where a driver of HGVs engaged on collecting milk from farms suffered frostbite in his little toe as a result of water seeping in very cold weather through a tiny unobserved hole where the toe-cap of his reinforced boots met the sole. Regulation 7 of the Personal Protective Equipment at Work Regulations 1992 provided that "every employer shall ensure that any personal protective equipment provided to his employees is maintained (including, replaced or cleaned as appropriate) in an efficient state, in efficient working order and in good repair." It was accepted that this imposed an absolute duty, but the question was whether the obligation did not relate solely to the risk in relation to which the protective equipment, the reinforced boots, was supplied, namely to protect against falling objects, stubbing etc. The Court of Appeal with a strong dissent held that the employer was not liable as this injury fell outside the risk to be protected against.

4. Ms Dugmore, a nurse devoted to nursing, picked up a box which had contained latex gloves while working for hospital Y and suffered a disabling anaphylactic attack which put paid to her career. Her allergy to latex had arisen through wearing latex gloves while working for hospital X in 1994, a date when the condition was not known. A person once sensitised cannot be desensitised, and when she suffered a severe reaction two years later, hospital X provided her with vinyl gloves. When she transferred to hospital Y in 1997 and told them of her condition, they too supplied her with vinyl gloves. The Court of Appeal held first that hospital X was not liable in negligence since, even given that as a health care provider it should know about these things better than most, there was no reason for it to know of the problem prior to the time of the first sensitisation in 1994, which was the cause of all the trouble. The Court then applied Reg.7(1) of the Control of Substances Hazardous to Health Regulations (now SI 1999/437) which provides that "Every employer shall ensure that the exposure of his employees to a substance hazardous to health is either prevented or, where this is not reasonably practicable, adequately controlled." It being agreed that latex was a substance hazardous to health, hospital X was found to have been in breach even prior to its knowledge of the danger: the duty was absolute, and it would have been reasonably practicable to prevent the sensitisation by supplying vinyl gloves instead of latex in the first place. Hospital Y on the other hand was not liable, not in negligence since she was so keen to carry on nursing that she would have ignored a warning to find a safer environment, and the employer was not bound to terminate her employment, and not under the regulations since it was not reasonably practicable to prevent exposure, and if it was not adequately controlled this did not cause the anaphylactic attack which could have occurred anywhere. *Dugmore v Swansea NHS Trust* [2003] 1 All E.R. 333.

5. Other important Regulations, apart from those mentioned in reg.12(5) above, include the Workplace (Health, Safety & Welfare) Regulations 1992 (SI 1992/3004), and the Personal Protective Equipment at Work Regulations (SI 1992/2996) and the Provision and Use of Work Equipment Regulations 1998 (SI 1998/2306), whose reg.11 replaces the famous s.14(1) of the Factories Act 1961 ("Every dangerous part of any machinery . . . shall be securely fenced") which generated so much judicial gloss. The Workplace Regulations cover, *inter alia*, Ventilation, Temperature, Lighting, Cleanliness, Room Dimensions, Workstations and Seating, Falls or Falling Objects, Windows, Skylights and Ventilators, Doors and Gates, Escalators and Moving Walkways, Ability to Clean Windows Safely, Sanitary Conveniences, Washing Facilities, Drinking Water, Accommodation for Clothing, Facilities for Rest and to Eat Meals.

6. Regulation 12 of the Workplace Regulations is frequently applied:

"(1) Every floor in a workplace and the surface of every traffic route in a workplace shall be of a construction such that the floor or surface of the traffic route is suitable for the purpose for which it is used.

(2) Without prejudice to the generality of para.(1), the requirements in that paragraph shall include requirements that—(a) the floor, or surface of the traffic route, shall have no hole or slope, or be uneven or slippery so as, in each case, to expose any person to a risk to his health or safety; and (b) every such floor shall have effective means of drainage where necessary.

(3) So far as is reasonably practicable, every floor in a workplace and the surface of every traffic route in a workplace shall be kept free from obstructions and from any article or substance which may cause a person to slip, trip or fall.

(4) In considering whether for the purposes of para.(2)(a) a hole or slope exposes any person to a risk to his health or safety—(a) no account shall be taken of a hole where adequate measures have been taken to prevent a person falling; and (b) account shall be taken of any handrail provided in connection with any slope.

(5) Suitable and sufficient handrails and if appropriate, guards shall be provided on all traffic routes which are staircases except in circumstances in which a handrail cannot be provided without obstructing the traffic route."

7. The Management of Health and Safety at Work Regulations 1999 (SI 1999/3242) used to exclude civil liability for breach except as to expectant mothers and young persons (reg.22); that Regulation has now been amended so that any employee may claim damages for breach of the provisions, notably the provision which requires employers to conduct "risk assessments": see Management of Health and Safety at Work and Fire Precautions (Workplace) Amendment Regulations 2003 (SI 2003/2457).

8. On August 21, 1998 a police motorcyclist got damages for hearing impairment due to wind noise while he was riding his motorcycle on duty. Under the Noise at Work Regulations 1989, more than 90dB is unacceptable. Is it relevant that wearing earmuffs prevents the cyclist hearing traffic noise? Soon we shall have claims from players in orchestras. Is it relevant that they should be able to hear each other?

Section 3.—Public Nuisance

BENJAMIN v STORR

Common Pleas (1874) L.R. 9 C.P. 400; 43 L.J.C.P. 162; 30 L.T. 362; 22 W.R. 631

Action by frontager against highway user in respect of financial loss

The defendant kept the horse-drawn vans in which he fetched goods to and from his auction rooms in Covent Garden standing in the narrow street outside the cafe which the plaintiff had recently opened next door. This made the cafe dark, and the smell of the horses' urine discommoded and deterred the plaintiff's customers.

The jury, instructed to say whether the obstruction was greater than was reasonable in point of time and manner, taking into consideration the interests of all parties, and without unnecessary inconvenience, awarded the plaintiff £75. This verdict was upheld.

Brett J.: This action is founded upon alleged wrongful acts by the defendants, *viz.*, the unreasonable use of a highway—unreasonable to such an extent as to amount to a nuisance. That alone would not give the plaintiff a right of action; but the plaintiff goes on to allege in his declaration that the nuisance complained of is of such a kind as to cause him a particular injury other than and beyond that suffered by the rest of the public, and therefore he claims damages against the defendants. The first point discussed was whether it was necessary that the plaintiff should show something more than an injury to his business, an actual injury to his property; and cases decided under the Lands Clauses Consolidation Act (8 & 9 Vict. c. 18) were cited. In this case I think the action is maintainable without showing injury to property. In the class of cases referred to, the action is brought to recover compensation for lands taken or injuriously affected; and there, of course, injury to property must be shown, and not merely injury to the trade of the occupier. Those cases, therefore, do not at all affect the present. Before the passing of the Lands Clauses Consolidation Act, by the common law of England, a person guilty of a public nuisance might be indicted; but, if injury resulted to a private individual, other and greater than that which was common to all the Queen's subjects, the person injured had his remedy by action. The cases referred to upon this subject show that there are three things which the plaintiff must substantiate, beyond the existence of the mere public nuisance, before he can be entitled to recover. In the first place, he must show a particular injury to himself beyond that which is suffered by the rest of the public. It is not enough for him to show that he suffers the same inconvenience in the use of the highway as other people do, if the alleged nuisance be the obstruction of a highway. The case of *Hubert v Groves* ((1794) 170 E.R. 308) seems to me to prove that proposition. There, the plaintiff's business was injured by the obstruction of a highway, but no greater injury resulted to him therefrom than to anyone else, and therefore it was held that the action would not lie. . . . Other cases show that the injury to the individual must be direct, and not a mere consequential injury; as, where one way is obstructed, but another (though possibly a less convenient one) is left open; in such a case the private and particular injury has been held not to be sufficiently direct to give a cause of action. Further, the injury must be shown to be of a substantial character, not fleeting or evanescent. If these propositions be correct, in order to entitle a person to maintain an action for damage caused by that which is a public nuisance, the damage must be particular, direct, and substantial. The question then is, whether the plaintiff here has brought himself within the rule so laid down.

The evidence on the part of the plaintiff that from the too long standing of horses and wagons of the defendants in the highway opposite his house, the free passage of light and air to his premises was obstructed, and the plaintiff was in consequence obliged to burn gas nearly all day, and so to incur expense. I think that brings the case within all the requirements I have pointed out; it was a particular, a direct, and a substantial damage. As to the bad smell, that also was a particular injury to the plaintiff, and a direct and substantial one. So, if by reason of the access to his premises being obstructed for an unreasonable time and in an unreasonable manner, the plaintiff's customers were prevented from coming to his coffee-shop, and he suffered a material diminution of trade, that might be a particular, a direct, and a substantial damage. . . .

Note:
Public nuisance is a crime because it is likely to cause at least widespread inconvenience. Stopping it is a matter for the state enforcement authorities. It would be intolerable if everyone inconvenienced could bring a private suit. The courts therefore allow a person to sue only if he can show damage specific to himself. This requirement of particular damage was strictly insisted on in the mid-nineteenth century, lest the construction of railways, which was necessarily disruptive, become too expensive (*Ricket v Metropolitan Railway* (1867) L.R. 2 H.L. 175) but proven business loss is now certainly recoverable.

In *Tate & Lyle v G.L.C.* [1983] 1 All E.R. 1159, HL, the Greater London Council had statutory authority to construct new terminals for the Woolwich Ferry, but did it in such a manner as to cause four times more siltation than necessary in the channel which led from the Thames to the plaintiff's jetty, used for loading and unloading sugar. The plaintiff's claim in negligence ("engaging simplicity") was rejected, but it obtained three-quarters of its dredging costs in public nuisance. Similar considerations allowed the courts in the United States to award damages to sea fishermen whose trade had been ruined by pollution caused by the defendant: *Union Oil Co v Oppen* 501 F.2d 558 (9th Cir. 1974).

More straightforward is *Woolfall v Knowsley B.C.* [1992] Times L.R. 319: a boy of 12 was injured on the highway when an aerosol exploded on a local authority rubbish tip. The tip was alight because the dustmen were on strike and the local authority did not want to exacerbate them by taking preventive action.

Question
Every evening people waiting at the bus-stop outside your house throw into your front garden the remnants of the fish-and-chips they have bought from a take-away close by. Have you a remedy against the bus company or the take-away?

WANDSWORTH LBC v RAILTRACK

Court of Appeal [2001] EWCA Civ 1236; [2002] Q.B. 756; [2002] 2 W.L.R. 512

Liability of occupier of railway bridge from which pigeons fouled the pavement below

Chadwick L.J.: Wandsworth London Borough Council is the highway authority in respect of that part of Balham High Road which adjoins Balham station. The street is crossed by a railway bridge which is now vested in Railtrack plc as part of its undertaking. The construction of the railway bridge is such that it provides a convenient roost to the numerous feral pigeons attracted to the area by the ready availability of food in the vicinity. The obvious consequences of pigeon infestation ensue, to the annoyance and inconvenience of pedestrians using the highway beneath the bridge. The judge found, "as a matter of fact and degree" that the pigeon infestation and the fouling caused by it amounted to a nuisance; that is to say that there was a substantial interference with the comfort and convenience of the public or a significant class of the public who use the footpaths or pavements. There is no challenge to that finding. Nor could there be; the evidence was overwhelming.

It is the duty of the Council, as local highway authority, to assert and protect the rights of the public to the use and enjoyment of Balham High Road, including the pavements provided for pedestrian use—see s.130(1) of the Highways Act 1980. In furtherance of that duty the Council has brought these proceedings against Railtrack plc as the owners of the bridge. The issue on this appeal is whether the judge was right to find, as he did, that Railtrack were liable for the public nuisance arising from the pigeon infestation.

The liability of a landowner for a public nuisance on or emanating from his land was recognised by this Court over one hundred years ago in *Attorney-General v Tod Heatley* [1897] 1 Ch. 560. The decision of this Court in *Tod Heatley* was approved by the House of Lords in *Sedleigh-Denfield v O'Callaghan* [1940] A.C. 880—see, in particular, the passage at page 899 in the speech of Lord Atkin, to which Lord Justice Kennedy has referred. Liability in public nuisance arises where the landowner has knowledge of the existence of a nuisance on or emanating from his land, where there are means reasonably open to him for preventing or abating it, and where he fails to take those means within a reasonable time. I agree with Lord Justice Kennedy that there is nothing in the subsequent decisions in this Court to which we were referred—*Slater v Worthington's Cash Stores (1930) Ltd* [1941] 1 K.B. 488, *Leakey v National Trust for Places of Historic Interest or Natural Beauty* [1980] 1 Q.B. 485 and *Holbeck Hall Hotel Ltd v Scarborough Borough Council* [2000] Q.B. 836—nor in the decision of the Privy Council in *Goldman v Hargrave* [1967] 1 A.C. 645 which throws doubt upon that as the test to be applied in a public nuisance case.

The three elements of knowledge, means to abate and failure to take those means are all present in the present case. In my view, the judge was plainly correct to find that liability in public nuisance had been established. I agree, also, that he was entitled to make an order for the payment of damages in addition to the declaration which he granted.

Question:
Was the claimant council not claiming in respect of purely economic loss?

MINT v GOOD

Court of Appeal [1951] 1 K.B. 517; 94 S.J. 822; [1950] 2 All E.R. 1159; 49 L.G.R. 495

Action by injured pedestrian against owner of property adjoining highway

The defendant owned two houses whose forecourts were separated from a public footpath by a low wall. He let the houses on weekly tenancies without reserving any right to enter for the purpose of inspection or repair. The plaintiff, a boy of ten, was using the footpath when the wall collapsed and injured him.

Stable J. found that the wall was in imminent danger of collapse, and that a competent person would have realised this after a reasonable inspection; accordingly the wall was technically a nuisance. But he dismissed the action on the ground that the defendant was not liable for it, since he had not reserved the right to enter the premises, and therefore had no control of the wall.

The plaintiff's appeal to the Court of Appeal was allowed in unreserved judgments.

Denning L.J.: The law of England has always taken particular care to protect those who use a highway. It puts on the occupier of adjoining premises a special responsibility for the structures which he keeps beside the highway. So long as those structures are safe, all well and good; but if they fall into disrepair, so as to be a potential danger to passers-by, then they are a nuisance, and, what is more, a public nuisance; and the occupier is liable to anyone using the highway who is injured by reason of the disrepair. It is no answer for him to say that he and his servants took reasonable care; for, even if he has employed a competent independent contractor to repair the structure, and has every reason for supposing it so be safe, the occupier is still liable if the independent contractor did the work badly: see *Tarry v Ashton* ((1876) 1 Q.B.D. 314).

The occupier's duty to passers-by is to see that the structure is as safe as reasonable care can make it; a duty which is as high as the duty which an occupier owes to people who pay to come on to his premises. He is not liable for latent defects, which could not be discovered by reasonable care on the part of anyone, nor for acts of trespassers of which he neither knew, nor ought to have known: see *Barker v Herbert* ([1911] 2 K.B. 633 at 645); but he is liable when structures fall into dangerous disrepair, because there must be some fault on the part of someone or other for that to happen; and he is responsible for it to persons using the highway, even though he was not actually at fault himself. That principle was laid down in this court in *Wringe v Cohen* ([1940] 1 K.B. 233), where it is to be noted that the principle is confined to "premises on a highway," and is, I think, clearly correct in regard to the responsibility of an occupier to passers-by.

The question in this case is whether the owner, as well as the occupier, is under a like duty to passers-by. I think that in many cases he is. In this case the judge found that the condition of the wall was a nuisance, and that a reasonable examination of the wall by a competent person would have detected the condition in which it was. That means that the duty of the landlord was not fulfilled. His duty was to see that the structure was as safe as reasonable care could make it. It was not so safe.

I agree, therefore, that the appeal should be allowed, and judgment entered accordingly.

Notes:

1. One starts with the proposition that if a person is hurt by something on the highway, he must first inquire whether the act which hurt him was incidental to the defendant's reasonable use of the highway. If it was, then, subject to *res ipsa loquitur*, he must prove carelessness in the actor. If, however, the damage is due to an act which the actor had no right to do on the highway at all, the victim can recover for foreseeable harm without having to prove carelessness.

2. People may also be hurt by things falling on to the highway from adjoining land. Some legal systems make the occupier of those premises strictly liable to the person injured. In England, however, there is no law of *res dejectae vel effusae* (see Buckland, *Textbook of Roman Law* 598). If a chattel such as Miss Stone's cricket ball falls into the highway, the person struck by it must prove negligence, but the chattel may help him by speaking for itself (*Byrne v Boadle* (1863) 2 H. & C. 722; 159 E.R. 299; but see *Walsh v Holst & Co* below, p.313).

3. The biggest things that fall into the highway (apart from airplanes and things falling from them, as to which liability is strict: Civil Aviation Act 1982, s.76) are trees and bits of houses; the law of England appears to distinguish between them. A house involves liability if, had a competent person looked at it just before it collapsed, he would have seen that it needed repair. A tree makes the occupier liable only if he should have procured a competent person to look at it, and that person would have seen that action was called for (*Caminer v Northern & London Investment Trust* [1951] A.C. 88; *British Road Services v Slater* [1964] 1 W.L.R. 498; *Quinn v Scott* [1965] 2 All E.R. 588). This is the difference between liability in nuisance and liability in negligence.

Now what are the grounds for distinction between a tree and a bit of a house? Is it that a house is used and a tree is not? (*Sedleigh-Denfield v O'Callaghan* [1940] A.C. 880). Is it because a house is always built and a tree is not always planted? (It would be absurd to distinguish between planted and self-sown trees, *Davey v Harrow Corp.* [1958] 1 Q.B. 60. Is it because a tree is uncommonly lovely and a house is commonly unlovely? Or is it because people are supposed to know about houses and not about trees, trees being subject, as houses are usually not, to *secret unobservable processes of nature*?

4. The italicised phrase occurs in *Wringe v Cohen* [1940] 1 K.B. 229, an action in respect of property damage between neighbours adjoining the highway. That case established that an occupier was liable if his house, or part of it, collapsed owing to want of repair, independently of the question whether he was negligent or not. It would be a defence to show that the collapse was caused by the act of a trespasser (and enemy bombers were treated as trespassers in *Cushing v Peter Walker & Son* [1942] 2 All E.R. 693) or a secret unobservable process of nature. The decision has been very adversely commented on, but, as Somervell L.J. said in the present case, "It is a plain decision, laying down plain principles." The French Civil Code, Art.1386, provides: "The owner of a building is liable for the damage caused by its collapse, if it collapses by reason of want of repair or fault in construction."

5. In English law we think of the occupier and not the owner as being the person responsible, but the principal case shows one of the great advantages of public nuisance as a ground of action. Once the plaintiff has been injured by a thing which can be characterised as a nuisance, he is in a better position than the plaintiff in negligence who has to look around for a person who *acted* badly. The plaintiff in nuisance only has to study the thing and he can catch anyone connected with that thing—here the landlord as well as the occupier. So if I fall into an unguarded trench dug illegally on the highway, I can sue not only the careless person who dug it, but also the perfectly careful person who procured the digging.

6. But the rules of public nuisance protect only those on the highway, that is, those outside buildings. People injured inside buildings must generally use the Occupiers' Liability Act 1957. For this purpose the landlord as well as the tenant may be the occupier (see *Wheat v Lacon*, above, p.35); even if he is not the occupier, the landlord may still be held liable to an injured visitor under the Defective Premises Act 1972, s.4 (above, p.38), provided that he is in breach of obligations owed, or deemed by s.4(4) to be owed, to the tenant. Note, however, that the landlord's liability under the Defective Premises Act 1972 extends also to persons outside the premises, while not, presumably, diminishing their rights, if wider, under the common law of which the principal case is an example. Indeed, *Mint v Good* was invoked by the Court of Appeal in *McAuley v Bristol CC* [1992] 1 All E.R. 749 so as to render the landlord liable to a tenant injured on a garden step which the landlord had power to repair (Defective Premises Act 1972, s.4(4)) though he was under no obligation to do so.

Chapter 4

CAUSATION

Section 1.—No Cause

McWILLIAMS v SIR WILLIAM ARROL & CO

House of Lords [1962] 1 W.L.R. 295; 106 S.J. 218; 1962 S.C.(HL) 70; 1962 S.L.T. 121;
[1962] 1 All E.R. 623

Action by widow against employer of husband

The pursuer appealed to the House of Lords from an order of the First Division of the Court of Session (1961 S.L.T. 265) affirming judgment given by the Lord Ordinary in favour of the defender. Her appeal was dismissed.

Lord Reid: My Lords, the appellant is the widow of William McWilliams, a steel erector who was killed on May 27, 1956, when he fell from a steel tower which was being erected in a shipyard occupied by the second respondents. The first respondents were his employers. McWilliams was setting up a working platform for riveters on the outside of the tower about seventy feet from the ground. This had to be placed on "needles" which are battens projecting some four feet from the tower. They were secured to the tower by lashings. A lashing of one of the needles was not properly fixed so that when the deceased put his weight on this needle it tilted and he fell to the ground. It is not clear whether he was responsible for not fixing it properly or not inspecting it, and in this action no fault is alleged against the respondents with regard to the needle.

The case made by the appellant is that both respondents were at fault in not providing safety belts. These belts have about fifteen feet of rope attached to them so that the end of the rope can be tied to some convenient part of the structure near where the man is working: then if he falls the rope prevents him from falling more than its length. It is not denied that if McWilliams had been wearing a safety belt when he fell he would not have been killed. The employers do not deny that it was general practice to provide such belts but they do not admit any duty to provide them. The courts below have held that they had this duty and also that the Factories Act 1937 required the second respondents to provide these belts. I need not consider whether this was right, because the main defence of both respondents is that if such belts had been available on the day of the accident McWilliams would not have worn one and, therefore, any failure to provide a belt was not the cause of his death. I shall assume in the case of both respondents that they were in breach of duty in not providing belts.

There can be no certainty as to whether the deceased would or would not have worn a belt on this day, but the defenders maintain that it is highly probable that he would not. Work on this tower had been proceeding for many weeks and at least for a good part of that time he had been doing work similar to that which he was doing when he fell. Throughout this period safety belts had to his knowledge been available in a hut near-by and it is clear that it was not his practice to wear a belt. Steel erectors were neither required nor exhorted to wear belts, and several witnesses with long experience say that they had never seen any steel erector wear a belt, and in particular that they had never seen McWilliams wear one. And there is evidence that the

205

condition of the belts showed that they had seldom if ever been used. But one witness says that
he saw McWilliams wearing a belt on two occasions when working in an exposed position. The
Lord Ordinary thought this extremely doubtful, but I am prepared to assume in the appellant's
favour that this evidence can be accepted. It was left to the discretion of each man to decide
whether to wear a belt, and it appears that the reason why belts were not generally worn was not
mere prejudice against them. They are cumbersome and some witnesses say they might be
dangerous in certain circumstances.

For some reason, the belts were taken away to another site two or three days before the
accident. So after that the defenders were in breach of their duty to provide belts. We do not
know whether the deceased knew that they had been removed, and there is nothing to suggest
that during those two or three days he may have considered changing his normal practice not to
wear a belt. So it appears to me to be a natural, and indeed almost inevitable, inference that he
would not have worn a belt on this occasion even if it had been available. And that inference is
strengthened by the general practice of other men not to wear belts.

It was argued that the law does not permit such an inference to be drawn because what a man
did on previous occasions is no evidence of what he would have done on a later similar occasion.
This argument was based on the rule that you cannot infer that a man committed a particular
crime or delict from the fact that he has previously committed other crimes or delicts. But even
that is not an unqualified rule, and there are reasons for that rule which would not apply to a case
like the present. It would not be right to draw such an inference too readily because people do
sometimes change their minds unexpectedly. But the facts of this case appear to me to be
overwhelming.

I would have had much more difficulty if the only evidence had been that there was a general
practice not to wear belts. One would assume, in the absence of evidence to the contrary, that the
deceased was a reasonable and careful man, and it may be that if the evidence proved that a
reasonable and careful man would not have worn a belt on such an occasion that would be
sufficient. But I would reserve my opinion about a case which merely depended on evidence of
general practice. I regard the evidence about general practice in this case as corroborating the
inference to be drawn from McWilliams' own past conduct.

The appellant founded on the case of *Roberts v Dorman Long & Co Ltd* ([1953] 1 W.L.R.
942). There a steel erector who was not wearing a safety belt was killed during the erection of
a steel building to which building regulations of 1948 applied. They required that belts should
be available which would "so far as practicable enable such persons who elect to use them to
carry out the work without risk of serious injury." The employers did have belts but they were
kept so far away from the site that they were held not to be available. One question in the case
was whether the employers' breach of statutory duty could be founded on in face of evidence of
a general practice to elect not to use such belts. Lord Goddard C.J. said: "I think that if a person
is under a duty to provide safety belts or other appliances and fails to do so, he cannot be heard
to say: 'Even if I had done so they would not have been worn.'" In my view, this is not correct.
"He cannot be heard to say" suggests to me personal bar or estoppel: indeed, I know of no other
ground on which a defender can be prevented from proving a fact vital for his defence. If I prove
that my breach of duty is no way caused or contributed to the accident I cannot be liable in
damages. And if the accident would have happened in just the same way whether or not I fulfilled
my duty, it is obvious that my failure to fulfil my duty cannot have caused or contributed to it.
No reason has ever been suggested why a defender should be barred from proving that his fault,
whether common law negligence or breach of statutory duty, had nothing to do with the accident.

It has been suggested that the decision of this House in *Bonnington Castings Ltd v Wardlaw*
([1956] A.C. 613) lays down new law and increases the burden on pursuers. I do not think so.
It states what has always been the law—a pursuer must prove his case. He must prove that the
fault of the defender caused, or contributed to, the danger which he has suffered. But proof need
not be by direct evidence. If general practice or a regulation requires that some safety appliance
shall be provided, one would assume that it is of some use, and that a reasonable man would use
it. And one would assume that the injured man was a reasonable man. So the initial onus on the
pursuer to connect the failure to provide the appliance with the accident would normally be
discharged merely by proving the circumstances which led to the accident, and it is only where

the evidence throws doubt on either of these assumptions that any difficulty would arise. Normally it would be left to the defender to adduce evidence, if he could, to displace these assumptions. So in practice it would be realistic, even if not theoretically accurate, to say that the onus is generally on the defender to show that the man would not have used the appliance even if it has been available. But in the end, when all the evidence has been brought out, it rarely matters where the onus originally lay, the question is which way the balance of probability has come to rest. . . .

Lord Devlin: . . . Mr Stott, for the appellant, based his case upon the proposition that the failure to provide the safety belt was the cause of the [workman's] death. In my opinion, this proposition is incomplete. There is a missing link. The immediate cause of the deceased's death was the fact that at the time of the fall he was not wearing a safety belt. The cause or reason he was not wearing a safety belt may have been the fact that one was not provided, but the failure to provide operates only through the failure to wear. The correct way of stating the appellant's case is, I think, as follows: The immediate cause of the deceased's death was that at the time of the fall he was not wearing a safety belt: but for the fault of his employers, he would have been wearing a safety belt: therefore the fault of his employers was an effective cause of his death. So stated, it is plain that the reason why the deceased was not wearing a safety belt must be a proper subject for inquiry. . . .

This question of the burden of proof is frequently important when what is in issue is what a dead workman in fact did. Without his evidence it may be difficult to prove that negligence by the employers was an effective cause of the death: once negligence is proved, the fact that the workman cannot be called to account for his actions often defeats the proof of contributory negligence. But in the present case the question is not what the deceased actually did but what he would have done in circumstances that never arose. Whether the workman is alive or dead, this cannot be proved positively as a matter of fact but can only be inferred as a matter of likelihood or probability. Even when the workman himself is perforce silent, there may be plenty of material, as there is in this case, from which an inference can be drawn one way or the other; and then the question of burden of proof is unimportant. . . .

Question

Was "death by falling" within the risk envisaged by the legislature when it required safety-belts to be provided? Did the defendant's failure to provide safety-belts enhance the risk of death by falling? Did it enhance the risk that McWilliams might fall to his death?

Notes:

1. A one-man cash guard employed by Securicor was shot and badly injured by a robber as he left a garage with the takings. Body armour would probably have avoided or mitigated the injuries, but the trial judge found that the claimant would not have worn it if it had been provided. The Court of Appeal reversed: the Personal Protective Equipment at Work Regulations, SI 1992/2966 (regs.4, 6, and especially 10) required the employer to ensure that body armour was provided *and used*, so it was irrelevant that the claimant would not have worn it if merely provided. *Henser-Leather v Securicor Cash Services* [2002] EWCA Civ 816.

2. In matters of causation the hypothetical is unavoidable. The question "Did X contribute to the occurrence of Y" may seem perfectly factual, a mere matter of history, but it really means "Would Y have happened without X," which is manifestly hypothetical: one is in the zone of the probable, not the provable.

In *McWilliams* the judges were confident that he would not have worn a safety-belt even if safety-belts had been dangled in front of him. But suppose he sometimes wore one and sometimes didn't, that he wore one on average once every four days. Would there be any basis for awarding one-fourth of the damages due to his death? Must the judge make up his mind one way or the other on whether McWilliams *would have worn* a belt or not, or can he hedge his bets and reflect in his award of damages the odds on or against belt-wearing on that day? Can we say that though the failure to provide safety belts probably didn't cause McWilliams to die (since he *probably* wouldn't have worn one), nevertheless it certainly deprived him of a chance of wearing one (which he *might* have taken), that even a chance of not being killed is worth having, and that it is consequently a harm to be denied that chance, the extent of the harm being related to the value of the chance? Can we in this way turn the causation problem into a damage question? See below p.214.

BOLITHO v CITY AND HACKNEY H.A.

House of Lords [1998] A.C. 232; [1997] 3 W.L.R. 1151; [1997] 4 All E.R. 771
(noted [1998] Camb. L.J. 248)

Claim against hospital for failing to prevent death of child

When a young patient had a breathing crisis the nurse called a doctor but the doctor failed to come (the battery in her pager being flat!) and the child died. Had the doctor come and intubated the child he would probably not have died, but the doctor said that she would not have intubated the child, and the question was whether her failure to do so (had she arrived) would have been negligent and whether this affected the question of causation.

Lord Browne-Wilkinson: . . .   Where, as in the present case, a breach of a duty of care is proved or admitted, the burden still lies on the plaintiff to prove that such breach caused the injury suffered (see *Bonnington Castings Ltd v Wardlaw* [1956] 1 All E.R. 615; [1956] A.C. 613 and *Wilsher v Essex Area H.A.* [1988] 1 All E.R. 871; [1988] A.C. 1074). In all cases, the primary question is one of fact: did the wrongful act cause the injury? But in cases where the breach of duty consists of an omission to do an act which ought to be done (*e.g.* the failure by a doctor to attend) that factual inquiry is, by definition, in the realms of hypothesis. The question is what would have happened if an event which by definition did not occur, had occurred. In a case of non-attendance by a doctor, there may be cases in which there is a doubt as to which doctor would have attended if the duty had been fulfilled. But in this case there was no doubt: if the duty had been carried out it would have either been Dr Horn or Dr Rodger, the only two doctors at St Bartholomew's who had responsibility for Patrick and were on duty. Therefore in the present case, the first relevant question is "what would Dr Horn or Dr Rodger have done if they had attended?" As to Dr Horn, the judge accepted her evidence that she would not have intubated. By inference, although not expressly, the judge must have accepted that Dr Rodger also would not have intubated: as a senior house officer she would not have intubated without the approval of her senior registrar, Dr Horn.

. . . in the present case, the answer to the question "what would have happened" is not determinative of the issue of causation. At the trial the defendants accepted that if the professional standard of care required any doctor who attended to intubate Patrick, Patrick's claim must succeed. Dr Horn could not escape liability by proving that she would have failed to take the course which any competent doctor would have adopted. A defendant cannot escape liability by saying that the damage would have occurred in any event because he would have committed some other breach of duty thereafter. I have no doubt that this concession was rightly made by the defendants. But there is some difficulty in analysing why it was correct. I adopt the analysis of Hobhouse L.J. in *Joyce v Merton Sutton and Wandsworth H.A.* (1996) 27 B.M.L.R. 124. In commenting on the decision of the Court of Appeal in the present case, he said (at 156):

> "Thus, a plaintiff can discharge the burden of proof on causation by satisfying the court *either* that the relevant person would in fact have taken the requisite action (although she would not have been at fault if she had not) *or* that the proper discharge of the relevant person's duty towards the plaintiff required that she take that action. The former alternative calls for no explanation since it is simply the factual proof of the causative effect of the original fault. The latter is slightly more sophisticated: it involves the factual situation that the original fault did not itself cause the injury but that this was because there would have been some further fault on the part of the defendants; the plaintiff proves his case by proving that his injuries would have been avoided if proper care had continued to be taken. In *Bolitho* the plaintiff had to prove that the continuing exercise of proper care would have resulted in his being intubated."

There were, therefore, two questions for the judge to decide on causation: (1) What would Dr Horn have done, or authorised to be done, if she had attended Patrick? and (2) If she would not have intubated, would that have been negligent? The *Bolam* test has no relevance to the first of those questions but is central to the second.

Puzzles

1. In a motor accident for which the defendant was responsible the plaintiff lost 30 per cent of the use of his left leg. Three years later gangsters shot him in the same leg and it had to be amputated. Did the defendant (who was clearly not liable for the amputation—*novus actus interveniens*) have to pay for 30 per cent of the leg for the rest of the plaintiff's life or only for the three years until it was amputated? *Baker v Willoughby* [1970] A.C. 467 said for life (but only for the loss of amenity which was thought to be continuing, not for the pain and suffering, which had come to an end).

2. A person who might have been expected to work until 1985 had an accident in 1973 owing to his employer's fault. This reduced his earning capacity by 50 per cent. In 1976 a disease quite unconnected with the accident incapacitated him totally. Does he get 50 per cent of his lost earnings for three years or for twelve? *Jobling v Associated Dairies* ([1982] A.C. 794) said for three.

In that case Lord Wilberforce drew "the conclusion that no general, logical, or universally fair rules can be stated which will cover, in a manner consistent with justice, cases of supervening events, whether due to tortious, partially tortious, non-culpable or wholly accidental events."

3. A school is under a duty not to let children out till 3.30 p.m., since that is when their mothers fetch them. One day the school lets a child out at 3.25 p.m., and at 3.29 p.m. the child is run over in the street. It is proved that on that day the mother would have been 15 minutes late. Is the school liable for causing the death of the child?

4. George is injured when Henry runs him over in the street. Henry wasn't looking where he was going and didn't apply the brakes at all. If he had been paying attention he could have braked and if the brakes had worked he would not have hit George. The brakes would not have worked, however, because Ian, a mechanic, had failed to fix them properly. Has either Henry or Ian contributed to George's injuries? Have both?

5. Consider the following from Lord Hoffmann in *South Australia Asset Corp. v York Montague* [1996] 3 All E.R. 365 at 373. In that case the plaintiffs lent money on the security of landed property carelessly overvalued by the defendant and would not have lent any money at all had the valuation been as accurate as they were entitled to expect. After they had made the loan on what was already insufficient security, the property market collapsed, the security became more than ever insufficient and the lender lost hand over fist.

On a simple view the causal link seemed established: the plaintiff would not have suffered this loss if the defendant's valuation had been as accurate as it should have been. Nevertheless his Lordship held that the defendant was liable not for the whole loss foreseeably suffered as a result of making the loan, but only for the amount by which the valuation exceeded the true value of the property at the time, that is, the amount by which the property was insufficient security. He emphasised that the questions of duty breached and loss caused are not discrete and completely severable; one may have to consider the scope of the duty breached in order to discover what consequences fall within it. "The real question is the kind of loss in respect of which the duty is owed."

He offered the following example:

"A mountaineer about to undertake a difficult climb is concerned about the fitness of his knee. He goes to a doctor who negligently makes a superficial examination and pronounces the knee fit. The climber goes on the expedition, which he would not have undertaken if the doctor had told him the true state of his knee. He suffers an injury which is an entirely foreseeable consequence of mountaineering, but has nothing to do with his knee. . . . it is damage which would not have occurred if he had been given correct information about his knee. He would not have gone on the expedition and would have suffered no injury. On what I have suggested is the more usual principle, the doctor is not liable. The injury had not been caused by the doctor's bad advice, because it would have occurred even if the advice had been correct." (at 371–72)

His Lordship instanced *The Empire Jamaica* [1956] 3 All E.R. 144, HL, where liability was denied when a vessel being navigated carefully by a captain not licensed to navigate at all was involved in a collision. The duty breached in that case was a statutory one, and with some, but not very much, plausibility one could say that the harm was not within the intended scope of the rule laid down about licences. (Compare *Gorris v Scott*, below, p.223). But the scope/purpose approach may be applicable even at common law. For example, it is negligent of a parent to let a child of ten have a loaded shot-gun, but what is the position if the child drops it on his aunt's foot? One might say that the harm was not within the scope of the duty broken, which was designed to prevent injury or fright due to the gun going off. This would be analogous to the German theory that the harm must fall within the protective purpose of the rule infringed.

Note:

Despite the odd puzzle, the basic principle is relatively simple. Once one has identified the respect in which the alleged tortfeasor is at fault, one asks whether it would have made any difference if he had behaved properly, if safety belts had been provided, if the doctor had arrived. If not, there is no liability: the claimant would have suffered the same harm anyway. Note that for this purpose one must clearly identify the respect in which the defendant was to blame: if, for example, he is castigated for failing to warn the claimant of a danger, it will be relevant to know whether the warning would have been heard or ignored. Other cases show that there is no liability for carelessly failing to rescue someone already dead (*The Ogopogo* [1971] 2 Lloyd's Rep. 410), or not diagnosing a person with an incurable disease, at least if there was no chance of alleviation (*Barnett v Kensington and Chelsea Hospital* [1968] 1 All E.R. 1068).

However, having thus considered the application of the "but for" test we must see how right an Australian judge was to deny that "the 'but for' (causa sine qua non) test ever was or should become the exclusive test of causation in negligence cases". The developments in this area, which are not yet over, have been dramatic.

We can start with *Bonnington Castings v Wardlaw* [1956] A.C. 613. The pursuer contracted pneumoconiosis as a result of inhaling silica dust, which came from two sources in the factory, a pneumatic hammer and swing grinders. The dust emanating from the pneumatic hammers involved no breach of duty by the employer, but that from the swing grinders did. Lord Reid held that "the employee must make it appear at least that, on a balance of probabilities, the breach of duty caused, *or materially contributed to*, his injury" (Italics added). Accordingly, even if there was enough "innocent" dust to have rendered the claimant sick, the addition of the guilty dust probably contributed to his progressive condition. It will be seen that the "but for" test is not satisfied here. Likewise, if I negligently make a drunk person drunker, and he causes an injury because he is as drunk as he now is, I cannot escape liability by saying that he was probably drunk enough anyway to have caused the injury.

This was to lay the ground for the decision in *Fairchild*, next following, that it was enough if the defendant's fault contributed, not to the actual occurrence of the harm, but to the risk of its occurrence, given that it did in fact occur. But this development went by way of *McGhee v National Coal Board* [1972] 3 All E.R. 1008, whose background is explained by Lord Hope in a luminous article significantly entitled "James McGhee—A Second Mrs Donoghue" [2003] Camb. L.J. 587. The pursuer developed dermatitis after a few days' work in the defender's warm brick kiln. Since no washing facilities were provided, which the defender admitted was a breach of duty, the claimant had to cycle home in the cold, still covered with brick dust. The experts were unable to say that the dermatitis would not have developed had he washed (as he would have done), but the House of Lords held the defender liable.

This decision, whose significance was not immediately seen, led to the following statement in *Wilsher*: "If it is an established fact that conduct of a particular kind creates a risk that injury will be caused to another or increases an existing risk that injury will ensue, and if the two parties stand in such a relationship that the one party owes a duty not to conduct himself in that way, and if the other party does suffer injury of the kind to which the risk related, then the first party is taken to have caused the injury by his breach of duty, even though the existence and extent of the contribution made by the breach cannot be ascertained." [1986] 3 All E.R. 801, 820, *per* Mustill LJ. In *Wilsher* a tiny baby born very prematurely had several congenital ailments which might well have caused the affliction of which his parents made complaint, but it might also have been due to the fact that the doctors had negligently hyperoxygenated him owing to a defect in the control machinery. When the House of Lords reversed the Court of Appeal's judgment for the claimant, Lord Bridge said in the course of his speech, with which all the other members of the House agreed, "*McGhee v National Coal Board* laid down no new principle of law whatever. On the contrary, it affirmed the principle that the onus of proving causation lies on the pursuer of plaintiff. Adopting a robust and pragmatic approach to the undisputed primary facts of the case, the majority concluded that it was a legitimate inference of fact that the defenders' negligence had materially contributed to the pursuer's injury."

In *Fairchild*, next following, the speeches in *McGhee* were subjected to detailed analysis of the kind described by Lord Steyn in *Rees* (above p.118) as "gruesome", and with the sole exception of Lord Hutton their Lordships decided that that case did indeed lay down a new proposition of law, *viz.* contribution to the risk of an injury which eventuates is in some cases as good as contribution to the actual occurrence of that injury and is therefore causally adequate. Lord Bridge was held to have been in error in his analysis, but the actual decision in *Wilsher* was approved, because that was not a case where a precondition laid down by Lord Bingham was satisfied, namely that any other cause of the injury could be discounted.

FAIRCHILD v GLENHAVEN FUNERAL SERVICES

House of Lords [2002] UKHL 22, [2002] 3 All E.R. 305

The facts as stated by Lord Hoffmann are as follows:

"The appellant Mr Matthews is suffering from a cancer (mesothelioma) caused by exposure to asbestos. Between 1973 and 1981 he was exposed to substantial quantities of asbestos dust in the course of successive employments by the two respondents, Associated Portland Cement and British Uralite. It is accepted that both employers were in breach of duty—the link between asbestos and cancer was well known by the mid-1960s—and that both exposures contributed substantially to the risk that he would contract the disease. But the precise mechanism by which asbestos causes cancer is unknown. It may be caused by the mutation of a single cell caused by a single asbestos fibre. At any rate, it is impossible to say that it was more likely to have been caused by the exposure to asbestos during employment with the one respondent rather than the other. And on that ground the Court of Appeal has held that Mr Matthews' claim must fail. It was said to be a rule of law that in order to succeed against either respondent, he must prove that, but for its breach of duty, he would not have contracted the disease."

Lord Nicholls of Birkenhead: My Lords, in the normal way, in order to recover damages for negligence, a plaintiff must prove that but for the defendant's wrongful conduct he would not have sustained the harm or loss in question. He must establish at least this degree of causal connection between his damage and the defendant's conduct before the defendant will be held responsible for the damage.

Exceptionally this is not so. In some circumstances a lesser degree of causal connection may suffice. This sometimes occurs where the damage flowed from one or other of two alternative causes. Take the well-known example where two hunters, acting independently of each other, fire their guns carelessly in a wood, and a pellet from one of the guns injures an innocent passer-by. No one knows, and the plaintiff is unable to prove, from which gun the pellet came. Should the law of negligence leave the plaintiff remediless, and allow both hunters to go away scot-free, even though one of them must have fired the injurious pellet?

Not surprisingly, the courts have declined to reach such an unjust decision: see *Summers v Tice* (1948) 199 P 2d 1, a decision of the Supreme Court of California, and *Cook v Lewis* [1951] S.C.R. 830, a decision of the Supreme Court of Canada. As between the plaintiff and the two hunters, the evidential difficulty arising from the impossibility of identifying the gun which fired the crucial pellet should redound upon the negligent hunters, not the blameless plaintiff. The unattractive consequence, that one of the hunters will be held liable for an injury he did not in fact inflict, is outweighed by the even less attractive alternative, that the innocent plaintiff should receive no recompense even though one of the negligent hunters injured him. It is this balance ('.. outweighed by ..') which justifies a relaxation in the standard of causation required. Insistence on the normal standard of causation would work an injustice. Hunting in a careless manner and thereby creating a risk of injury to others, followed by injury to another person, is regarded by the law as sufficient causal connection in the circumstances to found responsibility.

This balancing exercise involves a value judgment. This is not at variance with basic principles in this area of the law. The extent to which the law requires a defendant to assume responsibility for loss following upon his wrongful conduct always involves a value judgment. The law habitually *limits* the extent of the damage for which a defendant is held responsible, even when the damage passes the threshold 'but for' test. The converse is also true. On occasions the threshold 'but for' test of causal connection may be over-exclusionary. Where justice so requires, the threshold itself may be lowered. In this way the scope of a defendant's liability may be *extended*. The circumstances where this is appropriate will be exceptional, because of the adverse consequences which the lowering of the threshold will have for a defendant. He will be held responsible for a loss the plaintiff might have suffered even if the defendant had not been involved at all. To impose liability on a defendant in such circumstances normally runs counter to ordinary perceptions of responsibility. Normally this is unacceptable. But there are circumstances, of which the two hunters' case is an example, where this unattractiveness is outweighed by leaving the plaintiff without a remedy.

The present appeals are another example of such circumstances, where good policy reasons exist for departing from the usual threshold 'but for' test of causal connection. Inhalation of asbestos dust carries a risk of mesothelioma. That is one of the very risks from which an employer's duty of care is intended to protect employees. Tragically, each claimant acquired this fatal disease from wrongful exposure to asbestos dust in the course of his employment. A former employee's inability to identify which particular period of wrongful exposure brought about the onset of his disease ought not, in all justice, to preclude recovery of compensation.

So long as it was not insignificant, each employer's wrongful exposure of its employee to asbestos dust and, hence, to the risk of contracting mesothelioma, should be regarded by the law as a sufficient degree of causal connection. This is sufficient to justify requiring the employer to assume responsibility for causing or materially contributing to the onset of the mesothelioma when, in the present state of medical knowledge, no more exact causal connection is ever capable of being established. Given the present state of medical science, this outcome may cast responsibility on a defendant whose exposure of a claimant to the risk of contracting the disease had in fact no causative effect. But the unattractiveness of casting the net of responsibility as widely as this is far outweighed by the unattractiveness of the alternative outcome.

I need hardly add that considerable restraint is called for in any relaxation of the threshold 'but for' test of causal connection. The principle applied on these appeals is emphatically not intended to lead to such a relaxation whenever a plaintiff has difficulty, perhaps understandable difficulty, in discharging the burden of proof resting on him. Unless closely confined in its application this principle could become a source of injustice to defendants. There must be good reason for departing from the normal threshold 'but for' test. The reason must be sufficiently weighty to justify depriving the defendant of the protection this test normally and rightly affords him, and it must be plain and obvious that this is so. Policy questions will loom large when a court has to decide whether the difficulties of proof confronting the plaintiff justify taking this exceptional course. It is impossible to be more specific.

I should comment briefly on the much discussed case of *McGhee v National Coal Board* [1973] 1 W.L.R. 1. As I understand it, the decision of your Lordships' House is an example of the application of the approach discussed above. In the circumstances of that case the House departed from the usual threshold 'but for' test of causal connection and treated a lesser degree of causal connection as sufficient. The novelty in the decision lay in the adoption of this approach in this country and, further, in the type of claim to which this approach was applied: there, as with the present appeals, the field of industrial disease. Given the medical evidence in *McGhee*, it was not open to the House, however robustly inclined, to draw an inference that the employer's negligence had in fact caused or materially contributed to the onset of the dermatitis in the sense that, but for that negligence, the dermatitis would not have occurred. Instead, a less stringent causal connection was regarded as sufficient. It was enough that the employer had materially increased the risk of harm to the employee . . . when applying the principle described above the court is not, by a process of inference, concluding that the ordinary 'but for' standard of causation is satisfied. Instead, the court is applying a different and less stringent test. It were best if this were recognised openly.

Lord Hoffmann: I shall first consider the question in principle. It is axiomatic that the law will not impose liability to pay compensation for damage unless there is a relevant causal connection between the damage and the defendant's tort, breach of contract or statutory duty. But what amounts to a relevant causal connection?

Everyone agrees that there is no scientific or philosophical touchstone for determining the relevant causal connection in any particular case. The relevance of a causal connection depends upon the purpose of the inquiry. In the present case, the House is required to say what should be the relevant causal connection for breach of a duty to protect an employee against the risk of contracting (among other things) mesothelioma by exposure to asbestos.

It is frequently said that causation is a question of fact or a matter of common sense. Both of these propositions are true but they need to be analysed with some care in order to avoid confusion.

In my opinion, the essential point is that the causal requirements are just as much part of the legal conditions for liability as the rules which prescribe the kind of conduct which attracts liability or the rules which limit the scope of that liability. If I may repeat what I have said on another occasion, one is never simply liable, one is always liable *for* something—to make compensation for damage, the nature and extent of which is delimited by the law. The rules which delimit what one is liable for may consist of causal requirements or may be rules unrelated to causation, such as the foreseebility requirements in the rule in *Hadley v Baxendale* (1854) 9 Exch 341. But in either case they are rules of law, part and parcel of the conditions of liability. Once it is appreciated that the rules laying down causal requirements are not autonomous expressions of some form of logic or judicial instinct but creatures of the law, part of the conditions of liability, it is possible to explain their content on the grounds of fairness and justice in exactly the same way as the other conditions of liability.

In the law of negligence, for example, it has long been recognised that the imposition of a duty of care in respect of particular conduct depends upon whether it is just and reasonable to impose it. The same is true of causation. The concepts of fairness, justice and reason underlie the rules which state the causal requirements of liability for a particular form of conduct (or non-causal limits on that liability) just as much as they underlie the rules which determine that conduct to be tortious. And the two are inextricably linked together: the purpose of the causal requirement rules is to produce a just result by delimiting the scope of liability in a way which relates to the reasons why liability for the conduct in question exists in the first place. For example, if it is thought just and reasonable to impose a duty to take care to protect someone against harm caused by the informed and voluntary act of another responsible human being, it would be absurd to retain a causal requirement that the harm should not have been so caused. An extreme case of this kind was *Reeves v Commissioner of Police of the Metropolis* [2000] 1 A.C. 360, in which the defendant accepted that in the circumstances of the case, he owed a duty to take reasonable care to prevent a responsible human being from causing injury to himself. Your Lordships decided that in those circumstances it would be contradictory to hold that the causal requirements of the tort excluded liability for harm so caused. Thus the causal requirements are always adapted to conform to the grounds upon which liability is imposed. Again, it may be said that this is no more than common sense. But it is capable of rational explanation.

The question of principle is this: which rule would be more in accordance with justice and the policy of common law and statute to protect employees against the risk of contracting asbestos-related diseases? My Lords, as between the employer in breach of duty and the employee who has lost his life in consequence of a period of exposure to risk to which that employer has contributed, I think it would be both inconsistent with the policy of the law imposing the duty and morally wrong for your Lordships to impose causal requirements which exclude liability.

Lord Rodger of Earlsferry: Counsel urged that, if minded to apply some version of the principle in *McGhee*, the House should define its scope. Identifying, at an abstract level, the defining characteristics of the cases where it is, none the less, proper to apply the principle is far from easy. The common law naturally and traditionally shies away from such generalisations especially in a developing area of the law. But I would tentatively suggest that certain conditions are necessary, but may not always be sufficient, for applying the principle. All the criteria are satisfied in the present cases.

First, the principle is designed to resolve the difficulty that arises where it is inherently impossible for the claimant to prove exactly how his injury was caused. It applies, therefore, where the claimant has proved all that he possibly can, but the causal link could only ever be established by scientific investigation and the current state of the relevant science leaves it uncertain exactly how the injury was caused and, so, who caused it. *McGhee* and the present cases are examples. Secondly, part of the underlying rationale of the principle is that the defendant's wrongdoing has materially increased the risk that the claimant will suffer injury. It is therefore essential not just that the defendant's conduct created a material risk of injury to a class of persons but that it actually created a material risk of injury to the claimant himself. Thirdly, it follows that the defendant's conduct must have been capable of causing the claimant's injury. Fourthly, the claimant must prove that his injury was caused by the eventuation of the kind of risk created by the defendant's wrongdoing. In *McGhee*, for instance, the risk created by the defenders' failure was that the pursuer would develop dermatitis due to brick dust on his skin and he proved that he had developed dermatitis due to brick dust on his skin. By contrast, the principle does not apply where the claimant has merely proved that his injury could have been caused by a number of different events, only one of which is the eventuation of the risk created by the defendant's wrongful act or omission. *Wilsher* is an example. Fifthly, this will usually mean that the claimant must prove that his injury was caused, if not by exactly the same agency as was involved in the defendant's wrongdoing, at least by an agency that operated in substantially the same way. Sixthly, the principle applies where the other possible source of the claimant's injury is a similar wrongful act or omission of another person, but it can also apply where, as in *McGhee*, the other possible source of the injury is a similar, but lawful, act or omission of the same defendant.

Their Lordships all agreed on the justice of allowing the appeal.

Note:

Fairchild was all about risk. There is a correlative notion, namely "chance". We use the word "risk" when there is a chance of something bad happening; "chances", even if as remote as those in the National Lottery, relate to something good. While all the fuss was going on about risk, there was a concurrent excitement in terms of "chance". It started off with young Hotson falling out of a tree and hurting himself. That was no one's fault but his own, but when he went to the defendant hospital, they badly misdiagnosed his condition, effectively putting a Bandaid on his knee when it was his hip which had suffered a very severe injury. When he returned to the hospital some days later they realised their mistake but said it had made no difference since when he first came there was nothing they could have done which would have prevented his being a cripple for life. The trial judge held that while probably nothing effective could have been done there had been a one in four chance that prompt diagnosis and treatment would have cured him, so he awarded young Hotson one quarter of the damages he would have awarded had effective treatment clearly been possible. The Court of Appeal upheld this judgment but the House of Lords reversed [1997] 2 All E.R. 909: the claimant had failed to prove that it was more probable than not that treatment would have helped, since on the evidence it was three times more likely than not that it would have been futile. The hospital had not deprived him of a chance of cure, for in view of the severity of the injury, a matter of proven fact, he had had no such chance.

This decision was taken to show that in personal injury cases you had to prove an injury and not just the loss of the chance of avoiding it. That seems to be a matter of defining the appropriate kind of damage in such a suit, rather than one of causation. In *Fairchild*, by contrast, there was no doubt that sufficient damage had been suffered,

People have had difficulty reconciling this reading of *Hotson*, which may yet be disavowed, with cases where clearly it was sufficient for the claimant to show that the defendant had wrongfully caused him to lose a chance of something good. These are all cases of financial harm, starting with *Chaplin v Hicks* [1911] 2 K.B. 786. There the claimant had wrongfully been prevented from entering a final round of a beauty competition. The trial judge said he couldn't tell whether she would have won or not, but the Court of Appeal sent the case back and told him to appraise the chance that she would have done so. The same applies in tort—where the damage is financial. Thus in *Davies v Taylor* a widow claimed damages for loss of support from her late husband, killed by the defendant's negligence. It was proved that the husband was about to divorce her for adultery and probably would not have supported her. The House of Lords held clearly that the judge must determine what the chances were, even if they were less than evens, of a reconciliation taking place, and unless the chance was minimal, award proportional damages.

But economics is not physics, or even medicine, the worlds of Newton and of Adam Smith are worlds apart, even if they both speak of causes and results. There is a fundamental difference between *Davies* and *Hotson*. If I deprive you of a chance of monetary gain, I deprive you of a gain, though a lesser one than the gain you were deprived of the chance of making. The chance and the thing—the stake and the prize—are *in pari materia*, consubstantial, entirely comparable, in the way that the chance of not being crippled and being actually crippled are not. It is therefore quite inept to argue from *Chaplin* to *Hotson*, though Lord Bridge described the analogy as "superficially attractive" but one which there were formidable difficulties in the way of accepting. Lord Mackay also said that "it would be unwise in the present case to lay it down as a rule that a plaintiff could never succeed by proving loss of a chance in a medical negligence case. In *McGhee v National Coal Board* this House held that where it was proved that the failure to provide washing facilities for the pursuer at the end of his shift had materially increased the risk that he would contract dermatitis it was proper to hold that the failure to provide such facilities was a cause to a material extent of his contracting dermatitis and thus entitled him to damages from his employers for their negligent failure measured by his loss resulting from dermatitis. Material increase of the risk of contraction of dermatitis is equivalent to material decrease in the chance of escaping dermatitis. I think it unwise to do more than say that unless and until this House departs from the decision in *McGhee* your Lordships cannot affirm the proposition that in no circumstances can evidence of loss of a chance resulting from the breach of a duty of care found a successful claim of damages, although there was no suggestion that the House regarded such a chance as an asset in any sense."

We must wait and see how the House reacts to the appeal in *Gregg v Scott* [2002] EWCA Civ 1471, where the Court of Appeal was faced with a claim against a doctor by a patient whose malignant tumour grew during the delay due to the negligent doctor's failure to diagnose it as such, thereby reducing the chance of a cure from 42 per cent to 25 per cent. The Court dismissed the claim, Latham L.J. dissenting. Like Latham L.J., Mance L.J. was able to distinguish *Hotson*, but Simon Brown L.J., the trial judge in *Hotson*, felt bound by the House of Lords judgment in that case.

Section 2.—Directness and Foreseeability

Preliminary Note:

The previous cases in this chapter have dealt with the question whether the tortfeasor can be said to have caused the harm in issue. The next cases show that he may not be liable for harm though he has undeniably caused it.

In *Re an Arbitration between Polemis and Furness, Withy & Co* [1921] 3 K.B. 560 (a case whose very title shows that the parties were contractors) the Court of Appeal held the charterer of a vessel liable to the owner for its destruction when, during unloading at Casablanca, a plank carelessly knocked by a stevedore into the hold which was full of petrol vapour caused a wholly unexpected fire and the total loss of the vessel. The Court of Appeal held that since some harm was foreseeable as a result of the careless act, all the harm directly ensuing, even if not foreseeable, was to be compensated: there was liability for the direct consequences of negligence, even if they were not foreseeable.

Re Polemis was sunk by *The Wagon Mound (No.1)* immediately below, and should no longer be cited.

OVERSEAS TANKSHIP (U.K.) LTD v MORTS DOCK & ENGINEERING CO (THE WAGON MOUND)

Privy Council [1961] A.C. 388; [1961] 2 W.L.R. 126; 105 S.J. 85; [1961] 1 All E.R. 404; [1961] 1 Lloyd's Rep. 1

Action by frontager against highway user in respect of property damage

A large quantity of oil was carelessly allowed to spill from *The Wagon Mound*, a ship under the defendant's control, during bunkering operations in Sydney Harbour on October 30, 1951. This oil spread to the plaintiff's wharf about 200 yards away, where a ship, the *Corrimal*, was being repaired. The plaintiff asked whether it was safe to continue welding, and was assured (in accordance with the best scientific opinion) that the oil could not be ignited when spread on water. On November 1, a drop of molten metal fell on a piece of floating waste; this ignited the oil, and the plaintiff's wharf was consumed by fire.

Kinsella J. found that the destruction of the wharf by fire was a direct but unforeseeable consequence of the carelessness of the defendant in spilling the oil, but that some damage by fouling might have been anticipated. He gave judgment for the plaintiff [1958] 1 Lloyd's Rep. 575. The Full Court of the Supreme Court of New South Wales affirmed his decision [1959] 2 Lloyd's Rep. 697. The defendant appealed to the Judicial Committee of the Privy Council, and the appeal was allowed.

Viscount Simonds: . . . the authority of *Polemis* has been severely shaken though lip-service has from time to time been paid to it. In their Lordships' opinion it should no longer be regarded as good law. It is not probable that many cases will for that reason have a different result, though it is hoped that the law will be thereby simplified, and that in some cases, at least, palpable injustice will be avoided. For it does not seem consonant with current ideas of justice or morality that for an act of negligence, however slight or venial, which results in some trival foreseeable damage the actor should be liable for all consequences however unforeseeable and however grave, so long as they can be said to be "direct." It is a principle of civil liability, subject only to qualifications which have no present relevance, that a man must be considered to be responsible for the probable consequences of his act. To demand more of him is too harsh a rule, to demand less is to ignore that civilised order requires the observance of a minimum standard of behaviour.

This concept applied to the slowly developing law of negligence has led to a great variety of expressions which can, as it appears to their Lordships, be harmonised with little difficulty with the single exception of the so-called rule in *Polemis*. For, if it is asked why a man should be responsible for the natural or necessary or probable consequences of his act (or any other similar description of them) the answer is that it is not because they are natural or necessary or probable, but because, since they have this quality, it is judged by the standard of the reasonable man that he ought to have foreseen them. Thus it is that over and over again it has happened that in different judgments in the same case, and sometimes in a single judgment, liability for a consequence has been imposed on the ground that it was reasonably foreseeable or, alternatively, on the ground that it was natural or necessary or probable. The two grounds have been treated as coterminous, and so they largely are. But, where they are not, the question arises to which the wrong answer was given in *Polemis*. For, if some limitation must be imposed upon the consequences for which the negligent actor is to be held responsible—and all are agreed that some limitation there must be—why should that test (reasonable foreseeability) be rejected which, since he is judged by what the reasonable man ought to foresee, corresponds with the common conscience of mankind, and a test (the "direct" consequence) be substituted which leads to nowhere but the never-ending and insoluble problems of causation. "The lawyer," said Sir Frederick Pollock, "cannot afford to adventure himself with philosophers in the logical and metaphysical controversies that beset the idea of cause." Yet this is just what he has most unfortunately done and must continue to do if the rule in *Polemis* is to prevail. A conspicuous example occurs when the actor seeks to escape liability on the ground that the "chain of causation" is broken by a *"nova causa"* or *"novus actus interveniens."*

It is, no doubt, proper when considering tortious liability for negligence to analyse its elements and to say that the plaintiff must prove a duty owed to him by the defendant, a breach of that duty by the defendant, and consequent damage. But there can be no liability until the damage has been done. It is not the act but the consequence on which tortious liability is founded. Just as (as it has been said) there is no such thing as negligence in the air, so there is no such thing as liability in the air. Suppose an action brought by A for damage caused by the carelessness (a neutral word) of B, for example, a fire caused by the careless spillage of oil. It may, of course, become relevant to know what duty B owed to A, but the only liability that is in question is the liability for damage by fire. It is vain to isolate the liability from its context and to say that B is or is not liable, and then to ask for what damage he is liable. For his liability is in respect of that damage and no other. If, as admittedly it is, B's liability (culpability) depends on the reasonable foreseeability of the consequent damage, how is that to be determined except by the foreseeability of the damage which in fact happened—the damage in suit? And, if that damage is unforeseeable so as to displace liability at large, how can the liability be restored so as to make compensation payable?

But, it is said, a different position arises if B's careless act has been shown to be negligent and has caused some foreseeable damage to A. Their Lordships have already observed that to hold B liable for consequences however unforeseeable of a careless act if, but only if, he is at the same time liable for some other damage however trivial, appears to be neither logical nor just. This becomes more clear if it is supposed that similar unforeseeable damage is suffered by A and C but other foreseeable damage, for which B is liable, by A only. A system of law which would hold B liable to A but not to C for the similar damage suffered by each of them could not easily be defended. Fortunately, the attempt is not necessary. For the same fallacy is at the root of the proposition. It is irrelevant to the question whether B is liable for unforeseeable damage that he is liable for foreseeable damage, as irrelevant as would the fact that he had trespassed on Whiteacre be to the question whether he has trespassed on Blackacre. Again, suppose a claim by A for damage by fire by the careless act of B. Of what relevance is it to that claim that he has another claim arising out of the same careless act? It would surely not prejudice his claim if that other claim failed: it cannot assist it if it succeeds. Each of them rests on its own bottom, and will fail if it can be established that the damage could not reasonably be foreseen. We have come back to the plain common sense stated by Lord Russell of Killowen in *Bourhill v Young* ([1943] A.C. 92, 101). As Denning L.J. said in *King v Phillips* ([1953] 1 Q.B. 429 at 441): "there can be no doubt since *Bourhill v Young* that the test of *liability for shock* is foreseeability of *injury by shock.*" Their Lordships substitute the word "fire" for "shock" and endorse this statement of the law.

Their Lordships conclude this part of the case with some general observations. They have been concerned primarily to displace the proposition that unforeseeability is irrelevant if damage is "direct." In doing so they have inevitably insisted that the essential factor in determining liability is whether the damage is of such a kind as the reasonable man should have foreseen. This accords with the general view thus stated by Lord Atkin in *Donoghue v Stevenson*: "The liability for negligence, whether you style it such or treat it as in other systems as a species of 'culpa,' is no doubt based upon a general public sentiment of moral wrongdoing for which the offender must pay." It is a departure from this sovereign principle if liability is made to depend solely on the damage being the "direct" or "natural" consequence of the precedent act. Who knows or can be assumed to know all the processes of nature? But if it would be wrong that a man should be held liable for damage unpredictable by a reasonable man because it was "direct" or "natural," equally it would be wrong that he should escape liability, however "indirect" the damage, if he foresaw or could reasonably foresee the intervening events which led to its being done. Thus foreseeability becomes the effective test. In reasserting this principle their Lordships conceive that they do not depart from, but follow and develop, the law of negligence, as laid down by Baron Alderson in *Blyth v Birmingham Waterworks Co* ((1856) 11 Exch. 781 at 784; 156 E.R. 1047).

. . .

Their Lordships will humbly advise Her Majesty that this appeal should be allowed, and the respondents' action so far as it related to damage caused by the negligence of the appellants be dismissed with costs, but that the action so far as it related to damage caused by nuisance should be remitted to the Full Court to be dealt with as that court may think fit.

Questions
1. Did their Lordships deny that the spillage of oil caused the fire?
2. Could *you* defend a legal system which held "B liable to A but not to C for the similar damage suffered by each of them" if there was a contract or other special relationship between B and A but not between B and C or vice versa?
3. Does what the claimant complains of have to be merely foreseeable, or does it have to be a foreseeable *consequence* of the defendant's behaviour? If the latter, how do we escape from the "never-ending and insoluble problems of causation?

Notes:
1. Viscount Simonds said "it is not the hindsight of a fool; it is the foresight of the reasonable man which alone can determine responsibility." One of the characters in Congreve's *Love for Love* is named Foresight. He is described as "An illiterate old Fellow, peevish and positive, superstitious and pretending to understand Astrology, Palmistry, Physiognomy, Omens, Dreams &c."
2. In 1967 the *Torrey Canyon* collided with Land's End. The Royal Air Force attacked the oil slick with all its incendiary bombs and high explosives. They were unable to set it on fire. Doubtless another occasion on which the experts were very surprised.
3. In *Page v Smith* (above, p.110) Lord Lloyd debunked the famous phrase which Viscount Simonds (above, p.217) quoted so approvingly from Lord Denning's judgment in *King v Phillips*, itself now held to be erroneous. Indeed in *Page v Smith* [1995] 2 All E.R. 736 Lord Lloyd held, to Lord Goff's distress in *White* (above, p.108), that unforeseeable psychiatric harm was compensable if it resulted directly from negligence which threatened merely physical harm. *Polemis* rides again?
4. In *The Wagon Mound (No.2)* the same defendant was sued by the owners of the ship which was being repaired at Morts Dock. The trial judge held that there could be no recovery in negligence, since the fire was unforeseeable, but that unforeseeability of consequences was irrelevant in nuisance. The Privy Council held that there was no difference in this respect between nuisance and negligence, but found that the fire was foreseeable after all and gave judgment for the plaintiff in negligence ([1967] 1 A.C. 617, on appeal from [1963] 1 Lloyd's Rep. 402). (Appeals from the Antipodes have now been abolished.)
So the defendants paid the owner of the burnt ship. Could they then claim contribution (below p.286) from Morts Dock? That depends on whether Morts Dock would have been liable to the owners of the ship they were repairing. Now that the fire has been held to have been foreseeable, could one properly say that it was negligent of *The Wagon Mound's* engineer to let the oil spill, but not negligent of the wharf-owners to carry on welding? Probably one could, since liability depends on the unreasonableness of behaviour as well as the foreseeability of the results. Remember the words of Lord Reid: "If a real risk is one which would occur to the mind of a reasonable man . . . and which he would not brush aside as far-fetched, and if the criterion is to be what that reasonable man would have done in the circumstances, then surely he would not neglect such a risk if action to eliminate it presented no difficulty, involved no disadvantage and required no expense." ([1967] 1 A.C. 617 at 643–644).
The Wagon Mound (No.2) discusses how foreseeable the damage must be in order to satisfy the test laid down by *The Wagon Mound (No.1)*. As Lord Upjohn put it in *The Heron II* [1969] 1 A.C. 350 at 422, "the tortfeasor is liable for any damage which he can reasonably foresee may happen as a result of the breach however unlikely it may be, unless it can be brushed aside as far-fetched." According to *The Heron II* the rules of remoteness are different in contract and tort: a contractor is not, like the tortfeasor, liable for consequences which are just foreseeable, but only for those which are so foreseeable that one would actually have predicted them. Now although the rules of remoteness certainly operate differently depending on the features of the case in hand, it is far from clear that the distinction between contract and tort is the correct one to draw or that it is useful to spend time on such verbal formulae. If we accept that the outcome of a damages suit is a function of (a) the type of harm complained of, (b) the relationship between the parties and (c) the blameworthiness of the defendant, then we can be sure that liability for consequences will be more extensive if (a) the harm is physical, especially personal injury, (b) there is a special relationship, and (c) the defendant was greatly to blame. Whereas features (a) and (c) are often missing in contract cases, feature (b) is invariably present; in tort cases, on the other hand, (a) and (c) are usually present but (b) often is not (as in *The Wagon Mound* itself). In *Parsons v Uttley Ingham* [1978] Q.B. 791 the defendants sold the plaintiff a hopper for pig-food. Because its ventilator was stuck, the nuts inside went mouldy. The plaintiff's pigs got

a rare disease from the mouldy nuts and 254 of them died. Here was physical harm (as Lord Denning emphasised) caused by a careless breach of contract. The defendants were held liable.

SMITH v LEECH BRAIN & CO

Queen's Bench [1962] 2 Q.B. 405; [1962] 2 W.L.R. 148; 106 S.J. 77; [1961] 3 All E.R. 1159

Action by widow against employer of husband

Smith was employed by the defendant as labourer and galvaniser; his job was to remove galvanised articles from a tank of molten metal. One day in 1950 he was burnt on the lip by a drop of molten metal when a large object was immersed in the tank. The defendants were negligent in not providing adequate protection. Smith died of cancer in 1953. He had previously worked in a gasworks for nine years and was consequently at the time of the accident in a condition such that a burn or scratch might induce the malignancy from which he died.

Lord Parker C.J.: . . . Accordingly, I find that the burn was the promoting agency of cancer in tissues which already had a pre-malignant condition. In those circumstances, it is clear that the plaintiff's husband, but for the burn, would not necessarily ever have developed cancer. On the other hand, having regard to the number of matters which can be promoting agencies, there was a strong likelihood that at some stage in his life he would develop cancer. But that the burn did contribute to, or cause in part, at any rate, the cancer and the death, I have no doubt.

The third question is damages. Here I am confronted with the recent decision of the Privy Council in *Overseas Tankship (U.K.) Ltd v Morts Dock and Engineering Co Ltd (The Wagon Mound)* . But for that case, it seems to me perfectly clear that, assuming negligence proved, and assuming that the burn caused in whole or in part the cancer and the death, the plaintiff would be entitled to recover.

For my part, I am quite satisfied that the Judicial Committee in *The Wagon Mound* case did not have what I may call, loosely, the thin skull cases in mind. It has always been the law of this country that a tortfeasor takes his victim as he finds him. It is unnecessary to do more than refer to the short passage in the decision of Kennedy J. in *Dulieu v White & Sons*, where he said ([1901] 2 K.B. 669 at 679): "If a man is negligently run over or otherwise negligently injured in his body, it is no answer to the sufferer's claim for damages that he would have suffered less injury, or no injury at all, if he had not had an unusually thin skull or an unusually weak heart."

To the same effect is a passage in the judgment of Scrutton L.J. in *The Arpad* ([1934] p.189 at 202). But quite apart from those two references, as is well known, the work of the courts for years and years has gone on on that basis. There is not a day that goes by where some trial judge does not adopt that principle, that the tortfeasor takes his victim as he finds him. If the Judicial Committee had any intention of making an inroad into that doctrine, I am quite satisfied that they would have said so.

It is true that if the wording in the advice given by Lord Simonds in *The Wagon Mound* case is applied strictly to such a case as this, it could be said that they were dealing with this point. But, as I have said, it is to my mind quite impossible to conceive that they were.

The Judicial Committee were, I think, disagreeing with the decision in the *Polemis* case [and holding instead] that a man is no longer liable for the type of damage which he could not reasonably anticipate. The Judicial Committee were not, I think, saying that a man is only liable for the extent of damage which he could anticipate, always assuming the type of injury could have been anticipated.

In those circumstances, it seems to me that this is plainly a case which comes within the old principle. The test is not whether these employers could reasonably have foreseen that a burn would couse cancer and that he would die. The question is whether these employers could reasonably foresee the type of injury he suffered, namely, the burn. What, in the particular case, is the amount of damage which he suffers as a result of that burn depends upon the characteristics and constitution of the victim.

Accordingly, I find that the damages which the widow claims are damages for which the defendants are liable.

[His Lordship considered the question of damages, observed that he must make a substantial reduction from the figure taken for the dependency because of the fact that the plaintiff's husband might have developed cancer even if he had not suffered the burn, and awarded the plaintiff £3,064, 17s. Od.]

Questions

1. Was this a claim in respect of "immediate physical consequences" which were unforeseeable?

2. Was the claim in respect of damage of the same *type* as could have been foreseen?

3. Complete the following: "The test of liability for fire is foreseeability of injury by fire. The test of liability for cancer is foreseeability of injury by—."

4. Does the "thin-skull" rule apply every time some injury to the plaintiff is foreseeable and a different injury occurs?

5. If it be true, that policy is an element in questions of remoteness of damage, would it be right to make a distinction between claims for personal injury (this case) and property damage (*The Wagon Mound*)? If the claim is for purely financial loss, is the rule of remoteness likely to be applied in a manner favourable to the plaintiff. Would it be relevant that there was a special relationship between the parties?

Notes:

1. "You take your victim as you find him" is a perplexing saying in some ways. The principal case seems to hold that a claim for unforeseeable consequences of careless conduct is not defeated if their unforeseeability results from an unsuspected pre-existing susceptibility of the victim, given that some injury was foreseeably caused. The susceptibility is an old cause, not a new one such as involves discussion of *novus actus interveniens*. And the point is distinct from that of the rule that if one knows or should know of a particular susceptibility one may have to take extra steps to avoid damage: *Paris v Stepney B.C.* [1951] A.C. 367; *Haley v London Electricity Board* (above, p.160); *Walker v Northumberland C.C.* [1995] 1 All E.R. 737.

Note the words above—"given that some injury was foreseeably caused." This precondition for the application of the "thin-skull" rule was, according to Lord Goff in *White* (above, p.108), ignored by Lord Lloyd in *Page*. Lord Goff said: "The maxim only applies where liability as been established. . . . Lord Lloyd appears to have taken an exceptional rule relating to compensation and treated it as being of general application, thereby creating a wider principle of liability." ([1999] 1 All E.R. 1 at 17).

But there may be both old susceptibility and a new cause. In one case the plaintiff turned out to be tragically allergic to an anti-tetanus serum which was foreseeably injected after he suffered an abrasion on a ladder which was oily owing to the defendant employer's negligence. In upholding judgment for the plaintiff, the Court of Appeal said: " . . . the principle that a defendant must take the plaintiff as he finds him involves that if a wrongdoer ought reasonably to foresee that as a result of his wrongful act the victim may require medical treatment he is, subject to the principle of novus actus interveniens, liable for the consequences of the treatment applied although he could not reasonably foresee those consequences or that they could be serious." (*Robinson v Post Office* [1974] 2 All E.R. 737 at 750). Can this be reconciled with the decision for the defendant in a South African case where the victim of a traffic accident who was taking Parstellin as prescribed died as a result of eating a cheese sandwich, it not being known at that time that the drug and cheese made a fatal mixture? (*Alston v Marine & Trade Ins. Co* 1964 (4) S.A. 112).

2. The saying also sometimes works to the benefit of the defendant. If the young man whom the motorist injures has a secret ailment which would in any case have curtailed his working life, the motorist pays less by way of damages, just as the damages payable by Leech Brain to Mrs Smith reflected the fact that her late husband was a "poor life".

We have seen that a tortfeasor is not liable for harm which would have happened anyway. What if it would (probably) have happened later? The question was raised in *Chester v Afshar* [2002] Q.B. 356. The defendant doctor was negligent in failing to tell the claimant patient that the surgical operation he proposed involved a certain risk, say 1%, of serious damage. The operation was carefully conducted but the risk eventuated, and the patient was seriously harmed. Had she been told of the risk she would not have had the operation then and there, but might well have had it later. Had she had it later, the risk would be the same. Was the surgeon liable? The Court of Appeal held that he was, and this seems right, because though the risk remained the same in the substitute operation, the same harm was not at all likely to happen. Leave to appeal has been given.

3. Where personal injury is suffered and there is no intervening event, the injury has to be really freaky if the negligent person who caused it is to be let off. One can contrast two cases of employer's liability. In *Bradford v Robinson Rentals* [1967] 1 All E.R. 267 in the depths of the worst winter for years the plaintiff radio engineer was required to drive in unheated vans from Honiton to Bedford and back, a trip of 24 hours in two days; he suffered frostbite, a rare complaint in England, and recovered damages. In *Tremain v Pike* [1969] 3 All E.R. 1303 a farm worker contracted Well's disease or leptospirosis after coming into contact with the urine of rats which his employer had allowed to proliferate; the judge thought this a very unusual affliction, and gave judgment for the defendant. (In fact, there are over 100 cases of leptospirosis per year, about ten of them fatal, and it is now classed as an occupational disease).

4. It may be worth repeating that whereas thin skulls are quite rare, thin skins are very common. This means that the extension of the "thin-skull" rule from physical vulnerability to psychic susceptibility is no trivial step, but actually one that is out of harmony with the prevailing notion of foreseeability, itself closely connected with normality.

McGOVERN v BRITISH STEEL CORP.

Court of Appeal [1986] I.C.R. 608

Action for personal injuries against employer

A walkway on scaffolding 20 metres above the ground was bordered by toe-boards, planks eight inches broad and nine feet long, lying on their edge, one-and-a-half inches thick. Some time in the late morning one of these boards fell inwards and lay in the walkway, and the plaintiff, using the walkway for the fourth time that day, tripped over it. He was quite unharmed, and decided to replace the board (of which he later said that he could carry half-a-dozen without difficulty). In this apparently innocuous manoeuvre he ricked his back badly for reasons which remained entirely unexplained.

The trial judge found that the accident was unforeseeable in *The Wagon Mound* sense, and that there was therefore no liability at common law, but he gave judgment for the plaintiff on the ground of breach of reg.30(2) of the Construction (Working Places) Regulations 1966: "Every . . . gangway . . . shall be kept free from any unnecessary obstruction and material." The defendant's appeal was dismissed, Ralph Gibson L.J. dissenting.

Sir John Donaldson M.R.: I agree that the only live issues in this appeal are (a) causation—whether the injury suffered by the plaintiff was caused by the defendants' breach of regulation 30 of the Construction (Working Places) Regulations 1966, and (b) mischief—whether the injury suffered by the plaintiff was of a kind against which the regulation was intended to guard.

I start with the mischief issue. As Lord Reid said in *Grant v National Coal Board* ([1956] A.C. 649 at 661):

"In every case the problem is to ascertain the intention of Parliament from the terms of the statute . . . If the statute is only aimed at preventing a certain kind of injury, then it seems reasonable to hold (as in *Gorris v Scott*) that civil liability only results if that kind of injury is caused by a breach. But in this case there is no question of limitation to a particular kind of injury: . . . "

The same can, in my judgment, be said of the present case. The regulation is designed to avoid the mischief of obstruction in gangways. If injury is caused by the obstruction, it must fall within the regulation. The mischief issue is thus indistinguishable from that of causation.

I turn therefore to causation. The "but for" test was much canvassed in argument. However, it is of limited value. As the learned editors of *Clerk & Lindsell on Torts*, (15th ed., 1982) put it, at para. 11–37:

> "In the main the courts appear to isolate, first, the possible factors but for which the damage would not have been sustained, and then to pick out what appears to be the most responsible cause. The so-called 'but for' test serves an exclusionary purpose, namely, to reject from further consideration any factor which did not affect the event."

Is so happened that in *Millard v Serck Tubes Ltd* ([1969] 1 W.L.R. 211), the "but for" test was conclusive, because there was no other competing cause, but it is fallacious to rely upon it to establish positive causation where there is.

There is no doubt that the toe-board caused the plaintiff to trip and "but for" his having tripped he would never have noticed the toe-board, tried to move it or suffered his injury. However, it was quite clear that the trip did not cause him any injury. The chain of causation was broken. The starting point is thus, at the earliest, the time at which, having noticed the obstruction, he sought to remove it. The judge, who had the advantage of seeing and hearing the witness and getting a "feel" for the situation which is denied to us, concluded that it was very probable that if anyone saw the board they would take steps to move it out of the way. I therefore see no reason to disagree with the judge when he held that the presence of the board obstructing the gangway in breach of the regulation was a cause of the plaintiff trying to remove it. However, this is not sufficient unless the removal of the board was a cause of the plaintiff's injury.

I confess that it is this aspect which has given me the greatest difficulty. The toe-board was of no great weight and it is difficult to see why the accident happened at all. All would have been explained if it had emerged that the plaintiff tried to move the toe-board in a negligent manner, such as trying to break it in two for more convenient handling. Then his negligence and not the obstruction would have been the cause of his injury. But in the absence of any evidence of an intervening cause, I am driven to the conclusion that the removal of the board was the cause of the plaintiff's injury. How this came about is another matter. If, of course, the process of removal could not possibly by itself have caused the injury, the plaintiff would fail, but I do not think that that was the position. It looks as if the toe-board was jammed in some peculiar way such that, once it was moved, compressive forces were released and transmitted to the plaintiff causing the injury to his back. This is sufficient to establish the plaintiff's claim.

I would dismiss the appeal.

Notes:

In *Millard v Serck Tubes* [1968] 1 All E.R. 598, Salmon L.J. said "the fact that the accident occurred in an entirely unforeseeable way is wholly irrelevant in this case." The section of the Factories Act 1961 then in issue has been replaced by regulation 11 of the Provision and Use of Work Equipment Regulations 1998 (above, p.197), but it will still be necessary to determine whether a part of machinery is "dangerous" and for this purpose one really must ask whether any accident was foreseeable. Accordingly we have here an example of Lord Sumner's dictum that foreseeability "goes to culpability not to compensation", though in *The Wagon Mound* (above, p.216) that observation was said to be fundamentally false. Note, however, that in *Larner v British Steel* [1993] 4 All E.R. 102 the Court of Appeal denied that the test of foreseeability was relevant to determine whether a workplace was "safe", while accepting that liability could arise only "in relation to a plaintiff acting in a way that a human being may reasonably be expected to act in circumstances which may reasonably be expected to occur."

Question

The Regulation involved in *McGovern's* case has also been replaced. See reg.12(3) of the Workplace (Health, Safety and Welfare) Regulations 1992 (above, p.199). Would the decision be the same under the new Regulation?

Section 3.—The Risk Involved

GORRIS v SCOTT

Court of Exchequer (1874) L.R. 9 Exch. 125; 43 L.J. Ex. 92; 30 L.T. 431; 22 W.R. 575

Action by owner against carrier in respect of loss of property

Kelly C.B.: This is an action to recover damages for the loss of a number of sheep which the defendant, a shipowner, had contracted to carry, and which were washed overboard and lost by reason (as we must take it to be truly alleged) of the neglect to comply with a certain order made by the Privy Council, in pursuance of the Contagious Diseases (Animals) Act 1869. The Act was passed merely for sanitary purposes, in order to prevent animals in a state of infectious disease from communicating it to other animals with which they might come in contact. Under the authority of that Act, certain orders were made; amongst others, an order by which any ship bringing sheep or cattle from any foreign ports to ports in Great Britain is to have the place occupied by such animals divided into pens of certain dimensions, and the floor of such pens furnished with battens or foot-holds. The object of this order is to prevent animals from being overcrowded, and so brought into a condition in which the disease guarded against would be likely to be developed. This regulation has been neglected, and the question is, whether the loss, which we must assume to have been caused by that neglect, entitles the plaintiffs to maintain an action. The damage complained of here is something totally apart from the object of the Act of Parliament, and it is in accordance with all the authorities to say that the action is not maintainable.

Pigott B.: . . . The object, then, of the regulations which have been broken was, not to prevent cattle from being washed overboard, but to protect them against contagious disease . . . If, indeed, by reason of the neglect complained of, the cattle had contracted a contagious disease, the case would have been different. But as the case stands on this declaration, the answer to the action is this: Admit there has been a breach of duty; admit there has been a consequent injury; still the legislature was not legislating to protect against such an injury, but for an altogether different purpose; its object was not to regulate the duty of the carrier for all purposes, but only for one particular purpose.

Pollock B.: . . . Here no other negligence is alleged than the omission of that precaution; we must assume that the sheep were washed overboard merely in consequence of that omission and the question is whether the washing away gives a cause of action to the plaintiffs. Now, the Act of Parliament was passed *alio intuitu*; the recital in the preamble and the words of s.75 point out that what the Privy Council have power to do is to make such orders as may be expedient for the purpose of preventing the introduction and the spread of contagious and infectious diseases amongst animals. Suppose, then, that the precautions directed are useful and advantageous for preventing animals from being washed overboard, yet they were never intended for that purpose, and a loss of that kind caused by their neglect cannot give a cause of action.

Quote
  "It is one thing to say that if the damage suffered is of a kind totally different from that which it is the object of the regulation to prevent, there is no civil liability. But it is quite a different thing to say that civil liability is excluded because the damage, though precisely of the kind which the regulation was designed to prevent, happened in a way not contemplated by the maker of the regulation. The difference is comparable with that which caused the decision in *Overseas Tankship (U.K.) Ltd v Morts Dock & Engineering Co Ltd (The Wagon Mound)* ([1961] A.C. 388; above, p.216) to go one way and the decision in *Hughes v Lord*

Advocate ([1963] A.C. 837, next below) to go the other way." *Donaghey v Boulton & Paul Ltd* ([1968] A.C. 1 at 26, *per* Lord Reid).

Notes:

1. We have already seen that the purpose for which Parliament requires audited company accounts to be sent to shareholders can limit the scope of the common law duty of the accountants who prepare them (*Caparo v Dickman*, above, p.80). So, too, liability at common law for failure to take care in the exercise of statutory powers may be affected by the purpose for which the powers were conferred: *Peabody Donation Fund v Sir Lindsay Parkinson & Co* [1985] A.C. 210.

2. Consider in this context *Fytche v Wincanton Logistics* (above p.199 n.3) (boot designed to protect against impact causes frostbite), and *Corbett v Bond Pearce* (above p.83): the purpose of the solicitor's duty in taking testator's testamentary instructions is to protect the intended beneficiaries, not the testator's estate.

3. In 1973 the Merlins bought a substantial house on an estuary. The house became contaminated by particles emitted by a nuclear power station six miles away, and could be sold only at a very reduced price. Although the Nuclear Installations Act 1965 imposes an absolute duty on the operator of a nuclear installation regarding damage done by emissions from nuclear material to property as well as person, the judge held that the plaintiffs must fail, since the property was not physically damaged. *Merlin v British Nuclear Fuels* [1990] 3 All E.R. 711. Likewise when cargo oil escaped from a tanker in the Shetland Islands, the strict statutory liability of the tanker-owner did not extend to the financial loss of the only ferry company servicing the islands: *P & O Scottish Ferries v Braer Corp.* [1999] Times L.R. 171.

HUGHES v LORD ADVOCATE

House of Lords [1963] A.C. 837; [1963] 2 W.L.R. 779; 107 S.J. 232; [1963] 1 All E.R. 705; 1963 S.C.
(HL) 31; 1963 S.L.T. 150 (noted (1964) 80 L.Q.R. 1 at 145)

*Action by pedestrian against person working on highway in respect of
personal injury*

The defenders, acting under statutory powers, opened a manhole in an Edinburgh street in order to do underground telephone repairs. Above the manhole their workmen placed a tent, and round the tent they placed warning paraffin lamps. At five o'clock one winter evening all the workmen left for tea. The pursuer, a boy of eight, and his uncle, a boy of ten, came along, took a lamp and entered the manhole. As they emerged, the lamp was knocked into the hole and a violent explosion took place, with flames shooting 30 feet into the air. The pursuer was knocked back into the hole where he sustained serious burns.

The Lord Ordinary, after hearing evidence, gave judgment for the defenders, and this decision was upheld by the First Division of the Court of Session (Lord Carmont dissenting), 1961 S.C. 310. The pursuer's appeal to the House of Lords was allowed.

Lord Pearce: My Lords, the dangerous allurement was left unguarded in a public highway in the heart of Edinburgh. It was for the defenders to show by evidence that, although this was a public street, the presence of children there was so little to be expected that a reasonable man might leave the allurement unguarded. But, in my opinion, their evidence fell short of that, and the Lord Ordinary rightly so decided.

The defenders are therefore liable for all the foreseeable consequences of their neglect. When an accident is of a different type and kind from anything that a defender could have foreseen he is not liable for it (see *The Wagon Mound*). But to demand too great precision in the test of foreseeability would be unfair to the pursuer since the facets of misadventure are innumerable. . . . In the case of an allurement to children it is particularly hard to foresee with precision the exact shape of the disaster that will arise. The allurement in this case was the combination of a red paraffin lamp, a ladder, a partially closed tent, and a cavernous hole within it, a setting well fitted to inspire some juvenile adventure that might end in calamity. The obvious risks were burning and conflagration and a fall. All these in fact occurred, but unexpectedly the mishandled lamp instead of causing an ordinary conflagration produced a violent explosion. Did the explosion create an accident and damage of a different type from the misadventure and damage that could be foreseen? In my judgment it did not. The accident was but a variant of the foreseeable. It was, to quote the words of Denning L.J. in *Roe v Minister of Health* (above, p.166), "within the risk created by the negligence." No unforeseeable, extraneous, initial occurrence fired the train. The children's entry into the tent with the ladder, the descent into the hole, the mishandling of the lamp, were all foreseeable. The greater part of the path to injury had thus been trodden, and the mishandled lamp was quite likely at that stage to spill and cause a conflagration. Instead, by some curious chance of combustion, it exploded and no conflagration occurred, it would seem, until after the explosion. There was thus an unexpected manifestation of the apprehended physical dangers. But it would be, I think, too narrow a view to hold that those who created the risk of fire are excused from the liability for the damage by fire because it came by way of explosive combustion. The resulting damage, though severe, was not greater than or different in kind from that which might have been produced had the lamp spilled and produced a more normal conflagration in the hole.

I would therefore allow the appeal.

Section 4.—Intervening Act

THE OROPESA

Court of Appeal [1943] p.32; 112 L.J.P. 91; 168 L.T. 364; 74 Lloyd's Rep. 86; 59 T.L.R. 103; [1943] 1 All E.R. 211

Action by dependants of seaman against owners of colliding vessel

The *Manchester Regiment* and the *Oropesa* collided off Nova Scotia in December 1939. Both vessels were to blame, and both were badly damaged. The captain of the *Manchester Regiment* put 50 of his crew of 74 in a lifeboat and they reached the *Oropesa* in safety. Then, more than an hour after the collision, he decided to go and discuss the salvage of his ship with the captain of the *Oropesa*, already over a mile away. He embarked in a lifeboat with the rest of his crew. The lifeboat capsized in the heavy seas after half-an-hour and nine persons, including the plaintiffs' son, were drowned. The others reached the *Oropesa* and Nova Scotia in safety. The *Manchester Regiment* sank.

Langton J. gave judgment for the plaintiffs [1942] p.140, and the Court of Appeal dismissed the defendants' appeal.

Lord Wright: ... On the main question, the plaintiffs sue on the basis that the owners of the *Oropesa* owed a duty, not only to the owners of the *Manchester Regiment*, but also to her officers and crew, to navigate with care and skill so as not to injure them. Negligent navigation would obviously be a breach of that duty, and, therefore, it is said there was here a breach of duty towards the deceased. The defendants deny liability on the ground that there was no legal connection between the breach of duty and the death of the deceased. Certain well-known formulae are invoked, such as that the chain of causation was broken and that there was a *novus actus interveniens*. These phrases, sanctified as they are by standing authority, only mean that there was not such a direct relationship between the act of negligence and the injury that the one can be treated as flowing directly from the other. Cases have been cited which show great difference of opinion on the true answer in the various circumstances to the question whether the damage was direct or too remote. I find it very difficult to formulate any precise and all-embracing rule. I do not think that the authorities which have been cited succeed in settling that difficulty. It may be said that in dealing with the law of negligence it is possible to state general propositions, but when you come to apply those principles to determine whether there has been actionable negligence in any particular case, you must deal with the case on its facts.

What were the facts here? The master of the *Manchester Regiment* was faced with a very difficult proposition. His ship was helpless, without any means of propulsion or of working any of her important auxiliary apparatus, a dead lump in the water, and he had only the saving thought that she might go on floating so long as her bulkheads did not give way. He had great faith in his ship, but he realised that there was a heavy sea, with a heavy gale blowing and that he was in a very perilous plight. As Sir Robert Aske pointed out in his argument, the captain of a ship is guilty of a misdemeanour under s.220 of the Merchant Shipping Act 1894 if he "refuses or omits to do any lawful act proper and requisite to be done by him for preserving his ship from immediate loss, destruction or serious danger, or for preserving any person belonging to or on board ship from immediate danger to life or limb." In those circumstances the master decided to go to the *Oropesa* where, no doubt, he thought he would find valuable help and advice. Nobody suggests that he was acting unreasonably or improperly in doing so, or, indeed, that he was doing anything but his duty. Nor can anyone say that the deceased acted unreasonably in getting into the boat. If he had not obeyed the lawful orders of his captain, he would have committed a criminal offence under s.225(1)(b) of the Merchant Shipping Act 1894. If, therefore, the test is whether what was done was reasonable, there can be no question that the actions of both the master and the deceased were reasonable. Whether the master took exactly the right course is another matter. He may have been guilty of an error of judgment, but, as I read the authorities, that would not affect the question whether the action he took and its consequences flowed directly from the negligence of the *Oropesa*. I am not sure that Mr Sellers does not agree with that view, anyhow to some extent, but he also argued that the deceased was merely a spectator of the collision. He received no personal injury nor shock, and there was no need for special steps to be taken on his behalf in the emergency. That being so, in obeying the master's orders and getting into the boat, he was merely doing a voluntary act which was in no legal sense associated or connected with the negligence of the *Oropesa*. As for the master, Mr Sellers argued that what he did had no legal connection with the casualty. In my view, that is not a correct reading of the position. Having regard to the situation of the *Manchester Regiment* and those on board her, I think that the hand of the casualty lay heavily on her and that the conduct both of the master and of the deceased was directly caused by and flowed from it. There was an unbroken sequence of cause and effect between the negligence which caused the *Oropesa* to collide with the *Manchester Regiment*, and their action, which was dictated by the exigencies of the position. It cannot be severed from the circumstances affecting both ships. To that must be joined the duty which they were under in their positions as captain and sixth engineer.

There are some propositions which are beyond question in connection with this class of case. One is that human action does not *per se* sever the connected sequence of acts. The mere fact that human action intervenes does not prevent the sufferer from saying that injury which is due to that human action as one of the elements in the sequence is recoverable from the original wrongdoer. If the master and the deceased in the present case had done something which was outside the exigencies of the emergency, whether from miscalculation or from error, the plaintiffs would be debarred from saying that a new cause had not intervened. The question is not whether there was new negligence, but whether there was a new cause. To break the chain of causation it must be shown that there is something which I will call ultroneous, something unwarrantable, a new cause which disturbs the sequence of events, something which can be described as either unreasonable or extraneous or extrinsic. I doubt whether the law can be stated more precisely than that. Lord Haldane gave a fuller description in *Canadian Pacific Ry v Kelvin Shipping Co Ltd* ((1927) 138 L.T. 369 at 370), where the whole of the ultimate damage was due to a handling of the vessel after the collision. Lord Haldane said: " . . . what those in charge of the injured ship do to save it may be mistaken, but if they do whatever they do reasonably, although unsuccessfully, their mistaken judgment may be a natural consequence for which the offending ship is responsible, just as much as is any physical occurrence. Reasonable human conduct is part of the ordinary course of things which extends to the reasonable conduct of those who have sustained the damage and who are seeking to save further loss." . . . I think that is an important statement of principle—"if they do whatever they do reasonably, although unsuccessfully, their mistaken judgment may be a natural consequence for which the offending ship is responsible." Here it may be said that, even if the master of the *Manchester Regiment* was not doing quite the right thing, his mistake might be regarded as the natural consequence of the emergency in which he was placed by the negligence of the *Oropesa*. A mere voluntary act would clearly cause a breaking in the sequence of cause and effect as, for instance, in *The Amerika* ([1917] A.C. 38), one of the claims made by the Admiralty by way of damages for loss due to the collision was that they had paid bounties to relatives of members of the ship's crew who had lost their lives. It was held that those payments were purely voluntary. That is an extreme, but obvious, illustration of a loss resulting from a collision which did not impose any legal liability. It was a loss incurred by purely ultroneous conduct.

The real difficulty in the present case is the application of the principle, which is a question of fact. I agree entirely with Langton J. in the way in which he has dealt with the question. I am not prepared to say in all the circumstances that the fact that the deceased's death was due to his leaving the ship in the lifeboat and to the unexpected capsizing of that boat prevented his death being a direct consequence of the casualty. It was a risk, no doubt, but a boat would not generally capsize in those circumstances. In my opinion, the appeal should be dismissed.

Scott L.J.: I agree. We have been advised, as Langton J. was advised, that the position throughout in these happenings was one of critical danger to all those on board the *Manchester Regiment*. I am satisfied that the action taken by the master to save the lives of those for whom he was responsible was reasonable, and, therefore, that there was no break in the chain of causation. I agree entirely with the judgment which has just been delivered.

Questions

1. Suppose that the captain of the *Manchester Regiment* had been the only person drowned. Would his dependants have recovered?

2. Suppose that, owing to the unreasonable behaviour of the captain, the life-boats of the *Manchester Regiment* were incapable of being used, would the defendants have been liable to the dependants of persons drowned in consequence?

3. Suppose that, though the life-boats could be used, the captain of the *Manchester Regiment* unreasonably declined to allow the crew to leave the sinking ship; would the dependants of the crew recover from the defendants?

4. Lord Wright said that the deceased's death was a "direct" consequence of the casualty. Do you agree? Why did he say it?

Note:

When the question is asked whether the captain behaved "reasonably" or not, one is not asking whether he behaved without negligence, but whether his decision to act as he did, that decision having turned out to be wrong, was voluntary or not. If the decision was made in the stress of danger, it will not be really voluntary ("the hand of casualty lay heavily on her"), and it may be called a reasonable response to the emergency, notwithstanding that it turned out to be wrong. Behaviour which is unreasonable only in the sense of being careless is much less potent causally than a voluntary act even if that act can be called "reasonable." Though "*sciens*" is not "*volens*," voluntariness is affected by knowledge, perhaps dependent on it. Thus a failure to remedy a known defect or danger is a better insulator than a failure to discover it. For example, in *Taylor v Rover Co* [1966] 1 W.L.R. 1491, an employee was injured by a chisel which had carelessly been overhardened by the supplier's sub-contractor. The employer, however, had prior knowledge that the chisel was dangerous and had failed to remove it from circulation. Baker J. held that this insulated the supplier from possible liability. In *Lambert v Lewis* [1982] A.C. 225, on the other hand, where the plaintiffs were injured on the highway when a farmer's trailer came loose from his Land-Rover owing to a defect in the coupling, which had been badly designed by the manufacturer, the manufacturer was held liable to the victims although the farmer knew that the coupling was defective and dangerous. Would the results of *Taylor* and *Lambert* be the same under the Consumer Protection Act 1987?

Question
  Is there an explanation in terms of causation of s.1(4) of the Congenital Disabilities (Civil Liability) Act 1976 (above, p.117)?

WRIGHT v LODGE

Court of Appeal [1993] 4 All E.R. 299; [1993] R.T.R. 123

Claim for contribution by reckless lorry driver against stationary Mini-driver

Miss Shepherd was driving Miss Duncan and another friend eastwards towards Bury St. Edmunds on the A45 near midnight one foggy February night when her Mini spluttered to a halt on the unlit dual carriageway. It refused to start again, and three minutes later it was rear-ended by a Scania articulated lorry driven at quite excessive speed by Mr Lodge. After striking the Mini, a collision in which Miss Duncan was injured, the Scania went out of control, crossed the central reservation into the westbound carriageway and overturned. Three cars and a lorry collided with it. One of the car-drivers, Mr Wright, was injured, and another, Mr Kerek, was killed.

The lorry driver agreed to pay £6,900 to Miss Duncan, £10,000 to Mr Wright and £225,000 in respect of Mr Kerek. He now claimed contribution towards those payments from Miss Shepherd, the driver of the Mini.

The trial judge held that Miss Shepherd had been (slightly) negligent in not removing her stalled Mini from the carriageway and made her make a 10 per cent contribution towards the payment made by the lorry-driver to Miss Duncan. The lorry-driver's claim for contribution towards his payments to the other victims was dismissed, as was his appeal.

Parker L.J.: The judge's conclusions may be summarised as follows. (1) The fact that the Scania lorry crossed into the other carriageway was wholly attributable to the recklessness with which Mr Lodge was driving and was thus the sole cause of the injuries to them. (2) Miss Shepherd was negligent in failing, when the engine stopped, to get her passengers to push the Mini off the carriageway onto the verge, which would have been an easy task. (3) That negligence was partly, namely as to 10 per cent, causative of the initial impact on the Mini.

. . . we are faced with a situation that Miss Shepherd must be regarded as 10 per cent to blame for the impact with the Mini and thus for Miss Duncan's injuries. In these circumstances the contention of Mr Walker QC for Mr Lodge that she ought to be held responsible to the same degree in respect of the claims of Mr Wright and Mr Kerek appears to me to have great force. He presented it in this clear and simple form. (1) Mr Lodge's lorry went out of control because he had to brake and swerve violently in order to try to avoid the Mini. (2) The presence of the stationary Mini on the nearside lane of the eastbound carriageway was due to the negligence of Miss Shepherd. (3) Therefore it follows that the presence of the Scania on the westbound carriageway, and thus the injuries to Mr Wright and Mr Kerek, was in part caused by the negligence of Miss Shepherd. (4) Whether Mr Lodge's driving was negligent, grossly negligent, or reckless is irrelevant to the question whether Miss Shepherd's negligence was causative of the Scania's presence on the westbound carriageway. Given her initial negligence the question was simply whether the chain of causation had been broken by a *novus actus interveniens* and it had not. . . . As against this, Mr Douglas for Miss Shepherd put forward the equally clear and simple argument. (1) On an unlit road at night and in thick fog Mr Wright and Mr Kerek collided with an overturned Scania blocking the carriageway and thereby suffered personal injuries. (2) The question was: what was the cause or what were the causes of its presence there? (3) The judge had found and was entitled to find that the sole cause was the reckless driving of Mr Lodge.

That argument also appears to me to have considerable force.

In order to reach a conclusion upon the question as to which of the two arguments should prevail, it is in my view important to consider the nature of the claim in respect of Miss Duncan as compared with the claims in respect of Mr Wright and Mr Kerek.

In the case of Miss Duncan the foundation of the claim for contribution is that Miss Shepherd was in breach of a duty of care to her back-seat passenger. Proceeding on the basis, which I must, that the presence of the Mini constituted a danger to others proceeding eastbound, including persons negligently so driving, and that its presence there was due to negligence, the finding that, despite Mr Lodge's recklessness, negligence was partly the cause of Miss Duncan's injuries is clearly sustainable, although I am far from sure that I would have reached the same conclusion.

In the cases of Mr Wright and Mr Kerek however the position is different. Mr Lodge must establish that Miss Shepherd owed a duty of care to drivers on the westbound carriageway, that she was in breach of that duty of care in allowing the Mini to remain stationary on the nearside lane of the eastbound carriageway and that the breach of duty was, in part, causative of the presence of the upturned Scania in the westbound carriageway.

The differences in the two situations is of importance. It is clear that Miss Shepherd's passengers and others using the eastbound carriageway must have been within her reasonable contemplation as being likely to be affected by her omission to remove the Mini from the carriageway. She thus owed a duty of care to them. It is also clear that in some circumstances a driver on a dual carriageway will be under a duty of care to those on the opposite carriageway. If, for example, a driver in the fast lane of a dual carriageway were to stop without warning, those on the opposite carriageway would in my view be within the scope of the duty. It would be clear that such a stop would or might cause a following driver who was, owing to the presence of traffic there, unable to swerve into the slow lane, to swerve onto and over the central reservation into the path of a driver in the fast lane of the other carriageway. But in the present case Miss Shepherd was stationary with lights on in the nearside lane of the eastbound carriageway in thick fog which made it necessary for traffic to proceed at reduced speed. The situations are different.

Causation is also different. In the case of Miss Duncan there is an obvious connection between the presence of the Mini and the fact that it was struck from behind. The connection between its presence and the fact that the Scania went out of control and ended on its side in the westbound carriageway is in my view far from obvious. Suppose for example that the Scania, owing to its excessive speed and failure to observe the Mini until a very late stage had, instead of pulling over, proceeded upright across the westbound carriageway, through a brick wall into the driveway of a house and there injured a guest of the owners who was leaving after a dinner party. I would find it very hard to accept that such injuries were caused at all by the presence of the Mini.

In cases of this sort there is always much discussion on the question of foreseeability in relation to the duty of care, to causation and to remoteness and there have in the cases been many and different expressions as to the test or tests to be applied, but they must all be related to the facts of the cases in which they were expressed. There is in my view no single test. . . .

. . . Mr Walker submits that the judge misinterpreted *Rouse v Squires* [1973] 2 All E.R. 903. I do not myself consider that he did. *Rouse v Squires* recognised that there would be no liability, because no relevant danger, if an obstruction was only a danger to a reckless driver, and his reference to other cases and this case falling "the wrong side of the line" in my view show that he approached the matter correctly.

In any event approaching the matter as if he were a jury and taking a common sense view, he was, as we are, clearly entitled to conclude that the presence of the Scania in the westbound carriageway was wholly attributable to Mr Lodge's reckless driving. It was unwarranted and unreasonable. It was the violence of the swerve and braking which sent his lorry out of control. Such violence was due to the reckless manner in which he was driving and it was his reckless speed which resulted in the swerve, loss of control and headlong career onto, and overturn on, the westbound carriageway. It is true that it would not have been there had the Mini not obstructed the nearside lane of the eastbound carriageway but the passages which I have cited show clearly that this is not enough. It does not thereby necessarily become a legally operative cause. The subsequent conduct of Mr Lodge was such that any judge or jury could in my judgment exclude Miss Shepherd's conduct as being causative of the subsequent accident. The judge did exclude it and in my judgment he was right to do so.

I would dismiss the appeal.

Staughton L.J.: The critical question in these appeals is one of causation. Plainly the negligent driving of Mr Lodge was a relevant cause of the injuries to Mr Wright and the death of Mr Kerek. That has not been disputed. But the judge also found that Miss Shepherd was negligent in some degree.... The issue then is whether Miss Shepherd's negligence was also a relevant cause of Mr Wright's injuries and Mr Kerek's death. The judge held that it was not. But he did hold that Miss Shepherd's negligence was a relevant cause of the injury to her passenger, Miss Duncan— as, of course, was the negligence of Mr Lodge. Was it open to the judge to reach those conclusions?

It would not be difficult to produce a substantial anthology of authorities for three propositions. (i) Causation is not the same as remoteness. Foreseeability may be a useful guide, but it is by no means the true criterion. (ii) Causation depends on common sense, and not on theoretical analysis by a philosopher or metaphysician. (iii) Not every cause "without which not"—or "but for"—is regarded as a relevant cause in law. The judge or jury must choose, by the application of common sense, the cause (or causes) which are to be regarded as relevant.

In my judgment Hobhouse J. was entitled ... to find on the facts of this case that the negligence of Miss Shepherd was a relevant cause of the injury to Miss Duncan, but not of the injuries to Mr Wright and the death of Mr Kerek. I too would dismiss this appeal.

Questions

1. Was Lodge's reckless driving an intervening cause? If so, what did it intervene between?

2. Contribution may be claimed by D1 from D2 only where both are liable to the victim. Could the victims here have sued Miss Shepherd? If not, is the better reason

    (a)   that she was in breach of no duty to them,
    (b)   that though she was in breach of duty, her breach did not contribute to their harm, or
    (c)   that though her breach did contribute to their harm, their harm was too remote a consequence for her to be made liable to pay for it?

Notes:

1. In motorway pile-ups, which are normally caused by successive acts of bad driving, the person responsible for the initial accident tends to be liable for all the ensuing damage. In *Rouse v Squires* ([1973] 2 All E.R. 903) A, the driver of an articulated lorry, carelessly let it skid: it jack-knifed and blocked the slow and centre lanes. B, in a car, collided with it. C, in a lorry, drove past, parked and returned to help. D pulled his lorry up 15 feet short and illuminated the scene with his headlights. Five or ten minutes after the original accident E, driving too fast, braked too late and skidded into D's lorry which was pushed forward on to C, who was killed. E, held liable to C's widow, was able to claim 25 per cent contribution from A.

2. *Knightley v Johns* [1982] 1 All E.R. 851, CA is worth considering. The first defendant had negotiated the blind bend in a one-way tunnel in Birmingham and nearly reached the exit when he negligently crashed his car and blocked the tunnel. The police were called, but the inspector failed to obey standing orders and close off the entrance to the tunnel. When it began to fill with traffic, the inspector told the plaintiff constable to get on his bike and ride back up the tunnel to the entrance. As the plaintiff was doing this he was struck and badly injured by a car which had just entered the tunnel and was being driven quite carefully. The trial judge held that the original motorist was liable to the plaintiff policeman and that the police inspector was not, but the Court of Appeal reversed both holdings.

Stephenson L.J. said: "The ordinary course of things took an extraordinary course. The length and irregularities of the line leading from the first accident to the second have no parallel in the reported cases, in all of which the plaintiff succeeded in establishing the original wrongdoer's liability. It was natural, it was probable, it was foreseeable, it was indeed certain, that the police would come to the overturned car and control the tunnel traffic. It was also natural and probable and foreseeable that some steps would be taken in controlling the traffic and clearing the tunnel and some things be done that might be more courageous than sensible. The reasonable hypothetical observer would anticipate some human errors, some forms of what might be called folly, perhaps even from trained police officers, and some unusual and unexpected accidents in the course of their rescue duties. But would he anticipate such a result as this from so many errors as these, so many departures from the common sense procedure prescribed by the standing orders for just such an emergency as this?"

3. In *The Oropesa* (above, p.225) the intervening act was reasonable though misguided, and in *Wright v Lodge* it was recklessly dangerous. We can note the observation by Lord Hobhouse (the trial judge in *Wright*) that "Careless conduct may ordinarily be regarded as being within the range of normal human conduct when reckless conduct ordinarily would not" in a case in which, as we shall see below, p.242, the allegedly intervening act was quite intentional (*Reeves v Commissioner of Police* [1993] 3 All E.R. 897 at 925). We have considered some such cases already under the heading of "duty to protect", recalling, however, that in the *Dorset Yacht* case Lord Reid observed that " . . . the question is really one of remoteness of damage." The connecting factor is this, that conduct which one is under a particular duty to forestall—the "very thing" one should have guarded against—cannot be invoked as a *novus actus* even if it is deliberate. In *Reeves* although the decedent quite consciously seized the opportunity to commit suicide, it was negligent of the police to let him have the opportunity: they were to guard against exactly what he chose to do, because he was known to be apt to do it. In the House of Lords only Lord Hobhouse was for the defendant, on the ground that the suicide was the prisoner's own "free choice"; yet even he would not describe the suicide as a *novus actus* had a third party been affected.

Despite the categorical nature of Lord Simonds's acerbities in *The Wagon Mound* foreseeability is not a universal solvent. This can be seen in the attempts in *Lamb v Camden B.C.* [1981] 2 All E.R. 408, noted (1982) 98 L.Q.R. 23, to reconcile Lord Reid's statements in *Dorset Yacht* with the terms of *The Wagon Mound*. The plaintiff's tenant vacated her house near Hampstead Heath in 1973 when its foundations were weakened by a flood due to the defendant's contractors. Next summer the plaintiff returned from abroad and arranged for building work to start. On returning at Christmas the plaintiff evicted the squatters who had installed themselves in October, and put up some boarding. Next summer more squatters moved in and did damage to the tune of £30,000 before they were finally ousted two years later. This was the item in issue. The plaintiff's appeal from the dismissal of her claim was dismissed by the Court of Appeal.

4. In *A v Essex CC* [2003] EWCA Civ 1848 a boy and girl were placed with the claimants with a view to adoption. The boy had severe behavioural problems which the defendants did not disclose though the claimants had indicated that they would not accept such a child. The court held that the claimants would probably have declined the placement had they been informed, and granted damages for the damage done in the 14 months prior to the actual adoption, but not for the period thereafter, when the claimants knew what they were doing.

5. A carpenter was injured when a fellow workman deliberately pushed over the scaffolding on which he was standing. Even if the employer was in breach of safety regulations, this was a novus actus and the employer was not liable. *Horton v Taplin Contracts* [2002] EWCA Civ 1604.

6. In *Roberts v Bettany* ([2001] EWCA Civ 109) the defendants decided to clear part of an embankment behind their property, part of the colliery spoil heap on which the claimant's property was built. In 1991 their gardener lit a number of bonfires to dispose of the rubbish. An underground fire was discovered two or three months later and the local authority, having served an abatement notice, itself extinguished the fire and filled the space with inert material. The next year the claimant's property began to subside, and it was found that the infilling was inadequate. The judge struck out the claim on the ground that the excavation and infilling by the local authority constituted a novus actus interveniens, but the Court of Appeal reversed: the defendants had created a dangerous situation curable only by what the local authority tried to do, and this was not a case where the intervention turned the original act of negligence into merely part of the surrounding circumstances. This may seem surprising, but it is to be noted that it was actually the defendant's duty to effect the cure.

7. If you injure a person physically he is likely to need medical attention, and medical attention has its risks. So you will be liable if your victim's condition is aggravated by normal medical negligence. This was ignored in *Rahman v Arearose* [2001] Q.B. 351, but was restated in *Webb v Barclays Bank plc* [2001] EWCA Civ 1141 where the question was "whether, when an employee is injured in the service, and by the negligence, of her employer, his liability to her is terminated by the intervening negligence of a doctor brought in to treat the original injury, but who in fact made it worse." The answer was no. The claimant was injured owing to the fault of her employer, the first defendant, and had her leg amputated above the knee by the second defendant, who was negligent in proceeding to such an operation without properly advising the claimant. Her employer settled her claim in full and sought contribution from the second defendant. It was held that the second defendant's negligence did not break the chain of causation so as to terminate the first defendant's liability, so the second defendant was held liable to contribute to the extent of 75%.

8. In the cases excerpted so far in this section the harm complained of would not have occurred at all but for the act of the third party. In other cases harm for which the defendant is clearly responsible is prolonged or aggravated by an incompetent doctor, an indolent garage, a neurotic mother or a dilatory solicitor. Are there any grounds for distinguishing cases of the two types?

9. In *Salsbury v Woodland* (below, p.311) the Court of Appeal expressed relief that the judge's finding on causation was not questioned. Do you think that the facts of that case raised any difficult question of causation?

McKEW v HOLLAND & HANNEN & CUBITTS (SCOTLAND) LTD

House of Lords [1969] 3 All E.R. 1621; 8 K.I.R. 921; 1970 S.C. (HL) 20

Action by employee against employer for personal injuries

The pursuer, who had suffered a slight injury at work by reason of the defender's fault, which had made him stiff and weakened his left leg, went some days later to inspect a tenement flat, in the company of some members of his family. The stair was steep, with walls on either side, but no hand-rail. As the pursuer left the apartment with his daughter, he raised his right foot to go down the stairs. His left leg "went" and he was about to fall. Rather than fall, he jumped, and landed heavily on his right foot, breaking the right ankle and a bone in his left leg.

The Court of Session disallowed the claim for the consequences of the second accident, and the House of Lords dismissed the pursuer's appeal.

Lord Reid: My Lords, the appellant sustained in the course of his employment trivial injuries which were admittedly caused by the fault of the respondents. His back and hips were badly strained, he could not bend, and on several occasions his left leg suddenly "went away from" him. I take this to mean that for a short time he lost control of his leg and it became numb. He would have recovered from his injuries in a week or two but for a second accident in which he suffered a severe fracture of his ankle. The question in this case is whether the respondents are liable for the damage caused by this second accident. If they are so liable then damages have been agreed at £4,915; if they are not so liable then damages are agreed at £200, the sum awarded in the Court of Session. . . .

The appellant's case is that this second accident was caused by the weakness of his left leg which in turn had been caused by the first accident. The main argument for the respondents is that the second accident was not the direct or natural and probable or foreseeable result of their fault in causing the first accident.

In my view the law is clear. If a man is injured in such a way that his leg may give way at any moment he must act reasonably and carefully. It is quite possible that in spite of all reasonable care his leg may give way in circumstances such that as a result he sustains further injury. Then that second injury was caused by his disability which in turn was caused by the defender's fault. but if the injured man acts unreasonably he cannot hold the defender liable for injury caused by his own unreasonable conduct. His unreasonable conduct is novus actus interveniens. The chain of causation has been broken and what follows must be regarded as caused by his own conduct and not by the defender's fault or the disability caused by it. Or one may say that unreasonable conduct of the pursuer and what follows from it is not the natural and probable result of the original fault of the defender or of the ensuing disability. I do not think that foreseeability comes into this. A defender is not liable for a consequence of a kind which is not foreseeable. But it does not follow that he is liable for every consequence which a reasonable man could foresee. What can be foreseen depends almost entirely on the facts of the case, and it is often easy to foresee unreasonable conduct or some other novus actus interveniens as being quite likely. But that does not mean that the defender must pay for damage caused by the novus actus. It only leads to trouble that if one tries to graft on to the concept of foreseeability some rule of law to the effect that a wrongdoer is not bound to foresee something which in fact he could readily foresee as quite likely to happen. For it is not at all unlikely or unforeseeable that an active man who has suffered such a disability will take some quite unreasonable risk. But if he does he cannot hold the defender liable for the consequences.

So in my view the question here is whether the second accident was caused by the appellant doing something unreasonable. It was argued that the wrongdoer must take his victim as he finds him and that that applies not only to a thin skull but also to his intelligence. But I shall not deal with that argument because there is nothing in the evidence to suggest that the appellant is abnormally stupid. This case can be dealt with equally well by asking whether the appellant did something which a moment's reflection would have shown him was an unreasonable thing to do.

He knew that his left leg was liable to give way suddenly and without warning. He knew that this stair was steep and that there was no hand-rail. He must have realised, if he had given the matter a moment's thought, that he could only safely descend the stair if he either went extremely slowly and carefully so that he could sit down if his leg gave way, or waited for the assistance of his wife and brother-in-law. But he chose to descend in such a way that when his leg gave way he could not stop himself. . . .

But I think it right to say a word about the argument that the fact that the appellant made to jump when he felt himself falling is conclusive against him. When his leg gave way the appellant was in a very difficult situation. He had to decide what to do in a fraction of a second. He may have come to a wrong decision; he probably did. But if the chain of causation had not been broken before this by his putting himself in a position where he might be confronted with an emergency, I do not think that he would put himself out of court by acting wrongly in the emergency unless his action was so utterly unreasonable that even on the spur of the moment no ordinary man would have been so foolish as to do what he did. In an emergency it is natural to try to do something to save oneself and I do not think that his trying to jump in this emergency was so wrong that it could be said to be no more than an error of judgment. But for the reasons already given I would dismiss this appeal.

Notes:

1. Some commentators think that judgment should have been given for the pursuer subject to a deduction for contributory negligence. Yet there must come a time when "the buck passes" (as perhaps it did to the police in *Knightley v Johns* (above, p.230), to the employer in *Taylor v Rover Co* (above, p.227), and certainly to Mrs Lamb in Hampstead (above, p.231)). If the buck passes to a person, it may well pass from the previous holder. McKew had a gammy leg. He was to be paid for it. Of course it was likely to "go." He would never be perfectly steady on his feet. But that does not mean that he must never go upstairs or move about without a stick. It is up to him how he conducts his daily life: he is not the defendant's conditional pensioner, and if he falls over, he cannot look to a court to say that the defendant must pay him again just because the fall was quite foreseeable and his conduct perfectly reasonable.

Lord Reid agreed that McKew's fall was *foreseeable*, and observed that it would be wrong to say it was not. But is it not just as wrong to say that McKew's conduct was *unreasonable*? Is it not rather that the leg was now *his* problem to deal with, that the buck had passed to him, knowing as he did of his propensity to fall and being wholly in control of the situations in which that was apt to happen? Need one even say (not that Lord Reid did say it) that his going upstairs was voluntary?

It might have been held that the buck had passed in *Crown River Cruises v Kimbolton Fireworks* [1996] 2 Lloyd's Rep. 533. Debris from the first defendant's firework show on a barge on the Thames caused a fire on *The Surround*, a barge belonging to the plaintiff, moored about 200 yards away. The fire brigade, the second defendant, came to extinguish it and 20 minutes later thought they had done so; they then stayed in the vicinity for two more hours. Some time after they had gone, a sister barge returned and moored near *The Surround*, and in the early morning was found to be on fire. The judge found that the second fire was caused by the first and that the firemen's failure to extinguish the first fire was not a *novus actus* so as to insulate the first defendants from liability for the damage done by the second; he did, however, hold the fire brigade 75 per cent responsible.

There is an analogue for the notion that a time comes when the buck passes, that is, the idea that the person who negligently causes a dangerous situation ceases to be responsible for the ulterior consequences once the danger has come under the control of a third party who could and should defuse it. It is this: when a person has been misled by the defendant into acquiring a piece of property there comes a time when he can no longer charge the defendant with subsequent losses in value or indeed have to give credit for subsequent increases in value which might be thought to reduce the loss: it is *his* affair now, for good or ill. (*Hussey v Eels* [1990] 1 All E.R. 449). Thus in *Needler Financial Services v Taber* [2002] 3 All E.R. 501 the customer, owing to bad advice from the agent, left his occupational pension scheme and took out a personal pension with an insurer, which eventually produced a lower pension. Meanwhile, however, the insurer demutualised and gave the customer shares which he sold for over £7,000. Did he have to give credit for this bonus? No: the relevant question was whether the negligence that had caused the loss had also caused the profit in the sense that the latter had been part of a continuous transaction of which the former had been the inception. (See also *Primavera v Allied Dunbar Assurance plc* [2002] EWCA Civ 1327). What is true of unwanted property may also be true of unwanted problems, like McKew's gammy leg. Might it also be true of unwanted babies (*Rees v Darlington*, above p.118)?

2. McKew may have had a sore leg, but his mind was unimpaired. Not so in the notorious case of *Meah v McCreamer* [1985] 1 All E.R. 367, followed by [1986] 1 All E.R. 935 and [1986] 1 All E.R. 943: Meah,

a 26-year-old borstal graduate and ex-skinhead, was badly injured in a Jaguar driven by the very drunk McCreamer, since vanished. He suffered brain damage analogous to that resulting from leukotomy. Before the accident Meah had been self-indulgent and promiscuous in sexual matters but not generally violent or inconsiderate, but some three years after the accident he viciously attacked two women, and six months later, while on bail for those offences, raped and savaged a third. He was sentenced to life imprisonment and as a category A prisoner would probably not be released for very many years.

In the first suit Meah claimed damages from the driver for the imprisonment as well as the injury. The defendant insurer expressly disclaimed any argument arising from remoteness of damage or public policy, so the only question was whether there was a causal link between the injury and the crimes. The judge held that there was: the plaintiff would probably have committed, and perhaps have been jailed for, other minor crimes, but would not have committed such crimes as these but for the injury, though the injury would not have caused him to commit them had he not been a latent aggressive psychopath particularly susceptible to being so affected by such an injury. General damages of £60,000 were awarded, reduced by 25 per cent because it was careless of the plaintiff to travel with an obviously drunken driver.

Then two of the victims claimed damages from Meah, now richer by £45,000. There was no problem about liability, of course, and damages of £6,750 and £10,250 were awarded (as compared with £3,600 from the Criminal Injuries Compensation Board in the latter case; a Master awarded £12,500 to the third victim). There was the predictable howl of outraged ignorance in the Press: "Rapist Gets More Than Victims!"

Meah then claimed an indemnity from the defendant for the sums he had just been held liable to pay to his victims. At this stage the defendant did raise arguments of remoteness of damage and of public policy. On both grounds the judge dismissed Meah's claim.

It is important to note that the judge never held that Meah's imprisonment was not too remote a consequence of the injury, but it is clear that he would sooner have given damages for the imprisonment than for the loss resulting from Meah's having to pay his victims, and he was certain that the victims had no claim of their own against the driver.

Section 5.—Multiple Causes

Because a result (such as the French Revolution) may have many causes, harm may be due to a number of tortfeasors: indeed, the expansion of tort liability has made this a very frequent occurrence. Stevenson was the only person Mrs Donoghue could sue, but the Dorset Yacht Company could have sued the Borstal boys as well as the Home Office (above p.84) and Hedley Byrne already had a claim against Easipower (above p.57). Some attempts to find secondary tortfeasors have nearly succeeded: Caparo could, and did, sue Dickman for fraud as well as Touche Ross for negligence (above p.80), Marc Rich tried to get money from the surveyor as well as from the shipowner who was carrying the goods (above p.45), and in *Stovin* (above p.89) the question was whether the injured motorcyclist could have sued the highway authority as well as the negligent driver who ran into him.

Where more than one tortfeasor is involved, none of them is helped in the slightest by pointing to the liability of the others: it is no use blaming others if you yourself are to blame. The classic rule is that a person who is liable for harm is liable for all of it, no matter how many other people may also be liable for it. Naturally the victim may only recover up to the amount of his loss, and once he has been paid for it, all other tortfeasors are released from liability to him in damages (but not, as we shall see, from liability to contribute to the tortfeasor whose payment released them from liability to the victim). The rule is a good one because one of the tortfeasors may be insolvent or in hiding or have his liability contractually limited in amount; indeed this is generally the reason for suing the other.

Tortfeasors who cause separate harms are of course liable only for the harm they cause, but if the harm is indivisible in nature, they are each liable for it all. That, at any rate, was the traditional rule, found until recently in almost all legal systems. But the extension of liability has led to a backlash, and this rule of "joint and several liability", to give it its ugly name, has been brought into question.

Symptomatic is the remark of Stuart-Smith L.J. that the claimant "will be entitled to succeed if he can prove that the defendant's tortious conduct made a material contribution to his disability. But strictly speaking the defendant is liable only to the extent of that contribution."

(*Holtby v Brigham & Cowan* [2000] 3 All E.R. 421). This is revolutionary. "Material contribution to harm" comes from *Bonnington Castings v Wardlaw*, and "material contribution to the risk of harm" comes from *McGhee*, and in both cases, as well as in *Fairchild* (where there were multiple defendants), the claimant recovered his damages in full. Stuart-Smith L.J. attributes this to the fact that in those cases it was not argued that the defendant's liability should be less than full, but only in proportion to his contribution to the harm. Lord Bridge did however say in *Hotson* "if the plaintiff had proved on a balance of probabilities that the authority's negligent failure to diagnose and treat his injury promptly had materially contributed to the development of [the harm], I know of no principle of English law which would have entitled the authority to a discount from the full measure of damage to reflect the chance that, even given prompt treatment, [the harm] might well still have developed." He disapproved sternly of the decision in *Bagley* where the judge discounted the damages payable by a hospital which was liable for a still-birth by the chance (5 per cent) that in any case the child might not have been born alive. And it is certainly true that the claimant's victory in *Bonnington Castings* would be pyrrhic indeed if he could recover only to the extent of the defendant's contribution to his pneumoconiosis, since that was probably very small, if it could be measured at all.

What factors have triggered this revolution? One is surely the feeling that a person should not have to pay for harm which the victim has already suffered: causation cannot work backwards. This is illustrated by the decision that if you carelessly dent the wing of a car which is already dented you don't have to pay for the beating out and the respray (*Performance Cars v Abraham* [1962] 1 Q.B. 33). In other words if the victim has already suffered some harm, you need pay only for aggravating it. Take the case where X negligently injures Y who is then taken to hospital where Z, the doctor, makes his condition worse instead of improving it. Z is clearly not liable for the original injury but only for the aggravation (for which X is also liable).

The new doctrine that you are liable only in proportion to your contribution to the victim's harm originated in cases of progressive industrial diseases whose severity is increased by each successive exposure, be it to noise or to inhalation of polluted air or—in the case of asbestosis but not mesothelioma—asbestos fibres. In such cases it is clear that some harm had already been done when a later employer added to it, and at a pinch one can apportion responsibility between the successive employers who are at fault by asking how long the claimant was employed, and exposed to the noxious agent, by each of them.

But the novel doctrine is now applied much more widely, for example, in cases such as *Barrett* (above p.100) where a local authority takes an abused child into care and is sued for failing to treat it properly. Here the claimant was surely traumatised by the abuse he received at home, and, if the psychologists are right, predominantly so. In such cases the problems of attributing proportional responsibility are quite insoluble. In one case, for instance, the claimant had been abused at home and bullied at school until she was fourteen, when she was taken into care by the defendants. She was bullied again and then subjected to physical, emotional and sexual abuse by some of the defendant's staff. Unsurprisingly she had difficulties in her adult life. Buxton L.J. said "this is a case where the usual process of attributing responsibility between various causes to a large extent breaks down." "It was Mrs G's opinion that 80 per cent of the causation of the difficulty in her adult life lay in her experiences in care. Dr. A was at first of the view that her experiences in care were 20 per cent to blame for her problems." The judge was held to be right not to make an assessment in percentage terms, though he had invoked *Holtby*: it was a "jury question" and a "broad brush" approach was appropriate (*C v A Local Authority* [2001] EWCA Civ 302, [2001] 2 F.L.R. 33).

In cases of industrial disease the original contributions are made by another tortfeasor, but sometimes the defendant has operated on the claimant's congenital condition. Thus in the educational torts, such as *Phelps*, the student must already have been backward by the time the teacher is charged with failure to diagnose his dyslexia.

Stress at work has recently been added to the list of cases where proportional damages are awarded.. In *Hatton v Sutherland* [2002] 2 All E.R. 1 Hale L.J. said " . . . if it is established that the constellation of symptoms suffered by the claimant stems from a number of different extrinsic causes then in our view a sensible attempt should be made to apportion liability accordingly". There is no reason to distinguish these conditions from the chronological development of industrial diseases or disabilities. . . . Where the tortfeasor's breach of duty has exacerbated a pre-existing disorder or accelerated the effect of pre-existing vulnerability, the award of general damages for pain, suffering and loss of amenity will reflect only the exacerbation or acceleration. Further, the quantification of damages for financial losses must take some account of contingencies. In this context, one of those contingencies may well be the chance that the claimant would have succumbed to a stress-related disorder in any event. The judgment concluded that "Where the harm suffered has more than one cause, the employer should only pay for that proportion of the harm suffered which is attributable to his wrongdoing, unless the harm is truly indivisible. It is for the defendant to raise the question of apportionment"—a question not argued in *Barber v Somerset C.C.* [2004] UKHL 13, which in other respects approved the judgment of Hale L.J.

Two points should be noted. Hale L.J. speaks only of "extrinsic causes". This doubtless in order to preserve the "thin-skull" rule. But are we not very close indeed to rejecting that rule in the case where a contributory cause is the claimant's congenital condition? Secondly, exception is made for harm which is "truly indivisible". But in fact in these cases the harm is not divisible at all. In *Rahman v Arearose*, for example, the psychological condition of the claimant was not discerptible: he was not, like Hamlet, "but mad north-north-west", he was encompassingly mad, least of all half-mad plus half-mad. Yet the Court of Appeal was prepared to divide up his condition, and apportion liability accordingly. When the courts say that the result is divisible (though generally they avoid saying this in terms, but just proceed on this assumption) all they mean is that they can distinguish (and try to weigh, measure or appraise) the different causes. But the rule relates to the nature of the harm not to the conduct. Take death, for example. In their death David and Jonathan were not divided, but the death of each was certainly not divisible. Are we now to say that when two people kill a third the two each has half-killed him? The terms of the Fatal Accidents Act may make this difficult, but it is not the sole cause of the difficulty.

This novel habit of dividing up indivisible damage has one inconvenience, to put it no higher. Where two or more people are liable, the statute next following provides that the court may order that, as between themselves, they bear the loss in such proportion as it may find to be "just and equitable". But for the application of the Act the parties must be liable, on whatever ground, for "the same damage". In the cases just considered the division of the damage means that the parts are not "the same damage". To put it another way, the payment by the claimant for contribution must have released the party from whom the contribution is claimed, and this is only true when they are both liable for the same damage. The division therefore deprives the court of doing what is "just and equitable" between the tortfeasors, and may lead them as regards the victim of them both to do what may be neither just nor equitable, especially as the defendant is apt to be insured against liability and the claimant is unlikely to be insured against harm.

This criticism, that the novel practice ousts the just division permitted by the Act, does not apply when the defendant's liability is reduced by reason of the external factors mentioned by Hale L.J. which do not connote the liability of a third party. But if sufficient control is exercised over the question whether the defendant is liable at all, which is admittedly easier in the case of liabilities at common law rather than for breach of statutory duty, it would probably be right to allow the claimant to recover in full from a defendant who has contributed to the damage, provided that it is "truly indivisible", meaning "truly", not as in "Yours truly".

CIVIL LIABILITY (CONTRIBUTION) ACT 1978

1.—(1) Subject to the following provisions of this section, any person liable in respect of any damage suffered by another person may recover contribution from any other person liable in respect of the same damage (whether jointly with him or otherwise).

(2) A person shall be entitled to recover contribution by virtue of subsection (1) above notwithstanding that he has ceased to be liable in respect of the damage in question since the time when the damage occurred, provided that he was so liable immediately before he made or was ordered or agreed to make the payment in respect of which the contribution is sought.

(3) A person shall be liable to make contribution by virtue of subsection (1) above notwithstanding that he has ceased to be liable in respect of the damage in question since the time when the damage occurred, unless he ceased to be liable by virtue of the expiry of a period of limitation or prescription which extinguished the right on which the claim against him in respect of the damage was based.

(4) A person who has made or agreed to make any payment in bona fide settlement or compromise of any claim made against him in respect of any damage (including a payment into court which has been accepted) shall be entitled to recover contribution in accordance with this section without regard to whether or not he himself is or ever was liable in respect of the damage, provided, however, that he would have been liable assuming that the factual basis of the claim against him could be established.

(5) A judgment given in any action brought in any part of the United Kingdom by or on behalf of the person who suffered the damage in question against any person from whom contribution is sought under this section shall be conclusive in the proceedings for contribution as to any issue determined by that judgment in favour of the person from whom the contribution is sought.

(6) . . .

2.—(1) Subject to subsection (3) below, in any proceedings for contribution under section 1 above the amount of the contribution recoverable from any person shall be such as may be found by the court to be just and equitable having regard to the extent of that person's responsibility for the damage in question.

(2) Subject to subsection (3) below, the court shall have power in any such proceedings to exempt any person from liability to make contribution, or to direct that the contribution to be recovered from any person shall amount to a complete indemnity.

(3) Where the amount of the damages which have or might have been awarded in respect of the damage in question in any action brought in England and Wales by or on behalf of the person who suffered it against the person from whom the contribution is sought was or would have been subject to—

(a) any limit imposed by or under any enactment or by any agreement made before the damage occurred;

(b) any reduction by virtue of section 1 of the Law Reform (Contributory Negligence) Act 1945 or section 5 of the Fatal Accidents Act 1976; or

(c) any corresponding limit or reduction under the law of a country outside England and Wales;

the person from whom the contribution is sought shall not by virtue of any contribution awarded under section 1 above be required to pay in respect of the damage a greater amount than the amount of those damages as so limited or reduced.

. . .

6.—(1) A person is liable in respect of any damage for the purposes of this Act if the person who suffered it (or anyone representing his estate or dependants) is entitled to recover compensation from him in respect of that damage (whatever the legal basis of his liability, whether tort, breach of contract, breach of trust or otherwise).

Example:

A good instance of multiple liability is provided by *Clay v Crump* [1964] 1 Q.B. 533, CA. When an old building was being demolished prior to the erection of a new one, the site-owner asked the architect if one of its walls could be left standing. The architect unwisely agreed, and the demolition contractor, who should have known better, proceeded to demolish the walls which supported it. The building contractor then sent his men onto the site without checking it for safety, and one of them was injured when the remaining wall fell on him. The victim sued the site-owner, the architect, the demolition contractor and his employer. The site-owner was let off because it was reasonable for him, as an amateur, to trust the professionals, but the demolition contractor was held liable because he should have known that he was making the wall unsafe, the building contractor was held liable for sending his men to a place he should have known to be dangerous, and the architect was held liable because he failed to show the professional skill the others were relying on him to display. The plaintiff obtained judgment in full against all the defendants who were held liable, and was entitled to collect from them as he pleased. As between themselves, the defendants were liable in the following proportions: architect 42 per cent; demolition contractor 38 per cent; building contractor/employer 20%.

Questions

1. A mother out shopping with her toddler carelessly loses sight of him. He scampers into the street and is run over by a motorist who is not paying quite enough attention. The child would naturally sue the (insured) motorist rather than his (uninsured) mother. Until 1935 when the predecessor to this Act was passed, the insurer would pay and that would be that. Now this Act permits the motorist's insurer to claim contribution from the mother, unless the court is ready to hold that a mother owes no duty to her child to take care that it is not injured, as the courts of New York did in this very context (*Holodook v Spencer* (1974) 324 N.E.2d 338). Is this satisfactory? Or take *Jones v Wilkins* [2001] T.L.R. 89. On Easter Sunday the infant claimant was badly injured in a collision entirely due to the fault of the oncoming driver. The infant was on his mother's knee in the front seat of the car driven by his aunt, and was restrained only by the lapstrap of his mother's safety belt, which was worse than useless. The oncoming driver's insurer claimed contribution from both the aunt and the mother and they were both held liable as to 25 per cent. The aunt would have liability-insurance, but the mother? Could the aunt's insurer claim contribution from the mother? The relationship between apportionment under the 1945 and the 1978 Acts was interestingly discussed in relation to *Jones v Wilkins* in *Pride Valley Foods v Hall and Partners* [2001] EWCA Civ 1001 at [67] ff. (Sedley LJ).

2. Does a contribution claim lie between A, who negligently advises B that he must pay C, and C who receives the undue payment? The Court of Appeal so held in *Friends Provident Life Office v Hillier Parker May & Rowden* [1997] Q.B. 85. Why was this wrong? (The exuberance of the Court of Appeal has since been counteracted by the House of Lords in *Royal Brompton Hospital v Hammond* [2002] UKHL 14).

3. Reference was made above, (p.26) to *The Esso Bernicia* [1989] A.C. 643 where, owing to a manufacturing defect in a tug which was helping to berth an Esso tanker, the tanker collided with the terminal and much bunker oil was spilt. Under an agreement with other tanker operators, Esso had to pay huge sums of money to the terminal owner and the crofters whose sheep were poisoned. The House of Lords held that these sums could not be claimed in tort, as this was simply economic loss which was not consequent on the damage to Esso's property. Quite right, too. However, if the incident had occurred in England rather than North of the border, this enactment would unquestionably have allowed Esso to claim these very sums from the shipbuilders, because the shipbuilders were in law liable to the terminal operator and crofters for their property damage (not under the Directive, of course, but under *Donoghue v Stevenson*) and Esso was also liable to them—in contract, though not in tort, since not at fault. Do you think it right that an enactment built on the stilts of unjust enrichment should so pervert the sound principles of the law of tort?

4. In *The Nicholas H* (above, p.45) the plaintiff's cargo was sunk because the carrying ship was unseaworthy. The shipowner was liable in contract, but for an amount limited both by the contract and by statute. The cargo owner sued the surveyor for negligently permitting the ship to sail. If the surveyor had been held liable (he was not), could he have claimed contribution from the shipowner?

5. Publishing firms often seek to make their authors warrant that the manuscript contains nothing defamatory. Why do they do this when they would have a contribution claim against the author in the event of their being held liable for defamation?

Notes:

1. We have seen that though the insurer of property has no personal claim against the tortfeasor who by damaging the property triggers the insurer's liability to the insured, the doctrine of subrogation permits the insurer to exercise the insured's tort claim against the negligent party (above, p.52). In the result, and thanks to "equity," the insurer, though paid to take the risk of harm, gets an indemnity which the law of tort would deny him. This Act does something similar: it allows a tortfeasor who is rendered liable by his own fault to claim money from another tortfeasor, a result which the law of tort itself would never contemplate. In neither case need there be any special relationship between the claimant (insurer/tortfeasor) and the defendant tortfeasor, yet their claim for mere financial loss is met by equity and statute respectively. Both subrogation and contribution are misconceived, only superficially just, and lead to disagreeable results, not least of which is that the only persons allowed to sue a stranger for negligently exposing them to financial loss are subrogated insurers and contribution-claiming tortfeasors (and their insurers).

2. Despite this the courts are giving the Act a very wide interpretation. For example, contributory negligence is not a defence against fraud, yet apportionment by way of contribution has been ordered between a fraudulent and a negligent misrepresentor (*Downs v Chappell* [1996] 3 All E.R. 344 at 363, *per* Hobhouse L.J.).

3. The victim of a highway accident always sues the motorist involved, because the motorist is bound to be insured (and if he is not, the Motor Insurers Bureau will pay). The motorist's insurer then looks for someone to contribute towards the sums he had to pay the victim. Many of these contribution claims are wholly unmeritorious: thus in *Clough v Bussan* [1990] 1 All E.R. 431 the insurer tried to claim contribution from the police who had failed to react to the information that a traffic light in Bradford was malfunctioning; in *Coote v Stone* [1971] 1 All E.R. 657 from the insurer of a car parked illegally but not dangerously; in *Salsbury v Woodland* (below, p.311) from a neighbouring householder who had done nothing wrong. In all these cases the courts wisely rejected the (usually subrogated) private insurer's claim to contribution, but claims by insurers against highway authorities have unfortunately been more successful: indeed, had it not been for the bare majority in the House of Lords in *Stovin v Wise* (above, p.89) the highway authority would have had to pay the driver's insurer 30% of the damages due to her negligence. It will not, however, stop the practice of bringing such subrogated contribution claims for the courts have often endorsed and encouraged them, as if they were simply tort claims for personal injuries by an otherwise unindemnified human being rather than restitutionary claims for money paid by a greedy and disgruntled insurer temporarily out of pocket by reason of his contract with the insured. One recent case arose out of the Selby rail disaster, when a dozy motorist left the motorway and fell on to a railway line just as a fast train was approaching. His insurer (admittedly liable for £22 million) claimed contribution from the highway authority for not having a crash barrier 100 metres long rather than the 62.7 metres actually present (much more than the 30 metres regarded as minimum by the Department of Transport). The claim was dismissed, for although the highway authority did owe a duty to those apt to be injured by the inadequacy of the protection provided, the authority had not been negligent. (*Great North Eastern Railway v Hart* ([2003] EWHC 2450 (Q.B.)).

Before long we shall have a case where a drunk motorist's insurer tries to recoup itself from the host who made the driver drunk, a situation which has provoked exciting legal developments in the United States (where, however, unlimited mandatory liability insurance for drivers does not exist). See, for example, *Coulter v Superior Court* 577 p.2d 669 (Cal. 1978) and *Cory v Shierloh* 629 p.2d. 8 (Cal. 1981).

4. The existence of a contribution claim can have adverse effects on primary tort claims. In *Talbot v Berkshire C.C.* [1993] 4 All E.R. 9 the driver of a car, when sued by his passenger, claimed contribution (but not damages for his own injuries) from the highway authority, and obtained a contribution of one-third, both of them being held liable to the passenger. But when the driver sought to claim from the highway authority for his own injuries, it was held that he was barred by *res judicata*: by claiming contribution (not that he knew about it—it was his insurer's doing!) he had compromised his tort suit.

Talbot was politely trashed by Simon Brown L.J. in *C v Hackney L.B.C.* [1996] 1 All E.R. 973, but in *Bradford & Bingley v Seddon* [1999] 4 All E.R. 217 at 227, Auld L.J. said that his reasoning was "against the flow of modern jurisprudence in this court." Fortunately the House of Lords, reversing the Court of Appeal, held in in *Johnson v Gore Wood* [2001] 1 All E.R. 481 that a claim or defence should be struck out only if putting it forward really constituted an abuse: the question was not whether it could have been raised in the earlier suit, but whether it should have been. Though *Talbot* was not expressly disapproved, it seems unlikely to be followed; and the Court of Appeal seems to be heedful of their Lordships' views: *Toth v Ledger* [2002] P.I.Q.R. P1.

This ridiculous business of penalising litigants for not arguing the whole case when they are sued for part of it works both ways. In *Sellen v Bailey* [1999] R.T.R. 63, CA, there was a collision between cars driven by X and Y, in whose car the plaintiff was a passenger. X sued Y for damages and obtained the princely sum of £129.74, Y not bothering to appear but sending a prompt cheque after the hearing. The plaintiff then sued them both, and before anything was proved, X was granted an indemnity against Y, on the basis that as between the two of them the question of who was at fault had already been determined. If the aim is to curtail litigation it hardly seems sensible to make people defend a trivial claim to the hilt lest their failure to do so land them in a major liability.

Chapter 5

DEFENCES

Introduction

In a suit based on negligence, as we have seen, the plaintiff has to show that the defendant owed him a duty to take care not to injure him, that the defendant breached that duty by unreasonable conduct and that the harm complained of was not only a consequence of that conduct but a foreseeable consequence. If the plaintiff manages to show all this, how can he lose? How can a careless defendant escape liability for the foreseeable harm he was under a duty not to cause?

In some other torts the plaintiff has much less to prove. In a *trespass* suit, for example, he has only to show that the defendant laid hands on him or set foot on his premises. Such acts are often perfectly justifiable, so there are quite a lot of defences by which the defendant may justify them. Again, all the plaintiff need prove in a *defamation* suit is that the defendant said or wrote something nasty about him; but since the nasty statement may have been quite true, or something which, if true, needed to be said, or the expression of an honest opinion on a public matter which the defendant was entitled to express, several defences are open. Indeed, in these torts the main debate actually centres on the defence, whereas in negligence suits the principal problem is to establish the claim, by showing the duty, proving the breach and persuading the judge of its contribution to the occurrence of the harm, or the risk of its occurrence. Even when this has been done, however, a few defences are open to the defendant.

The first is that although he was to blame for the plaintiff's injuries, so, too, was the plaintiff himself. This was a complete defence until 1945, even where the defendant had been very much more to blame than the plaintiff, but in that year Parliament enacted that the plaintiff's fault was only to reduce his damages, not to defeat his claim. This is "contributory negligence", a phrase which should be used only where the negligence in question is that of the claimant himself, and not where it is the negligence of a secondary tortfeasor which has contributed to the harm in issue.

The second defence is consent. The very sensible principle is that you cannot complain of something you willingly accepted—in Latin, *volenti non fit injuria*. Consent is often embodied in a contract. If you have validly contracted to bear a risk, and the risk eventuates, you cannot shuffle off the ensuing loss and impose on your contractor a liability he has validly disclaimed. Agreements have some force. But not as much as they had. The Unfair Contract Terms Act 1977 invalidates a great many disclaimers and agreements to accept risks. The Act applies to agreements and notices in actual words, but the cognate common law defence may apply even though nothing is put in words: a person who voluntarily and needlessly exposes himself to a risk of harm emanating from the defendant may be taken as evidencing his consent to bear the consequences. Any such exposure will seem unreasonable to those who like a quiet life, so contributory negligence may apply as well as *volenti*; but whereas the former only reduces the extent of the defendant's liability, the latter extinguishes or suppresses it entirely, which is probably why the defence is handled with such caution by judges who like compromise (and have sometimes been hesitant about individual autonomy).

The third defence is illegality. Here again there is a Latin tag, *ex turpi causa non oritur actio*. The courts are there to mulct the wicked, not to reward or compensate them. Yet even criminals have their rights, especially the right not to be maimed. The defence tends to be raised where the parties are fellow-criminals and the activity dangerous as well as illegal, that is, in cases where elements of both consent and contributory negligence are also present.

Of the three defences, contributory negligence is by far the most common, perhaps because people are in fact clumsy more often than foolhardy or wicked, or more likely because in law its effects are less severe.

We have already seen cases where a defendant escaped liability for harm although his negligence had contributed to its occurrence, sometimes on the ground that he owed the claimant no duty, and it is quite common to deny the duty where the harm was deliberately caused by an assailant, arsonist or thief whose activities were facilitated by the defendant's negligence, sometimes on the ground that the deliberate intervention broke the causal link.

In *Reeves*, next below, the police admitted that they were under a duty to try to prevent the victim from deliberately killing himself and were in breach of that duty. In the light of this concession one judge of the Court of Appeal held that none of the defences *could* apply as a matter of law, and the majority of the House of Lords imposed liability subject only to contributory negligence.

REEVES v COMMISSIONER OF POLICE OF THE METROPOLIS

House of Lords [2000] 1 A.C. 360, [1999] 3 All E.R. 897, [1999] 3 W.L.R. 363

Action against custodian for failing to prevent suicide of detainee

Remanded in custody on charges of fraud and failure to answer to bail, Martin Lynch, 29 years old, was placed in a very bare cell at Kentish Town Police Station just before one o'clock. The doctor called by the police, who knew that he was a suicide risk and had consequently removed the belt with which he had tried to strangle himself earlier in the day, thought him quite sane. At 1.57 p.m. the police checked his well-being, but on the next visit only eight minutes later he was found irremediably unconscious: he had hanged himself by threading his shirt through the hatch in the door and the much smaller spy-hole above it. This was possible only because the glass lens was missing from the spy-hole and the flap of the hatch had been left open, contrary to standing orders.

Suit was brought under the Fatal Accidents Act by his unmarried partner for the benefit of their child. The trial judge dismissed the claim, but the Court of Appeal by a majority reversed and the House of Lords, Lord Hobhouse dissenting, gave judgment for the claimant subject to a reduction of 50 per cent for contributory negligence.

Lord Hope of Craighead: ... The commissioner accepts that he owed a duty of care to the deceased while he was in police custody. He also accepts that he was in breach of that duty, as the wicket gate was left open when the deceased was in the cell. But he submits that, as the deceased was of sound mind, his suicide in these circumstances did not give rise to a liability to his estate in damages. He seeks to distinguish this case from *Kirkham v Chief Constable of the Greater Manchester Police* [1990] 3 All E.R. 246), where the person who committed suicide was held to have been suffering from clinical depression when he took his own life while in police custody. His arguments on liability have been maintained in your Lordships' House on three grounds: *volenti non fit injuria, novus actus interveniens* and contributory negligence.

In my opinion it is necessary at the outset to identify the duty which was owed to the deceased by the commissioner. There is no doubt that the commissioner was right to concede that he owed a duty of care to the deceased while he remained in police custody. The deceased had been identified as a suicide risk, having on two previous occasions attempted to strangle himself with a belt after being placed in a cell. It was the commissioner's duty to take reasonable care not to provide him with the opportunity of committing suicide by making use of defects in his cell door. The risk was not that he would injure himself accidentally if given that opportunity, but that he would do so deliberately. That is the nature of an act of suicide by a person who is of sound mind. It is a deliberate act of self-destruction by a person who intends to end his own life. So I think that the commissioner's duty can most accurately be described as a duty to take reasonable care to prevent the deceased, while in police custody, from taking his own life deliberately.

It is unusual for a person to be under a duty to take reasonable care to prevent another person doing something to his loss, injury or damage deliberately. On the whole people are entitled to act as they please, even if this will inevitably lead to their own death or injury. As a general rule the common law duty of care is directed towards the prevention of accidents or of injury caused by negligence. The person to whom the duty is owed is, of course, under a corresponding duty to take reasonable care for his own safety. If he is in breach of that duty, his damages may be reduced on the ground of his contributory negligence. But if he injures himself by intentionally doing deliberately the very thing which the defendant is under a duty to prevent him doing negligently, he may find that he is unable to recover any damages. He may be found to have assumed the risk of injury, on the principle of *volenti non fit injuria*. Or it may be held that the chain of causation was broken by his deliberate act, in which case his claim will be defeated on the principle of *novus actus interveniens*. Or it may simply be that his loss, injury and damage will be held to have been caused wholly by his own fault, with the result that there will be no room even for a reduced award on the ground of contributory negligence.

But the duty of care may sometimes extend to preventing people injuring themselves deliberately. The person to whom the duty is owed may be unaware of the risks to which he will expose himself by his deliberate act. Or he may be too young to appreciate them, as in *Yachuk v Oliver Blais Co Ltd* [1949] 2 All E.R. 150, where petrol was sold to a child aged nine who was unaware of its dangerous properties, or *Hughes v Lord Advocate* [1963] 1 All E.R. 705, where the inquisitive children meddled with objects in the unattended shelter in the roadway without thought as to the consequences. Or he may be of unsound mind, with the result that he is at risk of doing something to himself which no rational person would do as he would appreciate that to do this would inevitably lead to injury. Or the risk that the person may commit an act of deliberate self-harm may be the result of something which the defendant has done or is doing to him.

That is the situation which may arise where a person who is of sound mind is deprived of his liberty and put in prison or detained in custody by the police. The duty of those who are entrusted with his custody is to take reasonable care for his safety while he remains in their hands. If it is known that he may engage in self-mutilation or suicide while he is in their custody, their duty is to take reasonable care to prevent him from engaging in these acts so that he remain free from harm until he is set at liberty. This duty is owed to the prisoner if there is that risk, irrespective of whether he is mentally disordered or of sound mind. It arises simply from the fact that he is being detained by them in custody and is known to be at risk of engaging in self-mutilation or of committing suicide.

This brings me to the first of the three arguments which the commissioner has advanced in his defence, which is *volenti non fit injuria*. I do not see how that principle can be applied to a case where the loss, injury or damage was caused by the deliberate act of self-harm which the defendant was under a duty to take reasonable care to prevent. The situation would be different if a defendant who was under a duty to prevent the plaintiff from sustaining injury by accident or negligently was faced with a claim for damages arising from an injury which the plaintiff, in full knowledge of the risks, had done to himself deliberately. It might then be said that he had voluntarily assumed the risk of injury. But that is not this case. The deceased did to himself the very thing that the commissioner was under a duty to take reasonable care to prevent while he remained in his custody. It is true that he deliberately exploited the situation which had been created by the commissioner's negligence. But that was the thing which the commissioner was under a duty to prevent, as it was the foreseeable consequence of his acting negligently.

Similarly, I do not see how what occurred in this case could be said to amount to a *novus actus interveniens*. There was no "new" act here at all. The act by which the deceased killed himself was the very act which the commissioner was under a duty to prevent by not leaving the wicket gate open when the deceased was in his cell and thus providing him with the means of hanging himself. The chain of causation was not broken. There was no "third factor", as explained by Hart and Honoré, *Causation in the Law* (2nd ed., 1985), p.000, which might have negatived a causal connection between the wrongful act and the harm to the deceased. Here the wrongful act was the cause of the harm because it created the opportunity for the deliberate act of self-harm. The suicide was a foreseeable consequence of the failure in duty which occurred when the deceased, who was a known suicide risk, was placed in a cell which provided him with the opportunity to carry out that act.

Lord Hobhouse (dissenting): . . . The suicide of Mr Lynch was foreseeable; it was within the scope of the duty of care owed by the defendant to Mr Lynch. If the plaintiff or some other person had an independent cause of action of their own against the defendant, say for nervous shock, in connection with what occurred that day in Kentish Town police station, the conduct of Mr Lynch would not make the loss suffered by such a person too remote. The Court of Appeal and your Lordships have been right to reject the defence of *novus actus*. But where, in my judgment, the majority of the Court of Appeal went wrong was to stop there. They rejected wholly any relevance of the second category of legal principle.

The second category of legal principle to which I must refer is that which relates to the responsibility of the plaintiff for that of which he complains. A number of principles are involved. First there is the fundamental principle of human autonomy. Where a natural person is not under any disability, that person has a right to choose his own fate. He is constrained in so far as his choice may affect others, society or the body politic. But, so far as he himself alone is concerned, he is entitled to choose. The choice to commit suicide is such a choice. A corollary of this principle is, subject to the important qualification to which I will refer, the principle that a person may not complain of the consequences of his own choices. This both reflects coherent legal principle and conforms to the accepted use of the word cause: the person's choice becomes, so far as he is concerned, the cause. The autonomy of the individual human confers the right and the responsibility.

To qualify as an autonomous choice, the choice made must be free and unconstrained—*i.e.* voluntary, deliberate and informed. If the plaintiff is under a disability, either through lack of mental capacity or lack or excess of age, the plaintiff will lack autonomy and will not have made a free and unconstrained choice. Child plaintiffs come into this category. Both as a matter of causation and the attribution of responsibility, their conduct does not (without more) remove the responsibility of the defendant or transfer the responsibility to the child plaintiff: see *Yachuk v Oliver Blais Co Ltd* [1949] 2 All E.R. 150. Similarly, plaintiffs suffering from a temporary or a more serious loss of mental capacity (see *Kirkham v Chief Constable of the Greater Manchester Police* [1990] 3 All E.R. 246), will not have made the requisite free and unconstrained choice. Where the plaintiff's lack of mental capacity has been caused by the defendant's breach of duty, the entitlement to recover is all the stronger. On the same basis choices made under constraint of circumstances, such as those made by rescuers or persons placed in immediate danger, will not carry with them the consequence that the choice was the sole cause of the subsequent injury to the plaintiff nor will it result in his bearing the sole responsibility for his injury: see *Haynes v Harwood* [1935] 1 K.B. 146, *cf. Cutler v United Dairies (London) Ltd* [1933] 2 K.B. 297. The same applies if the plaintiff's choice was vitiated by misinformation or lack of information. In the context of employment, the question of the reality of the employee's assent and his acceptance of risk has been the subject of many decisions; perhaps the most illuminating discussion for present purposes is to be found in *Imperial Chemical Industries Ltd v Shatwell* [1964] 2 All E.R. 999 at 1008–1009, *per* Lord Hodson where he stresses that the plaintiff's conduct cannot be described as voluntary unless he truly had a free choice. (The case also, like

Stapley v Gypsum Mines Ltd [1953] 2 All E.R. 478, illustrates the distinction between lack of care for one's own safety and the true acceptance of risk.) These qualifications are fundamental and are the basis of the decisions where a plaintiff has been held entitled still to sue notwithstanding his having made a choice which led to the event of which he complains.

The simplest way in which to express the relevant principles, both the basic principle of autonomy and the qualification, is in terms of causation. Both as a matter of the ordinary use of language and as a matter of law it is correct to say that the plaintiff's voluntary choice was *the* cause of his loss. Another partial expression of this principle is the maxim *volenti non fit injuria.* This maxim, originating from a rather different Roman law context, is a notorious source of confusion: see *Dann v Hamilton* [1939] 1 K.B. 509. In intentional torts it means consent by the plaintiff to the act which would otherwise be the tort. In the law of negligence it means the acceptance variously of the risk created by the defendant's negligence or of the risk of the defendant's negligence. In such cases it is probably best confined to cases where it can be said that the plaintiff has expressly or impliedly agreed to exempt the defendant from the duty of care which he would otherwise have owed (*Nettleship v Weston* [1971] 3 All E.R. 581), a formulation which, it will be appreciated, immediately brings the maxim into potential conflict with s.2 of the Unfair Contract Terms Act 1977. It will also be appreciated that so interpreted the maxim would only have an artificial application to the facts of the present case. The suggestion that Mr Lynch was agreeing to exempt the police authority from anything is both objectionable and wholly unrealistic.

But, my Lords, if the question raised by Mr Lynch's conduct is seen as a question of causation, these artificialities fall away. If Mr Lynch, knowing that the police officers had put him in a cell with a defective door and had failed to close the hatch, then voluntarily and deliberately, in full possession of his faculties, made the rational choice to commit suicide, principle and language say that it was his choice which was the cause of his subsequent death. He was not on the judge's findings, acting under any disability or compulsion. He made a free choice: he is responsible for the consequence of that choice.

Lord Hoffmann and **Lord Jauncey of Tullichettle** delivered opinions dismissing the appeal, and **Lord Mackay of Clashfern** agreed with **Lord Hoffmann** and **Lord Hope.**

Notes:

1. In *Orange v Chief Constable of West Yorkshire Police* [2002] Q.B. 347 the Court of Appeal held that the gaoler's duty to try to prevent suicide did not extend to all prisoners: only when they know or ought to know a prisoner to be a suicide risk must the prison authorities appraise him and take care to prevent him killing or injuring himself. Although the risk among prisoners was high, it would be wrong to treat all prisoners as suicide risks, for that would lead to an unacceptable level of control, bad for the authorities and the prisoners alike.

2. The state may be liable under the Human Rights Act if, whenever there is a death in custody (or elsewhere involving the police), it fails to undertake a satisfactory public inquiry in which the relatives can be heard (*R v Secretary of State, ex parte Amin* [2003] UKHL 51).

Section 1.—Contributory Negligence

LAW REFORM (CONTRIBUTORY NEGLIGENCE) ACT 1945

1.—(1) Where any person suffers damage as the result partly of his own fault and partly of the fault of any other person or persons, a claim in respect of that damage shall not be defeated by reason of the fault of the person suffering the damage, but the damages recoverable in respect thereof shall be reduced to such extent as the court thinks just and equitable having regard to the claimant's share in the responsibility for the damage: . . .

(2) Where damages are recoverable by any person by virtue of the foregoing subsection subject to such reduction as is therein mentioned, the court shall find and record the total damages which would have been recoverable if the claimant had not been at fault. . . .

4. The following expressions have the meanings hereby respectively assigned to them, that is to say—

"damage" includes loss of life and personal injury;
"fault" means negligence, breach of statutory duty or other act or omission which gives rise to a liability in tort or would, apart from this Act, give rise to the defence of contributory negligence.

Notes:

1. In determining the proportion by which the plaintiff's damages are to be reduced, attention must be paid to the respective blameworthiness of the parties as well as to the causative potency of their acts or omissions (for the position under the Contribution Act 1977, see above, p.236); after all, if attention were not paid to causative potency, a careless plaintiff would recover nothing from a defendant who was free from fault but strictly liable, and if blameworthiness were not taken into account the results would be unfair. Because a motor car is more powerful than a pedestrian, it is said that "it is rare for a pedestrian to be found more responsible than a driver unless the pedestrian had suddenly moved into the path of an oncoming vehicle, since the court had consistently placed a high burden on drivers to reflect the fact that the car was potentially a dangerous weapon." (*Eagle v Chambers* [2003] EWCA Civ 1107, [2003] Times L.R. 502). The reduction is to be by an amount that is "just and equitable" having regard to the claimant's responsibility for the harm. Since it is only regard that has to be had to the claimant's responsibility, it may not be just and equitable to make a deduction which precisely reflects it: thus in *Russell v Smith* (Q.B.D. June 30, 2003) the judge felt able to deduct only 50% from the damages payable to a cyclist who was 75% to blame for the accident. It has been suggested that it may not be just and equitable to reduce at all the damages payable by an employer to a mildly careless employee (*Hawkins v Ian Ross (Castings)* [1970] 1 All E.R. 180). It had, indeed, already been held, before the Act was passed, that an employee who made a careless mistake in the heat and stress of factory conditions was not, as against an occupier in breach of safety regulations, to be treated as careless (*Staveley Iron and Chemical Co v Jones* (below p.281), but this new approach is more extensive. Contrariwise, " . . . there is no principle of law which requires that, even where there is a breach of statutory duty in circumstances . . . where the intention of the statute is to provide protection, *inter alia*, against folly on the part of a workman, there cannot be 100% contributory negligence on the part of the workman" (*Jayes v IMI (Kynoch)* [1985] I.C.R. 155, 159, *per* Robert Goff L.J.).

But hearken to Sedley L.J.: " . . . *Jayes* should, in my respectful view, not be followed by judges of first instance and should not be relied upon by advocates in argument. The relevant principles are straightforward. Whether the claim is in negligence or for breach of statutory duty, if the evidence, once it has been appraised as the law requires, shows the entire fault to lie with the claimant there is no liability on the defendant. If not, then the court will consider to what extent, if any, the claimant's share in the responsibility for the damage makes it just and equitable to reduce his damages. The phrase '100% contributory negligence', while expressive, is unhelpful, because it invites the court to treat a statutory qualification of the measure of damages as if it were a secondary or surrogate approach to liability, which it is not. If there is liability, contributory negligence can reduce its monetary quantification, but it cannot legally or logically nullify it." (*Anderson v Newham College of Further Education* [2002] EWCA Civ 505, in which the deduction was reduced from 90% to 50%, the claimant having been extremely stupid and the defendant not at fault at all, but only in mild breach of a strict safety regulation). In between times the Court of Appeal had held *obiter* in *Pitts v Hunt* (below p.260) that 100% deduction was not possible, but in *Reeves* the trial judge and one of the members of the Court of Appeal were ready to allow it, and none of the members of the House of Lords took a position on the matter, save to say that to allow it would negate the breach of duty (which it would not).

Consider *Sousa v A & J Bull Ltd* [2001] EWCA Civ 1039. The trial judge imposed liability, subject to 30% contributory negligence, on the driver of a 38-ton lorry for running over the claimant who fell off a bicycle which he was pedalling with an adult on the cross-bar doing the steering. The bicycle wobbled as it drew out to overtake a stationary car, and the lorry pulled over to right lane of the dual carriageway and slowed down to about 25 mph. The Court of Appeal held that the defendant was not in breach of his duty of care and therefore not liable at all.

Contrast *Foster v Maguire* [2001] EWCA Civ 273: the defendant had parked his van and trailer on a straight stretch of dual carriageway, blocking the cycle lane and protruding 2.4 metres into the highway. The claimant, cycling with her head down in the morning rain, ran into it, not having looked up for 185 metres though she could have stopped in 10 metres. The trail judge held that the defendant was not negligent since he had not caused a danger to anyone using the highway in a way that persons could reasonably be expected to use it, but the Court of Appeal, by a majority, reversed, subject to 70% contributory negligence.

Although the Court of Appeal keeps saying that it is reluctant to interfere with the trial judge's apportionment, in fact it keeps doing so. To take two examples out of very many, it reduced to 50% a reduction of 75% in the damages awarded to a drunken guest who climbed on a table at a party organised by the defendant and cut his head on a revolving fan (*Brannan v Airtours* [1999] Times L.R. 73) and in *Morales v Eccleston* [1991] R.T.R. 151 where the claimant, 11 years old, was struck by the defendant's offside while he was kicking a ball in the middle of a busy street raised the deduction from 20 to 75%.

The reason there are so many appeals when any increase or diminution in the damages awarded can hardly be very great is that when there has been a payment into court it is not just the damages but also the costs, which may be much higher, which are in issue.

2. It is well established that contributory negligence, unlike defendant's negligence, need not be a breach of a duty to take care. The terms of *Tremayne v Hill* [1987] R.T.R. 131, CA are therefore puzzling. The defendant carelessly drove through a red light and ran over the plaintiff who was crossing the road where there was no pedestrian-crossing. In repelling the (impertinent) defence of contributory negligence, Sir Roger Ormrod said: "The only question . . . is whether the plaintiff owed any duty of care, either to himself or to other drivers on the road, to act in any way other than that which he did," and Ralph Gibson L.J. said: "The plaintiff was not shown to have been in breach of a self-regarding duty." Note, too, that in *Reeves* (above) Lord Hope spoke of contributory negligence as a breach of duty. This inaccuracy is venial, since one regularly speaks of the "duty to mitigate damage", which is not a duty at all (since breach of it is not actionable) but simply indicates that one cannot claim for an item of harm one could reasonably have avoided or of expenditure which need not have been incurred.

Misconception about the nature of contributory negligence can lead to mistakes. In *Sahib Foods v Paskin Kyriakides Sands* (CA, December 19, 2003) a fire which broke out in the preparation room of the claimant's food factory was able to spread because of the absence of fire-proof panels, the defendant having failed to advise on their installation, partly because one of the claimant's employees, X, had given him inaccurate and inadequate information about processes in the preparation room. The trial judge ignored this on the ground that neither the claimant nor X owed any duty to the defendant as regards this information, and held the defendant liable in full, but the Court of Appeal reduced the claimant's damages by two-thirds: it was enough that X's negligent misinformation was given in the course of his employment by the claimant.

3. Unlike the use of a Walkman or a cell-phone, failure to wear a seat-belt does not cause accidents, though it may aggravate injuries. Failure to wear a seat-belt is normally unreasonable and damages will be reduced if the defendant can show that it made a difference. Lord Denning suggested standard reductions of 15 per cent if the injuries would have been less serious, 25 per cent if they would have been avoided (*Froom v Butcher* [1976] Q.B. 286). The unlawfulness of failure to wear a seat-belt is of course irrelevant. A stationary moped-cyclist who suffered serious injuries owing to the atrocious driving of the drunk defendant was docked 10 per cent for not having his crash-helmet fastened: *Capps v Miller* [1989] 2 All E.R. 333, CA, but no deduction was made in the case of an unbelted taxi-driver, since it was reasonable (though unlawful) for him not to wear a belt in view of the risk of attack by passengers (*Jones v Morgan* [1994] C.L.Y.B. § 3344).

Contrariwise, if a driver is injured because the seat-belt is defective, the manufacturer may invoke his bad driving as contributory negligence (*Kaye v Alfa Romeo* (1984) 134 New L.J. 126—still law after the Consumer Protection Act 1987?), but where an ambulance had an accident which was not the driver's fault, the passenger in the back could not sue him for failing to ensure that she wore the seat-belt, since there were notices to say that she should. (*Eastman v South West Thames A.H.A.* [1991] Times L.R. 352, CA). The Highway Code makes it the driver's responsibility to see that seat-belts are worn by passengers under the age of 14. See *Jones v Wilkins* above p.238.

4. Contributory negligence must be pleaded by the defendant: *Fookes v Slaytor* [1979] 1 All E.R. 137, CA. This may, however, prove counterproductive, as General Cleaning Contractors found when they alleged that Christmas, the injured window-cleaner who was suing them, should have used wedges to immobilise a window-sash, and were themselves held liable for failing to provide them. ([1952] 2 All E.R. 1110, HL). Sometimes when judgment is rendered on liability the assessment of damages is deferred; in such a case, if contributory negligence has been pleaded but not ruled on, it may be raised in the assessment (*Maes Finance v AL Phillips* [1997] Times L.R. 157).

5. We have seen earlier the recent growth of the view that a defendant need not pay full damages if there were other causes of the claimant's injury or the chance of harm was less than 50%, but traditionally this Act provided the only means, apart from the doctrine of mitigation of damage, of giving the claimant something by way of damages for established harm, but less than the full amount. (Other systems are more flexible—in Switzerland damages may be reduced if the defendant was not greatly at fault, and in France judges have a *de facto* discretion because no final appeal lies on questions of *quantum*). The bare majority of the House of Lords was surely wrong, from this point of view, to hold that the Act cannot be invoked against a trespasser complaining of injuries unless the trespasser had been disregardful not only of the defendant's rights

but also of his own safety (*Westwood v Post Office* [1974] A.C. 1), not apparently followed in *Revill v Newbery* [1996] 1 All E.R. 291, where the Court of Appeal, holding an old man liable in damages for shooting in the direction of a young burglar (wrong in policy), reduced the damages by two-thirds (wrong in law). The courts are said to be unwilling to find that a young child has been contributorily negligent (*Gough v Thorne* [1966] 1 W.L.R. 1387), and the Pearson Commission recommended—in vain—that the defence of contributory negligence should not be available in the case of motor vehicle accidents where the victim was under the age of 12. But consider *Morales*, the case of the child kicking a football in the middle of a busy street, above n.1. In fact there are numerous cases where a motorist who has run over a small child has been held not liable at all, having had no reason to expect that the child would dart into the road so close that stopping was impossible.

There has, however, been a curious case where damages were apportioned at common law. In *Tennant Radiant Heat v Warrington Development Corp.* [1988] 1 E.G.L.R. 41 the plaintiff's premises were flooded because 20 rainwater outlets on the roof were blocked. As to 19 of them the defendant was to blame for neglecting his architect's advice, but the twentieth was the responsibility of the plaintiff himself who, though not at fault, was in breach of his covenant *vis-à-vis* the defendant. The Act did not apply because the plaintiff's breach of contract was not tortious, but he recovered 90 per cent of his damage, a decision regarded as problematic in *The Good Luck* [1989] 3 All E.R. 628 at 672.

6. Damages claimed for loss of support by dependants of a person killed by the defendant are reduced by the amount of carelessness of the deceased. A child's damages are not reduced by reason of the concurrent carelessness of a parent or guardian, but the parent or guardian may, at a pinch, be brought in as a third party by the tortfeasor and held liable to pay contribution (above, p.238). Neither a passenger in a vehicle nor its owner is affected by the contributory negligence of the driver unless he is driving as their servant or agent. Note, however, the position under s.1(7) of the Congenital Disabilities (Civil Liability) Act 1976, and consider the position if a child is born deformed as a result of a collision between a car negligently driven by the pregnant mother and one negligently driven by a stranger.

7. Rescuers are frequently and nobly indifferent to their own safety but their recovery is not often barred or limited on that account. In a case where the rescuer's negligence contributed to the emergency which called for the rescue, Boreham J. overcame his "distaste about finding a rescuer guilty of contributory negligence" (*Harrison v British Railways Board* [1981] 3 All E.R. 679).

8. The purpose of this Act is to split the loss between a careless plaintiff and a responsible defendant. Where two defendants are responsible, the loss is split between them under the 1978 Act, the Contribution Act (above, p.236). Where the cast includes two responsible defendants and a careless plaintiff as well, both Acts apply. Their interaction has caused trouble. In *Fitzgerald v Lane* [1988] 2 All E.R. 961, HL, the plaintiff walked briskly on to a pelican crossing when the lights were against him and was struck first by D1, a motorist carelessly proceeding South and then by D2, a motorist carelessly proceeding North. The trial judge held all three parties equally to blame, and gave the plaintiff judgment against each defendant for two-thirds of his claim, the defendants to contribute equally *inter se*. Given his apportionment of blame, this order was entirely correct. The Court of Appeal did not disturb the judge's evaluation of the respective faults, but nevertheless allowed the plaintiff only half of his claim. Although this was quite wrong, the House of Lords upheld the Court of Appeal's order, but only because it varied the apportionment of responsibility, finding that the claimant was twice as much to blame as either of the drivers, or to put it another way, as much to blame as both of them together.

What emerges from this mess is as follows. One must first appraise the plaintiff's contribution to his injuries in relation to the total event, taking into consideration only the conduct of those whose liability is established, and then decide by how much his damages should be docked in the light of his contribution. The plaintiff gets an order for damages in the resulting sum against all defendants who are liable, regardless of their individual contributions. Then one decides how, at the end of the day, after the plaintiff has made his collection as he chooses, the defendants are severally to bear the loss for which they are jointly liable. It will quite often happen that a plaintiff gets substantial damages from a defendant less blameworthy than himself, especially when there is another defendant who is more culpable than either. But that is the result of the principle that all defendants at all to blame are liable for the whole damage, except (thanks to this Act) to the extent that the victim has himself been to blame for it.

The two Acts may interact in another way. *Wall v Radford* [1991] 2 All E.R. 741 was a personal injury claim by one driver against another. In an earlier suit by the plaintiff's passenger, the two drivers had been held equally to blame. The judge held that it would be "an affront to justice" (!) if the plaintiff could reopen the question of liability or apportionment: her contributory negligence and its *quantum* had been concluded by the finding in the contribution proceedings. The practical effect of this dubious holding will be to prolong the trial of claims by an innocent plaintiff such as the passenger in this accident—a result quite characteristic of contribution claims between defendants.

9. The Contributory Negligence Act applies only where the defendant's conduct is tortious. Thus if the defendant has broken his contract without committing any tort, a plaintiff whose fault has conduced to the harm will recover all or nothing (*Quinn v Burch Bros* [1966] 2 Q.B. 370, affirming [1965] 3 All E.R. 801;

Lambert v Lewis all in the Court of Appeal, nothing in the House of Lords [1980] 1 All E.R. 978; [1981] 1 All E.R. 1185). Where the defendant's liability is purely contractual, Nourse L.J. has said: "It ought to have been perfectly obvious that the Law Reform (Contributory Negligence) Act 1945 was never intended to obtrude the defence of contributory negligence into an area of the law where it has no business to be" (*Barclays Bank v Fairclough Building* [1995] 1 All E.R. 289 at 306). It is actually far from obvious that contributory negligence is inapt in such cases, and it is to be regretted that the Law Commission has proposed that an additional Act be passed permitting apportionment where, but only where, the contractual duty breached by the defendant is one to take reasonable care or exercise reasonable skill or both. ("Contributory Negligence as a Defence in Contract", Law. Com. No.219 (1993)). Very often, of course, the defendant's breach will simultaneously constitute a tort, even though the harm is purely financial, and in such a case the Act applies and damages may be reduced, even if the plaintiff stresses the contractual nature of his claim (*Forsikringsaktieselskapet Vesta v Butcher* [1989] 1 All E.R. 402, HL, affirming [1988] 2 All E.R. 43. The High Court of Australia has refused to follow *Vesta* and allows the careless victim of a breach of a contractual duty of care to claim full damages even if he could have sued "in tort" and had his damages reduced (*Astley v Austrust Ltd* [1999] H.C.A. 6).

10. Since the legislature has seen fit to enact that "Contributory negligence is no defence in proceedings founded on conversion, or on intentional trespass to goods" (Torts (Interference with Goods) Act 1977, s. 11), and the courts have held that while it may be opposed to a claim under the Misrepresentation Act 1967, it is no defence to a claim for deceit (*Standard Chartered Bank v Pakistan National Shipping Corp.* [2003] 1 A.C. 959); it is still important to distinguish the cause of action being relied on. In cases of nuisance, where the plaintiff is complaining that the defendant's conduct is rendering life on the plaintiff's premises unbearable, the obvious defence in some cases is that the plaintiff was aware of the situation when he moved in. Traditionally, however, it is no defence that "the plaintiff came to the nuisance." See *Miller v Jackson* below, p.445. This is all the more peculiar as the defence of contributory negligence rests on a very general principle. For example, an award for unfair dismissal may be reduced if the applicant's conduct caused or contributed to the dismissal: Employment Rights Act 1996, s.123(6). In s.123(4) that Act separately preserves the cognate doctrine of mitigation of damage whereby one cannot claim damages in respect of an item of harm, otherwise compensable, if you could reasonably have prevented its occurrence. Here also one need only behave reasonably: one is not bound to martyrise oneself to save the defendant's pocket. Thus the mother who might lawfully have had an abortion may still claim for the expense of bringing up the handicapped child conceived owing to the negligent failure of a sterilisation operation (*Emeh v Kensington A.H.A.* [1984] 3 All E.R. 1044, CA).

11. The existence of this Act has induced the judges to reduce the scope of the defence of *volenti non fit injuria*, by which a plaintiff who has accepted the risk of the injury which has occurred is barred from recovery in respect of it. The reaction is perfectly understandable, but it is not wholly justifiable, since respect for the self-determination of the individual requires the legal system to make him suffer the consequences of *voluntarily* exposing himself to physical risk, even if it was not in the circumstances an *unreasonably* dangerous thing to do. As we shall see, the Act has also induced courts to downplay the total defence of unlawfulness or *ex turpi causa*.

12. A person who has taken out insurance against liability can naturally recover from his insurer in full although he was at fault in incurring the liability: that is the whole point of the policy (though he may have problems if his fault was very grave, like rape). So also a person who insures against his property being damaged or lost may recover under the policy though it was his fault the damage or loss occurred: a term in the policy that he must take care is construed as a term that he must not act recklessly (*W J Lane v Spratt* [1970] 2 Q.B. 480). But people other than insurers do not often promise to pay people for the consequences of their own carelessness, so indemnity clauses are rigorously construed (*Thompson v T Lohan Ltd* [1987] 2 All E.R. 631, CA) and will be invalid against a consumer unless reasonable (Unfair Contract Terms Act 1977, s.4).

13. In France motorists have been strictly liable for traffic accidents for over 60 years, but until recently had to pay only reduced damages if the victim had been careless. The widespread feeling that such a reduction was unfair led to a striking decision by the Court of Cassation that any reduction was unlawful. Subsequent legislation provides that the damages are not to be reduced unless the victim was himself at the wheel. In Britain where the victim can recover only if the motorist is at fault, we do not feel it unfair that damages should be reduced if the victim was also at fault, but it would be possible to argue that if one can recover from one's own insurer though one is at fault, one should equally be able to recover from someone else's insurer.

14. Although a victim's contributory negligence reduces his damages, his entitlement to social security benefits is unaffected. As will be seen below (p. 647 *et seq.*) the benefits he receives are now deducted *in toto* by the defendant from the damages awarded by the court and repaid to the state. Thus the victim who lost £10,000 in earnings and received £5,000 in benefits related to his incapacity for work will receive no damages under that head if he was 50 per cent contributorily negligent. Is this fair?

Section 2.—*Volenti Non Fit Injuria*

IMPERIAL CHEMICAL INDUSTRIES v SHATWELL

House of Lords [1965] A.C. 656; [1964] 3 W.L.R. 329; 108 S.J. 578; [1964] 2 All E.R. 999

Action by employee against employer in respect of personal injury

On the facts, sufficiently stated in the judgment of Lord Reid, Elwes J. gave judgment for the plaintiff, subject to a reduction of damages by 50 per cent for contributory negligence. The Court of Appeal affirmed this judgment. The defendant's appeal was allowed by the House of Lords.

Lord Reid: My Lords, this case arises out of the accidental explosion of a charge at a quarry belonging to the appellants which caused injuries to the respondent George Shatwell and his brother James, who were both qualified shot firers. On June 28, 1960, these two men and another shot firer, Beswick, had bored and filled fifty shot holes and had inserted electric detonators and connected them up in series. Before firing it was necessary to test the circuit for continuity. This should have been done by connecting long wires so that the men could go to a shelter some eighty yards away and test from there. They had not sufficient wire with them and Beswick went off to get more. The testing ought not to have been done until signals had been given so that other men could take shelter and these signals were not due to be given for at least another hour.

Soon after Beswick had left George said to his brother: "Must we test them?" meaning shall we test them, and James said "Yes." The testing is done by passing a weak current through the circuit in which a small galvanometer is included and if the needle of the instrument moves when a connection is made the circuit is in order. So George got a galvanometer and James handed two short wires to him. Then George applied the wires to the galvanometer and to the needle did not move. This showed that the circuit was defective so the two men went round inspecting the connections. They saw nothing wrong and George said that that meant there was a dud detonator somewhere, and decided to apply the galvanometer to each individual detonator. James handed two other wires to him and George used them to apply the galvanometer to the first detonator. The result was an explosion which injured both men.

This method had been regularly used without mishap until the previous year. Then some research done by the appellants showed that it might be unsafe and in October 1959, the appellants gave orders that testing must in future be done from a shelter and a lecture was given to all the shot firers, including the Shatwells, explaining the position. Then in December 1959, new statutory regulations were made (SI 1959/2259) probably because the Ministry had been informed of the results of the appellants' research. These regulations came into operation in February 1960, and the Shatwells were aware of them. But some of the shot firers appear to have gone on in the old way. An instance of this came to the notice of the management in May 1960, and the management took immediate action and revoked the shot firing certificate of the disobedient man, and told the other shot firers about this. George admitted in evidence that he knew all this. He admitted that they would only have had to wait ten minutes until Beswick returned with the long wires. When asked why he did not wait, his only excuse was that he could not be bothered to wait.

George now sues the appellants on the ground that he and his brother were equally to blame for this accident, and that the appellants are vicariously liable for his brother's conduct. He has been awarded £1,500, being half the agreed amount of his loss. There is no question of the appellants having been in breach of the regulations because the duty under the regulation is laid on the shot firer personally. So counsel for George frankly and rightly admitted that if George has sued James personally instead of suing his employer the issue would have been the same. If this decision is right it means that if two men collaborate in doing what they know is dangerous and is forbidden and as a result both are injured, each has a cause of action against the other.

The appellants have two grounds of defence, first that James's conduct had no causal connection with the accident, the sole cause being George's own fault, and secondly, *volenti non fit injuria*. I am of opinion that they are entitled to succeed on the latter ground but I must deal shortly with the former ground because it involves the decision of this House in *Stapley v Gypsum Mines Ltd* ([1953] A.C. 663), and I think that there has been some misunderstanding of that case. Stapley and a man named Dale were working together in the mine. They found that a part of the roof was dangerous. They tried to bring it down but failed. Then, contrary to the foreman's orders and to statutory regulations, they decided to go on with their ordinary work and Stapley went to work below that part of the roof. It fell on him and he was killed. The only issue before the House was whether the conduct of Dale had contributed to cause the accident, and the House decided by a majority that it had. There was little, if any, difference of opinion as to the principles to be applied; the difference was in their application to the facts of the case. The case gives authoritative guidance on the question of causation but beyond that it decides nothing. It clearly appears from the argument of counsel that the defence *volenti non fit injuria* was never taken and nothing about it was said by any of their Lordships.

Applying the principles approved in *Stapley's* case, I think that James's conduct did have a causal connection with this accident. It is far from clear that George would have gone on with the test if James had not agreed with him. But perhaps more important James did collaborate with him in making the test in a forbidden and unlawful way. His collaboration may not have amounted to much but it was not negligible. If I had to consider the allocation of fault I would have difficulty in finding both men equally to blame. If James had been suing in respect of his damage it would, I think, be clear that both had contributed to cause the accident but that the greater part of the fault must be attributed to George. So I do not think that the appellants could succeed entirely on this defence and I turn to consider their second submission.

The defence *volenti non fit injuria* has had a chequered history. At one time it was very strictly applied. Then the tide began to turn. The modern view can be seen emerging in the judgments of the majority in *Yarmouth v France* ((1887) 19 Q.B.D. 647). No one denied that a man who freely and voluntarily incurs a risk of which he has full knowledge cannot complain of injury if that risk materialises and causes him damage. The controversy was whether acceptance of the risk can (or must) be inferred from the mere fact that the man goes on working in full knowledge of the risk involved. The point was finally settled by this House in *Smith v Baker & Sons* ([1891] A.C. 325).

The *ratio* in *Smith v Baker and Sons* was, I think, most clearly stated by Lord Herschell: "The maxim is founded on good sense and justice. One who has invited or assented to an act being done towards him cannot, when he suffers from it, complain of it as a wrong. The maxim has no special application to the case of employer and employed, though its application may well be invoked in such a case." Then he pointed out that a person undertaking to do work which is intrinsically dangerous, notwithstanding that care has been taken to make it as little dangerous as possible, cannot if he suffers complain that a wrong has been done him. And then he continued: "But the argument for the respondents went far beyond this. The learned counsel contended that, even though there had been negligence on the part of the defendants, yet the risk created by it was known to the plaintiff; and inasmuch as he continued in the defendants' employment, doing his work under conditions, the risk of which he appreciated, the maxim, 'Volenti non fit injuria,' applied, and he could not recover." And later he said: "If, then, the employer thus fails in his duty towards the employed, I do not think that because he does not straightaway refuse to continue his service, it is true to say that he is willing that his employer should thus act towards him. I believe it would be contrary to fact to assert that he either invited or assented to the act or default which he complains of as a wrong."

More recently it appears to have been thought in some quarters that, at least as between master and servant, *volenti non fit injuria* is a dead or dying defence. That I think is because in most cases where the defence would now be available it has become usual to base the decision on contributory negligence. Where the plaintiff's own disobedient act is the sole cause of the injury it does not matter in the result whether one says 100 per cent contributory negligence or *volenti non fit injuria*. But it does matter in a case like the present. If we adopt the inaccurate habit of using the word "negligence" to denote a deliberate act done with full knowledge of the risk it is not surprising that we sometimes get into difficulties. I think that most people would say, without stopping to think of the reason, that there is a world of difference between two fellow-servants collaborating carelessly so that the acts of both contribute to cause injury to one of them, and two fellow-servants combining to disobey an order deliberately though they know the risk involved. It seems reasonable that the injured man should recover some compensation in the former case but not in the latter. If the law treats both as merely cases of negligence it cannot draw a distinction. But in my view the law does and should draw a distinction. In the first case only the partial defence of contributory negligence is available. In the second *volenti non fit injuria* is a complete defence if the employer is not himself at fault and is only liable vicariously for the acts of the fellow-servant. If the plaintiff invited or freely aided and abetted his fellow-servant's disobedience, then he was *volens* in the fullest sense. He cannot complain of the resulting injury either against the fellow-servant or against the master on the ground of his vicarious responsibility for his fellow-servant's conduct. I need not here consider the common case where the servant's disobedience puts the master in breach of a statutory obligation and it would be wrong to decide in advance whether that would make any difference. There remain two other arguments for the respondent which I must deal with.

It was argued that in this case it has not been shown that George had a full appreciation of the risk. In my view it must be held that he had. He knew that those better qualified than he was took the risk seriously. He knew that his employers had forbidden this practice and that it had then been prohibited by statutory regulation. And he knew that his employers were taking strong measures to see that the order was obeyed. If he did not choose to believe what he was told I do not think that he could for that reason say that he did not fully appreciate the risk. He knew that the risk was that a charge would explode during testing, and no shot firer could be in any doubt about the possible consequences of that.

Finally the respondent argues that there is a general rule that the defence of *volenti non fit injuria* is not available where there has been a breach of a statutory obligation. It would be odd if that were so. In the present case the prohibition of testing except from a shelter had been imposed by the appellants before the statutory prohibition was made. So it would mean that if the respondent had deliberately done what he did in full knowledge of the risk the day before the statutory prohibition was made this defence would have been open to the appellants, but if he had done the same thing the day after the regulation came into operation it would not . . .

I entirely agree that an employer who is himself at fault in persistently refusing to comply with a statutory rule could not possibly be allowed to escape liability because the injured workman had agreed to waive the breach.

I can find no reason at all why the facts that these two brothers agreed to commit an offence by contravening a statutory prohibition imposed on them as well as agreeing to defy their employer's orders should affect the application of the principle *volenti non fit injuria* either to an action by one of them against the other or to an action by one against their employer based on his vicarious responsibility for the conduct of the other. I would therefore allow this appeal.

Questions
1. Is there a big difference between doing something bad and doing something badly?
2. Should all those who agree to play Russian Roulette be liable to the loser's widow?
3. Lord Reid described "the habit of using the word 'negligence' to denote a deliberate act down in full knowledge of the risk" as "inaccurate". Was the House of Lords guilty of this inaccuracy in *Reeves* [above p.242]?
4. Can you reconcile Lord Reid's reference to "100 per cent contributory negligence" with the observations of Sedley L.J. in *Anderson v Newham College*, above p.246, n.1?

Notes:
1. The defence of *volenti* was upheld in a case where the trial judge had given judgment for the plaintiff subject to only 20 per cent contributory negligence. The facts were as follows: After some hours of heavy drinking in *The Blue Boar*, Murray suggested to Morris that they go for a spin in his private plane. Morris drove them to the airport and tried to help start the plane. The weather was so poor that flying at the club had been stopped. Murray unwisely took off down-wind, and wholly failed to control the plane thereafter. It crashed immediately. Murray was killed and Morris badly injured. (*Morris v Murray* [1991] 2 Q.B. 6; [1990] 3 All E.R. 801).

The Court of Appeal faced two problems. In *Dann v Hamilton* [1939] 1 K.B. 509, a case where a passenger had been injured by the negligence of a driver she knew to be drunk, Asquith J. had rejected the defence (a decision disapproved by Megaw L.J. in *Nettleship*, above, p.130). Secondly, in *Wooldridge v Sumner* [1962] 2 All E.R. 978 Diplock L.J. had doubted the application of the defence where the claim was based on negligence *simpliciter* (as he unsimply said).

The first difficulty was resolved by noting that if the drunkenness had been extreme and the need to travel trivial, even Asquith J. would not have objected to upholding the defence, and the second by distinguishing "special relationships" from cases of negligence *simpliciter*. Another problem was whether the plaintiff was not himself so drunk as to be unable to appreciate the risks of the flight. It was held that he knew what he was doing, and that his claim must be dismissed in its entirety.

2. One might suppose that if the defence of *volenti* ever operated in the non-participatory area, it would apply to a person who deliberately tried to kill himself. Lloyd L.J. was inclined so to hold in *Kirkham v Chief Constable* [1990] 3 All E.R. 246, where the police failed to notify the remand centre that the prisoner they were transferring was a suicide risk who required special supervision, but he held that Kirkham was not *volens* because, though not legally insane, he was clinically depressed and of diminished responsibility. Farquharson L.J. gave as a further reason that "the defence is inappropriate where the act of the deceased relied on is the very act which the duty cast on the defendant required him to prevent." This was the reason for the unsatisfactory decision in *Reeves* (above, p.242), where the defendant conceded that it was in breach of its duty to try to prevent the sane prisoner's suicide.

3. A convict called Dillon who deliberately set his cell on fire in a Scottish prison sued the authorities for his burns on the ground that their response to his companions' cries for help was unduly dilatory. His claim failed. Of course prisoners enjoy suing—a day in court is better than another day in the cell—but why was legal aid made available in such a case? Glen Hewson, another prisoner, collected £35,568 for injuries sustained when stones thrown by warders dislodged him from the 22–foot perimeter wire he had climbed in an attempt to break out. (See [1989] New L.J. 1104.) If *volenti* did not apply, why not contributory negligence?

4. A naval airman serving at a Navy posting in northern Norway drank himself into a stupor and suffocated in his own vomit after his mates had taken him to his cabin and put him in his bunk. The trial judge held that the Ministry of Defence should have controlled the amount of drinking on the base and reduced damages by 25 per cent. The Court of Appeal held that the defendant was not liable for allowing the deceased to drink too much: "To dilute self-responsibility and to blame one adult for another's lack of self-control is neither just nor reasonable and in the development of the law of negligence an increment too far." (*Barrett v Ministry of Defence* [1995] 3 All E.R. 87 at 95). It accepted, however, that his mates had failed to look after him properly once he had collapsed, and upheld judgment subject to a reduction of two-thirds.

5. Philip Morley, aged 24, went drinking with his fiancee and friends. After he had had six pints they decided to change pubs. She drove the Ford Escort. He left the car to answer a call of nature and was to rejoin the car on the other side of the tracks. As he approached it she started to drive off slowly. He climbed on the rear bumper. She then accelerated slightly, still in first gear, and adopted a zig-zag course on the empty road. He fell off and died of his injuries. His estate now claims on a personal accident policy excluding liability where death or injury resulted "directly or indirectly from . . . wilful exposure to needless peril . . . ". The Court, reversing the trial judge, made the insurer pay, refusing to characterise "his impulsive response to a practical joke . . . as wilful exposure to needless peril. In quality and degree his actions fell short of deliberate risk taking or recklessness of injury of which he was mindful." *Morley v United Friendly Ins.* [1993] 3 All E.R. 47 at 55. Receipt of the insurance money would have no effect on a claim against the fiancee under the Fatal Accidents Act. Would it be sensible to bring such a claim?

6. Legislators admit the existence of the defence. The Occupiers' Liability Act 1957, s.2(5) reads: "The common duty of care does not impose on an occupier any obligation to a visitor in respect of risks willingly accepted as his by the visitor (the question whether a risk was so accepted to be decided on the same principles as in other cases in which one person owes a duty of care to another)." The same is true of the 1984 Act, in relation to trespassers. It was this defence that barred the claim of the drunk student who broke into a swimming pool at night and got badly hurt by diving in at the shallow end: *Ratcliff v McConnell* [1999] 1 W.L.R. 670, CA: "The plaintiff was aware of the risk and willingly accepted it. Accordingly the defendants were under no duty towards him." The defence was also upheld at first instance in *Scott and Swainger v Associated British Ports*, where two adolescent glue-sniffers were injured while "surfing" on the defendant's trains, but the Court of Appeal on November 22, 2000 preferred to hold that the defendant was not in causative breach of duty, since no reasonable fence would have deterred the claimants. Simon Brown L.J. said, however, that he "would recognise that on certain facts a comparable duty would be owed by occupiers to trespassers who they know are consciously imperilling themselves on their land to that owed by police or prison officers to those known to be of suicidal tendency in their care."—He referred to *Reeves* [above p.242]; *Tomlinson* [above p.149] where admittedly the claimant could not be said to have taken a deliberate risk still lay in the future.

Acceptance of risk is also a specific defence to a claim under the Control of Pollution Act 1974, s.88. Note, however, that the Road Traffic Act 1988, s.149(3), provides that "the fact that a person so carried [*i.e.* carried in a vehicle whose use is such that a policy of insurance is required] has willingly accepted as his the risk of negligence on the part of the user shall not be treated as negativing any such liability of the user." This section reverses the effect of such decisions as *Birch v Thomas* [1972] 1 W.L.R. 294, CA, which will, however, remain useful to repel claims by pillion passengers on toboggans and by waterskiers against the motorman.

7. No statute was involved when a 17 year old arrested for a drunken brawl kicked his way out of the police van and jumped out when it was travelling at 25 m.p.h.: "Even a child would know what risk he was taking" and "In so far as his appreciation was lessened by his intake of alcohol, that was also his fault." *Sacco v Chief Constable* May 15, 1998, much discussed in *Vellino* [below, p.256].

8. In his *Last Journal*, Captain Scott wrote: "I do not regret this journey; we took risks, we knew we took them, things have come out against us, therefore we have no cause for complaint."

Question

A's dog and B's dog are fighting on the highway. C intervenes to separate them and is bitten by A's dog. *Volenti non fit injuria*? Is it different if they are fighting in C's garden? Is it different if B intervenes and is bitten by A's dog?

Section 3.—Agreement and Notice

UNFAIR CONTRACT TERMS ACT 1977

1.—(1) For the purposes of this Part of the Act, "negligence" means the breach—

(a) of any obligation, arising from the express or implied terms of a contract, to take reasonable care or exercise reasonable skill in the performance of the contract;
(b) of any common law duty to take reasonable care or exercise reasonable skill (but not any stricter duty);
(c) of the common duty of care imposed by the Occupiers' Liability Act 1957 or the Occupiers' Liability Act (Northern Ireland) 1957

. . .

(3) In the case of both contract and tort, sections 2 to 7 apply (except where the contrary is stated in section 6(4)) only to business liability, that is liability for breach of obligations or duties arising—

(a) from things done or to be done by a person in the course of a business (whether his own business or another's); or
(b) from the occupation of premises used for business purposes of the occupier;

and references to liability are to be read accordingly, but liability of an occupier of premises for breach of an obligation or duty towards a person obtaining access to the premises for recreational or educational purposes, being liability for loss or damage suffered by reason of the dangerous state of the premises, is not a business liability of the occupier unless granting that person such access for the purposes concerned falls within the business purposes of the occupier.

(4) In relation to any breach of duty or obligation, it is immaterial for any purpose of this Part of this Act whether the breach was inadvertent or intentional, or whether liability for it arises directly or vicariously.

2.—(1) A person cannot by reference to any contract term or to a notice given to persons generally or to particular persons exclude or restrict his liability for death or personal injury resulting from negligence.

(2) In the case of other loss or damage, a person cannot so exclude or restrict his liability for negligence except insofar as the term or notice satisfies the requirement of reasonableness.

(3) Where a contract term or notice purports to exclude or restrict liability for negligence a person's agreement to or awareness of it is not of itself to be taken as indicating his voluntary acceptance of any risk.

11. . . .

(3) In relation to a notice (not being a notice having contractual effect), the requirement of reasonableness under this Act is that it should be fair and reasonable to allow reliance on it, having regard to all the circumstances obtaining when the liability arose or (but for the notice) would have arisen.

(4) Where by reference to a contract term or notice a person seeks to restrict liability to a specified sum of money, and the question arises (under this or any other Act) whether the term or notice satisfies the requirement of reasonableness, regard shall be had in particular (but without prejudice to subsection (2) above in the case of contract terms) to—

    (a) The resources which he could expect to be available to him for the purpose of meeting the liability should it arise; and

    (b) how far it was open to him to cover himself by insurance.

(5) It is for those claiming that a contract term or notice satisfies the requirement of reasonableness to show that it does.

13.—(1) To the extent that this Part of this Act prevents the exclusion or restriction of any liability it also prevents—

    (a) making the liability or its enforcement subject to restrictive or onerous conditions;

    (b) excluding or restricting any right or remedy in respect of the liability, or subjecting a person to any prejudice in consequence of his pursuing any such right or remedy;

    (c) excluding or restricting rules of evidence or procedure;

and (to that extent) sections 2 and 5 to 7 also prevent excluding or restricting liability by reference to terms and notices which exclude or restrict the relevant obligation or duty.

14. In this Part of this Act—

"business" includes a profession and the activities of any government department or local or public authority;

. . .

"negligence" has the meaning given by section 1(1);

"notice" includes an announcement, whether or not in writing, and any other communication or pretended communication;

. . .

Notes:

1. The value-judgments of the draftsmen of the Act are clear enough: (i) personal injury is more serious than property damage (even a reasonable exclusion of liability for causing personal injury by negligence is void); (ii) conduct is particularly objectionable if it is careless (strict liability for even personal injury may be excluded, though not vicarious liability for negligence causing it); (iii) businesses are subject to greater liability than persons in private life.

2. The classic instance of the defence which this Act so severely restricts arises where a person is allowed to take a short cut across the land of another on the published terms that he is to have no claim against the occupier even if he is negligently injured. The Court of Appeal upheld this defence in *Ashdown v Williams* [1957] 1 Q.B. 409, and the legislator endorsed the decision in the Occupiers' Liability Act 1957, s.2(1). However, this extremely paternalistic Unfair Contract Terms Act originally invalidated any notice whereby the business occupier of premises (such as the farmer) purported to exempt himself from liability for personal injury suffered by a visitor, so farmers and others, quite happy to have people crossing their land provided they didn't sue, refused to let people cross their land at all. So in 1984 the legislator had to add the final words to s.1(3) above, though he cannot have needed to add them so cumbrously, and should have forestalled the need to add them at all. After all, people will not be generous if they get punished for trying to be helpful. Traffic victims in the United States used to sue the doctors who stopped to give them first aid—biting the hand that fed them—so the States rightly enacted "Good Samaritan" statutes to encourage doctors to be socially useful by rendering them legally immune.

3. Section 2(1) of this Act rendered arguable the claim by a junior hospital doctor that his employer could not lawfully put his health at risk by requiring him to do all the overtime he had contracted to be ready to do: *Johnstone v Bloomsbury H.A.* [1991] 2 All E.R. 293, CA. The employer of course owes a duty to the employee not unreasonably to endanger him, and the overtime clause might constitute a restriction of that duty; if so, it would be automatically invalid, even if otherwise reasonable, since damage to health was in issue. But why was the doctor not *volens* as to any injury to his health which might result from his continuing in employment under those terms? Would one not be *volens* if one continued to reside in a house one knew to be unsafe?

4. In *Smith v Eric S. Bush* [1989] 2 All E.R. 514, the House of Lords held that the Act applied to a disclaimer accompanying a valuer's report which misrepresented the condition of a dwelling, the Court of Appeal having held otherwise on the ground that, as in *Hedley Byrne* (above, p.57), the disclaimer prevented the duty from arising and did not simply purport to neutralise the effects of its breach. According to Lord Templeman: " . . . the 1977 Act requires that all exclusion notices which would in common law provide a defence to an action for negligence must satisfy the requirement of reasonableness."

5. Liability in tort may nevertheless be denied on the ground that a duty of care would be incompatible with a provision in a contract, even one to which the defendant is not a party. In the main contract for the reconstruction of a swimming-pool complex the plaintiff accepted the risk of fire, and the sub-contracts referred to this fact. The Court of Appeal held that neither the sub-contractor nor its employee who carelessly set the building alight were under any duty of care to the site-owner: *Norwich C.C. v Harvey* [1989] 1 All E.R. 1180. Although much may depend on the precise terms of the contract (see *British Telecommunications v James Thomson & Sons* [1999] 2 All E.R. 241, HL), remember that in *The Nicholas H* (above, p.45) the existence of contractual relations between the plaintiff and a third party may be a factor leading to the denial of a duty to take care, even in respect of physical harm to property.

Section 4.—Illegality

VELLINO v CHIEF CONSTABLE OF GREATER MANCHESTER

Court of Appeal [2001] EWCA Civ 1249; [2002] 3 All E.R. 78; [2002] 1 W.L.R. 218

The claimant was badly injured when he threw himself out of the window of his second-floor flat immediately after he was arrested yet again by the police, who knew of his propensity for self-defenestration and stood back while he indulged it.

Schiemann L.J.: The issue in this case is whether the police owe to an arrested person a duty to take care that he is not injured in a foreseeable attempt by him to escape from police custody. Elias J. concluded that the police owed no such duty. He found against the claimant on liability and the claimant appeals to this court . . . The judge held that it was foreseeable that the claimant would suffer physical injury in the circumstances of the present case and that the police knew that the claimant had a tendency to jump from a window in a manner which inevitably risked serious injury.

The judge said this in relation to the legal issues:

"Analytically there are two different questions, was there a duty of care and, if so, is the defendant prevented from recovering damages by the application of the principle ex turpi causa non oritur actio. In fact, however, in my judgment the two questions interrelate, but I will begin by considering them independently. There is no doubt that the police owe a duty of care to an arrested person. They must take reasonable care to ensure that he does not suffer physical injury as a consequence of their own acts, such as if they are driving carelessly, or the acts of a third party, but the question here is whether they owed any duty to protect him from himself, in circumstances where the conduct of the claimant involves the commission of a criminal offence at common law, *i.e.* whether they must take reasonable care to ensure he does not injure himself, as a consequence of his own deliberate decision to escape from custody."

It is common ground that under our law two persons can stand aside and watch a third jump to his death: there is no legal duty to rescue. Not all legal systems adopt that as their approach but for better or for worse that is the established position in English law. It is common ground that, prior to uttering the words "I arrest you", the police owed him no duty to prevent him hurting himself while trying to escape.

To suggest that the police owe a criminal the duty to prevent the criminal from escaping, and that the criminal who hurts himself while escaping can sue the police for the breach of that duty, seems to me self-evidently absurd. No policy reason has been suggested for the law adopting such a course. Mr Stockdale expressly disavowed this way of putting his case [but] I understood him to submit that the police are under a duty owed to the claimant to prevent him from sustaining foreseeable injury whilst foreseeably attempting to escape from custody. This with respect seems to me equally untenable: it would require the police to hold him in the loosest of grasps so that there was no danger of him wrenching his shoulder as he struggled to break free. Again no policy reason has been suggested for declaring this to be the law.

Moreover, even this formulation does not cover the present case. The claimant injured himself after he had escaped from custody, if by that one means containment by the police in some physical sense rather some jurisprudential concept.

The difficulties which Mr Stockdale had in formulating the duty of care would only be intensified if his concepts were expressed in terms of the criminal's rights. In contexts such as this the police duties to the criminal give rise to correlative rights in the criminal. It would be difficult without making oneself sound foolish to formulate a right in the criminal against the police not to be exposed to danger whilst escaping . . . Similarly in the context of prisoners there is in my judgment no right in a prisoner who hurts himself while leaping from a high boundary wall to be compensated on the basis that it is foreseeable that prisoners will try and escape and that if they leap off high walls they may well hurt themselves.

At the conclusion of the argument I was of the view that the appeal must fail essentially for the reasons given by the judge. He pointed out that there is an overlap between the considerations which go to the question "is there a duty?" and those which attend the defence of ex turpi causa. I agree. He based his decision on absence of duty rather than on that defence. So would I.

In the present circumstances I do not find it unjust to deny the claimant a right to damages. As I observed in *Sacco*'s case:

"Whether one expresses the refusal of a remedy as being based on absence of causation, absence of duty in these circumstances, absence of a breach of a wider duty, or as being based upon the application of a wider principle that a plaintiff as a matter of policy is denied recovery on tort when his own wrongdoing is so much part of the claim that it can not be overlooked, or because the plaintiff had voluntarily assumed the risk of it, is perhaps a matter of jurisprudential predilection on the part of the judge."

Like Elias J. I would find that in the present case that the officers did not owe the claimant any duty to bar his progress through the window.

I would therefore dismiss this appeal.

Sedley L.J. (dissenting): It is well settled that the court will refuse its aid to a claimant who, for example, sues on a contract tainted by fraud, at least where the defendant too was implicated in the fraud. Here it is readily apparent that if it were to adjudicate the court would be compounding the litigants' misconduct and permitting one of them to profit by his own wrongdoing. Where the dishonesty is unilateral, it is in general only the dishonest party who will be prevented from suing, and for a similar reason. Applied to tort actions, the principle has been recently applied in undiluted and undifferentiated form in the recent decisions of this court in *Pitts v Hunt* [1991] 1 Q.B. 24 and *Sacco v Chief Constable of South Wales Constabulary* [1998] CA Transcript 1382. *Sacco*'s case concerned a claimant who had jumped from a moving police van in which he was being conveyed in custody to the police station, and who accordingly lost his claim: Beldam L.J., who had also given the principal judgment in the former case, cited the rule in its early form as stated by Lord Mansfield C.J. in *Holman v Johnson* (1775) 1 Cowp 341 at 342: "No court will lend its aid to a man who founds his cause of action upon an immoral or illegal act."

... In most cases the doctrine of voluntary acceptance of risk will prevent a criminal from suing a fellow offender for, say, injuries negligently inflicted on him in the course of a robbery. But it cannot cover the case of a criminal who is wantonly shot, whether by armed police or by a fellow criminal, albeit while committing a crime. And suppose for a moment that the facts in *Sacco*'s case had been that the van had set off with the rear doors open and the drunk claimant seated by them without a firm police hold on him. There is no obvious reason why there should not have been a breach of the duty of care owed to him whether he fell out or jumped out, since in his drunken state either will have been foreseeable. A large share of the blame would have rested on him, drunk or not, if he had jumped, but little or none if he had fallen out. Given the ability of the law for over half a century to apportion blame, I see little substantial justice in such circumstances in sacrificing a judicial apportionment of responsibility on the altar of a doctrinaire refusal to adjudicate. There is no residual or underlying injustice in apportionment: indeed where it is the claimant who has effectively put the defendant in breach of duty, his contributory fault may extinguish his claim entirely.

The approach I have described was taken by the majority of the Court of Appeal (Evans and Millett L.JJ.) in *Revill v Newbery* [1996] Q.B. 567, in which an award of damages to a burglar who was shot by the occupier was upheld. Evans L.J. considered that to deny the claimant compensation for an assault which went beyond self-defence was a different thing from denying him the fruits of his crime and was akin to outlawing him. Millett L.J. took the view that in such a case there was simply no room for the turpitude doctrine. It was only Neill L.J. who, albeit concurring in the result, based himself on the Occupiers Liability Act 1984; but he too started from a common law position which excluded the turpitude doctrine. It is a common law case, and one which seems to me difficult to reconcile with the reasoning of the majority in *Pitts v Hunt*, the progenitor of *Sacco*'s case.

Equally significantly, in the field of what one can call ordinary personal injury litigation, the turpitude doctrine has been consciously eliminated by the courts on policy grounds. In road accident cases, for example, it is common enough to find that the injured claimant has contributed to the accident by speeding or driving with faulty brakes; but I know of no decision that such a claimant cannot sue another driver who has negligently caused his injuries. Nor can I see any justice in so deciding when the criminal law is there to deal with his criminality and the power to apportion damages will deal with his own contribution to his injuries ...

... The authorities are in my view not reconcilable: in their present state, as the Law Commission says, "it is difficult to predict an outcome or to explain the outcome in terms of the apparent rationale of the illegality defence". It is clear that since the passage of the 1945 Act the power to apportion liability between claimant and defendant in tort actions of all kinds has afforded a far more appropriate tool for doing justice than the blunt instrument of turpitude. In many cases, classically where both parties have been involved in a single criminal enterprise, the outcome would be the same. But the present case is unusual in that the offences committed by claimant and defendant, while causally connected, were not joint. The claimant's offence was able to be committed only because the constables' had been committed first. [It is not] the same situation as in *Sacco*'s case, where the sole causative act was the claimant's own. Albeit escape cases are a long way from the suicide cases, the logic of the law cannot properly differ. I consider that arresting officers owe a prisoner a duty not to afford both a temptation to escape and an opportunity of doing so when there is a known risk that the prisoner will do himself real harm, even if much of the blame for hurting himself will ultimately come to rest on the prisoner himself. That duty was breached in this case, and I do not believe that a legal system which shuts its eyes to such things is doing justice, especially-but not only-where the officers' neglect is also a crime. To deny the claimant redress in such a situation because of his own offending is both to make him an outlaw and to reward the misconduct of his captors.[!!!] To apportion responsibility, as Elias J. would have done had he not considered his path to be blocked by doctrine, is in my view to do justice.

While I respectfully accept that the exegesis of the present state of the law set out in the concluding passage of Sir Murray Stuart-Smith's judgment is the nearest one can come to a consistent account of it, for the reasons I have given I do not think that the authorities are consistent or, therefore, that it is an analysis that we are bound to adopt.

Sir Murray Stuart-Smith: I agree that this appeal should be dismissed for the reasons given by Schiemann L.J. I will also state my own reasons since we are not all in agreement. It is common ground that if the facts are such that the maxim ex turpi causa non oritur actio is applicable, it does not matter whether the correct legal analysis is that the defendants owed no duty of care, because the third limb of the test in *Caparo Industries plc v Dickman* [1990] 2 A.C. 605, namely that it is just fair and reasonable to impose a duty of care, is not satisfied, or that the maxim affords a free standing reason for holding that the cause of action does not arise or cannot be pursued. The question in this appeal therefore is whether the judge was correct in holding that the maxim did apply.

There are many statements of the principle to be found in the reports. In *Pitts v Hunt* [1991] 1 Q.B. 24 at 41 Beldam L.J. said, after reviewing the authorities:

"I have quoted . . . the considerations which have led courts to refuse on grounds of public policy to permit a person to enforce a claim to indemnity for they illustrate to my mind how the courts have adjusted the application of the maxim to changing social conditions . . . They establish, I believe, that it is the conduct of the person seeking to base his claim on an unlawful act which is determinative of the application of the maxim."

In *Sacco*, where the claimant sustained injury when he escaped from police custody by jumping from the police van, Beldam L.J. said:

"Finally, I would reject the submission that the decision in *Reeves v Metropolitan Police Comr* [2000] 1 A.C. 360 renders the judge's conclusion on public policy untenable. The actions of the deceased in that case were not unlawful, nor were they criminal. In *Scott v Brown Dearing McNab & Co* [1892] 2 Q.B. 724 at 728, [1891–4] All E.R. Rep 654 at 657, Lindley L.J. said of the maxim ex turpi causa non oritur actio: 'This old and well-known legal maxim is founded in good sense, and expresses a clear and well-recognised legal principle, which is not confined to indictable offences.' The rule was stated by Lord Mansfield C.J. in Holman v Johnson (1775) 1 Cowp 341 at 342, to be a rule of public policy that: 'No court will lend its aid to a man who founds his cause of action upon an immoral or illegal act.' There are many other statements to the same effect."

And Schiemann L.J., giving the second of three grounds upon which the claim failed, said:

"Second, he was engaged in a criminal act, namely attempting to escape from lawful custody. As a matter of legal policy, I see no reason to permit a man to recover damages against the police if he hurts himself as part of that illegal enterprise. The basis of such recovery must be either an allegation of a breach of a duty owed to him not to let him escape, or of a duty owed to him to take care that he does not hurt himself if he tries to escape. I see no reason to create such duties owed to him. It is common ground that the policy of the law is not to permit one criminal to recover damages from a fellow criminal who fails to take care of him whilst they are both engaged on a criminal enterprise. The reason for that rule is not the law's tenderness towards the criminal defendant, but the law's unwillingness to afford a criminal plaintiff a remedy in such circumstances. I see no reason why that unwillingness should be any the less because the defendant is a policeman and not engaged in any crime."

In *Cross v Kirkby* [2000] Times L.R. 268 Judge L.J. said: "In my judgment, where the claimant is behaving unlawfully, or criminally, on the occasion when his cause of action in tort arises, his claim is not liable to be defeated ex turpi causa unless it is also established that the facts which give rise to it are inextricably linked with his criminal conduct. I have deliberately expressed myself in language which goes well beyond questions of causation in the general sense."

In the *National Coal Board* case [1954] A.C. 546 their Lordships may have doubted whether the maxim ex turpi causa had any application in tort. Many decisions of this court since hold that it does.

From these authorities I derive the following propositions. (1) The operation of the principle arises where the claimant's claim is founded upon his own criminal or immoral act. The facts which give rise to the claim must be inextricably linked with the criminal activity. It is not sufficient if the criminal activity merely gives occasion for tortious conduct of the defendant. (2) The principle is one of public policy; it is not for the benefit of the defendant. Since if the principle applies, the cause of action does not arise, the defendant's conduct is irrelevant. There is no question of proportionality between the conduct of the claimant and defendant. (3) In the case of criminal conduct this has to be sufficiently serious to merit the application of the principle. Generally speaking a crime punishable with imprisonment could be expected to qualify. If the offence is criminal, but relatively trivial, it is in any event difficult to see how it could be integral to the claim. (4) The 1945 Act is not applicable where the claimant's action amounts to a common law crime which does not give rise to liability in tort.

Applying these principles it is common ground that the claimant has to rely on his criminal conduct in escaping lawful custody to found his claim. It is integral to the claim. The crime of escape is a serious one; it is a common law offence for which the penalty is at large. It is almost invariably punished by a sentence of imprisonment, although the length of the sentence is usually measured in months rather than years. In my judgment it is plainly a sufficiently serious offence for the purpose of the application of the maxim. I would have reached this conclusion in any event; but it accords with the judgments of the Court of Appeal in *Sacco*'s case.
[The Appeal Committee of the House of Lords refused permission to appeal]

Observation

A claim may be affected by the claimant's consent, his fecklessness of his wickedness. The parameters of these defences are not very neatly drawn. They often overlap. In cases where there is no overlap, *e.g.* where it was reasonable of the claimant to take a risk of harm or where the illegal activity was not dangerous, the courts are very cautious. There was a major overlap in *Pitts v Hunt* [1991] 1 Q.B. 24: Andrew Pitts, 18 years old, and Mark Hunt, two years younger, were on their way back from a club where they had drunk far too much, Pitts riding pillion on a 250 cc Suzuki driven by Hunt, unlicensed and uninsured but not inexperienced. With Pitts's vocal and active encouragement Hunt drove in a "reckless, irresponsible and idiotic" manner, weaving from side to side of the road at 50 mph, slaloming across the white lines and deliberately frightening the odd pedestrian by these antics. They were on the wrong side of the road as the second defendant's car approached them; he veered to the offside in order to avoid them, but when both parties sought to regain their proper side there was a collision in which Hunt was killed and Pitts seriously injured.

The defence of *volenti* was unavailable by reason of Road Traffic Act 1972, s.148(3), but the court applied the *ex turpi causa* doctrine and dismissed Pitts's claim.

Questions

1. Some courts have asked if in cases like these the defendant owed the claimant a duty and if so, what was its content. But surely the essence of the matter is that the claim is being dismissed because of the claimant's conduct or misconduct (as the espoused application of the Contributory Negligence Act demonstrates)? As to the level of duty, if one is blowing a safe in order to get at its contents, does the care to be

taken depend on whether one is acting pursuant to or contrary to the wishes of the owner? Can a burglar sensibly say that his fellow-burglar mishandled the Semtex? How much care did Hunt have to show to (a) the passenger, (b) oncoming drivers? Note that the Motor Insurers' Bureau rejects the claim of a passenger against the owner or driver of a vehicle he knew or must have known to be uninsured or stolen (*White v White* [2001] 2 All E.R. 43 (HL)). Does this reflect the defence of contributory negligence, or consent or illegality? Given this rule, why was Pitts advised to sue?

2. A doctor negligently fails to notice that a child *in utero* will be sadly handicapped, but the pregnancy is already so far advanced that abortion would be criminal (*Rance v Mid-Downs H.A.* [1991] 1 All E.R. 801.) What doctrine justifies the holding that the doctor is not answerable for the extra cost of maintaining the handicapped child?

Notes:

1. Earlier in the book we saw that unlawful as well as unreasonable behaviour might render a *defendant* liable, though often it does not. Unreasonable conduct on the part of the *plaintiff* may reduce or extinguish his claim, as we have already seen in this chapter. What if his conduct is unlawful?

Judges are naturally unwilling to award damages to plaintiffs they think should be in the dock. Bad people get less. This is reflected in the Latin tag *ex turpi causa non oritur actio*. As Diplock L.J. said in *Hardy v MIB* [1964] 2 All E.R. 742 at 750, it is concerned:

> "generally with the enforcement of rights by the courts, whether or not such rights arise under contract. All that the rule means is that the courts will not enforce a right which would otherwise be enforceable if the right arises out of an act committed by the person asserting the right . . . which is regarded by the court as sufficiently anti-social to justify the court's refusing to enforce that right."

Although it is of general application throughout the law, it has different effects in the different branches of the law of obligations. In contract, for example, if we agree that I shall kill your mother-in-law for £500 and I do kill her, I cannot claim the £500—judges will not reward a person for doing wrong: and if I change my mind, you cannot sue me for non-performance—the judges will not make a person pay for not doing wrong. These principles are so strong in contract law that they apply even if the illegality is quite technical and the parties morally innocent. In restitution the principle operates less fiercely. It is true that if I decide not to murder your mother-in-law, I can keep any down-payment you made me, not because I have earned it (since I have not), but because you will be disentitled from reclaiming it; here the normal right to reclaim is lost only if the claimant is tainted with turpitude. In *Tinsley v Milligan* [1993] 3 All E.R. 65 the House of Lords decided by a bare majority that transactional turpitude does not prevent the assertion of rights in property being reclaimed; even odder was their unanimity in discountenancing the "public conscience" test partly relied on by Beldam L.J. in *Pitts* and regularly utilised by the courts of Germany in applying § 826 BGB.

2. In tort cases the wickedness of the plaintiff plays a slighter role, because the interests traditionally in issue are basic—liberty, life and limb, property. Of course the liberty of criminals is at risk, since they are subject to arrest and imprisonment, but they are no longer hanged or beaten, even if their property may be confiscated (Proceeds of Crime Act 2002). So if I run someone over in the street, it can hardly be relevant that he was on his way to or from a robbery (unless in the former case he was claiming for lost swag or in the latter for damage to his booty). Convicted criminals have sometimes attempted to claim damages for the fact of their imprisonment: if Meah the rapist succeeded against his driver, it was only because of the way the defendant pleaded his case (see above, p.238), while the claim of Clunis against the health authority which left him uncontrolled and at liberty to kill a total stranger in a Tube station was unsuccessful, though he was of diminished responsibility (*Clunis v Camden & Islington H.A.* [1998] 3 All E.R. 180, CA—"We do not consider that the public policy that the court will not lend its aid to a litigant who relies on his own criminal or immoral act is confined to particular causes of action").

3. Recent years have seen a revival of the defence, whether because of a growing moralism in the courts or because of the restriction of other defences or because tort law now protects merely financial interests (the investor in a dodgy business?). Thus in *Burns v Edman* [1970] 2 Q.B. 541 a criminal had been killed in a motor accident for which the defendant was principally responsible. Not only was the claim for loss of life (then possible) reduced because the criminal's lot, like the policeman's, is not a happy one, but his widow and children were not allowed to claim for the loss of their share of the proceeds of his prevented crimes. Again, it has been held that a person running an illicit business cannot claim damages from a tortfeasor who interferes with it (*Columbia Pictures Indus. v Robinson* [1985] 3 All E.R. 338 at 379) and that if the proceeds of a cheque represent the fruits of a fraud in which he was implicated the payee whose endorsement has been forged cannot sue the bank which negligently cashes it and credits a third party (*Thackwell v Barclays Bank* [1986] 1 All E.R. 676). This last decision has been overruled by the Court of Appeal in *Webb v Chief*

Constable [2000] 1 All E.R. 209, in which the court ordered the police to return to the donee money representing the proceeds of the donor's drug-dealing—a shocking result apparently mandated by *Tinsley v Milligan*!

4. The defence may, however, be carried too far. Consider *Ashmore, Benson, Pease & Co v AV Dawson* [1973] 2 All E.R. 856, where the Court of Appeal dismissed a claim in respect of damage negligently caused to the plaintiffs' property while it was being carried by the defendants on a vehicle which, as the plaintiffs knew, was illegally and dangerously inadequate for the load. Lord Denning said: " . . . the question is whether the illegality prevents Ashmores from suing for that negligence. This depends on whether the contract itself was unlawful, or its performance was unlawful." But suppose a doctor agrees to perform an illegal abortion and carelessly injures the patient. Surely the patient would not be debarred from suing just because she knew the operation was unlawful?

5.—Immunity

Rules have exceptions, and it is nearly a rule that those who behave negligently are liable for the foreseeable harm they cause. One can therefore expect the odd exception. Sometimes such exceptions lurk under the holding "no duty"; sometimes, however, an exception for a class of person or for persons engaged on a specified activity is described as an "immunity". Thus until 1947 the Crown had immunity in all kinds of tort. However, in singling out a small group as exceptional, "immunity" may seem like "privilege" and be regarded as politically incorrect.

In 1988 the House of Lords held that the police could not be sued for negligence in their role as investigators of crime. The word "immunity" used in this connection ran into difficulties in Strasbourg (*Osman v United Kingdom* [1999] 1 F.L.R. 193) and though the view in that case that such an immunity infringed the right to a fair trial has been modified (*Z v United Kingdom* [2001] 2 F.L.R. 612) the "blanket" immunity of the police has gone.

In 1967 the House of Lords famously laid down in *Rondel v Worsley* [1969] 1 A.C. 191 that as regards his conduct in court a barrister could not be sued in negligence—that he was immune from suit—even if his gross incompetence or intoxication led to his client's loss of liberty. The immunity extended to acts of lawyers preparatory to the proceedings in courts, provided they were intimately connected with it (*Saif Ali v Sidney Mitchell & Co* [1980] A.C. 198), but to celebrate the new century the immunity was wholly removed (*Arthur J.S. Hall v Simons* [2000] 3 All E.R. 673).

But some immunities do remain, in particular the immunity of witnesses. As Lord Hobhouse put it in *Hall v Simons*:

> "It is illuminating to consider the conceptual basis in the trial process for the witness immunity. It is that the witness, although called by a party, is giving evidence to the court. The witness's duty is to tell the truth to the court regardless of the interests of the party who has called him or is asking him questions. The same scheme is spelled out in the new CPR regarding expert witnesses. An expert witness is in a special position similar to that of the advocate. He is selected and paid by the party instructing him. Part of his duties include advising the party instructing him. If that advice is negligently given the expert, like the lawyer, is liable. But once the expert becomes engaged on providing expert evidence for use in court (CPR 35.2; *Stanton v Callaghan* [2000] 1 Q.B. 75) his relationship to the court becomes paramount . . . and he enjoys the civil immunity attributable to that function."

When counsel urged that the immunity of the advocate was analogous to that of the witness and should therefore be retained, Lord Hoffmann said this: "A witness owes no duty of care to anyone in respect of the evidence he gives to the court. His only duty is to tell the truth. There seems to me no analogy with the position of a lawyer who owes a duty of care to his client. Nor is there in my opinion any analogy with the position of the judge. The judge owes no duty of care to either of the parties. He has only a public duty to administer justice in accordance with his oath. The fact that the advocate is the only person involved in the trial process who is liable to be sued for negligence is because he is the only person who has undertaken a duty of care to his client."

The following case shows the use of the concept in a case where there would normally be liability for negligence. One should also read *Taylor v Serious Fraud Office* below, p.540, which is in the chapter on defamation because liability in that tort is in principle so strict that the occasional immunity or "privilege" is inevitable, whether in the absolute form which bars suits even for malice or more frequently in the qualified form such that the privilege is lost if abused.

STANTON v CALLAGHAN

Court of Appeal [2000] Q.B. 75; [1999] 2 W.L.R. 745; [1998] 4 All E.R. 961

Claim by intending litigant against his expert witness for negligently weakening his evidence

When the partial underpinning undertaken to cure the subsidence of the plaintiff's house failed to work he retained the defendant, a civil and structural engineer, to advise. The defendant reported that total underpinning was now required. When his insurers declined to pay for this work, the plaintiff issued proceedings against them. About a month before the trial was due, the defendant met with the insurers' expert, as requested by the plaintiff, and they produced a joint statement proposing an alternative remedy at a third of the cost. Because of this the insurers paid a smallish sum into court and the plaintiff felt bound to accept it. In the event he was unable to sell his house for what it would have fetched if totally underpinned, and now sued the defendant for negligently advising that the cheaper remedy would work. The defendant's application to strike out the claim on the ground of witness immunity was rejected below, but granted by the Court of Appeal.

Chadwick L.J.: . . . There is, if I may say so, no difficulty in recognising the need for immunity in relation to the investigation and preparation of evidence in criminal proceedings, or in child abuse cases, in order to ensure that potential witnesses are not deterred from coming forward. For my part, however, I find it much more difficult to recognise an immunity founded on the need to ensure that witnesses are not deterred from giving evidence by the possibility of vexatious suits in a case where the witness is a professional man who has agreed, for reward, to give evidence in support of his opinion on matters within his own expertise; *a fortiori*, where the immunity is relied upon to protect the witness from suit by his own client, towards whom, prima facie, he owes contractual duties to be careful in relation to the advice which he gives.

It is important to keep in mind that expert witnesses have the safeguard, in common with other professional men, that they will not be held liable for negligent advice unless that advice is such as no reasonable professional, competent in the field and acting reasonably, could give. I find it difficult to believe that the pool of those who hold themselves out as ready to act as expert witnesses in civil cases, on terms as to remuneration which they must find acceptable, would dry up if expert witnesses could be held liable to those by whom they are instructed for failing to take proper care in reaching the opinions which they advance. Indeed, I would find it a matter of some surprise if expert witnesses offer their services at present on the basis that they cannot be held liable if their advice is negligent.

It is important, also, to keep in mind that immunity from suit, where liability would otherwise lie, constitutes an exception to the general law. The exception must be justified on some ground of public policy. The justification requires careful examination. If, as I think, immunity from suit in respect of negligent advice cannot be justified, in the case of a witness who has held himself out as ready to give expert evidence in the course of carrying on his profession, on the ground that, without protection against vexatious claims, the pool of experts willing to testify would dry up, the immunity cannot be recognised unless some more satisfactory basis for departing from the general law on the ground of public policy can be found.

What, then, is the position in relation to expert reports? It seems to me that the following propositions are supported by authority binding in this court: (i) an expert witness who gives evidence at a trial is immune from suit in respect of anything which he says in court, and that immunity will extend to the contents of the report which he adopts as, or incorporates in, his evidence; (ii) where an expert witness gives evidence at a trial the immunity which he would enjoy in respect of that evidence is not to be circumvented by a suit based on the report itself and (iii) the immunity does not extend to protect an expert who has been retained to advise as to the merits of a party's claim in litigation from a suit by the party by whom he has been retained in respect of that advice, notwithstanding that it was in contemplation at the time when the advice was given that the expert would be a witness at the trial if that litigation were to proceed. What, as it seems to me, has not been decided by any authority binding in this court is whether an expert is immune from suit by the party who has retained him in respect of the contents of a report which he prepares for the purpose of exchange prior to trial, say, to comply with directions given under Ord. 38, r. 37, in circumstances where he does not, in the event, give evidence at the trial; either because the trial does not take place or because he is not called as a witness.

If there is to be immunity in such circumstances, it must be founded on some identifiable ground of public policy. As Lord Wilberforce pointed out in *Saif Ali v Sydney Mitchell & Co (a firm)* [1978] 3 All E.R. 1033 at 1039. " . . . account must be taken of the counter policy that a wrong ought not to be without a remedy". Further, it must be recognised that the report prepared for the purposes of exchange prior to trial is likely to contain, or reflect, the initial advice as to the merits of the claim—advice which, as Bingham M.R. pointed out in *M (a minor) v. Newham London B.C.* [1994] 4 All E.R. 602 at 618, did not itself attract immunity.

In my view, the only ground of public policy that can be relied upon as a foundation for immunity in respect of the contents of an expert's report, in circumstances where no trial takes place and the expert does not give evidence, is that identified by Lord Morris of Borth-y-Gest in *Rondel v Worsley* [1967] 3 All E.R. 993 at 1014, "It has always been the policy of the law to ensure that trials are conducted without avoidable strains and tensions of alarm and fear."

The other grounds mentioned in the authorities, the need to ensure that potential witnesses are not deterred from coming forward and the need to avoid a multiplicity of actions, appear to me to have little or no relevance in the present context. The claim for immunity in a case like the present must, as it seems to me, be tested against the criteria: is the immunity necessary for the orderly management and conduct of the trial which is in prospect.

I am not persuaded that experts who, as part of their professional practice and for reward, offer their services as potential witnesses on matters within their expertise are prone to "strains and tensions of alarm and fear" at the stage at which they are preparing reports for exchange. I would not, myself, subscribe to the view that experts' reports would be any more or less helpfully drawn than they now are if the authors were or were not immune from suit by those who retain them in respect of the contents of those reports. But there does come a point at which the expert begins to take part in the management and conduct of the trial in advance of proceedings in court. . . .

It is of importance to the administration of justice, and to those members of the public who seek access to justice, that trials should take no longer than is necessary to do justice in the particular case; and that, to that end, time in court should not be taken up with a consideration of matters which are not truly in issue. It is in that context that experts are encouraged to identify, in advance of the trial, those parts of their evidence on which they are, and those on which they are not, in agreement. Provision for a joint statement, reflecting agreement after a meeting of experts has taken place, is made by Ord. 38, r.38. In my view, the public interest in facilitating full and frank discussion between experts before trial does require that each should be free to make proper concessions without fear that any departure from advice previously given to the party who has retained him will be seen as evidence of negligence. That as it seems to me, is an area in which public policy justifies immunity. The immunity is needed in order to avoid the tension between a desire to assist the court and fear of the consequences of a departure from previous advice.

In the present case the expert's report was made after, and as a result of, a meeting between the experts on each side. The report incorporated what had been agreed. On that ground, I agree with the judge's conclusion that Mr Callaghan and the other defendants are immune from suit by the plaintiffs in respect of the alleged negligence in agreeing the viability of the gap solution on December 14, 1989 and incorporating that agreement in the report delivered on December 18, 1989.

Notes:

1. Witness immunity covers the police when they give evidence in court, and to an extent when they are preparing the evidence they will give in court, but it does not extend to the planting of evidence or the fabrication of false evidence (*Darker v Chief Constable* [2001] 1 A.C. 435).

2. In *L v Reading BC* it was alleged that, during an investigation into an accusation by the claimant's wife, unsupported by evidence and later shown to be baseless, that he had abused their child, a police constable had lied to the claimant and misrepresented what he had said. The trial judge struck out the claim on the grounds of witness immunity, but the Court of Appeal reinstated it: each case where witness immunity was claimed must be determined on its own facts. [2001] EWCA Civ 346.

PART II

LIABILITY THROUGH OTHERS

INTRODUCTION

MANY of the plaintiffs we have encountered have been real people blood—after all, only real people can suffer personal injury—but very ... the defendants have been the actual individuals whose misbehaviour caused the injury. The defendants have usually been constructive non-entities, like the Britannia Hygienic Laundry Co Legal persons (that is, unnatural persons, or *moral* persons as the French rather perversely call them) enjoy all manner of legal incidents and attributes such as rights and powers and duties and liabilities, so they may be immensely significant in the metaworld of law, in which alone they have any being, but they cannot actually *do* anything in the world of perceptible fact. If you telephone a company and get an answer it will not be the company's voice that answers, for it cannot even speak: it will be its servant's voice, not his master's. We may say, if we like, that a legal person did something wrong, but we should realise that we are speaking shorthand or metaphor or nonsense, since legal persons cannot do anything whatsoever. However many vans the Britannia Hygienic Laundry Co may *own*, it cannot *drive* any of them; and though magistrates once convicted a company of driving without a permit (*Richmond B.C. v Pinn & Wheeler* (1989) 87 L.G.R. 659, DC), a company cannot knock over a single pedestrian. Physical harm can be positively caused only by physical acts of which notional creatures are incapable, but companies and corporations (especially local authorities) are very good at *not* doing things, so they can be personally caught for inaction if a duty to act is imposed, as it often is by statute (remember the Human Rights Act, and the safety regulations above p.195) and also at common law (employer, occupier, bailee). Incapable though they may be of acting, however, legal persons are perfectly capable of paying (for that is a legal act): so we can make them pay for those they pay to act for them.

Of those human beings who are lucky enough to have a job at all, a few are self-employed; the great majority, however, are employed by someone else, almost always by a legal non-entity rather than by another human being. But while the odd employer may still be human, there has never been an employee who was anything else. A company can no more be an employee than it can be a husband: dependent status is reserved for mankind. Of course you can get a company to do something for you or, more accurately, to get things done for you, through its employees or others, but you will be paying the company a fee rather than wages (the hallmark of employment), you will be a customer rather than an employer, and the company will be an independent contractor rather than your humble servant. The company's customers may well include other companies, but customers are often human beings, eagerly consuming the goods and services promised by companies and delivered by their employees or contractors.

Those being the facts, suppose that one were challenged to produce formal rules with the substantial effect that companies must pay for people but not *vice versa*. One could hardly do better than lay down that liability should attach to employers but not to customers, that one should be liable for one's permanent staff but not for any other bodies whom or which one might pay to do things or get things done—in brief, that there should be liability for employees but not for independent contractors. That is more or less the position in English law (and, indeed, in most other Western systems of law as well).

.. although in general an employer (even human) is liable for servants and a ,ustomer (even corporate) is not liable for contractors, one is not liable for everything one's servants do wrong, and one may in certain situations be liable for the misdoings of one's independent contractor.

An employer is liable for what his servant does only if the servant was acting in the course and scope of his employment at the time. Since the victim's claim is really that the defendant's business hurt him, he must establish a relationship between the servant's act and the master's business. The question will be whether the servant was just doing his job badly or not doing the job at all, doing his own thing instead. Considerations of time, place, equipment and purpose will all be relevant to this purely factual determination.

This vicarious liability of employer for employee is said to be a general principle. This is true in the sense that the victim need not set up any special relationship between himself and the employer. But it is not true that an employer is invariably liable for the torts of his employees in the course and scope of their employment. A special relationship between plaintiff and defendant may reduce or increase the defendant's liability. Thus if the defendant is the beneficiary of a valid exclusion or disclaimer clause or notice he cannot be made liable for an employee's tort. Yet recently, after holding that local authorities in the exercise of their child-care and educational functions were not personally liable either for breach of statutory duty (since the duty was not actionable in damages) nor for breach of a common law duty to take care in the exercise of their powers (since it would not be fair, just and reasonable so to interfere with their statutory discretion), the House of Lords, reversing the Court of Appeal on this very point, has held that they are vicariously liable for the negligence of the individuals they use in the performance of these functions (*Phelps v Hillingdon LBC* [2001] 2 A.C. 619). Given that the authorities cannot perform their functions at all except through individual social workers and teachers the circumvention of the principal rule, probably seen as unattractive, seems clear.

Now liability is only vicarious if it is imposed on a defendant though he himself is not in breach of any duty, but he may well be under a duty such that it can be broken by others than himself. The cases in English law where a person may be liable although his own organisation has operated flawlessly are exceptional and heterogeneous. First, a person may be subject to a statutory duty such as to make him liable if the required result is not brought about. Many health and safety regulations (above, p.195) are of such a kind. To take another instance, the property developer is liable under section 1 of the Defective Premises Act 1972 (above, p.34) if the house is badly built: it will not help him in the least to say that it was built by an independent company working under contract. So, too, the financier who has arranged for the supply of goods on credit may be liable to the consumer for the supplier's misrepresentation or breach of contract (Consumer Credit Act 1974, s.75). In each case it will be a question of construction whether the statute imposes a liability stern enough to catch the defendant when the fault lies with an independent third party.

Secondly, a contractor who has promised actual results may be liable despite his best efforts. For example, a defect in a building may be entirely attributable to the carelessness of the brick company, but the builder may still have to pay the customer (*Young & Marten v McManus Childs* [1969] 1 A.C. 454). Again it is a question of construction how strict a liability is assumed under the contract or imposed by it.

The judges are thus quite accustomed to making defendants pay damages where the blame attached not to them or to their staff but to an independent third party. Are there any such cases at common law, leaving aside statute and contract?

It seems that it is only for injuries on the highway that one may be liable to a complete stranger for the harm done to him by one's careless contractor. People who are simply using the highway are not caught by this extended liability (the driver does not answer for the mechanic), but those responsible for works on the highway or buildings alongside it may be liable if their contractors are incompetent in the work or the repairs (see the 1980 Act, above, p.154). These can be classified as instances of public nuisance (above, p.200). In private nuisance also one may have to answer for one's contractor's doings (below, p.318), but between neighbours-in-fact there is a special relationship, and a special relationship can give rise to higher as well as to lower liabilities or, which is the same thing, liabilities for wider or narrower ranges of assistants.

We must now slightly extend the cast of characters and concepts. Just as a person may loosely be called a "trustee" if he is trusted with property "for" another, so a person who does some act "for" another can be called an "agent." This term is too general to be of much use: after all, servants and independent contractors both do things "for" the person who pays them and we have seen that we must distinguish between them. We need to draw two further distinctions, one relating to the nature of the service performed, the other to the terms on which the service is performed. First, we distinguish those who are retained to do something in the world of fact from those who are retained to do something in the world of law: on the one hand, the airline which actually flies me across the Atlantic and, on the other, the travel agency which gets me the ticket. An agent in the latter sense is retained to transact rather than just to act. Such an agent (who may be either a servant or an independent contractor, often a firm) will render the principal liable for faults in the transaction: such faults characteristically take the form of misrepresentation and result in financial rather than physical harm. This liability is an outcrop of the main function of the agent-negotiator, which is to effect contractual relations between his principal and the other party, and it is here that we come across the notion of "authority" which is the source of the agent's power to do so.

But if one of the functions of an agent in this sense is to *create* obligations on behalf of the principal, another may be to *perform* obligations on his behalf or to execute his powers. In this sense the agent might be styled a "delegate," a person through whom the principal seeks to perform his obligations. In such a case, if the agent misperforms, the innocent principal may well be held liable for the agent's negligent breach of his duties or negligent exercise of his powers. Such a strong duty does not normally exist at common law in the absence of a special relationship such as bailment, but it may well arise, like special powers, under statute.

Secondly we must distinguish the business world from the social scene. Servants and independent contractors act because they are paid to. People who do things for others without any thought of payment (actually, even the "bob-a-job" boy scout) may well be independent, but they are not contractors. If such a service is unsolicited, the recipient will not be liable, but a person who asks another to do him a favour may well be responsible if his "agent" hurts a third party in the process, especially if he equips the "agent" with the means, as well as the occasion, of causing harm.

Some final points remain to be made. The first is that the liability of the superior is additional to the liability of the actual tortfeasor, not alternative to it. The workman who renders his employer liable remains personally liable. If we may use a forbidden language, not only *qui facit per alium facit per se* but *culpa tenet suos auctores*. Indeed, the workman is primarily liable, and liable in law (though rarely in fact) to pay his employer if his employer has to pay the victim (*Lister v Romford Ice & Cold Storage Co* [1957] A.C. 555). So many companies still go into compulsory liquidation (6,319 in 2002–2003) that it is very appealing to sue their officers and employees (for directors are employees!) since they may have some money left. This is rendered much easier now that tort has entered the field of economic transactions, for in fact most breaches of contract are attributable to misconduct on the part of the contractor's employees and the common law has readily allowed claimants to sue the employee in tort rather than his employer in contract. This was commonly done in order to circumvent exemption clauses which protected the contractor but not the employee (*Adler v Dickson* [1955] 1 Q.B. 158), but this unseemly device is unnecessary now that (a) such clauses are void as regards personal injury or death caused by negligence, personal or vicarious (Unfair Contract Terms Act, above, p.254) and (b) clauses not so void may be invoked by employees (Contracts (Rights of Third Parties) Act 1999, s.1(6)).

No exemption clause was involved in *Fairline Shipping Corp. v Adamson* [1975] Q.B. 180 but the director was held liable for failing in the company's duties as bailee, and it looked very much as if this would be extended so as to make a director liable for bad advice supplied by the company. A welcome stop has been put to this development by *Williams v Natural Life Health Foods* (above, p.62). Indeed we may well be moving in the direction of holding the employer solely liable and exculpating the employee for doing, albeit badly, only what he was employed to do: the Westfall Act in the United States has done this with regard to government employees, and France, by judicial decision, has done it more generally, except where the employee's conduct is criminal.

The second point is that a superior employee, such as the managing director of a company or a ranking civil servant, is not liable for employees lower down the hierarchy: only the master, the paymaster, is vicariously liable. Of course a managing director might be liable for unreasonably making or letting an inferior do something dangerous, but that would be a personal rather than an imputed liability.

That takes us to the third point. In each case one must consider all the possible bases of liability—the personal liability of the defendant as well as his vicarious liability both as employer and as principal. In one case, for example, an apprentice was bullied by a fellow-employee. The master was not liable in his capacity as the employer of the bully, since the bully was not acting in the scope of his employment, but he was personally liable as the employer of the plaintiff apprentice, for failing to take reasonable steps to protect him from the bully (*Hudson v Ridge Manufacturing Co* [1957] 2 Q.B. 348). Likewise, if the tortfeasor is an independent contractor, it is worth asking whether it was not careless of the defendant to select him for the task. Again, if an employee carelessly injures his mate while driving him to work, the employer will not be liable as employer, since driving to work is not driving at work; but if the driving was being done at the employer's request, the driver may well be the employer's "agent" and the employer will be liable as principal (*Vandyke v Fender* [1970] 2 Q.B. 292).

Chapter 6

EMPLOYEES

Section 1.—Employers and Employees

MONTGOMERY V JOHNSON UNDERWOOD LTD

Court of Appeal EWCA Civ 38; [2001] I.C.R. 819

Who is the employer of a worker supplied and paid by an employment agency?

Buckley J.: On 30 May 1995, a Carla Panter of [the employment agency] Johnson Underwood (JU) telephoned Mrs Montgomery and said she had a suitable position with a local company, Orenstein & Kopple Ltd (O&K). Hours of work and rate of pay were discussed and agreed. The next day Mrs Montgomery received JU's letter of confirmation and printed terms and conditions. In return she sent her P45 and bank details. On 1 June 1995, she started work at O&K. Thereafter JU caused payment for hours worked to be made directly into Mrs Montgomery's bank account. The amount was calculated in accordance with time sheets approved by O&K.

Mrs Montgomery worked on weekday afternoons and all was well for almost two-and-a-half years until late 1997. By then it seems that O&K was unhappy with Mrs Montgomery's use of its telephone for personal calls and asked JU to terminate the assignment. Mrs Johnson, a director of JU, duly attended O&K's office on 12 November 1997 and told Mrs Montgomery that it was over. She was offered another position but, so far as I am aware, did not pursue it.

Mrs Montgomery claimed compensation for unfair dismissal and named JU as the employer, subsequently adding O&K. Both respondents put in appearances and each denied that Mrs Montgomery was its employee. A preliminary issue was ordered and heard by the tribunal on 20 February 1998. In effect, the question was whether Mrs Montgomery was an employee of either of the respondents and thus whether either would be a proper respondent for the purpose of an unfair dismissal hearing.

The tribunal unanimously decided that: "There was no basis upon which to hold the applicant to have been an employee of the second respondent (O&K)." and that: "We are satisfied that the applicant was an employee of the first respondent (JU)."

O&K took no part in the appeal to this court and the only issue was the industrial tribunal's decision, supported by the majority of the EAT, that Mrs Montgomery was employed by JU.

The law

I consider the safest starting point to be the oft-quoted passage of MacKenna J. in *Ready Mixed Concrete (South East) Ltd v Minister of Pensions and National Insurance* [1968] 2 Q.B. 497 at 515:

> "A contract of service exists if these three conditions are fulfilled. (i) The servant agrees that, in consideration of a wage or other remuneration, he will provide his own work and skill in the performance of some service for his master. (ii) He agrees, expressly or

impliedly, that in the performance of that service he will be subject to the other's control in a sufficient degree to make that other master. (iii) The other provisions of the contract are consistent with its being a contract of service."

MacKenna J. made plain that provided (i) and (ii) are present (iii) requires that all the terms of the agreement are to be considered before the question as to the existence of a contract of service can be answered. As to (ii) he had well in mind that the early legal concept of control as including control over how the work should be done was relevant but not essential. Society has provided many examples, from masters of vessels and surgeons to research scientists and technology experts, where such direct control is absent. In many cases the employer or controlling management may have no more than a very general idea of how the work is done and no inclination directly to interfere with it. However, some sufficient framework of control must surely exist. A contractual relationship concerning work to be carried out in which the one party has no control over the other could not sensibly be called a contract of employment. MacKenna J. cited a passage from the judgment of Dixon J. in *Humberstone v Northern Timber Mills* [1949] 79 C.L.R. 389 from which I take the first few lines only: "The question is not whether in practice the work was in fact done subject to a direction and control exercised by any actual supervision or whether any actual supervision was possible but whether ultimate authority over the man in the performance of his work resided in the employer so that he was subject to the latter's order and directions."

Clearly as society and the nature and manner of carrying out employment continues to develop, so will the court's view of the nature and extent of "mutual obligations" concerning the work in question and "control" of the individual carrying it out.

I agree with Charles J. that since legislation, in effect, requires an employment agency to treat the individual as an employee for National Insurance and tax purposes, the fact they have done so takes the matter no further. I also agree with the judge that the tribunal appear to have taken little, if any, account of the absence of any review or grievance procedures as between the agency and Mrs Montgomery. These factors were present in the *McMeechan* case ([1997] I.C.R. 353) and doubtless played a not insignificant part in the final decision.

For my part, I would accept that an offer of work by an agency, even at another's workplace, accepted by the individual for remuneration to be paid by the agency, could satisfy the requirement of mutual obligation. I put it no higher because it would be necessary to look at the circumstances carefully and realistically. It may, for example, be more difficult to find that necessary mutuality in a very short assignment as opposed to one which was or had become more permanent. Since I have reached the conclusion that I have on "control", I prefer to say no more on this aspect of the matter, particularly as it was not really explored before the tribunal.

Finally, I would observe that there appears to be considerable uncertainty concerning the status of individuals who find work through employment agencies. This is apparent from the remarks of both the tribunal and the EAT. Their view seems to be shared by those in the agency business. Mrs Johnson, a director of JU, said in evidence before the tribunal: "Temps are not employed by the clients nor by us. We are not allowed to treat them as self-employed. I do not know what their status is. No one in the agency business knows the answer. They're in limbo."

I agree with the passage in the EAT's judgment in which they comment on this uncertainty:

" . . . it seems to us that it would be sensible for the relevant government department and Parliament to give further consideration to the position of employment agencies, their clients and the individuals who work for such clients on the introduction of the agency. We are of this view notwithstanding that in the Employment Relations Act 1999 an agency worker is defined and included within the definition of worker (see s.13 of that Act). Indeed, we comment that the power conferred by s.23 of that Act on the Secretary of State for Trade and Industry to extend the protection of employment legislation to a specified description of individuals might be put to important use in this respect. Continued confusion about whether there exists any protection at all in certain cases against unfair dismissal assists nobody."

Longmore L.J.: I agree. I was at one time during the hearing of the appeal somewhat troubled by the fact that Mr Samek's argument led to the conclusion that Mrs Montgomery was neither an employee nor an independent contractor. It is absurd to suppose that Mrs Montgomery as a telephonist working at O&K's office could be an independent contractor; it might be natural, therefore, to conclude that Mrs Montgomery was an employee and, if so, that she was an employee of JU, the employment agency.

Some such reasoning may lie behind the decisions of the employment tribunal and the EAT; but I am satisfied that this approach is wrong. In the context of a claim for unfair dismissal, an applicant must show that she (or he) is an employee of the defendant sued. In a case where (as here) the tribunal has found as a fact that there was "little or no control, direction or supervision", on the part of JU, a conclusion that Mrs Montgomery was the employee of JU cannot stand. Whatever other developments this branch of the law may have seen over the years, mutuality of obligation and the requirement of control on the part of the potential employer are the irreducible minimum for the existence of a contract of employment. Here, part of that irreducible minimum is absent and, accordingly, whatever contractual arrangements were enjoyed by Mrs Montgomery, she cannot have been an employee of JU.

Questions:

1. Given that the agency which paid and dismissed the claimant but not her employer, was she employed by the firm she worked for? Could that firm have dismissed her? What consideration did the firm provide for her work?

2. What if Mrs Montgomery (a) was injured at work by a breach of statutory duty imposed only on an employer, (b) negligently injured one of the firm's employees, (c) carelessly contributed to the damage to the firm's property due to the negligence of a third party?

Note:

In a case where the tribunal had found that there was both "control" and "mutuality of obligation" between the parties but nevertheless held that the worker was not employed by either the agency or the firm because that was inconsistent with the expressed intention of the parties, the Employment Appeal Tribunal allowed the appeal. A temporary worker could be the "employee" of the agency in respect of assignments actually worked, even if the worker was not entitled to employee status under the general terms of the engagement by the agency. *Dacas v Brook Street Bureau* (EAT/492/02, December 11, 2002). The requisite "mutuality" was well expressed in the dictum that "A contract of service implies an obligation to serve, and it comprises some degree of control by the master."

LANE v SHIRE ROOFING CO (OXFORD) LTD

Court of Appeal [1995] I.R.L.R. 493; [1995] Times L.R. 104

Claim for personal injury against alleged employer

The defendant contracted with Mr and Mrs Bird to reroof the porch on their house at Sonning Common, and agreed to pay the plaintiff £200 to do the actual work, which would take four days. The plaintiff fell off his ladder while cutting a slate. The Construction (Working Places) Regulations 1966, which could be invoked only by an employee, provided that where work could not be safely done from the ground or a permanent structure, a ladder could be used as an alternative to a scaffold or other means of support only if it was appropriate to do so and the ladder was sufficient and suitable for the purpose.

Henry L.J. discussed the accident and continued: The building contract in relation to that job had been entered into by the respondents, through Mr Whittaker, and the householders, Mr and Mrs Bird, for an agreed price of £389 (plus VAT). (As will be seen, the economic realities of that price were that if, to do it safely, scaffolding had to be hired and erected, the job would be loss-making to the respondents.) Mr Whittaker then visited the site with the appellant, agreed to pay him an all-in fee of £200 for the job, and discussed (as we shall see) with him what was necessary in the way of plant (using that phrase to embrace ladders, scaffolds and trestles) to do the job. And Mr Whittaker accepted in cross-examination that it was his responsibility to supply aids such as scaffolds and trestles.

The question is whether the respondents owed to the plaintiff the common law or statutory duty of an employer to his employees, or whether the appellant when doing that job was acting as an independent contractor. When it comes to the question of safety at work, there is a real public interest in recognising the employer/employee relationship when it exists, because of the responsibilities that the common law and statutes such as the Employers' Liability (Compulsory Insurance) Act 1969 places on the employer.

The judge was to find that the appellant was not an employee, but was an independent contractor. In that event the appellant would have been responsible for his own safety; the respondent would have owed him no duty of care, and would have had no responsibility (statutory or at common law) for the safety of the work done by the appellant. That was the context in which the question was asked.

We were taken through the standard authorities on this matter: *Ready Mixed Concrete (South East) Ltd v Minister of Pensions and National Insurance* [1968] 2 Q.B. 497; *Market Investigations Ltd v Minister of Social Security* [1969] 2 Q.B. 173; and *Ferguson v Dawson & Partners (Contractors) Ltd* [1976] I.R.L.R. 346, to name the principal ones. Two general remarks should be made. The overall employment background is very different today (and was, though less so, in 1986) than it had been at the time when those cases were decided. First, for a variety of reasons there are more self-employed and fewer in employment. There is a greater flexibility in employment, with more temporary and shared employment. Second, there are perceived advantages for both workman and employer in the relationship between them being that of independent contractor. From the workman's point of view, being self-employed brings him into a more benevolent and less prompt taxation regime. From the employer's point of view, the protection of employees' rights contained in the employment protection legislation of the 1970s brought certain perceived disincentives to the employer to take on full-time long-term employees. So even in 1986 there were reasons on both sides to avoid the employee label. But, as I have already said, there were, and are, good policy reasons in the safety at work field to ensure that the law properly categorises between employees and independent contractors.

That line of authority shows that there are many factors to be taken into account in answering this question, and, with different priority being given to those factors in different cases, all depends on the facts of each individual case. Certain principles relevant to this case, however, emerge.

First, the element of control will be important: who lays down what is to be done, the way in which it is to be done, the means by which it is to be done, and the time when it is done? Who provides (*i.e.* hires and fires) the team by which it is done, and who provides the material, plant and machinery and tools used?

But it is recognised that the control test may not be decisive—for instance, in the case of skilled employees, with discretion to decide how their work should be done. In such cases the question is broadened to whose business was it? Was the workman carrying on his own business, or was he carrying on that of his employers? The answer to this question may cover much of the same ground as the control test (such as whether he provides his own equipment and hires his own helpers) but may involve looking to see where the financial risk lies, and whether and how far he has an opportunity of profiting from sound management in the performance of his task (see *Market Investigations v Minister of Social Security, supra,* at 185).

And these questions must be asked in the context of who is responsible for the overall safety of the men doing the work in question. Mr Whittaker, of the respondents, was cross-examined on these lines and he agreed that he was so responsible. Such an answer is not decisive (though it may be indicative) because ultimately the question is one of law, and he could be wrong as to where the legal responsibility lies (see *Ferguson v Dawson, supra,* at 1219G).

The facts that the judge had to consider were as follows. The appellant was a builder/roofer/carpenter who had since 1982 traded as a one-man firm, P J Building. He had obtained self-employed fiscal status, with a right to the 714 tax exemption certificates issued by the Inland Revenue. As a one-man firm he solicited work through advertisements, and when engaged by clients would of course be responsible for estimating, buying in materials, and matters of that kind. But that work had dried up. His public liability insurance had lapsed. At the time he answered the respondents' advertisement he was usually working for others.

The respondent company (which was the corporate manifestation of its proprietor, Mr Whittaker) was a newly established roofing contractor. It was in its early days of trading, and Mr Whittaker did not wish to take on too many long-term employees—he considered it prudent and advantageous to hire for individual jobs. In September of 1986 he obtained a large roofing sub-contract in Marlow. He advertised for men to work that contract. The appellant answered that advertisement, and was employed by him at the daily rate of £45. He started work on that job at some time in September. It seems, though the evidence is not entirely clear on this, that that job was nearly over when, at the respondents' request, he left that job to do the Sonning Common porch re-roofing job. As he had been promised no work from the respondents after the Marlow job, it is right to consider the question whether he was an employee in the context of the Sonning Common job.

Mr Matthews, for the respondents, rightly distinguishes between a *Ferguson v Dawson* situation, where an employer engages men on "the lump" to do labouring work (where the men are clearly employees, whatever their tax status may be), and when a specialist sub-contractor is employed to perform some part of a general building contract. That team or individual clearly will be an independent contractor. He submits that the appellant in this case falls somewhere in between. With that I would agree, but would put this case substantially nearer "the lump" than the specialist sub-contractor. Though the degree of control that Mr Whittaker would use would depend on the need he felt to supervise and direct the appellant (who was just someone answering the advertisement) the question "Whose business was it?" in relation to the Sonning Common job could only in my judgment be answered by saying that it was the respondents' business and not the appellant's. In my judgment, therefore, they owed the duties of employers to the appellant. Consequently, for my part I would find that the first ground of appeal against the judge's judgment succeeds.

[His Lordship then held that it was not appropriate for this job to be done from a ladder and that the plaintiff should have damages, subject to a deduction of 50 per cent for contributory negligence. Auld and Nourse L.JJ. agreed]

Questions

1. Would the plaintiff have described himself as an employee? Would he have described the £200 as "wages"?

2. Was the plaintiff an employee while working on the Marlow job? If so, is that because other people were working with him or because it was a bigger job with more equipment provided?

3. If the plaintiff had dropped a slate on the head of one of the Bird children would the defendant have been liable? Would the defendant or the plaintiff or both of them have had insurance?

4. Was it relevant that the defendant was a company?

Notes:

1. The relationship of employer and employee may be relevant in many contexts other than vicarious liability in tort. For example, it was in the context of contempt of court that Lord Templeman observed: "An employee who acts for the company within the scope of his employment is the company" (*Re Supply of Ready Mixed Concrete (No.2)* [1995] 1 All E.R. 135 at 142), and of the first two cases in this chapter, the first concerned the vesting of copyright (for the employer usually owns what the employee creates in his employment) and the second the employer's duty to his employee rather than his liability to others for what the employee did.

2. It was only to be expected that the notion of "control", apt enough in the days when the employer was a human being like his employees, has yielded to the test of "integration" now that almost all employers are companies and not individuals.

3. In *Roe v Minister of Health* (above p.166) Lord Denning said: "I think that the hospital authorities are responsible for the whole of their staff, not only for the nurses and doctors, but also for the anaesthetists and the surgeons. It does not matter whether they are permanent or temporary, resident or visiting, whole-time or part-time. The hospital authorities are responsible for all of them. The reason is because, even if they are not servants, they are the agents of the hospital to give the treatment. The only exception is the case of

consultants or anaesthetists selected and employed by the patient himself. I went into the matter with some care in *Cassidy v Ministry of Health* [1951] 2 K.B. 343 and I adhere to all I there said." [Bear in mind that there is a special relationship between the claimant patient and the hospital where he is hurt.]

4. Not all those who are—or ought to be—under the control of others are employees. Examples are provided by policemen (servants of the public), ministers of religion (servants of God), children (out of control altogether), members of associations and subsidiary companies (not human). Some of these are now to be discussed.

POLICE ACT 1996

88—.(1) The chief officer of police for a police area shall be liable in respect of any unlawful conduct of constables under his direction and control in the performance or purported performance of their functions in like manner as a master is liable in respect of any unlawful conduct of his servants in the course of their employment, and accordingly shall, in the case of a tort, be treated for all purposes as a joint tortfeasor.

(2) There shall be paid out of the police fund—

(a) any damages or costs awarded against the chief officer of police in any proceedings brought against him by virtue of this section and any costs incurred by him in any such proceedings so far as not recovered by him in the proceedings; and
(b) any sum required in connection with the settlement of any claim made against the chief officer of police by virtue of this section, if the settlement is approved by the police authority.

Notes:
1. The chief constable's liability may be more extensive than that of a private employer: in *Weir v Bettison* [2003] EWCA Civ 111, [2003] I.C.R. 708 a constable who was quite improperly using a police van to help his girlfriend move house manhandled and pushed into the police van a youth who was rummaging in her possessions in the street.
2. In 2001–2002 the Metropolitan Police paid out £901,000 in civil damages, down from £3,217,000 in 1999–2000. Can this be the effect of *Thompson*, below p.639?

POWERS OF CRIMINAL COURTS (SENTENCING) ACT 2000

137. (1) Where—

(a) a child or young person (that is to say, any person aged under 18) is convicted of any offence for the commission of which a fine or costs may be imposed or a compensation order may be made, and
(b) the court is of the opinion that the case would best be met by the imposition of a fine or costs or the making of such an order, whether with or without any other punishment, the court shall order that the fine, compensation or costs awarded be paid by the parent or guardian of the child or young person instead of by the child or young person himself, unless the court is satisfied—
  (i) that the parent or guardian cannot be found; or
  (ii) that it would be unreasonable to make an order for payment, having regard to the circumstances of the case.

Notes:
Trade Unions: Trade unions used not to be liable in tort at all. When the immunity was removed, it had to be decided for what actions by which members they could be made to pay. They are now liable for even

wholly unauthorised industrial action undertaken by their officials or committees unless they immediately and formally repudiate it (Trade Union and Labour Relations (Consolidation) Act 1992, ss.20, 21).

Corporate Subsidiaries. Although companies incur vicarious liability for their employees, vicarious liability for their corporate subsidiaries has not developed properly: the subsidiary company cannot be an employee, not being human, and though it can be wholly owned, like a slave, it is not quite a thing such as an animal, for which liability has long been imposed. Liability for subsidiaries was proposed in the now defunct European Company Statute (see K. Hofstetter, "Parent Liability for Subsidiary Corporations: Evaluating European Trends" (1990) 39 I.C.L.Q. 576), but English law is very backward. In *Adams v Cape Industries* [1991] 1 All E.R. 929 at 1026, the Court of Appeal said: " . . . we do not accept as a matter of law that the court is entitled to lift the corporate veil as against a defendant company which is the member of a corporate group merely because the corporate structure has been used so as to ensure that the legal liability (if any) in respect of particular future activities of the group (and correspondingly the risk of enforcement of that liability) will fall on another member of the group rather than the defendant company. Whether or not this is desirable, the right to use a corporate structure in this manner is inherent in our corporate law."

However, in *Lubbe v Cape plc* [2000] 1 W.L.R. 1545, the House of Lords allowed South African employees who suffered asbestosis-related injuries to sue the parent company in England, not the natural or appropriate forum, because in South Africa the right professional and expert assistance was not available. In the event, Cape provided a compensation package of £21m. for 7,500 South African workers affected in the asbestos mines in Northern Cape and Limpopo provinces; 300 had already died (*The Times*, September 10, 2002).

MERSEY DOCKS & HARBOUR BOARD v COGGINS & GRIFFITH (LIVERPOOL) LTD

House of Lords [1947] A.C. 1; 115 L.J.K.B. 465; 175 L.T. 270; 62 T.L.R. 533; [1946] 2 All E.R. 345

Is the negligence of a crane driver imputed to the harbour authority which employs him to operate their crane or to the stevedores for whom he is actually operating it?

McFarlane was injured at Liverpool Docks when a crane-driver, Newall, carelessly drove into him. Newall was employed by the appellants who let crane and driver to the respondent stevedores under a contract providing that "the drivers so provided shall be the servants of the [respondent]." Newall himself gave evidence, and said: "I take no orders from anybody."

Croom-Johnson J. gave judgment against the crane-owners on the ground that Newall was in their employment at the time of the accident, and judgment in favour of the stevedores on the ground that he was not. The Court of Appeal dismissed the crane-owners' appeal [1945] K.B. 301, and their further appeal to the House of Lords was also dismissed.

Lord Macmillan: My Lords, the only question for your Lordships' determination is whether on the principle of *respondeat superior*, the responsibility for the negligence of the driver of the crane lies with the stevedores or with the appellant board, whom the plaintiff sued alternatively. The answer depends on whether the driver was acting as the servant of the stevedores or as the servant of the appellant board when he set the crane in motion. That the crane driver was in general the servant of the appellant board is indisputable. The appellant board engaged him, paid him, prescribed the jobs he should undertake and alone could dismiss him. The letting out of cranes on hire to stevedores for the purpose of loading and unloading vessels is a regular branch of the appellant board's business. In printed regulations and rates issued by the appellant board the cranes are described as "available for general use on the dock estate at Liverpool and Birkenhead" and as regards portable cranes the stipulated rates vary according as they are provided "with board's driver" or "without board's driver." Prima facie therefore it was as the servant of the appellant board that Newall was driving the crane when it struck the plaintiff. But it is always open to an employer to show, if he can, that he has for a particular purpose or on a particular occasion temporarily transferred the services of one of his general servants to another party so as to constitute him pro hac vice the servant of that other party with consequent liability for his negligent acts. The burden is on the general employer to establish that such a transference has been effected. Agreeing as I do with the trial judge and the Court of Appeal, I am of opinion that, on the facts of the present case, Newall was never so transferred from the service and control of the appellant board to the service and control of the stevedores as to render the stevedores answerable for the manner in which he carried on his work of driving the crane. The stevedores were entitled to tell him where to go, what parcels to lift and where to take them, that is to say, they could direct him as to what they wanted him to do; but they had no authority to tell him how he was to handle the crane in doing his work. In driving the crane, which was the appellant board's property confided to his charge, he was acting as the servant of the appellant board, not as the servant of the stevedores. It was not in consequence of any order of the stevedores that he negligently ran down the plaintiff; it was in consequence of his negligence in driving the crane, that is to say, in performing the work which he was employed by the appellant board to do.

Question

If one is not liable for one's independent contractor, would it not be odd if one were liable for one's independent contractor's servants?

Notes:

1. It is one thing to supply a manned machine, especially if it is the machine which does the harm; it is another thing to supply just men, especially if they are to man the machines of others. Nevertheless "Just as with employers who let out a man with a machine, so also with an employer who sends out a skilled man to do work for another, the general rule is that he remains the servant of the general employer throughout." *Savory v Holland & Hannen & Cubitts (Southern) Ltd* [1964] 1 W.L.R. 1158 at 1163, *per* Lord Denning M.R.

2. The same problem arises when the question is not "who is responsible *for* this person?" but rather "who is responsible *to* this person?", since employers owe a higher duty to their employees than, for example, an occupier owes to his visitors. "When the court had to decide whether a temporary or the general employer was vicariously liable for damage caused by an employee to a third party, the right of control was an appropriate test. But if the employee was injured the general employer remained liable to him. He was personally liable for the performance of his duty to the employee and could not avoid liability if he delegated it to another who performed it negligently: . . . *McDermid v Nash Dredging*" (below, p.302). So said by Beldam L.J. in *Morris v Breaveglen* in [1992] Times L.R. 657 (reported more fully at [1993] I.C.R. 766 and [1993] I.R.L.R. 350), where the plaintiff was sent to work for a construction company by the defendant "labour-only" sub-contractor and was injured while driving one of the construction company's dumpers, without having received from the defendant any instruction in how to drive it.

3. In cases where the actionable negligence of the "temporary employer" puts the general employer in breach of his duty to the employee (so that the injured employee could hold them both liable), the general employer may claim a full indemnity under the 1978 Act (above, p.236): *Nelhams v Sandells Maintenance* [1995] Times L.R. 339.

4. Note that rights regarding unfair dismissal and redundancy payments depend on "continuous employment" (see Employment Rights Act 1996, s.210).

5. It is quite common for a person to work for someone other than his employer. In order to extend the reach of anti-discrimination legislation the following statutory provision was thought necessary: "(1) This section applies to any work for a person ("the principal") which is available for doing by individuals ("contract workers") who are employed not by the principal himself but by another person, who supplies them under a contract made with the principal. (2) It is unlawful for the principal, in relation to work to which this section applies, to discriminate against a contract worker . . . " (Race Relations Act 1976, s.7). Note also the phrase "contract personally to do any work" under Disability Discrimination Act 1995, s.68(1), which apparently does not include managers who can get others to do the work: *Sheehan v Post Office Counters* [1999] I.C.R. 734 (EAT).

6. In *Interlink Express Parcels v Night Trunkers* [2001] EWCA Civ 360 the "borrowed servant" question arose in an unusual context. There was an agreement between the parties that Night Trunkers would supply employees of theirs to drive trucks belonging to Interlink Express, and the question was whether this agreement was not void and illegal on the ground that its performance entailed the commission of an offence under the Goods Vehicles (Licensing of Operators) Act 1995 which required the user of a vehicle to have a

licence. Interlink had such a licence but Night Trunkers did not. The statute provided that "the person whose servant or agent (is) the driver shall be deemed to be using the vehicle". So the question was whether the drivers supplied by Night Trunkers were the servants of Interlink. The trial judge held that they were not, but the Court of Appeal reversed, on the ground that Interlink had sufficient control over the drivers to turn them into "deemed temporary employees". This was said to be in accordance with the *Mersey Docks* case.

7. D, a firm of accountants, seconded an employee Y to serve as financial controller of a firm X. P, a bank, had lent a large sum of money to X on the basis of accounts submitted by D which were misleading by reason of the fraud of Y while working for X. Since X had a right to direct and control the way Y worked for it, it was held that D was not liable for the fraud of its employee while on secondment. *Royal Bank of Scotland v Bannerman Johnstone Maclay* 2003 S.C. 125 (O.H.).

Section 2.—Liability to Whom?

STAVELEY IRON & CHEMICAL CO v JONES

House of Lords [1956] A.C. 627; [1956] 2 W.L.R. 479; 100 S.J. 130; [1956] 1 All E.R. 403; [1956] 1 Lloyd's Rep. 65 (noted (1956) 72 L.Q.R. 158 at 522)

Action by employee against employer in respect of personal injury

The plaintiff, an experienced coremaker employed in the defendant's ironworks at Hollingwood, Derbyshire, was injured when a pan of cores being lifted by crane swung towards him and caught his arm against a railway truck. The crane-driver, Bertha Howett, had lowered the crab of the crane, from which hung four chains, over a pan of cores, and the plaintiff fixed two of the chains to his corners of the pan while an assistant (whom the plaintiff could not see for the height of the cores) fixed the other two to the remaining corners. Then, although she could not see clearly whether the crab was central, as was necessary to prevent the pan slewing sideways when lifted, she suddenly, without any signal and without testing the balance of the pan, lifted it, and caused the accident.

The plaintiff alleged that the defendant failed to provide a safe system of work or safe plant and equipment, but this claim was rejected. He further alleged that the crane-driver was negligent in not keeping a look-out to see that the crab was central over the pan, in raising the load when it was not safe to do so, and in failing to control the crane. The defendant pleaded that the plaintiff was contributorily negligent in not paying sufficient regard to the centralisation of the crab, in not instructing the crane-driver that the crab was not central, in not signalling to the crane driver to lower the crab, and in not standing clear of the pan.

Sellers J. gave judgment for the defendant. The Court of Appeal allowed the plaintiff's appeal, and entered judgment for him [1955] 1 Q.B. 474. The defendant's appeal to the House of Lords was dismissed.

Lord Reid: ... My Lords, it is proved that the proper practice is not to raise the load at once but only to take the weight on the chains and then to pause to see whether everything is in order. For some reason which she could not explain the crane-driver did not do this, and, if she had done, the lack of centring ought to have been noticed and the accident would almost certainly have been avoided. The question is whether her failure to pause in lifting the load was negligence for which the appellants, her employers, are responsible.

Sellers J. held that both Jones and the crane-driver were guilty of errors of judgment but not of negligence, but, at least as regards the crane-driver, I do not think that he applied the right test of negligence.

"I think there was some fault on the crane-driver's part, but I think there was at least as great, and probably greater, fault on the part of the plaintiff himself and, as I say, it raises quite acutely the question whether the court here ought to characterize this failure to do that which ought to have been done in the circumstances as acts of negligence—which would mean that the plaintiff would recover some damages, but only a proportion which is ultimately assessed to be his due having regard to his own conduct—or whether in circumstances such as this where there is team work, routine work, work which necessitates a close co-operation with both and where there is a mistake which results, but only just results, in an accident as here, whether it is more appropriate to regard them in such a case as this as errors of judgment on the part of both.

This seems to me to be based on the view that conduct which would amount to negligence if a stranger were injured may not amount to negligence if the person injured is a fellow servant. The abolition of the doctrine of common employment appears to me to make it necessary to hold that the test of negligence is the same whether the person injured is a fellow servant or a stranger: to hold otherwise would mean that if a servant causes damage then by reason of their common employment a fellow servant would not have as full a remedy against his master as a stranger would have.

The Court of Appeal reversed the decision of Sellers J., but different views were expressed on the law. Denning L.J., as I read his judgment, did not find it necessary to hold that the crane-driver was herself negligent. He said: "The employer is made liable, not so much for the crane-driver's fault, but rather for his own fault committed through her. . . . He acts by his servant; and his servant's acts are, for this purpose, to be considered as his acts. *Qui facit per alium facit per se*. He cannot escape by the plea that his servant was thoughtless or inadvertent or made an error of judgment. If he takes the benefit of a machine like this, he must accept the burden of seeing that it is properly handled. It is for this reason that the employer's responsibility for injury may be ranked greater than that of the servant who actually made the mistake."

My Lords, if this means that the appellants could be held liable even if it were held that the crane-driver was not herself guilty of negligence, then I cannot accept that view. Of course, an employer may be himself in fault by engaging an incompetent servant or not having a proper system of work or in some other way. But there is nothing of that kind in this case. Denning L.J. appears to base his reasoning on a literal application of the maxim *qui facit per alium facit per se*, but, in my view, it is rarely profitable and often misleading to use Latin maxims in that way. It is a rule of law that an employer, though guilty of no fault himself, is liable for damage done by the fault or negligence of his servant acting in the course of his employment. The maxims *respondeat superior* and *qui facit per alium facit per se* are often used, but I do not think that they add anything or that they lead to any different results. The former merely states the rule baldly in two words, and the latter merely gives a fictional explanation of it. . . .

Lord Morton of Henryton: . . . My Lords, what the court has to decide in the present case: Was the crane-driver negligent? If the answer is "Yes," the employer is liable vicariously for the negligence of his servant. If the answer is "No," the employer is surely under no liability at all. Cases such as this, where an employer's liability is vicarious, are wholly distinct from cases where an employer is under a personal liability to carry out a duty imposed upon him as an employer by common law or statute. In the latter type of case the employer cannot discharge himself by saying: "I delegated the carrying out of this duty to a servant, and he failed to carry it out by mistake or error of judgment not amounting to negligence." To such a case one may well apply the words of Denning L.J.: "[The employer] remains responsible even though the servant may, for some reason, be immune." These words, however, are, in my view, incorrect as applied to a case where the liability of the employer is not personal but vicarious. In such a case if the servant is "immune," so is the employer. . . .

Lord Tucker: . . . My Lords, I think I have already sufficiently indicated that I do not consider that recent legislation has in any way altered the standard of care which is required from workmen or employers or that the standard can differ according to whether the workman is being sued personally or his employer is being sued in respect of his acts or omissions in the course of his employment. It is true that, in accordance with what was said in this House in *Caswell's* case, there may be cases, such as those involving breach of statutory duty, where an employer who is in breach of his duty cannot be heard as against his own servant who has been injured thereby to say that some risky act due to familiarity with the work or some inattention resulting from noise or strain amounts to contributory negligence. In this respect it is possible the same act may have different consequences when the injured man is the plaintiff suing his employers and where the employer is being sued by a third party (including another employee) in respect of the same act or omission. This is not so illogical as may appear at first sight when it is remembered that contributory negligence is not founded on breach of duty (*cf. Nance v British Columbia Electric Ry Co Ltd* ([1951] A.C. 601) and *Lewis v Denye* ([1939] 1 K.B. 540 at 544) and the cases there referred to), although it generally involves a breach of duty, and that in Factory Act cases the purpose of imposing the absolute obligation is to protect the workmen against those very acts of inattention which are sometimes relied upon as constituting contributory negligence so that too strict a standard would defeat the object of the statute.

This doctrine cannot be used so as to require any modification in the standard of care required from a workman in relation to his fellow servants or other third parties or the resulting liability of his employers. . . .

Note:

In *Lister v Romford Ice & Cold Storage Co* [1957] A.C. 555 the House of Lords decided that an employer who had been held vicariously liable to servant A for the fault of servant B could recover from B the damages paid to A, even if the employer had insurance cover against such liability. It is true that the insurance companies have now agreed not to enforce their rights and that employers are not likely to, but in law Bertha Howett is liable to pay Jones, through their employer, the full amount of his damage, although the trial judge found that they were equally at fault. "Fair's fair," isn't it?

ROSE v PLENTY

Court of Appeal [1976] 1 W.L.R. 141; 119 S.J. 592; [1976] 1 All E.R. 97

Action by illicit passenger against driver's employer

Lord Denning M.R.: Mr Plenty was a milk roundsman employed at Bristol by the Co-operative Retail Services Ltd. He started working for them at Easter 1970. There were notices up at the depot making it quite clear that the roundsmen were not allowed to take children on the vehicles. One notice said: "Children and young persons *must not in any circumstances be employed by you* in the performance of your duties." Both employers and trade union did their utmost to stop it. No doubt Mr Plenty knew it was not allowed. But in spite of all these warnings, the practice still persisted. Boys used to hang about the depot waiting to be taken on and some of the roundsmen used to take them.

Soon after Mr Plenty started work as a milk roundsman a boy, Leslie Rose, who was just over 13, went up to Mr Plenty and asked if he could help him. Mr Plenty agreed to let him do it. The boy described his part in these words: "I would jump out of the milk float, grab the milk, whatever had to go into the house, collect the money if there was any there and bring the bottles back." That is what he did. The milk roundsman paid the boy six shillings for the weekends and four shillings for the week days. While the boy was going round some houses the roundsman would go to others. On June 21, 1970, unfortunately, there was an accident. After going to one house, the boy jumped on to the milk float. He sat there with one foot dangling down so as to be able to jump off quickly. But at that time the milk roundsman, I am afraid, drove carelessly and negligently. He went too close to the kerb. As the milk float went round the corner, the wheel caught the boy's leg. He tried to get his leg away, but he was dragged out of the milk float. His foot was broken with a compound fracture, but it was mended. So it was not very serious.

Afterwards he, by his father as his next friend, brought an action for damages against the roundsman and against his employers. The judge found that the milk roundsman was negligent, but he felt that the boy was old enough to bear some part of the blame himself. He assessed the responsibility for the accident at 75 per cent to the milk roundsman and 25 per cent to the boy. He assessed the total damages at £800. He gave judgment against the milk roundsman for three-quarters of it: £600. But he exempted the employers from any liability. He held that the roundsman was acting outside the scope of his employment and that the boy was a trespasser on the float. The boy, through his father, now appeals to this court. He says the employers are liable for the acts of their milk roundsman.

This raises a nice point on the liability of a master for his servant. I will first take the notices to the roundsmen saying they must not take the boys on. Those do not necessarily exempt the employers from liability. The leading case is *Limpus v London General Omnibus Co* (1862) 1 H. & C. 526; 158 E.R. 993. The drivers of omnibuses were furnished with a card saying they "must not on any account race with or obstruct another omnibus." Nevertheless the driver of one of the defendants' omnibuses did obstruct a rival omnibus and caused an accident in which the plaintiff's horses were injured. Martin B. directed the jury that, if the defendants' driver did it for the purposes of his employer, the defendants were liable, but if it was an act of his own, and in order to effect a purpose of his own, the defendants were not responsible. The jury found for the plaintiff. The Court of Exchequer Chamber held that the direction was correct. It was a very strong court which included Willes J. and Blackburn J. Despite the prohibition, the employers were held liable because the injury resulted from an act done by the driver in the course of his service and for the master's purposes. The decisive point was that it was *not* done by the servant for his own purposes, but for his master's purposes.

I will next take the point about a trespasser. The boy was a trespasser on the milk float so far as the employers were concerned. They had not given him any permission to be on the float and had expressly prohibited the milk roundsman from taking him on. There are two early cases where it was suggested that the employer of a driver is not liable to a person who is a trespasser on the vehicle. They are *Twine v Bean's Express Ltd* (1946) 62 T.L.R. 458 and *Conway v George Wimpey & Co Ltd (No.2)* [1951] 2 K.B. 266. But these cases are to be explained on other grounds and the statements about a trespasser are no longer correct. . . . So far as vehicles are concerned, I venture to go back to my own judgment in *Young v Edward Box & Co Ltd* [1951] 1 T.L.R. 789 at 793, when I said: "In every case where it is sought to make a master liable for the conduct of his servant the first question is to see whether the servant was liable. If the answer is Yes, the second question is to see whether the employer must shoulder the servant's liability." That way of putting it is, I think, to be preferred to the way I put it later in *Jones v Staveley Iron and Chemical Co Ltd* [1955] 1 Q.B. 474 at 480.

Applying the first question in *Young v Edward Box & Co Ltd*, it is quite clear that the driver, the milk roundsman, was liable to the boy for his negligent driving of the milk float. He actually invited the boy to ride on it. So the second question arises, whether his employers are liable for the driver's negligence. That does not depend on whether the boy was a trespasser. It depends, as I said in *Young v Edward Box & Co Ltd*, on whether the driver, in taking the boy on the milk float, was acting in the course of his employment.

In considering whether a prohibited act was within the course of the employment, it depends very much on the purpose for which it is done. If it is done for his employer's business, it is usually done in the course of his employment, even though it is a prohibited act. That is clear from *Limpus v London General Omnibus Co, Young v Edward Box & Co Ltd* and *Ilkiw v Samuels* [1963] 1 W.L.R. 991. But if it is done for some purpose other than his master's business, as, for instance, giving a lift to a hitchhiker, such an act, if prohibited, may not be within the course of his employment. Both *Twine v Bean's Express Ltd* and *Conway v George Wimpey & Co Ltd (No.2)* are to be explained on their own facts as cases where a driver had given a lift to someone else, contrary to a prohibition and not for the purposes of the employers. In the present case it seems to me that the course of the milk roundsman's employment was to distribute the milk, collect the money and to bring back the bottles to the van. He got or allowed his young boy to do part of that business which was the employers' business. It seems to me that although prohibited, it was conduct which was within the course of the employment; and on this ground I think the judge was in error. I agree it is a nice point in these cases on which side of the line the case falls; but, as I understand the authorities, this case falls within those in which the prohibition affects only the conduct within the sphere of the employment and did not take the conduct outside the sphere altogether. I would hold that the conduct of the roundsman was within the course of his employment and the masters are liable accordingly, and I would allow the appeal.

In parting with the case, it may be interesting to notice that this type of case is unlikely to arise so much in the future, since a vehicle is not to be used on a road unless there is in force an insurance policy covering, *inter alia*, injury to passengers.

Lawton L.J. (dissenting): Ever since 1946 employers of drivers have been entitled to arrange their affairs on the assumption that if they gave clear and express instructions to their drivers that they were not to carry passengers on the employers' vehicles, the employers would not be liable in law for any injury sustained by such passengers. They were entitled to make that assumption because of the decision of this court in *Twine v Bean's Express Ltd.* No doubt since 1946 employers when negotiating with their insurers have sought to get reductions in premiums and have done so because of the assumption which, so it seems to me, they were entitled to make about freedom from liability to unauthorised passengers. . . . If between 1946 and 1951 any employers had the kind of doubts about *Twine's* case which in more recent years have been expressed by academic writers, their minds would have been put at rest by another decision of this court in 1951, namely, *Conway v George Wimpey & Co Ltd (No.2)*. That was a case in which a lorry driver employed by a firm of contractors on a site where many other contractors were working, contrary to his express instructions, gave an employee of another firm of contractors a lift in his lorry. This man was injured while a passenger. The problem for the court was whether the injured man could claim against the employers of the lorry driver who have given him a lift. This court, in a unanimous decision, adjudged that the injured man could not claim. The leading judgment was given by Asquith L.J. and he gave his reason for saying that what the lorry driver had done had not been done in the course of his employment. He said, at p.276: "I should hold that taking men not employed by the defendants on to the vehicle was not merely a wrongful mode of performing the act of the class this driver was employed to perform, but was the performance of an act of a class which he was not employed to perform at all." These two cases have not been overruled by the House of Lords. Insurers have proceeded ever since on the assumption that these cases are properly decided. It would I think be most unfortunate if this court departed from clear decisions save on good and clear grounds. What has been submitted is that those two judgments should not be followed because when the driver of the milk float employed the boy to carry bottles for him, he was employing him to do acts which furthered the employers' business interests. In my judgment he was doing nothing of the sort. The driver had been employed to drive the milk float and deliver the milk. He had not been authorised to sub-contract his work. What he was doing was setting the boy to do the job for which he had been employed and for which he was getting paid. In my judgment in so doing he was acting outside the scope of his employment—just as in the same way as was the driver in *Conway v George Wimpey & Co Ltd (No.2)*.

If a general principle should be relied upon to justify my opinion in this case, I would adopt the same approach as Lord Greene M.R. in *Twine's* case. What duty did the employers owe to the boy? The plaintiff's counsel says: "Oh well, they put the driver with the milk float on the road: they put him into a position to take passengers if he were minded to disobey his instructions and therefore it is socially just that they should be responsible." I do not agree. When they put the driver with his float on the road they put him into a position where he had to take care not to injure those with whom he was reasonably likely to have dealings or to meet, that is all other road users and his customers. They expressly excluded anyone travelling as a passenger on his milk float. He was instructed specifically that he was not to carry passengers. Had he obeyed his instructions, he would not have had a passenger to whom he owed a duty of care. It was his disobedience which brought the injured boy into the class of persons to whom the employers vicariously owed a duty of care. He had not been employed to do anything of the kind. In my judgment, the injured boy has failed to establish that the employers owed him any duty of care.

I appreciate that in *Ilkiw v Samuels* [1963] 1 W.L.R. 991 . . . Diplock L.J. did say that a broad approach must be made to this problem. But the broad approach must not be so broad that it obscures the principles of law which are applicable. Therein lies the danger of too broad an approach. That can be illustrated by examining Diplock L.J.'s suggested general question, namely, what was the job on which he, the employee, was engaged for his employer? If that general question is asked without reference to the particular circumstances, the answer in *Twine's* case would have been to make Bean's Express liable for his injuries. The van driver in that case had been employed to drive carefully. He had not been employed to drive negligently. When Twine was injured the driver was doing the job he had been employed to do, namely, to drive. Unless this court is prepared to say that *Twine v Bean's Express Ltd* was wrongly decided, for my part I cannot see how that case can be distinguished from this. In the course of the argument an illustrative example was put to Mr Rawlins, the plaintiff's counsel. He was asked whether if in *Twine's* case the driver has asked the passenger to do some map reading for him in order that he could get more quickly to the place where in the course of his employment he wanted to go, whether that fact would have made the employers liable. Mr Rawlins said it would. In my judgment fine distinctions of that kind should have no place in our law, particularly in a branch of it which affects so many employers and their insurers. Having regard to what has been decided in the past, in my judgment it would be wrong now, without the authority either of the House of Lords or of Parliament not to follow the 1946 and 1951 cases. I would dismiss the appeal.

Scarman L.J. agreed with Lord Denning in allowing the appeal, not because the master's work was being advanced, but on the ground that the prohibitions did not limit the sphere of the roundsman's employment and that his disregard of them did not take him outside it. Scarman L.J. consequently approved of *Iqbal v London Transport Executive* (1973) 16 K.I.R. 329, which Lord Denning regarded as "out of line": in that case the employer was held not liable for a bus conductor who, to be helpful, tried to drive a bus.

Questions

1. Did Master Rose become one of the dairy's employees when Mr Plenty agreed to pay him for helping with his work?

2. Is it relevant whether or not Master Rose knew of the prohibitions?

3. Did the roundsman commit a tort against the boy by enlisting his assistance? If not, what is the relevance of asking whether he was or was not in the course of his employment in doing so?

4. The vicarious liability of an employer must be distinguished from his personal liability for breach of his own duty. Does Lawton L.J. not suggest that vicarious liability is excluded if the defendant is not in breach of a duty towards the claimant? What can you make of his expression "the class of persons to whom the employers vicariously owe a duty of care"?

5. Alf parks his car without permission in an awkward place on Bert's premises. Charlie, one of Bert's servants, has to extricate a lorry in order to make a delivery for Bert. In his manoeuvres Charlie carelessly collides with Alf's car. Is Bert liable to Alf? Is Charlie?

6. Were the Shatwell brothers (above, p.250) acting in the course and scope of their employment?

7. Does it follow from this case that an employer is now liable to a hitchhiker to whom the employee has, in breach of instructions prominently displayed on the dashboard, given a lift and whom the employee has injured through negligent driving?

8. Suppose that the dairy now claims an indemnity from Mr Plenty for breach of contract. What breach of contract would it allege?

9. Suppose that Mr Plenty, deviating from the milk-round, drove Master Rose into a wood and there abused him. Would the dairy be liable?

10. Supposing Master Rose to have been a trespasser (as he certainly was!), could he successfully invoke the Occupiers Liability Act 1984 (above, p.40)?

Note:

The House of Lords has considered the question when C, invited by B to enter A's premises, is a trespasser *vis-à-vis* A. If B had no actual authority to issue the invitation, it depends on whether A had made him look as if he had such authority (ostensible authority). C will be a trespasser if he knew or should have realised that B had no such authority. In *Ferguson v Welsh* [1987] 3 All E.R. 777 it was held that a demolition contractor who had been forbidden to subcontract nevertheless had, as a result of being invited on to the premises, ostensible authority to invite subcontractors on to the premises. It is clear, however, that unless B had actual authority, A may turn C off the premises on due notice.

Section 3.—For what Conduct?

CENTURY INSURANCE CO v NORTHERN IRELAND ROAD TRANSPORT BOARD

House of Lords [1942] A.C. 509; 111 L.J.P.C. 138; 167 L.T. 404; [1942] 1 All E.R. 491

Action against liability insurer by insured whose legal liability it denied

The Board provided Holmes, Mullin & Dunn Ltd with tankers and drivers for the delivery of petrol to their customers. On August 2, 1937, a driver, Davison, collected 300 gallons of petrol from that firm and drove the tanker to Catherwood's garage in Belfast. He backed the tanker into the garage, inserted the nozzle of the delivery pipe into the manhole of Catherwood's storage tank, and turned on the stop-cock on the side of the tanker. He then lit a cigarette and threw away the match. The match ignited some material on the ground, and the fire spread to the manhole. Catherwood attacked the manhole with a fire-extinguisher; Davison, without turning off the stop-cock, drove the tanker into the street. The fire followed the trail of petrol from the delivery pipe, and when it reached the tanker, the tanker exploded and did damage to Catherwood's car and the neighbouring houses.

The Board met the claims of those who suffered property damage and now sought to recover from their liability insurers, but the insurers denied cover on the ground that the Board had been under no liability to the victims because (a) the driver was not acting as their servant but as the servant of Holmes, Mullin & Dunn and (b) he was not acting in the course of his employment at the time he caused the fire. On the first point the appellants managed to persuade only one judge; on the second they failed before all nine.

Viscount Simon L.C.: . . . On the second question, every judge who has had to consider the matter in Northern Ireland agrees with the learned arbitrator in holding that Davison's careless act which caused the conflagration and explosion was an act done in the course of his employment. Admittedly, he was serving his master when he put the nozzle into the tank and turned on the tap. Admittedly, he would be serving his master when he turned off the tap and withdrew the nozzle from the tank. In the interval, spirit was flowing from the tanker to the tank, and this was the very delivery which the respondents were required under their contract to effect. Davison's duty was to watch over the delivery of the spirit into the tank, to see that it did not overflow, and to turn off the tap when the proper quantity had passed from the tanker. In circumstances like these, "they also serve who only stand and wait." He was presumably close to the apparatus, and his negligence in starting smoking and in throwing away a lighted match at that moment is plainly negligence in the discharge of the duties on which he was employed by the respondents. This conclusion is reached on principle and on the evidence, and does not depend on finding a decided case which closely resembles the present facts, but the decision of the English Court of Appeal twenty years ago in *Jefferson v Derbyshire Farmers Ltd* ([1921] 2 K.B. 281) provides a very close parallel. As for the majority decision, nearly sixty years before that, of the Exchequer Chamber in *Williams v Jones* ((1865) 3 H. & C. 602; 159 E.R. 668) it may be possible to draw distinctions, as the court in *Jefferson*'s case sought to do, but this House is free to review the earlier decision, and for my part I prefer the view expressed in that case by the minority, which consisted of Blackburn and Mellor JJ. The second question must also be answered adversely to the appellants, I move that the appeal be dismissed with costs. . . .

Notes:

1. In April 1954, eight coal-miners at the Whiterigg Colliery in West Lothian were injured in an explosion caused when one of them left the working-face during a lull in work, entered the "waste" and lit a cigarette.

The use of naked lights and the possession of matches or cigarettes was forbidden by statute. All five judges held that the employers were not liable for the smoker's negligence. *Kirby v NCB*, 1958 S.C. 514. Lord President Clyde said: "In the first place, if the master actually authorised a particular act, he is clearly liable for it. Secondly, where the workman does some work which he is appointed to do, but does it in a way which his master has not authorised and would not have authorised had he known of it, the master is nevertheless still responsible, for the servant's act is still within the scope of his employment. On the other hand, in the third place, if the servant is employed only to do a particular work or a particular class of work, and he does something outside the scope of that work, the master is not responsible for any mischief the servant may do to a third party. Lastly, if the servant uses his master's time or his master's place or his master's tools for his own purposes, the master is not responsible." *Ibid.* at 532–533.

2. Apprentices on day-release from their various employers were members of a joinery class at a technical college. Gregory and Llewendon had finished their assignment and went to tease and harass Powell, who was still working at the same bench as the plaintiff. Llewendon jabbed at Powell's handiwork and Gregory picked up a chisel, apparently in order to do likewise. Powell told him to put it down, and when Gregory failed to do so, grabbed for it. In the ensuing struggle the chisel flew into the air and hit the plaintiff in the eye. Gregory and Powell were held equally to blame but Powell's employer was held liable and Gregory's was not. *Duffy v Thanet D.C.* (1984) 134 New L.J. 680 (McCowan J.).

3. A person on the way to work has not yet arrived; the transit is *hors d'oeuvre*, for the course of employment has not yet started. Thus a master is not in general liable to those run over by his men on their way to work, or from it. However, the work may involve driving, as does that of a commercial traveller, so it may be held that the work started or stopped at home (*Elleanor v Cavendish Woodhouse* [1973] 1 Lloyd's Rep. 313). Lord Lowry hazarded a number of relevant propositions in *Smith v Stages* [1989] 1 All E.R. 833 at 851 in which the employer was held liable for the bad driving on a Bank Holiday of a peripatetic lagger returning to the Midlands after a week's assignment in Wales, the driver being paid wages for the time spent travelling plus the equivalent of the train fare. Furthermore, the driver may be bringing others to work at the employer's request; the driver may then make his master liable, not because he is doing his work, but because he is doing a job for the master—the master will be liable for him as agent, not as servant. See, in this connection, *Vandyke v Fender* [1970] 2 Q.B. 292. Those who leave work early may also take themselves outside the course of their employment: *Harrison v British Railways Board* [1981] 3 All E.R. 679 ("Mr Howard was no longer at work. He should have been, but he was not.") And this is so although he was allowed to use his employer's transport to go home in. By a bare majority, the Pearson Commission recommended that industrial injuries benefits should be extended to workers injured on the way to or from work. We can expect an intervention from Brussels on this point, but it is not really necessary. Since employers are required to carry insurance against liability to their employees, and motorists are required to have insurance against liability to those they carelessly injure on the highway, most disputes are between insurers of the two types.

4. To hold that a person is not vicariously liable does not mean that he is not liable at all, even where it is his servant who did the damaging act. If the management of Whiterigg colliery had known that miners were smoking and did nothing to stop it, they would be liable for breach of their own duty to take reasonable steps to prevent their employees being exposed to unnecessary danger. See *Hudson v Ridge Manufacturing Co* [1957] 2 Q.B. 348.

LISTER v HESLEY HALL

House of Lords [2001] UKHL 22, [2002] 1 A.C. 215, [2001] 2 W.L.R. 1311, [2001] 2 All E.R. 769

The claimants, who were boarders at the defendant's school for disturbed children and housed in an annexe under the care and control of a warden employed by the school, were serially abused by him.

Lord Steyn: . . . The central question before the House is whether the employers of the warden of a school boarding house, who sexually abused boys in his care, may be vicariously liable for the torts of their employee. The claims were advanced on two separate grounds. First, it was alleged that the employers were negligent in their care, selection and control of the warden. Secondly, the plaintiffs alleged that the employers were vicariously liable for the torts committed by the warden. . . . Vicarious liability is legal responsibility imposed on an employer, although he is himself free from blame, for a tort committed by his employee in the course of his employment.

Our law no longer struggles with the concept of vicarious liability for intentional wrongdoing. Thus the decision of the House of Lords in *Racz v Home Office* [1994] 2 A.C. 45 is authority for the proposition that the Home Office may be vicariously liable for acts of police officers which amounted to misfeasance in public office—and hence for liability in tort involving bad faith.

In my view the approach of the Court of Appeal in *Trotman v North Yorkshire County Council* [where a deputy headmaster sexually abused a vulnerable child during a holiday camp] was wrong. It resulted in the case being treated as one of the employment furnishing a mere opportunity to commit the sexual abuse. The reality was that the county council were responsible for the care of the vulnerable children and employed the deputy headmaster to carry out that duty on its behalf. And the sexual abuse took place while the employee was engaged in duties at the very time and place demanded by his employment. The connection between the employment and the torts was very close.

Employing the traditional methodology of English law, I am satisfied that in the case of the appeals under consideration the evidence showed that the employers entrusted the care of the children in Axeholme House to the warden. The question is whether the warden's torts were so closely connected with his employment that it would be fair and just to hold the employers vicariously liable. On the facts of the case the answer is yes. After all, the sexual abuse was inextricably interwoven with the carrying out by the warden of his duties in Axeholme House. Matters of degree arise. But the present cases clearly fall on the side of vicarious liability

Lord Clyde: I turn finally to the facts of the present case. It appears that the care and safekeeping of the boys had been entrusted to the respondents and they in turn had entrusted their care and safekeeping, so far as the running of the boarding house was concerned, to the warden. That gave him access to the premises, but the opportunity to be at the premises would not in itself constitute a sufficient connection between his wrongful actings and his employment. In addition to the opportunity which access gave him, his position as warden and the close contact with the boys which that work involved created a sufficient connection between the acts of abuse which he committed and the work which he had been employed to do. It appears that the respondents gave the warden a quite general authority in the supervision and running of the house as well as some particular responsibilities. His general duty was to look after and to care for, among others, the appellants. That function was one which the respondents had delegated to him. That he performed that function in a way which was an abuse of his position and an abnegation of his duty does not sever the connection with his employment. The particular acts which he carried out upon the boys have to be viewed not in isolation but in the context and the circumstances in which they occurred. Given that he had a general authority in the management of the house and in the care and supervision of the boys in it, the employers should be liable for the way in which he behaved towards them in his capacity as warden of the house. The respondents should then be vicariously liable to the appellants for the injury and damage which they suffered at the hands of the warden.

Lord Hobhouse of Woodborough: These appeals are described as raising a question of the vicarious liability for acts of sexual abuse by an employee . . . What these cases and *Trotman's* case in truth illustrate is a situation where the employer has assumed a relationship to the plaintiff which imposes specific duties in tort upon the employer and the role of the employee (or servant) is that he is the person to whom the employer has entrusted the performance of those duties. These cases are examples of that class where the employer, by reason of assuming a relationship to the plaintiff, owes to the plaintiff duties which are more extensive than those owed by the public at large and, accordingly, are to be contrasted with the situation where a defendant is simply in proximity to the plaintiff so that it is foreseeable that his acts may injure the plaintiff or his property and a reasonable person would have taken care to avoid causing such injury.

The fact that sexual abuse was involved does not distinguish this case from any other involving the care of the young and vulnerable and the duty to protect them from the risk of harm. The classes of persons or institutions that are in this type of special relationship to another human being include schools, prisons, hospitals and even, in relation to their visitors, occupiers of land. They are liable if they themselves fail to perform the duty which they consequently owe. If they entrust the performance of that duty to an employee and that employee fails to perform the duty, they are still liable. The employee, because he has, through his obligations to his employers, adopted the same relationship towards and come under the same duties to the plaintiff, is also liable to the plaintiff for his own breach of duty. The liability of the employers is a *vicarious* liability because the actual breach of duty is that of the employee. The employee is a tortfeasor. The employers are liable for the employee's tortious act or omission because it is to him that the employers have entrusted the performance of their duty. The employers' liability to the plaintiff is also that of a tortfeasor. I use the word "entrusted" in preference to the word "delegated" which is commonly, but perhaps less accurately, used. Vicarious liability is sometimes described as a "strict" liability. The use of this term is misleading unless it is used just to explain that there has been no *actual* fault on the part of the employers. The liability of the employers derives from their voluntary assumption of the relationship towards the plaintiff and the duties that arise from that relationship and their choosing to entrust the performance of those duties to their servant. Where these conditions are satisfied, the motive of the employee and the fact that he is doing something expressly forbidden and is serving only his own ends does not negative the vicarious liability for his breach of the "delegated" duty.

The duty which I have described is also to be found in relation to the loss of or damage to goods. The leading case in this connection is *Morris v C W Martin & Sons Ltd* [1966] 1 Q.B. 716, a case upon the liability of a bailee, already referred to by my noble and learned friend Lord Steyn. A bailor is a person who entrusts the possession and care of goods to the bailee. It is a legal relationship giving rise to common law obligations owed by the bailee to the bailor. Salmon L.J., referring to the duties of a bailee, said: "the act of stealing the fur was a glaring breach of the duty to take reasonable care to keep it safe—and this is negligence." Doing the opposite of what it is your duty to do is still a breach of that duty. My Lords, I feel it necessary to mention this because one of the arguments which was advanced by the respondents (and which has found some favour) has been that it cannot be a breach of a duty to take care of a child to abuse him. It is an exemplary and egregious breach of the servant's duty both to his employer and to the child. The appreciation that there are duties involved is at the heart of the analysis and the identification of the criteria for the existence or no of vicarious liability.

The decision in *Morris v C W Martin & Sons Ltd* was reasoned applying the principles of vicarious liability. All these cases illustrate the general proposition that, where the defendant has assumed a relationship to the plaintiff which carries with it a specific duty towards the plaintiff, the defendant is vicariously liable in tort if his servant, to whom the performance of that duty has been entrusted, breaches that duty.

Whether or not some act comes within the scope of the servant's employment depends upon an identification of what duty the servant was employed by his employer to perform. If the act of the servant which gives rise to the servant's liability to the plaintiff amounted to a failure by the servant to perform that duty, the act comes within "the scope of his employment" and the employer is vicariously liable. If, on the other hand, the servant's employment merely gave the servant the opportunity to do what he did without more, there will be no vicarious liability, hence the use by some authorities of the word "connection" to indicate something which is not a casual coincidence but has the requisite relationship to the employment of the tortfeasor (servant) by his employer: *Kirby v National Coal Board* 1958 S.C. 514; *Williams v A & W Hemphill Ltd* 1966 S.C.(HL) 31.

My Lords, the correct approach to answering the question whether the tortious act of the servant falls within or without the scope of the servant's employment for the purposes of the principle of vicarious liability is to ask what was the duty of the servant towards the plaintiff which was broken by the servant and what was the contractual duty of the servant towards his employer.

Lord Millett: . . . the precise terminology is not critical. What is critical is that attention should be directed to the closeness of the connection between the employee's duties and his wrongdoing and not to verbal formulae.

As my noble and learned friend Lord Steyn has observed, *Morris v Martin* has consistently been held to be an authority on vicarious liability generally and not confined to cases of bailment. So it is no answer to say that the employee was guilty of intentional wrongdoing, or that his act was not merely tortious but criminal, or that he was acting exclusively for his own benefit, or that he was acting contrary to express instructions, or that his conduct was the very negation of his employer's duty. The cases show that where an employer undertakes the care of a client's property and entrusts the task to an employee who steals the property, the employer is vicariously liable. But the theft must be committed by the very employee to whom the custody of the property is entrusted. He does more than make the most of an opportunity presented by the fact of his employment. He takes advantage of the position in which the employer has placed him to enable the purposes of the employer's business to be achieved. If the boys in the present case had been sacks of potatoes and the defendant, having been engaged to take care of them, had entrusted their care to one of its employees, it would have been vicariously liable for any criminal damage done to them by the employee in question, though not by any other employee. Given that the employer's liability does not arise from the law of bailment, it is not immediately apparent that it should make any difference that the victims were boys, that the wrongdoing took the form of sexual abuse, and that it was committed for the personal gratification of the employee.

In the present case the warden's duties provided him with the opportunity to commit indecent assaults on the boys for his own sexual gratification, but that in itself is not enough to make the school liable. The same would be true of the groundsman or the school porter. But there was far more to it than that. The school was responsible for the care and welfare of the boys. It entrusted that responsibility to the warden. He was employed to discharge the school's responsibility to the boys. For this purpose the school entrusted them to his care. He did not merely take advantage of the opportunity which employment at a residential school gave him. He abused the special position in which the school had placed him to enable it to discharge its own responsibilities, with the result that the assaults were committed by the very employee to whom the school had entrusted the care of the boys. I would hold the school liable.

I would regard this as in accordance not only with ordinary principle deducible from the authorities but with the underlying rationale of vicarious liability. Experience shows that in the case of boarding schools, prisons, nursing homes, old people's homes, geriatric wards, and other residential homes for the young or vulnerable, there is an inherent risk that indecent assaults on the residents will be committed by those placed in authority over them, particularly if they are in close proximity to them and occupying a position of trust.

I would hold the school vicariously liable for the warden's intentional assaults, not (as was suggested in argument) for his failure to perform his duty to take care of the boys. That is an artificial approach based on a misreading of *Morris v Martin*. The cleaners were vicariously liable for their employee's conversion of the fur, not for his negligence in failing to look after it. Similarly in *Photo Production v Securicor Transport Ltd* the security firm was vicariously liable for the patrolman's arson, not for his negligence. The law is mature enough to hold an employer vicariously liable for deliberate, criminal wrongdoing on the part of an employee without indulging in sophistry of this kind.

Lord Hope of Craighead concurred in a separate speech.

Note:

1. The principal importance of this decision is that it abandons the Salmond formula, repeated for over a century, according to which the employer was liable if the employee's wrongful conduct was either authorised by the employer or an improper way of doing what was authorised. The notion of "authority", central to the law of agency in transactional matters, is ill-suited to cases of personal injury or property damage. It led to the monstrous decision in *Keppel Bus Co v Sa'ad bin Ahmad* [1974] 2 All E.R. 700 where a bus conductor beat a passenger about the head with his ticket machine and Lord Kilbrandon was pleased to make the ludicrously inapposite observation that "there was no evidence which would justify the ascription of the act of the conductor to any authority, express or implied, vested in him by his employers."

2. That test has been replaced by the test of whether what the employee did was so closely connected with what he was supposed to be doing that it would be fair just and reasonable to hold his employer liable for the resulting harm to the claimant. There is nothing much wrong with that: it is really no looser than the test now properly abandoned.

3. Neither the abandonment of the old test nor its replacement is highlighted in the extracts given from the speeches in *Lister*. They have been chosen to indicate the confusion which runs through every single speech.

The confusion is between vicarious liability properly so called and the defendant's personal liability for breach of his own duty through the act of another.

It must be repeated that vicarious liability is a liability imposed on a person though he is not in breach of any duty he owes to the claimant, but rather because another person is in breach of *his* duty towards the claimant. It is not quite accurate for Lord Steyn to say "Vicarious liability is legal responsibility imposed on an employer although he himself is *free from blame*": it is legal responsibility imposed on an employer (though not only employers) although he is *not in breach of any duty*—for even if one is free from blame one may well be in breach of one's duty. After all one does not say that the liability of the building contractor is vicarious when his subcontractor's delinquency puts him in breach of his contractual duty to the customer to produce a satisfactory building: it is not vicarious because the contractor is in breach of his own duty, blameless though he is, and furthermore he is rendered so liable not only by his employees, but also by independent contractors whom he gets to help him perform his duty. Such cases also exist outside of contract, such as the duty of the sub-bailee to the known owner of the chattel for which he has undertaken responsibility.

The speeches in *Lister* modulate vertiginously between these two grounds of liability, which are quite distinct and should be kept so. Lord Hobhouse starts off splendidly by indicating the difference, but then we find him speaking of the employer's "vicarious liability for [the employee's] breach of the 'delegated' duty". But the equivocation is found in every speech.

On the facts of *Lister* it is clear that the school was in a very special relationship with the claimants and having undertaken responsibility for their welfare owed them a personal duty to see that they were properly looked after; the performance of this duty they delegated to the warden—he was to look after the children for the school; accordingly, they are answerable for its faulty performance, even though they themselves were in no way to blame—they were in breach of duty though not at fault. Lord Millett surely makes this point when he says that the situation would be the same if the boys had been sacks of potatoes.

Indeed, the equivocation already exists in *Morris v Martin* where the fur entrusted to the defendant bailee was stolen by an employee. It was made clear that the bailee was liable for the theft only if it was committed by the very employee to whom the fur was entrusted, not for theft by other furtive employees (for whom the presence of the fur would simply present an opportunity for making off with it). But it is also clear that if it had been entrusted to an independent contractor whose servant made off with it, the bailee would be liable to the customer (*British Road Services v Crutchley* [1968] 1 All E.R. 811). Now if the tortfeasor needn't be an employee at all, and if he is an employee must be the actual delegate, it seems clear that we are not in the area of vicarious liability properly so-called: we are in the area of the defendant bailee being put in breach of his (non-delegable) duty to the customer by the act of the person, employee or not, whom he retained to perform his duty.

These situations are inevitably triangular. Let the apices be C, the claimant, D, the defendant, and T, the tortfeasor. If C is in a special relationship with D, he can go directly to D and say: "You owed me a duty and though I realise that you yourself are not to blame, your duty to me was not performed but broken owing to the fault of the person to whom you delegated its performance". But C can only do this if D does indeed owe him a special duty arising out of a recognised relationship which generates it. Otherwise all C can say to D is "I recognise that you know nothing about me, I am a total stranger, but I am sorry to say that T torted me, in breach of his own, T's, duty to me, and because he was your employee acting in the course of his employment by you, you have to pay up for him." These two routes round the triangle really must be kept separate: if the defendant is not in breach of his duty to the claimant, his liability can only be vicarious, but he may be put in breach of his duty by the act of a third party, not necessarily an employee.

But the defendant may be in breach of a personal duty towards the claimant even though there is no special relationship between them. Take the case that a trucking firm in London sends an employee off in a truck to deliver cargo to a customer in Leeds, but the employee decides to go and see his girl friend in Bristol. If he runs over a pedestrian in Swindon his employer will not be liable: the employee is clearly frolicking and not in the course of his employment at all. But suppose that the truck has defective brakes as a result of poor maintenance, and it is because of that fault that the pedestrian in Swindon is run over; then the firm will be liable even if the driver is frolicking like crazy.

4. Decisions like *Lister* are not merely authorities, they also set up a trend. Thus in *Mattis v Pollock (t/a Flamingo's Nightclub)* [2003] EWCA Civ 887, [2003] 1 W.L.R. 2158 the owner of a nightclub who knew that his bouncer was capable of violence was liable to a person stabbed after the bouncer, following an altercation, had gone home to fetch a knife. Since this was the culmination of an incident which started in the nightclub and could not fairly and justly be treated in isolation, the Court of Appeal reversed the decision below that the connection was insufficiently close.

5. Shortly after deciding *Lister*, the House of Lords had occasion, in *Dubai Aluminium Co v Salaam* [2002] UKHL 45, [2003] 2 A.C. 366, to engage with vicarious liability once more, this time not that of the employer for an employee but that of a partnership for a fraudulent partner (of course if partners are partners in crime we call them conspirators and make them liable for all the harm resulting from the conspiracy—bad people pay more!). Section 10 of the Partnership Act 1890 provides that "Where, by any wrongful act or

omission of any partner acting in the ordinary course of the business of the firm, or with the authority of his co-partners, loss or injury is caused to any person not being a partner in the firm, or any penalty is incurred, the firm is liable therefor to the same extent as the partner so acting or omitting to act."

The facts involved a transactional tort (fraud) to which the Salmond test involving notions of authority might have been thought less inappropriate. However, Lord Nicholls said: "The underlying legal policy [of vicarious liability] is based on the recognition that carrying on a business enterprise necessarily involves risks to others. It involves the risk that others will be harmed by wrongful acts committed by the agents through whom the business is carried on. When those risks ripen into loss, it is just that the business should be responsible for compensating the person who has been wronged. This policy reason dictates that liability for agents should not be strictly confined to acts done with the employer's authority. Negligence can be expected to occur from time to time. Everyone makes mistakes at times Additionally, it is a fact of life, and therefore to be expected by those who carry on businesses, that sometimes their agents may exceed the bounds of their authority or even defy express instructions. It is fair to allocate risk of losses thus arising to the businesses rather than leave those wronged with the sole remedy, of doubtful value, against the individual employee who committed the wrong. To this end, the law has given the concept of "ordinary course of employment" an extended scope.

If, then, authority is not the touchstone, what is? Perhaps the best general answer is that the wrongful conduct must be so closely connected with acts the partner or employee was authorised to do that, for the purpose of the liability of the firm or the employer to third parties, the wrongful conduct *may fairly and properly be regarded* as done by the partner while acting in the ordinary course of the firm's business or the employee's employment. Lord Millett said as much in *Lister v Hesley Hall Ltd* [2002] 1 A.C. 215, 245.

In these formulations the phrases "may fairly and properly be regarded", "can be said", and "can fairly be regarded" betoken a value judgment by the court. The conclusion is a conclusion of law, based on primary facts, rather than a simple question of fact.

This "close connection" test focuses attention in the right direction. But it affords no guidance on the type or degree of connection which will normally be regarded as sufficiently close to prompt the legal conclusion that the risk of the wrongful act occurring, and any loss flowing from the wrongful act, should fall on the firm or employer rather than the third party who was wronged. This lack of precision is inevitable, given the infinite range of circumstances where the issue arises. The crucial feature or features, either producing or negativing vicarious liability, vary widely from one case or type of case to the next. Essentially the court makes an evaluative judgment in each case, having regard to all the circumstances and, importantly, having regard also to the assistance provided by previous court decisions. In this field the latter form of assistance is particularly valuable."

MORRIS v C W MARTIN & SONS LTD

Court of Appeal [1966] 1 Q.B. 716; [1965] 3 W.L.R. 276; 109 S.J. 451; [1965] 2 Lloyd's Rep. 63; [1965] 2 All E.R. 725

Action by owner of goods against person in lawful possession of them in respect of their loss by theft

The plaintiff wanted her mink stole cleaned, and delivered it to one Beder. Beder could not clean it himself, so with the plaintiff's agreement he delivered it to the defendants for that purpose. The contract between Beder and the defendants contained a clause limiting the defendants' liability in certain circumstances. The trial judge found that while Beder had the plaintiff's authority to sub-contract the job of cleaning the stole, he entered the sub-contract as principal and not as agent (in other words, the defendant was to invoice Beder, not the plaintiff). The defendant handed the fur to an employee, Morrissey, for cleaning, but he made off with it and it was never recovered.

The trial judge held himself bound by *Cheshire v Bailey* [1905] 1 K.B. 237 to give judgment for the defendants. The Court of Appeal allowed the plaintiff's appeal.

Lord Denning M.R.: . . . The case raises the important question of how far a master is liable for theft or dishonesty by one of his servants. If the master has himself been at fault in not employing a trustworthy man, of course he is liable. But what is the position when the master is not himself at fault at all?

The law on this subject has developed greatly over the years. During the nineteenth century it was accepted law that a master was liable for the dishonesty or fraud of his servant if it was done in the course of his employment *and* for his master's benefit. Dishonesty or fraud by the servant for his *own* benefit took the case out of the course of his employment. The judges took this simple view: No servant who turns thief and steals is acting in the course of his employment. He is acting outside it altogether. But in 1912 the law was revolutionised by *Lloyd v Grace, Smith & Co* ([1912] A.C. 716), where it was held that a master was liable for the dishonesty or fraud of his servant if it was done within the course of his employment, no matter whether it was done for the benefit of the master or for the benefit of the servant. Nevertheless, there still remains the question: What is meant by the phrase "in the course of his employment?" When can it be said that dishonesty or fraud of a servant, done for his *own* benefit, is in the course of his employment?

If you go through the cases on this difficult subject, you will find that, in the ultimate analysis, they depend on the nature of the duty owed by the master towards the person whose goods have been lost or damaged. If the master is under a duty to use due care to keep goods safely and protect them from theft and depredation, he cannot get rid of his responsibility by delegating his duty to another. If he entrusts that duty to his servant, he is answerable for the way in which the servant conducts himself therein. No matter whether the servant be negligent, fraudulent, or dishonest, the master is liable. But not when he is under no such duty. The cases show this:

(i) *Gratuitous bailment.* Suppose I visit a friend's house and leave my coat with his servant in the hall, so that my friend becomes a gratuitous bailee of it: see *Ultzen v Nicols* ([1894] 1 Q.B. 92). On my departure, I find my coat has gone. The servant who was entrusted with it has stolen it without my friend's fault. He has converted it, it may be said, in the course of his employment. But nevertheless my friend is not liable for the loss, because he was not under any duty to prevent it being stolen, but only to keep it as his own. "The law is not so unreasonable," said Holt C.J., "as to charge a man for doing such a friendly act for a friend": see *Coggs v Bernard* ((1703) 2 Ld.Raym. 909 at 914; 92 E.R. 107 at 110) and *Giblin v McMullen* ((1869) L.R. 2 P.C. 317), where it was assumed, rightly or wrongly, that the bank was a gratuitous bailee.

(ii) *Occupier's liability for visitor's belongings.* Suppose an actor leaves his belongings in his dressing-room. The porter negligently leaves the stage door unattended. A thief slips in and steals the actor's belongings. The porter was negligent in the course of his employment. But nevertheless the occupiers of the theatre are not liable for the loss, for the simple reason that they were under no duty to protect the actor's belongings from theft: see *Deyong v Shenburn* ([1946] K.B. 227) and *Edwards v West Herts. Group Hospital Management Committee* ([1957] 1 W.L.R. 415).

(iii) *Bailment for reward.* Once a man has taken charge of goods as a bailee for reward, it is his duty to take reasonable care to keep them safe; and he cannot escape that duty by delegating it to his servant. If the goods are lost or damaged, whilst they are in his possession, he is liable unless he can show—and the burden is on him to show—that the loss or damage occurred without any neglect or default or misconduct of himself or of any of the servants to whom he delegated his duty. This is clearly established by *Reeve v Palmer* ((1858) 5 C.B.(N.S.) 84; 141 E.R. 33), *Coldman v Hill* ([1919] 1 K.B. 443) and *Building and Civil Engineering Holidays Scheme Management Ltd v Post Office* ([1966] 1 Q.B. 247). The bailee, to excuse himself, must show that the loss was without any fault on his part or on the part of his servants. If he shows that he took due care to employ trustworthy servants, and that he and his servants exercised all diligence, and yet the goods were stolen, he will be excused: but not otherwise. Take a case where a cleaner hands a fur to one of his servants for cleaning, and it is stolen. If the master can prove that the thieves came in from outside and stole it without the fault of any of his servants, the master is not liable. But if it appears that the servant to whom he entrusted it was negligent in leaving the door unlocked—or collaborated with the thieves—or stole the fur himself, then the master is liable: see *Southcote's* case ((1601) 76 E.R. 1061); *United Africa Co Ltd v Saka Owoade* ([1955] A.C. 130) and *Reg. v Levy Bros Co Ltd* ([1961] S.C.R. 189).

(iv) *Contract to take care to protect the goods.* Although there may be no bailment, nevertheless circumstances often arise in which a person is under a contractual duty to take care to protect goods from theft or depredation: see, for instance, *Stansbie v Troman* ([1948] 2 K.B. 48). The most familiar case is the keeper of a boarding house or a private hotel. He is under an implied contract to take reasonable care for the safety of property brought into the house by a guest. If his own servants are negligent and leave the place open so that thieves can get in and steal he is liable: see *Dansey v Richardson* ((1854) 3 E. & B. 144; 118 E.R. 1095) and *Scarborough v Cosgrove* ([1905] 2 K.B. 805). So also if they are fraudulent and collaborate with the thieves. Again, when a job-master lets out a brougham and coachman, he undertakes impliedly that the coachman will take care to protect the goods in the brougham. If they are stolen owing to the coachman's negligence, the job-master is liable. So also if the coachman steals them himself.

(v) *Apparent authority of servant.* In *Lloyd v Grace, Smith & Co* a solicitor's clerk, acting within the *apparent* scope of his authority from his principals, accepted Mrs Lloyd's deeds so as to sell her cottages on her behalf and to call in a mortgage. When he accepted her instructions, he intended to misappropriate the deeds for his own benefit, and he did so. His principals were held liable. The essence of that case as stressed in all the speeches (and especially in the judgment of Scrutton J.) was that the clerk was acting within his *apparent* authority in receiving the deeds and thus his principals had them in their charge. In consequence of this *apparent* authority, the firm of solicitors were clearly under a *duty* to deal honestly and faithfully with Mrs Lloyd's property: and they could not escape that duty by delegating it to their agent. They were responsible for the way he conducted himself therein, even though he did it dishonestly for his own benefit.

(vi) *Where there is only opportunity to defraud.* There are many cases in the books where a servant takes the opportunity afforded by his service to steal or defraud another for his own benefit. It has always been held that the master is not on that account liable to the person who has been defrauded: see *Ruben v Great Fingall Consolidated* ([1906] A.C. 439). If a window cleaner steals a valuable article from my flat whilst he is working there, I cannot claim against his employer unless he was negligent in employing him: see *De Parrell v Walker* ((1932) 49 T.L.R. 37). In order for the master to be liable there must be some circumstances imposing a duty on the master: see *Coleman v Riches, per* Williams J. ((1855) 16 C.B. 104 at 121; 139 E.R. 695).

From all these instances we may deduce the general proposition that when a principal has in his charge the goods or belongings of another in such circumstances that he is under a duty to take all reasonable precautions to protect them from theft or depredation, then if he entrusts that duty to a servant or agent, he is answerable for the manner in which that servant or agent carries out his duty. If the servant or agent is careless so that they are stolen by a stranger, the master is liable. So also if the servant or agent himself steals them or makes away with them.

Diplock L.J.: ... The defendants cannot in my view escape liability for the conversion of the plaintiff's fur by their servant Morrissey. They accepted the fur as bailees for reward in order to clean it. They put Morrissey as their agent in their place to clean the fur and to take charge of it while doing so. The manner in which he conducted himself in doing that work was to convert it. What he was doing, albeit dishonestly, he was doing in the scope or course of his employment in the technical sense of that infelicitous but time-honoured phrase. The defendants as his masters are responsible for his tortious act.

Nor are we concerned with what would have been the liability of the defendants if the fur had been stolen by another servant of theirs who was not employed by them to clean the fur or to have the care or custody of it. The mere fact that his employment by the defendants gave him the opportunity to steal it would not suffice. The crucial distinction between *Lloyd v Grace, Smith & Co* ([1912] A.C. 716) and *Ruben v Great Fingall Consolidated* ([1906] A.C. 439) is that in the latter case the dishonest servant was neither actually nor ostensibly employed to warrant the genuineness of certificates for shares in the company which employed him. His fraudulent conduct was facilitated by the access which he had to the company's seal and documents in the course of his employment for another purpose: but the fraud itself which was the only tort giving rise to a civil liability to the plaintiffs was not committed in the course of doing that class of acts which the company had put the servant in its place to do.

I base my decision in this case on the ground that the fur was stolen by the very servant whom the defendants as bailees for reward had employed to take care of it and clean it.

Salmon L.J.: ... I accordingly agree with my Lords that the appeal should be allowed. I am anxious, however, to make it plain that the conclusion which I have reached depends upon Morrissey being the servant through whom the defendants chose to discharge their duty to take reasonable care of the plaintiff's fur. A bailee for reward is not answerable for a theft by any of his servants but only for a theft by such of them as are deputed by him to discharge some part of his duty of taking reasonable care. A theft by any servant who is not employed to do anything in relation to the goods bailed is entirely outside the scope of his employment and cannot make the master liable. So in this case, if someone employed by the defendants in another depot had broken in and stolen the fur, the defendants would not have been liable. Similarly in my view if a clerk employed in the same depot had seized the opportunity of entering the room where the fur was kept and had stolen it, the defendants would not have been liable. The mere fact that the master, by employing a rogue, gives him the opportunity to steal or defraud does not make the master liable for his depredations: *Ruben v Great Fingall Consolidated* ([1906] A.C. 439). It might be otherwise if the master knew or ought to have known that his servant was dishonest, because then the master could be liable in negligence for employing him. ...

Questions

1. You take your car to a garage for repair. When you go to pick it up, the garage owner says: "I'm very sorry. One of my men sneaked back last night after we were closed, got in with a duplicate key he had had made somewhere, took your car—it was the nicest one in the garage—and wrecked it." Is this, or should it be, a satisfactory answer? See *Leesh River Tea Co v British India Steam Navigation Co* [1967] 2 Q.B. 250 at 278, *per* Salmon L.J.

2. Do you agree with the following decisions?

   (a) Long-distance telephone calls costing nearly £1,500 were made from the plaintiff's office by a cleaner employed by the defendant cleaning firm. Although the cleaning contracted for included the cleaning and sterilisation of the plaintiff's telephones, the defendants were held not liable. *Heasmans v Clarity Cleaning* [1987] I.R.L.R. 286, CA—"borderline" (Palmer, *Bailment* (2nd ed., 1991), p.867).

   (b) In *Swiss Bank v Brink's-MAT* [1986] 2 Lloyd's Rep. 79 a security firm was held not liable for a valuable cargo stolen by robbers tipped off by an employee who learnt of its arrival while on the job.

   (c) P.C. McCarthy went to the plaintiff's flat to ask questions, produced his warrant card, threatened her with arrest unless she had sex with him and then assaulted and buggered her. The Chief Constable was held not liable, though the constable had to pay punitive damages (*Makanjuola v Commissioner for Police* [1990] 2 Admin. L.R. 214).

   (d) In order to further their pay claim, firemen on a go-slow took five times as long as usual to reach a fire at the plaintiff's premises, which consequently became a total loss. The firemen's employer was held not liable: *General Engineering Services v Kingston Corp.* [1988] 3 All E.R. 867, PC. Would the individual firemen have been liable? Does the *Capital and Counties* case (above, p.103) make a difference?

3. Does this case mean that a patient assaulted by a nurse may sue the hospital but that a patient assaulted by a floor-cleaner cannot?

4. Is there any connection between the two following statements?

   (a) The very bad act of a third party tends to insulate a previous tortfeasor from liability for further consequences (above, p.225).

   (b) The worse a servant's act is, the less likely is the master to be held vicariously responsible.

5. Morrissey was both the servant of Martin and their delegate. Martin would not have been liable for theft by a servant who was not also a delegate, but would have been liable for theft by a delegate who was not a servant: *British Road Services v Arthur Crutchley* [1968] 1 All E.R. 811. So was it relevant that Morrissey was a servant?

6. Beder also was a bailee. Was Martin his delegate?

7. Lord Denning makes this case turn on the relationship between the plaintiff and the defendant. Is this consistent with what he did in *Rose v Plenty* (above, p.283)?

Notes:

1. A 16 year old of mixed parentage was mercilessly harassed by fellow-employees during the five weeks he stayed at work: they burned him with a screwdriver, pinned racist notes to this clothing and called him simian names. The Employment Appeal Tribunal held that the employer was not liable under the Race Relations Act 1976, s.32(1), which provides that "Anything done by a person in the course of his employment shall be treated for the purposes of this Act . . . as done by his employer as well as by him, whether or not it was done with the employer's knowledge or approval . . . " The Court of Appeal reversed, Waite L.J. saying "It would be particularly wrong to allow racial harassment on the scale that was suffered by the complainant in this case at the hands of his workmates . . . to slip through the net of employer responsibility by applying to it a common law principle evolved in another area of law to deal with vicarious responsibility for wrongdoing of a wholly different kind." *Jones v Tower Boot Co* [1997] 2 All E.R. 406 at 416. Note that damages for personal injury, physical or mental, may be awarded by an industrial tribunal: *Sheriff v Klyne Tugs* [1999] I.R.L.R. 481.

In *Trotman v North Yorks CC* [1998] Times L.R. 550 the Court of Appeal held that a school was not liable to pupils sexually assaulted by the deputy headmaster during a school trip abroad, and said that *Morris v Martin* applied only in bailment cases. This decision was of course overruled in *Lister v Hesley Hall*.

2. When the Court of Appeal held that there could never be vicarious liability for an employee guilty of the tort of misfeasance in office, which calls for bad faith abuse of public powers, the House of Lords disagreed and said that vicarious liability might well exist: it all depended on the particular facts (*Racz v Home Office* [1994] 1 All E.R. 97.

3. In *Crédit Lyonnais v Export Credits Guarantee Department* [1999] 1 All E.R. 929 the House of Lords decided a point which, since it had never been raised before, is unlikely to have a great future. The plaintiff bank was conned out of £10 million by one Chong who corrupted Pillai, an employee of the defendant who, within his authority and in the course of his employment, issued documents which, to Pillai's knowledge, Chong was to use as part of his confidence trick on the bank. Although his participation in the scheme made Pillai liable to the bank as a joint tortfeasor with Chong, *i.e.* personally liable for Chong's actings, his "actions . . . in the course of his employment probably went no further than facilitating the deceit on the bank by Mr Chong." (at 936) The employer was not liable: a tortfeasor does not make his employer liable unless the whole of his tort, and not just a discrete part of it (whether the remainder consists of acts of his outside the scope of his employment or of acts of a third party), takes place in the course and scope of his employment.

4. In 1991 Nurse Allitt killed four children and injured nine others at Grantham Hospital Ward 4 and is now serving 13 life sentences. The Lincolnshire H.A. agreed to split £500,000 between 12 of the families. Katie's parents rejected an offer of £1.5 million and obtained a settlement of £2,125K in a hearing before Jowitt J. Was the health authority right to admit liability?

Theft

Judges are rather reluctant to hold one person liable for theft committed by another. This reluctance is justifiable on the ground that theft is a risk against which sensible owners insure themselves (so that plaintiffs are either stupid owners or insurers in disguise), though it is also true that employers can take out fidelity insurance against the risk of an employee's dishonesty. Conceptually the judicial reluctance may be expressed in two ways, or even three, for in addition to denying the duty or the causation, it may be held that in the circumstances it was not unreasonable not to guard against the theft which occurred.

If one person is to be liable for theft by another, then his duty must be the duty to take positive steps to protect the goods against theft. This is higher than the normal duty in tort, namely, to take care not to damage the goods. Such a higher duty can arise either by contract or by reason of an "undertaking" by the defendant followed by a "reliance" by the plaintiff. (Was there any "reliance" by the plaintiff on the defendant in the principal case, or only on Beder?) The undertaking-reliance duty will exist in every bailment situation *inter partes*, and will subsist though the contract be tainted by fraud or illegality. In the absence of such an undertaking, the higher duty will not rest on an employer (*Edwards v West Herts. Group Hospital Management Committee* [1957] 1 W.L.R. 415) or on a neighbour (*Perl v Camden L.B.C.* [1983] 3 All E.R. 161) or on an occupier (*Tinsley v Dudley* [1951] 2 K.B. 18). Goods which are lawfully on another's premises may be there by mere licence—a bicycle in a college bicycle shed—or because the occupier has possession of them—a bicycle being repaired at the bicycle shop. (For a case distinguishing parking ("May I leave it here?") and garaging ("Will you look after it?"), see *Ashby v Tolhurst* [1937] 2 K.B. 242.) In the second case the occupier is also bailee; the mental element necessary for possession being the same as that required to constitute an "undertaking" in tort.

Alternatively, one can say that, even if the defendant was careless, the voluntary and unlawful act of the thief breaks the chain of causation between the carelessness and the loss. This may be said when either there was no duty to guard or the duty was fulfilled (*Brook's Wharf & Bull Wharf v Goodman Bros* [1937] 1 K.B.

534), but it is difficult to say it when there has been a failure to guard, there being a contract or undertaking to do so (*Stansbie v Troman* [1948] 2 K.B. 348), since the theft which has intervened is the very thing that should have been guarded against; for the difficulties, see *Mercantile Credit Co v Hamblin* [1965] 2 Q.B. 242 at 275, and *Lamb v Camden L.B.C.* [1981] 2 All E.R. 408.

None of this, however, need mean that a person who is under a duty to guard and has fulfilled it either personally or through the servant to whom he has entrusted the job (*e.g.* a nightwatchman) should not still be liable for theft by one of his other servants. But the law is that he is not.

Wholly different considerations apply where the defendant has dealt with the thing in an unpermitted manner which results in its loss. They are discussed in the chapter on conversion and other torts to chattels, below p.484f.

Chapter 7

CONTRACTORS

Section 1.—The Employer

DAVIE v NEW MERTON BOARD MILLS LTD

House of Lords [1959] A.C. 604; [1959] 2 W.L.R. 331; 103 S.J. 177; [1959] 1 All E.R. 346; [1959] 2
Lloyd's Rep. 587 (noted (1958) 74 L.Q.R. 397)

Action by employee against employer in respect of personal injury

During his employment by the first defendants, the plaintiff wanted to separate two pieces of a machine; for this purpose he needed a drift, a pointed metal bar about a foot long. He went to a cupboard and chose one which was apparently sound, but at the second stroke of his hammer a piece of the drift broke off and entered his left eye. The drift was too hard to be safe, because the manufacturers, the second defendants, had given it the wrong heat treatment; once this was done, however, the defect in the drift was undiscoverable, short of a test which it would have been unreasonable to expect the employers to carry out. The employers had not bought the drift directly from the manufacturers but from a reputable middleman.

Ashworth J. gave judgment for the plaintiff against both defendants, the employers to be indemnified by the manufacturers [1957] 2 Q.B. 368. The employers' appeal to the Court of Appeal was allowed (Jenkins L.J. dissenting) [1958] 1 Q.B. 210. The workman's appeal to the House of Lords was dismissed.

Viscount Simonds: ... Before I turn to the examination of the cases by which it may be supposed that guiding authority is given, I would remind your Lordships that this action was founded in tort. The accident, it was said, was caused by the negligence of the respondents, their servants or agents, and their negligence consisted in this, that they failed to provide a suitable drift which could be hammered safely without the risk of pieces flying off. I have deliberately used the language of the statement of claim which has been repeatedly used in these proceedings. It may be relevant to observe that it is not strictly accurate. The accident occurred not through a failure to supply a suitable drift—a failure that could result in nothing—but through the supply of an unsuitable drift. Therein lay their alleged negligence, and I pause to analyse that allegation. It may mean one of two things. First, it may mean that it was the duty of the respondents to supply suitable drifts: they supplied an unsuitable one: they did not do their duty: therefore they were negligent. This is a bare statement of absolute obligation. But, secondly, it may mean that the supply of an unsuitable drift was due to a want of reasonable care on their part. It must, then, be shown wherein lay the want of reasonable care, and at once the question arises, for whose negligence, acts, I suppose, of omission and commission, the employer is liable in the long chain which ends with the supply by him of a tool to his workman but may begin with the delving of the raw material of manufacture in a distant continent. In the case before us the chain is long enough. The respondents were not guilty of any negligence nor was any servant or agent of theirs nor was the reputable firm who supplied the drifts, but at the end of the chain were the manufacturers. The respondents stood in no contractual relation to them: so little connection was there between them that it was long in dispute whether the fatal drift had been manufactured by them and delivered by them to the suppliers. But is is for their negligence in manufacture that the appellant would make the respondents liable. Remembering, my Lords, that the essence of the tort of negligence lies in the failure to take reasonable care, I am constrained to wonder how this thing can be. . . .

My Lords, I would begin with a reference to the familiar words of Lord Herschell in *Smith v Charles Baker & Sons* in which he describes the duty of a master at common law as "the duty of taking reasonable care to provide proper appliances, and to maintain them in a proper condition, and so to carry on his operations as not to subject those employed by him to unnecessary risk," words that are important both in prescribing the positive obligation and in negativing by implication anything higher. The content of the duty at common law, thus described by Lord Herschell, must vary according to the circumstances of each case. Its measure remains the same: it is to take reasonable care, and the subject-matter may be such that the taking of reasonable care may fall little short of absolute obligation. I find nothing in the earlier cases, in either the English or Scottish courts, to which our attention was called, that requires any qualification of this statement. . . .

But, my Lords, as I have said, the difficulty arises, not on the primary statement of liability, but upon the question for whom is the employer responsible. Clearly he is responsible for his own acts, and clearly, too, for those of his servants. To them at least the maxims *respondeat superior* and *qui facit per alium facit per se* will apply. It is the next step that is difficult. The employer is said to be liable for the acts of his "agents" and, with greater hesitation, for the acts of "independent contractors." My Lords, fortunately we are not troubled here with the word "agent." No one could say that a manufacturer who makes a tool and supplies it to a merchant who in turn sells it to an employer is in any sense an agent of the latter for providing his workman with a tool. Is he then an independent contractor? It is perhaps a striking commentary on the artificiality of this concept that it should for a moment be thought possible to regard as an independent contractor with an employer a manufacturer with whom he never contracted, of whom he may never have heard and from whom he may be divided in time and space by decades and continents. It may lead your Lordships to the conclusion that the liability of the employer in such a case can only be sustained if his obligation is absolute. But that *ex hypothesi* it is not.

As I have tried to show, the contention, as stated in its first form, that the employer is liable for the acts of himself, his servants and agents and, subject to whatever limitations might be thought fit, independent contractors, could not lead to success in this action: for the manufacturer could not by any legitimate use of language be considered the servant or agent of, or an independent contractor with, the employer who buys his manufactures in the market. It was then sought to reach the same result by a different road. The employer, it was said, was under a duty to take reasonable care to supply his workmen with proper plant and machinery. It was assumed that this included tools such as drifts, and I, too, will, without deciding it, assume it. It was then said that the employer could not escape responsibility by employing a third party, however expert, to do his duty for him. So far, so good. But then comes the next step—but I would rather call it a jump, and a jump that would unhorse any rider. Therefore, it was said, the employer is responsible for the defect in goods that he buys in the market, if it can be shown that that defect was due to the want of skill or care on the part of anyone who was concerned in its manufacture. But, my Lords, by what use or misuse of language can the manufacturer be said to be a person to whom the employer delegated a duty which it was for him to perform? How can it be said that it was as the delegate or agent of the employer that the manufacturer failed to exhibit due skill and care? It is, to my mind, clear that he cannot. . . .

. . . It was said that an employer might, instead of purchasing tools of a standard design, either from the manufacturer direct or in the market, order them to be made to his own design. If he did so and if they were defective and an accident resulted, it was clear (so the argument ran) that he would be responsible. I agree that he would, if the fault lay in the design and was due to lack of reasonable care or skill on his part. There is no reason why he should not. A more difficult question would arise if the defect was not due to any fault in design (for which the employer was responsible) but to carelessness in workmanship. But that is a far cry from the present case, and recognising, as I do, that in this area of the law there is a borderline of difficult cases, I do not propose to say more than I need. I must, however, refer to a case tried by Finnemore J. at Chester Assizes. No authority having been cited to him, he said ([1955] 1 W.L.R. 549 at 551):

"Employers have to act as reasonable people, they have to take reasonable care; but if they buy their tools from well-known makers, such as the second defendants are, they are entitled to assume that the tools will be proper for the purposes for which both sides intended them to be used, and not require daily, weekly or monthly inspection to see if in fact all is well." My Lords, a prolonged examination of the authorities could not have led him to a sounder conclusion.

One more thing I must say. It was at one time suggested—I do not use a more emphatic word, for learned counsel was rightly discreet in his approach—that the House should take into consideration the fact that possibly or even probably the employer would, but the workman would not, be covered by insurance, and for that reason should be the more ready to fasten upon the employer liability for an accident due neither to his nor to the workman's carelessness. I will only say that this is not a consideration to which your Lordships should give any weight at all in your determination of the rights and obligations of the parties. The legislature has thought fit in some circumstances to impose an absolute obligation upon employers. The Factories Acts and the elaborate regulations made under them testify to the care with which the common law has been altered, adjusted and refined in order to give protection and compensation to the workman. It is not the function of a court of law to fasten upon the fortuitous circumstance of insurance to impose a greater burden on the employer than would otherwise lie upon him.

For these reasons, therefore, which I will sum up by saying that the claim was against reason, contrary to principle, and barely supported by authority, I would dismiss the appeal with costs.

Lord Reid: . . . even if it were open on the authorities to reach a conclusion in favour of the appellant, I would think such a conclusion to be wrong in principle. A master's duty to his servant with regard to the safety of plant supplied should, I think, be regarded as a part of the law of tort. Vicarious liability is well recognised and I see no difficulty in principle in extending vicarious liability beyond liability for those who are, strictly speaking, servants, but it would, I think, be going far beyond anything reasonable to extend it to cover a case where there was no relationship whatever between the master and the negligent person or his employer at the time when the negligence occurred. Then I take the other possible way of regarding the master's duty. It was common at one time to regard it as depending on the contract of employment, and, indeed, it was this view which was largely responsible for the invention of the rule of common employment. No doubt this view leaves the court much scope, but I think that it has always been recognised that an implied term must at least be reasonable. I could understand that it might be thought reasonable to make the master absolutely liable in certain cases. This has been done extensively by statute. But it seems to me wholly unreasonable to make the master's liability depend on the conduct of the servants of some person who may be a complete stranger. . . .

Where, then, is the line to be drawn? On the one hand it appears that an employer is liable for the negligence of an independent contractor whom he has engaged to carry out one of what have been described as his personal duties on his own premises and whose work might normally be done by the employer's own servant—at least if the negligent workmanship is discoverable by reasonable inspection. On the other hand, for the reasons which I have given, I am of opinion that he is not liable for the negligence of the manufacturer of an article which he has bought, provided that he has been careful to deal with a seller of repute and has made any inspection which a reasonable employer would make. That leaves a wide sphere regarding which it is unnecessary, and it would, I think, be undesirable, to express any opinion here. Various criteria have been suggested, and it must be left for the further development of the law to determine which is correct. In my judgment this appeal should be dismissed.

Lord Tucker: . . . My Lords, I do not think that the introduction of the independent contractor into this discussion presents any difficulty. It may well be that in some cases the employer may delegate the performance of his obligations in this sphere to someone who is more properly described as a contractor than a servant, but this will not affect the liability of the employer, he will be just as much liable for his negligence as for that of his servant. Such a contractor is entrusted by the employer with the performance of the employer's personal duty. But this does not mean that every person with whom the employer may have entered into some contractual relationship connected with the manufacture or supply of some machinery, appliance or tool which is ultimately used in his business automatically becomes a person entrusted by the employer with the performance of his common law duty. Still less can the negligence of some person with whom the employer has never been in contact contractually or otherwise, or of whom perhaps he has never even heard, be imputed to him. . . .

Notes:

1. The law on the precise point decided in this case was changed 10 years later by the Employers' Liability (Defective Equipment) Act 1969, which rendered the employer liable for personal injury suffered by an employee in consequence of a defect in equipment provided by the employer which was due to the fault of a "third party," "third party" including an unidentifiable manufacturer (*Cullum v Anill Hire* (Raymond Kidwell QC, June 9, 1986), and "equipment" including a ship in which the employee serves (*The Derbyshire* [1987] 3 All E.R. 1068, HL) and even a flagstone which the employee was to lay (*Knowles v Liverpool C.C.* [1993] 4 All E.R. 321, HL). The statutory requirement of fault on the part of the manufacturer may be satisfied by the mere fact that the equipment was defective under the Consumer Protection Act 1987, which also allows the employee to require the employer's supplier (and the employer himself?), on pain of personal liability, to reveal the name of his supplier, the manufacturer or the importer into the E.C. (Directive, above p.27).

2. The same year saw the enactment of the Employers' Liability (Compulsory Insurance) Act 1969 which requires employers to take out the insurance against liability to his employees which Viscount Simonds insisted on ignoring. It differs in two respects from the requirement that persons who put a motor vehicle on a highway have insurance: there is no civil liability for breach (*Richardson v Pitt-Stanley*, above, p.188), and the cover required is not unlimited, £5 million being adequate for the employer (SI 1998/2573).

3. *Davie* remains an illuminating case, however. The outcome was far from being as obvious as the opinions assert. The person who lets out tools on hire used to warrant that they were as fit as care and skill could make them, that is, that they were not defective by reason of any want of care or skill (*White v John Warwick* [1953] 1 W.L.R. 1285); the warranty of the lessor is now statutory and absolute, like that of the seller of goods (Supply of Goods and Services Act 1982, s.9). It would have been perfectly easy to imply into the relationship of employer and employee an undertaking by the employer that equipment provided by him would be safe and suitable. The opinions gain plausibility by insisting that the case was one of tort, not because there are not contractual duties merely to take care (rather than guarantee a result) or because there are no strict liabilities in tort, but because whereas the higher duty appears more natural in contract, the duty in tort tends to be only the duty to take care, through oneself and one's servants, unless there is some very good reason why it should be higher.

Question

An employer who notes that the skylight in his factory needs mending has an independent builder/glazier come to fix it. The work is apparently well done, but three days later in quite a severe storm the glass falls out and strikes an employee working below. Is the employer liable (a) as employer, (b) as occupier (i) at common law, (ii) under Regulations?

McDERMID v NASH DREDGING AND RECLAMATION CO

House of Lords [1987] A.C. 906; [1987] 3 W.L.R. 212; [1987] I.C.R. 917; [1987] 2 All E.R. 878; [1987] 2 Lloyd's Rep. 201 (noted [1988] Camb.L.J. 11; (1986) 49 M.L.R. 781)

Action for personal injury by employee against employer

The plaintiff was employed by the defendant as a deckhand on a tug, whose captain was employed by a third party (the defendant's parent company). The plaintiff's job was to untie the hawsers attaching the tug to a dredger and then to knock twice on the wheelhouse door to tell the captain that it was safe to start the tug. One day the captain started the tug before the knocks were given, and the plaintiff, pulled into the sea by the snaking ropes, suffered a serious leg injury.

The trial judge held that the captain was to be treated as the defendant's servant, even if he were not. The Court of Appeal held the defendant liable, even though the captain was not their servant [1986] Q.B. 965. The House of Lords unanimously dismissed the defendant's appeal.

Lord Brandon: My Lords, the Court of Appeal regarded the case as raising difficult questions of law on which clear authority was not easy to find. With great respect to the elaborate judgment of that court, I think that it has treated the case as more difficult than it really is. A statement of the relevant principle of law can be divided into three parts. First, an employer owes to his employee a duty to exercise reasonable care to ensure that the system of work provided for him is a safe one. Second, the provision of a safe system of work has two aspects: (a) the devising of such a system and (b) the operation of it. Third, the duty concerned has been described alternatively as either personal or non-delegable. The meaning of these expressions is not self-evident and needs explaining. The essential characteristic of the duty is that, if it is not performed, it is no defence for the employer to show that he delegated its performance to a person, whether his servant or not his servant, whom he reasonably believed to be competent to perform it. Despite such delegation the employer is liable for the non-performance of the duty.

In the present case the relevant system of work in relation to the plaintiff was the system for unmooring the tug *Ina*. In the events which occurred the defendants delegated both the devising and the operating of such system to Captain Sas, who was not their servant. An essential feature of such system, if it was to be a safe one, was that Captain Sas would not work the tug's engines ahead or astern until he knew that the plaintiff had completed his work of unmooring the tug. The system which Captain Sas devised was one under which the plaintiff would let him know that he had completed that work by giving two knocks on the outside of the wheelhouse. I have already said that I agree with the Court of Appeal that there was scope, on the evidence, for a finding that that system was not a safe one. I shall assume, however, in the absence of any contrary finding by Staughton J., that that system, as devised by Captain Sas, was safe. The crucial point, however, is that, on the occasion of the plaintiff's accident, Captain Sas did not operate that system. He negligently failed to operate it in that he put the tug's engines astern at a time when the plaintiff had not given, and he, Captain Sas, could not therefore have heard, the prescribed signal of two knocks by the plaintiff on the outside of the wheelhouse. For this failure by Captain Sas to operate the system which he had devised, the defendants, as the plaintiff's employers, are personally, not vicariously, liable to him.

It was contended for the defendants that the negligence of Captain Sas was not negligence in failing to operate the safe system which he had devised. It was rather casual negligence in the course of operating such system, for which the defendants, since Captain Sas was not their servant, were not liable. I cannot accept that contention. The negligence of Captain Sas was not casual but central. It involved abandoning the safe system of work which he had devised and operating in its place a manifestly unsafe system. In the result there was a failure by the defendants, not in devising a safe system of work for the plaintiff, but in operating one.

On these grounds, which while not differing in substance from those relied on by the Court of Appeal are perhaps more simply and directly expressed, I agree with that court that the defendants are liable to the plaintiff.

Questions

1. Would Lord Brandon have held the defendant liable if the reason the tug started had been (a) that Captain Sas had had a sudden heart attack and fallen against the wheel, (b) that another deckhand, whether or not employed by the defendant, had deliberately given the signal to start?

2. Is the operation of a system of work delegated to every person working under the system?

3. Is there any reason why an entrepreneur should not arrange to have each workman employed by a different company? See *Porr v Shaw, The Marabu Porr* [1979] 2 Lloyd's Rep. 331, CA.

4. In the *Mersey Docks* case (above, p.279) the trial judge gave judgment against the crane-owner and in favour of the stevedores. Suppose that the victim had been one of the stevedores' employees. In the light of the principal case, would such a judgment be correct?

Note:

A computer consultant sent by his U.K. employer to Saudi Arabia to work on premises owned and operated by Aramco tripped on the floor, from which a tile had been removed to permit access to the wiring system below. The Court of Appeal held that the U.K. employer could not be held liable for daily events of this kind taking place so far away, especially when the premises were under the control of a reputable firm. *Cook v Square D* [1992] I.C.R. 262. For other cases of employer's liability for injuries to workmen on customer's premises see *Clay v Crump* (above p.237), *Andrews v Initial Cleaning Services* (above p.148) and especially the Court of Appeal's decision in *Fairchild* [2002] 1 W.L.R. 1052.

Section 2.—The Carrier

RIVERSTONE MEAT CO PTY LTD v LANCASHIRE SHIPPING CO LTD

House of Lords [1961] A.C. 807; [1961] 2 W.L.R. 269; 105 S.J. 148; [1961] 1 All E.R. 495; [1961] 1 Lloyd's Rep. 57 (noted (1962) 78 L.Q.R. 364)

Action by cargo owner against carrier for damage to goods

The trial judge dismissed the action [1959] 1 Q.B. 74; the Court of Appeal affirmed [1960] 1 Q.B. 536; the House of Lords allowed the plaintiff's appeal.

Lord Radcliffe: My Lords, I have no doubt that this case is important in its implications and that it has merited the full consideration that it has received at all its hearings. Nevertheless, it appears to me that the answer to be returned to the problem it raises depends upon a very short question, what kind of obligation is imported by the words "shall be bound . . . to exercise due diligence to make the ship seaworthy" that appears in Article III (1) of the Rules scheduled to the Australian Sea Carriage of Goods Act 1924. As we know, these are in fact the Hague Rules. Read them in one way, the answer must necessarily be for the appellants, the cargo owners: read them in another, it must be for the respondents, the carriers.

The relevant facts are of the simplest. Cargo has been damaged in the course of a voyage and it was damaged because the ship on which it was carried was unseaworthy. The unseaworthiness was caused by the carelessness of a fitter employed by skilled repairers working for the carriers. The work that they were doing was in connection with the ship's No.2 special survey and annual load-line survey, in other words, work which was reasonably required in order to keep the ship in a seaworthy condition.

Now, I am quite satisfied that, treating the carriers as a legal person, a limited company whose mind, will and actions are determined by its officers and servants, they did nothing but what they should have done as responsible and careful persons in the carrying business. They were not themselves in the repairing business and there is no reason why they should have been, but they were mindful of their duty to have their ship in good order for its voyage or voyages and they not only entrusted her to a ship-repairing company of repute for reception in dry-dock but also employed an experienced and competent marine superintendent to act on their behalf. He, in his turn, acted with more than usual caution in requiring all the ship's storm-valves to be opened up for inspection and, although it was the carelessness of one of the repairers' fitters that left one of these valves ineffectively closed, it was ordinary prudent practice to entrust the work of closing up to a fitter and not to subject such work to an independent inspection.

I see no ground, therefore, for saying that the carriers themselves were negligent in anything that they did. If the content of their obligation is that they should, as a legal person, observe the standard of reasonable care that would be required at common law in a matter of this sort, which involves skilled and technical work, and if there is nothing more in their obligation than that, then I should not regard them as in default or, consequently, as liable to the cargo owners. Full and instructive as are the several judgments of the members of the Court of Appeal, I do not think that in the end they amount to more than an acceptance of this standard of obligation and a drawing of the necessary conclusion from the facts.

But there is, on the other hand, a way of looking at the intrinsic nature of the obligation that is materially different from this. It is to ask the question, when there has been damage to cargo and that damage is traceable to unseaworthiness of the vessel, whether that unseaworthiness is due to any lack of diligence in those who have been implicated by the carriers in the work of keeping or making the vessel seaworthy. Such persons are then agents whose diligence or lack of it is attributable to the carriers. An inquiry on these lines is not concerned with the distinctions between carelessness on the part of officers or servants of the carriers or their supervising agents, on the one hand, and carelessness on the part of their contractors or those contractors' contractors, on the other. The carriers must answer for anything that has been done amiss in the work. It is the work itself that delimits the area of the obligation, just as it is the period "before or at the beginning of the voyage" that delimits the time at which any obligation imputed to the carriers can be thought to begin. If these last points are borne in mind, I think that the difficulties about "an almost unlimited retrogression" (see *W Angliss & Co (Australia) Proprietary Ltd v P & O Steam Navigation Co* ([1927] 2 K.B. 456 at 461)) tend to disappear: for there is a point in each case at which defective work is not the work of any agent of the carrier and the duty to be diligent is no more than a duty to be skilled and careful in inspection. But the inspection that is relevant in such a case is not merely the carrier's inspection of his contractor's work: it is inspection on the part of anyone working for the carrier who is concerned to make sure that he does not accept defective materials or use defective tools.

If one had to choose between these two alternatives without any background in the way of previous authority or opinion with regard to the interpretation of this section of the Hague Rules, I think it would be very difficult to know which way one ought to turn. The natural meaning of the words does not seem to me to accord well with either reading. Whatever the responsibility is, it is imposed on the carrier and no one else—that is clear—but it is equally clear that no one would regard the carrier as being in the wrong merely because he gets whatever requires to be done, inspection, survey or work, done for him by someone else. If the respondents' reading is adopted, the one that has commended itself to McNair J. and the Court of Appeal, one must treat the words "due diligence to make the ship seaworthy" as if they were equivalent to "due diligence to see that the ship is made seaworthy," and that is not the same thing. On the other hand, the reading for which the appellants contend is not in truth consistent with the grammatical meaning of the words they have to rely upon, for the exercise of due diligence to which the carrier would be held would include the performance or omission of acts that were not in law the acts of the carrier at all.

Such general considerations as occur to me appear to favour the cargo owner's claim. He is not in any sense behind the scenes with regard to what is done to the vessel or how or when it is done. His concern with it begins and ends with the loading and discharge of his goods. The carrier, on the other hand, must have some form of ownership of the vessel and some measure of responsibility for seeing that it is fit and in proper condition for the carriage undertaken. He may qualify that responsibility by stipulation, if the law allows him to; or the law may write out the terms of his responsibility for him; but within those limits the responsibility is there. I should regard it as unsatisfactory, where a cargo owner has found his goods damaged through a defect in the seaworthiness of the vessel, that his rights of recovering from the carrier should depend on particular circumstances in the carrier's situation and arrangements with which the cargo owner has nothing to do; as, for instance, that liability should depend upon the measure of control that the carrier had exercised over persons engaged on surveying or repairing the ship or upon such questions as whether the carrier had, or could have done, whatever was needed by the hands of his own servants or had been sensible or prudent in getting it done by other hands. Carriers would find themselves liable or not liable, according to circumstances quite extraneous to the sea carriage itself. . . .

Lord Keith of Avonholm: . . . The obligation is a statutory obligation imposed in defined contracts between the carrier and the shipper. There is nothing novel in a statutory obligation being held to be incapable of delegation so as to free the person bound of liability for breach of the obligation, and the reasons for this become, I think, more compelling where the obligation is made part of a contract between parties. We are not faced with a question in the realm of tort, or negligence. The obligation is a statutory contractual obligation. The novelty, if there is one, is that the statutory obligation is expressed in terms of an obligation to exercise due diligence, etc. There is nothing, in my opinion, extravagant in saying that this is an inescapable personal obligation. The carrier cannot claim to have shed his obligation to exercise due diligence to make his ship seaworthy by selecting a firm of competent ship repairers to make his ship seaworthy. Their failure to use due diligence to do so is his failure. The question, as I see it, is not one of vicarious responsibility at all. It is a question of statutory obligation. Perform it as you please. The performance is the carrier's performance. As was said in a corresponding case under the Harter Act: "The Act requires due diligence in the work itself"—*The Colima* (82 F. 665 (D.C.N.Y. 1897)). Ample other authority in the same direction had already been cited by my noble and learned friends. I am only concerned here to say that it seems to me to proceed on sound principle. I should only add that when I refer to repairers I include sub-contractors brought on to the ship by the repairers to enable them to perform the work which they contracted to do. Their failure, in my opinion, must also be the failure of the carrier on whom the statutory duty rests, unless in some very exceptional circumstances their employment can be said to be without any authority, express or implied, of the carrier, a case which can be considered if ever it arises. . . .

Notes:

1. The Hague Rules have been updated, but the duty "to exercise due diligence" remains unchanged: Carriage of Goods by Sea Act 1971, Sch. Art.III(1).

2. The carrier of goods, like the warehouseman, the dry-cleaner and the repairman, is a bailee. The common-law duty of the bailee, though it may be expressed in terms of reasonable care or due diligence, always tends to be rather higher than it sounds. Thus the burden of disproof of breach of duty lies on the defendant (below, p.504), and the duty is a duty to take positive, though reasonable, steps to guard the goods from harm, and not just the usual duty to take reasonable care not to damage them. For a lucid and detailed exposition of the law of bailment in a case of carriage of goods by sea, see Lord Hobhouse in *The Starsin* [2003] UKHL 12, [132] to [135]: "The sub-bailment creates a specific bailor/bailee relationship between the sub-bailee and the goods owner. It is not the same as the 'neighbour/foresight' relationship exemplified by *Donoghue v Stevenson* and the duties created are not the same."

3. "The law has repeatedly drawn a distinction between bailments and licenses, the former requiring a transfer of possession and a voluntary acceptance of the common law duty of safekeeping, the latter amounting to no more than a grant of permission to the user of a chattel to leave it on the licensor's land on the understanding that neither possession shall be transferred nor responsibility for guarding the chattel accepted. The distinction is easy to state but difficult to draw, or, rather, it is difficult to place specific cases on one side or the other." *per* Rix L.J. in *The Rigoletto* [2000] 2 Lloyd's Rep. 532, where indeed Chadwick L.J. dissented from the view that the operator of a secure compound in a dockyard was the bailee of the seven Lotus Esprits placed there under licence by the stevedore who certainly had possession of the vehicles prior to their being loaded for export.

4. The Court of Appeal has said that a warehouseman is liable to the bailor if the goods are stolen in consequence of the carelessness of nightwatchmen supplied by an independent security firm. *BRS v Arthur V Crutchley* [1968] 1 All E.R. 811. Does it follow that the warehouseman would be equally liable if the goods were damaged by rainwater entering in consequence of the carelessness of the building firm which constructed or repaired the warehouse?

5. We have seen a case of authorised sub-bailment already (*Morris v Martin*, above, p.293). In *Metaalhandel JA Magnus BV v Ardfields Transport* [1988] 1 Lloyd's Rep. 197 the defendant contracted with the plaintiff to collect and store some tungsten tubing belonging to the plaintiff, but as his own warehouse was full, the defendant subcontracted the job to Jones, without objection by the plaintiff. Jones's security system was lax, and the goods were stolen. The judge stated that though the defendant had never taken actual physical possession of the goods (and therefore did not have the burden of disproof of negligence) he was, as quasi-bailee, subject to a non-delegable duty; but the ground on which he gave judgment for the plaintiff was that the defendant had failed to ascertain whether Jones's premises and system were secure, that is, breach of the obligation of reasonable care implied into a contract to provide a service (Supply of Goods and Services Act 1982, s.13), so it is not clear that the defendant would have been liable for merely occasional fault on the part of the delegate.

6. A double quasi-bailment was involved in *Transcontainer v Custodian Security* [1988] 1 Lloyd's Rep. 128, CA, where the plaintiff carrier had subcontracted the collection and actual carriage of brandy from

France to England where it was stolen from a security park operated by the dock company and guarded by the defendant security firm, whose careless servant allowed it to be stolen. Though the defendant was not a bailee, the Court would have held him liable to the owner, but not to the present plaintiff, who had become liable for a huge sum by way of excise duty, for he neither owned nor possessed the goods, as required for a negligence claim by *The Aliakmon* [1986] A.C. 785. Whether it would have been enough had the plaintiff had a "right to possession" was left undetermined: the answer should be "no".

Questions
　1. Why do textbooks on Contract not have a chapter on vicarious liability?
　2. In *Re Polemis* (noted above, p.215) the plank which so surprisingly caused the loss of the vessel was carelessly knocked into the hold by a stevedore who was certainly not an employee of the charterer. Why, then, was the charterer held liable? (Liability for stevedores is well laid out by Robert Goff L.J. in *The Aliakmon* [1985] 2 All E.R. 44 at 78). Note that the person who *charters* a vessel (or coach or plane) is not a bailee but simply has a contractual right to use it and, within limits, to direct its staff, who remain the servants of the owner. By contrast, the person who *hires* a self-drive car does become a bailee of it.
　3. Would the shipowner in *The Nicholas H* (above, p.45) have been in breach of his duty to the cargo-owner if the decision in *Riverstone* (sometimes referred to as *The Muncaster Castle*) had been the other way?

ROGERS v NIGHT RIDERS

Court of Appeal [1983] R.T.R. 324; (1984) 134 New L.J. 61; [1983] C.A.T. 22

Action by customer against minicab firm for personal injuries

The plaintiff was injured while travelling in a minicab owned and driven by L. when, owing to a defective door-catch, the door flew open, struck a parked car and slammed shut again. The minicab had been sent by the defendant firm in response to a telephone call by the plaintiff's mother. The defendant owned no cabs and employed no drivers, but had a list of independent driver-owners such as L. who agreed to pay the defendant a weekly sum for the hire of a car-radio and to collect customers as instructed by the defendant. The driver kept the whole fare paid by the customer.

Eveleigh L.J.: ... In my opinion, this is not a case where we are concerned to consider vicarious liability or whether there is liability for the act of an independent contractor. We are concerned to consider a case of primary duty on the part of the defendants. It was never suggested, and it was not put to the plaintiff, that she knew that the defendants were simply a kind of post box to put her in touch with someone else with whom she would be able to make an independent contract. On the facts of this case, in my opinion, the defendants undertook to provide a car and driver to take the plaintiff to her destination. They did not undertake, and neither did she request them, to put her in touch with someone else who would undertake this obligation. Now in those circumstances of undertaking to provide a car and its driver to take her to her destination the defendants could foresee that she might be injured if the vehicle were defective, and so they owed a duty arising out of this relationship to take care to see that the vehicle was safe. They relied upon the driver to do this. Whether he was a servant or an independent contractor matters not, he was a third person upon whom they relied to perform their duty arising from their relationship with the plaintiff, and it is well-established law that such a duty cannot be delegated.

Dunn L.J.: agreed.
　The firm Night Riders or A1 Cars hold themselves out to the general public as a car hire firm and they undertook to provide a hire-car to take the plaintiff to Euston Station. In those circumstances, they owed the plaintiff a duty to take reasonable steps to ensure that the car was

reasonably fit for that purpose. It matters not whether the duty is put in contract or in tort, either way it is a duty they could not delegate to a third person so as to evade responsibility if the car was not fit for that purpose. There was no suggestion in the evidence in the court below, and it was never put to the plaintiff, that she was told of the true position of the firm, that is to say, the car did not belong to them and that the firm was no more than a booking agent for owner-driven cars over which they had no control. If there had been such evidence and if the true nature of the defendants' business had been known to the plaintiff, then the situation would have been different. But so far as the plaintiff was concerned, she was dealing with a car-hire firm not a mere booking agency and, accordingly, the defendants were under a primary duty to her.

For those reasons, and the reasons given by Eveleigh L.J., I too would allow the appeal.

Notes:

1. Readers should be warned that no authority supports this unprincipled and unreserved decision whose practical effect is doubtless to render minicabs as expensive as the taxicabs which the Yellow Pages inform the world minicabs are not.

2. The contract here was not one of *hire* of the vehicle. Had it been a contract of hire, it would certainly have contained a warranty that the vehicle was not defective for want of care (now a strict warranty under Supply of Goods and Services Act 1982, s.9). But it was not a contract of hire, and the plaintiff's erroneous supposition that it was would not make it one. The contract was not a contract of *carriage*, either, whatever the plaintiff supposed. Had it been a contract of carriage, the words of Lord Radcliffe in *Barkway v South Wales Transp.* would apply: " . . . a carrier's obligation to his passenger, whether it be expressed in contract or in tort, is to provide a carriage that is as free from defects as the exercise of all reasonable care can make it" ([1950] 1 All E.R. 392 at 403). But the carrier is liable in tort because he actually carries, and in contract because he promises to carry. Here the defendant did not carry and did not promise to carry. In one case, admittedly, a freight forwarder was held to be a carrier (*Claridge & Holt v King & Ramsay* (1920) 3 L.L.R. 197 (Bailhache J.)), but it had announced, contrary to the fact, that it owned and operated a fleet of liners whereas there was nothing in our case to estop the defendant from asserting that it had not undertaken to carry the plaintiff or even to provide a vehicle which it owned or manned. It is the defendant's assumpsit, not the plaintiff's assumption, which imposes responsibility. In any case the plaintiff here had not relied on any such supposed undertaking: she simply wanted a ride to the station. The contact—or contract—here was so marginal that it is not easy to discern the consideration. Certainly the plaintiff was not to pay the defendant, but doubtless the agreement was "If you agree to pay the driver, I shall send one to pick you up." The defendant here was a sort of telephone commissionnaire, the modern equivalent of the man in the street you ask to call you a taxi. The idea that business efficiency requires the implication into such a contract of such a heavy duty as the court here found is ludicrous. Doubtless the contract would now fall under s.12 of the Supply of Goods and Services Act 1982, with the result that, under s.13, "there is an implied term that the supplier will carry out the service with reasonable care and skill." The service here, however, was to get the driver to call, and that service was punctiliously performed.

3. But even if one took a different view of the *contract* involved, one could not conclude that the defendant owed any such duty in *tort* as was here held. After all, the defendant was not even the occupier of the defective vehicle—and a person is not turned into an occupier by the visitor's erroneous supposition that he is one.

4. The decision has been the subject of comment. In *Aiken v Stewart Wrightson* [1995] 3 All E.R. 449 at 471 Potter J. said of it: " . . . the situation would have been different if the true nature of the defendants' business and method of operation had been known to the plaintiff", and Lord Slynn has described it as a "difficult case but one where the Court of Appeal was entitled to find that the obligation undertaken was one which could be performed by another and where the defendants remained liable for the performance of the service with reasonable skill and care." He said this in *Wong Mee Wan v Kwan Kin Travel Services* [1995] 4 All E.R. 745 at 751, PC, where the plaintiff's daughter was drowned owing to the carelessness of the operator of a speedboat negligently permitted to man it by a company which the defendant engaged to perform in China the travel arrangements which it had undertaken in Hong Kong. Lord Slynn said: "The plaintiff's claim does not amount to an implied term that her daughter would be reasonably safe. It is a term simply that reasonable skill and care would be used in rendering the services to be provided under the contract."

5. Despite facts like those in the case just mentioned, people often travel in order to have fun, and the Package Travel, Package Holidays and Package Tours Regulations 1992 (SI 1992/3288) are there to help them if, as is so often the case, they are disappointed. Reg.27 provides that specified offences give rise to no civil (*i.e.* tort) liability, but contractual liability is certainly assured, especially by reg.15(1), which makes the "other party liable to the consumer for the proper performance of the obligations under the contract, irrespective of whether such obligations are to be performed by that party or by other suppliers of services."

It is reported that two women were able to sue the tour company in respect of sexual harassment by waiters in their resort hotel. At common law the tour operator does not normally guarantee the safety, as opposed to the availability, of the accommodation provided: *Wilson v Best Travel* [1993] 1 All E.R. 353.

Question
Would the result in *Rogers*, the principal case, have been the same if the plaintiff's injury had arisen solely by reason of L.'s negligent driving? If not, why not?

Section 3.—The Occupier

GREEN v FIBREGLASS LTD

Assizes [1958] 2 Q.B. 245; [1958] 3 W.L.R. 71; 102 S.J. 472; [1958] 2 All E.R. 521

Action by visitor against occupier in respect of personal injury

The plaintiff was caretaker of a building in Newcastle in which the defendants rented some offices; she contracted with the defendants to have their offices regularly cleaned, and this she did with the aid of charwomen employed by herself.

On July 31, 1956, the plaintiff was dusting an electric fire in the defendants' offices when she received severe electrical burns, as a consequence of which the fingers of her right hand had to be amputated. There was nothing wrong with the fire itself, and it was switched off at the wall; but although the heating element was cold, it was charged with electricity. This was due to the fault of the reputable electrical contractors who had rewired the offices five years previously at the instance of the defendants, for they had used only red wires instead of the distinctive red, black and green wires then commonly used precisely in order to avoid this danger.

The plaintiff's action against the occupier was dismissed.

Salmon J.: The question arises whether the defendants are responsible for the negligent wiring which caused this accident. I have held that the plaintiff was not a servant of the defendants; at the time of the accident she was the defendants' invitee. It is clearly settled that the defendants, as invitors, owe a duty to exercise due care for the safety of their invitee, the plaintiff. An invitor must use reasonable care to prevent damage from an unusual danger of which he knows or ought to know: *Indermaur v Dames* ((1866) L.R. 1 C.P. 274). What is reasonable care must depend upon the circumstances of each particular case. When the defendants took over these offices in 1951 they knew nothing about the wiring; the wiring, for all they knew, might then have been dangerously defective. They took the precaution, however, of having the offices completely rewired by Cairns (Newcastle) Ltd I find that this company was, and the defendants reasonably believed them to be, a long-established firm with a high reputation as electrical contractors. It is obvious that unless the electrical wiring of any premises is put into a safe condition, anyone using the premises may be exposed to danger of an unusual kind. Electrical wiring, however, is a matter for expert electrical contractors and is not ordinarily carried out by the occupier himself. How were the defendants to fulfil their duty to use reasonable care? I cannot think it was incumbent on them to send one of their directors or servants to a Polytechnic to take a course in electrical engineering and then attempt the rewiring themselves. In my view, they would discharge their duty of care by employing reputable and competent experts; and this they did. Nor had the defendants at any time thereafter any reason to suppose that the experts had been negligent, or that the electrical installation was unsafe.

This case seems to me to be indistinguishable from *Haseldine v Daw & Son Ltd* ([1941] 2 K.B. 343), in which it was held that the owners of lifts discharge their duty of care to invitees by employing competent experts to attend to the lift for them. In that case, the lift in question became dangerous by reason of the negligence of one of the expert's servants and the plaintiff thereby suffered damage. It was held by the Court of Appeal that the defendants were not liable for the negligence of the servants of their independent contractor experts. Mr Stanley Price, on behalf of the plaintiff, has sought to distinguish that decision on the ground that in the present case the defendants did not employ experts to make regular inspections of the electrical installation. I am not impressed by that point. An ordinarily prudent man, it is true, would have his lift regularly examined and serviced by an expert. I cannot believe, however, that an ordinarily prudent man who had had his premises wholly rewired by experts would think of having the wiring examined within five years of its installation unless there was any special reason, such as an apparent fault, for him to do so. Here, there was no such reason. *Haseldine v Daw & Son Ltd* was distinguished, but no doubt was cast upon it, by du Parcq L.J. in *Woodward v Mayor of Hastings* ([1945] K.B. 174 at 182), and by Parker J. in *Bloomstein v Railway Executive* ([1952] 2 All E.R. 418). Those were cases where the safety of the invitee depended upon the careful performance of some act which called for no technical knowledge or experience but upon acts which the courts held that the invitor could and should have done himself and which he neglected to do. In such cases, the invitor is liable for his neglect to do the act. It is no excuse for his failure to do that act that, for purposes of his own, he chooses to employ an independent contractor who has neglected to perform the act or to perform it carefully. du Parcq L.J. and Parker J. reaffirmed that in the *Haseldine v Daw* class of case—to which the present case, in my judgment, clearly belongs—the invitor, because of his inherent lack of technical knowledge or experience, discharges his duty of care to the invitee, not by attempting to do the act himself but by employing a properly qualified independent contractor to do it for him. In another context, *Phillips v Britannia Hygienic Laundry Co Ltd* ([1923] 2 K.B. 832) and *Stennett v Hancock* ([1939] 2 All E.R. 578) are illustrations of the same principle.

It is well settled that generally in an action for negligence a man is not vicariously liable for the carelessness of an independent contractor. There are, of course, cases where, by virtue of a contract or by the operation of law, an obligation may be imposed on a man to do an act, or to ensure that it is done and done carefully. In such cases, the defendant cannot shelter behind any independent contractor whom he may have employed. If he breaches the obligation he is liable, not in negligence but in contract, as in *Maclenan v Segar* ([1917] 2 K.B. 325), or by reason of some breach of duty other than a duty to take care, as in *Dalton v Angus* ((1881) 6 App. Cas. 740). The master, too, owes special duties to his servant which he cannot delegate. Those duties, however, spring from the nature of the contract of service. I can find no authority for holding that an invitor owes the same duty to his invitee as a master does to his servant. "Ever since *Quarman v Burnett* ((1840) 6 M. & W. 499; 151 E.R. 509) it has been considered settled law that one employing another is not liable for his collateral negligence unless the relation of master and servant existed between them. So that a person employing a contractor to do work is not liable for the negligence of that contractor or his servants. On the other hand, a person causing something to be done, the doing of which casts on him a duty, cannot escape from the responsibility attaching on him of seeing that duty performed by delegating it to a contractor": *Dalton v Angus, per* Lord Blackburn (at 829). It is important to observe that the duty cast upon the defendant in that case was not a duty to take care but a duty not to let down the plaintiff's adjoining buildings whilst excavating on his own land, the plaintiff having acquired a right of support by twenty years' enjoyment of such support.

Hughes v Percival ((1883) 8 App.Cas. 443), *Honeywill & Stein Ltd v Larkin Bros Ltd* ([1934] 1 K.B. 191) and *Black v Christchurch Finance Co Ltd* ([1894] A.C. 48) are exceptional cases because there the defendants were employing contractors to do extra-hazardous acts, that is, acts which in their very nature involve in the eyes of the law special danger to others. It may be that such cases, like the master and servant cases, are an exception to the general rule that persons employing a contractor are not vicariously liable for his negligence or for the negligence of his servants. . . .

. . . With great diffidence, I doubt whether it is helpful to import into this branch of the law the conception of warranty. That seems to me to belong exclusively to the law of contract. The obligation of an invitor to an invitee has nothing to do with the law of contract or quasi-contract, but is part of the law of tort. The invitee's cause of action lies in negligence and nothing else.

The only obligation of the invitor in essence is an obligation imposed by law to take reasonable care and nothing more. In each case the question must be posed: How ought that obligation to be performed? The answer to that question must depend on the particular facts of each case. If, as in the present case and in *Haseldine v Daw & Son Ltd*, some act is to be performed which calls for special knowledge and experience which the invitor cannot be expected to possess, then, in my judgment, he fulfils his duty of care as a prudent man by employing a qualified and reputable expert to do the act.

In my judgment, it follows that the claim fails against the present defendants. I would add that on the facts as I have found them it would appear that there could have been no answer to the claim had it been brought against Cairns (Newcastle) Ltd.

Note:
See now Occupiers' Liability Act 1957, s.2(4)(b), above, p.000.

Questions
1. If, in *Glasgow Corp. v Muir* (above, p.155), the question was whether it was foreseeable that the person carrying the urn might drop it, why in this case was the question not asked whether it was foreseeable that the electrical contractor might do his job badly?

2. Would the result have been any different if the plaintiff had been a secretary employed by the defendant? Does *Davie*'s case help us to answer this? See *Cook v Broderip* (1968) 112 S.J. 193. Not being an employee, Mrs Green would fall outside the terms of the Employers' Liability (Defective Equipment) Act 1969. If she had been an employee, would the statute have allowed her to recover?

3. Suppose I call a tree-felling firm to come and trim the trees on my estate. I see one of their workmen astride a limb which he is busily sawing through at a point between himself and the trunk of the tree. I must clearly warn visitors, such as the postman, on whom he and the limb are likely to fall, but am I liable to the workman himself if I fail to warn him? *Ferguson v Welsh* [1987] 3 All E.R. 777, HL suggests not, as perhaps does *Roles v Nathan* (above, p.162).

Section 4.—The Organiser of Dangerous Works

SALSBURY v WOODLAND

Court of Appeal [1970] 1 Q.B. 324; [1969] 3 W.L.R. 29; 113 S.J. 327; [1969] 3 All E.R. 863

Action in respect of personal injuries by highway user against adjacent occupier

Telephone wires led from a pole on the far side of the highway to the eaves of a house 40 feet away. The first defendant, who had just bought the house, wanted a large hawthorn tree, some 25 feet high, eradicated by an expert. The second defendant, apparently competent, undertook the task at the instance of the first defendant's wife, but mismanaged it so badly that a branch of the falling tree broke the wires near the house and they fell across the highway. The plaintiff who had been watching from next door saw that the wires were a danger to traffic and went on to the road to try to remove them, but before he could do anything the third defendant rounded the corner at speed. To avoid being struck by the wires with which the third defendant collided, the plaintiff flung himself down on the grass verge, an act which, thanks to a pre-existing back condition, caused him fairly severe injuries.

The trial judge gave judgment for the plaintiff against all three defendants, *i.e.* the occupier, the tree-feller and the motorist. The occupier's appeal was allowed, that of the motorist dismissed.

Widgery L.J.: ... It is trite law that an employer who employs an independent contractor is not vicariously responsible for the negligence of that contractor. He is not able to control the way in which the independent contractor does the work, and the vicarious obligation of a master for the negligence of his servant does not arise under the relationship of employer and independent contractor. I think that it is entirely accepted that those cases—and there are some—in which an employer has been held liable for injury done by the negligence of an independent contractor are in truth cases where the employer owes a direct duty to the person injured, a duty which he cannot delegate to the contractor on his behalf. The whole question here is whether the occupier is to be judged by the general rule, which would result in no liability, or whether he comes within one of the somewhat special exceptions—cases in which a direct duty to see that care is taken rests upon the employer throughout the operation.

This is clear from authority; and for convenience I take from *Salmond on Torts* this statement of principle: "One thing can, however, be said with confidence: the mere fact that the work entrusted to the contractor is of a character which may cause damage to others unless precautions are taken is not sufficient to impose liability on the employer. There are few operations entrusted to an agent which are not capable, if due precautions are not observed, of being sources of danger and mischief to others; and if the principal was responsible for this reason alone, the distinction between servants and independent contractors would be practically eliminated from the law." I am satisfied that that statement is supported by authority, and I adopt it for the purpose of this judgment.

One can compare at once that statement with the statement of principle upon which the judge relied ... he said: "The principal, unlike the employer, is not liable for incidental acts of negligence during the work; for instance, dropping a hammer on someone's head; but he is liable if the very act he orders to be done contains in it a risk of injury to others, and someone is injured as a result of the contractor's negligence as a consequence of that risk. In this case"—he meant the instant case—"there can be no doubt that there was an inherent risk of injury to others when the tree was felled unless proper care was taken to get rid of the risk." I make two observations upon those words of the judge. First, the evidence makes it perfectly clear that the tree could have been felled by a competent contractor, using proper care, without any risk of injury to anyone. The undisputed evidence of an expert was that the proper way to fell it, in its confined situation, was to lop the branches respectively until there was left a stump of only eight to ten feet in height. All that could be done without any danger to anyone, if, at any rate, all appropriate precautions were taken, and the resultant stump eight to ten feet high could then have been winched out of the ground, again without risk to anyone. So when the judge referred to it as being an operation in which "there was an inherent risk," he was, in my view, putting the matter too high. If he meant that there was a risk which even due care could not avoid, he was, in my judgment, quite wrong upon the undisputed evidence that was before him.

Secondly, I would venture to criticise the statement of principle which he applied as being too wide. Taken literally, it would mean that the fare who hired a taxicab to drive him down the Strand would be responsible for negligence of the driver en route because the negligence would be negligence in the very thing which the contractor had been employed to do. No one is disposed to suggest that the liability of the employer is that high; and although the judge reinforced himself by certain observations of Romer L.J. in *Penny v Wimbledon U.D.C.* ([1899] 2 Q.B. 72 at 78), in my opinion, the test which he applied was far too stringent.

In truth, according to the authorities there are a number of well-determined classes of case in which this direct and primary duty upon an employer to see that care is taken exists. Two such classes are directly relevant for consideration in the present case. The first class concerns what have sometimes been described as "extra-hazardous acts"—acts commissioned by an employer which are so hazardous in their character that the law has thought it proper to impose this direct obligation on the employer to see that care is taken. An example of such a case is *Honeywill & Stein Ltd v Larkin Bros* ([1934] 1 K.B. 191). Other cases which one finds in the books are cases where the activity commissioned by the employer is the keeping of dangerous things within the rule in *Rylands v Fletcher* [below, p.453] and where liability is not dependent on negligence at all.

I do not propose to add to the wealth of authority on this topic by attempting further to define the meaning of "extra-hazardous acts"; but I am confident that the act commissioned in the present case cannot come within that category. The act commissioned in the present case, if done with ordinary elementary caution by skilled men, presented no hazard to anyone at all.

The second class of case, which is relevant for consideration, concerns dangers created in a highway. There are a number of cases on this branch of the law, a good example of which is *Holliday v National Telephone Co* ([1899] 2 Q.B. 392). These, on analysis, will all be found to be cases where work was being done in a highway and was work of a character which would have been a nuisance unless authorised by statute. It will be found in all these cases that the statutory powers under which the employer commissioned the work were statutory powers which left upon the employer a duty to see that due care was taken in the carrying out of the work, for the protection of those who passed on the highway. In accordance with principle, an employer subject to such a direct and personal duty cannot excuse himself, if things go wrong, merely because the direct cause of the injury was the act of the independent contractor.

This again is not a case in that class. It is not a case in that class because in the instant case no question of doing work in the highway, which might amount to a nuisance if due care was not taken, arises. In my judgment, the present case is clearly outside the well defined limit of the second class to which I have referred. Mr Bax, accordingly, invited us to say that there is a third class into which the instant case precisely falls, and he suggested that the third class comprised those cases where an employer commissions work to be done *near* a highway in circumstances in which, if due care is not taken, injury to passers-by on the highway may be caused. If that be a third class of case to which the principle of liability of the employer applies, no doubt the present case would come within that description. The question is, is there such a third class?

Reliance was placed primarily on three authorities. The first was *Holliday v National Telephone Co* ([1899] 2 Q.B. 392). That was a case of work being done in a highway by undertakers laying telephone wires. The injury was caused by the negligent act of a servant of the independent contractor who was soldering joints in the telephone wires. The cause of the injury was the immersion of a defective blow-lamp in a pot of solder, and the pot of solder was physically upon the highway—according to the report, on the footpath. The Earl of Halsbury L.C., holding the employers responsible for that negligence, in my view, on a simple application of the cases applicable to highway nuisance to which I have already referred, said (at p.399): "Therefore works were being executed in proximity to a highway, in which in the ordinary course of things an explosion might take place." Mr Bax drew our attention to the phrase "in proximity to a highway" and submitted that that supported his contention on this point. I am not impressed by that argument, because the source of danger in *Holliday's* case was itself on the highway.

The second case relied upon was *Tarry v Ashton* ((1876) 1 Q.B.D. 314). That was a case where a building adjoining the highway had attached to it a heavy lamp, which was suspended over the footway and which was liable to be a source of injury to passers-by if allowed to fall into disrepair. It fell into disrepair, and injury was caused. The defendant sought to excuse himself by saying that he had employed a competent independent contractor to put the lamp into good repair and that the cause of the injury was the fault of the independent contractor. Mr Bax argued that that case illustrated the special sympathy with which the law regards passers-by on the highway. He said that it demonstrated that the law has always been inclined to give special protection to persons in that category and so supported his argument that any action adjacent to the highway might be subject to special rights. But, in my judgment, that is not so. *Tarry v Ashton* seems to me to be a perfectly ordinary and straightforward example of a case where the employer was under a positive and continuing duty to see that the lamp was kept in repair. That duty was imposed upon him before the contractor came and after the contractor had gone; and on the principle that such a duty cannot be delegated the responsibility of the employer in that case seems to me to be fully demonstrated. I cannot find that it produces on a side-wind, as it were, anything in support of Mr Bax's contention.

The last case relied upon was *Walsh v Holst & Co Ltd* ([1958] 1 W.L.R. 800), a decision of this court. In that case the occupier of premises adjoining the highway was carrying out works of reconstruction, which involved knocking out large areas of the front wall. He employed for that purpose a contractor, who employed a sub-contractor. It was obvious to all that such an operation was liable to cause injury to passers-by by falling bricks unless special precautions against that eventuality were taken. Indeed, very considerable precautions were taken. However, on a day when the only workman employed was an employee of the sub-contractor, one brick escaped the protective net, fell in the street and injured a passer-by. The passer-by sued the occupier, the contractor, and the sub-contractor, relying on the doctrine of *res ipsa loquitur*. In my judgment, the only thing decided by that case was that on those facts the precautions which had been taken against such an injury rebutted the presumption of negligence which might otherwise have arisen under the doctrine of *res ipsa loquitur*. . . .

Accordingly, in my judgment, there is no third class of cases of the kind put forward by Mr Bax; and it was for those reasons that I concurred in the court's decision that the occupier's appeal should be allowed and the judgment against him set aside. . . .

Questions

1. Would you describe an accident of the sort that happened to the plaintiff as falling within the traffic risk or the householder's risk, as understood by insurers?

2. What if the branch had fallen into the neighbour's garden and (a) damaged the greenhouse, (b) injured the neighbour himself?

3. What was the source in *Tarry v Ashton* of the non-delegable duty to keep the lamp in repair? Compare *Mint v Good* (above, p.202).

4. In *Rowe v Herman* [1997] 1 W.L.R. 1390 the plaintiff fell over some metal plates on the highway outside the defendant's house, left there by the building contractor who had just finished building a garage for the defendant. The plaintiff's claim against the defendant-occupier was struck out by the Court of Appeal. How is the plaintiff to discover whom to sue? If the occupier had been held liable, would he have had a claim against the builder? If so, on what basis or bases?

Notes:

1. One justification for the very different treatment of employee and independent contractor is that the latter, being in business for himself, is much more likely to be substantial and insured than the individual in employment. Furthermore, the contractor will very often *be* a business whereas an employee is invariably a mere human being. In the principal case the tree-feller, if not actually moonlighting, seems to have been in business in the smallest possible way, and he would surely have been bankrupted if the motorist's liability insurer had chosen to exercise his right to claim contribution under the 1978 Act.

2. Widgery L.J. referred to *Honeywill & Stein v Larkin Brothers* [1934] 1 K.B. 191. It is a strange case. The plaintiffs did some work in a cinema, obtained the permission of the cinema company to have the work photographed and then contracted with the defendants to go to the cinema and do the photography. In doing so, the defendants' employee carelessly set light to the curtains and caused a fire. The plaintiffs paid the cinema company's bill for the damage but on suing to recover this sum from the defendants they met the trumpery defence that they need not have paid the cinema company at all. The Court of Appeal held that the plaintiffs had indeed been liable to the cinema company for the negligence of the defendants, independent contractors though they were, since the task (which in those days involved igniting magnesium powder on a tin tray) was extra hazardous. It is hardly surprising that a decision on such facts has not proved very fertile.

3. *Honeywill* was referred to in *Bottomley v Todmorden Cricket Club* [2003] EWCA Civ 1575. In an aside Brooke L.J. said: "It is therefore not necessary, even if it was appropriate for us at this level, to consider the criticisms of *Honeywill v Larkin* made by Mason J. in the High Court of Australia in *Stevens v Brodribb Sawmilling Co Pty Ltd* 160 C.L.R. 16, 30. *Honeywill v Larkin* is binding on us, although it may well be that the House of Lords today would prefer to avoid subtle distinctions between what is and is not 'extra-hazardous' and would follow Mason J. when he said: '[T]he traditional common law response to the creation of a special danger is not to impose strict liability but to insist on a higher standard of care in the performance of an existing duty.' "

The facts in *Bottomley* were that at a fundraising event organised by the Cricket Club on their premises the Club had retained a two-man stunt team, Chaos Encounter (CE), who proposed to put on a pyrotechnic display. The claimant was a volunteer assistant enlisted by CE who was badly burnt when a gunpowder charge which he was inserting into a mortar tube exploded. CE had no liability insurance, so the claimant sued the club. The Court of Appeal adhered to the erroneous view that the Occupiers' Liability Act did not mean what it said when it explicitly replaced the common law as regards "things done or omitted to be done" on the premises (see above p.40) and accepted the peculiar view of Lord Goff (above p.148) that an occupier owed no duty under the Act to the employees of independent contractors working on the premises, but found an exception where what the occupier was permitting to be done on his land for his benefit was very dangerous. Here the club had failed adequately to check the competence of CE, and was accordingly liable.

4. The habit of the English lawyers of describing the person who pays a firm to provide a service as its "employer" hardly helps us distinguish between independent contractors and true employees. The firm providing the service would itself describe the person to whom it provides it as its "customer", not its "employer"; it might assist students if they did likewise.

5. Widgery L.J. referred to *Rylands v Fletcher* (below, p.453). In *Cambridge Water v Eastern Counties Leather* [1994] 1 All E.R. 53 at 75–76 Lord Goff said this: "It can be argued that the rule in *Rylands v Fletcher* . . . should . . . be treated as a developing principle of strict liability from which can be derived a general rule of strict liability for damage caused by ultra-hazardous operations, on the basis of which persons conducting such operations may properly be held strictly liable for the extraordinary risk to others involved in such operations . . . Even so, there is much to be said for the view that the courts should not be proceeding down the path of developing such a general theory."

Rylands v Fletcher has been described as a case of liability for the fault of independent contractors (*Dunne v North Western Gas Board* [1964] 2 Q.B. 806 at 831), and indeed in Australia has been "absorbed by the principles of ordinary negligence" on that basis (*Burnie Port Auth. v General Jones Pty* (1994) 120 A.L.R. 42 at 67). See the *Transco* case below p.463.

Section 5.—The Owner

ORMROD v CROSVILLE MOTOR SERVICES LTD (MURPHIE, THIRD PARTY)

Court of Appeal [1953] 1 W.L.R. 1120; 97 S.J. 570; [1953] 2 All E.R. 753

Actions for personal injury and property damage arising out of a highway accident

There was a collision in fog between an Austin Healey car, belonging to Murphie, the third party, and a bus owned by one defendant and driven by the other. Both vehicles were damaged, and personal injuries were suffered by both the male plaintiff, who was driving the Austin Healey, and the female plaintiff, his wife and passenger. When sued by the plaintiffs in respect of their personal injuries, the bus company claimed the cost of repairing its bus from Murphie.

Devlin J. held that the accident was caused solely by the fault of the male plaintiff and dismissed the personal injury claims. He then held that Murphie was responsible for the male plaintiff's negligence and made him pay for the repairs to the bus ([1953] 1 W.L.R. 409).

The plaintiffs were taking Murphie's car to Monte Carlo for him, where he was driving another car in the Rally; thereafter they were all to go on holiday together. On the way to Monte Carlo the plaintiffs were going to visit friends in Bayeux; the accident took place on the way to the Channel port.

Murphie appealed, as did the plaintiffs. The Court of Appeal dismissed Murphie's appeal on point of liability, but subsequently, on hearing further evidence, allowed the plaintiffs' appeals, holding that the two drivers were equally to blame.

Singleton L.J.: . . . It has been said more than once that a driver of a motor-car must be doing something for the owner of the car in order to become an agent of the owner. The mere fact of consent by the owner to the use of a chattel is not proof of agency; but the purpose for which the car was being taken down the road on the morning of the accident was either that the car should be used by the owner or that it should be used for the joint purposes of the owner and the plaintiffs when it reached Monte Carlo.

In those circumstances, it appears to me that the judgment of Devlin J. that at the time of the accident the male plaintiff was the agent of the third party was right, and the third party's appeal on that head should be dismissed.

Denning L.J.: It has often been supposed that the owner of a vehicle is only liable for the negligence of the driver if that driver is his servant acting in the course of his employment. But that is not correct. The owner is also liable if the driver is his agent, that is to say, if the driver is, with the owner's consent, driving the car on the owner's business or for the owner's purposes. In the present case the driver was, by mutual arrangement, driving the car partly for his own purposes and partly for the owner's purposes. The owner wanted the car taken to Monte Carlo, and the driver himself wanted to go with his wife to Monte Carlo, and he intended to visit friends in Normandy on the way. On this account he started two or three days earlier than he would have done if he had been going solely for the owner's purposes. Mr Scholefield Allen says that this should exempt the owner from liability for the driver's negligence, because the accident might never have happened if he had started later. He says that the owner would not have been liable for any negligence of the driver on the trip from Calais to Normandy and should not be liable for negligence on the early start. I do not think this argument is correct. The law puts an especial responsibility on the owner of a vehicle who allows it out on to the road in charge of someone else, no matter whether it is his servant, his friend, or anyone else. If it is being used wholly or partly on the owner's business or for the owner's purposes, then the owner is liable for any negligence on the part of the driver. The owner only escapes liability when he lends it out or hires it out to a third person to be used for purposes in which the owner has no interest or concern: see *Hewitt v Bonvin* ([1940] 1 K.B. 188). That is not this case. The trip to Monte Carlo must be considered as a whole, including the proposed excursion to Normandy, and, as such, it was undertaken with the owner's consent for the purposes of both of them, and the owner is liable for any negligence of the driver in the course of it. I agree that the appeal should be dismissed.

(At first instance)

Devlin J.: . . . It is clear that there must be something more than the granting of mere permission in order to create liability in the owner of a motor-car for the negligence of the driver to whom it has been lent. But I do not think that it is necessary to show a legal contract of agency. It is in an area between the two that this case is to be found, and it may be described as a case where, in the words of du Parcq L.J., there is a "social or moral" obligation to drive the owner's car ([1940] 1 K.B. 196). Mr Ormrod was under such a duty as this; for if he had not driven the car as arranged, then the third party would have had a legitimate grievance. I think that the arrangement amounted to a request to Mr Ormrod to drive the car. He who complies with such a request is the agent of the other, since he who makes the request has an interest in its being done. In this case the car was wanted for the purpose of a joint holiday; that was enough to give the third party an interest in the arrival of the car, so that the driving became an act done for his benefit. In the case of mere permission the person permitting has no interest in whether the act is done or not.

Questions

1. Could Mrs Ormrod have claimed damages for her personal injuries from Murphie?

2. Was Ormrod an "independent contractor" of Murphie's?

3. Could Murphie claim (a) damages, (b) statutory contribution, (c) a quasi-contractual indemnity from Ormrod in respect of the damages paid by Murphie to the bus company? Would Warbey face any extra difficulties if he brought an action of relief against the person to whom he lent his car (*Monk v Warbey*, above, p.194)?

4. Would Murphie's claim against the defendants for damage to his Austin Healey be reduced by reason of Ormrod's negligence?

5. Suppose, in *Salsbury v Woodland* (above, p.311), that instead of paying a tree-feller the occupier had asked his adolescent son or house-guest to cut down the hawthorn tree. Would the occupier be liable?

6. If a hitch-hiker sues the employer of the person who gives him a lift, could one impute the driver's negligence to the hitch-hiker on the basis that the driver was his agent?

Note:

The seeds planted by Lord Denning at the end of his judgment came to harvest in *Launchbury v Morgans* [1971] 2 Q.B. 245. A husband frequently used his wife's car to go to work and to go drinking with his friends thereafter. His wife had asked him to get a friend to drive him home when he was the worse for ... one such evening he did so. The friend drove off at 90 mph in the wrong direction and collided with ... husband and friend were killed, the plaintiff passengers injured. The question was whether the wife ... liable. The trial judge and a majority of the Court of Appeal held that she was. According to Lord Denning the wife would have been liable even if she had not asked her husband to procure a substitute driver, because she had an "interest or concern" in the return of her car (and of her husband), and the return of her husband and her car was what the friend was engaged on or for.

The House of Lords, in distinctly acid judgments, unanimously reversed ([1973] A.C. 127). It was emphasised that there were no special common law rules for cars and that in order to make the owner liable the driver, if not his servant, must be shown to be his agent. Not everyone who does something in the interests of another is his agent: an agent is a person who does something at another's request. It must be a request rather than a permission, and in order to discover which it is it may be useful to ask whether the alleged principal had any interest in the matter: after all, you *ask* people to do things for you, you *let* them do things for themselves, and letting someone do something, even with your property, does not make you liable for his negligence.

Of course A may be liable for B's driving of C's car—as in *Launchbury v Morgans* the friend was certainly the agent of the husband—on this see *Nottingham v Aldridge* ([1971] 2 Q.B. 739).

It may be useful to place this doctrine of agency in the context of the other rules relating to liability for traffic accidents.

Where A, a pedestrian, suffers personal injury because of the bad driving by B of C's car, A can sue C if:

(1) C was careless in allowing B to drive (because C should have known that either B or the car was dangerous);

(2) C is B's employer, and B was driving in the course of his employment;

(3) C has *asked* B (servant or not) to drive the car (*Carberry v Davies* [1968] 1 W.L.R. 1103; [1968] 2 All E.R. 817);

(4) C has *permitted* B (whoever he is) to drive the car (on any business whatever), and neither B nor C has a policy covering the liability of either to A.

The last-mentioned head of liability comes from the decision of the Court of Appeal in *Monk v Warbey* [above, p.194] to the effect that a person injured by an uninsured and insolvent driver whom the owner has permitted to drive can sue the owner for breach of his statutory duty not to cause or permit another person to use a motor vehicle on a road unless a policy is in force with regard to it. Such insurance has been required since 1930, and it has had a profound effect on the law of tort. Originally the only liability which was required to be covered was liability for causing personal injury to those outside the vehicle or carried for hire. Later, insurance was required against liability for personal injury to gratuitous passengers as well. Finally, thanks to an unsatisfactory development (which comes to us, of course, from Brussels), insurance is now required against liability for property damage as well as personal injury (SI 1987/2171). The development is unsatisfactory because people normally take out accident insurance on their own property but not on their bodies, and it is wasteful to have the same risk covered by two policies.

In *Ormrod* it was property damage for which the owner was held liable, though he was not then required to have insurance cover against such liability, and perhaps had none. Accordingly, it is questionable in terms of policy, and should not be extended, as it was (in favour of an injured passenger) in *Scarsbrook v Mason* [1961] 3 All E.R. 767, doubted by Oliver L.J. in *S v Walsall M.D.C.* [1995] 3 All E.R. 294 (a case on whether a local authority is answerable to a child in its care for the negligence of foster-parents). Now that mandatory insurance has been extended to property damage, it is no longer necessary, as it was in *Ormrod*, to prove that the driver was asked, rather than just permitted, to drive, for if insurance cover is lacking, the owner will be liable under *Monk v Warbey*, though only for the amount irrecoverable from the driver (or the Motor Insurers' Bureau which now meets claims for over £300 in respect of property damage done by an uninsured (but not a hit-and-run) driver, provided the claimant himself has the mandatory cover).

Insurance policies often cover the liability not just of the owner/insured himself but also that of anyone driving the vehicle with his permission. Such a person, though not a party to the policy, and therefore unable at common law to claim on it, has a statutory right to the promised indemnity, and it is neither necessary nor useful to sue the owner at all. The victim can now sue the tortfeasor's insurer directly under the European Communities (Rights against Insurers) Regulations 2002 (SI 2002/3061), and hold the insurer liable to the extent he is liable to his insured. If the insurer is not liable to his insured, the driving was without insurance and the victim can sue the Motor Insurers Bureau.

Section 6.—Other Cases

ible in tort for the negligence of a subcontracting plasterer? No, said the
F Estates v Church Comm'rs [1989] A.C. 177, but he may be under a
ork.

wood (above, p.31) the Court of Appeal in holding, contrary to the law
se of Lords on appeal, that the local authority owed the purchaser of a
care in the passing of plans for its construction, had to ask whether the
duty was broken by the error of an independent firm of structural engineers which it consulted.
Nicholls L.J. said:

> "It seems to me that the common law duty of care would be in danger of being emasculated,
> and its purpose partly defeated, if the local authority's liability for the negligence of those
> advising it were to depend on whether the authority had decided to go outside for advice
> rather than dealing with the matter 'in house.' I can see no justification for so concluding."
> [1990] 2 All E.R. 269 at 298.

The question may become important now that local authorities are encouraged to retain
independent contractors to do what previously was done "in house." Consider, in this context,
the duty of the council landlord which retains an independent contractor to repair a relevant
defect in tenanted premises: Defective Premises Act 1972, s.4 (above, p.38).

3. In *Luxmoore-May v Messenger May Baverstock* [1990] 1 All E.R. 1067, CA a provincial
auctioneer failed to realise that the pictures submitted for sale by the plaintiff could well be by
Stubbs and sold them for a price very much lower than they soon afterwards fetched. Their duty,
though contractual, was to take reasonable care about the sale. They had taken advice from a
local person they often consulted (but did not employ as a member of their staff) and also
consulted Christie's in London. The auctioneer would have been liable for the negligence of their
local consultant, whom they often used, but not, it appears, for any negligence of the London
experts.

4. A mortgagee which arranges for a valuation/survey of a house on which it is asked to lend
money is not normally responsible for the negligence of the nominated valuer/surveyor: *Smith v
Eric S Bush* [1989] 2 All E.R. 514 at 536 *per* Lord Griffiths.

5. In *Rivers v Cutting* [1982] 3 All E.R. 69, CA it was held that the police who have the power
to arrange for the removal of a motor vehicle from the highway are not answerable for the
negligence of the firm they arrange to remove it.

6. In *Alcock v Wraith* [1991] Times L.R. 600, CA, plaintiff and defendant lived in adjacent
terraced houses with a continuous slate roof. In replacing the slates on the defendant's roof with
concrete tiles, the defendant's builder made a very bad join with the plaintiff's roof, and rain got
into the plaintiff's house. The defendant was held liable for the damage, on the basis that the job
was a notoriously difficult one which presented a special risk (!), and was akin to doing work on
a party wall, Neill L.J. saying that "it did not matter whether the claim was framed in negligence,
trespass or nuisance". But surely the true reason is that plaintiff and defendant were actual
neighbours: the defendant (as opposed to the builder) would not have been liable to one of the
plaintiff's house-guests whose belongings got soaked. Compare *Balfour v Barty-King* [1957] 1
Q.B. 496, where the defendant's plumber caused a fire which spread to the plaintiff's premises
next door, and see *Johnson v BJW Property Developments* [2002] 3 All E.R. 574, [2002] EWHC
(TCC) 1131.

7. Before the havoc at Lloyd's wrought by hurricanes and pollution in the United States,
members' agents used to delegate to managing agents the function of effecting underwriting on
behalf of the "names" with whom the members' agents had a contract: the members' agents
were responsible to the names for the faults of the managing agents: *Henderson v Merrett
Syndicates* [1994] 3 All E.R. 506 at 535—in contract, but not in tort (*Aiken v Stewart Wrightson*
[1995] 3 All E.R. 449).

PART III

TRESPASS

INTRODUCTION

THE tort of negligence is quite young by the standards of the common law, but it has thrived so mightily and grown so lusty that one could be forgiven for wondering whether there was room left for any other tort at all. Negligence is always trying to edge out the other torts in the hope of elevating into a completely general and comprehensive principle its own proposition that it is actionable *unreasonably* to cause *foreseeable* harm to another. As Lord Templeman felt forced to say " . . . the tort of negligence has not yet subsumed all torts and does not supplant the principles of equity or contradict contractual promises or complement the remedy of judicial review or supplement statutory rights." (*China and South Sea Bank v Tan* [1989] 3 All E.R. 839 at 841). Although we have seen that in Australia the rule in *Rylands v Fletcher* "has been absorbed into the principles of ordinary negligence" (above, p.466) and shall later have to record the sad death of detinue (below, p.502), a few torts have just managed to resist the cuckoo in the nest. Trespass has survived in part. Trespass existed long before negligence—long enough, indeed, to figure in the 1611 version of the Lord's Prayer. Trespass has its principle, too. Its principle is that any *direct invasion* of a *protected right* by a *positive act* is wrongful and actionable, subject to justification. This needs a word of explanation.

The first wrongdoers a system has to catch are the worst—the footpad, the highwayman, the kidnapper, the burglar and the thief. They should be brought before the King's Bench forthwith. If there is no police force to prosecute them, the victim must be encouraged to bring suit. This was done by the writ of trespass. In sanctioning these miscreants, the law was protecting the citizen's interests in bodily safety, security from attack, liberty of movement and possession of property. These are very important interests (which are missing?). So important are they that perhaps they should be protected against *all* invasions, not just criminal invasions, and not just those invasions which result in provable harm. It would be too much, however, if everyone whose conduct somehow resulted in such an invasion were held liable, so a doubly restrictive device was adopted: the invasion had to result *directly* from a *positive act*. If the invasion was *indirect*, however foreseeable, there was no liability in trespass, and there was no liability in trespass for *omissions*, however clear the duty to act. Those who had encompassed the plaintiff's ruin by indirection or occasioned it by indolence might well be liable in some other form of action, but trespassers they were not.

This trespass system was not a bad one in a society where parties could not be witnesses and where the jury consequently knew nothing but the *res gestae*. Most invasions in fact cause actual damage, and the jury could always award very small sums if no damage was caused. Again, most acts which directly cause an invasion are acts likely to cause such an invasion, even if they are not actually designed to produce it. However, some invasions do not involve any damage (shaking your fist at a bouncer, tip-toeing through a stubble-field), and sometimes an act directly results in an invasion which is neither designed nor foreseeable (a gamekeeper aiming at a pheasant hits a concealed picnicker). Thus trespass not only failed to catch some scoundrels (the ones who sat idly by or who caused indirect harm), but also caught some people who were quite innocent.

There was bound to be a categorical conflict between negligence, with its insistence on unreasonableness of conduct and foreseeability of harm, and trespass, with its emphasis on positive action and directness of invasion. The conflict was joined in *Fowler v Lanning* [1959] 1 Q.B. 426. The plaintiff asserted simply that the defendant shot him. There could hardly be a terser statement of a claim in trespass. "He shot" establishes the positive act: "shot me" establishes the direct invasion. It entails, however, no assertion that there was anything unreasonable about the defendant's conduct, or that the plaintiff's being shot was a foreseeable result of the defendant's shooting. Diplock J. held that this statement of claim disclosed no cause of action: Fowler must allege and prove that it was either intentionally or negligently that Lanning shot him.

This means that a person is not responsible for an unintended invasion (a) if his conduct was reasonable, or (b) even supposing his conduct was unreasonable, if the invasion was an unforeseeable consequence of it (*The Wagon Mound*, above, p.216). It is no longer sufficient that the act be positive—it must be unreasonable; or that the invasion be direct—it must be foreseeable. To this extent the rules of negligence have completely trumped those of trespass, at least so far as actual damage is concerned.

That leaves intended invasions. Here the rules of trespass remain unimpaired, especially the vital rule that it is not for the plaintiff to show that the defendant's conduct was unreasonable but rather for the defendant to justify it. When the plaintiff has established an intentional invasion against his will, he will recover damages unless the defendant can establish a justification. This is the most important, as well as the oldest, rule in the book. The Cheetham Cricket Club (above, p.141) was not liable for hitting Miss Stone because they did not intend to touch her at all, and what they did was reasonable; but no one in Britain, *no one*, can justify deliberately touching even a hair on Miss Stone's head, or entering her garden—much less depriving her of her liberty—merely on the ground that it was reasonable to do so, or on the more insidious ground that he reasonably thought he was entitled to do so. Trespass trips up the zealous bureaucrat, the eager policeman and the officious citizen; indeed, punitive damages can be awarded against the first two. It is not enough to *think* you are entitled; you must actually *be* entitled. Sometimes you will be entitled because of what you reasonably think (*e.g.* a policeman's power to arrest criminals extends to arresting those he reasonably but erroneously believes guilty); sometime not (a bailiff may enter A's house to find B; but only if B is actually there: *Southam v Smout* [1964] 1 Q.B. 308).

This point has to be insisted on, since it is in danger of being overlooked. The law of tort does not have one function only; few things do. It is true that most tort claimants want compensation for harm caused to them by someone else and that in this sense (and in this sense only) the main function of the law of tort is to ordain such compensation. It has another function, however, which, though traditional, has rarely been more important than now, namely to vindicate constitutional rights. Not every infraction of a right causes damage. That is precisely why the law of trespass does not insist on damage. But if jurists believe that damage is of the essence of a tort claim, they will regard trespass as anomalous, deride it as antiquated, ignore the values it enshrines and proceed to diminish the protection it affords to the rights of the citizen. When constitutional rights are in issue what matters is whether they have been infringed, not whether the defendant can really be blamed for infringing them. But if jurists think of negligence as the paradigm tort (and they do so for no better reason than that a great many people are mangled on the highway) they will regard it as the overriding principle of the law of tort that you do not have to pay unless you were at fault (and, equally, that you always have to pay if you were at fault); the old cases where liability was imposed despite the absence of fault (or not imposed despite its presence) are then to be restricted or overruled as vestigial exceptions. If a defendant can say that he acted reasonably, a negligence lawyer will let him off, without bothering to distinguish the reasonable but erroneous belief that the projected behaviour was *authorised* from the reasonable but erroneous belief that it was *safe*.

It is especially important in Britain to make this distinction, because we can sue officials and the government, local or central, as if they were private persons. Officials are no less liable by reason of their office. That is all very well and good. But at common law they are no more liable either; and that may not be so good, for it means that if you diminish the circumstances under which the citizen can sue another citizen you likewise diminish the circumstances under which the citizen can sue the state or its officials. Fortunately one can still claim punitive damages from an official who behaves outrageously; but one should also be able to claim damages from an official who, though behaving reasonably after the manner of officials, has nevertheless invaded those basic rights which are protected by the law of trespass. For it must be remembered (or learnt) that those who invade our rights generally do so on reasonable grounds, that is, for our own good or for someone else's good or for the public good (which may, perhaps, be no one's).

It was stated in the previous paragraph that at common law officials are no more liable than private persons (though they can be liable for misfeasance in office and may have to pay punitive damages). The Human Rights Act 1998, however, does expose public bodies to a more extensive liability, since it is only for them that it is unlawful to act in contravention of the specified Convention rights. Language in terms of rights has not hitherto been characteristic of negligence discourse in England (as opposed to Germany, but not France), but liability in trespass turns precisely on the invasion of the plaintiff's rights in liberty, person and possessions, given that no damage need be proved and that reasonableness of conduct is not a defence. Unsurprisingly, therefore, a number of human rights cases involve trespasses of one kind or another.

Thus in one case the police entered the complainant's house while her ex-husband was removing property from it. This was to prevent a breach of the peace, a justification acceptable to the English courts (*McLeod v Metropolitan Police Commissioner* [1994] 4 All E.R. 553, CA). The Strasbourg Court held that while the common law power to enter for that purpose was legitimate and clear enough to be in "accordance with the law" under Art.8, the actual entry in this case was disproportionate to any legitimate aim of preventing disorder since the police knew that the occupier was not at home and that the risk of disorder was slight. There was thus a violation of Art.8 by the police. *McLeod v United Kingdom* (1999) 5 B.H.R.C. 364.

Again, when a stepfather thumped his nine-year-old stepson for indiscipline and was prosecuted for assault occasioning bodily harm—severe bruising—under s.47 of the Offences Against the Person Act 1861, the jury acquitted him. It was held in Strasbourg that the United Kingdom was in breach of Art.3 in failing to provide adequate protection against such ill-treatment. *A v United Kingdom* (1999) 5 B.H.R.C. 137.

The effect of the Human Rights Act on private law is less than clear, but it is devoutly to be hoped that its existence will not diminish the applicability of our own dear trespass law, our home-made way of protecting basic rights. It is true that while the defendants subject to the Act are less numerous, the rights protected by it are much wider than those protected by trespass law and that a human rights violation, unlike trespass, does not call for a positive act, but the damages sanction under the Act is much less satisfactory, especially as, if our courts are to follow the Strasbourg court in the matter, punitive damages will be unavailable for human rights violations. It would therefore be intolerable if the consideration that a body was guilty of unlawful behaviour under the Act led to the conclusion that it was not liable in the common law of trespass.

The person who has committed a trespass must justify it. In creating the grounds of justification, the law is doing what it did in *Watt v Hertfordshire C.C.* (above, p.144); it balances the interests of the plaintiff against the interests sought to be furthered by the defendant. But here the rules are a little more precise, partly because they were formed under a system of strict pleading, and partly because there must be stricter limitations on those who intentionally invade the interests of others than on those who merely imperil them.

There is no reason to suppose that the categories of justification are closed, but they should be extended with the greatest caution, since every extension of a defence constitutes an erosion of a right. The present justifications exist for the purposes of promoting the most important interests—maintenance of public order, enforcement of the law, and preservation of life and property—and they frequently overlap. In addition, an act cannot be unlawful if it is authorised by the legislature, a judge or a proper custom.

Order is the precondition of justice: without public order social life is impossible. Thus anyone may stop a person committing, or from committing, a breach of the peace (*Albert v Lavin* [1982] A.C. 546). But even when order is not threatened the law must be enforced: criminals must be caught however orderly they are. When they are caught in the act, there are not too many problems, but once they have got away, it is less clear that a crime has been committed and whether the suspects are guilty. A policeman may safely arrest a person whom he reasonably suspects of having committed certain crimes, but a private person had better let a policeman do any arresting that needs to be done, since if he does it himself he must show that the offence in question was actually committed. In other words, the private citizen must not only be reasonable about the suspect; he must be right about the crime. These powers are now largely statutory (below, p.380). Arrest by warrant is safer, provided it is the person named in it who is arrested; here there is a second ground of justification—the order of a magistrate. There may, of course, also be a statutory power. May one trespass to land in order to catch a thief? It would be idle to say that a person who is subject to arrest can be taken only at home or on the highway. Thus policemen may enter premises if they have reasonable grounds for supposing the suspect to be there. There is, of course, no common law power to go on premises to look for evidence, but some striking statutory powers exist and have given cause for concern (*Inland Revenue Commissioners v Rossminster Ltd* [1980] A.C. 952).

If you can thus justify a trespass against a man who threatens the public, you can also justify one against a man who threatens you. Self-defence against aggressor, defence of property against burglar and thief are of course permitted. But now we happen upon a peculiarity. Under the old system of pleading, only trespassers could be thrown off land and only assailants could be struck in self-defence: in other words, if B used force against A in defence of person or property, B's liability depended on whether A was a trespasser or not. "Trespassers" must therefore include not only those who ought to be held liable in damages but also those whom one may evict or strike in self-defence. Now we see why a person who has no right to stay on land must be called a trespasser even if he came there without any negligence at all and even if he is doing no harm whatever. Likewise a person must be called an assailant if he appeared to be about to strike, whatever his real intentions may have been.

Take a famous case about whether someone was guilty of assault. S and T had exchanged disobliging words in the street; T put his hand on the hilt of his sword, rather like the man in the Western going for his gun, but said as he did so "If 'twere not assize-time I should not take such language from you." The main question was whether T's behaviour constituted an assault, but of course T was not being sued for assault— even in the seventeenth century you didn't sue someone for not hitting you; T was suing S for battery, because S had then actually drawn his sword and poked T in the eye with it. But whether S was guilty of battery for blinding T depended on whether T was guilty of assault. In the event T won, despite his act of putting his hand to his sword, since it was clear from what he said that he was not going to draw it (*Tuberville v Savage* (1669) 1 Mod. 3; 86 E.R. 684).

In these cases one justifies self-defence by calling the other party a wrongdoer. But suppose my neighbour's prize cat is about to eat my canary; if the cat got the bird, my neighbour might well not be responsible, but I would surely be justified in hurling a brickbat at the cat in order to deter it, and I would not be liable to its owner if I hit it and caused it injury. Suppose that an accidental fire breaks out on my neighbour's land; if it appears likely to spread to my land, I can surely go on to his land to dig a fire-trench (though doubtless it would be better to call the Fire Brigade).

Now suppose that the danger in no way comes from the plaintiff, as the cat and fire did. A fire breaks out in my own house; may I seize my neighbour's fire-extinguisher and use it? This does not seem a wrongful thing to do, but it does seem that I should pay for the use of his thing. French law would unhesitatingly impose liability on the principle that one must not enrich himself (by cutting down fire damage) at the expense of another. English law has only two alternatives—to say (contrary to our belief) that the act was wrongful, or to say that it was not, and leave the plaintiff with the loss (contrary to our wish). The courts of England dislike the defence of necessity ("the tyrant's plea"), though it has its place in emergencies, but it was vigorously rejected in a case where squatters in council property said that they had nowhere else to live and that this was due to the council's breach of duty: *Southwark v Williams* ([1971] Ch. 734, CA).

What of protection of property from loss? Must a storekeeper permit a child to leave his store with a thing its mother has stolen? Surely not. The Theft Act 1978, to be sure, empowers anyone to arrest a person who is dishonestly making off with goods without paying for them as required or expected, but there must also be some power at common law to retake chattels from someone in wrongful possession of them, and to enter land to retake stolen chattels or things which have been put there by the occupier.

But at this point self-defence or protection of property tends to become self-help; it is not preventing loss but remedying it; that is what the courts are for, and when the courts have a role, they like it to be an exclusive one. The legislature agrees with them, for it has enacted that a court order is required by an owner who wants to take back his goods from a hire-purchaser in default who has paid a third of the price (Consumer Credit Act 1974, s.90(1)), and also by a landlord who wants to evict a tenant on the expiry of the tenancy (Protection from Eviction Act 1977, ss.2 and 3). That a mortgagee may re-enter without a court order is regarded as anomalous (*Ropaigealach v Barclays Bank plc* [1999] 4 All E.R. 235, CA).

One very important overriding qualification attaches to all these common law powers. They must be exercised reasonably. A person who would be lawfully arrested if he were told the reason is unlawfully arrested if he is not (PACE, s.28, below, p.381). A trespasser who would go when asked may sue if pushed. A court will not order a stranger to return your thing if you have not demanded it (*Clayton v Le Roy* [1911] 2 K.B. 1031); you may not take it back yourself in the absence of that courtesy.

There is no similar principle that statutory or contractual powers must be exercised reasonably. Granted that such a power exists, it may be exercised "for a good reason or a bad reason or no reason at all," *Chapman v Honig* [1963] 2 Q.B. 502 at 520, *per*

Pearson L.J. But the law is not as helpless as it sounds. For although the judges will not admit that there is an overriding duty to exercise such powers reasonably, they are in a position to say exactly what those powers are, by construing the statute or contract in question. Except in an unusual case, the document will be held to grant the power conditionally on its reasonable use. Thus in one case the defendants had a power under statute to pull down the plaintiff's house. They did so. The plaintiff claimed damages for trespass. He recovered. The court held that there was in the statute an implied qualification of the power, namely, that notice of its intended exercise must be given. It would certainly have been reasonable for the defendant to have given notice, but the statute said nothing about it (*Cooper v Wandsworth Board of Works* (1863) 143 E.R. 414).

Finally, judges and magistrates, who spend so much of their time causing people to be laid by the heels or locked up, have very considerable immunity from strict liability in trespass (see below, p.385).

These are the legal justifications which a defendant may adduce if he has deliberately invaded one of the plaintiff's protected interests and is therefore guilty of false imprisonment, assault, battery, or trespass to land or goods. But no justification is required if the plaintiff consented to the invasion: *volenti non fit injuria*. One boxer cannot sue another for a fair blow. There may be disputes of fact about the existence of the consent: did the suspect agree to go to the police station when asked to help, or was he taken willy nilly? Or about the extent of the licence—you may come here but not go there. Or about its duration—can the theatre manager eject a patron before the show is over? Or about the mode of exercise—does the patient consent to the surgeon's use of a dirty scalpel? Or about its validity—perhaps the consent was induced by fraud, or the invasion agreed to was illegal (can the masochist sue the sadist?). There may also be questions of law—can consent be given by a servant against his master's will (was Master Rose a trespasser?, above, p.283), and what if there was apparently consent but really none?

HUMAN RIGHTS ACT 1998

[for the text, see above p.000]

Notes:

1. It is slightly odd that the *Human* Rights Act is so-called: the very first case where the Court of Appeal issued a declaration that a statutory provision was incompatible with the Act involved a pawnbroking company. (The House of Lords found no incompatibility: *Wilson v First County Trust* [2003] UKHL, [2003] 4 All E.R. 97).

2. The First Protocol protects a (natural or legal) person's *possessions*. This includes intangible assets. Consider the following case. A 22-year lease which Mr Stretch had entered with the Dorchester Borough Council required him to erect buildings for light industrial use and entitled him to an extension for a further 21 years. When he applied for this extension he was told that it could not be granted because the original grant was beyond the council's powers. Proceedings before the English courts were unavailing (*Stretch v West Dorset CC* (1998) 96 L.G.R. 637), but the Court in Strasbourg held unanimously that the council had behaved disproportionately in defeating his legitimate expectations, and for this breach of his rights under Art.1 of the First Protocol awarded him €31,000 for his pecuniary loss and €5,000 for non-pecuniary loss (!). (Application No. 44277/98).

3. Whereas the law of trespass requires that the defendant (public or private) have committed a positive act invasive of one of the protected rights (liberty, person and property in possession), the law as developed by the Court of Human Rights in Strasbourg imposes on public bodies some positive obligations. Not only must they take steps to protect citizens threatened by other citizens with grievous bodily harm (*Osman*), but

they must conduct a proper inquiry into every case where there is a death in custody but also where there is no public involvement in a suspicious death or serious injury (*Menson v UK* (47916/99)).

In the event of failure to meet this requirement, which may extend to facilitating the involvement of close relatives, those relatives may have a "free-standing" claim under s.7(1)(a) of the Act, and obtain damages or further relief (see Jackson J. in *R. v Home Office, Ex p Wright and Bennett* (2001) U.K.H.R.R. 1399). It is not easy for a tort lawyer to see such relatives as falling within the category of "victims" as required for a claim under the Act.

Chapter 8

THE CAUSE OF ACTION

Section 1.—Trespass in Context

(i) Trespass and Negligence

LETANG v COOPER

Court of Appeal [1965] 1 Q.B. 232; [1964] 3 W.L.R. 573; 108 S.J. 519; [1964] 2 Lloyd's Rep. 339; [1964] 2 All E.R. 929

Claim against motorist for personal injuries

The defendant appealed from a judgment for the plaintiff by Elwes J., who held that the plaintiff's claim was not time-barred [1964] 2 Q.B. 53. The appeal was allowed.

Lord Denning M.R.: On July 10, 1957, the plaintiff was on holiday in Cornwall. She was staying at an hotel and thought she would sunbathe on a piece of grass where cars were parked. While she was lying there the defendant came into the car park driving his Jaguar motor-car. He did not see her. The car went over her legs and she was injured.

On February 2, 1961, more than three years after the accident, the plaintiff brought this action against the defendant for damages for loss and injury caused by (1) the negligence of the defendant in driving a motor-car and (2) the commission by the defendant of a trespass to the person.

The sole question is whether the action is statute-barred. The plaintiff admits that the action for negligence is barred after three years, but she claims that the action for trespass to the person is not barred until six years have elapsed. The judge has so held and awarded her £575 damages for trespass to the person.

Under the Limitation Act 1939 the period of limitation was six years in all actions founded "on tort"; but, in 1954, Parliament reduced it to three years in actions for damages for personal injuries, provided that the actions come within these words of section 2(1) of the Law Reform (Limitation of Actions, etc.) Act 1954, "actions for damages for negligence, nuisance or breach of duty (whether the duty exists by virtue of a contract or of a provision made by or under a statute or independently of any contract or any such provision) where the damages claimed by the plaintiff for the negligence, nuisance or breach of duty consist of or include damages in respect of personal injuries to any person."

The plaintiff says that these words do not cover an action for trespass to the person and that therefore the time bar is not the new period of three years, but the old period of six years.

The argument, as it was developed before us, became a direct invitation to this court to go back to the old forms of action and to decide this case by reference to them. . . .

I must decline, therefore, to go back to the old forms of action in order to construe this statute. I know that in the last century Maitland said "the forms of action we have buried, but they still rule us from their graves" (see Maitland, *Forms of Action* (1909), p.296), but we have in this century shaken off their trammels. These forms of action have served their day. They did at one time form a guide to substantive rights; but they do so no longer. Lord Atkin, in *United Australia Ltd v Barclays Bank Ltd* ([1941] A.C. 1 at 29), told us what to do about them: "When these ghosts of the past stand in the path of justice clanking their mediaeval chains the proper course for the judge is to pass through them undeterred."

The truth is that the distinction between trespass and case is obsolete. We have a different sub-division altogether. Instead of dividing actions for personal injuries into trespass (direct damage) or case (consequential damage), we divided the causes of action now according as the defendant did the injury intentionally or unintentionally. If one man intentionally applies force directly to another, the plaintiff has a cause of action in assault and battery, or, if you so please to describe it, in trespass to the person. "The least touching of another in anger is a battery," *per* Holt C.J. in *Cole v Turner* ((1704) 87 E.R. 907). If he does not inflict injury intentionally, but only unintentionally, the plaintiff has no cause of action today in trespass. His only cause of action is in negligence, and then only on proof of want of reasonable care. If the plaintiff cannot prove want of reasonable care, he may have no cause of action at all. Thus, it is not enough nowadays for the plaintiff to plead that "the defendant shot the plaintiff." He must also allege that he did it intentionally or negligently. If intentional, it is the tort of assault and battery. If negligent and causing damage, it is the tort of negligence.

The modern law on this subject was well expounded by Diplock J. in *Fowler v Lanning* ([1959] 1 Q.B. 426, above, p.322), with which I fully agree. But I would go this one step further: when the injury is not inflicted intentionally, but negligently, I would say that the only cause of action is negligence and not trespass. If it were trespass, it would be actionable without proof of damage; and that is not the law today.

In my judgment, therefore, the only cause of action in the present case, where the injury was unintentional, is negligence and is barred by reason of the express provision of the statute. . . .

Notes:

1. Lord Denning held in the alternative that a claim in trespass would also have fallen within the statutory phrase "breach of duty" and thus be subject to the time-bar of three and not six years. The House of Lords has now said that he was wrong on this point: a claim for deliberate battery (in the case, sexual abuse and rape) is not one for "breach of duty" and is accordingly subject to the residual six-year time-bar which, unlike the three-year period under the 1980 Limitation Act, cannot be extended by the courts. (*Stubbings v Webb* [1993] 1 All E.R. 322. Lord Griffiths said: " . . . I should not myself have construed 'breach of duty' as including a deliberate assault. The phrase lying in juxtaposition with 'negligence' and 'nuisance' carries with it the implication of a breach of duty of care not to cause personal injury, rather than an obligation not to infringe any legal right of another person. If I invite a lady to my house one would naturally think of a duty to take care that the house is safe but would one really be thinking of a duty not to rape her?"

The House accordingly held, reversing the Court of Appeal, that the plaintiff, aged over 30 when the writ was issued, could not sue her stepfather and stepbrother for sexual assaults and rape which took place 18 to 28 years previously. Was this consistent with the Convention on Human Rights? The Commission in Strasbourg held that there was a breach by the U.K., but the Court disagreed ((1997) 23 E.H.R.R. 213) and held by a majority that there was no breach of Art.6(1) and unanimously that there was no breach of Art.8.

2. But now that *Lister* has held that an innocent superior may be liable for abuses committed by an inferior, a new twist has been added which it was sought to unravel in *KR v Bryn Alyn Community* [2003] EWCA Civ 85 at [97] to [108], [2003] 3 W.L.R. 107. The Court of Appeal held that "in the absence of some provable allegation of systemic negligence of the [employer], . . . its employees' deliberate abuse does not fall within s.11 and is therefore governed by a non-extendable six-year period of limitation rather than an extendable three-year period." But if we refer back to the discussion of *Lister* (above, p.288) we may see an argument that the deliberate abuse by the employee constitutes a breach of duty on the part of the employer, even if the employer is not negligent at all. If so, then the employer is liable for personal injuries due to a breach of duty, and the limitation period for the claim against him (though not the employee) should be an extensible three years from the date of knowledge once majority has been attained.

3. While doubtless we are much cleverer than our predecessors, since they are dead and we are not, nevertheless there is much to be learnt from them, so the aspersions of Lord Denning, following Lord Atkin, on the old forms of action should be taken with a grain of salt.

(ii) Trespass and Wilful Wrongs

WAINWRIGHT v HOME OFFICE

House of Lords, [2003] UKHL 53, [2003] 3 W.L.R. 1137, [2003] 4 All E.R. 969

Invasion of privacy and causing of emotional distress

When the claimants, mother and son, went to visit their son and brother in prison they were told that they must be searched for drugs. The mother was emotionally distressed by the experience of having to undress in front of an uncurtained window and the son, whose private parts were actually touched, suffered post-traumatic stress disorder.

Lord Hoffmann: . . . the question is whether the searches themselves or the manner in which they were conducted gave the Wainwrights a cause of action.

The judge found two causes of action, both of which he derived from the action for trespass. As Diplock L.J. pointed out in *Letang v Cooper* [1965] 1 Q.B. 232, 243, trespass is strictly speaking not a cause of action but a form of action. It was the form anciently used for a variety of different kinds of claim which had as their common element the fact that the damage was caused directly rather than indirectly; if the damage was indirect, the appropriate form of action was the action on the case. After the abolition of the forms of action trespass is no more than a convenient label for certain causes of action which derive historically from the old action for trespass vi et armis. One group of such causes of action is trespass to the person, which includes the torts of assault, battery and false imprisonment, each with their own conditions of liability.

Battery involves a touching of the person with what is sometimes called hostile intent (as opposed to a friendly pat on the back) but which Robert Goff L.J. in *Collins v Wilcock* [1984] 1 W.L.R. 1172, 1178 redefined as meaning any intentional physical contact which was not "generally acceptable in the ordinary conduct of daily life": see also *Wilson v Pringle* [1987] Q.B. 237. Counsel for the Home Office conceded that touching Alan's penis was not acceptable and was therefore a battery.

That, however, was the only physical contact which had occurred. The judge nevertheless held that requiring the Wainwrights to take off their clothes was also a form of trespass to the person. He arrived at this conclusion by the use of two strands of reasoning. First, he said that a line of authority starting with *Wilkinson v Downton* [1897] 2 Q.B. 57, which I shall have to examine later in some detail, had extended the conduct which could constitute trespass to the utterance of words which were "calculated" to cause physical (including psychiatric) harm. There was in his view little distinction between words which directly caused such harm and words which induced someone to act in a way which caused himself harm, like taking his own clothes off. So inducing Alan to take off his clothes and thereby suffer post-traumatic stress disorder was actionable.

The judge recognised, however, that in the cases upon which he relied the claimant had suffered a recognised psychiatric injury. Mrs Wainwright had not. It seemed to him illogical to deny her a remedy for distress because her constitution was sufficiently robust to protect her from psychiatric injury. So the second strand of his reasoning was that the law of tort should give a remedy for any kind of distress caused by an infringement of the right of privacy protected by article 8 of the European Convention for the Protection of Human Rights and Fundamental Freedoms. At the time of the incident the Human Rights Act 1998 had not yet come into force but the judge considered that he was justified in adapting the common law to the Convention by analogy with the principle by which, even before the 1998 Act, the courts interpreted statutes so as to conform, if possible, to the Convention.

The judge therefore found in favour of both Wainwrights. He awarded Mrs Wainwright damages of £2,600, divided into £1,600 "basic" and £1,000 aggravated damages, and Alan £4,500, divided into £3,500 basic and £1,000 aggravated. The award to Alan did not distinguish between the damages for the battery and the injury caused by having to strip.

The Court of Appeal did not agree with the judge's extensions of the notion of trespass to the person and did not consider that (apart from the battery, which was unchallenged) the prison officers had committed any other wrongful act. So they set aside the judgments against the Wainwrights with the exception of the damages for battery, to which they attributed £3,750 of the £4,500 awarded by the judge.

The Wainwrights appeal to your Lordships' House. Their counsel put the case in two ways. The first was that, in order to enable the United Kingdom to conform to its international obligations under the Convention, the House should declare that there is (and in theory always has been) a tort of invasion of privacy under which the searches of both Wainwrights were actionable and damages for emotional distress recoverable. This does not give retrospective effect to the Human Rights Act 1998. It accepts that the Convention, at the relevant time, operated only at the level of international law. Indeed, the argument (if valid) would have been equally valid at any time since the United Kingdom acceded to the Convention. Alternatively, counsel proposed that if a general tort of invasion of privacy seemed too bold an undertaking, the House could comply with the Convention in respect of this particular invasion by an extension of the principle in *Wilkinson v Downton* [1897] 2 Q.B. 57.

My Lords, let us first consider the proposed tort of invasion of privacy. Since the famous article by Warren and Brandeis (The Right to Privacy (1890) 4 Harvard L.R. 193) the question of whether such a tort exists, or should exist, has been much debated in common law jurisdictions. Warren and Brandeis suggested that one could generalise certain cases on defamation, breach of copyright in unpublished letters, trade secrets and breach of confidence as all based upon the protection of a common value which they called privacy or, following Judge Cooley (Cooley on Torts, 2nd ed. (1888), p.29) "the right to be let alone". They said that identifying this common element should enable the courts to declare the existence of a general principle which protected a person's appearance, sayings, acts and personal relations from being exposed in public.

Courts in the US were receptive to this proposal and a jurisprudence of privacy began to develop. It became apparent, however, that the developments could not be contained within a single principle; not, at any rate, one with greater explanatory power than the proposition that it was based upon the protection of a value which could be described as privacy. Dean Prosser, in his work on The Law of Torts, 4th ed. (1971), p.804, said that: "What has emerged is no very simple matter . . . it is not one tort, but a complex of four. To date the law of privacy comprises four distinct kinds of invasion of four different interests of the plaintiff, which are tied together by the common name, but otherwise have almost nothing in common except that each represents an interference with the right of the plaintiff 'to be let alone'."

Dean Prosser's taxonomy divided the subject into (1) intrusion upon the plaintiff's physical solitude or seclusion (including unlawful searches, telephone tapping, long-distance photography and telephone harassment) (2) public disclosure of private facts and (3) publicity putting the plaintiff in a false light and (4) appropriation, for the defendant's advantage, of the plaintiff's name or likeness. These, he said, at p.814, had different elements and were subject to different defences.

The need in the U.S. to break down the concept of "invasion of privacy" into a number of loosely-linked torts must cast doubt upon the value of any high-level generalisation which can perform a useful function in enabling one to deduce the rule to be applied in a concrete case. English law has so far been unwilling, perhaps unable, to formulate any such high-level principle. There are a number of common law and statutory remedies of which it may be said that one at least of the underlying values they protect is a right of privacy. Sir Brian Neill's well known article "Privacy: a challenge for the next century" in Protecting Privacy (ed. B Markesinis, 1999) contains a survey. Common law torts include trespass, nuisance, defamation and malicious falsehood; there is the equitable action for breach of confidence and statutory remedies under the Protection from Harassment Act 1997 and the Data Protection Act 1998. There are also extra-legal remedies under Codes of Practice applicable to broadcasters and newspapers. But there are gaps; cases in which the courts have considered that an invasion of privacy deserves a remedy which the existing law does not offer. Sometimes the perceived gap can be filled by judicious development of an existing principle. The law of breach of confidence has in recent years undergone such a process: see in particular the judgment of Lord Phillips of Worth Matravers M.R. in *Campbell v MGN Ltd* [2003] Q.B. 633. On the other hand, an attempt to create a tort of telephone harassment by a radical change in the basis of the action for private nuisance in *Khorasandjian v Bush* [1993] Q.B. 727 was held by the House of Lords in *Hunter v Canary Wharf Ltd* [1997] A.C. 655 to be a step too far. The gap was filled by the 1997 Act.

What the courts have so far refused to do is to formulate a general principle of "invasion of privacy" (I use the quotation marks to signify doubt about what in such a context the expression would mean) from which the conditions of liability in the particular case can be deduced. The reasons were discussed by Sir Robert Megarry V-C in *Malone v Metropolitan Police Comr* [1979] Ch. 344, 372–381.

The absence of any general cause of action for invasion of privacy was again acknowledged by the Court of Appeal in *Kaye v Robertson* [1991] F.S.R. 62, in which a newspaper reporter and photographer invaded the plaintiff's hospital bedroom, purported to interview him and took photographs. The law of trespass provided no remedy because the plaintiff was not owner or occupier of the room and his body had not been touched. Publication of the interview was restrained by interlocutory injunction on the ground that it was arguably a malicious falsehood to represent that the plaintiff had consented to it. But no other remedy was available.

There seems to me a great difference between identifying privacy as a value which underlies the existence of a rule of law (and may point the direction in which the law should develop) and privacy as a principle of law in itself. The English common law is familiar with the notion of underlying values—principles only in the broadest sense—which direct its development. A famous example is *Derbyshire County Council v Times Newspapers Ltd* [1993] A.C. 534, in which freedom of speech was the underlying value which supported the decision to lay down the specific rule that a local authority could not sue for libel. But no one has suggested that freedom of speech is in itself a legal principle which is capable of sufficient definition to enable one to deduce specific rules to be applied in concrete cases. That is not the way the common law works.

Furthermore, the coming into force of the Human Rights Act 1998 weakens the argument for saying that a general tort of invasion of privacy is needed to fill gaps in the existing remedies. Sections 6 and 7 of the Act are in themselves substantial gap fillers; if it is indeed the case that a person's rights under Art.8 have been infringed by a public authority, he will have a statutory remedy. For these reasons I would reject the invitation to declare that since at the least 1950 there has been a previously unknown tort of invasion of privacy.

I turn next to the alternative argument based upon *Wilkinson v Downton* [1897] 2 Q.B. 57. This is a case which has been far more often discussed than applied. Thomas Wilkinson, landlord of the Albion public house in Limehouse, went by train to the races at Harlow, leaving his wife Lavinia behind the bar. Downton was a customer who decided to play what he would no doubt have described as a practical joke on Mrs Wilkinson. He went into the Albion and told her that her husband had decided to return in a horse-drawn vehicle which had been involved in an accident in which he had been seriously injured. The story was completely false and Mr Wilkinson returned safely by train later that evening. But the effect on Mrs Wilkinson was dramatic. Her hair turned white and she became so ill that for some time her life was thought in danger. The jury awarded her £100 for nervous shock and the question for the judge on further consideration was whether she had a cause of action.

The difficulty in the judge's way was the decision of the Privy Council in *Victorian Railway Comrs v Coultas* (1888) 13 App. Cas. 222, in which it had been said that nervous shock was too remote a consequence of a negligent act (in that case, putting the plaintiff in imminent fear of being run down by a train) to be a recoverable head of damages. RS Wright J. distinguished the case on the ground that Downton was not merely negligent but had intended to cause injury. Quite what the judge meant by this is not altogether clear; Downton obviously did not intend to cause any kind of injury but merely to give Mrs Wilkinson a fright. The judge said, however, at p.59, that as what he said could not fail to produce grave effects "upon any but an exceptionally indifferent person", an intention to cause such effects should be "imputed" to him.

By the time ... the law was able comfortably to accommodate the facts of *Wilkinson v Downton* [1897] 2 Q.B. 57 in the law of nervous shock caused by negligence it was unnecessary to fashion a tort of intention or to discuss what the requisite intention, actual or imputed, should be. Commentators and counsel have nevertheless been unwilling to allow *Wilkinson v Downton* to disappear beneath the surface of the law of negligence. Although, in cases of actual psychiatric injury, there is no point in arguing about whether the injury was in some sense intentional if negligence will do just as well, it has been suggested (as the claimants submit in this case) that damages for distress falling short of psychiatric injury can be recovered if there was an intention to cause it. This submission was squarely put to the Court of Appeal in v *Wong v Parkside Health NHS Trust* [2001] EWCA Civ 1721; *The Times*, December 7, 2001 and rejected. Hale L.J. said that before the passing of the Protection from Harassment Act 1997 there was no tort of intentional harassment which gave a remedy for anything less than physical or psychiatric injury. That leaves *Wilkinson v Downton* with no leading role in the modern law.

I do not resile from the proposition that the policy considerations which limit the heads of recoverable damage in negligence do not apply equally to torts of intention. If someone actually intends to cause harm by a wrongful act and does so, there is ordinarily no reason why he should not have to pay compensation. But I think that if you adopt such a principle, you have to be very careful about what you mean by "intend".

If ... one is going to draw a principled distinction which justifies abandoning the rule that damages for mere distress are not recoverable, imputed intention will not do. The defendant must actually have acted in a way which he knew to be unjustifiable and intended to cause harm or at least acted without caring whether he caused harm or not. Lord Woolf C.J., as I read his judgment, at [2002] Q.B. 1334, 1350, paras 50–51, might have been inclined to accept such a principle. But the facts did not support a claim on this basis. The judge made no finding that the prison officers intended to cause distress or realized that they were acting without justification in asking the Wainwrights to strip. He said, at para.83, that they had acted in good faith and, at para.121, that:

> "The deviations from the procedure laid down for strip-searches were, in my judgment, not intended to increase the humiliation necessarily involved but merely sloppiness."

Even on the basis of a genuine intention to cause distress, I would wish, as in *Hunter*'s case [1997] A.C. 655, to reserve my opinion on whether compensation should be recoverable. In institutions and workplaces all over the country, people constantly do and say things with the intention of causing distress and humiliation to others. This shows lack of consideration and appalling manners but I am not sure that the right way to deal with it is always by litigation. The Protection from Harassment Act 1997 defines harassment in s.1(1) as a "course of conduct" amounting to harassment and provides by s.7(3) that a course of conduct must involve conduct on at least two occasions. If these requirements are satisfied, the claimant may pursue a civil remedy for damages for anxiety: s.3(2). The requirement of a course of conduct shows that Parliament was conscious that it might not be in the public interest to allow the law to be set in motion for one boorish incident. It may be that any development of the common law should show similar caution.

In my opinion, therefore, the claimants can build nothing on *Wilkinson v Downton* [1897] 2 Q.B. 57. It does not provide a remedy for distress which does not amount to recognized psychiatric injury and so far as there may a tort of intention under which such damage is recoverable, the necessary intention was not established.

Lord Scott of Foscote: The essence of the complaint of each claimant is that he or she was subjected to conduct by the prison officers at Armley Prison, Leeds, that was calculated to, and did, cause humiliation and distress. The main issue is whether this conduct was tortious. The important issue of principle is not, in my opinion, whether English common law recognises a tort of invasion of privacy. As Lord Hoffmann has demonstrated, whatever remedies may have been developed for misuse of confidential information, for certain types of trespass, for certain types of nuisance and for various other situations in which claimants may find themselves aggrieved by an invasion of what they conceive to be their privacy, the common law has not developed an overall remedy for the invasion of privacy. The issue of importance in the present case is whether the infliction of humiliation and distress by conduct calculated to humiliate and cause distress, is without more, tortious at common law. I am in full agreement with the reasons that have been given by Lord Hoffmann for concluding that it is not. Nor, in my opinion, should it be. Some institutions, schools, university colleges, regiments and the like (often bad ones) have initiation ceremonies and rites which newcomers are expected to undergo. Ritual humiliation is often a part of this. The authorities in charge of these institutions usually object to these practices and seek to put an end to any excesses. But why, absent any of the traditional nominate torts such as assault, battery, negligent causing of harm etc, should the law of tort intrude? If a shop assistant or a bouncer or barman at a club is publicly offensive to a customer, the customer may well be humiliated and distressed. But that is no sufficient reason why the law of tort should be fashioned and developed with a view to providing compensation in money to the victim.

Whether today, the Human Rights Act 1998 having come into effect, conduct similar to that inflicted on Mrs Wainwright and Alan Wainwright, but without any element of battery and without crossing the line into the territory of misfeasance in public office, should be categorised as tortious must be left to be decided when such a case arises. It is not necessary to decide now whether such conduct would constitute a breach of Art.8 or of Art.3 of the Convention.

I, too, would dismiss these appeals.

Lord Bingham, **Lord Hope** and **Lord Hutton** agreed.

Note:
The tort of trespass protects one's right to exclusive possession of land and chattels (including letters and files) as well as one's physical integrity, and the tort of nuisance guarantees a certain tranquillity at home, but trespass requires a positive act of physical invasion and you need an interest in the land to be able to sue in nuisance. These requirements at common law have not been relaxed, but in another head of liability mentioned by Lord Hoffmann there has been a great development. This is *breach of confidence*. It was, as he says, equitable in origin, in the sense that if you trusted someone with a "secret", he could be enjoined from disclosing it, unless it was already public knowledge or such disclosure was in the public interest, rather narrowly defined.

Expansion has been in two directions: information need no longer be confided in order to be treated as confidential, and damages may be awarded. In *Douglas v Hello!* [2003] 3 All E.R. 996 the defendant magazine, in order to meet the insatiable concern of the idle to learn about the doings and misdoings of "celebrities", published photographs furtively taken by a rascally paparazzo of the wedding of Ms Catherine Zeta-Jones, who had taken every measure to control the photography of this exciting event by granting *OK!*, doubtless for a consideration, the exclusive right to publish the pictures, and who was distressed beyond measure to be shown to the fanzine-buying public in the act of eating a piece of her own bridal cake. It was clear that the "information" about how the wedding looked was "secret", until so wickedly disclosed by *Hello!*, so the human victims received £3,750 each for their distress, which will not go far towards their next weddings, and *OK!* received over £1 million for its commercial loss and expenses.

Then a married star footballer raised the question whether the young woman with whom he spent an intimate night or two was entitled to tell the press how much she enjoyed the experience. The trial judge issued an injunction against the press (for you are not allowed to publish what you must have known was obtained by your informant in breach of confidence), but the injunction was lifted by the Court of Appeal (*A v B* [2002] 2 All E.R. 545).

Finally in this trio of demands for justice there was a claim for damages by a famous denizenne of the catwalk, the press having published the fact that, contrary to her public pronouncements, she had a drug problem and was having treatment for it. She has appealed to the House of Lords from the negative judgment of the Court of Appeal, so we may have some clarification (*Campbell v Mirror Group* [2003] 1 All E.R. 224).

Note that these are all claims against defendants who told the truth. The law of defamation (see below p.519f) sees to it that if what is said would make the average reader think worse of a person, that person can obtain damages unless the defendant can prove that what he said was true, that he had a special privilege to say it or was only giving his personal opinion.

The Human Rights Act is much ventilated in these cases. That is not because the press, not being a public body, is directly bound to respect the citizen's private life, protected under Art.8, though perhaps the court as a public body might be bound to protect the citizen against the press's invasion of that right; it is because another Convention right (Art.10) is freedom of expression, available to everyone, but subject to restriction "for the protection of the reputation or rights of others". This is a right to which the "court must have particular regard" (Human Rights Act 1998, s.12) when considering whether or not to grant relief which might affect it, "any privacy code" being taken into account. The courts have held that while freedom of expression is a powerful card, it is not the ace of trumps, and the rights of expression and privacy have to be balanced against each other. Nothing has been made of Art.17, which according to the Human Rights Act s.1(1) is to be read in conjunction with the Convention rights. It provides that "Nothing in this Convention may be interpreted as implying for any ... person any right to engage in any activity or perform any act aimed at the destruction of any of the rights and freedoms set forth herein or at their limitation to a greater extent than is provided for in the Convention."

PROTECTION FROM HARASSMENT ACT 1997

1.—(1) A person must not pursue a course of conduct—

(a) which amounts to harassment of another, and
(b) which he knows or ought to know amounts to harassment of the other.

(2) For the purposes of this section, the person whose course of conduct is in question ought to know that it amounts to harassment of another if a reasonable person in possession of the same information would think the course of conduct amounted to harassment of the other.
(3) Subsection (1) does not apply to a course of conduct if the person who pursued it shows—

(a) that it was pursued for the purpose of preventing or detecting crime,
(b) that it was pursued under any enactment or rule of law or to comply with any condition or requirement imposed by any person under any enactment, or
(c) that in the particular circumstances the pursuit of the course of conduct was reasonable.

2.—(1) A person who pursues a course of conduct in breach of s.1 is guilty of an offence.
(2) A person guilty of an offence under this section is liable on summary conviction to imprisonment for a term not exceeding six months, or a fine not exceeding level 5 on the standard scale, or both.
3.—(1) An actual or apprehended breach of s.1 may be the subject of a claim in civil proceedings by the person who is or may be the victim of the course of conduct in question.
(2) On such a claim, damages may be awarded for (among other things) any anxiety caused by the harassment and any financial loss resulting from the harassment.
7.—(2) References to harassing a person include alarming the person or causing the person distress.
(3) A "course of conduct" must involve conduct on at least two occasions.
(3A) A person's conduct on any occasion shall be taken, if aided, abetted, counselled or procured by another—

(a) to be conduct on that occasion of the other (as well as conduct of the person whose conduct it is); and
(b) to be conduct in relation to which the other's knowledge and purpose, and what he ought to have known, are the same as they were in relation to what was contemplated or reasonably foreseeable at the time of the aiding, abetting, counselling or procuring.

(4) "Conduct" includes speech.

Notes:
    1. As Hale L.J. said in *Wong v Parkside Health NHS Trust* [2001] EWCA Civ 1721, [2003] 3 All E.R. 932, "Parliament has provided a civil remedy, which includes damages for anxiety, as well as a criminal remedy in the 1997 Act. No doubt the concept of 'a course of conduct ... which amounts to harassment' will be

developed in decisions under that Act. Until that Act came into force, there was power to restrain by injunction conduct which might result in the tort of intentional infliction of harm or otherwise threaten the claimant's right of access to the courts, but there was no right to damages for conduct falling short of an actual tort."

2. Companies cannot sue under the Protection from Harassment Act, but their threatened employees may. *Daiichi Ltd v Stop Huntingdon Animal Cruelty* [2003] EWHC (Q.B.) 2337.

3. Harassment is most likely to be prolonged when the parties are neighbours (*Wood v Hills*, CA, October 15, 2003), family members (*Lomas v Parle* [2003] EWCA Civ 1804, or fellow-employees (*Wong*—above). Proximity is required for friction . . .

4. In family matters the situation is complex. Leaving aside criminal proceedings, "the victim of domestic violence has some choice of civil remedies. Protection may be sought under s.42 of the Family Law Act and under s.3 of the Protection from Harassment Act 1997. In our experience s.42 is the more usual choice. One attraction of the Family Law Act may lie in the court's ability to attach a power of arrest to the non-molestation injunction, whilst s.3(3) of the Protection from Harassment Act necessitates a separate application for a warrant for arrest in the event of breach of the court's injunction.

On the other hand s.3(2) of the Protection from Harassment Act offers the prospect of compensatory damages, which may be attractive in cases where the perpetrator has the means to satisfy an award. There would seem to be no bar on concurrent applications under both ss.42 and s.3 of these two Acts. In that event the application should be issued in the same court, consolidated and tried by a judge with jurisdiction in both civil and family." (*Lomas v Parle* [2003] EWCA Civ 1804). Note that the offence created by the 1997 Act is an arrestable one.

5. Newspapers may be guilty of harassment "by publishing racist criticism of a person which was foreseeably likely to stimulate a racist reaction on the part of their readership and to cause her distress." There had been two articles criticising "a black clerk" in the police station for reporting racist remarks by two sergeants who were then demoted; indignant readers' letters had been published. But "harassment was not to be given an interpretation which restricted the right of freedom of expression, especially by the press, save in so far as that was necessary to achieve a legitimate aim." *Thomas v News Group Newspapers* [2001] EWCA Civ 1233, *The Times* July 25, 2001

6. You must be civil to civil servants, or you may be prosecuted for harassment, as Mr Baron found. He had written a monstrous letter addressed to the complainant's subordinate and on being told he must communicate only with the Benefits Centre, he wrote a rude letter to the complainant personally followed by another over four months later, indicating that he would cross-examine her severely on her evidence that his claim had been fraudulent. His conviction under the Protection from Harassment Act was upheld by the Crown Court and the Divisional Court. *Baron v Crown Prosecution Service* (DivCt, June 13, 2000)

7. "Conduct" apparently does not include litigation. When persons guilty of copyright and trade mark infringement claimed that by suing and bankrupting them Microsoft were guilty of infringing the Protection from Harassment Act, it was found that there was only a single act—namely a late night telephone call—which could constitute harassment, so the claim was dismissed. *Tuppen v Microsoft Corp.* Q.B.D. (Douglas Brown J., July 16, 2000).

Section 2.—False Imprisonment

"In one sense it is true to say that the tort of false imprisonment has two ingredients; the fact of imprisonment and the absence of lawful authority to justify it . . . But as I understand the law, the gist of the action of false imprisonment is the mere imprisonment. The plaintiff need not prove that the imprisonment was unlawful or malicious; he established a prima facie case if he proves he was imprisoned by the defendant." So said Neill L.J. in *C v Mirror Group Newspapers* [1996] 4 All E.R. 511 at 517.

(i) The Act

BIRD v JONES

Queen's Bench (1845) 7 Q.B. 742; 15 L.J.Q.B. 82; 5 L.T.(o.s.) 406; 10 J.P. 4; 9 Jur. 870; 115 E.R. 668

The plaintiff obtained a verdict in a trial before Lord Denman C.J. The defendant sought a new trial on the ground of misdirection. A new trial was ordered, Lord Denman C.J. dissenting.

Patteson J.: This was an action of trespass for an assault and false imprisonment. The pleas were: as to the assault, *son assault demesne*; as to the imprisonment, that the plaintiff, before the imprisonment, assaulted the defendant, wherefore the defendant gave him into custody. The replication was *de injuria* to each plea. This puts in issue, as to the first plea, who committed the first assault; and, as to the second, whether the imprisonment was before or after the assault, if any, committed by the plaintiff. . . .

Now the facts of this case appear to be as follows. A part of Hammersmith Bridge which is ordinarily used as a public footway was appropriated for seats to view a regatta on the river, and separated for that purpose from the carriage way by a temporary fence. The plaintiff insisted on passing along the part so appropriated, and attempted to climb over the fence. The defendant, being clerk of the Bridge Company, seized his coat, and tried to pull him back: the plaintiff, however, succeeded in climbing over the fence. The defendant then stationed two policemen to prevent, and they did prevent, the plaintiff from proceeding forwards along the footway; but he was told that he might go back into the carriage way, and proceed to the other side of the bridge, if he pleased. The plaintiff would not do so, but remained where he was above half an hour: and then, on the defendant still refusing to suffer him to go forwards along the footway, he endeavoured to force his way, and, in so doing, assaulted the defendant: whereupon he was taken into custody.

It is plain from these facts that the first assault was committed by the defendant when he tried to pull the plaintiff back as he was climbing over the fence: and, as the jury have found the whole transaction to have been continuous, the plaintiff would be entitled to retain the verdict which he has obtained on the issue as to the first plea. Again, if what passed before the plaintiff assaulted the defendant was in law an imprisonment of the plaintiff, that imprisonment was undoubtedly continuous, and the assault by the plaintiff would not have been before the imprisonment as alleged in the second plea, but during it, and in attempting to escape from it: and the plaintiff would, in that case, be entitled to retain the verdict which he has obtained on the issue as to the second plea. But, if what so passed was not in law an imprisonment, then the plaintiff ought to have replied the right of footway and the obstruction by the defendant, and that he necessarily assaulted him in the exercise of the right, and, not having so replied, is not entitled to the verdict. So that the case is reduced to the question, whether what passed before the assault by the plaintiff was or was not an imprisonment of the plaintiff in point of law.

I have no doubt that, in general, if one man compels another to stay in any given place against his will, he imprisons that other just as much as if he locked him up in a room: and I agree that it is not necessary, in order to constitute an imprisonment, that a man's person should be touched. I agree, also, that the compelling a man to go in a given direction against his will may amount to imprisonment. But I cannot bring my mind to the conclusion that, if one man merely obstructs the passage of another in a particular direction, whether by threat of personal violence or otherwise, leaving him at liberty to stay where he is or to go in any other direction if he pleases, he can be said thereby to imprison him. He does him wrong, undoubtedly, if there was a right to pass in that direction, and would be liable to an action on the case for obstructing the passage, or of assault, if, on the party persisting in going in that direction, he touched his person, or so threatened him as to amount to an assault. But imprisonment is, as I apprehend, a total restraint of the liberty of the person, for however short a time, and not a partial obstruction of his will, whatever inconvenience it may bring on him. The quality of the act cannot, however, depend on the right of the opposite party. If it be an imprisonment to prevent a man passing along the public highway, it must be equally so to prevent him passing further along a field into which he has broken by a clear act of trespass.

. . . Upon the whole, I am of opinion that the only imprisonment proved in this case was that which occurred when the plaintiff was taken into custody after he had assaulted the defendant, and that the second plea was made out; I therefore think that the rule for a new trial ought to be made absolute.

Lord Denman C.J. (dissenting): A company unlawfully obstructed a public way for their own profit, extorting money from passengers, and hiring policemen to effect this purpose. The plaintiff, wishing to exercise his right of way, is stopped by force, and ordered to move in a direction which he wished not to take. He is told at the same time that a force is at hand ready to compel his submission. That proceeding appears to me equivalent to being pulled by the collar out of the one line and into the other.

There is some difficulty perhaps in defining imprisonment in the abstract without reference to its illegality; nor is it necessary for me to do so, because I consider these acts as amounting to imprisonment. That word I understand to mean any restraint of the person by force. . . .

I had no idea that any person in these times supposed any particular boundary to be necessary to constitute imprisonment, or that the restraint of a man's person from doing what he desires ceases to be an imprisonment because he may find some means of escape.

. . . As long as I am prevented from doing what I have a right to do, of what importance is it that I am permitted to do something else? How does the imposition of an unlawful condition show that I am not restrained? If I am locked in a room, am I not imprisoned because I might effect my escape through a window, or because I might find an exit dangerous or inconvenient to myself, as by wading through water or by taking a route so circuitous that my necessary affairs would suffer by delay?

It appears to me that this is a total deprivation of liberty with reference to the purpose for which he lawfully wished to employ his liberty: and, being effected by force, it is not the mere obstruction of a way, but a restraint of the person. The case cited as occurring before Lord Chief Justice Tindal, as I understand it, is much in point. He held it an imprisonment where the defendant stopped the plaintiff on his road till he had read a libel to him. Yet he did not prevent his escaping in another direction.

It is said that, if any damage arises from such obstruction, a special action on the case may be brought. Must I then sue out a new writ stating that the defendant employed direct force to prevent my going where my business called me, whereby I sustained loss? And, if I do, is it certain that I shall not be told that I have misconceived my remedy, for all flows from the false imprisonment, and that should have been the subject of an action of trespass and assault? For the jury properly found that the whole of the defendant's conduct was continuous: it commenced in illegality; and the plaintiff did right to resist it as an outrageous violation of the liberty of the subject from the very first.

Notes:

1. This is the first decision we have had under the old system of pleading, and it is very illustrative.

First, the plaintiff was not, as might be thought on a cursory reading, complaining of being held up on Hammersmith Bridge for half an hour. He was complaining of having had to spend a night in jail after being arrested by the defendant for breach of the peace.

Secondly, the decision turned entirely on the pleadings. The question was not whether the plaintiff was entitled to recover on the facts—he was, indeed—but whether the replication framed for him by his counsel was appropriate in view of the facts.

2. As to the substance, students will recall the tort of public nuisance, and the rule that a person cannot sue unless he has suffered some particular damage as a result of the illegal obstruction (above, p.200). The plaintiff here had not. If this obstruction had been held to constitute an imprisonment, that rule would have been wholly subverted, because in an action of false imprisonment no damage has to be proved.

3. A person is entitled to abate a thing which is a nuisance. That is why the plaintiff did no wrong in climbing over the fence. That is why he might have retained his verdict in assault against the defendant. But the defendant had stopped assaulting him by the time the plaintiff tried to force his way past; at that stage the defendant had stopped being an assailant and was merely a nuisance. People often are a nuisance, but you cannot hit them even so, though you may hit your gaoler. To put it differently, you may use force against people in order to get *out* but not in order to get *past*. On this point Patteson J. was surely in error when he said "if what so passed was not in law an imprisonment, then the plaintiff ought to have replied the right of footway and the obstruction by the defendant, and that he necessarily assaulted him in the exercise of the right."

4. We may take it that Bird won the argument on assault but lost on false imprisonment. Today he would not be entitled to proceed to trial by jury, which is available for the latter but not the former tort. The lawyers for a woman who had been raped were therefore clever to claim that the rape amounted to imprisonment, to obtain a jury trial and achieve an award of £50,000. Was this good law? Were the damages punitive? Juries have also been obtained by persons suing for being strip-searched while visiting inmates at Franklands Prison ([1992] New L.J. 337), and by Araceli Buenavista, who emphasised the restriction on her liberty of movement when suing on facts quite like those of *Godwin v Uzoigwe* [1992] Times L.R. 300. In *Godwin* the defendant couple with five children had brought the plaintiff as a sixteen year old from Nigeria, exploited her

as a household drudge for two and a half years and kept her virtually confined to the house without money, proper clothes or social intercourse of any kind: the Court of Appeal reduced the damages from £25,000 to £20,000.

MURRAY v MINISTRY OF DEFENCE

House of Lords [1988] 1 W.L.R. 692; [1988] 2 All E.R. 521 (noted [1988] Camb.L.J. 332)

The case concerned the lawfulness of the manner in which military personnel arrested the plaintiff in Ulster, where special rules and practices obtain. The precise facts are irrelevant to the purpose for which the following extract is cited.

Lord Griffiths: . . . Although on the facts of this case I am sure that the plaintiff was aware of the restraint on her liberty from 7.00 a.m., I cannot agree with the Court of Appeal that it is an essential element of the tort of false imprisonment that the victim should be aware of the fact of denial of liberty. The Court of Appeal relied on *Herring v Boyle* ((1834) 149 E.R. 1126) for this proposition which they preferred to the view of Atkin L.J. to the opposite effect in *Meering v Grahame-White Aviation Co Ltd* ((1919) 122 L.T. 44). *Herring v Boyle* is an extraordinary decision of the Court of Exchequer: a mother went to fetch her 10-year-old son from school on December 24, 1833 to take him home for the Christmas holidays. The headmaster refused to allow her to take her son home because she had not paid the last term's fees, and he kept the boy at school over the holidays. An action for false imprisonment brought on behalf of the boy failed. In giving judgment Bolland B. said:

> " . . . as far as we know, the boy may have been willing to stay; he does not appear to have been cognizant of any restraint, and there was no evidence of any act whatsoever done by the defendant in his presence. I think that we cannot construe the refusal to the mother in the boy's absence, and without his being cognizant of any restraint, to be an imprisonment of him against his will . . . "

I suppose it is possible that there are schoolboys who prefer to stay at school rather than go home for the holidays but it is not an inference that I would draw, and I cannot believe that on the same facts the case would be similarly decided today. In *Meering v Grahame-White Aviation Co Ltd* the plaintiff's employers, who suspected him of theft, sent two of the works police to bring him in for questioning at the company's offices. He was taken to a waiting-room where he said that if he was not told why he was there he would leave. He was told he was wanted for the purpose of making inquiries about things that had been stolen and he was wanted to give evidence; he then agreed to stay. Unknown to the plaintiff, the works police had been instructed not to let him leave the waiting-room until the Metropolitan Police arrived. The works police therefore remained outside the waiting-room and would not have allowed the plaintiff to leave until he was handed over to the Metropolitan Police, who subsequently arrested him. The question for the Court of Appeal was whether on this evidence the plaintiff was falsely imprisoned during the hour he was in the waiting-room, or whether there could be no "imprisonment" sufficient to found a civil action unless the plaintiff was aware of the restraint on his liberty. Atkin L.J. said:

> "It appears to me that a person could be imprisoned without his knowing it. I think a person can be imprisoned while he is asleep, while he is in a state of drunkenness, while he is unconscious, and while he is a lunatic. Those are cases where it seems to me that the person might properly complain if he were imprisoned, though the imprisonment began and ceased while he was in that state. Of course, the damages might be diminished and would be affected by the question whether he was conscious of it or not. . . . It is quite unnecessary

to go on to show that in fact the man knew that he was imprisoned. If a man can be imprisoned by having the key turned upon him without his knowledge, so he can be imprisoned if, instead of a lock and key or bolts and bars, he is prevented from, in fact, exercising his liberty by guards and warders or policemen. They serve the same purpose. Therefore it appears to me to be a question of fact. It is true that in all cases of imprisonment so far as the law of civil liberty is concerned that 'stone walls do not a prison make,' in the sense that they are not the only form of imprisonment, but any restraint within defined bounds which is a restraint in fact may be an imprisonment."

I agree with this passage. In the first place it is not difficult to envisage cases in which harm may result from unlawful imprisonment even though the victim is unaware of it. Dean William L. Prosser gave two examples in "False Imprisonment: Consciousness of Confinement" (1955) 55 Col.L.Rev. 847, in which he attacked § 42 of the American Law Institute's Restatement of the Law of Torts, which at that time stated the rule that "there is no liability for intentionally confining another unless the person physically restrained knows of the confinement."

The Restatement of the Law of Torts has now been changed and requires that the person confined "is conscious of the confinement or is harmed by it" (see Restatement of the Law, Second, Torts 2d (1965) § 35, p.52).

If a person is unaware that he has been falsely imprisoned and has suffered no harm, he can normally expect to recover no more than nominal damages, and it is tempting to redefine the tort in the terms of the present rule in the American Law Institute's Restatement of the Law of Torts. On reflection, however, I would not do so. The law attaches supreme importance to the liberty of the individual and if he suffers a wrongful interference with that liberty it should remain actionable even without proof of special damage. . . .

Questions

1. X strikes Y a severe blow which renders Y unconscious for five minutes. Is X guilty of false imprisonment as well as battery?

2. Given that harm due to very improper conduct may be compensable even if the conduct is not strictly speaking trespassory (above, p.334), are courts and writers sufficiently distinguishing the question what conduct should be actionable from the question what conduct should be physically resistible? Does the latter question arise in the case of a person oblivious of his confinement?

3. In *Roberts v Chief Constable* [1999] 2 All E.R. 326 the plaintiff, lawfully arrested, was detained in a cell for over two hours beyond the point when his detention should have been reviewed. He obtained damages, Clarke L.J. saying (at 333) "A sum of £500 is substantially more than I would have awarded to compensate the respondent for false imprisonment for a period of 2 hours 20 minutes during which he was asleep, especially in circumstances in which if a review had been carried out at 5.25 a.m., his detention would have been lawful." How much would you have awarded as *compensatory* damages?

ROBINSON v BALMAIN NEW FERRY CO LTD

Privy Council [1910] A.C. 295; 79 L.J.P.C. 84; 26 T.L.R. 143

The plaintiff, a lawyer, obtained a verdict for £100 from a jury before Darley C.J. The defendant sought to have the verdict set aside. The High Court of Australia, reversing the Supreme Court of New South Wales, did set it aside, and the plaintiff's appeal to the Judicial Committee of the Privy Council was unsuccessful.

Lord Loreburn L.C.: . . . The plaintiff paid a penny on entering the wharf to stay there till the boat should start and then be taken by the boat to the other side. The defendants were admittedly always ready and willing to carry out their part of this contract. Then the plaintiff changed his mind and wished to go back. The rules as to the exit from the wharf by the turnstile required a penny for any person who went through. This the plaintiff refused to pay, and he was by force prevented from going through the turnstile. He then claimed damages for assault and false imprisonment.

There was no complaint, at all events there was no question left to the jury by the plaintiff's request, of any excessive violence, and in the circumstances admitted it is clear to their Lordships that there was no false imprisonment at all. The plaintiff was merely called upon to leave the wharf in the way in which he contracted to leave it. There is no law requiring the defendants to make the exit from their premises gratuitous to people who come there upon a definite contract which involves their leaving the wharf by another way; and the defendants were entitled to resist a forcible passage through their turnstile.

The question whether the notice which was affixed to these premises was brought home to the knowledge of the plaintiff is immaterial, because the notice itself is immaterial.

When the plaintiff entered the defendants' premises there was nothing agreed as to the terms on which he might go back, because neither party contemplated his going back. When he desired to do so the defendants were entitled to impose a reasonable condition before allowing him to pass through their turnstile from a place to which he had gone of his own free will. The payment of a penny was a quite fair condition, and if he did not choose to comply with it the defendants were not bound to let him through. He could proceed on the journey he had contracted for.

Under these circumstances their Lordships consider that, when the defendants at the end of the case submitted that there ought to be a nonsuit, the learned judge ought to have nonsuited the plaintiff. Their Lordships are glad that they can thus arrive, in accordance with law, at this decision, because they regard the plaintiff's conduct as thoroughly unreasonable in this case.

Questions

1. Was the plaintiff's complaint (a) "He shut me in," or (b) "He wouldn't let me out"?

2. Suppose that the plaintiff had no penny at all. Would he have to stay there for ever without being able to bring an action for false imprisonment? Would it matter whether he knew a penny to be exigible on exit?

3. Suppose that the plaintiff had a sixpence, and the defendants declined to change it for him, though they could?

4. The owner of a mansion looks out of his window and sees his two Dobermann Pinscher dogs growling at the bottom of an apple tree, which contains an infant trespasser. He does not call off the dogs, and the child remains there all night. Is there any liability for false imprisonment? Is there any liability at all?

5. Does this decision justify an occupier of land in clamping a vehicle parked under a notice saying that parking is prohibited, that parked cars will be clamped and that such cars will be released on payment of a sum of money? See below p.405.

6. Persons remanded in custody after being charged with crimes are entitled after a certain period of time to be released on bail, possibly subject to conditions. It is the duty of the Crown Prosecution Service to bring the accused before the Crown Court shortly before the custody time limit arrives. In *Olutu v Home Office* [1997] 1 All E.R. 385 the CPS failed to do so, with the result that the accused was in custody for 81 days beyond the limit. "Once the custody time limit had expired, the plaintiff was . . . unlawfully detained . . . " (*per* Lord Bingham C.J. at 391), but it was held that the prison governor was not liable since he was holding the plaintiff under a court order and was not entitled to release her until a further court order was made, and that the CPS was not liable because the Regulations imposing the duty on them were not intended to create any civil cause of action. Is this somewhat surprising result consistent with Art.5 of the European Convention on Human Rights (above, p.97)?

DAVIDSON v CHIEF CONSTABLE OF NORTH WALES

Court of Appeal [1994] 2 All E.R. 597 (noted [1994] Camb.L.J. 433)

The plaintiff and her friend were looking at cassettes in a shop. They selected one, and her friend took it to the cash desk and paid for it. He returned to the cassette counter and chatted with her for a while. The store detective, Mrs Yates, then started to observe them, and when they left the shop with the cassette, she concluded that it had not been paid for. They went to a cafe opposite and Mrs Yates phoned for the police. She told them of her suspicions, and they arrested the plaintiff and her friend for shoplifting.

The plaintiff sued the police and Mrs Yates for false imprisonment, but the judge withdrew the case from the jury when the police testified that in making the arrest they had exercised their own judgment about what Mrs Yates had told them.

The plaintiff's appeal was dismissed in unreserved judgments by the Court of Appeal.

Sir Thomas Bingham M.R.: ... the question which arose for the decision of the learned judge in this case whether there was information properly to be considered by the jury as to whether what Mrs Yates did went beyond laying information before police officers for them to take such action as they thought fit and amounted to some direction, or procuring, or direct request, or direct encouragement that they should act by way of arresting these defendants. He decided that there was no evidence which went beyond the giving of information. Certainly there was no discussion of any kind as to what action the police officers should take.

The crux of Mr Clover's submission is that this case is different from the case in which an ordinary member of the public gives information to a police officer because this is a store detective, somebody better informed than an ordinary member of the public as to what was likely to happen upon making a complaint, and somebody with a very clear intention and expectation as to what would happen. No doubt the store detective did have an intention and expectation as to what would happen. The fact remains that the learned judge to my mind quite correctly held that what Mrs Yates did and said in no way went beyond the mere giving of information, leaving it to the officers to exercise a discretion which on their unchallenged evidence they did as to whether they should take any action or not.

In those circumstances the learned judge was, I think, entirely correct to withdraw the matter from the jury since it seems to me inevitable that had he left it to the jury, and had the jury found for the plaintiff, that verdict would have been open to challenge in this court which would have led to its being overruled. I, therefore, dismiss this appeal.

Staughton L.J.: Section 24(6) of the Police and Criminal Evidence Act 1984 provides that where a constable has reasonable grounds for suspecting that an arrestable offence has been committed he may arrest without a warrant anyone whom he has reasonable grounds for suspecting to be guilty of the offence. That applied to PC Walker, who was the person who physically arrested Miss Davidson and Mr Halford. On that ground proceedings against the police were abandoned. That subsection could not apply to Mrs Yates, the store detective, because she was not a constable. In other circumstances she might have had the power of arrest under s.24(4), which enables any person to arrest without a warrant anyone whom he has reasonable grounds for suspecting to be committing such an offence. At the time of the arrest the offence, if there had been one, was no longer being committed.

Section 24(5) might have applied to Mrs Yates. That provides that when an arrestable offence has been committed a person may arrest without a warrant anyone whom he has reasonable grounds to suspect is guilty of it. But there had been no offence committed in this case. So Mrs Yates had no power of arrest by the time that these two persons were in the cafe.

Was there any evidence to go to the jury that she did arrest Miss Davidson and Mr Halford? It was not she who physically detained them. That was PC Walker. She was not even there; but she had given information to the police officers and had pointed out Miss Davidson and Mr Halford to them.

In those circumstances, like Sir Thomas Bingham M.R., I would refer to the passage in the judgment of Barry J. in *Pike v Waldrum and Peninsular & Oriental Steam Navigation Company* [1952] 1 Lloyd's Rep. 431 at 454:

"The authorities cited to me, to which I need not refer in detail, establish quite clearly to my mind that the person who requests a police officer to take some other person into custody may be liable to an action for false imprisonment; not so if he merely gives information upon which the constable decides to make an arrest."

Whether a request by itself is sufficient to make a person liable does not arise in this case. What is clear in the passage I have read is that merely giving information is not enough. That does not give rise to false imprisonment. Mrs Yates did no more than that. However much one may look at evidence and analyse what possible consequences might or would arise from the information which she gave, the fact is that all she did was give the information.

I too would dismiss this appeal.

Question:
Did Jones arrest Bird?

HARNETT v BOND

House of Lords [1925] A.C. 669; 94 L.J.K.B. 569; 133 L.T. 482; 89 J.P. 182; 41 T.L.R. 509; [1925] All E.R.Rep. 110

The plaintiff was an inmate of Malling Place, a licensed house for lunatics run by Dr Adam, the second defendant. He was granted a month's leave, but Dr Adam had the power to reconfine him during that period. On the second day the plaintiff went to the offices of the Commissioners of Lunacy and saw one of the Commissioners, Bond, the first defendant. Bond came to the conclusion that the plaintiff was not fit to be at large, so he telephoned Dr Adam to send a car and detained the plaintiff until it arrived three hours later. Back at Malling Place Dr Adam examined the plaintiff and decided that he was insane. The plaintiff was confined in various institutions for the next nine years, but then he escaped and was found to be quite sane.

The jury found that the plaintiff had not been of unsound mind at the time the first defendant had detained him in the Commissioners' offices with a view to his further detention at Malling Place. The judge instructed them that in fixing the damages to be paid by the first defendant they might take account of the subsequent period of confinement. The jury gave a verdict for the plaintiff for £5,000 against Bond alone and for £20,000 against both defendants.

The Court of Appeal directed judgment for Dr Adam on the ground that there was no evidence that he had failed to exercise reasonable care and that he would not be liable unless he had so failed; they also ordered a new trial against Bond, the Commissioner.

The plaintiff's appeal to the House of Lords was dismissed.

Viscount Cave L.C.: ... It is not disputed that, on the assumption that the findings of the jury as to the appellant's mental condition on December 14, 1912, were correct, Dr Bond had no right to cause the appellant to be detained at the office pending the arrival of Dr Adam's car, and is liable in damages for that illegal detention. But those damages must, on the authorities, be confined to such as were the direct consequence of the wrong committed; and to hold that the detention of the appellant at the offices for a few hours was the direct cause, not only of his being retaken and conveyed to Malling Place, but also of his being confined in that and other houses until October 1921 appears to me to be impossible. ... The retaking and confinement were the independent acts of Dr Adam, and each of them was a *novus actus interveniens* sufficient to break the chain of causation.

Note:
Likewise, liability for false arrest (but not, of course, for malicious prosecution) ends, when the magistrate, before whom the prisoner must be promptly brought, remands him in custody.

Section 3.—Assault

READ v COKER

Common Pleas (1853) 13 C.B. 850; 22 L.J.C.P. 201; 21 L.T.(o.s.) 156; 17 Jur. 990; 1 W.R. 413; 138 E.R. 1437

The plaintiff was a paper-stainer in financial difficulties and in arrears with his rent. The defendant purchased his equipment and paid the rent under an agreement which secured to the plaintiff a weekly allowance. One day the defendant told the plaintiff to leave the premises, and when the plaintiff refused, the defendant collected together some of his workmen who mustered round the plaintiff, tucking up their sleeves and aprons, and threatened to break the plaintiff's neck if he did not leave. The plaintiff did leave, and now brought an action of trespass for assault.

At the trial Talfourd J. left it to the jury to say whether there was an intention on the part of the defendant to assault, and whether the plaintiff was apprehensive of personal violence if he did not retire. The jury found for the plaintiff, damages one farthing. The defendant asked for a new trial on the grounds of misdirection by the judge.

Byles Serjt. (*arguendo*) That which was proved as to the first count, clearly did not amount to an assault. [JERVIS C.J.: It was as much an assault as a sheriff's officer being in a room with a man against whom he has a writ, and saying to him "You are my prisoner," is an arrest.] To constitute an assault, there must be something more than a threat of violence. An assault is thus defined in Buller's *Nisi Prius*, p.15: "An assault is an attempt or offer, by force or violence, to do a corporal hurt to another, as, by pointing a pitchfork at him, when standing within reach; presenting a gun at him [within shooting distance]; drawing a sword, and waving it in a menacing manner, &c., *The Queen v Ingram* (1712) 1 Salk. 384; 91 E.R. 335. But no words can amount to an assault, though perhaps they may in some cases serve to explain a doubtful action,—1 Hawk.P.C. 133; as, if a man were to lay his hand upon his sword, and say, 'If it were not assize time, he would not take such language': the words would prevent the action from being construed to be an assault, because they show he had no intent to do him any corporal hurt at that time: *Tuberville v Savage* (1669) 1 Mod. 3; 86 E.R. 684." So, in Selwyn's *Nisi Prius*, (11th ed.), 26, it is said: "An assault is an attempt, with force or violence, to do a corporal injury to another, as, by holding up a fist in a menacing manner; striking at another with a cane or stick, though the party striking may miss his aim; drawing a sword or bayonet; throwing a bottle or glass with intent to wound or strike; presenting a gun at a person who is within the distance to which the gun will carry; pointing a pitchfork at a person who is within reach,—*Genner v Sparks* (1705) 6 Mod. 173; 1 Salk. 79; 87 E.R. 928—or by any other similar act, accompanied with such circumstances as denote at the time an intention coupled with a present ability,—see *Stephens v Myers* (1830) 4 C. & P. 349; 172 E.R. 735—of using actual violence, against the person of another." So, in 3 Bl.Comm. 120, an assault is said to be "an attempt or offer to beat another, without touching him; as, if one lifts up his cane or his fist, in a threatening manner, at another; or strikes at him but misses him; this is an assault, *insultus*, which Finch (L. 202) describes to be 'an unlawful setting upon one's person.'" [JERVIS C.J.: If a man comes into a room, and lays his cane on the table, and says to another, "If you don't go out, I will knock you on the head," would not that be an assault?] Clearly not: it is a mere threat, unaccompanied by any gesture or action towards carrying it into effect. The direction of the learned judge as to this point was erroneous. He should have told the jury that, to constitute an assault, there must be an attempt, coupled with a present ability to do personal violence to the party; instead of leaving it to them, as he did, to say what the plaintiff thought, and not what they (the jury) thought was the defendant's intention. There must be some act done denoting a present ability and an intention to assault.

Jervis C.J.: . . . If anything short of actual striking will in law constitute an assault, the facts here clearly showed that the defendant was guilty of an assault. There was a threat of violence exhibiting an intention to assault, and a present ability to carry the threat into execution. . . .

Rule discharged on first count.

BALL v AXTEN

Nisi Prius (1866) 4 F. & F. 1019; 176 E.R. 890

There was an altercation between a farmer and the defendant who was hunting without permission on his land. The defendant struck a blow at the farmer's dog, and hit his wife who was trying to protect it.

Lord Cockburn C.J.: . . . even though the defendant had not aimed the blow at the woman, there was no doubt an assault. . . .

Question:
   An assault, as the judge said, or a battery? Or just negligence? Does it matter?

Section 4.—Battery

GIBBONS v PEPPER

King's Bench (1695) 1 Ld.Raym. 38; 4 Mod. 404; 2 Salk. 637; 91 E.R. 922

Per curiam: . . . for if I ride upon a horse, and J.S. whips the horse, so that he runs away with me and runs over any other person, he who whipped the horse is guilty of the battery, and not me. But if I by spurring was the cause of such accident, then I am guilty. In the same manner, if A takes the hand of B and with it strikes C, A is the trespasser and not B.

FAGAN v METROPOLITAN POLICE COMMISSIONER

Queen's Bench Division [1969] 1 Q.B. 439; [1968] 3 W.L.R. 1120; [1968] 3 All E.R. 443; 52 Cr.App.R. 700 (noted (1969) 85 L.Q.R. 162)

Prosecution for assaulting police constable in the execution of his duty

As Fagan was parking his car at the direction of a police constable, the car came to rest on the constable's foot. Urged by the constable to back off, Fagan became abusive and switched off the engine before eventually complying.

   Fagan was convicted by the Willesden Magistrates of assaulting a police constable in the execution of his duty, and his appeal to Middlesex Quarter Sessions was dismissed, as was his present appeal to the Divisional Court, Bridge J. dissenting.

James J. (with whom **Lord Parker C.J.** agreed): . . . The justices . . . were left in doubt whether the mounting of the wheel on to the officer's foot was deliberate or accidental. They were satisfied, however, beyond all reasonable doubt that the appellant "knowingly, provocatively and unnecessarily" allowed the wheel to remain on the foot after the officer said "Get off, you are on my foot." They found that, on these facts, an assault was proved. . . .

In our judgment, the question arising, which has been argued on general principles, falls to be decided on the facts of the particular case. An assault is any act which intentionally—or possibly recklessly—causes another person to apprehend immediate and unlawful personal violence. Although "assault" is an independent crime and is to be treated as such, for practical purposes today "assault" is generally synonymous with the term "battery," and is a term used to mean the actual intended use of unlawful force to another person without his consent. On the facts of the present case, the "assault" alleged involved a "battery." Where an assault involved a battery, it matters not, in our judgment, whether the battery is inflicted directly by the body of the offender or through the medium of some weapon or instrument controlled by the action of the offender. An assault may be committed by the laying of a hand on another, and the action does not cease to be an assault if it is a stick held in the hand and not the hand itself which is laid on the person of the victim. So, for our part, we see no difference in principle between the action of stepping on to a person's toe and maintaining that position and the action of driving a car on to a person's foot and sitting in the car while its position on the foot is maintained.

To constitute this offence, some intentional act must have been performed; a *mere* omission to act cannot amount to an assault. Without going into the question whether words alone can constitute an assault, it is clear that the words spoken by the appellant could not alone amount to an assault; they can only shed a light on the appellant's action. For our part, we think that the crucial question is whether, in this case, the act of the appellant can be said to be complete and spent at the moment of time when the car wheel came to rest on the foot, or whether his act is to be regarded as a continuing act operating until the wheel was removed. In our judgment, a distinction is to be drawn between acts which are complete—though results may continue to flow—and those acts which are continuing. Once the act is complete, it cannot thereafter be said to be a threat to inflict unlawful force on the victim. If the act, as distinct from the results thereof, is a continuing act, there is a continuing threat to inflict unlawful force. If the assault involves a battery and that battery continues, there is a continuing act of assault. For an assault to be committed, both the elements of *actus reus* and *mens rea* must be present at the same time. The "*actus reus*" is the action causing the effect on the victim's mind. . . . The "*mens rea*" is the intention to cause that effect. It is not necessary that *mens rea* should be present at the inception of the *actus reus*; it can be superimposed on an existing act. On the other hand, the subsequent inception of *mens rea* cannot convert an act which has been completed without *mens rea* into an assault.

In our judgment, the justices at Willesden and quarter sessions were right in law. On the facts found, the action of the appellant may have been initially unintentional, but the time came when, knowing that the wheel was on the officer's foot, the appellant (i) remained seated in the car so that his body through the medium of the car was in contact with the officer, (ii) switched off the ignition of the car, (iii) maintained the wheel of the car on the foot, and (iv) used words indicating the intention of keeping the wheel in that position. For our part, we cannot regard such conduct as mere omission or inactivity. There was an act constituting a battery which at its inception was not criminal because there was no element of intention, but which became criminal from the moment the intention was formed to produce the apprehension which was flowing from the continuing act. The fallacy of the appellant's argument is that it seeks to equate the facts of this case with such a case as where a motorist has accidentally run over a person and, that action having been completed, fails to assist the victim with the intent that the victim should suffer.

We would dismiss this appeal.

Bridge J.: I fully agree with my Lords as to the relevant principles to be applied. No mere omission to act can amount to an assault. Both the elements of *actus reus* and *mens rea* must be present at the same time, but the one may be superimposed on the other. It is in the application of these principles to the highly unusual facts of this case that I have, with regret, reached a different conclusion from the majority of the court. I have no sympathy at all for the appellant, who behaved disgracefully; but I have been unable to find any way of regarding the facts which satisfied me that they amounted to the crime of assault. This has not been for want of trying; but at every attempt I have encountered the inescapable question: after the wheel of the appellant's car had accidentally come to rest on the constable's foot, what was it that the appellant *did* which constituted the act of assault? However the question is approached, the answer which I feel obliged to give is: precisely nothing. The car rested on the foot by its own weight and remained stationary by its own inertia. The appellant's fault was that he omitted to manipulate the controls to set it in motion again.

Neither the fact that the appellant remained in the driver's seat nor that he switched off the ignition seem to me to be of any relevance. The constable's plight would have been no better, but might well have been worse, if the appellant had alighted from the car leaving the ignition switched on. Similarly, I can get no help from the suggested analogies. If one man accidentally treads on another's toe or touches him with a stick, but deliberately maintains pressure with foot or stick after the victim protests, there is clearly an assault; but there is no true parallel between such cases and the present case. It is not, to my mind, a legitimate use of language to speak of the appellant "holding" or "maintaining" the car wheel on the constable's foot. The expression which corresponds to the reality is that used by the justices in the Case Stated. They say, quite rightly, that he "allowed" the wheel to remain.

With a reluctantly dissenting voice, I would allow this appeal and quash the appellant's conviction.

Question

In *Fagan* there was contact but no act. Sometimes there is act and harm but no contact. In *Kaye v Robertson* (above, p.333) Glidewell L.J. said "I am prepared to accept that it may well be the case that if a bright light is deliberately shone into another person's eyes and injures his sight, or damages him in some other way, this may be in law a battery." Whereas in *R. v Ireland* [1997] 4 All E.R. 225 at 236 Lord Steyn said " . . . it is not feasible to enlarge the generally accepted legal meaning of what is a battery to include the circumstances of a silent caller who causes psychiatric harm." If harm is caused in these ways, does it matter whether the conduct amounts to a battery or not?

WILSON v PRINGLE

Court of Appeal [1987] Q.B. 237; [1986] 2 All E.R. 440; [1986] 3 W.L.R. 1; 130 S.J. 468

Claim for personal injuries sustained in juvenile horseplay

The plaintiff and defendant, 13-year-old classmates, were walking down the school corridor after a maths class, the plaintiff being in front, when the defendant pulled at the sports bag which the plaintiff was carrying over his right shoulder. The plaintiff fell and suffered a nasty hip injury. The defendant pleaded that the incident was "ordinary horse-play between pupils in the same school and the same class."

The judge held that the defendant was so clearly liable for trespass on these averments that he gave the plaintiff leave to proceed to judgment without a trial, under Order 14. On the defendant's appeal, the Court of Appeal gave him leave to defend.

Croom-Johnson L.J. delivered the judgment of the Court. . . .

It is not possible, even if it were desirable, to ignore the distinction between torts of negligence and torts of trespass strictly so called. This distinction has to be borne in mind in view of a submission made on behalf of the defendant, which would have had the effect of blurring the lines of demarcation between the two causes of action. In a situation (such as the present) in which both causes of action are sought to be raised it is necessary to be as precise as possible in seeing which of the facts giving rise to that situation are appropriate to which cause of action. . . .

The defendant in the present case has sought to add to the list of necessary ingredients. He has submitted that before trespass to the person will lie it is not only the touching that must be deliberate but the infliction of injury. The plaintiff's counsel, on the other hand, contends that it is not the injury to the person which must be intentional, but the act of touching or battery which precedes it: as he put it, what must be intentional is the application of force and not the injury. In support of his contention, counsel for the defendant has relied on passages in the judgments in *Fowler v Lanning* [1959] 1 Q.B. 426 and *Letang v Cooper* [above, p.329].

[His Lordship discussed those cases.]

In our view, the submission made by counsel for the plaintiff is correct. It is the act and not the injury which must be intentional. An intention to injure is not essential to an action for trespass to the person. It is the mere trespass by itself which is the offence.
. . .

Nevertheless, it still remains to indicate what is to be proved by a plaintiff who brings an action for battery. Robert Goff L.J.'s judgment [in *Collins v Wilcock* [1984] 3 All E.R. 374] is illustrative of the considerations which underlie such an action, but it is not practicable to define a battery as "physical contact which is not generally acceptable in the ordinary conduct of daily life."

In our view, the authorities lead one to the conclusion that in a battery there must be an intentional touching or contact in one form or another of the plaintiff by the defendant. That touching must be proved to be a hostile touching. That still leaves unanswered the question, when is a touching to be called hostile? Hostility cannot be equated with ill-will or malevolence. It cannot be governed by the obvious intention shown in acts like punching, stabbing or shooting. It cannot be solely governed by an expressed intention, although that may be strong evidence. But the element of hostility, in the sense in which it is now to be considered, must be a question of fact for the tribunal of fact. It may be imported from the circumstances. Take the example of the police officer in *Collins v Wilcock*. She touched the woman deliberately, but without any intention to do more than restrain her temporarily. Nevertheless, she was acting unlawfully and in that way was acting with hostility. She was acting contrary to the woman's legal right not to be physically restrained. . . .

In our judgment the judge took too narrow a view of what has to be proved in order to make out a case of trespass to the person. It will be apparent that there are a number of questions which must be investigated in evidence.

Accordingly we would allow this appeal, and give unconditional leave to defend.

Questions

1. Was young Wilson claiming for injury to his person or for an invasion of his rights? Which was involved in *Collins v Wilcock* [1984] 3 All E.R. 374?

2. Do you think that Master Pringle's conduct was unreasonable? Do you think that Master Wilson's injury was foreseeable? Do you think that the answers to these questions should matter? Do you think they mattered to the Court of Appeal? Consider *Mullin* (above, p.138).

3. Alter the facts. As Master Pringle is poised to pounce, Master Wilson turns round and sees him; as Master Pringle is in the act of pouncing, Master Wilson punches him in the face, unexpectedly breaking his nose. Can Master Wilson justify his action as being in self-defence? If so, does that not prove that Master Pringle was guilty of trespassory assault?

4. Is an unwelcome kiss or other blandishment, actuated by love, properly to be described as "hostile"? Is it a trespass? Can its recipient repel it by force? Can its recipient sue for damages?

Note:

See the stately speech of Lord Goff in *F v West Berks. H.A.*, below, p.393, where he defends his view in *Collins v Wilcock* and expresses disagreement with the supposed requirement of "hostility" in *Wilson v Pringle*. Note that in *Wainwright v Home Office* (above, p.331) Lord Hoffmann spoke indifferently of the two views as to what constitutes an actionable battery.

NASH v SHEEN

Queen's Bench, *The Times*, March 13, 1953

The plaintiff went to the defendant's hairdressing establishment to obtain a "permanent wave" in her hair. The defendant applied a "tone rinse" which not only dyed the plaintiff's hair an unpleasing colour, but also provoked a painful rash all over her body. The plaintiff did not allege that the rash was a foreseeable consequence of the application of the dye.

Hilbery J.: His Lordship said that the first question to be considered was whether what was applied to the hair, which was called in the trade a "tone-rinse," was applied without the plaintiff's express consent and was a trespass. . . . It was quite clear that she went to the salon for a permanent wave, and he (his Lordship) did not believe that Mrs Nash consented to the application of the colouring matter . . . in his view that was a trespass. Even on the defendant's account it was plain that the plaintiff never gave consent to the application of any dye or colouring matter to her hair.

The plaintiff recovered £437 damages, including £50 for "her appearance being altered in a way which was distressing to her."

Questions
1. Is this decision still good law after (a) *Fowler v Lanning*, (b) *Wilson v Pringle*, (c) *Collins v Wilcock*?
2. Here there was a contract between the parties. Would it be an implied term of that contract (a) that nothing be applied to the plaintiff's head save what she asked for, or (b) that the defendant should take reasonable care not to apply detrimental substances to her head, or (c) both?
3. Would it have been a trespass if the hairdresser had applied the permanent wave substance in a concentrated form?
4. Did the plaintiff not consent, though mistakenly, to the application of the substance in the hairdresser's hand?
5. Would it have been a trespass if the hairdresser had reasonably thought that the substance being applied was a permanent wave solution?
6. If I go to a hospital for a vaccination and am injected with a contraceptive drug or *vice versa*, need I prove fault on the part of the hospital if I get (a) pregnant, (b) smallpox, (c) neither?

Section 5.—Trespass to Land

(i) Title to Sue

HARPER v CHARLESWORTH

King's Bench (1825) 4 B. & C. 574; 3 L.J.(o.s.) K.B. 572; 107 E.R. 1174

The defendant claimed to be exercising a public right of footway across land in Staffordshire which belonged to the Crown. The plaintiff paid the Crown 20s. per year in respect of the land, and hunted over it during the appropriate months; he also allowed others to pasture on the land.

At the trial before Garrow B., the jury found a verdict for the plaintiff. The defendant obtained a rule nisi for judgment notwithstanding the verdict, on the ground that the plaintiff was not rightfully in possession of the land in question, inasmuch as since he had no claim against the

Crown, he was a mere intruder on Crown land, and could not maintain trespass. The rule was discharged.

Bayley J.: I think that . . . the Crown might at any time, without notice, have removed him from that possession and occupation. Then it becomes a question, whether a person having the actual possession of Crown land can maintain trespass against a mere wrongdoer? Generally speaking, actual possession is sufficient to entitle a party to maintain trespass against a wrongdoer. . . . Apply that doctrine to this case: the plaintiff had no title to enable him to maintain an ejectment, because he had not a legal conveyance from the Crown; but still . . . he would be entitled, by reason of his actual possession, to maintain trespass against a wrongdoer. . . .

DELANEY v TP SMITH LTD

Court of Appeal [1946] K.B. 393; 115 L.J.K.B. 406; 175 L.T. 187; 62 T.L.R. 398; 90 S.J. 296;
[1946] 2 All E.R. 23

The defendant owned a dwelling-house which was bombed. It was agreed orally that the plaintiff should enter as tenant when the repairs were completed, which was expected to be in December 1944. In that month, the plaintiff entered clandestinely. One week later the defendant forcibly ejected him and his belongings. In the county court the defendant pleaded that the oral tenancy could not be relied on by the plaintiff, by reason of section 40 of the Law of Property Act 1925, which requires contracts for an interest in land to be evidenced by a memorandum in writing. The county court judge held that the defendant's justification for the trespass was defeated by proof of the agreement, despite its informality. The defendant appealed, and his appeal was allowed.

Tucker L.J.: . . . It is no doubt true that a plaintiff in an action of trespass to land need only in the first instance allege possession. This is sufficient to support his action against a wrongdoer, but it is not sufficient as against the lawful owner, and in an action against the freeholder the plaintiff must at some stage of the pleadings set up a title derived from the defendant. . . . I think the plaintiff was at some stage bound to rely on the oral agreement of tenancy. . . .

WHITE v BAYLEY

Common Pleas (1861) 10 C.B.(N.S.) 227; 142 E.R. 438

The plaintiff was employed by the trustees of the Swedenborg Society under a contract by which he was to be paid £75 per year for managing and living in premises rented by the trustees in Bloomsbury Street; the agreement was terminable on six months' notice. The ground floor of the premises was used as a book-shop, the first floor as a library and reading-room for the Society, while the upper floors were a residence for the plaintiff and his family. Over the shop stood the words "Swedenborg Society", and on the door-posts "William White, Bookseller and Publisher." The trustees gave notice to quit forthwith, and they took possession of the premises for a time until the plaintiff forcibly re-entered. Then the trustees obtained an injunction in Chancery, compelling the plaintiff to give up possession. In his action of trespass the plaintiff was nonsuited, and his motion for a new trial refused.

Byles J.: The first count of the declaration complains of a trespass *quare clausum fregit*. That clearly does not lie unless the plaintiff has some estate in the land. . . . I agree with my Brother Willes in thinking that the plaintiff had the use but not the occupation of the premises: and I do not think he could have maintained trespass *quare clausum fregit* even against a stranger. But, assuming the effect of the agreement to have been to give him any estate at all, the utmost it could amount to would be a tenancy at will. . . .

Willes J.: . . . though generally speaking the relation of master and servant or principal and agent may, where the servant or agent has been guilty of misconduct, be terminated at a moment, if such an arrangement as this were held to vest in the servant or agent an interest in the employer's premises, the servant might set his employer at defiance, and, though the latter were perfectly justified in putting an end to the relation of master and servant between them, the former might insist upon holding on as a tenant until the expiration of a regular notice to quit. . . .

Questions
1. Do you think that Byles J. would have nonsuited the plaintiff if the plaintiff had been suing a burglar?
2. The police want to search the room of X, who is a lodger in Y's house. Do the police, if they have no warrant, require the permission of X as well as Y? If Y gives his permission, can X sue him for (a) trespass, (b) breach of contract?

Note:
Trespass to the *person* involves no question of title to sue; only the person imprisoned, battered or assaulted may claim. But when the alleged trespass is to a piece of *property*, the question who can sue in respect of it is very important.

Title to sue in trespass is based on possession. That sounds very simple; it sounds as if one merely had to look at the factual relation of the person and the thing, and ask whether the plaintiff was in control of the thing. One does have to look at that, for if he did not have control, the plaintiff cannot sue. This was confirmed in *Simpson v Fergus*, October 15, 1999, CA. The plaintiff's predecessor ran a guest-house backing on to a service road over which other residents had a right of way. He sought to colonise the grass verge, to which no one had a paper title, by marking out parking bays, putting up "Private" notices and chasing off non-guests who parked there. Having bought the guest-house, the plaintiff sought an injunction to prevent the residents parking there. The Court of Appeal vacated the injunction: possession had not been established, since intention to exclude was not enough, though fencing might well have been. Fencing was admittedly impractical here, but the standard required was not to be lowered just because it was difficult to meet.

But even if a person had adequate control, he cannot always sue, for the defendant may be entitled to have the possession from him, either because he owns it or because he is entitled to it under a contract with the plaintiff. Thus it comes about that we have the confusing observations that "possession is title as against a wrongdoer," and that the defendant's plea of "not possessed" means "not possessed as against the defendant." Conversely, a plaintiff who has never actually taken possession of land may be held to have sufficient control to bring suit. In *Portland Managements v Harte* [1977] Q.B. 306 at 316, Scarman L.J. took it to be clear law that " . . . when an owner of land is making a case of trespass against a person alleged to be in possession, all that the owner has to prove is his title and an intention to regain possession. If the defendant to the action either admits his ownership or is faced with evidence, which the court accepts, that the plaintiff is in fact the owner, then the burden is on the defendant to confess and avoid; that is to say, to set up a title or right to possession consistent with the fact of ownership vested in the plaintiff." Not long afterwards the same judge said "Trespass is of course a wrong not to ownership, but to possession." *Hesperides Hotel v Aegean Turkish Holidays* [1978] Q.B. 205 at 231.

When four students occupied a large flat in Hornsey Lane, N.6 and were held to be licensees and not tenants, Lord Bridge said: "Each occupant had a contractual right, enforceable against the appellants, to prevent the number of persons permitted to occupy the flat at any one time exceeding four. But this did not give them exclusive possession of the kind which is distinctive of a leasehold interest. Having no estate in land, they could not sue in trespass. Their remedy against intruders would have been to persuade the appellants to sue as plaintiffs or to join the appellants as defendants by way of enforcement of their contractual rights." *AG Securities v Vaughan* [1988] 3 All E.R. 1058 at 1061.

Certain difficulties follow from deciding too much on the question of title to sue. So accustomed were the judges of the nineteenth century to saying that a servant never had possession (lest it be used against the master) that there was some doubt whether the chambermaid could sue a burglar who entered her bedroom. Now perhaps it does not matter, since such an entry is probably a wilful act calculated to cause physical harm such that, if physical harm ensues, the chambermaid can sue the burglar in negligence.

DUTTON v MANCHESTER AIRPORT

Court of Appeal [2002] Q.B. 133, [1999] 3 W.L.R. 524, [1999] 2 All E.R. 675

Action for possession by gratuitous licensee against trespassers in possession

Arthur's Wood is a National Trust property near Manchester Airport. In order to create a second runway the operators of the Airport needed to lop and fell some trees in the wood, which the defendants had occupied so as to prevent this. Shortly thereafter the Airport obtained from the National Trust a gratuitous licence to enter the wood for the limited purpose in question. The airport thereupon sought an order for possession. It was granted by Steel J., and the defendants appealed. Their appeal was dismissed, Chadwick L.J. dissenting most cogently.

Laws L.J.: In my judgment the true principle is that a licensee not in occupation may claim possession against a trespasser if that is a necessary remedy to vindicate and give effect to such rights of occupation as by contract with his licensor he enjoys. This is the same principle as allows a licensee who is in *de facto* possession to evict a trespasser. There is no respectable distinction, in law or logic, between the two situations. An estate owner may seek an order whether he is in possession or not. So, in my judgment, may a licensee, if other things are equal. In both cases, the plaintiff's remedy is strictly limited to what is required to make good his legal right. The principle applies although the licensee has no right to exclude the licensor himself. Elementarily he cannot exclude any occupier who, by contract or estate, has a claim to possession equal or superior to his own. Obviously, however, that will not avail a bare trespasser.

In this whole debate, as regards the law of remedies in the end I see no significance as a matter of principle in any distinction drawn between a plaintiff whose right to occupy the land in question arises from title and one whose right arises only from contract. In every case the question must be, what is the reach of the right, and whether it is shown that the defendant's acts violate its enjoyment. If they do, and (as here) an order for possession is the only practical remedy, the remedy should be granted. Otherwise the law is powerless to correct a proved or admitted wrongdoing; and that would be unjust and disreputable. The underlying principle is in the Latin maxim (for which I make no apology) *"ubi ius, ibi sit remedium"*.

Chadwick L.J. (dissenting): It is against that background that I consider the question whether the airport company has shown that it has a right to possession of the relevant part of Arthur's Wood which is of the quality necessary to support the order for possession made in these proceedings and the writ of possession issued consequent upon that order. It is essential to keep in mind that it is not contended by the airport company that it is, or ever has been, in actual possession of the wood (or of any part of it) to the exclusion of the appellants. It has been common ground that the appellants had entered the wood and encamped there before the licence of June 22, 1998 was granted. This is not a case in which the plaintiff can rely on its own prior possession to recover possession of land from which it has been ousted. The airport company must rely on the title (if any) which it derives under the licence.

It is plain, therefore, that the licence of June 22, 1998, whatever its terms, could not confer on the airport company a right to exclusive possession of the surface of Arthur's Wood. It could not do so because the National Trust had no power to grant such a right. The airport company do not contend otherwise. In those circumstances the question is whether some right enjoyed by the airport company under the licence of June 22, 1998 (being a right less than a right to exclusive possession) can be the basis for an order for possession—that is to say, for an order in rem—made under Ord. 113.

It has long been understood that a licensee who is not in exclusive occupation does not have title to bring an action for ejectment. The position of an action for ejectment—the forerunner of the present action for recovery of land—as well as an action for trespass can only be brought by a person who is in possession or who has a right to be in possession. Further, that possession is synonymous, in this context, with exclusive occupation—that is to say occupation (or a right to occupy) to the exclusion of all others, including the owner or other person with superior title (save in so far as he has reserved a right to enter).

In the present case the question is not whether the agreement of June 22, 1998 creates a tenancy or a licence. It does not create a tenancy, for it is a gratuitous agreement under which no rent is payable. Nor, in the present case, is the question whether the airport company, as occupier under a licence, has exclusive possession or a right to exclusive possession. That question is determined by the inability of the National Trust, in the exercise of its statutory powers, to grant a right to exclusive possession. The question is whether a person who has a right to occupy under a licence but who does not have any right to exclusive possession can maintain an action to recover possession.

The lessee, having a right to exclusive possession, could, before entry into possession, maintain an action for ejectment. A licensee, if he did not have a right to exclusive possession, could not bring ejectment. A tenant or a licensee who was in actual possession—that is to say in occupation in circumstances in which he had exclusive possession in fact—could maintain an action for trespass against intruders; but that is because he relied on the fact of his possession and not on his title.

The licence in the present case, as it seems to me, is a clear example of a personal permission to enter the land and use it for some stipulated purpose. In my view, it would be contrary to what Windeyer J. described as "long-established law" to hold that it conferred on the airport authority rights to bring an action in rem for possession of the land to which it relates.

There was no material, in the present case, on which the judge could reach the conclusion that the airport company was in de facto possession of the relevant part of Arthur's Wood; and, for my part, I do not think that she did reach that conclusion. She treated the question as one which turned on the construction of the licence. In my view the judge was in error when she held, in the passage to which I have already referred, that:

"The licence gives the right of possession and this is, I am satisfied, a right of possession which does not give absolute title, but it does nevertheless give a power against trespassers."

She did not make the distinction, essential in cases of this nature, between a plaintiff who is in possession and who seeks protection from those who seek to interfere with that possession; and a plaintiff who has not gone into possession but who seeks to evict those who are already on the land. In the latter case (which is this case) the plaintiff must succeed by the strength of his title; not on the weakness (or lack) of any title in the defendant.

I would have allowed this appeal.

Kennedy L.J. agreed with **Laws L.J.**, basing his decision exclusively on RSC Ord. 113 (which had been authoritatively stated to have no substantive effect).

Notes:

1. The courts seem almost as cavalier with the law as Swampy and his friends, whose obstructive tactics they are determined to frustrate. Consider, in addition to the present case, *R. v Chief Constable, Ex p Central Electricity Generating Board* (below, p.389) and *Minister of Transport v Williams* (below, p.622), the former of which (like the present case) is simply wrong (and has been said to be so) while the latter is as objectionable as the dissent indicates. *Percy v Hall* [1996] 4 All E.R. 523 is another disgraceful decision: it held lawful an arrest for breach of an unlawful byelaw protecting a GCHQ post—a byelaw which the Ministry continued to enforce after it had been held unlawful by a court—see *Secretary of State v Percy* [1999] 1 All E.R. 732.

2. *Dutton* was distinguished and implicitly disapproved in *Countryside Residential v Tugwell* [2000] 34 E.G. 87, a case on very similar facts, apart from a marginally different contract between the estate owner and the claimant.

3. A person who has a right to be on another's land is not suable in trespass, but he may become a trespasser if he exceeds the right whereby his presence is justified or uses it for a purpose other than that for

which it was granted. One might then speak of an abuse of right. If the right is a contractual one, it is a matter of the extent of the occupier's valid consent, but if the right is one which exists at law, as is the case with the public right to use the highway, the limits must be laid down by law. In the next following case we see once again the introduction of the test of "reasonableness" to supplant the more specific rules which existed in earlier times.

DIRECTOR OF PUBLIC PROSECUTIONS v JONES

House of Lords [1999] 2 A.C. 240; [1999] 2 W.L.R. 625; [1999] 2 All E.R. 257

Were the defendants trespassing by assembling peaceably on the verge of the highway near Stonehenge?

A group of more than twenty people, including the defendants, gathered peaceably on the grass verge of the A344 very close to Stonehenge, knowing that a prohibitory order had been issued under the Public Order Act 1986 which permits such orders as regards an assembly "held on land to which the public has only a limited right of access" which exceeds "the limits of the public's right of access". The defendants, who refused to move on when requested by a police officer, were arrested, charged and convicted with taking part in a trespassory assembly. The convictions were quashed by the Crown Court but reinstated by the Divisional Court. The defendants' appeal to the House of Lords was allowed, Lord Slynn and Lord Hope dissenting.

Lord Irvine of Lairg L.C.: My Lords, this appeal raises an issue of fundamental constitutional importance: what are the limits of the public's right of access to the public highway? Are these rights so restricted that they preclude in all circumstances any right of peaceful assembly on the public highway? . . .

I do not accept that, to be lawful, activities on the highway must fall within a rubric incidental or ancillary to the exercise of the right of passage. The meaning of Lord Esher M.R.'s judgment in *Harrison*'s case [1893] 1 Q.B. 142 at 146–147, is clear: it is not that a person may use the highway only for passage and repassage and acts incidental or ancillary thereto; it is that any "reasonable and usual" mode of using the highway is lawful, provided it is not inconsistent with the general public's right of passage. I understand Collins L.J.'s acceptance in *Hickman v Maisey* [1900] 1 Q.B. 752 at 757–758, of Lord Esher M.R.'s judgment in *Harrison*'s case in that sense.

Nor can I attribute any hard core of meaning to a test which would limit lawful use of the highway to what is incidental or ancillary to the right of passage. In truth very little activity could accurately be described as "ancillary" to passing along the highway; perhaps stopping to tie one's shoe lace, consulting a street-map, or pausing to catch one's breath. But I do not think that such ordinary and usual activities as making a sketch, taking a photograph, handing out leaflets, collecting money for charity, singing carols, playing in a Salvation Army band, children playing a game on the pavement, having a picnic, or reading a book, would qualify. These examples illustrate that to limit lawful use of the highway to that which is literally "incidental or ancillary" to the right of passage would be to place an unrealistic and unwarranted restriction on common-place day-to-day activities. The law should not make unlawful what is commonplace and well accepted.

Nor do I accept that the broader modern test which I favour materially realigns the interests of the general public and landowners. It is no more than an exposition of the test Lord Esher M.R. proposed in 1892. It would not permit unreasonable use of the highway, nor use which was obstructive. It would not, therefore, afford carte blanche to squatters or other uninvited visitors. Their activities would almost certainly be unreasonable or obstructive or both. Moreover the test of reasonableness would be strictly applied where narrow highways across private land are concerned, for example, narrow footpaths or bridle paths, where even a small gathering would be likely to create an obstruction or a nuisance.

Nor do I accept that the "reasonable user" test is tantamount to the assertion of a right to remain, which right can be acquired by express grant, but not by user or dedication. That recognition, however, is in no way inconsistent with the "reasonable user" test. If the right to use the highway extends to reasonable user not inconsistent with the public's right of passage, then the law does recognise (and has, at least since Lord Esher M.R.'s judgment in *Harrison*'s case, recognised) that the right to use the highway goes beyond the minimal right to pass and repass. That user may in fact extend, to a limited extent, to roaming about on the highway, or remaining on the highway. But that is not of the essence of the right. That is no more than the scope which the right might in certain circumstances have, but always depending on the facts of the particular case. On a narrow footpath, for example, the right to use the highway would be highly unlikely to extend to a right to remain, since that would almost inevitably be inconsistent with the public's primary right to pass and repass.

I conclude therefore the law to be that the public highway is a public place which the public may enjoy for any reasonable purpose, provided the activity in question does not amount to a public or private nuisance and does not obstruct the highway by unreasonably impeding the primary right of the public to pass and repass; within these qualification there is a public right of peaceful assembly on the highway.

Since the law confers this public right, I deprecate any attempt artificially to restrict its scope. It must be for the magistrates in every case to decide whether the user of the highway under consideration is both reasonable in the sense defined and not inconsistent with the primary right of the public to pass and repass. In particular, there can be no principled basis for limiting the scope of the right by reference to the subjective intentions of the persons assembling. Once the right to assemble within the limitations I have defined is accepted, it is self-evident that it cannot be excluded by an intention to exercise it. Provided an assembly is reasonable and non-obstructive, taking into account its size, duration and the nature of the highway on which it takes place, it is irrelevant whether it is premeditated or spontaneous; what matters is its objective nature. To draw a distinction on the basis of anterior intention is in substance to reintroduce an incidentality requirement. For the reasons I have given, that requirement, properly applied, would make unlawful commonplace activities which are well accepted. Equally, to stipulate in the abstract any maximum size or duration for a lawful assembly would be an unwarranted restriction on the right defined. These judgments are ever ones of fact and degree for the court of trial.

Lord Hutton: . . . I am of opinion that the holding of a public assembly on a highway can constitute a reasonable user of the highway and accordingly will not constitute a trespass and I would allow the appeal. But I desire to emphasise that my opinion that this appeal should be allowed is based on the finding of the Crown Court that the assembly in which the defendants took part on this particular highway, the A344, at this particular time, constituted a reasonable user of the highway. I would not hold that a peaceful and non-obstructive public assembly on a highway is always a reasonable user and is therefore not a trespass . . .

Lord Clyde: . . . The matter is essentially one to be judged in light of the particular facts of the case. But I am prepared to hold that a peaceful assembly which does not obstruct the highway does not necessarily constitute a trespassory assembly . . .

Lord Slynn (dissenting): . . . On existing authority, I consider that the law is clear. The right is restricted to passage and reasonable incidental uses associated with passage . . .

Lord Hope of Craighead (dissenting): The assembly which was said by the police to have formed on this occasion was undoubtedly a peaceful and non-obstructive one and, as it was on the grass verge of a road which was vested in the statutory highway authority, it may reasonably be said to have been doing no harm to anyone. But the consequences of accepting that anyone who was behaving in this way was exercising the public's right of access to the highway—was doing so as of right and not by mere tolerance—would have implications far beyond the facts of this case. It would affect the position of every private owner of land throughout the country over which there is a public right of way, irrespective of whether this is a made-up road or a footpath or bridleway. The right of assembly which Mr Fitzgerald was seeking to establish was what would be described in the terms of property law as a right to remain. I wish to stress that the purpose for which the defendants were seeking to remain where they had gathered is not material in this context. Any member of the public may use a highway for passage in the exercise of the public right whatever his reason may be for doing so. In the same way, if such a thing as a public right to assemble and remain in one place on the highway were to be recognised, the purpose of those who wished to exercise it would be immaterial. If it was an unlawful purpose it could be stopped on that ground. But if it was lawful there would be nothing to prevent those who wished to exercise it from remaining where they were for however long they wished, whatever their number and whatever their purpose might be in doing so.

It is not difficult to see that to admit a right in the public in whatever numbers to remain indefinitely in one place on a highway for the purpose of exercising the freedom of the right to assemble could give rise to substantial problems for landowners in their attempts to deal with the activities of demonstrators, squatters and other uninvited visitors. It would amount to a considerable extension of the rights of the public as against those of both public and private landowners which would be difficult for the courts to control by reference to any relevant principle. The margin between what is and what is not a nuisance is an imprecise one, as to which he who wishes to put a stop to it may be in difficulty in obtaining an immediate remedy. The test of reasonable use of the highway as such is consistent with the rule that the public's right of way is essentially a right of passage. It is also consistent with the law as to the kind of user which must be shown in order to show that a public right of way has been constituted over the land of the proprietor. The proposition that the public is entitled to do anything on the highway which amounts in itself to a reasonable user may seem at first sight to be an attractive one. But it seems to me to be tantamount to saying that members of the public are entitled to assemble, occupy and remain anywhere upon a highway in whatever numbers as long as they wish for any reasonable purpose, so long as they do not obstruct it. I do not think that there is any basis in the authorities for such a fundamental rearrangement of the respective rights of the public and of those of public and private landowners.

(ii) The Act

SMITH v STONE

King's Bench (1647) Sty. 65; 82 E.R. 533

Smith brought an action of trespasse against Stone pedibus ambulando, the defendant pleads this speciall plea in justification, *viz.* that he was carried upon the land of the plaintiff by force, and violence of others, and was not there voluntarily, which is the same trespasse, for which the plaintiff brings his action. The plaintiff demurs to this plea: in this case Roll Iustice said, that it is the trespasse of the party that carried the defendant upon the land, and not the trespasse of the defendant: as he that drives my cattel into another mans land is the trespassor against him, and not I who am owner of the cattell.

BASELY v CLARKSON

Common Pleas (1681) 3 Lev. 37; 83 E.R. 565

Difference *inter* trespass involuntary, and *per* mistake.

Trespass for breaking his closs called the *balk* and the *hade*, and cutting his grass, and carrying it away. The defendant disclaims any title in the lands of the plaintiff, but says that he hath a *balk* and *hade* adjoining to the balk and hade of the plaintiff, and in mowing his own land he involuntarily and by mistake mowed down some grass growing upon the balk and hade of the plaintiff, intending only to mow the grass upon his own *balk* and *hade*, and carried the *grass, &c. quae est eadem, &c. Et quod ante emanationem brevis* he tendered to the plaintiff 2s. in satisfaction, and that 2s. was a sufficient amends. Upon this the plaintiff demurred, and had judgment; for it appears the fact was voluntary, and his intention and knowledge are not traversable; they cannot be known.

Note:
    " . . . the fact was voluntary. . . . " Presumably, "fact" is a mistranslation of "fait" and means "act."
    A balk is a strip of ground left unploughed between two ploughed areas to serve as a boundary. A hade appears to be the same thing. "Where great Balkes betwixt Lands, Hades, Meares, or Divisions betwixt Land and Land are left," Blithe, *English Improvement*, 13 (1649).

PEACOCK v YOUNG

Queen's Bench (1869) 21 L.T. 527

During an election at Wisbech in which he was a candidate, the defendant allowed his enthusiastic and rather rowdy supporters to pull him along in his carriage, in which he was standing and waving his hat. He told them not to do any damage, but they smashed the windows of the plaintiff's furniture shop. The plaintiff obtained a verdict in the county court, but the defendant appealed and his appeal was allowed.

Cockburn C.J.: . . . The judge says that if he had stopped the procession and got out of his carriage, there might have been an end put to the whole proceedings of the mob. I may take it, therefore, as found, that Mr Young was guilty of an act of imprudence, and that is all that is found. But I cannot see, because a gentleman canvassing in the course of his electioneering is accompanied by a crowd of people, that they are therefore his agents, he doing nothing intentionally to encourage them. If he does some act which is no more than an imprudence, he cannot be held responsible for what the mob may do in consequence, in an action of trespass, which this is substantially.

Question
    Were the borstal boys in the *Dorset Yacht Co* case (above, p.84) the agents of the Home Office?

Note:
    In the 300,000 acres of Exmoor, the League Against Cruel Sports owned 23 "sanctuaries," unfenced areas averaging 52 acres each, or about 500 yards square. Some of the Devon and Somerset Staghounds (the dogs, not the members) used to enter the sanctuaries in pursuit of deer, without doing any damage to any of the plaintiff's property. The League sued the joint Masters of the Hounds for damages for several such trespasses and sought an injunction against further trespasses. Park J. issued an injunction in respect of one sanctuary, restraining (on pain of imprisonment) the defendants by themselves, their servants or agents, or mounted followers, from causing or permitting hounds to enter or cross the property. Damages totalling £180 for six trespasses were awarded. *League Against Cruel Sports v Scott* [1985] 2 All E.R. 489.
    The judge said "Where a master of staghounds takes out a pack of hounds and deliberately sets them in pursuit of a stag or hind knowing that there is a real risk that in the pursuit hounds may enter or cross prohibited land, the master will be liable for trespass if he intended to cause the hounds to enter such land or if by his failure to exercise proper control over them he causes them to enter such land." The Masters were held responsible for the mounted followers but not the followers on foot or in cars, because they had a power of control over the former and not over the latter.

Questions:
  1. Was it the hounds or the masters who were the trespassers?
  2. If trespass is an intentional tort (see Lord Denning above, p.329), why was the master's failure to control the followers relevant? And if the tort was negligence, why was the absence of damage not relevant?
  3. Should the court have discussed the question of the use to which the plaintiffs were putting their property? Was it really in order to protect their property that the plaintiffs brought suit?
  4. If advertising material is delivered to the house of a person who has stated that he does not wish to receive it is this a trespass if the delivery is (a) made manually, (b) by mail?

Further Note:
  Suppose that a local authority wants to clear gypsies off land which belongs to third parties. It cannot obtain an injunction against them as trespassers, because it is not their land, but it can obtain a court order under certain conditions if the activities of the gypsies constitute a statutory nuisance under what is now s.79, Environmental Protection Act 1990 (*Bradford City M.C. v Brown* (1986) 84 L.G.R. 731) and it has standing under s.222 of the Local Government Act 1972 to seek an injunction against the continued commission of a crime: the gypsies' activities might constitute a public nuisance, for example, or the alarming offence contained in s.40 of the Local Government (Misc.Prov.) Act 1982 which can apparently be committed by two glue-sniffers quietly sniffing glue in a deserted playground (*Sykes v Holmes* (1985) 84 L.G.R. 355).

(iii) The Invasion

ANCHOR BREWHOUSE DEVELOPMENTS v BERKLEY HOUSE (DOCKLANDS DEVELOPMENTS)

Chancery Division [1987] 2 E.G.L.R. 173; [1987] 38 Building Law Reports 82

Suit to prevent further oversailing by crane booms

Scott J.: I have before me an application by three plaintiffs for injunctions to restrain tower cranes erected and operated by the defendants from oversailing their respective properties.

The matter concerns a highly prestigious development site to the south of Tower Bridge in London. . . . For the purpose of developing its site the defendant, or one of its contractors, has been using and is using a number of tower cranes. A tower crane is static. When not in use the boom or jib of the crane must be left free to swing, like a weather vane, in the wind. Otherwise there is a danger that the crane may collapse in a high wind. So the boom must be left free-swinging.

Both when free-swinging and when in use the booms swing over the respective properties of the plaintiffs. This, the plaintiffs contend, is trespass. They say that they have given no permission for the booms to swing over their respective properties and that they want the trespasses stopped. They have called upon the defendant to desist, but without avail, and they therefore come to the court for injunctive relief.

The case for injunctive relief, save in one respect, is not based upon any actual or apprehended damage to the plaintiffs' respective proprietary interests. The plaintiffs seek injunctions simply on the footing that they are owners of their properties and that trespass has been committed and is threatened to be continued.

The defendant resists the plaintiffs' claim on two grounds. First, the defendant contends that there is no trespass at all. It is denied that an infringement of air space at the height at which the booms of the tower cranes pass over the plaintiffs' properties represents trespass. It is contended that, at most, the infringement of air space might represent nuisance. But damage is a necessary ingredient of the tort of nuisance and, in the absence of damage, there can be no nuisance. So, it is said, there is no tort being committed. Liability is denied.

If that is wrong and if oversailing booms do constitute trespass, the defendant contends, secondly, that it ought not to be subjected to injunctions restraining the use of the cranes in the manner I have described. The trespass, if that is what it is, does no actual damage to the plaintiffs. Use of static tower cranes is virtually essential for the commercial development of this important site. The defendant has found itself in danger of being injuncted through no fault of its own. The plaintiffs stood by and allowed the tower cranes to be erected and used. For all these reasons, it is submitted, the plaintiffs ought not to be granted injunctive relief but should be left to damages at common law.

The first question with which I must deal is whether the oversailing cranes are committing trespass or whether the invasion of air space by tower cranes sounds only in nuisance.

The question whether invasion of air space is as much trespass as invasion on or beneath the surface of land is a matter which has been the subject of judicial and academic examination for some time. The first comprehensive modern review of authority is to be found in the decision of McNair J. in *Kelsen v Imperial Tobacco Co* [1957] 2 Q.B. 334. That case concerned an advertising sign erected by the defendant which projected into the air space above the plaintiff's property. The plaintiff sought a mandatory injunction for the removal of the sign on the grounds that its presence above his property constituted trespass. The defendants alleged that if the presence of the sign constituted a tort at all it could be only nuisance. McNair J. held that there was a trespass.

Mr Moss, for the defendant, relies heavily on the judgment of Griffiths J. (as he then was) in *Bernstein v Skyviews & General Ltd* [1978] Q.B. 479. This was a case in which the defendant used an overflying aeroplane in order to obtain aerial photographs of Lord Bernstein's country residence. Lord Bernstein alleged that in so doing the defendant was trespassing in his air space and invading his right to privacy. He sued for damages. Griffiths J. was not prepared to hold that the invasion of air space by an overflying aircraft represented trespass. He referred to the previous authorities, in particular to *Kelsen v Imperial Tobacco Co* and said this:

> "I do not wish to cast any doubts upon the correctness of the decision upon its own particular facts. It may be a sound and practical rule to regard any incursion into the air space at a height which may interfere with the ordinary user of the land as a trespass rather than a nuisance. Adjoining owners then know where they stand; they have no right to erect structures overhanging or passing over their neighbours' land and there is no room for argument whether they are thereby causing damage or annoyance to their neighbours about which there may be much room for argument and uncertainty."

But wholly different considerations arise when considering the "passage of aircraft at a height which in no way affects the user of the land." Griffiths J. continued:

> "The problem is to balance the rights of an owner to enjoy the use of his land against the rights of the general public to take advantage of all that science now offers in the use of air space. This balance is in my judgment best struck in our present society by restricting the rights of an owner in the air space above his land to such height as is necessary for the ordinary use and enjoyment of his land and the structures upon it, and declaring that above that height he has no greater rights in the air space than any other member of the public."

Mr Moss fastened on the learned judge's reference to balancing the rights of an owner against the rights of the public and contended that it justified a whole new appraisal of ownership in so far as it extended to all space above the property owned.

In my view, it would be an incorrect use of authority to extract Griffiths J.'s approach to the difficult question of overflying aircraft and to seek to apply that approach to the invasion of air space in general. Griffiths J. was dealing with an argument that the incursion by an aircraft into the air space above the plaintiff's land represented trespass. He was not prepared to accept that that was necessarily so. But he accepted in the first passage I cited that adjoining owners had no right to erect structures projecting over their neighbours' land.

What is complained of in the present case is infringement of air space by a structure positioned upon a neighbour's land. The defendant has erected tower cranes on its land. Attached to each tower crane is a boom which swings over the plaintiffs' land. The booms invade the air space over the plaintiffs' land. Each boom is part of the structure on the defendant's land. The tort of trespass represents an interference with possession or with the right to possession. A landowner is entitled, as an attribute of his ownership of the land, to place structures on his land and thereby to reduce into actual possession the air space above his land. If an adjoining owner places a structure on his (the adjoining owner's) land that overhangs his neighbour's land, he thereby takes into his possession air space to which his neighbour is entitled. That, in my judgment, is trespass. It does not depend upon any balancing of rights.

The difficulties posed by overflying aircraft or balloons, bullets or missiles, seem to me to be wholly separate from the problem which arises where there is invasion of air space by a structure placed or standing upon the land of a neighbour. One of the characteristics of the common law of trespass is, or ought to be, certainty. The extent of proprietary rights enjoyed by landowners ought to be clear. It may be that, where aircraft or overflying missiles are concerned, certainty cannot be achieved. I do not wish to dissent at all from Griffiths J.'s approach to that problem in the *Bernstein* case. But certainty is capable of being achieved where invasion of air space by tower cranes, advertising signs and other structures are concerned. In my judgment, if somebody erects on his own land a structure, part of which invades the air space above the land of another, the invasion is trespass.

Mr Martin has submitted that if I am satisfied, as I am, that the oversailing booms of the cranes are committing trespass and if it is the case, as it is, that the trespass is threatened to be continued by the defendant, the plaintiffs are entitled to an injunction as of course. An injunction is a discretionary remedy, but it is well settled that the discretion must be exercised in accordance with judicial precedent and principle and there is authority for Mr Martin's submission that a trespass threatened to be continued will be restrained by injunction as of course.

There is a sense in which the grant of an injunction against trespass enables a landowner to behave like a dog in a manger. I am not suggesting that these plaintiffs are so behaving but the conclusion that even if they are, they are nonetheless entitled to their injunction sticks a little in my gullet. It would be possible for the law to be that the court should not grant an injunction to restrain a trifling trespass if it were shown to be reasonable and sensible that the trespass be allowed to continue for a limited period upon payment of substantial and proper damages. But I do not think it is open to me to proceed on that footing. There is too much authority in the way. The authorities establish, in my view, that the plaintiffs are entitled as of course to injunctions to restrain continuing trespass.

For these reasons, reached with some regret, I grant the injunctions as asked.

Note:

One reason given by Scott J. for granting the injunction was that the effect of refusing it would be to allow a legal wrong to continue unabated for which the plaintiff could repeatedly claim damages. This reason (though not the grant of the injunction) was criticised by the Court of Appeal in *Jaggard v Sawyer* [1995] 2 All E.R. 189 at 201, 206: if the court awards damages in lieu of an injunction, as it may under the Act of 1858 (Lord Cairns' Act, now Supreme Court Act 1981, s.50), such an award either compensates the plaintiff for future harm due to the wrong (*per* the Master of the Rolls) or bars further suit on the basis of *res judicata* (*per* Millett L.J.). It may seem (as Mrs Jaggard objected) to be playing with words when the latter said: " . . . it is not the award of damages which has the practical effect of licensing the defendant to commit the wrong, but the refusal of injunctive relief. Thereafter the defendant may have no right to act in the manner complained of, but he cannot be prevented from doing so. . . . It has always been recognised that the practical consequence of withholding injunctive relief is to authorise the continuance of an unlawful state of affairs . . . " The award of an injunction is not "of course" (*i.e.* automatic), but "usually turns on the question: would it in all the circumstances be oppressive to the defendant to grant the injunction to which the plaintiff is prima facie entitled?" (at 208).

We can test whether Millett L.J. is correct to say that the refusal of the injunction/award of damages does not license the defendant to commit the wrong. The facts of that case concerned the use of a private road. Suppose Mrs Jaggard now physically obstructs Mr Sawyer from using the road by standing in his way. Could Mr Sawyer use force to get past? He would surely only have a defence to a claim for assault and battery if he has a right to use the road. But how could such a right at law arise from equity's refusal of an injunction to stop him trespassing by using the road?

PERERA v VANDIYAR

Court of Appeal [1953] 1 W.L.R. 672; 97 S.J. 332; [1953] 1 All E.R. 1109

The plaintiff was tenant of the defendant's flat, and protected by the Rent Restriction Acts. On October 8, 1952, the defendant cut off the gas and electricity. The plaintiff remained there for two days with his wife and child but without heat or light, and then went to stay with friends. He returned when the utilities were reconnected on October 14.

The plaintiff claimed damages for breach of the tenancy agreement, for which the county court judge awarded £25 general damages and £3 10s. special damages. At the instance of the judge, the plaintiff amended his claim to include an averment that the acts "were done with the intent to evict the plaintiff and did cause the eviction of the plaintiff," whereupon the judge awarded a further £25 punitive damages. The defendant's appeal against the award of this further sum was allowed by the Court of Appeal.

Romer L.J.: . . . The county court judge, after assessing £25 as being the amount which, in his view, would be the right amount to award by way of damages for breach of contract, then held that a further £25 should be added on a certain basis. That basis was, in his own words, that the action of the defendant in cutting off the gas and electricity was a deliberate and malicious tort. That the defendant's action was deliberate is plain, and that it was malicious is, I think, reasonably plain, but I cannot for myself see that it amounted to a tort. It did not constitute an interference with any part of the demised premises and, therefore, could not be regarded as a trespass. It was merely a breach of contract, the object of which was to persuade or induce the tenant to go. That is not a tort. What the defendant did in *Lavender v Betts* ([1942] 2 All E.R. 72) was a tort, because it was a trespass. Although the intention of the defendant here was precisely the same as the intention proved in that case, the defendant in *Lavender v Betts* resorted to trespass for the purpose of getting his own way. It was not because he formed an intention to evict that damages were awarded in *Lavender v Betts*. They were awarded because he trespassed upon his tenant's property.

Eviction might, in certain circumstances, be a tort, and certainly would be if it involved also trespass, but the mere intention to evict cannot, as I see it, be a tort nor does it become a tort merely because the person who forms the intention hopes to give effect to it by interfering with the tenant's contractual rights. That is what the defendant here did, and in respect of that the first sum of £25 was awarded against him. But he did not bring himself into the area of tort which would justify the awarding of a further sum under the head of punitive damages. Accordingly, though perhaps with some reluctance, I agree that the judgment of the judge went too far in awarding the second sum of £25 . . .

Note:

In *McCall v Abelesz* [1976] Q.B. 585 Lord Denning said that the outcome of this case would be different today, now that damages for mental distress may be awarded for breach of contract (see above, p.112). But the Court of Appeal has now held that such damages may not be awarded to a tenant for breach of the covenant of quiet enjoyment in a lease (*Branchett v Beaney* [1992] 3 All E.R. 910), and in any case the damages in *Perera* were awarded as exemplary damages, unavailable in a contract suit since *Addis v Gramophone Co* [1909] A.C. 488. Since *McCall* declined to hold that the Protection from Eviction Act 1977 had made harassment of a tenant into a tort as well as an offence, there still seems to be a difference between cases like *Drane v Evangelou* [1978] 2 All E.R. 437 where there was a physical trespass and *Perera* where there was not.

Where the landlord is guilty of a physical trespass, exemplary damages may be awarded against him under the second head of *Rookes v Barnard* (see below, p.642) because he is evicting the tenant in order to get more money from his successor (as in *Millington v Duffy* (1984) 17 H.L.R. 232). This principle is carried forward in ss.27 and 28 of the Housing Act 1988, which imposes liability "in the nature of a liability in tort" on a landlord who harasses a residential occupier with the intention of making him give up occupation, the measure of damages if the tenant is not reinstated being the enhancement in value of his interest in the property by reason of its being vacant: in *Tagro v Cafane* [1991] 2 All E.R. 235, CA the plaintiff obtained £31,000 under this head as well as £15,538 for trespass to her goods. The courts may, however, mitigate these damages in the light of the tenant's conduct (s.27(7)), and they take the view that such damages are designed to strip the landlord of his profit, not to fine him, as exemplary damages would do. (*Osei-Bonsu v Wandsworth L.B.C.* [1999] 1 All E.R. 265).

Chapter 9

DEFENCES

Section 1.—Consent

(i) Existence

CHATTERTON v GERSON

Queen's Bench [1981] Q.B. 432; [1980] 3 W.L.R. 1003; [1981] 1 All E.R. 257 (noted
(1981) 97 L.Q.R. 113)

Action by patient against doctor for personal injury

The plaintiff, suffering great pain after a hernia operation, was referred to the defendant, a
specialist in the treatment of chronic intractable pain. The defendant gave her a spinal injection,
which helped the pain for a while but then made her numb in the right leg. Pain returned. The
defendant gave a second spinal injection which made the pain no better and the numbness worse.
There was dispute regarding the explanation given by the defendant to the plaintiff about the
nature and probable effect of the injections.

Bristow J.: . . . It is clear law that in any context in which consent of the injured party is a
defence to what would otherwise be a crime or a civil wrong, the consent must be real. Where,
for example a woman's consent to sexual intercourse is obtained by fraud, her apparent consent
is no defence to a charge of rape. It is not difficult to state the principle or to appreciate its good
sense. As so often, the problem lies in its application.

No English authority was cited before me of the application of the principle in the context of
consent to the interference with bodily integrity by medical or surgical treatment. . . .

In my judgment what the court has to do in each case is to look at all the circumstances and
say, "Was there a real consent?" I think justice requires that in order to vitiate the reality of
consent there must be a greater failure of communication between doctor and patient than that
involved in a breach of duty if the claim is based on negligence. When the claim is based on
negligence the plaintiff must prove not only the breach of duty to inform but that had the duty
not been broken she would not have chosen to have the operation. Where the claim is based on
trespass to the person, once it is shown that the consent is unreal, then what the plaintiff would
have decided if she had been given the information which would have prevented vitiation of the
reality of her consent is irrelevant.

In my judgment once the patient is informed in broad terms of the nature of the procedure
which is intended, and gives her consent, the consent is real, and the cause of the action on which
to base a claim for failure to go into risks and implications is negligence, not trespass. Of course,
if information is withheld in bad faith, the consent will be vitiated by fraud. Of course, if by some
accident, as in a case in the 1940s in the Salford Hundred Court where a boy was admitted to
hospital for tonsilectomy and due to administrative error was circumcised instead, trespass would
be the appropriate cause of action against the doctor, though he was as much the victim of the

error as the boy. But in my judgment it would be very much against the interests of justice if actions which are really based on a failure by the doctor to perform his duty adequately to inform were pleaded in trespass.

In this case in my judgment even taking Miss Chatterton's evidence at its face value she was under no illusion as to the general nature of what an intrathecal injection of phenol solution nerve block would be, and in the case of each injection her consent was not unreal. I should add that getting the patient to sign a pro forma expressing consent to undergo the operation "the effect and nature of which have been explained to me," as was done here in each case, should be a valuable reminder to everyone of the need for explanation and consent. But it would be no defence to an action based on trespass to the person if no explanation had in fact been given. The consent would have been expressed in form only, not in reality . . .

Notes:

1. Nowadays consent must be real and free. In *St. George's NHS Trust v S* [1998] 3 All E.R. 673 a woman who for days had strenuously resisted surgical intervention despite her life-threatening condition was subjected to a Caesarean operation. "Under the pressure of an exhausting and emotionally charged situations, and faced with the court order, S ceased to offer any resistance. This was not consent but submission." (at 684). For more facts see below, p.398.

2. If consent to treatment has been given and the consent is withdrawn, the treatment must stop even if the patient's decision is life-threatening, provided that the patient is mentally competent. To continue the treatment is a trespass: *Re B* [2002] EWHC 429, [2002] 2 All E.R. 449. Likewise the anticipatory refusal of consent in an "advance directive" is inherently revocable and revocation will be easily inferred: *HE v A Hospital NHS Trust* [2003] EWHC 1017, [2003] 2 F.L.R. 408.

3. The accused, pretending to have medical qualifications and relevant training, as he had not, persuaded several women to take part in a breast cancer survey during which he felt their breasts. Accused of indecent assault, he claimed that they had consented, but the women said they had consented only because they thought he was medically qualified. There was no evidence of sexual motive, and despite a defence that the women were not misled as to the identity of the accused or the nature of the act in question, his conviction (and sentence of nine months), was upheld. *R. v Tabassum* [2000] 2 Cr.App.Rep. 328, [2000] T.L.R. 418.

4. The claimant in an "approved school" acted as a rent-boy and consented to repeated buggery. The Criminal Injuries Compensation Board rejected his claim on the ground that the activities were consensual and not a crime of violence. This decision was quashed. Consent did not prevent it being a crime of violence when it was an indecent assault occasioning harm: minor indecent assaults (*e.g.* mere stroking) might not be crimes of violence even against a child. *R. v Criminal Injuries Compensation Appeals Panel, Ex parte B.* Collins J., June 30, 2000.

5. In several countries the patient's right to know can increase the doctor's duty to tell. Under the slogan of "informed consent" patients there may claim damages when an operation, though sensibly proposed and carefully conducted, goes sour, on the basis that if they had known of the inherent risks they would not have agreed to the operation at all, and since they were not told, their consent to it was not valid. In Britain it is sufficient if, in providing information about hazards intrinsic to the treatment proposed, the doctor or surgeon conducts himself in accordance with a responsible body of medical opinion which takes due account of the plaintiff's right to make the final decision: *Sidaway v Royal Bethlem Hospital* [1985] A.C. 871, but as we have seen, the House of Lords in *Bolitho* (above, p.164) has made it clear that it is prepared to appraise the *bien-fondé* of the medical opinion proffered by the defendant's expert.

(ii) Duration

HURST v PICTURE THEATRES LTD

Court of Appeal [1915] 1 K.B. 1; 83 L.J.K.B. 1837; 111 L.T. 972; 58 S.J. 739

Claim by cinemagoer for extrusion from cinema

The plaintiff, having paid the entrance fee (as the jury found), entered the defendant's cinema and took a proper seat. The attendant alleged that he had not paid, and asked him to leave. The plaintiff declined. The defendant's manager called a policeman. The policeman refused to act. The defendant's doorkeeper then ejected the plaintiff.

At a trial before Channell J. and a jury, the plaintiff had a verdict, damages £150. The defendant appealed to the Court of Appeal, who dismissed the appeal (Phillimore L.J. dissenting).

Buckley L.J.: ... The proposition which Mr Mackinnon sets out to affirm is that if a man has paid for his seat at the opera, or the theatre, and has entered and taken his seat, and is behaving himself quite properly, it is competent to the proprietors of the theatre, merely because they choose so to do, to call upon him to withdraw before he has seen the performance for the enjoyment of which he has paid; that what he has obtained for his money is a mere revocable licence to come upon the land of the proprietor of the theatre, and that the proprietor may, simply because he chooses, say "I revoke your licence; go." If that proposition be true, it involves startling results. Kennedy L.J. has suggested one. Suppose that there be sitting in the stalls a man who is a constant patron of the opera or the theatre, to whom the management pay great deference, whether from his rank or his habit of attendance: he goes to the management and says, "I do not like the person sitting in front of me or next to me; ask him to go." It would be competent to the management to go to that person and say, "Please go; you cannot have your money back, go." Further, if the proposition is right, it follows that, having let the seat to A, the management may come to A at the end of the first act or before and say "I revoke your licence, go," and he has to go. The management may let the seat to B for the rest of the performance, and at the end of the second act or sooner they may come to B and say, "I revoke your licence, go." He will have to go, and they may let the seat a third time to C. Those consequences ensue from this proposition if it be well founded. It was for that reason I said at the outset of my remarks that it seems to me, when the point comes to be considered, it is contrary to good sense. Next it is to my mind contrary also to good law. The proposition is based upon the well-known decision in *Wood v Leadbitter* ((1845) 13 M. & W. 838; 153 E.R. 351). Let me at the outset say what *Wood v Leadbitter* seems to me to have decided. It affirmed that a mere licence, whether or not it be under seal, by which I mean a licence not coupled with an interest or a grant whether it be under seal or not, is revocable. It affirmed also that if there be a licence coupled with an interest coupled with a grant, it is not, or at any rate in general is not, revocable. For those two propositions, I read these two sentences from the case of *Wood v Leadbitter* (at 844): "A mere licence is revocable; but that which is called a licence is often something more than a licence; it often comprises or is connected with a grant, and then the party who has given it cannot in general revoke it, so as to defeat his grant, to which it was incident. It may further be observed, that a licence under seal (provided it be a mere licence) is as revocable as a licence by parol; and, on the other hand, a licence by parol, coupled with a grant, is as irrevocable as a licence by deed, provided only that the grant is of a nature capable of being made by parol."

...

What is the grant in this case? The plaintiff in the present action paid his money to enjoy the sight of a particular spectacle. He was anxious to go into a picture theatre to see a series of views or pictures during, I suppose, an hour or a couple of hours. That which was granted to him was the right to enjoy looking at a spectacle, to attend a performance from its beginning to its end. That which was called the licence, the right to go upon the premises, was only something granted to him for the purpose of enabling him to have that which had been granted him, namely, the right to see. He could not see the performance unless he went into the building. His right to go into the building was something given to him in order to enable him to have the benefit of that which had been granted to him, namely, the right to hear the opera, or see the theatrical performance, or see the moving pictures as was the case here. So that here there was a licence coupled with a grant. If so, *Wood v Leadbitter* does not stand in the way at all. A licence coupled with a grant is not revocable; *Wood v Leadbitter* affirmed as much.

The position of matters now is that the court is bound under the Judicature Act to give effect to equitable doctrines. The question we have to consider is whether, having regard to equitable considerations, *Wood v Leadbitter* is now law meaning that *Wood v Leadbitter* is a decision which can be applied in its integrity in a court which is bound to give effect to equitable considerations. In my opinion, it is not. . . . The present Lord Parker, then Parker J., in the case of *Jones v Earl of Tankerville*, says this ([1909] 2 Ch. 440 at 443): "An injunction restraining the revocation of the licence, when it is revocable at law, may in a sense be called relief by way of specific performance, but it is not specific performance in the sense of compelling the vendor to do anything. It merely prevents him from breaking his contract, and protects a right in equity which but for the absence of a seal would be a right at law, and since the Judicature Act it may well be doubted whether the absence of a seal in such a case can be relied on in any court." What was relied on in *Wood v Leadbitter*, and rightly relied on at that date, was that there was not an instrument under seal, and therefore there was not a grant, and therefore the licensee could not say that he was not a mere licensee, but a licensee with a grant. That is now swept away. It cannot be said as against the plaintiff that he is a licensee with no grant merely because there is not an instrument under seal which gives him a right at law.

There is another way in which the matter may be put. If there be a licence with an agreement not to revoke the licence, that, if given for value, is an enforceable right. If the facts here are, as I think they are, that the licence was a licence to enter the building and see the spectacle from its commencement until its termination, then there was included in that contract a contract not to revoke the licence until the play had run to its termination. It was then a breach of contract to revoke the obligation not to revoke the licence. . . .

The defendants had, I think, for value contracted that the plaintiff should see a certain spectacle from its commencement to its termination. They broke that contract and it was a tort on their part to remove him. They committed an assault upon him by law. It was not of a violent kind, because, like a wise man, the plaintiff gave way to superior force and left the theatre. They sought to justify the assault by saying that they were entitled to remove him because he had not paid. He had paid, the jury have so found. Failing on that question of fact, they say that they were entitled to remove him because his licence was revocable. In my opinion, it was not. There was, I think, no justification for the assault here committed. Under the circumstances it was for the jury to give him such a sum as was right for the assault which was committed upon him, and for the serious indignity to a gentleman of being seized and treated in this way in a place of public resort. The jury have found that he was originally in the theatre as a spectator, that the assault was committed upon him, and that it was a wrongful act.

Questions

1. May a cinema owner eject a young couple kissing quietly in the back row?

2. Suppose the ticket had said (a) on its face, and (b) in tiny print on the back, "The management reserves the right to eject any person who refuses, when asked, to leave," could the management safely eject a person on the grounds mentioned by Buckley L.J. at the beginning of his judgment?

3. Why was there any difficulty in the case, given that the defendant's act was admittedly a breach of contract and therefore wrongful?

4. £150 in 1915 money is nearly £6,000 in 2002 money. Do you think the damages which the jury awarded were aggravated or exemplary?

Note:

In *Winter Garden Theatre (London) v Millennium Productions* [1947] A.C. 173 at 188 Viscount Simon said this:

"The effect of a licence by A to permit B to enter upon A.'s land or to use his premises for some purpose is in effect an authority which prevents B. from being regarded as a trespasser when he avails himself of the licence (*Thomas v Sorrell* (1673) 124 E.R. 1098). Such a licence may fall into one of various classes. It may be a purely gratuitous licence in return for which A gets nothing at all, *e.g.* a licence to B to walk across A's field. Such a gratuitous licence would plainly be revocable by notice given by A to B. Even in that case, however, notice of revocation conveyed to B. when he was in the act of crossing A's field could not turn him into a trespasser until he was off the premises, but his future right of crossing would thereupon cease. There is another class of licences which may be called licences for value, in which B, gives consideration for the permission he obtains from A, and this last class may be further subdivided. In some cases the consideration may be given once for all, as for example by the payment of a capital sum or by conferring a single benefit at the beginning. In other cases, the consideration may take the form of a periodic payment. There is yet a third variant of a licence for value which constantly occurs, as in the sale of a ticket to enter premises and witness a particular event, such as a ticket for a seat at a particular performance at a theatre or for entering private ground to witness a day's sport. In this last class of case, the implication of the arrangement, however it may be classified in law, plainly is that the ticket entitles the purchaser to enter and, if he behaves himself, to remain on the premises until the end of the event which he has paid his money to witness. Such, for example, was the situation which gave rise to the decision of the Court of Appeal in *Hurst v Picture Theatres*. I regard this case as rightly decided, and repudiate the view that a licensor who is paid for granting his licensee to enter premises in order to view a particular event, can nevertheless, although the licensee is behaving properly, terminate the licence before the event is over, turn the licensee out, and leave him to an action for the return of the price of his ticket. The licence in such a case is granted under contractual conditions, one of which is that a well-behaved licensee shall not be treated as a trespasser until the event which he has paid to see is over, and until he has reasonable time thereafter to depart, and in *Hurst v Picture Theatres*, where these rights were disregarded and the plaintiff was forced to leave prematurely substantial damages for assault and false imprisonment rightly resulted."

Yet the apparently excellent decision in *Hurst* must have limits. For example, suppose I contract with a decorator that he should paint my study. He comes and starts working. When he has painted half of it, I tell him I do not like the quality of his work (which is excellent), and that he must take his brushes and go. He declines to go, on the ground that he has invested money on the paint on the wall. I can surely throw him out after the lapse of a reasonable time. For a case where an injunction was issued to prevent a person exercising his contractual right to enter the land of another, see *Thompson v Park* [1944] 1 K.B. 408, which was clearly right on the facts, though the reasons have attracted much flak (*Verrall v Great Yarmouth B.C.* [1980] 1 All E.R. 839).

In *Hounslow v Twickenham Garden Developments* ([1971] Ch. 233) a borough sought an injunction to remove from their site some building contractors whose employment they had tried to terminate. Megarry J. refused the injunction on the ground that it was not clear that the purported termination was contractually valid. He observed that a person who had a contractual right to remain on property could not be physically evicted by the occupier bound by that contract, even if the contract were not specifically enforceable, and held that a court would never issue an injunction to evict such a person. It is to be hoped that neither observation will be treated as authoritative, for they give far too much effect to the mere existence of a contract. The effect of a contract depends on the strength of the right it purports to limit—a point Megarry J. himself recognised in discussing *White & Carter (Councils) Ltd v McGregor* ([1962] A.C. 413). The learned judge also cast some doubt on the case next following.

VAUGHAN v HAMPSON

Court of Exchequer (1875) 33 L.T. 15

The defendant, who was a solicitor for a bankrupt, called a general meeting of the creditors, which was attended by the plaintiff, who was acting as proxy for two of them. The defendant ejected him from the meeting, and the plaintiff sued for damages for assault and battery. The defendant pleaded that the plaintiff was a trespasser whom he ejected without unnecessary force. The plaintiff replied that he was a proxy for two of the creditors, and lawfully refused to leave when asked. The defendant demurred to this replication, and his demurrer was overruled.

Cleasby B.: The question is whether or not the plaintiff was a trespasser on the occasion in question. We are of opinion that he was not. He was, on the contrary, one of the number of persons who went to the defendant's office by invitation to attend a meeting of creditors, in order to discuss what steps should be taken in the matter of the liquidation proceedings against the bankrupt, for some of whose creditors the plaintiff was acting as the solicitor and duly appointed proxy on the occasion. The defendant had given the plaintiff leave and licence to be present, and the latter therefore had a right, coupled with an interest, entitling him to be on the defendant's premises. Our judgment must be for the plaintiff.

Pollock B.: I do not think that any question arises here as to whether the defendant had or not any authority as chairman of the meeting to turn the plaintiff out. No such allegation appears in the plea. This case is not governed, in my opinion, by that of *Wood v Leadbitter* ((1845) 13 M. & W. 838; 153 E.R. 351), on which Mr Herschell seemed to rely as an authority in favour of the defendant here. In that case there was a contract for pleasure. In the present case, as my brother Cleasby had said, a right coupled with an interest in the plaintiff to be where he was.

Amphlett B.: I am of the same opinion; and I will only add that if we could come to any other conclusion I think it would be a great scandal to the law.

Note:

In *Wandsworth LBC v A* [2000] 1 W.L.R. 1246, a headmaster banned the mother of a pupil from entering the school premises without giving her an opportunity to rebut the allegations on which he based his decision. The trial judge enjoined her from reentering the school, but the Court of Appeal vacated the injunction and held that the mother's licence (whatever it was) was such that in order for the decision to revoke it to be valid it must be consistent with public law, *i.e.* fair: it was not revocable peremptorily for no reason assigned. This seems to be a very odd decision.

Less odd is *Porter v Commissioner of Police*, October 20, 1999, CA. The plaintiff went to the showroom of the electricity board, as she was surely licensed to do, in order to complain of their failure to connect power to her new home. She made a scene and refused to leave till her wishes were complied with. When the police were called they tried for 45 minutes to persuade her to leave before finally removing her forcibly and provoking a scuffle. The plaintiff was arrested and charged with assault on the officer she bit. In her claim for assault, battery, wrongful arrest, false imprisonment and malicious prosecution (the charge was dropped by the CPS) the judge held that (1) she was guilty of trespass in remaining on the premises when asked to leave; (2) the officers were entitled to remove her at the request of the occupier, and there was no evidence of unreasonable force; (3) the arrest for breach of the peace was justified; (4) the bitten officer had a reasonable belief in the guilt of the plaintiff. These questions were therefore not left to the jury, and the plaintiff's appeal was dismissed on every point.

(iii) Content

BURNARD v HAGGIS

Court of Common Pleas (1863) 14 C.B. (N.S.) 45; 2 New Rep. 126; 32 L.J.C.P. 189; 8 L.T. 320; 9 Jur. (N.S.) 1325; 11 W.R. 644; 143 E.R. 360

Claim against bailee for damage to bailed property

The plaintiff let out horses for riding at 7s. 6d., and for jumping at one guinea. The defendant, an infant undergraduate at Trinity College, Cambridge, with rooms in Rose Crescent, went to the plaintiff's stable and asked for a horse for riding to be delivered to Green Street (where his friend Bonner lived). The charge was 7s. 6d. and it was clear that the horse was not to be used for jumping. Bonner, mounted on the plaintiff's mare, and the defendant, otherwise mounted, went out riding over the fields towards Grantchester. Bonner put the plaintiff's mare to a wattle fence and a stake entered her, causing a wound of which she subsequently died.

The plaintiff recovered £30 in the county court, and the defendant's appeal was dismissed.

Willes J.: . . . It appears to me that the act of riding the mare into the place where she received her death-wound was as much a trespass, notwithstanding the hiring for another purpose, as if, without any hiring at all, the defendant had gone into a field and taken the mare out and hunted her and killed her. It was a bare trespass, not within the object and purpose of the hiring. It was not even an excess. It was doing an act towards the mare which was altogether forbidden by the owner. . . .

Byles J.: ... I am of the same opinion. Here the mare was let for the specific purpose of a ride along the road, and for the purpose of being ridden only by the defendant. The defendant not only allows his friend to mount, but allows him to put the mare to a fence for which he was told she was unfit. Quite independently, therefore, of the question of necessaries, the defendant is clearly responsible for the wrong done.

Question

In *Lord Camoys v Scurr* (1840) 9 C. & p.383; 173 E.R. 879, the defendant obtained the plaintiff's horse from the plaintiff's agent for sale for the purpose of trial. The defendant tried it and asked a nobleman's groom to try it also. The horse ran away with the groom and was killed. Coleridge J. said: "The defendant had this mare for the purpose of trying her and I think that he was entitled to put a competent person on the mare to try her." Or a person appearing to be competent? Would this apply to the trial of a car?

Note:

This case is not really as simple as it looks. It is difficult to believe that the mere permitting the horse to be jumped could constitute a trespass, but the giving of the horse to Bonner to ride might well be. "There are many bailments in which the bailee is entitled to make a sub-bailment: the repairer of a motor-car for instance, can often quite reasonably send away a part of it to another firm for repairs; a carrier of goods may need to entrust them to another carrier for part of the journey; a hirer may himself often, quite lawfully, sub-hire the goods. It all depends on the circumstances of the particular case," *per* Denning L.J. in *Edwards v Newland & Co* [1950] 2 K.B. 534 at 542.

The liability of a bailee who has deviated from the terms of his holding is absolute in the sense that he becomes an all-risks insurer for the goods. It is not necessary that the damage be a foreseeable consequence of the deviation; if the goods are damaged *during* the deviation, the bailee must pay (*Lilley v Doubleday* (1881) 7 Q.B.D. 510), just as he must if he keeps them too long (*Mitchell v Ealing* [1978] 2 All E.R. 779). In the normal case, the bailee will have promised, as a matter of contract, to adhere to the terms of the holding. Such a promise would not, as a matter of contract, be binding if the contract were illegal, but the bailee might still be liable for deviating from the terms of his holding as a matter of tort.

BYRNE v KINEMATOGRAPH RENTERS SOCIETY LTD

Chancery [1958] 1 W.L.R. 762; 102 S.J. 509; [1959] 2 All E.R. 579

Action for economic loss caused by unlawful means

The plaintiff cinema-owner was blacklisted and put out of business by the defendant film-distributors whose employees had gone to the plaintiff's cinema not to see the film but simply to check on the number of patrons. The plaintiff claimed damages on the theory that the defendants had deliberately injured him in his trade by means of illegal acts, namely trespasses.

Harman J.: ... It is alleged by the plaintiff that the investigation conducted by K.R.S. through Belton and his emissaries was illegal because it involved acts of trespass on the plaintiff's property. It was argued that the 23 visits of Pinder or Lewis and their assistants to the County Cinema which I have described were all acts of trespass because they went into the cinema not for the purpose for which alone the public was invited to attend but for a different purpose, namely, to obtain evidence against the plaintiff. I cannot think there is anything in this point. The cinema was open to the public who were invited to go in and take tickets, and this is what Pinder and Lewis and their assistants did. Their motives in taking the tickets are, I think, immaterial from this point of view. They did nothing they were not invited to do, and in my judgment it cannot be said that because they may not have wished to see the performance but were merely interested in the numbers on the tickets or in counting the number of patrons they committed acts of trespass. ...

Questions

1. Suppose that Pinder had injured himself on a nail on one of the seats. Could he recover from the present plaintiff?

2. Suppose that, after their entry to the cinema, the plaintiff had discovered that Pinder and Lewis had come to count the patrons and tickets so as to give evidence inimical to his interests. He asks them to leave. They refuse. He ejects them. Would they succeed in an action of assault? If not, would that be because (a) the contract was induced by fraud, (b) though it was not, equity would not in the circumstances think of ordering specific enforcement, (c) there was an implied term in the contract, or (d) *Hurst's* case was wrongly decided? Would the plaintiff have to give them their money back?

3. Was this a claim in trespass? If not, why not?

Note:

"A person is guilty of burglary if— . . . (b) having entered any building . . . as a trespasser he steals . . . anything in the building . . . or inflicts . . . on any person therein any grievous bodily harm" (Theft Act 1968, s.9(1)). The term "trespasser" in this enactment is bound to provoke some discussion in the coming years, but great care must be taken before transposing to private law the decisions of criminal courts on such texts. For instance, *mens rea* in relation to the trespass is required for burglary, that is, the accused must have known, or as good as known, that he was trespassing: such knowledge is quite irrelevant in private law.

(iv) Mistake

ARMSTRONG v SHEPPARD & SHORT LTD

Court of Appeal [1959] 2 Q.B. 384; [1959] 3 W.L.R. 84; 123 J.P. 401; 103 S.J. 508; [1959] 2 All E.R. 651

The defendant building contractors wanted to construct a sewer under a pathway at the back of the plaintiff's house. The plaintiff did not know that he owned this land, and when he was asked by the defendants if he had any objection to their constructing the proposed sewer, he said that he had none. The sewer was built. When the plaintiff discovered that he owned the land, he asked the defendants to remove the sewer. They did not, and continued to discharge effluent through it. The county court judge refused the injunction requested by the plaintiff, but awarded him 20s. damages for trespass. The plaintiff appealed and the defendant cross-appealed.

As to the plaintiff's appeal, the Court of Appeal held that no injunction should be granted because the plaintiff was suffering only trivial damage, and in any case he had tried to deceive the court by denying that he ever gave permission for the construction of the sewer. The cross-appeal also failed.

Evershed M.R.: . . . in an action of common law trespass, it does not, in the circumstances here, matter that the plaintiff was unaware of his proprietary rights when he gave permission: the thing is done: and it has had the lawful justification (in so far as this case is concerned) that it was done with the approval of the man who now tries to complain about it. It follows from that conclusion (as [his counsel] conceded) that [the plaintiff] cannot complain of the presence in the land now of the physical things, the manhole and the pipes. . . .

[His Lordship turned to the trespass by means of the discharge of effluent.] First, if the subject-matter which is alleged to have been granted, is an interest in land, then it cannot be done by parol only. Of course, a licence coupled with a grant, if it is effectively done, will no doubt be irrevocable. But there is nothing in the authorities that [defendant's counsel] cited to support the view that a right to pass water through another's land—which is, as I conceive, a proprietary right—is capable of grant by parol. But, secondly, such a permission to pass effluent down a man's land no doubt might be, as a matter of contract, properly covered as between one individual and another. . . . In my judgment . . . a licence of that kind if it is to be irrevocable during the plaintiff's tenure, must have the necessary qualities of a contract, binding upon the parties: it must be supported by consideration, and must in other respects be the subject of a contract. . . .

. . . by well-established principle the licensee does not become necessarily a trespasser the moment the licensor says "The licence is at an end": the alleged trespasser is allowed a reasonable time . . . to discontinue the act which thereby would become a trespass. . . .

Note:

Although the injunction was refused and damages were awarded, the damages were awarded at common law and not under Lord Cairns' Act in lieu of the injunction, the Act not having been invoked at all. See above, p.361.

Questions

1. Do you accept the distinction between an act which would constitute a continuing trespass and a series of acts which would constitute repeated trespasses?

2. Was the plaintiff merely estopped from complaining about the presence of the pipes?

Section 2.—Law and Order

HUSSIEN v CHONG FOOK KAM

Privy Council [1970] A.C. 942; [1970] 2 W.L.R. 441; [1969] 3 All E.R. 1626

Lord Devlin: . . . This is an appeal in an action for false imprisonment. The two plaintiffs in the action were arrested on July 11, 1965, held in custody overnight and brought before the magistrate on July 12, when he made an order for their retention for seven days for further investigation. On the next day the plaintiffs were released, the police having found that there was not sufficient evidence to proceed against either of them. It was agreed that the false imprisonment, if any, was brought to an end by the magistrate's order. The plaintiffs' action was dismissed in the High Court of Malaysia but was successful on appeal in the Federal Court of Malaysia, where judgment was given in their favour for damages of $2,500 each. From this judgment the defendants have appealed to the Board.

The police inquiry began with a complaint made at the Mentakab police station at 10.15 p.m. on July 10. The complainant stated that at 9.15 p.m., when he was driving home with four friends in his car, he passed a lorry, coming in the opposite direction, with a trailer loaded with timber. As he passed a piece of timber fell off the lorry, hitting his windscreen and two of the men in the car. One of the men died. The lorry did not stop. Police inquiries led them to conclude that the incident had occurred as stated and that the lorry involved in it was numbered PC 8200. . . . it is not disputed that the police had reasonable grounds for reaching this conclusion. Directions were given that the lorry PC 8200 was to be stopped and detained.

At 7.55 a.m. on July 11, PC 22927 of Bukit Tinggi police station found the lorry stationary in front of a coffee shop about a quarter of a mile from the police station. He found and detained the two plaintiffs, one of whom admitted to being the driver of the lorry and the other the attendant. The corporal in charge of the station arrived 10 minutes later. According to his evidence (the police evidence generally was accepted by the trial judge) one of the plaintiffs "asked me what wrong he had done. I told him that I had received instructions from Mentakab to detain him on suspicion of a fatal road accident case." This was said in the hearing of the other plaintiff. About 1 p.m. the area inspector from Mentakab and his superior officer, the district superintendent—these are the two individual defendants in the action—arrived at the coffee shop. They interrogated both plaintiffs there. The one who said he was the driver said that they had not met with an accident. The evidence is not very clear, but it is reasonable to infer that he meant by that that they were not at the scene of the accident at the relevant time, for both men were asked to give an account of their movements. The police officers did not regard their explanations as satisfactory and it was decided that they should be taken to Mentakab police station for further investigation. Since an attendant in a lorry is frequently an alternate driver and the police felt doubt about which man was the driver at the relevant time, both men were treated alike. They left about 3 p.m. and arrived at Mentakab at about 5 p.m. Their story was that on the evening in question they had bought food at a shop in Mentakab and that one of them had had his hair cut at a barber's shop. They were taken to the two shops where they pointed out to the police two witnesses, but the witnesses were reluctant to answer any questions. At 6.15 p.m. they were taken back to the police station where, as already recorded, they spent the night and were brought before the magistrate on the following morning ...

An arrest occurs when a police officer states in terms that he is arresting or when he uses force to restrain the individual concerned. It occurs also when by words or conduct he makes it clear that he will, if necessary, use force to prevent the individual from going where he may want to go. It does not occur when he stops an individual to make inquiries. The moment when it occurred in this case was between 8.05 and 9 a.m. on July 11 when the corporal told the plaintiffs of the existing suspicion and said that he had instructions to detain them.

At that point of time the police had good reason to suspect that one or other of the plaintiffs was driving the lorry from whose trailer the piece of timber fell. But there is a wide gap between a suspicion that one of the plaintiffs was the man driving the lorry and a suspicion that he was driving it recklessly or dangerously. The trial judge did not acknowledge the existence of such a gap. He said in his judgment—"Suspicion focused reasonably enough on the said lorry and it goes without saying on the driver." Granted that the fall of the timber is of itself some evidence of insecure loading, and granted also that it would be reckless driving to drive at any speed or in any manner a lorry with a trailer which the driver knew or ought to have known to be insecurely loaded, the police had in their Lordships' opinion no reasonable grounds for suspecting that either plaintiff had any knowledge, actual or constructive, of the state of the load. Likewise, there was nothing at all to suggest that the lorry was at the time of the accident being driven in a dangerous manner. Mr Gratiaen has argued that a driver ought to satisfy himself before he sets off that his load is secure. No doubt he ought to notice an obvious danger of collapse, but the fall of a single piece of timber is no evidence of that. Mr Gratiaen has relied strongly—and it is a strong point—on the fact that the lorry did not stop after the accident. But here again their Lordships must, with respect, differ from the trial judge when he describes it as "clearly a hit and run case." It is quite possible that the fall of a single piece of timber from the trailer might not be noticed at the time, and even if it were and the plaintiffs speculated about it, it might not occur to them that it would lead to the unusual consequences that happened here. Their Lordships concluded that the suspicion that the plaintiffs or either of them was guilty of reckless driving was not reasonable.

... Suspicion in its ordinary meaning is a state of conjecture or surmise where proof is lacking: "I suspect but I cannot prove." Suspicion arises at or near the starting-point of an investigation of which the obtaining of prima facie proof is the end. When such proof has been obtained, the police case is complete; it is ready for trial and passes on to its next stage. It is indeed desirable as a general rule that an arrest should not be made until the case is complete. But if arrest before that were forbidden, it could seriously hamper the police. To give power to arrest on reasonable suspicion does not mean that it is always or even ordinarily to be exercised. It means that there is an executive discretion. In the exercise of it many factors have to be considered besides the strength of the case. The possibility of escape, the prevention of further crime and the obstruction of police inquiries are examples of those factors with which all judges who have had to grant or refuse bail are familiar. There is no serious danger in a large measure of executive discretion in the first instance because in countries where common law principles prevail the discretion is subject indirectly to judicial control. There is first the power, which their Lordships have just noticed, to grant bail. There is secondly the fact that in such countries there is available only a limited period between the time of arrest and the institution of proceedings; and if a police officer institutes proceedings without prima facie proof, he will run the risk of an action for malicious prosecution. The ordinary effect of this is that a police officer either has something substantially more than reasonable suspicion before he arrests or that, if he has not, he has to act promptly to verify it. In Malaysia the period available is strictly controlled by the Code. Under section 28 the suspect must be taken before a magistrate at the latest within 24 hours. If the investigation cannot be completed in 24 hours and there are grounds for believing that the accusation or information is well founded, under section 117 the magistrate may order the detention of the accused for a further period not exceeding 15 days in the whole. By allowing 15 days after arrest for investigation, the Code shows clearly that it does not contemplate prima facie proof as a prerequisite for arrest.

Their Lordships have not found any English authority in which reasonable suspicion has been equated with prima facie proof. In *Dumbell v Roberts* ([1944] 1 All E.R. 326), Scott L.J. said (at p.329): "The protection of the public is safeguarded by the requirement, alike of the common law and, so far as I know, of all statutes, that the constable shall before arresting satisfy himself that there do in fact exist reasonable grounds for suspicion of guilt. That requirement is very limited. The police are not called upon before acting to have anything like a prima facie case for conviction; . . . " There is another distinction between reasonable suspicion and prima facie proof. Prima facie proof consists of admissible evidence. Suspicion can take into account matters that could not be put in evidence at all. There is a discussion about the relevance of previous convictions in the judgment of Lord Wright in *McArdle v Egan* ((1934) 150 L.T. 412). Suspicion can take into account also matters which, though admissible, could not form part of a prima facie case. Thus the fact that the accused has given a false alibi does not obviate the need for prima facie proof of his presence at the scene of the crime; it will become of considerable importance in the trial when such proof as there is is being weighed perhaps against a second alibi; it would undoubtedly be a very suspicious circumstance.

Their Lordships have developed the distinction between reasonable suspicion and prima facie proof because of its materiality at a later stage. The plaintiffs when interrogated denied that they were at the place of the accident. The police, who had admittedly good ground for suspecting that it was the plaintiffs' lorry which was in fact involved, must be credited with equally good grounds for suspecting that the alibi was false. When checked, no corroboration was found for it. These facts, added to the failure to stop, were enough in their Lordships' opinion to raise at this later stage a reasonable suspicion that the plaintiffs were concerned in a piece of reckless driving. But the case falls far short of prima facie proof.

Mr Gratiaen . . . , accepting the arrest as being made in the morning of July 11, invited the Board, if it is open to them to do so, to reduce the damages. Undoubtedly their Lordships' conclusion affects the amount of the damages. It is not merely that it cuts in half the period of false imprisonment and excises in particular the night at the police station. Much more important, it alters the character of the arrest. It becomes a premature arrest rather than one that was unjustifiable from first to last. The police made the mistake of arresting before questioning; if they had questioned first and arrested afterwards, there would have been no case against them.

Question

" . . . if [the police] had questioned first and arrested afterwards, there would have been no case against them." But what power had the police to detain the plaintiffs while the questions were being put to them? Or would a refusal to stay for questioning be in itself a suspicious circumstance which, added to the others, would justify an arrest?

Note:

Lord Devlin emphasises that, given that there are reasonable grounds for suspicion, the policeman has an "executive discretion" whether to arrest or not. Only if this discretion is abused, and not just if it is exercised unreasonably, will the policeman be liable for arresting the suspect. Thus it was not an abuse to arrest a person because she was more likely to confess in the police-station: *Holgate-Mohammed v Duke* [1984] 1 All E.R. 1054, HL.

In *Castorina v Chief Constable* [1988] New L.J.R. 180, CA, in which a verdict of £4,500 for an arrest which was "premature" in this sense was overturned, Woolf L.J. said " . . . there are three questions to be answered:

1. Did the arresting officer suspect that the person who was arrested was guilty of the offence? The answer to this question depends entirely on the findings of fact as to the officer's state of mind.

2. Assuming the officer had the necessary suspicion, was there reasonable cause for that suspicion? This is a purely objective requirement to be determined by the judge if necessary on the facts found by a jury.

3. If the answer to the two previous questions is in the affirmative, then the officer has a discretion which entitles him to make an arrest and the question in relation to that discretion is whether it has been exercised in accordance with the principles laid down by Lord Greene M.R. in *Associated Provincial Picture Houses v Wednesbury Corp.* [1948] 1 K.B. 223."

In a case where the only ground for suspicion was information supplied by a police informant, the trial judge held that there were no reasonable grounds for arrest, only to be reversed by the Court of Appeal, which admitted that extreme caution should be observed in such cases (*James v Chief Constable of South Wales*, April 16, 1991, CA)).

4. *Hussien* was treated as establishing that "the threshold for suspicion on which an officer could arrest was a low one" by the judge in *Matin v Commissioner of Police (No.1)*, Q.B. June 18, 2001. Do you agree?

POLICE AND CRIMINAL EVIDENCE ACT 1984

PART I

POWERS TO STOP AND SEARCH

1.—(1) A constable may exercise any power conferred by this section—

(a) in any place to which at the time when he proposes to exercise the power the public or any section of the public has access, on payment or otherwise, as of right or by virtue of express or implied permission; or

(b) in any other place to which people have ready access at the time when he proposes to exercise the power but which is not a dwelling.

(2) Subject to subsections (3) to (5) below, a constable—

(a) may search—
   (i) any person or vehicle;
   (ii) anything which is in or on a vehicle, for stolen or prohibited articles . . . ; and

(b) may detain a person or vehicle for the purpose of such a search.

(3) This section does not give a constable power to search a person or vehicle or anything in or on a vehicle unless he has reasonable grounds for suspecting that he will find stolen or prohibited articles.

(4) If a person is in a garden or yard occupied with and used for the purposes of a dwelling or on other land so occupied and used, a constable may not search him in the exercise of the power conferred by this section unless the constable has reasonable grounds for believing—

(a) that he does not reside in the dwelling; and

(b) that he is not in the place in question with the express or implied permission of a person who resides in the dwelling.

(5) . . .

(6) If in the course of such a search a constable discovers an article which he has reasonable grounds for suspecting to be a stolen or prohibited article . . . , he may seize it.

. . .

Code A of the Code of Practice came into force in April 2003. Breach of its terms by the police gives rise to no civil liability but may lead to the exclusion of evidence. "Powers to stop and search must be used fairly, responsibly, with respect for people being searched and without unlawful discrimination . . . " (para.1.1) There must be "reasonable grounds for suspicion" that the person stopped has in his possession "prohibited articles" such as offensive weapons or bladed or pointed articles. "Reasonable grounds for suspicion" is explained in paras 2.1–2.11, the test being partly subjective—genuine suspicion—and partly objective—would a reasonable person entertain such a suspicion? Good reasons do not include a person's race, age, appearance or previous conviction. Citizens need not answer questions and may walk away if not detained, but their answers may provide grounds for detention and search. A person who consents to being searched may still not be searched unless there is a legal power to do so. There are specific powers outside PACE which do not depend on reasonable suspicion (paras 2.12–2.29).

PART II

POWERS OF ENTRY, SEARCH AND SEIZURE

Search warrants

8. . . .

15.—(1) This section and section 16 below have effect in relation to the issue to constables under any enactment, including an enactment contained in an Act passed after this Act, of warrants to enter and search premises; and an entry on or search of premises under a warrant is unlawful unless it complies with this section and section 16 below.

(2) Where a constable applies for any such warrant, it shall be his duty—

(a) to state—
   (i) the ground on which he makes the application; and
   (ii) the enactment under which the warrant would be issued;
(b) to specify the premises which it is desired to enter and search; and
(c) to identify, so far as is practicable, the articles or persons to be sought.

(3) An application for such a warrant shall be made *ex parte* and supported by an information in writing.

(4) The constable shall answer on oath any question that the justice of the peace or judge hearing the application asks him.

(5) A warrant shall authorise an entry on one occasion only.

(6) A warrant—

(a) shall specify—
   (i) the name of the person who applies for it;
   (ii) the date on which it is issued;
   (iii) the enactment under which it is issued; and
   (iv) the premises to be searched; and
(b) shall identify, so far as is practicable, the articles or persons to be sought.

(7) Two copies shall be made of a warrant.

(8) The copies shall be clearly certified as copies.

16.—(1) A warrant to enter and search premises may be executed by any constable.

(2) Such a warrant may authorise persons to accompany any constable who is executing it.

(3) Entry and search under a warrant must be within one month from the date of its issue.

(4) Entry and search under a warrant must be at a reasonable hour unless it appears to the constable executing it that the purpose of a search may be frustrated on an entry at a reasonable hour.

(5) Where the occupier of premises which are to be entered and searched is present at the time when a constable seeks to execute a warrant to enter and search them, the constable—

(a) shall identify himself to the occupier and, if not in uniform, shall produce to him documentary evidence that he is a constable;

(b) shall produce the warrant to him; and

(c) shall supply him with a copy of it.

(6) . . .

(7) If there is no person present who appears to the constable to be in charge of the premises, he shall leave a copy of the warrant in a prominent place on the premises.

(8) A search under a warrant may only be a search to the extent required for the purpose for which the warrant was issued. . . .

Entry and search without search warrant

17.—(1) Subject to the following provisions of this section, and without prejudice to any other enactment, a constable may enter and search any premises for the purpose—

(a) of executing—
  (i) a warrant of arrest issued in connection with or arising out of criminal proceedings; or
  (ii) a warrant of commitment issued under section 76 of the Magistrates' Courts Act 1980;

(b) of arresting a person for an arrestable offence;

(c) of arresting a person for an offence under—
  (i) section 1 (prohibition of uniforms in connection with political objects) of the Public Order Act 1936;
  (ii) any enactment contained in sections 6 to 8 or 10 of the Criminal Law Act 1977 (offences relating to entering and remaining on property);
  (iii) section 4 of the Public Order Act 1986 (fear or provocation of violence);
  (iiia) section 163 of the Road Traffic Act 1988 (c 52) (failure to stop when required to do so by a constable in uniform);
  (iv) section 76 of the Criminal Justice and Public Order Act 1994 (failure to comply with interim possession order);

(ca) of arresting, in pursuance of section 32(1A) of the Children and Young Persons Act 1969, any child or young person who has been remanded or committed to local authority accommodation under section 23(1) of that Act;

(cb) of recapturing any person who is, or is deemed for any purpose to be, unlawfully at large while liable to be detained—
  (i) in a prison, remand centre, young offender institution or secure training centre, or
  (ii) in pursuance of [section 92 of the Powers of Criminal Courts (Sentencing) Act 2000] (dealing with children and young persons guilty of grave crimes), in any other place;]

(d) of recapturing [any person whatever] who is unlawfully at large and whom he is pursuing; or

(e) of saving life or limb or preventing serious damage to property.

(2) Except for the purpose specified in paragraph (e) of subsection (1) above, the powers of entry and search conferred by this section—

(a) are only exercisable if the constable has reasonable grounds for believing that the person whom he is seeking is on the premises; and . . .

(3) The powers of entry and search conferred by this section are only exercisable for the purposes specified in subsection (1)(c)(ii) or (iv) above by a constable in uniform.

(4) The power of search conferred by this section is only a power to search to the extent that is reasonably required for the purpose for which the power of entry is exercised.

(5) Subject to subsection (6) below, all the rules of common law under which a constable has power to enter premises without a warrant are hereby abolished.

(6) Nothing in subsection (5) above affects any power of entry to deal with or prevent a breach of the peace.

19.—(1) The powers conferred by subsections (2), (3) and (4) below are exercisable by a constable who is lawfully on any premises.

(2) The constable may seize anything which is on the premises if he has reasonable grounds for believing—

(a) that it has been obtained in consequence of the commission of an offence; and

(b) that it is necessary to seize it in order to prevent it being concealed, lost, damaged, altered or destroyed.

(3) The constable may seize anything which is on the premises if he has reasonable grounds for believing—

(a) that it is evidence in relation to an offence which he is investigating or any other offence; and

(b) that it is necessary to seize it in order to prevent the evidence being concealed, lost, altered or destroyed.

PART III

ARREST

24.—(1) The powers of summary arrest conferred by the following subsections shall apply—

(a) to offences for which the sentence is fixed by law;

(b) to offences for which a person of 21 years of age or over (not previously convicted) may be sentenced to imprisonment for a term of five years (or might be so sentenced but for the restrictions imposed by section 33 of the Magistrates' Courts Act 1980); and

(c) to the offences listed in Schedule 1A, and in this Act "arrestable offence" means any such offence.

(4) Any person may arrest without a warrant—

(a) anyone who is in the act of committing an arrestable offence;
(b) anyone whom he has reasonable grounds for suspecting to be committing such an offence.

(5) Where an arrestable offence has been committed, any person may arrest without a warrant—

(a) anyone who is guilty of the offence;
(b) anyone whom he has reasonable grounds for suspecting to be guilty of it.

(6) Where a constable has reasonable grounds for suspecting that an arrestable offence has been committed, he may arrest without a warrant anyone whom he has reasonable grounds for suspecting to be guilty of the offence.

(7) A constable may arrest without a warrant—

(a) anyone who is about to commit an arrestable offence;
(b) anyone whom he has reasonable grounds for suspecting to be about to commit an arrestable offence.

25.—(1) Where a constable has reasonable grounds for suspecting that any offence which is not an arrestable offence has been committed or attempted, or is being committed or attempted, he may arrest the relevant person if it appears to him that service of a summons is impracticable or inappropriate because any of the general arrest conditions is satisfied.

(2) In this section "the relevant person" means any person whom the constable has reasonable grounds to suspect of having committed or having attempted to commit the offence or of being in the course of committing or attempting to commit it.

(3) The general arrest conditions are—

(a) that the name of the relevant person is unknown to, and cannot be readily ascertained by, the constable;
(b) that the constable has reasonable grounds for doubting whether a name furnished by the relevant person as his name is his real name;
(c) that—
    (i) the relevant person has failed to furnish a satisfactory address for service; or
    (ii) the constable has reasonable grounds for doubting whether an address furnished by the relevant person is a satisfactory address for service;
(d) that the constable has reasonable grounds for believing that arrest is necessary to prevent the relevant person—
    (i) causing physical injury to himself or any other person;
    (ii) suffering physical injury;
    (iii) causing loss of or damage to property;
    (iv) committing an offence against public decency; or
    (v) causing an unlawful obstruction of the highway;
(e) that the constable has reasonable grounds for believing that arrest is necessary to protect a child or other vulnerable person from the relevant person.

. . .

28.—(1) Subject to subsection (5) below, where a person is arrested, otherwise than by being informed that he is under arrest, the arrest is not lawful unless the person arrested is informed that he is under arrest as soon as is practicable after his arrest.

(2) Where a person is arrested by a constable, subsection (1) above applies regardless of whether the fact of the arrest is obvious.

(3) Subject to subsection (5) below, no arrest is lawful unless the person arrested is informed of the ground for the arrest at the time of, or as soon as is practicable after, the arrest.

(4) Where a person is arrested by a constable, subsection (3) above applies regardless of whether the ground for the arrest is obvious.

(5) Nothing in this section is to be taken to require a person to be informed—

(a) that he is under arrest; or

(b) of the ground of the arrest,

if it was not reasonably practicable for him to be so informed by reason of his having escaped from arrest before the information could be given.

29. Where for the purpose of assisting with an investigation a person attends voluntarily at a police station or at any other place where a constable is present or accompanies a constable to a police station or any such other place without having been arrested—

(a) he shall be entitled to leave at will unless he is placed under arrest;

(b) he shall be informed at once that he is under arrest if a decision is taken by a constable to prevent him from leaving at will.

30.—(1) Subject to the following provisions of this section, where a person—

(a) is arrested by a constable for an offence; or

(b) is taken into custody by a constable after being arrested for an offence by a person other than a constable,

at any place other than a police station, he shall be taken to a police station by a constable as soon as practicable after the arrest.

(10) Nothing in subsection (1) above shall prevent a constable delaying taking a person who has been arrested to a police station if the presence of that person elsewhere is necessary in order to carry out such investigation as it is reasonable to carry out immediately.

31. Where—

(a) a person—

(i) has been arrested for an offence; and

(ii) is at a police station in consequence of that arrest; and

(b) it appears to a constable that, if he were released from that arrest, he would be liable to arrest for some other offence,

he shall be arrested for that other offence.

117. Where any provision of this Act—

(a) confers a power on a constable; and

(b) does not provide that the power may only be exercised with the consent of some person, other than a police officer,

the officer may use reasonable force, if necessary, in the exercise of the power.

Note:
Many trespassory acts are legitimated by this important enactment—acts of false imprisonment, battery, trespass to goods and trespass to land.

Section 1: Note that these powers may not be exercised in dwellings at all, or in gardens attached to dwellings unless the person is probably trespassing. The stopping and searching of a person otherwise lawful is rendered unlawful by the policeman's refusal to give his name and section on request by the person stopped (s.2(3)(a)). *Osman v DPP* [1998] Times L.R. 681.

Section 8, 15(1): While it is possible to seek judicial review of the magistrate's decision to issue a search warrant, it is greatly preferable for the complainant to sue in trespass for wrongful seizure: *R. v Chief Constable, Ex p.Fitzpatrick* [1998] 1 All E.R. 65, Div.Ct.

Section 15(1): Note that breach of the statutory requirements renders the entry unlawful, and that some of the requirements cannot be satisfied until after the entry itself. This is a version of the doctrine of trespass *ab initio*, derided by Lord Denning in *Chic Fashions (West Wales) Ltd v Jones* [1968] 2 Q.B. 299, but resuscitated by him in *Cinnamond v British Airports Auth.* [1980] 2 All E.R. 368. Although material unlawfully seized is not automatically inadmissible as evidence (*R. v Sang* [1979] 2 All E.R. 1222), material seized during a search which is unlawful (as under s.16 where the complete warrant is not produced and a copy supplied) may not be retained and must be returned: *R. Chief Constable of Lancs., Ex p.Parker* [1993] 2 All E.R. 56.

Section 17(1)(d) "pursuing" means what it says and does not include "going to look for" or, indeed, "going to apprehend": *D'Souza v DPP* [1992] 4 All E.R. 545, HL.

Section 17(6): Note that the common law power to enter premises with a view to preventing or quelling a breach of the peace remains unimpaired, and applies to private as well as public premises, provided the officer is satisfied that there is a real and imminent risk of a breach of the peace. However, when the police entered the home of Mrs McLeod, a very doughty litigant, and the Court of Appeal found that this was lawful (*McLeod v Commissioner of Police* [1994] 4 All E.R. 553), the Strasbourg Court held that the entry was disproportionate, and awarded Mrs McLeod satisfaction (but not damages) (*McLeod v United Kingdom* [1998] 2 F.L.R. 1048).

Section 19: Cowan, sentenced to $12\frac{1}{2}$ years for offences against children brought suit against the police for having seized, after lawfully arresting him, the car in which the offences were allegedly committed. [1999] Times L.R. 632. Statutory authority for the seizure was dubious, since the Act defined "premises" as including a vehicle and gave power to seize anything on the premises but not the premises themselves (*i.e.* the vehicle). More worrying than an interpretation favourable to the police (moveable premises could be seized) is the aside that quite apart from statute the common law gave the police power to seize the vehicle. This must be based on the disgraceful decision in *Chic Fashions (West Wales) v Jones* (above) which should be held to have been displaced by PACE. Indeed that was what the Divisional Court held in *R (Rottman) v Commissioner of Police* [2001] EWHC Admin 576, where Brooke L.J. said "I find it quite impossible to interpret Part II of PACE as providing any saving for the common law power [to search premises on effecting an arrest] . . . While it is true that s.18 contains no provision comparable to s.17(5) ('all the rules of common law under which a constable has power to enter premises without a warrant are hereby abolished'), it appears to me that Parliament intended s.18 to provide in codified form for the full extent of a constable's power to enter and search premises after an arrest (for the purposes identified in that section), and intended it to be limited to police inquiries into domestic offences." But the House of Lords (Lord Hope dissenting) held to the contrary [2002] 2 A.C. 692, and resoundingly endorsed *Chic Fashions* (above) and its younger brother (same father in law), *Ghani v Jones* [1970] 1 Q.B. 693.

Section 24: The existence of reasonable grounds is a question for the court and not for the jury. *Ward v Chief Constable* [1997] Times L.R. 660.

Section 24(5): Compare subsections 5 and 6. The restriction on the citizen's right to arrest a suspect (namely that the arrestable offence has actually been committed) stems from *Walters v WH Smith & Sons* [1914] 1 K.B. 595. See *Davidson v Chief Constable*, above, p.342, *R. v Self* [1992] 3 All E.R. 476 and the critical note by Spencer, [1992] Camb.L.J. 405.

Section 25: If a constable makes an arrest for an offence which he mistakenly believes to be arrestable ("You're nicked for obstruction") he cannot invoke the general arrest conditions, and this is true even if good grounds for arrest or detention were, to his knowledge, available. *Edwards v DPP* (1993) 97 Cr.App.R. 301: "giving correct information as to the reason for an arrest is a matter of the utmost constitutional significance." Motive is apparently different from reason, since it has been held that an arrest otherwise justified is not rendered unlawful by the fact that it is motivated by a collateral purpose, as in *R. v Chalkley* [1998] 2 All E.R. 155 where the police wanted the person arrested out of the way so that they could plant a surveillance device.

Section 25(6): Anyone may stop a person committing a breach of the peace (*Albert v Lavin* [1982] A.C. 546). Perhaps "arrest" is not quite the right word to describe the act of using reasonable force for this purpose, but it was used by the Court of Appeal in *R. v Howell* [1982] Q.B. 416 at 427: " . . . the word 'disturbance' when used in isolation cannot constitute a breach of the peace. We are emboldened to say that there is a breach of the peace whenever harm is actually done or is likely to be done to a person or in his presence to his property or a person is in fear of being so harmed through an assault, an affray, a riot, an unlawful assembly or other disturbance. It is for this breach of the peace, when done in his presence, or the reasonable apprehension of it that a constable, or anyone else, may arrest an offender without warrant." Lord Denning's observation in *R. v Chief Constable of Devon, Ex p.Central Elec. Generating Board* that it is a breach of the peace "whenever a person who is lawfully carrying out work is unlawfully and physically prevented by another from doing it" has been held erroneous in *Percy v DPP* [1995] 3 All E.R. 124 which confirmed *R. v Howell* and applied it to cases of binding over by magistrates who must now find that violence creating a real risk of breach of the peace was beyond reasonable doubt a natural consequence of the defendant's conduct. *Nicol v DPP* ([1995] Times L.R. 607) has added that the risk of breach of the peace must be due to the unreasonable conduct of the defendant rather than to the unreasonable reactions of others. Belief in the imminence of a breach of the peace must be reasonable, as it was not on the facts of *Foulkes v Chief Constable* [1998] 3 All E.R. 705 where the person apprehended was intent on reentering the family home against the wishes of his wife who had locked him out. Beldam L.J. said (at 711) "There must, I consider, be a sufficiently real and present threat to the peace to justify the extreme step of depriving of his liberty a citizen who is not at the time acting unlawfully."

Section 26 (not quoted) abolishes all other statutory powers of arrest with warrant except those granted in the 23 enactments listed in Sch.2.

Section 28(3): Did Purchas L.J. accurately reflect the terms of this provision when he said, in *Abbassy v Comm'r of Police* [1990] 1 All E.R. 193 at 202 "The question whether the person arrested was reasonably informed of the reason for that arrest is ultimately a question for the jury."

In *Ghafar v Chief Constable* (CA, May 12, 2000) G was driving without wearing a seat-belt. When the police asked him for his name and address he refused to give them, and said he had no driving licence to indicate his identity. He was then arrested with the words "until I can verify your name and address". It was enough to justify the arrest that an offence (not wearing a seat-belt) had apparently been committed and that one of the general arrest conditions (failure to give name and address) had occurred, and this had been communicated to the claimant, so that there had been compliance with s.28(3).

The requirements of s.28(3) were not, however, met in *Wilson v Chief Constable* (CA, Nov 23, 2000, Thorpe L.J. dissenting). The claimant was reasonably suspected of having cashed a forged cheque at a bank. Prior to his arrest for theft he was asked only where he had been at the relevant time and whether he had been into a bank. It was held, reversing the trial judge, that the arrest was unlawful (for the twelve minutes before the full reasons were given in the police station): where the facts were known to the police and could have been made known to arresting officers, it was unfair to arrest for an unidentified offence that took place at some unspecified time and place. An arresting officer's minimum obligation was to give a suspect sufficient information as to the nature of the arrest to allow the suspect sufficient opportunity to respond."

Section 28(3) makes it clear that an arrest is not lawful unless the person arrested is informed of the reason for the arrest as soon as practicable. The detention under arrest becomes lawful when the reasons are given, and no damages may be awarded for any subsequent period: *Lewis v Chief Constable* [1991] 1 All E.R. 206, CA. More problematic is the holding of the Divisional Court that a policeman who fails to give reasons when practicable may nevertheless prosecute the arrestee for assaulting him in the execution of his duty prior to that time: *DPP v Hawkins* [1988] 3 All E.R. 673. What would be the case of an assault between the time when it became practicable to give reasons and the time when they were actually given?

Note that in a prosecution for obstructing the police in connection with an arrest it is for the police to prove that the arrest obstructed was lawful (*Riley v DPP* [1990] Crim. L.R. 422); furthermore, a police constable who lays hands on a person he mistakenly believes to have been arrested by a colleague is acting outside the course of his duty, and consequently cannot complain of being struck (*Kerr v DPP* [1994] Times L.R. 459).

Section 31: What is the mischief against which this section is directed?

Further Notes:

1. The Act deals with summary arrests, but there may be problems with warrants also. In *McGrath v Chief Constable* [2001] UKHL 39 a person properly arrested in Scotland falsely gave his name as that of the claimant, and it was under that name that the villain was charged and pleaded guilty. He jumped bail and a warrant was issued in the name of the claimant, and he was arrested as he got off the boat from Ireland. Though the claimant was not the person charged, whom the sheriff wished to have arrested, the House of Lords, reversing the Court of Appeal of Northern Ireland, dismissed the claim for false imprisonment. It treated *Evans* (below, p.385) as irrelevant, as involving a mistake of law on the part of the governor, whereas here there was a mistake of fact, and relying on *Hoye v Bush* from 1840, which hardly seems relevant, since it decided that the arrest of the right person was wrongful, since it was not he but his father who was named in the warrant. It is intolerable that a person not intended to be arrested should have no redress when he is arrested.

2. The same should be true when a person is arrested for something which was not, as the police thought, an offence at all (certainly if a mistake of law is to be treated differently from a mistake of fact). That was the case in *Percy v Hall* [1997] Q.B. 924 where the bye-law under which the arrest was effected (for the

150th time) was later held invalid. It should be an irrelevance that the police were not at fault, given that the claimant was not at liberty, and should have been. *Percy v Hall*, outrageous though it is, has not been disavowed.

3. In one case police had the impertinence to contend that a person cannot complain of the unlawfulness of his arrest or detention if he subsequently pleads guilty to the offence in question. The trial judge actually accepted this monstrous contention, and the reversal by the Court of Appeal was extremely unenthusiastic. It is clear that a plea of guilty prejudices one's chances of a jury trial against the police: *Hill v Chief Constable of South Yorkshire* [1990] 1 All E.R. 1046, in which Purchas L.J. remarked that "where statutory provisions which provide rights to police constables to interfere with the liberty of the subject are concerned those provisions ought to be construed strictly against those purporting to exercise those rights."

4. In *Simpson v Chief Constable* [1991] Times L.R. 121 a coal-miner who had been convicted of maliciously wounding a policeman sued for assault by the same policeman. The trial judge and one member of the Court of Appeal would have dismissed the claim on the ground that it was an abuse of court procedure, as an attempt to question the final decision of another court. This device had been used successfully in *Hunter* (above, p.188) where the Birmingham Six were prevented from raising in a civil court the question whether the police had beaten them up in order to extract their confessions. *Some* final decisions should be subjected to collateral as well as frontal attack!

Simpson also made the point that an arrest was not rendered unlawful simply because undue force was used by the arrester: though an action for assault may well succeed, no claim for false imprisonment lies in such circumstances and therefore there will be no right to trial by jury. (County Courts Act 1984, s.66(3)).

PACE gives the citizen other rights, invasion of which does not constitute a trespass, such as the right to consult a solicitor (s.58), to have a person informed of the arrest (s.56), to have copies of material seized by the police (s.22). If contraventions of such rights are to be actionable the citizen must persuade the court that a claim for breach of statutory duty arises (and also prove that appropriate damage ensued). On this the Act is silent, but s.67(10) states that breach of the Code of Practice, while admissible in evidence, gives rise to no civil claim. In Part IV of PACE, which concerns detention by the police, s.34(1) lays down that "A person arrested for an offence shall not be kept in police detention except in accordance with the provisions of this Part of this Act." In a case where the requisite review of custody was not carried out in time, "The respondent's claim was not for damages for breach of duty to carry out a review at 5.25 a.m. but for false imprisonment". *Roberts v Chief Constable* [1999] 2 All E.R. 326.

Indirect Imprisonment

It is not only the detainer who may be liable for a person's loss of liberty: quite apart from malicious prosecution (below, p.628) maliciously to procure a person's arrest is actionable (*Roy v Prior* [1970] 2 All E.R. 729, H.L.) as is the malicious procurement of a search warrant—*Gibbs v Rea* [1998] A.C. 786, PC) and indeed there may be liability for negligently causing a prolongation of detention, as the police discovered when in delivering to prison a person sentenced to nine days they supplied the governor with a document suggesting erroneously that the detention had started on that very day, with the result that the plaintiff was released later than was proper. *Clarke v Chief Constable* [1999] Times L.R. 440.

CRIMINAL LAW ACT 1967

3.—(1) A person may use such force as is reasonable in the circumstances in the prevention of crime, or in effecting or assisting in the lawful arrest of offenders or suspected offenders or of persons unlawfully at large.

(2) Subsection (1) above shall replace the rules of the common law on the question when force used for a purpose mentioned in the subsection is justified by that purpose.

MAGISTRATES' COURTS ACT 1980

125D. . . .

(2) A warrant to which this subsection applies . . . may be executed by a constable even though it is not in his possession at the time.

(3) Subsection (2) above applies to

(a) a warrant to arrest a person in connection with an offence . . .

(4) Where by virtue of this section a warrant is executed by a person not in possession of it, it shall, on the demand of the person arrested, committed or detained . . . be shown to him as soon as practicable.

JUSTICES OF THE PEACE ACT 1997

51.—No action shall lie against any justice of the peace or justice's clerk in respect of any act or omission of his—

(a) in the execution of his duty
    (i) as such a justice; or
    (ii) as such a clerk exercising, by virtue of any statutory provision, any of the functions of a single justice; and
(b) with regard to any matter within his jurisdiction.

52.—An action shall lie against any justice of the peace or justice's clerk in respect of any act or omission of his—

(a) in the purported execution of his duty
    (i) as such a justice; or
    (ii) as such a clerk exercising, by virtue of any statutory

provision, any of the functions of a single justice; but

(b) with regard to any matter which is not within his jurisdiction if, but only if, it is proved that he acted in bad faith.

Court orders

Imprisonment is of course justified by a court order, much as arrest is justified by a warrant. But the matter is not entirely straightforward.

Suppose that the order is vacated on appeal: the Strasbourg court has said that "A period of detention will in principle be lawful if it is carried out pursuant to a court order. A subsequent finding that the court erred under domestic law in making the order will not necessarily retrospectively affect the validity of the intervening period of detention." *Benham* (1996) 22 E.H.R.R. 293 at 322. We shall note later, however, that a hospital was held liable in trespass for performing an operation which a judge had declared lawful. See *St. George's NHS Trust v S* [1998] 3 All E.R. 673 at 702 (below, p.398).

R. v Governor of Brockhill Prison, Ex p.Evans (No.2) [1998] 4 All E.R. 993, CA, is a difficult case. In 1982 a certain meaning was attributed by the Divisional Court to the rather obscure statutory provisions for the computation of the permissible period of detention of a person who, after being in custody pending trial, was sentenced for several different offences. In 1996 the Divisional Court reinterpreted those provisions with the result of shortening the period of permissible detention. Between the dates of the two conflicting decisions the plaintiff was held in prison for a period which was perfectly proper under the view prevailing at the time but longer than that permitted by the subsequent reinterpretation of the law. The governor was held liable: the plaintiff had been kept in durance vile for 59 days more than was now recognised to be lawful. Lord Woolf M.R. said this (at 996): "The appeal raises issues of importance involving two principles which are deeply embedded in our law. The first is that any authoritative decision of the courts stating what is the law operates retrospectively. The decision does not only state what the law is from the date of the decision, it states what it has always been. This is the position even if in setting out the law the court overrules an earlier decision which took a totally different view of the law. The second principle is that a person imprisoned without lawful authority is entitled to damages irrespective of any question of fault on the part of the person responsible for the imprisonment."

The House of Lords upheld the Court of Appeal's judgment for the claimant, emphasising that false imprisonment was a tort of strict liability and that it was irrelevant that the governor was blameless: he had made what was later to be held to be a mistake. *R. v Governor of Brockhill Prison, Ex p.Evans (No.2)* [2001] 2 A.C. 19.

However in *Olutu v Home Office* [1997] 1 All E.R. 385, CA, the governor of the prison received the plaintiff under a court order which was valid until replaced by a subsequent court order to which the plaintiff was entitled but which the governor was under no duty to procure, that being the duty of the CPS. No such order was sought. Although the continued detention of the plaintiff was unlawful the governor was not liable, since the existing court order protected him, and the CPS was not liable since their statutory duty entailed no civil liability for breach.

That is by no means the only case where a person unlawfully imprisoned went without redress. In *Quinlan v Governor of Swaleside Prison* [2003] 1 All E.R. 1173 the judge in the Crown Court couldn't do his sums and sentenced the claimant to two years and six months imprisonment instead of the intended two years and three months. Owing to the characteristic bureaucratic incompetence of the Criminal Appeal Office this was not brought to the notice of the courts until the two years and six months had been served. There was no liability (a) on the governor, because the court order as written justified his keeping, indeed required him to keep, the claimant confined for the period stated in the order, or (b) the Registrar, because he was protected by the Crown Proceedings Act 1947, s.2(5) which provides that "No proceedings shall lie against the Crown . . . in respect of anything done or omitted to be done by a person while discharging or purporting to discharge . . . and responsibilities which he has in connection with the execution of judicial process."

It is manifestly wrong that a person who was locked up when he should have been at liberty should obtain no damages, and it is quite unsatisfactory to hold that the person locking him up was not liable because he was not at fault and that those who were at fault are not liable. The governor should be held liable; the money will come from public funds. We shall see later that a similar problem exists with regard to arrest.

CIVIL PROCEDURE ACT 1997

7. (1) The court may make an order under this section for the purpose of securing, in the case of any existing or proposed proceedings in the court—

(a) the preservation of evidence which is or may be relevant, or
(b) the preservation of property which is or may be the subject-matter of the proceedings or as to which any question arises or may arise in the proceedings.

(3) Such an order may direct any person to permit any person described in the order, or secure that any person so described is permitted—

(a) to enter premises in England and Wales, and
(b) while on the premises, to take in accordance with the terms of the order any of the following steps.

(4) Those steps are—

(a) to carry out a search for or inspection of anything described in the order, and
(b) to make or obtain a copy, photograph, sample or other record of anything so described.

Note:

This puts on a statutory footing the judicial invention of "Anton Piller orders", now called "search orders". Since the role of the policeman was played by the plaintiff's solicitor, such orders were capable of abuse, even though the applicant had to give an undertaking in damages which might render him liable for excessive or oppressive conduct (*Columbia Picture Industries v Robinson* [1986] 3 All E.R. 338 at 371, where the judge said that he would not regard as "freely and effectively given" any consent to the removal of property not particularly specified in the order unless the party's own solicitor were present).

In *Lock International v Beswick* [1989] 3 All E.R. 373 at 384 Hoffmann J. said:

"The making of an intrusive order even against a guilty defendant is contrary to normal principles of justice and can only be done where there is a paramount need to prevent a denial of justice to the plaintiff. The absolute extremity of the court's powers is to permit a search of a defendant's dwelling house, with the humiliation and family distress which that frequently involves."

Not long thereafter the Vice-Chancellor was faced with a case where a woman, in bed with her children but otherwise alone, was knocked up at 7.15 a.m. by a man unknown to her waving an Anton Piller order, demanding admission and forbidding her to speak to anyone (for a week!) except a lawyer (naturally unavailable at that hour). The solicitors paid up £10,000 for each individual and £2,000 for each company involved. While accepting that "in suitable and strictly limited cases, Anton Piller orders furnish courts with a valuable aid in their efforts to do justice between two parties" the Vice-Chancellor laid down stern conditions regarding their exercise (*Universal Thermosensors v Hibben* [1992] 3 All E.R. 257).

The procedure in one case came before the European Commission for Human Rights, which by the barest of majorities (6–5) held that there had been no unjustifiable infringement of Art.8 of the Convention: "Everyone has the right to respect for his private and family life, his home and his correspondence." *Chappell v U.K.* [1989] 2 E.C.H.R. 543.

HAGUE v DEPUTY GOVERNOR OF PARKHURST PRISON
WELDON v HOME OFFICE

House of Lords [1992] 1 A.C. 58; [1991] 3 W.L.R. 340; [1991] 3 All E.R. 733 (noted [1992] Camb.L.J. 12)

Action by convicts for unlawful treatment in prison

Lord Jauncey of Tullichettle: My Lords, these two appeals arise out of actions by convicted prisoners in respect of incidents during their confinement. In *Hague's* case the prisoner sought judicial review of a decision of the deputy governor of Parkhurst Prison to segregate him and thereafter to transfer him to Wormwood Scrubs for continued segregation. He claimed certain declarations as well as damages for false imprisonment. The Divisional Court dismissed the application (see [1990] 3 W.L.R. 1210) but on appeal the Court of Appeal held, *inter alia* (1) that he was entitled to a declaration that his continued segregation in Wormwood Scrubs on the authority of the deputy governor of Parkhurst was unlawful, (2) that a breach of the Prison Rules 1964 (SI 1964/388) could not found a private law claim for damages by a prisoner, and (3) that a convicted prisoner could only succeed in an action for false imprisonment in respect of his detention in prison if he was kept in intolerable conditions which, so far as Hague was concerned, was not the case (see [1990] 3 All E.R. 687). In *Weldon's* case the prisoner claimed damages for false imprisonment in respect of his confinement overnight in a strip cell in the prison in which he was serving a sentence. The Court of Appeal dismissed an appeal against a refusal to strike out the claim, being of the view that the facts disclosed an arguable case of false imprisonment either on the grounds that he had been unlawfully deprived of his residual liberty or that he had been kept in intolerable conditions. Hague appealed on the grounds (1) that a breach of the Prison Rules sounded in damages, and (2) that the reasons given by the Court of Appeal in *Weldon's* case for refusing to strike out the claim were sound. The Home Office appealed in *Weldon's* case on the ground that a convicted prisoner serving a sentence could not maintain an action of damages for false imprisonment against the prison authorities. There was no challenge to the declaration granted to Hague by the Court of Appeal. . . .

Lord Bridge: . . . The starting point is section 12(1) of the Prison Act 1952 which provides:

"A prisoner, whether sentenced to imprisonment or committed to prison on remand pending trial or otherwise, may be lawfully confined in a prison."

This provides lawful authority for the restraint of the prisoner within the defined bounds of the prison by the governor of the prison, who has the legal custody of the prisoner under section 13, or by any prison officer acting with the governor's authority. Can the prisoner then complain that his legal rights are infringed by a restraint which confines him at any particular time within a particular part of the prison? It seems to me that the reality of prison life demands a negative answer to this question. Certainly in the ordinary closed prison the ordinary prisoner will at any time of day or night be in a particular part of the prison, not because that is where he chooses to be, but because that is where the prison regime requires him to be. He will be in his cell, in the part of the prison where he is required to work, in the exercise yard, eating meals, attending education classes or enjoying whatever recreation is permitted, all in the appointed place and at the appointed time and all in accordance with a more or less rigid regime to which he must conform. Thus the concept of the prisoner's "residual liberty" as a species of freedom of movement within the prison enjoyed as a legal right which the prison authorities cannot lawfully restrain seems to me quite illusory. The prisoner is at all times lawfully restrained within closely defined bounds and if he is kept in a segregated cell, at a time when, if the rules had not been misapplied, he would be in the company of other prisoners in the workshop, at the dinner table or elsewhere, this is not the deprivation of his liberty of movement, which is the essence of the tort of false imprisonment, it is the substitution of one form of restraint for another.

In my opinion, to hold a prisoner entitled to damages for false imprisonment on the ground that he has been subject to a restraint upon his movement which was not in accordance with the Prison Rules would be, in effect, to confer on him under a different legal label a cause of action for breach of statutory duty under the rules. Having reached the conclusion that it was not the intention of the rules to confer such a right, I am satisfied that the right cannot properly be asserted in the alternative guise of a claim to damages for false imprisonment.

I turn next to the question posed by the example of a prisoner locked in a shed by fellow prisoners. I think the short answer to this question is given by Taylor L.J. who said in *Hague*'s case [1990] 3 All E.R. 687 at 707:

> "In such a situation an action for false imprisonment would surely lie (for what it was worth), since the fellow prisoners would have no defence under section 12 of the Prison Act 1952."

The prisoner locked in the shed is certainly restrained within defined bounds and it is *nihil ad rem* that if he were not locked in the shed, he would be locked in his cell or restrained in accordance with the prison regime in some other part of the prison. The restraint in the shed is unlawful because the fellow prisoners acted without the authority of the governor and it is only the governor, who has the legal custody of the prisoner, and persons acting with the authority of the governor who can rely on the provisions of s.12(1).

This consideration also leads to the conclusion that a prison officer who acts in bad faith by deliberately subjecting a prisoner to a restraint which he knows he has no authority to impose may render himself personally liable to an action for false imprisonment as well as committing the tort of misfeasance in public office. Lacking the authority of the governor, he also lacks the protection of s.12(1). . . .

There remains the question whether an otherwise lawful imprisonment may be rendered unlawful by reason only of the conditions of detention.

I sympathise entirely with the view that the person lawfully held in custody who is subjected to intolerable conditions ought not to be left without a remedy against his custodian, but the proposition that the conditions of detention may render the detention itself unlawful raises formidable difficulties. If the proposition be sound, the corollary must be that when the conditions of detention deteriorate to the point of intolerability, the detainee is entitled immediately to go free. It is impossible, I think, to define with any precision what would amount to intolerable conditions for this purpose. . . . The law is certainly left in a very unsatisfactory state if the legality or otherwise of detaining a person who in law is and remains liable to detention depends on such an imprecise criterion and may vary from time to time as the conditions of his detention change.

The logical solution to the problem, I believe, is that if the conditions of an otherwise lawful detention are truly intolerable, the law ought to be capable of providing a remedy directly related to those conditions without characterising the fact of the detention itself as unlawful. I see no real difficulty in saying that the law can provide such a remedy. Whenever one person is lawfully in the custody of another, the custodian owes a duty of care to the detainee. If the custodian negligently allows, or *a fortiori*, if he deliberately causes, the detainee to suffer in any way in his health he will be in breach of that duty. But short of anything that could properly be described as a physical injury or an impairment of health, if a person lawfully detained is kept in conditions which cause him for the time being physical pain or a degree of discomfort which can properly be described as intolerable, I believe that could and should be treated as a breach of the custodian's duty of care for which the law should award damages. For this purpose it is quite unnecessary to attempt any definition of the criterion of intolerability. It would be a question of fact and degree in any case which came before the court to determine whether the conditions to which a detainee had been subjected were such as to warrant an award of damages for the discomfort he had suffered. In principle I believe it is acceptable for the law to provide a remedy on this basis. . . . In practice the problem is perhaps not very likely to arise.

Lord Ackner: My Lords, a person lawfully held in custody who is subjected to intolerable conditions, must, of course, have a remedy against his custodian. This clearly can include the following: (a) an action in tort against a prison authority for damages for negligence where, for example, the intolerable conditions cause him to suffer injury to his health; (b) where the facts fit, an action in tort for damages for assault; (c) where malice can be established, an action for misfeasance in the exercise of a public office; and (d) the termination of such conditions by judicial review.

I accept, however . . . that an otherwise lawful imprisonment is not rendered unlawful by reason only of the conditions of detention, thereby providing a prisoner with a potential action for the tort of false imprisonment. . . .

Note:
    The Human Rights Act empowers and requires our courts to provide prisoners with a remedy if they have been subjected to "inhuman or degrading treatment to punishment" contrary to Art.3.

Preliminary Note:
    The next case is included because it highlights the relevance of the common law of trespass and its defences to the exercise of civil liberties and the maintenance of public order in the face of contested progress. It must be noted immediately that, for all that Lord Denning describes his judgment, characteristically monosyllabic in style and authoritarian in substance, as a "definitive legal mandate" to the Chief Constable, it quite misrepresents the law and is cavalier in its treatment of precedent.

R. v CHIEF CONSTABLE OF DEVON AND CORNWALL, Ex p.CENTRAL ELECTRICITY GENERATING BOARD

Court of Appeal [1982] Q.B. 458; [1981] 3 W.L.R. 967; [1981] 3 All E.R. 826

Action to require police to remove demonstrators inhibiting petitioner's performance of statutory functions on private land of third party

Lord Denning M.R.: The coast of Cornwall is beautiful. Much of the inland is ugly. It is despoiled by china clay workings. Not far from them there is open farmland with small villages dotted around. Pleasant enough but not outstanding. The Central Electricity Generating Board view this as a possible site for a nuclear power station. They wish to survey it so as to compare it with other possible sites. The farmer objected to the survey. So did the villagers. They took up a stand against it. But on being told by the courts that it was unlawful for them to obstruct the survey, they desisted. They moved off the site. They obeyed the law. But then groups of outsiders came in from far and wide. They had no local connection with the place. They came anonymously. They would not disclose their identity. They would not give their names and addresses. They flouted the law. They wilfully obstructed the survey. Can these newcomers be moved off the site so that they obstruct no more? Can the board move them off? Or, if the board cannot do it, can the police be called in to help? The chief constable feels that he cannot use his force for the purpose. It would put his men in a bad light with the local inhabitants. What then is to be done?

[His Lordship quoted from the affidavit of Chief Inspector Bradley: "In the circumstances there is no reason whatsoever for the Police to suspect or have any grounds to believe that a breach of the peace is anticipated, the demonstrators are acting in a very "passive" manner and in no way are they committing a breach of the peace."]

Now I am afraid that I cannot share the view taken by the police. English law upholds to the full the right of people to demonstrate and to make their views known so long as all is done peaceably and in good order (see *Hubbard v Pitt* ([1976] Q.B. 161). But the conduct of these demonstrators is not peaceful or in good order. By wilfully obstructing the operations of the board, they are deliberately breaking the law. Every time they lie down in front of a rig, or put their foot or umbrella down to stop a hole being drilled, or sit on the hole, they are guilty of an offence for which they could be fined up to £50 for every occasion. They must know it is unlawful. They must know of the injunctions granted against the farmers and the local residents. Yet they persist in going on with their unlawful conduct, knowing full well that it is unlawful. Is the law powerless to stop them? Can these people avoid the process of the law by not giving their names and addresses, so that neither a summons nor a writ can reach them? Can they avoid it by bringing in one group after another? I think not. These obstructors should not be in any better position than those against whom injunctions have been obtained. The arm of the law is long enough to reach them despite their attempts to avoid it.

In the first place, I must say that the leaflet issued by the organisers is completely erroneous. The board and their contractors are entitled to manhandle the obstructors so as to move them out of the way. Every person who is prevented from carrying out his lawful pursuits is entitled to use self-help so as to prevent any unlawful obstruction: see *Holmes v Bagge* (1853) 118 E.R. 629 at 631 *per* Lord Campbell C.J. He must, of course, not use more force than is reasonably necessary; but there is no doubt whatever that he can use force to do it.

I go further. I think that the conduct of these people, their criminal obstruction, is itself a breach of the peace. There is a breach of the peace whenever a person who is lawfully carrying out his work is unlawfully and physically prevented by another from doing it. He is entitled by law peacefully to go on with his work on his lawful occasions. If anyone unlawfully and physically obstructs the worker, by lying down or chaining himself to a rig or the like, he is guilty of a breach of the peace. Even if this were not enough, I think that their unlawful conduct gives rise to a reasonable apprehension of a breach of the peace. It is at once likely that the lawful worker will resort to self-help by removing the obstructor by force from the vicinity of the work so that he obstructs no longer. He will lift the recumbent obstructor from the ground. This removal would itself be an assault and battery, unless it was justified as being done by way of self-help. Long years ago Holt C.J. declared that "the least touching of another in anger is a battery" (see *Cole v Turner* (1704) 90 E.R. 958). *Salmond on Torts* (17th ed., 1977), p.120 adds that even anger is not essential. An "unwanted kiss may be a battery." So also the lifting up of a recumbent obstructor would be a battery unless justified as being done in the exercise of self-help. But in deciding whether there is a breach of the peace or the apprehension of it, the law does not go into the rights or wrongs of the matter, or whether it is justified by self-help or not. Suffice it that the peace is broken or is likely to be broken by one or another of those present. With the result that any citizen can, and certainly any police officer can, intervene to stop breaches.

If I were wrong on this point, if there was here no breach of the peace or apprehension of it, it would give a licence to every obstructor and every passive resister in the land. He would be able to cock a snook at the law as these groups have done. Public works of the greatest national importance could be held up indefinitely. This cannot be. The rule of law must prevail. . . .

Notwithstanding all that I have said, I would not give any orders to the chief constable or his men. It is of the first importance that the police should decide on their own responsibility what action should be taken in any particular situation.

It is plain that the board can use self-help so as to get rid of this wilful obstruction. To me the obvious solution would be to erect a fence around their place of work, a barbed-wire entanglement if need be, so as to prevent the obstructors getting anywhere near the operations. This is just common sense, so that they should not be a danger to themselves or to others. If they should try and break through the fence, or rush it, the battle would be on. There would be the clearest possible breach of the peace, the police would move in, arrest them, and take them before the magistrates. So I would say to the board, put up a fence and get on with your work. Stand no more of this obstruction.

Lawton L.J.: This appeal has two aspects, the general and the particular. The general can be described as follows: can those who disapprove of the exercise by a statutory body of statutory powers frustrate their exercise on private property by adopting unlawful means, not involving violence, such as lying down in front of moving vehicles, chaining themselves to equipment and sitting down where work has to be done. Such means are sometimes referred to as passive resistance. The answer is an emphatic No. If it were otherwise, there would be no rule of law. Parliament decides who shall have statutory powers and under what conditions and for what purpose they shall be used. Those who do not like what Parliament has done can protest, but they must do so in a lawful manner. What cannot be tolerated, and certainly not by the police, are protests which are not made in a lawful manner.

A statutory body can use the minimum of force reasonably necessary to remove those obstructing the exercise of their statutory powers from the area where work has to be carried out. This is the common law remedy of abatement by self-help; but it would involve the statutory body taking the law into its own hands and is, as Lord Wright said in *Sedleigh-Denfield v O'Callaghan* ([1940] A.C. 880 at 911), much to be discouraged. There are many reasons why self-help should be discouraged. Disputes are likely to arise whether the minimum amount of force reasonably necessary was used. In my judgment, based on my understanding of human nature and a long experience of the administration of criminal justice, the most important reason for not using self-help, if any other remedy can be used effectively, is that as soon as one person starts to, or makes to, lay hands on another there is likely to be a breach of the peace.

On the evidence it seems likely that the board will have to use self-help if they are to perform their statutory duties at Luxulyan. Civil proceedings have been ineffective. Prosecutions for offences under ss.280 and 281(2) of the Town and Country Planning Act 1971 would serve no useful purpose. When they do decide to use self-help and fix a day for doing so, they should inform the local police who will no doubt be present in sufficient numbers to ensure as best they can that breaches of the peace do not occur and, if they do, that those responsible are removed from the site.

In my judgment this is not a case for making an order of mandamus against the chief constable. It is a case for co-operation between the board and the chief constable and the use of plenty of common sense by all concerned, including those who are on the site obstructing the board's functions.

I would dismiss the appeal.

Notes:

1. As authority for his observation that "Every person who is prevented from carrying out his lawful pursuits is entitled to use self-help so as to prevent any unlawful obstruction" Lord Denning invokes *Holmes v Bagge*. What actually happened in that case was that the plaintiff was making a peaceful protest against a game of cricket by lying down on the pitch. He was gently removed by the visiting team and gently deposited beyond the boundary. Nevertheless his claim for battery was successful. Hardly a good authority for Lord Denning's proposition!

2. He also said that "There is a breach of the peace whenever a person who is lawfully carrying out his work is unlawfully and physically prevented by another from doing it". This has subsequently been described and disregarded as "erroneous" (*e.g. Percy v DPP* [1995] 3 All E.R. 124), but one may test it by considering another Victorian protester, Citizen Bird (*Bird v Jones*, above, p.337). In crossing Hammersmith Bridge Citizen Bird was unquestionably carrying out a lawful pursuit. Subaltern Jones physically and unlawfully obstructed him. Yet Citizen Bird was not allowed to "get rid of this wilful obstruction" by using self-help. Nor was there any suggestion that Subaltern Jones was guilty of breach of the peace by obstructing Citizen Bird; it would have been absurd to suggest it. Nor, as the Chief Constable had rightly supposed, were the Cornish protesters guilty of breach of the peace.

3. This cavalier attitude to the law seems to have been shared by the entire court. Templeman L.J., for example, states that "Any person who wilfully obstructs the board in the exercise of their powers also commits a tort" (at 837). Whatever tort can this be? Does he suppose that section 280(9) of the Town and Country Planning Act 1971 (now s.325(2) of the Town and Country Planning Act 1990), (the sole source of the incantation that the protesters' passive activities were "unlawful") gives a right of action in damages? Or was he obliquely predicting the majority decision of the Court of Appeal in *Minister of Transport v Williams* [1993] Times L.R. 627, that a person guilty of wilful obstruction under Highways Act 1980, s.303, was also guilty of the tort of causing loss by unlawful means and was therefore enjoinable, and then subject to the sanction, not provided for the offence itself, of imprisonment for breach of the injunction?

4. Lawton L.J. spoke of the "common law remedy of abatement by self-help". On the given facts one might well ask "Abatement of *what*?" The authority he cited related to the right of a person whose property was under threat from a situation on his neighbour's land to go on to that land to defuse the danger. Hardly a powerful analogy? The court's readiness to endorse self-help by the board, a public body, against conduct only doubtfully tortious contrasts displeasingly with their extreme reluctance in other cases to approve of self-help by a citizen who is undeniably the victim of a clear tort. See below, p.412.

5. Note that the police could now arrest the protesters under the general arrest conditions of PACE, s.25 (above, p.380). It appears that the Cornish protesters had the consent of the occupiers to be there. In the absence of such consent, what they did would now be a trespassory assembly (Criminal Justice and Public Order Act 1994, s.70, introducing new s.14A into the Public Order Act 1986). Indeed, two or more persons present on land in the open air "with the common purpose of . . . disrupting a lawful activity" may be arrested without warrant for not leaving or reentering when directed to leave, but again their presence must be trespassory (s.69). A single person is guilty of aggravated trespass and summarily arrestable if he trespasses on land in the open air and does "anything" with the intention of disrupting or obstructing a lawful activity there or on adjoining land (s.68).

Section 3.—Protection of the Weak-Minded

MENTAL HEALTH ACT 1983

136.—(1) If a constable finds in a place to which the public have access a person who appears to him to be suffering from mental disorder and to be in immediate need of care or control, the constable may, if he thinks it necessary to do so in the interests of that person or for the protection of other persons, remove that person to a place of safety within the meaning of section 135 above.

(2) A person removed to a place of safety under this section may be detained there for a period not exceeding 72 hours for the purpose of enabling him to be examined by a registered medical practitioner and to be interviewed by an approved social worker and of making any necessary arrangements for his treatment or care.

139.—(1) No person shall be liable, whether on the ground of want of jurisdiction or on any other ground, to any civil or criminal proceedings to which he would have been liable apart from this section in respect of any act purporting to be done in pursuance of this Act or any regulations or rules made under this Act, . . . unless the act was done in bad faith or without reasonable care.

(2) No civil proceedings shall be brought against any person in any court in respect of any such act without the leave of the High Court . . . ;

Note:
  Until 1983 s.139(2) continued with the words: "and the High Court shall not give leave under this section unless satisfied that there is substantial ground for the contention that the person to be proceeded against has acted in bad faith or without reasonable care." What do you infer from the omission of these words in 1983?

  Their effect can be noted in *Carter v Commissioner for Police* [1975] 2 All E.R. 33. Early one morning the plaintiff, who had been born in Jamaica, telephoned the police, as she had done on several previous occasions, to complain of the behaviour of her neighbours in the council block. Four or five policemen arrived and took her to the police station and then to a hospital where doctors found that she was not suffering from any mental disturbance and never had been. The plaintiff maintained that she was calm and collected throughout, while the police asserted that she had been screaming and shouting. Cairns L.J. said: "What seems to me impressive in this case is that one has all these police officers in complete agreement with each other."(!) Lawton L.J. said: " . . . what possible explanation can there be for these police officers behaving as they are said to have behaved? There could not be any rational explanation for them to take a woman who was calm, collected and had done nothing wrong at all, and a stranger to them, into custody." The plaintiff was refused leave to sue (and thus to cross-examine the police).

Re F, F v WEST BERKSHIRE H.A.

House of Lords [1990] 2 A.C. 1; [1989] 2 W.L.R. 1025; [1989] 2 All E.R. 545
(noted (1990) 53 M.L.R. 91)

Lawfulness of sterilisation of subnormal adult incapable of safe
pregnancy or motherhood

F, aged 36, had been a voluntary in-patient in a mental hospital since she was 14. Sometimes aggressive, she could be happy, sad or afraid, but she had only a five-year-old's mental capacity and the verbal ability of a child of two. She was now having a sexual relationship with a male patient at the hospital, but would be quite unable to cope with pregnancy and parturition. As contraception by pills and devices would be either ineffective or dangerous, it was proposed to sterilise her by tying off her Fallopian tubes, a proceeding which all the judges agreed was in her best interests.

Lord Bridge of Harwich: . . . I propose an order in the following terms. (1) It is declared that the operation of sterilisation proposed to be performed on the plaintiff being in the existing circumstances in her best interests can lawfully be performed on her despite her inability to consent to it. . . .

  The issues canvassed in argument before your Lordships revealed the paucity of clearly defined principles in the common law which may be applied to determine the lawfulness of medical or surgical treatment given to a patient who for any reason, temporary or permanent, lacks the capacity to give or to communicate consent to that treatment. It seems to me to be axiomatic that treatment which is necessary to preserve the life, health or well-being of the patient may lawfully be given without consent. But, if a rigid criterion of necessity were to be applied to determine what is and what is not lawful in the treatment of the unconscious and the incompetent, many of those unfortunate enough to be deprived of the capacity to make or communicate rational decisions by accident, illness or unsoundness of mind might be deprived of treatment which it would be entirely beneficial for them to receive.

  Moreover, it seems to me of first importance that the common law should be readily intelligible to and applicable by all those who undertake the care of persons lacking the capacity to consent to treatment. It would be intolerable for members of the medical, nursing and other professions devoted to the care of the sick that, in caring for those lacking the capacity to consent to treatment, they should be put in the dilemma that, if they administer the treatment which they believe to be in the patient's best interests, acting with due skill and care, they run the risk of being held guilty of trespass to the person, but, if they withhold that treatment, they may be in breach of a duty of care owed to the patient. If those who undertake responsibility for the care of incompetent or unconscious patients administer curative or prophylactic treatment which they believe to be appropriate to the patient's existing condition of disease, injury or bodily malfunction or susceptibility to such a condition in the future, the lawfulness of that treatment should be judged by one standard, not two. It follows that if the professionals in question have acted with due skill and care, judged by the well-known test laid down in *Bolam v Friern Hospital Management Committee* [above, p.165] they should be immune from liability in trespass, just as they are immune from liability in negligence. The special considerations which apply in the case of the sterilisation of a woman who is physically perfectly healthy or of an operation on an organ transplant donor arise only because such treatment cannot be considered either curative or prophylactic.

Lord Goff of Chieveley: My Lords, the question in this case is concerned with the lawfulness of a proposed operation of sterilisation on the plaintiff, F, a woman of 36 years of age, who by reason of her mental incapacity is disabled from giving her consent to the operation. It is well established that, as a general rule, the performance of a medical operation on a person without his or her consent is unlawful, as constituting both the crime of battery and the tort of trespass to the person. Furthermore, before Scott Baker J. and the Court of Appeal, it was common ground between the parties that there was no power in the court to give consent on behalf of F to the proposed operation of sterilisation, or to dispense with the need for such consent.

It follows that, as was recognised in the courts below, if the operation on F is to be justified, it can only be justified on the applicable principles of common law. The argument of counsel revealed the startling fact that there is no English authority on the question whether as a matter of common law (and if so in what circumstances) medical treatment can lawfully be given to a person who is disabled by mental incapacity from consenting to it. Indeed, the matter goes further, for a comparable problem can arise in relation to persons of sound mind who are, for example, rendered unconscious in an accident or rendered speechless by a catastrophic stroke. All such persons may require medical treatment and, in some cases, surgical operations. All may require nursing care. In the case of mentally disordered persons, they may require care of a more basic kind, dressing, feeding and so on, to assist them in their daily life, as well as routine treatment by doctors and dentists. It follows that, in my opinion, it is not possible to consider in isolation the lawfulness of the proposed operation of sterilisation in the present case. It is necessary first to ascertain the applicable common law principles and then to consider the question of sterilisation against the background of those principles.

I start with the fundamental principle, now long established, that every person's body is inviolate. As to this, I do not wish to depart from what I myself said in the judgment of the Divisional Court in *Collins v Wilcock* [1984] 3 All E.R. 374 and in particular from the statement that the effect of this principle is that everybody is protected not only against physical injury but against any form of physical molestation.

Of course, as a general rule physical interference with another person's body is lawful if he consents to it; though in certain limited circumstances the public interest may require that his consent is not capable of rendering the act lawful. There are also specific cases where physical interference without consent may not be unlawful: lawful arrest, self-defence, the prevention of crime and so on. As I pointed out in *Collins v Wilcock* (at 378), a broader exception has been created to allow for the exigencies of everyday life: jostling in a street or some other crowded place, social contact at parties and such like. This exception has been said to be founded on implied consent, since those who go about in public places, or go to parties, may be taken to have impliedly consented to bodily contact of this kind. Today this rationalisation can be regarded as artificial; and, in particular, it is difficult to impute consent to those who, by reason of their youth or mental disorder, are unable to give their consent. For this reason, I consider it more appropriate to regard such cases as falling within a general exception embracing all physical contact which is generally acceptable in the ordinary conduct of everyday life.

In the old days it used to be said that, for a touching of another's person to amount to a battery, it had to be a touching "in anger" (see *Cole v Turner* (1704) 90 E.R. 948 *per* Holt C.J.); and it has recently been said that the touching must be "hostile" to have that effect (see *Wilson v Pringle* [above, p.348]). I respectfully doubt whether that is correct. A prank that gets out of hand, an over-friendly slap on the back, surgical treatment by a surgeon who mistakenly thinks that the patient has consented to it, all these things may transcend the bounds of lawfulness, without being characterised as hostile. Indeed, the suggested qualification is difficult to reconcile with the principle that any touching of another's body is, in the absence of lawful excuse, capable of amounting to a battery and a trespass. Furthermore, in the case of medical treatment, we have to bear well in mind the libertarian principle of self-determination which, to adopt the words of Cardozo J. (in *Schloendorff v Society of New York Hospital* (1914) 211 N.Y. 125 at 126), recognises that—

> "Every human being of adult years and sound mind has a right to determine what shall be done with his own body; and a surgeon who performs an operation without his patient's consent, commits an assault. . . . "

. . . On what principle can medical treatment be justified when given without consent? We are searching for a principle on which, in limited circumstances, recognition may be given to a need, in the interests of the patient, that treatment should be given to him in circumstances where he is (temporarily or permanently) disabled from consenting to it. It is this criterion of a need which points to the principle of necessity as providing justification.

That there exists in the common law a principle of necessity which may justify action which would otherwise be unlawful is not in doubt. But historically the principle has been seen to be restricted to two groups of cases, which have been called cases of public necessity and cases of private necessity. The former occurred when a man interfered with another man's property in the public interest, for example (in the days before we could dial 999 for the fire brigade) the destruction of another man's house to prevent the spread of a catastrophic fire, as indeed occurred in the Great Fire of London in 1666. The latter cases occurred when a man interfered with another's property to save his own person or property from imminent danger, for example when he entered on his neighbour's land without his consent in order to prevent the spread of fire onto his own land.

There is, however, a third group of cases, which is also properly described as founded on the principle of necessity and which is more pertinent to the resolution of the problem in the present case. These cases are concerned with action taken as a matter of necessity to assist another person without his consent. To give a simple example, a man who seizes another and forcibly drags him from the path of an oncoming vehicle, thereby saving him from injury or even death, commits no wrong. But there are many emanations of this principle to be found scattered through the books. These are concerned not only with the preservation of the life or health of the assisted person, but also with the preservation of his property (sometimes an animal, sometimes an ordinary chattel) and even to certain conduct on his behalf in the administration of his affairs. Where there is a pre-existing relationship between the parties, the intervener is usually said to act as an agent of necessity on behalf of the principal in whose interests he acts, and his action can often, with not too much artificiality, be referred to the pre-existing relationship between them. Whether the intervener may be entitled either to reimbursement or to remuneration raises separate questions which are not relevant to the present case.

We are concerned here with action taken to preserve the life, health or well-being of another who is unable to consent to it. Such action is sometimes said to be justified as arising from an emergency. . . . In truth, the relevance of an emergency is that it may give rise to a necessity to act in the interests of the assisted person without first obtaining his consent. Emergency is however not the criterion or even a prerequisite; it is simply a frequent origin of the necessity which impels intervention. The principle is one of necessity, not of emergency.

We can derive some guidance as to the nature of the principle of necessity from the cases on agency of necessity in mercantile law. . . . From them can be derived the basic requirements, applicable in these cases of necessity, that, to fall within the principle, not only (1) must there be a necessity to act when it is not practicable to communicate with the assisted person, but also (2) the action taken must be such as a reasonable person would in all the circumstances take, acting in the best interests of the assisted person.

On this statement of principle, I wish to observe that officious intervention cannot be justified by the principle of necessity. So intervention cannot be justified when another more appropriate person is available and willing to act; nor can it be justified when it is contrary to the known wishes of the assisted person, to the extent that he is capable of rationally forming such a wish. . . . But as a general rule, if the above criteria are fulfilled, interference with the assisted person's person or property (as the case may be) will not be unlawful. Take the example of a railway accident, in which injured passengers are trapped in the wreckage. It is this principle which may render lawful the actions of other citizens, railway staff, passengers or outsiders, who rush to give aid and comfort to the victims: the surgeon who amputates the limb of an unconscious passenger to free him from the wreckage; the ambulance man who conveys him to hospital; the doctors and nurses who treat him and care for him while he is still unconscious. Take the example of an elderly person who suffers a stroke which renders him incapable of speech or movement. It is by virtue of this principle that the doctor who treats him, the nurse who cares for him, even the relative or friend or neighbour who comes in to look after him will commit no wrong when he or she touches his body.

The two examples I have given illustrate, in the one case, an emergency and, in the other, a permanent or semi-permanent state of affairs. Another example of the latter kind is that of a mentally disordered person who is disabled from giving consent. I can see no good reason why the principle of necessity should not be applicable in his case as it is in the case of the victim of a stroke. Furthermore, in the case of a mentally disordered person, as in the case of a stroke victim, the permanent state of affairs calls for a wider range of care than may be requisite in an emergency which arises from accidental injury. When the state of affairs is permanent, or semi-permanent, action properly taken to preserve the life, health or well-being of the assisted person may well transcend such measures as surgical operation or substantial medical treatment and may extend to include such humdrum matters as routine medical or dental treatment, even simple care such as dressing and undressing and putting to bed.

The distinction I have drawn between cases of emergency and cases where the state of affairs is (more or less) permanent is relevant in another respect. We are here concerned with medical treatment, and I limit myself to cases of that kind. Where, for example, a surgeon performs an operation without his consent on a patient temporarily rendered unconscious in an accident, he should do no more than is reasonably required, in the best interests of the patient, before he recovers consciousness. I can see no practical difficulty arising from this requirement, which derives from the fact that the patient is expected before long to regain consciousness and can then be consulted about longer term measures. The point has however arisen in a more acute form where a surgeon, in the course of an operation, discovers some other condition which, in his opinion, requires operative treatment for which he has not received the patient's consent. In what circumstances he should operate forthwith, and in what circumstances he should postpone the further treatment until he has received the patient's consent, is a difficult matter . . . which it is not necessary for your Lordships to consider in the present case.

But where the state of affairs is permanent or semi-permanent, as may be so in the case of a mentally disordered person, there is no point in waiting to obtain the patient's consent. The need to care for him is obvious; and the doctor must then act in the best interests of his patient, just as if he had received his patient's consent so to do. Were this not so, much useful treatment and care could, in theory at least, be denied to the unfortunate. It follows that, on this point, I am unable to accept the view expressed by Neill L.J. in the Court of Appeal, that the treatment must be shown to have been necessary. Moreover, in such a case, as my noble and learned friend Lord Brandon has pointed out, a doctor who has assumed responsibility for the care of a patient may not only be treated as having the patient's consent to act, but also be under a duty so to act.

In these circumstances, it is natural to treat the deemed authority and the duty as interrelated. But I feel bound to express my opinion that, in principle, the lawfulness of the doctor's action is, at least in its origin, to be found in the principle of necessity. This can perhaps be seen most clearly in cases where there is no continuing relationship between doctor and patient. The "doctor in the house" who volunteers to assist a lady in the audience who, overcome by the drama or by the heat in the theatre, has fainted away is impelled to act by no greater duty than that imposed by his own Hippocratic oath. Furthermore, intervention can be justified in the case of a non-professional, as well as a professional, man or woman, who has no pre-existing relationship with the assisted person, as in the case of a stranger who rushes to assist an injured man after an accident. In my opinion, it is the necessity itself which provides the justification for the intervention.

I have said that the doctor has to act in the best interests of the assisted person. In the case of routine treatment of mentally disordered persons, there should be little difficulty in applying this principle. In the case of more serious treatment, I recognise that its application may create problems for the medical profession; however, in making decisions about treatment, the doctor must act in accordance with a responsible and competent body of relevant professional opinion, on the principles set down in *Bolam v Friern Hospital Management Committee* [above, p.165]. No doubt, in practice, a decision may involve others besides the doctor. It must surely be good practice to consult relatives and others who are concerned with the care of the patient. Sometimes, of course, consultation with a specialist or specialists will be required; and in others, especially where the decision involves more than a purely medical opinion, an inter-disciplinary team will in practice participate in the decision. It is very difficult, and would be unwise, for a court to do more than to stress that, for those who are involved in these important and sometimes difficult decisions, the overriding consideration is that they should act in the best interests of the person who suffers from the misfortune of being prevented by incapacity from deciding for himself what should be done to his own body in his own best interests.

In the present case, your Lordships have to consider whether the foregoing principles apply in the case of a proposed operation of sterilisation on an adult woman of unsound mind, or whether sterilisation is (perhaps with one or two other cases) to be placed in a separate category to which special principles apply. . . . Even so, while accepting that the principles which I have stated are applicable in the case of sterilisation, the matters relied on by counsel provide powerful support for the conclusion that the application of those principles in such a case calls for special care. There are other reasons which support that conclusion. It appears, for example, from reported cases in the United States that there is a fear that those responsible for mental patients might (perhaps unwittingly) seek to have them sterilised as a matter of administrative convenience. Furthermore, the English case of *Re D (A Minor) (Wardship: Sterilisation)* [1976] 1 All E.R. 326, provides a vivid illustration of the fact that a highly qualified medical practitioner, supported by a caring mother, may consider it right to sterilise a mentally retarded girl in circumstances which prove, on examination, not to require such an operation in the best interests of the girl. Matters such as these, coupled with the fundamental nature of the patient's organs with which it is proposed irreversibly to interfere, have prompted courts in the United States and in Australia to pronounce that, in the case of a person lacking the capacity to consent, such an operation should only be permitted with the consent of the court. Such decisions have of course been made by courts which have vested in them the *parens patriae* jurisdiction, and so have power, in the exercise of such jurisdiction, to impose such a condition. They are not directly applicable in this country, where that jurisdiction has been revoked; . . .

Lord Griffiths, not dissenting, would "declare that on grounds of public interest an operation to sterilise a woman incapable of giving consent on grounds of either age or mental incapacity is unlawful if performed without the consent of the High Court."

Notes:

1. In *B v Croydon H.A.* [1995] 1 All E.R. 683 Hoffmann L.J. said: "The general law is that an adult person of full mental capacity has the right to choose whether to eat or not. Even if the refusal to eat is tantamount to suicide, as in the case of a hunger strike, he cannot be compelled to eat or forcibly fed. On the other hand, if a person lacks the mental capacity to choose, by the common law the medical practitioner who has him in his care may treat him (and by this I include the artificial administration of food) according to his clinical judgment of the patient's best interests. In addition, under s.63 of the Mental Health Act 1983 the consent of a patient is not required for "any medical treatment given to him for the mental disorder from which he is suffering . . . " In that case nasogastric tube feeding of a patient compulsorily detained under s.3 was held to constitute "medical treatment" for the psychopathic disorder which had led her, deprived of the means of cutting and burning herself, to refuse food until her weight was reduced to 32 kg.

2. However, in *Re C* [1994] 1 All E.R. 819 the court declined to permit the amputation of a possibly fatally gangrenous limb when a paranoidal schizophrenic patient in Broadmoor would not consent to the operation,

and refused to allow the prison authorities to force-feed a prisoner who was putting his life at risk by hunger-strike (*Secretary of State v Robb* [1994] Times L.R. 522).

3. Much more problematic is the order made, under conditions of extreme urgency, by Sir Stephen Brown P., in *Re S* [1992] 4 All E.R. 671, that a Caesarian operation might be performed on a patient with the strongest religious objections to it where there was otherwise a very grave risk of death to both the patient and the foetus.

4. Dissent by a minor to surgical intervention may be overridden by the consent of the person with parental authority: *Re R* [1991] 4 All E.R. 177; *Re J* [1992] Times L.R. 243.

5. In *St. George's Healthcare NHS Trust v S* [1998] 3 All E.R. 673 the autonomy of the adult capable of consent was resoundingly reasserted by the Court of Appeal. S was pregnant and very ill with a condition threatening to her life and that of the foetus. She was perfectly clear-headed and adamant against any surgical intervention. Nevertheless the social worker had her admitted to a mental hospital for assessment. This was unlawful since there was no true belief that S might be mentally ill. Though the application was not duly completed, the hospital was protected by statute because it appeared to be so. S was then transferred to a normal hospital and despite repeated expressions of strong dissent subjected to a Caesarian operation. This was quite unlawful and her detention and treatment there were actionable, notwithstanding that the treatment proceeded in accordance with a declaration issued *ex parte* by Hogg J. "While it may be available to defeat any claim based on aggravated or exemplary damages, in the extraordinary circumstances of this case, the declaration provides no defence to the claim for damages for trespass against St. George's Hospital", the reason being that a declaration affects only the parties and only by way of estoppel which cannot bind an absent party. The case is noted at [1998] Camb. L.J. 438.

Question

Section 30 of the Fire Services Act 1947 empowers fire authorities to enter land for the purpose of extinguishing fires. Was statutory authority required?

R. v BOURNEWOOD COMMUNITY AND MENTAL HEALTH NHS TRUST

House of Lords [1999] 1 A.C. 458; [1998] 3 W.L.R. 107; [1998] 3 All E.R. 289

Justification of detention, if any, of compliant person informally admitted to mental hospital

Some of those in mental hospitals on any day consent to being there. Some 13,000 are there against their will, having been "sectioned." About 22,000 others who neither consent nor dissent are there "informally." L was one of the latter. He had spent 30 of his 48 years resident in the Bournewood Hospital, and in 1994 was discharged temporarily into the community. He was well looked after by paid carers, the Enderbys. One day at the Day Centre L became so agitated as to be a danger to himself and others. He was taken by his social worker to the Hospital where a psychiatrist decided that he needed in-patient treatment, but that in view of his compliance he need not be "sectioned." L made no attempt to leave, but had he done so, the staff would have stopped him and they refused to allow his carers to visit him for several days.

L applied for judicial review of the decision to detain him in hospital and for a writ of habeas corpus and damages for wrongful imprisonment. The trial judge dismissed the claim, but the Court of Appeal allowed it, awarded 1p damages and ordered his release. The House of Lords allowed the Trust's appeal on the ground that if L had been detained the detention was justified by necessity, but differed on the question whether he had indeed been detained.

Lord Goff of Chieveley: . . . When, on July 22, Mr L became agitated and acted violently, an emergency in any event arose which called for intervention, as a matter of necessity, in his best interests and, at least in the initial stages, to avoid danger to others. Plainly it was most appropriate that the appellant trust, and Dr Manjhubashini in particular, should intervene in these circumstances; certainly Mr and Mrs Enderby, as Mr L's carers, could not assert any superior position. . . . I have no doubt that all the steps in fact taken, as described by Dr Manjubhashini, were in fact taken in the best interests of Mr L and, in so far as they might otherwise have constituted an invasion of his civil rights, were justified on the basis of the common law doctrine of necessity.

I wish to add that the latter statement is as true of any restriction upon his freedom of movement as then occurred, as it is of any touching of his person. There were times during the episode when it might be said that Mr L was "detained" in the sense that, in the absence of justification, the tort of false imprisonment would have been committed. I have particularly in mind the journey by ambulance from the Day Centre to the Accident and Emergency Unit. But that journey was plainly justified by necessity, as must frequently be so in the case of removal to hospital by ambulance of unfortunate people who have been taken ill or suffered injury and as a result are incapacitated from expressing consent.

Finally, the readmission of Mr L to hospital as an informal patient under s.131(1) of the 1983 Act could not, in my opinion, constitute the tort of false imprisonment. His readmission, as such, did not constitute a deprivation of his liberty. As Dr Manjubhashini stated in para.9 of her affidavit, he was not kept in a locked ward after he was admitted and the fact that she, like any other doctor in a situation such as this, had it in her mind that she might thereafter take steps to detain him compulsorily under the Act, did not give rise to his detention in fact at any earlier date. Furthermore his treatment while in hospital was plainly justified on the basis of the common law doctrine of necessity. It follows that none of these actions constituted any wrong against Mr L.

For these reasons, I would allow the appeal.

Lord Steyn: . . . In my view the issue of detention must be considered and determined before one can turn to the issue of justification: see *Hague v Deputy Governor of Parkhurst Prison, Weldon v Home Office* [1991] 3 All E.R. 733 at 743, and *Collins v Wilcock* [1984] 3 All E.R. 374, *per* Robert Goff L.J. This is consistent with the rule that if a plaintiff proves an imprisonment, the burden is on the defendant to show that it was lawful. Moreover, the element of detention or imprisonment is a pure issue of fact for the jury and the element of justification is one in which the judge has a role to play: see *Dallison v Caffery* [1964] 2 All E.R. 610. The two issues must therefore be kept separate. If instead one turns straightaway to the lawfulness of the conduct of a defendant, one is not concentrating on the right question, namely *whether conduct which as a matter of fact amounts to detention or imprisonment is justified in law.* It is therefore essential in the present case to determine in the first place whether in the common law sense, as explained in the decided cases, there has been a detention of L. Only if this question is answered in the affirmative, is it right to turn to the question of the lawfulness of the detention. To start with an inquiry into the lawfulness of conduct, or to conflate the two issues, is contrary to legal principle and authority. And such an approach tends to erode legal principles fashioned for the protection of the liberty of the individual.

It is unnecessary to attempt a comprehensive definition of detention. In my view, this case falls on the wrong side of any reasonable line that can be drawn between what is or what is not imprisonment or detention. The critical facts are as follows. (1) When, on July 22, 1979 at the Day Centre, L became agitated and started injuring himself, he was sedated and then physically supported and taken to the hospital. Even before sedation he was unable to express dissent to his removal to hospital. (2) Health care professionals exercised effective power over him. If L had physically resisted, the psychiatrist would immediately have taken steps to ensure his compulsory admission. (3) In hospital, staff regularly sedated him. That ensured that he remained tractable. This contrasts with the position when he was with carers; they seldom resorted to medication and then only in minimal doses. (4) The psychiatrist vetoed visits by the carers to L. She did so, as she explained to the carers, in order to ensure that L did not try to leave with them. The psychiatrist told the carers that L would be released only when she, and other health care professionals, deemed it appropriate. (5) While L was not in a locked ward, nurses closely monitored his reactions. Nurses were instructed to keep him under continuous observation and did so.

Counsel for the trust and the Secretary of State argued that L was in truth always free not to go to the hospital and subsequently to leave the hospital. This argument stretches credulity to breaking point. The truth is that for entirely bona fide reasons, conceived in the best interests of L, any possible resistance by him was overcome by sedation, by taking him to hospital and by close supervision of him in hospital and, if L had shown any sign of wanting to leave, he would have been firmly discouraged by staff and, if necessary, physically prevented from doing so. The suggestion that L was free to go is a fairy tale.

At one stage counsel for the trust suggested that L was not detained because he lacked the necessary will, or more precisely the capacity to grant or refuse consent. That argument was misconceived. After all, an unconscious or drugged person can be detained: see *Murray v Ministry of Defence* [1988] 2 All E.R. 521 at 528–529, *per* Lord Griffiths. In my view L was detained because the healthcare professionals intentionally assumed control over him to such a degree as to amount to complete deprivation of his liberty.

It is now necessary to consider whether there was lawful authority to justify the detention and any treatment of L.

Lord Nolan: ... I am satisfied that the respondent trust and its medical staff behaved throughout, not only in what they judged to be the best interests of Mr L, but in strict accordance with their common law duty of care and the common law principle of necessity.

The first question before your Lordships, however, is whether it is correct to describe Mr L as having been detained during the period of his informal admission to the Bournewood Hospital; for if not, the appellant trust has no case to answer. Owen J. considered that Mr L was not detained. He said that Mr L—

"has at all times been free to leave because that is a consequence of an informal admission, and he will continue to be free to leave until Dr. Manjubhashini or somebody else takes steps to 'section' him or otherwise prevent him leaving."

The Court of Appeal did not accept this view. They said:

"We do not consider that the judge was correct to conclude that L was 'free to leave'. We think that it is plain that, had he attempted to leave the hospital, those in charge of him would not have permitted him to do so."

My Lords, upon this point I agree with the Court of Appeal. Mr L, was closely monitored at all times so as to ensure that he came to no harm. It would have been wholly irresponsible for those monitoring him to let him leave the hospital until he had been judged fit to do so.

Before your Lordships counsel for the appellant trust accepted that Owen J. might have been wrong in describing Mr L as being "free to leave". He submitted, however, that in so far as Mr L's liberty was constrained, the constraint arose from his illness rather than from the wishes or actions of the hospital staff. Alternatively he submitted that the question of detention could not arise unless and until Mr L tried to leave.

My Lords, in my judgment these submissions must fail in the light of the appellant trust's own evidence.

After quoting from this the Court of Appeal concluded:

"Mr and Mrs Enderby had looked after L, as one of the family, for over three years. They had made it plain that they wanted to take him back into their care. It is clear that the hospital was not prepared to countenance this. If they were not prepared to release L into the custody of his carers they were not prepared to let him leave the hospital at all. He was and is detained there."

My Lords, with that conclusion too I agree. I have laid some stress on the point not only because the individual's right to liberty, and the remedy of habeas corpus, lie at the heart of our law but because if Mr L, in the circumstances which I have described, was not detained then (leaving aside the question of his treatment, which is not in issue) there was no ground in law upon which the hospital and its staff could be called upon to justify their unwillingness to release him. I find it hard to believe that the medical profession in general would regard that as a satisfactory state of affairs.

In the event, as I have said, I am satisfied that this justification has been fully made out, and I would allow the appeal on that basis.

Section 4.—Self-Defence

ANONYMOUS CASE

Assizes (1836) 2 Lew.C.C. 48; 168 E.R. 1075

Parke B. (to the jury): . . . When a man strikes at another, within a distance capable of the latter being struck, nature prompts the party struck to resist it, and he is justified in using such a degree of force as will prevent a repetition. . . .

ANDERSON v MARSHALL

Court of Session (1835) 13 S.1130

The defender was a London businessman who was having difficulties with a firm in Peterhead. At the request of that firm, the pursuer wrote the defender a letter, to which the defender did not reply. The pursuer then wrote another letter, accusing the defender of behaving in a cowardly manner and using other injurious language which he underlined. The defender, on receipt of this letter, went to the pursuer's shop and struck him, not doing any injury.

Lord President Hope (to the jury): This is a case in which there are faults on both sides; and the first fault was committed by the pursuer, in addressing a letter to the defender, containing expressions which, to say the least of them, were extremely ill-judged and foolish. There could be none more intemperate or worse chosen than that which imputed cowardly conduct to the defender. And there were other words of a very insulting character. The defender acted instantaneously, on receipt of the letter; and, if he had merely gone to the pursuer's shop, and abused him, by applying those epithets which he employed, I should have thought there was no ground for a finding in favour of the pursuer at all. But the defender went farther than this, and, in the heat of the moment, he struck the pursuer with his hand. It is my duty to inform you that no verbal provocation whatever can justify a blow. The law on this point is inflexible. I conceive, therefore, that there must be a verdict for the pursuer. But, as verbal provocation is a good ground for mitigating damages, and as the pursuer does not come before you with clean hands, I should conceive that sufficient reparation would be made in this case by a small award of damages. On the proper amount to be awarded you will decide.

The jury found for the pursuer; damages 1s.

Note:
  In *Bullerton*, reported by R. Burns at [1992] New L.J. 1725, the defendant in the Crown Court, charged with causing grievous bodily harm, had for some months been receiving obscene telephone calls from a person unknown. With the aid of a friendly electronic engineer he devised a "screech-box" which when

activated sent a piercing sound down the line. This partially deafened the complainant (who now identified himself) and provoked tinnitus. The judge withdrew the defence of self-defence from the jury, and the Court of Appeal held that this was correct, since "physical force may not be used to prevent psychological harm". The judge's decision to discharge the accused was approved. The Court did, however, say that it should have been left to the jury to say whether the accused's actions were not the use of reasonable force in the protection of his property, namely his telephone number, which for business reasons he could not change!

TOWNLEY v RUSHWORTH

Queen's Bench Divisional Court (1963) 62 L.G.R. 95; 107 S.J. 1004

Prosecution for assault

This was an appeal from conviction for assault. The appeal was allowed.

The Mental Health Act 1959, s.31(1), provided that: "An application for the admission of a patient to a hospital under this Part of this Act, duly completed in accordance with the foregoing provisions of this Part of this Act, shall be sufficient authority for the applicant, or any person authorised by the applicant, to take the patient and convey him to the hospital."

Lord Parker of Waddington C.J.: . . . Shortly, what happened in this case was as follows: on April 22, 1963, the defendant's wife signed a form of emergency application; that form bore the words "This application is founded on the medical recommendation forwarded herewith," and it clearly contemplated that, in the case of an emergency certificate, the one medical practitioner would make a medical recommendation for admission on a form, and that that recommendation would be, as it were, annexed to the wife's application.

Having made out the form, the defendant's wife handed it to a Dr Hardman, who had been the defendant's medical adviser. Although it is not found in the case, I assume that Dr Hardman deliberately refrained from making the recommendation to be attached to that application until he had in fact seen the defendant. On that same day the doctor went along armed with the wife's application and with a form of recommendation which he would fill up if he felt the condition of the defendant was such that he should do so. He went to the house with a brother-in-law of the defendant, and with two police constables, Kaylor and Major. When they arrived at the house, Dr Hardman went in first; the defendant heard somebody moving about and then, when told who it was, he told the doctor to get out. Thereupon the doctor went to the door and brought in the other three. The defendant at once said: "You have no right to come in here. You need two doctors. I am going to my bedroom, you can get out." With that he went upstairs to his bedroom. Dr Hardman and the other three followed him up to the bedroom and, in the bedroom, Dr Hardman referred to the form of emergency application which he had in his hand, and told the defendant that he, the doctor, was afraid that he, the defendant, would have to go to hospital for a little while whether he wished or not. The defendant then got angry, said: "It's a put up show and a conspiracy to get me out of the way." Then Dr Hardman went even further; he said to the defendant and to the police constables present that he would have to give the defendant an injection with a sedative, and thereupon left the room to prepare the injection.

While the injection was being prepared the defendant, who was with the other three men in the bedroom, said that he wished to telephone the chief constable, no doubt to remonstrate. Thereupon one of the police constables, Kaylor, stood between the defendant and the door to prevent him from leaving. The defendant tried to push the police constable away and the police constable took the defendant by the arm. At that moment the other police constable, Major, seeing a sort of scuffle going on, came across, as the defendant apparently thought, to strike him, and before he was struck the defendant succeeded in freeing his arm and levelling a fist blow at Major which, most unfortunately, fractured his nose. After that had occurred Dr Hardman came in, administered the injection and called for an ambulance and then, and then only, did he fill up the recommendation to be attached to the application.

In those circumstances the first question that arises is whether these four men, and in particular police constable Major, were lawfully in the defendant's house and were acting lawfully in keeping him there with a view to taking him against his will to a hospital for observation. In my judgment it is quite clear, and indeed it is conceded, that since the application form was not at the time duly completed by the addition of Dr Hardman's medical certificate, none of those persons there had any lawful authority to restrain the patient and convey him to hospital. Indeed, they were trespassers in the house. It is as I have said most unfortunate, because I am sure that Dr Hardman had refrained from filling up the recommendation because he honestly wanted to see whether it was a proper case in which to make the recommendation, and he could not say that until he had seen the defendant during that visit. . . .

Here is a case where as the facts turned out, there were four trespassers in the house without any lawful authority, who had been told to get out and had failed to do so—trespassers whom the defendant in the first instance at any rate was not prepared to eject forcibly because he retired; he said he was going to his bedroom, and he went up to his bedroom. He was then pursued; he was told that whether he liked it or not he was going to be taken away, and for that purpose he was going to have an injection and he was further told, while the injection was being prepared, that he was not at liberty even to leave his bedroom; and one officer forcibly restrained him from leaving the bedroom.

Unless it is to be said that a householder is to sit down and submit, not only to his liberty being infringed in his own house, but also to assault by injection, and to his liberty being removed in hospital, I cannot say that to hit out with the fist is an unreasonable use of force.

It is of course, a question of fact for the justices, and this court would hesitate to interfere, but in the present case I am in very grave doubt, from the very wording of the case, what the justices really did have in mind. It may be that they were considering the question whether there were reasonable grounds for belief that police constable Major was going to strike the defendant and were not taking into consideration the full picture that I have tried to outline. It may be also that they were saying to themselves: "well, the fact that the application did not have the recommendation attached at the time was really a mere formality, and the defendant ought to have submitted to his removal." It is, at any rate, those ambiguities in the finding in the case which make me feel justified in saying that although this is a question of fact for the justices, they must have misdirected themselves by not considering the full picture on the basis that these four men were there without any lawful authority. In these circumstances I feel that in this unfortunate case the only course is to quash the conviction.

Quote:
  "Lay not that flattering unction to your soul,
  That not your trespass but my madness speaks."

Hamlet, III.iv.

Questions
  1. Would the defendant have been guilty of assault if the doctor had previously completed his recommendation?
  2. Did the defendant know that the doctor had not completed his recommendation?
  3. Why do you think that this prosecution was brought?

Notes:
  1. The accused was not nobody. He was Sir John Barton Townley, M.A. (Cantab., Downing College), D.Lit. (Sorbonne), knighted for founding many youth (Rydal) clubs, and dying aged 76 in 1990. A member of the Royal and Ancient, he listed his hobbies in *Who's Who*. They included boxing. (*ex rel. Geoffrey Samuel*).
  2. "To order a man who has done no wrong out of his home is without question drastic" (*per* Ralph Gibson L.J. in *Wiseman v Simpson* [1988] 1 All E.R. 245 at 255), but it can be done, and is very frequently done, by a "non-molestation order" under Part IV of the Family Law Act 1996. Such an order may be obtained *ex parte* by an "associated person", very widely defined in s.62, and may have a power of arrest for breach attached to it.

3. If one believes that Townley would have been rightly convicted had the critical document been signed, one will have some difficulty with *Blackburn v Bowering* [1994] 3 All E.R. 380, where the Court of Appeal apparently held that if you are unaware that the person about to detain you is a court officer with power to do so, physical resistance on your part does not amount to assault; it is not that ignorance is a defence, but rather that there is no assault at all. "The prosecution have to prove that he was guilty of assault, and they do not do that merely by proving that a person whom he believed to be gratuitously seizing him was in fact doing so in the execution of his duty." (*per* Roch L.J. at 386). Surely this is not so in private law, where the question must be who is entitled to strike, not who is at fault in striking. Thus we do not know whether the pugilistic Townley realised that the move towards him was unauthorised: all that mattered was that it was not authorised. In *Regina v McKoy* [2002] EWCA Crim 1628, [2002] T.L.R. 264 the accused erroneously supposed that when the policeman laid a hand on him during a domestic dispute he was being arrested. He reacted violently, and was convicted. The conviction was reversed and his appeal allowed by the Court of Appeal: the restraint was unlawful and he was entitled to resist, even if he thought it was lawful.

Section 5.—Protection of Property

Preliminary Note:

In *DPP v Jones* (above p.355) it was held that persons peaceably meeting on the highway without causing any obstruction were not trespassing. This was in the context of a criminal prosecution for "trespassory assembly", so the question was not whether there was a defence to the trespass but whether it was a trespass at all. The distinction may arise in private law, however, when a defendant has a right to invade property in the claimant's possession: the invasion is a trespass, the defendant's right to do what he did a defence. Such cases have sometimes involved the highway, since the subsoil of the highway is vested in the landowners on either side—not that their property right is of much use to them since the public are entitled to drive up and down it (but only to get to their destination!), and now, after *DPP v Jones*, to meet there for discussions or demonstrations. Thus landowners had a defence to a charge of battery when they physically "moved on" persons using the highway that ran over their land for purposes other than passage and repassage, such as acting as scare-pheasants. It was made clear that the public right to go on the highway was limited by the purpose for which it was being exercised.

There may be other public rights. Thus the Countryside and Rights of Way Act 2000 entitles citizens to roam over private land which is "open country", though the right exists only for recreational purposes. The purpose, as is often the case, defines the extent of the right. (May one hunt for buried treasure?) The Secretary of State has power under s.3 to extend the right to "coastal land", including land adjacent to the foreshore, but seems not yet to have done so. As to the foreshore, therefore, the old common law may still apply.

There is a public right to go on the foreshore in connection with fishing and navigation (you do not trespass, or rather, you have a defence, if you are landing your catch or avoiding death by drowning—see *Southport Corp.* below p.410), and in *Anderson v Alnwick DC* [1993] 1 W.L.R. 1156 it was held that one might go on the foreshore to dig for lugworms, this being ancillary to the fishing right, provided that the lugworms were to be used for fishing and not for commercial purposes. A similar question arose whether persons were entitled to go beachcombing, for picking up flotsam (which does not involve abandonment) and jetsam (which does). The property in question was coal washed up on the Northumbrian coast, worth, it was said, about £100,000 per year. In *Beckett v Lyons* [1967] Ch. 449 it was held that there was no such right. Indeed it was not clear that there was any common law right to go on the foreshore, even from the sea, in order to bathe in the sun or the water, for "It is well known that in relation to the English foreshore many activities, including walking thereon, bathing therefrom, and beach-combing, have been generally tolerated by the Crown as owner of the foreshore, without at any time giving rise to any legal right in the public to continue them." Once the Secretary exercises his power, there will be such a right by statute, though "recreational purposes" will doubtless not extend to collecting coal for sale.

Yet when people have been doing something for a long time, they get to believe that they are entitled to do it. This is what an Austrian jurist called "the normative effect of facts." But if what people have been doing is an invasion of the rights of others, the law has to be cautious in holding that it is now justified. The rule is delicate: if the landowner has given permission for the doing of the thing, he can withdraw that permission, unless there was a contract not to (the good reason being that he will not give permission at all if he is not free to withdraw it). And if he does not know about it, he can stop it. But if he knows about it and does nothing, merely tolerates it, a right to continue doing it may be acquired by those using his land. This is very old law: if A has been crossing B's land in the past year the Roman praetor would enjoin B from preventing him doing so, provided A's crossing was not *vi clam or precario*, (by force, secretly or with permission), the very words used by Lord Bingham in 2003, holding that the use by residents of a piece of council land for sports purpose was not permitted by the council but merely tolerated, so that after twenty years the land could be registered as a town or village green and the sports activities continue. *R. (on the application of Beresford) v City of Sunderland* [2003] UKHL 60.

COLLINS v RENISON

King's Bench (1754) Say. 138; 96 E.R. 830

The plaintiff brought an action of trespass for assault, alleging that the defendant had overturned a ladder upon which the plaintiff was standing and threw the plaintiff from it on to the ground. The defendant pleaded: "that he was in possession of a certain garden; and that the plaintiff, against the will of the defendant, erected a ladder in the garden, and went up the ladder, in order to nail a board to the house of the plaintiff; and that the defendant forbid the plaintiff so to do, and desired him to come down; and that upon the plaintiff's persisting in nailing the board, he gently shook the ladder, which was a low ladder, and gently overturned it, and gently threw the plaintiff from it upon the ground, thereby doing as little damage as possible to the plaintiff."

The plaintiff demurred to the defendant's plea, and the demurrer was upheld.

Ryder C.J.: Such force, as was used in the present case, is not justifiable in the defence of possession of land. The overturning of the ladder could not answer the purpose of removing the plaintiff out of the garden; since it only left him upon the ground at the bottom of the ladder, instead of being upon it.

Notes:

1. Renison could not justify what he did by reference to his right as occupier right to extrude trespassers, for that is a right to evict, to disembarrass and disencumber the land, and what he did had the opposite effect. The occupier's right to extrude trespassers applies to trespassing objects as well. In the modern world those objects are generally motor cars. Clearly one is entitled to have it removed, but that costs money. May one clamp it? The trouble is that clamping does not remove the vehicle and disencumber the land: rather the reverse.

The Court of Appeal wrestled with this problem in *Arthur v Anker* [1997] Q.B. 564, and came up with an elegant solution: that the trespasser was deemed to consent to the clamping if there was a notice forbidding trespassing which fixed a reasonable fee for removal of the clamp and information about how to contact the clamper. A subsequent Court of Appeal did not seem to realise that the consent was deemed to be given, and supposed that it must actually be given, and imposed liability on the clamper when the trespasser failed (or said she failed) to see the notice, it being temporarily obscured by a truck. *Vine v Waltham Forest LBC* [2000] 4 All E.R. 169.

The question is now resolved by governmental intervention of a characteristic variety: you now need *official permission* to clamp a trespassing car. The Private Security Industry Act 2001 makes it an offence for any occupier to immobilise a vehicle unless he has a licence from a quango set up for the purpose (Sch. 2 para.3). This applies, however, only where the immobilisation is effected by affixing an immobilisation device. Occupiers of land are still, remarkably enough, free to close and lock their gates though this prevents, and is intended to prevent, the exit of a trespassing car. This is because there is no tort which calls for justification: locking the gate is not a trespass to the car, as clamping is, because there is no touching, and it is not a conversion since the occupier is not asserting any title to the vehicle.

2. As Collins had doubtless found, it may be impossible for a person to repair or maintain his house without going a foot or two on to his neighbour's land in order to erect scaffolding or whatever. At common law the neighbour is perfectly entitled to refuse permission to enter, and to evict the householder if he comes on, though the principal case shows that the courts might be a little unsympathetic. Nowadays Collins could invoke the rather complex procedures of the Access to Neighbouring Land Act 1992, and obtain a right to do what he did. Again, if one wishes to build a wall at the edge of one's property, legislation was required to give one the right to put the footings under the neighbour's land and to enter the land for that purpose. The right is subject to conditions and carries the obligation to minimise inconvenience and pay for any loss or damage caused by the exercise of the right. See the Party Wall etc. Act 1996, s.7.

3. It is characteristic of English law to permit property owners (like the League Against Cruel Sports, above, p.358, or Anchor Brewhouse, above, p.359) to behave in a bloody-minded manner if they choose. Thus in one case an outgoing tenant had left on the landlord's premises some chattels which he had hired from the plaintiff. When the plaintiff asked for them back, the landlord refused either to bring the chattels to the front door or to permit the plaintiff to enter the premises to fetch them (*British Economical Lamp Co* (1913) 29 T.L.R. 386).

4. Was that decision for the defendant treated as obsolete or merely ignored in *Saleslease v Davis* [1999] 1 W.L.R. 1664? The defendant's tenant had taken MoT equipment on hire from the plaintiff. After both the tenancy and the hire had been terminated the defendant refused to let the plaintiff have the equipment unless he paid certain sums (for which he was not liable). The defendant's conduct being held wrongful without discussion, the argument turned on the question of damages. The majority held that no loss had been proved, since the plaintiff could have relet the equipment only to a very special customer of whose existence the defendant had no reason to know.

Perhaps the 1913 case was indeed thought obsolete, since in *Miller v Jackson* [1977] 3 All E.R. 338 at 342 Lord Denning had said that such conduct on the part of the occupier was no longer lawful and he said the same in the *Capital Finance Co* case (below, p.502). But what tort is it? According to *England v Cowley* (below, p.498) it is not conversion to prevent a person having access to his chattel. Is the owner of the chattel entitled, against the will of the occupier, to come on to the premises to collect his property? Is that the sort of self-help the law should encourage?

The Shropshire police seem to think so, for in the summer of 1995 they arrested (for theft!) a woman who refused to return a ball which the neighbour's kids had yet again kicked into her garden. It is to be hoped that she got swingeing damages (from the police, not the neighbour—see *Davidson*, above, p.342).

Question

One Webb, taking part in a demonstration, sat on the bonnet of the Minister's car. The car drove off and the plaintiff was injured. He obtained nearly £8,000 damages. Do you agree that there was "no conceivable justification" for the driver's action? Was the Minister bound to tolerate being immobilised? Was the plaintiff not trespassing to the car, and liable to be ousted from his position on it? (*The Independent*, October 10, 1992).

Was it this decision which prompted the Legal Aid Board (on the advice of a barrister) to support the claim (costs about £50,000) by "Dodger Gedge"? While his drunken mates in combat uniform were attacking the car in which the terrified Sarah Field was sitting—one trying to get through the sunroof, another kicking at the windscreen—Gedge lay down in front of the car so as to facilitate their efforts. Ms Field drove off and Gedge lost his leg. AND sued! His suit failed. Not, one supposes, because of *volenti*, but because the law permits those falsely imprisoned to regain their liberty even at the corporeal expense of the person falsely imprisoning them. The question is NOT whether it is reasonable to exercise this right but whether, given that one is entitled to exercise it, the mode of exercise was reasonable. Doubtless the Minister had to warn Webb before driving off, but having done so he was entitled to proceed, given that he could not reverse. Ms Field was not even under any obligation to warn.

WHATFORD v CARTY

Queen's Bench Divisional Court, *The Times*, October 29, 1960

The appellants, head keeper and game-keepers on the Copped Hall Estate, Epping Forest, laid three informations against the respondent for assault, under Offences against the Person Act 1861, s.42. The justices dismissed the information on the ground that the respondent had no case to answer. The appeal was dismissed.

Lord Parker C.J.: ... On Sunday, November 22, 1959, in broad daylight, the respondent was seen by the appellants on a part of the Copped Hall Estate, armed with a bow and arrow. Having seen him, they apparently traced his motor-cycle and went and waited by it until he returned. The moment he got there without any bag, the first appellant took his bow and arrows away from him and handed them to the third appellant, whereupon the respondent said "You are not going to have my bow" and went for the appellants. He pushed the first appellant into a ditch, kicked the second appellant on the leg, took hold of the third appellant and pushed him into a hedge. Unfortunately he kicked their dog and the dog bit him.

His Lordship said that at the end of this momentous case the justices came to the conclusion that the respondent had no case to answer and dismissed the informations. His Lordship entirely agreed. It had been admitted that the first appellant had no right to take the bow and arrows. What was said was that once he had taken them peaceably, it was an offence in law for the respondent to attempt to repossess the weapons without making a request for them, and, presumably, without giving a reasonable time for the request to be complied with.

His Lordship thought that it would be wrong to divide up this little episode, which must have taken a matter of seconds, into stages of that sort. It seemed to him that the appellants must have taken the bow and arrows almost before the respondent knew what it was all about. The moment they did, he said "You are not having my bow," and repossession almost immediately took place. The position was perfectly clearly stated in *Russell on Crime*: "If one come forcibly and take away another's goods the owner may oppose him at once, for there is no time to make a request."

Secondly, it has been said that at any rate the assault on the second appellant was not justified because he never handled the bow or the arrows; but the answer to that was that all three appellants were acting in concert.

Finally, it had been said that there was no evidence that the assaults were committed to regain possession of the weapons, but the respondent's immediate reaction was "You are not having my bow."

In his Lordship's view the justices were amply justified in coming to the conclusion they did and would dismiss the appeal.

Note:

In its Eighteenth Report, Cmnd. 4774, (1971) the Law Reform Committee said "This is a field of law which touches very closely the ordinary man's conception of his fundamental rights and in our view it is of the essence of a good law on the subject that it should allow self-help where the majority of the community would consider it reasonable." (para.122).

CRESSWELL v SIRL

Court of Appeal [1948] 1 K.B. 241; [1948] L.J.R. 654; 63 T.L.R. 620; 112 J.P. 69; 91 S.J. 653; [1947] 2 All E.R. 730; 46 L.G.R. 109 (noted (1947) 64 L.Q.R. 39 at 436)

Action for shooting plaintiff's dog

A farmer's son was woken one night by the sound of barking. He went out and found two excited dogs noisily worrying the sheep. He went back for advice and a gun, and returned with a relative to find that the dogs had by now penned the sheep in a corner of a field and were still worrying them. They flashed a light onto the dogs and the dogs started towards them. When they were about 40 yards away, the defendant fired, and the plaintiff's dog was killed.

The county court judge gave judgment for the plaintiff, on the ground that the killing of the dog could be justified only if it was actually attacking the stock at the time and there was no other method of deterring it.

The defendant's appeal to the Court of Appeal was allowed, and the case was remitted to the county court.

Scott L.J.: This is the judgment of the court. This case is of interest since it has involved a consideration by the court—after an interval of more than 100 years—of the law relating to the justification for the shooting of another's dog. It is also, we think, of no little public importance. To shoot a dog is hateful to anyone fond of animals. On the other hand, those who keep dogs in the country or take dogs to the country are under a real and serious obligation not to allow their dogs to chase sheep or cattle. Even if the sheep or cattle are not physically attacked, serious injury may be done to them if they are frightened and chased, particularly when (as in the present case) the ewes are in lamb or the cattle in calf. . . .

The learned county court judge treated as a conclusive test of the defendant's liability in question whether at the moment of shooting, the plaintiff's dogs were actually attacking the sheep; and since at that moment, the dogs had admittedly left the sheep and were approaching the defendant and his brother-in-law, he found, on the application of this test, in favour of the plaintiff.

The learned judge derived his test from the case of *Janson v Brown* (1807) 170 E.R. 869, before Lord Ellenborough C.J. in 1807 . . . But since that date, and particularly since the date of *Kirk v Gregory* ((1876) 1 Ex.D. 55), the law generally relating to the justification of acts of trespass has been appreciably developed and defined. For the rule that the property in question must be actually under attack has been substituted the more generous rule that it must be in real or imminent danger; and for the absolute criterion that the act of trespass must be shown—in the light of subsequent events—to have been necessary for the preservation of the property has been substituted the more relative standard of reasonable necessity, namely, that any reasonable man would, in the circumstances of the case, have concluded that there was no alternative to the act of trespass if the property endangered was to be preserved. . . .

The whole matter fell to be considered by this court in the case of *Cope v Sharpe (No.2)* ([1912] 1 K.B. 496). In that case the question was whether the defendant was justified in doing certain acts of trespass on the plaintiff's land for the purpose of preventing the spread of heath fire and consequent loss and damage to the property of the defendant's master. In that case it was shown that the fire never in fact damaged the property of the defendant's master and would not have done so even if the preventive measures adopted by the defendant had not in fact been taken. The risk and danger to the property in question had, however, been "real and imminent" and the steps taken by the defendant, trespassing for the purpose on the plaintiff's land, were held by the jury to have been unnecessary in fact, but nevertheless to have been reasonably necessary. On these findings this court held that the defendant had made out his plea of justification. "The test, I think"—said Buckley L.J.—"is whether . . . there was such real or imminent danger to his" (that is, the defendant's master's) "property as that he was entitled to act and whether his acts were reasonably necessary in the sense of being acts which a reasonable man would properly do to meet a real danger." And Kennedy L.J. said that danger had been found by the jury to have been "so far imminent that any reasonable person in the circumstances of the defendant would act reasonably in treating it as necessary to adopt the method for the preservation of the property in jeopardy which the defendant adopted."

In our view, the principle underlying the judgment of this court in *Cope v Sharpe* is one of general application to justification of acts of trespass and we do not think that the older cases cited to the county court judge should be regarded as laying down any special rules appropriate to the case of shooting dogs. . . .

We come to the conclusion that the law applicable to the facts of the present case is less narrow than the county court judge holds in his judgment. Chasing by dogs which causes any real or present danger of serious harm to the animals chased constitutes an "attack" which entitles the owner to take effective measures of prevention. We think the relevant rules of law may be thus stated: (1) The onus of proof is on the defendant to justify the preventive measure of shooting the attacking dogs. (2) He has, by proof, to establish two propositions, but each proposition may be established in either of two ways: *Proposition No.1*: That at the time of shooting, the dog was either (a) actually (in the above sense) attacking the animals in question, or (b) if left at large would renew the attack so that the animals would be left presently subject to real and imminent danger unless renewal was prevented. *Proposition No.2*: That either (a) there was in fact no practicable means, other than shooting, of stopping the present attack or preventing such renewal, or (b) that the defendant, having regard to all the circumstances in which he found himself, acted reasonably in regarding the shooting as necessary for the protection of the animals against attack or renewed attack. . . .

In the circumstances . . . we think that the proper course . . . is to refer the matter back to His Honour with the following directions: If the learned judge finds that the defendant has established both propositions in either of the alternative ways open to him, he should enter judgment for the defendant; but if he finds that the defendant has not so established both propositions, the plaintiff will sustain her judgment.

Note:

In *Sorrell v Paget*, below, p.506, the defendant was held entitled (1) to remove the plaintiff's cow from a railway line just before the arrival of an express train, and (2) when it went into one of his fields, to remove it and detain it to protect his cattle from the risk of infection. The justifications for these prima facie trespasses were not discussed, but were doubtless (1) necessity, and (2) protection of property and distress damage feasant.

ANIMALS ACT 1971

. . .

9.—(1) In any civil proceedings against a person (in this section referred to as the defendant) for killing or causing injury to a dog it shall be a defence to prove—

(a) that the defendant acted for the protection of any livestock and was a person entitled to act for the protection of that livestock; and
(b) that within 48 hours of the killing or injury notice thereof was given by the defendant to the officer in charge of a police station.

(2) For the purposes of this section a person is entitled to act for the protection of any livestock if, and only if—

(a) the livestock or the land on which it is belongs to him or to any person under whose express or implied authority he is acting; and
(b) the circumstances are not such that liability for killing or causing injury to the livestock would be excluded by section 5(4) of this Act.

(3) Subject to subsection (4) of this section, a person killing or causing injury to a dog shall be deemed for the purposes of this section to act for the protection of any livestock if, and only if, either—

(a) the dog is worrying or is about to worry the livestock and there are no other reasonable means of ending or preventing the worrying; or
(b) the dog has been worrying livestock and is not under the control of any person and there are no practical means of ascertaining to whom it belongs.

(4) For the purposes of this section, the condition stated in either of the paragraphs of the preceding subsection shall be deemed to have been satisfied if the defendant believed that it was satisfied and had reasonable ground for that belief.

(5) For the purposes of this section—

(a) an animal belongs to any person if he owns it or has it in his possession; and
(b) land belongs to any person if he is the occupier thereof.

Question

How lengthy do you think the Civil Code of England would be if the article relating to liability for killing dogs were as long as this? What rules would apply if I poisoned my neighbour's cat which had made repeated forays into my chicken-run?

Notes:

1. The reader will be glad to learn from the definition in section 11 that "livestock" (a very difficult and abstract concept) includes not only mules but also hinnies. A hinny is a mule whose parents are a male horse and a female donkey instead of the other way round. What a lot one has to know in order to understand an English enactment prompted by a statutory body (the Law Commission) whose duty is to simplify the law.

2. Suppose my neighbour's cat is about to pounce on my canary. I throw a brickbat at the cat and kill it. The statute does not apply, for two reasons: (a) a canary is not "livestock", as defined and (b) a cat is not a dog ("dog" not being defined). Then what rule does apply? Answer: the common law rule laid down prior to the enactment of the statute. What facts underlay the cases in which that rule was laid down? Answer: dogs threatening livestock (then called "cattle"). This illustrates an important point, namely that while statutory rules are never applied by analogy, judge-made rules always are. The implication is that since the range of application of judge-made rules cannot be contained by the court that lays them down, it may be wise, when a rule is wanted for very specific fact-situations only, to leave it to the legislature. In the light of this it might be worth considering (a) *White v Jones* (above, p.65), (b) *Arthur v Anker* (above, p.405).

SOUTHPORT CORPORATION v ESSO PETROLEUM Co

Queen's Bench [1953] 3 W.L.R. 773; 118 J.P. 1; 97 S.J. 764; [1952] 2 All E.R. 1204; 52 L.G.R. 22; [1953] 2 Lloyd's Rep. 414 (noted (1955) 71 L.Q.R. 6)

Action for pollution of seashore by oil intentionally discharged

The master of the defendant's tanker deliberately discharged a large amount of oil on to the sea not far from the plaintiffs' foreshore. He did this because the tanker had run aground and he was concerned for the possible loss of life. The plaintiffs claimed the clean-up cost.

Devlin J. gave judgment for the defendants on the ground that the plaintiffs must prove negligence and had failed to do so. The plaintiffs' appeal to the Court of Appeal was allowed (Morris L.J. dissenting) on the ground that the defendants must disprove negligence and had failed to do so [1954] 2 Q.B. 182. The House of Lords allowed the defendants' appeal on the ground that the plaintiffs had failed to establish the facts alleged in their pleadings [1956] A.C. 218.

Devlin J.: . . . In my judgment the plaintiffs have a good cause of action in trespass or nuisance subject to the special defences raised by the defendants which I shall next consider.

On the first of these, if one seeks an analogy from traffic on land, it is well established that persons whose property adjoins the highway cannot complain of damage done by persons using the highway unless it is done negligently: *Gayler & Pope Ltd v Davies (B) & Son Ltd* ([1924] 2 K.B. 75). . . .

But there is hardly need to search for exact authority, for the point is covered by two dicta, which may be *obiter* but which bear the great authority of Lord Blackburn and which lay down the same rule on land and water. In *Fletcher v Rylands* ((1866) L.R. 1 Ex. 265 at 286) Blackburn J. said: "Traffic on the highways, whether by land or sea, cannot be conducted without exposing those whose persons or property are near it to some inevitable risk; and that being so, those who go on the highway, or have their property adjacent to it, may well be held to do so subject to their taking upon themselves the risk of injury from that inevitable danger." The judge then went on to say that such persons could not recover "without proof of want of care or skill occasioning the accident." In *River Wear Commissioners v Adamson* ((1877) 2 App.Cas. 743 at 767) Lord Blackburn said: "My Lords, the common law is, I think, as follows—property adjoining to a spot on which the public have a right to carry on traffic is liable to be injured by that traffic. In this respect there is no difference between a shop, the railings or windows of which may be broken by a carriage on the road, and a pier adjoining to a harbour or a navigable river or the sea, which is liable to be injured by a ship. In either case the owner of the injured property must bear his own loss, unless he can establish that some other person is in fault, and liable to make it good. . . ."

The defence of necessity would have called for close examination if in fact it had been based solely on the saving of property and if in law I had thought that the plaintiffs' rights of ownership in the foreshore were unqualified by their proximity to the sea. But the facts of this case, when examined, show that the peril said to justify the discharge of the cargo is that the ship was in imminent danger of breaking her back. The consequence of that would be not merely that the ship herself would become a total loss, but that in the circumstances of this case the lives of the crew would be endangered. The safety of human lives belongs to a different scale of values from the safety of property. The two are beyond comparison and the necessity for saving life has at all times been considered a proper ground for inflicting such damage as may be necessary upon another's property. I think, therefore, that if I am wrong in the application of the principle which I have taken from Lord Blackburn, the defence in this case can equally well be put on the ground of necessity.

It is, of course, an answer to either of these defences if the predicament in which the ship found herself was due to her own negligence. Indeed, in the principle I am applying it is necessary, as Lord Blackburn said, for the plaintiffs to prove negligence, and so my examination of the law results in the conclusion that this action is to be treated in the same way as any running-down or collision case in which the plaintiff alleges negligence. . . .

Notes:

1. A dangerous psychopath entered the plaintiff's gun-shop in Northampton after closing hours one evening. He armed himself with guns, loaded them and fired them several times. The police decided to flush him out, and fired a canister of CS gas into the shop. A bad fire ensued, and it took time to put it out because there was no fire engine handy, though a comparable military vehicle had previously been standing by. *Rigby v Chief Constable of Northants.* [1985] 2 All E.R. 985. The trespass was held justifiable by necessity, but the police were held liable as it was unreasonable of them to use the inflammatory canister in the absence of any fire-fighting vehicle.

2. Owners of tankers and other vessels from which oil is discharged are now liable regardless of negligence for any damage done, including clean-up costs: Merchant Shipping Act 1995, ss.153, 154. The only defence (s.154) is that the event was due to the act of a third party, neither servant nor agent, with intent to do damage.

McPHAIL v PERSONS UNKNOWN

Court of Appeal [1973] Ch. 447; [1973] 3 W.L.R. 71; 117 S.J. 448; 72 L.G.R. 93; [1973]
3 All E.R. 393 (noted (1973) 89 L.Q.R. 458)

Action against squatters for possession of private dwelling

The owner of a house sought an order for possession against persons who had broken into it and were squatting in it. The trial judge granted the order and the defendants appealed, asking for a stay of execution on the ground that they had nowhere else to live. The Court of Appeal held that it had no power to grant such a stay.

Lord Denning M.R.: . . .

2. The law as to squatters

What is a squatter? He is one who, without any colour of right, enters on an unoccupied house or land, intending to stay there as long as he can. He may seek to justify or excuse his conduct.

He may say that he was homeless and that this house or land was standing empty, doing nothing. But this plea is of no avail in law. As we said in *London Borough of Southwark v Williams* [1971] Ch. 734 at 744:

"If homelessness were once admitted as a defence to trespass, no one's house could be safe. . . . So the courts must, for the sake of law and order, take a firm stand. They must refuse to admit the plea of necessity to the hungry and the homeless; and trust that their distress will be relieved by the charitable and the good."

(i) The remedy of self-help

Now I would say this at once about squatters. The owner is not obliged to go to the courts to obtain possession. He is entitled, if he so desires, to take the remedy into his own hands. He can go in himself and turn them out without the aid of the courts of law. This is not a course to be recommended because of the disturbance which might follow. But the legality of it is beyond question. The squatters were themselves guilty of the offence of forcible entry contrary to the statute of 1381 [now repealed]. When they broke in, they entered "with strong hand" which the statute forbids. They were not only guilty of a criminal offence. They were guilty of a civil wrong. They were trespassers when they entered, and they continued to be trespassers so long as they remained there. The owner never acquiesced in their presence there. So the trespassers never gained possession. The owner, being entitled to possession, was entitled forcibly to turn them out: see *Browne v Dawson* (1840) 113 E.R. 950. As Sir Frederick Pollock put it in his book on Torts:

"A trespasser may in any case be turned off land before he has gained possession, and he does not gain possession until there has been something like acquiescence in the physical fact of his occupation on the part of the rightful owner."

Even though the owner himself should use force, then, so long as he uses no more force than is reasonably necessary, he is not himself liable either criminally or civilly. He is not liable criminally because it was said in the old times that none of the statutes of forcible entry apply to the expulsion by the owner of the tenant at will: . . . but, even if this is no longer true, in any case the statutes only apply to the expulsion of one who is in possession: see *R. v Child* (1846) 2 Cox C.C. 102. They do not apply to the expulsion of a trespasser who has no possession. The owner was not civilly liable because the owner is entitled to turn out a trespasser using force, no more than is reasonably necessary: see *Hemmings v Stoke Poges Golf Club* [1920] 1 K.B. 720.

(ii) The remedy by action

Although the law thus enables the owner to take the remedy into his own hands, that is not a course to be encouraged. In a civilised society, the courts should themselves provide a remedy which is speedy and effective; and thus make self-help unnecessary. The courts of common law have done this for centuries. The owner is entitled to go to the court and obtain an order that the owner "do recover" the land, and to issue a writ of possession immediately.

3. The position of tenants

I must point out, however, that I have referred so far only to squatters who enter without any colour of title at all. It is different with a tenant who holds over after his term has come to an end or after he has been given notice to quit. His possession was lawful in its inception. Even after the tenancy is determined, there is high authority for saying that the owner is not entitled to take the law into his own hands and remove the tenant by force. He should go to the court and get an order for possession. Otherwise he is guilty of a criminal offence. . . .

Note:

1. The scope for self-help by those wishing to regain the use of their landed property from a trespasser in occupation of it was reduced by the Criminal Law Act 1977, and then slightly extended by the Criminal Justice and Public Order Act 1994, ss.72, 74. The only persons who may legitimately use main force and helpers for this purpose are the "displaced residential occupier" (the person who returns home to find a trespasser *in situ*) and now the "protected intending occupier" (most individual owners, lessees, licensees, but not corporate bodies: new s.12A). Even such people, however, would do better to call the police, who have power at their instance to proceed to an eviction. Others require a court order.

2. The common law allows one to lop branches of trees which overhang one's land and cut roots which intrude into it. One may also demolish an encroaching wall, at least if dangerous (*Co-operative Wholesale Soc'y v British Railways Board* [1995] Times L.R. 695), charging the neighbour for the cost of demolition, but not reinstatement. Doubtless one may move, but not use, a discrete chattel which is on one's land without one's consent, and if unsolicited goods have been delivered one's powers are greater (Unsolicited Goods and Services Act, 1971). These rules justify what would prima facie be a trespass to property.

3. One may also be justified in going on to one's neighbour's land in order to abate a nuisance there. Though Mark and Dolores Leach went much too far in 1992 when they broke down a fence and strangled the neighbour's parrot whose continual screeching at up to 90dB had been making their lives a misery for years (*The Independent*, October 10, 1992), surely one should be able to go on to a neighbour's land to defuse a persistently noisy burglar alarm? The courts, however, seem to be mounting a campaign against the use of the common law power of abatement (*e.g. Billson v Residential Apartments* [1992] 1 All E.R. 141, HL; noted [1991] Camb. L.J. 401). This is in line with their attitude to defence of property (which itself is sadly out of line with public attitudes), as witness *Revill v Newbery* [1996] 1 All E.R. 291, where the Court of Appeal upheld an award of damages to a 29-year-old burglar shot by an 80-year old trying to protect his allotment (could the old man claim it back under a compensation order?). The courts even went so far in *Burton v Winters* [1993] 3 All E.R. 847 as to send Miss Burton to jail for *two years* for insisting on her property rights in breach of an injunction. That judgment (resting on a misreading of Blackstone and the citation of "authority" from Iowa) held that one may abate only in emergencies—otherwise one must go to court (and wait and wait and wait)—and if the courts refuse to help, you may not help yourself. This provides the (wrong) answer to the question raised by *Jaggard v Sawyer* (above, p.361) whether the refusal of an injunction (whether or not accompanied by an award of damages) legally as well as practically deprives the applicant of his property rights.

4. Owners of copyright are afforded, subject to notifying the police in advance, a certain right of self-help ("probably only good against the feeblest suitcase-salesman", W.R. Cornish, *Intellectual Property* (5th ed., 2003), p.66). They are entitled to seize infringing copies, but only if they are displayed in a public place or on public premises temporarily occupied as a place of business. No force may be used, and the police must be informed. (Copyright, Designs and Patents Act 1988, s.100).

5. In *Monsanto v Tilly* [1999] Times L.R. 829, CA, the defendants pleaded that since they were acting in the interest of protecting the public against genetically modified crops they were entitled to uproot crops which the plaintiff had planted under licence from the farmer who owned the land. Having held that the plaintiff could sue for trespass to the crops once uprooted and also (*sed quaere*) for trespass to the land, the court dismissed the defence of justification. The defendants' invocation of *F v West Berkshire H.A.* (above, p.393) was inappropriate because here Monsanto could (not that it would) have given consent. Destruction of private property in the public interest was permissible only in very restricted circumstances, and then only on payment of compensation (*Burmah Oil* [1964] 2 All E.R. 348), but *Southwark L.B.C. v Williams* [referred to in *McPhail*, above, p.411] was particularly in point. Indeed, the defence was so hopeless and the issue of the merits of genetic modification so incapable of being tried in a court of justice that the defence must be struck out, despite the defendants' claim that they were entitled to have a hearing on the merits, citing *Barrett* (above, p.100) and *Osman v U.K.* (1998) 5 B.H.R.C. 293.

PROTECTION FROM EVICTION ACT 1977

3.—(1) Where any premises have been let as a dwelling under a tenancy which is neither a statutorily protected tenancy nor an excluded tenancy, and—

(a) the tenancy . . . has come to an end, but
(b) the occupier continues to reside in the premises or part of them,

it shall not be lawful for the owner to enforce against the occupier, otherwise than by proceedings in the court, his right to recover possession of the premises.

Note:
Indeed even a landlord who has obtained an order of possession from the court may not himself resume possession of the premises but must await the execution of a warrant of possession by the bailiff (*Haniff v Robinson* [1993] 1 All E.R. 185, where the tenant obtained judgment for over £28,000). Some surprise was caused by the decision of the Court of Appeal in *Ropaigealach v Barclay's Bank* [1999] 4 All E.R. 235 that, subject to the Criminal Law Act 1977, a mortgagee could move into the mortgaged property when payments were in arrears, notwithstanding that if it had applied for an order of possession the court could have adjourned the claim or stayed execution.

CONSUMER CREDIT ACT 1974

90.—(1) At any time when—

(a) the debtor is in breach of a regulated hire-purchase or a regulated conditional sale agreement relating to goods, and
(b) the debtor has paid to the creditor one-third or more of the total price of the goods, and
(c) the property in the goods remains in the creditor,

the creditor is not entitled to recover possession of the goods from the debtor except on an order of the court.
91.—If goods are recovered by the creditor in contravention of section 90—

(a) the regulated agreement, if not previously terminated, shall terminate, and
(b) the debtor shall be released from all liability under the agreement, and shall be entitled to recover from the creditor all sums paid by the debtor under the agreement.

92.—(1) Except under an order of the court, the creditor or owner shall not be entitled to enter any premises to take possession of goods subject to a regulated . . . agreement. . . .
(3) An entry in contravention of subsection (1) . . . is actionable as a breach of statutory duty.

Abandoned Property
Abandoned shopping and luggage trolleys may be taken into possession by local authorities: Environmental Protection Act 1990, s.99 and Sch.4.
The powers of the police to remove motor vehicles are contained in the Removal and Disposal of Motor Vehicles Regulations 1986 (SI 1986/183); see *Rivers v Cutting* [1982] 3 All E.R. 69.
What of this case? A car was stolen when its owner was on holiday. A friend informed the police and gave his telephone number. The police then found the car which had been abandoned by the thieves, and had it taken to a garage. The following day the friend complained that he had not been contacted when the car was found. The garage then invoiced the owner for the storage charges and said the car would be sold if they were not paid. The Court of Appeal held that the power of the police was not limited to cars which had actually been abandoned, but covered cars which appeared to have been abandoned. But should that cover a car which had been abandoned by a thief when the police knew that it had not been abandoned by the owner? *Clarke v Chief Constable* [2001] EWCA Civ 1169, [2002] R.T.R. 5, [2001] T.L.R. 544.

PART IV

LAW BETWEEN NEIGHBOURS

INTRODUCTION

IN *Donoghue v Stevenson* Lord Atkin chose to designate as "neighbours" the people we should have in mind as likely to be affected by whatever it is we are doing. Such people may be said to be neighbours-in-law, but in fact our real neighbours are actually the people next door or upstairs. Of course they are likely to be affected by what we do, indeed, so likely to be affected that whatever we do, we cannot avoid having some adverse effect on them. We cannot live or work or do the other things we are entitled to do without producing noise and smells and other emanations which will percolate into the neighbours' zone of being. So we have the rule—we have to have it—that while we must not make their lives a misery, they cannot complain of every noise or smell we make. This is a whole different scenario from the relationship of neighbours-in-law.

There was a special régime for actual neighbours long before *Donoghue v Stevenson* enunciated its general principle, and if students have some difficulty in understanding the present law, this is not just because "This cause of action is immersed in undefined uncertainty", as Erle C.J. observed in 1867, but partly also because there is a tension between the general negligence principle and the old law of nuisance which deviated in several respects from the twin principles of "liability for fault" and "no liability without fault." We have seen a similar problem in trying to reconcile the rules of trespass with those of negligence, where also the difference is as much one of function as of history.

The personal relationship in space of neighbours-in-fact reflects a relationship of contiguity or vicinity between the plots of land they occupy. One may therefore ask whether the function of the tort of nuisance is to protect the land or the persons on it. persons on it. The House of Lords in *Hunter* gave a categorical answer: it is to protect the land. This may seem odd, for the trend has been to use the law of negligence for cases of actual damage to land, and to leave to the law of nuisance only cases of noise and smells which, though doubtless capable of rendering a res. less des., can really only offend human beings with ears and nose.

But here as elsewhere the Human Rights Act is having its say. The common law of nuisance may protect only the house, but Art.8 of the Convention requires respect for the home. It is true that the duty of respect is imposed only on public bodies, but that duty may call for proactive steps, including protecting the tranquillity of the home from disturbance by third parties. Nor need the disturbance come from next door, as the cases on aircraft noise show. Perhaps therefore we should analyse the cases, even the common law cases, in terms of the claimant's right to relative enjoyment of his property rather than in terms of his relationship with his neighbours—not too dramatic a shift of emphasis, given that it is mainly those close to you who can make your life a misery. If we focus on the claimant's right in this way, we will be readier to accept (a) the grant of injunctions even if there is no actual harm, and (b) the downplaying of any need for fault in the defendant.

As to the common law between neighbours-in-fact some old instances of strict liability have been qualified and some old cases of non-liability have been modified. Here are two instances. It used to be the law that if your buildings were subverted by the roots of my tree I had to pay you, regardless. The Court of Appeal has now said that

I have to pay only if the result was foreseeable, if I failed to take proper steps against it (*Solloway v Hampshire C.C.*, below, p.442). Here the old rule of strict liability has been qualified by the introduction of the requirements of negligence. By contrast, I used not to be liable to you if some danger on my land, which arose without any of my doing, caused harm to your land. Nowadays I have to take reasonable steps to prevent such harm—and bear the expense. The first step was to say that if the trouble was on my land for a period, then by not removing it I had "continued" it (*Sedleigh-Denfield v O'Callaghan* [1940] A.C. 880 (Lord Atkin!)) but now liability is based openly on my negligence in not removing it (though not quite the negligence we know and love) (*Leakey v National Trust*, below, p.437).

The infusion of negligence principles has taken place mainly in cases where one neighbour has caused or permitted *actual damage* to another's property, rather than in those cases where the plaintiff is complaining of smell, noise, dust, etc. *Donoghue v Stevenson* has had relatively little effect on cases of the latter type, which are usually claims for an injunction rather than damages. On the other hand, in cases of *personal injury*, the principles of negligence reign supreme, and if one is injured, it matters relatively little whether or not one was at home at the time or whether the cause of the injury arose from activities next door rather than in the street. The democratic principle is that one's body should not be better protected simply by reason of one's property relations (and much of nuisance law is akin to property relations, and in consequence affected by the traditional unreasonableness—at any rate, lack of concern with reasonableness—characteristic of the English law of property).

But even where the principles of negligence have made themselves felt, attention is still paid to the fact that the relationship between actual neighbours is a very "special" one. It will be easy to find that neighbourly duties are non-delegable, that one can sue one's neighbour for what his contractors, and not just his employees, do on his land. Thus if the tree in *Salsbury v Woodland* (above, p.311) had fallen on the neighbour's greenhouse instead of harming the neighbour's son in the street outside, the occupier who retained the tree-fellers would probably have had to pay.

Two instances can be given of deviation from general principle in this area. First, normal notions of contributory negligence or contributory fault do not apply. Thus one can buy a house right next to an established cricket field and then complain that people are playing cricket on it (*Miller v Jackson*, below, p.445). The reason for this exceptional rule was that otherwise a person who started his noisome activity when his artisan neighbours were complaisant could continue it even when the sensitive bourgeoisie moved in, and this might be contrary to the public interest in embourgeoisement. Now that we have administrative measures to prevent unpleasant activities, this unsatisfactory old rule of private law could well disappear. Secondly, although in general "one takes the plaintiff as one finds him," in disputes between neighbours this is qualified. It would be wrong if my freedom of activity on my own land were to be constrained by reason of the neurotic sensibility of the the person next door.

Another contrast between negligence and nuisance can be seen in their relation to public law. We have seen, in cases such as *Barrett* and *Phelps* (above p.100) how negligence has moved into public law, the relations between government and individuals, rendering local authorities ever more liable. Public law, by contrast, is threatening to take over the law of nuisance in its most distinctive area.

For example, when Parliament has authorised an activity or installation people in the neighbourhood who are annoyed by it may, depending on the construction of the statute and subject to questions of compensation for expropriation, find themselves without a remedy. By contrast, when a local authority grants planning permission, the environment may be changed in fact, but it cannot otherwise affect the rights of the inhabitants

(*Wheeler v JJ Saunders* [1995] 2 All E.R. 697). On the other hand, local authorities can be very helpful to those with complaints about noisy or noisome neighbours.

If your neighbours are being a real nuisance these days, you don't issue a writ, you phone the local authority, and if you phone often enough and cry havoc, they will let slip their formidable powers to deal with "statutory nuisances" (below, p.431). In this way you will not only get the nuisance stopped, you may get a compensation order into the bargain: much better, quicker and cleaner than a private law suit for damages. Those barons of the modern age, the local authorities, are the vigilantes of the environment: only in the rare case where the noisome activity is agreeable to the local politicians (oil refinery (*Halsey v Esso Petroleum* [1961] 2 All E.R. 145); brothel (*Thompson-Schwab v Costaki* [1956] 1 All E.R. 652); go-kart racing (*Tetley v Chitty* [1986] 1 All E.R. 663)), or the problem is too hot to handle (*Hussain v Lancaster C.C.* [1999] 4 All E.R. 125) does the private lawsuit really answer.

Disputes between neighbours, the lawyer's nightmare, are as fractious and bad-tempered as disputes within the home: both generally involve "fault", or at least lack of forbearance, on both sides, and are nearly as likely to lead to violence, sometimes fatal (murder and suicide). Alternative dispute resolution is not likely to help in such cases, so litigation is resorted to and persisted in to the bitter end. The Protection from Harassment Act 1997 permits the deployment of criminal procedures in both cases. Although there is no statutory provision for ouster orders as there is in family matters, there have been cases where a person has been enjoined from going within a certain distance of the claimant's home, with the result that he has to move out of his own home or be imprisoned for contempt. Even the choice of reluctantly leaving the area is not unconstrained, since you may have difficulty selling your house if you have had problems with your neighbour, a matter you are bound to disclose to a prospective purchaser (see *McMeekin v Long* [2003] 2 E.G.L.R. 81).

"Disputes among neighbours could become a thing of the past under laws that came into force yesterday". So wrote *The Times* Legal Correspondent on October 14, 2003. She was surely being unduly sanguine in this reference to the Land Registration Act 2002, which admittedly facilitates the swift and conclusive determination of the precise line of demarcation between adjacent properties, and thereby reduces the probable incidence of boundary disputes, hitherto adjusted in the forum of trespass rather than nuisance. But high hedges have been just as much of a problem. Robert Frost reminded us that "good fences make good neighbours", but while there were legal restrictions on the height of fences, until the Anti-Social Behaviour Act 2003 there was nothing that could be done about the exuberant *cupressus leylandii*, the cause of much grief to many whose flowers withered and died in its shadow. The Act empowers local authorities to deal with complaints if a hedge—two or more evergreen or semi-evergreen trees or shrubs—is over two metres high (s.66–73). The same Act extends the powers and duties of local authorities regarding noise under the Noise Act 1996, and even permits the closure of licensed premises if the noise from them constitutes a public nuisance (s.40–41).

One very famous case involving actual damage—the flooding of a mine—is *Rylands v Fletcher* (below, p.453), whose relationship to nuisance has been ambiguous. The High Court of Australia has held that it has now been absorbed into the ordinary law of negligence, but the House of Lords, having clarified the relationship between *Rylands* and nuisance in the *Cambridge Water Co* case, refused to follow the Australians, and decided to retain this time-honoured head of liability, with certain adjustments. See *Transco*, below p.463.

Chapter 10

NUISANCE

Section 1.—Title to Sue

HUNTER v CANARY WHARF

House of Lords [1997] A.C. 655; [1997] 2 W.L.R. 684; [1997] 2 All E.R. 426 (noted [1997] Camb. L.J. 453; (1998) 61 M.L.R. 870; (1997) 113 L.Q.R. 515)

690 inhabitants of properties in the Isle of Dogs, East London, sued in respect of the interruption of television reception owing to the existence of the skyscraper known as Canary Wharf (later to attract the attentions of Irish bombers) and of the irruption of dust caused by its construction. The Court of Appeal held that while mere residents could sue even if they did not have exclusive possession of the affected land, no claim lay in respect of the interruption of television signals. The House of Lords (apart from Lord Cooke) was of a different opinion on the first of these points.

Lord Goff of Chieveley: On the authorities as they stand, an action in private nuisance will only lie at the suit of a person who has a right to the land affected. Ordinarily, such a person can only sue if he has the right to exclusive possession of the land, such as a freeholder or tenant in possession, or even a licensee with exclusive possession. Exceptionally this category may include a person in actual possession who has no right to be there; and in any event a reversioner can sue in so far his reversionary interest is affected. But a mere licensee on the land has no right to sue.

The question therefore arises whether your Lordships should be persuaded to depart from established principle, and recognise such a right in others who are no more than mere licensees on the land. At the heart of this question lies a more fundamental question, which relates to the scope of the law of private nuisance. Here, I wish to draw attention to the fact that although, in the past, damages for personal injury have been recovered at least in actions of public nuisance, there is now developing a school of thought that the appropriate remedy for such claims as these should lie in our now fully developed law of negligence, and that personal injury claims should be altogether excluded from the domain of nuisance. The most forthright proponent of this approach has been Professor Newark in his article. "The Boundaries of Nuisance" (1949) 65 L.Q.R. 480. Furthermore, it is now being suggested that claims in respect of physical damage to the land should also be excluded from private nuisance (see, *e.g.* the article by Mr Conor Gearty, "The Place of Private Nuisance in a Modern Law of Torts" [1989] C.L.J. 214). In any event, it is right for present purposes to regard the typical cases of private nuisance as being those concerned with interference with the enjoyment of land and, as such, generally actionable only by a person with a right in the land. Characteristic examples of cases of this kind are those concerned with noise, vibrations, noxious smells and the like. The two appeals with which your Lordships are here concerned arise from actions of this character.

For private nuisances of this kind, the primary remedy is in most cases an injunction, which is sought to bring the nuisance to an end, and in most cases should swiftly achieve that objective. The right to bring such proceedings is, as the law stands, ordinarily vested in the person who has exclusive possession of the land. He or she is the person who will sue, if it is necessary to do so. Moreover he or she can, if thought appropriate, reach an agreement with the person creating the nuisance, either that it may continue for a certain period of time, possibly on the payment of a sum of money, or that it shall cease, again perhaps on certain terms including the time within which the cessation will take place. The former may well occur when an agreement is reached between neighbours about the circumstances in which one of them may carry out major repairs to his house which may affect the other's enjoyment of his property. But the efficacy of arrangements such as these depends upon the existence of an identifiable person with whom the creator of the nuisance can deal for this purpose. If anybody who lived in the relevant property as a home had the right to sue, sensible arrangements such as these might in some cases no longer be practicable.

Moreover, any such departure from the established law on this subject, such as that adopted by the Court of Appeal in the present case, faces the problem of defining the category of persons who would have the right to sue. The Court of Appeal adopted the not easily identifiable category of those who have a "substantial link" with the land, regarding a person who occupied the premises "as a home" as having a sufficient link for this purpose. But who is to be included in this category? It was plainly intended to include husbands and wives, or partners, and their children, and even other relatives living with them. But is the category also to include the lodger upstairs, or the au pair girl or resident nurse caring for an invalid who makes her home in the house while she works there? If the latter, it seems strange that the category should not extend to include places where people work as well as places where they live, where nuisances such as noise can be just as unpleasant or distracting. In any event, the extension of the tort in this way would transform it from a tort to land into a tort to the person, in which damages could be recovered in respect of something less serious than personal injury and the criteria for liability were founded not upon negligence but upon striking a balance between the interests of neighbours in the use of their land. This is, in my opinion, not an acceptable way in which to develop the law.

Lord Hoffmann: The concept of nuisance as a tort against land has recently been questioned by the decision of the Court of Appeal in *Khorasandjian v Bush* [1993] 3 All E.R. 669. The plaintiff was a young woman aged 18 living with her mother. The defendant was a former friend who pestered her with telephone calls. In the ordinary sense of the word, he was making a nuisance of himself. The problem was to find a cause of action which could justify the grant of an injunction to stop him. A majority of the Court of Appeal (Peter Gibson J. dissenting) held that she was entitled to sue in nuisance.

This is based upon a fundamental mistake about the remedy which the tort of nuisance provides. It arises, I think, out of a misapplication of an important distinction drawn by Lord Westbury L.C. in *St Helen's Smelting Co v Tipping* (1865).

St Helen's Smelting Co v Tipping was a landmark case. It drew the line beyond which rural and landed England did not have to accept external costs imposed upon it by industrial pollution. But there has been, I think, some inclination to treat it as having divided nuisance into two torts, one of causing "material injury to the property", such as flooding or depositing poisonous substances on crops, and the other of causing "sensible personal discomfort", such as excessive noise or smells. In cases in the first category, there has never been any doubt that the remedy, whether by way of injunction or damages, is for causing damage to the land. It is plain that in such a case only a person with an interest in the land can sue. But there has been a tendency to regard cases in the second category as actions in respect of the discomfort or even personal injury which the plaintiff has suffered or is likely to suffer. On this view, the plaintiff's interest in the land becomes no more than a qualifying condition or springboard which entitles him to sue for injury to himself.

If this were the case, the need for the plaintiff to have an interest in land would indeed be hard to justify. But the premise is quite mistaken. In the case of nuisances "productive of sensible personal discomfort", the action is not for causing discomfort to the person but, as in the case of the first category, for causing injury to the land. True it is that the land has not suffered "sensible" injury, but its utility has been diminished by the existence of the nuisance. It is for an unlawful threat to the utility of his land that the possessor or occupier is entitled to an injunction and it is for the diminution in such utility that he is entitled to compensation.

Once it is understood that nuisances "productive of sensible personal discomfort" do not constitute a separate tort of causing discomfort to people but are merely part of a single tort of causing injury to land, the rule that the plaintiff must have an interest in the land falls into place as logical and, indeed, inevitable.

Lord Hope of Craighead and **Lord Lloyd of Berwick** delivered concurring speeches; **Lord Cooke of Thorndon** dissented on the question of title to sue.

Notes:

1. The claim for interference with television reception would have failed in any case, for the interruption was due, not to any activity of the defendants (as to which the question was left open), but to the existence of their building. Vital though televiewing is, seeing in daylight is even more important, but even so you are free to build in England so as to block the light getting into your neighbour's building, unless it has been there for 20 years, in which case he must be left with a reasonable amount.

2. The Court of Appeal has held that a "tolerated trespasser" ("a recent, somewhat bizarre, addition to the dramatis personae of the law", *per* Clarke L.J.) could sue the landlord in nuisance when cockroaches entered the apartment from the common parts of the building. A "tolerated trespasser" is a former tenant whose tenancy has been brought to an end but who remains there with the consent of the previous landlord on payment of the rent, failing which a further court order can be obtained or a suspended one enforced. Such a person cannot claim under the Defective Premises Act 1972, since there is no longer any tenancy, but her continued exclusive occupation, though terminable, is enough for title to sue in nuisance. *Pemberton v Southwark LBC* [2000] 3 All E.R. 924.

3. A block of flats let on, long lease had already been damaged by the roots of the defendant's plane tree when the claimant bought the freehold with a view to managing it through a subsidiary company. The defendant refused to fell the tree. Could the plaintiff sue? Yes: *Delaware Mansions v Westminster CC* [2001] 4 All E.R. 737 (HL). Even if no fresh damage was done after the claimant's purchase of the property, it was a continuing nuisance, and provided that the claimant had informed the defendant of the problem without any effective response, he could sue for the remedial costs. Although the result is not objectionable, there are some very regrettable features in the reasoning of the single speech in the House of Lords.

4. The device of the "continuing nuisance" may render the Human Rights Act applicable to a nuisance which started before it came into force. In *McKenna v British Aluminium* (Birmingham District Registry, January 16, 2002) Neuberger J., refused to strike out a claim by over thirty children that they had suffered mental distress and physical harm from the emissions from the defendant's factory. The defence that the claim was hopeless in the light of *Hunter* (as it was, on two distinct grounds) was repelled, because of the human rights aspect.

5. Between the decision of the Court of Appeal in *Khorosandjian* and its overruling in *Hunter* claims in nuisance were frequently brought by small children: the reason was that they could obtain legal aid, since, unlike the bourgeois owners of the property, they had no money. Nice work, no? Now, of course, the kids can sue for breach of their human rights in their home, but this is not so useful since their parents can get legal aid if there is a human rights angle to the claim.

Section 2.—The Elements

BAMFORD v TURNLEY

Court of Exchequer Chamber (1862) 3 B. & S. 66; 31 L.J.Q.B. 286; 6 L.T. 721;
9 Jur.(N.S.) 377; 10; W.R. 803; 122 E.R. 27

Action for damages for smoke and smell from brick-works

The plaintiff complained of the smoke and smell arising from the burning of bricks by the defendant on his land not far from the plaintiff's house. At the trial, Lord Cockburn C.J. directed the jury, on the authority of *Hole v Barlow* (1858) 4 C.B. (N.S.) 334; 140 E.R. 1113, that if they thought that the spot was convenient and proper, and the burning of bricks was, under the circumstances, a reasonable use by the defendant of his own land, the defendant would be entitled to a verdict, independently of the small matter of whether there was an interference with the plaintiff's comfort thereby. The jury accordingly found a verdict for the defendant. The plaintiff moved for a rule calling upon the defendant to show cause why a verdict should not be entered for the plaintiff for 40s., but the Court of Queen's Bench (Cockburn C.J., Wightman, Hill and Blackburn JJ.) refused the rule. The plaintiff appealed to the Court of Exchequer Chamber, who allowed the appeal and entered judgment for the plaintiff, Pollock C.B. dissenting.

Williams J.: . . . if the true doctrine is, that whenever, taking all the circumstances into consideration, including the nature and extent of the plaintiff's enjoyment before the acts complained of, the annoyance is sufficiently great to amount to a nuisance according to the ordinary rule of law, an action will lie, whatever the locality may be, then surely the jury cannot properly be asked whether the causing of the nuisance was a reasonable use of the land.

If such a question is proper for their consideration in an action such as the present, for a nuisance by emitting corrupted air into the plaintiff' house, we can see no reason why a similar question should not be submitted to the jury in actions for other violations of the ordinary rights of property; *e.g.* the transmission by a neighbour of water in a polluted condition. But certainly it would be difficult to maintain, as the law now stands, that the jury, in such an action, ought to be told to find for the defendant if they thought that the manufactory which caused the impurity of the water was built on a proper and convenient spot, and that the working of it was a reasonable use by the defendant of his own land. Again, where an easement has been gained in addition to the ordinary rights of property, *e.g.* where a right has been gained to the lateral passage of light and air, no one has ever suggested that the jury might be told, in an action for obstructing the free passage of the light and air, to find for the defendant if they were of opinion that the building which caused the obstruction was erected in a proper and convenient place, and in the reasonable enjoyment by the defendant of his own land. And yet, on principle, it is difficult to see why such questions should not be left to the jury if *Hole v Barlow* was well decided.

We are, however, of opinion that the decision in that case was wrong. . . .

Pollock C.B. (dissenting): The question in this case is, whether the direction of the Lord Chief Justice, professing to be founded on the decision of the Court of Common Pleas in *Hole v Barlow*, was right, and in my judgment substantially it was right, *viz.*, taking it to have been as stated in the case, *viz.*, "that if the jury thought that the spot was convenient and proper, and the burning of the bricks was, under the circumstances, a reasonable use by the defendant of his own land, the defendant would be entitled to a verdict." I do not think that the nuisance for which an action will lie is capable of any legal definition which will be applicable to all cases and useful in deciding them. The question so entirely depends on the surrounding circumstances—the place where, the time when, the alleged nuisance, what, the mode of committing it, how, and the duration of it, whether temporary or permanent, occasional or continual—as to make it impossible to lay down any rule of law applicable to every case, and which will also be useful in assisting a jury to come to a satisfactory conclusion: it must at all times be a question of fact with reference to all the circumstances of the case.

Most certainly in my judgment it cannot be laid down as a legal proposition or doctrine, that anything which, under any circumstances, lessens the comfort or endangers the health or safety of a neighbour, must necessarily be an actionable nuisance. That may be a nuisance in Grosvenor Square which would be none in Smithfield Market, that may be a nuisance at midday which would not be so at midnight, that may be a nuisance which is permanent and continual which would be no nuisance if temporary or occasional only. A clock striking the hour, or a bell ringing for some domestic purpose, may be a nuisance, if unreasonably loud and discordant, of which the jury alone must judge; but although not unreasonably loud, if the owner, from some whim or caprice, made the clock strike the hour every 10 minutes, or the bell ring continually, I think a jury would be justified in considering it to be a very great nuisance. In general, a kitchen chimney, suitable to the establishment to which it belonged, could not be deemed a nuisance, but if built in an inconvenient place or manner, on purpose to annoy the neighbours, it might, I think, very properly be treated as one. The compromises that belong to social life, and upon which the peace and comfort of it mainly depend, furnish an indefinite number of examples where some apparent natural right is invaded, or some enjoyment abridged, to provide for the more general convenience or necessities of the whole community; and I think the more the details of the question are examined the more clearly it will appear that all that the law can do is to lay down some general and vague proposition which will be no guide to the jury in each particular case that may come before them.

I think the word "reasonable" cannot be an improper word, and too vague to be used on this occasion . . . If the act complained of be done in a convenient manner, so as to give no unnecessary annoyance, and be a reasonable exercise of some apparent right, or a reasonable use of the land, house or property of the party under all the circumstances, in which I include the degree of inconvenience it will produce, then I think no action can be sustained, if the jury find that it was reasonable—as the jury must be taken to have found that it was reasonable that the defendant should be allowed to do what he did, and reasonable that the plaintiff should submit to the inconvenience occasioned by what was done. And this gets rid of the difficulty suggested in the judgment just read by my brother Williams; because it cannot be supposed that a jury would find that to be a reasonable act by a person which produces any ruinous effect upon his neighbours. . . .

. . . in my opinion the judgment of the court below ought to be affirmed.

Bramwell B.: I am of opinion that this judgment should be reversed.

The plaintiff has a prima facie case. The defendant has infringed the maxim *sic utere tuo ut alienum non laedas*. Then, what principle or rule of law can he rely on to defend himself? It is clear to my mind that there is some exception to the general application of the maxim mentioned. The instances put during the argument, of burning weeds, emptying cesspools, making noises during repairs, and other instances which would be nuisances if done wantonly or maliciously, nevertheless may be lawfully done. It cannot be said that such acts are not nuisances, because, by the hypothesis, they are; and it cannot be doubted that, if a person maliciously and without cause made close to a dwelling-house the same offensive smells as may be made in emptying a cesspool, an action would lie. Nor can these cases be got rid of as extreme cases, because such cases properly test a principle. . . . There must be, then, some principle on which such cases must be excepted. It seems to me that that principle may be deduced from the character of these cases, and is this, *viz.*, that those acts necessary for the common and ordinary use and occupation of land and houses may be done, if conveniently done, without subjecting those who do them to an action. This principle would comprehend all the cases I have mentioned, but would not comprehend the present, where what has been done was not the using of land in a common and ordinary way, but in an exceptional manner—not unnatural nor unusual, but not the common and ordinary use of land. There is an obvious necessity for such a principle as I have mentioned. It is as much for the advantage of one owner as of another; for the very nuisance the one complains of, as the result of the ordinary use of his neighbour's land, he himself will create in the ordinary use of his own, and the reciprocal nuisances are of a comparatively trifling character. The convenience of such a rule may be indicated by calling it a rule of give and take, live and let live.

Then can this principle be extended to, or is there any other principle which will comprehend, the present case?

It is said that it is lawful because it is for the public benefit. Now, in the first place, that law to my mind is a bad one which, for the public benefit, inflicts loss on an individual without compensation. But further, with great respect, I think this consideration misapplied in this and in many other cases. The public consists of all the individuals of it, and a thing is only for the public benefit when it is productive of good to those individuals on the balance of loss and gain to all. So that if all the loss and all the gain were borne and received by one individual, he on the whole would be a gainer. But whenever this is the case—whenever a thing is for the public benefit, properly understood—the loss to the individuals of the public who lose will bear compensation out of the gains of those who gain. It is for the public benefit there should be railways, but it would not be unless the gain of having the railway was sufficient to compensate the loss occasioned by the use of the land required for its site; and accordingly no one thinks it would be right to take an individual's land without compensation to make a railway. It is for the public benefit that trains should run, but not unless they pay their expenses. If one of those expenses is the burning down of a wood of such value that the railway owners would not run the train and burn down the wood if it were their own, neither is it for the public benefit they should if the wood is not their own. If, though the wood were their own, they still would find it compensated them to run trains at the cost of burning the wood, then they obviously ought to compensate the owner of such wood, not being themselves, if they burn it down in making their gains. So in like way in this case a money value indeed cannot easily be put on the plaintiff's loss, but it is equal to some number of pounds or pence, £10, £50, or what not: unless the defendant's profits are enough to compensate this, I deny that it is for the public benefit he should do what he has done; if they are, he ought to compensate.

The only objection I can see to this reasoning is, that by injunction or by abatement of the nuisance a man who would not accept a pecuniary compensation might put a stop to works of great value, and much more than enough to compensate him. This objection, however, is comparatively of small practical importance; it may be that the law ought to be amended, and some means be provided to legalise such cases, as I believe is the case in some foreign countries on giving compensation; but I am clearly of opinion that, though the present law may be defective, it would be much worse, and be unjust and inexpedient, if it permitted such power of inflicting loss and damage to individuals, without compensation, as is claimed by the argument for the defendant.

ST. HELEN'S SMELTING CO v TIPPING

House of Lords (1865) 11 H.L.Cas. 642, 35 L.J.Q.B. 66; 12 L.T. 776; 29 J.P. 579;
11 Jur.(N.S.) 785; 13 W.R. 1083; 11 E.R. 1483

Action for damage to garden by pollution from smelting works

The plaintiff bought a valuable estate in June 1860. In September 1860 the defendant began very extensive smelting operations on land a mile and a half away. Its use prior to that time was uncertain, but the vapours now emanating from the defendant's works were destroying the plaintiff's shrubs and trees.

At the trial, Mellor J. laid down the law to the jury in the following terms: "That every man is bound to use his own property in such a manner as not to injure the property of his neighbour, unless, by the lapse of a certain period of time, he has acquired a prescriptive right to do so. But the law does not regard trifling inconveniences; every thing must be looked at from a reasonable point of view; and, therefore, in an action for nuisance to property by noxious vapours arising on the land of another, the injury to be actionable must be such as visibly to diminish the value of the property and the comfort and enjoyment of it. That, in determining that question the time, locality, and all the circumstances should be taken into consideration; that in counties where great works have been erected and carried on, which are the means of developing the national wealth, persons must not stand on extreme rights and bring actions in respect of every matter of annoyance, as, if that were so, business could not be carried on in those places."

The jury found a verdict for the plaintiff, damages £361 18s. 4½d. The defendant sought a new trial on the ground of misdirection, but was unsuccessful in the Queen's Bench (1863) 122 E.R. 588, in the Court of Exchequer Chamber (1864) 122 E.R. 591, and finally in the House of Lords.

Lord Westbury L.C.: . . . My Lords, in matters of this description it appears to me that it is a very desirable thing to mark the difference between an action brought for a nuisance upon the ground that the alleged nuisance produces material injury to the property, and an action brought for a nuisance on the ground that the thing alleged to be a nuisance is productive of sensible personal discomfort. With regard to the latter, namely, the personal inconvenience and inter-ference with one's enjoyment, one's quiet, one's personal freedom, anything that discomposes or injuriously affects the senses or the nerves, whether that may or may not be denominated a nuisance, must undoubtedly depend greatly on the circumstances of the place where the thing complained of actually occurs. If a man lives in a town, it is necessary that he should subject himself to the consequences of those operations of trade which may be carried on in his immediate locality, which are actually necessary for trade and commerce, and also for the enjoyment of property, and for the benefit of the inhabitants of the town and of the public at large. If a man lives in a street where there are numerous shops, and a shop is opened next door to him, which is carried on in a fair and reasonable way, he has no ground for complaint, because to himself individually there may arise much discomfort from the trade carried on in that shop. But when an occupation is carried on by one person in the neighbourhood of another, and the result of that trade, or occupation, or business, is a material injury to property, then there unquestion-ably arises a very different consideration. I think, my Lords, that in a case of that description, the submission which is required from persons living in society to that amount of discomfort which may be necessary for the legitimate and free exercise of the trade of their neighbours, would not apply to circumstances the immediate result of which is sensible injury to the value of the property.

Now, in the present case, it appears that the plaintiff purchased a very valuable estate, which lies within a mile-and-a-half from certain large smelting works. What the occupation of these copper smelting premises was anterior to the year 1860 does not clearly appear. The plaintiff became the proprietor of an estate of great value in the month of June 1860. In the month of September 1860 very extensive smelting operations began on the property of the present appellants, in their works at St. Helen's. Of the effect of the vapours exhaling from those works upon the plaintiff's property, and the injury done to his trees and shrubs, there is abundance of evidence in the case.

My Lords, the action has been brought upon that, and the jurors have found the existence of the injury; and the only ground upon which your Lordships are asked to set aside that verdict, and to direct a new trial, is this, that the whole neighbourhood where these copper smelting works were carried on, is a neighbourhood more or less devoted to manufacturing purposes of a similar kind, and there it is said, that inasmuch as this copper smelting is carried on in what the appellant contends is a fit place, it may be carried on with impunity, although the result may be the utter destruction, or the very considerable diminution, of the value of the plaintiff's property. My Lords, I apprehend that that is not the meaning of the word "suitable," or the meaning of the word "convenient," which has been used as applicable to the subject. The word "suitable" unquestionably cannot carry with it this consequence, that a trade may be carried on in a particular locality, the consequence of which trade may be injury and destruction to the neighbouring property. Of course, my Lords, I except cases where any prescriptive right has been acquired by a lengthened user of the place.

On these grounds, therefore, shortly, without dilating farther upon them (and they are sufficiently unfolded by the judgment of the learned judges in the court below), I advise your Lordships to affirm the decision of the court below, and to refuse the new trial, and to dismiss the appeal with costs.

Notes:

1. These Victorian cases are fascinatingly set in the social-historical context by J.P.S. McLaren in "Nuisance Law and the Industrial Revolution—Some Lessons from Social History" (1983) 3 O.J.L.S. 155. See also A.W.B. Simpson, *Leading Cases in the Common Law* (1995), 163–194.

2. In his outstanding decision of *Halsey v Esso Petroleum Co.* [1961] 1 W.L.R. 683, Veale J. said this: " . . . liability for nuisance by harmful deposits could be established by proving damage by the deposits to the property in question, provided of course that the injury was not merely trivial. Negligence is not an ingredient of the cause of action, and the character of the neighbourhood is not a matter to be taken into consideration. On the other hand, nuisance by smell and noise is something to which no absolute standard can be applied. It is always a question of degree whether the interference with comfort or convenience is sufficiently serious to constitute a nuisance. The character of the neighbourhood is very relevant and all relevant circumstances have to be taken into account."

3. Of course, if prolonged discomfort is caused, the value of the property will diminish; it cannot have been the intention of Lord Westbury to permit a plaintiff to pretend that his discomfort was intolerable on the mere ground that it had economic effects. Accordingly, his distinction must refer to physical damage to property, and not to mere economic loss. But surely if disamenity is treated as diminution in value and cases of actual physical damage are siphoned off into negligence law the result will be that nuisance will be left with nothing but economic harm?

4. In *Halsey's* case the plaintiffs' life had been made a misery for five years by the constant noise, dirt and nocturnal commotion from the oil depot near their house in Fulham; all they got by way of damages was £200. In *Bone v Seale* [1975] 1 All E.R. 787 (referred to rather ambiguously by Lord Lloyd in *Hunter* ([1997] 2 All E.R. 426 at 444)) the plaintiff occupiers had been disgusted for 12 years by the nauseating smells emanating from a village pig-farm but were unable to prove any diminution of value in their property. The judge awarded them £500 *per year*, a total of £6,000 each, but the Court of Appeal reduced the award to a lump sum of £1,000. In both cases an injunction was granted as well as damages.

Question

Can a person recover from a neighbour who has installed a petrol station the amount by which his fire insurance premiums have consequently gone up? Consider *Merlin v British Nuclear Fuels* [1990] 3 All E.R. 711, which refused compensation when a house was rendered unsaleable by radiation from a nuclear power station). Also *C & G Homes Ltd v Secretary of State*, *The Independent*, November 6, 1990 where the health authority was proposing to instal mental convalescents in two houses on an estate covered by a restrictive covenant binding purchasers not to cause or permit any act "which may become a nuisance, annoyance, danger or detriment", and the Court of Appeal held that impaired marketability did not fall within the covenant.

WATT v JAMIESON

Court of Session, 1954 S.C. 56

Action for damage to walls by vapour from domestic installation

The pursuer, an advocate and proprietor of the upper floors of 3, Moray Place, Edinburgh, claimed £3,050 from the defender, a solicitor, and proprietor of the lower floors of 4, Moray Place. The defender had installed a gas water storage heater, the flue of which he connected to the vent in the gable common to the two houses. This flue discharged $2\frac{1}{2}$ gallons of water every six hours, and alarming symptoms of damage appeared on the interior and exterior walls of the pursuer's house. The defender pleaded that the action was irrelevant on the ground that there was no liability for the normal natural and familiar use of property and that this was such a use. A proof before answer was allowed.

Lord President Cooper: ... From these and other pronouncements I deduce that the proper angle of approach to a case of alleged nuisance is rather from the standpoint of the victim of the loss or inconvenience than from the standpoint of the alleged offender; and that, if any person so uses his property as to occasion serious disturbance or substantial inconvenience to his neighbour or material damage to his neighbour's property, it is in the general case irrelevant as a defence for the defender to plead merely that he was making a normal and familiar use of his own property. The balance in all such cases has to be held between the freedom of a proprietor to use his property as he pleases and the duty on a proprietor not to inflict material loss or inconvenience on adjoining proprietors or adjoining property; and in every case the answer depends on considerations of fact and degree. I cannot accept the extreme view that in order to make a relevant case of nuisance it is always necessary for the pursuer to aver that the type of user complained of was *in itself* non-natural, unreasonable and unusual. Especially when (as in this case) the so-called "locality" principle applies, it must be accepted that a certain amount of inconvenience, annoyance, disturbance and even damage must just be accepted as the price the pursuer pays for staying where he does in a city tenement. The critical question is whether what he was exposed to was *plus quam tolerabile* when due weight has been given to all the surrounding circumstances of the offensive conduct and its effects. If that test is satisfied, I do not consider that our law accepts as a defence that the nature of the user complained of was usual, familiar and normal. *Any* type of use which in the sense indicated above subjects adjoining proprietors, to substantial annoyance, or causes material damage to their property, is prima facie not a "reasonable" use. . . .

Notes:

1. As Lord Fraser said in reference to this case " . . . the fact that the proper approach is from the standpoint of the victim does not mean that the question of fault on the part of the alleged offender can be completely disregarded, so as to make him an insurer . . . " (*RHM Bakeries (Scotland) v Strathclyde R.C.* 1985 S.L.T. 214 at 218, HL).

2. Prior to the decision in the next case it had indeed been the view that what counts is the effect on the plaintiff rather than the fault of the defendant. Thus in *Sampson v Hodson-Pressinger* [1981] 3 All E.R. 710 it had been held that the perfectly normal use of premises which, owing to their defective construction or insulation, caused insufferable noise on adjacent premises did constitute a nuisance, a decision which had to be sidelined by the Court of Appeal in *Baxter* [1999] 1 All E.R. 237, 243 upheld in the next case.

3. When the defendants were demolishing buildings which had a party wall with the premises where the plaintiffs had a recording studio, the vibration from the demolition work caused the collapse of a seal above where a chimney breast had been removed on the plaintiff's premises. Unknown to anyone a large quantity of dust and debris had accumulated above the seal; it fell on to the plaintiff's recording equipment and damaged it. Held: There was no negligence since the presence of such debris was unsuspected, but there was liability in nuisance for the damage to the claimant's moveable property. *Video London Sound Studios v Asticus* (Technology and Construction Court, March 3, 2001).

Question

Because of a recent laryngeal operation the defendant downstairs cannot sleep without snoring so stertorously as to wake up her neighbours above and keep them awake. What is to be done? Earplugs for the folk upstairs, the convalescent to sleep only during the day? Or would you follow David Steel J. who overturned a county court decision that a woman had to move because she had made her neighbours' lives a total misery by shouting and swearing, banging at night and making rude gestures? The judge said that to evict her for her repeated antisocial behaviour would breach her rights under the Disability Discrimination Act: "The overwhelming preponderance of her bizarre and unwelcome behaviour is attributable to her mental illness, which forms her disability." (See *The Times*, April 1, 2003: Lewis Smith, "Judge lets abusive neighbour keep home".)

BAXTER v CAMDEN L.B.C. [reported along with SOUTHWARK L.B.C. v MILLS]

House of Lords [2001] 1 A.C. 1; [1999] 3 W.L.R. 939; [1999] 4 All E.R. 449

Can the normal daily use of a dwelling constitute a nuisance?

In 1992 Miss Baxter became the defendant's tenant in the first-floor flat in a three-storey Victorian house which had been horizontally subdivided in 1975 consistently with building regulations then in force. The sound insulation was so poor that the noise from the flats above and below her subjected Miss Baxter to intolerable discomfort although the occupants, whose tenancy antedated hers, were using them in an absolutely normal manner.

Her claim against her landlord was dismissed by every judge who heard it.

Lord Millett: . . . The law of nuisance is concerned with balancing the conflicting interests of adjoining owners. It is often said to be encapsulated in the Latin maxim *sic utere tuo ut alienum non laedas*. This suggests a strict liability, but in practice the law seeks to protect the competing interests of both parties so far as it can. For this purpose it employs the control mechanism described by Lord Goff of Chieveley in *Cambridge Water Co Ltd v Eastern Counties Leather plc* [1994] 1 All E.R. 53 at 70, as "the principle of reasonable user—the principle of give and take".

The use of the word "reasonable" in this context is apt to be misunderstood. It is no answer to an action for nuisance to say that the defendant is only making reasonable use of his land. As Jessel M.R. insisted in *Broder v Saillard* (1876) 2 Ch.D. 692 at 701–702 that is not the question. What is reasonable from the point of view of one party may be completely unreasonable from the point of view of the other. It is not enough for a landowner to act reasonably in his own interest. He must also be considerate of the interest of his neighbour. The governing principle is good neighbourliness, and this involves reciprocity. A landowner must show the same consideration for his neighbour as he would expect his neighbour to show for him. The principle which limits the liability of a landowner who causes a sensible interference with his neighbour's enjoyment of his property is that stated in by Bramwell B. in *Bamford v Turnley* (1862).

[His Lordship quoted the passage from the speech of Bramwell B. (above, p.425) from "There must be . . . live and let live."]

It is true that Bramwell B. appears to justify his conclusion by the fact that the resulting nuisances are normally of a comparatively trifling character, and that is not the present case. But he cannot have intended the defence to be confined to such cases. Trifling nuisances have never been actionable, and Bramwell B was searching for the principle which exempts from liability activities which would otherwise be actionable. His conclusion was that two conditions must be satisfied: the acts complained of must (i) "be necessary for the common and ordinary use and occupation of land and houses" and (ii) must be "conveniently done", that is to say done with proper consideration for the interests of neighbouring occupiers. Where these two conditions are satisfied, no action will lie for that substantial interference with the use and enjoyment of his neighbour's land that would otherwise have been an actionable nuisance.

In my opinion Tuckey L.J. ([1999] 1 All E.R. 237 at 244), was correct in stating that the ordinary use of residential premises without more is not capable of amounting to a nuisance. As he rightly explained, this is why adjoining owner-occupiers are not liable to one another if the party wall between their flats is not an adequate sound barrier so that the sounds of everyday activities in one flat substantially interfere with the use and enjoyment of the other.

Counsel for Miss Baxter is prepared to argue if necessary that the tenants of the other flats could be held liable to her in nuisance. In this he would be wrong; their activities are not merely reasonable, they are the necessary and inevitable incidents of the ordinary occupation of residential property. They are unavoidable if those tenants are to continue in occupation of their flats. But his primary submission is that the council is liable in nuisance as the common landlord. In this he is, in my opinion, plainly wrong.

Once the activities complained of have been found to constitute an actionable nuisance, more than one party may be held legally responsible. The person or persons directly responsible for the activities in question are liable, but so too is anyone who authorised them. Landlords have been held liable for nuisances committed by their tenants on this basis. It is not enough for them to be aware of the nuisance and take no steps to prevent it. They must either participate directly in the commission of the nuisance, or they must be taken to have authorised it by letting the property: see *Malzy v Eichholz* [1916] 2 K.B. 308. But they cannot be held liable in tort for having authorised the commission of an actionable nuisance unless what they have authorised is an actionable nuisance. The logic of the proposition is obvious. A landlord cannot be liable to an action for authorising his tenant to do something that would not be actionable if he did it himself.

Counsel for Miss Baxter relies on the fact that the council not only let the adjoining flats for residential occupation but did so without first installing adequate sound insulation. It thereby authorised the use of the flats for residential occupation in circumstances which, the argument runs, inevitably caused a nuisance. But in my opinion this takes the matter no further. What Miss Baxter must show, but cannot show, is that they inevitably caused an actionable nuisance. The council has no obligation to soundproof her property to keep noise out, whether it emanates from her neighbours or from traffic or aircraft. It is under no positive duty to her to soundproof the adjoining flats in order to keep the noise in; such a duty could only arise by statute or contract. It is under no duty to bring the nuisance to an end, whether by regaining possession of the flats or by soundproofing the premises, unless it is an actionable nuisance.

My Lords, I would not wish to be thought indifferent to Miss Baxter's plight. I have the greatest sympathy for her. But the fact remains that she took a flat on the first floor of a house, knowing that the ground and second floors were also occupied as residential flats, and expecting their occupants to live normal lives. That is all that they are doing. She has no cause to complain of their activities, which mirror her own; or of the council for having permitted them by letting the adjoining flats. Her real complaint is, and always has been, of the absence of adequate sound insulation. Her complaint, however well founded, cannot be redressed by the law of tort; any remedy must lie in statute or contract.

My Lords, these appeals illuminate a problem of considerable social importance. No one, least of all the two councils concerned, would wish anyone to live in the conditions to which the tenants in these appeals are exposed. For the future, building regulations will ensure that new constructions and conversions have adequate sound insulation. But the huge stock of pre-war residential properties presents an intractable problem. Local authorities have limited resources, and have to decide on their priorities. Many of their older properties admit damp and are barely fit for human habitation. The London Borough of Southwark has estimated that it would cost £1.271 billion to bring its existing housing stock up to acceptable modern standards. Its budget for 1998–1999 for major housing schemes was under £55 million. The average cost of installing sound installation in the flats in Casino Avenue is £8,000 per flat. There are 34 similar flats in the estate, so that the total cost would be about £272,000. The borough-wide cost could be of the order of £37 million. The relevant local residents' association has considered that the installation of sound insulation is not a priority need.

These cases raise issues of priority in the allocation of resources. Such issues must be resolved by the democratic process, national and local. The judges are not equipped to resolve them. All that we can do is to say that there is nothing in the relevant tenancy agreements or current legislation, or in the common law, which would enable the tenants to obtain redress through the courts.

I would dismiss both appeals.

Lord Hoffmann delivered a speech to like effect, and **Lord Slynn, Lord Steyn** and **Lord Clyde** agreed with them both.

Note:

The House of Lords did not engage with the question whether, had the use of the flats above and below been a nuisance, it would have been a defence to the landlord that the "plaintiff came to the nuisance." The Court of Appeal held that it would: the *Sturges v Bridgman* principle (see *Miller v Jackson* below, p.445) does not apply as regards claims by tenant against landlord: the tenant takes the premises subject to any nuisances emanating from other property of the landlord's at the time.

ENVIRONMENTAL PROTECTION ACT 1990

Statutory Nuisances

79.—(1) Subject to subsections (1A) to (6A) below, the following matters constitute "statutory nuisances" for the purpose of this Part, that is to say—

(a) any premises in such a state as to be prejudicial to health or a nuisance;
(b) smoke emitted from premises so as to be prejudicial to health or a nuisance;

(c) fumes or gases emitted from premises so as to be prejudicial to health or a nuisance;
(d) any dust, steam, smell or other effluvia arising on industrial, trade or business premises and being prejudicial to health or a nuisance;
(e) any accumulation or deposit which is prejudicial to health or a nuisance;
(f) any animal kept in such a place or manner as to be prejudicial to health or a nuisance;
(g) noise emitted from premises so as to be prejudicial to health or a nuisance;
(ga) noise that is prejudicial to health or a nuisance and is emitted from or caused by a vehicle, machinery or equipment in a street;
(h) any other matter declared by any enactment to be a statutory nuisance;

and it shall be the duty of every local authority to cause its area to be inspected from time to time to detect any statutory nuisances which ought to be dealt with under s.80 below and, where a complaint of a statutory nuisance is made to it by a person living within its area, to take such steps as are reasonably practicable to investigate the complaint.
. . .
(4) Subsection (1)(c) above does not apply in relation to premises other than private dwellings.
(6A) Subsection (1)(ga) above does not apply to noise made—

(a) by traffic, . . .
(c) by a political demonstration . . .

(7) . . . "person responsible" in relation to a statutory nuisance, means the person to whose act, default or sufferance the nuisance is attributable;
. . .
(9) In this Part "best practicable means" is to be interpreted by reference to the following provisions—

(a) "practicable" means reasonably practicable having regard among other things to local conditions and circumstances, to the current state of technical knowledge and to the financial implications;
(b) the means to be employed include the design, installation, maintenance and manner and periods of operation of plant and machinery, and the design, construction and maintenance of buildings and structures;
(c) the test is to apply only so far as compatible with any duty imposed by law;
(d) the test is to apply only so far as compatible with safety and safe working conditions, and with the exigencies of any emergency or unforeseeable circumstances;

and, in circumstances where a code of practice under section 71 of the Control of Pollution Act 1974 (noise minimisation) is applicable, regard shall also be had to guidance given in it.
   80.—(1) Where a local authority is satisfied that a statutory nuisance exists, or is likely to occur or recur, in the area of the authority, the local authority shall serve a notice ("an abatement notice") imposing all or any of the following requirements—

(a) requiring the abatement of the nuisance or prohibiting or restricting its occurrence or recurrence;
(b) requiring the execution of such works, and the taking of such other steps, as may be necessary for any of those purposes,

and the notice shall specify the time or times within which the requirements of the notice are to be complied with.
   (2) . . . the abatement notice shall be served—

(a) except in a case falling within paragraph (b) or (c) below, on the person responsible for the nuisance;

(b) where the nuisance arises from any defect of a structural character, on the owner of the premises;

(c) where the person responsible for the nuisance cannot be found or the nuisance has not yet occurred, on the owner or occupier of the premises.

(3) A person served with an abatement notice may appeal against the notice to a magistrates' court within the period of twenty-one days beginning with the date on which he was served with the notice.

(4) If a person on whom an abatement notice is served, without reasonable excuse, contravenes or fails to comply with any requirement or prohibition imposed by the notice, he shall be guilty of an offence.

(5) Except in a case falling within subsection (6) below, a person who commits an offence under subsection (4) above shall be liable on summary conviction to a fine not exceeding level 5 on the standard scale together with a further fine of an amount equal to one-tenth of that level for each day on which the offence continues after the conviction.

(6) A person who commits an offence under subsection (4) above on industrial, trade or business premises shall be liable on summary conviction to a fine not exceeding £20,000.

(7) Subject to subsection (8) below, in any proceedings for an offence under subsection (4) above in respect of a statutory nuisance it shall be a defence to prove that the best practicable means were used to prevent, or to counteract the effects of, the nuisance.

(8) The defence under subsection (7) above is not available—

(a) in the case of a nuisance falling within paragraph (a), (d), (e), (f) or (g) of section 79(1) above except where the nuisance arises on industrial, trade or business premises;

(aa) in the case of a nuisance falling within paragraph (ga) of section 79(1) above except where the noise is emitted from or caused by a vehicle, machinery or equipment being used for industrial, trade or business purposes;

(b) in the case of a nuisance falling within paragraph (b) of section 79(1) above except where the smoke is emitted from a chimney; and

(c) in the case of a nuisance falling within paragraph (c) or (h) of section 79(1) above.

Notes:

1. Perhaps rather surprisingly, premises are not "prejudicial to health" under s.79(1)(a) just because they are dangerous (*R. v Bristol C.C., Ex p. Everett* [1999] 2 All E.R. 193—steep staircase in nineteenth century house). But noise can be injurious to health (*Southwark L.B.C. v Ince* (1989) 21 H.L.R. 504).

2. Section 80 imposes a duty on the local authority to issue an abatement notice when it finds that a statutory nuisance exists: it is not enough for it to decide to monitor the situation. *R. v Carrick D.C., Ex p. Shelley* [1996] Times L.R. 231.

3. A compensation order may be made against those found guilty of offences under the Act (*Botross v Hammersmith & Fulham L.B.C.* [1994] Times L.R. 558). But whereas an order for costs must be made in favour of a successful claimant (s.82(12)), a compensation order should be made only in "simple cases" (*Davenport v Walsall M.B.C.* (1994) 93 L.G.R. 268). Nevertheless the procedure laid down in s.82 of the Act "is intended to provide ordinary people, numbered amongst whom are those who are disadvantaged (whether by reason of their health or their financial circumstances or otherwise) with a speedy and effective remedy for circumstances which will often have an adverse effect (or a potentially adverse effect) upon their health and/or the health of their children." *Hall v Kingston upon Hull Council* [1999] 2 All E.R. 609 at 624. Note that failure to comply with an abatement notice, though an offence, gives rise to no civil liability: *Issa v Hackney LBC* [1997] 1 All E.R. 999, CA. See also above, p.182.

4. Under the Noise Act 1996 a local authority may issue a warning notice if a complaint is received from a person present in a dwelling that excessive noise is being made in another dwelling between the hours of 11 p.m. and 7 a.m. When a warning notice has been issued, it is an offence if excessive noise is emitted from that dwelling during the period specified in it. An officer of the local authority may enter the offending dwelling and remove any equipment apparently being or having been used in the emission of the noise; so, too, where there is power to abate a statutory nuisance under s.79(1)(g).

Question

How does the regime of statutory nuisances square with the view of the House of Lords in *Hunter* that nuisance has no role to play in personal injury cases?

Section 3.—Malice

HOLLYWOOD SILVER FOX FARM LTD v EMMETT

King's Bench [1936] 2 K.B. 468; 105 L.J.K.B. 829; 155 L.T. 288; 52 T.L.R. 611; 80 S.J. 488; [1936] 1 All E.R. 825

Action for damage to breeding silver foxes by needless gunfire on defendant's premises

The plaintiff's managing director, Captain Chandler, set up the plaintiff company to breed silver foxes, and erected at the boundary of his land and adjacent to the highway a sign saying "Hollywood Silver Fox Farm." This annoyed his neighbour, the defendant, who was developing the adjoining land as a housing estate, and thought that the sign would deter potential buyers. Emmett accordingly asked Captain Chandler to remove the sign and when Captain Chandler refused he threatened to shoot along the boundary. This was a serious threat since, as Emmett knew, the effect of loud noises on vixens is to deter mating, impede whelping and provoke infanticide. On four subsequent evenings the threat was carried out by the defendant's son, and damage done. Macnaghten J. gave judgment for the plaintiff in damages, and also issued an injunction.

Macnaghten J.: . . . In these circumstances the decision of the Court of King's Bench in *Keeble v Hickeringill* ((1706) 11 East 574n.; 103 E.R. 1127; 90 E.R. 906), if it be well founded, is a clear authority that the defendant has committed an actionable wrong. In that case the plaintiff, the owner of a duck decoy, brought an action against the defendant for shooting at and disturbing the ducks in his decoy. The jury found a verdict for the plaintiff and the question whether the action was maintainable was argued before the Full Court.

During the argument there was some question whether the defendant had actually trespassed on the plaintiff's land, and according to the report in 11 Mod., p.74, Lord Holt said: "But suppose the defendant had shot in his own ground, if he had occasion to shoot, it would have been one thing; but to shoot on purpose to damage the plaintiff is another thing and a wrong."

The court decided that the action was maintainable and judgment was entered for the plaintiffs.

Mr Roche submitted that the defendant was entitled to shoot on his own land, and that even if his conduct was malicious he had not committed any actionable wrong. In support of his argument, Mr Roche relied mainly on the decision of the House of Lords in the case of *Bradford Corp. v Pickles* ([1894] A.C. 587). In that case the Corporation of Bradford sought to restrain Mr Pickles from sinking a shaft on land which belonged to him because, according to their view, his object in sinking the shaft was to draw away from their land water which would otherwise come into their reservoirs. Mr Pickles, they said, was acting maliciously, his sole object being to do harm to the Corporation. The House of Lords decided once and for all that in such a case the motive of the defendant is immaterial.

In the case of *Allen v Flood* ([1898] A.C. 587 [below, p.519] Lord Herschell, commenting on the decision in *Bradford Corp. v Pickles*, said: "It has recently been held in this House, in the case of *Bradford Corp. v Pickles*, that acts done by the defendant upon his own land were not actionable when they were within his legal rights, even though his motive were to prejudice his neighbour. The language of the noble and learned Lords was distinct. The Lord Chancellor said: 'This is not a case where the state of mind of the person doing the act can affect the right. If it was a lawful act, however ill the motive might be, he had a right to do it. If it was an unlawful act, however good the motive might be, he would have no right to do it.' The statement was confined to the class of cases then before the House; but I apprehend that what was said is not applicable only to rights of property, but is equally applicable to the exercise by an individual of his other rights."

Mr Roche argued that in the present case the defendant had not committed any nuisance at all in the legal sense of the term, and he referred to the case of *Robinson v Kilvert* ((1889) 41 Ch.D. 88). In that case a complaint was made by the tenant of the ground floor of a building that the tenant of the basement was making the basement so warm that the brown paper which he kept on the ground floor suffered damage, and it was held by the Court of Appeal that no actionable wrong had been committed by the defendant, in that the heating was not of such a character as would interfere with the ordinary use of the rest of the house. Mr Roche submitted that the keeping of a silver fox farm is not an ordinary use of land, and that the shooting would have caused no alarm to the animals which are usually to be found on farms in Kent or done them any harm.

Apart from the case of *Keeble v Hickeringill* there is authority for the view that in an action for nuisance by noise the intention of the person making the noise must be considered. In *Christie v Davey* ([1893] 1 Ch. 316 at 326) the plaintiffs, Mr and Mrs Christie, and the defendant lived side by side in semi-detached houses in Brixton. Mrs Christie was a teacher of music, and her family were also musical, and throughout the day sounds of music pervaded their house and were heard in the house of their neighbour. The defendant did not like the music that he heard, and by way of retaliation he took to making noises himself, beating trays and rapping on the wall. North J. delivered judgment in favour of the plaintiffs and granted an injunction restraining the defendant from causing or permitting any sounds or noises in his house so as to vex or annoy the plaintiffs or the occupiers of their house. In the course of his judgment, he said at page 326, after dealing with the facts as he found them, "The result is that I think I am bound to interfere for the protection of the plaintiffs. In my opinion the noises which were made in the defendant's house were not of a legitimate kind. They were what, to use the language of Lord Selborne in *Gaunt v Fynney*, 'ought to be regarded as excessive and unreasonable.' I am satisfied that they were made deliberately and maliciously for the purpose of annoying the plaintiffs." Then come the significant words: "If what has taken place had occurred between two sets of persons both perfectly innocent, I should have taken an entirely different view of the case. But I am persuaded that what was done by the defendant was done only for the purpose of annoyance, and in my opinion it was not a legitimate use of the defendant's house to use it for the purpose of vexing and annoying his neighbours."

. . .

The cases to which I have referred were decided before the decision of the House of Lords in *Bradford Corp. v Pickles*; and the question therefore arises whether those cases must now be considered as overruled. It is to be observed that in *Allen v Flood* Lord Watson discussed fully the case of *Keeble v Hickeringill* and said with reference to that case: "No proprietor has an absolute right to create noises upon his own land, because any right which the law gives him is qualified by the condition that it must not be exercised to the nuisance of his neighbours or of the public. If he violates that condition he commits a legal wrong, and if he does so intentionally he is guilty of a malicious wrong, in its strict legal sense."

In my opinion the decision of the House of Lords in *Bradford Corp. v Pickles* has no bearing on such cases as this. I therefore think that the plaintiff is entitled to maintain this action. I think also that in the circumstances an injunction should be granted restraining the defendant from committing a nuisance by the discharge of firearms or the making of other loud noises in the vicinity of the Hollywood Silver Fox Farm during the breeding season—namely, between January 1 and June 15—so as to alarm or disturb the foxes kept by the plaintiffs at the said farm, or otherwise to injure the plaintiff company.

Background Reading:
    For the social and legal setting of *Bradford v Pickles* see Taggart, *Private Property and Abuse of Rights in Victorian England* (2002).

Questions

1. In view of the terms of the injunction issued, do you think that the defendant could safely shoot any rabbits there might actually be close to the boundary?

2. What kind of harm was in issue in (a) this case, (b) the *Pickles* case, (c) *Christie v Davey?* Do you think the differences are relevant?

3. Since the damage done here was physical (dead silver foxes), should the law of negligence have been applied? What would the result have been?

Note on Malicious Acts of Third Parties:

1. In *Smith v Scott* ([1973] Ch. 314) the plaintiffs had to move out of their house because the problem family next door had made their life intolerable by noise and vandalism. An injunction was naturally issued against the family (but then where do they go?). The local authority which had installed them as tenants was held not liable, although they had known the nature of the tenants they installed. The local authority did not authorise the nuisance because they had inserted a clause forbidding the tenants to create a nuisance, and the nuisance did not result from the purposes for which the premises were let, but only from the persons to whom they were let; there was no duty under *Donoghue v Stevenson* to take care to choose tenants who would not cause harm to their neighbours.

2. Is *Smith v Scott* still good law? If so, according to Hirst L.J., it was decisive in favour of the defendant local authority in *Hussain v Lancaster City Council* [1999] 4 All E.R. 125. The plaintiff freeholders of a shop had long been subjected to intolerable harassment, including physical damage, by racist thugs from the housing estate nearby, many of whom were tenants of the defendant council. The council had power as landlord to dispossess tenants, even secure tenants, if they created a nuisance, as well as a power (if not a duty) in its capacity as highway authority to enjoin any conduct which infringed the rights of the public to use and enjoy the highway. Hirst L.J. said:

> "In the present case the acts complained of unquestionably interfered persistently and intolerably with the plaintiffs' enjoyment of the plaintiffs' land, but they did not involve the tenants' use of the tenants' land and therefore fell outside the scope of the tort. Turning to the ambit of the landlord's responsibility for his tenants' acts of nuisance, *Smith v Scott* is decisive authority in favour of [the council] provided it still holds good."

The claim against the council in negligence for failing to exercise its powers over the thugs, whether as tenants or as persons abusing the highway, was dismissed by the Court of Appeal on the ground that it would not be fair, just and reasonable to hold the council liable, especially in the light of the words of Lord Browne-Wilkinson that " . . . the courts should proceed with great care before holding liable in negligence those who have been charged by Parliament with the task of protecting society from the wrongdoing of others" ([1995] 3 All E.R. 353, 382). Is it not arguable that the council, as a public authority, might be held under a duty to exercise its powers so as to prevent the gross invasion of the claimant's right under Art.8 of the Convention on Human Rights?

3. Since landlords are not in possession of tenanted premises, they are not primary defendants as regards unauthorised nuisances emanating from those premises, but if the persons on the premises who are making the plaintiff's life a misery are not tenants but only licensees or trespassers, possession (and consequent control) remains in the occupier, and if he "adopts" their presence with their known proclivities, he may well be held liable for what they do. In *Lippiatt v South Gloucestershire Council* [1999] 4 All E.R. 149, in which the dictum of Hirst L.J. given above was doubted and not followed, the defendant had provided facilities (toilets, skips, water points) for travellers who for more than two years had an unauthorised encampment on local authority land—the verge of the A46—whence they made damaging forays on to the plaintiff's farm. It was held that *Hussain* was distinguishable and that on the striking-out motion "It is reasonably arguable that the continuing presence of the travellers on the council's land constituted a nuisance to the plaintiffs' use and enjoyment of their rights in their land, even though the travellers' activities involved using the council's land as a launching pad for repeated acts of trespass on the plaintiffs' land" (*per* Mummery L.J. at 159). The slightly slender authorities relied on were *A.-G. v Corke* [1933] Ch. 89 where, on rather similar facts, an injunction was issued by a puisne judge on the basis of public nuisance and *Rylands v Fletcher*, and *Thompson-Schwab v Costaki* [1956] 1 All E.R. 652, CA, where the plaintiff obtained an injunction against the defendant in respect of the offensive goings-on on the highway outside the defendant's brothel of the prostitutes and their clients.

4. In *Lippiatt*, unlike the authorities relied on, the claim was for damages only (since by the time of the trial the travellers had been moved on), but there was certainly an element of duration in the harmful situation and though the travellers were trespassers, their presence had been tolerated. Neither fact was present in *Smith v Littlewoods Organisation* [1987] 1 All E.R. 710, HL, where the occupier was held not liable for

failing to guard against unexpected trespassers who deliberately set a fire on the premises which escaped and burnt the property of the pursuer.

Section 4.—Inaction

LEAKEY v NATIONAL TRUST FOR PLACES OF HISTORIC INTEREST OR NATURAL BEAUTY

Court of Appeal [1980] Q.B. 485; [1980] 2 W.L.R. 65; [1980] 1 All E.R. 17; 78 L.G.R. 100

Action by owner of house threatened by natural collapse of defendant's hillside

Burrow Mump is a conical hill in Somerset, remarkable enough to be owned by the National Trust. Centuries ago a bit of the West side of the Mump had been sliced off so as to accommodate the plaintiffs' seventeenth-century cottages. For years there had been small falls of earth from the Mump on to the plaintiffs' property directly below, but the summer drought and autumn rains of 1976 caused a really large crack to appear, presaging a major collapse. The National Trust denied liability, but when a serious fall occurred it was required by interlocutory injunction to take the steps necessary to prevent falls of soil. At the trial to determine who was to bear the cost of these works, eventually totalling £6,000-odd, the judge held that once the National Trust knew that the condition of its property, wholly natural though it was, constituted a threat to the plaintiffs' property, the Trust came under a duty to take reasonable steps to prevent damage to them.

The injunction sought was refused, but the defendants were held liable in damages of £50 and £2.

The defendants' appeal was dismissed, the plaintiffs' cross-appeal abandoned.

Megaw L.J.: This appeal from the judgment of O'Connor J. ([1978] Q.B. 849) raises questions which are of importance in the development of English law. The learned judge held that the defendants are liable to the plaintiffs in damages, on a claim framed in nuisance, based on the fact that soil and other detritus had fallen from property owned and occupied by the defendants onto the plaintiffs' properties. It was accepted by the parties that the instability of the defendants' land which made it liable, and which had caused, and was likely to continue to cause, falls of detritus on the plaintiffs' land, was not caused by, nor was it aggravated by, any human activities on the defendants' land. It was caused by nature: the geological structure, content and contours of the land, and the effect thereon of sun, rain, wind and frost and suchlike natural phenomena. It was held by the learned judge, and is not now in dispute, that, at least since 1968, the defendants knew that the instability of their land was a threat to the plaintiffs' property because of the possibility of falls of soil and other material. Although requested by the plaintiffs to take steps to prevent such falls, the defendants had not taken any action, because they held the view, no doubt on legal advice, that in law they were under no liability in respect of any damage which might be caused to neighbouring property in consequence of the natural condition of their own property and the operation of natural forces thereon.

O'Connor J. has held that that view of the law is wrong. He based his decision on the judgment of the Judicial Committee of the Privy Council in *Goldman v Hargrave* ([1967] 1 A.C. 645). The main issue in this appeal is whether *Goldman v Hargrave* accurately states the law of England. If it does, the appeal fails, and the defendants are liable . . .

The relevant facts of *Goldman v Hargrave* were simple. A redgum tree, 100 feet high, on the defendant's land was struck by lightning and caught fire. The defendant caused the land around the burning tree to be cleared and the tree was then cut down and sawn into sections. So far there could be no complaint that the defendant had done anything which he ought not to have done or left undone anything which he ought to have done, so as in any way to increase the risk which had been caused by this act of natural forces setting fire to the tree. Thereafter the defendant (this was the state of the facts on which the Judicial Committee based their decision) did not do anything which he ought not to have done. He took no positive action which increased the risk of the fire spreading. But he failed to do something which he could have done without any substantial trouble or expenses, which would, if done, have eliminated or rendered unlikely the spreading of the fire, that is, to have doused with water the burning or smouldering sections of the tree as they lay on the ground. Instead the defendant chose to allow or encourage the fire to burn itself out. Foreseeably (again it was the forces of nature and not human action), the weather became even hotter and a strong wind sprang up. The flames from the tree spread rapidly through the defendant's land to the land of neighbours where it did extensive damage to their properties.

The judgment of the Board was delivered by Lord Wilberforce. It was held that the risk of the consequence which in fact happened was foreseeable. This, it is said, "was not really disputed". The legal issue was then defined:

" . . . the case is not one where a person has brought a source of danger on to his land, nor one where an occupier has so used his property as to cause a danger to his neighbour. It is one where an occupier, faced with a hazard accidentally arising on his land, fails to act with reasonable prudence so as to remove the hazard. The issue is therefore whether in such a case the occupier is guilty of legal negligence, which involves the issue whether he is under a duty of care, and, if so, what is the scope of that duty."

It is to my mind clear, from this passage and other passages in the judgment, that the duty which is being considered, and which later in the judgment is held to exist, does not involve any distinction of principle between what, in another sphere of the law, used to be known as misfeasance and non-feasance. A failure to act may involve a breach of the duty, though, since the duty which emerges is a duty of reasonable care, the question of misfeasance or non-feasance may have a bearing on the question whether the duty has been broken. It is to my mind clear, also, that no distinction is suggested in, or can properly be inferred from, the judgment as between a hazard accidentally arising on the defendant's land which, on the one hand, gives rise to a risk of damage to a neighbour's property by the encroachment of fire and, on the other hand, gives rise to such a risk by the encroachment of the soil itself, falling from the bank onto the neighbour's land. There is no valid distinction, to my mind, between an encroachment which consists, on the one hand, of the spread of fire from a tree on fire on the land, and, on the other hand, of a slip of soil or rock resulting from the instability of the land itself, in each case, the danger of encroachment, and the actual encroachment, being brought about by the forces of nature . . .

I return to the judgment in *Goldman v Hargrave*. The law of England as it used to be is set out in the following passage:

" . . . it is only in comparatively recent times that the law has recognised an occupier's duty as one of a more positive character than merely to abstain from creating, or adding to, a source of danger or annoyance. It was for long satisfied with the conception of separate or autonomous proprietors, each of which was entitled to exploit his territory in a 'natural' manner and none of whom was obliged to restrain or direct the operations of nature in the interest of avoiding harm to his neighbours."

The judgment of the Board then goes on to review the development of the law which, as the Board held, had changed the law so that there now exists "a general duty of occupiers in relation to hazards occurring on their land, whether natural or man-made."

That change in the law, in its essence and in its timing, corresponds with, and may be viewed as being a part of, the change in the law of tort which achieved its decisive victory in *Donoghue v Stevenson*, though it was not until eight years later, in the House of Lords decision in *Sedleigh-Denfield v O'Callaghan* ([1940] A.C. 880), that the change as affecting the area with which we are concerned was expressed or recognised in a decision binding on all English courts, and, even then, the full, logical effect of the decision in altering what had hitherto been thought to be the law was not immediately recognised. But *Goldman v Hargrave* has now demonstrated what that effect was in English law . . .

In the *Sedleigh-Denfield* case, a local authority had trespassed on the defendant's land, without the defendant's knowledge or consent, and had placed a culvert in a ditch on that land. By the improper placing of a grid at the mouth of the culvert, instead of further back, those who did the work created a danger of flooding which would be likely to spread to the plaintiff's land. The defendant, through his servants, came to know what had been done. He should have realised that it created a real risk of flooding of his neighbour's land. He did nothing. A heavy rainstorm caused the ditch to flood, because of the trespasser's work. The plaintiff's land was damaged. The House of Lords held that the defendant was liable. The defendant himself had not done anything which was an "unnatural user" of his land. He had not himself brought anything "unnatural" onto his land. But when he knew or ought to have known of the risk of flood water from his land encroaching on his neighbour's land he had done nothing towards preventing it. Prevention could have been achieved without any great trouble or expense.

The approval by the House of Lords in the *Sedleigh-Denfield* case of Scrutton L.J.'s judgment in the *Job Edwards* case ([1924] 1 K.B. 341) meant . . . that it was thereafter the law of England that a duty existed under which the occupier of land might be liable to his neighbour for damage to his neighbour's property as a result of a nuisance spreading from his land to his neighbour's land, even though the existence and the operative effect of the nuisance were not caused by any "non-natural" use by the defendant of his own land. But the liability was not a strict liability such as that which was postulated by the House of Lords in *Rylands v Fletcher* [below, p.453] as arising where damage was caused to another by an "unnatural" user of land. The obligation postulated in the *Sedleigh-Denfield* case, in conformity with the development of the law in *Donoghue v Stevenson*, was an obligation to use reasonable care. A defendant was not to be liable as a result of a risk of which he neither was aware nor ought, as a reasonably careful landowner, to have been aware . . .

This leads on to the question of the scope of the duty. This is discussed, and the nature and extent of the duty is explained, in the judgment in *Goldman v Hargrave*. . . . The defendant's duty is to do that which is reasonable for him to do. The criteria of reasonableness include, in respect of a duty of this nature, the factor of what the particular man, not the average man, can be expected to do, having regard, amongst other things, where a serious expenditure of money is required to eliminate or reduce the danger, to his means. Just as, where physical effort is required to avert an immediate danger, the defendant's age and physical condition may be relevant in deciding what is reasonable, so also logic and good sense require that, where the expenditure of money is required, the defendant's capacity to find the money is relevant. But this can only be in the way of a broad, and not a detailed, assessment; and, in arriving at a judgment on reasonableness, a similar broad assessment may be relevant in some cases as to the neighbour's capacity to protect himself from damage, whether by way of some form of barrier on his own land or by way of providing funds for expenditure on agreed works on the land of the defendant.

Take, by way of example, the landowner through whose land a stream flows. In rainy weather, it is known, the stream may flood and the flood may spread to the land of neighbours. If the risk is one which can readily be overcome or lessened, for example by reasonable steps on the part of the landowner to keep the stream free from blockage by flotsam or silt carried down, he will be in breach of duty if he does nothing or does too little. But if the only remedy is substantial and expensive works, then it might well be that the landowner would have discharged his duty by saying to his neighbours, who also know of the risk and who have asked him to do something about it, "You have my permission to come onto my land and to do agreed works at your expense," or, it may be, "on the basis of a fair sharing of expense." In deciding whether the landowner had discharged his duty of care, if the question were thereafter to come before he had discharged his duty of care, the question of reasonableness of what had been done or offered would fall to be decided on a broad basis, in which, on some occasions, there might be included an element of obvious discrepancy of financial resources.

Shaw L.J.: . . . Why should a nuisance which has its origin in some natural phenomenon and which manifests itself without any human intervention cast a liability on a person who has no other connection with that nuisance than the title to the land on which it chances to originate? This view is fortified inasmuch as a title to land cannot be discarded or abandoned. Why should the owner of land in such a case be bound to protect his neighbour's property and person rather than that the neighbour should protect his interests against the potential danger?

The old common law duty of a landowner on whose land there arose a nuisance from natural causes only, without any human intervention, was to afford a neighbour whose property or person was threatened by the nuisance a reasonable opportunity to abate that nuisance. This entailed (1) that the landowner should on becoming aware of the nuisance give reasonable warning of it to his neighbour, (2) that the landowner should give to the neighbour such access to the land as was reasonably requisite to enable him to abate the nuisance.

The principle was relatively clear in its application and served in broad terms to do justice between the parties concerned. The development of "the good neighbour" concept has however blurred the definition of rights and liabilities between persons who stand in such a relationship as may involve them in reciprocal rights and liabilities.

It has culminated in the judgment of the Privy Council in *Goldman v Hargrave*.

. . . with diffident reluctance I would dismiss the appeal.

Cumming-Bruce L.J. agreed with **Megaw L.J.**

Questions

1. The defendant in *Goldman v Hargrave* was an elderly man who lived alone on a 600–acre grazing property near Gidgegannup. When the lightning struck on the Saturday, he took active steps to deal with the situation: he called for the assistance of the local fire officer (for in hot dry countries the risk of fire is always in the forefront of people's minds) and bulldozed the area around the tree he had cut down. On the Tuesday he went to Perth and it was in his absence that the wind got up and fanned the embers into flames. Hundreds of acres round about were devastated. But take the facts as given by Megaw L.J. Would the plaintiff have suffered the same damage if the defendant had been away on holiday, and would the defendant have been liable (a) if no one was left on his premises, (b) there was only a housekeeper, (c) there was no one but a house-guest from town?

2. Does *Leakey* apply in cases of discomfort or only in cases of damage or threatened damage?

3. Does *Leakey* involve that if pheasants spontaneously nest on my land in great numbers, I am to be at the expense of a game-keeper to protect my neighbour's crops?

4. Does the variable duty laid down mean that the plaintiff must take the defendant as he finds him? Is this especially appropriate in cases of neighbours in the true sense? See *Vaughan v Menlove* (1837) 3 Bing. N.C. 468; 132 E.R. 490.

5. Consider the relationship of the *ratio* of this case and the *ratio* of *Stephens v Anglian Water Auth.* (note 3, below), namely that you may drain your own land even if you know that that will cause actual property damage to your neighbour.

Notes:

1. That the National Trust should have to pay to protect the Leakeys from the operation of the law of gravity is absurd enough, but at least the Leakeys were being bombarded by bits of the defendant's property. In *Holbeck Hall v Scarborough B.C.* gravity operated the other way, so to speak: the plaintiff's hotel fell into the sea. Although marine encroachment is notoriously difficult to prevent, as King Canute was well aware, the trial judge held the defendant council, which had control of the strip of land between the plaintiff's hotel and the sea, liable for failure to heed the advice of their geophysical experts that they should spend yet more money on seaworks (1998) 57 Constr. L.R. 113). But how could it possibly be right that plaintiffs who had profited for many years from having a hotel with a beautiful view of the nearby sea should be granted compensation from public funds when the sea takes its revenge? The Court of Appeal reversed the decision below, not because no duty was owed by the defendant council but only because the duty under *Goldman/Leakey* is only a "measured" one, and it would be too much to require the defendant to incur the great expense involved ([2000] Q.B. 836). One hopes that the Strasbourg Court would also hold that the council was not required to protect the claimant's property under the First Protocol.

2. The collapse of buildings (unlike things falling from on high) had figured frequently in the law reports, and the law was clear: if *activities* on the defendant's land caused the collapse of his neighbour's land (or

his house, if it had been there long enough to acquire an easement of support) the defendant was strictly liable: negligence was not at issue. But the collapse had to result from an act, activity or operation (usually excavation): there was no liability at all if the defendant had done nothing and it was a purely natural landslip, even one the defendant could have prevented. In *Holbeck Hall* the trial judge said he would have preferred the old law, but that "it would be . . . a serious blot on any rational system of law to tolerate, and unworkable in practice, to attempt to accommodate anomalies of the kind which would follow from a rule which perpetuated a distinction between the duties of uphill and downhill neighbours". Such is the absurdity to which the injustice of *Leakey*, stemming from the "let it all hang out" attitude inherent in *Goldman*, can lead. Could one here deploy the distinction drawn by Lord Hoffmann in *Marcic* (below p.450) between the law relating to private neighbours and that relating to the expenditure of public funds? The role of a coastal protection agency is surely not so different from that of a sewerage authority.

3. The old law drew a distinction between digging and shoring up in the sense that you were liable for digging even if you were not negligent and not liable for not shoring up even if you were, and it drew another distinction whose days are perhaps equally numbered, the distinction between digging and draining.

In *Langbrook Properties v Surrey C.C.* [1969] 3 All E.R. 1424 the defendants were doing excavation work pursuant to their statutory functions near a site which the plaintiffs were developing. The excavations were kept dry by pumping and the pumping abstracted water from under the plaintiffs' land, which caused buildings there to settle. It was held that the defendants were not liable even if the damage might have been avoided with reasonable care. Plowman J. reviewed the authorities. They clearly established that a landowner has no absolute right to water support as he does to support by land, though in none of them had the defendant by negligent abstraction caused actual damage to property. The judge added that if abstraction of water was not actionable if one intended to cause injury (*Bradford v Pickles* [1895] A.C. 587) it could hardly be actionable if one did not.

The Court of Appeal has endorsed his view that one has an absolute right to drain one's land, though not to dig holes in it, in *Stephens v Anglian Water Auth.* [1987] 3 All E.R. 379, where on very similar facts the plaintiff sued only "in negligence". The court's view that the case was covered by *Pickles* is perhaps a little cavalier, since there is surely a relevant difference between a complaint that one has not received water one hoped for and a complaint that one's house is falling about one's ears. Not cited was a decision of the Court of Appeal on March 21, 1984 where the plaintiff's house settled after the defendant had knocked down the house next door; the settlement took place not because the latter house had been propping up the former but because its presence had been preventing the evaporation of water. Dillon L.J. said "I can see no reason in law or sense why the right of support should be curtailed where what has impaired support is the removal by the dominant owner by some act on his own land of water in the clay sub-soil under the plaintiff's building" (*Brace v SE Regional Housing Assoc'n.* [1984] C.A.T. 20).

Langbrook Properties was not cited in *Home Brewery v Davis & Co* [1987] 1 All E.R. 637 (Piers Ashworth Q.C.). Here also the defendants had waterlogged land, but instead of draining it they filled it in. The result was that (1) subsequent rainfall was retained on the plaintiff's land up the hill because it could not percolate through the defendant's land as theretofore, and (2) water in an osier bed was squeezed back on to the plaintiff's land. It was held that the defendants were liable for (2), but not for (1) since their conduct was reasonable. The latter qualification is surprising; even more so is the hint that the defendant might be liable even if his conduct was reasonable (*per* Rattee J. in *Palmer v Bowman* [2000] 1 All E.R. 22 at 35, CA.

If one is entitled to drain one's land whatever the external effects, one might have supposed that one would be free to spray one's crops so long as none of the herbicide or pesticide escaped. Not so. Farmer Walter sprayed his rape crop at a time which seemed good to him despite the counterindications noted by the manufacturer, and his neighbours' bees were poisoned when they came to crop his rape and vice versa. Farmer Walter was held liable because he had broken a duty of care. If he had given longer warning he might have avoided liability (*Tutton v AD Walter Ltd* [1985] 3 All E.R. 757).

4. Quite often a building subsides not because of deliberate draining, but because the encroaching roots of a neighbour's tree dry out the subsoil. What is the law here? In *Morgan v Khyatt* [1964] 1 W.L.R. 475, Lord Evershed, speaking for the Privy Council, said " . . . it has . . . long been established as a general proposition that an owner of land may make any natural use of it; but also (and by way of qualification of the general rule) that if an owner of land grows or permits the growth on his land in the natural way of trees whose roots penetrate into adjacent property and thereby cause and continue to cause damage to buildings upon that property, he is liable for the tort of nuisance to the owner of that adjacent property." In that case, Viscount Simonds approved, *arguendo*, *Davey v Harrow Corp.* [1958] 1 Q.B. 60, where Lord Goddard had said " . . . if trees encroach, whether by branches or roots, and cause damage, an action for nuisance will lie . . . " (at 73).

Now in *Leakey* Megaw L.J. also approved of *Davey* but added a proviso requiring in the defendant knowledge, actual or constructive, of both the encroachment and the damage likely to be caused. The Court of Appeal has now endorsed that qualification and has given judgment for the defendant in a case where the defendant's tree unquestionably caused the plaintiff's house to settle when its roots reached a quite unexpected pocket of clay under the house and dehydrated it in unusual weather conditions (*Solloway v Hants. C.C.* (1981) 79 L.G.R. 449). The questions to be asked are (1) was there a foreseeable risk that the encroachment of these tree roots would cause damage to the plaintiff's house, and (2) were there any reasonable precautions which the defendants could have taken to prevent or minimise that risk? Dunn L.J. said this: "Although it was not necessary for the decision the proviso suggested by Megaw L.J. puts nuisance by encroachment of tree roots and branches into the same category as any other nuisance not brought about by human agency. It is consistent with *Sedleigh-Denfield v O'Callaghan* [1940] A.C. 880, and confines the strict liability for nuisance to cases where there has been some non-natural user of the land as stated in *Rylands v Fletcher* (1868) L.R. 3 H.L. 330."

This significant change in the basis of liability also means that the judge cannot simply ask "On whose land was this tree?" (not that that is always an easy question, especially where the tree is on the highway—see *Hurst v Hampshire C.C.* (1997) 96 L.G.R. 27, CA), but must inquire into the defendant's geological knowledge, arboreal skills and financial resources. For a case from Hampstead Garden Suburb where the judge had to balance the aesthetic drawbacks of cutting down a century-old oak, with the risk of consequent "heave," the practicalities of encircling the roots, and the efficacy of lopping its limbs, and ignored the fact that the defendants (reasonably) believed that they were not responsible for the tree, see *Russell v Barnet L.B.C.* [1984] 2 E.G.L.R. 44; (1984) 271 EG 699 at 779).

It is a matter for great regret that in *Delaware Mansions* [2001] 4 All E.R. 737 the single speech in the House of Lords enthusiastically endorsed the decision in *Solloway* precisely on the ground that it harmonised the law of tree roots with the law of negligence as laid down in *Goldman v Hargrave*. Warming to the theme of reasonableness, the speech held that "a reasonable landowner would notify the neighbour as soon as tree root damage was suspected" and that "the defendant is entitled to notice and a reasonable opportunity of abatement before liability for remedial expenditure can arise." This new and unnecessary gloss had to be applied by the Court of Appeal in *LE Jones v Portsmouth CC* [2002] EWCA Civ 1723.

It is worth noting that there have been more cases on tree roots in the 25 years since *Solloway* than in the five centuries prior to that silly decision, and that, so far as can be seen, *Solloway* is the only case where the claimant failed to recover. The litigation results from *Solloway*'s determination that there must be *one* rule for all cases of "nuisance", and that that rule must be the rule of negligence. To analogise tree roots with escaping fire and falling debris is to indulge in an uncomfortably higher level of abstraction. Note the very sensible observation of Lord Hoffmann in *Marcic* (below), reversing the Court of Appeal which had relied on previous cases: " . . . the cases are not about general principles of the law of nuisance. They are cases about sewers." Likewise the earlier cases imposing strict liability on the owner of the tree whose roots did damage were not about general principles of the law of nuisance: they were cases about tree roots. It has been said that nuisance is "protean" (meaning not "nutritious" but "taking many shapes"); it does not need to have a universal solvent.

5. In *Loftus-Brigham v Ealing LBC* [2003] EWCA Civ 1490 the dehydration of the soil beneath the claimant's house was due not only to the defendant's trees but to the claimant's own creepers. The trial judge's judgment for the defendant was reversed by the Court of Appeal and remanded: he should have asked whether the tree roots materially contributed to the damage, because "the rules of causation were the same in nuisance and negligence". If the tree roots were a contributory cause of the harm, would there be a defence of contributory negligence, or shall we see a replay of the *Tennant Radiant Heat* case (above p.248).

6. Another sensible old rule of the common law has gone as a result of *Leakey*: in *Green v Lord Somerleyton* [2003] EWCA Civ 198 the Court of Appeal chided the trial judge for following *Thomas & Evans v Mid-Rhondda Co-operative Society* [1941] 1 K.B. 381 and holding that an upstream landowner owed no duty to control the natural flow of water from his land on to his neighbour's.

7. It is worth asking why, when dry-rot is so sadly a common natural phenomenon in England, there was no case about its spread until *Bradburn v Lindsay* [1983] 2 All E.R. 408, where the defendant was held liable for not taking steps to prevent its spreading next door when she knew of its existence on her property. She was also held bound to weatherproof the party wall which became exposed to the elements when her house was demolished with her consent by the local authority. As the West German Basic Law pithily observes (and enacts) "Property obliges" (Art.14(2)). Then in *Rees v Skerrett* [1997] EWCA Civ 760 the crack damage to the claimant's wall after the demolition of the defendant's adjoining property was more likely due to suction damage from the wind than to withdrawal of support, but it was said that the wind damage could be said to result from the weight of the unsupported building and therefore be due to the withdrawal of support, which generated an absolute liability. Even apart from that, however, *Leakey* required the defendant to do all that was reasonable to prevent damage to his neighbour, and so the defendant was liable on that ground. Mild concern was voiced that liability might be being extended . . .

8. It will be seen that the effect of *Donoghue v Stevenson* has been to reduce the pockets of strict liability and of non-liability which used to be a significant feature of the tort of nuisance. Admittedly one can see the aesthetic appeal of applying *Donoghue v Stevenson* to actual neighbours as well as neighbours-in-law, but are neighbourly feelings in fact going to be advanced if George, whose kids have broken Harry's window

while playing ball in their own back garden, can refuse to pay unless Harry proves that George was at fault in letting them do so?

9. Note that a nuisance next door may not only cause you damage, as in *Leakey*, but also make you liable for nuisance! An abatement notice may be served on premises prejudicial to health even if the cause of the condition is situated on other premises: *Pollway Nominees v Havering L.B.C.* (1989) 88 L.G.R. 192, DC. Consider the consequences in private law.

Section 5.—Authorised Activities

MANCHESTER CORP. v FARNWORTH

House of Lords [1930] A.C. 17; 99 L.J.K.B. 83; 142 L.T. 145; 94 J.P. 62; 46 T.L.R. 85;
73 S.J. 818; 27 L.G.R. 709; [1929] All E.R. Rep. 90

The plaintiff was a farmer at Barton-on-Irwell whose fields were destroyed by the poisonous fumes emitted from the chimneys of an electric power station erected and operated by the defendant corporation. The defendants pleaded that they were empowered to set up the station by s.32, Manchester Corporation Act 1914.

Talbot J. gave judgment for the defendant. The Court of Appeal (Lawrence L.J. dissenting) granted an injunction and damages [1929] 1 K.B. 533. On appeal by the Corporation, the House of Lords dismissed the appeal, and varied the order by declaring that the plaintiff should have damages until the injunction ceased to be suspended or was dissolved, that the injunction be suspended for one year, with liberty to the defendants to apply for dissolution of the injunction on establishing that all reasonable modes of preventing mischief to the plaintiff had been exhausted and on their submitting to adopt the most effective modes of avoiding such mischief and to replace them by other reasonable but more effective modes of prevention subsequently discovered.

Viscount Dunedin: . . . The serious character of the nuisance naturally makes one reflect on the magnitude of the nuisance which would be caused by stations far bigger than this one, and that such stations are likely in the near future to be established is certain. That brings me to say a word or two on what I conceive to be the well settled law on such matters. The cases are numerous . . . I believe their whole effect may be expressed in a very few sentences. When Parliament has authorised a certain thing to be made or done in a certain place, there can be no action for nuisance caused by the making or doing of that thing if the nuisance is the inevitable result of the making or doing so authorised. The onus of proving that the result is inevitable is on those who wish to escape liability for nuisance, but the criterion of inevitability is not what is theoretically possible but what is possible according to the state of scientific knowledge at the time, having also in view a certain common sense appreciation, which cannot be rigidly defined, of practical feasibility in view of situation and of expense.

Now it is true that in this case we can hold so far that by their callous indifference in planning the construction of the station to all but its own efficiency, the defendants have not discharged the onus incumbent on them . . .

Viscount Sumner: . . . My Lords, the conclusion to which a close examination of the evidence has forced me is that the defendants have not shown that a generating station, such as the legislature contemplated in 1914, whatever that may have been, could not have been erected then and cannot be used now without causing a nuisance, but that they have failed to show that they have used all reasonable diligence and taken all reasonable steps and precautions to prevent their operations from being a nuisance to their neighbours, and this for two reasons. (1) At the time of the erection their responsible officers never directed their minds to the prevention of the nuisance, which it was quite obvious might occur, but (2) they were under the impression that, for all practical purposes, so long as their plant was efficiently and successfully conducted, the neighbours must endure their consequent injuries with such stoicism as they could muster. The proof of this is writ large in their answers generally . . .

Notes:

1. The common law of nuisance is a limitation on activities on one's own land. If one cannot keep 200 horses on one's own land without causing intolerable inconvenience to the neighbours, then the common law says one cannot keep them there at all. But if the legislature has said that something is to be done, the common law cannot say that it is not to be done. What the common law can say is that the thing must be done so as to cause the least damage consistent with its being done. Accordingly, where the defendant in a nuisance case has acted under statutory authority, the common law can demand only that he have acted reasonably so as to minimise the harm; proof of reasonable care will exonerate him, but the proof of that is on him.

The law was stated in four propositions by Webster J. in *Department of Transport v North West Water* [1983] 1 All E.R. 892 at 895, approved by the House of Lords on successful appeal at [1983] 3 All E.R. 273:

> "1. In the absence of negligence, a body is not liable for a nuisance which is attributable to the exercise by it of a duty imposed on it by statute;
> 2. It is not liable in those circumstances even if by statute it is expressly made liable, or not exempted from liability, for nuisance.
> 3. In the absence of negligence, a body is not liable for a nuisance which is attributable to the exercise by it of a power conferred by statute if, by statute, it is not expressly either made liable, or not exempted from liability, for nuisance.
> 4. A body is liable for a nuisance by it attributable to the exercise of a power conferred by statute, even without negligence, if by statute it is expressly either made liable, or not exempted from liability, for nuisance." "Negligence" is here "used in a special sense so as to require the undertaker, as a condition of obtaining immunity from action, to carry out the work and conduct the operation with all reasonable regard and care for the interests of other persons . . . "

2. In the absence of statutory authority from Westminster, planning permission from a local authority is almost always required for any change in the use of land. The question is whether a use for which planning permission has been granted may be enjoined by the courts. The answer is that it can. In *Wheeler v Saunders* [1995] 2 All E.R. 697 the defendants were enjoined from using the authorised newly-erected pig-styes which inevitably made life in the plaintiff's house and holiday cottages intolerable. The court did not disapprove of an earlier case in which Buckley J., while saying that planning permission is not a licence to commit nuisance and that a planning authority has no jurisdiction to authorise nuisance, nevertheless refused an injunction against a round-the-clock dockyard which made life grim for inhabitants by the heavy traffic it attracted, on the ground that the nature of the neighbourhood had been changed by the exercise of the permission (*Gillingham B.C. v Medway (Chatham) Dock Co* [1992] 3 All E.R. 923).

3. Those who suffer from what would be an actionable nuisance but for the fact that it is due to authorised public works executed with proper care may well (but do not necessarily) have a claim to statutory compensation for "injurious affection" from the Lands Tribunal pursuant to the Compulsory Purchase Act 1965, s. 10. "The remedy is given because Parliament by authorising the works has prevented damage caused by them from being actionable, and the compensation is given as a substitute for damages at law." (*per* Scott L.J. in *Horn v Sunderland Corp.* [1941] 2 K.B. 26.

Thus in *Wildtree Hotels v Harrow LBC* [2000] 3 All E.R. 289 the House of Lords held that although temporary loss of value resulting from the careful execution of authorised works calls for compensation, and although noise and vibrations affecting the amenity value of the land must be regarded as injury to the land just as much as physical damage, statutory compensation was not payable for personal discomfort resulting from the execution of the works because such discomfort is not an actionable nuisance unless the work, whether authorised or not, is inconsiderately executed (*Andreae v Selfridge* [1938] Ch. 1) and compensation is payable only if the statutory authorisation is the only reason that damages cannot be claimed.

4. Statutory authority can of course be overcome if one goes to Strasbourg. Thus in *Hatton v UK* [2002] 1 F.C.R. 732 the Third Section of the Court of Human Rights held that each of the claimants who had been disturbed by the noise of authorised night flights from Heathrow should receive £4,000 for nonpecuniary damage. The Grand Chamber, however, by a majority reversed, and held that the statutory permission fell within the state's margin of appreciation. (Application No. 36022/97)

5. In *Dennis v Ministry of Defence* [2003] EWHC 793 there was no statutory authority for the flights of Harrier jump jets from RAF Wittering. They started in 1969. In 1984 the claimants purchased an estate

two miles distant with a Carolean Grade I listed mansion on it. They now claimed that the noise from the aircraft had reduced the capital value of their estate and had prevented them from developing it commercially(!). Buckley J. dismissed the argument that the airbase had been there when the claimants moved in, and said that the public interest in training combat pilots could be taken into account only as regards the remedy. So he refused an injunction but awarded the claimants £950,000 for economic loss, past and future, and loss of amenity. The loss of amenity figure was £50,000—much more than was awarded to another wealthy groundling in *Farley v Skinner* [2002] 2 A.C. 732 against the surveyor who failed to tell him that aircraft from Gatwick were apt to fly over the house he was minded to buy in its vicinity.

Section 6.—Established Activities

MILLER v JACKSON

Court of Appeal [1977] Q.B. 966; [1977] 3 W.L.R. 20; 121 S.J. 287; [1977] 3 All E.R. 338 (noted (1977) 93 L.Q.R. 481; (1978) 94 L.Q.R. 178

Action by incomer to enjoin established village cricketing

In 1972 houses were built in an empty field next to a village cricket ground which had been in use for nearly 70 years. That summer the plaintiffs bought one of the houses; its garden wall was only 102 feet from the wicket, so cricket balls kept sailing over it, and they complained bitterly. The cricket club erected the highest possible wire fence atop the wall and instructed the batsmen to try to keep the ball low, but even so five more balls came over in 1975. The plaintiffs refused offers to instal unbreakable glass and to cover the whole garden with a safety net, and sought an injunction to prevent the defendants playing cricket in such a matter that cricket balls came into the plaintiffs' garden. At the trial it appeared that cricket could not be played there at all without the occasional ball going over. The trial judge granted the injunction. The defendants appealed. Although it was held, Lord Denning dissenting, that the defendants were guilty of nuisance notwithstanding that the plaintiffs were aware of the defendants' well-established activity at the time they bought their house, the defendants' appeal was allowed, Geoffrey Lane L.J. dissenting.

Lord Denning M.R.: . . . It has been often said in nuisance cases that the rule is *sic utere tuo ut alienum non laedas*. But that is a most misleading maxim. Lord Wright put it in its proper place in *Sedleigh-Denfield v O'Callaghan* [1940] A.C. 880 at 903:

"[It] is not only lacking in definiteness but is also inaccurate. An occupier may make in many ways a use of his land which causes damage to the neighbouring landowners, and yet be free from liability . . . a useful test is perhaps what is reasonable according to the ordinary usages of mankind living in society, or, more correctly, in a particular society."

I would, therefore, adopt this test: is the use by the cricket club of this ground for playing cricket a reasonable use of it? To my mind it is a most reasonable use. Just consider the circumstances. For over 70 years the game of cricket has been played on this ground to the great benefit of the community as a whole, and to the injury of none. No one could suggest that it was a nuisance to the neighbouring owners simply because an enthusiastic batsman occasionally hit a ball out of the ground for six to the approval of the admiring onlookers. Then I would ask: does it suddenly become a nuisance because one of the neighbours chooses to build a house on the very edge of the ground, in such a position that it may well be struck by the ball on the rare occasion when there is a hit for six? To my mind the answer is plainly No. The building of the house does not convert the playing of cricket into a nuisance when it was not so before. If and in so far as any damage is caused to the house or anyone in it, it is because of the position in which it was built. Suppose that the house had not been built by a developer, but by a private owner. He would be in much the same position as the farmer who previously put his cows in the field. He could not complain if a batsman hit a six out of the ground and, by a million to one chance, it struck a cow or even the farmer himself. He would be in no better position than a spectator at Lord's or the Oval or at a motor rally. At any rate, even if he could claim damages for the loss of the cow or the injury, he could not get an injunction to stop the cricket. If the private owner could not get an injunction, neither should a developer or a purchaser from him.

It was said, however, that the case of the physician's consulting-room was to the contrary (*Sturges v Bridgman* (1879) 11 Ch.D. 852). But that turned on the old law about easements and prescriptions, and so forth. It was in the days when rights of property were in the ascendant and not subject to any limitations except those provided by the law of easements. But nowadays it is a matter of balancing the conflicting interests of the two neighbours. That was made clear by Lord Wright in *Sedleigh-Denfield v O'Callaghan*, when he said: "A balance has to be maintained between the right of the occupier to do what he likes with his own and the right of his neighbour not to be interfered with."

In this case it is our task to balance the right of the cricket club to continue playing cricket on their cricket ground, as against the right of the householder not to be interfered with. On taking the balance, I would give priority to the right of the cricket club to continue playing cricket on the ground, as they have done for the last 70 years. It takes precedence over the right of the newcomer to sit in his garden undisturbed. After all he bought the house four years ago in mid-summer when the cricket season was at its height. He might have guessed that there was a risk that a hit for six might possibly land on his property. If he finds that he does not like it, he ought, when cricket is played, to sit on the other side of the house or in the front garden, or go out; or take advantage of the offers the club have made to him of fitting unbreakable glass, and so forth. Or, if he does not like that, he ought to sell his house and move elsewhere. I expect there are many who would gladly buy it in order to be near the cricket field and open space. At any rate he ought not to be allowed to stop cricket being played on this ground.

This case is new. It should be approached on principles applicable to modern conditions. There is a contest here between the interest of the public at large and the interest of a private individual. The *public* interest lies in protecting the environment by preserving our playing fields in the face of mounting development, and by enabling our youth to enjoy all the benefits of outdoor games, such as cricket and football. The *private* interest lies in securing the privacy of his home and garden without intrusion or interference by anyone. In deciding between these two conflicting interests, it must be remembered that it is not a question of damages. If by a million-to-one chance a cricket ball does go out of the ground and cause damage, the cricket club will pay. There is no difficulty on that score. No, it is a question of an injunction. And in our law you will find it repeatedly affirmed that an injunction is a discretionary remedy. In a new situation like this, we have to think afresh as to how discretion should be exercised. On the other hand, Mrs Miller is a very sensitive lady who has worked herself up into such a state that she exclaimed to the judge: "I just want to be allowed to live in peace. Have we got to wait until someone is killed before anything can be done?"

If she feels like that about it, it is quite plain that, for peace in the future, one or other has to move. Either the cricket club have to move, but goodness knows where. I do not suppose for a moment there is any field in Lintz to which they could move. Or Mrs Miller must move elsewhere. As between their conflicting interests, I am of opinion that the public interest should prevail over the private interest. The cricket club should not be driven out. In my opinion the right exercise of discretion is to refuse an injunction; and, of course to refuse damages in lieu of an injunction. Likewise as to the claim for past damages. The club were entitled to use this ground for cricket in the accustomed way. It was not a nuisance, nor was it negligence of them so to run it. Nor was the batsman negligent when he hit the ball for six. All were doing simply what they were entitled to do. So if the club had put it to the test, I would have dismissed the claim for damages also. But as the club very fairly say that they are willing to pay for any damage, I am content that there should be an award of £400 to cover any past or future damage.

I would allow the appeal, accordingly.

Geoffrey Lane L.J.: . . . Was there here a use by the defendants of their land involving an unreasonable interference with the plaintiffs' enjoyment of *their* land? There is here in effect no dispute that there has been and is likely to be in the future an interference with the plaintiffs' enjoyment of no. 20 Brackenridge. The only question is whether it is unreasonable. It is a truism to say that this is a matter of degree. What that means is this. A balance has to be maintained between on the one hand the rights of the individual to enjoy his house and garden without the threat of damage and on the other hand the rights of the public in general or a neighbour to engage in lawful pastimes. Difficult questions may sometimes arise when the defendants' activities are offensive to the sense, for example by way of noise. Where, as here, the damage or potential damage is physical the answer is more simple. There is, subject to what appears hereafter, no excuse I can see which exonerates the defendants from liability in nuisance for what they have done or from what they threaten to do. It is true no one has yet been physically injured. That is probably due to a great extent to the fact that the householders in Brackenridge desert their gardens whilst cricket is in progress. The danger of injury is obvious and is not slight enough to be disregarded. There is here a real risk of serious injury.

There is, however, one obviously strong point in the defendants' favour. They or their predecessors have been playing cricket on this ground (and no doubt hitting sixes out of it) for 70 years or so. Can someone by building a house on the edge of the field in circumstances where it must have been obvious that balls might be hit over the fence, effectively stop cricket being played? Precedent apart, justice would seem to demand that the plaintiffs should be left to make the most of the site they have elected to occupy with all its obvious advantages and all its equally obvious disadvantages. It is pleasant to have an open space over which to look from your bedroom and sitting room windows, so far as it is possible to see over the concrete wall. Why should you complain of the obvious disadvantages which arise from the particular purpose to which the open space is being put? Put briefly, can the defendants take advantage of the fact that the plaintiffs have put themselves in such a position by coming to occupy a house on the edge of a small cricket field, with the result that what was not a nuisance in the past now becomes a nuisance? If the matter were *res integra*, I confess I should be inclined to find for the defendants. It does not seem just that a long-established activity, in itself innocuous, should be brought to an end because someone chooses to build a house nearby and so turn an innocent pastime into actionable nuisance. Unfortunately, however, the question is not open. In *Sturges v Bridgman* (1879) 11 Ch.D. 852 this very problem arose. The defendant had carried on a confectionery shop with a noisy pestle and mortar for more than 20 years. Although it was noisy, it was far enough away from neighbouring premises not to cause trouble to anyone, until the plaintiff, who was a physician, built a consulting-room on his own land but immediately adjoining the confectionery shop. The noise and vibrations seriously interfered with the consulting-room and became a nuisance to the physician. The defendant contended that he had acquired the right either at common law or under the Prescription Act 1832 by uninterrupted use for more than 20 years to impose the inconvenience. It was held by the Court of Appeal, affirming the judgment of Jessel M.R. that use such as this which was, prior to the construction of the consulting-room, neither preventible or actionable, could not found a prescriptive right. That decision involved the assumption, which so far as one can discover has never been questioned, that it is no answer to a claim in nuisance for the defendant to show that the plaintiff brought the trouble on his own head by building or coming to live in a house so close to the defendant's premises that he would inevitably be affected by the defendant's activities, where no one had been affected previously. See also *Bliss v Hall* (1848) 132 E.R. 758. It may be that this rule works injustice, it may be that one would decide the matter differently in the absence of authority. But we are bound by the decision in *Sturges v Bridgman* and it is not for this court as I see it to alter a rule which has stood for so long . . .

Cumming-Bruce L.J. agreed with Geoffrey Lane L.J. that the defendants were liable in negligence and nuisance, and that *Sturges v Bridgman* was binding. He agreed, however, with Lord Denning M.R. that no injunction should be granted.

Note:

Here the plaintiff was seeking to enjoin a group activity in the interests of private repose (and safety). So it was also in *Kennaway v Thompson* [1981] Q.B. 88; noted (1981) 97 L.Q.R. 3, where the plaintiff had built a nice house by a man-made lake on which the defendant club was just beginning to organise water-skiing and speed-boat racing. By the time of the lawsuit noise organised by the defendants was making life intolerable for the plaintiff. The trial judge refused an injunction, but granted damages of £15,000 in lieu. The Court of Appeal reversed on the basis of a late Victorian decision which held that a mid-Victorian Act permitting the grant of damages in lieu of an injunction had not altered the early Victorian practice of granting an injunction to stop a nuisance in all but very exceptional cases (*Shelfer v City of London Electric Lighting Co* [1895] 1 Ch. 287). None of the reluctance evinced by Scott J. in the *Anchor Brewhouse* case (aerial trespass, above, p.359) marked the Court of Appeal in *Elliott v Islington B.C.* [1990] Times L.R. 517 when it refused to discharge a mandatory injunction that a chestnut tree which was damaging the plaintiff's wall be removed: "it was wrong to deprive individuals of their rights for the public benefit." In *Kennaway*, it must be said, the injunction was very qualified in its terms, on the basis that only the excessive noise could be enjoined—a principle which also applies in claims for damages (*Tate & Lyle Indus. v G.L.C.* [1983] 1 All E.R. 1159; *Andreae v Selfridge* [1937] 3 All E.R. 255). However, in *Tetley v Chitty* [1986] 1 All E.R. 663, where residents of Rochester were complaining of the noise from a go-kart track on land across the Medway which the local authority had leased to a go-kart club, go-kart racing was totally enjoined.

The local authority, having leased out the land, was no longer in occupation of it, but was held liable because excessive noise was a very predictable consequence of the use for which the land had been let (contrast *Smith v Scott* above, p.436). A landlord who creates a condition on the premises which renders a nuisance inevitable remains liable, even after he has disposed of his interest; and the person who acquires his interest may become liable for the nuisance although he did not create it. This emerges (rather obscurely) from *Sampson v Hodson-Pressinger* [1981] 3 All E.R. 710; noted [1982] Camb.L.J. 38. Here X sold the plaintiff a 99 year lease of a flat, and then constructed a terrace/roof-garden above it for use with the upstairs flat, then vacant, in which he sold a 99 year lease to the first defendant. X then sold the reversion of the whole building to the second defendant. The terrace was badly tiled and the sound of persons walking and talking on it quite normally was intolerable in the plaintiff's sitting room. The decision that the occupant of the flat was liable although she was doing absolutely nothing abnormal cannot stand with *Baxter* (above, p.429) but the second defendant was held liable because he knew of the trouble when he bought the freehold and because by accepting rent he was authorising the nuisance. Likewise the landlord was held liable in *Toff v McDowell* (1993) 25 H.L.R. 650 when the tenants had done nothing but use the leased flat quite normally, but in that case the landlord had removed the floor-covering and that had made the tenants' noise intolerable for the plaintiff below. The judge, in addition to making the defendant pay £6,000 for past noise, ordered payment of a further £12,000 unless within three months he reinstated the flooring.

In both these cases an injunction was refused. The interplay of the remedies of injunction and damages has been a source of fascination especially to law-and-economics people, excited by the relationship between neighbours-in-fact, parties who can in principle negotiate, whether before or after the grant of an injunction. The American literature is enormous, but Rabin, "Nuisance Law: Rethinking Fundamental Assumptions" (1977) 63 Virginia L. Rev. 1299 is very accessible. For England one can consult Tromans, "Nuisance— Prevention or Payment" [1982] Camb.L.J. 87. One idea adopted in Arizona but unlikely to be followed by English courts is to grant an injunction on the terms that the claimant compensate the party enjoined.

Lord Denning naturally referred to the other great cricket case, *Bolton v Stone* (above, p.141), noting that Lord Porter had said that in the circumstances of that case "nuisance cannot be established unless negligence is proved". He did not add that Lord Porter said, contrary to the fact, that this point had been conceded by plaintiff's counsel. See Birkenhead, *Walter Monckton* (London, 1969) 267, cited by E. Grayson, "Sporting Legal Lotteries" [1994] New L.J. 788 at 789.

MARCIC v THAMES WATER UTILITIES

House of Lords [2003] UKHL 66; [2003] 3 W.L.R. 1603; [2004] 1 All E.R. 135

Claim by flooded householder that the sewerage authority was required by the common law of nuisance and by the Human Rights Act to upgrade the sewage system

Lord Hoffmann: Thames Water Utilities Ltd ("Thames") is a statutory sewerage undertaker. Mr Marcic has a house in Stanmore, within the area for which Thames is responsible. Since 1992

Mr Marcic's garden has suffered periodic flooding. The reason for the flooding is that the sewers in his street are overloaded. At the time they were laid, the surface and foul water sewers were adequate. But many more houses have since been built. Each has the right to connect itself to the existing sewers: section 106 of the Water Industry Act 1991. The result of the overload is that in heavy rain the surface water sewer becomes so full that the water overflows through the gullies into Mr Marcic's low lying garden. Still worse, the surface water enters the foul sewer and causes sewage to flow back onto his property through his foul drain. Since 1992 the garden has been regularly flooded. Only Mr Marcic's private flood defence system, constructed at a cost of some £16,000, has prevented the water from entering the house.

Thames has a statutory duty, under s.94(1) of the 1991 Act:

"(a) to provide, improve and extend such a system of public sewers (whether inside its area or elsewhere) and so to cleanse and maintain those sewers as to ensure that that area is and continues to be effectually drained; and

(b) to make provision for the emptying of those sewers and such further provision (whether inside its area or elsewhere) as is necessary from time to time for effectually dealing, by means of sewage disposal works or otherwise, with the contents of those sewers."

Mr Marcic, however, has not attempted to enforce this duty. The reason is that Chapter II of the 1991 Act contains an exclusive code for the enforcement of, among others, the duty under s.94(1). Section 18(8) makes it clear that the statutory remedies are the only remedies available for an act or omission which constitutes a contravention of duties enforceable under s.18. So all that Mr Marcic could do by way of enforcement of the s.94(1) duty was to make a complaint to the Director, in which case it would be the duty of the Director to consider the complaint and take such steps, if any, as he thought appropriate: see s.30.

Mr Marcic chose not the avail himself of this route. Instead, he issued a writ claiming an injunction and damages for nuisance. Section 18(8) does not exclude any "remedies available in respect of [an] act or omission otherwise than by virtue of constituting . . . a contravention [of a duty enforceable under s.18]." It follows that if the failure to improve the sewers to meet the increased demand gives rise to a cause of action at common law, it is not excluded by the statute. The question is whether there is such a cause of action.

The flooding has not been due to any failure on the part of Thames to clean and maintain the existing sewers. Nor are they responsible for the increased use. They have, as I have said, a statutory duty to accept whatever water and sewage the owners of property in their area choose to discharge. The omission relied upon by Mr Marcic as giving rise to an actionable nuisance is their failure to construct new sewers with a greater capacity.

Until the decision of the Court of Appeal in this case, there was a line of authority which laid down that the failure of a sewage authority to construct new sewers did not constitute an actionable nuisance. The only remedy was by way of enforcement of the statutory duty now contained in s.94(1) of the 1991 Act. The earlier acts also had a special procedure for enforcement which the courts held to be exhaustive. The existence of this procedure for the enforcement of statutory duties did not exclude common law remedies for common law torts, such as a nuisance arising from failure to keep a sewer properly cleaned. But the courts consistently held that failure to construct new sewers was not such a nuisance.

The principal authorities for this last proposition were three cases in the late nineteenth century. Mr Marcic can therefore have a cause of action in nuisance only if these authorities are no longer good law. The Court of Appeal decided that they should no longer be followed. They said that the earlier cases had been overtaken by developments in the concept of "adopting" or "continuing" a nuisance which enabled one to say, in appropriate circumstances, that a sewerage undertaker had a common law duty to lay new sewers in order to prevent overloaded old ones from flooding neighbouring properties.

The cases relied upon by the Court of Appeal are those in which it has been held that a land owner may have a duty to take positive steps to remove a source of nuisance which he did not himself create. The leading case is of course *Sedley-Denfield v O'Callaghan* [1940] A.C. 880, in which the potential source of the nuisance was created by a trespasser. Attempts to distinguish cases in which the damage arose from natural causes (lightning or natural weathering of rocks and soil) failed in *Goldman v Hargrave* [1967] 1 A.C. 645 and *Leakey v National Trust* [1980] Q.B. 685. The present law is that, as Denning L.J. said in the *Pride of Derby* case by reference to *Sedleigh-Denfield*, "a person may 'continue' a nuisance by adopting it, or in some circumstances by omitting to remedy it."

In other words, the four cases are not about general principles of the law of nuisance. They are cases about sewers.

The Court of Appeal said that since the four cases were decided, the law of nuisance had been "radically extended" by the *Sedleigh-Denfield* case. The *Goldman* and *Leakey* cases were said to have made a "significant extension" to the law. It is true that they rejected a distinction between acts of third parties and natural events which Lord Wilberforce said (at p.661) was "well designed to introduce confusion into the law" and lacked "any logical foundation." Both cases also discussed in greater detail the extent of the duty to remedy a potential nuisance. Otherwise, however, they were applications of the *Sedleigh-Denfield* principle. [But the earlier "cases are not about general principles of the law of nuisance. They are cases about sewers."]

Why should sewers be different? If the *Sedleigh-Denfield* case lays down a general principle that an owner of land has a duty to take reasonable steps to prevent a nuisance arising from a known source of hazard, even though he did not himself create it, why should that not require him to construct new sewers if the court thinks it would have been reasonable to do so?

The difference in my opinion is that the *Sedleigh-Denfield*, *Goldman* and *Leakey* cases were dealing with disputes between neighbouring land owners simply in their capacity as individual landowners. In such cases it is fair and efficient to impose reciprocal duties upon each landowner to take whatever steps are reasonable to prevent his land becoming a source of injury to his neighbour. Even then, the question of what measures should reasonably have been taken may not be uncomplicated. As Lord Wilberforce said in *Goldman*'s case ([1967] 1 A.C. 645, 663, the court must (unusually) have regard to the individual circumstances of the defendant. ... the court in such cases is performing its usual function of deciding what is reasonable as between the two parties to the action. But the exercise becomes very different when one is dealing with the capital expenditure of a statutory undertaking providing public utilities on a large scale. The matter is no longer confined to the parties to the action. If one customer is given a certain level of services, everyone in the same circumstances should receive the same level of services. So the effect of a decision about what it would be reasonable to expect a sewerage undertaker to do for the plaintiff is extrapolated across the country. This in turn raises questions of public interest. Capital expenditure on new sewers has to be financed; interest must be paid on borrowings and privatised undertakers must earn a reasonable return. This expenditure can be met only be charges paid by consumers. Is it in the public interest that they should have to pay more? And does expenditure on the particular improvements with which the plaintiff is concerned represent the best order of priorities?

These are decisions which courts are not equipped to make in ordinary litigation. It is therefore not surprising that for more than a century the question of whether more or better sewers should be constructed has been entrusted by Parliament to administrators rather than judges.

The 1991 Act makes it even clearer than the earlier legislation that Parliament did not intend the fairness of priorities to be decided by a judge. It intended the decision to rest with the Director, subject only to judicial review. It would subvert the scheme of the 1991 Act if the courts were to impose upon the sewerage undertakers, on a case-by-case basis, a system of priorities which is different from that which the Director considers appropriate.

That leaves only the question of whether the remedies provided under the 1991 Act do not adequately safeguard Mr Marcic's Convention rights to the privacy of his home and the protection of his property. The judge, who found for Mr Marcic on this ground, did not have the benefit of the decision of the Grand Chamber of the European Court of Human Rights in *Hatton v United Kingdom* (July 8, 2003) (unreported). That decision makes it clear that the Convention does not accord absolute protection to property or even to residential premises. It requires a fair balance to be struck between the interests of persons whose homes and property are affected and the interests of other people, such as customers and the general public. National institutions, and particularly the national legislature, are accorded a broad discretion in choosing the solution appropriate to their own society or creating the machinery for doing so. There is no reason why Parliament should not entrust such decisions to an independent regulator such as the Director. He is a public authority within the meaning of the 1998 Act and has a duty to act in accordance with Convention rights. If (which there is no reason to suppose) he has exceeded the broad margin of discretion allowed by the Convention, Mr Marcic will have a remedy under s.6 of the 1998 Act. But that question is not before your Lordships. His case is that he has a Convention right to have the decision as to whether new sewers should be constructed made by a court in a private action for nuisance rather than by the Director in the exercise of his powers under the 1991 Act. In my opinion there is no such right.

I would therefore allow the appeal and dismiss the action.

Lord Nicholls and **Lord Hope** also delivered speeches in favour of allowing the appeal; **Lord Steyn** and **Lord Scott** agreed with **Lord Nicholls** and **Lord Hoffmann**.

Chapter 11

RYLANDS v FLETCHER

RYLANDS v FLETCHER

House of Lords (1868) L.R. 3 H.L. 330; 37 L.J.Ex. 161; 19 L.T. 220; 33 J.P. 70

Action for damages for flooding of plaintiff's mine by water from defendant's artificial millpond

Near Ainsworth in Lancashire the defendants had a mill whose water supply they wanted to improve. They obtained permission from Lord Wilton to construct a reservoir on his land and retained reputable engineers to do it. Unknown to the defendants, the plaintiff, who had a mineral lease from Lord Wilton, had carried his workings to a point not far distant, though separated by the land of third parties. In the course of construction the engineers came across some disused mine shafts and did not seal them properly, with the result that when the completed reservoir was filled, water flowed down those shafts and into the plaintiff's coal-mine, causing damage later agreed at £937.

The arbitrator stated a special case for the Court of Exchequer, which found for the defendants (Bramwell B. dissenting) ((1865) 3 H. & C. 774; 159 E.R. 737). The plaintiff took a writ of error to the Court of Exchequer Chamber, which gave him judgment. The defendants' appeal to the House of Lords was dismissed.

In the House of Lords

Lord Cairns L.C.: . . . The reservoir of the defendants was constructed by them through the agency and inspection of an engineer and contractor. Personally, the defendants appear to have taken no part in the works, or to have been aware of any want of security connected with them. As regards the engineer and the contractor, we must take it from the case that they did not exercise, as far as they were concerned, that reasonable care and caution which they might have exercised, taking notice, as they appear to have taken notice, of the vertical shafts filled up in the manner which I have mentioned. However, my Lords, when the reservoir was constructed, and filled, or partly filled, with water, the weight of the water bearing upon the disused and imperfectly filled-up vertical shafts, broke through those shafts. The water passed down them and into the horizontal workings, and from the horizontal workings under the close of the defendants it passed on into the workings under the close of the plaintiff, and flooded his mine causing considerable damage, for which this action was brought.

The Court of Exchequer . . . was of opinion that the plaintiff had established no cause of action. The Court of Exchequer Chamber, before which an appeal from the judgment was argued, was of a contrary opinion, and the judges there unanimously arrived at the conclusion that there was a cause of action, and that the plaintiff was entitled to damages.

My Lords, the principles on which this case must be determined appear to me to be extremely simple. The defendants, treating them as the owners or occupiers of the close on which the reservoir was constructed, might lawfully have used that close for any purpose for which it might in the ordinary course of the enjoyment of land be used; and if, in what I may term the natural user of that land, there had been any accumulation of water, either on the surface or underground, and if, by the operation of the laws of nature, that accumulation of water had passed off into the close occupied by the plaintiff, the plaintiff could not have complained that that result had taken place. If he had desired to guard himself against it, it would have lain upon him to have done so, by leaving, or by interposing, some barrier between his close and the close of the defendants in order to have prevented that operation of the laws of nature.

As an illustration of that principle, I may refer to a case which was cited in the argument before your Lordships, the case of *Smith v Kenrick* in the Court of Common Pleas ((1849) 7 C.B. 515; 137 E.R. 105).

On the other hand if the defendants, not stopping at the natural use of their close, had desired to use it for any purpose which I may term a non-natural use, for the purpose of introducing into the close that which in its natural condition was not in or upon it, for the purpose of introducing water either above or below ground in quantities and in a manner not the result of any work or operation on or under the land—and if in consequence of their doing so, or in consequence of any imperfection in the mode of their doing so, the water came to escape and pass off into the close of the plaintiff, then it appears to me that that which the defendants were doing they were doing at their own peril; and, if in the course of their doing it, the evil arose to which I have referred, the evil, namely, of the escape of the water and its passing away to the close of the plaintiff and injuring the plaintiff, then for the consequence of that, in my opinion, the defendants would be liable. As the case of *Smith v Kenrick* is an illustration of the first principle to which I have referred, so also the second principle to which I have referred is well illustrated by another case in the same court, the case of *Baird v Williamson* ((1863) 15 C.B. (N.S.) 376; 143 E.R. 831), which was also cited in the argument at the Bar.

My Lords, these simple principles, if they are well founded, as it appears to me they are, really dispose of this case.

The same result is arrived at on the principles referred to by Blackburn J. in his judgment in the Court of Exchequer Chamber, where he states the opinion of that court as to the law in these words: "We think that the rule of law is, that the person who, for his own purposes, brings on his land and collects and keeps there anything likely to do mischief if it escapes, must keep it in at his peril; and if he does not do so, is prima facie answerable for all the damage which is the natural consequence of its escape. He can excuse himself by showing that the escape was owing to the plaintiff's default; or, perhaps, that the escape was the consequence of *vis major*, or the act of God; but as nothing of this sort exists here, it is unnecessary to inquire what excuse would be sufficient. The general rule, as above stated, seems on principle just. The person whose grass or corn is eaten down by the escaping cattle of his neighbour, or whose mine is flooded by the water from his neighbour's reservoir, or whose cellar is invaded by the filth of his neighbour's privy, or whose habitation is made unhealthy by the fumes and noisome vapours of his neighbour's alkali works, is damnified without any fault of his own; and it seems but reasonable and just that the neighbour who has brought something on his own property (which was not naturally there), harmless to others so long as it is confined to his own property, but which he knows will be mischievous if it gets on his neighbour's, should be obliged to make good the damage which ensues if he does not succeed in confining it to his own property. But for his act in bringing it there no mischief could have accrued, and it seems but just that he should at his peril keep it there, so that no mischief may accrue, or answer for the natural and anticipated consequence. And upon authority this we think is established to be the law, whether the things so brought be beasts, or water, or filth, or stenches."

My Lords, in that opinion, I must say I entirely concur. Therefore, I have to move your Lordships that the judgment of the Court of Exchequer Chamber be affirmed, and that the present appeal be dismissed with costs.

Lord Cranworth: My Lords, I concur with my noble and learned friend in thinking that the rule of law was correctly stated by Blackburn J. in delivering the opinion of the Exchequer Chamber. If a person brings, or accumulates, on his land anything which if it should escape, may cause damage to his neighbour, he does so at his peril. If it does escape, and cause damage, he is responsible, however careful he may have been, and whatever precautions he may have taken to prevent the damage. . . .

In the Court of Exchequer Chamber (1866) L.R. 1 Ex. 265

Blackburn J.: . . . The plaintiff, though free from all blame on his part, must bear the loss, unless he can establish that it was the consequence of some default for which the defendants are responsible. The question of law therefore arises, what is the obligation which the law casts on a person who, like the defendants, lawfully brings on his land something which, though harmless whilst it remains there, will naturally do mischief if it escape out of his land. It is agreed on all hands that he must take care to keep in that which he has brought on the land and keeps there, in order that it may not escape and damage his neighbours, but the question arises whether the duty which the law casts upon him, under such circumstances, is an absolute duty to keep it in at his peril, or is, as the majority of the Court of Exchequer have thought, merely a duty to take all reasonable and prudent precautions, in order to keep it in, but no more. If the first be the law, the person who has brought on his land and kept there something dangerous, and failed to keep it in, is responsible for all the natural consequences of its escape. If the second be the limit of his duty, he would not be answerable except on proof of negligence, and consequently would not be answerable for escape arising from any latent defect which ordinary prudence and skill could not detect.

Supposing the second to be the correct view of the law, a further question arises subsidiary to the first, *viz.*, whether the defendants are not so far identified with the contractors whom they employed, as to be responsible for the consequences of their want of care and skill in making the reservoir in fact insufficient with reference to the old shafts, of the existence of which they were aware, though they had not ascertained where the shafts went to.

We think that the true rule of law is [here follows the passage cited by Lord Cairns L.C., above, p.454]. . . .

. . . But it was said by Martin B. that when damage is done to personal property, or even to the person, by collision, either upon land or at sea, there must be negligence in the party doing the damage to render him legally responsible; and this is no doubt true, and as was pointed out by Mr Mellish during his argument before us, this is not confined to cases of collision, for there are many cases in which proof of negligence is essential, as for instance, where an unruly horse gets on the footpath of a public street and kills a passenger: *Hammack v White* ((1862) 11 C.B.(N.S.) 588; 142 E.R. 926); or where a person in a dock is struck by the falling of a bale of cotton which the defendant's servants are lowering, *Scott v London Dock Company* ((1865) 3 H. & C. 596; 159 E.R. 665); and many other similar cases may be found. But we think these cases distinguishable from the present. Traffic on highways, whether by land or sea, cannot be conducted without exposing those whose persons or property are near it to some inevitable risk; and that being so, those who go on the highway, or have their property adjacent to it, may well be held to do so subject to their taking upon themselves the risk of injury from that inevitable danger; and persons who by the licence of the owner pass near to warehouses where goods are being raised or lowered, certainly do so subject to the inevitable risk of accident. In neither case, therefore, can they recover without proof of want of care or skill occasioning the accident; and it is believed that all the cases in which inevitable accident has been held an excuse for what prima facie was a trespass, can be explained on the same principle, *viz.*, that the circumstances were such as to show that the plaintiff had taken that risk upon himself. But there is no ground for saying that the plaintiff here took upon himself any risk arising from the uses to which the defendants should choose to apply their land. He neither knew what these might be, nor could he in any way control the defendants, or hinder their building what reservoirs they liked, and storing up in them what water they pleased, so long as the defendants succeeded in preventing the water which they there brought from interfering with the plaintiff's property.

The view which we take of the first point renders it unnecessary to consider whether the defendants would or would not be responsible for the want of care and skill in the persons employed by them, under the circumstances stated in the case.

We are of opinion that the plaintiff is entitled to recover, . . .

Note:

Rylands v Fletcher is not accepted in Scotland, but in the United States it was the starting point of a liability without fault for the consequences of "ultraharzardous" (now "abnormally dangerous") activities, a development which Lord Goff viewed with reserve in the *Cambridge Water Co* case, below p.000. In Australia it has been absorbed into the general principles of negligence law: *Burnie Port Authority v General*

Jones Pty (1994) 120 A.L.R. 42, discussed in *Transco*, below p.463. It is worth noting that Australia had already allowed claims for personal injury to be brought under *Rylands v Fletcher* and had extended the range of non-delegable duties (*Kondis v State Transport Authority* (1984) 55 A.L.R. 225). One oddity of the *Burnie* decision (which had to do with fire, to which *Rylands* does not obviously apply), is that the majority of the court, having absorbed *Rylands* into negligence law, gave judgment for the claimant while the minority, upholding *Rylands* with its supposedly strict liability, were for the defendant.

RICKARDS v LOTHIAN

Privy Council [1913] A.C. 263; 82 L.J.P.C. 42; 108 L.T. 225; 29 T.L.R. 281; 57 S.J. 281; [1911–13] All E.R. Rep. 71

Action by subjacent tenant against landlord in respect of property damage caused by escaping water

The plaintiff leased second-floor offices in a building occupied by the defendant. One morning he found his stock-in-trade seriously damaged by water. This water came from a fourth-floor lavatory basin, whose outlet had been plugged with nails, soap, pen-holders and string, and whose tap had been turned fully on. The defendant's caretaker testified that all was well at 10.20 the previous evening.

The jury found that the defendant was careless in not providing a lead safe on the floor under the basin, but that the plugging of the outlet and the turning of the tap "was the malicious act of some person." The county court judge at Melbourne entered judgment for the plaintiff. On appeal by the defendant, the Supreme Court of Victoria reversed the judgment, but the High Court of Australia reinstated it. The defendant's appeal to the Judicial Committee of the Privy Council was allowed.

Lord Moulton: ... Their Lordships are of opinion that all that is ... laid down as to a case where the escape is due to "*vis major* or the King's enemies" applies equally to a case where it is due to the malicious act of a third person, if indeed that case is not actually included in the above phrase ... a defendant cannot in their Lordships' opinion be properly said to have caused or allowed the water to escape if the malicious act of a third person was the real cause of its escaping without any fault on the part of the defendant.

It is remarkable that the very point involved in the present case was expressly dealt with by Bramwell B. in delivering the judgment of the Court of Exchequer in *Nichols v Marsland* ((1876) 2 Ex.D. 1). He says: "What has the defendant done wrong? What right of the plaintiff has she infringed? She has done nothing wrong. She has infringed no right. It is not the defendant who let loose the water and sent it to destroy the bridges. She did indeed store it, and store in in such quantities that if it was let loose it would do as it did, mischief. But suppose a stranger let it loose, would the defendant be liable? If so, then if a mischievous boy bored a hole in a cistern in any London house, and the water did mischief to a neighbour, the occupier of the house would be liable. That cannot be. Then why is the defendant liable if some agent over which she has no control lets the water out? ... I admit that it is not a question of negligence. A man may use all care to keep the water in ... but would be liable if through any defect, though latent, the water escaped. ... But here the act is that of an agent he cannot control."

Following the language of this judgment their Lordships are of opinion that no better example could be given of an agent that the defendant cannot control than that of a third party surreptitiously and by a malicious act causing the overflow. ...

Their Lordships ... are of opinion that a defendant is not liable on the principle of *Fletcher v Rylands* for damage caused by the wrongful acts of third persons.

But there is another ground upon which their Lordships are of opinion that the present case does not come within the principle laid down in *Fletcher v Rylands*. It is not every use to which land is put that brings into play that principle. It must be some special use bringing with it increased danger to others, and must not merely be the ordinary use of the land or such a use as is proper for the general benefit of the community. To use the language of Lord Robertson in *Eastern and South African Telegraph Co v Cape Town Tramways Companies* ([1902] A.C. 393), the principle of *Fletcher v Rylands* "subjects to a high liability the owner who uses his property for purposes other than those which are natural." This is more fully expressed by Wright J. in his judgment in *Blake v Woolf* ([1898] 2 Q.B. 426). In that case the plaintiff was the occupier of the lower floors of the defendant's house, the upper floors being occupied by the defendant himself. A leak occurred in the cistern at the top of the house which without any negligence on the part of the defendant caused the plaintiff's premises to be flooded. In giving judgment for the defendant Wright J. says: "The general rule as laid down in *Rylands v Fletcher* is that prima facie a person occupying land has an absolute right not to have his premises invaded by injurious matter, such as large quantities of water which his neighbour keeps upon his land. That general rule is, however, qualified by some exceptions, one of which is that, where a person is using his land in the ordinary way and damage happens to the adjoining property without any default or negligence on his part, no liability attaches to him. The bringing of water on to such premises as these and the maintaining a cistern in the usual way seems to me to be an ordinary and reasonable user of such premises as these were; and, therefore, if the water escapes without any negligence or default on the part of the person bringing the water in and owning the cistern, I do not think that he is liable for any damage that may ensue." . . .

Their Lordships are in entire sympathy with these views. The provision of a proper supply of water to the various parts of a house is not only reasonable, but has become, in accordance with modern sanitary views, an almost necessary feature of town life. It is recognised as being so desirable in the interests of the community that in some form or other it is usually made obligatory in civilised countries. Such a supply cannot be installed without causing some concurrent danger of leakage or overflow. It would be unreasonable for the law to regard those who install or maintain such a system of supply as doing so at their own peril, with an absolute liability for any damage resulting from its presence even when there has been no negligence. It would be still more unreasonable if, as the respondent contends, such liability were to be held to extend to the consequences of malicious acts on the part of third persons. In such matters as the domestic supply of water or gas it is essential that the mode of supply should be such as to permit ready access for the purpose of use, and hence it is impossible to guard against wilful mischief. Taps may be turned on, ball-cocks fastened open, supply pipes cut, and waste-pipes blocked. Against such acts no precaution can prevail. It would be wholly unreasonable to hold an occupier responsible for the consequences of such acts which he is powerless to prevent, when the provision of the supply is not only a reasonable act on his part but probably a duty. Such a doctrine would, for example, make a householder liable for the consequences of an explosion caused by a burglar breaking into his house during the night and leaving a gas tap open. There is, in their Lordships' opinion, no support either in reason or authority for any such view of the liability of a landlord or occupier. In having on his premises such means of supply he is only using those premises in an ordinary and proper manner, and, although he is bound to exercise all reasonable care, he is not responsible for damage not due to his own default, whether the damage be caused by inevitable accident or the wrongful acts of third persons. . . .

The appeal must therefore be allowed and judgment entered for the defendant. . . .

Question

Does this decision mean that the occupier is not liable for unforeseeable escapes?

Note:

This decision confutes the view of the court in *Humphries v Cousins* (1877) 2 C.P.D. 239 that "the prima facie right of every occupier of a piece of land is to enjoy that land free from all invasion of filth or other matter coming from any artificial structure on land adjoining [and that the liability of defendants] is independent of what they may know or not know of the state of their own property, and independent of the care or want of care which they may take of it." A century later the Court of Appeal had to reverse a trial judge who held the occupier of an upper floor liable for the escape from a blocked drain of a large quantity of sewage which fouled the stock of the plaintiff below: *WH Smith v Daw*, March 31, 1987, CA.

Flooding from upstairs is quite a common occurrence, but the courts are reluctant to impose liability for escapes due to the act of a stranger even where the occupier has arguably been careless in not preventing access: see *King v Liverpool Corp.* [1986] 3 All E.R. 544 (no duty); and negligence is not presumed, at any rate for a first escape (*Hawkins v Dhawan* (1987) 19 H.L.R. 232, CA.) Where water escapes from a pipe vested in a water authority, however, the authority is strictly liable for all consequent damage: Water Industry Act 1991, s.209.

READ v J LYONS & Co

House of Lords [1947] A.C. 156; [1947] L.J.R. 39; 175 L.T. 413; 62 T.L.R. 646; [1946] 2 All E.R. 471

Action by visitor against occupier in respect of personal injury

By agreement with the Minister of Supply the defendants undertook the management and control of the Elstow Ordnance Factory where they made high-explosive shells for the government. The plaintiff was directed to work as an inspector in the factory, and when she was lawfully in the shell-filling shop on August 31, 1942, there was an explosion which killed one person and injured several others, including the plaintiff.

She did not plead or try to prove that the defendants were negligent, but averred merely that she was lawfully present in the place where the defendants were manufacturing high-explosive shells which they knew to be dangerous things and that she suffered damage when one of them exploded.

The plaintiff succeeded before Cassels J. The defendants' appeal to the Court of Appeal was allowed [1945] 1 K.B. 216. The plaintiff's appeal to the House of Lords was dismissed.

Viscount Simon: My Lords, the simple question for decision is whether in these circumstances the respondents are liable, without any proof or inference that they were negligent, to the appellant in damages, which have been assessed at £575 2s. 8d. for her injuries. Cassels J. who tried the case, considered that it was governed by *Rylands v Fletcher* and held that the respondents were liable, on the ground that they were carrying on an ultra-hazardous activity and so were under what is called a "strict liability" to take successful care to avoid causing harm to persons whether on or off the premises. The Court of Appeal (Scott, MacKinnon, and du Parcq L.JJ.) reversed this decision, Scott L.J. in an elaborately reasoned judgment holding that a person on the premises had, in the absence of any proof of negligence, no cause of action, and that there must be an escape of the damage-causing thing from the premises and damage caused outside before the doctrine customarily associated with the case of *Rylands v Fletcher* can apply. I agree that the action fails.

Now, the strict liability recognised by this House to exist in *Rylands v Fletcher* is conditioned by two elements which I may call the condition of "escape" from the land of something likely to do mischief if it escapes, and the condition of "non-natural use" of the land. . . . It is not necessary to analyse this second condition on the present occasion, for in the case now before us the first essential condition of "escape" does not seem to me to be present at all. "Escape," for the purpose of applying the proposition of *Rylands v Fletcher*, means escape from a place where the defendant has occupation of or control over land to a place which is outside his occupation or control. Blackburn J. several times refers to the defendant's duty as being the duty of "keeping a thing in" at the defendant's peril, and by "keeping in" he does not mean preventing an explosive substance from exploding but preventing a thing which may inflict mischief from escaping from the area which the defendant occupies or controls.

. . . I hold that the appellant fails for the reason that there was no "escape" from the respondents' factory. I move that the appeal be dismissed with costs.

Lord Macmillan: My Lords, nothing could be simpler than the facts in this appeal; nothing more far-reaching than the discussion of fundamental legal principles to which it has given rise. . . .

. . . The doctrine of *Rylands v Fletcher*, as I understand it, derives from a conception of mutual duties of adjoining or neighbouring landowners and its congeners are trespass and nuisance. If its foundation is to be found in the injunction *sic utere tuo ut alienum non laedas*, then it is manifest that it has nothing to do with personal injuries. The duty is to refrain from injuring not *alium* but *alienum*. The two prerequisites of the doctrine are that there must be the escape of something from one man's close to another man's close and that that which escapes must have been brought upon the land from which it escapes in consequence of some non-natural use of that land, whatever precisely that may mean. Neither of these features exists in the present case. . . .

Your Lordships' task in this House is to decide particular cases between litigants and your Lordships are not called upon to rationalise the law of England. That attractive if perilous field may well be left to other hands to cultivate. It has been necessary in the present instance to examine certain general principles advanced on behalf of the appellant because it was said that consistency required that these principles should be applied to the case in hand. Arguments based on legal consistency are apt to mislead for the common law is a practical code adapted to deal with the manifold diversities of human life, and as a great American judge has reminded us, "the life of the law has not been logic; it has been experience." For myself, I am content to say that in my opinion no authority has been quoted from case or textbook which would justify your Lordships, logically or otherwise, in giving effect to the appellant's plea. I would accordingly dismiss the appeal.

Lord Simonds: . . . I turn then to the first question which raises the familiar problem of strict liability, a phrase which I use to express liability without proof of negligence. Here is an age-long conflict of theories which is to be found in every system of law. "A man acts at his peril," says one theory. "A man is not liable unless he is to blame," answers the other. It will not surprise the students of English law or of anything English to find that between these theories a middle way, a compromise, has been found. For it is beyond question that in respect of certain acts a man will be liable for the harmful consequences of those acts, be he never so careful, yet in respect of other acts he will not be liable unless he has in some way fallen short of a prescribed standard of conduct. It avails not at all to argue that because in some respects a man acts at his peril, therefore in all respects he does so. There is not one principle only which is to be applied with rigid logic to all cases. To this result both the infinite complexity of human affairs and the historical development of the forms of action contribute. . . . Yet I would venture to say that the law is that, subject to certain specific exceptions which I will indicate, a man is not in the absence of negligence liable in respect of things, whether they are called dangerous or not, which he has brought or collected or manufactured upon his premises, unless such things escape from his premises and, so escaping, injure another, and I would leave it open whether, even in the event of such escape, he is liable (still in the absence of negligence) for personal injury as distinguished from injury to some proprietary interest.

My Lords, in this branch of the law it is inevitable that reference should be made to what Blackburn J. said in *Fletcher v Rylands* and what Lord Cairns L.C. said in *Rylands v Fletcher*. In doing so I think it is of great importance to remember that the subject-matter of that action was the rights of adjoining landowners and, though the doctrine of strict liability there enforced was illustrated by reference to the responsibility of the man who keeps beasts, yet the defendant was held liable only because he allowed, or did not prevent, the escape from his land on to the land of the plaintiff of something which he had brought on to his own land, and which he knew or should have known was liable to do mischief if it escaped from it. . . .

This is in harmony with the development of a strictly analogous branch of the law, the law of nuisance, in which also negligence is not a necessary ingredient in the case. For if a man commits a legal nuisance it is no answer to his injured neighbour that he took the utmost care not to commit it. There the liability is strict, and there he alone has a lawful claim who has suffered an invasion of some proprietary or other interest in land. To confine the rule in *Rylands v Fletcher* to cases in which there has been an escape from the defendants' land appears to me consistent and logical. For the present purpose it is sufficient to say negatively that the appellant being on the respondents' premises cannot hold them liable for the damage suffered by her unless she alleges and proves negligence by them in their manufacture of explosives. . . .

Lord Uthwatt: My Lords, the appellant does not allege either negligence or lack of skill on the part of the respondents. Her case is that by reason of the dangerous nature of the business which involved the risk of explosion they owed to her a duty to safeguard her from any harm resulting from its dangerous character. . . .

Is there any good reason consistent with respect for the rights of dominion and user incident to the occupation of land, and with an appreciation of the position of an invitee, for subjecting the occupier carrying on a dangerous but lawful business to an absolute duty to safeguard the invitee from harm? I can see none. In carrying on such a business the occupier may be doing something which is not common, but he is not doing anything which is out of the ordinary course of affairs or which is concealed from the invitee. He is in no way abusing his right to use his land. To subject him to an absolute duty to an invitee would be to my mind to impose an unreasonable limitation on the due exercise of that right. But the relation between the parties is the governing consideration and it is the incidents which the law attaches to that relation that are in question. I do not think that the invitee, any more than the occupier, would assume that, by reason only of the dangerous nature of the business carried on, the occupier guaranteed him freedom from harm. If that be so it is against reason that the law, whose function it is to give effect to reasonable expectations, should impose such a guarantee. A measure of care determined by the degree of danger is in my opinion the utmost that either party would envisage and, in my opinion, the law demands that and no other standard of duty. This denial of absolute liability to an invitee is indeed not inconsistent with the assertion—I do not make it—of an absolute duty towards persons who suffer harm outside the occupier's premises. Matters happening within one's own bounds are one thing and matters happening outside those bounds are an entirely different thing. In the latter case the personal relation is absent and the occupier's dominion over and right to use his land have to be reconciled with the rights of others to use or be present on adjoining lands not subject to his dominion. Unless compelled by authority to come to a contrary conclusion I would, therefore, reject the appellant's contention.

There is no authority which directly supports that contention. The appellant, to some extent, relied on the animal cases, but they are of no real help. Her sheet anchor was *Rylands v Fletcher.* That case on the facts related only to the duty which an occupier of land—nuisance and negligence not being involved and trespass treated as not being involved—owed to an occupier of other land in respect of an intrusion from the land of the one to the land of the other. The accommodation between occupiers of land there laid down was that things liable to escape must be kept by an occupier within his bounds unless their presence within those bounds was due to a natural use of his land. The liability and the excuse both relate to the use of land as affecting other land. I do not regard *Rylands v Fletcher* as laying down any principle other than a principle applicable between occupiers in respect of their land or as reflecting an aspect of some wider principle applicable to dangerous businesses or dangerous things.

Note:

As Scott L.J. said at the outset of his excellent judgment in the Court of Appeal, "This case is elemental. It goes to the roots of the common law." Its result he paraphrased by saying " . . . our law of torts is concerned not with activities but with acts." The case decided conclusively that a person injured on the land of another must prove negligence in that other, failing the intervention of the legislature or the attack of a wild beast. But in effect it did more than that. If *Donoghue v Stevenson* laid down that negligence is normally sufficient for liability, this case asserts that it is normally necessary. And what could be more important than that?

Question:

A tenant's premises are flooded with water which (a) comes on to the premises because the landlord's gutter is blocked, and (b) stays on the premises because the landlord's drain is blocked. The tenant can recover for (a) but not for (b) (*Duke of Westminster v Guild* 1984 3 All E.R. 144, 152). Is this rational?

CAMBRIDGE WATER Co v EASTERN COUNTIES LEATHER PLC

House of Lords [1994] 2 A.C. 264; [1994] 2 W.L.R. 53; [1994] 1 All E.R. 53; [1994] 1 Lloyd's Rep. 335 (noted (1995) 111 L.Q.R. 445; [1994] Camb.L.J. 216)

Claim by owner of water-well against polluter of ground-water

The defendants produced high-class leather goods in an old-established and well-managed business situated in a village near Cambridge where light industry had been going on for centuries. In order to degrease the raw skins they used quite large quantities of chemicals, analogous to domestic stain removers, familiarly called "perk" and "trike". Until 1976 these chemicals were delivered in barrels which were emptied into the cleaning machines and then dumped in a field awaiting collection. A certain quantity of the chemicals naturally got spilt on the factory floor and leaked into the field. Unsuspected by anyone, the seeping chemical formed immiscible pools many metres underground and slowly drifted in the aquifer.

In 1979 the plaintiffs bought a water well over a mile away, having tested it for purity, and supplied the water from it to Cambridge residents. Although there was not the slightest risk to health, Brussels issued a Directive requiring it to be forbidden for water to be sold for domestic use if it contained more than the slightest trace of chemicals such as perk and trike. The plaintiffs then discovered that the water in their well contained a great deal more than the permitted trace, and eventually proved that much of it came from the defendant's land. They claimed the cost of relocating the well, over a million pounds.

Ian Kennedy J. dismissed the claim, holding that there was no liability in negligence, since no one could have known that letting the chemical seep away could cause any harm, no liability in nuisance since the harm was unforeseeable, and no liability under *Rylands v Fletcher*, since the defendant's use of its land was not "non-natural".

The plaintiffs appealed solely on the basis of *Rylands v Fletcher*, but the Court of Appeal ignored this and gave judgment for the plaintiff on the basis of a nuisance case variously reported from 1885, holding in terms that "The actor acts at his peril . . . The owner's right is to have . . . water come to him in an uncontaminated condition." The House of Lords unanimously allowed the defendant's appeal, holding that unforeseeable damage was not compensable under *Rylands v Fletcher*, but that if the damage had been foreseeable the defendants would have been liable, even if not negligent, since their use was indeed "non-natural".

Lord Goff of Chieveley: . . . It is necessary to consider the question whether foreseeability of harm of the relevant type is an essential element of liability either in nuisance or under the rule in *Rylands v Fletcher*. I shall take first the case of nuisance. . . .

It is, of course, axiomatic that in this field we must be on our guard, when considering liability for damages in nuisance, not to draw inapposite conclusions from cases concerned only with a claim for an injunction. This is because, where an injunction is claimed, its purpose is to restrain further action by the defendant which may interfere with the plaintiff's enjoyment of his land, and ex hypothesi the defendant must be aware, if and when an injunction is granted, that such interference may be caused by the act which he is restrained from committing. It follows that these cases provide no guidance on the question whether foreseeability of harm of the relevant type is a prerequisite of the recovery of damages for causing such harm to the plaintiff. In the present case, we are not concerned with liability in damages in respect of a nuisance which has arisen through natural causes, or by the act of a person for whose actions the defendant is not responsible, in which cases the applicable principles in nuisance have become closely associated with those applicable in negligence: see *Sedleigh-Denfield v O'Callaghan* [1940] 3 All E.R. 349 and *Goldman v Hargrave* [1966] 2 All E.R. 989. We are concerned with the liability of a person where a nuisance has been created by one for whose actions he is responsible. Here, as I have said, it is still the law that the fact that the defendant has taken all reasonable care will not of itself exonerate him from liability, the relevant control mechanism being found within the principle of reasonable user. But it by no means follows that the defendant should be held liable for damage of a type which he could not reasonably foresee; and the development of the law of negligence in the past sixty years points strongly towards a requirement that such foreseeability should be a prerequisite of liability in damages for nuisince, as it is of liability in negligence. For if a plaintiff is in ordinary circumstances only able to claim damages in respect of personal injuries where he can prove such foreseeability on the part of the defendant, it is difficult to see why, in common justice, he should be in a stronger position to claim damages for interference with the enjoyment of his land where the defendant was unable to foresee such damage. Moreover, this appears to have been the conclusion of the Privy Council in *The Wagon Mound (No.2)* [1966] 2 All E.R. 709. The facts of the case are too well known to require repetition, but they gave rise to a claim for damages arising from a public nuisance caused by a spillage of oil in Sydney Harbour. Lord Reid, who delivered the advice of the Privy Council, considered that, in the class of nuisance which included the case before the Board, foreseeability is an essential element in determining liability. . . .

It is widely accepted that this conclusion has settled the law to the effect that foreseeability of harm is indeed a prerequisite of the recovery of damages in private nuisance, as in the case of public nuisance.

Having regard to the step which this House has already taken in *Read v Lyons* to contain the scope of liability under the rule in *Rylands v Fletcher*, it appears to me to be appropriate now to take the view that foreseeability of damage of the relevant type should be regarded as a prerequisite of liability in damages under the rule. It would moreover lead to a more coherent body of common law principles if the rule were to be regarded essentially as an extension of the law of nuisance to cases of isolated escapes from land, even though the rule as established is not limited to escapes which are in fact isolated. I wish to point out, however, that in truth the escape of the water has not been an isolated escape, but a continuing escape resulting from a state of affairs which has come into existence at the base of the chalk aquifer underneath ECL's premises. Classically, this would have been regarded as a case of nuisance; and it would seem strange if, by characterising the case as one falling under the rule in *Rylands v Fletcher*, the liability should thereby be rendered more strict in the circumstances of the present case.

Turning to the facts of the present case, it is plain that, at the time when the PCE was brought onto ECL's land, and indeed when it was used in the tanning process there, nobody at ECL could reasonably have foreseen the resultant damage which occurred at CWC's borehole at Sawston.

In the result, since those responsible at ECL could not at the relevant time reasonably have foreseen that the damage in question might occur, the claim of CWC for damages under the rule in *Rylands v Fletcher* must fail.

I turn to the question whether the use by ECL of its land in the present case constituted a natural use, with the result that ECL cannot be held liable under the rule in *Rylands v Fletcher*. In view of my conclusion on the issue of can deal with this point shortly. . . .

Fortunately, I do not think it is necessary for the purposes of the present case to attempt any redefinition of the concept of natural or ordinary use. This is because I am satisfied that the storage of chemicals in substantial quantities, and their use in the manner employed at ECL's premises, cannot fall within the exception. For the purpose of testing the point, let it be assumed that ECL was well aware of the possibility that PCE, if it escaped, could indeed cause damage, for example by contaminating any water with which it became mixed so as to render that water undrinkable by human beings. I cannot think that it would be right in such circumstances to exempt ECL from liability under the rule in *Rylands v Fletcher* on the ground that the use was natural or ordinary. The mere fact that the use is common in the tanning industry cannot, in my opinion, be enough to bring the use within the exception, nor the fact that Sawston contains a small industrial community which is worthy of encouragement or support. Indeed I feel bound to say that the storage of substantial quantities of chemicals on industrial premises should be regarded as an almost classic case of non-natural use; and I find it very difficult to think that it should be thought objectionable to impose strict liability for damage caused in the event of their escape. It may well be that, now that it is recognised that foreseeability of harm of the relevant type is a prerequisite of liability in damages under the rule, the courts may feel less pressure to extend the concept of natural use to circumstances such as those in the present case; and in due course it may become easier to control this exception, and to ensure that it has a more recognisable basis of principle. For these reasons, I would not hold that ECL should be exempt from liability on the basis of the exception of natural use.

However, for the reasons I have already given, I would allow ECL's appeal with costs before your Lordships' House and in the courts below.

Notes:

When the House of Lords reversed the decision of the Court of Appeal industrialists, if not environmental-ists, must have breathed a sigh of relief. But the relief may be short-lived, because the second part of Lord Goff's judgment, which severely restricts substantive defences to liability, will prove much more significant in practice than the first part, which goes only to remoteness. After all, *The Wagon Mound* itself, which also substituted a test of foreseeability for the test of directness, has not had much effect. It is a safe prediction that persons whose property is damaged by the emission of industrial matter from neighbouring premises will now recover damages regardless of whether the defendant firm was careless or not as regards the escape. The unforeseeable (and if foreseeable, unpreventable) act of a stranger may remain a defence, under the first part of *Rickards v Lothian*, but the second part will be restricted to escapes from domestic premises.

The perk and trike were wasted, no doubt, but they were not "waste". "Waste products" may be products but waste itself is not, and liability for waste is different from liability for products, though Brussels is interested in both. See Environmental Protection Act 1990, s.73(6). A European Directive on civil liability for causing or failing to prevent environmental damage may soon be expected.

TRANSCO PLC v STOCKPORT METROPOLITAN BOROUGH COUNCIL

House of Lords [2003] UKHL 61; [2003] 3 W.L.R. 1467, [2004] 1 All E.R. 589

Is Rylands v Fletcher still good law?

Without any fault on the part of the defendant council, which owned a housing estate including a tower block containing 66 apartments, a great deal of water escaped through a crack in the very large pipe which fed the tanks in the basement of the tower and eventually ran downhill and washed away the embankment along which a railway line had run and in which the claimant had laid a high pressure gas main. The gas main was thus vulnerably exposed and as a matter of urgency the claimant took remedial measures for which it now claims reimbursement.

Lord Bingham of Cornhill: In this appeal the House is called upon to review the scope and application, in modern conditions, of the rule of law laid down by the Court of Exchequer Chamber, affirmed by the House of Lords, in *Rylands v Fletcher* (1866) L.R. 1 Exch 265; (1868) LR 3 HL 330. . . . Few cases in the law of tort or perhaps any other field are more familiar, or have attracted more academic and judicial discussion, than *Rylands v Fletcher*.

In the course of his excellent argument for the council, Mr Mark Turner Q.C. canvassed various ways in which the rule in *Rylands v Fletcher* might be applied and developed in future, without however judging it necessary to press the House to accept any one of them. The boldest of these courses was to follow the trail blazed by a majority of the High Court of Australia in *Burnie Port Authority v General Jones Property Ltd* (1994) 120 A.L.R. 42 by treating the rule in *Rylands v Fletcher* as absorbed by the principles of ordinary negligence. In reaching this decision the majority were influenced by the difficulties of interpretation and application to which the rule has undoubtedly given rise (pp.52–55), by the progressive weakening of the rule by judicial decision (pp.54–55), by recognition that the law of negligence has been very greatly developed and expanded since *Rylands v Fletcher* was decided (pp.55–65) and by a belief that most claimants entitled to succeed under the rule would succeed in a claim for negligence anyway (pp. 65–67).

Coming from such a quarter these comments of course command respect, and they are matched by expressions of opinion here. There is a theoretical attraction in bringing this somewhat anomalous ground of liability within the broad and familiar rules governing liability in negligence. This would have the incidental advantage of bringing the law of England and Wales more closely into line with what I understand to be the law of Scotland. Consideration of the reported English case law over the past 60 years suggests that few if any claimants have succeeded in reliance on the rule in *Rylands v Fletcher* alone.

I would be willing to suppress an instinctive resistance to treating a nuisance-based tort as if it were governed by the law of negligence if I were persuaded that it would serve the interests of justice to discard the rule in *Rylands v Fletcher* and treat the cases in which it might have been relied on as governed by the ordinary rules of negligence. But I hesitate to adopt that solution for four main reasons. First, there is in my opinion a category of case, however small it may be, in which it seems just to impose liability even in the absence of fault. In the context of then recent catastrophes *Rylands v Fletcher* itself was understandably seen as such a case. With memories of the tragedy at Aberfan still green, the same view might now be taken of *Attorney General v Cory Brothers and Co Ltd* [1921] 1 A.C. 521 even if the claimants had failed to prove negligence, as on the facts they were able to do. I would regard *Rainham Chemical Works Ltd v Belvedere Fish Guano Co Ltd* [1921] 2 A.C. 465, and *Cambridge Water Co v Eastern Counties Leather plc* [1994] 2 A.C. 264 (had there been foreseeability of damage), as similarly falling within that category. Second, it must be remembered that common law rules do not exist in a vacuum, least of all rules which have stood for over a century during which there has been detailed statutory regulation of matters to which they might potentially relate. With reference to water, s.209 of the Water Industry Act 1991 imposes strict liability (subject to certain exemptions) on water undertakers and Sch.2 to the Reservoirs Act 1975 appears to assume that on facts such as those of *Rylands v Fletcher* strict liability would attach. Third, although in *Cambridge Water* [1994] 2 A.C. 264, 283–285, the possibility was ventilated that the House might depart from *Rylands v Fletcher* in its entirety, it is plain that this suggestion was not accepted. Instead, the House looked forward to a more principled and better controlled application of the existing rule. Fourth, while replacement of strict *Rylands v Fletcher* liability by a fault-based rule would tend to assimilate the law of England and Wales with that of Scotland, it would tend to increase the disparity between it and the laws of France and Germany. Having reviewed comparable provisions of French and German law, van Gerven, Lever and Larouche (*Cases, Materials and Text on National, Supranational and International Tort Law (2000)*, p.205) observe: "Even if the contours of the respective regimes may differ, all systems studied here therefore afford a form of strict liability protection in disputes between neighbouring landowners." The authors indeed suggest (p.205) that the English rule as laid down in *Rylands v Fletcher* is "the most developed of these regimes".

There remains a third option, which I would myself favour: to retain the rule, while insisting upon its essential nature and purpose; and to restate it so as to achieve as much certainty and clarity as is attainable, recognising that new factual situations are bound to arise posing difficult questions on the boundary of the rule, wherever that is drawn.

The rule in *Rylands v Fletcher* is a sub-species of nuisance, which is itself a tort based on the interference by one occupier of land with the right in or enjoyment of land by another occupier of land as such. From this simple proposition two consequences at once flow. First, as very clearly decided by the House in *Read v J Lyons & Co Ltd* [1947] A.C. 156, no claim in nuisance or under the rule can arise if the events complained of take place wholly on the land of a single occupier. There must, in other words, be an escape from one tenement to another. Second, the claim cannot include a claim for death or personal injury, since such a claim does not relate to any right in or enjoyment of land.

It has from the beginning been a necessary condition of liability under the rule in *Rylands v Fletcher* that the thing which the defendant has brought on his land should be "something which . . . will naturally do mischief if it escape out of his land" ((1865) L.R. 1 Exch 265, 279 *per* Blackburn J). . . . The practical problem is of course to decide whether in any given case the thing which has escaped satisfies this mischief or danger test, a problem exacerbated by the fact that many things not ordinarily regarded as sources of mischief or danger may nonetheless be capable of proving to be such if they escape. I do not think this condition can be viewed in complete isolation from the non-natural user condition to which I shall shortly turn, but I think the cases decided by the House give a valuable pointer. In *Rylands v Fletcher* itself the courts were dealing with what Lord Cranworth ((1868) L.R. 3 H.L. 330, 342) called "a large accumulated mass of water" stored up in a reservoir, and I have touched on the historical context of the decision above. *Rainham Chemical Works* [1921] 2 A.C. 465, 471, involved the storage of chemicals, for the purpose of making munitions, which "exploded with terrific violence". In *Attorney General v Cory Brothers and Co Ltd* [1921] 1 A.C. 521, 525, 530, 534, 536, the landslide in question was of what counsel described as an "enormous mass of rubbish", some 500,000 tons of mineral waste tipped on a steep hillside. In *Cambridge Water* [1994] 2 A.C. 264 the industrial solvents being used by the tannery were bound to cause mischief in the event, unforeseen on the facts, that they percolated down to the water table. These cases are in sharp contrast with those arising out of escape from a domestic water supply (such as *Carstairs v Taylor* (1871) L.R. 6 Exch 217, *Ross v Fedden* (1872) 26 L.T. 966 or *Anderson v Oppenheimer* (1880) 5 Q.B.D. 602) which, although decided on other grounds, would seem to me to fail the mischief or danger test. Bearing in mind the historical origin of the rule, and also that its effect is to impose liability in the absence of negligence for an isolated occurrence, I do not think the mischief or danger test should be at all easily satisfied. It must be shown that the defendant has done something which he recognised, or judged by the standards appropriate at the relevant place and time, he ought reasonably to have recognised, as giving rise to an exceptionally high risk of danger or mischief if there should be an escape, however unlikely an escape may have been thought to be.

No ingredient of *Rylands v Fletcher* liability has provoked more discussion than the requirement of Blackburn J. ((1866) L.R. 1 Exch 265, 280) that the thing brought on to the defendant's land should be something "not naturally there", an expression elaborated by Lord Cairns ((1868) L.R. 3 H.L. 330, 339) when he referred to the putting of land to a "non-natural use". Read literally, the expressions used by Blackburn J. and Lord Cairns might be thought to exclude nothing which has reached the land otherwise than through operation of the laws of nature. But such an interpretation has been fairly described as "redolent of a different age", and in *Read v J Lyons & Co Ltd* [1947] A.C. 156, 169, 176, 187 and *Cambridge Water* at p 308 the House gave its imprimatur to Lord Moulton's statement in *Rickards v Lothian* [1913] A.C. 263, 280: "It is not every use to which land is put that brings into play that principle. It must be some special use bringing with it increased danger to others, and must not merely be the ordinary use of the land or such a use as is proper for the general benefit of the community."

I think it clear that ordinary user is a preferable test to natural user, making it clear that the rule in *Rylands v Fletcher* is engaged only where the defendant's use is shown to be extraordinary and unusual. This is not a test to be inflexibly applied: a use may be extraordinary and unusual at one time or in one place but not so at another time or in another place I also doubt whether a test of reasonable user is helpful, since a user may well be quite out of the ordinary but not unreasonable, as was that of *Rylands*, *Rainham Chemical Works* or the tannery in *Cambridge Water*. Again, as it seems to me, the question is whether the defendant has done something which he recognises, or ought to recognise, as being quite out of the ordinary in the place and at the time when he does it. An occupier of land who can show that another occupier of land has brought or kept on his land an exceptionally dangerous or mischievous thing in extraordinary or unusual circumstances is in my opinion entitled to recover compensation from that occupier for any damage caused to his property interest by the escape of that thing, subject to defences of Act of God or of a stranger, without the need to prove negligence.

By the end of the hearing before the House, the dispute between the parties had narrowed down to two questions: had the council brought on to its land at Hollow End Towers something likely to cause danger or mischief if it escaped? and was that an ordinary user of its land? Applying the principles I have tried to outline, I think it quite clear that the first question must be answered negatively and the second affirmatively, as the Court of Appeal did: [2001] EWCA Civ 212.

It is of course true that water in quantity is almost always capable of causing damage if it escapes. But the piping of a water supply from the mains to the storage tanks in the block was a routine function which would not have struck anyone as raising any special hazard. In truth, the council did not accumulate any water, it merely arranged a supply adequate to meet the residents' needs. The situation cannot stand comparison with the making by Mr Rylands of a substantial reservoir. Nor can the use by the council of its land be seen as in any way extraordinary or unusual. It was entirely normal and routine. I am satisfied that the conditions to be met before strict liability could be imposed on the council were far from being met on the facts here.

Lord Hoffmann: Liability in nuisance is strict in the sense that one has no right to carry on an activity which unreasonably interferes with a neighbour's use of land merely because one is doing it with all reasonable care. If it cannot be done without causing an unreasonable interference, it cannot be done at all. But liability to pay damages is limited to damage which was reasonably foreseeable.

It is tempting to see, beneath the surface of the rule, a policy of requiring the costs of a commercial enterprise to be internalised; to require the entrepreneur to provide, by insurance or otherwise, for the risks to others which his enterprise creates. That was certainly the opinion of Bramwell B, who was in favour of liability when the case was before the Court of Exchequer: (1865) 3 H. & C. 774. He had a clear and consistent view on the matter: see *Bamford v Turnley* [above, p.423]. But others thought differently. They considered that the public interest in promoting economic development made it unreasonable to hold an entrepreneur liable when he had not been negligent. On the whole, it was the latter view—no liability without fault—which gained the ascendancy. With hindsight, *Rylands v Fletcher* can be seen as an isolated victory for the internalisers. The following century saw a steady refusal to treat it as laying down any broad principle of liability.

To summarise the very limited circumstances to which the rule has been confined: First, it is a remedy for damage to land or interests in land. As there can be few properties in the country, commercial or domestic, which are not insured against damage by flood and the like, this means that disputes over the application of the rule will tend to be between property insurers and liability insurers. Secondly, it does not apply to works or enterprises authorised by statute. That means that it will usually have no application to really high risk activities. As Professor Simpson points out ([1984] 13 J Leg Stud 225) the Bradfield Reservoir was built under statutory powers. In the absence of negligence, the occupiers whose lands had been inundated would have had no remedy. Thirdly, it is not particularly strict because it excludes liability when the escape is for the most common reasons, namely vandalism or unusual natural events. Fourthly, the cases in which there is an escape which is not attributable to an unusual natural event or the act of a third party will, by the same token, usually give rise to an inference of negligence. Fifthly, there is a broad and ill-defined exception for "natural" uses of land. It is perhaps not surprising that counsel could not find a reported case since the Second World War in which anyone had succeeded in a claim under the rule. It is hard to escape the conclusion that the intellectual effort devoted to the rule by judges and writers over many years has brought forth a mouse.

In *Burnie Port Authority v General Jones Pty Ltd* (1994) 179 C.L.R. 520 a majority of the High Court of Australia lost patience with the pretensions and uncertainties of the rule and decided that it had been "absorbed" into the law of negligence. Your Lordships have been invited by the respondents to kill off the rule in England in similar fashion. It is said, first, that in its present attenuated form it serves little practical purpose; secondly, that its application is unacceptably vague ("an essentially unprincipled and ad hoc subjective determination" said the High Court (at p.540) in the *Burnie* case) and thirdly, that strict liability on social grounds is better left to statutory intervention.

There is considerable force in each of these points. It is hard to find any rational principle which explains the rule and its exceptions. In *Read v J Lyons & Co Ltd* [1947] A.C. 156, 175 Lord Macmillan said with Scottish detachment "your Lordships are not called upon to rationalise the law of England" but in *RHM Bakeries (Scotland) Ltd v Strathclyde Regional Council* 1985 S.C. (HL) 17, 41 Lord Fraser of Tullybelton described the suggestion that the rule formed part of the law of Scotland as "a heresy which ought to be extirpated". And the proposition that strict liability is best left to statute receives support from the speech of Lord Goff of Chieveley in the *Cambridge Water* case [1994] 2 A.C. 264, 305: "Like the judge in the present case, I incline to the opinion that, as a general rule, it is more appropriate for strict liability in respect of operations of high risk to be imposed by Parliament than by the courts. If such liability is imposed by statute, the relevant activities can be identified and those concerned can know where they stand. Furthermore, statute can where appropriate lay down precise criteria establishing the incidence and scope of such liability."

An example of statutory strict liability close to home is s.209 of the Water Industry Act 1991: "(1) Where an escape of water, however caused, from a pipe vested in a water undertaker causes loss or damage, the undertaker shall be liable, except as otherwise provided in this section, for the loss or damage . . . (3) A water undertaker shall not incur any liability under subs.(1) above in respect of any loss or damage for which the undertaker would not be liable apart from that subsection and which is sustained . . . (b) by any public gas supplier within the meaning of Pt.I of the Gas Act 1986 . . . "

This provision is designed to avoid all argument over which insurers should bear the loss. Liability is far stricter than under the rule in *Rylands v Fletcher*. There is no exception for acts of third parties or natural events. The undertaker is liable for an escape "however caused" and must insure accordingly. On the other hand, certain potential claimants like public gas suppliers (now called public gas transporters) must insure themselves. The irony of the present case is that if the leak had been from a high pressure water main, belonging to the North West Water Authority, a much more plausible high-risk activity, there could have been no dispute. Section 209(3)(b) would have excluded a statutory claim and the authority's statutory powers would have excluded the rule in *Rylands v Fletcher*.

But despite the strength of these arguments, I do not think it would be consistent with the judicial function of your Lordships' House to abolish the rule. It has been part of English law for nearly 150 years and despite a searching examination by Lord Goff of Chieveley in the *Cambridge Water* case [1994] 2 A.C. 264, 308, there was no suggestion in his speech that it could or should be abolished. I think that would be too radical a step to take.

It remains, however, if not to rationalise the law of England, at least to introduce greater certainty into the concept of natural user which is in issue in this case.

In my opinion the Court of Appeal was right to say that it was not a "non-natural" user of land. I am influenced by two matters. First, there is no evidence that it created a greater risk than is normally associated with domestic or commercial plumbing. True, the pipe was larger. But whether that involved greater risk depends upon its specification. One cannot simply assume that the larger the pipe, the greater the risk of fracture or the greater the quantity of water likely to be discharged. I agree with my noble and learned friend Lord Bingham of Cornhill that the criterion of exceptional risk must be taken seriously and creates a high threshold for a claimant to surmount. Secondly, I think that the risk of damage to property caused by leaking water is one against which most people can and do commonly insure. This is, as I have said, particularly true of Transco, which can be expected to have insured against any form of damage to its pipe. It would be a very strange result if Transco were entitled to recover against the council when it would not have been entitled to recover against the Water Authority for similar damage emanating from its high pressure main.

Lord Scott of Foscote: In or around 1966 North West Gas Board laid a 16 inch high pressure gas main in and along a railway embankment then owned by the British Railways Board. The gas main was laid pursuant to a Deed of Grant dated 3 November 1966. Transco plc, the appellant before the House, is the successor of North West Gas Board. So the gas main is Transco's gas main. The railway embankment belongs now to the respondent, the Stockport Metropolitan Borough Council. It is accepted that, as between the two parties, Transco and its predecessors are, and have been at all times material to this litigation, entitled to maintain their gas pipe in the council's embankment and to the support of the gas pipe by the earth beneath it.

The council is the owner also of an 11 storey block of 66 flats, Hollow End Towers, not far from the embankment. The block of flats had already been built at the time when Transco's gas pipe was laid in the embankment. The water supply to the block of flats is carried from the water authority's mains via a 3 inch internal diameter asbestos cement pipe. This supply pipe is the council's pipe. Its maintenance is, therefore, the council's responsibility. It is not contended that the supply pipe was in any way unusual in its dimensions for the supply of water to an 11 storey block of 66 flats.

The land lying between the block of flats and the embankment, too, is owned by the council. The area had been used by the council in the 1950s for landfilling and has since been grassed over.

... whatever else may be said of the rule in *Rylands v Fletcher* the rule does not come into play unless there has been an escape from the defendant's land of whatever it is that has caused the damage. That essential element of escape is absent in the present case. The water flowing from the fractured pipe accumulated in a part of the old landfill site and then made its way to the embankment. It began its "escape" on the council's property, accumulated on the council's property and eventually damaged the embankment, also the council's property. It is in respect of the damage to the embankment that Transco seeks damages.

The "escape" issue was specifically addressed by the trial judge. I would readily accept that if, in a case to which the rule in *Rylands v Fletcher* applies, the damage done by the escaped substance is damage to servient land over which there is an easement and the damage interferes with the enjoyment of the easement, the proprietor of the easement is as well entitled to claim the cost of repairing the servient land as is the owner of the land. But if the easement is an easement over the defendant's own land, the land onto which the defendant has brought the substance which has caused the damage, a *Rylands v Fletcher* claim is, in my opinion, barred by *Read v Lyons*. If the *Read v Lyons* plaintiff had left her car parked in the factory car park and the car had been damaged by the explosion, the reasoning of their Lordships would have barred her recovery for that damage. There would have been no "escape". Nor would the case have been any different if the parked car had belonged to someone else, a neighbour who had had an easement to park it on the factory car park. Proof of negligence would have been necessary for recovery.

In my opinion, therefore, Transco's *Rylands v Fletcher* case fails by reason of its failure to satisfy the "escape" condition of liability that was re-confirmed by this House in *Read v Lyons*.

Lord Hobhouse delivered a concurring speech, as did **Lord Walker of Gestingthorpe**, who agreed with the reasons given by **Lord Bingham** and **Lord Hoffmann**. **Lord Scott** also agreed with the reasons given by **Lord Bingham, Lord Hoffmann** and **Lord Walker**.

Preliminary Note:

"Liability for the damage caused by the spread of fire has traditionally been a separate form of liability outside the traditional causes of action in negligence, nuisance or under *Rylands v Fletcher*" (*Johnson v BJW Property* [2002] 3 All E.R. 575, 585, *per* Judge Thornton Q.C.).

One of the distinctions between liability for fire and liability under *Rylands v Fletcher* is that liability for fire extends to personal injury, as in *Ribee v Norrie* [2000] EWCA Civ 275 (fire negligently started in communal room by lodger).

MASON v LEVY AUTO PARTS OF ENGLAND LTD

Assizes [1967] 2 Q.B. 530; [1967] 2 W.L.R. 1384; 111 S.J. 234; [1967] 2 All E.R. 62; [1967] 1 Lloyd's Rep. 372 (noted (1967) 83 L.Q.R. 324)

The defendants kept in their yard large stacks of wooden cases containing greased or wrapped machinery, as well as quantities of petroleum, acetylene and paint. At noon one fine day a fire broke out for an unknown reason, and could not be controlled before it had done damage to the plaintiff's adjoining garden.

MacKenna J.: ... I come now to the law, beginning with s.86 of the Fires Prevention (Metropolis) Act 1774, whose obscure provisions were foreseeably invoked by the defendants.

The section provides that: " . . . no action, suit, or process whatever shall be had, or prosecuted, against any person in whose house, chamber, stable, barn, or other building, or on whose estate any fire shall . . . accidentally begin, nor shall any recompense be made by such person for any damage suffered thereby; any law, usage, or custom to the contrary notwithstanding. . . . "

. . .

If under the statute the householder may no longer be presumed to have caused the fire, must he be presumed, even rebuttably, to have caused it negligently? I would have said not.

One case only is in the plaintiff's favour, decided by Judge Malcolm Wright QC, in the county court, namely, *Hyman (Sales) Ltd v Benedyke & Co Ltd* ([1957] 2 Lloyd's Rep. 601). But that case is, I think, to be explained as a decision on a bailee's liability to his bailor, which may perhaps be an exception to the general rule prescribed by the Fires Prevention (Metropolis) Act 1774.

In my judgment the plaintiff's first point fails. There is no burden on the defendants of disproving negligence.

Has the plaintiff proved that the defendants were negligent, which is his second point? Or has he brought the case within *Rylands v Fletcher* or any similar principle of liability, which is his third point?

In his particulars the plaintiff charges the defendants with providing no adequate means of detecting or extinguishing fire. I do not think that either of these charges was proved. The defendants were under no duty to maintain a constant lookout for fire, and this fire was in any case detected at an early stage by the defendants' workmen. The appliances recommended by the fire brigade had been provided, and if it proved impossible to control or extinguish the fire by these means that is not the fault of the defendants for failing to provide more or better equipment. Such appliances are, anyhow, intended only as first-aid. That they were ineffective to control or extinguish this fire is not proof of any culpable failure to provide more adequate equipment. Then it is said that the crates were so closely stacked "that there was no reasonable access between them for fire-fighting purposes." That was true of some parts of the yard, but I have no reason to suppose that if it had been otherwise this fire would have been controlled.

As I see it, the plaintiff's real case against the defendants is in the allegation that they "so used their land by cluttering it with combustible material closely packed that the plaintiff's land was endangered." That, like the plaintiff's other allegations, is put against the defendants in alternative ways, including negligence, nuisance, allowing a dangerous thing, namely, fire, to escape from their land, and as a failure so to use their land as not to harm the plaintiff.

I shall consider it under the two last of these heads, beginning, as one must, with *Musgrove v Pandelis* ([1919] 2 K.B. 43) [where petrol in the carburettor of the defendants' garaged car ignited when his servant started it, but no harm would have been done to the plaintiff's flat above if the servant had turned off the petrol flow from the tank as he should]. Bankes L.J. reasoned thus: (a) there were at common law three separate heads of liability for damage done by fire originating on a man's property, "(i) for the mere escape of the fire; (ii) if the fire was caused by the negligence of himself or his servants, or by his own wilful act; (iii) on the principle of *Rylands v Fletcher*." (b) *Filliter v Phippard* decided that the statute did not cover the second case. (c) "Why," Bankes L.J. asked, "if that is the law as to the second head of liability, should it be otherwise as to the third head, the liability on the principle of *Rylands v Fletcher*?" The answer, I would have said with respect, is obvious enough. There were not three heads of liability at common law but only one. A person from whose land a fire escaped was held liable to his neighbour unless he could prove that it had started or spread by the act of a stranger or of God. *Filliter*'s case had given a special meaning to the words "accidental fire" used in the statute, holding that they did not include fires due to negligence, but covered only cases of "a fire produced by mere chance, or incapable of being traced to any cause." But it does not follow, because that meaning may be given to "accidental," that the statute does not cover cases of the *Rylands v Fletcher* kind where the occupier is held liable for the escape though no fault is proved against him. In such cases the fire may be "produced by mere chance" or may be "incapable of being traced to any cause." Bankes L.J. was making a distinction unknown to the common law, between "the mere escape of fire" (which was his first head) and its escape under *Rylands v Fletcher* conditions (which was his third), and was imputing an intention to the legislature of exempting from liability in the former case and not in the latter. In holding that an exemption given to accidental fires, "any law, usage, or custom to the contrary notwithstanding," does not include fires for which liability might be imposed upon the principle of *Rylands v Fletcher*, the Court of Appeal went very far. But it is my duty to follow them unless *Musgrove*'s case has been overruled, or unless its principle does not apply to the facts proved here.

Musgrove's case has not been overruled, that is certain. . . .

What then, is the principle? As Romer L.J. in *Collingwood*'s case pointed out ([1936] 3 All E.R. 200), it cannot be exactly that of *Rylands v Fletcher*. A defendant is not held liable under *Rylands v Fletcher* unless two conditions are satisfied: (i) that he has brought something on to his land likely to do mischief if it escapes, which has in fact escaped, and (ii) that those things happened in the course of some non-natural user of the land. But in *Musgrove*'s case the car had not escaped from the land, neither had the petrol in its tank. The principle must be, Romer L.J. said, the wider one on which *Rylands v Fletcher* itself was based, "*sic utere tuo.* . . . "

If, for the rule in *Musgrove*'s case to apply, there need be no escape of anything brought on to the defendant's land, what must be proved against him? There is, it seems to me, a choice of alternatives. The first would require the plaintiff to prove (1) that the defendant had brought something on to his land likely to do mischief if it escaped; (2) that he had done so in the course of a non-natural user of the land; and (3) that the thing had ignited and that the fire had spread. The second would be to hold the defendant liable if (1) he brought on to his land things likely to catch fire, and kept them there in such conditions that if they did ignite the fire would be likely to spread to the plaintiff's land; (2) he did so in the course of some non-natural use; and (3) the things ignited and the fire spread. The second test is, I think, the more reasonable one. To make the likelihood of damage if the thing escapes a criterion of liability, when the thing has not in fact escaped but has caught fire, would not be very sensible.

So I propose to apply the second test, asking myself the two questions: (i) did the defendants in this case bring to their land things likely to catch fire, and keep them there in such conditions that if they did ignite the fire would be likely to spread to the plaintiff's land? If so, (ii) did the defendants do these things in the course of some non-natural user of the land?

I have no difficulty in answering "yes" to the first of those questions, but the second is more troublesome. I feel the difficulty which any judge must feel in deciding what is a non-natural user of the land, and have prepared myself for answering the question by reading what is said about it in *Salmond on Torts* (14th ed., 1965), pp.450–452, and in *Winfield on Torts* (7th ed., 1963), pp.449–452. Thus conditioned, I would say that the defendants' use of their land in the way described earlier in this judgment was non-natural. In saying that, I have regard (i) to the quantities of combustible material which the defendants brought on their land: (ii) to the way in which they stored them: and (iii) to the character of the neighbourhood.

It may be that those conditions would also justify a finding of negligence. If that is so, the end would be the same as I have reached by a more laborious, and perhaps more questionable, route.

Notes:

1. If a fire properly (and therefore deliberately) lit in a grate escapes without negligence there is no liability, but it was different where the grate had been reconstructed by an independent contractor who removed the existing fire-bricks and failed to replace them with adequate insulating material (*Johnson v BJW Property Developments* [2002] 3 All E.R. 574).

2. If negligence on the part of anyone lawfully on the premises causes the fire or conduces to its escape, the occupier is liable. (*Ribee v Norrie* (lodger; [2000] EWCA Civ 275); *Balfour v Barty-King* (independent contractor, [1957] 1 Q.B. 496)). Consider also *H & N Emanuel v Greater London Council* [1971] 2 All E.R. 836, which contains some worrying asides.

3. Most people who have an interest in a building keep it insured against fire. Where insurance so fully covers loss, there is less need for the law of tort to intervene: indeed, the curtailment of strict liability for the escape of fire was contemporaneous with the rise of the insurance companies in the eighteenth century, the 1774 Act having been preceded by one in 1708, when the memory of the Great Fire of London (which gave Wren the chance of building St. Paul's Cathedral) was not yet extinct. The law as now established will still be used by two classes of person, first, the householder who has underinsured (a large class of persons in times of rapidly increasing building costs) and, secondly, the insurer who has paid the householder and is exercising his rights of subrogation. It is impossible to tell which is which, because insurance companies sue in the name of the person insured.

In one case where the landlord's insurer tried to sue the tenant whose carelessness had caused the premises to be burnt, it was held that the tenant was exempted from liability by the clause in the lease whereby the landlord promised to keep the premises insured (with a contribution from the tenant) and to use the proceeds for reinstatement. (*Mark Rowlands v Berni Inns* [1985] 3 All E.R. 473, CA).

Under a fire policy the insurance company pays only the value of the property up to the policy limit; it does not pay for the loss caused to the insured by reason of his inability to use the property until it is repaired or rebuilt. To recover for such loss the owner requires a consequential loss policy or an action in tort.

PART V

ANIMALS

INTRODUCTION

ANIMALS are anomalies. They are things, not people. But, like people, these things are self-propelled; cattle-chattels *stray*—to taste the grass on the far side of the fence or to tangle with a Jaguar on the highway. And, like people, they *attack*—animals bite and scratch, butt and gore. Animals are both tiresome and dangerous. Even so, pre-industrial society can hardly make the keeper of an animal pay for all the damage it does. Animals are too useful. Alive or dead they give milk and meat, strength and warmth. Or some do. So the law, as is its function, makes distinctions.

The first distinction was between straying and attacking. As to straying, it mattered both whither and whence. If cattle strayed on to the highway, the keeper used not to be liable even if he was careless; if they strayed on to private land, the keeper was liable even if he was not careless; if they strayed there from the highway, the person who took them on to the highway was liable only if he was careless. Each rule had a separate justification, but the first has been reprobated by modern people who think the highway is for cars not cows, and their view has prevailed. As to attacking, it mattered what kind of species the animal belonged to; the tiger and the lamb may have the same Creator but they call for different rules. The keeper was not liable to a person attacked by a domesticated animal unless he knew that it was given to attacks of that kind, but a person who kept a wild beast, even a docile one, was liable for all the damage it did.

The subject has fascinated law reformers because it seems unduly complicated, but the Animals Act 1971 resulting from the study and recommendations of the Law Commission maintains most of the old distinctions and most of the old rules.

Readers of this book who have noted the extent to which the general principles of liability for negligence have subverted existing rules adapted to particular subject-matters such as family, property and governmental administration will not be surprised to learn that the general principles have also entered this area with considerable effect. (See, for example, *Bativala v West* [1970] 1 Q.B. 716 and *Draper v Hodder* [1972] 2 Q.B. 556.) This no doubt reflects the view of the Goddard Committee which said that: "There should be no special rules as to damage done by animals." (Cmd. 8746 (1953), para. 5.) Considering the distinctive qualities of animals mentioned above, it is hard to see why special rules should be avoided or, indeed, how they could be. As Lord Simonds, speaking of the compartmentalised development of the law of torts, rather charmingly said in *Read v Lyons* (above, p.458), "beasts have travelled in a compartment of their own".

Chapter 12

ANIMALS

ANIMALS ACT 1971

1.—(1) The provisions of sections 2 to 5 of this Act replace—

(a) the rules of the common law imposing a strict liability in tort for damage done by an animal on the ground that the animal is regarded as *ferae naturae* or that its vicious or mischievous propensities are known or presumed to be known;

(b) subsections (1) and (2) of section 1 of the Dogs Act 1906 as amended by the Dogs (Amendment) Act 1928 (injury to cattle or poultry); and

(c) the rules of the common law imposing a liability for cattle trespass.

(2) Expressions used in those sections shall be interpreted in accordance with the provisions of section 6 (as well as those of section 11) of this Act.

2.—(1) Where any damage is caused by an animal which belongs to a dangerous species, any person who is a keeper of the animal is liable for the damage, except as otherwise provided by this Act.

(2) Where damage is caused by an animal which does not belong to a dangerous species, a keeper of the animal is liable for the damage, except as otherwise provided by this Act, if—

(a) the damage is of a kind which the animal, unless restrained, was likely to cause or which, if caused by the animal, was likely to be severe; and

(b) the likelihood of the damage or of its being severe was due to characteristics of the animal which are not normally found in animals of the same species or are not normally so found except at particular times or in particular circumstances; and

(c) those characteristics were known to that keeper or were at any time known to a person who at that time had charge of the animal as that keeper's servant or, where that keeper is the head of a household, were known to another keeper of the animal who is a member of that household and under the age of 16.

3. Where a dog causes damage by killing or injuring livestock, any person who is a keeper of the dog is liable for the damage, except as otherwise provided by this Act.

4.—(1) Where livestock belonging to any person strays on to land in the ownership or occupation of another and—

(a) damage is done by the livestock to the land or to any property on it which is in the ownership or possession of the other person; or

(b) any expenses are reasonably incurred by that other person in keeping the livestock while it cannot be restored to the person to whom it belongs or while it is detained in pursuance of section 7 of this Act, or in ascertaining to whom it belongs;

the person to whom the livestock belongs is liable for the damages or expenses, except as otherwise provided by this Act.

(2) For the purposes of this section any livestock belongs to the person in whose possession it is.

5.—(1) A person is not liable under sections 2 to 4 of this Act for any damage which is due wholly to the fault of the person suffering it.

(2) A person is not liable under section 2 of this Act for any damage suffered by a person who has voluntarily accepted the risk thereof.

(3) A person is not liable under section 2 of this Act for any damage caused by an animal kept on any premises or structure to a person trespassing there, if it is proved either—

(a) that the animal was not kept there for the protection of persons or property; or
(b) (if the animal was kept there for the protection of persons or property) that keeping it there for that purpose was not unreasonable.

(4) A person is not liable under section 3 of this Act if the livestock was killed or injured on land on to which it had strayed and either the dog belonged to the occupier or its presence on the land was authorised by the occupier.

(5) A person is not liable under section 4 of this Act where the livestock strayed from a highway and its presence there was a lawful use of the highway.

(6) In determining whether any liability for damage under section 4 of this Act is excluded by subsection (1) of this section the damage shall not be treated as due to the fault of the person suffering it by reason only that he could have prevented it by fencing; but a person is not liable under that section where it is proved that the straying of the livestock on to the land would not have occurred but for a breach by any other person, being a person having an interest in the land, of a duty to fence.

6.—(1) The following provisions apply to the interpretation of sections 2 to 5 of this Act.

(2) A dangerous species is a species—

(a) which is not commonly domesticated in the British Islands; and
(b) whose fully grown animals normally have such characteristics that they are likely, unless restrained, to cause severe damage or that any damage they may cause is likely to be severe.

(3) Subject to subsection (4) of this section, a person is a keeper of an animal if—

(a) he owns the animal or has it in his possession; or
(b) he is the head of a household of which a member under the age of 16 owns the animal or has it in his possession.

and if at any time an animal ceases to be owned by or to be in the possession of a person, any person who immediately before that time was a keeper thereof by virtue of the preceding provisions of this subsection continues to be a keeper of the animal until another person becomes a keeper thereof by virtue of those provisions.

(4) Where an animal is taken into and kept in possession for the purpose of preventing it from causing damage or of restoring it to its owner, a person is not a keeper of it by virtue only of that possession.

(5) Where a person employed as a servant by a keeper of an animal incurs a risk incidental to his employment he shall not be treated as accepting it voluntarily.

Questions

1. Does s.2(1) alter the result of *Weller & Co v Foot and Mouth Disease Research Institute* [1966] 1 Q.B. 569, where cattle-auctioneers were unable to recover for trading losses suffered when cattle movement in the area was stopped after the defendants carelessly let a nasty foreign foot-and-mouth disease virus escape from their laboratory?

2. Am I liable under s.2(2) when my cat eats my neighbour's goldfish?

3. If a stranger maliciously releases a tiger from a zoo, is the zoo liable for the expenses of the police in warning the population and catching the tiger?

4. How can damage *caused* by an animal ever be *due* wholly to the fault of the person to whom it is done? What would you say if a man afflicted with severe schizophrenia climbed the perimeter fence of the tiger enclosure in order to converse with the big cats and was badly mauled by one of them?

5. What about bees?

6. Section 2(2)(b) speaks of "animals of the same species." In the case of an Alsatian dog, does this mean "Alsatian" or "dog"? See *Hunt v Wallis* [1991] Times L.R. 237.

7. If one knows that one's dog, being large, has a tendency to attack other dogs, is one liable to the owner of the other dog, knocked over in the canine aggression? Yes: *Smith v Ainger* [1990] Times L.R. 433, CA. How would you have justified the trial judge's judgment for the defendant which the Court of Appeal overturned? And do you agree with the Court of Appeal that "it is unrealistic to distinguish between a bite and a buffet"?

8. In 1999 nearly 7,000 postal delivery workers were menaced by dogs, and nearly one in ten was off work for a day or more. Do you suppose that many of them obtained damages?

Notes:

1. We have an instance of the application of the Act in the extempore opinions of the Court of Appeal in *Cummings v Granger* [1977] Q.B. 397, reversing judgment for the plaintiff below. The plaintiff trespassed one night in the defendant's scrapyard and was badly bitten by the untrained Alsatian guard dog which she knew was allowed to roam at large there. Section 2(2)(a): The damage was a bite. This Alsatian was not likely to bite, but any bite would likely be severe. Section 2(2)(b): This dog was a perfectly normal Alsatian. Like other Alsatians, however, it was excitable (and hence likely to bite) when used as a guard dog ("particular circumstances"). Section 2(2)(c): The defendant knew that the dog was excitable when on guard. The requirements of s.2 were accordingly satisfied and the defendant was liable unless he could establish a defence. Section 5(1): The damage was partly, but not wholly, due to the fault of the plaintiff. Section 5(2): The plaintiff did not voluntarily accept the risk of this damage by entering premises without permission when she knew this was apt to excite the dog. Section 5(3): The plaintiff was a trespasser, and although the dog was kept there to protect property (s.5(3)(a)), it was not unreasonable to keep it there for that purpose (s.5(3)(b)).

2. In *Cummings*, therefore, the keeper was in principle liable for damage done by the dog behaving quite normally *in the circumstances* (like all other Alsatians it was excitable, and so likely to bite, when on guard duty).

Several judges have been loth to accept that Parliament really intended to impose strict liability for the harm, even if likely or likely to be severe, done by a perfectly normal domesticated animal behaving quite normally for its kind in abnormal circumstances, especially as the existence of those circumstances need not be known to the keeper. The matter was very controverted by reason of the convoluted draftsmanship of s.2(2)(b), but it has now been determined by the majority of the House of Lords that the *Cummings* reading is the right one. The case involved horses of exemplary character which were terrified by some unknown event and panicked, as any horses would do; they broke out of the field and rushed headlong down the highway into the claimant's car, killing themselves and injuring him (*Mirvahedy v Henley* [2003] UKHL 16, [2003] 2 All E.R. 401). The judgments are not recommended reading.

3. Lord Justice, a true thoroughbred, was nervous and unpredictable. On one occasion he lunged into his horse-box instead of entering it in a docile manner, and crushed the arm of the plaintiff groom. Lord Justice was not vicious, but his unpredictability was a "characteristic not normally found in horses" and was known to the defendant owner, so the plaintiff's claim succeeded. Similar success would probably not have attended her concurrent claim for negligence. *Wallace v Newton* [1982] 2 All E.R. 106 (Park J.).

4. "Particular circumstances" were held to include the "territorial susceptibilities" of the bull-mastiff Max, who bit a boy who approached as Max was being loaded into the back of a car (*Cutts v Betts* [1990] 1 All E.R. 769).

5. When the postman got off his moped to deliver mail for the Paul family, their 100-pound Rottweiler called Boots came up to him. The postman turned tail and Boots chased him 100 yards down the driveway. The postman then fell over and hurt himself. His claim failed. *Chauhan v Paul* February 19, 1998, CA. There was no evidence that the defendants knew that Boots had any propensity to chase though he was given to jumping up to show his good nature. He was not dangerous but "friendly, albeit sometimes boisterous", a "gentle giant" rather apt, "like Tigger", to "bounce". Furthermore, he behaved well in court. (The postman should have read his Shakespeare:

"To fly the boar before the boar pursues
Were to incense the boar to follow us
And make pursuit when he did mean no chase."
Richard III, III.2)

6. Apparently if an actress falls off a camel her injuries are damage caused by the animal which, being of a dangerous species, renders its keeper strictly liable to her: *Tutin v Mary Chipperfield Promotions* (Cantley J., May 23, 1980).

7. In *Cox v McIntosh* [1992] C.L.Y.B. § 1523 the defendant's Rottweiler twice entered the garden of the 89-year-old plaintiff and savaged her dog. She saw the effect of the first attack and the actuality of the second, with great distress. Damages of £100 *per* incident were awarded in addition to vet's fees, but for want of a medical report no shock damages. This was said to be a trespass to P's goods, to wit her dog.[?]

8. The problem of stray dogs is addressed by ss.149, 150 of the Environmental Protection Act 1990. Section 149(5) provides: "A person claiming to be the owner of a dog seized under this section shall not be entitled to have the dog returned to him unless he pays all the expenses incurred by reason of its detention and such further amount as is for the time being prescribed." Seizure is by a dog-catcher appointed by the local authority; he has no power to seize dogs on private property without the consent of the occupier.

PART VI

TORTS TO CHATTELS

INTRODUCTION

IF England had a rational system of law there would be no need for a special section on torts to chattels and this chapter could be entirely suppressed. It is quite true that goods get lost or stolen as well as damaged, and that commercial wrongdoing is not exactly like dangerous behaviour, but the tort of negligence can perfectly well embrace cases where a person has been indirectly deprived of a physical asset and the tort of trespass can cope with cases of forthright snatching. In a rational system this would be quite adequate, for a plaintiff who had lost goods would obtain *tort* damages from a defendant only if he was to blame for their loss.

Two conditions would have to be fulfilled before the role of tort could be so sensibly restricted: first, the law of property must provide a means whereby the owner of goods can get them back from whoever is in possession of them without any right to retain them; secondly, the law of contract, rather than the law of tort, must regulate the right of contractors to the property they contract about. Neither condition is satisfied in England.

Property

The common law has no special remedy for the owner of a thing who wishes to claim it back from the person in possession of it. This gap has therefore to be filled by a remedy in tort. Unfortunate consequences ensue. The first is to introduce into tort law an area of liability without fault: this is unavoidable, because however innocent a person may be in acquiring possession of a thing, he must deliver it up to the true owner unless he has some special right to retain it. The second consequence is to raise problems about who may sue: in a property remedy we would naturally define the plaintiff in terms of his *ownership* or other property right, but when the remedy is in tort one tends to regard the plaintiff's *loss* as a necessary and sufficient criterion of eligibility to sue. This may, thirdly, give rise to to multiple plaintiffs when different people have concurrent interests in the thing. Tort has its own problems, as we have seen, when several people suffer loss as a result of injury to person or property, but these problems will be greatly extended if we make tort perform a property role as well. Fourthly, what of the plaintiff's behaviour? In tort cases his contributory negligence has a role to play in reducing the damages he obtains. This can hardly happen in a property remedy: the owner either gets his thing back or he doesn't. Fifthly, what of the defendant? In a property remedy we would insist that the defendant be in actual possession of the thing: after all, an owner who wants his thing back must sue the person who actually has it. In a tort suit we would be more interested in the defendant's past behaviour—what did he do with the thing?—than in his present position or possession. Sixthly, if the owner, not being bound to sue the present possessor, can sue all those through whose hands the goods have passed, there will be grave problems of multiple defendants. We have seen what happens in proper tort cases—the victim may sue any or all of the tortfeasors until he has been paid off, and then those who have paid more than their fair share can claim contribution from those who have paid less (above, p.236)—but one cannot simply apply this solution to litigation about lost property. Finally, what order is the judge to make? In tort cases he orders the defendant to pay monetary compensation, but in a property remedy he may have to order specific restitution, and if that is impossible he will be tempted to order the defendant to pay the value of the thing even if that differs from the sum which he would award as compensation. These are the problems which arise when tort takes on the role of property law.

Contract

The second condition required for rationality is that tort should not encroach on the role of contract. Where two people are in a voluntary relationship about a thing, the terms of that relationship should control their reciprocal rights in the thing. This is true whether the contract envisages a transfer of the ownership of the thing (as in sale) or only of its possession (as in contracts for hire, repair, carriage, etc., all those relationships so usefully called "bailments" in the common law). One would expect a special relationship to make a difference, here as elsewhere: the man you *trust* with a thing (as every equity lawyer knows) is in a different position towards you from the man who just happens to come by your thing. If you pretend to apply the same rules to such different situations, you will have either to bend the rules or to put up with bad results.

Let us test this by contrasting two possessors, one who holds the thing under a contract with the owner and one who does not. If A takes his car to the B garage for repair, a bailment arises between A and B: A has trusted B with his car (more accurately, with the possession of his car). If B now wrongfully sells the car to C and delivers it to him, C will be in possession of A's car, as B was, but C's position *vis-à-vis* A will be different from B's, because A has not trusted C with the car. There is no relationship between A and C, except that C has A's thing, whereas the relationship between A and B is very special, because A permitted B to have his thing.

As we shall see, B is guilty of conversion for selling the car and C is likewise guilty of conversion for buying it, but let us ignore that fact for the moment and concentrate on the differences which arise because of the presence or absence of a contract with the owner. First, B, knowing that the car is not his, must be under a duty to take steps to protect it from harm. C, not knowing that the car is not his, cannot be under any duty to protect it or even to refrain from damaging it: a person who reasonably believes that he owns a car can hardly be liable for wrecking it. Secondly, if the car is destroyed and the possessor receives the insurance money or damages from the tortfeasor responsible, B must—but C will not—hold this money in trust for A in priority to his own creditors. Thirdly, if A demands his car from B, B must, one would have thought, hand it over without the slightest demur regarding A's title to the car: after all, B has promised to return the car to A, and his promise is not conditional on the car's actually belonging to A (though of course B will be bound to give it up to the true owner on demand). C, on the other hand, had never seen A, let alone promised him to return the car, so he can insist that A prove his entitlement. Finally, one can see that unless C is actually in possession when A makes demand on him, C should be under no liability to A at all, whereas if B has ceased to be in possession through his wrongful act he will be liable whenever A makes demand on him. These instances sufficiently show that one cannot treat all possessors as equal: much depends on whether the possessor received the thing directly from the claimant or not, that is, on whether there is a special relationship or not. These differences have been rather ignored by English law, which still holds possessors of both types liable in conversion.

Before we turn to the actual English law we must say a word about ownership and possession. The distinction is basically simple: ownership is a legal right, possession a physical fact. The owner is entitled to a thing, whether he has it or not; the possessor has it, whether he is entitled to it or not. Proudhon, the revolutionary, put the point in a neat but nasty way: the husband owns, the lover possesses.

The matter does not stay so simple for long. First, possession is easily proved by witnesses, whereas ownership can only be established by laborious examination of the ownership of predecessors. One is therefore tempted to let a plaintiff rely on his possession rather than require him to establish ownership. Secondly, possession needs to be protected as a matter of public order. Expropriation may be unjust, but dispossession is unruly, so we must give a remedy to people whose possession is invaded, sometimes even if it is invaded by the owner: as Sohm said, the justice of ownership yields to the order of possession.

But now see what we have done. If we let the possessor as such regain or retain possession, possession has itself become a ground of entitlement: the fact of possession gives rise to the right to possess. But ownership itself is important mainly because it gives rise to the right to possess. The concept of "right to possess" thus becomes a sort of half-way house between ownership and possession, blurring both. But it is worse than that, for a right to possess may arise from a contract as well as from ownership and possession, for example, the purchaser of goods to whom delivery has been promised. (And a contract may transfer an owner's right to possess, as when a finance company lets a car on hire-purchase.)

Thus there is a confusion between the categories of property, contract and tort, and also a blurring of the concepts of ownership and possession and of the distinction between the right to possess which arises from each of them and the right to possess which arises from a contract. A case in 1963 (below, p.494) shows how wretchedly the law of England in this area operates. The bona fide purchaser of a stolen car took it to his garage for repair. It was swiped from the garage by a man who thought it belonged to the finance company which employed him. In fact it belonged to an associated company, so he gave the car back to it, the rightful owner. In his suit against the employer, the bona fide purchaser recovered the full value of a car he never owned and which he was in any case about to lose!

This amazing result was reached at a time when there were three torts operating in the area—trespass, detinue and conversion. We need a word about each, since although detinue has been abolished, no existing right of action has thereby been impaired.

As we have seen in an earlier chapter, a person who intentionally interferes with goods in the possession of another is guilty of *trespass* and is liable for any resulting harm unless he can justify his interference. The proper plaintiff in a trespass action is the person in actual possession of the goods at the time; unfortunately people with only a right to possess have sometimes been allowed to sue. It is also unfortunate that people who have misbehaved with a chattel entrusted to them have sometimes been held liable in trespass; such people should be liable on the ground that they cannot excuse their inability to return the thing, but they have not invaded anyone's possession, so they should not be liable as *trespassers*.

A person who treats goods as if they were his when they are not is liable to be sued in *conversion*. This is said to turn on the defendant's *denial of the plaintiff's title*. Some explanation is required.

If I sell a person's goods without his consent, I should certainly be liable to him: it would be quite wrong for me, however innocent I was, to keep the price of someone else's goods. Again, if I buy goods from someone not empowered to sell them, and they do not become mine, I should obviously have to give them up to the true owner: it would be quite wrong for me, however innocent I was, to keep someone else's goods. Thus the seller and the buyer of a third party's goods are rightly held liable to the true owner, though for quite different reasons. The common lawyers, however, with their characteristic penchant for false analysis, decided that there was only one reason, namely that buyer and seller alike were guilty of a denial of the true owner's title. Once this false rationalisation is made, two results follow. First, the buyer becomes liable even if he no longer has the goods, because now the wrong is thought to consist in the purchase, not in the retention after demand. Secondly, the auctioneer becomes liable, although he doesn't keep the price of the goods he sells. This is extremely odd. Just as the auctioneer's very job is to sell other people's goods, so the carrier's is to carry them. Now if A gives B's goods to C for carriage, C is not liable to B for carrying them, so why should Z be strictly liable to Y for selling goods which X has given him for sale? The answer given, forsooth, is that in selling the goods as X's he is denying Y's title to them. Note that the liability of purchaser and seller is strict in the sense that they are liable however carefully they may have checked the title of their vendor or principal. A possessor who refuses to hand over the thing to a person entitled to demand it also commits conversion, and other acts which result in the loss of the goods may be construed as denials of the claimant's title, though in some cases the defendant must have knowledge that he was doing wrong. However, conversion always required a positive act: losing a thing or letting it get stolen might lead to liability in detinue, but it did not constitute conversion until the 1977 Act, which abolished detinue, came into force (below, p.502).

To be able to bring a claim in conversion it is neither necessary nor sufficient to own the thing: what is required is a "right to immediate possession." Any person who has such a right may sue, even if his right arises only by contract; a person who has no such right cannot sue, even if he is the owner. An owner may give up his right to immediate possession by contracting it away; whether he has actually given it up depends on the bailment—the gratuitous lender is always entitled to repossess, as is the bailor whose bailee has misconducted himself, so in such cases bailors can sue notwithstanding the bailment.

Detinue, which has now been abolished, could be brought by a bailor against his bailee or by a person entitled to possess a thing against the person in actual possession of it. This form of action was especially useful to a claimant who wanted the goods themselves rather than money damages, since only in detinue could the judge order specific delivery. If the defendant no longer had the thing, he obviously could not hand it over, but the bailee would be liable in damages if his inability to return the thing was due to his positive act, such as giving it to someone else, or his failure to look after it properly. Detinue thus had two advantages: it gave rise, as against a possessor, to a right to have the thing back, and it made a bailee liable for carelessly ceasing to possess. The 1977 Act allows a judge to order the redelivery of the thing in any appropriate case, and it turns the wrongful failure to look after a thing into an act of conversion. So detinue has gone only in name.

In 1967 the Lord Chancellor asked the Law Reform Committee to consider the law of detinue and conversion; trespass was added to the brief at the Committee's request, and in 1971 the Committee produced its Eighteenth Report (Cmnd. 4774), with the following principal recommendations:

(1) that the three existing torts should be replaced by a new tort;

(2) that in general there should continue to be liability wherever there was liability under any of the old torts, and that in particular the strict liability imposed in conversion should remain;

(3) that any person with a possessory or proprietary interest in the chattel (other than a purely equitable interest) should be entitled to sue;

(4) that the measure of recovery in each case should be the amount of the plaintiff's loss;

(5) that so far as possible all interested parties should be brought into the suit, and that the defendant should therefore be permitted to show that others had a better interest than the plaintiff;

(6) that contributory negligence should not be a defence;

(7) that the court should have discretion to order the return of the chattel as an alternative to payment of damages;

(8) that remedies in this tort should continue to concur with remedies for breach of contract.

By no means all of these recommendations are implemented in the Torts (Interference with Goods) Act 1977. Only detinue is abolished: tort liability in conversion and trespass remains exactly as before. Certainly the Act introduces "wrongful interference with goods" but this is not a new tort, it is just a new name, a simple way of referring to all torts which involve lost or damaged goods, not only conversion and trespass but also negligence and any other tort. Such a term was useful because the Act applies to all such torts a number of new rules, mainly procedural in character. One such rule empowers a judge to order specific delivery in any suitable case. Another rule, which provides that a claimant's title is extinguished on full payment or settlement, will be useful where there are several possible defendants. Where there are several possible claimants, it is best if they all join in a single suit, so that each can receive the right amount. Provision is therefore made for the amalgamation of suits begun in different courts. Further, the defendant is allowed to mention, and the plaintiff may be required to disclose, the existence of other possible claimants: these may forfeit their rights if they fail, after notification, to join in the suit. If a second claimant appears after a first claimant has already been paid, the first must account for any excess to the second, and if this results in overpayment to the second, he must hand over the excess to the wrongdoer. Indeed, if the two claimants are bailor and bailee, no second action in respect of damage to the chattel is possible: *O'Sullivan v Williams* [1992] 3 All E.R. 385.

Two proposals in particular were not implemented by the Act: (1) that anyone could sue if he had a possessory or proprietary interest in the goods, and (2) that the the measure of recovery in all cases should be the amount of the plaintiff's loss. It is therefore necessary, in order to ascertain the existing law on these important topics, to familiarise oneself with the law as it was before the Act. A good starting-place would be *IBL Ltd v Coussens* [1991] 2 All E.R. 145, CA, which also shows that the Act is taken to have introduced (2) above; the *Kuwait Airways* case, below p.511, goes a good way towards adopting (4).

The first case given below is rather exceptional in this chapter, since it involved a good deal of money (as share transactions often do), but though one will find references to a case involving gold bullion, a good part of which the Bank of England had managed to mislay (*U.S.A. and Republic of France v Dollfus Mieg et cie.* [1952] A.C. 582), most chattels are not worth very much and consequently not worth much in the way of lawyers' fees or judges' time. It will be noted that in several of the cases that follow the opinions were extempore and not very powerfully reasoned, a fact which may in itself have contributed to the rather confused state of the law.

Chapter 13

TORTS TO CHATTELS

Section 1.—Title to Sue

(i) Conversion

MCC PROCEEDS INC v LEHMAN BROS. INTERNATIONAL (EUROPE)

Court of Appeal [1998] 4 All E.R. 675

Owner in equity sues good faith purchaser from legal owner

Macmillan Inc, to whose rights the plaintiff had succeeded, owned shares in Berlitz. As part of the deeply dishonest machinations of the repulsive Robert Maxwell who fatally fell off his yacht in 1991, Macmillan transferred these shares into the name of BIT, a nominee also controlled by Maxwell: the effect was that BIT became trustee of the shares for Macmillan. Without Macmillan's knowledge BIT pledged those shares to the defendant LB as part of a deal. On default by BIT the defendant LB sold the pledged shares to Shearson Lehman which was unaware of the prior shenanigans. A prior action against Shearson Lehman had failed after a trial lasting 117 days. This action also failed.

Mummery L.J.: . . . Sir Patrick Neill submitted that MCC Proceeds, as successor to Macmillan, has good causes of action against LB for conversion of the five share certificates.

Some of the legal propositions relied on to support this argument were not disputed. It is helpful to record those in order to define and restrict the area of dispute on the law.

(1) Conversion is a common law action, tortious in form, imposing strict liability for a wrongful interference with the right to possession of a chattel. It consists of any act of wilful interference, without lawful justification, with any chattel in any manner inconsistent with the right of another whereby that other is deprived of the use and possession of it . . .

(2) Share certificates are personal chattels and can properly be the subject of a claim in conversion for which full damages can be recovered to the extent of the loss, not just nominal damages for the value of the share certificates as pieces of paper. The damages are the value of the shares at the date of conversion.

(3) A person has title to sue for conversion if he has either actual possession or an immediate legal right to possession of the goods at the time of conversion. It is not necessary to prove ownership. A bailee at will has an immediate right to possession sufficient to bring a conversion claim.

(4) A bailor, under a bailment of goods for a fixed period, has an immediate right to possession when the person holding the goods acts in a manner repugnant to the agreement under which the goods are held.

The dispute has centred on the following further legal propositions formulated by Sir Patrick Neill.

(1) A person with an equitable interest in goods can sue for conversion if he has an immediate right to possession. Reliance was placed on *International Factors Ltd v Rodriguez* [1979] 1 All E.R. 17.

(2) The bona fide purchaser of a chattel is liable in conversion, unless he can rely on a relevant statutory exception or on a conclusive estoppel.

(3) Legal ownership of a chattel by the defendant converter does not preclude a conversion claim against him. Thus a person with a legal title to goods can be sued in conversion by one who has an immediate right to possession of them.

(4) There was a "reversionary interest" in the share certificates for which Macmillan is entitled to claim damages, even if not entitled to sue in conversion for some technical reason. On this point particular reliance was placed on *Mears v London and South Western Ry Co* (1862) 142 E.R. 1029 and *Transcontainer Express Ltd v Custodian Security Ltd* [1988] 1 Lloyd's Rep. 128 at 137. This type of claim had not been abolished by the 1977 Act. It was covered by the broad language of s.1(d).

Applying those propositions to this case, it was submitted that Macmillan had beneficial ownership of the share certificates under the nominee agreement, coupled with a right to call for the return of the certificates at any time; that it therefore had title to sue for conversion; that the fact that BIT had the bare legal title to the certificates did not prevent Macmillan from asserting a conversion claim against BIT; that the fact that LB were innocent of wrongdoing by BIT and of Macmillan's interest in the certificates did not provide any defence nor did the fact that LB acquired a legal title to the certificates from BIT; that BIT converted the certificates when they were wrongfully delivered to LB by way of pledge and that, by operation of s.11(2) of the 1977 Act, the receipt of the certificates by LB was also a conversion.

In my judgment, the conversion claim is misconceived in law and it would be vexatious and an abuse of the process of the court for MCC Proceeds to pursue that claim against LB.

It will be necessary to analyse some of the authorities cited in argument by counsel in both sides. It is convenient at this stage to summarise the reasons for my conclusion.

(1) It was held in the first action that the effect of the nominee agreement was to create a trust of the shares in Berlitz for the benefit of Macmillan. The legal title to the shares was vested in BIT as trustee. BIT was not agent or bailee for Macmillan. The certificates, which evidenced BIT's legal title to the shares, were in BIT's name and in BIT's possession by virtue of BIT's rights as legal owner. Macmillan's interest in the shares and in the certificates, which evidenced the title to those shares, was an equitable interest only: Macmillan did not have actual possession of the certificates or an immediate right to possession of them or a reversionary interest of the kind relied on as an alternative title.

(2) Pursuant to blank stock transfer forms duly executed on its behalf, BIT, the trustee and registered holder, validly transferred the legal title in the shares and the share certificates evidencing their ownership to LB. It was held in the first action that LB was the bona fide purchaser from the legal owner, BIT, of the legal estate in the shares without notice of any breach of trust by BIT or of any claim by Macmillan and therefore acquired a good title to the shares and the certificates deposited as security, free of adverse claims, thereby extinguishing Macmillan's prior equitable interest. The result was that Macmillan had no legal right to the return of the shares or of the certificates from LB.

(3) A claim for conversion of goods is not maintainable by a person who only has an equitable interest in them against another who has acquired the legal title to the goods, as a bona fide purchaser for value without notice of the prior equitable claim. Such an interest has been overreached and extinguished. The fact that BIT acted without authority and in breach of trust in charging the shares to LB in the first place is not relevant to the claim by MCC Proceeds for conversion against LB. The validity of LB's title acquired from BIT cannot be challenged since, even if, as between BIT and Macmillan, BIT acted wrongfully and in breach of trust, legal title

would nevertheless pass to LB as bona fide purchaser without notice, free of Macmillan's claim and also free of a claim by its successor, MCC Proceeds.

A sound foundation for embarking on an analysis of the relevant authorities is to be found in F. W. Maitland, *Equity a Course of Lectures* (1929), pp.46–47, where he vividly illustrated the fundamental conceptual distinction, sometimes difficult to draw in practice, between a trust and a bailment. The distinction is of particular importance, in a case such as this, where the rights of innocent third parties are affected by a party to the relationship acting in breach of his legal or equitable duty. Maitland brought what he described as an 'almost metaphysical distinction' to life by the following example from the law of sale:

> "A is the bailor, B is the bailee of goods; B sells the goods to X, the sale not being authorised by the terms of the bailment and not being made in market overt or within the Factors Acts. X, though he purchases in good faith, and though he has no notice of A's rights, does not get a good title to the goods. A can recover them from him; if he converts them to his use he wrongs A. Why? Because he bought them from one who was not owner of them. Turn to the other case. T is holding goods as trustee of S's marriage settlement. In breach of trust he sells them to X; X buys in good faith and has no notice of the trust. X gets a good title to the goods. T was the owner of the goods; he passed his rights to X; X became the owner of the goods and S has no right against X—for it is an elementary rule, to which I must often refer hereafter, that trust rights can not be enforced against one who has acquired legal (*i.e.* common law) ownership *bona fide*, for value, and without notice of the existence of those trust rights. Here you see one difference between the bailee and the trustee." (Author's emphasis).

In my judgment, a full appreciation of the ramifications of that statement of fundamental principle is critical to the analysis of the conversion claim advanced by MCC Proceeds and of the authorities relied on in support of it. As already pointed out, BIT was registered with legal title to the Berlitz shares. It was trustee of those shares under the terms of the nominee agreement. There was no separate bailment of the share certificates in the provisions of the nominee agreement or otherwise. Share certificates are documents which serve as evidence of title. They were as much held in trust by BIT as the shares themselves. This means that, in principle, any disposition of the legal title to the shares and the certificates in favour of a bona fide purchaser for value without notice of the equitable interest of the beneficiary (Macmillan) in the shares or in the certificates, would give that purchaser a good legal title to the shares *and* to the certificates, thus protecting him against *all* claims by the beneficiary whose interest has been overreached.

Do any of the authorities or statutory provisions cited invalidate this analysis of the legal position? In my judgment, they do not. My comments on the state of the law on conversion, as revealed in the authorities cited, are as follows.

(1) Viscount Cave L.C. in *Performing Right Society Ltd v London Theatre of Varieties Ltd* [1924] A.C. 1 at 14 rejected the contention that the position of equitable owners had been changed by the fusion of law and equity in the Judicature Acts.

More recently Lord Brandon in *Leigh & Sillavan Ltd v Aliakmon Shipping Co Ltd, The Aliakmon* [1986] 2 All E.R. 145 at 151 rejected as insupportable the proposition that "a person who has the equitable ownership of goods is entitled to sue in tort for negligence anyone who by want of care causes them to be lost or damaged without joining the legal owner as a party to the action". He explained the position in these words:

> "There may be cases where a person who is the equitable owner of certain goods has also a possessory title to them. In such a case he is entitled, by virtue of his possessory title rather than his equitable ownership, to sue in tort for negligence anyone whose want of care has caused loss of or damage to the goods without joining the legal owner as a party to the action: see, for instance, *Healey v Healey* [1915] 1 K.B. 938. If, however, the person is the equitable owner of the goods and no more, then he must join the legal owner as a party to

the action, either as co-plaintiff if he is willing or as co-defendant if he is not. This has always been the law in the field of equitable ownership of land and I see no reason why it should not also be so in the field of equitable ownership of goods."

(3) In *International Factors Ltd v Rodriguez* [1979] 1 All E.R. 17, a company controlled by the defendant factored debts to the plaintiff company and it was agreed that the company would hold all cheques sent to it on trust for the plaintiff and immediately hand them over to the plaintiff. The defendant paid four cheques made out to the company into the company's account. The defendant was held liable for conversion of the cheques.

Sir David Cairns, with whose ex tempore judgment Bridge L.J. agreed, said:

"For the proposition that a person with an equitable title to goods can sue in conversion, assistance is derived from the decision of Shearman J. in *Healey v Healey* . . . It is perhaps curious that that is the only decision that counsel has been able to discover of a cestui que trust being entitled to sue in conversion, but it seems to me that since the fusion of law and equity that is sound law."

This passage is not, in my judgment, the ratio of the decision: it is not binding on this court and it is not good law.

On the facts of the case it was not necessary to hold that the plaintiff could succeed on the strength of an equitable title alone. As appears from the judgment the effect of the agreement was that, as soon as one of the cheques came into the possession of the company, there arose not only a trust for the plaintiffs but also an obligation "of immediately handing over the cheque itself to the plaintiffs" (see [1979] 1 All E.R. 17 at 20). This feature of the case formed the basis of the judgment of Buckley L.J., who agreed with Sir David Cairns and Bridge L.J. that the appeal should be dismissed. All three members of the court agreed that the plaintiffs were entitled to have the cheques "handed directly to them". This conferred "on the plaintiffs . . . an immediate right to possession of any such cheque quite sufficient to support a cause of action in conversion against anyone who wrongfully deals with the cheque in any other manner" per Buckley L.J. who added:

" . . . whether or not an enforceable trust would attach immediately on the payment of any debt direct to the company by cheque, whether or not an immediate trust would attach to such a cheque, I think that there is a contractual right here for the plaintiffs to demand immediate delivery of the cheque to them, and that that is a sufficient right to possession to give them a status to sue in conversion."

In my judgment, there was no disagreement on this point among the members of the court. The references in the judgment of Sir David Cairns to the title of an equitable owner were not necessary for the decision on the case and were *obiter*.

The short answer to MCC Proceeds' claim is to be found rooted deep in English legal history: conversion is a common law action and the common law did not recognise the equitable title of the beneficiary under a trust. It recognised only the title of the trustee, as the person normally entitled to immediate possession of the trust property. MCC Proceeds' claim for conversion cannot be maintained, as its predecessor in title, Macmillan, had only an equitable title to the share certificates and the shares.

I would like to acknowledge the assistance given on the conversion point by Professor Tettenborn, "Trust Property and Conversion: An Equitable Confusion" (1996) 55 Camb. L.J. 36.

LORD v PRICE

Court of Exchequer (1873) L.R. 9 Exch. 54; 43 L.J. Ex. 49; 30 L.T. 271; 22 W.R. 318

Action against innocent remover from seller's possession of goods bought but not paid for by plaintiff

The plaintiff bought two lots of cotton at an auction. He thereby became owner of them. The terms of the sale were that payment should be made immediately after the auction, but the plaintiff paid only the deposit. He collected one lot, but when he returned for the other, he discovered that the defendant had taken it in mistake for a lot which he had purchased at the same sale.

The plaintiff was nonsuited at the Passage Court, Liverpool. He moved for a new trial, but the rule was discharged.

Bramwell B.: I am of opinion that this rule must be discharged, on the ground that the action cannot be maintained without a right of present possession in the plaintiff. Here there is no evidence that the plaintiff had any right of possession; that right was in the vendor, who was entitled to retain possession of the goods until the balance of the purchase-money was paid, and, on non-payment, to resell the goods and recoup himself for any loss sustained on re-sale. Therefore, if the goods were tortiously removed (and there is no evidence that the vendor assented to their removal) it is manifest that the vendor could have maintained an action. But it cannot be that two men can be entitled at the same time to maintain an action of trover for the same goods. It is, therefore, abundantly manifest that the vendor could, and that the plaintiff cannot, maintain this action.

Whether, by paying the balance of the price now, or tendering it, the buyer can, either in an action of trover or by a special action on the case, have any remedy at Common Law in his own name, or whether he is limited to an action in the name of the vendor, it is not necessary now to pronounce. It is sufficient to say that, on the facts shewn here, the plaintiff cannot recover.

Note:
It seems very hard that the owner of goods should not be able to get them from a person who possesses them and has no title to them. But if the plaintiff had been allowed to recover in this action, he would have been in the very happy position of having a bale of cotton (or its value) for which he had not paid and for which he could not be made to pay. Conversion actions cannot be regarded as involving just the plaintiff and the defendant. Here the plaintiff could not sue because he did not have possession of the goods at the time of the defendant's act, and he did not at that time have the right to their immediate, that is, unconditional, possession. He could only get possession by paying the vendor the balance of the price. But Bramwell B. was wrong in saying that it is never possible for two persons to have the right to maintain conversion in respect of the same goods at the same time. Whenever there is a bailment such that the bailor may resume possession on demand, either party to the bailment may sue a stranger in conversion. (*Nicolls v Bastard* (1835) 2 Cr. M. & R. 659; 150 E.R. 279 Parke B., *arguendo*).

If the vendor had *delivered* the cotton to the defendant by mistake, then the plaintiff could have maintained his action; for the act of the vendor would have destroyed his lien for the price (*Chinery v Viall* (1860) 5 H. & N. 288; 157 E.R. 1192). On the other hand, if the vendor had delivered the cotton to the defendant pursuant to a second sale, he would be liable to the plaintiff in conversion, but the defendant would not be, since the second purchaser from a vendor left in possession obtains, if in good faith, a good title on delivery, *i.e.* is not liable in conversion (Sale of Goods Act 1979, s.24).

On the facts as they were, there seems little reason to doubt that if the plaintiff had paid the price to the auctioneer, he could then demand the goods of the defendant, and, if he did not deliver them up, sue him for the conversion constituted by the refusal to deliver. But if the defendant had sold them already, he would have to find the person with the goods, or a person who had had dealings with them after the payment of the price, as the plaintiff must have had title to sue at the moment of the conversion founded upon.

(ii) Trespass

WILSON v LOMBANK LTD

Assizes [1963] 1 W.L.R. 1294; [1963] 1 All E.R. 740

Action by bona fide purchaser of stolen car against unauthorised repossessor who returned it to true owner

The plaintiff unsuspectingly bought a Renault Dauphine car from a person who had no right to sell it. He took it to his garage for repairs. The defendant's servant saw it there, and thought it belonged to the finance company which employed him. He accordingly took it, without the assent of the garage owner. In fact it belonged to another finance company, to whom the defendant then returned it.

The plaintiff was held entitled to recover the value of the car as repaired.

Hinchcliffe J.: ... It is in these circumstances that the plaintiff submits that he was in possession of the motor-car; that the defendants had no right to take the car away; and that since the plaintiff was in possession and the defendants had no legal title, it is not open to the defendants to assert that the title rests in another person. In other words, the plaintiff says that possession here is title.

The defendants, through their counsel, Mr Fox-Andrews, present an interesting argument. They concede that an action for trespass in respect of a personal chattel would lie if, at the time of the taking of the chattel, the plaintiff was in possession of it. It is submitted that a person is in possession in law if he has actual possession, constructive possession, or an immediate right to possession. In the circumstances of this case Mr Fox-Andrews contends that the plaintiff did not have actual possession and he did not have constructive possession, since the motor-car was in the hands of a garage for repairs. And he further submits that the plaintiff did not have an immediate right to possession since this is something which only arises in the case of a gratuitous bailment, which this was not. Furthermore, it is submitted that because the motor-car was in for repairs, the garage had a lien on it, and therefore the plaintiff could not have had an immediate right of possession.

Mr Fox-Andrews further submits that even if the plaintiff did have an immediate right of possession, his claim is defeated by virtue of the fact that on April 16, 1960, the defendants returned the motor-car to the true owners. . . .

Mr Best, on behalf of the plaintiff, agrees that "possession" includes constructive possession; the right to immediate possession; and, of course, actual possession. Mr Best relies on *United States of America and Republic of France v Dolfus Mieg et Cie SA and Bank of England*, and he draws my attention to . . . the speech of Lord Porter ([1952] A.C. 582 at 611): . . . "the better opinion is, I think, that where the bailor can at any moment demand the return of the object bailed, he still has possession."

Mr Best also submits that as to the question of lien, here there was a monthly account between the plaintiff and the Haven Garage Co Ltd. The repairs had been completed. The motor-car was on the forecourt awaiting collection and there therefore was an implied term between the plaintiff and the Haven Garage that there was to be no lien.

I have summarised the submissions as briefly as I can, and I hope accurately. Giving those submissions the best consideration I can, in my judgment the plaintiff was in possession of the car; not only did he have the right to immediate possession, but I do not think that in the circumstances of this case he ever lost possession of the car. In my view the plaintiff at all times could have demanded the return of the car, and I would, with respect, like to adopt the words of Lord Porter in his speech which I have just quoted. I do not think there was a lien on the motor-car, having regard to the course of dealing between the plaintiff and the Haven Garage over a period of eight years, during which time there existed this monthly credit. On the view I have formed, that the plaintiff never lost possession of the motor-car, it seems to me that the defendants wrongfully took the car and that the plaintiff is entitled to recover damages.

As to the damages, the plaintiff submits that he is entitled to recover the sum of £470, that is to say, the amount that he paid for the motor-car, plus the cost of the repairs—£27 14s., plus the loss of profit that he would have made. The defendants submit that only the cost of the repairs is recoverable. I am of the opinion that the plaintiff is entitled to recover the full value of the article wrongfully taken by the defendants. Here the full value was £470. To that sum there should be added the sum of £27 14s., the cost of the repairs. I am not prepared to speculate what the loss of profit would have been. In my judgment the plaintiff is entitled to recover the total of those two sums.

Note:

The holding that the plaintiff was still in actual possession of the car when it was in the garage is questionable (Palmer, *Bailment* (2nd ed., 1991), p.341, n.19); so is the holding that an immediate right to possession is enough to enable one to sue in trespass (as opposed to conversion); so is the measure of damages awarded.

Questions

1. Could the plaintiff have sued in conversion?
2. What is the measure of damages in (a) conversion, (b) trespass?
3. What is the value of a car? How much damage does a person suffer if he loses the use of a car which he has no right to retain, or property which he is in fact soon going to lose? (See *Burmah Oil v Lord Advocate* [1964] 2 All E.R. 348 at 362.)
4. If the owner of the car could sue both the plaintiff and the defendant in conversion, would they be tortfeasors "liable in respect of the same damage?" (See above, p.236) If so, how much damage has an owner suffered who has got his thing back? How would that damage be divided as between the plaintiff and the defendant? (The decision in *Honourable Society of the Middle Temple v Lloyds Bank* [1999] Times L.R. 91, in which two parties liable for separate conversions were held to be in a contribution relationship, may not be a good authority for cases involving chattels, since the item converted was a cheque, and cheques, though convertible, are different: money, which is what cheques really are, is divisible in a way that things are not, which explains why contributory negligence, not normally a defence to a conversion claim, is exceptionally a defence to a claim for conversion of a cheque. On cheques, see below, p.501).

Section 2.—The Act of Conversion

HIORT v BOTT

Court of Exchequer (1874) L.R. 9 Exch. 86; 43 L.J.Ex. 81; 30 L.T. 25; 22 W.R. 414

Action against fraud's dupe for facilitating theft of goods

The plaintiffs were corn-merchants in Hull who occasionally used a broker named Grimmett. The defendant was a licensed victualler in Birmingham who had never had any dealings with either of them. He was therefore surprised one day to receive from the plaintiffs an invoice for 83 quarters of barley said to have been ordered by him through Grimmett, and a delivery order empowering him to collect them from the railway station. Grimmett had indeed put in the order, but as a fraud. A day or two later Grimmett called on the defendant, said that it was all a mistake, and asked the defendant to endorse over the delivery order so that it could be put right. The defendant did endorse over the delivery order and gave it to Grimmett. Grimmett collected the barley, sold it and made off with the proceeds.

The jury found that the defendant had no intention of appropriating the barley to his own use, but was anxious to correct a supposed error, with a view to returning the barley to the plaintiffs. Archibald J. directed a verdict for the defendant with leave to the plaintiffs to move to enter a verdict for £180, the value of the barley. The plaintiffs obtained a rule accordingly, and the rule was made absolute by the Court of Exchequer. That is, the plaintiffs won.

Bramwell B.: . . . I think the plaintiffs are entitled to recover; though, so far as concerns the defendant, whose act was well meant, I regret the result. Mr Bosanquet gave a good description of what constitutes a conversion when he said that it is where a man does an unauthorised act which deprives another of his property permanently or for an indefinite time. The expression used in the declaration is "converted to his own use"; but that does not mean that the defendant consumed the goods himself; for, if a man gave a quantity of another person's wine to a friend to drink, and the friend drank it, that would no doubt be as much a conversion of the wine as if he drank it himself. Now here the defendant did an act that was unauthorised. There was no occasion for him to do it; for the delivery order made the barley deliverable to the order of the consignor or consignee, and if the defendant had done nothing at all it would have been delivered to the plaintiffs. And there is no doubt that by what he did he deprived the plaintiffs of their property; because, by means of this order so indorsed, Grimmett got the barley and made away with it, leaving the plaintiffs without any remedy against the railway company, who had acted according to the instructions of the plaintiffs in delivering the barley to the order of the consignee. The case, therefore, stands thus: that by an unauthorised act on the part of the defendant, the plaintiffs have lost their barley, without any remedy except against Grimmett, and that is worthless. It seems to me, therefore, that this was assuming a control over the disposition of these goods, and causing them to be delivered to a person who deprived the plaintiffs of them. The conversion is therefore made out.

Various ingenious cases were put as to what would happen if, for instance, a parcel were left at your house by mistake, and you gave it to your servant to take back to the person who left it there, and the servant misappropriated it. Probably the safest way of dealing with that case is to wait until it arises; but I may observe that there is the difference between such a case and the present one, that where a man delivers a parcel to you by mistake, it is contemplated that if there is a mistake, you will do something with it. What are you to do with it? Warehouse it? No. Are you to turn it into the street? That would be an unreasonable thing to do. Does he not impliedly authorise you to take reasonable steps with regard to it—that is, to send it back by a trustworthy person? And when you say, "Go and deliver it to the person who sent it," are you in any manner converting it to your own use? That may be a question. But here the defendant did not send the order back; but at Grimmett's request indorsed it to him, though, no doubt, as the jury have found, with a view to the barley being returned to the plaintiffs. There is therefore a distinction between the case put and the present one. And there is also a distinction between the case of *Heugh v London and North Western Ry* ((1870) L.R. 5 Ex. 51), which was cited for the defendant, and the present case; because there it was taken that the plaintiff authorised the defendants to deliver the goods to a person applying for them, if they had reasonable grounds for believing him to be the right person.

On these considerations I think the plaintiffs are entitled to recover. But I must add one word. This is an action for conversion, and I lament that such a word should appear in our proceedings, which does not represent the real facts, and which always gives rise to a discussion as to what is, and what is not, a conversion. But supposing the case were stated according to a non-artificial system of pleading, thus: "We, the plaintiffs, had at the London and North Western Railway station certain barley. We had sent the delivery order to you, the defendant. You might have got it, if you were minded to be the buyer of it; you were not so minded, and therefore should have done nothing with it. Nevertheless, you ordered the London and North Western Railway Co to deliver it, without any authority, to Grimmett, who took it away." Would not that have been a logical and precise statement of a tortious act on the part of the defendant, causing loss to the plaintiffs? It seems to me that it would. I think, but not without some regret, that this rule should be made absolute, to enter the verdict for the plaintiffs.

Cleasby B.: . . . It should be particularly noticed in this case that the plaintiffs had not, by what they had done, placed the defendant in any position of difficulty, as is often the case with an involuntary bailee (an expression often used in the argument) who has received property into his possession for a purpose which cannot, as it afterwards appears, be exactly carried into effect, and who does his best and acts in a reasonable manner for carrying into effect the purpose of the bailment. In such cases the bailee has a duty to perform in relation to the goods, and he is placed in a difficulty in the discharge of that duty by the default of the plaintiff, who ought not to be allowed to complain if, under that difficulty, the bailee has acted in a manner which is considered reasonable and proper.

But no difficulty of that sort arises here, . . .

It is also to be observed that the present case is different from a class of cases referred to in the argument, in which some act is done to goods, such as shoeing a horse, packing goods, or forwarding them on. In these cases no act is done having reference to the property in the goods or the right to the possession of them. The act is consistent with the title of any person. But in the present case the act of the defendant transfers the title to the possession of the goods, so as to cause them to be lost to the real owner.

. . .

It was not left to the jury in this case to say whether the conduct of the defendant was reasonable and proper, but I do not think that this was necessary. No objection was made in the argument that this had not been done; but it was unnecessary, because to transfer voluntarily the title to the possession of goods, in which you have no interest whatever, to a third person is, in my opinion, under the circumstances of the present case, obviously improper and unreasonable; and that is the ground of my judgment.

Questions

1. Did the defendants in this case behave reasonably? Would it be reasonable for them to behave in the same way today?

2. Would you describe the defendant's conduct as a cause of the plaintiff's loss?

3. Suppose that the defendants had wired the plaintiffs to discover if delivery to Grimmett were in order. Could they recover the cost of the telegram? See *The Winson* [1982] A.C. 939.

4. In *Elvin & Powell v Plummer Roddis* (1934) 50 T.L.R. 158 the same fraud was tried with equal success, with a bundle of coats worth £350 instead of a delivery order. Hawke J. said: "If persons were involuntary bailees and had done everything reasonable they were not liable to pay damages if something which they did resulted in the loss of the property," and gave judgment for the defendant. Which case would you follow if a similar fraud involved a diamond ring? The matter is discussed in that treasure-house of learning Palmer, *Bailment* (2nd ed., 1991), pp.689–697.

Note:

One can sympathise with Baron Bramwell's lamenting the use of the word "conversion" for it is not really an appropriate description of many of the acts which constitute conversion in law, especially now that conversion embraces loss of goods by a bailee (s.2(2) of the 1977 Act, below, p.502). But a literal conversion did take place in the interesting California case of *Moore v Regents of the University of California* 51 Cal.3d 120; 271 Cal.Rptr. 146; (1990) 793 P.2d 479, where the question was rather whether what had been converted was property *at all*.

The plaintiff, suffering from hairy-cell leukaemia, agreed to the removal of his enlarged spleen, an operation which greatly improved his condition. From the organ thus removed the doctor took a sample of the cells, and used them to isolate a cell-line from which the research laboratory was able to develop many profitable products, patented by the University. The plaintiff claimed damages on the basis of conversion, lack of informed consent, breach of fiduciary duty and an accounting. The doctor was held liable for breach of his fiduciary duty to inform his patient of what he was doing and obtain informed consent to it, but the claims in conversion against the others were dismissed: research scientists could hardly be expected to trace the pedigree of all the material they worked on. The dissent strongly objected to the denial of a conversion claim, arguing that the cells were obviously property, for had they been stolen from the laboratory, the laboratory could clearly have sued the thief. All this objection shows, however, is that the cells were susceptible of being trespassed to, not that they were capable of being converted.

The plaintiff in that case was seeking the profits made by the defendants from his spleen, whose removal had cost him no loss. In *Dobson v North Tyneside H.A.* [1996] 4 All E.R. 474 the plaintiffs wanted to sue for wrongful death and needed the decedent's brain for evidentiary purposes. The defendant hospital had had possession of the brain, for when the decedent had succumbed to a brain tumour the neuropathologist appointed by the coroner to effect an autopsy preserved the brain in paraffin and delivered it to the defendant for storage with a view to a histological examination which in fact never took place. By the time proceedings were started the defendant had already disposed of the brain. It was held that the plaintiffs had no arguable claim: legal representatives (as opposed to next-of-kin) had a right to the possession of a cadaver for the sole purpose of interment, and though conversion might lie for human parts which had, after separation, been the object of work and skill, this was not the case where a brain had simply been bottled. [The point was not taken that conversion lies only if the plaintiffs had a right to immediate possession at the time of the alleged conversion, whereas here the brain had probably been disposed of before the plaintiffs took out letters of administration].

ENGLAND v COWLEY

Court of Exchequer (1873) L.R. 8 Exch. 126; 42 L.J. Ex. 80; 28 L.T. 67; 21 W.R. 337

Priority between distraining landlord and repossessing mortgagee

Miss Morley owed money to both the defendant and the plaintiff. The defendant was her landlord, and she owed him six months' rent; the plaintiff had lent her money which she had not repaid. The dispute between them was over Miss Morley's furniture, which the plaintiff was empowered to take by a Bill of Sale signed by Miss Morley, and which the defendant could distrain on at common law, but only while the goods were on the premises and only during the hours of daylight. The plaintiff had put a man in the house in early August, and after sunset on the eleventh he sent round two men with vans to pick up the furniture. The defendant forbade them to take it away, and stationed a policeman at the gate to make sure they did not.

A verdict was entered for the defendant on instructions by Bramwell B., and this decision was upheld by the Court of Exchequer.

Bramwell B.: . . . I think no action is maintainable, because the defendant did no act, but only threatened that, in a certain event, he would do something. The plaintiff should either have proceeded with the removal of the goods, or at least have commenced to remove them, leaving the defendant to stop him at his peril, when there might have been a cause of action of some sort. But further, even if the defendant had prevented the removal of the goods by physical force, I do not think trover would have been maintainable. The substance of that action is the same as before the Common Law Procedure Act, 1852, and although in the form of declaration there given in Sch.B the words used are, "converted to his own use, or wrongfully deprived the plaintiff of the use and possession of the plaintiff's goods," the gist of the action is the conversion, as for example, by consuming the goods or by refusing the true owner possession, the wrong-doer having himself at the time a physical control over the goods. Now here the defendant did not "convert" the goods to his own use, either by sale or in any other way. Nor did he deprive the plaintiff of them. All he did was to prevent, or threaten to prevent, the plaintiff from using them in a particular way. "You shall not remove them," he said, but the plaintiff still might do as he pleased with them in the house. Assume that there was actual prevention, still I think this action cannot be maintained. Take some analogous cases, by way of illustration. A man is going to fight a duel, and goes to a drawer to get one of his pistols. I say to him, "You shall not take that pistol of yours out of the drawer," and hinder his doing so. Is that a conversion of the pistol by me to my own use? Certainly not. Or, again, I meet a man on horseback going in a particular direction, and say to him, "You shall not go that way, you must turn back"; and make him comply. Who could say that I had been guilty of a conversion of the horse? Or I might prevent a man from pawning his watch, but no one would call that a conversion of the watch by me. And really this case is the same with these. Illustrations of my meaning might be easily multiplied. The truth is that, in order to maintain trover, a plaintiff who is left in possession of the goods must prove that his dominion over his property has been interfered with, not in some particular way, but altogether; that he has been entirely deprived of the use of it. It is not enough that a man should say that *something* shall not be done by the plaintiff; he must say that *nothing* shall. Now here there was no interference with the plaintiff's rights except the statement by the defendant that he would prevent the goods from being removed. This is not sufficient to furnish a basis for the present action. For it must be remembered that if the defendant is liable at all, it is for the value of the goods. But how unjust that would be! The plaintiff's man was left in possession. Miss Morley could not legally take away the goods. If she did, the plaintiff could maintain an action against her for their wrongful removal. Yet he is also to be able to recover their full value against the defendant. Moreover, I cannot but think that the jury really negatived all idea of conversion. "If you are of opinion," they were told, "that the defendant did not deprive the plaintiff of his goods, did not take possession of, nor assume dominion over them, but merely prevented the plaintiff from removing them from one place to another, allowing the plaintiff to remain in possession of them if he liked," then there is no cause of action. The jury answered this question in favour of the defendant. There had, therefore, been no general assertion of right to the exclusion of the plaintiff.

Questions
    1. Would the answer have been the same if the defendant had had no claim in respect of the property whose removal he prohibited? Would it be the same if he had not owned the premises on which the goods were situated?
    2. How far was the consideration that the measure of damages in conversion was then the whole value of the goods a factor which led to this result?
    3. What would have happened if, the following morning, the plaintiff's man had stopped the defendant from taking possession of the goods?
    4. Did the plaintiff act unreasonably?

Notes:
    1. This decision makes it clear that, whereas clamping a trespassing car is itself a trespass, locking the gate, which involves no physical touching but equally prevents its exit, is not a conversion of the vehicle.
    2. In *Bird v Jones* (above, p.337) a similar attempt to use a form of strict liability failed, since the proper remedy for a person obstructed on the highway is public nuisance and not false imprisonment. Given that the plaintiff here had suffered financial loss by the improper act of the defendant but could not sue him in conversion, what form of action could he use?

RH WILLIS & SON v BRITISH CAR AUCTIONS

Court of Appeal [1978] 1 W.L.R. 438; [1978] 2 All E.R. 392

Action against auctioneer by owner of property sold without authority

Croucher, a publican, paid the plaintiff motor dealers £350 towards a car priced at £625, and they let him have it on hire-purchase terms, making it clear that he must not sell it before the balance was paid. Croucher nevertheless took the car to the defendant auctioneers and asked them to sell it for at least £450. The highest bid at the auction was only £410. After the auction Croucher was asked in the defendants' office if he would accept the £410, and after the defendants had reduced their commission he did so. Croucher went bankrupt, the purchaser and the car disappeared, and the plaintiffs sued the defendants for conversion.

The plaintiffs obtained judgment for £275 in the county court, and the Court of Appeal dismissed the defendants' appeal.

Lord Denning M.R.: ... The question that arises is the usual one: which of the two innocent persons is to suffer? Is the loss to fall on the motor car dealers? They have been deprived of the £275 due to them on the car. Or on the auctioneer? They sold it believing that Mr Croucher was the true owner. In answering that question in cases such as this, the common law has always acted on the maxim: *nemo dat quod non habet*. It has protected the property rights of the true owner. It has enforced them strictly as against anyone who deals with the goods inconsistently with the dominion of the true owner. Even though the true owner may have been very negligent and the defendant may have acted in complete innocence, nevertheless the common law held him liable in conversion. Both the "innocent acquirer" and the "innocent handler" have been hit hard. That state of the law has often been criticised. It has been proposed that the law should protect a person who buys goods or handles them in good faith without notice of any adverse title, at any rate where the claimant by his own negligence or otherwise has largely contributed to the outcome. Such proposals have however been effectively blocked by the decisions of the House of Lords in the last century of *Hollins v Fowler* (1875) L.R. H.L. 757 and in this century of *Moorgate Mercantile Co Ltd v Twitchings* [1977] A.C. 890, to which I may add the decision of this court in *Central Newbury Car Auctions Ltd v Unity Finance Ltd* [1957] 1 Q.B. 371.

In some instances the strictness of the law has been mitigated by statute, as for instance, by the protection given to private purchasers by the Hire Purchase Acts. But in other cases the only way in which the innocent acquirers or handlers have been able to protect themselves is by insurance. They insure themselves against their potential liability. This is the usual method nowadays. When men of business or professional men find themselves hit by the law with new and increasing liabilities, they take steps to insure themselves, so that the loss may not fall on one alone, but be spread among many. It is a factor of which we must take account: see *Post Office v Norwich Union Fire Insurance Society Ltd* [1967] 2 Q.B. 363 at 375 and *Morris v Ford Motor Co Ltd* [1973] Q.B. 792 at 801.

The position of auctioneers is typical. It is now, I think, well established that if an auctioneer sells goods by knocking down his hammer at an auction and thereafter delivers them to the purchaser—then although he is only an agent—then if the vendor has no title to the goods, both the auctioneer and the purchaser are liable in conversion to the true owner, no matter how innocent the auctioneer may have been in handling the goods or the purchaser in acquiring them: see *Barker v Furlong* [1891] 2 Ch. 172 at 181, *per* Romer J. and *Consolidated Co v Curtis & Son* [1892] 1 Q.B. 495. This state of the law has been considered by the Law Reform Committee in 1966 as to innocent acquirers (Twelfth Report, Transfer of Title to Chattels, Cmnd. 2958); and in 1971 as to innocent handlers (Eighteenth Report, Conversion and Detinue, Cmnd. 4774). But Parliament has made no change in it; no doubt it would have done so in the Torts (Interference with Goods) Act 1977 if it had thought fit to do so.

Such is the position with sales "under the hammer." What about sales which follow a "provisional bid?" I see no difference in principle. In each case the auctioneer is an intermediary who brings the two parties together and gets them to agree on the price. They are bound by the conditions of sale which he has prepared. He retains the goods in his custody. He delivers them to the purchaser on being paid the price. He pays it over to the vendor and deducts his commission. So in principle, I think that on a "provisional bid" an auctioneer is liable in conversion, just as when he sells under the hammer. There are two decisions, however, which suggest a difference. In those two cases it was held that the auctioneer was not liable in conversion, because he had not actually effected the sale. It had been made by the parties themselves. I doubt whether those decisions are correct. Although the auctioneer had not actually effected the sale, his intervention in each case was an efficient cause of the sale and he got his commission for what he did. To my mind those two decisions are a departure from the principles stated by Blackburn J. in *Hollins v Fowler*. That is the principle which should guide us, especially as it was inferentially accepted by the House of Lords. I cannot help thinking that in those two cases the courts were anxious to protect the auctioneer, as an innocent handler, from the strictness of the law. In doing so they introduced fine distinctions which are difficult to apply. I do not think we should follow those two cases today, especially when regard is had to the insurance aspect to which I now turn. It is clear that the auctioneers insure against both kinds of sale equally. On every one of the sales, under the hammer or on provisional bids, the auctioneers charge an "indemnity fee" to the purchaser. He has to pay a premium of £2 on each vehicle purchased. In return for it the auctioneers, British Car Auctions Ltd, through an associate company, the Omega Insurance Co Ltd, insures the purchaser against any loss he may suffer through any defect in title of the seller. So if the true owner comes along and retakes the goods from the purchaser or makes him pay damages for conversion, the auctioneers (through their associate company) indemnify the purchaser against the loss. The premium thus charged by the auctioneers (through their associate company) is calculated to cover the risk of the seller having no title or a defective title. That risk is the same no matter whether the true owner sues the auctioneer or the purchaser. The auctioneer collects £2 from every purchaser to cover that risk. We are told it comes to £200,000 a year. Seeing that they receive these sums, they ought to meet the claims of the true owners out of it. This system is the commercial way of doing justice between the parties. It means that all concerned are protected. The true owner is protected by the strict law of conversion. He can recover against the innocent acquirer and the innocent handler. But those innocents are covered by insurance so that the loss is not borne by any single individual but is spread through the community at large. The insurance factor had a considerable influence on the Law Reform Committee. In view of it they did not recommend any change in the law. So also it may properly have an influence on the courts in deciding issues which come before them.

My conclusion is that, where goods are sold by the intervention of an auctioneer, under the hammer or as a result of a provisional bid, then if the seller has no title, the auctioneer is liable in conversion to the true owner. I would dismiss the appeal accordingly.

Note:

This case shows that when goods are sold without the owner's consent, the seller commits a tort. The buyer usually commits a tort as well. It is common to describe the buyer's position in terms of the law of property—"the buyer acquires no better title to the goods than the seller had" (Sale of Goods Act 1979, s.21); this is precisely equivalent to saying that the buyer is just as liable as the seller. In certain situations, however, an exception is made and the buyer does get a better title than the seller; in other words, the buyer is sometimes not liable although the seller had no authority to sell. For example, although one is normally liable to the finance company if one buys goods, however innocently, from a person who has taken them on hire-purchase terms, an exception is made if the chattel in question is a motor vehicle and the buyer is not a dealer (Hire Purchase Act 1964, s.27). The rules are too complicated to go into here, but they may be found in the Twelfth Report of the Law Reform Committee (Cmnd. 2958 (1966)). The Committee's principal recommendation, still unimplemented, was that people in good faith should not be liable for buying goods in a shop or at a public auction.

This would go some way (though by a different route) towards the position in modern civilian systems. Both France and Germany have abandoned the Roman rule *nemo dat quod non habet* (s.21 of the Sale of Goods Act 1979) and have provided that a buyer in good faith can acquire property from a non-owner (Code civil, Art.2279: "*En fait de meubles, possession vaut titre*"; BGB § 932). Both systems make special provision for the case of lost or stolen goods: in other words, the person who has trusted another with his property cannot get it back from a third party who buys it in good faith from the—dare one say it?—trustee. And this is the position in that green and leafy branch of English law called "equity." Conversion, however, is the wrong end of that dry old stick, the common law, and *nemo dat quod non habet* still has sway, subject to various statutory exceptions. The *MCC Proceeds* case (above, p.489) shows the categorical conflict between the common law principle of *nemo dat* and the equitable principle of protecting the good faith purchaser, a conflict resolved in favour of the latter.

2. In *Marcq v Christie's* [2003] EWCA Civ 731, [2003] 3 All E.R. 561 a pretty Dutch painting by Jan Steen, *The Backgammon Players*, which had been stolen from the claimant, was delivered by X to the defendant for the purposes of sale by auction. At auction it remained unsold and the defendant redelivered it to X, having no reason to believe that he was not the true owner. The claim was dismissed. As Tuckey L.J. said: "the authorities indicate that an auctioneer who receives goods from their apparent owner and simply redelivers them to him when they are unsold is not liable in conversion provided he has acted in good faith and without knowledge of any adverse claim to them. The auctioneer intends to sell and if he does so will incur liability if he delivers the goods to the buyer. But his intention does not make him liable; it is what he does in relation to the goods which determines liability. Mere receipt of the goods does not amount to conversion. In receiving the goods from and redelivering them to their apparent owner the auctioneer in such a case has only acted ministerially. He has in the event merely changed the position of the goods and not the property in them."

3. In *Hiort v Bott* (above, p.495) all the defendant did was to handle a document, but he was held liable for the conversion of the barley to which it related. Unidentified money cannot be converted, but one may be liable for converting a document which relates to money (for a superb off-the-cuff exposé see Diplock L.J. in *Marfani & Co v Midland Bank* [1968] 1 W.L.R. 956 at 970–973). The Law Reform Committee considered the question and said: "It is true that a claim against a banker for conversion of a cheque has a somewhat

artificial air, because what the true owner is in substance complaining about is that the bank has diverted his money, and if it were theoretically possible the obvious claim would be for the conversion of the money. But . . . We are satisfied that the present application of the law of conversion to such instruments is sound in principle and is not merely a legal fiction." (Eighteenth Report (Cmnd. 4774), para.98).

Sound in principle it may be, but it would be impossible in practice if bankers, who spend all their time paying out on cheques (*i.e.* buying them) and collecting on them (*i.e.* selling them), were vulnerable to a conversion claim every time they accepted a cheque from a person not entitled to it. Bankers therefore have protection of two kinds. First, cheques are negotiable instruments, and unless their negotiability has been impaired in some way, the acquiring bank can often obtain a better title than the person presenting it. Secondly, bankers now have statutory protection in most cases if they can prove that they acted normally and without negligence (Bills of Exchange Act 1882, ss.60, 80; Cheques Act 1957, s.4).

In modern times the value of property may be greatly enhanced if its owner obtains permission to use it in certain ways (licences, planning permissions, etc.). It is sometimes possible for a person to appropriate such a benefit to himself without handling the property to which it relates or even any document vested in the other party. In such a case there should be liability if the conduct is improper, but conversion is not the right tort since in conversion claims guilty knowledge is not a prerequisite. *Douglas Valley Finance Co v Hughes* [1969] 1 Q.B. 738 is an interesting case in this connection.

TORTS (INTERFERENCE WITH GOODS) ACT 1977

2.—(1) Detinue is abolished.

(2) An action lies in conversion for loss or destruction of goods which a bailee has allowed to happen in breach of his duty to his bailor (that is to say it lies in a case which is not otherwise conversion, but would have been detinue before detinue was abolished).

CAPITAL FINANCE COMPANY LTD v BRAY

Court of Appeal [1964] 1 W.L.R. 323; 108 S.J. 95; [1964] 1 All E.R. 603

Action against hire-purchaser for failure to return goods temporarily and wrongfully repossessed by finance company

The plaintiff let a car on hire-purchase terms to the defendant, and when the defendant defaulted on his payments, repossessed the car in the middle of the night. The defendant immediately informed them, correctly, that they had no right to repossess the car without a court order, since he had paid more than one-third of the purchase price, and threatened to bring an action to recover all that he had paid. The plaintiffs returned the car, and the defendant used it without paying. Nine months later, on March 1, 1963, the plaintiffs demanded the return of the car to one of three addresses within 10 days, and payment of the outstanding instalments of £89. The defendant did nothing. On April 11 the company claimed the return of the car on the basis of the original contract. The defendant answered that the contract was terminated by the illegal repossession of the car, and counter-claimed for the £113 he had paid. The plaintiff added a claim in detinue and damages for detention up to the time of the hearing.

The county court judge gave judgment for the plaintiff on the ground of the defendant's failure to return the car as demanded, and gave damages from the date of that failure up to the date on which the plaintiff initiated proceedings. The defendant appealed, and the Court of Appeal allowed his appeal; the defendant had judgment on the counterclaim.

Lord Denning M.R.: Now comes the point in the case. What was the position after March 1, 1963? Was there a wrongful detention of the car by Bray so as to give rise to a claim in detinue? The judge held that there was. The key sentence in his judgment in this: "When, however, in response to the plaintiffs' solicitor's letter of March 1, 1963, he failed to deliver the car on March 11, as demanded, then it seems to me a claim arose in detinue." While I agree with much of the judgment, I cannot agree with this. This claim in detinue was only raised at the last moment and I do not think the judge had the benefit of the authorities as we have had. In my judgment the letter of March 1 was not a sufficient demand to found a claim in detinue. It was a demand to deliver up in accordance with the hire-purchase agreement. It demanded delivery up by Bray at his own expense to one of three named places, Edinburgh, Waterloo Place in London, or Stone Buildings, Lincoln's Inn. But once the hire-purchase agreement was determined and not reinstated, Bray was under no obligation to take the goods to the finance company. He could leave the goods at his house until the owner came to collect them. He would not be guilty of any unlawful detention unless, when the owner came to collect them, he prevented him taking possession of them. It is rather like the case which was put in argument. Suppose a trader leaves some article on my premises—it may be a photograph or even a grand piano—hoping I will buy it. If I am unwilling to buy it, he cannot demand that I post the picture back to him or that I load the grand piano on a haulage contractor's van and take it back to him. I can leave it where it is. Or I can put it out of my way, if I like, without being guilty of any wrongdoing at all. If he comes to collect it, I must let him have it: but that is all. There is no obligation on a person who has another person's goods to return them to him, except by contract. The rule is accurately stated in *Salmond on Torts*, (13th ed.), p.264: "No one is bound, save by contract, to take a chattel to the owner of it. His only obligation is not to prevent the owner from getting it when he comes for it." That has been the law ever since the case to which we were referred of *Clements v Flight* ((1846) 153 E.R. 1090). The judgment of the court makes it quite clear that, in order that there should be a wrongful detention of goods, the defendant must withhold the goods and prevent the plaintiff from having possession of them. He is not bound to be active and send the goods back unless there is an obligation by contract to do so. It seems to me, therefore, that this demand of March 1, 1963, was not a good demand such as to found a claim in detinue. It did not merely demand delivery up. It demanded that the hirer should take the car back to one of these three addresses. He was under no obligation to do so.

The only way in which a claim in detinue might be made here was the way Mr Shaw put it. He said that if a man uses a car in defiance of the owner's rights, that may give a claim in detinue. I agree. It may. No doubt after receiving the letter of March 1, 1963, Bray had no right to use the car. The owners had withdrawn their consent to it. And if he did use it after March 1, 1963, there might be a claim to detinue. But what evidence of that is there here? There is no evidence of any use by Bray after March 1, 1963. It was argued that the judge inferred use from that time: but I am not all sure that he did. In any event if he did, there was no evidence of it: and I do not think it should be inferred. So there is no claim on that score.

This means that in my judgment the cross appeal should be allowed and the claim of the finance company should be dismissed. Bray is entitled to the £113 on his counterclaim.

Questions

1. Debts are payable at the domicile of the creditor. Why is there a different rule where the object of a debt is a chattel?

2. Suppose that, after March 1, the car had been stolen from Bray's garage, the door of which he had failed to lock. Would he be liable? Suppose that it is not clear whether Bray was careless or not. Would he have to prove that he was not, or must the plaintiffs prove that he was?

3. Lord Denning said elsewhere in his judgment that Bray was not liable to pay for the use of the car between the time it was returned to him and the time it was demanded back from him. Can this be right?

4. Lord Denning said that Bray might have been liable in detinue if he had used the car after March 1. Would he be liable now that detinue has been abolished? If so, under what head of liability?

5. *Wincanton v P & O TransEuropean* [2001] EWCA 227 also raised the question of the interface of bailment and contract. It involved 2,847 pallets and the claim was for over £35,000. The defendant was a carrier who uplifted from the claimant's warehouse goods belonging to X, there being a contract of carriage between the defendant and X and a contract of storage between the claimant and X, but no contract of any kind between the claimant and the defendant. The uplifted goods were stacked on pallets which the claimant hired from Y, the pallets not being identifiable otherwise than as belonging to Y. The defendant delivered the pallets with the goods on them to X's customers, but never returned any pallets to the claimant, who now alleged that the defendant was a bailee of the pallets and therefore under a duty to return them or their equivalent. It was held by the Court of Appeal, reversing the trial judge, that the (sub)bailment to the defendant came to an end when the defendant delivered the goods on the pallets to X's customers, and that

it was consequently under no further duty as regards the pallets. The claimant was seeking "to impose on the defendant a duty which could only have been imposed by contract." (at [24]).

HOUGHLAND v R R LOW (LUXURY COACHES) LTD

Court of Appeal [1962] 1 Q.B. 694; [1962] 2 W.L.R. 1015; 106 S.J. 243; [1962] 2 All E.R. 159
(noted (1963) 79 L.Q.R. 19)

Action for loss of luggage on charabanc outing

The plaintiff and her husband were old age pensioners who went on a trip to Jersey organised by the Good Companions Club. Back in Southampton, the party boarded one of the defendant's coaches to return to Hoylake, Cheshire, and the plaintiff's suitcase was put in the boot along with the others. After a tea-stop at Ternhill, Shropshire, the coach would not start again. Three hours later the relief coach arrived and the luggage was transferred, the passengers unloading it without supervision and the defendant's driver packing it expertly in the boot. At Hoylake the plaintiff's suitcase could not be found.

The plaintiff claimed "delivery up of the said suitcase and the contents thereof or £82 10s. their value." Alternatively she claimed damages in a similar amount on the grounds of negligence. The county court judge found that it was probably at Ternhill that the suitcase was either taken or lost, and gave judgment for the plaintiff. The defendant appealed, and the Court of Appeal dismissed the appeal in unreserved judgments.

Ormerod L.J.: The objection made to the judgment, as I understand it, is that, as this was a gratuitous bailment, the high degree of negligence required, otherwise called gross negligence in some of the cases, has not been established; that the judge made no finding of negligence, and that, in the circumstances, the judgment should not stand. I am bound to say that I am not sure what is meant by the term "gross negligence" which has been in use for a long time in cases of this kind. There is no doubt, of course, that it is a phrase which has been commonly used in cases of this sort since the time of *Coggs v Bernard*, when the distinction was made in a judgment of Lord Holt C.J. ((1703) 92 E.R. 107), which has been frequently referred to and cited; but as we know from the judgment of Lord Chelmsford in *Giblin v McMullen* ((1869) L.R. 2 P.C. 317 at 336), that it was said, after referring to the use of the term "gross negligence" over a long period: "At last, Lord Cranworth (then Baron Rolfe) in the case of *Wilson v Brett* ((1843) 152 E.R. 757) objected to it, saying that he "could see no difference between negligence and gross negligence; that it was the same thing, with the addition of a vituperative epithet." And this critical observation has been since approved of by other eminent judges."

For my part, I have always found some difficulty in understanding just what was "gross negligence," because it appears to me that the standard of care required in a case of bailment, or any other type of case, is the standard demanded by the circumstances of that particular case. It seems to me that to try and put a bailment, for instance, into a watertight compartment—such as gratuitous bailment on the one hand, and bailment for reward on the other—is to overlook the fact that there might well be an infinite variety of cases, which might come into one or the other category. The question that we have to consider in a case of this kind, if it is necessary to consider negligence, is whether in the circumstances of this particular case a sufficient standard of care has been observed by the defendants or their servants.

Supposing that the claim is one in detinue, then it would appear that once the bailment has been established, and once the failure of the bailee to hand over the articles in question has been proved, there is a prima facie case, and the plaintiff is entitled to recover, unless the defendant can establish to the satisfaction of the court a defence; and that, I think, is very clear from the words used by Bankes L.J. in *Coldman v Hill* ([1919] 1 K.B. 443 at 449) in a passage that appears to me to be important in this case: "I think the law still is that if a bailee is sued in detinue only, it is a good answer for him to say that the goods were stolen without any default on his part, as the general bailment laid in the declaration pledges the plaintiff to the proof of nothing except that the goods were in the defendant's hands and were wrongfully detained." So far, so good, but it is, of course, in those circumstances for the defendants to establish affirmatively, not only that the goods were stolen, but that they were stolen without default on their part; in other words, that there was no negligence on their part in the care which they took of the goods.

Willmer L.J.: . . . The burden was on the defendants to adduce evidence in rebuttal. They could discharge that burden by proving what in fact did happen to the suitcase, and by showing that what did happen happened without any default on their part. They certainly did not succeed in doing that, for the judge was left in the position that he simply did not know what did happen to the suitcase.

Alternatively, the defendants could discharge the burden upon them by showing that, although they could not put their finger on what actually did happen to the suitcase, nevertheless, whatever did occur occurred notwithstanding all reasonable care having been exercised by them throughout the whole of the journey. Clearly the judge was not satisfied that they had proved the exercise of any such degree of care throughout the whole of the journey . . .

Notes:

1. There is no harm in saying that a bailee of whatever nature must take reasonable care in all the circumstances, provided that it is remembered that the relevant circumstances include not only the circumstances surrounding the *loss* but also those surrounding the *bailment*. The inception of a voluntary relationship controls its consequences. If that is forgotten, dire things will happen, because there is a real difference between the person who does a favour—like looking after your cat while you are away—and the person performing a service by way of trade. The Civil Codes insist that a gratuitous depositee is liable only for gross negligence (French Civil Code, Art.1927: German Civil Code, § 690). But the distinction between gratuitous and remunerated bailments is not really the right one, since a businessman may not make a separate charge for a particular service. In *Coughlin v Gillison* [1899] 1 Q.B. 145 at 149, Collins L.J. suggested that liability might be higher in bailments of mutual benefit, but in *Andrews v Home Flats* [1946] 2 All E.R. 698, Scott L.J. preferred to ask whether the transaction was a "business arrangement." That seems a very good test, and brings it into line with *Hedley Byrne*, above, p.57.

2. The duty of the bailee to look after the goods does not depend on the existence of a contract with the owner (*Gilchrist Watt & Sanderson Pty v York Products Pty* [1970] 1 W.L.R. 1262, PC; *Morris v Martin* (above, p.293)), but a contract very commonly does exist, and it may contain an exemption or limitation clause which purports to protect the bailee. Such a clause, if reasonable, is not invalidated by the Unfair Contract Terms Act 1977 (above, p.254). In the case of an authorised sub-bailment, there may be a difference between the terms of the bailment and sub-bailment respectively. The question then is whether the sub-bailee who knew that they were not the bailee's goods may rely on the terms on which he accepted the goods or only on such terms as the bailor can be taken to have assented to. The Privy Council has now opted for the latter solution: *The Pioneer Container* [1994] 2 All E.R. 250.

That case involved the question whether a sub-bailee could rely on the terms under which he accepted the goods from the bailee or only such terms as the bailor had "authorised" the bailee to agree to. Having held (rather unsatisfactorily) that the latter was the correct analysis (as in *Morris v Martin*, above p.293) Lord Goff said that the sub-bailee must be aware that the goods were the property of someone other than the bailee. This observation has been taken too extensively. In *Marcq* Tuckey L.J. said that it was "obvious . . . that if you are to owe duties to someone else you should know or at least have some means of knowing of his existence" ([2003] 3 All E.R. at 575). Now it may well be true that if you accept goods from X believing him to be the owner you do not owe Y, the unsuspected true owner, the duty of a *bailee*, that is a duty to protect the thing from *loss*, but you certainly owe him a duty to take care not to *damage* the goods by carelessness, and if you positively convert it (as the defendant in *Marcq* did not) you will be liable to whoever emerges from the woodwork and shows that he had an immediate right to possession of the thing. It is true that the Torts (Interference with Goods) Act 1977 treats it as a conversion (rather than detinue, just abolished) if a bailee allows goods to be lost in breach of his duty to *his* bailor [emphasis supplied]; so perhaps, for conversion purposes, the duty not to allow goods to be lost cannot be owed to a third party.

3. That a duty of care may be owed by a bailee to an unsuspected third party was the decision in *Awad v Pillai* [1982] R.T.R. 266, where the claimant had bailed his car to X to have it repaired. X lent it to the defendant, saying that it belonged to him and was fully insured. The defendant damaged the car by careless driving. The Court of Appeal held that the defendant owed the owner of the car, unknown though he was, a duty to take care not to damage it and was liable for breach of that duty.

4. *AVX v EGM Solders* (*The Times*, July 7, 1982) involved the question whether you could be liable for damaging goods which you believed to be your own. The defendants were expecting to receive from the plaintiffs a single package of tiny solder spheres which were being returned to them as sub-standard goods and which the defendants were naturally going to scrap on arrival. However, at the same time as the plaintiffs handed that package to carriers for delivery to the defendants, they also handed them 21 other packages addressed to their own depot, containing brand new capacitors for sale to customers. By error the carriers delivered all 22 packages to the defendants with a delivery note indicating that the defendants were the consignees of the whole consignment. The defendant's storeman asked his boss what to do with the goods on arrival from the plaintiffs and was told the scrap them. Scrapped they were, or at any rate inextricably intermingled and commercially destroyed, to the tune of $100,000 and more.

Staughton J. treated this as a case of "unconscious bailment" and held the defendant liable. As Tuckey L.J. pointed out in *Marcq* there was no need to speak of bailment at all. "A person who destroys goods which are self-evidently not his in the mistaken belief that they are must be liable [in negligence]". The difficulty in the case is the finding that the defendants were negligent at all, for the goods were certainly not "self-evidently" not the defendant's. Furthermore, your view of the merits of Staughton J.'s decision may be affected by the considerations (i) that the claimants at interest were not the owners of the goods but their insurers, and (ii) that the carriers, whose entire fault it was, had a limitation clause in their contract with the claimants. Consider *The Nicholas H* (above p.45).

5. Normally the bailee has the burden of proving that he was not negligent. What the effect of an exemption clause on the burden of proof may be is not clear now that the substantive doctrine of fundamental breach has gone (*Photo Production v Securicor* [1980] A.C. 827).

6. In *Lervold v Chief Constable of Kent* [1994] C.L.Y.B. §3385 the plaintiff drifted ashore in his boat, and was lawfully arrested by the police. During his detention his boat was looted by humans and damaged by natural forces. He sued the police for failure to look after his property, and their attempts to have the claim struck out failed at all three instances. What was the source of the duty of the police?

SORRELL v PAGET

Court of Appeal [1950] 1 K.B. 252; 65 T.L.R. 595; 93 S.J. 631; [1949] 2 All E.R. 609

Liability of finder for death of cow in his keeping

The plaintiff and defendant had adjoining farms alongside the main London to Dover railway line. The plaintiff's heifer kept straying. One morning the defendant found it on the railway line, drove it off, and delivered it, with a protest, to the plaintiff's servants. That very evening at dusk the defendant saw it on the railway line again, telephoned the station and had the *Golden Arrow* stopped. He drove the heifer into his own stubble field, where it went to sleep. During the night or early morning the beast left that field, went along the highway, and entered a field where the defendant kept his T.T. herd. The defendant removed it, put it in a barn and fed it on hay and water. He did not inform the plaintiff. Four days later the plaintiff discovered its whereabouts and sent two men to fetch it. The defendant demanded £2 salvage and one shilling per day for keep. No money was offered to him, so he kept the heifer. Three days later the heifer died, having been driven mad, according to the plaintiff, by the defendant's negligence.

The county court judge held that the taking possession of the heifer was not wrongful, that the refusal to deliver up was not wrongful, and that the plaintiff had failed to prove negligence; he accordingly gave judgment for the defendant. The plaintiff appealed to the Court of Appeal, and his appeal was dismissed in unreserved judgments.

Bucknill L.J.: The first question that arises is: Did the defendant commit any wrong to the plaintiff when he took possession of the plaintiff's heifer? In my opinion he did not. It was getting dark at the time and the defendant, rightly, in my opinion, in the interests of the plaintiff and his heifer and of the common safety of the public using the railway, drove the heifer again for the second time that day off the railway and, on this occasion, into one of his own fields, which the county court judge has described as a place of "comparative safety." Unfortunately, that night the heifer escaped from that field on to a highway and thence strayed into another field of the defendant where was his T.T. herd. The defendant saw the heifer there in the morning to his dismay, because he was anxious to keep his herd free from all possible infection. The defendant then impounded the heifer in his barn. I think that the second question in the case is: Was he entitled to do so? In my opinion he was. He fed the heifer with baled hay and gave it water. Since, apparently, the plaintiff and the defendant were not on good terms, the defendant did not communicate with the plaintiff and tell him that the heifer was in his barn.

The third question is whether, when the plaintiff ascertained that his heifer was in the defendant's barn and sent his men to fetch her, the defendant was wrong in refusing to hand over the heifer. The county court judge has dealt with that point in his judgment where he said: "No actual money was offered to the defendant for the keep or damage. He told the men to go and get the whole of the money, keep and compensation. It was open to the men to do one of two things: hand the defendant three shillings"—I think he must mean 1s. a day—"for keep, or go away and return, and tender the keep money. It had been argued that they should be excused because they were told to go and get the money. There was never in this case any kind of offer to pay any sum at all, and therefore no legal tender." I think that the learned judge's view there was right.

During the course of the case a discussion took place as to the use of the word "salvage." There is no doubt that, strictly speaking, salvage on land is not a recognised head of claim in the common law as it is by maritime law, at sea. I need only refer to the judgment of Bowen L.J. in *Falcke v Scottish Imperial Insurance Co* ((1886) 34 Ch.D. 234 at 248) to show what is the position. He said: "The general principle is, beyond all question, that work and labour done or money expended by one man to preserve or benefit the property of another do not according to English law create any lien upon the property saved or benefited, nor, even if standing alone, create any obligation to repay the expenditure. Liabilities are not to be forced upon people behind their backs any more than you can confer a benefit upon a man against his will." Then he goes on to deal with maritime salvage. Unfortunately, in this case, although it is admitted that the defendant did ask for salvage, there is nothing in the judge's notes to show that he was asked what he meant by salvage. There is no evidence to show that he made any claim for damage apart from salvage, and I think he clearly would be entitled to damage if he could prove it; damage, for instance, done by the heifer in getting into this field and grazing, and possible damage to the herd. But, assuming that the defendant was putting forward a claim, which included a claim for salvage proper, and that such a claim was not recognisable by law, I think that the cases do establish that it was the duty of the plaintiff to make a tender in respect of any damage done by the animal. He never did make a tender, and until the tender was made the defendant was justified in keeping the heifer in the barn.

The only other point is whether the defendant was negligent in keeping the heifer in that barn for a week before it died. If she was lawfully there, it was for the plaintiff to prove that the defendant was negligent, and that the death of the animal was the result of that negligence. That is a question of fact. It was a question which, I suspect, was argued with great vigour before the judge, and he has come to the conclusion, as he says in his judgment, that "the plaintiff has not got anywhere near proving that the animal died as a result of the defendant's fault. I am satisfied that the barn was a large, well-ventilated one and a suitable place to impound the animal." He was satisfied that she had been properly attended to all the time she was alive. So the plaintiff failed on this issue. For these reasons, in my judgment, this appeal should be dismissed.

Questions

1. What is the principal difference between this case and the last case?

2. Why was it not a trespass for the defendant to remove the plaintiff's heifer from the railway line? Would it have been a trespass if the defendant had left the heifer on the highway instead of putting it in his field?

3. Why did the defendant not have the burden of disproving negligence?

4. Suppose that a car is left parked on my property where I have erected a notice saying "No Parking." May I put the car on the highway? If so, is that the result of the principal case? Suppose, in putting it there, I damage the car. Must I disprove negligence? Suppose I put it in a safe position on the highway and a motorist carelessly drives into it? Suppose I put it in a place where parking is prohibited and it is lawfully

removed by the authorities and the owner is charged £150 for release? (For the common law as to clamping trespassory cars, see *Arthur v Anker* (above, p.405).)

Notes:

1. The commonest ground of lien (that is, the right to detain a chattel until a money claim is paid) arises from the repair of chattels. Here the defendant had no such lien, because he did not improve the cow; he only fed it (*Re Southern Livestock Producers* [1964] 1 W.L.R. 24). For the circumstances in which the repairer's lien can be asserted against the owner of the chattel when the chattel was received from someone else, see *Tappenden v Artus* [1964] 2 Q.B. 185. Only an innkeeper has a lien over stolen goods (*Marsh v Commissioner of Police* [1944] W.N. 204, where the inn was The Ritz Hotel).

2. Changes in the law relating to the seizure and detention of stray livestock are contained in the Animals Act 1971, s.7. It appears to apply only if the stray animal is taken on land occupied by the person seizing it, and therefore it would not apply on the facts of the principal case. Under the Act, the person detaining the livestock is bound to inform the police and the owner, if known, within 48 hours, to treat the beast properly (there is no mention of burden of proof) and to return it on payment of a sum sufficient to satisfy any claim under s.4 of the Act for damage done by the beast. A power of sale after 14 days is given.

Section 3.—The Remedies

TORTS (INTERFERENCE WITH GOODS) ACT 1977

1. In this Act "wrongful interference," or "wrongful interference with goods," means—

    (a) conversion of goods (also called trover),
    (b) trespass to goods,
    (c) negligence so far as it results in damage to goods or to an interest in goods,
    (d) subject to section 2, any other tort so far as it results in damage to goods or to an interest in goods.

. . .

3.—(1) In proceedings for wrongful interference against a person who is in possession or in control of the goods relief may be given in accordance with this section, so far as appropriate.

    (2) The relief is—

    (a) an order for delivery of goods, and for payment of any consequential damages, or
    (b) an order for delivery of the goods, but giving the defendant the alternative of paying damages by reference to the value of the goods, together in either alternative with payment of any consequential damages, or
    (c) damages.

    (3) Subject to rules of court—

    (a) relief shall be given under only one of paragraphs (a), (b) and (c) of subsection (2),
    (b) relief under paragraph (a) of subsection (2) is at the discretion of the court, and the claimant may choose between the others.

    (4) If it is shown to the satisfaction of the court that an order under subsection (2)(a) has not been complied with, the court may—

    (a) revoke the order, or the relevant part of it, and

(b) make an order for payment of damages by reference to the value of the goods.

(5) Where an order is made under subsection (2)(b) the defendant may satisfy the order by returning the goods at any time before execution of judgment, but without prejudice to liability to pay any consequential damages.

(6) An order for delivery of the goods under subsection (2)(a) or (b) may impose such conditions as may be determined by the court, or pursuant to rules of court, and in particular, where damages by reference to the value of the goods would not be the whole of the value of the goods, may require an allowance to be made by the claimant to reflect the difference.

For example, a bailor's action against the bailee may be one in which the measure of damages is not the full value of the goods, and then the court may order delivery of the goods, but require the bailor to pay the bailee a sum reflecting the difference.

. . .

7.—(1) In this section "double liability" means the double liability of the wrongdoer which can arise—

(a) where one of two or more rights of action for wrongful interference is founded on a possessory title, or
(b) where the measure of damages in an action for wrongful interference founded on a proprietary title is or includes the entire value of the goods, although the interest is one of two or more interests in the goods.

(2) In proceedings to which any two or more claimants are parties, the relief shall be such as to avoid double liability of the wrongdoer as between those claimants.

(3) On satisfaction, in whole or in part, of any claim for an amount exceeding that recoverable if subsection (2) applied, the claimant is liable to account over to the other person having a right to claim to such extent as will avoid double liability.

(4) Where, as the result of enforcement of a double liability, any claimant is unjustly enriched to any extent, he shall be liable to reimburse the wrongdoer to that extent.

For example, if a converter of goods pays damages first to a finder of the goods, and then to the true owner, the finder is unjustly enriched unless he accounts over to the true owner under subsection (3); and then the true owner is unjustly enriched and becomes liable to reimburse the converter of the goods.

8.—(1) The defendant in an action for wrongful interference shall be entitled to show, in accordance with rules of court, that a third party has a better right than the plaintiff as respects all or any part of the interest claimed by the plaintiff, or in right of which he sues, and any rule of law (sometimes called jus tertii) to the contrary is abolished.

(2) Rules of court relating to proceedings for wrongful interference may—

(a) require the plaintiff to give particulars of his title,
(b) require the plaintiff to identify any person who, to his knowledge, has or claims any interest in the goods,
(c) authorise the defendant to apply for directions as to whether any person should be joined with a view to establishing whether he has a better right than the plaintiff, or has a claim as a result of which the defendant might be doubly liable,
(d) where a party fails to appear on an application within paragraph (c), or to comply with any direction given by the court on such an application, authorise the court to deprive him of any right of action against the defendant for the wrong either unconditionally, or subject to such terms or conditions as may be specified.

(3) Subsection (2) is without prejudice to any other power of making rules of court.

. . .

11.—(1) Contributory negligence is no defence in proceedings founded on conversion or on intentional trespass to goods.

. . .

Notes:

1. Section 7 will rarely be invoked, for where the concurrent interests are those of bailor and bailee, settlement with either bars the claim of the other: *O'Sullivan v Williams* [1992] 3 All E.R. 385, CA.

2. A situation which is economically analogous, though different in legal analysis, arises every time an insured motor car is damaged by negligence. Both the owner's insurer and the owner himself have an interest in the claim against the negligent party (or his insurer), the former for the insured loss and the latter for the uninsured loss (the "excess" under the policy). Here again there is a double interest, though only one claim. If the negligent party or his insurer settles with the owner for the uninsured loss or has judgment entered against him, is the claim for the insured loss by the owner's subrogated insurer barred on the ground that the claim has been finally litigated or compromised? The courts have shown themselves quite accommodating to the subrogated insurer in such cases. See *Buckland v Palmer* [1984] 3 All E.R. 554, CA.

3. Section 11(1) is a very silly piece of legislation. It has already had to be disapplied in suits against a banker where he is by statute liable only on proof of negligence (Banking Act 1979, s.47; and see above, p. 249).

But worse, it bars judicial reversal of the very bad common law rule that a person who carelessly facilitates the theft of his goods can nevertheless sue a third party bona fide purchaser. An owner of goods may sometimes be estopped from denying that the person from whom the defendant purchased the goods was authorised to sell them, but carelessness does not ground such an estoppel unless the plaintiff owed the defendant a duty to be careful, which is hardly ever the case, except in cases of representation, as the defendant is usually a stranger and the harm in issue financial only.

Thus in *Moorgate Mercantile Co v Twitchings* [1977] A.C. 890 the defendants bought a car which was offered to them for sale; before buying it they had checked with H.P. Information but had drawn a blank because the plaintiffs had carelessly failed to register the fact that the car was theirs and that it was the subject of a hire-purchase transaction. All their Lordships agreed that if the plaintiffs had owed the defendants a duty to take care to register their interest (which a bare majority denied), then the action in conversion must fail. But if a third member of the House had held that the plaintiffs owed the defendants a duty to take care, and the plaintiffs had accordingly lost their suit, would this not be an instance of "contributory negligence" now barred by the Act?

4. The Act states in s.3(2)(b) that damages are to be "by reference to the value of the goods." It does not say on what date the goods are to be valued, yet this is important because goods depreciate and appreciate even if their physical condition remains constant, as often it does not. The previous alternatives were the date of the wrongful act and the date of judgment. Now, astonishingly, the Court of Appeal has held that such date must be chosen as will produce a figure which represents the plaintiff's actual loss (*IBL Ltd v Coussens* [1991] 2 All E.R. 133). This is to ignore the distinctive proprietary nature of the tort as well as the words of the Act, bearing in mind the legislator's refusal to adopt the proposal of the Law Reform Committee that the measure of recovery be the plaintiff's loss.

THE WINKFIELD

Court of Appeal [1902] P. 42; 71 L.J.P. 21; 85 L.T. 668; 50 W.R. 246; 18 T.L.R. 176; 46 S.J. 163;
9 Asp.M.L.C. 259; [1900–3] All E.R. Rep. 346

Claim by bailee for negligent destruction of bailed goods

The *Winkfield* negligently collided with the *Mexican*, which was carrying mails to South Africa. The Postmaster-General claimed the full value of the mails lost, although he was under no liability to their owners.

His claim was successful on appeal.

Collins M.R.: . . . I am of opinion that . . . the law is that in an action against a stranger for loss of goods caused by his negligence, the bailee in possession can recover the value of the goods, although he would have had a good answer to an action by the bailor for damages for the loss of the thing bailed.

It seems to me that the position, that possession is good against a wrongdoer and that the latter cannot set up the *jus tertii* unless he claims under it, is well established in our law, and really concludes this case against the respondents. As I shall show presently, a long series of authorities establishes this in actions of trover and trespass at the suit of a possessor. And the principle being the same, it follows that he can equally recover the whole value of the goods in an action on the case for their loss through the tortious conduct of the defendant. I think it involves this also, that the wrongdoer who is not defending under the title of the bailor is quite unconcerned with what the rights are between the bailor and bailee, and must treat the possessor as the owner of the goods for all purposes quite irrespective of the rights and obligations as between him and the bailor.

I think this position is well established in our law, though it may be that reasons for its existence have been given in some of the cases which are not quite satisfactory. I think also that the obligation of the bailee to the bailor to account for what he has received in respect of the destruction or conversion of the thing bailed has been admitted so often in decided cases that it cannot now be questioned; and, further, I think it can be shown that the right of the bailee to recover cannot be rested on the grounds suggested in some of the cases, namely, that he was liable over to the bailor for the loss of the goods converted or destroyed. It cannot be denied that since the case of *Armory v Delamirie* ((1722) 93 E.R. 664), not to mention earlier cases from the Year Books onward, a mere finder may recover against a wrongdoer the full value of the thing converted. That decision involves the principle that as between possessor and wrongdoer the presumption of law is, in the words of Lord Campbell in *Jeffries v Great Western Ry* ((1856) 119 E.R. 680), "that the person who has possession has the property." In the same case he says: "I am of opinion that the law is that a person possessed of goods as his property has a good title as against every stranger, and that one who takes them from him, having no title in himself, is a wrongdoer, and cannot defend himself by showing that there was title in some third person, for *against a wrongdoer possession is title*. The law is so stated by the very learned annotator in his note to *Wilbraham v Snow*" ((1670) 85 E.R. 624). Therefore it is not open to the defendant, being a wrongdoer, to inquire into the nature or limitation of the possessor's right, and unless it is competent for him to do so the question of his relation to, or liability towards, the true owner cannot come into the discussion at all; and, therefore, as between those two parties full damages have to be paid without any further inquiry. The extent of the liability of the finder to the true owner not being relevant to the discussion between him and the wrongdoer, the facts which would ascertain it would not have been admissible in evidence, and therefore the right of the finder to recover full damages cannot be made to depend upon the extent of his liability over to the true owner. To hold otherwise would, it seems to me, be in effect to permit a wrongdoer to set up a *jus tertii* under which he cannot claim. But, if this be the fact in the case of a finder, why should it not be equally the fact in the case of a bailee? Why, as against a wrongdoer, should the nature of the plaintiff's interest in the thing converted be any more relevant to the inquiry, and therefore admissible in evidence, than in the case of a finder? It seems to me that neither in one case nor the other ought it to be competent for the defendant to go into evidence on that matter. . . .

Question
This rule was confirmed by the Privy Council on an appeal from Singapore in *The Jag Shakti* [1986] 1 All E.R. 480 at 485. Is it still good law in England after s.8 of the 1977 Act?

KUWAIT AIRWAYS CORP. v IRAQI AIRWAYS CO

House of Lords [2002] UKHL 19, [2002] 2 A.C. 883, [2002] 3 All E.R. 209

Liability of a transferee for impounded chattels accepted from an immune sovereign state

In August 1990 when the Iraqis invaded Kuwait and purported to annex it, they snaffled ten aircraft belonging to the claimant; the Iraqi government then handed them over to the defendant who proceeded to use them as its own, in good faith, believing their government to be acting within its powers. Six of the planes were taken by the defendant to Iran on the orders of the government, while four remained in Iraq at Mosul and were bombed to bits by the allies.

According to Iraqi law the good faith usurper of goods is liable for their physical destruction only if it would not have occurred "but for" the usurpation. That was not the case of the "Mosul four", for which accordingly the defendant was not liable, but the "Iran Six" were not damaged, and the defendant was held liable for converting them.

Lord Nicholls of Birkenhead: Conversion of goods can occur in so many different circumstances that framing a precise definition of universal application is well nigh impossible. In general, the basic features of the tort are threefold. First, the defendant's conduct was inconsistent with the rights of the owner (or other person entitled to possession). Second, the conduct was deliberate, not accidental. Third, the conduct was so extensive an encroachment on the rights of the owner as to exclude him from use and possession of the goods. The contrast is with lesser acts of interference. If these cause damage they may give rise to claims for trespass or in negligence, but they do not constitute conversion.

... Bowen L.J., whose judgments are invariably instructive, was scathingly dismissive of the idea that substantial damages should be awarded in an action for wrongful detention of goods when there has been no substantial loss. He said: "You do not give damages in an action for detention in poenam; it is not a paternal correction inflicted by the court, but simply compensation for the loss ... I cannot think that the law could really lay down anything so ridiculous as that a man should be compensated whether he suffered damages or not."

This approach has been adopted by the Court of Appeal on several occasions. In 1966 it was applied in *Wickham Holdings v Brooke House Motors Ltd* [1967] 1 W.L.R. 295, 299–300. In refusing to award damages measured by reference to the value of the Rover car converted by the garage dealer, Lord Denning M.R. said that the plaintiff finance company was "only entitled to what it has lost by the wrongful act of the defendants". Again, in *Brandeis Goldschmidt & Co Ltd v Western Transport Ltd* [1981] Q.B. 864, 870: failing evidence of loss resulting from the wrongful detention of copper, the court awarded only nominal damages. Having acquired the copper for use as a raw material in its business, the fall in the market value of the copper occasioned the plaintiff no loss. Brandon L.J. could not see why there should be any universally applicable rule for assessing damages for wrongful detention of goods: "Damages in tort are awarded by way of monetary compensation for a loss or losses which a plaintiff has actually sustained." This view was echoed by the Court of Appeal in *IBL Ltd v Coussens* [1991] 2 All E.R. 133, 139, 142.

I have no hesitation in preferring and adopting this view of the present state of the law. The aim of the law, in respect of the wrongful interference with goods, is to provide a just remedy. Despite its proprietary base, this tort does not stand apart and command awards of damages measured by some special and artificial standard of its own. The fundamental object of an award of damages in respect of this tort, as with all wrongs, is to award just compensation for loss suffered. Normally ("prima facie") the measure of damages is the market value of the goods at the time the defendant expropriated them. This is the general rule, because generally this measure represents the amount of the basic loss suffered by the plaintiff owner. He has been dispossessed of his goods by the defendant. Depending on the circumstances some other measure, yielding a higher or lower amount, may be appropriate. The plaintiff may have suffered additional damage consequential on the loss of his goods. Or the goods may have been returned.

I turn to consider the purpose sought to be achieved by the tort of conversion. Conversion is the principal means whereby English law protects the ownership of goods. Misappropriation of another's goods constitutes conversion. Committing this tort gives rise to an obligation to pay damages. Payment of damages may have proprietary consequences. Payment of damages assessed on the footing that the plaintiff is being compensated for the whole of his interest in the goods extinguishes his title: see s.5 of the Torts (Interference with Goods) Act 1977. Further, when the defendant is in possession of the plaintiff's goods the remedies available to the plaintiff include a court order that the goods be delivered up: see s.3.

Consistently with its purpose of providing a remedy for the misappropriation of goods, liability is strict. As Diplock L.J. said in *Marfani & Co Ltd v Midland Bank Ltd* [1968] 1 W.L.R.

956, 970–971, one's duty to one's neighbour is to refrain from doing any voluntary act in relation to his goods which is a usurpation of his property or possessory rights in them. Whether the defendant still has the goods or their proceeds matters not. Nor does it matter whether the defendant was a thief or acted in the genuine and reasonable belief the goods were his. Baron Cleasby's aphorism, uttered in 1872 in *Fowler v Hollins* L.R. 7 Q.B. 616, 639, still represents the law: "persons deal with the property in chattels or exercise acts of ownership over them at their peril." This, he observed, was regarded as a salutary rule for the protection of property.

Some aspects of this rule have attracted criticism. Vindication of a plaintiff's proprietary interests requires that, in general, all those who convert his goods should be accountable for benefits they receive. They must make restitution to the extent they are unjustly enriched. The goods are his, and he is entitled to reclaim them and any benefits others have derived from them. Liability in this regard should be strict subject to defences available to restitutionary claims such as change of position: see *Lipkin Gorman v Karpnale Ltd* [1991] 2 A.C. 548. Additionally, those who act dishonestly should be liable to make good any losses caused by their wrongful conduct. Whether those who act innocently should also be liable to make good the plaintiff's losses is a different matter. A radical reappraisal of the tort of conversion along these lines was not pursued on these appeals. So I shall say nothing more about it.

The existing principle of strict liability as described above is deeply ingrained in the common law. It has survived at least since the days of Lord Mansfield in *Cooper v Chitty* (1756) 1 Burr 20. The hardship it may cause to those who deal innocently with a person in possession of goods has long been recognised. Blackburn J. noted this in the leading case of *Fowler v Hollins* (1875) L.R. 7 H.L. 757, 764. The hardship arises especially for innocent persons who no longer have the goods. There has been some statutory amelioration of the principle, in the Factors Acts and elsewhere, but in general the principle endures.

Consistently with this principle, every person through whose hands goods pass in a series of conversions is himself guilty of conversion and liable to the owner for the loss caused by his misappropriation of the owner's goods. His liability is not diminished by reason, for instance, of his having acquired the goods from a thief as distinct from the owner himself. In such a case, it may be said, looking at the successive conversions overall, the owner is no worse off as a result of the acts of the person who acquired the goods from the thief. Such a person has not "caused" the owner any additional loss.

In one sense this is undoubtedly correct. The owner had already lost his goods. But that is really nothing to the point for the purposes of assessing damages for conversion. By definition, each person in a series of conversions wrongfully excludes the owner from possession of his goods. This is the basis on which each is liable to the owner. That is the nature of the tort of conversion. The wrongful acts of a previous possessor do not therefore diminish the plaintiff's claim in respect of the wrongful acts of a later possessor. Nor, for a different reason, is it anything to the point that, absent the defendant's conversion, someone else would wrongfully have converted the goods. The likelihood that, had the defendant not wronged the plaintiff, somebody would have done so is no reason for diminishing the defendant's liability and responsibility for the loss he brought upon the plaintiff.

Where, then, does this leave the simple "but for" test in cases of successive conversion? I suggest that, if the test is to be applied at all, the answer lies in keeping in mind, as I have said, that each person in a series of conversions wrongfully excludes the owner from possession of his goods. The exclusionary threshold test is to be applied on this footing. Thus the test calls for consideration of whether the plaintiff would have suffered the loss in question had he retained his goods and not been unlawfully deprived of them by the defendant. The test calls for a comparison between the owner's position had he retained his goods and his position having been deprived of his goods by the defendant. Loss which the owner would have suffered even if he had retained the goods is not loss "caused" by the conversion. The defendant is not liable for such loss.

For these reasons I consider KAC's claims in respect of the Iran Six do not fail at the threshold stage. Had KAC not been unlawfully deprived of its goods by IAC KAC would not have suffered any of the heads of loss it is now claiming. Had KAC retained possession of the Iran Six, the aircraft would not have been evacuated to Iran.

The parties presented to the House extensive written and oral arguments on whether the test for liability for consequential loss in cases of conversion is reasonable foreseeability as distinct from whether the loss arises naturally and directly from the wrong. By consequential loss I mean loss beyond that represented by the value of the goods. The route I have followed in reaching my conclusions on KAC's claims under this head makes it strictly unnecessary to express any opinion on this point. Nevertheless, in the absence of clear authority, I ought to state my view briefly.

Expressed in terms of the traditional guideline principles, the choice is between confining liability for consequential loss to damage which is "foreseeable", as distinct from damage flowing "directly and naturally" from the wrongful conduct. In practice, these two tests usually yield the same result. Where they do not, the foreseeability test is likely to be the more restrictive. The prevalent view is that the more restrictive test of foreseeability is applicable to the torts of negligence, nuisance and *Rylands v Fletcher*: see the two *Wagon Mound* cases [1961] A.C. 388 and [1967] 1 A.C. 617 and *Cambridge Water Co v Eastern Counties Leather plc* [1994] 2 A.C. 264. The Court of Appeal recently applied this test to the tort of conversion, apparently without any contrary argument, in *Saleslease Ltd v Davis* [1999] 1 W.L.R. 1664, although the members of the court differed in the application of the principle to the facts of the case.

In contrast, the less restrictive test is applicable in deceit. The more culpable the defendant the wider the area of loss for which he can fairly be held responsible: see the discussion by my noble and learned friend Lord Steyn in *Smith New Court Securities Ltd v Scrimgeour Vickers (Asset Management) Ltd* [1997] A.C. 254, 279–285.

This bifurcation causes difficulty with the tort of conversion. Dishonesty is not an essential ingredient of this wrong. The defendant may be a thief, or he may have acted wholly innocently. Both are strictly liable. But it seems to me inappropriate they should be treated alike when determining their liability for consequential loss. Parliament, indeed, has recognised that for some purposes different considerations should apply to persons who steal goods, or knowingly receive stolen goods, and persons who can show they bought the goods in good faith. In respect of the tort of conversion the Limitation Act 1980 prescribes different limitation provisions for these two types of cases: see ss.3 and 4.

I have already mentioned that, as the law now stands, the tort of conversion may cause hardship for innocent persons. This suggests that foreseeability, as the more restrictive test, is appropriate for those who act in good faith. Liability remains strict, but liability for consequential loss is confined to types of damage which can be expected to arise from the wrongful conduct. You deal with goods at the risk of discovering later that, unbeknown to you, you have not acquired a good title. That is the strict common law principle. The risk is that, should you not have acquired title, you will be liable to the owner for the losses he can expect to have suffered as a result of your misappropriation of his goods. That seems the preferable approach, in the case of a person who can prove he acted in the genuine belief the goods were his. A person in possession of goods knows where and how he acquired them. It is up to him to establish he was innocent of any knowing wrongdoing. This is the approach Parliament has taken in s.4 of the Limitation Act 1980.

Persons who knowingly convert another's goods stand differently. Such persons are acting dishonestly. I can see no good reason why the remoteness test of "directly and naturally" applied in cases of deceit should not apply in cases of conversion where the defendant acted dishonestly.

Lord Hoffmann: My Lords, it would be an irrational system of tort liability which did not insist upon there being some causal connection between the tortious act and the damage. But causal connections can be of widely differing kinds. ... There is no uniform causal requirement for liability in tort. Instead, there are varying causal requirements, depending upon the basis and purpose of liability. One cannot separate questions of liability from questions of causation. They are inextricably connected. One is never simply liable; one is always liable for something and the rules which determine what one is liable for are as much part of the substantive law as the rules which determine which acts give rise to liability. It is often said that causation is a question of fact. So it is, but so is the question of liability. Liability involves applying the rules which determine whether an act is tortious to the facts of the case. Likewise, the question of causation is decided by applying the rules which lay down the causal requirements for that form of liability to the facts of the case.

In the case of conversion, the causal requirements follow from the nature of the tort. The tort exists to protect proprietary or possessory rights in property; it is committed by an act inconsistent with those rights and it is a tort of strict liability. So conversion is "a taking with the intent of exercising over the chattel an ownership inconsistent with the real owner's right of possession": per Rolfe B in *Fouldes v Willoughby* (1841) 8 M. & W. 540, 550. And the person who takes is treated as being under a continuing strict duty to restore the chattel to its owner. It follows, first, that it is irrelevant that if IAC had not taken possession of the aircraft, someone else would have done so. Secondly, it is irrelevant that, having taken possession, IAC would have been prevented from restoring the aircraft (even if it had wished to do so) by circumstances beyond its control: the orders of the Iraqi Government and their detention in Iran. The liability is strict. Thus the causal questions are answered by reference to the nature of the liability.

When one comes to consequential loss, the causal requirements are different. The primary purpose of conversion is to protect the proprietary or possessory interest in the chattel. Thus the cost of putting the aircraft into repair or paying a ransom for their recovery from Iran is part of the damage or expenditure incurred in mitigation of the damage to the proprietary interest. But when one comes to real consequential losses, such as the cost of hiring substitute aircraft, the cost of financing the purchase of new ones and loss of profit, there is no reason why causal requirements which are considered fair in other cases of consequential loss flowing from wrongful acts should not also be applied. For the reasons given by Lord Nicholls of Birkenhead, I would agree that these requirements are in principle satisfied in respect of the hire of substitute aircraft and the loss of profits, but that although the failure of IAC to restore the aircraft was a necessary condition of the decision to buy a new fleet, that decision was a voluntary act which on conventional principles made the causal connection with IAC's tortious conduct insufficient.

WICKHAM HOLDINGS LTD v BROOKE HOUSE MOTORS LTD

Court of Appeal [1967] 1 W.L.R. 295; [1967] 1 All E.R. 117

Measure of damages in suit by finance company against purchaser from hirer

A finance company sued for conversion of a car in respect of which only £274.50 was still due under the hire-purchase contract. The trial judge gave judgment for £440, *i.e.* the full value of the car at the time of the conversion plus £75 as damages for detention. The amount of the judgment was reduced on appeal.

Lord Denning M.R.: ...

Even so, there remains the important question: what is the proper measure of damage? It is a familiar situation. The hirer of a motor car, who has got it on hire-purchase, wrongfully sells it to someone else. The hiring is thereupon automatically determined. The finance company claims the return of the car and damages for detention or, alternatively, damages for conversion. In such a case the finance company in my opinion is not entitled to the full value of the car. The finance company is only entitled to what it has lost by the wrongful act of the defendant. I am well aware, of course, that prima facie in conversion the measure of damages is the value of the goods at the date of the conversion. That does not apply, however, where the plaintiff, immediately prior to the conversion, has only a limited interest in the goods: see *Edmonson v Nuttall* (1864) 114 E.R. 113 at 118–119, *per* Willes J. Take this case. The hirer had a most valuable interest in the car. He had paid already £615 10s. towards the purchase price and had the right to buy it outright on paying another £274 10s. The interest of the finance company was limited correspondingly. Its interest was limited to securing the payment of the outstanding £274 10s. It is entitled to be compensated for the loss of that interest, and no more. This was so held by Channell J., in the well known case of *Belsize Motor Supply Co v Cox* [1914] 1 K.B. 244. As Winn L.J., pointed out in the course of the argument, immediately prior to the wrongful sale, the high probability was that the finance company would only get out of this transaction another £274 10s.; either because Mr Pattinson would complete the purchase, or because a purchaser would pay the "settlement figure." That is all that the finance company has lost and all that it should recover. It would be most unjust that the finance company should recover twice as much as it has lost.

I base my decision on this. In a hire-purchase transaction there are two proprietary interests, the finance company's interest and the hirer's interest. If the hirer wrongfully sells the goods or the benefit of the agreement in breach of the agreement, then the finance company are entitled to recover what they have lost by reason of this wrongful act. That is normally the balance outstanding on the hire-purchase price; but they are not entitled to more than they have lost.

I would, therefore, allow the appeal. The judgment below should be varied by substituting for the figure of £440, the sum of £274 10s. We were told, however, that the finance company has claimed another instalment of £54 10s. from Mr Pattinson, and has received it. So this must come off too.

Questions

1. If the Post Office in *The Winkfield* could recover more than it had lost, why not the finance company in this case?

2. The trial judge awarded £75 as damages for detention. Why could the plaintiff not retain this sum?

3. Would it now be right to say that a hire-purchaser has a transferable "proprietary interest" even if the contract forbids both the transfer of possession and the assignment of any contract rights? What kind of interest does the hire-purchaser have—a chose in possession or a chose in action?

4. The X Co lets a car on hire-purchase to A. B steals it and wrecks it. Can the X Co sue B (a) in trespass, (b) in conversion, (c) at all? How much can be recovered from B by (a) the X Co, (b) A? Suppose that the X Co and A had each insured the car under separate policies. How much would each receive from his insurer? If the X Co received the full value of the car from its insurer, would A still owe anything under the hire-purchase contract?

5. If the fact that the auctioneer is insured is a good reason for making him pay though he is not to blame (*Willis*, above, p.499), why is it not a good reason for making him pay too much?

Notes:

1. In distraining on X's property for non-payment of VAT the defendant bailiffs auctioned off for £178 a cash-register which X said was his. In fact X had taken it on hire-purchase terms from the plaintiff: the plaintiff owned it and X owed £1,200 on it. The plaintiff was able to recover only the market value of the thing, taken to be £178, and not, as the trial judge had held, the sum of £950 which X's default rendered the plaintiff liable to pay to the factors to whom they had assigned the right to receive the instalments (*Chubb Cash v John Crilley & Son* [1983] 2 All E.R. 294, CA).

2. In *Hillesden Securities v Ryjak* [1983] 2 All E.R. 184 the plaintiffs obtained much more than the value of the chattel. They got £13,282.50 as well as the Rolls Royce which the defendants had bought from their lessee in September 1980, when its value was £7,500, and continued to use despite demand in February 1981 until returning it in December 1982. As the car was a profit-making asset in the plaintiff's hands the defendants were treated as if they were hiring the vehicle for £115 per week.

3. In *Indian Herbs (UK) v Hadley & Ottoway*, January 21, 1999, CA a seller who had retained title to goods against full payment of the price wrongfully repossessed them when part of the price had been paid. The seller, though still owner, was thus guilty of conversion, since the buyer had an immediate right of possession (*i.e.* actual possession plus contractual right to retain them till the balance of payment was due). The plaintiff was not, however, entitled to the full value of the goods since he had not yet paid part of the price.

4. On the measure of damages see two articles by A. Tettenborn, "Damages in Conversion—the Exception or the Anomaly?" [1993] Camb.L.J. 128 and "Reversionary Damage to Chattels" [1994] Camb. L.J. 326. For damages in cases of infringement of rights to intellectual, as opposed to physical, property, see Cornish, *Intellectual Property* (4th ed., 1999), pp.73–76.

PART VII

DEFAMATION

INTRODUCTION

I⊤ is when important interests come into conflict—"the conflict between right and right" was how Hegel described tragedy—that law gets difficult and fascinating. We have seen some such tensions before: in the tort of false arrest the suspect's interest in liberty is in conflict with the policemen's interest in repressing crime; when a trespassing car gets clamped, there is a stand-off between the car-owner's interest in his vehicle and the site owner's concern for unencumbered land; in conversion claims there is the stasis between the owner's interest in regaining his property and the third party purchaser's concern to keep it.

In defamation the conflict is between your interest in what people think of you and my interest in telling them what I think of you. Defamation is arguably the most difficult of all torts. It is certainly the oddest. For instance, defamation is the only tort in which (a) liability is extinguished by the death of either party, (b) trial by jury is available at the instance of either party, and (c) there is a one-year time-bar. These are marginal matters, perhaps, but defamation is odd at the very core. Here is a plaintiff complaining of being misrepresented. Well, we know what must be shown in a normal claim for misrepresentation: *Hedley Byrne* (above, p.57) told us. The plaintiff must prove (a) that the statement was false, that it was a *mis*representation; (b) that the defendant was wrong to say it, in breach of a duty (not so easy to establish); (c) that the plaintiff suffered proven harm as a foreseeable result. Now change just one thing. Suppose that the representation is *critical of the plaintiff.* "Untune one string," as Shakespeare nearly says, "and hark what discord follows!" In the case of *such* a representation the plaintiff need prove *none* of the above: he can get damages (swingeing damages!) for a statement made to others without showing that the statement was untrue, without showing that the statement did him the slightest harm, and without showing that the defendant was in any way wrong to make it (much less that the defendant owed him any duty of any kind). Are we still in the law of tort? Note, too, that the damage wrought by the publication of defamatory matter is either emotional hurt or financial harm or both, neither of which lies at the heart of the traditional law of tort.

In *Hedley Byrne* cases it is the person spoken *to* who sues, whereas in defamation it is the person spoken *about.* In the latter case, if the words are not defamatory, the tort is called malicious falsehood, a tort free from the incidental features of defamation mentioned above, and naturally requiring proof of falsehood, damage and, most difficult of all, malice. It can, of course, also be used where the words are indeed defamatory: thus governmental units (which cannot, after all, suffer emotional hurt) must resort to this tort, since they are no longer permitted to harass critical citizens by deploying the condign rules of defamation against them (*Derbyshire C.C. v Times Newspapers* [1993] 1 All E.R. 1011). Although malice is usually required for this tort, negligence may be enough if the communication is in breach of a duty of care owed to the person referred to, as where an ex-employer writes an unreasonably depreciatory reference about an ex-employee (*Spring v Guardian Assurance* [1994] 3 All E.R. 129, HL); even so, the plaintiff must establish fault in the defendant.

Not so in defamation. Accordingly, the crucial question in this chapter, on which the rest of it depends, is "Were the words defamatory?" That involves discovering the meaning of the words. Even in dictionaries words have more than one meaning: in the varied contexts of life words can mean almost anything. Since the parties usually disagree about the meaning to be accorded to the words in issue, it is for the jury, which is not bound to accept the view of either, to decide what "the" meaning is, that is, the meaning that would be attributed to it by the normal, if not perfectly reasonable, reader or auditor. When can words be said to be very likely to cause normal people to think worse of the plaintiff? The answer is, when they are critical of his conduct, his competence or his character, for the addressee of such reflections is apt—such is the frailty of human nature—to visit the victim with hatred, ridicule or contempt. In law, uttered words are held to mean what the addressee would reasonably have supposed the utterer to have intended to convey; in fact people understand what they read and hear in the light of what they already know and believe, and they may know more than the speaker or writer; it is thus quite possible for words to be defamatory of a person although the publisher had no idea that such a person even existed, let alone that the words defamed him.

The matter has to be "published" to a third party—you can be as rude as you like if no one is listening (subject to *Wilkinson v Downton*)—and "publication" at common law meant simply contributing to other people's awareness of the imputation in question. The common law did exempt booksellers and lending libraries, provided they had no reason to suspect that the material was defamatory, but now the Defamation Act 1996 provides more widely (read section 1 with care!) that a person other than the author, editor or commercial publisher who contributes to the publication of a defamatory statement has a defence if he had no reason to believe that he was doing so and acted with reasonable care. Even so, a great many actionable publications take place. The text of a book is published by the author of a manuscript to his typist, by the author to the publisher, by the publisher to the printer, and by the publisher to the purchaser. And a person is liable for every publication he intended, even, it is now said, for foreseeable repetitions (*Slipper v BBC* [1991] 1 All E.R. 165, CA).

Thus liability in defamation is extremely easy to incur, especially if you say anything interesting. But there are defences.

The first defence is "justification" or truth. The law has an extraordinary regard for truth, and just as it makes a person liable for a white lie, it makes a person immune in respect of a black truth. Truth is a total defence, in the sense that it rebuts the presumption that what the defendant said was false. It is thus irrelevant why the defendant published the unpalatable fact; the plaintiff has no right to a reputation based on concealment; put otherwise, the public has a right to know all. Truth may out. To this there is now one exception: if a person's conviction for an offence is "spent" by the lapse of the appropriate period, a malicious reference to it is actionable despite its truth (Rehabilitation of Offenders Act 1974, s.8). Apart from this a defendant who makes a single imputation goes free if he proves it to be substantially true, that is, if he justifies its "sting"; where the words of which the plaintiff makes complaint contain several imputations, failure to justify them all is not fatal to the defendant "if the words not proved to be true do not materially injure the plaintiff's reputation having regard to the truth of the remaining charges" (Defamation Act 1952, s.5); and if the plaintiff complains of one of several charges in the same publication the defendant can justify others which have a "common sting".

This being so, can the defendant say "Well, I find I can't prove that what I said was true, but there were true things I might have said which would have done no more harm than what I did say?" Not really. It is true that if he pleads justification and fails, the jury, on determining the damages, may take account of any evidence properly before them. "Thus a defence of partial justification, though it may not prevent the plaintiff from succeeding on the issue of liability, may be of great importance on the issue of damages" (*Pamplin v Express Newspapers (No.2)* [1988] 1 All E.R. 282 at 286). This is, however, a dangerous strategy. If the defendant does not seek to justify what he actually said, he can only lead evidence about such of the plaintiff's behaviour as is publicly known, so as to show that he had not much reputation to lose (*Plato Films v Speidel* [1961] A.C. 1090). This is not justification but mitigation. A considerable extension was proposed, on the basis that "the plaintiff is not entitled to damages for injury to his reputation beyond what he would be entitled to if all facts affecting or liable to affect his reputation (at the time that damages fall to be assessed), in relation to the sector of his life to which the defamatory statement relates, were matters of public notoriety": "The defendant may . . . lead evidence . . . as to specific facts which if they were then generally known would affect the plaintiff's reputation in relation to the relevant sector of his life." This was clause 11 of the Draft Defamation Bill 1995. Most of the Bill became law in the Act of 1996 (below, p.537), but this particular provision was struck out, and one can well imagine why our Honourable Members were unhappy about it. They proceeded to replace it with a section of benefit only to themselves as Members, for it empowers an individual Member to waive the privilege of Parliament (which by barring inquiry by the courts into goings-on in Parliament entailed that a Member couldn't sue for statements about what he did there). There is some justice in the world, however, for the very Member for whose benefit the substitution was engineered, one Neil Hamilton, was hoist with his own (actually Lord Hoffmann's) petard: he found to his dismay and downfall that in the lawsuit which the new section enabled him to bring the jury was persuaded that he had indeed taken money in return for raising apparently disinterested questions in the House.

Secondly, there is the defence of privilege. In some situations communication is so important that its flow must not be impeded by fear of lawsuits. Thus in Parliament and the courts speech is absolutely privileged, and an action in respect of words spoken there is foredoomed: the people who make our law have protected themselves, with good reason, from its effects. In other cases communications are protected only if they were made bona fide: the privilege is qualified in the sense that it is open to the plaintiff to show, if he can, that the occasion was abused. Of course the defendant will be liable if he knew that what he was saying was false, but "malice" will be established also if he was using the occasion just to hurt the plaintiff. To test whether or not an individual has a privilege in a particular situation, imagine that X comes to you and says "Look, I know this bad thing about Z. Should I tell Y?"; if as a reasonably sensitive and responsible member of society you would think it right that X should tell Y, and Y is the right person to tell, X's communication to him is privileged.

This common law privilege was of little use to newspapers and television companies, since hardly any of what they publish is of interest to the whole world. They did have, however, a statutory privilege to publish fair and accurate reports of the proceedings and decisions of various public bodies and meetings, and to communicate notices from certain public officers; sometimes this privilege is conditional on their publishing a reasonable statement from the plaintiff by way of explanation or contradiction. This protection was needed because it is no defence that you were just repeating, with proper attribution, what others had said. This qualified privilege is now extended by the Defamation Act 1996, s.15 to the reports and statements listed in Sch.1.

Much more important, however, is the judicial widening of qualified privilege at common law in the *Reynolds* case, below, p.548. Although it appears to confirm the existing law, it in fact liberalises it considerably, so that a newspaper which behaves with proper circumspection in publishing matters of public interest, at any rate political matters, will probably no longer be liable just because it was misled as to the actual facts. The House of Lords declined to go quite as far as the High Court of Australia which laid down that in such matters the newspaper would not be liable if it proved that it had acted with reasonable care, and stopped far short of the position adopted by the Supreme Court of the United States which held it unconstitutional to impose liability in damages on the media, perhaps on anyone, for speaking out on a matter of public concern unless the plaintiff proved that what was said was false and that he was at fault in saying it; even so, damages are limited to proved loss unless actual malice is shown, as it must be by a public figure who wants any damages at all.

As to pure opinion, however, anyone is free to say what he thinks on matters of public interest, however daft his opinion may be and however prejudicial to others. Public discussion of matters of public interest should be encouraged. But not public error. So the defence of "fair comment" applies only to comments, not to facts. If one gets one's facts wrong, one is strictly liable for stating them; but if the facts are right, then any honest comment is protected. Truth is the criterion of fact, honesty of opinion. The distinction between statement and comment—important because reasonableness of statement is insufficient and reasonableness of comment is not required—appears to be whether the addressee would suppose he was being given a piece of information or a personal value-judgment.

Many people are dissatisfied by the present law of defamation in England. It seems to give too much protection to reputation and to impose too great a restriction on the freedom of speech. Reputation, the cousin of respectability, is now regarded as less important than it was, since one is not supposed to care what other people think. Freedom of speech, on the other hand, is now regarded as more important than it was: to the utilitarian view that its effects are good ("the truth shall make you free") is added the more modern hedonistic view that self-expression is fun. In our sober—nay, solemn—world, it is probably the former idea which lies behind s.12 of the Human Rights Act 1998 which requires the courts to be particularly scrupulous when thinking of granting any relief which might affect the exercise of the right to freedom of expression.

Dissatisfaction with the law doubtless explains the number of committees convened in the past fifty years to suggest improvements. In certain respects the 1996 Act (which is not a product of the Law Commission) is better than its predecessor of 1952, whose procedure of "offer of amends" remained a dead letter. The new proposals about offers to make amends and summary disposal seem to be working.

Some of these provisions clearly could not have been introduced by the judges, but the courts could arguably have done more to prevent the law becoming as absurd, complex and unfair as it is, without resigning themselves to saying, as Diplock L.J. did, that the law of defamation "has passed beyond redemption by the courts" ([1968] 2 Q.B. 157 at 179). Other judicial observations include the following: "The law of defamation has attained a degree of refinement and sophistication beside which the equitable doctrine of constructive trust is a model of clarity and simplicity." (Millett L.J. in *Gillick v BBC* [1996] E.M.L.R. 267 at 274), or Parker L.J.'s reluctance to "embody into the tangled web of the law of defamation as it presently exists yet further absurdity" (*Brent Walker v Time Out* [1991] 2 All E.R. 753 at 761). It is true that in 1996 the valiant Master of the Rolls grasped the nettle and bit on the bullet of absurdly high jury damages (deplored in Strasbourg in *Tolstoy Miloslavsky v United Kingdom* (1995) 20 E.H.R.R. 442) by reducing to a mere £75,000 the award of £350,000 made by a doubtless musical jury to Elton John for some trivial aspersion which can have done him no harm whatsoever. Yet this was more than fifty years after MacKinnon L.J. said "I have been struck by the contrast between the frequent niggardliness of verdicts in cases of personal injury and the invariable profuseness in claims for defamation. A soiled reputation seems assured of more liberal assuagement than a compound fracture" (*Groom v Crocker* [1939] 1 K.B. 194 at 231). Yet it would be sanguine to suppose that the conflict between right to reputation and right to express oneself is soluble. If in 1647 (!) the author of a work on slander, then recently rendered actionable in the secular courts, said that such actions had brought "as much grist to the mill, if not more, than any one branch of the law whatsoever" (Baker, *Introduction to English Legal History* (2nd ed., 1979), p.368), in the year 2002 128 actions for defamation were started in the High Court, as against five only for nuisance, trespass, fraud, malicious prosecution, assault and conspiracy (there were 827 for personal injuries, 268 for other negligence claims: remember that most claims for less than £50,000 must go to the county courts). Apart from defamation cases, the following are tried in the High Court: claims for professional negligence, Fatal Accident Act claims, claims based on fraud and undue influence, claims for malicious prosecution or false imprisonment and other claims against the police. (Practice Direction 29, para.2.6)

The defects of the present law arise because it uses a single remedy, the action for damages, in order to perform three distinct purposes; (a) to permit people to clear their reputation from unfounded allegations; (b) to allow people to claim compensation for the harm they suffer because others have abused their freedom of speech, and (c) to repress gratuitous vituperation, scurrilous disparagement and malignant calumny.

Only for (b) is damages the appropriate remedy. For (a) we need a procedure for retraction or correction, and for (c) we need the public stocks.

It is worth noting briefly the different kinds of damage done by our law of defamation. It protects the wicked such as Robert Maxwell from disclosure of their misdeeds. It induces the greedy to sue and tempts them to tamper with the evidence: three recent victims are Jonathan Aitken, imprisoned for provoking perjury, Jeffrey Archer, who attempted to do so, and Neil Hamilton, proved venal and mendacious. Such litigation takes up the time of honest citizens who as jurymen have to endure hours of vacuous argument and lying testimony. It takes up the time of judges when there are real problems to be dealt with, and disputes to be resolved more serious than that between Berkoff and Burchill (below, p.525). Finally, libel lawyers have to be put on the bench in order to deal with defamation cases; in doing so they seem to find it hard to suppress the hieratic lore from which they so profited at the Bar, so that the law becomes ever more complex, and once there they have to decide cases from other areas of law, for which their dismal specialisation does not always seem to stand them in very good stead.

Chapter 14

DEFAMATION

Section 1.—What is Defamatory?

BERKOFF v BURCHILL

Court of Appeal [1996] 4 All E.R. 1008

Neill L.J.: This appeal raises questions as to the meaning of the word "defamatory" and as to the nature of an action for defamation.

The facts can be stated quite shortly. The plaintiff, Mr Steven Berkoff, is an actor, director and writer who is well known for his work on stage, screen and television. The first defendant, Miss Julie Burchill, is a journalist and writer who at the material times was retained to write articles about the cinema for the *Sunday Times*. The second defendants, Times Newspapers Ltd, are the publishers of the *Sunday Times*.

In the issue of the *Sunday Times* dated January 30, 1994 Miss Burchill wrote a review of the film "The Age of Innocence". In the course of the review, in a general reference to film directors, Miss Burchill wrote: " . . . film directors, from Hitchcock to Berkoff, are notoriously hideous-looking people . . . " Nine months later Miss Burchill returned to the same theme in a review of the film "Frankenstein". In this review, which was published in the issue of the *Sunday Times* dated November 6, 1994, Miss Burchill described a character in the film called "the Creature". She wrote:

> "The Creature is made as a vessel for Waldman's brain, and rejected in disgust when it comes out scarred and primeval. It's a very new look for the Creature—no bolts in the neck or flat-top hairdo—and I think it works; it's a lot like Stephen Berkoff, only marginally better-looking."

The defendants then issued a summons pursuant to RSC Ord. 14A seeking an order that the following question of law might be determined: " . . . whether the meaning pleaded in paragraph 6 of the Statement of Claim . . . is capable of being defamatory . . . " The summons also included an application for an order that if it were determined that the meaning was not defamatory the action should be dismissed.

I am not aware of any entirely satisfactory definition of the word "defamatory". It may be convenient, however, to collect together some of the definitions which have been used and approved in the past.

(1) The classic definition is that given by Lord Wensleydale (then Parke B.) in *Parmiter v Coupland* (1840) 151 E.R. 340 at 341–342. He said that in cases of libel it was for the judge to give a legal definition of the offence which he defined as being:

> "A publication, without justification or lawful excuse, which is calculated to injure the reputation of another, by exposing him to hatred, contempt, or ridicule . . . "

It is to be noted that in *Tournier v National Provincial Union Bank of England Ltd* [1924] 1 K.B. 461 at 477, Scrutton L.J. said that he did not think that this "ancient formula" was sufficient

525

in all cases, because words might damage the reputation of a man as a business man which no one would connect with hatred, ridicule or contempt. Atkin L.J. expressed a similar opinion ([1924] 1 K.B. 461 at 486–487):

"I do not think that it is a sufficient direction to a jury on what is meant by 'defamatory' to say, without more, that it means: Were the words calculated to expose the plaintiff to hatred, ridicule or contempt, in the mind of a reasonable man? The formula is well known to lawyers, but it is obvious that suggestions might be made very injurious to a man's character in business which would not, in the ordinary sense, excite either hate, ridicule, or contempt—for example, an imputation of a clever fraud which, however much to be condemned morally and legally, might yet not excite what a member of a jury might understand as hatred, or contempt."

(2) In *Scott v Sampson* (1882) 8 Q.B.D. 491 Cave J. explained the nature of the right which is concerned in an action for defamation (8 Q.B.D. 491 at 503):

"Speaking generally the law recognizes in every man a right to have the estimation in which he stands in the opinion of others unaffected by false statements to his discredit; and if such false statements are made without lawful excuse, and damage results to the person of whom they are made, he has a right of action."

But the word "discredit" is itself incapable of precise explication. Nevertheless, in *Youssoupoff v Metro-Goldwyn-Mayer Pictures Ltd* (1934) 50 T.L.R. 581 Scrutton L.J. said that he thought that it was difficult to improve upon the language of this definition.

(3) In *Sim v Stretch* [1936] 2 All E.R. 1237 at 1240 Lord Atkin expressed the view that the definition in *Parmiter v Coupland* was probably too narrow and that the question was complicated by having to consider the person or class of persons whose reaction to the publication provided the relevant test. He concluded this passage in his speech:

" . . . after collating the opinions of many authorities I propose in the present case the test: would the words tend to lower the plaintiff in the estimation of right-thinking members of society generally?"

(4) In *Drummond-Jackson v British Medical Association* [1970] 1 All E.R. 1094; [1970] 1 W.L.R. 688 the Court of Appeal was concerned with an article in a medical journal which, it was suggested, impugned the plaintiff's reputation as a dentist. Lord Pearson said:

" . . . words may be defamatory of a trader or business man or professional man, although they do not impute any moral fault or defect of personal character. They [can] be defamatory of him if they impute lack of qualification, knowledge, skill, capacity, judgment or efficiency in the conduct of his trade or business or professional activity . . . "

It is therefore necessary in some cases to consider the occupation of the plaintiff.

(5) In *Youssoupoff v Metro-Goldwyn-Mayer Pictures Ltd* (1934) 50 T.L.R. 581 at 587 Slesser L.J. expanded the *Parmiter v Coupland* definition to include words which cause a person to be shunned or avoided. He said:

" . . . not only is the matter defamatory if it brings the plaintiff into hatred, ridicule, or contempt by reason of some moral discredit on [the plaintiff's] part, but also if it tends to make the plaintiff be shunned and avoided and that without any moral discredit on [the plaintiff's] part. It is for that reason that persons who have been alleged to have been insane, or to be suffering from certain diseases, and other cases where no direct moral responsibility could be placed upon them, have been held to be entitled to bring an action to protect their reputation and their honour."

Slesser L.J. added, in relation to the facts in that case:

"One may, I think, take judicial notice of the fact that a lady of whom it has been said that she has been ravished, albeit against her will, has suffered in social reputation and in opportunities of receiving respectable consideration from the world."

(6) The Faulks Committee in their report recommended that for the purpose of civil cases the following definition of defamation should be adopted (para.65):

"Defamation shall consist of the publication to a third party of matter which in all the circumstances would be likely to affect a person adversely in the estimation of reasonable people generally."

It will be seen from this collection of definitions that words may be defamatory, even though they neither impute disgraceful conduct to the plaintiff nor any lack of skill or efficiency in the conduct of his trade or business or professional activity, if they hold him up to contempt, scorn or ridicule or tend to exclude him from society. On the other hand, insults which do not diminish a man's standing among other people do not found an action for libel or slander. The exact borderline may often be difficult to define.

The case for Mr Berkoff is that the charge that he is "hideously ugly" exposes him to ridicule, and/or alternatively, will cause him to be shunned or avoided. . . . It was suggested that these two passages would reduce the respect with which he was regarded. The words complained of might affect Mr Berkoff's standing among the public, particularly theatre-goers, and among casting directors.

It may be that in some contexts the words "hideously ugly" could not be understood in a defamatory sense, but one has to consider the words in the surroundings in which they appear. This task is particularly important in relation to the second article.

It is trite law that the meaning of words in a libel action is determined by the reaction of the ordinary reader and not by the intention of the publisher, but the perceived intention of the publisher may colour the meaning. In the present case it would, in my view, be open to a jury to conclude that in the context the remarks about Mr Berkoff gave the impression that he was not merely physically unattractive in appearance but actually repulsive. It seems to me that to say this of someone in the public eye who makes his living, in part at least, as an actor, is capable of lowering his standing in the estimation of the public and of making him an object of ridicule.

I confess that I have found this to be a far from easy case, but in the end I am satisfied that it would be wrong to decide this preliminary issue in a way which would withdraw the matter completely from the consideration of a jury.

I would dismiss the appeal.

Millett L.J. (dissenting): Many a true word is spoken in jest. Many a false one too. But chaff and banter are not defamatory, and even serious imputations are not actionable if no one would take them to be meant seriously. The question, however, is how the words would be understood, not how they were meant, and that issue is pre-eminently one for the jury. So, however difficult it may be, we must assume that Miss Julie Burchill might be taken seriously. The question then is: is it defamatory to say of a man that he is "hideously ugly".

Mr Berkoff is a director, actor and writer. Physical beauty is not a qualification for a director or writer. Mr Berkoff does not plead that he plays romantic leads or that the words complained of impugn his professional ability. In any case, I do not think that it can be defamatory to say of an actor that he is unsuitable to play particular roles.

How then can the words complained of injure Mr Berkoff's reputation? They are an attack on his appearance, not on his reputation. It is submitted on his behalf that they would cause people "to shun and avoid him" and would "bring him into ridicule". Ridicule, it will be recalled, is the second member of a well-known trinity.

The submission illustrates the danger of trusting to verbal formulae. Defamation has never been satisfactorily defined. All attempted definitions are illustrative. None of them is exhaustive. All can be misleading if they cause one to forget that defamation is an attack on reputation, that is on a man's standing in the world.

The cases in which words have been held to be defamatory because they would cause the plaintiff to be shunned or avoided, or "cut off from society", have hitherto been confined to allegations that he suffers from leprosy or the plague or the itch or is noisome and smelly (see *Villers v Monsley* (1769) 95 E.R. 886). I agree with Phillips L.J. and for the reasons which he gives that an allegation of ugliness is not of that character. It is a common experience that ugly people have satisfactory social lives—Boris Karloff is not known to have been a recluse—and it is a popular belief for the truth of which I am unable to vouch that ugly men are particularly attractive to women.

I have no doubt that the words complained of were intended to ridicule Mr Berkoff, but I do not think that they made him look ridiculous or lowered his reputation in the eyes of ordinary people. There are only two cases which have been cited to us which are at all comparable. In *Winyard v Tatler Publishing Co Ltd, The Independent*, August 16, 1991 it was held to be defamatory to call a professional beautician "an ugly harridan", not because it reflected on her professional ability, but because some of her customers might not wish to be attended by an ugly beautician. I find the decision difficult to understand, since the reasoning suggests that the cause of action would more properly be classified as malicious falsehood rather than defamation, so that actual loss of custom would have to be proved.

The other case is *Zbyszko v New York American Inc* (1930) 228 App. Div. 277. A newspaper published a photograph of a particularly repulsive gorilla. Next to it appeared a photograph of the plaintiff above the caption: "Stanislaus Zbyszko, the Wrestler, Not Fundamentally Different from the Gorilla in Physique." The statement of claim alleged that this had caused the plaintiff to be shunned and avoided by his wife (who presumably had not noticed her husband's physique until it was pointed out to her by the newspaper), his relatives, neighbours, friends and business associates, and had injured him in his professional calling. The Appellate Division of the New York Supreme Court held that the caption was capable of being defamatory. The case was presumably cited to us as persuasive authority. I find it singularly unpersuasive except as a demonstration of the lengths of absurdity to which an enthusiastic New York lawyer will go in pleading his case.

The line between mockery and defamation may sometimes be difficult to draw. When it is, it should be left to the jury to draw it. Despite the respect which is due to the opinion of Neill L.J., whose experience in this field is unrivalled, I am not persuaded that the present case could properly be put on the wrong side of the line. A decision that it is an actionable wrong to describe a man as "hideously ugly" would be an unwarranted restriction on free speech. And if a bald statement to this effect would not be capable of being defamatory, I do not see how a humorously exaggerated observation to the like effect could be. People must be allowed to poke fun at one another without fear of litigation. It is one thing to ridicule a man; it is another to expose him to ridicule. Miss Burchill made a cheap joke at Mr Berkoff's expense; she may thereby have demeaned herself, but I do not believe that she defamed Mr Berkoff.

If I have appeared to treat Mr Berkoff's claim with unjudicial levity it is because I find it impossible to take it seriously. Despite the views of my brethren, who are both far more experienced than I am, I remain of the opinion that the proceedings are as frivolous as Miss Burchill's article. The time of the court ought not to be taken up with either of them. I would allow the appeal and dismiss the action.

Phillips L.J.: My conclusion is that a statement that a person is hideously ugly does not fall into that category of statements that are defamatory because they tend to make people shun or avoid the plaintiff.

Where the issue is whether words have damaged a plaintiff's reputation by exposing him to ridicule, that question has to be considered in the light of the actual words used and the circumstance in which they are used. There are many ways of indicating that a person is hideously ugly, ranging from a simple statement of opinion to that effect, which I feel could never be defamatory, to words plainly intended to convey that message by way of ridicule. The words used in this case fall into the latter category. Whether they have exposed the plaintiff to ridicule to the extent that his reputation has been damaged must be answered by the jury. The preliminary point raised by the defendants cannot be answered in the affirmative and this appeal should be dismissed.

Question:
The Court did not decide that the words imputing ugliness were actually defamatory, only that they were capable of being so held and that it should be left to the jury to decide. But how can a jury possibly know whether the claimant's reputation has actually been damaged?

LEWIS v DAILY TELEGRAPH LTD

House of Lords [1964] A.C. 234; [1963] 2 W.L.R. 1063; 107 S.J. 356; [1963] 2 All E.R. 151

Just before Christmas 1958, the *Daily Mail* published a paragraph headed "Fraud Squad Probe Firm" and the *Daily Telegraph* one headed "Inquiry on Firm by City Police," both on the front page. The paragraphs identified the corporate plaintiff as the company in question and the individual plaintiff as its chairman.

The plaintiffs alleged that the words were defamatory in their ordinary and natural meaning, and this the defendants did not dispute. But the plaintiffs said that the words in their ordinary meaning indicated that the plaintiffs were guilty of, or were suspected by the police of being guilty of, fraud or dishonesty, whereas the defendants said the words meant only that there was an inquiry on foot, and this meaning they sought to justify as being true.

Salmon J. rejected the defendants' submission that the meaning put on the words by the plaintiffs was impossible, and instructed the jury that they might find that the words meant what the plaintiffs said they meant. He did not point out the absence of cogent evidence of financial loss, and asked them only two questions: (1) whether they found for the plaintiffs or for the defendants, and (2) if for the plaintiffs, what damages. In the first action, against the *Daily Telegraph*, the jury awarded £25,000 to the chairman and £75,000 to the company; in the second action, against the *Daily Mail*, a different jury awarded £17,000 to the chairman and £100,000 to the company. It was accepted that the size of the awards indicated that the juries took the words to impute guilt and not merely suspicion.

The Court of Appeal allowed the defendants' appeals, and ordered new trials [1963] 1 Q.B. 340. The plaintiffs' appeal to the House of Lords was dismissed.

Lord Hodson: ... The defendants having admitted that the words are defamatory in their ordinary meaning have always maintained that their ordinary meaning does not go so far as to include actual guilt or fraud. They have sought to justify by proving that an inquiry was in fact held, not by proving actual suspicion of fraud.

This is the gist of the whole case. Salmon J., who tried both pairs of actions, took the view that the words were capable of imputing guilt of fraud. Davies L.J. was inclined to the same opinion, and my noble and learned friend, Lord Morris of Borth-y-Gest, has expressed the same opinion as Salmon J. Holroyd Pearce L.J. and Havers J. took the contrary view. In view of this difference of judicial opinion, one naturally hesitates before expressing a concluded opinion of one's own, but after listening to many days of argument I am myself satisfied that the words cannot reasonably be understood to impute guilt. Suspicion, no doubt, can be inferred from the fact of the inquiry being held if such was the case, but to take the further step and infer guilt is, in my view, wholly unreasonable. This is to draw an inference from an inference and to take two substantial steps at the same time.

. . .

It has been argued before your Lordships that suspicion cannot be justified without proof of actual guilt on the analogy of the rumour cases such as *Watkin v Hall* ((1868) L.R. 3 Q.B. 396). Rumour and suspicion do, however, essentially differ from one another. To say something is rumoured to be the fact is, if the words are defamatory, a republication of the libel. One cannot defend an action for libel by saying that one has been told the libel by someone else, for this might be only to make the libel worse. The principle as stated by Blackburn J. in *Watkin v Hall* is that a party is not the less entitled to recover damages from a court of law for injurious matter published concerning him because another person previously published it. It is wholly different with suspicion. It may be defamatory to say that someone is suspected of an offence, but it does not carry with it that that person has committed the offence, for this must surely offend against the ideas of justice which reasonable persons are supposed to entertain. If one repeats a rumour one adds one's own authority to it and implies that it is well founded, that is to say, that it is true. It is otherwise when one says or implies that a person is under suspicion of guilt. This does not imply that he is in fact guilty but only that there are reasonable grounds for suspicion, which is a different matter.

Having reached the conclusion that the innuendo should not have been left to the jury as a separate issue and that the natural and ordinary meaning of the words does not convey actual guilt of fraud, I agree with the Court of Appeal that there must be a new trial for the learned judge left the question to the jury "Did they find for plaintiffs or defendants?" without a direction that the words were incapable of the extreme meaning which I have rejected. . . .

The responsibility of the judge to exclude a particular meaning which the plaintiff seeks to ascribe to words in their natural or ordinary meaning is, I think clearly established by the decision of this House in *Capital and Counties Bank Ltd v Henty & Sons* ((1882) 7 App.Cas. 741). Henty & Sons had sent out a circular to a number of their customers giving notice that they would not receive in payment cheques drawn on any of the vouchers of the bank. There was no evidence to support the innuendo that the words imputed insolvency to the bank, and it was held that in their natural and ordinary meaning the words were not libellous. Lord Blackburn said (at 776): "Since Fox's Act at least, however the law may have been before, the prosecutor or plaintiff must also satisfy a jury that the words are such, and so published, as to convey the libellous imputation. If the defendant can get either the court or the jury to be in his favour, he succeeds. The prosecutor, or plaintiff, cannot succeed unless he gets both the court and the jury to decide for him." . . .

Lord Devlin: . . . If it is said of a man that he is a fornicator the statement cannot be enlarged by innuendo. If it is said of him that he was seen going into a brothel, the same meaning would probably be conveyed to nine men out of ten. But the lawyer might say that in the latter case a derogatory meaning was not a necessary one because a man might go to a brothel for an innocent purpose. An innuendo pleading that the words were understood to mean that he went there for an immoral purpose would not, therefore, be ridiculous. To be on the safe side, a pleader used an innuendo whenever the defamation was not absolutely explicit. That was very frequent, since scandalmongers are induced by the penalties for defamation to veil their meaning to some extent. . . . I have said that a derogatory implication might be easy or difficult to detect; and, of course, it might not be detected at all, except by a person who was already in possession of some specific information. Thus, to say of a man that he was seen to enter a named house would contain a derogatory implication for anyone who knew that the house was a brothel but not for anyone who did not. . . .

The real point, I think, that Mr Milmo makes is that whether the libel is looked at as a statement or as a rumour, there is no difference between saying that a man is suspected of fraud and saying that he is guilty of it. It is undoubtedly defamatory, he submits, to say of a man that he is suspected of fraud, but it is defamatory only because it suggests that he is guilty of fraud: so there is no distinction between the two. This is to me an attractive way of putting the point. On analysis I think that the reason for its attraction is that as a maxim for practical application, though not as a proposition of law, it is about three-quarters true. When an imputation is made in a general way, the ordinary man is not likely to distinguish between hints and allegations, suspicion and guilt. It is the broad effect that counts and it is no use submitting to a judge that he ought to dissect the statement before he submits it to the jury. But if on the other hand the distinction clearly emerges from the words used it cannot be ignored. If it is said of a man: "I do not believe that he is guilty of fraud but I cannot deny that he has given grounds for suspicion," it seems to me to be wrong to say that in no circumstances can they be justified except by the speaker proving the truth of that which he has expressly said he did not believe. It must depend on whether the impression conveyed by the speaker is one of frankness or one of insinuation. Equally, in my opinion, it is wrong to say that, if in truth the person spoken of never gave any cause for suspicion at all, he has no remedy because he was expressly exonerated of fraud. A man's reputation can suffer if it can truly be said of him that although innocent he behaved in a suspicious way; but it will suffer much more if it said that he is not innocent.

It is not, therefore, correct to say as a matter of law that a statement of suspicion imputes guilt. It can be said as a matter of practice that it very often does so, because although suspicion of guilt is something different from proof of guilt, it is the broad impression conveyed by the libel that has to be considered and not the meaning of each word under analysis. A man who wants to talk at large about smoke may have to pick his words very carefully if he wants to exclude the suggestion that there is also a fire; but it can be done. One always gets back to the fundamental question: what is the meaning that the words convey to the ordinary man: you cannot make a rule about that. They can convey a meaning of suspicion short of guilt; but loose talk about suspicion can very easily convey the impression that it is a suspicion that is well founded.

In the libel that the House has to consider there is, however, no mention of suspicion at all. What is said is simply that the plaintiff's affairs are being inquired into. That is defamatory, as is admitted, because a man's reputation may in fact be injured by such a statement even though it is quite consistent with innocence. I dare say that it would not be injured if everybody bore in mind, as they ought to, that no man is guilty until he is proved so, but unfortunately they do not. It can be defamatory without it being necessary to suggest that the words contained a hidden allegation that there were good grounds for inquiry. A statement that a woman has been raped can affect her reputation, although logically it means that she is innocent of any impurity: *Yousoupoff v Metro-Goldwyn-Mayer Pictures Ltd* ((1934) 50 T.L.R. 581). So a statement that a man has been acquitted of a crime with which in fact he was never charged might lower his reputation. Logic is not the test. But a statement that an inquiry is on foot may go further and may positively convey the impression that there are grounds for the inquiry, that is, that there is something to suspect. Just as a bare statement of suspicion may convey the impression that there are grounds for belief in guilt, so a bare statement of the fact of an inquiry may convey the impression that there are grounds for suspicion. I do not say that in this case it does; but I think that the words in their context and in the circumstances of publication are capable of conveying that impression. But can they convey an impression of guilt? Let it be supposed, first, that a statement that there is an inquiry conveys an impression of suspicion; and, secondly, that a statement of suspicion conveys an impression of guilt. It does not follow from these two suppositions that a statement that there is an inquiry conveys an impression of guilt. For that, two fences have to be taken instead of one. While, as I have said, I am prepared to accept that the jury could take the first, I do not think that in a case like the present, where there is only the bare statement that a police inquiry is being made, it could take the second in the same stride. If the ordinary sensible man was capable of thinking that wherever there was a police inquiry there was guilt, it would be almost impossible to give accurate information about anything: but in my opinion he is not. I agree with the view of the Court of Appeal. . . .

In the result I think that all your Lordships are now clearly of the opinion that the judge must rule whether the words are capable of bearing each of the defamatory meanings, if there be more than one, put forward by the plaintiff. . . .

Lord Morris of Borth-y-Gest (dissenting on this point): . . . My Lords, I turn to consider the question whether the words were capable of bearing the meaning that the affairs of the company and/or its subsidiaries were conducted fraudulently or dishonestly. I do not understand any of your Lordships to be of the view that the words were not capable of bearing the meaning that the police suspected that the affairs of the company or its subsidiaries were conducted fraudulently or dishonestly: nor did I understand any submission to be made that the words were not so capable.

It is a grave thing to say that someone is fraudulent. It is a different thing to say that someone is suspected of being fraudulent. How much less wounding and damaging this would be must be a matter of opinion depending upon the circumstances. Similarly in the case of the personal plaintiff the submission is made that the words, while capable of bearing some of the alleged meanings, were not capable of bearing the meanings that Mr Lewis had been guilty of fraud or dishonesty in connection with the affairs of the company or its subsidiaries or had caused or permitted the affairs to be conducted fraudulently or dishonestly.

My Lords, the only question that now arises is not whether the words did bear but whether they were capable of bearing the meanings to which I have referred. What could ordinary reasonable readers think? Some, I consider, might reasonably take the view that there was just an inquiry to find out whether or not there had been any fraud or dishonesty. Some, I consider, might reasonably take the view that the words meant that there was an inquiry because the police suspected that there had been fraud or dishonesty. Some, I consider, might reasonably take the view that the words meant that there was an inquiry because there had been fraud or dishonesty which occasioned or required the inquiry by the police. Some, I consider, might reasonably take the view that the words meant that the inquiry was either (a) because there had been fraud or dishonesty or (b) because of a suspicion that there had been.

My Lords, it is not for me to say what I think was the meaning which the words conveyed to the ordinary reasonable reader of a newspaper, nor is it for me to express any opinion as to what conclusion a jury should reach as to this matter, but I do not consider that that meaning which involved that there had been fraud or dishonesty was a meaning which the jury should have been prohibited from considering on the basis that it was a meaning of which the words were not capable. I do not think that it can be said that 12 jurors could not reasonably have come to the conclusion that the words bore the meaning now being considered.

. . .

My Lords, it was for the jury to determine what they consider was the meaning that the words would convey to ordinary men and women: we have only to decide as to the limits of the range of meanings of which the words were capable. For the reasons that I have given I have the misfortune to differ from your Lordships as to this very important part of the case. I consider that the learned judge was fully entitled to leave the matter to the jury in the way in which he did, and I consider that his directions concerning liability were clear and correct and fair. . . .

Questions

1. Lord Reid said this: "To my mind, there is a great difference between saying that a man has behaved in a suspicious manner and saying that he is guilty of an offence, and I am not convinced that you can only justify the former statement by proving guilt. I can well understand that if you say there is a rumour that X is guilty you can only justify it by proving that he is guilty, because repeating someone else's libellous statement is just as bad as making the statement directly. . . . " Is the difference not simply between saying "A thinks B is guilty" and saying "A says B is guilty?" If this is true, is the difference as material as is suggested? And which is wrong—the rumour or the suspicion rule?

2. Why did the juries award such enormous damages, very much higher in real terms than the £500,000 awarded in 1987 to Jeffrey Archer who was alleged to have used the services of a prostitute?

3. Can a person be libelled by an obvious misprint? (*e.g.* the General who was referred to as battle-scared (or bottle-scarred)).

Notes:

1. *Lewis* was invoked by both sides in *Stern v Piper* [1996] 3 All E.R. 385, a claim brought against the *Sunday Mail* which had published on its city page an article about the plaintiff (the biggest bankrupt in British history) containing, without endorsing, certain allegations made in an affirmation which a solicitor had submitted to a court in support of his claim against the plaintiff for some £3 million.

The defendant sought to justify its article by quoting from those allegations, *i.e.* was saying "I was only saying what X said." The trial judge had held that "If all the article does is to report that a claim is being made by one protagonist against another in an action in legal proceedings, the party against whom that claim is made can be met, if he sues for defamation, with the defence that the report is a true one." The Court of Appeal reversed and struck out the defendant's pleadings.

Simon Brown L.J. makes it clear, as does the decision itself, that the "repetition" rule is designed to *prevent* the jury finding that the newspaper was merely reporting, not adopting, the allegations in question. In other words, even if it is made crystal clear—so that the jury is unanimously of opinion that no one could think otherwise—that the defendant is merely reporting the fact that so-and-so has said X and not taking any position about whether X is the case or not, the defendant must be held liable if X is defamatory and there is no privilege. One will look in vain in the judgments for any reason—apart from the existing law, itself quite unreasonable—for this restriction on the jury's right to determine the meaning of the article being sued on. The Court of Appeal refused to extend by a jot or tittle the decisions binding on it to the effect that one is entitled to report that a writ has been issued and to report what a judge has said in open court.

The situation was made even worse in *Shah v Standard Chartered Bank* [1998] 4 All E.R. 155 (marginally modified in *Chase v News Group Newspapers* [2002] EWCA Civ 1772), on the basis that your words impute reasonable suspicion rather than guilt, the question was whether you must, in the absence of privilege, prove objective facts supporting your suspicion or whether "it is permissible to rely on what you have been told by someone else". It was held that it was not enough to say "I have reasonable grounds to suspect that X is guilty, because Y told me that X is guilty and because I know that Y is honest and reliable": Y must be brought into court to substantiate what he said. It will be plain that this does not in the least follow from the view of Simon Brown L.J. given above. There is, however, a gleam of hope: now that newspapers may reply on qualified privilege (see *Reynolds* below, p.548) they may, in appropriate circumstances, safely repeat an allegation if they take care to dissociate themselves from its truth: *Al-Fagih v HH Saudi Research & Marketing* [2001] EWCA Civ 1634.

2. In 1988 the Master of the Rolls observed that "the practice and procedure . . . in . . . claims for defamation is the last refuge of complexity and technicality in the law" (*Singh v Gillard* [1988] New L.J. 144). This is inferable from s.7 of the Act of 1996: "In defamation proceedings the court shall not be asked to rule whether a statement is arguably capable, as opposed to capable, of bearing a particular meaning or meanings attributed to it." Now the practice is being modified, and one judge has even put the meaning of the words to the jury as a preliminary question before hearing any evidence. It remains the case that the jury can only decide whether or not the words were actually defamatory if the judge has previously ruled that they were capable of being defamatory. Almost everything is capable of being defamatory, it seems: the House of Lords has been criticised for its holding in *Capital and Counties Bank v Henty* (above, p.530); Lord Morris thought the trial judge right in *Lewis v Daily Telegraph*; and recently, applying a new rule, the Court of Appeal held that assertions that a small family company was on the verge of bankruptcy were capable of defaming its directors (*Aspro Travel v Owners Abroad Group* [1995] 4 All E.R. 728). A tendency is perceptible to hold that words are defamatory if they are apt to cause harm: that is regrettable, for defamation is a social rather than a commercial question, and the tort of malicious falsehood is available for statements which cause damage to a person without reflecting badly on his character or competence. Accordingly claims by companies are suspect: "The court needed to be alert to the possibility of corporate entities being 'put up' to bring claims for libel in respect of allegations truly reflecting upon individuals", *per* Eady J. in *Elite Model Management v BBC* (May 25, 2001). And where a subsidiary company is "defamed" the holding company, which is only a shareholder, cannot sue unless there is an implication of management. Furthermore, a company, unlike an individual, must have some reputation in the jurisdiction, though if it does, damage is presumed. *Per* Eady J. in *Multigroup Bulgaria v Oxford Analytica* [2001] E.M.L.R. 28.

3. Although in fact words may mean different things to different people, in law they have a "natural and ordinary meaning", and it is this, in the absence of a legal innuendo explaining a latent significance, which is the test of whether a newspaper article is defamatory or not. In *Charleston v News Group Newspapers* [1995] 2 All E.R. 313 the plaintiffs (as so often) were television actors, playing a blameless married couple in *Neighbours*. Pornographers devised a computer game in which their faces were superimposed on bodies of other actors and actresses intently engaged in deplorable intimacies. The *News of the World* reproduced two stills from the game with the headline "Strewth! What's Harold up to with our Madge?". The plaintiffs alleged that many readers of such newspapers got no further than the headlines and that such persons would suppose that the plaintiffs had lent themselves to the depicted practices. The House of Lords did not dissent from this, but held that the test was what the ordinary, reasonable, fair-minded reader would understand, and that such a person would proceed to read the text, which clearly counteracted the defamatory effect of the headline and pictures. This holding (accepted by all nine judges!) is criticised in "Libel and Pornography" (1995) 58 Mod. L. Rev. 752 by Peter Prescott Q.C., a specialist in media and entertainment law.

4. It is now safe to say, until the conviction is "spent", that a person was guilty of an offence if he has been convicted by a court in the United Kingdom (Civil Evidence Act 1968, s.13(1)); in other words, a person erroneously convicted cannot establish his innocence in a defamation suit. Had other recommendations of the Law Reform Committee been implemented, an acquittal would be conclusive of innocence, which would have been equally bad, but for different reasons (Fifteenth Report, Cmnd. 3391 (1967), draft clause 3(1)). For example, it would have prevented the insurance company proving that the insured who had been acquitted of arson had deliberately set fire to the insured property: *Radcliffe v National Farmers Mutual Ins. Soc'y* [1993] C.L.Y.B. § 708.

Section 2.—Reference to the Plaintiff

E. HULTON & CO v JONES

House of Lords [1910] A.C. 20; 79 L.J.K.B. 198; 101 L.T. 831; 26 T.L.R. 128; 54 S.J. 116;
[1908–10] All E.R. Rep. 29

The defendants published in the *Sunday Chronicle* an article by their Paris correspondent describing a motor festival at Dieppe. It contained the following passages: "Upon the terrace marches the world, attracted by the motor races—a world immensely pleased with itself, and minded to draw a wealth of inspiration—and, incidentally, of golden cocktails—from any scheme to speed the passing hour . . . 'Whist! there is Artemus Jones with a woman who is not his wife, who must be, you know—the other thing!' whispers a fair neighbour of mine excitedly into her bosom friend's ear. Really, is it not surprising how certain of our fellow-countrymen behave when they come abroad? Who would suppose, by his goings on, that he was a churchwarden at Peckham? No one, indeed, would assume that Jones in the atmosphere of London would take on so austere a job as the duties of a churchwarden. Here, in the atmosphere of Dieppe on the French side of the Channel, he is the life and soul of a gay little band that haunts the Casino and turns night into day, besides betraying a most unholy delight in the society of female butterflies."

The plaintiff was a barrister on the North Wales Circuit who was baptised as Thomas Jones but on confirmation took, on the ground of its distinctiveness, the additional name of Artemus. Until being called to the Bar in 1901 he had contributed signed articles to the defendant's paper, but he accepted that the writer of the article and the editor of the paper knew nothing of him and that they did not intend the article to refer to him. Witnesses called by the plaintiff testified that they took the article to refer to him.

The jury awarded £1,750 damages, and Channell J. entered judgment for the plaintiff in that amount. The defendant's appeal to the Court of Appeal was dismissed (Fletcher Moulton L.J. dissenting) [1909] 2 K.B. 444. The defendant further appealed to the House of Lords, and that appeal was also dismissed in unreserved judgments.

Lord Loreburn L.C.: My Lords, I think this appeal must be dismissed. A question in regard to the law of libel has been raised which does not seem to me to be entitled to the support of your Lord ships. Libel is a tortious act. What does the tort consist in? It consists in using language which others knowing the circumstances would reasonably think to be defamatory of the person complaining of and injured by it. A person charged with libel cannot defend himself by showing that he intended in his own breast not to defame, or that he intended not to defame the plaintiff, if in fact he did both. He has none the less imputed something disgraceful and has none the less injured the plaintiff. A man in good faith may publish a libel believing it to be true, and it may be found by the jury that he acted in good faith believing it to be true, and reasonably believing it to be true, but that in fact the statement was false. Under those circumstances he has no defence to the action, however excellent his intention. If the intention of the writer be immaterial in considering whether the matter written is defamatory, I do not see why it need be relevant in considering whether it is defamatory of the plaintiff. The writing, according to the old form, must be malicious, and it must be of and concerning the plaintiff.

It is suggested that there was a misdirection by the learned judge in this case. I see none. He lays down in his summing-up the law as follows: "The real point upon which your verdict must turn is, ought or ought not sensible and reasonable people reading this article to think that it was a mere imaginary person such as I have said—Tom Jones, Mr Pecksniff as a humbug, Mr Stiggins, or any of that sort of names that one reads of in literature used as types? If you think any reasonable person would think that, it is not actionable at all. If, on the other hand, you do not think that, but think that people would suppose it to mean some real person—those who did not know the plaintiff of course would not know who the real person was, but those who did know of the existence of the plaintiff would think that it was the plaintiff—then the action is maintainable, subject to such damages as you think under all the circumstances are fair and right to give the plaintiff."

I see no objection in law to that passage.

Questions

1. Is the true question (a) whether the defendant intended to be understood as referring to the plaintiff; (b) whether the words used by the defendant fitted the plaintiff; or (c) whether reasonable people might believe that the defendant was intending to refer to the plaintiff? Is your answer affected by the fact that mere vulgar abuse is not actionable, and by the result of *Blennerhasset v Novelty Sales Services Ltd* (1933) 175 L.T.J. 393?

2. The jury awarded £1,750 in 1909. In the values of 2003 this represents nearly £90,000. Libel damages are not taxed. Do you think that anyone who knew Artemus Jones believed the libel, or that anyone who did not know him cared in the least? Did Artemus Jones embellish his reputation by this lawsuit?

Notes:

1. The decision in the House of Lords was given in unreserved judgments. Accordingly, the careful judgments in the Court of Appeal should be read, especially the furious dissenting judgment of Fletcher Moulton L.J., who said: "It is . . . to my mind, settled law that a defendant is not guilty of libel unless he wrote and published the defamatory words 'of and concerning the plaintiff'—in other words, unless he intended them to refer to the plaintiff. . . . To say that when the common law required it to be alleged and proved that the defendant wrote and published the words of and concerning the plaintiff it meant only that it must be shewn that some people might think so is, to my mind, to give up all pretence of interpreting language and arbitrarily to create new torts which the law never did and should not now recognize as such. . . . If this be the law, then a person who makes a statement about Mr A.B. which is perfectly true, but which if not true would be libellous, can be made liable to every person of the name of A.B. except the person of and concerning whom the words were written. . . . It cannot be pretended that any actual damage has been suffered by the plaintiff."

Farwell L.J. approached the question from the point of view of recklessness and carelessness in the publication: " . . . [the defendant] has, therefore, for his own purpose chosen to assert a fact of a person bearing the very unusual name of Artemus Jones, recklessly, and caring not whether there was such a person or not, or what the consequences might be to him. . . . " He also said: "If the libel was true of another person and honestly aimed at and intended for him, and not for the plaintiff, the latter has no cause of action, although all his friends and acquaintances may fit the cap on him."

(In *Newstead v London Express* [1940] 1 K.B. 377, the case of the Camberwell bigamist, the Court of Appeal disapproved this last remark, and gave damages to a person in respect of a statement true of someone else; thus the consequence followed which Fletcher Moulton L.J. foretold and Farwell L.J. denied and both regarded as absurd. It has happened more recently, too. The weekly *Dog World* reported that "Stephen King" had traumatised a dog called Mitch by pulling on his choke chain and swinging him about. This was true of Stephen Barry King, subsequently prosecuted by the RSPCA, but entirely false as to Stephen Geoffrey King, the claimant, who was a highly respected dog trainer and animal lover. Compensation was paid. *King v Dog World* (Eady J., October 13, 2003).

Are pictures like names? Morland J. thought so in a case where the claimant looked very much like the woman provocatively displayed in an advertisement for a porno website in a Sunday newspaper, but he held that it would be disproportionate to subject the right of expression under Art.10 of the Human Rights Convention to a duty to ascertain that there was no one else who looked like the person whose picture one portrayed. *O'Shea v MGN Ltd* [2001] E.M.L.R. 40.

2. The "offer to make amends" in the Defamation Act 1996 is a distinct improvement on the dead letter of section 4 of the Act of 1952. The offer must be to publish a correction/apology in respect of the statement complained of and to pay compensation, to be fixed, if not agreed, by a judge (alone) on normal principles. If the offer is rejected, an action will fail unless the claimant can prove that the defendant knew or ought to have known that the statement was false and defamatory of him.

3. After the success of *The Second Mrs Tanqueray* Sir Arthur Pinero decided to write a play about *The Notorious Mrs—*, but he wanted to be sure that there was no first Mrs—. He looked through *Crockford's*

Clerical Dictionary, and was struck by the name of Canon Flood-Jones; he therefore called his play *The Notorious Mrs Ebbsmith*. His caution did him no good, for there was a lady of that improbable name who considered herself defamed.

4. Artemus Jones was mentioned by name, or, more accurately, the name Artemus Jones was mentioned. The name of the plaintiff in *Morgan v Odhams Press* ([1971] 1 W.L.R. 1239) was not. All the newspaper had said was that Miss X had been kidnapped by a dog-doping gang and kept in a flat in Finchley during a specified week. The plaintiff had in fact had Miss X staying with him in his flat in Willesden the previous week, and claimed that people who knew this fact would suppose that the newspaper was saying that he was connected with the gang. The jury awarded him £4,750. The Court of Appeal reversed on the ground that the plaintiff must find in the words used some key or pointer to him. The House of Lords disagreed with this, and ordered a new trial on damages only: the jury might reasonably find that readers of the *Sun* would ignore the discrepancies of time and place, and think of the plaintiff while reading the story. A further point arose. One of the plaintiff's witnesses said that though he thought the story referred to the plaintiff he did not believe it. Lord Reid said of this, with the emphatic approval of Lord Morris: "It was argued that . . . no tort is committed by making a defamatory statement about X to a person who utterly disbelieves it. That is plainly wrong." So we now have powerful authority for the ludicrous proposition that a person may be sued for making a true statement about X which anyone can, despite its terms, suppose to be a false statement about Y.

5. Another extraordinary case of reference is *Boston v Bagshaw* ([1966] 1 W.L.R. 1126). The defendants broadcast the true statement that at a recent auction a man had bid for pigs, given his name as Boston of Rugeley, and made off with the pigs without paying. The true Boston of Rugeley claimed damages and nearly got them. Is it defamatory of X to say that a person masquerading as X has done something disgraceful? Is it defamatory of X to masquerade as X and do something disgraceful?

6. It is actionable to be rude about an unspecified person and then identify him later, as is shown by the very thrilling case of *Hayward v Thompson* [1981] 3 All E.R. 450.

7. "I venture to think that it is a mistake to lay down a rule as to libel on a class, and then qualify it with exceptions. The only relevant rule is that in order to be actionable the defamatory words must be understood to be published of and concerning the plaintiff. It is irrelevant that the words are published of two or more persons if they are proved to be published of him, and it is irrelevant that the two or more persons are called by some generic or class name. There can be no law that a defamatory statement made of a firm, or trustees, or the tenants of a particular building is not actionable, if the words would reasonably be understood as published of each member of the firm or each trustee or tenant. The reason why a libel published of a large or indeterminate number of persons described by some general name generally fails to be actionable is the difficulty of establishing that the plaintiff was, in fact, included in the defamatory statement, for the habit of making unfounded generalisations is ingrained in ill-educated or vulgar minds, or the words are occasionally intended to be a facetious exaggeration." So said Lord Atkin in *Knupffer v London Express Newspaper* [1944] A.C. 116.

8. In *Riches v News Group Newspapers* [1985] 2 All E.R. 845 the defendant repeated a besieged madman's grotesque allegations against "the Banbury CID", accusing them, *inter alia*, of raping his wife. Then 10 of the 11 male members of the Banbury CID sued. The jury awarded each of them £300 compensatory damages and £25,000 exemplary damages, a total of £253,000. The Court of Appeal ordered a new trial on exemplary damages; not only was this sum excessive (though there was evidence that the publication was reckless and designed—"EXCLUSIVE"—to improve the circulation of the *News of the World*) but only a single sum by way of such damages should be awarded, to be divided equally between the plaintiffs. For a review of the role of judges when exemplary damages are claimed, see now *John v MGN Ltd* [1996] 2 All E.R. 35.

9. Would it be defamatory to say "With only two or three exceptions, successful plaintiffs in defamation suits in the past fifteen years have been the scum and froth of civil society". Would it be true?

10. In France, a newspaper which refers to a person, even in a non-defamatory way, is bound, on pain of a fine, to allow that person the right of reply (Law of the Press, July 29, 1881, Art.13). The Faulks Committee dismissed this idea as one "which entitles a person, who may be without merits, to compel a newspaper to publish a statement extolling his non-existent virtue." (para.623). Now an E.C. Directive (97/36 of June 30, 1997) had amended Directive 89/552 so as to make it provide in Art.23(1): "Without prejudice to other provisions adopted by Member States under civil, administrative or criminal law, any natural or legal person, regardless of nationality, whose legitimate interests, in particular reputation and good name, have been damaged by an assertion of incorrect facts on a television programme must have a right of reply or equivalent remedies . . . " Is Britain compliant?

11. Note that under our own dear system no plaintiff *ever* leaves court with his reputation cleared: even the award of massive damages is no indication that what the defendant said was false, only that the defendant did not prove it to be true, quite a different matter: in other words, the successful plaintiff may be every bit as bad as the defendant said and as subsequent events prove when the truth finally emerges (Maxwell, Sutcliffe, Archer . . .).

DEFAMATION ACT 1996

Responsibility for publication

1.—(1) In defamation proceedings a person has a defence if he shows that—

(a) he was not the author, editor or publisher of the statement complained of,
(b) he took reasonable care in relation to its publication, and
(c) he did not know, and had no reason to believe, that what he did caused or contributed to the publication of a defamatory statement.

(2) For this purpose "author", "editor" and "publisher" have the following meanings, which are further explained in subsection (3)—

"author" means the originator of the statement, but does not include a person who did not intend that his statement be published at all;
"editor" means a person having editorial or equivalent responsibility for the content of the statement or the decision to publish it; and
"publisher" means a commercial publisher, that is, a person whose business is issuing material to the public, or a section of the public, who issues material containing the statement in the course of that business.

(3) A person shall not be considered the author, editor or publisher of a statement if he is only involved—

(a) in printing, producing, distributing or selling printed material containing the statement;
(b) in processing, making copies of, distributing, exhibiting or selling a film or sound recording . . . containing the statement;
(c) in processing, making copies of, distributing or selling any electronic medium in or on which the statement is recorded, or in operating or providing any equipment, system or service by means of which the statement is retrieved, copied, distributed or made available in electronic form;
(d) as the broadcaster of a live programme containing the statement in circumstances in which he has no effective control over the maker of the statement;
(e) as the operator of or provider of access to a communications system by means of which the statement is transmitted, or made available, by a person over whom he has no effective control.

In a case not within paragraphs (a) to (e) the court may have regard to those provisions by way of analogy in deciding whether a person is to be considered the author, editor or publisher of a statement.

(4) Employees or agents of an author, editor or publisher are in the same position as their employer or principal to the extent that they are responsible for the content of the statement or the decision to publish it.

(5) In determining for the purposes of this section whether a person took reasonable care, or had reason to believe that what he did caused or contributed to the publication of a defamatory statement, regard shall be had to—

(a) the extent of his responsibility for the content of the statement or the decision to publish it,
(b) the nature or circumstances of the publication, and

(c) the previous conduct or character of the author, editor or publisher.

Offer to make amends

2.—(1) A person who has published a statement alleged to be defamatory or another may offer to make amends under this section.

(2) The offer may be in relation to the statement generally or in relation to a specific defamatory meaning which the person making the offer accepts that the statement conveys ("a qualified offer").

(3) An offer to make amends—

(a) must be in writing,
(b) must be expressed to be an offer to make amends under section 2 of the Defamation Act 1996, and
(c) must state whether it is a qualified offer and, if so, set out the defamtory meaning in relation to which it is made.

(4) An offer to make amends under this section is an offer—

(a) to make a suitable correction of the statement complained of and a sufficient apology to the aggrieved party,
(b) to publish the correction and apology in a manner that is reasonable and practicable in the circumstances, and
(c) to pay to the aggrieved party such compensation (if any), and such costs, as may be agreed or determined to be payable.

The fact that the offer is accompanied by an offer to take specific steps does not affect the fact that an offer to make amends under this section is an offer to do all the things mentioned in paragraphs (a) to (c).

(5) An offer to make amends under this section may not be made by a person after serving a defence in defamation proceedings brought against him by the aggrieved party in respect of the publication in question.

(6) An offer to make amends under this section may be withdrawn before it is accepted; and a renewal of an offer which has been withdrawn shall be treated as a new offer.

3.—(1) If an offer to make amends under section 2 is accepted by the aggrieved party, the following provisions apply.

(2) The party accepting the offer may not bring or continue defamation proceedings in respect of the publication concerned against the person making the offer, but he is entitled to enforce the offer to make amends, as follows.

(3) If the parties agree on the steps to be taken in fulfilment of the offer, the aggrieved party may apply to the court for an order that the other party fulfil his offer by taking the steps agreed.

(4) If the parties do not agree on the steps to be taken by way of correction, apology and publication, the party who made the offer may take such steps as he thinks appropriate, and may in particular—

(a) make the correction and apology by a statement in open court in terms approved by the court, and
(b) give an undertaking to the court as to the manner of their publication.

(5) If the parties do not agree on the amount to be paid by way of compensation, it shall be determined by the court on the same principles as damages in defamation proceedings.

The court shall take account of any steps taken in fulfilment of the offer and (so far as not agreed between the parties) of the suitability of the correction, the sufficiency of the apology and whether the manner of their publication was reasonable in the circumstances, and may reduce or increase the amount of compensation accordingly.

(6) If the parties do not agree on the amount to be paid by way of costs, it shall be determined by the court on the same principles as costs awarded in court proceedings.

. . .

(10) Proceedings under this section shall be heard and determined without a jury.

4.—(1) If an offer to make amends under section 2, duly made and not withdrawn, is not accepted by the aggrieved party, the following provisions apply.

(2) The fact that the offer was made is a defence (subject to subsection (3)) to defamation proceedings in respect of the publication in question by that party against the person making the offer.

A qualified offer is only a defence in respect of the meaning to which the offer related.

(3) There is no such defence if the person by whom the offer was made knew or had reason to believe that the statement complained of—

(a) referred to the aggrieved party or was likely to be understood as referring to him, and
(b) was both false and defamatory of that party;

but it shall be presumed until the contrary is shown that he did not know and had no reason to believe that was the case.

(4) The person who made the offer need not rely on it by way of defence, but if he does he may not rely on any other defence.

If the offer was a qualified offer, this applies only in respect of the meaning to which the offer related.

(5) The offer may be relied on in mitigation of damages whether or not it was relied on as a defence.

8.—(1) In defamation proceedings the court may dispose summarily of the plaintiff's claim in accordance with the following provisions.

(2) The court may dismiss the plaintiff's claim if it appears to the court that it has no realistic prospect of success and there is no reason why it should be tried.

(3) The court may give judgment for the plaintiff and grant him summary relief (see section 9) if it appears to the court that there is no defence to the claim which has a realistic prospect of success, and that there is no other reason why the claim should be tried. Unless the plaintiff asks for summary relief, the court shall not act under this subsection unless it is satisfied that summary relief will adequately compensate him for the wrong he has suffered.

(5) Proceedings under this section shall be heard and determined without a jury.

9.—(1) For the purposes of section 8 (summary disposal of claim) "summary relief" means such of the following as may be appropriate—

(a) a declaration that the statement was false and defamatory of the plaintiff;
(b) an order that the defendant publish or cause to be published a suitable correction and apology;
(c) damages not exceeding £10,000 or such other amount as may be prescribed by order of the Lord Chancellor;
(d) an order restraining the defendant from publishing or further publishing the matter complained of.

(2) The content of any correction and apology, and the time, manner, form and place of publication, shall be for the parties to agree.

If they cannot agree on the content, the court may direct the defendant to publish or cause to be published a summary of the court's judgment agreed by the parties or settled by the court in accordance with rules of court.

If they cannot agree on the time, manner, form or place of publication, the court may direct the defendant to take such reasonable and practicable steps as the court considers appropriate.

17.—(1) In this Act—

"publication" and "publish", in relation to a statement, have the meaning they have for the purposes of the law of defamation generally, but "publisher" is specially defined for the purposes of section 1; "statement" means words, pictures, visual images, gestures or any other method of signifying meaning; . . .

Notes:

1. When a surfer accessed a message from a newsgroup on the Internet this was publication at common law by the service provider; it could not defend under section 1 of the Act since it had knowledge of the defamatory nature of the message and could have removed it. *Godfrey v Demon Internet* [1999] 4 All E.R. 342. The defendant ended up paying £150,000.

2. The offer of amends procedure appears to be working. In *Milne v Express Newspapers* [2002] EWHC 2564 and [2003] EWHC 1843 the defendant's unqualified offer was rejected by the claimant who proceeded to sue on the basis that the defendant "had reason to believe" that what was published was false (s.4(3)). The claim was dismissed and the defence held good: the person rejecting the offer must show actual bad faith, negligence or constructive knowledge being insufficient.

3. The summary procedure is useful. Note, however, that the claimant is entitled to elect for it, and the judge may, if he chooses, issue a declaration of falsity and order the publication of an apology, neither of which is possible at the successful conclusion of a trial. It is not surprising that Dr. Loutchansky opted for summary disposal of his claim: what he really wanted was not damages, but a declaration of falsity. The judge is not, however, bound to oblige.

4. The Act provides that claims must normally be brought within one year of publication (s.5). However, every time a person reads, hears or accesses the information this is a new publication and time starts to run afresh, though damages may be awarded only for the extra harm resulting.

5. The curious incident of the Act, like the hound of the Baskervilles which did not bark in the night-time, is what it omits. See above, p.521.

Section 3.—Privilege

TAYLOR v SERIOUS FRAUD OFFICE

House of Lords [1999] 2 A.C. 177; [1998] 3 W.L.R. 1040; [1998] 4 All E.R. 801

Communications between those investigating crime

A lawyer employed by the Serious Fraud Office suspected the plaintiff of being involved with F, S and D in a major fraud. She wrote to the Attorney-General for the Isle of Man, stating her suspicions and inviting him to exercise his power to call the plaintiff for interview. When F was prosecuted, the Serious Fraud Office had to supply his lawyers with its files, including the letter to the Attorney-General, and F's lawyers showed it to the plaintiff whom they wanted to call as a witness. The plaintiff now sued for defamation in respect of that letter.

The Court of Appeal upheld the dismissal of the claim on the basis that absolute immunity attached to communications between those investigating crime. The House of Lords agreed unanimously that the claim should be dismissed on that ground as well as on the ground (preferred by Lord Lloyd) that documents disclosed for the purpose of trials, criminal as well as civil, could not be used for collateral purposes.

Lord Hoffmann: The two principles in debate are each well established and the question before your Lordships is the extent of their reach. The concept of an implied undertaking originated in the law of discovery in civil proceedings. A solicitor or litigant who receives documents by way of discovery is treated as if he had given an undertaking not to use them for any purpose other than the conduct of the litigation. As Hobhouse J. pointed out in *Prudential Assurance Co Ltd v Fountain Page Ltd* [1991] 3 All E.R. 878 at 885, the undertaking is in reality an obligation imposed by operation of law by virtue of the circumstances in which the document or information is obtained. The reasons for imposing such an obligation were explained by Lord Keith of Kinkel in *Home Office v Harman* [1982] 1 All E.R. 532 at 540;

> "Discovery constitutes a very serious invasion of the privacy and confidentiality of a litigant's affairs. It forms part of English legal procedure because the public interest in securing that justice is done between parties is considered to outweigh the private and public interest in the maintenance of confidentiality. But the process should not be allowed to place on the litigant any harsher or more oppressive burden than is strictly required for the purpose of securing that justice is done."

The question in this appeal is whether the public interest in the administration of justice requires the application of an analogous principle to documents disclosed by the prosecution to the defence in criminal proceedings.

Likewise, the core of the principle of immunity from suit is not in doubt. By the end of the nineteenth century it was settled that persons taking part in a trial—the judge, the advocates, the witnesses—could not be sued for anything written or spoken in the course of the proceedings. The immunity was absolute and could not be defeated even by proof of malice. The reason for the immunity was explained by Fry L.J. in a well-known passage in *Munster v Lamb* (1883) 11 Q.B.D. 588 at 607:

> "Why should a witness be able to avail himself of his position in the box and to make without fear of civil consequences a false statement, which in many cases is perjured, and which is malicious and affects the character of another? The rule of law exists, not because the conduct of those persons ought not of itself to be actionable, but because if their conduct was actionable, actions would be brought against judges and witnesses in cases in which they had not spoken with malice, in which they had not spoken with falsehood. It is not a desire to prevent actions from being brought in cases where they ought to be maintained that has led to the adoption of the present rule of law; but it is the fear that if the rule were otherwise, numerous actions would be brought against persons who were merely discharging their duty. It must always be borne in mind that it is not intended to protect malicious and untruthful persons, but that it is intended to protect persons acting bonâ fide, who under a different rule would be liable, not perhaps to verdicts and judgments against them, but to the vexation of defending actions."

In *Watson v M'Ewan* [1905] A.C. 480, the House of Lords extended the immunity to statements made by the witness to a party and his legal advisers with a view to giving evidence. The question in this case is whether the immunity extends more generally to statements made to or by investigators for the purposes of a criminal investigation.

It will be noticed that although both principles are concerned with public policy in securing the proper administration of justice, the interests which they are intended to protect are somewhat different and this is reflected in differences in their scope. The implied undertaking in civil proceedings is designed to limit the invasion of privacy and confidentiality caused by compulsory disclosure of documents in litigation. It is generated by the circumstances in which the documents have been disclosed, irrespective of their contents. It excludes all collateral use, whether in other litigation or by way of publication to others. On the other hand, the undertaking may be varied or released by the courts if the interests of justice so require and, unless the court otherwise orders, ceases to apply when the documents have been read to or by the court, or referred to, in proceedings in open court.

The immunity from suit, on the other hand, is designed to encourage freedom of speech and communication in judicial proceedings by relieving persons who take part in the judicial process from the fear of being sued for something they say. It is generated by the circumstances in which the statement was made and it is not concerned with its use for any purpose other than as a cause of action. In this respect, however, the immunity is absolute and cannot be removed by the court or affected by subsequent publication of the statement.

While therefore the effect of the two principles may occasionally overlap, it is easy to think of cases in which one would apply but not the other. For example, a statement protected by the immunity may be disclosed on discovery and subsequently read out in court. The implied undertaking would cease to apply and anyone would be free to publish the statement but it still could not form the basis of a cause of action.

Nevertheless, there is some degree of interaction between the two principles. The implied undertaking prevents, so far as possible, the publication or dissemination of disclosed documents and therefore restricts the extent to which damage can be caused by defamatory statements which they may contain. In this sense, the injustice which may be caused by the fact that such defamatory statements are protected by the immunity is reduced.

In my opinion, therefore, the disclosure of documents by the prosecution as unused material under its common law obligations did generate an implied undertaking not to use them for any collateral purpose. I think that Sir Michael Davies was right to strike out the action for the reasons which he gave.

In view of the opinion I have expressed on the implied undertaking, it is not strictly necessary for me to consider the ground upon which the Court of Appeal dismissed the appeal, namely immunity from suit. Nevertheless, the question was fully argued before your Lordships and I think it is right to deal with it. It could easily have happened that the documents were read in open court. I think it would be right for your Lordships to decide whether in that case the plaintiff would have been entitled to rely upon them for the purposes of an action in libel.

There is no doubt that the claim for absolute immunity in respect of statements made by one investigator to another, or by an investigator to a person helping with the inquiry, or to an investigator by a person helping the inquiry who is not intended to be called as a witness is a novel one. So far as I know, it is not a category of absolute immunity which has been considered before. But it should not for that reason be rejected. Again, I would imagine that the reason why this question now arises for the first time is that before the broadening of the prosecution's disclosure obligation, such letters and memoranda, internal to the investigation, would never have seen the light of day. At any rate, the question is now whether they fall within the underlying rationale for the existence of immunity from suit.

Thus the test is a strict one; necessity must be shown, but the decision on whether immunity is necessary for the administration of justice must have regard to the cases in which immunity has been held necessary in the past, so as to form part of a coherent principle.

Approaching the matter on this basis, I find it impossible to identify any rational principle which would confine the immunity for out of court statements to persons who are subsequently called as witnesses. The policy of the immunity is to enable people to speak freely without fear of being sued, whether successfully or not. If this object is to be achieved, the person in question must know at the time he speaks whether or not the immunity will attach. If it depends upon the contingencies of whether he will be called as a witness, the value of the immunity is destroyed. At the time of the investigation it is often unclear whether any crime has been committed at all. Persons assisting the police with their inquiries may not be able to give any admissible evidence; for example, their information may be hearsay, but none the less valuable for the purposes of the investigation. But the proper administration of justice requires that such people should have the same inducement to speak freely as those whose information subsequently forms the basis of evidence at a trial.

When one turns to the position of investigators, it seems to me that the same degree of necessity applies. It would be an incoherent rule which gave a potential witness immunity in respect of the statements which he made to an investigator but offered no similar immunity to the investigator if he passed that information to a colleague engaged in the investigation or put it to another potential witness. In my view it is necessary for the administration of justice that investigators should be able to exchange information, theories and hypotheses among themselves and to put them to other persons assisting in the inquiry without fear of being sued if such statements are disclosed in the course of the proceedings. I therefore agree with the test proposed by Drake J. in *Evans v London Hospital Medical College* [1981] 1 All E.R. 715 at 721; [1981] 1 W.L.R. 184 at 192:

> "The protection exists only where the statement or conduct is such that it can fairly be said to be part of the process of investigating a crime or a possible crime with a view to a prosecution or a possible prosecution in respect of the matter being investigated."

This formulation excludes statements which are wholly extraneous to the investigation—irrelevant and gratuitous libels—but applies equally to statements made by persons assisting the inquiry to investigators and by investigators to those persons or to each other.

As the policy of the immunity is to encourage freedom of expression, it is limited to actions in which the alleged statement constitutes the cause of action. In *Marrinan v Vibart* [1962] 3 All E.R. 380; [1963] 1 Q.B. 528 the Court of Appeal held that the immunity in respect of statements made in court or with a view to a prosecution could not be circumvented by alleging that it formed part of a conspiracy with other witnesses to give false evidence. That seems to me to be right. On the other hand, the immunity does not apply to actions for malicious prosecution where the cause of action consists in abusing legal process by maliciously and without reasonable cause setting the law in motion against the plaintiff. It does not matter that an essential step in setting the law in motion was a statement made by the defendant to a prosecuting authority or even the court: see *Roy v Prior* [1970] 2 All E.R. 729.

Actions for defamation and for conspiracy to give false evidence plainly fall within the policy of the immunity and actions for malicious prosecution fall outside it. In between, there is some disputed ground. In *Evans v London Hospital Medical College* Drake J. held that it precluded reliance on the statement in an action for negligence in which it was alleged that a carelessly prepared post mortem report had led to the plaintiff being unjustifiably arrested and charged with murder. I express no view on this case, which I think might nowadays have been decided on the ground that the defendants owed the plaintiff no duty of care. But I am satisfied that the Court of Appeal was right in holding that the statements relied upon in this case were protected by absolute immunity and for that reason also I would dismiss the appeal.

Notes:

1. As this decision shows, the privilege which attaches to the occasion of a communication must be distinguished from (but may be concurrent with) the immunity or privilege which may attach to a document so as to render it inadmissible as evidence of what was communicated. Thus one may not found a libel suit on a document compulsorily disclosed in prior litigation (*Riddick v Thames Board Mills* [1977] 3 All E.R. 677). This was extended in *Hasselblad (G.B.) v Orbinson* [1985] 1 All E.R. 173. The defendant bought a camera manufactured by the plaintiff and then complained to the shop that the plaintiff refused to repair it because it had come from an unauthorised dealer. The shop sent the letter to its supplier, the supplier sent it to the European Commission which it had previously notified of the plaintiff's possible breach of Article 86 of the Treaty of Rome, and the Commission, as it was bound to do, sent a copy of it to the plaintiff. The plaintiff sued for defamation. The Court of Appeal held that the absolute privilege which attaches to evidence given to a judicial or quasi-judicial body did not apply since the Commission's procedure rendered it administrative rather than in any way judicial, but that Hasselblad should be prevented from using the letter as the foundation of a libel suit as it had been mandatorily disclosed to it for a limited purpose. The suit therefore collapsed. Those who ask, with May L.J., why qualified privilege was not sufficient protection for the defendant may ponder the words of Sir John Donaldson M.R.: "It is only the very rich, the very foolish, the very malicious or the very dedicated who will knowingly put themselves in a position in which they have to defend a libel action, even with the benefit of qualified privilege as a defence. The anxieties would be enormous and, even if ultimately successful, the difference between actual and recoverable costs would be very substantial indeed." May L.J. was struck by the fact that no similar case had come up in any of the other Member States of the EEC. That is because none of them has a law of defamation as dotty as ours, or as susceptible of wicked abuse.

2. Although absolute privilege was extended in the principal case, and extended further in *Mahon v Rahn* [2000] 4 All E.R. 41, where it was held to cover a letter from a bank to the Serious Fraud Office with regard to the question whether a person was a fit and proper person to carry on investment business, libel lawyers on the bench seem to dislike it very much, perhaps because any extension tends to diminish the take of libel lawyers still in practice. Thus *Hasselblad* has been rather frowned upon ("a very special decision reached

on its very special facts"—*Waple v Surrey C.C.* [1998] 1 All E.R. 624 at 633), and absolute privilege has been denied to communications to the Parole Board by a woman accused of lying by a prisoner convicted of rape (*Daniels v Griffiths* [1997] Times L.R. 613). It has also been denied to communications by a local authority to the Department of Health, pursuant to guidelines issued by the latter, about a social worker who had been removed from work with children (*S v Newham L.B.C.* [1998] F.L.R. 1061, CA, where Lord Woolf complacently observed of the risk of hassle that "Today this danger can and should be substantially reduced by court management of litigation".) Again absolute privilege was denied to a local authority solicitor who, trying to be helpful to a woman unhappy at the removal into foster care of her adopted child, wrote a response to an inquiry from the woman's solicitor. Taking the view that litigation was not yet in view and that "It is the form, not the substance with which the court is traditionally concerned in cases of this type" the court ignored the argument that absolute privilege would be justified because "the proper performance by council staff of their child welfare functions has an inherent tendency to produce dissatisfied parties, emotional upset, occasional outbursts, frustration and a desire to blame others for adverse outcomes": the court found a justification for not increasing the scope of absolute privilege in the fact that Parliament quite frequently did so (*Waple v Surrey CC* [1998] 1 All E.R. 624). The situation is hardly one where the risk of malice is great enough that complainants should be allowed to try to establish it at the price of almost certain failure and certain cost to the courts (as well as money for libel lawyers!). The courts which were in the past wise enough to protect local authorities, the targets of grudge, against claims for negligence should do likewise when they are harassed by libel actions.

3. Distinguishable yet again is "public interest immunity", which prevents the disclosure in court of documents which the court believes should not be seen by the jury. For many years the courts held that such immunity attached to the files of the Police Complaints Authority by reason of the kind of document they were rather than the kind of information they contained. This was very unfair to private litigants, for, as Lord Taylor L.C.J. well said in *Ex p. Coventry Newspapers* [1993] 1 All E.R. 86 at 95: "If . . . documents appear to point clearly towards corruption on the part of named police officers, it is surely not to be tolerated that those same officers should continue to mulct the press in damages whilst the courts disable their adversaries from an effective defence by withholding the documents from them." Shortly thereafter, happily, the House of Lords held that such documents do not *ipso facto* attract immunity from production: *R. v Chief Constable of West Midlands, Ex p. Wiley* [1994] 3 All E.R. 420.

WATT v LONGSDON

Court of Appeal [1930] 1 K.B. 130; 98 L.J.K.B. 711; 142 L.T. 4; 45 T.L.R. 619; 73 S.J. 544; [1929] All E.R. Rep. 284

Longsdon was liquidator of the Scottish Petroleum Company. He received from Browne, manager of their office in Casablanca, a letter relating that Watt, the managing director, had been living in sin for two months with the housemaid, who was described as old, deaf and nearly blind and was said to dye her hair; the letter also stated that Watt had planned to seduce Mrs Browne. Longsdon sent this letter to Singer, the chairman of the board of directors. Longsdon also replied to Browne, saying that he had long suspected Watt of immorality and that, in his view, Mrs Watt (whom he knew well, as she had nursed him through an illness) ought to be told; he himself would tell her, if only Browne would obtain a sworn statement, by bribery, if need be. Before that statement was obtained, Watt himself returned to England, and Longsdon sent Browne's original letter to Mrs Watt. The result was a separation and proceedings for divorce.

Watt sued Longsdon in respect of the publications to Singer, Browne and Mrs Watt. The learned judge held that the occasion of all three publications was privileged, and held further that there was no evidence of malice fit to be left to the jury. The plaintiff appealed; the Court of Appeal allowed his appeal and ordered a new trial.

Scrutton L.J.: This case raises, amongst other matters, the extremely difficult question, equally important in its legal and social aspect, as to the circumstances, if any, in which a person will be justified in giving to one partner to a marriage information which that person honestly believes to be correct, but which is in fact untrue, about the matrimonial delinquencies of the other party to the marriage. The question becomes more difficult if the answer in law turns on the existence or non-existence of a social or moral duty, a question which the judge is to determine, without any evidence, by the light of his own knowledge of the world, and his own views on social morality, a subject-matter on which views vary in different ages, in different countries, and even as between man and man. . . .

The learned judge appears to have taken the view that the authorities justify him in holding that if "there is an obvious interest in the person to whom a communication is made which causes him to be a proper recipient of a statement," even if the party making the communication had no moral or social duty to the party to whom the communication is made, the occasion is privileged. . . . He has therefore found in the present case that the occasion of each of the three communications, to Singer, to the wife, and to Browne, was privileged, and that there is no evidence of excess of communication or of malice to be left to the jury.

By the law of England there are occasions on which a person may make defamatory statements about another which are untrue without incurring any legal liability for his statements. These occasions are called privileged occasions. But communications made on these occasions may lose their privilege: (1) they may exceed the privilege of the occasion by going beyond the limits of the duty or interest, or (2) they may be published with express malice, so that the occasion is not being legitimately used, but abused. . . . The question whether the occasion was privileged is for the judge, and so far as "duty" is concerned, the question is: Was there a duty, legal, moral, or social, to communicate? As to legal duty, the judge should have no difficulty; the judge should know the law; but as to moral or social duties of imperfect obligation, the task is far more troublesome. The judge has no evidence as to the view the community takes of moral or social duties. Is the judge merely to give his own view of moral and social duty, though he thinks a considerable portion of the community hold a different opinion? Or is he to endeavour to ascertain what view "the great mass of right-minded men" would take? It is not surprising that with such a standard both judges and text-writers treat the matter as one of great difficulty in which no definite line can be drawn. . . .

. . . In 1855, in *Harrison v Bush* ((1855) 119 E.R. 509), Lord Campbell C.J. giving the judgment of the Court of Queen's Bench accepted a principle stated thus: "A communication made bona fide upon any subject-matter in which the party communicating has an interest, or in reference to which he has a duty, is privileged, if made to a person having a corresponding interest or duty, although it contain criminatory matter which, without this privilege, would be slanderous and actionable." This is the first of a series of statements that both parties, the writer and the recipient, must have a corresponding interest or duty. . . . Lord Atkinson in *Adam v Ward* ([1917] A.C. 309 at 334) expresses it thus: "It was not disputed, in this case on either side, that a privileged occasion is, in reference to qualified privilege, an occasion where the person who makes a communication has an interest or a duty, legal, social, or moral, to make it to the person to whom it is made, and the person to whom it is so made has a corresponding interest or duty to receive it. This reciprocity is essential." With slight modifications in particular circumstances, this appears to me to be well-established law, but, except in the case of communications based on common interest, the principle is that either there must be interest in the recipient and a duty to communicate in the speaker, or an interest to be protected in the speaker and a duty to protect it in the recipient. Except in the case of common interest justifying intercommunication, the correspondence must be between duty and interest. There may, in the common interest cases, be also a common or reciprocal duty. It is not every interest which will create a duty in a stranger or volunteer. . . .

In *Stuart v Bell* ([1891] 2 Q.B. 341) there was a difference of opinion . . . Stanley, the explorer, and his valet, Stuart, were staying with the mayor of Newcastle, Bell. The Edinburgh police made a very carefully worded communication to the Newcastle police that there had been a robbery in Edinburgh at an hotel where Stuart was staying, and it might be well to make very careful and cautious inquiry into the matter. The Newcastle police showed the letter to the mayor, who after consideration showed it to Stanley, who dismissed Stuart. Stuart sued the mayor. Lindley and Kay L.JJ. held that the mayor had a moral duty to communicate, and Stanley a material interest to receive the communication; Lopes L.J. held that in the circumstances there was no moral duty to communicate, though in some circumstances there might be such a duty in a host towards a guest. I myself should have agreed with the majority, but the difference of opinion between such experienced judges shows the difficulty of the question.

In my opinion Horridge J. went too far in holding that there could be a privileged occasion on the ground of interest in the recipient without any duty to communicate on the part of the person making the communication. But that does not settle the question, for it is necessary to consider, in the present case, whether there was, as to each communication, a duty to communicate, and an interest in the recipient.

First as to the communication between Longsdon and Singer, I think the case must proceed on the admission that at all material times Watt, Longsdon and Browne were in the employment of the same company, and the evidence afforded by the answer to the interrogatory put in by the plaintiff that Longsdon believed the statements in Browne's letter. In my view on these facts there was a duty, both from a moral and a material point of view, on Longsdon to communicate the letter to Singer, the chairman of his company, who, apart from questions of present employment, might be asked by Watt for a testimonial to a future employer. Equally, I think Longsdon receiving the letter from Browne, might discuss the matter with him, and ask for further information, on the ground of a common interest in the affairs of the company, and to obtain further information for the chairman. I should therefore agree with the view of Horridge J. that these two occasions were privileged, though for different reasons. Horridge J. further held that there was no evidence of malice fit to be left to the jury, and, while I think some of Longsdon's action and language in this respect was unfortunate, as the plaintiff has put in the answer that Longsdon believed the truth of the statements in Browne's and his own letter, I do not dissent from his view as to malice. As to the communications to Singer and Browne, in my opinion the appeal should fail.

The communication to Mrs Watt stands on a different footing. I have no intention of writing an exhaustive treatise on the circumstances when a stranger or a friend should communicate to husband or wife information he receives as to the conduct of the other party to the marriage. I am clear that it is impossible to say he is always under a moral or social duty to do so; it is equally impossible to say he is never under such a duty. It must depend on the circumstances of each case, the nature of the information, and the relation of speaker and recipient. It cannot, on the one hand, be the duty even of a friend to communicate all the gossip the friend hears at men's clubs or women's bridge parties to one of the spouses affected. On the other hand, most men would hold that it was the moral duty of a doctor who attended his sister in law, and believed her to be suffering from a miscarriage, for which an absent husband could not be responsible, to communicate that fact to his wife and the husband. . . . If this is so, the decision must turn on the circumstances of each case, the judge being much influenced by the consideration that as a general rule it is not desirable for anyone, even a mother in law, to interfere in the affairs of man and wife. Using the best judgment I can in this difficult matter, I have come to the conclusion that there was not a moral or social duty in Longsdon to make this communication to Mrs Watt such as to make the occasion privileged, and that there must be a new trial so far as it relates to the claim for publication of a libel to Mrs Watt.

Questions

1. If a statement is false, how can there ever be a duty to communicate it?

2. Would the outcome of the case have been the same if Longsdon had sent the defamatory letter in response to an inquiry from Mrs Watt whether he had any news of her husband? Or asking if what she had heard about him were true? Or asking if he could help her obtain evidence for a forthcoming divorce suit? If there were a privilege in any of these cases, what would be its source?

3. If A defames B to C, and B retaliates by defaming A to C, can B, when sued by A, claim (a) that he had any kind of duty to make the statement in question, and (b) that C had any interest in hearing it? See *Turner v MGM Pictures Ltd* [1950] 1 All E.R. 449, HL, and note 3 below. If one is defamed on the internet may one publish a defamatory reply in the same medium?

4. Would it be safe for a disgruntled customer to write to the manager of a store that in his view its employees (or a named employee) were incompetent and insolent?

5. Is it not odd that speech is free only where there is a duty to speak or to listen? Can you think of a better technique than qualified privilege to distinguish socially desirable communications from gratuitous gossip and mere muck-raking?

6. How do you like the court's holding that while the employer was entitled to know of the employee's alleged shenanigans, the wife was not? What if the plaintiff had told the defendant truly and in confidence that he had had an affair in Morocco, and the defendant, in breach of this confidence, had told the wife? See *Stephens v Avery* [1988] 2 All E.R. 99.

Notes:

1. As Blackburn J. said in *Davies v Snead* ((1870) L.R. 5 Q.B. 608 at 611): "where a person is so situated that it becomes right in the interests of society that he should tell to a third person certain facts, then if he bona fide and without malice does tell them it is a privileged communication." The test of the existence of privilege is objective: it must be right in the interests of society, and it is not enough that the defendant honestly supposed that it was right; furthermore, the person to whom he makes the communication must be the right person to receive it, and it is not enough that the defendant should honestly think that he is. If these objective criteria are satisfied, then the defendant is protected if he honestly believed what he said, even if he got his facts wrong. Indeed, if he got his facts wrong, privilege is the only possible defence, even if the matter is one of public interest.

2. A businessman who dictates a letter "publishes" its contents to his secretary. If the letter was destined for a third party, privilege attaches to the dictation if actual publication to that third party would be privileged. If the letter is addressed to the plaintiff, there is the difficulty that since publication to the party defamed is not a tort at all, it cannot strictly be called privileged; even so, the dictation of such a letter appears to be privileged unless the letter was quite unwarranted. If the secretary has any particular interest in the subject-matter, the dictation may be privileged in its own right, but otherwise no privilege attached to the dictation situation as such. *Bryanston Finance v de Vries* [1975] Q.B. 703 contains a fascinating conflict of opinion on the matter between Lord Denning and Lord Diplock.

(It might be better to say that there is no publication at all between businessman and secretary, just as there is none between husband and wife (Spencer [1975] Camb. L.J. 195): if the only "publication" is to an unmarried cohabitant fully conversant with the situation (neighbour problems), an attempt to base a libel suit on it may be struck out as an abuse: *Wallis v Valentine* [2002] EWCA Civ 1034. And what of communication to the *plaintiff's* agent? If the plaintiff asks his solicitor to make inquiry of the defendant and the defendant replies in a manner allegedly defamatory of the plaintiff, should one not be able to deny publication? See the facts of *Waple*, above p.544.

3. It will be seen that the common law of qualified privilege is not very homogeneous.

(a) "Duty/interest" and "common interest" do not fit well together. This was exemplified in a case where the Bar Council wrote a letter to barristers erroneously suggesting that the claimant was not a firm of solicitors qualified to instruct barristers (*Kearns v Bar Council* [2003] EWCA Civ 331). Simon Brown L.J. said he would prefer to drop the "common interest" label and ask whether the communication took place within a pre-existing relationship, such as clearly exists between the Bar Council and the Bar, since communication within such a relationship should be more free, less readily held to be actionable. If you are communicating to a total stranger, it may be sensible to ask whether you were under any sort of duty to do so. But was Mrs Watt a total stranger to Longsdon?

(b) A subspecies of privilege which it is not easy to accommodate is the right of verbal self-defence, to return insult for insult, like for like. This seems to fit in with neither the "duty/interest" nor the "common interest" cases. Perhaps that is why, like other instances of self-help these days, it is being downplayed. A good example is *Baldwin v Rusbridger* [2001] E.M.L.R. 47. The defendant journalist and newspaper, having been held liable for defamation, commented on the decision against them and in doing so repeated the original libel. After holding that they were under no duty to publish this (!), the judge repelled the defence that that they were replying to an attack on them in court by the claimant's counsel. The judge noted that counsel's remarks were covered by absolute privilege (what is the relevance of that in this context?), and that the defendants' comments fell outside "the narrow confines of the 'reply to attack'", given the powerful arguments of public policy against extending to journalists the privilege of attacking those who had criticised them in the courts of law. Those arguments were not specified, and one wonders what they could be, apart, of course, from the Barristers and Courts Protection Scheme.

Or consider *Watts v Times Newspapers* [1996] 1 All E.R. 152. The newspaper published two articles suggesting that the plaintiff, a writer, was a plagiarist. Alongside the articles they published a photograph of a quite different Nigel Watts, a property developer. The property developer insisted that the newspaper publish an apology to himself, containing words which were again defamatory of the plaintiff, who sued both the newspaper and the property developer's solicitors in respect of this further publication. It was held that the developer had qualified privilege arising out of self-defence (though actually it was not the plaintiff writer who had defamed him), but that the newspaper did not (since it was rather the original defamer than the subsequent defamed). Nor is *Fraser-Armstrong v Hadow* [1994] Times L.R. 35, CA free from difficulty, for Staughton L.J. said "It did not seem . . . to be a proper motive to seek to defend oneself if the attacks made by the plaintiff were true", and Simon Brown L.J. said it did not matter whether one said that there was no privilege to protect oneself against justified attack or that it was malicious to do so. It matters a good deal as to burden of proof, for one thing, and there are others, such as, what if one unreasonably believes that the attack is unjustified? A solicitor may, however, be entitled to respond defamatorily to attacks on his client (*Regan v Taylor*, March 9, 2000, CA).

4. As the principal case shows, the plaintiff in a defamation suit who is suing on a statement published on a privileged occasion must prove malice. As held in *Stuart v Bell*, mentioned above, p.545, a reference sent to a potential employer about a past employee is privileged. Accordingly the employee who wishes to sue in defamation, *i.e.* who wants to benefit from the rules that he need not prove falsehood or damage but cannot prove malice, will be thwarted. Does this entail that if he *can* prove falsehood and damage, he cannot sue at all, short of proving malice, even if he can establish negligence? The Court of Appeal said so in *Spring v Guardian Assurance* [1993] 2 All E.R. 273, reversing the trial judge, but they were themselves reversed by the House of Lords [1994] 3 All E.R. 129.

5. We shall see later that anyone may freely *comment* on matters of public interest (below, p.557). Newspapers may also *report* certain matters of public interest, including what people said at public meetings of specified types, without falling foul of the general rule that to repeat a defamation is to become liable for it. The matters which may be so reported are listed in Schedule 1 to the Defamation Act 1996, those in Part II thereof being protected only if the defendant refuses or neglects, when requested by the plaintiff, to publish "in a suitable manner a reasonable letter or statement by way of explanation or contradiction". Reports of proceedings must be "fair and accurate" and it is for the jury to decide, if two views are possible, whether a report is indeed fair and accurate and whether the matter is of public interest and the publication for the public benefit (as required by s.15(3) of the Act) *Kingshott v Associated Kent Newspapers* [1991] 2 All E.R. 99.

REYNOLDS v TIMES NEWSPAPERS

House of Lords [2001] 2 A.C. 127; [1999] 3 W.L.R. 1010; [1999] 4 All E.R. 609 (noted (2000) 116 L.Q.R. 185)

Publication by newspaper of politically significant but inaccurate facts

The defendant newspaper published an article implying that the plaintiff, then Taoiseach (Prime Minister) of Eire, had lied to the Dáil (House of Representatives) there. At the trial which, because of errors in the summing-up, was ultimately remanded for retrial, the jury found that the newspaper had failed to prove that this was true (but awarded no damages), and the judge ruled that the publication was not covered by qualified privilege. On the newspaper's cross-appeal, the Court of Appeal held that although the newspaper could be said to have had a duty to publish and that what it published was of interest to the public so that the duty/interest test was satisfied, it failed a third test, now enunciated for the first time, a test relating to the circumstances of the publication: the editor should have sought an explanation from the plaintiff before printing what it did and had failed to mention the explanation given by the plaintiff to the Dáil.

The House of Lords held, Lord Steyn and Lord Hope dissenting, that the question of privilege was concluded by the decision of the Court of Appeal, though the third test applied by it was superfluous.

Lord Nicholls of Birkenhead: My Lords, this appeal concerns the interaction between two fundamental rights: freedom of expression and protection of reputation. The context is newspaper discussion of a matter of political importance. Stated in its simplest form, the newspaper's contention is that a libellous statement of fact made in the course of political discussion is free from liability if published in good faith. Liability arises only if the writer knew the statement was not true or if he made the statement recklessly, not caring whether it was true or false, or if he was actuated by personal spite or some other improper motive. Mr Reynolds' contention, on the other hand, is that liability may also arise if, having regard to the source of the information and all the circumstances, it was not in the public interest for the newspaper to have published the information as it did. Under the newspaper's contention the safeguard for those who are defamed is exclusively subjective: the state of mind of the journalist. Under Mr Reynolds' formulation, there is also an objective element of protection.

The jury verdict took the form of answers to questions. The jury decided that the defamatory allegation of which Mr Reynolds complained was not true. So the defence of justification failed. The jury decided that Mr Ruddock was not acting maliciously in writing and publishing the words complained of, nor was Mr Witherow. So, if the occasion was privileged, and that was a question for the judge, the defence of qualified privilege would succeed. The defendants unsuccessfully contended for a wide qualified privilege at common law for "political speech". The judge ruled that publication of the article was not privileged.

The Court of Appeal set aside the verdict, finding and judgment of the court below and ordered a new trial. The Court of Appeal also considered whether the defendants would be able to rely on qualified privilege at the retrial. The court held they would not. Your Lordships' House gave leave to the defendants to appeal against this ruling, since it raised an issue of public importance. That is the issue now before your Lordships.

The defence of qualified privilege must be seen in its overall setting in the law of defamation. Historically the common law has set much store by protection of reputation. Publication of a statement adversely affecting a person's reputation is actionable. The plaintiff is not required to prove that the words are false. Nor, in the case of publication in a written or permanent form, is he required to prove he has been damaged. But, as Littledale J. said in *M'Pherson v Daniels* (1829) 109 E.R. 448: " . . . the law will not permit a man to recover damages in respect of an injury to a character which he either does not, or ought not, to possess." Truth is a complete defence. If the defendant proves the substantial truth of the words complained of, he thereby establishes the defence of justification. With the minor exception of proceedings to which the Rehabilitation of Offenders Act 1974 applies, this defence is of universal application in civil proceedings. It avails a defendant even if he was acting spitefully.

The common law has long recognised the "chilling" effect of this rigorous, reputation-protective principle. There must be exceptions. At times people must be able to speak and write freely, uninhibited by the prospect of being sued for damages should they be mistaken or misinformed. In the wider public interest, protection of reputation must then give way to a higher priority.

One established exception is the defence of comment on a matter of public interest. This defence is available to everyone, and is of particular importance to the media. The freedom of expression protected by this defence has long been regarded by the common law as a basic right, long before the emergence of human rights conventions. In 1863 Crompton J. observed in *Campbell v Spottiswoode* 122 E.R. 288 at 291: "It is the right of all the Queen's subjects to discuss public matters . . . " The defence is wide in its scope.

It is important to keep in mind that this defence is concerned with the protection of comment, not imputations of fact. If the imputation is one of fact, a ground of defence must be sought elsewhere. Further, to be within this defence the comment must be recognisable as comment, as distinct from an imputation of fact. The comment must explicitly or implicitly indicate, at least in general terms, what are the facts on which the comment is being made.

The defence of honest comment on a matter of public interest, then, does not cover defamatory statements of fact. But there are circumstances, in the famous words of Parke B. in *Toogood v Spyring* (1834) 149 E.R. 1044; All E.R. Rep 735 at 738 when the "common convenience and welfare of society" call for frank communication on questions of fact. In *Davies v Snead* (1870) L.R. 5 Q.B. 608 at 611 Blackburn J. spoke of circumstances where a person is so situated that it "becomes right in the interests of society" that he should tell certain facts to another. There are occasions when the person to whom a statement is made has a special interest in learning the honestly held views of another person, even if those views are defamatory of someone else and cannot be proved to be true. When the interest is of sufficient importance to outweigh the need to protect reputation, the occasion is regarded as privileged.

Sometimes the need for uninhibited expression is of such a high order that the occasion attracts absolute privilege, as with statements made by judges or advocates or witnesses in the course of judicial proceedings. More usually, the privilege is qualified in that it can be defeated if the plaintiff proves the defendant was actuated by malice.

Over the years the courts have held that many common form situations are privileged. Classic instances are employment references, and complaints made or information given to the police or appropriate authorities regarding suspected crimes. The courts have always emphasised that the categories established by the authorities are not exhaustive. The list is not closed. The established categories are no more than applications, in particular circumstances, of the underlying principle of public policy. The underlying principle is conventionally stated in words to the effect that there must exist between the maker of the statement and the recipient some duty or interest in the making of the communication. Lord Atkinson's dictum, in *Adam v Ward* [1917] A.C. 309 at 334, much quoted:

> " . . . a privileged occasion is . . . an occasion where the person who makes a communication has an interest or a duty, legal, social, or moral, to make it to the person to whom it is made, and the person to whom it is so made has a corresponding interest or duty to receive it. This reciprocity is essential."

The requirement that both the maker of the statement and the recipient must have an interest or duty draws attention to the need to have regard to the position of both parties when deciding whether an occasion is privileged. But this should not be allowed to obscure the rationale of the underlying public interest on which privilege is founded. The essence of this defence lies in the law's recognition of the need, in the public interest, for a particular recipient to receive frank and uninhibited communication of particular information from a particular source. That is the end the law is concerned to attain. The protection afforded to the maker of the statement is the means by which the law seeks to achieve that end. Thus the court has to assess whether, in the public interest, the publication should be protected in the absence of malice.

In determining whether an occasion is regarded as privileged the court has regard to all the circumstances. And circumstances must be viewed with today's eyes. The circumstances in which the public interest requires a communication to be protected in the absence of malice depend upon current social conditions. The requirements at the close of the twentieth century may not be the same as those of earlier centuries or earlier decades of this century.

Frequently a privileged occasion encompasses publication to one person only or to a limited group of people. Publication more widely, to persons who lack the requisite interest in receiving the information, is not privileged. But the common law has recognised there are occasions when the public interest requires that publication to the world at large should be privileged. In *Cox v Feeney* (1863) 176 E.R. 445 Cockburn C.J. approved an earlier statement by Lord Tenterden C.J. that "a man has a right to publish, for the purpose of giving the public information, that which it is proper for the public to know". Whether the public interest so requires depends upon an evaluation of the particular information in the circumstances of its publication. Through the cases runs the strain that, when determining whether the public at large had a right to know the particular information, the court has regard to all the circumstances. The court is concerned to assess whether the information was of sufficient value to the public that, in the public interest, it should be protected by privilege in the absence of malice.

This issue has arisen several times in the context of newspapers discharging their important function of reporting matters of public importance.

In *Blackshaw v Lord* [1983] 2 All E.R. 311, the Court of Appeal rejected a claim to generic protection for a widely stated category: "fair information on a matter of public interest" A claim to privilege must be more precisely focused. In order to be privileged publication must be in the public interest. Whether a publication is in the public interest or, in the conventional phraseology, whether there is a duty to publish to the intended recipients, there the readers of the *Daily Telegraph*, depends upon the circumstances, including the nature of the matter published and its source or status.

I turn to the appellants' submissions. The newspaper seeks the incremental development of the common law by the creation of a new category of occasion when privilege derives from the subject matter alone: political information. Political information can be broadly defined as information, opinion and arguments concerning government and political matters that affect the people of the United Kingdom. Malice apart, publication of political information should be privileged regardless of the status and source of the material and the circumstances of the publication. The newspaper submitted that the contrary view requires the court to assess the public interest value of a publication, taking these matters into account. Such an approach would involve an unpredictable outcome. Moreover, it would put the judge in a position which in a free society ought to be occupied by the editor. Such paternalism would effectively give the court an undesirable and invidious role as a censor or licensing body.

These are powerful arguments, but I do not accept the conclusion for which the newspaper contended. My reasons appear from what is set out below.

My starting point is freedom of expression. The high importance of freedom to impart and receive information and ideas has been stated so often and so eloquently that this point calls for no elaboration in this case. At a pragmatic level, freedom to disseminate and receive information on political matters is essential to the proper functioning of the system of parliamentary democracy cherished in this country. This freedom enables those who elect representatives to Parliament to make an informed choice, regarding individuals as well as policies, and those elected to make informed decisions. Freedom of expression will shortly be buttressed by statutory requirements. Under s.12 of the 1998 Act, the court is required, in relevant cases, to have particular regard to the importance of the right to freedom of expression. The common law is to be developed and applied in a manner consistent with Art.10 of the European Convention for the Protection of Human Rights and Fundamental Freedoms, and the court must take into account relevant decisions of the European Court of Human Rights (see ss.6 and 2). To be justified, any curtailment of freedom of expression must be convincingly established by a compelling countervailing consideration, and the means employed must be proportionate to the end sought to be achieved.

Likewise, there is no need to elaborate on the importance of the role discharged by the media in the expression and communication of information and comment on political matters. It is through the mass media that most people today obtain their information on political matters. Without freedom of expression by the media, freedom of expression would be a hollow concept. The interest of a democratic society in ensuring a free press weighs heavily in the balance in deciding whether any curtailment of this freedom bears a reasonable relationship to the purpose of the curtailment. In this regard it should be kept in mind that one of the contemporary functions of the media is investigative journalism. This activity, as much as the traditional activities of reporting and commenting, is part of the vital role of the press and the media generally.

Reputation is an integral and important part of the dignity of the individual. It also forms the basis of many decisions in a democratic society which are fundamental to its well-being: whom to employ or work for, whom to promote, whom to do business with or to vote for. Once besmirched by an unfounded allegation in a national newspaper, a reputation can be damaged for ever, especially if there is no opportunity to vindicate one's reputation. When this happens, society as well as the individual is the loser. For it should not be supposed that protection of reputation is a matter of importance only to the affected individual and his family. Protection of reputation is conducive to the public good. It is in the public interest that the reputation of public figures should not be debased falsely. In the political field, in order to make an informed choice, the electorate needs to be able to identify the good as well as the bad. Consistently with these considerations, human rights conventions recognise that freedom of expression is not an absolute right. Its exercise may be subject to such restrictions as are prescribed by law and are necessary in a democratic society for the protection of the reputations of others.

The crux of this appeal, therefore, lies in identifying the restrictions which are fairly and reasonably necessary for the protection of reputation. Leaving aside the exceptional cases which attract absolute privilege, the common law denies protection to defamatory statements, whether of comment or fact, proved to be actuated by malice, in the *Horrocks v Lowe* sense [see below, p.554]. This common law limitation on freedom of speech passes the "necessary" test with flying colours. This is an acceptable limitation. Freedom of speech does not embrace freedom to make defamatory statements out of personal spite or without having a positive belief in their truth.

In the case of statements of opinion on matters of public interest, that is the limit of what is necessary for protection of reputation. Readers and viewers and listeners can make up their own minds on whether they agree or disagree with defamatory statements which are recognisable as comment and which, expressly or implicitly, indicate in general terms the facts on which they are based.

With defamatory imputations of fact the position is different and more difficult. Those who read or hear such allegations are unlikely to have any means of knowing whether they are true or not. In respect of such imputations, a plaintiff's ability to obtain a remedy if he can prove malice is not normally a sufficient safeguard. Malice is notoriously difficult to prove. If a newspaper is understandably unwilling to disclose its sources, a plaintiff can be deprived of the material necessary to prove, or even allege, that the newspaper acted recklessly in publishing as it did without further verification. Thus, in the absence of any additional safeguard for reputation, a newspaper, anxious to be first with a "scoop", would in practice be free to publish seriously defamatory misstatements of fact based on the slenderest of materials. Unless the paper chose later to withdraw the allegations, the politician thus defamed would have no means of clearing his name, and the public would have no means of knowing where the truth lay. Some further protection for reputation is needed if this can be achieved without a disproportionate incursion into freedom of expression.

This is a difficult problem. No answer is perfect. Every solution has its own advantages and disadvantages. Depending on local conditions, such as legal procedures and the traditions and power of the press, the solution preferred in one country may not be best suited to another country. The appellant newspaper commends reliance upon the ethics of professional journalism. The decision should be left to the editor of the newspaper. Unfortunately, in the United Kingdom this would not generally be thought to provide a sufficient safeguard. In saying this I am not referring to mistaken decisions. From time to time mistakes are bound to occur, even in the best regulated circles. Making every allowance for this, the sad reality is that the overall handling of these matters by the national press, with its own commercial interests to serve, does not always command general confidence.

As highlighted by the Court of Appeal judgment in the present case, the common law solution is for the court to have regard to all the circumstances when deciding whether the publication of particular material was privileged because of its value to the public. Its value to the public depends upon its quality as well as its subject matter. This solution has the merit of elasticity. As observed by the Court of Appeal, this principle can be applied appropriately to the particular circumstances of individual cases in their infinite variety. It can be applied appropriately to all information published by a newspaper, whatever its source or origin.

Hand in hand with this advantage goes the disadvantage of an element of unpredictability and uncertainty. The outcome of a court decision, it was suggested, cannot always be predicted with certainty when the newspaper is deciding whether to publish a story. To an extent this is a valid criticism. A degree of uncertainty in borderline cases is inevitable. This uncertainty, coupled with the expense of court proceedings, may "chill" the publication of true statements of fact as well as those which are untrue. The chill factor is perhaps felt more keenly by the regional press, book publishers and broadcasters than the national press. However, the extent of this uncertainty should not be exaggerated. With the enunciation of some guidelines by the court, any practical problems should be manageable. The common law does not seek to set a higher standard than that of responsible journalism, a standard the media themselves espouse. An incursion into press freedom which goes no further than this would not seem to be excessive or disproportionate. The investigative journalist has adequate protection.

My conclusion is that the established common law approach to misstatements of fact remains essentially sound. The common law should not develop "political information" as a new "subject matter" category of qualified privilege, whereby the publication of all such information would attract qualified privilege, whatever the circumstances. That would not provide adequate protection for reputation. Moreover, it would be unsound in principle to distinguish political discussion from discussion of other matters of serious public concern. The elasticity of the common law principle enables interference with freedom of speech to be confined to what is necessary in the circumstances of the case. This elasticity enables the court to give appropriate weight, in today's conditions, to the importance of freedom of expression by the media on all matters of public concern.

Depending on the circumstances, the matters to be taken into account include the following. The comments are illustrative only. (1) The seriousness of the allegation. The more serious the charge, the more the public is misinformed and the individual harmed, if the allegation is not true. (2) The nature of the information, and the extent to which the subject matter is a matter of public concern. (3) The source of the information. Some informants have no direct knowledge of the events. Some have their own axes to grind, or are being paid for their stories. (4) The steps taken to verify the information. (5) The status of the information. The allegation may have already been the subject of an investigation which commands respect. (6) The urgency of the matter. News is often a perishable commodity. (7) Whether comment was sought from the plaintiff. He may have information others do not possess or have not disclosed. An approach to the plaintiff will not always be necessary. (8) Whether the article contained the gist of the plaintiff's side of the story. (9) The tone of the article. A newspaper can raise queries or call for an investigation. It need not adopt allegations as statements of fact. (10) The circumstances of the publication, including the timing.

This list is not exhaustive. The weight to be given to these and any other relevant factors will vary from case to case. Any disputes of primary fact will be a matter for the jury, if there is one. The decision on whether, having regard to the admitted or proved facts, the publication was subject to qualified privilege is a matter for the judge. This is the established practice and seems sound. A balancing operation is better carried out by a judge in a reasoned judgment than by a jury. Over time, a valuable corpus of case law will be built up.

In separate speeches **Lord Cooke of Thorndon** and **Lord Hobhouse** concurred, **Lord Steyn** and **Lord Hope of Craighead** dissented as to the result.

Notes:

1. It has become clear that the *Reynolds* qualified privilege is not really a derivative or extension of the qualified privilege previously recognised at common law: it is "sui generis" (Lord Phillips in *Loutchansky v Times Newspapers* [2002] 1 All E.R. 652, 665), and "applies only to media publications" (Simon Brown L.J. in *Kearns v Bar Council*, [2003] 2 All E.R. 534, 536).

One important distinction is this: the common law privilege attached to the occasion of publication and in a case where such privilege did attach, care in the publication was irrelevant: there was no requirement of, for example, verification of the matter communicated. Thus in *Watt v Longsdon* (previous case) nothing was made of the fact that Watt did not wait to check the truth of the allegations from Casablanca. Under *Reynolds*, by contrast, where the privilege attaches not to the occasion but to the publication, verification or the attempt to verify is an essential feature of the question whether the press behaved properly. Again, the common law privilege was ousted only by malice, by abuse of the privilege, whereas in the *Reynolds* situation the question of malice appears to be totally absorbed in the question whether the defendant behaved in accordance with proper journalistic practice.

There are drawbacks, too, in treating the *Reynolds* privilege as related to the "duty/interest" of the previous common law. It is true that as in negligence law, the "duty" notion does call up a picture of the right standard of conduct, which is crucial under *Reynolds*, but the word also connotes a notion of obligation, which is quite inappropriate in this context. This may have led the trial judge in *Loutchansky* to suggest that the press must show that it had a duty to publish in the sense that it would be open to criticism if it failed to do so. The Court of Appeal held that he had applied too strict a test ([2002] 1 All E.R. 652).

Again, it may be due to the "duty" analysis that the courts have held that evidence which came to the notice of the defendant after the date of publication is inadmissible (*Loutchansky*). But might the question whether the public had a right to know not depend on all the information available at the time of the trial? However, the "right to know", which one might have supposed to be the corollary of "duty", if one is to use that term, has been severely downplayed (as it was in the context of the patient's "right to know" as opposed to the doctor's "duty" to volunteer information: see *Sidaway* [1985] 1 A.C. 871).

2. There are also some conceptual difficulties with the decision that the test of privilege as regards the publication of matters of political concern remains that of "duty/interest". In this case the jury had found that it was not true that Reynolds had lied to the Dáil. How then could there possibly be any *duty* to publish or *interest* in receiving this falsehood? But instead of seeking to prove the truth of their assertions, defendants may rely on privilege, a defence where truth is irrelevant: privilege attaches to a communication if *on the supposition* (which may be true or false) *that what was said was true* it was right in all the circumstances to say it to the persons to whom and in the manner in which the communication was made, hurtful though the fact alleged might be. Here, had it been the case that Reynolds had in fact lied to the Dáil, can there be any doubt that the publication would have been privileged, *i.e.* that the public was "entitled to know" the (supposed) fact? Lord Nicholls said "An article . . . faces an uphill task in claiming privilege if the allegation proves to be false . . . " Who is doing the proving in question? Or are we back at the old folly of supposing that anything hurtful is presumably false?

3. Lord Hobhouse said oddly: "This case is concerned with the problems which arise from the publication of factual statements which are not correct—*i.e.* do not conform to the truth. This case is not concerned with freedom of expression and opinion. . . . There is no human right to disseminate information that is not true." Contrary to this assertion, there is (or ought to be) a right in certain circumstances to say what you honestly believe to be true. What are those circumstances—given that we do not know whether what was said was true or not? The Court of Appeal was perhaps right to advert to the circumstances in their "circumstantial" test (which they held not satisfied), additional to that of "duty/interest" (which was met in the case in hand).

4. When defendant's counsel suggested a rule to the effect that privilege be defeated if the plaintiff showed that the defendant's conduct in publishing was unreasonable Lord Nicholls said that it was "a moot point" whether "this test would differ substantially from the common law test". Is this not very odd? How can a test in terms of "duty/interest", excluding the circumstantial test adopted by the Court of Appeal and rejected by the House of Lords, be analogised to a test of reasonableness of the particular defendant's conduct?

5. The suggestion by defendant's counsel was close to that adopted by the High Court of Australia. Lord Steyn rejected the Australian solution on the ground that it "would involve a radical re-writing of our law of defamation". A radical rewriting is exactly what is called for. And what is the House of Lords for, anyway? If it is true that its adoption would involve a radical rewriting of the law, how can Lord Nicholls's observation that it would not make any substantial difference be correct?

HORROCKS v LOWE

House of Lords [1975] A.C. 135; [1974] 2 W.L.R. 282; 118 S.J. 149; [1974] 1 All E.R. 662; 72 L.G.R. 251 (noted (1974) 37 M.L.R. 692).

At a meeting of the Bolton town council the defendant, a Labour alderman, proposed that the plaintiff, a Conservative councillor, be removed from a committee because of his interests as a property developer. In a heated speech the defendant reminded the council that it had had to pay £17,000 compensation to the Conservative Club because the plaintiff's company had refused to release a restrictive covenant on land leased by the council to the Club.

The trial judge held that the occasion was privileged but that the defendant, being in the grip of gross and unreasonable prejudice, was guilty of malice, although he really believed what he was saying and was not actuated by any personal spite or ill-will against the plaintiff. He gave judgment for the plaintiff, damages £400. The defendant's appeal to the Court of Appeal was allowed unanimously, on the ground that a defendant who believed in the truth of what he said on a privileged occasion could not normally be held liable ([1972] 3 All E.R. 1098). The plaintiff's appeal to the House of Lords was dismissed unanimously.

Lord Diplock: . . . Mr Lowe and other members of the Labour caucus took the view that because of his personal interest in the development of land in Bolton Mr Horrocks ought not to be a member of the Management and Finance Committee. He had expressed this view at the meeting of that committee on October 27, 1969 but was powerless to obtain acceptance of it by the committee because of the Conservative majority on the committee and in the council itself. He gave notice that he intended to raise the matter again at the council meeting on 5th November on the occasion of the statement by Alderman Telford about the Bishops Road site. This he did and what he said at that meeting of the council is the slander in respect of which this action has been brought. It consisted in large part of a recital of what he understood to be the facts about the Bishops Road affair. It was hard hitting criticism of Mr Horrocks's conduct. The sting of it was in the words quoted by Stirling J.:

> "I don't know how to describe his attitude whether it was brinkmanship, megalomania or childish petulance . . . I suggest that he has misled the town, the Leader of the party and his political and club colleagues some of whom are his business associates. I therefore request that he be removed from the Committee to some other where his undoubted talents can be used to the advantage of the Corporation."

My Lords, as a general rule, English law gives effect to the ninth commandment that a man shall not speak evil falsely of his neighbour. It supplies a temporal sanction: if he cannot prove that defamatory matter which he published was true, he is liable in damages to whomsoever he has defamed, except where the publication is oral only, causes no damage and falls outside the categories of slander actionable *per se*. The public interest that the law should provide an effective means whereby a man can vindicate his reputation against calumny has nevertheless to be accommodated to the competing public interest in permitting men to communicate frankly and freely with one another about matters with respect to which the law recognises that they have a duty to perform or an interest to protect in doing so. What is published in good faith on matters of these kinds is published on a privileged occasion. It is not actionable even though it be defamatory and turns out to be untrue. With some exceptions which are irrelevant to the instant appeal, the privilege is not absolute but qualified. It is lost if the occasion which gives rise to it is misused. For in all cases of qualified privilege there is some special reason of public policy why the law accords immunity from suit—the existence of some public or private duty, whether legal or moral, on the part of the maker of the defamatory statement which justifies his communicating it or of some interest of his own which he is entitled to protect by doing so. If he uses the occasion for some other reason he loses the protection of the privilege.

So, the motive with which the defendant on a privileged occasion made a statement defamatory of the plaintiff becomes crucial. The protection might, however, be illusory if the onus lay on him to prove that he was actuated solely by a sense of the relevant duty or a desire to protect the relevant interest. So he is entitled to be protected by the privilege unless some other dominant and improper motive on his part is proved. "Express malice" is the term of art descriptive of such a motive. Broadly speaking, it means malice in the popular sense of a desire to injure the person who is defamed and this is generally the motive which the plaintiff sets out to prove. But to destroy the privilege the desire to injure must be the dominant motive for the defamatory publication; knowledge that it will have that effect is not enough if the defendant is nevertheless acting in accordance with a sense of duty or in bona fide protection of his own legitimate interests.

The motive with which a person published defamatory matter can only be inferred from what he did or said or knew. If it be proved that he did not believe that what he published was true this is generally conclusive evidence of express malice, for no sense of duty or desire to protect his own legitimate interests can justify a man in telling deliberate and injurious falsehoods about another, save in the exceptional case where a person may be under a duty to pass on, without endorsing, defamatory reports made by some other person.

Apart from those exceptional cases, what is required on the part of the defamer to entitle him to the protection of the privilege is positive belief in the truth of what he published or, as it is generally though tautologously termed, "honest belief." If he publishes untrue defamatory matter recklessly, without considering or caring whether it be true or not, he is in this, as in other branches of the law, treated as if he knew it to be false. But indifference to the truth of what he publishes is not to be equated with carelessness, impulsiveness or irrationality in arriving at a positive belief that it is true. The freedom of speech protected by the law of qualified privilege may be availed of by all sorts and conditions of men. In affording to them immunity from suit if they have acted in good faith in compliance with a legal or moral duty or in protection of a legitimate interest the law must take them as it finds them. In ordinary life it is rare indeed for people to form their beliefs by a process of logical deduction from facts ascertained by a rigorous search for all available evidence and a judicious assessment of its probative value. In greater or less degree according to their temperaments, their training, their intelligence, they are swayed by prejudice, rely on intuition instead of reasoning, leap to conclusions on inadequate evidence and fail to recognise the cogency of material which might cast doubt on the validity of the conclusions they reach. But despite the imperfection of the mental process by which the belief is arrived at it may still be "honest," *i.e.* a positive belief that the conclusions they have reached are true. The law demands no more.

Even a positive belief in the truth of what is published on a privileged occasion—which is presumed unless the contrary is proved—may not be sufficient to negative express malice if it can be proved that the defendant misused the occasion for some purpose other than that for which the privilege is accorded by the law. The commonest case is where the dominant motive which actuates the defendant is not a desire to perform the relevant duty or to protect the relevant interest, but to give vent to his personal spite or ill-will towards the person he defames. If this be proved, then even positive belief in the truth of what is published will not enable the defamer to avail himself of the protection of the privilege to which he would otherwise have been entitled. There may be instances of improper motives which destroy the privilege apart from personal spite. A defendant's dominant motive may have been to obtain some private advantage unconnected with the duty or the interest which constitutes the reason for the privilege. If so, he loses the benefit of the privilege despite his positive belief that what he said or wrote was true.

Judges and juries should, however, be very slow to draw the inference that a defendant was so far actuated by improper motives as to deprive him of the protection of the privilege unless they are satisfied that he did not believe that what he said or wrote was true or that he was indifferent to its truth or falsity. The motives with which human beings act are mixed. They find it difficult to hate the sin but love the sinner. Qualified privilege would be illusory, and the public interest that it is meant to serve defeated, if the protection which it affords were lost merely because a person, although acting in compliance with a duty or in protection of a legitimate interest, disliked the person whom he defamed or was indignant at what he believed to be that person's conduct and welcomed the opportunity of exposing it. It is only where his desire to comply with the relevant duty or to protect the relevant interest plays no significant part in his motives for publishing what he believes to be true that "express malice" can properly be found.

There may be evidence of the defendant's conduct on occasions other than that protected by the privilege which justifies the inference that on the privileged occasion too his dominant motive in publishing what he did was personal spite or some other improper motive, even though he believed it to be true. But where, as in the instant case, conduct extraneous to the privileged occasion itself is not relied on, and the only evidence of improper motive is the content of the defamatory matter itself or the steps taken by the defendant to verify its accuracy, there is only one exception to the rule that in order to succeed the plaintiff must show affirmatively that the defendant did not believe it to be true or was indifferent to its truth or falsity. Juries should be instructed and judges should remind themselves that this burden of affirmative proof is not one that it lightly satisfied.

The exception is where what is published incorporates defamatory matter that is not really necessary to the fulfilment of the particular duty or the protection of the particular interest on which the privilege is founded. Logically it might be said that such irrelevant matter falls outside the privilege altogether. But if this were so it would involve the application by the court of an objective test of relevance to every part of the defamatory matter published on the privileged occasion; whereas, as everyone knows, ordinary human beings vary in their ability to distinguish that which is logically relevant from that which is not and few, apart from lawyers, have had any training which qualifies them to do so. So the protection afforded by the privilege would be illusory if it were lost in respect of any defamatory matter which on logical analysis could be shown to be irrelevant to the fulfilment of the duty or the protection of the right on which the privilege was founded. As Lord Dunedin pointed out in *Adam v Ward* the proper rule as respects irrelevant defamatory matter incorporated in a statement made on a privileged occasion is to treat it as one of the factors to be taken into consideration in deciding whether, in all the circumstances, an inference that the defendant was actuated by express malice can properly be drawn. As regards irrelevant matter the test is not whether it is logically relevant but whether, in all the circumstances, it can be inferred that the defendant either did not believe it to be true or, though believing it to be true, realised that it had nothing to do with the particular duty or interest on which the privilege was based, but nevertheless seized the opportunity to drag in irrelevant defamatory matter to vent his personal spite, or for some improper motive. Here, too, judges and juries should be slow to draw this inference.

My Lords, what is said by members of a local council at meetings of the council or of any of its committees is spoken on a privileged occasion. The reason for the privilege is that those who represent the local government electors should be able to speak freely and frankly, boldly and bluntly, on any matter which they believe affects the interests or welfare of the inhabitants. They may be swayed by strong political prejudice, they may be obstinate and pig-headed, stupid and obtuse; but they were chosen by the electors to speak their minds on matters of local concern and so long as they do so honestly they run no risk of liability for defamation of those who are the subjects of their criticism.

In the instant case Mr Lowe's speech at the meeting of the Bolton borough council was on matters which were undoubtedly of local concern. With one minor exception the only facts relied on as evidence from which express malice was to be inferred had reference to the contents of the speech itself, the circumstances in which the meeting of the council was held and the material relating to the subject-matter of Mr Lowe's speech which was within his actual knowledge or available to him on enquiry. The one exception was his failure to apologise to Mr Horrocks when asked to do so two days later. A refusal to apologise is at best but tenuous evidence of malice, for it is consistent with a continuing belief in the truth of what he said. Stirling J. found it to be so in the case of Mr Lowe.

So the judge was left with no other material on which to found an inference of malice except the contents of the speech itself, the circumstances in which it was made and, of course, Mr Lowe's own evidence in the witness box. Where such is the case the test of malice is very simple. It was laid down by Lord Esher himself, as Brett L.J. in *Clark v Molyneux* (1873) 3 Q.B.D. 237. It is: has it been proved that the defendant did not honestly believe that what he said was true, *i.e.* was he either aware that it was not true or indifferent to its truth or falsity? But however gross, however unreasoning the prejudice it does not destroy the privilege unless it has this result. If what it does is to cause the defendant honestly to believe what a more rational or impartial person would reject or doubt he does not thereby lose the protection of the privilege.

My Lords, in his judgment Stirling J. rejected the inference that Mr Lowe was actuated by personal spite against Mr Horrocks. He found, however, that Mr Lowe was—

"so anxious to have the plaintiff removed from the Management and Finance Committee that . . . he did not consider fairly and objectively whether the evidence that he had of the plaintiff's conduct over Bishops Road came anything like far enough to justify his conclusions or comments."

. . . The other matters referred to by the learned judge as showing Mr Lowe to be grossly and unreasonably prejudiced might have warranted the inference that he was indifferent to the truth or falsity of what he said, if his own evidence as to his belief had been unconvincing. But it was an inference the judge, who heard and saw Mr Lowe in the witness box, did not feel able to draw. "I am prepared," he said "to accept what the defendant reiterated in his evidence that he believed and still believes that everything he said was true and justifiable."

However prejudiced the judge thought Mr Lowe to be, however irrational in leaping to conclusions unfavourable to Mr Horrocks, this crucial finding of Mr Lowe's belief in the truth of what he said on that privileged occasion entitled him to succeed in his defence of privilege. The Court of Appeal so held. I would myself do likewise and dismiss this appeal.

Questions

1. If it is proposed at a meeting that the holder of an office be removed from it on the ground that he is unfit to continue in it, is it possible without defaming him (a) to make the proposal, (b) to speak in its favour, (c) to vote for it? Does it matter whether the alleged unfitness is moral, intellectual, political or physical?

2. In this fine speech Lord Diplock said that "no sense of duty . . . can justify a man in telling deliberate and injurious falsehoods about another, save in the exceptional case where a person may be under a duty to pass on, without endorsing, defamatory reports made by some other person." Is the case really so exceptional after *Reynolds*?

Notes:

1. Since Lord Denning could not persuade the other members of the Court of Appeal in *Riddick v Thames Board Mills* [1977] Q.B. 881 that an employer should not have to pay when one of his employees defames another to a third, the usual rules of vicarious liability apply in defamation: a principal or employer, although entirely free from fault, is liable if his agent or servant utters actionable defamations in the scope of his authority or the course of his employment. This remains true where the occasion of publication is privileged

and the defamation is actionable only because the subordinate is malicious. In such a case principal and agent or master and servant are joint tortfeasors.

2. This does not, however, apply in all cases of joint publication. If A and B jointly draft and send a letter, that is doubtless a joint publication such that if there were no privilege both would be liable; but if privilege does prima facie attach to the communication, B, if innocent, will not be rendered liable just because A is malicious. This is true whether B is an equal or a subordinate. *Egger v Viscount Chelmsford* [1965] 1 Q.B. 248, CA.

3. What if the words in question are held to mean X but the defendant meant Y? Is there malice if the defendant really believed Y but not X? No: *Loveless v Earl* [1998] Times L.R. 695 (where it appears to have been because of a word-processing error that the letter in question failed to represent the defendant's intention).

4. The Public Interest Disclosure Act 1998 is designed to prevent employees from being deterred from "whistle-blowing". Whistle-blowing generally involves telling the boss that a fellow-employee is misbehaving. The Act protects the whistle-blower against retaliatory conduct by the employer but does nothing to protect him against the fellow-employee, necessarily defamed. Fortunately *Watt v Longsdon* (above, p.544) makes it clear that the communication will be covered by qualified privilege, naturally rebuttable by proof of subjective malice.

Section 4.—Fair Comment

CHENG v TSE WAI CHUN PAUL

Court of Final Appeal, Hong Kong, November 13, 2000: [2000] H.K.C.F.A. 88; [2003] 3 H.K.L.R.D. 418; [2001] H.K.E.C. 57

"Fair comment" and "malice"

The trial judge instructed the jury that even if the defendants honestly held the opinions they uttered on a television programme the defence of fair comment was unavailable if their motives were "other than just speaking as critics or commentators". The appeal of the individual defendants, whom the jury found liable, was allowed on the ground of misdirection and the case was remanded for a new trial.

Lord Nicholls of Birkenhead NPJ: This is an appeal in a defamation action. It raises an important point on the defence of fair comment. The title of this defence is misleading. Comment, or honest comment, would be a more satisfactory name. In this judgment I adhere, reluctantly, to the traditional terminology.

In order to identify the point in issue I must first set out some non-controversial matters about the ingredients of this defence. These are well established. They are fivefold. First, the comment must be on a matter of public interest. Public interest is not to be confined within narrow limits today: see Lord Denning in *London Artists Ltd v Littler* [1969] 2 Q.B. 375, 391.

Second, the comment must be recognisable as comment, as distinct from an imputation of fact. If the imputation is one of fact, a ground of defence must be sought elsewhere, for example, justification or privilege. Much learning has grown up around the distinction between fact and comment. For present purposes it is sufficient to note that a statement may be one or the other, depending on the context. Ferguson J. gave a simple example in the New South Wales case of *Myerson v Smith's Weekly* (1923) 24 S.R. (N.S.W.) 20, 26: "To say that a man's conduct was dishonourable is not comment, it is a statement of fact. To say that he did certain specific things and that his conduct was dishonourable is a statement of fact coupled with a comment."

Third, the comment must be based on facts which are true or protected by privilege: see, for instance, *London Artists Ltd v Littler* [1969] 2 Q.B. 375, 395. If the facts on which the comment purports to be founded are not proved to be true or published on a privilege occasion, the defence of fair comment is not available.

Next, the comment must explicitly or implicitly indicate, at least in general terms, what are the facts on which the comment is being made. The reader or hearer should be in a position to judge for himself how far the comment was well founded.

Finally, the comment must be one which could have been made by an honest person, however prejudiced he might be, and however exaggerated or obstinate his views. It must be germane to the subject matter criticised. Dislike of an artist's style would not justify an attack upon his morals or manners. But a critic need not be mealy-mouthed in denouncing what he disagrees with. He is entitled to dip his pen in gall for the purposes of legitimate criticism.

These are the outer limits of the defence. The burden of establishing that a comment falls within these limits, and hence within the scope of the defence, lies upon the defendant who wishes to rely upon the defence.

That is not the end of the matter. Even when a defendant has brought his case within these limits, he will not necessarily succeed. The plaintiff may still defeat ("rebut") the defence by proving that when he made his comment the defendant was, in the time-hallowed expression, "actuated by malice".

The question raised by this appeal concerns the meaning of malice in the context of the defence of fair comment. On this, two matters are clear. First, unlike the outer limits (as I have called them) of the defence of fair comment, which are objective, malice is subjective. It looks to the defendant's state of mind. Second, malice covers the case of the defendant who does not genuinely hold the view he expressed. In other words, when making the defamatory comment the defendant acted dishonestly. He put forward as his view something which, in truth, was not his view. It was a pretence. The law does not protect such statements. Within the objective limits mentioned above, the law protects the freedom to express opinions, not vituperative make-believe.

The point of principle raised by this appeal, crucial to the outcome of the action, is whether, in contemplation of law, malice may exist in this context even when the defendant positively believed in the soundness of his comment. More specifically, the issue is whether the purpose for which a defendant stated an honestly held opinion may deprive him of the protection of the defence of fair comment; for instance, if his purpose was to inflict injury, as when a politician seeks to damage his political opponent, or if he was simply acting out of spite.

One would have expected that this basic issue in respect of the much-used defence of fair comment would have been settled long ago. This is not so. The meaning of malice has been comprehensively analysed in relation to the defence of qualified privilege, most notably in the speech of Lord Diplock in *Horrocks v Lowe* [1975] A.C. 135. But no similar exposition has been undertaken regarding fair comment.

Before turning to the authorities I shall go back to first principles. Proof of malice is the means whereby a plaintiff can defeat a defence of fair comment where a defendant is abusing the defence. Abuse consists of using the defence for a purpose other than that for which it exists. The purpose for which the defence of fair comment exists is to facilitate freedom of expression by commenting on matters of public interest. This accords with the constitutional guarantee of freedom of expression. And it is in the public interest that everyone should be free to express his own, honestly held views on such matters, subject always to the safeguards provided by the objective limits mentioned above. These safeguards ensure that defamatory comments can be seen for what they are, namely comments as distinct from statements of fact. They also ensure that those reading the comments have the material enabling them to make up their own minds on whether they agree or disagree. The public interest in freedom to make comments within these limits is of particular importance in the social and political fields. Professor Fleming stated the matter thus in his invaluable book on *The Law of Torts*, 9th edition, p.648:

> " . . . untrammelled discussion of public affairs and of those participating in them is a basic safeguard against irresponsible political power. The unfettered preservation of the right of fair comment is, therefore, one of the foundations supporting our standards of personal liberty."

The purpose and importance of the defence of fair comment are inconsistent with its scope being restricted to comments made for particular reasons or particular purposes, some being regarded as proper, others not. Especially in the social and political fields, those who make public comments usually have some objective of their own in mind, even if it is only to publicise and advance themselves. They often have what may be described as an "ulterior" object. Frequently their object is apparent, but not always so. They may hope to achieve some result, such as promoting one cause or defeating another, elevating one person or denigrating another. In making their comments they do not act dispassionately, they do not intend merely to convey information. They have other motives.

The presence of these motives, and this is of crucial importance for present purposes, is not a reason for excluding the defence of fair comment. The existence of motives such as these when expressing an opinion does not mean that the defence of fair comment is being misused. It would make no sense, for instance, if a motive relating to the very feature which causes the matter to be one of public interest were regarded as defeating the defence.

On the contrary, this defence is intended to protect and promote comments such as these. Liberty to make such comments, genuinely held, on matters of public interest lies at the heart of the defence of fair comment. That is the very object for which the defence exists. Commentators, of all shades of opinion, are entitled to "have their own agenda". Politicians, social reformers, busybodies, those with political or other ambitions and those with none, all can grind their axes. The defence of fair comment envisages that everyone is at liberty to conduct social and political campaigns by expressing his own views, subject always, and I repeat the refrain, to the objective safeguards which mark the limits of the defence.

Nor is it for the courts to choose between "public" and "private" purposes, or between purposes they regard as morally or socially or politically desirable and those they regard as undesirable. That would be a highly dangerous course. That way lies censorship. That would defeat the purpose for which the law accords the defence of freedom to make comments on matters of public interest. The objective safeguards, coupled with the need to have a genuine belief in what is said, are adequate to keep the ambit of permissible comment within reasonable bounds.

One particular motive calls for special mention: spite or ill will. This raises a difficult point. I confess that my first, instinctive reaction was that the defence of fair comment should not be capable of being used to protect a comment made with the intent of injuring another out of spite, even if the person who made the comment genuinely believed in the truth of what he said. Personal spite, after all, is four square within the popular meaning of malice. Elsewhere the law proscribes conduct of this character; for instance, in the field of nuisance, as exemplified by the well known case of the householder who made noises on musical instruments with the intention of annoying his neighbour (*Christie v Davey* [1893] 1 Ch. 316).

On reflection I do not think the law should attempt to ring-fence comments made with the sole or dominant motive of causing injury out of spite or, which may come to much the same, causing injury simply for the sake of doing so. In the first place it seems to me that the postulate on which this problem is based is a little unreal. The postulate poses a problem which is more academic than practical. The postulate is that the comment in question falls within the objective limits of the defence. Thus, the comment is one which is based on fact; it is made in circumstances where those to whom the comment is addressed can form their own view on whether or not the comment was sound; and the comment is one which can be held by an honest person. This postulate supposes, further, that the maker of the comment genuinely believes in the truth of his comment. It must be questionable whether comments, made out of spite and causing injury, are at all likely to satisfy each and every of these requirements. There must be a query over whether, in practice, there is a problem here which calls for attention.

Moreover, in so far as this situation is ever likely to arise, it is by no means clear that the underlying public interest does require that the person impugned should have a remedy. Take the case of a politician or a journalist who genuinely believes that a minister is untrustworthy and not fit to hold ministerial office. Facts exist from which an honest person could form that view. The politician or journalist states his view, with the intention of injuring the minister. His reason for doing so was a private grudge, derived from a past insult, actual or supposed. I am far from persuaded that the law should give the minister a remedy. The spiteful publication of a defamatory statement of fact attracts no remedy if the statement is proved to be true. Why should the position be different for the spiteful publication of a defamatory, genuinely held comment based on true fact?

There is a further consideration. The law of defamation is, in all conscience, sufficiently complex, even tortuous, without introducing further subtle distinctions which will be hard to explain to a jury. The concept of intent to injure is easy enough. But, as already noted, intent to injure is not inconsistent with the purpose for which the defence of fair comment exists. So, if spite and cognate states of mind are to be outlawed for the purposes of this defence, the directions to the jury would have to be elaborate and sophisticated.

The combination of all these factors seems to me to point convincingly away from treating spiteful comments as forming a category of their own. This is, of course, very much a question of policy.

I now turn to the authorities. . . . As already indicated, there is no decision directly on the point now under consideration. It is no doubt for this reason that textbook writers have sought to fill the gap by resorting to the decision of the House of Lords in *Horrocks v Lowe* [1975] A.C. 135, even though that case related to a different defence, the defence of qualified privilege. In the absence of any clear guidance, it is temptingly easy to assume that malice must bear the same meaning in all respects for both defences. It is essential, therefore, to consider the reasoning which underlies Lord Diplock's authoritative analysis of malice for the purposes of the defence of qualified privilege, with a view to seeing how far it is applicable to the defence of fair comment. As will appear, I believe that misapplication of this analysis is largely responsible for the erroneous statements of the law in some of the textbooks.

In a much-quoted passage, at page 150, Lord Diplock said this:

"Even a positive belief in the truth of what is published on a privileged occasion . . . may not suffice to negative express malice if it can be proved that the defendant misused the occasion for some purpose other than that for which the privilege is accorded by the law. The commonest case is where the dominant motive which actuates the defendant is not a desire to perform the relevant duty or to protect the relevant interest, but to give vent to his personal spite or ill will towards the person he defames."

Lord Diplock continued by noting that there may be other improper motives which destroy the privilege. He instanced the case where a defendant's dominant motive may have been to obtain "some private advantage unconnected with the duty or the interest which constitutes the reason for the privilege".

Lord Diplock's observations are in point to the extent that they enunciate the principle that express malice is to be equated with use of a privileged occasion for some purpose other than that for which the privilege is accorded by the law. The same approach is applicable to the defence of fair comment. Beyond that his observations do not assist in the present case, because the purposes for which the law has accorded the defence of qualified privilege and the defence of fair comment are not the same. So his examples of misuse of qualified privilege cannot be carried across to fair comment without more ado. Instances of misuse of qualified privilege may not be instances of misuse of fair comment. What amounts to misuse of fair comment depends upon the purposes for which that defence exists.

I must make good my statement that the purposes for which the two defences exist are not the same. The rationale of the defence of qualified privilege is the law's recognition that there are circumstances when there is a need, in the public interest, for a particular recipient to receive frank and uninhibited communication of particular information from a particular source: see *Reynolds v Times Newspapers Ltd* [1999] 3 W.L.R. 1010, 1017. Traditionally, these occasions have been described in terms of persons having a duty to perform or an interest to protect in providing the information. If, adopting the traditional formulation for convenience, a person's dominant motive is not to perform this duty or protect this interest, he is outside the ambit of the defence. For instance, if a former employer includes defamatory statements in an employment reference with the dominant purpose of injuring the former employee, the former employer is misusing the privileged occasion and this will vitiate his defence of qualified privilege.

The rationale of the defence of fair comment is different, and is different in a material respect. It is not based on any notion of performance of a duty or protection of an interest. As already noted, its basis is the high importance of protecting and promoting the freedom of comment by everyone at all times on matters of public interest, irrespective of their particular motives. In the nature of things the instances of misuse of privilege highlighted by Lord Diplock (for example, "some private advantage unconnected with the duty or interest which constitutes the reason for the privilege") are not necessarily applicable to fair comment. A failure to appreciate this has, I fear, led some textbook writers into the error of suggesting that parts of Lord Diplock's observations are equally applicable to the defence of fair comment even though they lack the rationale on which the observations were founded.

My conclusion on the authorities is that, for the most part, the relevant judicial statements are consistent with the views which I have expressed as a matter of principle. To summarise, in my view a comment which falls within the objective limits of the defence of fair comment can lose its immunity only by proof that the defendant did not genuinely hold the view he expressed. Honesty of belief is the touchstone. Actuation by spite, animosity, intent to injure, intent to arouse controversy or other motivation, whatever it may be, even if it is the dominant or sole motive, does not of itself defeat the defence. However, proof of such motivation may be evidence, sometimes compelling evidence, from which lack of genuine belief in the view expressed may be inferred. Proof of motivation may also be relevant on other issues in the action, such as damages.

It is said that this view of the law would have the undesirable consequence that malice would bear different meanings in the defences of fair comment and qualified privilege, and that this would inevitably cause difficulty for juries. I agree that if the term "malice" were used, there might be a risk of confusion. The answer lies in shunning that word altogether. Juries can be instructed, regarding fair comment, that the defence is defeated by proof that the defendant did not genuinely believe the opinion he expressed. Regarding qualified privilege, juries can be directed that the defence is defeated by proof that the defendant used the occasion for some purpose other than that for which the occasion was privileged. This direction can be elaborated in a manner appropriate to the facts and issues in the case.

Notes:

1. Any belief that this clear judgment does away with problems relating to the defence of "fair comment" or "honest opinion" will evaporate on even a cursory reading of *Branson v Bower* [2002] Q.B. 737, where an article by the defendant, author of an unauthorised life of Richard Branson, contained the sentence "Revenge rather than self-righteousness has motivated Richard Branson's latest bid to run Britain's Lottery." The trial judge held that in context the words could only be seen as fair comment, and the Court of Appeal agreed with his withdrawal of that question from the eventual jury. The result was that at the trial the claimant would have to prove that Mr Bower did not honestly believe what he was saying but was only pretending.

One slight difficulty in the case was the line of authority that to impute regrettable motives went beyond comment. Thus in *Campbell v Spottiswoode* (1862) 122 Eng.Rep. 288 Cockburn C.J. said to the jury: "A public writer is fully entitled to comment upon the conduct of a public man. But it cannot be said that because a man is a public man a public writer is entitled not only to pass a judgment upon his conduct, but to ascribe to him corrupt and dishonest motives." A century later, however, Lord Denning said: "Even if the words did convey the imputation, by way of comment, that the plaintiff's conduct was dishonest, insincere or hypocritical, the defence of fair comment was still available." (*Slim v Daily Telegraph* [1968] 2 Q.B. 157, 169), and this was in line with the view of the Faulks Committee that "Any special limitation of the defence of comment in cases where base or sordid motives are imputed should be abolished" (Cmnd. 5909 (1975) para. 161).

2. There is, however, another problem, namely the connection between the comment, if it is held to be such, and the facts on which it is based. As the judge in *Branson* said: "It might be thought to be imposing undue restrictions on free speech if a defendant only has the defence of fair comment in circumstances where he has remembered to identify, even perhaps in the heat of public debate, the facts which led him to hold those views about the claimant. That may be so, but at least the law is clear in this respect. It has long been recognised at common law."

KEMSLEY v FOOT

House of Lords [1952] A.C. 345; [1952] 1 T.L.R. 532; 96 S.J. 165; [1952] 1 All E.R. 501

Another newspaper proprietor complains of criticism

An article written by the defendant and published in the *Tribune* of March 10, 1950, stated "The prize for the foulest piece of journalism perpetrated in this country for many a long year, and that is certainly saying something, must go to Mr Herbert Gunn, editor of the *Evening Standard*, and all those who assisted him in the publication of an attack on John Strachey last week", and proceeded with a savage attack on the *Evening Standard*. This was not the matter complained of, since Viscount Kemsley, the plaintiff, had no connection whatever with the *Evening Standard*. His complaint was that the article appeared under the headline "Lower than Kemsley", and he alleged that in the context of the article this headline conveyed the message that he "used his position as a director of newspaper companies to procure the publication of statements he knew to be false and that his name was a byword in this respect." The defendants in para.5 of their pleadings claimed that the words were "fair comment made in good faith and without malice upon a matter of public interest namely the control by the plaintiff of . . . newspapers."

The plaintiff applied to strike out this defence. The Master refused. On appeal by the plaintiff, Parker J. ordered the paragraph struck out. The Court of Appeal allowed the defendant's appeal and restored the Master's order [1951] 2 K.B. 34. The plaintiff's appeal to the House of Lords was dismissed.

Lord Porter: . . . It is not, as I understand, contended that the words contained in that article are fact and not comment: rather it is alleged that they are comment with no facts to support it. The question for your Lordships' decision is, therefore, whether a plea of fair comment is only permissible where the comment is accompanied by a statement of facts upon which the comment is made and to determine the particularity with which the facts must be stated. . . .

The question in all cases is whether there is a sufficient substratum of fact stated or indicated in the words which are the subject-matter of the action, and I find my view well expressed in the remarks contained in *Odgers on Libel and Slander* (6th ed., 1929), p.166. "Sometimes, however," he says, "it is difficult to distinguish an allegation of fact from an expression of opinion. It often depends on what is stated in the rest of the article. If the defendant accurately states what some public man has really done, and then asserts that 'such conduct is disgraceful,' this is merely the expression of his opinion, his comment on the plaintiff's conduct. So, if without setting it out, he identifies the conduct on which he comments by a clear reference. In either case, the defendant enables his readers to judge for themselves how far his opinion is well founded; and, therefore, what would otherwise have been an allegation of fact becomes merely a comment. But if he asserts that the plaintiff has been guilty of disgraceful conduct, and does not state what that conduct was, this is an allegation of fact for which there is no defence but privilege or truth. The same considerations apply where a defendant has drawn from certain facts an inference derogatory to the plaintiff. If he states the bare inference without the facts on which it is based, such inference will be treated as an allegation of fact. But if he sets out the facts correctly, and then gives his inference, stating it as his inference from those facts, such inference will, as a rule, be deemed a comment. But even in this case the writer must be careful to state the inference as an inference, and not to assert it as a new and independent fact; otherwise, his inference will become something more than a comment, and he may be driven to justify it as an allegation of fact."

But the question whether an inference is a bare inference in this sense must depend upon all the circumstances. Indeed, it was ultimately admitted on behalf of the appellant that the facts necessary to justify comment might be implied from the terms of the impugned article . . . The exact meaning is not, in my opinion, for your Lordships but for the jury. All I desire to say is that it is at least arguable that the words directly complained of imply as fact that Lord Kemsley is in control of a number of known newspapers and that the conduct of those newspapers is in question. Had the contention that all the facts justifying the comment must appear in the article been maintainable, the appeal would succeed, but the appellant's representatives did not feel able to and, I think, could not support so wide a contention. The facts they admitted, might be implied, and the respondents' answer to their contention is: "We have pointed to your press. It is widely read. Your readers will and the public generally can know at what our criticism is directed. It is not bare comment; it is comment on a well-known matter, much better known, indeed, than a newly printed book or a once-performed play." . . .

Notes:

1. This lawsuit is one of the silliest in the book, even in this chapter of the book: if, as Lord Porter says, the plaintiff was not contending that "the words contained in the article are fact and not comment," what possible point was the plaintiff making? That there is some *tertium quid* between fact and comment? That comment has to be part of a commentary? Students who read judgments ought to realise (a) that judges must respond to the arguments of counsel, however stupid and silly, and (b) counsel may have to make stupid and silly arguments if their clients insist on their prosecuting the claim, appeal, etc. That is not to say that counsel only make stupid and silly arguments when obliged to, but in any case the judges have to respond, and their responses get into the casebooks, and so it proceeds as if the question raised were real and important, which commonly it is not.

2. *Kemsley v Foot* figures in a much more important case concerning an angry letter from the defendant in the *Daily Telegraph*. He pleaded only fair comment, and would therefore be liable if what he wrote was held to be fact. The judge withdrew the case from the jury on the ground that it could be nothing but comment, but the House of Lords reversed. *Telnikoff v Matusevitch* [1991] 4 All E.R. 817. The letter was in rebuttal of an article by the plaintiff in a prior issue of the *Daily Telegraph*. People reading the letter and article in conjunction would realise that the defendant was simply criticising the views expressed in the article, but a person reading the letter on its own might be misled as to what those views actually were. Against the dissent of Lord Ackner, who held that this was unduly to restrict the defence of fair comment, the House held that the letter must be read on its own, since that is how people would read it: the writer must make clear what facts he was commenting on. Thus in deciding whether the words were fact or comment, rather than whether, if comment, they were fair, the jury could not consider the article, though it could have done so had the defendant pleaded justification and tried to say that the plaintiff's views actually were as the defendant suggested. Students may ask themselves whether the £240,000 eventually awarded to the plaintiff should really have turned on this dodgy decision by the House. It didn't do Telnikoff much good, however, since when he pursued the defendant to the United States, whither their employer had sent him, and tried to enforce the English judgment there the Supreme Court of Maryland decided that it was repugnant to state law: (1997) 347 Md. 561, 702 A.2d 230—a very good opinion, noting that "present Maryland defamation law is totally different from English defamation law in virtually every significant respect."

Question

What can Lord Kemsley have sought to achieve, or to indulge, by bringing this lawsuit at the expense of so much time and money?

Note:

Kemsley and other press barons, possibly the nastiest of all types of tycoon, have no compunction about suing for what other people print. Not just the barons either, for the baronettes and fly-by-knights of the dailies and weeklies are also prompt to take the legal system for a ride, if possible. When the editor of the uppity *Sunday Times* sued the former editor of the *Sunday Telegraph* for some fatuous triviality, he got all of £1,000 (*Neill v Worsthorne*, January 1990—costs estimated at £130,000 mainly to lawyers). The unspeakable Maxwell, who had the gall to celebrate his unjust victory over *Private Eye* (£55,000) by getting his hacks to write a book about it (see *Maxwell v Pressdram* [1977] 1 All E.R. 656), had over 100 writs for libel outstanding when he drowned—he was uneager for the truth to emerge, and our law of libel was there to help him suppress it. One is reminded of Lord Bernstein, the TV mogul, suing the people who photographed his house, of Hedley Byrne, the advertising agents, complaining of misrepresentation, of Caliban seeing his face in the glass. A pity that it was not Maxwell's tabloid that had to pay £500,000 to Jeffrey Archer, politician and writer, for saying that he had used the services of a prostitute when he had only paid her to leave the country. Another sensitive familiar of the law courts was the tycoon Sir James Goldsmith, ludicrously characterised by a judge as an "ordinary citizen" (*Goldsmith v Sperrings* [1977] 2 All E.R. 557 at 566; *Goldsmith v Pressdram* [1987] 3 All E.R. 485).

The publicity and drama of the court are naturally alluring to actors and actresses. Liberace had the nerve to sue the *Daily Mirror* for calling him "fruit-flavoured" (a word whose meaning the judge had to have explained to him) and collected £8,000 for this unveiled allusion to his manifest and ultimately fatal proclivities; Telly Savalas exacted a load of money from those who suggested a habit of arriving on set late and unsober; and an actress who sued one of Maxwell's papers for featuring her as "Wally of the Week" and describing her as having a "big bum" got £10,000, though not for long, as this verdict was reversed by the Court of Appeal which sent the case back for a further waste of everyone's time (*Cornwell v Myskow* [1987] 2 All E.R. 504).

Politicians are another class of person whom ambition or success has rendered insensitive to all but criticism and whose taste for publicity does not seem to have inured them to any obloquy. One prime minister was not ashamed to resort to a defamation suit in order to silence the only member of the opposition, and he was supported therein by the Privy Council, a success not publicised in the law reports (*Jeyaretnam v Lee*, February 24, 1982). Those in power in Singapore continue relentlessly to deploy the law of defamation in order to suppress criticism. The leader of the opposition was made to pay the then Prime Minister another £8,000 in September 1997 (*Goh v Jeyaretnam*), and a fellow M.P. was held liable for £3.75 million in suits by government ministers. We in Britain must be grateful to the House of Lords for deciding in *Derbyshire C.C. v Times Newspapers* [1993] 1 All E.R. 1011 that the government itself cannot sue for defamation (only for malicious falsehood on proof of malice and damage). That decision, however, left it open for ministers themselves to sue. Fortunately *Reynolds* (above) goes some way to protect journalists and others in respect of imputations (and not just comments) honestly believed and properly published on political matters.

Even those whose familiarity with the courts should have led them to know better seem unable to resist the lure of issuing a writ. We would have forgotten that Mr Justice Popplewell was once said to have fallen asleep on the bench if he had not sued the paper which suggested he had, and Douglas Draycott Q.C. may well be remembered for suing the BBC for suggesting that he had been negligent in conducting an appeal from Satpal Ram's conviction for murder, although the convict himself could not have sued him even if the allegation had been true.

Disgusting though all these proceedings are, one might ask why the law should not provide a forum in which really awful people can gird at each other with a chance of scooping the pool? After all, counsel at the libel bar, scandalously overpaid though they are for an activity entirely without social merit, are paid by the parties themselves (or is it by newspaper readers?). But the judges are paid by decent people, and they have better things to do. Worse still, ordinary people get caught up in these despicable goings-on, dragged away from their activities and pleasures to attend as jurymen to boring harangues, lying testimony and idiotic instructions. In the *Orme* case about the "Moonies," the trial with jury lasted no less than 100 days, and the appeal was expected to last 50. This prompted two eminent judges to move in a debate in the House of Lords that a judge should have discretion to decide whether there should be a jury or not. It remains the rule, however, that unless there are masses of documents (rather than the 118 witnesses in the *Orme* trial) either party to a defamation suit has the right to demand trial by jury (Supreme Court Act 1981, s.69(1); *Viscount de l'Isle v Times Newspapers* [1987] 3 All E.R. 499).

No jury was empanelled in the suit brought by McDonalds, the fast-food chain, against two unwaged Greenpeaceniks for distributing a "fact-sheet" severely critical of the environmental and social effects of McDonalds' production and supply practices: plaintiff's counsel successfully argued that the facts were too complicated (though not for the unrepresented defendants!). Yet if honest citizens did not have to waste their time appraising McDonalds' business methods, Bell J., surely appointed for more public service, had to spend no fewer than 313 days in court, ending on December 13, 1996, listening to over a hundred witnesses and studying 40,000 documents. On June 19, 1997 the judge held that while the defendants (unrepresented and unemployed) had failed to establish their principal allegations—that the plaintiff's food was poisonous and that its purchasing practices impoverished developing countries and diminished their forests—it was the case that its advertising practices were exploitative of children and that their staff were poorly paid. On March 31, 1999 the Court of Appeal upheld the judgment, subject to a reduction to £40,000 of the £60,000 damages awarded below, rejecting the argument that honest criticism of multinational corporations on a matter of public interest should not be actionable.

DEFAMATION ACT 1952

6. In an action for libel or slander in respect of words consisting partly of allegations of fact and partly of expressions of opinion, a defence of fair comment shall not fail by reason only that the truth of every allegation of fact is not proved if the expression of opinion is fair comment having regard to such of the facts alleged or referred to in the words complained of as are proved.

Question

1. How valuable is the right to comment on matters of public interest if one is liable for unavoidable errors of fact?

Note:

In *Broadway Approvals v Odhams Press* [1964] 2 All E.R. 904 the trial judge proposed to ask the jury "Could a fair-minded man in good faith have held the opinion expressed having regard to such of the facts referred to in the article as are proved?" but after argument said instead to the jury "And, needless to say, if the facts are untrue, then the criticism based upon those facts cannot by its very nature be fair, can it?" ([1965] 2 All E.R. at 535).

The matter is perplexing. If the commentator states as facts the facts on which he is commenting (as *Telnikoff* makes necessary) then those facts must be proved to be true or it must be shown that the defendant had a privilege to state them as he did on that occasion; it cannot be enough that he was repeating what someone else had said on an occasion then privileged. It is, however, a rule of pleading that the defendant must specify in his pleadings the facts he was relying on in making his comment (even if he did not publish those facts). Why should he have to prove that *those* facts, as opposed to those he stated in his publication, are true?

Unfortunately there was authority to the effect that he must, but in *Brent Walker v Time Out* [1991] 2 All E.R. 753 (where Parker L.J. was reluctant "to embody into the tangled web of the law of defamation as it presently exists yet further absurdity") the question was even more peculiar. It was whether a defendant might *plead* as fact on which his comment was based what a witness had said in court and was therefore (as to the witness) absolutely privileged, or whether he must show that if he had repeated that evidence (instead of simply relying on it) he would have had the protection of qualified privilege as having given a fair and accurate report of the proceedings in which it was uttered. Despite the quoted observation of Parker L.J. the court held that the defendant must show that the facts he was forced to plead would have been privileged if he had published them, as he did not.

Although the outcome is regrettable as allowing yet another murky individual to gag the press by deploying this absurd tort, the luminous prose of Bingham L.J. deserves quotation:

> "The civil law of libel is primarily concerned to provide redress for those who are the subject of false and defamatory factual publications. Thus in the simplest case A will be entitled to relief against B if B publishes a defamatory factual statement concerning A which B cannot show to be true. The law is not primarily concerned to provide redress for those who are the subject of disparaging expressions of opinion, and freedom of opinion is (subject to necessary restrictions) a basic democratic right. It is, however, plain that certain statements which might on their face appear to be expressions of opinion (as where, for example, a person is described as untrustworthy, unprincipled, lascivious or cruel) contain within themselves defamatory suggestions of a factual nature. Thus the law has developed the rule already mentioned that comment may only be defended as fair if it is comment on facts (meaning true facts) stated or sufficiently indicated. Failing that, the comment itself must be justified.
>
> Since the general rule is that comment, to be fair, must be on facts which are shown to be true, it might be said that such comment could never be based on statements which, although made on a privileged occasion, were shown to be false or not shown to be true. But neither party to this appeal has argued for such a result and rightly not, for it would be inconsistent with the reasoning in *Wason*'s, *Mangena*'s and *Addis*'s cases already discussed. Effectively, therefore, the issue concerns the width of the 'privileged occasion' exception to the general rule. Is it enough to sustain comment otherwise fair that the statement commented upon (even if false or not provable to be true) was made on an occasion of privilege? Or must the publisher meet the additional requirement, ordinarily incumbent on a publisher reporting a communication made on an occasion of privilege, of showing that his report of it is fair and accurate?
>
> In agreement with the learned deputy judge I accept the plaintiffs' submission that the publisher must meet this additional requirement. The wisdom in the public interest of permitting fair comment on statements made on privileged occasions (even if those statements are false or not proven to be true) is in my view clear, but the rule is an exception to the principle that comment (to be defensible) must be on facts, meaning true facts, or must be justified, and I am not persuaded that there is any public benefit in widening this exception. It would indeed be anomalous if a report lacking the qualities necessary to sustain a defence of privilege could nonetheless sustain a defence of fair comment. The point is not met by saying that comment based on a report lacking these qualities would be vulnerable to a reply of malice, since it is not hard to imagine circumstances in which a report, although not fair and accurate, would be untainted by any improper motive. The reporter might, for example, have heard and recorded a damaging accusation but left before its convincing refutation."

Note on Damages

As we have seen, juries in England have long awarded ridiculous sums of money in defamation cases (Scottish juries, unsurprisingly, had never awarded more than £50,000 until they found that Fr Noel Barry and Annie Clinton had been unjustifiably credited with sexual misdeeds and awarded them £165,000). Artemus Jones was more than handsomely paid off, as was Lewis of the Rubber Improvement Co; more recently a life peer was awarded £1.5 million and the wife of the Yorkshire Ripper £600,000. The Court of Appeal was very reluctant to interfere, so Rules passed under the Courts and Legal Services Act 1990 gave them power (not only in defamation cases, unfortunately) to reduce jury damages, a power the Court used somewhat hesitantly to reduce to £110,000 the £250,000 awarded to Esther Rantzen ([1993] 4 All E.R. 975). Then the European Court of Human Rights unanimously held that the award of £1.5 million was in breach of Count Tolstoy's right of expression under Art.10 of the Convention (*Tolstoy Miloslavsky v United Kingdom* (1995) 20 E.H.R.R. 442), although Lord Aldington had offered to settle (for a mere £300,000), as have other victorious plaintiffs (thus Graham Souness, awarded £750,000, accepted £100,000; and the inventor of a revolutionary wing-sailed trimaran, awarded £1.485 million against the *Yachting World* which had been rude about it, settled for £160,000—plus costs of £600,000).

Welcome though the legislative intervention was, the Court itself has now acted decisively in *John v MGN Ltd* [1996] 1 All E.R. 35, where the £350,000 awarded by the jury to Elton John was reduced to £75,000 and the Master of the Rolls delivered a masterly judgment holding:

(1) that while juries must not be referred to previous jury awards in defamation cases, they could be referred to sums awarded by the Court of Appeal, and might, in order to check that the sum awarded was reasonable, be referred to awards in personal injury cases, it being open to counsel and the court to indicate what, in their view, was a proper bracket within which the award should fall.

(2) As to exemplary damages, the jury must be told that they could be awarded only where the defendant must not only have published with a view to material gain, but must have suspected that the words were untrue and deliberately refrained from taking obvious steps which, if taken, would have confirmed that suspicion. Nor must such damages exceed the minimum sum required to teach the defendant and others that tort does not pay.

However "The decision in *John*'s case has not succeeded in its avowed purpose", as Sedley L.J. said, dissenting in *Kiam v MGN* [2002] 2 All E.R. 219, 238, where the majority upheld a jury verdict for £105,000, well outside the judge's bracket of £40,000 to £80,000; it was relevant that in *Heil v Rankin* [2001] Q.B. 272 the Court had raised awards in personal injury cases up to a maximum of £200,000 for pain and suffering. That was regarded by Eady J. as the maximum in *Lillie v Newcastle C.C.* [2002] EWHC 1600, and he awarded it against the four draftsmen of a Report commissioned by the City Council into alleged child abuse: the draftsmen stated matters they knew to be false and they could not therefore invoke the privilege which protected the Council which broadcast the Report. However, in *Campbell v Newsgroup Newspapers* [2002] E.W.C.A. 1143 the Court of Appeal sought to reassert its authority, and in a judgment to which it attached an Appendix reviewing and appraising earlier awards, reduced the jury's damages from £350,000 to £30,000.

Yet an award of the equivalent of £533,000 (reduced from a jury verdict of £1.2 million) was recently upheld by the Privy Council on appeal from Jamaica in a case where the life of a former Rhodes Scholar and President of the Oxford Union was blighted by the defendant newspaper's baseless allegations of bribery while he was Minister of Tourism. *Gleaner Co v Abrahams* [2003] UKPC 55.

The huge damages awarded in England have naturally attracted plaintiffs from abroad who can prove publication here. After all, even publications like *Hello!* cross frontiers. Where can suit be brought? Under the Brussels Convention compensation for damage wherever it arises can be claimed at the domicile of the defendant, but courts in other places of publication may award damages only in respect of publications within their jurisdiction which are shown to be harmful to reputation there. Case C–68/93 *Shevill v Presse Alliance* [1993] All E.R. E.C.) 289.

But it is not the lure of damages alone which makes England the libel capital of the world just as Reno, Nevada was the divorce capital of the United States for quite a time. Let us quote Lord Hoffmann, dissenting, in *Berezovsky v Michaels* [2000] 2 All E.R. 986 at 1004: "the notion that Mr Berezovsky, a man of enormous wealth, wants to sue in England in order to secure the damages appropriate to compensate him for being lowered in the esteem of persons in this country who have heard of him is something which would be taken seriously only by a lawyer. The common sense of the matter is that he wants the verdict of an English court that he has been acquitted of the allegations in the article, for use wherever in the world his business may take him. He does not want to sue in the United States because he considers it too likely that he will lose. He does not want to sue in Russia for the unusual reason that other people might think it was too likely that he would win. He says that success in the Russian courts would not be adequate to vindicate his reputation because it might be attributed to his corrupt influence over the Russian judiciary." The bare majority in the House of Lords held that the distribution in England of nearly 2,000 copies of Forbes Magazine (as against three-quarters of a million in the United States) of an article alleging in strong terms that the claimant was a criminal of the worst kind entitled our judges to hale the American publishers into court here to defend themselves against a claim by a non-resident whose links with Britain were not at all strong. Even if Mr Berezovsky wins his claim, however, he will not have vindicated his reputation, it will simply be that the defendants have failed to prove what they alleged.

Final Note:

Bringing libel damages into relation with personal injury damages highlights the absurdity of defamation, a clear case of tort gone wrong. If personal injury claims often arise from tragedy, defamation suits frequently end in it. Oscar Wilde paid dearly for prosecuting Lord Queensberry, and though the equally flamboyant Whistler was successful in his libel suit against the critic Ruskin ("flinging a pot of paint in the public's face"), he was bankrupted by it. It was the defendant who went bankrupt when Dr Smith sued his partner, Dr Alanah Houston, for slandering him in the hearing of their patients in the waiting room: the jury award of £160,000 was reduced to £50,000 by the Court of Appeal, but Dr Smith obtained only £1,000—plus a bill for £184,000 from his solicitor. Other successful plaintiffs who rued the day they sued include Lord Aldington with his unsatisfied judgment for £1.5 million against Count Tolstoy and Patricia Eaton whose colleague at school accused her of predatory tactics.

Bill Roache also. The surprisingly numerous viewers of *Coronation Street* may know that for over thirty years he played the role of Ken Barlow. In 1991 *The Sun* published an article which derided him as boring and greatly disliked by the cast. Roache refused as inadequate the £50,000 which *The Sun* paid into court, with the result that when the jury awarded him precisely that sum he became liable for *The Sun*'s costs from the time of payment in, some £116,000. He then sued his lawyers, unsuccessfully, at a cost of £80,000, the judge accepting that Roache had not been motivated by greed [!]. Eight years after the jury award he filed for bankruptcy.

Unsuccessful plaintiffs can regret it too. We need hardly mention the egregious Neil Hamilton whose disastrous suit against Al Fayed (a true case of *Snake v Mongoose*) fascinated the nation in late 1999. Earlier a doctor who sued Channel Four for branding him as a charlatan was met at the trial by substantiating evidence against him; his case collapsed and he had to withdraw from practice owing £750,000 in costs. (*British Medical Journal*, May 18, 1996, May 24, 1997, as reported in [1997] New L.J. 1620). It is not clear whether it was greed or some cognate cardinal sin such as pride which prompted Jonathan Aitken to persuade his daughter to give perjured evidence in his libel suit against *The Guardian*, but it cost him his freedom, since he was sentenced to eighteen months in jail for conspiracy to pervert the course of justice and perjury. This was the successful politician who announced: "If it falls to me to start a fight to cut out the cancer of bent and twisted journalism in our country with the simple sword of truth and the trusty shield of British fair play, so be it. I am ready for the fight." Aitken obtained no damages, unlike Lord Archer who was awarded and received £500,000; but it later transpired that he too had sought to persuade others to lie in court on his behalf.

The fact is that the defamation business taints all those who come into contact with it, not just those who claim damages but also those who receive fees for practising their noisome métier, like the firm famous for its involvement which has proudly announced that it will take libel claims on a "no win, no fee" basis. This true public-spiritedness enabled the firm to collect a success fee of £200,000 for acting on behalf of Joe Rahamim, but gratifyingly it had unrecoverable costs estimated at over £1.5 million in the unsuccessful suit against *Private Eye* by its client John Stuart Condliffe. See *Private Eye* for November 16–29, 2001 and *The Times*, September 30, 2003.

PART VIII

DECEPTION AND OTHER WRONGFUL CONDUCT

INTRODUCTION

PREVIOUS chapters have mainly concentrated on a single tort. Now, however, we face a host of torts—deceit, malicious falsehood, passing-off, inducing breach of contract, intimidation, interference with contract, causing loss by wrongful means, conspiracy and abuse of power. They can perhaps be grouped together loosely as the "economic torts", but the use of the word "economic" here certainly requires some explanation.

Tort law has primarily been concerned with the physical rather than the economic. The law of *trespass*, as we have seen, protects only what is tangible—persons and property; liability in *nuisance* depends on one's having an effect on land; only things can be the subject of *conversion*; even *defamation* is primarily concerned with the individual's social standing, not his wealth. So, too, the paradigmatic case of tortious *negligence* is when dangerous conduct has caused physical harm, and even modern liabilities, such as product or even environmental liability, may be restricted to cases of damage to person or property.

But if the thrust is towards the physical the scope of these torts embraces the economic. Conversion is applied to cheques. Companies can sue for defamation. A hotel can complain of nuisance. And in a personal injury claim one naturally recovers not only for pain and suffering but also for the economic aspects of the injury—increased outgoings in the form of medical treatment, decreased income from inability to work.

Thus much of what is meat to the lawyer is gravy to the economist: their interests overlap considerably. Nevertheless, they are not identical. A lawyer is not apt to speak of "human resources", does not regard the human being as primarily a unit of production and consumption, and sees more to justice than the maximisation of distributable wealth. Just as a literary critic would not think a book good simply because it sells well, so a lawyer acting as such is apt to regard the needless death of a baby rather differently from the professional economist. It is not *because* of their economic aspects that we protect human interests as we do: the human being is a value *per se* and *an sich*, a vulnerable value, one to be protected against wounds.

Now suppose that the consequences of the defendant's conduct are *only* economic. What position is the law of tort to adopt? As the recent writhings of the law of negligence clearly testify, the protection offered is rather hesitant. At a time when, despite the decline of capitalism and the fall of Marxism, wealth, important as it is, is still publicly treated as all-important, as the only thing that counts (perhaps because it can be counted), this hesitancy may seem eccentric, but irrational it is not.

Irrational is the last word one could apply to the German Civil Code, yet in its hesitancy to impose liability in tort for causing harm which is purely economic that Code is very like English law. According to its principal paragraph, § 823(1) BGB, *damage* calls for compensation if it results from the negligent or deliberate invasion of a *right*; the rights specified are life, body, health, freedom and property—very like the interests protected against direct invasion by our law of trespass. The compensable damage resulting from such invasions naturally includes the economic consequences to the victim, but since the right to earn one's living or the right to keep or enhance one's wealth are not among the rights specified, no protection against the negligent or even intentional invasion of mere economic interests is offered by this principle. This does not, however, mean that one can never sue for pure economic harm, for another paragraph in the tort section, § 826 BGB, provides that "It is actionable intentionally to cause harm to another in a morally offensive manner", and the "harm" here need not result from the invasion of a right, the wrong of the defendant making up for the right of the plaintiff. In sum, you don't have to pay for making someone poorer unless you meant to *and* the way you did it was disgusting. The worse you behave the more you have to pay for.

In this chapter we find the decisions which respond to the problem to which the German solution lies in § 826.

We mentioned as not being covered the "right to earn one's living". But what exactly is this interest in earning? How should it be analysed? We can hardly say that there is a legal *right* to one's living in the way that there is a right in property, because although neither interest is unqualified, the former is qualified almost to the point of extinction by the existence of a similar right in one's competitors. For example, even the littlest of the Three Bears can properly speak of "*my* bowl of porridge," for they have separate bowls. If they ate from a communal bowl, as all traders and earners do, he could not speak of "*my* bowl of porridge," for it is not. Nor could he speak of "*my* next spoonful," since, if the biggest bear eats quickly, there won't be one. Even the "right to dip in the bowl" is not a useful notion, because the biggest bear must have an identical right and may leave nothing. All that "right to dip in the bowl" suggests is that there may be circumstances where it is a wrong in the biggest bear to prevent baby bear from dipping; we must discover what those circumstances are.

Of course, if anything can be discovered which can be called "property" or a "right", even if it is not a thing in fact or a right in the general law, it tends to be more strongly protected. Thus an author's copyright, an inventor's patent and a tradesman's registered trade-mark are very strongly protected. A trade secret and an unregistered mark or name are protected less strongly, but still quite well. So also with a "right." An employer has a right to the services of his employee during the period of the contract, but not after that period, however likely it may be that the employee would remain. He can therefore sue a competitor who lures his employee away during that period, not one who offers the employee a larger salary at the end of it. But in the absence of anything which can, however transferentially, be called "property" or a "right", the interest in earning one's living appears to be merely an expectation of benefit from a third party—the hope that the public will come and buy or that the next job application will prove more fruitful.

We can look at the matter another way. Robinson Crusoe had a *body* of his own and could own *things*—indeed he was the monarch of all he surveyed—but he couldn't make any money till Man Friday came along, for until then there was no one to buy his property, no one to pay him wages for his work, no one to pay him interest for the use of any money he had with him. Money comes from others; in actuality, leaving aside the monetary benefits one gets from the state and the tax one has to pay it, the money most people get comes from their employer and is spent on goods and services. Accordingly while you can take direct action against a person's body or property (and trespass deals with that), to ruin a person financially the action you take must be indirect, through another person, the source of his earnings or profits. If you want to close the pub, you get at the supplier, the clientele or the staff.

The fact that you can only strike at a person through others (unless you can delude or blackmail him into wasting his own money) lends a certain complexity to these torts. England has not yet quite evolved a general principle comparable with that of § 826

BGB, but it may be useful to consider the cases which follow on the view that it is actionable to cause *intentional harm* to another by *wrongful* means. That may seem tautologous, but it is not. The reason it is not tautologous is that these situations are triangular, and wrongfulness is a quality attaching to straight lines. Thus we must examine the line between the plaintiff and the defendant to discover if the latter intended to hurt the plaintiff; and, in order to discover whether he used wrongful means, we must examine *both* the other sides of the triangle, both that linking the defendant and the third party, whom we call "X," and that linking the third party with the plaintiff.

Let us first examine the line between X and the defendant, bearing in mind that all that is done is designed by the defendant. If the defendant gets X to commit a wrong against the plaintiff, the defendant will be liable just as where A tells B to strike C, or sets his dog on him. If what X does at the defendant's instigation is a tort, the defendant is liable as a joint tortfeasor; if the defendant gets X to break his contract with the plaintiff (*e.g.* persuades X to dismiss him without notice), the defendant is equally liable, for the tort of inducing breach of contract. The only difference is that, whereas the defendant is taken to know the general law of tort, he must be proved to have knowledge or suspicion of the contract between X and the plaintiff. Note particularly that in such cases X will always have broken his contract *deliberately* if not freely; and if there is one kind of breach of contract which is wrongful, it must be the deliberate breach, whatever contract lawyers may say (and it will probably be an anticipatory breach anyway).

Now let us suppose that X is in a position to hurt the plaintiff without committing any wrong (*e.g.* to give him notice or to stop frequenting his shop). If the defendant persuades him to do so by lawful means, there will be no liability, save in the very rare case where both the defendant and X are actuated solely by "disinterested malevolence." But the means of persuasion used by the defendant on X must be studied. For example, he may have *misled* X into hurting the plaintiff. Those lies will constitute wrongful means; what in a two-party situation is called deceit is called malicious falsehood in a three-party situation. Or, absent fraud, the defendant may have used duress, may have *threatened* X with some evil if he did not hurt the plaintiff. If the evil threatened would be a wrong against X if it were committed, then those threats are wrongful means, whether the evil threatened would be a tort or a breach of contract. But if the evil threatened is one which the defendant is at liberty to produce, then there is no use of wrongful means so far as the line between X and the defendant is concerned. In either case, of course, the plaintiff will suffer harm only if X hurts him, in consequence of being taken in by the lie or coerced by the threat.

Now suppose that the defendant, in his aim of hurting the plaintiff, strikes *at* X instead of *through* him. Rather than threaten to assault the plaintiff's customers if they remain loyal, the defendant actually batters them. Rather than threaten to break his contract, he deliberately breaks it in order to hurt the plaintiff. There again we have wrongful means successfully employed to harm the plaintiff, and the defendant is liable (to the plaintiff as well as to X).

This basic common law is overlaid and obscured by statutes which outlaw commercial excess or legitimise industrial action. Even so, it is a pity that in most tort courses cases such as those in this chapter are rather over-shadowed by regular negligence cases, for while the rules of negligence just give people "out", as it were, like an umpire in a cricket match, these decisions lay down the rules of the game, rules as a basis for action, determining what is permitted and what is not. They are therefore concerned with the limits of freedom, rather like those cases which turn on defences to trespass claims: but here the freedom of action is, and should be, very much greater, because the plaintiff is complaining of only financial harm, not of an invasion of one of his primary rights.

The common law principles, developed at rather a high level of abstraction, apply to all cases where one person has deliberately caused financial loss to another. Legislation is needed if one wants to make distinctions between losing wages and losing profits, that is, between jobs and businesses, or between the various means of interference, such as withdrawal of labour, cutting off of supplies or dissuasion of customers.

Chapter 15

ECONOMIC MISCONDUCT

EDGINGTON v FITZMAURICE

Court of Appeal (1885) 29 Ch.D. 459; 55 L.J.Ch. 650; 1 T.L.R. 326; 53 L.T. 369; 33 W.R. 911

Action by subscriber against issuer of bonds

The Rev. Charles Edgington, a shareholder of the Army & Navy Provision Market (Ltd), received a prospectus issued by the defendant officers of that company, inviting him to subscribe for debenture bonds, and he did so, to the amount of £1,500. The prospectus stated that the sums were wanted "To enable the society to complete the present alterations and additions to the buildings and to purchase their own horses and vans . . . and to further develop the arrangements at present existing for the direct supply of cheap fish from the coast." It also stated that the society had purchased a London property subject to a mortgage on which £21,500 was out-standing, repayable in instalments.

The plaintiff now seeks the return of his £1,500 on the ground of fraud.

Bowen L.J.: This is an action for deceit, in which the plaintiff complains that he was induced to take certain debentures by the misrepresentations of the defendants, and that he sustained damage thereby. The loss which the plaintiff sustained is not disputed. In order to sustain his action he must first prove that there was a statement as to facts which was false; and secondly, that it was false to the knowledge of the defendants, or that they made it not caring whether it was true or false. For it is immaterial whether they made the statement knowing it to be untrue, or recklessly, without caring whether it was true or not, because to make a statement recklessly for the purpose of influencing another person is dishonest. It is also clear that it is wholly immaterial with what object the lie is told. That is laid down in Lord Blackburn's judgment in *Smith v Chadwick* ((1884) 9 App.Cas. 201), but it is material that the defendant should intend that it should be relied on by the person to whom he makes it. But, lastly, when you have proved that the statement was false, you must further show that the plaintiff has acted upon it and has sustained damage by so doing; you must show that the statement was either the sole cause of the plaintiff's act, or materially contributed to his acting. . . .

The alleged misrepresentations were three. First, it was said that the prospectus contained an implied allegation that the mortgage for £21,500 could not be called in at once, but was payable by instalments. I think that upon a fair construction of the prospectus it does so allege; and therefore that the prospectus must be taken to have contained an untrue statement on that point; but it does not appear to me clear that the statement was fraudulently made by the defendants. It is therefore immaterial to consider whether the plaintiff was induced to act as he did by that statement.

Secondly, it is said that the prospectus contains an implied allegation that there was no other mortgage affecting the property except the mortgage stated therein. I think there was such an implied allegation, but I think it is not brought home to the defendants that it was made dishonestly; accordingly, although the plaintiff may have been damnified by the weight which he gave to the allegation, he cannot rely on it in this action: for in an action of deceit the plaintiff must prove dishonesty. Therefore if the case had rested on these two allegations alone, I think it would be too uncertain to entitle the plaintiff to succeed.

But when we come to the third alleged misstatement I feel that the plaintiff's case is made out. I mean the statement of the objects for which the money was to be raised. These were stated to be to complete the alterations and additions to the buildings, to purchase horses and vans, and to develop the supply of fish. A mere suggestion of possible purposes to which a portion of the money might be applied would not have formed a basis for an action of deceit. There must be a misstatement of an existing fact: but the state of a man's mind is as much a fact as the state of his digestion. It is true that it is very difficult to prove what the state of a man's mind at a particular time is, but if it can be ascertained it is as much a fact as anything else. A misrepresentation as to the state of a man's mind is, therefore, a misstatement of fact. Having applied as careful consideration to the evidence as I could, I have reluctantly come to the conclusion that the true objects of the defendants in raising the money were not those stated in the circular. I will not go through the evidence, but looking only to the cross-examination of the defendants, I am satisfied that the objects for which the loan was wanted were misstated by the defendants, I will not say knowingly, but so recklessly as to be fraudulent in the eye of the law.

Then the question remains: Did this misstatement contribute to induce the plaintiff to advance his money. Mr Davey's argument has not convinced me that they did not. He contended that the plaintiff admits that he would not have taken the debentures unless he had thought they would give him a charge on the property, and therefore he was induced to take them by his own mistake, and the misstatement in the circular was not material. But such misstatement was material if it was actively present to his mind when he decided to advance his money. The real question is, what was the state of the plaintiff's mind, and if his mind was disturbed by the misstatement of the defendants, and such disturbance was in part the cause of what he did, the mere fact of his also making a mistake himself could make no difference. It resolves itself into a mere question of fact. I have felt some difficulty about the pleadings, because in the statement of claim this point is not clearly put forward, and I had some doubt whether this contention as to the third misstatement was not an afterthought. But the balance of my judgment is weighed down by the probability of the case. What is the first question which a man asks when he advances money? It is, what is it wanted for? Therefore I think that the statement is material, and that the plaintiff would be unlike the rest of his race if he was not influenced by the statement of the objects for which the loan was required. The learned judge in the court below came to the conclusion that the misstatement did influence him, and I think he came to a right conclusion.

Questions

1. In what ways is it possible *carelessly* to misrepresent one's present intentions?

2. " . . . if his mind was disturbed by the misstatement of the defendants, and such disturbance was in part the cause of what he did, the mere fact of his also making a mistake himself could make no difference." Would this be true where the defendants' misstatement was not deceitful but careless?

3. Normally the buyer of land who has exchanged contracts forfeits his deposit if he doesn't complete (unless the deposit is penal under *Workers Trust & Merchant Bank v Dojap Investments* [1993] 2 All E.R. 370). In *Goff v Gauthier* (1991) 62 P. & C.R. 388 the buyer, unable to complete, got his deposit back by showing that he only exchanged because the vendor had said that if he didn't do so, the vendor would withdraw. What else did the buyer have to establish apart from the mere fact that the vendor made that statement? Note that in *Smith New Court v Scrimgeour Vickers* (below, p.578) the deceitful representation was simply that a third party was contending for the purchase of the shares in question.

Notes:

1. Here the defendant told lies directly to the plaintiff. Cases below will show the defendant lying to others about the plaintiff (*Joyce v Sengupta* (below, p.580); *Martin v Watson* (below, p.628), or deluding others about his products (*Erven Warnink*, below, p.584) or about himself (*Lonrho v Fayed*, below, p.619). The law doesn't like liars; tell fibs to the court and you may forfeit your equitable remedies. Economists don't like liars, either, since misinformed people cannot make proper choices.

2. In cases like the present the House of Lords confirmed four years later that "To found an action for damages there must be a contract and breach, or fraud" (*Derry v Peek* (1889) 14 App.Cas. 337 at 347 *per* Lord Bramwell). Seventy-five years thereafter *Hedley Byrne v Heller & Partners* (above, p.57) showed that there was a middle ground of liability where there was neither contract nor fraud, but a special relationship and negligence. Does the tort of deceit still have a role? Yes, just as contract does. For just as there are special

relationships where there is no contract (as in *Hedley Byrne* itself) and therefore no possible guarantee liability, so there may be fraud where there is no special relationship, and therefore no possible liability for mere negligence.

We have seen that the duty to take care is more easily found where an answer is given to a particular questioner than when a statement is made to the world at large (above, p.57). Again, a duty is not apt to be found unless the statement is made on a business occasion. There are accordingly many situations where statements are made but no duty to take care arises; a person who suffers loss from reliance on such a statement may have to prove fraud in order to recover damages, but if he proves fraud, he will certainly recover. Is there any advantage, if one is in a duty situation, in trying to prove that the defendant was not just negligent but fraudulent, that not only should he not have believed what he said but that he actually did not? There may be advantages with regard to damages (aggravated? not exemplary: *Doyle v Olby (Ironmongers)* [1969] 2 Q.B. 158, contributory negligence (for the liar can hardly complain that his dupe was gullible—*Standard Chartered Bank v Pakistan National Shipping Corp.* [2002] UKHL 43, [2003] 1 A.C. 959, [2002] 1 All E.R. 173 or the defence of illegality (*Saunders v Edwards* [1987] 2 All E.R. 651 at 659–660).

3. In *East v Maurer* ([1991] 2 All E.R. 733; noted (1992) 108 L.Q.R. 386; [1992] Camb.L.J. 9) the defendant sold the plaintiff one of his two hairdressing salons in Bournemouth after stating that he had no intention of running the other. In fact he continued to run the other and ruined the plaintiff's trade. He was held liable to pay the plaintiff all she had lost, including the profits she would have made in the other business she would have bought and run had she not been induced to buy the defendant's hairdressing business. Had the defendant *promised* not to compete, instead of just misstating his intention, the plaintiff could have had the profits she would have made out of the business she bought from him. That is one difference between the contractual and the tortious measure of damages.

4. Although the Misrepresentation Act 1967 is available only to a contractor induced to contract by a misrepresentation, the measure of recovery is tortious and not contractual. Neither fraud nor negligence need be proved: the defendant must exculpate himself by showing that he did believe and had reasonable grounds for believing what he said. Thus the defendant may be liable although even negligence is not established against him. That makes it outrageous that the extent of his liability is held to be the same as that of a proven liar, for he must pay for all consequent loss, even if unforeseeable "unless otherwise too remote": *Royscot Trust v Rogerson* [1991] 3 All E.R. 294, CA; noted (1991) 107 L.Q.R. 547. The statute was ill-conceived and ill-drafted, but there is no reason why it should be so ill-construed. Reservations about this decision were expressed in *Smith New Court v Scrimgeour Vickers* (next below) but it was applied in *Spice Girls Ltd v Aprilia World Service* [2001] E.M.L.R. 8.

5. It seems that proof of causation may be somewhat relaxed in misrepresentation cases, especially where there is deceit. Lord Mustill once said: "As a matter of common sense . . . the [defendant] will have an uphill task in persuading the court that the . . . misstatement of circumstances satisfying the test of materiality had made no difference. There is ample material . . . in the general law . . . to suggest that there is a presumption in favour of a causative effect" (*Pan Atlantic Insurance v Pine Top Insurance* [1994] 3 All E.R. 581 at 619). This presumption was applied in *Country NatWest Bank v Barton* [1999] Times L.R. 567 where the Court of Appeal reversed the trial judge's decision and held that it would be presumed until rebuttal by the misrepresentor that a statement likely to play a part in the decision of a reasonable person did in fact play such a part. It need not be the sole inducement. A statement could not be said to have played a part if the representee had already made up his mind, but it might have induced him to persevere when otherwise he would not. Furthermore, a false answer to a relevant inquiry might confirm a belief spontaneously entertained and then be held to have induced all the consequences of the belief so confirmed.

6. In *Williams v Natural Life Health Foods* (above p.62) it was held that a person is liable for negligent advice or information only is he had assumed responsibility for it, which would not be the case where the claimant had relied on the principal who supplied him with the information rather than the agent who originated it. In *Standard Chartered Bank v Pakistan National Shipping* (above n.2) it was made clear that this did not apply to fraudulent misrepresentations: "No one can escape liability for his fraud by saying 'I wish to make it clear that I am committing this fraud on behalf of someone else and I am not to be personally liable'." At [22].

7. But the subjective element in deceit is very strong. "To establish liability in deceit it is incumbent on the representee to show that the representor intended his statement to be understood by the representee in the sense in which it is false. In most cases this is not a problem because if the representor claims that he intended his words to bear a meaning they do not then he is not likely to be believed. But where a representation is ambiguous then the representee must do more than show that in its ordinary meaning the representation was false." So held by the Court of Appeal in *Goose v Wilson Sandford & Co* [2001] 3 Lloyd's Rep. PN 189, referring to the Privy Council in *Akerhielm v De Mare* [1959] A.C. 789: "The question is not whether the defendant in any given case honestly believed the representation to be true in the sense assigned to it by the court on an objective consideration of its truth or falsity, but whether he honestly believed the representation to be true in the sense in which he understood it albeit erroneously when it was made."

SMITH NEW COURT SECURITIES LTD v SCRIMGEOUR VICKERS (ASSET MANAGEMENT) LTD

House of Lords [1997] A.C. 254; [1996] 3 W.L.R. 1051; [1996] 4 All E.R. 769
(noted [1997] Camb. L.J. 17)

Damages for deceit

For most of 1989 Ferranti shares were grossly overvalued since the stock market was unaware that the firm had been the victim of a massive fraud which reduced its net worth by nearly half and its income by nearly two-thirds. Some time before this became known, the plaintiffs were interested in buying 28 million Ferranti shares from the defendants, at 78p if they were for immediate resale or at a higher price for retention. 78p being unacceptable to the defendants, the plaintiffs agreed to purchase the shares for 82¼p, the defendants having stated that other parties were eager to buy them, though they knew that this was not true. The sale went through on July 21, the market price of the shares plummeted in September when the fraud on Ferranti became public knowledge, and in December the plaintiffs, who could realise only £11,788,204 for the shares for which they had paid the defendants £24,141,424, discovered that they had been misled.

The trial judge awarded the plaintiffs nearly £11 million, but the Court of Appeal reduced this to £1,196,010, reckoning that at the time of purchase the value of the shares was only 4p less than the price paid for them. The House of Lords unanimously reinstated the judgment at first instance.

Lord Steyn: That brings me to the question of policy whether there is a justification for differentiating between the extent of liability for civil wrongs depending on where in the sliding scale from strict liability to intentional wrongdoing the particular civil wrong fits in. It may be said that logical symmetry and a policy of not punishing intentional wrongdoers by civil remedies favour a uniform rule. On the other hand, it is a rational and defensible strategy to impose wider liability on an intentional wrongdoer. The exclusion of heads of loss in the law of negligence, which reflects considerations of legal policy, does not necessarily avail the intentional wrongdoer. Such a policy of imposing more stringent remedies on an intentional wrongdoer serves two purposes. First it serves a deterrent purpose in discouraging fraud. Counsel for Citibank argued that the sole purpose of the law of tort generally, and the tort of deceit in particular, should be to compensate the victims of civil wrongs. That is far too narrow a view. Professor Glanville Williams identified four possible purposes of an action for damages in tort: appeasement, justice, deterrence and compensation (see "The Aims of the Law of Tort" (1951) 4 C.L.P. 137). He concluded (p.172):

> "Where possible the law seems to like to ride two or three horses at once; but occasionally a situation occurs where one must be selected. The tendency is then to choose the deterrent purpose for torts of intention, and the compensatory purpose for other torts."

And in the battle against fraud civil remedies can play a useful and beneficial role. Secondly, as between the fraudster and the innocent party, moral considerations militate in favour of requiring the fraudster to bear the risk of misfortunes directly caused by his fraud. I make no apology for referring to moral considerations. The law and morality are inextricably interwoven. To a large extent the law is simply formulated and declared morality. And, as *Oliver Wendell Holmes, The Common Law* (1968), p.106 observed, the very notion of deceit with its overtones of wickedness is drawn from the moral world.

For more than a hundred years at least English law has adopted a policy of imposing more extensive liability on intentional wrongdoers than on merely careless defendants.

Eventually, the idea took root that an intentional wrongdoer is not entitled to the benefit of the reasonable foreseeability test of remoteness. He is to be held liable in respect of "the actual damage directly flowing from the fraudulent inducement": It was, however, not until the decision of the Court of Appeal in *Doyle v Olby (Ironmongers) Ltd* that the governing principles were clearly laid down. By fraudulent misrepresentation the defendant induced the plaintiff to buy a business. The trial judge awarded damages to the plaintiff on the basis of a contractual measure of damages, *i.e.* the cost of making good the representations. The Court of Appeal ruled that this was an error and substituted a higher figure assessed on the basis of the tort measure, *i.e.* restoration of the status quo ante. Lord Denning M.R. explained ([1969] 2 All E.R. 119 at 122):

> "In contract, the damages are limited to what may reasonably be supposed to have been in the contemplation of the parties. In fraud, they are not so limited. The defendant is bound to make reparation for all the actual damage directly flowing from the fraudulent inducement. The person who has been defrauded is entitled to say: 'I would not have entered into this bargain at all but for your representation. Owing to your fraud, I have not only lost all the money I paid you, but, what is more, I have been put to a large amount of extra expense as well and suffered this or that extra damages.' All such damages can be recovered: and it does not lie in the mouth of the fraudulent person to say that they could not reasonably have been foreseen."

The logic of the decision in *Doyle v Olby (Ironmongers) Ltd* justifies the following propositions.

(1) The plaintiff in an action for deceit is not entitled to be compensated in accordance with the contractual measure of damage, *i.e.* the benefit of the bargain measure. He is not entitled to be protected in respect of his positive interest in the bargain.

(2) The plaintiff in an action for deceit is, however, entitled to be compensated in respect of his negative interest. The aim is to put the plaintiff into the position he would have been in if no false representation had been made.

(3) The practical difference between the two measures was lucidly explained in a contemporary case note on *Doyle v Olby (Ironmongers) Ltd* (see Treitel "Damages for Deceit" (1969) 32 M.L.R. 558–559). The author said:

> "If the plaintiff's bargain would have been a bad one, even on the assumption that the representation was true, he will do best under the tortious measure. If, on the assumption that the representation was true, his bargain would have been a good one, he will do best under the first contractual measure (under which he may recover something even if the actual value of what he has recovered is greater than the price)."

(4) Concentrating on the tort measure, the remoteness test whether the loss was reasonably foreseeable had been authoritatively laid down in *The Wagon Mound* in respect of the tort of negligence a few years before *Doyle v Olby (Ironmongers) Ltd* was decided: *Overseas Tankship (U.K.) Ltd v Morts Dock and Engineering Co Ltd, The Wagon Mound* [1961] 1 All E.R. 404; [1961] A.C. 388. *Doyle v Olby (Ironmongers) Ltd* settled that a wider test applies in an action for deceit.

(5) The dicta in all three judgments, as well as the actual calculation of damages in *Doyle v Olby (Ironmongers) Ltd*, make it clear that the victim of the fraud is entitled to compensation for all the actual loss directly flowing from the transaction induced by the wrongdoer. That includes heads of consequential loss.

(6) Significantly in the present context the rule in the previous paragraph is not tied to any process of valuation at the date of the transaction. It is squarely based on the overriding compensatory principle, widened in view of the fraud to cover all direct consequences. The legal measure is to compare the position of the plaintiff as it was before the fraudulent statement was made to him with his position as it became as a result of his reliance on the fraudulent statement.

Notes:

1. Nine years after the claimant had had a vasectomy he started cohabiting with the defendant. She became pregnant three years later and alleged that the child was his. Believing this, he spent some £90,000 supporting the defendant and the child, only to discover that the child was not his. Could he sue the defendant for the tort of deceit? Stanley Brunton J. "unhesitatingly" held that he could: the courts' reluctance to discover contractual obligations within the family on the ground of absence of "intention to create legal relations" was not in point here. *P v B* [2001] 1 F.L.R. 1041, [2001] Fam Law 422.

2. A claimant who had been fraudulently induced into a contract from which he made a profit could claim damages on the basis that had he not been deceived he could have entered into an even more profitable contract. *Clef Aquitaine SARL v Laporte Minerals* [2000] 3 All E.R. 493.

JOYCE v SENGUPTA

Court of Appeal [1993] 1 W.L.R. 337; [1993] 1 All E.R. 897

Action for damages for malicious falsehood

The first defendant wrote an article, which the second defendant published prominently in its *Today* newspaper, to the effect that one of Princess Anne's maids, of whom details were given, had stolen her royal employer's private letters and handed them to a national newspaper. The article clearly referred to the plaintiff, who now claimed compensatory and exemplary damages as well as an injunction.

The judge struck out the plaintiff's statement of claim, but the Court of Appeal allowed the action to proceed.

Sir Donald Nicholls V.-C.: Miss Joyce's case is that the article contains several serious untruths regarding her: contrary to what is said in the article, she did not steal the letters, she was not banned from rooms containing confidential documents, she was not dismissed in consequence, she was not required to undertake that she would not discuss the letters and she was not on bad terms with the Princess. She has left her employment with Princess Anne. She did so on May 5, 1989, following a letter of resignation written months earlier in January 1989, but her resignation was for personal reasons unconnected with the statements in the *Today* article.

Miss Joyce asserts that the article was published maliciously: Mr Sengupta who wrote the article and the sub-editor who chose the headline "ROYAL MAID STOLE LETTERS" were recklessly indifferent about the truth or falsity of the serious allegations. Mr Sengupta took no steps to check the police suspicions on which he says he relied; he did not speak to the plaintiff, he made no independent investigations, he did not even await the outcome of the fingerprint tests mentioned in the article.

Miss Joyce claims damages. The article falsely portrays her as untrustworthy. This has damaged her future employment prospects. She also claims exemplary damages, and an injunction against repetition.

Before turning to the issues raised by the appeal I should comment briefly on the difference between defamation and malicious falsehood. The remedy provided by the law for words which injure a person's reputation is defamation. Words may also injure a person without damaging his reputation. An example would be a claim that the seller of goods or land is not the true owner. Another example would be a false assertion that a person has closed down his business. Such claims would not necessarily damage the reputation of those concerned. The remedy provided for this is malicious falsehood, sometimes called injurious falsehood or trade libel. This cause of action embraces particular types of malicious falsehood such as slander of title and slander of goods, but it is not confined to those headings.

Falsity is an essential ingredient of this tort. The plaintiff must establish the untruth of the statement of which he complains. Malice is another essential ingredient. A genuine dispute about the ownership of goods or land should not of itself be actionable. So a person who acted in good faith is not liable. Further, since the object of this cause of action is to provide a person with a remedy for a false statement made maliciously which has caused him damage, at common law proof of financial loss was another essential ingredient. The rigour of this requirement was relaxed by statute. I shall have to return to the question of damages at a later stage. For present purposes it is sufficient to note that if a plaintiff establishes that the defendant maliciously made a false statement which has caused him financial damage, or in respect of which he is relieved from proving damage by the Defamation Act 1952, the law gives him a remedy. The false statement may also be defamatory, or it may not. As already mentioned, it need not be defamatory. Conversely, the fact that the statement is defamatory does not exclude a cause of action for malicious falsehood, although the law will ensure that a plaintiff does not recover damages twice over for the same loss.

It is as plain as a pikestaff that, had legal aid been available for libel, this action would have been a straightforward defamation action. In an action for malicious falsehood the plaintiff has to take on the burden of proving that the words were false and that in publishing them the defendant was actuated by malice. It would make no sense for Miss Joyce to take on this burden. If this had been a defamation action she would not have to prove malice, and if the newspaper wished to put in issue the truth of the defamatory assertions it would have to plead and prove justification as a defence. . . .

So far as the statement of claim is concerned I am satisfied that, although open to criticism here and there, it does disclose the essentials of a cause of action for malicious falsehood. . . . Essentially, the plaintiff's case on malice is that the defendants went ahead and published the police suspicions as though they were fact and did so without taking any steps to check or verify them. This showed a calculated, reckless indifference to the truth or falsity of the allegations. Malice is to be inferred from the grossness and falsity of the assertions and the cavalier way they were published. In my view the pleading raises an arguable issue, and it does so in terms sufficient to inform the defendants of the case against them.

I turn to the points raised regarding damages. The plaintiff claims, first, that she suffered financial loss in consequence of the *Today* article. Having regard to the nature and prominence of the assertions in the article, her chances of finding work in any employment requiring trust and confidence have been diminished. Secondly, she relies on s.3 of the Defamation Act 1952, which provides:

> "(1) In an action for slander of title, slander of goods or other malicious falsehood, it shall not be necessary to allege or prove special damage—(a) if, the words upon which the action is founded are calculated to cause pecuniary damage to the plaintiff and are published in writing or other permanent form; or (b) if the said words are calculated to cause pecuniary damage to the plaintiff in respect of any office, profession, calling, trade or business held or carried on by him at the time of the publication . . . "

The plaintiff relies on para.(a). She alleges that the article was likely to cause pecuniary damage to her by seriously prejudicing her opportunity to obtain other employment requiring trust and confidence.

On this interlocutory appeal it would be wholly inappropriate for us to attempt to go into the detail of the evidence which may properly be called in support of these claims. Suffice to say, on the first claim the plaintiff will need to give particulars of the financial loss she claims to have suffered sufficient to ensure that the defendants will not be taken by surprise by any evidence she may adduce on the amount of her loss.

As to the second claim, this is an allegation of general damage. In support of this claim the plaintiff cannot adduce evidence of actual loss (see Lord Denning M.R. in *Calvet v Tomkies* [1963] 3 All E.R. 610 at 611). I do not accept, however, that in consequence the award under this head must necessarily be nominal only. In *Fielding v Variety Inc.* [1967] 2 All E.R. 497 the malicious falsehood lay in falsely describing the 'Charlie Girl' show in London as a disastrous flop. Only nominal damages of £100 were awarded in that case because there was no likelihood of the words damaging the success of the show in London or prejudicing the chances of a production in the United States. That case is not authority for the proposition that, in the absence of evidence of actual loss, a plaintiff who relies on s.3 can recover only nominal damages. The whole purpose of s.3 was to give the plaintiff a remedy in malicious falsehood despite the difficulty of proving actual loss. A plaintiff is seldom able to call witnesses to say they ceased to deal with him because of some slander that had come to their ears. In consequence actions for malicious falsehood had become extremely rare. Section 3 was enacted to right this injustice. The section would fail in its purpose if, whenever relied on, it could lead only to an award of nominal damages.

The plaintiff claims, thirdly, that as a consequence of the article she suffered anxiety, distress and injury to her feelings. Mr Browne submitted that this third head of damages is irrecoverable as a matter of law and should be struck out. Mr Robertson QC contended that, although at common law proof of pecuniary damage was an essential ingredient of the tort, once pecuniary loss is established, or a claim under s.3 is made out, a plaintiff is entitled to recover his whole loss. If he suffered mental distress, the law will include an award of damages under this head also. . . . [The] state of the authorities suggests that damages for anxiety and distress are not recoverable for malicious falsehood. If that is the law it could lead to a manifestly unsatisfactory and unjust result in some cases. Take the example I gave earlier of a person who maliciously spreads rumours that his competitor's business has closed down. Or the rumour might be that the business is in financial difficulty and that a receiver will soon be appointed. The owner of the business suffers severe financial loss. Further, because of the effect the rumours are having on his business he is worried beyond measure about his livelihood and his family's future. He suffers acute anxiety and distress. Can it be right that the law is unable to give him any recompense for this suffering against the person whose malice caused it? Although injury to feelings alone will not found a cause of action in malicious falsehood, ought not the law to take such injury into account when it is connected with financial damage inflicted by the false-hood?

The point bristles with problems, not all of which were explored in argument. One possibility is that in an action for malicious falsehood damages are limited to financial loss. That would mark out a clear boundary, but it would suffer from the drawback of failing to do justice in the type of case I have mentioned. I instinctively recoil from the notion that in no circumstances can an injured plaintiff obtain recompense from a defendant for understandable distress caused by a false statement made maliciously. However, once it is accepted there are circumstances in which non-pecuniary loss, or some types of non-pecuniary loss, can be recovered in a malicious falsehood action, it becomes extremely difficult to define those circumstances or those types of loss in a coherent manner. It would be going too far to hold that all non-pecuniary loss suffered by a plaintiff is recoverable in a malicious falsehood action, because that would include injury to reputation at large. The history of malicious falsehood as a cause of action shows it was not designed to provide a remedy for such injury: the remedy for such loss is an action for defamation in which, incidentally, damages for injury to feelings may be included in a general award of damages (see *Fielding v Variety Inc* [1967] 2 All E.R. 497 at 500, 502).

Nor would these difficulties be solved by rejecting damages for distress as a separate head of loss in a malicious falsehood action but permitting distress to be taken into account as an aggravating factor. On this footing the judge or jury could take injury to feelings into account when awarding a lump sum of damages "in the round". I do not see how, *if only pecuniary loss is recoverable*, the amount awarded can be increased to reflect the plaintiff's distress. That would be a contradiction in terms. It would be to award damages for distress in a disguised fashion. If distress can inflame the damages recoverable for pecuniary loss, the difference between awarding aggravated damages for that reason and awarding damages for distress as a separate head of loss is a difference of words only.

[In *Khodaparast v Shad* [2000] 1 All E.R. 545 the Court of Appeal in unreserved judgments held that though damages for loss of reputation could not be awarded in a claim for malicious falsehood (and the judge had "correctly identified the distinction between defamation and malicious falsehood", *per* Otton L.J. at 557), nevertheless aggravated damages could be, and had rightly been awarded, since "Malicious falsehood is a species of defamation" (*per* Stuart-Smith L.J. at 556).]

Notes:

1. This tort may be put to novel uses, as in *Kaye v Robertson* [1991] F.S.R. 62 (above p.333), where it was the sole legal basis for enjoining a newspaper from publishing as a "genuine interview" with a television star the information obtained by a journalist who intruded into the privacy of the hospital room where the star lay in semi-conscious eclipse. But it is no new tort. Not long after Shakespeare died, a publican sued the defendant for saying that if he gave his mare malt to eat it would piss better beer than the plaintiff's (*Dickes v Fienne* (1639) March 59; 82 E.R. 411)); the action failed because the plaintiff could not prove any loss of custom, but it would succeed nowadays because of that regrettable tradesman's charter, s.3 of the Defamation Act 1952.

2. The tort thus often takes the form of slander of goods or disparagement of their quality. It is not always easy to tell disparagement of property from defamation of person. This is "one of the grey areas of the common law," *per* Cooke P., in *Bell-Booth Group v Att-Gen* [1983] 3 N.Z.L.R. 148 at 153. Lord Halsbury once said: "Could it be gravely argued that to say of a fishmonger that he was in the habit of selling decomposed fish would not be a libel upon him in the way of his trade? And, if so, would it not be a mere juggle with language to alter the form of that allegation to say that all the fish in A's shop is decomposed?" (*Linotype Co v British Empire Typesetting Machine Co* (1899) 15 T.L.R. 524 at 526). Yet if the goods in question had been canned fish, it is not clear that there would have been a defamation. It would perhaps have been better if corporations had not been allowed to sue in defamation, but had been limited to this tort which guards not honour but wealth, which is all they have.

The problem arose again in *Patterson v ICN Photonics* [2003] EWCA Civ 343 where a doctor wrote to the patrons of a beauty salon where a laser device manufactured by the claimants was used to remove wrinkles, saying that it was surprising that the Health Authority allowed it to be used without medical supervision. The trial judge held that this was defamatory of the manufacturer, but the Court of Appeal held that it was only slander of goods.

3. The requirement of malice is naturally satisfied where the defendant had no belief in the truth of what he said, but it may possibly extend to the case where, though he believed what he said, he had no interest in saying it. There is a case in Coke (4 Co.Rep. 17a; 76 E.R. 899) where it is observed that to say "You are a bastard" is actionable, whereas to say "You are a bastard, and I am the true heir" is not, even if it is false. In the second case the words demonstrate the interest claimed by the speaker. A consumers' association presumably has an interest in communicating to its members the characteristics of the goods tested. We come here quite close to qualified privilege in defamation, but here, of course, the privilege should be wider.

4. After the ironically-named Access to Justice Act 1999 individuals will have no incentive to follow Miss Joyce in claiming for malicious falsehood rather than defamation, since neither can now be funded by the Community Legal Service (hitherto legal aid, available for the former but not for the latter).

5. Posh Spice certainly believed that what she said was true when she went to the claimant's shop which was selling memorabilia of her distinguished husband, David Beckham, and complained in a loud voice that they were unauthorised. This exciting event was naturally picked up and much ventilated by the media. Was Mrs Beckham, mother of Brooklyn, answerable for the publicity in the media? Yes, it was quite foreseeable, and it had been held in *Slipper v BBC* [1991] 1 Q.B. 283 that a defamer was accountable for foreseeable republications. *McManus v Beckham* [2002] EWCA Civ 939, [2002] 4 All E.R. 497.

6. As between competitors, the scope of the tort was rather cut down by the House of Lords in *White v Mellin* [1895] A.C. 154. There the defendant, Timothy White the chemist, had bought from the plaintiff who manufactured it some bottles of an invalid food. To these bottles the defendant physically attached leaflets singing the praises of another proprietary food in which he had an interest. When the plaintiff, who sought an injunction, failed to establish a contract to sell his goods in the form in which they were delivered, he was non-suited. The Court of Appeal allowed his appeal ([1894] 3 Ch. 276), but the House of Lords upheld the trial judge. Lord Shand said: "when all that is done is making a comparison between the plaintiff's goods and goods of the person issuing the advertisement, and the statement made is that the plaintiff's goods are inferior in quality or inferior, it may be, in some special qualities, I think this cannot be regarded as a disparagement of which the law will take cognisance." In *De Beers Abrasive Products v International General Electric Co* [1975] 2 All E.R. 599, Walton J. presents a useful review of the authorities and offers the test "Did the defendant make observations about the plaintiffs' product in relation to his own which a reasonable person would take as being seriously intended?" If so, and if malice is shown, an action will lie.

7. Comparative advertising was banned or discountenanced in many countries of the European Community, an attitude that favoured producers over consumers. The Council has now issued Directive on Comparative Advertising 97/55 of October 6, 1997 amending Directive 84/450 on Misleading Advertising. It is less liberal than many would like. See W.R. Cornish, *Intellectual Property* (5th ed., 2003), pp.632, 715f., and Ohly & Spence, *The Law of Comparative Advertising* (2000). The use of a competitor's trademark, without which it is not easy to do comparative advertising, used to be forbidden. It is now permitted by the Trade Marks Act 1994, s.10(6), provided that such use is consistent with honest practices and neither takes unfair advantage of nor is detrimental to the distinctive character of the mark.

8. In *Vodafone v Orange* [1996] Times L.R. 526; [1997] F.S.R. 34 the defendant's advertising campaign used the slogan: "On average, Orange users save £20 per month in comparison with Vodafone's or Cellnet's equivalent tariffs". The plaintiff's claim for malicious falsehood was "hopeless", since what the defendant said was true as understood in its natural and ordinary meaning, and the claim for trademark infringement failed. This was "honest practice" under s.10(6) of the Trade Marks Act of 1994. An advertisement which was significantly misleading would not be consistent with honest practice, as was held against both parties to *Emaco v Dyson Appliances* [1999] Times L.R. 93, a dispute between manufacturers of vacuum cleaners.

Questions

1. Miss Joyce claimed exemplary damages as well as damages for distress. Was she likely to obtain them? See above, p.580.

2. On December 3, 1988, Edwina Currie, Under-Secretary of State for Health for only ten days more, stated publicly that most egg production in England was contaminated by salmonella. Egg sales dropped by more than half. Egg producers issued writs against Mrs Currie. For how many reasons do you think such claims would fail? Do you think the issuing solicitors knew that? (The feeble government produced £19 million!)

3. The agents for a famous jazz violinist arranged a concert schedule for him without authority, and in cancelling those fixtures told the concert hall managers that the violinist was seriously ill and probably would never tour again. This statement, passed on to members of the public, was a complete fabrication. Then the authorised schedule of concerts was published, some of them on the same dates, though not in the same venues, as previously announced. The plaintiff sued for malicious falsehood and for defamation.

Why did he sue for both, and what was the outcome? See *Grappelli v Derek Block (Holdings)* [1981] 2 All E.R. 272.

ERVEN WARNINK BV v TOWNEND (J) & SONS (HULL)

House of Lords [1979] A.C. 731; [1979] 3 W.L.R. 68; (1979) 123 S.J. 472; [1979] 2 All E.R. 927; [1980] R.P.C. 31 (noted (1980) 43 M.L.R. 336)

Suit by producers of advokaat against producer of drink falsely described as advokaat

Advocaat differs from egg-flip in being made with spirits rather than with fortified wine, which is cheaper. In 1974, in order to profit from the popularity of advocaat, the defendants decided to call their egg-flip "Keeling's Old English Advocaat". They thereby made a hole in the market for true advocaat, in which the plaintiffs had a very large share, almost all the competitors being from the Netherlands also.

The trial judge found that while no one buying Keeling's drink would suppose that he was buying Warnink's advocaat or indeed any Dutch advocaat, many people did suppose, as Keeling's intended, that the drink they were buying was advocaat rather than egg-flip.

The trial judge granted an injunction. The Court of Appeal allowed the defendant's appeal, but the House of Lords restored the injunction.

Lord Diplock: My Lords, this is an action for "passing off," not in its classic form of a trader representing his own goods as the goods of somebody else, but in an extended form first recognised and applied by Danckwerts J. in the Champagne case (*Bollinger v Costa Brava Wine Co Ltd* ([1960] Ch. 262)). . . .

My Lords, the findings of fact accepted by the Court of Appeal and not challenged in your Lordships' House . . . seem to me to disclose a case of unfair, not to say dishonest, trading of a kind for which a rational system of law ought to provide a remedy to other traders whose business or goodwill is injured by it.

Unfair trading as a wrong actionable at the suit of other traders who thereby suffer loss of business or goodwill may take a variety of forms, to some of which separate labels have become attached in English law. Conspiracy to injure a person in his trade or business is one, slander of goods another, but most protean is that which is generally and nowadays, perhaps misleadingly, described as "passing off." The forms that unfair trading takes will alter with the ways in which trade is carried on and business reputation and goodwill acquired. Emerson's maker of the better mousetrap if secluded in his house built in the woods would today be unlikely to find a path beaten to his door in the absence of a costly advertising campaign to acquaint the public with the excellence of his wares.

The action for what has become known as "passing off" arose in the nineteenth century out of the use in connection with his own goods by one trader of the trade name or trade mark of a rival trader so as to induce in potential purchasers the belief that his goods were those of the rival trader. Although the cases up to the end of the century had been confined to the deceptive use of trade names, marks, letters or other indicia, the principle had been stated by Lord Langdale M.R. as early as 1842 as being: "A man is not to sell his own goods under the pretence that they are the goods of another man . . . " (*Perry v Truefitt* (1842) 6 Beav. 66 at 73; 49 E.R. 749 at 752). At the close of the century in *Reddaway v Banham* ([1896] A.C. 199), it was said by Lord Herschell that what was protected by an action for passing off was not the proprietary right of the trader in the mark, name or get-up improperly used. Thus the door was opened to passing-off actions in which the misrepresentation took some other form than the deceptive use of trade names, marks, letters or other indicia; but as none of their Lordships committed themselves to identifying the legal nature of the right that was protected by a passing-off action it remained an action sui generis which lay for damage sustained or threatened in consequence of a misrepresentation of a particular kind.

Reddaway v Banham, like all previous passing-off cases, was one in which Banham had passed off his goods as those of Reddaway, and the damage resulting from the misrepresentation took the form of the diversion of potential customers from Reddaway to Banham. Although it was a landmark case in deciding that the use by a trader of a term which accurately described the composition of his own goods might nevertheless amount to the tort of passing off if that term were understood in the market in which the goods were sold to denote the goods of a rival trader, *Reddaway v Banham* did not extend the nature of the particular kind of misrepresentation which gives rise to a right of action in passing off beyond what I have called the classic form of misrepresenting one's own goods as the goods of someone else nor did it provide any rational basis for an extension.

This was left to be provided by Lord Parker of Waddington in *AG Spalding & Bros v AW Gamage Ltd* ((1915) 32 R.P.C. 273 at 284). In a speech which received the approval of the other members of this House, he identified the right the invasion of which is the subject of passing-off actions as being the "property in the business or goodwill likely to be injured by the misrepresentation." The concept of goodwill is in law a broad one which is perhaps best expressed in the words used by Lord Macnaghten in *Inland Revenue Comrs. v Muller & Co.'s Margarine Ltd* ([1901] A.C. 217 at 223): "It is the benefit and advantage of the good name, reputation and connection of a business. It is the attractive force which brings in custom."

The goodwill of a manufacturer's business may well be injured by someone else who sells goods which are correctly described as being made by that manufacturer but being of an inferior class or quality are misrepresented as goods of his manufacture of a superior class or quality. This type of misrepresentation was held in *AG Spalding & Bros v AW Gamage Ltd* to be actionable and the extension to the nature of the misrepresentation which gives rise to a right of action in passing off which this involved was regarded by Lord Parker as a natural corollary of recognising that what the law protects by a passing-off action is a trader's property in his business or goodwill . . .

My Lords, *AG Spalding & Bros v AW Gamage Ltd* and the later cases make it possible to identify five characteristics which must be present in order to create a valid cause of action for passing off: (1) a misrepresentation (2) made by a trader in the course of trade, (3) to prospective customers of his or ultimate consumers of goods or services supplied by him, (4) which is calculated to injure the business or goodwill of another trader (in the sense that this is a reasonably foreseeable consequence) and (5) which causes actual damage to a business or goodwill of the trader by whom the action is brought or (in a quia timet action) will probably do so.

In seeking to formulate general propositions of English law, however, one must be particularly careful to beware of the logical fallacy of the undistributed middle. It does not follow that because all passing-off actions can be shown to present these characteristics, all factual situations which present these characteristics give rise to a cause of action for passing off. True it is that their presence indicates what a moral code would censure as dishonest trading, based as it is on deception of customers and consumers of a trader's wares, but in an economic system which has relied on competition to keep down prices and to improve products there may be practical reasons why it should have been the policy of the common law not to run the risk of hampering competition by providing civil remedies to everyone competing in the market who has suffered damage to his business or goodwill in consequence of inaccurate statements of whatever kind that may be made by rival traders about their own wares. The market in which the action for passing off originated was no place for the mealy mouthed: advertisements are not on affidavit; exaggerated claims by a trader about the quality of his wares, assertions that they are better than those of his rivals, even though he knows this to be untrue, have been permitted by the common law as venial "puffing" which gives no cause of action to a competitor even though he can show that he has suffered actual damage in his business as a result.

Parliament, however, beginning in the nineteenth century has progressively intervened in the interests of consumers to impose on traders a higher standard of commercial candour that the legal maxim caveat emptor calls for, by prohibiting under penal sanctions misleading descriptions of the character or quality of goods; but since the class of persons for whose protection the Merchandise Marks Acts 1887 to 1953 and even more rigorous later statutes are designed are not competing traders but those consumers who are likely to be deceived, the Acts do not themselves give rise to any civil action for breach of statutory duty on the part of a competing trader even though he sustains actual damage as a result: *Cutler v Wandsworth Stadium Ltd* ([1949] A.C. 398); and see *London Armoury Co Ltd v Ever Ready Co (Great Britain) Ltd* ([1941] 1 K.B. 742). Nevertheless the increasing recognition by Parliament of the need for more rigorous standards of commercial honesty is a factor which should not be overlooked by a judge confronted by the choice whether or not to extend by analogy to circumstances in which it has not previously been applied a principle which has been applied in previous cases where the circumstances although different had some features in common with those of the case which he has to decide. Where over a period of years there can be discerned a steady trend in legislation which reflects the view of successive Parliaments as to what the public interest demands in a particular field of law, development of the common law in that part of the same field which has been left to it ought to proceed on a parallel rather than a diverging course. . . .

My Lords, in the Champagne case [*Bollinger v Costa Brava Wine Co* [1959] 3 All E.R. 800] the class of traders between whom the goodwill attaching to the ability to use the word "champagne" as descriptive of their wines was a large one, 150 at least and probably considerably more, whereas in the previous English cases of shared goodwill the number of traders between whom the goodwill protected by a passing-off action was shared had been two . . .

It seems to me, however, as it seemed to Danckwerts J., that the principle must be the same whether the class of which each member is severally entitled to the goodwill which attaches to a particular term as descriptive of his goods is large or small. The larger it is the broader must be the range and quality of products to which the descriptive term used by the members of the class has been applied, and the more difficult it must be to show that the term had acquired a public reputation and goodwill as denoting a product endowed with recognisable qualities which distinguish it from others of inferior reputation that compete with it in the same market. The larger the class the more difficult it must also be for an individual member of it to show that the goodwill of his own business has sustained more than minimal damage as a result of deceptive use by another trader of the widely-shared descriptive term. As respects subsequent additions to the class, mere entry into the market would not give any right of action for passing off; the new entrant must have himself used the descriptive term long enough on the market in connection with his own goods and have traded successfully enough to have built up a goodwill for his business.

Of course it is necessary to be able to identify with reasonable precision the members of the class of traders of whose products a particular word or name has become so distinctive as to make their right to use it truthfully as descriptive of their product a valuable part of the goodwill of each of them; but it is the reputation that that type of product itself has gained in the market by reason of its recognisable and distinctive qualities that has generated the relevant goodwill. So if one can define with reasonable precision the type of product that has acquired the reputation, one can identify the members of the class entitled to share in the goodwill as being all those traders whose have supplied and still supply to the English market a product which possesses those recognisable and distinctive qualities.

It cannot make any difference in principle whether the recognisable and distinctive qualities by which the reputation of the type of product has been gained are the result of its having been made in, or from ingredients produced in, a particular locality or are the result of its having been made from particular ingredients regardless of the provenance, though a geographical limitation may make it easier (a) to define the type of product, (b) to establish that it has the qualities which are recognisable and distinguish it from every other type of product that competes with it in the market and which have gained for it in the market a reputation and goodwill and (c) to establish that the plaintiff's own business will suffer more than minimal damage to its goodwill by the defendant's misrepresenting his product as being of that type.

In the instant case it is true that all but a very small portion of the alcoholic egg drink which gained for the name "advocaat" a reputation and goodwill on the English market was imported from the Netherlands where, in order to bear that name, the ingredients from which it was made had to conform to the requirements of official regulations applicable to it in that country; but that is merely coincidental, for it is not suggested that an egg and spirit drink made in broad conformity with the Dutch official recipe for "advocaat," wherever it is made or its ingredients produced, is not endowed with the same recognisable and distinctive qualities as have gained for "advocaat" its reputation and goodwill in the English market.

So, on the findings of fact by Goulding J. the type of product that has gained for the name "advocaat" on the English market the reputation and goodwill of which Keelings are seeking to take advantage by misrepresenting that their own product is of that type is defined by reference to the nature of its ingredients irrespective of their origin. The class of traders of whose respective businesses the right to describe their products as advocaat forms a valuable part of their goodwill are those who have supplied and are supplying on the English market an egg and spirit drink in broad conformity with an identifiable recipe. The members of that class are easily identified and very much fewer in number than in the Champagne, Sherry or Scotch Whisky cases. Warnink with 75 per cent of the trade have a very substantial stake in the goodwill of the name "advocaat" and their business has been showed to have suffered serious injury as a result of Keelings putting on the English market in competition with Warnink and at a cheaper price an egg and wine based drink which they miscall advocaat instead of egg-flip which is its proper name.

My Lords, all the five characteristics that I have earlier suggested must be present to create a valid cause of action in passing off today were present in the instant case. Prima facie, as the law stands today, I think the presence of those characteristics is enough, unless there is also present in the case some exceptional feature which justifies, on grounds of public policy, withholding from a person who has suffered injury in consequence of the deception practised on prospective customers or consumers of his product a remedy in law against the deceiver. On the facts found by the judge, and I stress their importance, I find no such exceptional feature in the instant case.

I would allow this appeal and restore the injunction granted by Goulding J.

Notes:

1. In *Consorzio del Prosciutto di Parma v Marks & Spencer* [1991] R.P.C. 351 at 368, in which the plaintiffs unsuccessfully sought to argue that it was wrongful of the defendants to market as "Parma ham" Parma ham which was prepackaged in slices when in Italy only ham sliced in the presence of the customer could lawfully be sold as "Parma ham", Nourse L.J. said:

"Although the well-known speeches of Lord Diplock and Lord Fraser of Tullybelton in *Warnink v Townend* are of the highest authority, it has been my experience, and it is now my respectful opinion, that they do not give the same degree of assistance in analysis and decision as the classical trinity of

(1) a reputation (or goodwill) acquired by the plaintiff in his goods, name, mark, etc., (2) a misrepresentation by the defendant leading to confusion (or deception), causing (3) damage to the plaintiff."

The Parma ham people proceeded to sue Asda, deploying a Euro-argument that their registered designation of origin entitled them to prevent Asda's sales. The argument was rejected: the ham was the genuine article. *Consorzio del Prosciutto di Parma v Asda* [1998] Times L.R. 48 and 773. The House of Lords stayed the proceedings and referred the Euro-question to Luxembourg. The ECJ held that prescriptions as to slicing (otherwise than in a restaurant or retail sale) were indeed included in the protected designation of origin of "Prosciutto di Parma" under Regulation 2081/92, that although this was presumptively tantamount to a quantitative restriction on the importation of goods within the Community, it was justified as a proportionate protection of the rights of the Consorzio, but that since the Commission had not published the restriction in the *Official Journal*, businesses were not bound by it. (Case C–108/01, E.C.R. 2003 I–05121). The transparency of the judgment may be sampled: "Regulation No.2081/92 must be interpreted as not precluding the use of a PDO from being subject to the condition that operations such as the slicing and packaging of the product take place in the region of production, where such a condition is laid down in the specification."

2. A skirmish in the Great Hamburger War reached the courts. Burgerking put advertisements in London Tube trains headed "It's Not Just Big, Mac" and asserting that Burgerking burgers were 100 per cent beef. More than half the thousand travellers polled said they took the advertisements to be for McDonald's "Big Mac" hamburgers, one in ten thinking they could be had at Burgerking outlets. The trial judge found that passing-off was established but that, for want of malice, trade libel was not (*McDonald's Hamburgers v Burgerking (U.K.)* [1986] F.S.R. 45). The Court of Appeal ordered an enquiry as to damages (likely to be costly to the plaintiff) for the passing-off ([1987] F.S.R. 112).

3. If a person's competitors are restrained, his market position is strengthened, even if their competition is unfair. But the competition so restrained does not benefit the public if customers do not get what they are led to expect. Deception is therefore an important component of this tort. Thus there was no liability in *Bostik v Sellotape G.B.* [1994] Times L.R. 14, even though the defendant's product, once unwrapped, was indistinguishable from the plaintiff's; it was, however, encased in opaque packaging, so no one would buy it in the erroneous belief that it was indeed the plaintiff's product. Indeed, even where the defendant had actually copied the plaintiff's wheelchair cushions, there was no passing-off because the buyers were healthcare specialists who would not be taken in: *Hodgkinson & Corby v Wards Mobility Services* [1994] 1 W.L.R. 1564. If there is no deception, there is no liability for taking advantage of a market created by a competitor. For example, by means of a very expensive advertising campaign which stressed the muscularity of yesteryear, Cadbury Schweppes created public demand in Australia for their drink "Solo". The defendant decided to horn in on this market with his own drink "Pub Squash", also deliberately associated with macho nostalgia. He was not liable since no one was misled into thinking that Pub Squash was Solo. *Cadbury Schweppes v Pub Squash Co* [1981] 1 All E.R. 213, PC. In the light of this, consider the observation of Jacob J. in *Hodgkinson & Corby v Wards Mobility Services* [1995] F.S.R. 169 at 175: "At the heart of passing off lies deception or its likelihood ... Never has the tort shown even a slight tendency to stray beyond cases of deception. Were it to do so, it would enter the field of honest competition ... "

4. Confusion may arise from the honest use of one's own name. In *William Grant & Sons v Glen Catrine Bonded Warehouse* [1999] Times L.R. 356, Lord Cameron affirmed "the principle that where a trader had established that a name under which his goods were sold had come to denote the goods made by that trader and not the goods made by anyone else, then provided that the necessary element of confusion was satisfied, even the bona fide use on goods of a genuine personal or geographic name by another trader might be restrained." The pursuer sold Grant's Whisky and the defender sold, abroad, Grant's Vodka and Grant's Gin. Confusion was also found likely in *Reckitt & Coleman v Borden* [1990] 1 All E.R. 873; noted [1990] Camb.L.J. 403 where the House of Lords held that the plaintiffs had for so long been the sole firm to market real lemon juice in plastic lemons that the average unobservant supermarket shopper was bound to suppose that any lemon juice so packaged was the plaintiff's, and that consequently no competitor could lawfully sell lemon juice in such a container unless he took extraordinary (that is, impossible) steps to avoid any such mistake. The plaintiffs could not, of course, have registered the plastic lemon as a trademark, so the common law here confirmed a *de facto* monopoly which statute would not have endorsed.

5. Now, however, since the Trade Marks Act 1994 the plastic lemon (and the Coca-Cola bottle) could be registered as a trademark. This Act, implementing E.C. Directive 89/104, extends both what is eligible to be registered as a trade-mark and the protection given to registered marks. Section 1(1) provides "In this Act a 'trade mark' means any sign capable of being represented graphically which is capable of distinguishing goods or services of one undertaking from those of other undertakings." [Does this include "champagne"?] "A trade mark may, in particular, consist of words (including personal names), designs, letters, numerals or the shape of goods or their packaging."

There is less emphasis on deceiving the public, for although likelihood of confusion is required for the use of a similar mark on similar goods to constitute an infringement (s.10(2)), it is also an infringement to use a similar sign in relation to goods or services *not* similar to those for which the mark is registered if such use takes unfair advantage of or is detrimental to the distinctive character and repute of the trade mark (s.10(3)). The Act will evidently reduce the importance of the common law tort of passing-off, but not destroy its utility in certain cases.

6. In *Bristol Conservatories v Conservatories Custom Built* [1989] R.P.C. 455, CA; noted (1990) 106 L.Q.R. 564 the defendant, in soliciting business, had used a portfolio of photographs of the plaintiff's work as if the work were his own. Sometimes called "reverse passing-off," this is clearly actionable. There is a comparable complementarity in copyright law, where moral rights include the right to be identified as the creator of a work and the right not to have the work of others attributed to one. See Cornish, *Intellectual Property* (5th ed., 2003, p.464).

7. A defendant who had purchased in Italy and sold in Britain razors which he did not know were counterfeit was nevertheless held liable in damages for infringement of trademark and passing-off: *Gillette UK v Edenwest* [1994] R.P.C. 279. For the infringement of other intellectual property rights some statutory protection is afforded to those without fault. See Cornish, *Intellectual Property* (5th ed., 2003) pp.76, 632.

8. There is a fine account of the development of the tort of passing off by Laddie J. in *Irvine v Talksport* [2002] 2 All E.R. 414, 419–426. The case involved false endorsement, not character merchandising; his decision was reversed as to damages by the Court of Appeal [2003] 2 All E.R. 881.

LUMLEY v GYE

Queen's Bench (1853) 2 E. & B. 216; 22 L.J.Q.B. 463; 17 Jur. 827; 1 W.R. 432; 118 E.R. 749

Suit against impresario for poaching prima donna under exclusive contract to plaintiff

The plaintiff was manager of Her Majesty's Theatre and the defendant ran The Royal Italian Opera, Covent Garden; the dispute was over a prima donna, Richard Wagner's niece Johanna.

The law was decided on demurrer, *i.e.* on the defendant's objection that the plaintiff's declaration disclosed no cause of action. The first count stated that the plaintiff contracted and agreed with Johanna Wagner to perform in his theatre for a certain time, with a condition amongst others, that she should not sing or use her talents elsewhere during the term without the plaintiff's consent in writing: yet the defendant, well knowing the premises, and maliciously intending to injure the plaintiff, whilst the agreement with Wagner was still in force, and before the expiration of the term, enticed and procured Wagner to refuse to perform: by means of which enticement and procurement of the defendant, Wagner wrongfully refused to perform, and did not perform during the term.

The plaintiff had judgment on the demurrer, but since the defendant had obtained leave to plead as well as demur, the case went to trial on the facts and the plaintiff lost. The contract between the plaintiff and Wagner is contained in *Lumley v Wagner* (1852) 42 E.R. 687.

Erle J.: ... The question raised upon this demurrer is, whether an action will lie by the proprietor of a theatre against a person who maliciously procures an entire abandonment of a contract to perform exclusively at the theatre for a certain time; whereby damage was sustained? And it seems to me that it will. The authorities are numerous and uniform, that an action will lie by a master against a person who procures that a servant should unlawfully leave his service. The principle involved in those cases comprises the present; for, there, the right of action in the master arises from the wrongful act of the defendant in procuring that the person hired should break his contract, by putting an end to the relation of employer and employed; and the present case is the same. If it is objected that this class of actions for procuring a breach of contract of hiring rests upon no principle, and ought not to be extended beyond the cases heretofore decided, and that, as those have related to contracts respecting trade, manufacturers or household service, and not to performance at a theatre, therefore they are no authority for an action in respect of a contract for such performance; the answer appears to me to be, that the class of cases referred to rests upon the principle that the procurement of the violation of the right is a cause of action, and that, when this principle is applied to a violation of a right arising upon a contract of hiring, the nature of the service contracted for is immaterial. It is clear that the procurement of the violation of a right is a cause of action in all instances where the violation is an actionable wrong, as in violations of a right to property, whether real or personal, or to personal security: he who procures the wrong is a joint wrong-doer, and may be sued, either alone or jointly with the agent, in the appropriate action for the wrong complained of. Where a right to the performance of a contract has been violated by a breach thereof, the remedy is upon the contract against the contracting party; and, if he is made to indemnify for such breach, no further recourse is allowed; the action for this wrong, in respect of other contracts than those of hiring are not numerous; but still they seem to me sufficient to show that the principle has been recognised. . . . This principle is supported by good reason. He who maliciously procures a damage to another by violation of his right ought to be made to indemnify; and that, whether he procures an actionable wrong or a breach of contract. He who procures the non-delivery of goods according to contract may inflict an injury, the same as he who procures the abstraction of goods after delivery; and both ought on the same ground to be made responsible. The remedy on the contract may be inadequate, as where the measure of damages is restricted; or in the case of non-payment of a debt where the damage may be bankruptcy to the creditor who is disappointed, but the measure of damages against the debtor is interest only; or, in the case of the non-delivery of the goods, the disappointment may lead to a heavy forfeiture under a contract to complete a work within a time, but the measure of damages against the vendor of the goods for non-delivery may be only the difference between the contract price and the market value of the goods in question at the time of the breach. In such cases, he who procures the damage maliciously might justly be made responsible beyond the liability of the contractor.

With respect to the objection that the contracting party had not begun the performance of the contract, I do not think it a tenable ground of defence. The procurement of a breach of the contract may be equally injurious, whether the service has begun or not, and in my judgment ought to be equally actionable.

The result is that there ought to be, in my opinion, judgment for the plaintiff.

Wightman J.: . . . It was undoubtedly prima facie an unlawful act on the part of Miss Wagner to break her contract, and therefore a tortious act of the defendant maliciously to procure her to do so; and, if damage to the plaintiff followed in consequence of that tortious act of the defendant, it would seem, upon the authority of the two cases referred to . . . as well as upon general principle, that an action on the case is maintainable. . . .

Crompton J. used the illuminating phrase "wrongfully and maliciously, or, which is the same thing, with notice."

Coleridge J. (dissenting strongly): . . . there would be such a manifest absurdity in attempting to trace up the act of a free agent breaking a contract to all the advisers who may have influenced his mind, more or less honestly, more or less powerfully, and to make them responsible civilly for the consequences of what after all is his own act, and for the whole of the hurtful consequences of which the law makes him directly and fully responsible, that I believe it will never be contended for seriously. . . . To draw a line between advice, persuasion, enticement and procurement is practically impossible in a court of justice.

Grace Note:

Johanna Wagner was not the only donna traviata at the time, and Lumley was not always the innocent party. Jenny Lind, the Swedish Nightingale, had an exclusive contract with Drury Lane but sang at Her Majesty's Theatre in a performance of Meyerbeer's *Robert le Diable*, attended by Queen Victoria and Mendelssohn. The Queen wrote about it in her diary, and Jenny Lind paid £2,500 for breach of contract.

There is a fine description of the background to the dispute in Waddams, "Johanna Wagner and the Rival Opera Houses", 117 L.Q.Rev. 431 (2001), and in his *Dimensions of Private Law* (2003) pp.23–39.

Questions

1. Was it a material factor that the defendant here was trying to appropriate a benefit the plaintiff had secured for himself by contract? Would the answer be the same if the defendant had been the prima donna's manager who, on second thoughts, believed that it would not be in her professional interests to sing at the plaintiff's theatre?

2. What is the difference between saying "Break your contract, and I shall pay you more" and saying "You will earn more if you break your contract"? Should there be a difference in the two cases? If so, is the difference that between advising a person not to fulfil his contract and procuring that he does not?

3. If the defendant had kidnapped Miss Wagner in order to prevent her appearance at the plaintiff's theatre, could the plaintiff sue Miss Wagner for breach of contract? Could he sue the defendant?

Notes:

1. This tort can be approached in two ways, as the contrasting judgments of Erie C.J. and Wightman J. show, by concentrating either on the plaintiff's right or on the wrong of the defendant. Lord Macnaghten did the former in *Quinn v Leathem* [1901] A.C. 495 at 510: "A violation of a legal right committed knowingly is a cause of action, and . . . it is a violation of a legal right to interfere with contractual relations recognised by law if there be no sufficient justification for the interference." Lord Haldane in *Jasperson's* case concentrated on the defendant's wrong: "What was laid down long ago in *Lumley v Gye* reaches all wrongful acts done intentionally to damage a particular individual, and actually damaging him." ([1923] A.C. 709 at 712). Lord Haldane's analysis is preferable, especially after *Rookes v Barnard* (below, p.605) where it was held that even though no "right" of the plaintiff had been infringed, he could sue a defendant who by threatening to break his contract with another had procured that other to hurt him. Lord Macnaghten's formula has led to a deplorable expansion of this tort (see below, p.612), so much so that the Master of the Rolls, in reversing a distinguished trial judge, felt bound to say "In concentrating on the right, it seems to me that the judge did take his eye off the wrong" (*Law Debenture Trust v Ural Caspian Oil* [1995] 1 All E.R. 157 at 167). The facts were that Leisure bought four companies and promised the plaintiff (a) to pay it certain proceeds the companies might receive and (b) to exact a similar promise from anyone it sold the companies to. Leisure then sold the companies to Hilldon without exacting any such promise, and Hilldon likewise sold them to Caspian, all parties being fully aware of Leisure's promise to the plaintiff. Hilldon was accordingly (i) liable in damages for inducing breach of Leisure's contract with the plaintiff, and (ii) liable, if still in control of the companies, to be enjoined to retransfer them to Leisure. Caspian had not induced any breach of contract by Hilldon, since Hilldon itself had not made any promise to the plaintiff or anyone else: Caspian had, however, by acquiring the companies frustrated the plaintiff's right to require Hilldon to retransfer them to Leisure. The trial judge held that Caspian's knowing interference with the plaintiff's right to an injunction against Hilldon was enough and was ready to allow the trial to go forward against Caspian on this basis. The Court of Appeal reversed (while not condoning the conduct of these *personnes morales*): it is not the knowing invasion of *every* right of a plaintiff which involves liability. Although Caspian had knowingly destroyed the plaintiff's right to obtain an injunction, it had done no wrong in buying property which, until enjoined, Hilldon was free to sell.

Yet it is not only contractual rights which can be actionably interfered with by third parties. Or to put it another way, breach of duties other than those arising from contract may be actionably induced. Statutory duties (if actionable by the plaintiff), equitable duties . . .

2. In the classical version of this tort the defendant uses no wrongful means against the promise-breaker: Gye did not lie to Johanna or threaten to beat her, he just offered her a raise, and there is nothing wrong with that. But what it was offered for made it not simply a raise but a bribe, for he persuaded her to do what they both knew was wrong: it was a kind of commercial adultery. But suppose that wrongful means are used, Suppose Gye had threatened Miss W with g.b.h. if she sang for Lumley as promised. Of course there would be liability, but it would not be liability for inducing breach of contract, since Gye would be just as liable if there had been no breach at all, for example, if Miss Wagner had been entirely free not to sing for Lumley, but would in fact have done so, but for the unlawful threat. Gye's liability would be for causing intentional harm by wrongful means, not for inducing breach of contract.

In such a case it is not simply inelegant to emphasise the contract and breach, but positively harmful. Despite anything to the contrary in cases given below, to cause an involuntary breach of contract is not wrongful in itself: there should be no liability for causing an involuntary breach of contract unless unlawful means are used, and if unlawful means are used there is liability whether a contract is broken or not. The tort under *Lumley v Gye* is of *persuading* a contractor to defect. Of course that is a wrong, and because it is a wrong it may constitute wrongful means for the other tort, as where, in order to hurt A, the defendant persuades B to break his contract with C (as in *Merkur Island*, below, p.612).

3. This well-established tort has been deployed against extractors of trade secrets and other confidences (*British Industrial Plastics v Ferguson*, [1938] 4 All E.R. 504); against persons persuading agents to exceed the terms of their agency (*Jasperson v Dominion Tobacco Co* [1923] A.C. 709); against a tenant who

persuaded other tenants not to pay their rent because the building was in bad repair (*Camden Nominees v Forcey* [1940] Ch. 353): and against a person who offered to buy the Aintree racecourse for development from a person who had promised not to sell it for that purpose (*Sefton (Earl) v Topham's Ltd* [1964] 1 W.L.R. 1408, reversed on other, very odd grounds [1967] 1 A.C. 50).

A modern example is *Rickless v United Artists* [1987] 1 All E.R. 699, CA. Pursuant to contracts between his loan-out company and various production companies, Peter Sellers starred in the *Pink Panther* films on the terms that his performance would not be used for any other film without his consent; after his death the defendants knowingly obtained clips and take-outs from the production companies and were held liable to assignees of the loan-out company for using them to make another film.

4. For individuals, employment is the most important contract. Employees are commonly members of a union. Loyalty to the union may well conflict with obedience to the employer. Union officials would be powerless if they were liable simply for getting their members to break their contracts of employment, by striking or otherwise. Accordingly, ever since 1906, in order to protect what we refrain from calling the right to strike, certain conduct which would otherwise have been actionable under *Lumley v Gye* has been legitimised if done "in contemplation or furtherance of a trade dispute" (Trade Union and Labour Relations (Consolidation) Act 1992, s.219).

Since union members are employees rather than suppliers, the immunity originally attached only to inducing breach of contracts of employment. But then the courts very tiresomely held that if one got A's employees not to cooperate in the performance of A's contract of supply with B, one might be liable to B for inducing breach of the contract of supply (*Thomson (D.C.) & Co Ltd v Deakin* [1952] Ch. 646), so Parliament extended the immunity to cover inducing breach of commercial contracts. The immunity has since been reduced again by outlawing "secondary action", *i.e.* inducing breach of contracts of employment with an employer other than the firm you're actually quarrelling with, except in the course of lawful picketing (Trade Union and Labour Relations (Consolidation) Act 1992, s.224). Note that if the supply of goods or services to an individual (not a company!) is affected by industrial action tortious against anyone else, the individual may obtain a court order to prevent any further inducement to continue the industrial action; in this case there is no need for the individual to be entitled to the goods or services in question, *i.e.* no contract to which he is a party need have been breached. (Trade Union and Labour Relations Act 1992, s.235A, introduced by Trade Union Reform and Employment Rights Act 1993, s.22). Given that the reduction of the immunities involves that more means are now wrongful and that, as we shall see, a defendant guilty of causing intended harm by wrongful means is liable regardless of *Lumley v Gye*, the courts should stop striving to find that a breach of a contract to which the plaintiff was a party has been "induced". A hint that they may be doing so is inferable from *Middlebrook Mushrooms* [1993] I.C.R. 612, containing a welcome reminder that this tort, if unduly expanded, may conflict with the right of self-expression contained in Art.10 of the European Convention of Human Rights: the trial judge had enjoined employees of a mushroom grower from standing outside a supermarket and trying to dissuade potential customers from buying their employer's mushrooms, a decision the Court of Appeal was very right to reverse.

5. This tort also has the honour of giving rise to the largest award of damages in history. A Texas jury awarded Pennzoil (a Texas company) the sum of $10,530,000,000 ($10.53 bn.) against Texaco (a New York company) for interfering, by offering a higher price, with Pennzoil's contract to buy stock in Getty Oil (729 S.W.2d. 768 (Tex.App. 1987)). Texaco, unable to raise even the interest on this sum, filed for bankruptcy and finally agreed to pay Pennzoil $3,000,000,000. Very arguably, Texaco should not have been held liable at all, since when its offer was accepted by Getty, Texaco had no idea that Getty was already bound to Pennzoil.

6. "Inducement" may perhaps fall short of "persuasion", but it must be more than ready acquiescence in X's breach of contract with the claimant. In *Unique Pub Properties v Licensed Wholesale Co* (Ch.D. Oct 13, 2003) publicans who had agreed to buy all their beer from the claimant approached the defendant, to whom the claimant had sent a list of the relevant publicans, for supplies, which the defendant delivered. The judge refused to issue an interlocutory injunction since it would require the defendant to quiz potential purchasers.

7. The defendant must have realised that what he was doing was wrong. Thus in *British Industrial Plastics v Ferguson* [1940] 1 All E.R. 479 Doherty, an ex-employee of the plaintiffs, went to the defendants, in the same line of business, and said to Ferguson, the manager, that his knowledge might be of use to them. Ferguson was aware of the risk of trade secrets, but sent Doherty to his patent agents to see if the process disclosed was patentable, thinking that if it was patentable it couldn't be a trade secret. MacKinnon L.J. in the Court of Appeal said that "*A priori* I should find it difficult to imagine that anyone could be so stupid" but that the judge had "vindicated the honesty of Ferguson at the expense of his intelligence." Ferguson had behaved stupidly but not dishonestly and so was not liable.

Take a more recent case: On leaving the claimant's employment X took with her to the new employer in the same line of business a list of 151 of the claimant's clients, complete with contact details. This was a gross breach of contract and confidence on the part of X. The new employer, the second defendant, used the list to contact those clients to say that X had joined the firm, but was held not liable since she had simply not realised that what she was doing was wrong. *Thomas v Pearce and Darlows* (CA, February 10, 2000).

MOGUL STEAMSHIP CO v McGREGOR, GOW & CO

House of Lords [1892] A.C. 25; 61 L.J.Q.B. 295; 66 L.T. 1; 56 J.P. 101; 40 W.R. 337; 8 T.L.R. 182; 7 Asp.M.L.C. 120, Court of Appeal (1889) 23 Q.B.D. 598; 58 L.J.Q.B. 465; 61 L.T. 820; 53 J.P. 709; 37 W.R. 756; 5 T.L.R. 658; 6 Asp.M.L.C. 455, Queen's Bench (1888) 21 Q.B.D. 544

Suit by ruined competitor against cartel of shipowners

On the facts given in the judgment of Bowen L.J., the plaintiffs failed at first instance, and on appeal to the Court of Appeal (Lord Esher M.R. dissenting), and on further appeal to the House of Lords.

In the Court of Appeal

Bowen L.J.: We are presented in this case with an apparent conflict or antinomy between two rights that are equally regarded by the law—the right of the plaintiffs to be protected in the legitimate exercise of their trade, and the right of the defendants to carry on their business as seems best to them, provided they commit no wrong to others. The plaintiffs complain that the defendants have crossed the line which the common law permits; and inasmuch as, for the purposes of the present case, we are to assume some possible damage to the plaintiffs, the real question to be decided is whether, on such an assumption, the defendants in the conduct of their commercial affairs have done anything that is unjustifiable in law. The defendants are a number of shipowners who formed themselves into a league or conference for the purpose of ultimately keeping in their own hands the control of the tea carriage from certain Chinese ports, and for the purpose of driving the plaintiffs and other competitors from the field. In order to succeed in this object, and to discourage the plaintiffs' vessels from resorting to those ports, the defendants during the "tea harvest" of 1885 combined to offer to the local shippers very low freights, with a view of generally reducing or "smashing" rates, and thus rendering it unprofitable for the plaintiffs to send their ships thither. They offered, moreover, a rebate of 5 per cent to all local shippers and agents who would deal exclusively with vessels belonging to the Conference, and any agent who broke the condition was to forfeit the entire rebate on all shipments made on behalf of any and every one of his principals during the whole year—a forfeiture of rebate or allowance which was denominated as "penal" by the plaintiffs' counsel. It must, however, be taken as established that the rebate was one which the defendants need never have allowed at all to their customers. It must also be taken that the defendants had no personal ill-will to the plaintiffs, nor any desire to harm them except such as is involved in the wish and intention to discourage by such measures the plaintiffs from sending rival vessels to such ports. The acts of which the plaintiffs particularly complained were as follows: First, a circular of May 10, 1885, by which the defendants offered to the local shippers and their agents a benefit by way of rebate if they would not deal with the plaintiffs, which was to be lost if this condition was not fulfilled. Secondly, the sending of special ships to Hankow in order by competition to deprive the plaintiffs' vessels of profitable freight. Thirdly, the offer at Hankow of freights at a level which would not repay a shipowner for his adventure, in order to "smash" freights and frighten the plaintiffs from the field. Fourthly, pressure put on the defendants' own agents to induce them to ship only by the defendants' vessels, and not by those of the plaintiffs. It is to be observed with regard to all these acts of which complaint is made that they were acts that in themselves could not be said to be illegal unless made so by the object with which, or the combination in the course of which, they were done; and that in reality what is complained of is the pursuing of trade competition to a length which the plaintiffs consider oppressive and prejudicial to themselves. We were invited by the plaintiffs' counsel to accept the position from which their argument started—that an action will lie if a man maliciously and wrongfully conducts himself so as to injure another in that other's trade. Obscurity resides in the language used to state this proposition. The terms "maliciously," "wrongfully," and "injure" are words all of which have accurate meanings, well known to the law, but which also have a popular and less precise signification, into which it is necessary to see that the argument does not imperceptibly slide. An intent to "injure" in strictness means more than an intent to harm. It connotes an intent to do wrongful harm. "Maliciously," in like manner, means and implies an intention to do an act which is wrongful, to the detriment of another. The term "wrongful" imports in its turn the infringement of some right. The ambiguous proposition to which we were invited by the plaintiffs' counsel still, therefore, leaves unsolved the question of what, as between the plaintiffs and defendants, are the rights of trade. For the purpose of clearness, I desire, as far as possible, to avoid terms in their popular use so slippery, and to translate them into less fallacious language wherever possible.

The English law, which in its earlier stages began with but an imperfect line of demarcation between torts and breaches of contract, presents us with no scientific analysis of the degree to which the intent to harm, or, in the language of the civil law, the *animus vicino nocendi*, may enter into or affect the conception of a personal wrong: see *Chasemore v Richards* ((1859) 11 E.R. 140). All personal wrong means the infringement of some personal right. "It is essential to an action in tort," say the Privy Council in *Rogers v Rajendro Dutt* ((1860) 15 E.R. 78), "that the act complained of should under the circumstances be legally wrongful as regards the party complaining; that is, it must prejudicially affect him in some legal right; merely that it will, however indirectly, do a man harm in his interests, is not enough." What, then, were the rights of the plaintiffs as traders as against the defendants? The plaintiffs had a right to be protected against certain kinds of conduct; and we have to consider what conduct would pass this legal line or boundary. Now, intentionally to do that which is calculated in the ordinary course of events to damage, and which does, in fact, damage another in that other person's property or trade, is actionable if done without just cause or excuse. Such intentional action when done without just cause or excuse is what the law calls a malicious wrong (see *Bromage v Prosser* ((1825) 107 E.R. 1051); *Capital and Counties Bank v Henty, per* Lord Blackburn ((1882) 7 App.Cas. 741 at 772)). The acts of the defendants which are complained of here were intentional, and were also calculated, no doubt, to do the plaintiffs damage in their trade. But in order to see whether they were wrongful we have still to discuss the question whether they were done without any just cause or excuse. Such just cause or excuse the defendants on their side assert to be found in their own positive right (subject to certain limitations) to carry on their own trade freely in the mode and manner that best suits them, and which they think best calculated to secure their own advantage.

What, then, are the limitations which the law imposes on a trader in the conduct of his business as between himself and other traders? There seem to be no burdens or restrictions in law upon a trader which arise merely from the fact that he is a trader, and which are not equally laid on all other subjects of the Crown. His right to trade freely is a right which the law recognises and encourages, but it is one which places him at no special disadvantage as compared with others. No man, whether trader or not, can, however, justify damaging another in his commercial business by fraud or misrepresentation. Intimidation, obstruction, and molestation are forbidden; so is the intentional procurement of a violation of individual rights, contractual or other, assuming always that there is no just cause for it. The intentional driving away of customers by show of violence: *Tarleton v M'Gawley* ((1793) 170 E.R. 153); the obstruction of actors on the stage by preconcerted hissing: *Clifford v Brandon* ((1810) 170 E.R. 1183); *Gregory v Brunswick* ((1843) 134 E.R. 866); the disturbance of wild fowl in decoys by the firing of guns: *Carrington v Taylor* ((1809) 103 E.R. 1126) and *Keeble v Hickeringill* ((1706) 103 E.R. 1127); the impeding or threatening servants or workmen: *Garret v Taylor* ((1620), 79 E.R. 485); the inducing persons under personal contracts to break their contracts: *Bowen v Hall* ((1881) 6 Q.B.D. 333); *Lumley v Gye* ((1853) 2 E. & B. 216; 118 E.R. 749; above, p.589); all are instances of such forbidden acts. But the defendants have been guilty of none of these acts. They have done nothing more against the plaintiffs than pursue to the bitter end a war of competition waged in the interest of their own trade. But we were told that competition ceases to be the lawful exercise of trade, and so to be a lawful excuse for what will harm another, if carried to a length which is not fair or reasonable. The offering of reduced rates by the defendants in the present case is said to have been "unfair". This seems to assume that, apart from fraud, intimidation, molestation, or obstruction of some other personal right *in rem* or *in personam*, there is some natural standard of "fairness" or "reasonableness" (to be determined by the internal consciousness of judges and juries) beyond which competition ought not in law to go. There seems to be no authority, and I think, with submission, that there is no sufficient reason for such a proposition. It would impose a novel fetter upon trade. The defendants, we are told by the plaintiffs' counsel, might lawfully lower rates provided they did not lower them beyond a "fair freight," whatever that may mean. But where is it established that there is any such restriction upon commerce? And what is to be the definition of a "fair freight"? It is said that it ought to be a normal rate of freight, such as is reasonably remunerative to the shipowner. But over what period of time is the average of this reasonable remunerativeness to be calculated? All commercial men with capital are acquainted with the ordinary expedient of sowing one year a crop of apparently unfruitful prices, in order by driving competition away to reap a fuller harvest of profit in the future; and until the present argument at the bar it may be doubted whether shipowners or merchants were ever deemed to be bound by law to conform to some imaginary "normal" standard of freights or prices or that Law Courts had a right to say to them in respect of their competitive tariffs, "Thus far shalt thou go and no further." To attempt to limit English competition in this way would probably be as hopeless an endeavour as the experiment of King Canute. But on ordinary principles of law no such fetter on freedom of trade can in my opinion be warranted. A man is bound not to use his property so as to infringe upon another's right. *Sic utere tuo ut alienum non laedas*. If engaged in actions which may involve danger to others, he ought, speaking generally, to take reasonable care to avoid endangering them. But there is surely no doctrine of law which compels him to use his property in a way that judges and juries may consider reasonable: see *Chasemore v Richards* (1859) 7 H.L.C. 349). If there is no such fetter upon the use of property known to the English law, why should there be any such a fetter upon trade?

It is urged, however, on the part of the plaintiffs, that even if the acts complained of would not be wrongful had they been committed by a single individual, they become actionable when they are the result of concerted action among several. In other words, the plaintiffs, it is contended, have been injured by an illegal conspiracy. Of the general proposition, that certain kinds of conduct not criminal in any one individual may become criminal if done by combination among several, there can be no doubt. The distinction is based on sound reason, for a combination may make oppressive or dangerous that which if it proceeded only from a single person would be otherwise, and the very fact of the combination may show that the object is simply to do harm and not to exercise one's own just rights. In the application of this undoubted principle it is necessary to be very careful not to press the doctrine of illegal conspiracy beyond that which is necessary for the protection of individuals or of the public; and it may be observed in passing that as a rule it is the damage wrongfully done, and not the conspiracy, that is the gist of actions on the case for conspiracy: see *Skinner v Gunton* ((1668) 85 E.R. 249). But what is the definition of an illegal combination? It is an agreement by one or more to do an unlawful act, or to do a lawful act by unlawful means: *O'Connell v The Queen* ((1844) 8 E.R. 1061); *R. v Parnell* ((1881) 14 Cox Crim.Cas. 508); and the question to be solved is whether there has been any such agreement here. Have the defendants combined to do an unlawful act? Have they combined to do a lawful act by unlawful means? A moment's consideration will be sufficient to show that this new inquiry only drives us back to the circle of definitions and legal propositions which I have already traversed in the previous part of this judgment. The unlawful act agreed to, if any, between the defendants must have been the intentional doing of some act to the detriment of the plaintiffs' business without just cause or excuse. Whether there was any such justification or excuse for the defendants is the old question over again, which, so far as regards an individual trader, has been already solved. Assume that what is done is intentional, and that it is calculated to do harm to others. Then comes the question, Was it done with or without "just cause or excuse"? If it was bona fide done in the use of a man's own property, in the exercise of a man's own trade, such legal justification would, I think, exist not the less because what was done might seem to others to be selfish or unreasonable: see the summing-up of Erle J. and the judgment of the Queen's Bench in *R. v Rowlands* ((1851), 117 E.R. 1439). But such legal justification would not exist when the act was merely done with the intention of causing temporal harm, without reference to one's own lawful gain, or the lawful enjoyment of one's own rights. The good sense of the tribunal which had to decide would have to analyse the circumstances and to discover on which side of the line each case fell. But if the real object were to enjoy what was one's own, or to acquire for one's self some advantage in one's property or trade, and what was done was done honestly, peaceably, and without any of the illegal acts above referred to, it could not, in my opinion, properly be said that it was done without just cause or excuse. One may with advantage borrow for the benefit of traders what was said by Erle J. in *R. v Rowlands*, of workmen and of masters: "The intention of the law is at present to allow either of them to follow the dictates of their own will, with respect to their own actions, and their own property; and either, I believe, has a right to study to promote his own advantage, or to combine with others to promote their mutual advantage."

Lastly, we are asked to hold the defendants' Conference or association illegal, as being in restraint of trade. The term "illegal" here is a misleading one. Contracts, as they are called, in restraint of trade, are not, in my opinion, illegal in any sense, except that the law will not enforce them. It does not prohibit the making of such contracts; it merely declines, after they have been made, to recognise their validity. The law considers the disadvantage so imposed upon the contract a sufficient shelter to the public. . . . No action at common law will lie or ever has lain against any individual or individuals for entering into a contract merely because it is in restraint of trade. . . . If peaceable and honest combinations of capital for purposes of trade competition are to be struck at, it must, I think, be by legislation, for I do not see that they are under the ban of the common law.

In the result, I agree with Lord Coleridge C.J., and differ, with regret, from the Master of the Rolls. The substance of my view is this, that competition, however severe and egotistical, if unattended by circumstances of dishonesty, intimidation, molestation, or such illegalities as I have above referred to, gives rise to no cause of action at common law. I myself should deem it to be a misfortune if we were to attempt to prescribe to the business world how honest and peaceable trade was to be carried on in a case where no such illegal elements as I have mentioned exist, or were to adopt some standard of judicial "reasonableness," or of "normal" prices, or "fair freights," to which commercial adventures, otherwise innocent, were bound to conform.

In my opinion, accordingly, this appeal ought to be dismissed with costs.

Fry L.J.: . . . It was forcibly urged upon us that combinations like the present are in their nature calculated to interfere with the course of trade, and that they are, therefore, so directly opposed to the interest which the state has in freedom of trade, and in that competition which is said to be the life of trade, that they must be indictable. It is plain that the intention and object of the combination before us is to check competition; but the means it uses is competition, and it is difficult, if not impossible, to weigh against one another the probabilities of the employment of competition on the one hand and its suppression on the other; nor is it easy to say how far the success of the combination would arouse in others the desire to share in its benefits, and by competition to force a way into the magic circle. . . . To draw a line between fair and unfair competition, between what is reasonable and unreasonable, passes the power of the courts. . . .

Lord Esher M.R. (dissenting): . . . the act of the defendants in lowering their freights far beyond a lowering for any purpose of trade—that is to say, so low that if they continued it they themselves could not carry on trade—was not an act done in the exercise of their own free right of trade, but was an act done evidently for the purpose of interfering with, *i.e.* with intent to interfere with, the plaintiffs' right to a free course of trade, and was therefore a wrongful act as against the plaintiffs' right; and as injury ensued to the plaintiffs, they had also in respect of such act a right of action against the defendants. The plaintiffs, in respect of that act, would have had a right of action if it had been done by one defendant only. . . .

In the House of Lords

Lord Halsbury L.C.: . . . upon a review of the facts, it is impossible to suggest any malicious intention to injure rival traders, except in the sense that in proportion as one withdraws trade that other people might get, you, to that extent, injure a person's trade when you appropriate the trade to yourself. If such an injury, and the motive of its infliction, is examined and tested, upon principle, and can be truly asserted to be a malicious motive within the meaning of the law that prohibits malicious injury to other people, all competition must be malicious and consequently unlawful, a sufficient *reductio ad absurdum* to dispose of that head of suggested unlawfulness. . . .

Lord Bramwell: . . . what is the definition of "fair competition"? What is unfair that is neither forcible nor fraudulent . . . ?

At first instance

Lord Coleridge C.J.: . . . It must be remembered that all trade is and must be in a sense selfish; trade not being infinite, nay, the trade of a particular place or district being possibly very limited, what one man gains another loses. In the hand to hand war of commerce, as in the conflicts of public life, whether at the Bar, in Parliament, in medicine, in engineering, (I give examples only), men fight on without much thought of others except a desire to excel or to defeat them. Very lofty minds, like Sir Philip Sidney with his cup of water, will not stoop to take an advantage, if they think another wants it more. Our age, in spite of high authority to the contrary, is not without its Sir Philip Sidneys; but these are counsels of perfection which it would be silly indeed to make the measure of the rough business of the world as pursued by ordinary men of business. The line is in words difficult to draw, but I cannot see that these defendants have in fact passed the line which separates the reasonable and legitimate selfishness of traders from wrong and malice. . . .

Notes:

1. Whether or not he was recalling Hobbes's remark that "Force and fraud are in war the two cardinal virtues" (*Leviathan*, Part II Ch. 13), Lord Bramwell's brutal question marks the heart of this important decision; where no specific right has been infringed, everything in trade is fair save force and fraud. Unfair competition is not unlawful; only unlawful competition is. It is a strong case, for the tactics used by the Conference were implacably used and cripplingly effective—predatory price-cutting, "fighting-ships" and pressure on agents. It is curious that Lord Esher M.R. in his dissent focused on the first of these—the short-term uneconomic lowering of freights—when the law of contract was based on the view that a man might charge what he liked for his goods or services (see Lord Bramwell in *Manchester, Sheffield & Lincolnshire Ry v Brown* (1883) 8 App.Cas. at 716). In their other methods, the Conference sailed closer to the wind. By shadowing rival ships, they risked a liability of public nuisance which had been incurred by London bus companies for similar practices (*Green v London General Omnibus Co* (1859) 7 C.B.(N.S.) 290; 141 E.R. 828). In their approaches to the agents, they risked liability under *Lumley v Gye*.

2. The French courts did not believe, with Fry L.J., that it passed their power to say what was reasonable in matters of competition and what was not. They developed, as a matter of pure case law, an extensive system of control of *concurrence déloyale*. When the judges in Germany declined to do likewise, the legislature passed a special Act in very general terms in 1909 (*unlauterer Wettbewerb*), which the German judges now apply in addition to the rules of tort: "A person who in the course of business for purposes of competition acts in a manner which offends against good morals is liable to be enjoined or cast in damages." (Note that if Lord Bramwell's "force" could be extended to cover any "abuse of power" and his "fraud" to include all "dirty tricks," most offences against good morals would be reached.)

3. At the very time of the *Mogul* case, the United States Congress was passing the *Sherman Act*: "Every contract, combination in the form of trust or otherwise, or conspiracy in restraint of trade or commerce . . . is declared to be illegal," and any person suffering business loss in consequence may now recover threefold damages in a civil action. This Act was to keep competition alive; to keep it fair, Congress enacted the Federal Trade Commission Act in 1914, whereunder "Unfair methods of competition in commerce, and unfair or deceptive acts or practices in commerce, are declared unlawful." The regulatory device is an administrative tribunal empowered to enjoin and fine, and not the civil action for damages. Some of the

several states, unlike England, evolved a prima facie tort theory from the following dictum of Bowen L.J.: "Now intentionally to do that which is calculated in the ordinary course of events to damage, and which does, in fact, damage another, is actionable if done without just cause or excuse." But even this principle is incapable of producing a tort of unfair competition which has had, therefore, to develop from the rule that it is wrongful to take away someone's trade by selling your goods as his (passing-off; see above p.584).

4. Although the unfairness of competition depends on the deception of the consumer, it seems to be the competitor rather than the consumer who benefits from the remedies. It is true that the consumer is not necessarily hurt by being misled; what he gets may not be what he expects, but it may be just as good; and if it is cheaper, the result of the tort of passing-off is to give a remedy to the producer of the more expensive item. This lack of interest in the consumer can also be observed in the courts' treatment of agreements not to compete. Such an agreement was invalid at common law (that is, the parties were free to compete though they had promised not to) if the restraint was unreasonable either as to the party who sought release from it or as against the public, that is, the consumer. In fact, however, the former criterion was applied in very many more cases than the latter.

In tort Britain was very slow in providing remedies for the consumer, but has moved swiftly in recent years. Breaches of Community law must be remediable in the national courts (*Courage v Crehan* [2002] Q.B. 507 (E.C.J.)), but Community law strikes only at practices that affect the Community market, not the local one. In this respect the Competition Act has a wider application. But as to damages, the 1998 Act was coy in the extreme: consider s.60(6)(b) below. The Enterprise Act 2002 has put teeth into the Competition Act 1998 by providing that damages may be claimed not only before the courts but also before the Competition Appeal Tribunal (s.58, 58A), a finding of breach by the Office of Fair Trading being binding on the courts and a precondition to a claim before the Tribunal. Furthermore, new s.47B permits specified bodies such as the Consumer Association to bring claims for damages on behalf of at least two consenting individuals provided that the goods or services they ordered were not ordered in the course of a business.

COMPETITION ACT 1998

2.—(1) Subject to section 3, agreements between undertakings, decisions by associations of undertakings or concerted practices which—

(a) may affect trade within the United Kingdom, and
(b) have as their object or effect the prevention, restriction or distortion of competition within the United Kingdom,

are prohibited unless they are exempt in accordance with the provisions of this Part.

(2) Subsection (1) applies, in particular, to agreements, decisions or practices which—

(a) directly or indirectly fix purchase or selling prices or any other trading conditions;
(b) limit or control production, markets, technical development or investment;
(c) share markets or sources of supply;
(d) apply dissimilar conditions to equivalent transactions with other trading parties, thereby placing them at a competitive disadvantage;
(e) make the conclusion of contracts subject to acceptance by the other parties of supplementary obligations which, by their nature or according to commercial usage, have no connection with the subject of such contracts.

(3) Subsection (1) applies only if the agreement, decision or practice is, or is intended to be, implemented in the United Kingdom.

(4) Any agreement or decision which is prohibited by subsection (1) is void.

18.—(1) Subject to section 19, any conduct on the part of one or more undertakings which amounts to the abuse of a dominant position in a market is prohibited if it may affect trade within the United Kingdom.

(2) Conduct may, in particular, constitute such an abuse if it consists in—

(a) directly or indirectly imposing unfair purchase or selling prices or other unfair trading conditions;

(b) limiting production, markets or technical development to the prejudice of consumers;
(c) applying dissimilar conditions to equivalent transactions with other trading parties, thereby placing them at a competitive disadvantage;
(d) making the conclusion of contracts subject to acceptance by the other parties of supplementary obligations which, by their nature or according to commercial usage, have no connection with the subject of the contracts.

60.—(1) The purpose of this section is to ensure that so far as is possible (having regard to any relevant differences between the provisions concerned), questions arising under this Part in relation to competition within the United Kingdom are dealt with in a manner which is consistent with the treatment of corresponding questions arising in Community law in relation to competition within the Community.

(2) At any time when the court determines a question arising under this Part, it must act (so far as is compatible with the provisions of this Part and whether or not it would otherwise be required to do so) with a view to securing that there is no inconsistency between—

(a) the principles applied, and decision reached, by the court in determining that question; and
(b) the principles laid down by the Treaty and the European Court, and any relevant decision of that Court, as applicable at that time in determining any corresponding question arising in Community law.

(3) The court must, in addition, have regard to any relevant decision or statement of the Commission.
. . .
(6) In subsections (2)(b) and (3), "decision" includes a decision as to—

(a) the interpretation of any provision of Community law;
(b) the civil liability of an undertaking for harm caused by its infringement of Community law.

ALLEN v FLOOD

House of Lords [1898] A.C. 1; 67 L.J.Q.B. 119; 77 L.T. 717; 62 J.P. 595; 46 W.R. 258; 14 T.L.R. 125; 42 S.J. 149

Suit by carpenters against boilermaker trade-unionist for blighting their job prospects

The *Sam Weller* was under repair by the Glengall Iron Co in the Regent Dock at Millwall; the woodwork was being done by shipwrights, including the plaintiffs Flood and Taylor, members of the tiny Shipwrights' Provident Union, and the ironwork was being done by about 40 boilermakers, belonging to the huge Independent Society of Boiler Makers and Iron and Steel Ship Builders, whose London delegate was the defendant Allen. The boilermakers discovered that Flood and Taylor had been employed on ironwork by another company and wired for Allen, who came and talked to the boilermakers. He then told the company's manager that the boilermakers would go on strike unless Flood and Taylor were dismissed. Flood and Taylor were dismissed that very day. It was assumed that all the contracts were determinable at will.

Kennedy J. ruled that there was no evidence of conspiracy, or of intimidation or coercion or of breach of contract. The jury found that Allen maliciously induced the Glengall Co to discharge

Flood and Taylor from their employment, and also not to engage them again, and that each plaintiff had suffered damage amounting to £20.

After consideration, Kennedy J. gave judgment for the plaintiffs for £40 [1895] 2 Q.B. 21. The Court of Appeal (Lord Esher M.R., Lopes and Rigby L.JJ.) affirmed that decision [1895] 2 Q.B. 21, in judgments whose effect is stated by the headnote, which reads: "An action will lie against a person who maliciously induces a master to discharge a servant from his employment if injury ensues thereby to the servant, though the discharge by the master does not constitute a breach of the contract of employment. An action will also lie for maliciously inducing a person to abstain from entering into a contract to employ another, if injury ensues thereby to that other."

Allen appealed to the House of Lords. The case was argued before Lord Halsbury L.C., and Lords Watson, Herschell, Macnaghten, Morris and Shand. Eight judges answered a summons to attend (Hawkins, Mathew, Cave, North, Wills, Grantham, Lawrance and Wright JJ.) and the case was reargued before all of them, with the addition of Lord Ashbourne and Lord James of Hereford. The appeal was allowed (Lords Watson, Herschell, Macnaghten, Shand, Davey and James of Hereford; Lord Halsbury L.C., Lord Ashbourne and Lord Morris dissenting). Of the judges who wrote opinions at the request of the House, only Wright and Mathew JJ. were in favour of the defendant. Accordingly, of the 21 judges who wrote opinions on this case, only eight were in favour of the defendant who ultimately won.

Lord Watson: ... There are, in my opinion, two grounds only upon which a person who procures the act of another can be made legally responsible for its consequences. In the first place, he will incur liability if he knowingly and for his own ends induces that other person to commit an actionable wrong. In the second place, where the act induced is within the right of the immediate actor, and is therefore not wrongful in so far as he is concerned, it may yet be to the detriment of a third party; and in that case ... the inducer may be held liable if he can be shown to have procured his object by the use of illegal means directed against that third party. . . . [The iron-men] were not under any continuing engagement to their employers, and, if they had left their work and gone out on strike, they would have been acting within their right, whatever might be thought of the propriety of the proceeding. Not only so; they were, in my opinion, entitled to inform the Glengall Iron Company of the step which they contemplated, as well as of the reasons by which they were influenced, and that either by their own mouth, or as they preferred, by the appellant as their representative. . . .

Lord Herschell: ... I can imagine no greater danger to the community than that a jury should be at liberty to impose the penalty of paying damages for acts which are otherwise lawful, because they choose, without any legal definition of the term, to say that they are malicious . . . [His Lordship referred to the "fair-minded man" test propounded by Wills J., below, p.604] . . . this suggested test makes men's responsibility for their actions depend on the fluctuating opinions of the tribunal before whom the case may chance to come as to what a right-minded man ought or ought not to do in pursuing his own interests. . . . It was said that there seemed to be no good reason why, if an action lay for maliciously inducing a breach of contract, it should not equally lie for maliciously inducing a person not to enter into a contract. So far from thinking it a small step from the one decision to the other, I think there is a chasm between them. . . . Even . . . if it can be said without abuse of language that the employers were "intimidated and coerced" by the appellant, even if this be in a certain sense true, it by no means follows that he committed a wrong or is under any legal liability for his act. Everything depends on the nature of the representation or statement by which the pressure was exercised. The law cannot regard the act differently because you choose to call it a threat or coercion instead of an intimation or warning.

I understood it to be admitted at the Bar . . . that it would have been perfectly lawful for all the ironworkers to leave their employment and not to accept a subsequent engagement to work in the company of the plaintiffs. [His Lordship discussed the cases.] In all of them the act complained of was in its nature wrongful; violence, menaces of violence, false statements . . . everything depends on the nature of the act, and whether it is wrongful or not . . . I am aware of no ground for saying that competition is regarded with special favour by the law. . . . Even if a misrepresentation by the appellant to the Glengall Company would be sufficient in any circumstances to afford a right of action to the plaintiffs, I think it could be scarcely contended that it could do so, unless the misrepresentation were wilful and intentional. . . .

Lord Macnaghten: . . . Even if I am wrong in my view of the evidence and the verdict, if the verdict amounts to a finding that Allen's conduct was malicious in every sense of the word, and that he procured the dismissal of Flood and Taylor, that is, that it was his act and conduct alone which caused their dismissal, and if such a verdict were warranted by the evidence, I should still be of opinion that judgment was wrongly entered for the respondents. I do not think that there is any foundation in good sense or in authority for the proposition that a person who suffers loss by reason of another doing or not doing some act which that other is entitled to do or to abstain from doing at his own will and pleasure, whatever his real motive may be, has a remedy against a third person who, by persuasion or some other means not in itself unlawful, has brought about the act or omission from which the loss comes, even though it could be proved that such person was actuated by malice towards the plaintiff, and that his conduct if it could be inquired into was without justification or excuse.

The case may be different where the act itself to which the loss is traceable involves some breach of contract or some breach of duty, and amounts to an interference with legal rights. There the immediate agent is liable, and it may well be that the person in the background who pulls the strings is liable too, though it is not necessary in the present case to express any opinion on that point.

But if the immediate agent cannot be made liable, though he knows what he is about and what the consequences of his action will be, it is difficult to see on what principle a person less directly connected with the affair can be made responsible unless malice has the effect of converting an act not in itself illegal or improper into an actionable wrong. But if that is the effect of malice, why is the immediate agent to escape? Above all, why is he to escape where there is no one else to blame and no one else is answerable? And yet many cases may be put of harm done out of malice without any remedy being available at law. Suppose a man takes a transfer of a debt with which he has no concern for the purpose of ruining the debtor, and then makes him bankrupt out of spite, and so intentionally causes him to lose some benefit under a will or settlement—suppose a man declines to give a servant a character because he is offended with the servant for leaving—suppose a person of position takes away his custom from a country tradesman in a small village merely to injure him on account of some fancied grievance not connected with their dealings in the way of buying and selling—no one, I think, would suggest that there could be any remedy at law in any of those cases. But suppose a customer, not content with taking away his own custom, says something not slanderous or otherwise actionable or even improper in itself to induce a friend of his not to employ the tradesman any more. Neither the one nor the other is liable for taking away his own custom. Is it possible that the one can be made liable for inducing the other not to employ the person against whom he has a grudge? If so, a fashionable dressmaker might now and then, I fancy, be plaintiff in a very interesting suit. The truth is that questions of this sort belong to the province of morals rather than to the province of law. Against spite and malice the best safeguards are to be found in self-interest and public opinion. Much more harm than good would be done by encouraging or permitting inquiries into motives when the immediate act alleged to have caused the loss for which redress is sought is in itself innocent or neutral in character, and one which anybody may do or leave undone without fear of legal consequences. Such an inquisition would, I think, be intolerable, to say nothing of the probability of injustice being done by juries in a class of cases in which there would be ample room for speculation and wide scope for prejudice.

In order to prevent any possible misconstruction of the language I have used I should like to add that in my opinion the decision of the case can have no bearing on any case which involves the element of oppressive combination. The vice of that form of terrorism commonly known by the name of "boycotting," and other forms of oppressive combination, seems to me to depend on considerations which are, I think, in the present case conspicuously absent.

As regards authority, there is, I think, very little to be said. It is hardly necessary to go further back than *Lumley v Gye* in 1853. There is not much help to be found in the earlier cases that were cited at the Bar, not even, I think, in the great case about frightening ducks in a decoy, whatever the true explanation of that decision may be [*Keeble v Hickeringill* (1706) 103 E.R. 1127; 90 E.R. 906; 91 E.R. 659; 88 E.R. 898 at 945]. In *Lumley v Gye* it was held that an action would lie for procuring a person to break a contract for personal service. The subsequent cases of *Bowen v Hall* (1881) 6 Q.B.D. 333) and *Temperton v Russell* ([1893] 1 Q.B. 715) are authorities for the proposition that the principle is not confined to contracts for personal service. There is no doubt much to be said for that proposition. But the judgment under appeal does not depend on *Lumley v Gye* or on any decision before or after that case. . . .

Lord Shand: . . . One of the learned judges—the late Cave J.—has expressed the opinion that if a butler who, for some reason or another, has made up his mind that he will no longer continue in service with the cook, with whom he has been in the same employment, should intimate his resolution to the employer, and the services of the cook should thereupon be dispensed with, the cook will have in law a claim of damages against the butler. If this view were sound, then the plaintiffs in this case might be entitled to succeed. Indeed, I have always thought throughout the course of the argument that the case put by the learned judge is perhaps the simplest form in which the very question now under discussion could be raised. But, with great deference to the opinion of the learned judge, no such claim could arise in such circumstances, because it cannot be truly said that on the part of the butler there was either an unlawful act, or unlawful means used in the doing of a lawful act. A servant is surely entitled, for any reason sufficient in his judgment, or even from caprice, I should say, to resolve that he will no longer continue, after the expiry of a current engagement, in service with another servant in the same employment. This being unquestionable, the only limitation on his right to act is that he must not use unlawful means to induce his employer to dispense with the services of his fellow-servant. Should his master ask him the reason for his giving up the service, he is surely entitled to give the true reason, leaving the master to act as he thinks best in determining with which of the two servants he will part; and the notion of a claim of damages by his fellow-servant would be extravagant. It can make no difference that he thinks it right at his own hand to inform his master of the resolution he has taken, and I must add, with reference to what I have immediately to say, that this action being lawful, and no unlawful means being used in carrying it out, the motive, even if it be personal ill-will to another, would not, in my opinion, create liability to a claim of damages.

Coming now directly to the merits of the question in controversy in the case, the argument of the plaintiffs and the reasons for the opinions of the majority of the consulted judges seem to me to fail, because, although it is no doubt true that the plaintiffs were entitled to pursue their trade as workmen "without hindrance," their right to do so was qualified by an equal right, and indeed the same right, on the part of other workmen. The hindrance must not be of an unlawful character. It must not be by unlawful action. Amongst the rights of all workmen is the right of competition. In the like manner and to the same extent as a workman has a right to pursue his work or labour without hindrance, a trader has a right to trade without hindrance. That right is subject to the right of others to trade also, and to subject him to competition—competition which is in itself lawful, and which cannot be complained of where no unlawful means (in the sense I have already explained) have been employed. The matter has been settled in so far as competition in trade is concerned by the judgment of this House in the *Mogul Steamship Co* case ([1892] A.C. 25; [above, p.593]). I can see no reason for saying that a different principle should apply to competition in labour. In the course of such competition, and with a view to secure an advantage to himself, I can find no reason for saying that a workman is not within his legal rights in resolving that he will decline to work in the same employment with certain other persons, and in intimating that resolution to his employers.

It is further to be observed, distinguishing the case from one in which a contract might have subsisted between the plaintiffs and their employers for a definite period, or for the work, it might be, on a particular ship until the whole was completed (in which case the refusal to continue to give the work would be a breach of contract on the employers' part), that there was here no such breach of contract. The employers' act in dispensing with the services of the plaintiffs at the end of the day was a lawful act on their part. The defendant induced them only to do what they were entitled to do, and, in the absence of any fraud or other unlawful means used to bring this about, the action fails.

As already fully explained, there was no case of malice in the ordinary sense of the term, as meaning personal ill-will, presented to the jury; but I agree with those of your Lordships who hold that, even if such a motive had existed in the mind of the defendant, this would not have created liability in damages. On the grounds already stated, I think the defendant only exercised a legal right in intimating that the boiler-makers would leave work if the plaintiffs were continued; he used no fraud or illegal means in the assertion of that right; and the exercise by a person of a legal right does not become illegal because the motive of action is improper or malicious: *Bradford Corp. v Pickles* ([1895] A.C. 587) and the *Mogul Steamship Co* case . . .

Lord Davey: . . . Nor can I agree that there is no legal difference between persuasion to break a contract and persuasion not to enter a contract. . . . In the one case there is a violation of right; in the other case there is not. . . . It was, however, argued that the act of the appellant in the present case was a violation of the right which every man has to pursue a lawful trade and calling, and that the violation of this right is actionable. I remark in passing that, if this be so, the right of action must be independent of the question of malice, except in the legal sense. The right which a man has to pursue his trade or calling is qualified by the equal right of others to do the same and compete with him, though to his damage. And it is obvious that a general abstract right of this character stands on a different footing from such a private particular right as the right to performance of a contract into which one has entered. A man has no right to be employed by any particular employer, and has no right to any particular employment if it depends on the will of another. . . .

Lord Morris (dissenting): . . . The plaintiffs were only day-labourers, but with a certainty of their employment being continued *de die in diem* for a considerable time. In my opinion it is actionable to disturb a man in his business by procuring the determination of a contract at will, or even by preventing the formation of a contract, when the motive is malicious and damage ensues. . . .

The following are extracts from the opinions of judges who were asked to state them.

Hawkins J. (for the plaintiff): . . . I can imagine a state of things in which the defendant might have rightfully, in the bona fide exercise of a privilege or a duty, done and said what he did, but having acted and spoken under the prompting of malice or bad motive, those actions and words were wrongful, and without any privilege to excuse or justify them. . . .

Mathew J. (for the defendant): . . . in the judgments under review, no distinction is drawn between inducing a breach of contract and preventing a contract from being entered into. It seems to me the distinction is all-important. . . . I am not aware of any authority for the proposition that the law recognises a man's interest in his trade, profession or business as analogous to property in land or to a right created by contract. . . .

Cave J. (for the plaintiff): . . . It was asked by one of your Lordships, "If a cook says to her master, 'Discharge the butler or I leave you,' is that actionable?" With submission I say that it is, if the master does discharge the butler in consequence; and I hardly understand why it should not be. . . . Another question put in the course of the argument was this: "Will an action lie if A, out of ill-will to B, induces C not to leave him a legacy?" I answer, Certainly not, because there is no such recognised trade or profession as that of a legacy-hunter. . . . [Allen's] motive was not to secure the work they were then doing . . . but to punish the respondents for what they had previously done. . . .

North J. (for the plaintiff) held that there was no distinction to be drawn between a contract for a determinate time and a contract determinable at will, provided that, as a matter of fact, it was probable that the contractual relationship would not be determined: . . . one can readily divine what the answer of a layman would be who was told that the law made a distinction between the two cases, and the officious intermeddling of Allen would be justifiable in the one but not in the other. . . .

Wills J. (for the plaintiff): . . . If no interference with ancient lights . . . be involved, a man may erect upon his own land a building which may ruin his neighbour's industry exercised upon the adjoining land. No action could be maintained, though it were demonstrated that his only purpose in making the erection was to spite and damage his neighbour. . . . Equally any right given by contract may be exercised against the giver by the person to whom it is granted, no matter how wicked, cruel or mean the motive may be which determines the enforcement of the right . . . I think the question whether the act complained of was malicious would depend upon whether the defendant had in pursuing his own interests done so by such means and with such disregard of his neighbour as no honest and fair-minded man ought to resort to. . . . The distinction between inducing people to break contracts and inducing them not to enter into contracts cannot, in my opinion, be ignored; but it appears to me that it is one of circumstance rather than one of essence. . . .

Note:

This is arguably the most important case in the book, and it is certainly the one which was most argued, and on which most judicial opinions were written, the speeches extending to nearly 200 pages. The background of the participants is splendidly laid out in Heuston, "Judicial Prosopography," (1986) 102 L.Q.R. 90. The case is important because it has to do with freedom. It holds that, whatever morality may say, in law one is free to beggar one's neighbour provided one neither does anything unlawful oneself nor gets anyone else to do anything unlawful. The boilermen were free to stay away from work the next day, and the docks manager was free to dispense with the carpenters' services. Had the docks manager been bound to let the carpenters continue working, Allen would have been liable under *Lumley v Gye*, and had the boilermen been bound to continue working, he would have been liable under the next following case. Is it unfair in this area that as people's rights increase, so their freedom of action is restricted? After all, in contract, rights and obligations are reciprocal . . . If the decision had gone the other way, then in every case of industrial strife a jury would have been permitted to find that the acts of the defendants, workmen or masters, had been malicious in the sense that they had some motive of which the jury disapproved: it was better that injustice be done in shipyards and factories than in Her Majesty's courts.

On one view the decision is simply an application of the *ratio* of the *Mogul* case: both cases involved the deliberate infliction of purely economic loss without the use of any unlawful means. But in other respects the cases are very different. Mogul was a company, Flood a human being. In *Mogul* the plaintiff was complaining of lost freight, in *Allen v Flood* of lost wages. While Mogul lost cargoes, Flood lost his job.

Should an individual's job not be better protected than a company's trading profits? Under special legislation nowadays it is, but the labour legislation, originating in 1906, tended to equate "trade and business" with "employment" and a person's right to dispose of his capital with his right to dispose of his labour, though in collateral respects it distinguished the contract of employment from contracts of other kinds. The common law, which is curiously reluctant to distinguish between companies and individuals, is certainly capable, as we saw in the chapter on vicarious liability, of distinguishing the contract of employment from the contracts under which independent persons and non-persons obtain their income. Perhaps it should be done so in the present case.

Another distinction between *Mogul* and *Allen v Flood* is that there were several defendants in the former case and only one in the latter. In *Mogul* the defendants were palpably acting in their own group interests at the expense of Mogul's. In *Allen v Flood* the single defendant's motivation was held immaterial. *Quinn v Leathem* [1901] A.C. 495 involved several defendants acting in concert not to advance their own interests (so the jury found) but to hurt the plaintiff out of malevolence. The defendants wanted the plaintiff, a meat wholesaler, to fire his existing employees and replace them with union members. This the plaintiff refused to do, though he was perfectly willing for them to join the union and indeed was prepared to pay their fines and dues. The defendants were not satisfied with this and struck at him by getting their men at his best retail customer to refuse to handle any more meat from the plaintiff and by paying three of his men to quit their jobs. No breach of contract was induced or threatened, but the defendants were held liable. This is the tort of civil conspiracy, on which see *Lonrho v Fayed*, below, p.619.

ROOKES v BARNARD

House of Lords [1964] A.C. 1129; [1964] 2 W.L.R. 269; 108 S.J. 93; [1964] 1 All E.R. 367; [1964] 1 Lloyd's Rep. 28

Suit against members of plaintiff's previous union for causing him to lose his job by an improper strike-threat

The plaintiff was employed by B.O.A.C. as a skilled draughtsman at London Airport. He left his union, the Association of Engineering and Shipbuilding Draughtsmen, after a dispute. There was a meeting of the airport branch of the union, at which a resolution was passed that B.O.A.C. should be informed that all labour would be withdrawn unless the plaintiff were removed from the design office. The defendants spoke in favour of this resolution; two of them were employed by B.O.A.C. and the third, Silverthorne, was a union official. In consequence of this resolution, B.O.A.C. first suspended and then dismissed the plaintiff, with the lawful period of notice. Agreements between B.O.A.C. and the union provided for 100 per cent union membership, and also that there should be neither strike nor lock-out. By reason of the conceded fact that this last term was incorporated in the individual contracts of employment, the threat by the employees to withhold their labour constituted a threat to break their contracts.

The trial took place before Sachs J. and a jury, who returned a verdict for the plaintiff for £7,500 after an instruction permitting them to award exemplary damages [1961] 3 W.L.R. 438. The Court of Appeal reversed this decision on the ground that the tort of intimidation was limited to threats of violence, and was not satisfied with threats to break contracts [1963] 1 Q.B. 623. The House of Lords allowed the plaintiff's appeal on the merits, but remanded the case for retrial on the point of damages. (The case was later settled for £4,000 plus costs ([1966] 1 Q.B. 176).)

Lord Reid: ... This case raises the question whether it is a tort to conspire to threaten an employer that his men will break their contracts with him unless he dismisses the plaintiff, with the result that he is thereby induced to dismiss the plaintiff and cause him loss. The magnitude of the sum awarded by the jury shows that the appellant had every prospect of retaining his employment with B.O.A.C. if the respondents and the other conspirators had not interfered: leaving the Trade Disputes Act 1906 out of account, if B.O.A.C. had been induced to dismiss the appellant in breach of their contract with him then there is no doubt that the respondents would have committed a tort and would have been liable in damages (*Lumley v Gye*). Equally, there is no doubt that men are entitled to threaten to strike if that involves no breach of their contracts with their employer, and they are not trying to induce their employer to break any contract with the plaintiff. The question in this case is whether it was unlawful for them to use a threat to break their contracts with their employer as a weapon to make him do something which he was legally entitled to do but which they knew would cause loss to the plaintiff.

The first contention of the respondents is very far reaching. They say there is no such tort as intimidation. That would mean that, short of committing a crime, an individual could with impunity virtually compel a third person to do something damaging to the plaintiff which he does not want to do but can lawfully do: the wrongdoer could use every kind of threat to commit violence, libel or any other tort, and the plaintiff would have no remedy. And a combination of individuals could do the same, at least if they acted solely to promote their own interests. It is true that there is no decision of this House which negatives that argument. But there are many speeches in this House and judgments of eminent judges where it is assumed that that is not the law and I have found none where there is any real support for this argument. It has often been stated that if people combine to do acts which they know will cause loss to the plaintiff, he can sue if either the object of the conspiracy is unlawful or they use unlawful means to achieve it. In my judgment, to cause such loss by threat to commit a tort against a third person if he does not comply with their demands is to use unlawful means to achieve their object.

That brings me to the second argument for the respondents, which raises a more difficult question. They say that there is a distinction between threats to commit a tort and threats to break a contract. They point out that a person is quite entitled to threaten to do something which he has a legal right to do and they say that breach of contract is a private matter between the contracting parties. If the plaintiff cannot sue for loss to him which results from an actual breach of a contract to which he is not a party, why, they ask, should he be entitled to sue for loss which results from a threat to break a contract to which he is not a party?

A somewhat similar argument failed in *Lumley v Gye*. The defendant had induced a singer to break her contract with the plaintiff and he knew that this would cause loss to the plaintiff. The plaintiff had his action against the singer for breach of contract and he was held also to have a cause of action against the defendant for the tort of unjustifiably interfering so as to cause him loss. The fact that the direct cause of the loss was a breach of contract to which the defendant was not a party did not matter. So, too, the plaintiff's action in the present case does not sound in contract: in fact there was no breach of contract because B.O.A.C. gave in.

The appellant in this case could not take a benefit from contracts to which he was not a party or from any breach of them. But his ground of action is quite different. The respondents here used a weapon in a way which they knew would cause him loss, and the question is whether they were entitled to use that weapon—a threat that they would cause loss to B.O.A.C. if B.O.A.C. did not do as they wished. That threat was to cause loss to B.O.A.C. by doing something which they had no right to do, breaking their contracts with B.O.A.C. I can see no difference in principle between a threat to break a contract and a threat to commit a tort. If a third party could not sue for damage caused to him by the former I can see no reason why he should be entitled to sue for damage caused to him by the latter. A person is no more entitled to sue in respect of loss which he suffers by reason of a tort committed against someone else than he is entitled to sue in respect of loss which he suffers by reason of breach of a contract to which he is not a party. What he sues for in each case is loss caused to him by the use of an unlawful weapon against him—intimidation of another person by unlawful means. So long as the defendant only threatens to do what he has a legal right to do he is on safe ground. At least if there is no conspiracy he would not be liable to anyone for doing the act, whatever his motive might be, and it would be absurd to make him liable for threatening to do it but not for doing it. But I agree with Lord Herschell (*Allen v Flood*) that there is a chasm between doing what you have a legal right to do and doing what you have no legal right to do, and there seems to me to be the same chasm between threatening to do what you have a legal right to do and threatening to do what you have no legal right to do. It must follow from *Allen v Flood* that to intimidate by threatening to do what you have a legal right to do is to intimidate by lawful means. But I see no good reason for extending that doctrine. Threatening a breach of contract may be a much more coercive weapon than threatening a tort, particularly when the threat is directed against a company or corporation, and, if there is no technical reason requiring a distinction between different kinds of threats, I can see no other ground for making any such distinction. . . .

Intimidation of any kind appears to me to be highly objectionable. The law was not slow to prevent it when violence and threats of violence were the most effective means. Now that subtler means are at least equally effective I see no reason why the law should have to turn a blind eye to them. We have to tolerate intimidation by means which have been held to be lawful but there I would stop. Accordingly, I would hold that on the facts found by the jury the respondents' actions in this case were tortious. . . .

Questions

1. A contracts to sell to B some goods of which he has a monopoly; he then discovers that B *plans* to deliver them to C, whom A hates. A deliberately, and with the intention of hurting C, refuses to deliver the promised goods to B. Can C sue A? Does it make any difference if B has *contracted* to deliver the goods in question to C, and A knows this?

2. What is the difference between this case and *Allen v Flood*, above, p.599? If the difference is that here the defendants had a contractual right to continued employment, do you think it fair that their freedom of action should be correspondingly curtailed?

Notes:

1. This decision caused a fearful furore. Perhaps it was not perfectly understood. Or perhaps the objectors were lucid but malignant. The general proposition that A is liable for using unlawful pressure on B so as to

hurt C is surely acceptable. Doubtless there might be circumstances in which such action by A might be justified, but a justification is called for. Parliament immediately provided an immunity: conduct like that of Barnard and his mates was not to be actionable if done in contemplation or furtherance of a trade dispute. See below, p.00.

2. In this case Rookes was hurt when B.O.A.C. yielded to the defendants' pressure, but B.O.A.C. itself was unscathed. Commonly, however, the person leant on does suffer harm by complying with the demands of the person doing the leaning, often by conferring a benefit on him: thus the traveller enriches the highwayman and the policeman collects the protection money from the porno-dealer. Can the victim of blackmail or duress reclaim what he has paid?

In *Universe Tankships v International Transport Workers' Federation* [1982] 2 All E.R. 67; noted [1983] Camb. L.J. 43 at 47, a trade union blacked a ship and exacted a sum as the price of its release. Unless legitimised by statute, the blacking would have been tortious (inducing the tug-men to break their contracts of employment with the harbour authorities); if so legitimised, the House of Lords held, the restitutionary claim was also barred. A pretty variant, which divided the judges six-three, arose in *Dimskal Shipping Co v ITF* [1991] 4 All E.R. 871. In Sweden, where such an action was legitimate, ITF coerced shipowners into signing contracts, expressed to be subject to English law. The shipowners made payments under these contracts and now claimed their money back. "Money back" is, of course, a restitutionary claim, not a claim under a contract, but it cannot be claimed if the contract under which the money was paid is valid. The House held that the validity of the contract depended on English law and *that therefore* the restitutionary claim must succeed. The italicised words seem to constitute a *non sequitur*.

3. In *Inshore Services (International) v NFFO Services* [2001] EWCA Civ 1722 B, an employee of the defendant fishermen's association wrote a letter to H threatening to disrupt H's survey of Morecambe Bay if H went through with its plan, not yet a firm contract, to use a vessel belonging to Inshore. Inshore's vessel had already set off for the project when H decided, to avoid trouble, to use another vessel. It was found that B was indifferent as to the lawfulness of the steps threatened, and that such "eye-closing" was as relevant to the tort of intentionally causing harm by wrongful means as to the tort of inducing breach of contract (*Emerald Construction Co v Lowthian* [1966] 1 WLR 691).

4. It may be useful to recapitulate the effect of the last four cases excerpted: there is no liability simply for frustrating a person's economic prospects, even by bringing pressure on third parties (*Mogul, Allen v Flood*), but in doing so not only must you eschew the use of force and fraud, you must also respect people's binding engagements, your own (*Rookes*) as well as other people's (*Lumley v Gye*). If one recognises that one's liberty to beggar one's neighbour is conditioned upon one's using no unlawful means, it is far from clear that any further common law liability is required. In fact no further liability has ever been imposed, but methods have been used which are objectionable and pregnant with danger, exemplified in the next case.

TORQUAY HOTEL CO v COUSINS

Court of Appeal [1969] 2 Ch. 106; [1969] 2 W.L.R. 289; (1969) 113 S.J. 52; [1969] 1 All E.R. 522
(noted (1970) 86 L.Q.R. 189; (1968) 31 M.L.R. 555; (1969) 32 M.L.R. 435)

Hotelier sues trade unionist for preventing deliveries of fuel

Angry at what they took to be an intervention by the manager of the plaintiff's Imperial Hotel in a dispute they were having with another hotel in the area, the defendant union officials telephoned Esso, with whom the Imperial Hotel had a bulk contract for the delivery of oil, and said that no further deliveries should be made. Esso told the manager that there was little point in ordering further oil since none could be delivered as the tanker drivers, being members of the defendant union, would not cross the picket lines. Instead, the manager ordered oil from Alternative Fuels, who made a delivery in the temporary absence of the pickets; the defendants then telephoned the firm and threatened unspecific repercussions if further deliveries were attempted. After a solicitor's letter to the defendants, the manager ordered 3,000 gallons of oil from Esso; that oil was delivered but the defendants refused to give any undertaking that further deliveries would not be stopped.

Stamp J. granted an interlocutory injunction restraining the named defendants from "doing any act which, whether directly or indirectly, causes or procures a breach or breaches by any supplier of fuel oil of contracts made now or hereafter by such supplier with the plaintiff company for the delivery of oil to the plaintiff company, and picketing at or near the entrance or entrances near the Imperial Hotel for the purpose of persuading drivers of oil tankers not to deliver fuel oil there." ([1969] 2 Ch. 106 at 112).

The defendants' appeal to the Court of Appeal was dismissed, subject to the injunction being vacated as to the defendant union.

Lord Denning M.R.: ... The reason why the Imperial Hotel apply for an injunction is essentially *quia timet*. No oil has in fact been stopped from reaching the Imperial Hotel: but the Imperial Hotel fear that the union and their officials will try to stop it unless the court intervenes. To obtain an injunction, the plaintiffs must show that the defendants are proposing to do something unlawful.

Many grounds of unlawfulness have been canvassed before us, including breach of contract, conspiracy and intimidation. The judge put the case on the broad ground that the defendants were proposing, without justification, to interfere with the contractual relations of the Imperial Hotel. He granted an injunction to restrain the defendants from procuring a breach by any supplier of oil of contracts made or hereafter to be made for delivery of fuel-oil to the hotel. On the appeal the argument covered many points which I will take in order.

The Imperial Hotel had a contract with Esso under which the Imperial Hotel agreed to buy their total requirements of fuel-oil from Esso for one year, the quantity being estimated at 120,000 gallons, to be delivered by road tank wagon at a minimum of 3,000 gallons a time. Under the contract there was a *course of dealing* by which the Imperial Hotel used to order 3,000 gallons every week or 10 days, and Esso used to deliver it the next day. But there was a *force majeure* or *exception clause* which said that: "neither party shall be liable for any failure to fulfil any term of this agreement if fulfilment is delayed, hindered or prevented by any circumstance whatever which is not within their immediate control, including ... labour disputes."

It is plain that, if delivery was hindered or prevented by labour disputes, as, for instance, because their drivers would not cross the picket line, Esso could rely on that exception clause as a defence to any claim by Imperial. They would not be liable in damages. And I am prepared to assume that Esso would not be guilty of a breach of contract. But I do not think that would exempt the trade union officials from liability if they unlawfully hindered or prevented Esso from making deliveries. The principle of *Lumley v Gye* [above, p.589] extends not only to inducing breach of contract, but also to preventing the performance of it. That can be shown by a simple illustration taken from the books. In *Lumley v Gye*, Miss Wagner, an actress, was engaged by Mr Lumley to sing at Her Majesty's Theatre. Mr Gye, who ran Covent Garden, procured her to break her contract with Mr Lumley by promising to pay her more: see *Lumley v Wagner* ((1852) 1 De G.M. & G. 604). He was held liable to Mr Lumley for inducing a breach of contract. In *Poussard v Spiers & Pond* ((1876) 1 Q.B.D. 410) Madam Poussard was under contract with Spiers to sing in an opera at the Criterion Theatre. She fell sick and was unable to attend rehearsals. Her non-performance, being occasioned by sickness, was not a breach of contract on her part: but it was held to excuse the theatre company from continuing to employ her. Suppose now that an ill-disposed person, knowing of her contract, had given her a potion to make her sick. She would not be guilty of a breach herself. But undoubtedly the person who administered the potion would have done wrong and be liable for the damage suffered by them. So here I think the trade union officials cannot take advantage of the *force majeure* or exception clause in the Esso contract. If they unlawfully prevented or hindered Esso from making deliveries, as ordered by Imperial, they would be liable in damages to Imperial, notwithstanding the exception clause.

The principles of law

The principle of *Lumley v Gye* is that each of the parties to a contract has a "right to the performance" of it: and it is wrong for another to procure one of the parties to break it or not to perform it. That principle was extended a step further by Lord Macnaghten in *Quinn v Leathem* ([1901] A.C. 495), so that each of the parties has a right to have his "contractual relations" with the other duly observed. "It is," he said at 510, "a violation of legal right to interfere with contractual relations recognised by law if there be no sufficient justification for the interference." That statement was adopted and applied by a strong board of the Privy Council in *Jasperson v*

Dominion Tobacco Co ([1923] A.C. 709). It included Viscount Haldane and Lord Sumner. The time has come when the principle should be further extended to cover "deliberate and direct interference with the execution of a contract without that causing any breach." That was a point left open by Lord Reid in *Stratford (JT) & Son Ltd v Lindley* ([1965] A.C. 269 at 324). But the common law would be seriously deficient if it did not condemn such interference. It is this very case. The principle can be subdivided into three elements:

First, there must be *interference* in the execution of a contract. The interference is not confined to the procurement of a *breach* of contract. It extends to a case where a third person *prevents* or *hinders* one party from performing his contract, even though it be not a breach.

Second, the interference must be deliberate. The person must know of the contract or, at any rate, turn a blind eye to it and intend to interfere with it: see *Emerald Construction Co v Lowthian* [1966] 1 W.L.R. 691.

Third, the interference must be *direct*. Indirect interference will not do. Thus, a man who "corners the market" in a commodity may well know that it may prevent others from performing their contracts, but he is not liable to an action for so doing. A trade union official, who calls a strike on proper notice, may well know that it will prevent the employers from performing their contracts to deliver goods, but he is not liable in damages for calling it. *Indirect* interference is only unlawful if unlawful means are used. I went too far when I said in *Daily Mirror Newspapers Ltd v Gardner* ([1968] 2 Q.B. 762 at 782) that there was no difference between direct and indirect interference. On reading once again *Thomson (D.C.) & Co Ltd v Deakin* ([1952] Ch. 646), with more time, I find there is a difference. Morris L.J., at 702, there draws the very distinction between "*direct* persuasion to breach of contract" which is unlawful in itself: and "the intentional bringing about of a breach by *indirect* methods involving wrongdoing." This distinction must be maintained, else we should take away the right to strike altogether. Nearly every trade union official who calls a strike—even on due notice, as in *Morgan v Fry* ([1968] 2 Q.B. 710)—knows that it may prevent the employers from performing their contracts. He may be taken even to intend it. Yet no one has supposed hitherto that it was unlawful: and we should not render it unlawful today. A trade union official is only in the wrong when he procures a contracting party *directly* to break his contract, or when he does it indirectly *by unlawful means*.

I must say a word about unlawful means, because that brings in another principle. I have always understood that if one person deliberately interferes with the trade or business of another and does so by unlawful means, that is, by an act which he is not at liberty to commit, then he is acting unlawfully, even though he does not procure or induce any actual breach of contract. If the means are unlawful, that is enough. Thus in *Rookes v Barnard* ([1964] A.C. 1129) (as explained by Lord Reid in *Stratford v Lindley* [1965] A.C. 269 at 325, and Lord Upjohn, at p. 337) the defendants interfered with the employment of Rookes—and they did it by unlawful means, namely, by intimidation of his employers—and they were held to be acting unlawfully, even though the employers committed no breach of contract as they gave Rookes proper notice. And in *Stratford v Lindley* ([1965] A.C. 269), the defendants interfered with the business of Stratford—and they did it by *unlawful means*, namely, by inducing the men to *break their contracts* of employment by refusing to handle the barges—and they were held to be acting unlawfully, even in regard to *new business* of Stratford which was not the subject of contract. Lord Reid said, at 324: "The respondents' action made it practically impossible for the appellants to do any new business with the barge hirers. It was not disputed that such interference is tortious if any unlawful means are employed."

This point about unlawful means is of particular importance when a place is declared "black." At common law it often involves the use of unlawful means. Take the Imperial Hotel. When it was declared "black," it meant that the drivers of the tankers would not take oil to the hotel. The drivers would thus be induced to break their contracts of employment. That would be unlawful at common law. The only case in which "blacking" of such a kind is lawful is when it is done "in contemplation or furtherance of a trade dispute", for in that event, the act of inducing a breach of a contract of employment is a lawful act which is not actionable at the suit of anyone. Seeing that the act is lawful, it must, I think, be lawful for the trade union officials to tell the employers and their customers about it. And this is so, even though it does mean that those people are compelled to break their commercial contracts. The interference with the commercial contracts is only indirect, and not direct: see what Lord Upjohn said in *Stratford v Lindley* [1965] A.C. 269 at 337. So, if there had been a "trade dispute" in this case, I think it would have protected the trade union officials when they informed Esso that the dispute with Imperial was an "official dispute" and said that the hotel was "blacked"....

Seeing that there was no "trade dispute" this case falls to be determined by the common law. It seems to me that the trade union officials deliberately and directly interfered with the execution of the contract between the Imperial Hotel and Esso. They must have known that there was a contract between the Imperial Hotel and Esso. Why otherwise did they on that very first Saturday afternoon telephone the bulk plant at Plymouth? They may not have known with exactitude all the terms of the contract. But no more did the defendants in *Stratford v Lindley*, at 332. They must also have intended to prevent the performance of the contract. That is plain from the telephone message: "Any supplies of fuel-oil will be stopped being made." And the interference was direct. It was as direct as could be—a telephone message from the trade union official to the bulk plant.

Take next the supplies from Alternative Fuels. The first wagon got through. As it happened, there was no need for the Imperial Hotel to order any further supplies from Alternative Fuels. But suppose they had given a further order, it is quite plain that the trade union officials would have done their best to prevent it being delivered. Their telephone messages show that they intended to prevent supplies being made by all means in their power. By threatening "repercussions" they interfered unlawfully with the performance of any future order which Imperial Hotel might give to Alternative Fuels. And the interference was direct again. It was direct to Alternative Fuels. Such interference was sufficient to warrant the grant of an injunction *quia timet*....

Other wrongs were canvassed, such as conspiracy and intimidation, but I do not think it necessary to go into these. I put my decision on the simple ground that there is evidence that the defendants intended to interfere directly and deliberately with the execution of the existing contracts by Esso and future contracts by Alternative Fuels so as to prevent those companies supplying oil to the Imperial Hotel. This intention was sufficiently manifest to warrant the granting of an injunction.

Russell L.J.: . . . The bulk supply contract between Esso and the Imperial Hotel was such as might be expected for an establishment the size of the latter. It was argued that the exception clause had the effect that Esso could not be in breach of its supply contract if failure to deliver was due to labour disputes. In my view, the exception clause means what it says and no more: it *assumes* a failure to fulfil a term of the contract—*i.e.* a breach of contract—and excludes liability—*i.e.* in damages—for that breach in stated circumstances. It is an exception from liability for non-performance rather than an exception from obligation to perform. If over a considerable period Esso failed to deliver for one of the stated reasons it seems to me that the hotel would be entitled to repudiate the contract on the ground of failure by Esso to carry out its terms: otherwise the hotel would be unable to enter into another bulk supply contract until the Esso contract was time expired. I will not repeat the facts as to Esso and Alternative Fuels, but it seems to me that, as they appear at present, they demonstrate an attitude on the part of the union officials of willingness directly to induce breaches of contract for the supply of fuel oil to the Imperial Hotel in order to carry out a policy of punishing Mr Chapman for his temerity in being critical of the union. This justifies a continuance of the injunction pending trial....

Winn L.J.: . . . The evidence does not establish that in consequence any quantity of fuel which had been ordered was not delivered: no breach of contract by Esso was induced. However, the argument of Mr Pain that clause 10 of the written contract between Esso and the hotel company for a year's supply would have operated to prevent a failure or failures to deliver ordered instalments of fuel thereunder from being a breach does not seem to me to be sound. As I construe the clause it affords only an immunity against any claim for damages; it could not bar a right to treat the contract as repudiated by continuing breach: despite the clause Esso could well have been held to have committed a breach by non-delivery and Mr Pedley came close to committing a tort of the *Lumley v Gye* type.

It is not necessary in the instant case to consider to what extent the principle of that case may cover conduct which Lord Reid described in *Stratford v Lindley* ([1965] A.C. 269 at 324) as "deliberate and direct interference with the execution of a contract without that causing any breach." For my part I think that it can at least be said, with confidence, that where a contract between two persons exists which gives one of them an optional extension of time or an optional mode for his performance of it, or of part of it, but, from the normal course of dealing between them, the other person does not anticipate such postponement, or has come to expect a particular mode of performance a procuring of the exercise of such an option should, in principle, be held actionable if it produces material damage to the other contracting party.

It was one of Mr Pain's main submissions that mere advice, warning or information cannot amount to tortious procurement of breach of contract. Whilst granting *arguendi causa* that a communication which went no further would, in general, not, in the absence of circumstances giving a particular significance, amount to a threat or intimidation, I am unable to understand why it may not be an inducement. In the ordinary meaning of language it would surely be said that a father who told his daughter that her fiancé had been convicted of indecent exposure, had thereby induced her, with or without justification, by truth or by slander, to break her engagement. A man who writes to his mother-in-law telling her that the central heating in his house has broken down may thereby induce her to cancel an intended visit.

The court is not concerned in this case with any indirect procuring of breach, or non-performance of a contract, or with the adoption of indirect means to produce such a result: it is therefore not appropriate to consider whether such a mode of procuring such a result is only actionable, as Mr Pain submitted, where unlawful means, involving, for example, breaches of contract, or actionable breaches of contract, are involved.

Note:

Take the confident dictum of Winn L.J. He says that if (i) B has an option under a contract with A, and (ii) B plans to exercise the option and A expects him to, and (iii) C persuades B not to and A suffers loss, then A can sue C. This, if true, would mean that one may not by a surprise offer of a large wage persuade a long-standing and valuable employee to give notice to the employer who expected to retain and exploit him. This cannot be. The dictum is fundamentally false. It is also irreconcilable with *Allen v Flood*, a decision of rather greater authority, which counsel should force the courts to face one of these days before liberty has gone beyond recall.

Winn L.J. is wrong on "inducing" and he is wrong on "breach." As to the latter it is simply perverse (and as English as the Mad Hatter) to say that a man who has promised to deliver if possible has promised to deliver whether delivery is possible or not, with an immunity in the latter eventuality. As to the former, the defendants certainly *prevented* Esso from performing (and, as they used unlawful means, they should be liable), but they did not *induce* Esso not to perform. My mother-in-law is certainly induced to defer her visit by the indication of a chilly welcome, but that is because she could come if she nevertheless chose. Esso could not have delivered oil if they had chosen; their being told made no difference. After all, if I tie a man up and tell him not to move, it is the rope and not my instruction which induces immobility. Only Tweedledum would say the man was not moving because he had been told not to.

The defendants were rightly held liable, given that there was no trade dispute, but the proper ground of liability is for causing intended harm to the plaintiff by unlawful means, namely persuading Esso's men to break their contracts of employment. Had there been a trade dispute, then under the existing law the defendants should have been immune, for to induce breach of a contract *of employment* was then not unlawful. Indeed Lord Denning, though on erroneous grounds, correctly held that if there had been a trade dispute they would have been immune, whereas Winn L.J. managed to be wrong on that point also. Given a trade dispute with the plaintiff, conduct such as the defendant's in this case (secondary action) was lawful from 1906 until 1990, when the Employment Act withdrew the previous immunity.

Lord Denning held that the defendants were liable for directly interfering with the plaintiff's contractual expectations. The distinction between directness and indirectness is inappropriate, dangerous and incomprehensible. This can be seen from Lord Denning's judgment itself. For he holds that on the facts the interference was direct, and says that had there been a trade dispute the interference would have been indirect. But the existence of a trade dispute cannot conceivably make indirect what in its absence would be direct interference. So what is direct and what is indirect? If it is indirect, as Lord Denning says, to suborn the personnel and pre-empt the goods (and presumably to block the road) required for the execution of a contract for the delivery of goods, it seems that the only direct interference is an approach, perhaps through agents, to the contractor himself.

The proper and useful distinction is not between directness and indirectness, but between persuasion and prevention, between getting a man not to perform his contract and causing him not to. If you *persuade* a man not to do something he would otherwise have done, you are liable only if he was bound to do it; if he is not bound to do it, he must be free not to do it and you must be free to persuade him not to do it by all lawful means. (Of course, in our case Esso were not free not to deliver oil when they could, and if the defendants had persuaded Esso not to deliver oil when they could, Esso would have been in breach and the defendants consequently liable under *Lumley v Gye*.) If you *prevent* a man doing something, you are liable only if you use wrongful means, and if you use wrongful means you are liable whether or not he was bound to do it. Accordingly, even if Esso had guaranteed delivery of oil to Imperial, come what might, the defendants here would not be liable under *Lumley v Gye*; they would be liable on another principle, if they used wrongful means, as they did, by threatening to induce or inducing Esso's drivers to disobey orders.

The court here has treated a case of using unlawful means to cause harm to expectations as a case of interfering directly with contractual relations, a thing said to be wrongful in itself; by ignoring the unlawfulness of the means used, they have extended liability in a way contrary to authority and inimical to freedom. The dicta in this case suggest that you are liable for persuading a contractor not to do what is expected of him; but the very point decided in *Allen v Flood* was that it was not tortious to discourage a person from maintaining an existing contract which would otherwise have been maintained. It appears that *Allen v Flood* was not cited to the Court of Appeal, and it was certainly not cited by them. It would be gratifying if the present decision could be regarded as having being rendered *per incuriam*. Unfortunately the same is true of the next case. . . .

MERKUR ISLAND SHIPPING v LAUGHTON

House of Lords [1983] 2 A.C. 570; [1983] I.C.R. 490; [1983] 2 W.L.R. 778; [1983] 2 All E.R. 189
(noted (1983) 46 M.L.R. 632)

Action by owner of chartered ship prevented from sailing by trade unionists

The plaintiff's ship was let on a time-charter to X and on sub-charter to Y who contracted with Z to have it towed out of port. The ship was unable to leave port, however, because the defendants, in furtherance of their dispute with the plaintiff, persuaded Z's men not to do the towing. The charter provided that the ship was to proceed with the utmost dispatch, so performance was disrupted though no breach was caused. The trial judge granted an interlocutory injunction which was upheld by the Court of Appeal [1983] 1 All E.R. 334; the defendants' appeal to the House of Lords was dismissed.

Lord Diplock: . . . My Lords, your Lordships have had the dubious benefit during the course of the argument in this appeal of having been referred once more to many of those cases, spanning more than a century, that were the subject of analysis in the judgment of Jenkins L.J. in *Thomson (D.C.) & Co v Deakin* ([1952] Ch. 646) and led to his statement of the law as to what are the essential elements in the tort of actionable interference with contractual rights by blacking. That statement has, for 30 years now, been regarded as authoritative, and for my part, I do not think that any benefit is gained by raking over once again the previous decisions. The elements of the tort as stated by Jenkins L.J. were (at 697):

> " . . . first, that the person charged with actionable interference knew of the existence of the contract and intended to procure its breach; secondly, that the person so charged did definitely and unequivocally persuade, induce or procure the employees concerned to break their contracts of employment with the intent I have mentioned; thirdly, that the employees so persuaded, induced or procured did in fact break their contracts of employment; and, fourthly, that breach of the contract forming the alleged subject of interference ensued as a necessary consequence of the breaches by the employees concerned of their contracts of employment."

DC Thomson & Co v Deakin was a case in which the only interference with contractual rights relied on was procuring a *breach* by a third party of a contract between that third party and the plaintiff. That is why in the passage that I have picked out for citation Jenkins L.J. restricts himself to that form of actionable interference with contractual rights which consists of procuring an actual breach of the contract that formed the subject matter of interference; but it is evident from the passages in his judgment which precede the passage I have cited . . . that Jenkins L.J., though using the expression "breach," was not intending to confine the tort of actionable interference with contractual rights to the procuring of such non-performance of primary obligations under a contract as would necessarily give rise to secondary obligations to make monetary compensation by way of damages. All prevention of due performance of a primary obligation under a contract was intended to be included even though no secondary obligation to make monetary compensation thereupon came into existence, because the secondary obligation was excluded by some *force majeure* clause.

If there were any doubt about this matter, it was resolved in 1969 by the judgments of the Court of Appeal in *Torquay Hotel Co v Cousins* [above, p.607]. That was a case in which the contract the performance of which was interfered with was one for the delivery of fuel. It contained a *force majeure* clause excusing the seller from liability for non-delivery if delayed, hindered or prevented by, *inter alia*, labour disputes. Lord Denning M.R. stated the principle thus:

> " . . . there must be *interference* in the execution of a contract. The interference is not confined to the procurement of a *breach* of contract. It extends to a case where a third person *prevents* or *hinders* one party from performing his contract, even though it be not a breach." (Lord Denning's emphasis.)

Parliamentary recognition that the tort of actionable interference with contractual rights is as broad as Lord Denning M.R. stated in the passage I have just quoted is, in my view, to be found in s.13(1) of the 1974 Act itself, which refers to inducement not only "to break a contract," but also "to interfere with its performance," and treats them as being *pari materia*.

So I turn to the four elements of the tort of actionable interference with contractual rights as Jenkins L.J. stated them, but substituting "interference with performance" for "breach," except in relation to the breaking by employees of their own contracts of employment where such breach has as its necessary consequence the interference with the performance of the contract concerned.

[His Lordship considered the facts] . . . I accordingly agree with the Court of Appeal that the shipowners, on the evidence that was before Parker J., have made out a strong prima facie case that the ITF committed the common law tort of actionable interference with contractual rights.

I should mention that the evidence also establishes a prima facie case of the common law tort, referred to in ss.13(2) and (3) of the 1974 Act, of interfering with the trade or business of another person by doing unlawful acts. To fall within this genus of torts the unlawful act need not involve procuring another person to break a subsisting contract or to interfere with the performance of a subsisting contract. . . .

Note:
Each one of the first three paragraphs cited contains an error. As to the first, there is nothing in the speech of Jenkins L.J. to justify the supposition that he would have envisaged imposing liability for causing disruption of a contract without causing a breach of it, much less granting an action to a frustrated *debtor*. As to the second, doubt does remain despite the decision in *Torquay Hotel*, because of the three judges in that case only Lord Denning made his decision on the basis that there was no breach. As to the third, it is absurd to state that when Parliament accords immunity for certain conduct it is thereby endorsing the liability from which the immunity is accorded. From a judge who proceeds to berate the Parliamentary draftsman and say, truly enough, "Absence of clarity is destructive of the rule of law," this is sorry work indeed.

The defendants' conduct, it was held, was wrongful at common law under two heads—indirect interference with the charterparty by unlawful means, namely inducing the tugmen to break their contracts of employment, and interference with the plaintiff's business by the same unlawful means. While there was statutory immunity for the latter tort there was at the time none for the former (!). Both sets of lawmakers are to blame for this foolishness.

Questions:

1. If in *Lumley v Gye* it was the plaintiff's right to Miss Wagner's services which was interfered with, what right of the plaintiff's was interfered with here?

2. How many contracts were interfered with? Could both parties to each of them sue the defendant? Which party was targeted by the defendant?

TRADE UNION AND LABOUR RELATIONS (CONSOLIDATION) ACT 1992

219.—(1) An act done by a person in contemplation or furtherance of a trade dispute is not actionable in tort on the ground only—

(a) that it induces another person to break a contract or interferes or induces another person to interfere with its performance, or

(b) that it consists in his threatening that a contract (whether one to which he is a party or not) will be broken or its performance interfered with, or that he will induce another person to break a contract or interfere with its performance.

(2) An agreement or combination by two or more persons to do or procure the doing of an act in contemplation or furtherance of a trade dispute is not actionable in tort if the act is one which if done without any such agreement or combination would not be actionable in tort.

Note:

Section 219(1)(a) grants immunity from liability under *Lumley v Gye* (inducing) and *Torquay Hotel Co v Cousins* (interference). Section 219(1)(b) grants immunity from liability under *Rookes v Barnard*. Section 219(2) grants immunity from liability under *Quinn v Leathem* (above, p.591).

If in fact there is a trade dispute, as defined in s.244, conduct qualifies for immunity if the actor genuinely believed it would help his side (*Express Newspapers v McShane* [1980] 1 All E.R. 65). As Lord Diplock said in *NWL Ltd v Woods* [1979] 3 All E.R. 614 at 624, "Immunity . . . is not forfeited by being stubborn or pig-headed."

The immunity is, however, withdrawn if any of the specified acts is done in the course of picketing which is not rendered lawful by s.220, and by ss.222–226, if (1) any of the reasons for the act is (a) an employer's possible employment of a non-union member or refusal to discriminate against him, or (b) his supposed dismissal of an employee for unofficial strike action, or (2) if the act (a) constitutes secondary action other than lawful picketing, *i.e.* action against an employer not party to the trade dispute, or (b) is done in connection with a recognition dispute.

EDWIN HILL & PARTNERS v FIRST NATIONAL FINANCE CORP.

Court of Appeal [1989] 1 W.L.R. 225; [1988] 3 All E.R. 801

Suit by architect against mortgagee of site for causing his dismissal by developer/mortgagor

The defendant bank had lent a great deal of money to Pulver, a solicitor-developer, one of whose companies was called Leakcliff, with a view to the development of a site on the Waterloo Road, London. Both Pulver and Leakcliff had agreed with the plaintiff firm that it should act as the architect for any development of the site. When the loan was seriously outstanding the defendant decided that, rather than call in the loan (which would in any case have terminated the plaintiff's contract), it would finance the development itself, on condition that the plaintiff firm was replaced by different architects. Pulver and Leakcliff accordingly terminated their arrangement with the plaintiff.

The trial judge held that the defendant was justified in causing the plaintiff's contract to be broken, and the plaintiff's appeal to the Court of Appeal was unanimously dismissed.

[The judgment below has been considerably edited.]

Stuart-Smith L.J.: In the course of an admirably clear and concise judgment the judge made the following important findings and in so doing held that four of the five necessary ingredients of the tort of wrongful interference with contract were established: (1) that there was direct interference by the defendants with the plaintiffs contract with Leakcliff. There was inducement, pressure and procuration. Mr Pulver only dispensed with their services because the defendants insisted that he did so; (2) that the defendants knew that the plaintiffs were employed by Leakcliff under a binding contract to the end of the development and had sufficient knowledge that their conduct would interfere with that contract; (3) that the defendants intended to bring the plaintiffs' contract to an end. In this connection the judge found (a) that the defendants had decided to finance the "build-out" by about February 20, 1979 and that it was an integral part of the decision that the plaintiffs should not be the architects, (b) that the defendants knew that Mr Pulver had no effective choice but to dismiss the plaintiffs; it was not just foreseeable, but an inevitable consequence of their decision; (4) that the defendants' interference had caused damage to the plaintiffs.

But he held that the plaintiffs failed on the last ingredient, namely that the defendants' conduct must not have been justified. It is in relation to this conclusion that the plaintiffs appeal.

. . . Counsel for the defendants submitted that the judge's approach was correct. He contended that where the interferer's conduct is within the ambit or compass of his legal rights he is justified. By this phrase he means that if the defendants, instead of exercising their full legal rights of calling for repayment of the loan and exercising their powers of sale or appointment of a receiver, reach some accommodation with the mortgagor, which is more beneficial both to themselves and the mortgagor, they should not be held to lose the justification which they would have had if they had exercised the remedies available to them in the strict sense.

Alternatively he submits that the question of justification should be approached by what he called the "broad brush" approach adumbrated by Romer L.J. in *Glamorgan Coal Co Ltd v South Wales Miners' Federation* [1903] 2 K.B. 545. This is a convenient starting point for a consideration of the authorities. Romer L.J. said (at 574):

> "I respectfully agree with what Bowen L.J. said [in *Mogul Steamship Co Ltd v McGregor Gow & Co* (above, p.590)] when considering the difficulty that might arise whether there was sufficient justification or not: 'The good sense of the tribunal which had to decide would have to analyze the circumstances and to discover on which side of the line each case fell.' I will only add that, in analyzing or considering the circumstances, I think that regard might be had to the nature of the contract broken; the position of the parties to the contract; the grounds for the breach; the means employed to procure the breach; the relation of the person procuring the breach to the person who breaks the contract; and I think also to the object of the person in procuring the breach. But, though I deprecate the attempt to define justification, I think it right to express my opinion on certain points in connection with breaches of contract procured where the contract is one of master and servant. In my opinion, a defendant sued for knowingly procuring such a breach is not justified of necessity merely by his showing that he had no personal animus against the employer, or that it was to the advantage or interest of both the defendant and the workman that the contract should be broken."

When the case reached the House of Lords [1905] A.C. 239, nothing was said by any members of the House to suggest that this was the wrong approach. . . .

Thus the following matters have been held not to amount to justification. (1) Absence of malice or ill-will or intention to injure the person whose contract is broken: *Smithies v National Association of Operative Plasterers* [1909] 1 K.B. 310 and *South Wales Miners' Federation v Glamorgan Coal Co Ltd* [1905] A.C. 239; (2) The commercial or other best interests of the interferer or the contract breaker: *Read v Friendly Society of Operative Stonemasons* [1902] 2 K.B. 88, 732, the *Glamorgan* case [1905] A.C. 239, *Pratt v British Medical Association* [1919] 1 K.B. 244, and *De Jetley Marks v Lord Greenwood* [1936] 1 All E.R. 863; (3) The fact that A has broken his contract with X does not of itself justify X in revenge procuring a breach of an independent contract between A and B: *Smithies v National Association of Operative Plasterers* [1909] 1 K.B. 310 at 337.

On the other side of the line justification has been said to exist where (1) there is a moral duty to intervene, as for example in *Brimelow v Casson* [1924] 1 Ch. 302, where it was held that the defendants were justified in their actions since they owed a duty to their calling and its members to take all necessary steps to compel the plaintiff to pay his chorus girls a living wage so that they were not driven to supplement their earnings through prostitution, (2) where the contract interfered with is inconsistent with a previous contract with the interferer: see *per* Buckley L.J. in *Smithies*'s case [1909] 1 K.B. 310 at 337:

> "No doubt there are circumstances in which A is entitled to induce B to break a contract entered into by B with C. Thus, for instance, if the contract between B and C is one which B could not make consistently with his preceding contractual obligations towards A, A may not only induce him to break it, but may invoke the assistance of a Court of Justice to make him break it. If B having agreed to sell a property to A subsequently agrees to sell it to C, A of course may restrain B by injunction from carrying out B's contract with C, and the consequence may ensue that B will be liable to C in damages for breaking it."

Counsel for the plaintiffs submits that although the judge posed the correct test, namely whether the defendants had an equal or superior right to that of the plaintiffs, he reached the wrong conclusion in law, because he confused the defendants' commercial interests with the required legal right sustainable under the civil law deriving from their contract. He accepted that if the defendants had exercised their rights under the legal charge, such exercise might have had the effect of interfering with the plaintiff's contract and had that been the case the defendants would have been justified. For example, if they had called in the loan and exercised their power of sale, this would have had the inevitable consequence of putting an end to the plaintiff's contract; but such action would have been justified. But, he submits, if for their own commercial advantage they elect not to exercise any of their legal rights but instead adopt a course of conduct which intentionally interferes with the plaintiffs' contract, they are not justified and must pay.

The submission of counsel for the plaintiffs to us is to the effect that the words "sufficient justification for interference with plaintiff's right must be an equal or superior right in themselves" must be confined to the exercise of that right by the defendant. But I can find no warrant for this proposition and in my judgment it confuses right with the remedies available to protect the right.

Why, it may be asked, should the defendants be justified in interfering with the plaintiffs' contract if they exercise their power of sale as mortgagee in possession, but not if by agreement they permit the mortgagor to conduct the sale in the hope of achieving a better deal for both? Why should they be justified if they appoint a receiver, who has power to build-out the development and appoint architects, but not if they agree to finance the mortgagor to perform this task? I cannot find any logical answer to these questions.

Moreover, I think it would be undesirable if the law were to insist that a mortgagee in such a position should exercise his strict legal rights if he is to be justified in interference with contracts between the mortgagor and third parties, and could not be justified if he reached some sensible and reasonable accommodation which may be to the benefit of both himself and the mortgagor, but which has the same effect on the third parties' contract. The accommodation is designed to protect or defend the mortgagee's equal or superior right as a secured creditor, who had in this case financed the entire purchase and development of the site so far. And the accommodation was reached against the background of the remedy of sale or the appointment of a receiver. There can be no doubt that these rights existed once a formal demand for payment was made, a demand which could not have been met.

Justification for interference with the plaintiff's contractual right based on an equal or superior right in the defendant must clearly be a legal right. Such right may derive from property real or personal or from contractual rights. Property rights may simply involve the use and enjoyment of land or personal property. To give an example put in argument by Sir Nicolas Browne-

Wilkinson V.-C., if X carries on building operations on his land, they may to the knowledge of X interfere with a contract between A and B to carry out recording work on adjoining land occupied by A. But, unless X's activity amounts to a nuisance, he is justified in doing what he did. Alternatively, the law may grant legal remedies to the owner of property to act in defence or protection of his property; if in the exercise of these remedies he interferes with a contract between A and B of which he knows, he will be justified. If instead of exercising those remedies he reaches an accommodation with A, which has a similar effect of interfering with A's contract with B, he is still justified notwithstanding that the accommodation may be to the commercial advantage of himself or A or both. The position is the same if the defendant's right is to a contractual as opposed to a property right, provided it is equal or superior to the plaintiff's rights. In my judgment that is the position in this case; I therefore agree with the judge's conclusion and would dismiss the appeal.

In these circumstances it is not necessary to deal with the cross-appeal on the issue of intent. But, since I have reached a clear conclusion on this matter, in deference to counsel's argument I propose to state it shortly. The submission of counsel for the defendants was that the necessary intention to interfere with the plaintiff's contract is not established unless the defendant's conduct is aimed at the plaintiff and there is a desire to injure him. In support of this proposition he relied on the dictum of Evershed M.R. in *DC Thomson & Co Ltd v Deakin* [1952] Ch. 646 at 676–677.

I cannot accept this submission. It plays no part in the formulation of the tort propounded by Jenkins or Morris L.JJ. Jenkins L.J.'s statement of the tort was indorsed by the House of Lords in *Merkur Island Shipping Corp. v Laughton* (above, p.607). Moreover it seems to me to be directly contrary to the binding authority of the Court of Appeal in *Smithies v National Association of Operative Plasterers* [1909] 1 K.B. 310 at 316, where there was an express finding of fact that the defendants did not intend to injure the plaintiff or the dismissed workman Gibbs; yet nevertheless the claim succeeded.

Notes:

1. Stuart-Smith L.J.'s final remarks on this last requirement were quoted in an important case which shows that this tort has got entirely out of control. In *Millar v Bassey* [1994] E.M.L.R. 44 the famous singer had contracted with Dreampace to make a recording and the plaintiff had contracted with Dreampace to provide the requisite technical and musical back-up. All the arrangements were made, the hi-fi boys and the musicians were ready and willing, but the slim lady refused to sing, thereby putting Dreampace in breach of its contract with the plaintiffs.

The trial judge struck out the claim for want of an allegation that Miss Bassey's actions were directed against the plaintiffs: "It would not be enough to show at trial that [Miss Bassey] had broken her contract with [Dreampace] and that the natural consequence was that [Dreampace] broke its contract with the plaintiffs. The plaintiffs would have to show that [Miss Bassey's] act . . . was directed against them." The Court of Appeal by a majority reversed this decision and allowed the case to go to trial. Peter Gibson L.J., dissenting, identified the issue as being "Must the conduct of the defendant . . . be aimed directly at the plaintiff, the contracting party who suffers damage, in the sense that the defendant intends that the plaintiff's contract should be broken, or is it sufficient that the conduct should have the natural and probable consequence that the plaintiff's contract be broken?"

Now it must be noted that Miss Bassey did not persuade Dreampace to dismiss the musicians. All she did was to refuse to sing. There could really be no question of liability under *Lumley v Gye*, even after *Thomson v Deakin* had so unfortunately extended it (before the tort of intentionally causing loss by wrongful means was recognised): Jenkins L.J. himself would not have held Bowater's drivers liable for refusing to deliver to Thomson. Accordingly, the only tort for which Miss Bassey could possibly have been held liable is the tort of intentionally causing loss by wrongful means, and for such liability two matters have to be established, one of law and one of fact: (1) that a deliberate breach of contract (as opposed to the threat or inducement of one) constitutes wrongful means for this purpose, a matter rather controverted, and (2) that the defendant was aiming at the plaintiff. Where the defendant has actually persuaded a contractor not to perform, this last requirement need not be emphasised, since in such a case the victim is bound to be in the defendant's sights, even if only to obtain from him some advantage the defendant wished to get for himself, but once the tort is expanded into merely causing a breach of contract or interfering with one, it really must be insisted upon, because then the tort is simply that of causing loss by wrongful means in disguise. That Miss Bassey should even arguably be liable to all the plaintiffs simply for failure to perform her contract with Dreampace is an astonishing result, which demands a radical rethinking of the steps which led to it.

2. The example given by the Vice-Chancellor in the principal case of building operations, not in themselves a nuisance, which disturb recording under contract on neighbouring premises is an instance not of *inducing* breach of contract (as *Lumley v Gye* was), but at most of causing breach, for which no liability should exist in the absence of unlawful means (when it is immaterial whether or not there was any contract, breached or not). It is probably, however, an instance of the false tort of "interference with contractual relations" (see *Merkur Island Shipping* case (above, p.612)). If tort liability is to be expanded to cover cases of causing breach and of interference without breach, two consequences follow: first, the defence of justification will have to be greatly extended, and secondly, unlike the case where the defendant had knowingly induced a breach, the defendant must be shown to have been aiming at the plaintiff.

This is not to say that there should not be a defence of justification even in the classic case of inducing a known breach by direct persuasion. It is an error to suppose that all contracts are equally binding: it depends very much what interests are involved. If only money is involved, well and good; but if human interests are at stake, it is different. For example, if a pregnant woman contracts to have a lawful abortion I certainly cannot be sued by the disappointed clinic if I persuade her to break her word and keep the baby.

3. Stuart-Smith L.J. at the end of his judgment discounts the requirement that the defendant's conduct be "aimed at" the plaintiff and actuated by "a desire to injure him". The latter element may not be requisite in the tort of causing harm by wrongful means, but the former certainly is. Were it not so, we would be back with *Beaudesert*, peremptorily disavowed in *Lonrho v Shell* (above, p.186), of which Deane J. said in *Northern Territory v Mengel* (1995) 69 A.J.L.R. 527 at 553, cited by Mullany, (1995) 111 L.Q.R. 586: "There is no compelling reason in principle or policy for denying the existence of a cause of action in circumstances where a defendant has intentionally done a positive act, in contravention of the customary criminal law or of some statutory prohibition, which has, as an inevitable consequence, caused loss or harm to the plaintiff", but it is not the law. In one case, however, "targeting" is not required: under section 235A of the Trade Union and Labour Relations (Consolidation) Act 1992, introduced by the Trade Union Reform and Employment Rights Act 1993, if any individual's supplies of goods or services, whether contracted for or not, are interrupted or delayed as the likely effect of any person's tortious inducement of another to participate in unlawful industrial action, he may go to court not to obtain damages, admittedly, only an order which will put a stop to the conduct incriminated.

4. The question identified at (1) in note 1 above arose in *The Kaliningrad* [1997] 2 Lloyd's Rep. 35. To simplify the facts slightly, D chartered his vessel to X who then agreed to subcharter it to P as from February 14, for at least one voyage to the U.S.A. and back. On February 13, the defendant, having learnt the identity of P, one of his competitors on that route, "withdrew" the vessel. This put X in breach of his contract with P. P sued D for inducing that breach. After citing Jenkins L.J. in *Thomson (D.C.) & Co Ltd v Deakin* (inevitably) Rix J. rather unhelpfully held that D's "tort was of the variety of direct persuasion, procurement or inducement or direct invasion of another's contractual rights . . . by refusing to deliver the vessel into the head charter, [D] made it impossible for [X] to provide the vessel down the chain of charterers and ultimately to [P], and so procured a breach of contract." This will not do. Since on the facts no one had been *persuaded* by anyone to break their contract, it was not a *Lumley v Gye* case at all, but since, unlike *Millar v Bassey*, D here was unquestionably aiming at P, the only question was whether the means he used to cause the harm, namely the deliberate breach of his own obligation to continue providing X with the vessel, was unlawful or not. This question went unanswered.

The judge did, however, say that if, contrary to his view, X had promised D not to subcharter to P, he would not have held D liable. On the correct analysis that this was a case of causing intentional loss by wrongful means, this is quite right: X's repudiation of his obligations to P would have entitled P to terminate his own obligation to let X continue using the vessel, and his withdrawal of it would not have been wrongful at all. On the false analysis that D was in principle liable under *Lumley v Gye*, D's exercise of his contractual right to withdraw the vessel would have to be seen as a justification in the sense of *Edwin Hill* above p.614.

5. The question left unanswered by Rix J. in *The Kaliningrad* was addressed by Rix L.J. in *Stocznia Gdanska v Latvian Shipping Co* [2002] EWCA Civ 859, [2002] Lloyd's Rep. 436. D had promised X to keep Y in funds, and Y had contracted to pay for ships to be built by the claimant. D refused to provide Y with the promised funds, with the aim of causing Y to breach its contract with the claimant and the aim also, if not the predominant aim, of causing harm to the claimant. The judge held that D had not *directly* induced Y to breach its contract with the claimant, but held that it had *indirectly* done so. The wrongful conduct required for "indirect inducement" was D's deliberate breach of its contract with X to keep Y in funds. "Where a defendant wrongly, that is to say, by unlawful means, withholds that which is necessary to another party to fulfil his contract with a claimant, and does so with the requisite knowledge of that contract and with the requisite intention, I do not see why the ingredients of the tort have not been fulfilled." Here the defendant "must by its own actions have intended to injure the [claimant]". This distinguished the case from *Millar v Bassey* (above, n.1), cited by the judge.

Questions

1. Suppose that, to Miss Bassey's knowledge, Dreampace had retained in addition to numerous electronic wizards one double-bassist, two drummers and fiddlers three, and that it was solely to deprive the aspiring bassist of his engagement that she refused to sing: would all the others be able to sue her, too?

2. In the principal case, did the defendant induce the breach of the developer's contract with the plaintiff or merely cause it to be broken? What would the position have been if the defendant had simply foreclosed?

LONRHO PLC v FAYED

Court of Appeal [1990] 2 Q.B. 479; [1989] 3 W.L.R. 631; [1989] 2 All E.R. 65; House of Lords, [1991] 3 W.L.R. 188; [1991] 3 All E.R. 303 (noted [1992] Camb.L.J. 15)

Action against successful competitor for boasting to umpire

Lonrho and Fayed both wanted to acquire Harrods, the well-known department store. Lonrho made the first bid, but the Minister referred that bid to the Monopolies and Mergers Commission and this stopped Lonrho from proceeding until the Commission reported back to the Minister. Fayed then made a bid, and would likewise have been prevented from pursuing it if the Minister had referred it to the Commission, but he did not do so because, according to Lonrho, he was deceived by Fayed and his advisers as to Fayed's commercial standing and backing. Fayed was thus enabled to acquire the store while Lonrho were still barred from bidding.

Lonrho sued Fayed's advisers in negligence (claiming that though they believed what they said, they ought to have known better). Pill J. struck out this completely hopeless claim ([1990] 1 Q.B. 490), and no appeal was brought against that. Lonrho also sued for interference with their trade by false statements made fraudulently by Fayed and recklessly by his advisers. In unreserved opinions here reported, the Court of Appeal reinstated that claim. The defendants' appeal to the House of Lords on this point was dismissed.

Dillon L.J.: . . . The third cause of action alleged in the statement of claim is the common law tort of wrongful interference with trade or business. The existence of such a tort is conceded by the defendants. Reference can be made to the speech of Lord Diplock in *Merkur Island Shipping Corp. v Laughton* [1983] 2 A.C. 570 at 609–610, where he said:

> "In anticipation of an argument that was addressed to your Lordships on the stage 3 point, I should mention that the evidence also establishes a prima facie case of the common law tort, of interfering with the trade or business of another person by doing unlawful acts. To fall within this genus of torts the unlawful act need not involve procuring another person to break a subsisting contract or to interfere with the performance of a subsisting contract. Where, however, the procuring of another person to break a subsisting contract is the unlawful act involved, this is but one species of the wider genus of tort."

There are also references to this tort in *JT Stratford & Son Ltd v Lindley* [1965] A.C. 269. Lord Reid said (at 324):

> "In addition to interfering with existing contracts the respondents' action made it practically impossible for the appellants to do any new business with the barge-hirers. It was not disputed that such interference with business is tortious, if any unlawful means are employed."

But, although those statements indicate that the tort is a recognised tort, they cannot be taken as comprehensive definitions of what constitutes that tort.

There are several what may be called established exceptions to the generality of those definitions. In particular, although it is not relevant on the facts of the present case, the speech of Lord Diplock in *Lonrho Ltd v Shell Petroleum Co Ltd* [1982] A.C. 173 at 187 establishes that the mere fact that a person has suffered injury in his business by an act of the defendant which is illegal in the sense of being in breach of a statutory prohibition does not automatically entitle the injured person to bring an action within this tort to recover damages for the injury. The complainant still has to show that on its true construction the statute which imposed the prohibition gave rise to a civil remedy. That has to be considered in the light of the principles examined in *Cutler v Wandsworth Stadium Ltd* [1949] A.C. 398. Furthermore, in *RCA Corp. v Pollard* [1983] Ch. 135 at 153 Oliver L.J. sets out cogently that the action does not lie where the damage complained of is merely economic damage as an incidental result of the breach of a prohibition in a statute not designed to protect the interests of a class to which the plaintiff belongs.

It is submitted to us that, even with this tort, it must have been the predominant purpose of the tortfeasor to injure the victim rather than to further the tortfeasor's own financial ends. I do not accept that . . . predominant purpose to injure is required where the tortious act relied on is injury by wrongful interference with a third party's contract with the victim or by intimidation of a third party to the detriment of the victim, nor should it in my view be required where the wrongful interference has been by the practice of fraud on a third party, aimed specifically at the plaintiff, as it was put by Oliver L.J. in *RCA Corp. v Pollard* at 151. . . .

It also has to be proved by a plaintiff who seeks to rely on this tort, as counsel conceded for Lonrho, that the unlawful act was in some sense directed against the plaintiff or intended to harm the plaintiff. The origin of those phrases is the oft-quoted passage in the speech of Lord Watson in *Allen v Flood* [1898] A.C. 1 at 96, which was applied by the majority of this court (Buckley and Kennedy L.JJ.) in *National Phonograph Co v Edison-Bell Consolidated Phonograph Co* [1908] 1 Ch. 335. In that case the fraud was clearly directed against the plaintiff. . . .

Here the existence of this tort is recognised, but the detailed limits of it have to be refined. I regard it as right and, indeed, essential that this should be done on the actual facts as they emerge at the trial rather than on a set of hypotheses, more or less wide, in very comprehensive pleadings. . . .

There are many other issues which fall to be investigated, which are also, in my judgment, matters for investigation at the trial, such as whether the business interest which Lonrho claims to have had and which it claims has been injured by the allegedly tortious acts is a sufficient business interest to support the tort which is alleged, and whether the nature of the damage which Lonrho claims to have suffered is damage properly recoverable for that tort in the particular circumstances of this case. I have no doubt at all that these are all matters which must be investigated at the trial of the action. I underline that this tort is still in the process of judicial definition. This is not, therefore, so far as this cause of action is concerned, a proper case for striking out.

Ralph Gibson L.J.: The tort of unlawful interference in business may still be described in our law as new. It is, of course, more familiar to us when the unlawful means used is intimidation or procuring the breach of or interference with a contract. It is not, I think, disputed by the defendants that if the unlawful means alleged in this case had been fraudulent misstatements made to the Secretary of State for Trade and Industry and denigrating the plaintiffs, Lonrho plc, the action might arguably fall within the definition of the tort, but it was contended that the use of fraudulent misstatements to the Secretary of State, which served only to improve the reputation and standing and the supposed assets of the Fayed brothers could not, as a matter of law, be held to have been directed against Lonrho.

It is submitted for the defendants that there was no sufficient pleading of sufficient intention in the defendants to ground any tort, even the tort of unlawful interference with business, and that an essential element of that specific tort must be that of predominant intention to injure the plaintiffs. There is no allegation of such predominant intention. It is a question of law whether proof of such an element is required. But for my part, and in agreement with Dillon L.J., I do not accept it. It is not a requirement, as I understand the cases, of the tort when the unlawful means employed is intimidation or procuring a breach of contract. I see no reason to introduce such a requirement where the unlawful means employed is fraudulent misrepresentation.

It was also contended that the unlawful means used to the Secretary of State must be itself demonstrably actionable as a complete cause; and that in this case that is not pleaded as an alleged fact, because it is not said that there was any financial loss suffered by the Secretary of State. For my part I do not accept that fraudulent misrepresentations used to a public official in the circumstances alleged in this case cease to be unlawful means for the purposes of the tort of unlawful interference with business because there is no identifiable financial loss caused in addition to the fact that a public official has been caused to do by the fraud what otherwise he would not have done, or not to do what otherwise he would have done. . . .

Woolf L.J.: . . . The tort relied on by Lonrho plc of unlawful interference is still, in my view, of uncertain ambit, albeit that its existence is now beyond doubt and certain of its features are clearly defined. This coupled with the fact that in this case fraud is pleaded and relied on by Lonrho are matters which have influenced me into coming to my conclusion that I agree that this appeal should be allowed for the reasons given.

That said, I should make it clear that I have two reservations. My first reservation is whether the fraudulent misrepresentations relied on by Lonrho are sufficiently direct to be capable of amounting to the interference with the plaintiff's business which is needed for the purposes of the tort. I say this for two reasons: (1) the fraud relied on consisted of alleged misrepresentations as to the qualities of the Fayed brothers and not as to the shortcomings of Lonrho; (2) it is not suggested that the misrepresentations caused the Secretary of State for Trade and Industry to take any action or to desist from any action as against Lonrho. Instead it is alleged that the Secretary of State was influenced not to take action against the Fayeds.

My second reservation is whether the business asset which Lonrho alleges has been damaged is in fact capable of being a business interest for the purpose of a tort of unlawful interference. The business asset identified in para.16(1) of the statement of claim is Lonrho's desire to exploit an opportunity to acquire House of Fraser plc by bidding for shares in the company without "competition" from the Fayeds. Whether or not particular conduct is capable of amounting to interference and what is or is not capable of being a business asset which is protected by the tort is very much a question of fact and degree subject to parameters which are in the process of being settled by the courts as a matter of law. . . .

[In dismissing Fayed's appeal from this decision the House of Lords also reinstated the plaintiff's claim for conspiracy which had been struck out below in deference to the supposed view of the House of Lords in *Lonrho v Shell* [1982] A.C. 173 that even where unlawful means were used there could be no liability in conspiracy unless the conspirators were principally actuated by a desire to harm the plaintiff rather than to advantage themselves.]

Lord Bridge said: " . . . Where conspirators act with the predominant purpose of injuring the plaintiff and in fact inflict damage on him, but do nothing which would have been actionable if done by an individual acting alone, it is in the fact of their concerted action for that illegitimate purpose that the law, however anomalous it may now seem, finds a sufficient ground to condemn their action as illegal and tortious. But when conspirators intentionally injure the plaintiff and use unlawful means to do so, it is no defence for them to show that their primary purpose was to further or protect their own interests; it is sufficient to make their action tortious that the means used were unlawful."

Notes:

1. Once again we have a defendant telling lies, conduct clearly wrongful, and a holding, as regards the tort of deliberately causing loss by wrongful means, that the defendant need not be shown to have intended primarily to hurt the plaintiff who was in his sights. Now it is perfectly true that in deceit, that is, where the defendant tells lies directly to the plaintiff (rather than as here, to a third party), it need not be shown that the defendant intended to cause any harm to the plaintiff—"it is wholly immaterial with what object the lie is told" (Bowen L.J. in *Edgington v Fitzmaurice* (above, p.575)—only that the plaintiff should react in a certain way. But in such a case there is no problem of identifying the plaintiff—he is the person the defendant

is actually addressing. Likewise in the other cases instanced by Dillon L.J., namely intimidation and inducing breach of contract, to which one can add malicious falsehood: there again there is no problem in identifying the plaintiff, for in the first case the defendant is saying "Sack the plaintiff, or else . . . ", in the second (properly understood) the plaintiff is the (only) person entitled to the benefit of which the defendant is seeking to deprive him, and in malicious falsehood the plaintiff is the person about whom the defendant is telling lies. The identification of the plaintiff in all these cases is inherent in the structure. In the genus tort of wrongfully causing loss, however, the identification of the plaintiff is indeed a problem, and it can be done only by referring to the harmful intention of the defendant.

2. Apart from lies, what else is "wrongful means" for the purpose of this tort? In *Minister of Transport v Williams* [1993] Times L.R. 627 the defendants were wilfully obstructing the extension of the M3 motorway and so guilty of an offence under the Highways Act 1980, s.303. As they were doubtless aiming at the Department of Transport and seeking to cause it trouble and consequent expense, an injunction was issued against them (as it could not have been for mere offence in itself) on the ground that they were proposing to continue committing the tort of intentionally causing him loss by unlawful means. Dillon L.J. said that "anything which was illegal under any statute provided the unlawful means".

3. *Conspiracy.* Lord Bridge describes it as "anomalous" that A and B should be liable if they conspire together to harm C (rather than to advantage themselves) whereas neither would be liable if he acted on his own. Yet in the *Mogul* case (above, p.593) Bowen L.J. said: "The distinction is based on sound reason, for a combination may make oppressive or dangerous that which if it proceeded only from a single person would be otherwise" and Lord Lindley said: "Laws adapted to individuals not acting in concert with others require modification and extension if they are to be applied with effect to large bodies of persons acting in concert. The English law of conspiracy is based upon and is justified by this undeniable truth." (*South Wales Miners Federation v Glamorgan Coal Co* [1905] A.C. 239 at 252). In his speech in *Lonrho v Shell* [1982] A.C. 173 (disavowed on the main point by *Lonrho v Fayed*), Lord Diplock sought to trash Bowen L.J.'s observation by noting that nowadays some individual firms are very big and powerful, quite as big and powerful as a lot of small firms banding together. But did Bowen L.J. suggest that two pygmies were bigger than one giant or one pygmy? Would McGregor Gow by itself have been able to ruin the Mogul Steamship Co? Would the threat to withdraw the labour of one draughtsman have swayed B.O.A.C. and made it fire Rookes? Why is a boycott effective? Has it ceased to be so? What is a lynch mob? Does the principle of "two against one isn't fair" depend on the size of the one? Was it absurd of the EC Treaty to distinguish between agreements between two or more firms and abuse by one (Arts 81 and 82), as indeed does our Competition Act 1998 (ss.2 and 18)?

4. Conspiracy was alleged in *Yukong Line v Rendsburg Corp. (No.2)* [1998] 4 All E.R. 82 where the plaintiff was a creditor of a company and in order to frustrate his claim the defendants removed the company's funds from the jurisdiction. This removal—in their own interests—was in conscious breach of the fiduciary duty owed by one of them to the company. Toulson J. held that in an unlawful act conspiracy the unlawful act must be actionable by the victim and that was not the case here, since the plaintiff could not found on breach of a fiduciary duty owed not to him but only to the company. In *Lonrho v Fayed*, by contrast, he noted that the unlawful act—lying to the Minister—was individually actionable.

5. After reading this chapter, do you agree with the remark of Lord Templeman ([1991] 3 All E.R. 303 at 314) that "the ambit and ingredients of the torts of conspiracy and unlawful interference may hereafter require further analysis and reconsideration by the courts"? How would you redefine them, consistently with maintaining the proper degree of freedom of action in business affairs?

Chapter 16

ABUSE OF PUBLIC AND CIVIL POWERS

THREE RIVERS DISTRICT COUNCIL v BANK OF ENGLAND

House of Lords, [2001] UKHL 16, [2003] 2 A.C. 1, [2001] 2 All E.R. 513

Suit by 6,019 depositors who lost their money in the collapse of the Bank of Credit and Commerce International against the Bank of England for misuse of its regulatory powers in authorising BCCI to accept deposits and for failing to close it down sooner than it did

This extract sets out the requirements of the tort of misfeasance in public office, the sole basis of the complaint after the ruling that the depositors acquired no rights under the Community Directive. In a subsequent hearing the House, by a bare majority, decided that the case should proceed to trial, and reversed the decision of the courts below to strike out the claim.

Lord Steyn: The tort of misfeasance in public office is traceable to the 17th century: *Turner v Sterling* (1671) 2 Vent 25. But the first solid basis for this new head of tort liability, based on an action on the case, is to be found in *Ashby v White* (1703), best reported in 1 Smith's LC (13th ed.) 253. The view ultimately prevailed that an action would lie by an elector who was wilfully denied a right to vote by a returning officer. Despite the recognition of the tort in a number of cases in the 18th and 19th centuries, the Court of Appeal in 1907 denied the existence of the tort in *Davis v Bromley Corpn* [1908] 1 K.B. 170. But by 1981 the Privy Council described the tort as "well established": *Dunlop v Woollahra Municipal Council* [1982] A.C. 158, 172f. An examination of the ingredients of the tort was still required. The first step towards that goal was the judgments in the Court of Appeal in *Bourgoin SA v Ministry of Agriculture, Fisheries and Food* [1986] Q.B. 716. The present case is the first occasion on which the House has been called on to review the requirements of the tort in a comprehensive manner.

The rationale of the tort is that in a legal system based on the rule of law executive or administrative power "may be exercised only for the public good" and not for ulterior and improper purposes: *Jones v Swansea City Council* [1990] 1 W.L.R. 54, 85f, *per* Nourse L.J.

It is now possible to consider the ingredients of the tort. That can conveniently be done by stating the requirements of the tort in a logical sequence of numbered paragraphs.

(1) *The defendant must be a public officer.* It is the office in a relatively wide sense on which everything depends. Thus a local authority exercising private-law functions as a landlord is potentially capable of being sued: *Jones v Swansea City Council* [1990] 1 W.L.R. 54. In the present case it is common ground that the Bank satisfies this requirement.

(2) The second requirement is the *exercise of power as a public officer.* This ingredient is also not in issue. The conduct of the named senior officials of the Banking Supervision Department of the Bank was in the exercise of public functions. Moreover, it is not disputed that the principles of vicarious liability apply as much to misfeasance in public office as to other torts involving malice, knowledge or intention: *Racz v Home Office* [1994] 2 A.C. 45.

(3) The third requirement concerns the *state of mind of the defendant.* The case law reveals two different forms of liability for misfeasance in public office. First there is the case of targeted malice by a public officer, *i.e.* conduct specifically intended to injure a person or persons. This type of case involves bad faith in the sense of the exercise of public power for an improper or

ulterior motive. The second form is where a public officer acts knowing that he has no power to do the act complained of and that the act will probably injure the plaintiff. It involves bad faith inasmuch as the public officer does not have an honest belief that his act is lawful.

In the most important modern case in England the existence of the two forms of the tort was analysed and affirmed: *Bourgoin SA v Ministry of Agriculture, Fisheries and Food* [1986] Q.B. 716. The present case is not one of targeted malice. If the action in tort is maintainable it must be in the second form of the tort. It is therefore necessary to consider the distinctive features of this form of the tort. The remainder of my judgment will be directed to this form of the tort.

The basis for the action lies in the defendant taking a decision in the knowledge that it is an excess of the powers granted to him and that it is likely to cause damage to an individual or individuals. It is not every act beyond the powers vesting in a public officer which will ground the tort. The alternative form of liability requires an element of bad faith. This leads to what was a disputed issue. Counsel for the Bank pointed out that there was no precedent in England before the present case which held recklessness to be a sufficient state of mind to ground the tort. Counsel argued that recklessness was insufficient. Clarke J. lucidly explained the reason for the inclusion of recklessness [1996] 3 All E.R. 558, 581: "The reason why recklessness was regarded as sufficient by all members of the High Court in *Northern Territory v Mengel*, 69 A.L.J.R. 527 is perhaps most clearly seen in the judgment of Brennan J. It is that misfeasance consists in the purported exercise of a power otherwise than in an honest attempt to perform the relevant duty. It is that lack of honesty which makes the act an abuse of power."

The Court of Appeal accepted the correctness of this statement of principle. This is an organic development, which fits into the structure of our law governing intentional torts. The policy underlying it is sound: reckless indifference to consequences is as blameworthy as deliberately seeking such consequences. It can therefore now be regarded as settled law that an act performed in reckless indifference as to the outcome is sufficient to ground the tort in its second form.

Initially, counsel for the plaintiffs argued that in this context recklessness is used in an objective sense. But, understandably, the argument became more refined during the oral hearing and counsel for the plaintiffs accepted that only reckless indifference in a subjective sense will be sufficient. This concession was rightly made. The plaintiff must prove that the public officer acted with a state of mind of reckless indifference to the illegality of his act.

(4) *Duty to the plaintiff.* The question is who can sue in respect of an abuse of power by a public officer. Counsel for the Bank argued that in order to be able to claim in respect of the second form of misfeasance, there must be established "an antecedent legal right or interest" and an element of "proximity". Clarke J. did not enunciate a requirement of proximity. He observed [1996] 3 All E.R. 558, 584: "If an officer deliberately does an act which he knows is unlawful and will cause economic loss to the plaintiff, I can see no reason in principle why the plaintiff should identify a legal right which is being infringed or a particular duty owed to him, beyond the right not to be damaged or injured by a deliberate abuse of power by a public officer."

The majority in the Court of Appeal held that "the notion of proximity should have a significant part to play in the tort misfeasance, as it undoubtedly has in the tort of negligence." Counsel for the Bank argued that both requirements are essential in order to prevent the tort from becoming an uncontrollable one. It would be unwise to make general statements on a subject which may involve many diverse situations. What can be said is that, of course, any plaintiff must have a sufficient interest to found a legal standing to sue. Subject to this qualification, principle does not require the introduction of proximity as a controlling mechanism in this corner of the law. The state of mind required to establish the tort, as already explained, as well as the special rule of remoteness hereafter discussed, keeps the tort within reasonable bounds. There is no reason why such an action cannot be brought by a particular class of persons, such as depositors at a bank, even if their precise identities were not known to the bank. The observations of Clarke J. are correct.

In agreed issue 4 the question is raised whether the Bank is capable of being liable for the tort of misfeasance in public office to plaintiffs who were potentially depositors at the time of any relevant act or omission of misfeasance by the Bank. The majority in the Court of Appeal and Auld L.J. held that this issue is unsuitable for summary determination. In my view this ruling was correct.

(5) *Causation.* Causation is an essential element of the plaintiffs' cause of action. It is a question of fact. The majority in the Court of Appeal and Auld L.J. held that it is unsuitable for summary determination. That is plainly correct.

(6) *Damage and remoteness.* The claims by the plaintiffs are in respect of financial losses they suffered. These are, of course, claims for recovery of consequential economic losses. The question is when such losses are recoverable. On the assumption that the other requirements can be established, counsel for the plaintiffs argued that the plaintiffs should be able to recover all reasonably foreseeable losses suffered by them. Counsel for the Bank argued that the rule is more restrictive. He supported the conclusion of the majority in the Court of Appeal. The judge had held that the plaintiffs must prove that the Bank actually foresaw the losses to the plaintiffs as a probable consequence. This part of the judgment at first instance provided the reason for the judge refusing to allow the proposed amendments and striking out the claims. The majority observed that the "formulation, however, may have been too favourable to the plaintiffs. In view of the stringent requirements of the tort of misfeasance in public office, the more appropriate question may be: 'Is it reasonably arguable that the Bank at any stage made an unlawful and dishonest decision knowing at the time that it would cause loss to the plaintiffs?' To that question, in the light of our analysis of the evidence, the answer is plainly 'No'."

Counsel for the Bank adopted this formulation as his primary submission. In the alternative he submitted that the test stated by Clarke J. should be adopted.

Taking into account all the matters advanced the choice before the House can be narrowed down. So far as the majority was minded to adopt a stricter test that Clarke J., encapsulated in the words "knowing at the time that [the decision] would cause damage to the plaintiffs", they went too far. A test of knowledge or foresight that a decision would cause damage does not readily fit into the standard of proof generally required in the law of tort, and specifically in the case of intentional torts. Moreover, this test unnecessarily emasculates the effectiveness of the tort. The real choice is therefore between the test of knowledge that the decision would probably damage the plaintiff (as enunciated by Clarke J.) and the test of reasonable foreseeability (as contended for by counsel for the plaintiffs).

It is true that Clarke J. made new law. He relied on the special nature of the tort. He reasoned from legal principle. But apart from the *Mengel* case there has however been no judicial support for a foreseeability test. And there has been no academic criticism of the view of Clarke J. that a test of foreseeability is not enough in this tort. Given that his ground-breaking first instance judgment has been pored over by many judicial and academic eyes, this is a factor of some significance. Nevertheless, it is necessary to consider the merits of the competing solutions from the point of view of principle and legal policy.

Enough has been said to demonstrate the special nature of the tort, and the strict requirements governing it. This is a legally sound justification for adopting as a starting point that in both forms of the tort the intent required must be directed at the harm complained of, or at least to harm of the type suffered by the plaintiffs. This results in the rule that a plaintiff must establish not only that the defendant acted in the knowledge that the act was beyond his powers but also in the knowledge that his act would probably injure the plaintiff or person of a class of which the plaintiff was a member. In presenting a sustained argument for a rule allowing recovery of all foreseeable losses counsel for the plaintiffs argued that such a more liberal rule is necessary in a democracy as a constraint upon abuse of executive and administrative power. The force of this argument is, however, substantially reduced by the recognition that subjective recklessness on the part of a public officer in acting in excess of his powers is sufficient. Recklessness about the consequences of his act, in the sense of not caring whether the consequences happen or not, is therefore sufficient in law. This justifies the conclusion that the test adopted by Clarke J. represents a satisfactory balance between the two competing policy considerations, namely enlisting tort law to combat executive and administrative abuse of power and not allowing public officers, who must always act for the public good, to be assailed by unmeritorious actions.

Lord Millett: ... I have had the advantage of reading in draft the speeches of my noble and learned friends, Lord Steyn and Lord Hutton, with which I am in full agreement. It may, however, be helpful if I set out in my own words what I consider to be the elements of the tort of misfeasance in public office.

The tort is an intentional tort which can be committed only by a public official. From this two things follow. First, the tort cannot be committed negligently or inadvertently. Secondly, the core concept is abuse of power. This in turn involves other concepts, such as dishonesty, bad faith, and improper purpose. These expressions are often used interchangeably; in some contexts one will be more appropriate, in other contexts another. They are all subjective states of mind.

It is important to bear in mind that excess of power is not the same as abuse of power. Nor is breach of duty the same as abuse of power. The two must be kept distinct if the tort is to be kept separate from breach of statutory duty, which does not necessarily found a cause of action. Even a deliberate excess of power is not necessarily an abuse of power. Just as a deliberate breach of trust is not dishonest if it is committed by the trustee in good faith and in the honest belief that it is for the benefit of those in whose interests he is bound to act, so a conscious excess of official power is not necessarily dishonest. The analogy is closer than may appear because many of the old cases emphasise that the tort is concerned with the abuse of a power granted for the benefit of and therefore held in trust for the general public.

The tort is generally regarded as having two limbs. The first limb, traditionally described as "targeted malice", covers the case where the official acts with intent to harm the plaintiff or a class of which the plaintiff is a member. The second is said to cover the case where the official acts without such intention but in the knowledge that his conduct will harm the plaintiff or such a class. I do not agree with this formulation. In my view the two limbs are merely different ways in which the necessary element of intention is established. In the first limb it is established by evidence; in the second by inference.

The rationale underlying the first limb is straightforward. Every power granted to a public official is granted for a public purpose. For him to exercise it for his own private purposes, whether out of spite, malice, revenge, or merely self-advancement, is an abuse of the power. It is immaterial in such a case whether the official exceeds his powers or acts according to the letter of the power: see *Jones v Swansea City Council* [1990] 1 W.L.R. 1453. His deliberate use of the power of his office to injure the plaintiff takes his conduct outside the power, constitutes an abuse of the power, and satisfies any possible requirements of proximity and causation.

The rationale of the second limb is not so transparent. The element of knowledge which it involves is, in my opinion, a means of establishing the necessary intention, not a substitute for it. But intention does not have to be proved by positive evidence. It can be inferred. Proof that the official concerned knew that he had no power to act as he did and that his conduct would injure the plaintiff is only the first step in establishing the tort. But it may and will usually be enough for the necessary intention, and therefore of the requisite state of mind, to be inferred. The question is: why did the official act as he did if he knew or suspected that he had no power to do so and that his conduct would injure the plaintiff? As Oliver L.J. said in *Bourgoin SA v Ministry of Agriculture, Fisheries and Food* [1986] Q.B. 716, 777: "If an act is done deliberately and with knowledge of its consequences, I do not think that the actor can sensibly say that he did not 'intend' the consequences or that the act was not 'aimed' at the person who, it is known, will suffer loss."

As that case demonstrates, the inference cannot be rebutted by showing that the official acted not for his own personal purposes but for the benefit of other members of the public. An official must not knowingly exceed his powers in order to promote some public benefit at the expense of the plaintiff.

It will be seen from this that the real difference between the two limbs lies in the starting point. If the plaintiff can establish the official's subjective intention to exercise the power of his office in order to cause him injury, he does not need to establish that the official exceeded the terms of the powers conferred upon him. If, on the other hand, the plaintiff can establish that the official appreciated that he was acting in excess of the powers conferred upon him and that his conduct would cause injury to the plaintiff, the inference that he acted dishonestly or for an improper purpose will be exceedingly difficult and usually impossible to rebut. Moreover, as Blanchard J. pointed out in *Garrett v Attorney General* [1997] 2 N.Z.L.R. 332, 350, the consequences of his actions will usually be obvious enough to the official concerned, who can then be taken to have intended the damage he caused. I also agree with him that intention includes subjective recklessness, that is to say (to adopt his words at p 349) a "conscious disregard for the interests of those who will be affected by" the exercise of the power.

It is not, of course, necessary that the official should foresee that his conduct will certainly harm the plaintiff. Nothing in life is certain. Equally, however, I do not think that it is sufficient that he should foresee that it will probably do so. The principle in play is that a man is presumed to intend the natural and probable consequences of his actions. This is the test laid down by Mason C.J. writing for the majority of the High Court of Australia and Brennan J. in *Northern Territory v Mengel* 69 A.L.J.R. 527, *viz.* that it should be calculated (in the sense of likely) in the ordinary course of events to cause injury. But the inference cannot be drawn unless the official did foresee the consequences. It is not enough that he ought to have foreseen them if he did not do so in fact.

In the present case most (and perhaps all) of the complaints made by the plaintiffs are of the Bank's failure to act. Even their complaint that the Bank of England ought not to have granted BCCI initial authorisation is essentially a complaint that officials of the Bank failed to exercise an independent judgment and to apply the relevant criteria.

The parties are agreed that there is no conceptual difference between sins of omission and sins of commission. This may be so; but factually there is a great difference between them. It is no accident that the tort is misfeasance in public office, not nonfeasance in public office. The failure to exercise a power is not in itself wrongful. It cannot be equated with acting in excess of power. The tort is concerned with preventing public officials from acting beyond their powers to the injury of the citizen, not with compelling them to exercise the powers they do have, particularly when they have a discretion whether to exercise them or not. ...

In conformity with the character of the tort, the failure to act must be deliberate, not negligent or inadvertent or arising from a misunderstanding of the legal position. In my opinion, a failure to act can amount to misfeasance in public office only where (i) the circumstances are such that the discretion whether to act can only be exercised in one way so that there is effectively a duty to act; (ii) the official appreciates this but nevertheless makes a conscious decision not to act; and (iii) he does so with intent to injure the plaintiff or in the knowledge that such injury will be the natural and probable consequence of his failure to act.

Although we heard argument directed to the requirement of proximity and in particular the suggested need for the plaintiff to establish "an antecedent legal interest" or, as I would prefer to put it, "a legally protected interest", I cannot see that this presents a problem in the present case. The statutory powers in question were conferred on the Bank of England for the protection of actual and potential depositors, and any member of either class can satisfy the requirement.

Note:

Delroy Denton, an immigrant with a record of appalling violent crime in Jamaica, was allowed to remain in the country owing to the misconduct of an immigration officer, one Brian Fotheringham, who, in cahoots with Scotland Yard, arranged for Denton to stay in the country as a police informer; the police helped out by seeing to it that he was not properly tried and sentenced for the crimes for which he was arrested here during the delay in removal organised by Fotheringham. Eventually Denton killed Zena Laws by stabbing her after assaulting her sexually. This suit against the Home Office and the police was brought by her representatives.

Simon Brown L.J. said this: "To commit the tort of misfeasance in a public office otherwise than by way of targeted malice, the tortfeasor must be proved to have acted with subjective reckless indifference both to the illegality of his act and as to the probability that harm will result from it. The critical question arising before us is whether the claimant must prove too that it was him or a particular class of which he was a member who would probably be harmed, or whether it is sufficient to prove merely that someone would probably be harmed and in the event it was him?" The Court of Appeal decided that proximity was not required. "As for the defendants' argument that it would be very strange if the claim could proceed on the basis of misfeasance in public office (which requires that the harm should be foreseen) in circumstances where it would fail in negligence (which only requires that the harm should be reasonably foreseeable), I see nothing strange in this at all: a claim in misfeasance postulates that the claimant can prove altogether more blameworthy conduct than in a negligence action; it is unsurprising that the law should decline to impose a further limiting requirement akin to proximity." *Akenzua v Secretary of State* [2002] EWCA Civ 1470, [2003] 1 All E.R. 35.

SUTTON v JOHNSTONE

Exchequer Chamber (1785) 1 Term Rep. 544; 99 E.R. 1243

Action by naval captain against commodore who had him court-martialled

The defendant was a commodore of the British fleet, engaged in warfare with the French in the West Indies. After one engagement, he ordered the captains of his ships to slip their cables and pursue a squadron of the French. The plaintiff, one of those captains, failed to do so, because his top-mast was damaged. The defendant had the plaintiff imprisoned for two years, and court-martialled for delaying the public service and for disobeying orders.

At trials at Guildhall, the plaintiff had a verdict for £5,000 on the first occasion and £6,000 on the second. The defendant moved in arrest of judgment, but the Court of Exchequer discharged the rule (1785) 1 Term Rep. 501; 99 E.R. 1220. The defendant brought error to the Exchequer Chamber and succeeded. The plaintiff brought error to the House of Lords, and the decision of the Court of Exchequer Chamber was affirmed (1787) 1 Term Rep. 784; 99 E.R. 1377.

Lord Mansfield C.J. and Lord Loughborough C.J.: . . . There is no similitude or analogy between an action of trespass, or false imprisonment, and this kind of action. An action of trespass is for the defendant's having done that, which, upon the stating of it, is manifestly illegal. This kind of action is for a prosecution, which, upon the stating of it, is manifestly legal. The essential ground of this action is, that a legal prosecution was carried on without a probable cause. We say this is emphatically the essential ground; because every other allegation may be implied from this; but this must be substantively and expressly proved, and cannot be implied. From the want of probable cause, malice may be, and most commonly is, implied. The knowledge of the defendant is also implied. From the most express malice, the want of probable cause cannot be implied.

A man, from a malicious motive, may take up a prosecution for real guilt, or he may, from circumstances which he really believes, proceed upon apparent guilt; and in neither case is he liable to this kind of action.

The question of probable cause is a mixed proposition of law and fact. Whether the circumstances alleged to show it probable, or not probable, are true and existed, is a matter of fact; but whether, supposing them true, they amount to a probable cause, is a question of law . . .

We have no difficulty to give our opinion, that, in law, the commodore had a probable cause to bring the plaintiff to a fair and impartial trial . . . The person unjustly accused is not without his remedy . . . Reparation is done to him by an acquittal.

Notes:

1. Damages for malicious prosecution tend to be much higher than those for wrongful arrest. This is because the arrest ends when the suspect is brought to court, as he soon is or should be: if he is remanded in custody, even if the constable so wishes and requests, subsequent confinement is the act of the court, not the constable. The malicious prosecutor, however, is liable for the whole period of confinement until the case is dropped or there is an acquittal or the reversal of a conviction.

2. In *Martin v Watson* ([1995] 3 All E.R. 559, noted [1996] Camb.L.J. 8) the defendant told the police that the plaintiff had exposed himself to her over the garden fence. This was a deliberate lie. When the plaintiff was prosecuted, the Crown Prosecution Service offered no evidence and the case against him was dismissed.

Judge Goodman gave judgment for the plaintiff for £3,500, which the House of Lords reinstated after the Court of Appeal by a majority had allowed the defendant's appeal on the ground that she could not be liable for malicious prosecution since she was not technically the prosecutor. In the Court of Appeal McCowan L.J., dissenting, said: " . . . this was plainly not a case where the complainant simply laid the facts before the police officer for him to take such action as he thought fit. Indeed, she did not lay the facts before him at all: she laid lies. She actively misled the police into taking criminal proceedings against the plaintiff by a series of false allegations . . . There was no evidence against him other than hers." ([1994] 2 All E.R. 606 at 627).

3. One might see this as a case where the defendant, in order to cause harm to the plaintiff, had told lies to a third party, just as in *Lonrho v Fayed* (above, p.619). In the same way it is a tort maliciously to procure the issuance of a search warrant (*Gibbs v Rea* [1998] A.C. 786). But once a prosecution is on foot and the third party is a judge, there is a problem, for whatever the Ten Commandments may say about not bearing false witness (and, like adultery, it would not be forbidden were it not widely practised!), you are not liable in English law for telling lies about your enemy in court. That is why there is no liability for maliciously opposing bail (*Gizziano v Chief Constable* [1998] Times L.R. 264): the prosecution has begun.

4. "The essential feature of malicious prosecution is an abuse of the process of the court. If that has occurred it is immaterial that the abuse has involved giving evidence in a court of law." (*per* Lord Keith, [1995] 3 All E.R. 559 at 569). It is not, however, immaterial what the outcome of the prosecution is: had Martin been convicted as a result of Ms Watson's lies to the police, he would not have been able to sue her, since claimants suing for having been prosecuted must show that the prosecution ended in their favour.

5. It is a further requirement of the tort of malicious prosecution that there have been no reasonable and probable causes for it. This question is for the judge. As Lord Bramwell said in *Abrath v North Eastern Ry* (1886) 11 App.Cas. 247 at 252: "A man brings an action for a malicious prosecution: he gives evidence which shews or goes to shew that he is innocent. You may tell the jury over and over again that that is not the question, but they never or very rarely can be got to understand it. They think that it is not right that a man should be prosecuted when he is innocent, and in the end they pay him for it." The requirement cannot be sidelined by suing for misfeasance in office, where malice is enough: *McDonagh v Commissioner of Police, The Times*, December 28, 1989. The different claims must be kept distinct. Thus while the Crown Prosecution Service may be liable for abuse of public power (*Bennett v Commissioner of Police* [1997] Times L.R. 523) it is not liable in negligence (absent, arguably, a specific undertaking of responsibility— *Welsh v Chief Constable* [1993] 1 All E.R. 692, as understood in *Elguzouli-Daf v Commissioner of Police* [1995] 1 All E.R. 833 at 845), and a claim for negligence must not be dressed up as one for malicious prosecution: *Thacker v Crown Prosecution Service* [1997] Times L.R. 699. Likewise a claim for abuse of power will be struck out if the pleadings disclose no more than negligence: *Barnard v Restormel B.C.* [1998] 3 P.L.R. 27, where the plaintiff was suing the council for rejecting his application for planning permission, for which it would not be liable for merely acting unreasonably (*Lam v Brennan* [1997] 3 P.L.R. 22).

6. If one is convicted and the conviction is not overturned, there is not much one can do about it. Malicious prosecution is impossible and any "collateral attack" on the conviction is virtually foredoomed (*Smith v Linskills* [1996] 2 All E.R. 353), though perhaps it may be possible to get round this by saying that one is not suing the defendant for negligently causing the conviction but for negligently losing the chance that the conviction might not have taken place (*Acton v Graham Pearce* [1997] 3 All E.R. 909).

7. In this connection one should consider again the cases of *Stanton v Callaghan* (above, p.263) and *Taylor v Serious Fraud Office* (above, p.540).

Questions

1. If the store detective in *Davidson* (above, p.342) had known that the cassette had been paid for, would she have been liable for *false arrest?*

2. Can the victim of rape sue a person who concocts a false alibi for the rapist and furnishes the police with it? The Court of Session reversed the sheriff's decision that she could (*B v Burns*, 1994 S.L.T. 250).

SPEED SEAL PRODUCTS v PADDINGTON

Court of Appeal [1985] 1 W.L.R. 1327; [1986] 1 All E.R. 91; [1986] F.S.R. 309; 135 New L.J. 935
(noted [1986] Camb.L.J. 200; (1986) 102 L.Q.R. 9)

Counterclaim in allegedly abusive lawsuit

After working for the plaintiff on the design of oil-pipe couplings, the defendant left that employment and set up in business on his own. When he applied for a patent for an oil-pipe coupling and started advertising it, the plaintiff sought an injunction to prevent further advertise-ment or use of information allegedly confidential. In addition to defending, the defendant applied to bring a counterclaim for the tort of abuse of court process.

The trial judge struck out the plaintiff's claim as unlikely to succeed, and allowed the defendant to counterclaim for damages. The plaintiff's appeal was allowed on the first point but not on the second.

Fox L.J.: ... The proposed counterclaim asserts that the action was brought in bad faith for the ulterior motive of damaging the defendants' business, and not for the protection of any legitimate interest of the plaintiffs. ...

The plaintiffs' contentions on this part of the case are, broadly, as follows. (i) The nature of the motive with which an act is done does not make the act unlawful (see *Bradford Corp. v Pickles* [1895] A.C. 587). (ii) To bring legal proceedings is *per se* a lawful act. It is wrongful only if the proceedings are brought without reasonable and probable cause. (iii) There is no absence of reasonable and probable cause, at least where the alleged abuse is an action, unless such action has determined in favour of the person who is alleging the tortious act.

Now in the present case, say the plaintiffs, the proceedings have not determined in favour of the defendants. And further, there is no pleaded allegation that the plaintiffs commenced or continued the action without reasonable and probable cause. Accordingly, it is contended the counterclaim is not sustainable.

The defendants' response to that is as follows. They say, first, that if the allegations in the draft counterclaim are proved at the trial, they will establish the following: (i) that the plaintiffs started the action without any bona fide belief in its chance of success; (ii) that the plaintiffs intended to use and did use the existence of the action as a weapon to persuade the defendants' potential customers not to deal with them; (iii) that the defendants have suffered and, they emphasise, are still suffering serious damage as a result.

It would, say the defendants, be a serious defect in the law if it were powerless to protect the defendants in the original action itself on proof of those facts. They are suffering continuing damage and there should be no delay.

The defendants accept that, so far as the tort of malicious prosecution is concerned, it is necessary for the person asserting the tort to prove (a) the commencement of a suit, (b) malice, (c) damage to that person, (d) absence of reasonable and proper cause for the suit and (e) termination of the suit in that person's favour.

The defendants contend that, on the true construction of the pleading, absence of reasonable and probable cause is in fact pleaded, and that, in any event, the defect can be cured by amendment. And, so far as the requirement of determination of the proceedings is concerned, there is no reason why the point should not await the trial of the counterclaim. If at that stage the defendants cannot establish prior termination, they will fail.

But, quite apart from these contentions, the defendants advance a further argument. They say that there is a tort of abuse of process of the court established by *Grainger v Hill* (1838) 132 E.R. 769. In that case the plaintiff had borrowed £80 from the defendants on the mortgage of a ship which he owned. The debt was repayable on September 28, 1837. The defendants, being apparently apprehensive as to their security, decided in November 1836 (*i.e.* before the debt was repayable) to possess themselves of the ship's register, without which the plaintiff could not go to sea. They therefore called on the plaintiff to pay the debt (which was not due) and threatened to arrest him if he failed to pay. The defendants then made an affidavit of debt and sued out a writ of capias indorsed for bail in the sum of some £95, and sent in two sheriff's officers with the writ to the plaintiff, who was ill in bed and attended by a surgeon. One of the officers then told the plaintiff that they had not come to take him but to get the ship's register, but that if he failed to deliver the register either they must take him or leave one of the officers with him. The plaintiff, being unable to procure bail and being alarmed, gave up the register. The plaintiff claimed damages for the loss of voyages which he could not undertake because of the loss of the register, and also the recovery of the register.

The plaintiff succeeded at the trial, and there was an appeal to the Exchequer Chamber, which dismissed it. Tindal C.J. said (at 773):

"The second ground urged for a nonsuit is, that there was no proof of the suit commenced by the Defendants having been terminated. But the answer to this, and to the objection urged in arrest of judgment, namely, the omission to allege want of reasonable and probable cause for the Defendants' proceeding, is the same: that this is an action for abusing the process of the law, by applying it to extort property from the Plaintiff, and not an action for malicious arrest or malicious prosecution, in order to support which action the termination of the previous proceeding must be proved ... "

Tindall C.J. went on to say that, the complaint being that the process of the law had been abused, it was "immaterial whether the suit which that process commenced has been determined or not, or whether or not it was founded on reasonable and probable cause."

Park J. said that the argument as to the omission to prove the determination of the defendant's suit and to allege want of reasonable and probable cause for it proceeded on an erroneous analogy between the case and an action for malicious arrest (see 132 E.R. 773). Bosanquet J. said that "the process was enforced for an ulterior purpose" (at 774).

It is clear that the court distinguished the case from one of malicious prosecution, and accordingly rejected the arguments based on non-determination of the original proceedings. It regarded the wrong as abuse of the process. And the abuse, as I understand it, was that the purpose of the original proceeding was not the recovery of the debt (which was not due) but the extortion of the register.

Grainger v Hill has not been much referred to in the subsequent authorities, but it has not been disapproved.

In *Goldsmith v Sperrings Ltd* [1977] 2 All E.R. 566 at 574, Lord Denning M.R. (in a dissenting judgment) said:

"What may make it [the legal process] wrongful is the purpose for which it is used. If it is done in order to exert pressure so as to achieve an end which is improper in itself, then it is a wrong known to the law. This appears distinctly from the case which founded this tort. It is *Grainger v Hill* ... "

And Scarman L.J. said (at 582):

"In the instant proceedings the defendants have to show that the plaintiff has an ulterior motive, seeks a collateral advantage for himself beyond what the law offers, is reaching out 'to effect an object not within the scope of the process': *Grainger v Hill* ... "

The American Second Restatement of the Law of Tort (1977) § 682 states the following principle, under the heading "Abuse of Process":

"One who uses a legal process, whether criminal or civil, against another primarily to accomplish a purpose for which it is not designed, is subject to liability to the other for harm caused by the abuse of process."

Grainger v Hill is cited in the Restatement for the proposition that termination of the proceeding in favour of the plaintiff need not be shown.

It seems to me that if allegations of fact pleaded in the draft counterclaim are established at the trial, the decision in *Grainger v Hill* provides a basis for an arguable case that there has been an actionable abuse of the process of the court. I express no view as to the strength of the defendants' case. It is enough to say that I think that a sufficiently arguable case has been demonstrated to justify giving leave to amend the defence by adding a counterclaim, as asked. It will be open to the defendants to support it by such arguments as may be available, whether based on *Grainger v Hill* or not.

Questions

1. Is this decision reconcilable with the rule that no claim for damages lies in respect of false evidence given with a view to litigation?

2. Is it relevant (or is it the case) that while the public has an interest in the prosecution of those suspected of crime it has no comparable interest in civil litigation?

Notes:

1. There may be liability in damages for threatening to bring proceedings for infringement of intellectual property rights (*e.g.* Trademarks Act 1994, s.21), or even the Olympic symbol (Olympic Symbol, etc., (Protection) Act 1995, s.16).

2. The abuse of litigation is well shown in *Fitzroy v Cave* [1905] 2 K.B. 364. The plaintiff obtained from five of the defendant's creditors an assignment of their debts, on the terms that after collection he would pay them the net proceeds. On cross-examination the plaintiff admitted that his sole purpose in suing was to bankrupt the defendant in order to have him removed from the board of directors of the Cork Mineral Development Company. The trial judge dismissed the claim as savouring of maintenance and as being otherwise contrary to public policy, but the Court of Appeal reversed: "I fail to see that we have anything to do with the motives which actuated the plaintiff." This was only 30 years after the assignment of debts, previously banned as suspect, was legitimated. Even now an assignment can be avoided if the purpose is deplorable (*Trendtex Trading Corp. v Crédit Suisse* [1981] 3 All E.R. 520, HL).

3. An attempt to deploy the law of negligence in the area of litigation was foiled in *Business Computers International v Registrar of Companies* [1987] 3 All E.R. 465, where the plaintiff company was unaware that it was being wound up because the petitioner had carelessly sent the papers to the wrong address: "The safeguards against impropriety are to be found in the rules and procedure that control litigation and not in tort." (Scott J.)

4. In *Connolly-Martin v Davis* [1999] Times L.R. 431 it was held that a barrister owed no duty to his client's opponent when advising his client about the validity of an undertaking or indeed giving an undertaking without his client's authority.

METALL UND ROHSTOFF AG v DONALDSON LUFKIN & JENRETTE INC

Court of Appeal [1990] 1 Q.B. 391; [1989] 3 W.L.R. 563; [1989] 3 All E.R. 14

The defendants had agreed with the plaintiff's broker that disastrous losses incurred by one Glaser, trusted by the plaintiffs but acting in fraud of them to the knowledge of the broker, should be met by foreclosing on the plaintiff's assets under the pretence that Glaser's losses were for the plaintiff's account. The broker having broken, the plaintiff sued the defendants for inducing the broker to break his contract with the plaintiffs and conspiring with him to cause it loss.

The defendants' conduct in the litigation, which is in issue in this excerpt, was of a piece with its prior conduct, and consistent with the current morality of American financial institutions, namely, deceptive, evasive and impenitent.

Slade L.J.: . . . The recent decision of this court in *Speed Seal Products Ltd v Paddington* (above, p.629) establishes that it is at least well arguable that there exists a tort of abuse of the process of the court of a nature established by the decision of the Court of Common Pleas in *Grainger v Hill* (1838) 132 E.R. 769.

The present case is of a rather different nature. . . .

The substance of the complaint against the defendants is that they abused the process of the court by adducing false evidence and submitting a false case for the primary purpose of defeating claims by the plaintiff in the proceedings to the return of their metal and other assets and to prevent the defendants from dealing with such assets in the meantime.

No doubt the adduction of false evidence and the submission of a false case for the purpose of sustaining or defeating a claim in legal proceedings may subject the guilty plaintiff or defendant (as the case may be) to sanctions by way of a penal order for costs or even a prosecution for perjury. In our judgment, however, it does not expose him to an action for damages in tort under the principle of *Grainger v Hill*.

No authority has been cited to us which satisfies us that it does. If the use of court process is to expose a party to liability under this principle, the process must, in our judgment, have been used for a predominant purpose "outside the ambit of the legal claim upon which the Court is asked to adjudicate." Relief in tort under the principle of *Grainger v Hill* is not, in our judgment, available against a party who, however dishonestly, presents a false case for the purpose of advancing or sustaining his claim or defence in civil proceedings. This may well cause hardship to an injured party who cannot be sufficiently compensated by an appropriate order for costs.

However, if there is a gap in the law it rests on sound considerations of public policy, as does the rule of law which gives immunity to witnesses against civil actions based on the falsity of evidence given in judicial proceedings. If the position were otherwise, honest litigants might be deterred from pursuing honest claims or defences and honest witnesses might be deterred from giving evidence (*cf.* generally *Business Computers International Ltd v Registrar of Companies* [1987] 3 All E.R. 465 at 469, *per* Scott J. and the cases there cited).

In short we agree with the judge, for much the same reasons as his, that the facts relied on do not raise an arguable case that there was an abuse of process falling within the *Grainger v Hill* principle.

Perhaps implicitly recognising his difficulties in this context, counsel for the plaintiff in his reply focused particular attention on a quite different, alternative way of putting its case on this issue. He sought to rely on a tort or alleged tort having ingredients distinct and different from those constituting a *Grainger v Hill* type abuse of process, namely a tort of malicious institution of proceedings. . . .

Although we have not heard full argument on this point, we have great doubt whether any general tort of maliciously instituting civil proceedings exists. The courts have countenanced claims by a plaintiff complaining of a malicious and unjustified arrest or of malicious and unjustified institution of bankruptcy or liquidation proceedings, but the cases have not (to our knowledge) gone beyond these limited categories. There are dicta suggesting that in the case of an ordinary civil action, however maliciously and unjustifiably brought, the successful defendant has no cause of action in tort (see *Johnson v Emerson* (1871) L.R. 6 Exch. 329 at 372, *per* Martin B. and *Quartz Hill Consolidated Gold Mining Co v Eyre* (1883) 11 Q.B.D. 674 at 684, *per* Brett M.R.). We also have great doubt whether, in a case such as the present, the defendants could fairly be regarded as having instituted proceedings or set the law in motion, as would presumably be necessary for this tort if it does exist. There might, we accept, be cases in which a defendant launched a counterclaim independent of the plaintiff's claim against him and truly to be understood as a cross-action. Then the counterclaiming defendant could perhaps be treated as a plaintiff.

Note:

In *Gregory v Portsmouth City Council* (1997) 96 L.G.R. 569, CA, the plaintiff was barred from council activities as a result of disciplinary proceedings which the courts later held flawed. He claimed damages. The discussion was in terms of malicious prosecution. Simon Brown L.J. noted that such a claim had never lain except for criminal prosecutions and civil insolvency proceedings, and was not minded to extend it: "The tort had certain curious features (particularly in the civil sphere), even as it presently operated, and it might be doubted whether after all these years the courts should react creatively to proposals for its extension in any way whatever." Robert Walker L.J., agreeing that the claim be struck out, suggested that a person such as the plaintiff could have a claim in conspiracy, defamation or malicious falsehood. Schiemann L.J. dissented strongly, regarding the case as one where, allegedly, "The Council itself maliciously hauled the plaintiff before a tribunal which it knew had no power to hear the allegations against him, prevented him from having a fair hearing and then maliciously suspended him from office. All this, it is said, cost the plaintiff money in fees and damaged his health and reputation." He found it wrong that the law of tort should afford no remedy just because the old law of malicious prosecution required that the proceedings be before an actual court, not a mere tribunal, and that if the proceedings were not criminal, they must have to do with bankruptcy—restrictions which neither of the majority judges found happy or logical.

The House of Lords dismissed the plaintiff's appeal. Lord Steyn emphasised that malicious prosecution had the "distinctive feature . . . that the defendant has abused the coercive power of the state" (at 565), and noted that it had "never been extended to disciplinary proceedings of any kind" (at 566), in which, indeed, there may not be even a duty of care (*Calveley v Chief Constable* [1989] 1 All E.R. 1025, HL). The case for extending the tort to include civil proceedings generally was stronger, but not, in view of the coverage afforded by the torts of defamation, malicious prosecution, conspiracy and misfeasance in office, yet established. Here Mr Gregory was complaining, in addition to pecuniary loss, recoverable in all these torts, of damage to reputation which is compensable in defamation, of course, and in malicious prosecution, but not in malicious falsehood (where aggravated damages may now be awarded—*Khodaparast v Shad*, above, p.532) or conspiracy, while malice, at least in the sense of knowing abuse, is a requirement in all these torts, even in defamation where qualified privilege exists.

PART IX

DAMAGES

Chapter 17

DAMAGES

INTRODUCTION

THE foregoing pages have been more concerned with the question whether a defendant is liable than with the question how much he has to pay, in other words, with liability rather than damages. Yet in practice, if not in theory, damages are extremely important—especially to practitioners: they are, indeed, the "bottom line", what it's all about. Although a few torts like trespass and libel are actionable even if no damage is proved, in most torts (unlike breaches of contract) there is no liability unless there is harm, and it has to be quantified. Indeed the importance of liability turns on the question of quantum.

To give an example, the European Directive on Product Liability (above, p.27) was ostensibly designed to remedy the distortion of competition which allegedly arose as a result of the fact that producers in different Member States were subject to different rules as to liability. The Directive consequently harmonised the rules of liability, more or less, but since no attempt was made towards harmonising the rules of damages, this did nothing or very little towards solving the supposed problem. The rules of damages still vary enormously—German producers pay nothing in respect of grief when the product proves fatal, and not much for loss of support, British producers did not (at the time) have to pay for the medical treatment needed by the injured victim, and French producers pay even for mere economic loss due to a defect. It matters a great deal how much you have to pay—and how much you get—and that is why we spend so much time on the really preliminary question whether or not you have to pay—or are entitled to get—anything at all.

Sometimes harm is over and done with when the trial takes place—the building has burnt down—and it will be a matter of proof how much it amounts to, despite difficulties of valuation. But a trial does not put an end to pain or terminate the need for medical treatment, so the court must deal with continuing or future losses. In deference to the English desire to put an end to litigation we award a lump sum once for all, and since no one really knows how the situation will develop, we have to rely on unsure estimates. The lump sum may turn out to be overgenerous or inadequate. But lump sums present another problem. A capital sum awarded now for recurrent future losses produces interest in the meantime (unless it is wasted) so the sum awarded must be smaller than the amount one thinks the claimant should ultimately have: the sum must be discounted. The amount of this discount depends on the rate of interest the capital sum will attract. Furthermore, (although it is true that there is a relationship between interest rates and inflation) the cost of living keeps rising from year to year, with the result that the same number of pounds (or Euros) buys less as the years progress. The House of Lords dealt with this problem in what is one of the most important (and least interesting) decisions of recent years, namely *Wells v Wells* [1998] 3 All E.R. 481. The best way of ensuring that the claimant gets the amount of money he will need for recurrent losses is to give him inflation-proof money, or what it would cost him now to buy government index-linked bonds. But since such bonds produce less interest than the investments which claimants were previously presumed to make, the discount on the capital sum is smaller with the result that the award must now be greater than it previously was. The decision to reduce the discount rate to 3 per cent caused an *increase* in one of the cases of £300,000. A puisne judge has since applied a rate of 2 per cent.

The question of damages for personal injury and death has agitated the Law Commission over the past few years. In addition to the reports on Psychiatric Illness (Law Com. no. 249), Wrongful Death (Law Com. No.263) and Aggravated, Exemplary and Restitutionary Damages (Law Com. No.247) reports have been published on Structured Settlements, Interim and Provisional Damages (Law Com. No.224), Non-Pecuniary Loss (Law Com. No.257) and Collateral Benefits, including Medical, Nursing and Other Expenses (Law Com. No.262), the last three pursuant to Consultation Papers 125, 140 and 147 respectively.

Of these, the most dramatic is the Report on Non-Pecuniary Loss which proposes that the higher courts should set guidelines so as to increase by between 50 and 100 per cent the damages presently awarded in cases of serious injury, that is, those now fetching £3,000 or more. The Report is unpersuasive. While emphasising the importance of "public perceptions", it denies any role to the jury (though treating the jury decision in *Girvan* (below, p.643) as a useful instance of public perception). While stating that there is no demonstrably right view on quantum, its proposal to increase damages in line with inflation presupposes that the previous view was correct. It reports that victims of very serious injuries suffer more than they expected and that they would like more money, and regards these as telling arguments. It appeals to corrective justice while infringing the principle of distributive justice by increasing the disparity of treatment between those who receive damages and those who have no solvent defendant to sue.

Astonishingly the Court of Appeal has responded to this impertinent "invitation" (backed by a threat of legislation which the Law Commission is fortunately unable to implement), and gave modified effect to the proposals: awards of less than £10,000 (as against £3,000) remain unaffected and those in the most serious cases are to be increased by a third (rather than doubled), with a suggested maximum of £200,000. (*Heil v Rankin* [2001] Q.B. 272). Note that these increases are in respect of pain and suffering and loss of amenity only, awards in respect of material loss having already been hugely increased by *Wells v Wells*.

By contrast, the proposals regarding structured settlements were sensible and have already been implemented by the Damages Act 1996 (which also presaged *Wells v Wells*). It is worth noting that the excellent device of structured settlement, with its flexible and tax-efficient combination of capital payment and annuity, was not invented by the courts or the legislature, much less the Law Commission. It was the product of lawyers and accountants working with a surprisingly co-operative Inland Revenue. Structured settlements are generally reached by negotiation between the parties, but if a case does have to come to court, the court can now, with the consent of the parties, order a structured settlement rather than lump sum damages.

Two distinctions should be borne in mind when the cases in the chapter are being considered. The first is the French distinction between *dommage matériel* and *dommage moral*, the first being the kind of harm an economist would understand because he can count it and the second being the sort of harm he cannot understand because it is human. Giving a monetary equivalent for the former is rather easier (though future losses require prediction), while for the latter there are now *Guidelines for the assessment of general damages in personal injury cases*, compiled for the Judicial Studies Board, published by Blackstone and packed in every judge's lunchbag. The second distinction is that between losing something good and incurring something bad, which applies to both *dommage moral* (loss of amenity, extra pain) and *dommage matériel* (loss of income, increased expenditure).

This being the background, the following cases deal with other problems such as how to determine the plaintiff's loss, how to put a money value on it, and whether his gross loss should be reduced with reference to benefits which he would not have received had he not been hurt.

Section 1—Punitive Damages

THOMPSON v COMMISSIONER OF POLICE OF THE METROPOLIS

Court of Appeal, [1998] Q.B. 498; [1997] 3 All E.R. 762; [1997] 3 W.L.R. 403

Damages payable by the police for trespass to the person and malicious prosecution

Lord Woolf M.R.: In a number of recent cases members of the public have been awarded very large sums of exemplary damages by juries against the Commissioner of Police of the Metropolis for unlawful conduct towards them by the police. As a result these two appeals have been brought by the Commissioner. The intention is to clarify the directions which a judge should include in a summing up to assist the jury as to the amount of damages, particularly exemplary damages, which it is appropriate for them to award a plaintiff who is successful in this type of action.

The damages which were awarded to Mr Hsu were £220,000, of which £20,000 were compensatory, including aggravated damages, and £200,000 exemplary damages. The damages were for wrongful arrest, false imprisonment and assault. In the case of Miss Thompson the jury awarded £1,500 as compensatory, including, aggravated, damages and £50,000 exemplary damages. We examined the facts in some detail and are very conscious that in both cases the conduct of the police officers involved can only be described as outrageous and totally inconsistent with their responsibilities.

[*Lord Woolf considered decisions of the Court of Appeal in cases of defamation—see above p.567*].

[Although] it does not follow that what was said in the context of an action for defamation can be directly applied to the different class of cases now being considered it is when the jury have to consider whether there should be an award of aggravated damages as additional compensation that the award in this class of case is more analogous to that in defamation proceedings. As the Law Commission point out there can be a penal element in the award of aggravated damages. However, they are primarily to be awarded to compensate the plaintiff for injury to his proper pride and dignity and the consequences of his being humiliated. This injury which is made worse for the plaintiff because it is more difficult to excuse when the malicious motives, spite or arrogance on the part of the police: see *Rookes v Barnard* [1964] A.C. 1129, 1221 et seq., *per* Lord Devlin.

In this category of case the excessive awards are being paid out of public money (though police forces other than the Metropolitan do take out insurance) and could well result in a reduction in the resources of the police available to be used for activities which would benefit the public. It must at present be very difficult for a jury to understand the distinction between aggravated and exemplary damages when there is such a substantial overlap between the factors which provide the sole justification for both awards. The extent to which juries fluctuate in the awards which they make indicates the difficulties which they have. On the other hand there are arguments which can be advanced to justify the retention of the use of juries in this area of litigation. Very difficult issues of credibility will often have to be resolved. It is desirable for these to be determined by the plaintiff's fellow citizens rather than judges, who like the police are concerned in maintaining law and order. Similarly the jury because of their composition, are a body which is peculiarly suited to make the final assessment of damages, including deciding whether aggravated or exemplary damages are called for in this area of litigation and for the jury to have these important tasks is an important safeguard of the liberty of the individual citizen.

While there is no formula which is appropriate for all cases and the precise form of a summing up is very much a matter within the discretion of the trial judge, it is suggested that in many cases it will be convenient to include in a summing up on the issue of damages additional directions on the following lines. We think it may often be wise to take the jury's verdict on liability before they receive directions as to quantum.

(1) It should be explained to the jury that save in exceptional situations damages are only awarded as compensation and are intended to compensate the plaintiff for any injury or damage which he has suffered. They are not intended to punish the defendant.

(2) As the law stands at present compensatory damages are of two types. (a) Ordinary damages which we would suggest should be described as basic, and (b) aggravated damages. Aggravated damages can only be awarded where they are claimed by the plaintiff and where there are aggravating features about the defendant's conduct which justify the award of aggravated damages.

(3) The jury should be told that the basic damages will depend on the circumstances and the degree of harm suffered by the plaintiff. But they should be provided with an appropriate bracket to use as a starting point.

(4) In a straightforward case of wrongful arrest and imprisonment or malicious prosecution the jury should be informed of the approximate figure to be taken as the correct starting point for basic damages for the actual loss of liberty or for the wrongful prosecution, and also given an approximate ceiling figure. It should be explained that these are no more than guideline figures based on the judge's experience and on the awards in other cases and the actual figure is one on which they must decide.

(5) In a straightforward case of wrongful arrest and imprisonment the starting point is likely to be about £500 for the first hour during which the plaintiff has been deprived of his or her liberty. After the first hour an additional sum is to be awarded, but that sum should be on a reducing scale so as to keep the damages proportionate with those payable in personal injury cases and because the plaintiff is entitled to have a higher rate of compensation for the initial shock of being arrested. As a guideline we consider, for example, that a plaintiff who has been wrongly kept in custody for 24 hours should for this alone normally be regarded as entitled to an award of about £3,000. For subsequent days the daily rate will be on a progressively reducing scale.

(6) In the case of malicious prosecution the figure should start at about £2,000 and for prosecution continuing for as long as two years, the case being taken to the Crown Court, an award of about £10,000 could be appropriate. If a malicious prosecution results in a conviction which is only set aside on an appeal this will justify a larger award to reflect the longer period during which the plaintiff has been in peril and has been caused distress.

(8) If the case is one in which aggravated damages are claimed and could be appropriately awarded, the nature of aggravated damages should be explained to the jury. Such damages can be awarded where there are aggravating features about the case which would result in the plaintiff not receiving sufficient compensation for the injury suffered if the award were restricted to a basic award. Aggravating features can include humiliating circumstances at the time of arrest or any conduct of those responsible for the arrest or the

prosecution which shows that they had behaved in a high-handed, insulting, malicious or oppressive manner either in relation to the arrest or imprisonment or in conducting the prosecution. Aggravating features can also include the way the litigation and trial are conducted.

(9) The jury should then be told that if they consider the case is one for the award of damages other than basic damages then they should usually make a separate award for each category.

(10) We consider that where it is appropriate to award aggravated damages the figure is unlikely to be less than a £1,000. In the ordinary way we would not expect the aggravated damages to be as much as twice the basic damages except perhaps where, on the particular facts, the basic damages are modest.

(11) It should be strongly emphasised to the jury that the total figure for basic and aggravated damages should not exceed what they consider is fair compensation for the injury which the plaintiff has suffered. It should also be explained that if aggravated damages are awarded such damages, though compensatory and not intended as a punishment, will in fact contain a penal element as far as the defendant is concerned.

(12) Finally the jury should be told that though it is not normally possible to award damages with the object of punishing the defendant, exceptionally this is possible where there has been conduct, including oppressive or arbitrary behaviour, by police officers which deserves the exceptional remedy of exemplary damages. It should be explained to the jury: (a) that if the jury are awarding aggravated damages these damages will have already provided compensation for the injury suffered by the plaintiff as a result of the oppressive and insulting behaviour of the police officer and, inevitably, a measure of punishment from the defendant's point of view; (b) that exemplary damages should be awarded if, but only if, they consider that the compensation awarded by way of basic and aggravated damages is in the circumstances an inadequate punishment for the defendants; (c) that an award of exemplary damages is in effect a windfall for the plaintiff and, where damages will be payable out of police funds, the sum awarded may not be available to be expended by the police in a way which would benefit the public (this guidance would not be appropriate if the claim were to be met by insurers); (d) that the sum awarded by way of exemplary damages should be sufficient to mark the jury's disapproval of the oppressive or arbitrary behaviour but should be no more than is required for this purpose.

(13) Where exemplary damages are appropriate they are unlikely to be less than £5,000. Otherwise the case is probably not one which justifies an award of exemplary damages at all. In this class of action the conduct must be particularly deserving of condemnation for an award of as much as £25,000 to be justified and the figure of £50,000 should be regarded as the absolute maximum, involving directly officers of at least the rank of superintendent.

(14) In an appropriate case the jury should also be told that even though the plaintiff succeeds on liability any improper conduct of which they find him guilty can reduce or even eliminate any award of aggravated or exemplary damages if the jury consider that this conduct caused or contributed to the behaviour complained of.

The figures given will of course require adjusting in the future for inflation. We appreciate that the guideline figures depart from the figures frequently awarded by juries at the present time. However they are designed to establish some relationship between the figures awarded in this area and those awarded for personal injuries. In giving guidance for aggravated damages we have attached importance to the fact that they are intended to be compensatory and not punitive.

The appeals were test cases brought because of the size of some awards being made by juries in cases against the police. The court has provided guidance as to directions which in future should be given by judges to juries which should produce greater consistency and certainty as to awards and, in particular, avoid the award of excessive sums to plaintiffs as exemplary damages which are awarded as a civil punishment.

In the future the judge will include in his summing up a bracket for basic damages, an indication that the award for aggravating circumstances should not normally exceed the amount of the basic damages (except where the basic damages are modest) and it would require the most exceptional circumstances for aggravated damages to be as much as twice the basic damages. In the case of exemplary damages the conduct must be particularly deserving of punishment to justify an award of £25,000 and £50,000 should be regarded as the absolute maximum.

Notes:

1. In *Clarke v Chief Constable* [1999] Times L.R. 440 the jury awarded £750 for wrongful arrest and £150 for assault but only £500 for malicious prosecution, having asked the judge whether they might go below the starting figure he had given them of £2,000. The Court of Appeal raised the £500 to £2,000. Henry L.J. dissented on the ground that the Courts and Legal Services Act 1990, s.8 did not empower the court to increase a jury award found inadequate, that neither *Rantzen* nor *Thompson* said it did, that the award in question was not totally erroneous or clearly wrong and that the plaintiff's improper conduct could rightly reduce the compensatory damages even if it did not conduce to the prosecution.

2. An award of £125,000 for assault, false imprisonment and malicious prosecution was reduced by the Court of Appeal to £50,000 in *Gerald v Commissioner of Police* [1998] Times L.R. 401. It was said that damages for trauma falling short of physical or mental injury should be regarded as aggravated damages rather than as part of the basic award, especially now that aggravated and, indeed, punitive damages were to be related to the basic award. £50,000 is also the sum for which Scotland Yard settled with Silcott, whose conviction for murder was overturned.

3. Until 1964 it had been thought that punitive damages could be awarded by the jury in any case where the defendant had behaved outrageously. In that year Lord Devlin in *Rookes v Barnard* [1964] 1 All E.R. 367, on a point not discussed in the Court of Appeal or adverted to by his brethren, who merely agreed with him, held that they could be awarded only in two categories—where the defendant was a public official who abused his authority and where the defendant was cynically out for profit. This provoked an unprecedented reaction in the Court of Appeal: "Lord Devlin's whole approach was based on a fundamental fallacy" (Salmon L.J.); "the decision was clearly wrong and must be treated as delivered *per incuriam*" (Phillimore L.J.); "The new doctrine is hopelessly illogical and inconsistent" (Lord Denning, who then proceeded to instruct judges below him to ignore the House of Lords' decision!). *Broome v Cassell* [1971] 2 All E.R. 187. On appeal five of the seven judges in the House repelled these criticisms without really refuting them ([1972] 1 All E.R. 801).

4. Next, a very differently constituted Court of Appeal held that no punitive damages could be awarded unless the tort in question was one in which such damages had been awarded before 1964. (*AB v South West Water Services* [1993] 1 All E.R. 609). This extraordinary and totally unprincipled decision meant that no such damages could be awarded in the more modern torts (discrimination, harassment, misfeasance in public office) where perhaps they would be most desirable.

5. The Law Commission then got into the act and found to their surprise that they were unable to obtain any consensus among their "consultees". They eventually proposed that both *Rookes* and *AB v South West Water Services* be reversed, and that the award of punitive damages be removed from the jury (contrary to *Thompson*). The Government promptly indicated that it was not minded to legislate on the matter.

6. Next came the House of Lords decision in *Kuddus v Chief Constable* [2001] 3 All E.R. 193, which is to be praised for what it did decide, namely to overrule *AB v South West Water*, but cannot be criticised for what it did not decide, since counsel agreed not to question *Rookes v Barnard* or raise the matter whether punitive damages could be awarded against a defendant whose liability was purely vicarious. Those members of the House who evinced any view about these more general matters had different views: Lord Nicholls and Lord Hutton were favourable to the institution, while Lord Scott was adamantly against it—unsurprisingly, since he started out his speech with a *petitio principii*: "My Lords, the function of an award of damages in our civil justice system is to compensate the claimant for a wrong done to him." There is, however, one residual peculiarity: although punitive damages are now available for the tort of misfeasance in public office, and although it was fairly clear that the defendant's constable, who forged a citizen's signature on a document professing to be an abandonment of a complaint, was guilty of that tort, punitive damages may still not be payable because the constable's conduct, though disgraceful, was not "oppressive" in the sense of *Rookes v Barnard*. That, at any rate, was hinted at by at least two of their Lordships.

7. Like the decision in *Murphy* (above p.31), the question of punitive damages has divided the common law world. The *Rookes* position has not been followed in Canada, Australia or New Zealand. Indeed, the Privy Council on appeal from New Zealand, has held that punitive damages may exceptionally be awarded in cases of negligence, and that conscious recklessness or open-eyed risk-taking is not required, provided that the conduct was really outrageous. Lord Nicholls spoke of England "still toiling in the chains of *Rookes v Barnard*" [at 44]. Two dissentients, emphasising that these damages are punitive, were of the view that there must be subjective recklessness: *A v Bottrill* [2002] UKPC 44. It is true that since punitive damages are not known North of the Border (as aggravated damages are not) nor on the far side of the Channel, one can hardly say that they are an indispensable feature of any legal system. Nevertheless in the United States they are a well-established institution, though the federal government has protected itself against them and they

are subject to restriction in various ways in the several states, whose power to award punitive damages has recently been severely restricted by the Supreme Court: in *State Farm Mutual Auto Insurance Co v Campbell* 123 S.Ct. 1513, 155 L.Ed. 585 (2003) it overruled a decision of the Supreme Court of Utah to reinstate the jury award of $145 million punitive damages which the trial judge had reduced to $25 million plus $1 million as compensation. By a majority the U.S. Supreme Court held that the award was an "irrational and arbitrary deprivation of the property of the defendant".

The extreme distaste of continental jurisdictions for punitive damages may be seen in the astonishing provision in the EC Regulation on the law applicable to non-contractual obligations with international aspects (*Rome II*) that "The application of a provision of the law designated by this Regulation which has the effect of causing non-compensatory damages, such as exemplary or punitive damages, to be awarded shall be contrary to Community public policy." Britain had already determined that a judgment obtained abroad be wholly unenforceable here if it provided for a multiple of compensatory damages: Protection of Trading Interests Act 1980, s.5. This was to bar attempts to enforce claims on American judgments for triple damages under antitrust or racketeering legislation.

7. In England the jury was abolished in negligence cases by Lord Denning in *Ward v James* [1965] 1 All E.R. 653, but survives in cases of false imprisonment, malicious prosecution and defamation. In personal injury cases Scotland still occasionally uses the civil jury which England bestowed on it in the year of Waterloo. In *Girvan v Inverness Farmers (No.2)* 1998 S.C.(HL) 1 an appeal was made to the House of Lords from a second jury award, the first having been vacated as excessive and the case remanded by the Inner House. The first jury awarded *solatium* (general damages for pain and suffering) of £120,000, the second £95,000. The House held that the second award could not be interfered with, a 100 percent excess being acceptable.

8. The Copyright, Designs and Patents Act 1988 provides in s.97(2) that "The court may in an action for infringement of copyright having regard to all the circumstances, and in particular to—(a) the flagrancy of the infringement, and (b) any benefit accruing to the defendant by reason of the infringement, award such additional damages as the justice of the case may require." In *Redrow Homes v Betts Bros.* [1998] 1 All E.R. 385 at 391, which held that additional damages could not be claimed along with an account of profits, Lord Jauncey declined to decide whether additional damages were punitive or compensatory.

Section 2.—Personal Injuries

H WEST & SON v SHEPHARD

House of Lords [1964] A.C. 326; [1963] 2 W.L.R. 1359; 107 S.J. 454; [1963] 2 All E.R. 625

Damages for permanently comatose victim's loss of amenity

The plaintiff, a woman of 41 years of age, was dreadfully injured in a street accident brought about by the negligence of the defendant's servant. She suffered from cerebral atrophy and paralysis of all four limbs. She could not speak, but was able to move her right hand, and changes in her facial expression testified to a capacity to distinguish different foods and recognise people. She needed constant hospital nursing, and there was no prospect of improvement during the five years she was expected to live.

Paull J. gave £500 for loss of expectation of life, and £17,500 general damages. This sum he reached by referring to *Wise v Kaye* [1962] 1 Q.B. 638, where the Court of Appeal had upheld an award of £15,000 to a plaintiff rendered permanently unconscious.

The defendant's appeal to the Court of Appeal was dismissed, and his further appeal to the House of Lords was also dismissed (Lord Reid and Lord Devlin dissenting).

Lord Reid (dissenting): ... I can go straight to the question of general importance—What is the basis on which damages for serious injuries are awarded? The determination of that question in the ordinary case where the injured person is fully conscious of his disability will go far to decide how to deal with a case like *Wise v Kaye* ([1962] 1 Q.B. 638) where the injured person was wholly unconscious with no prospect of ever regaining consciousness or like the present case where the respondent is only conscious to a slight extent.

In the ordinary case of a man losing a leg or sustaining a permanent internal injury, he is entitled to recover in respect of his pain and suffering: if he is fortunate in suffering little pain he must get a smaller award. So it is not disputed that where an injured person does not suffer at all because of unconsciousness he gets no award under this head. Nothing was awarded in Wise's case and nothing has been awarded in this case. On the other hand no one doubts that damages must be awarded irrespective of the man's mental condition or the extent of his suffering where there is financial loss. That will cover the cost of treatment or alleviation of his condition just as much as it covers the cost of repairing or renewing his property. And it will cover loss of earning power: there may be a question whether some deduction should be made where his outgoings will be less than they would have been if there had been no accident, so as to reach his net financial loss, but that does not arise in the present case.

The difficulty is in connection with what is often called loss of amenity and with curtailment of his expectation of life. If there had been no curtailment of his expectation of life the man whose injuries are permanent has to look forward to a life of frustration and handicap and he must be compensated, so far as money can do it, for that and for the mental strain and anxiety which results. But I would agree with Sellers L.J. in Wise's case that a brave man who makes light of his disabilities and finds other outlets to replace activities no longer open to him must not receive less compensation on that account.

There are two views about the true basis for this kind of compensation. One is that the man is simply being compensated for the loss of his leg or the impairment of his digestion. The other is that his real loss is not so much his physical injury as the loss of those opportunities to lead a full and normal life which are now denied to him by his physical condition—for the multitude of deprivations and even petty annoyances which he must tolerate. Unless I am prevented by authority I would think that the ordinary man is, at least after the first few months, far less concerned about his physical injury than about the dislocation of his normal life. So I would think that compensation should be based much less on the nature of the injuries than on the extent of the injured man's consequential difficulties in his daily life. It is true that in practice one tends to look at the matter objectively and to regard the physical loss of an eye or a limb as the subject for compensation. But I think that is because the consequences of such a loss are very much the same for all normal people. If one takes the case of injury to an internal organ, I think the true view becomes apparent. It is more difficult to say there that the plaintiff is being paid for the physical damage done to his liver or stomach or even his brain, and much more reasonable to say that he is being paid for the extent to which that injury will prevent him from living a full and normal life and for what he will suffer from being unable to do so.

If that is so, then I think it must follow that if a man's injuries make him wholly unconscious so that he suffers none of these daily frustrations or inconveniences, he ought to get less than the man who is every day acutely conscious of what he suffers and what he has lost. I do not say that he should get nothing. This is not a question that can be decided logically. I think that there are two elements, what he has lost and what he must feel about it, and of the two I think the latter is generally the more important to the injured man. To my mind there is something unreal in saying that a man who knows and feels nothing should get the same as a man who has to live with and put up with his disabilities, merely because they have sustained comparable physical injuries. It is no more possible to compensate an unconscious man than it is to compensate a dead man. The fact that the damages can give no benefit or satisfaction to the injured man and can only go to those who inherit the dead man's estate would not be a good reason for withholding damages which are legally due. But it is, in my view, a powerful argument against the view that there is no analogy between a dead man and a man who is unconscious and that a man who is unconscious ought to be treated as if he were fully conscious.

It is often said that it is scandalous that it should be cheaper to kill a man than to maim him, and that it would be monstrous if the defendant had to pay less because in addition to inflicting physical injuries he had made the plaintiff unconscious. I think that such criticism is misconceived. Damages are awarded not to punish the wrongdoer but to compensate the person injured, and a dead man cannot be compensated. Loss to his estate can be made good, and we can give some compensation to those whom he leaves behind. Perhaps we should do more for them—but not by inflating the claim of the dead man's executor, for then the money may go to undeserving distant relatives or residuary legatees or even to the Treasury if he dies intestate and without heirs. And it is already the case that it may benefit the defendant to injure the plaintiff more severely. If he is injured so severely that he can only live a year or two at most the damages will be much less than if he is less severely injured so that he may survive for many years.

Coming to the facts of this case I would reduce the general damages of £17,500. I would consider separately the objective and the subjective element arising from the respondent's injuries. Accepting that in view of her shortened expectation of life £17,500 would be a fair sum if the respondent were fully conscious of her position. I would think that not more than £5,000 of that ought to be attributed to the actual physical injuries, and then the question is to what extent the respondent is conscious and suffering. Unfortunately we have nothing to go by except three medical reports and on this matter they do not take us very far. It would seem that the respondent has some but not very much appreciation of her surroundings and she seems to suffer no pain. I think that perhaps £4,000 would be appropriate here. And then perhaps insufficient attention has been given to expense which her husband may incur in tending her and providing amenities if her condition should improve slightly. So I would substitute a figure in the region of £10,000 for the sum of £17,500 which has been awarded.

Lord Devlin also dissented.

Lord Morris: . . . The fact of unconsciousness is therefore relevant in respect of and will eliminate those heads or elements of damage which can only exist by being felt or thought or experienced. The fact of unconsciousness does not, however, eliminate the actuality of the deprivations of the ordinary experiences and amenities of life which may be the inevitable result of some physical injury. . . .

Lord Tucker agreed with Lord Morris.

Lord Pearce: . . . The loss of happiness of the individual plaintiffs is not, in my opinion, a practicable or correct guide to reasonable compensation in cases of personal injury. A man of fortitude is not made less happy because he loses a limb. . . .

Quote

> "Of old when folk lay sick and sorely tried
> The doctors gave them physic, and they died.
> But here's a happier age: for now we know
> Both how to make men sick and keep them so."

Hilaire Belloc

Notes:

1. This decision has not been followed in Australia (*Skelton v Collins* (1966) 115 C.L.R. 94 (less)) or New York (*McDougald v Garber* 73 N.Y.2d 246; (1989) 536 N.E.2d 372 (nothing)), but in *Lim v Camden & Islington H.A.* [1979] 2 All E.R. 910 the House of Lords declined to overrule it, leaving that to the legislature. In 1976 the Pearson Commission recommended that "non-pecuniary [sic] damages should no longer be recoverable for permanent unconsciousness"; the Law Commission in 1999 recommended that they should be retained.

By contrast, the Pearson Commission's main proposal about non-economic loss is entirely unacceptable: no damages whatever for the first three months of pain, suffering and loss of amenity. But the first three months are the worst; that is when people pain and suffer most; indeed, there is often no pain at all thereafter—19 out of 20 injured workmen are back at work before the three months are up. Quite so. The saving in pay-outs would be immense. What would be done with the money thus saved? Most of it would go to those whose awards are already very large, but not quite large enough to make up fully for the fancy job they no longer do. Did the Commission not realise that money is the great divider, suffering the great equaliser? Why ignore so much human harm while meeting every money loss? Is getting and spending more important than feeling? Is it because personal injury *costs* or because it *hurts* that it rated a Royal Commission? If the former, why was property damage not included in their brief? Or did the Commission just feel that damages *in* money must be damages *for* money? At any rate the recommendation is nauseating in its implications and miserable in its effect—to free the rapist and the minor thug from all civil responsibility. Principle ousted by slide-rule.

2. Just as in claims for economic loss (*dommage matériel*) one can distinguish an increase in expenditure from a reduction in income, so in claims for human harm (*dommage moral*) one can distinguish extra misery (pain and suffering) and reduced happiness (loss of amenity). This may offer a more helpful analysis than the distinction between the objective and the subjective aspects of harm ("what he has lost and what he must feel about it" in Lord Reid's phrase). It might also help to support the majority view in the principal case.

Questions:

1. Is there a real difference between (a) a life with neither pain nor pleasure, and (b) no life at all, with regard to (i) tort damages, (ii) an annuity, (iii) the withdrawal of treatment on which continued "life" depends? (*Airedale NHS Trust v Bland* [1993] 1 All E.R. 821).

2. Should you get more damages for being unconscious for longer?

General Note:

The facts of *West v Shephard* are not very common, though there are said to be 650 new cases of permanent vegetative state each year, or about 1,500 in total (not that the figures seem consistent!). More normal cases call for some observations:

Economic Loss

A. *Lost income*

(1) *For how long?* Although one victim's normal earning life may not be shortened, another may die early as a result of his injuries. Can such a victim claim only what he would have earned during the years now left to him, or can he also claim what he would have earned, and not spent on himself, during the years of which he has been deprived? The House of Lords opted for the latter solution in *Pickett v British Rail Engineering* [1980] A.C. 136, which leads to tiresome discussions about how much the claimant would have spent on himself/actual dependants/possible dependants, etc. This claim no longer transmits to the victim's estate.

(2) *How much?*

(i) Income is taxed and damages are not. So the defendant makes good only the plaintiff's "take-home" pay. As to tax this was decided in *Gourley's* case [1956] A.C. 185 and as to contractual pension contributions by *Dews v NCB* [1987] 2 All E.R. 545, HL.

(ii) People's income often rises as they grow older because of (a) inflation and (b) promotion and seniority. The courts generally ignore (a) (*Auty v NCB* [1985] 1 All E.R. 930, CA), and take account of (b).

(iii) Future gains are birds in the bush, while present damages are birds in the hand. Folk-wisdom operates. Courts award a plaintiff less than he would probably have earned, because he might not have earned it.

(iv) The plaintiff is receiving money now in place of income and expenditure in the future. A discount is therefore applied. On the other hand, he is receiving money now that he was entitled to receive when he was injured, or, in deference to Englishry, at the moment he formally demanded it. He must therefore obtain interest, a matter which has given rise to not very interesting discussion.

(3) *Earnings, ability to earn, or ability to work?* If the victim continues to receive wages during his incapacity to work (and he has a statutory right now to a maximum of £59.95 *per* week for 28 weeks, paid by the employer) he suffers no "loss of earnings" with which to charge the tortfeasor. But what of a person who may well keep his job but whose disablement would make it difficult for him to find another job should the need arise? Here the courts may award damages for "loss of earning capacity". These are called "*Smith v Manchester*" damages, after the case at (1974) 17 K.I.R. 1,

confirmed in *Moeliker v Reyrolle* [1977] 1 All E.R. 9, CA. Such damages may be substantial (£35,000 in *Foster v Tyne & Wear C.C.* [1986] 1 All E.R. 567) and should always be considered (*Robson v Liverpool C.C.* [1993] P.I.Q.R. Q78).

Some people, of course, work without being paid. The housewife is the classic example. Until recently the housewife had no claim for her inability to do the housework. The husband, on the other hand, was able to claim something for the loss of her assistance in the home. The husband's action is abolished by the Administration of Justice Act 1982, s.2. Section 9 of the same enactment makes the tortfeasor liable for the victim's inability to perform gratuitous family services, but applies to Scotland only. English courts have applied the rule regardless: *Lowe v Guise* [2002] EWCA Civ 197, [2002] Q.B. 1369.

B. Increased outgoings

(1) *Medical expenses.* Although treatment under the National Health Service is free, patients who go to a private specialist can send the bill to the defendant (Law Reform (Personal Injuries) Act of 1948, s.2(4)). For the Criminal Injuries Compensation Authority, however, not only must the bill be reasonable but it must have been reasonable to incur it: Scheme, para.35(c).

(2) *Nursing.* The plaintiff may need attention after leaving hospital. Having a nurse to live in costs a lot. Having a member of the family do the nursing costs the patient nothing (though it may cost the family something if the carer gives up a job to do the nursing). The rule in England is that the victim may claim the reasonable value of services provided gratuitously by a relative or friend, but not if the person rendering the services was himself the tortfeasor (*Hunt v Severs* [1994] 2 All E.R. 385; where the House of Lords on the last-mentioned ground reduced the award by £81,429, (which indicates the value of such services). The Law Commission proposes that *Hunt v Severs* be reversed, but one may wonder whether a person who was at fault in causing a need should really get paid for meeting it. The care must be for the victim personally: a businessman cannot claim for the gratuitous services rendered by his wife to his business during his indisposition (*Hardwick v Hudson* [1999] 3 All E.R. 426).

PARRY v CLEAVER

House of Lords [1970] A.C. 1; [1969] 2 W.L.R. 821; [1969] 1 All E.R. 555; [1969] 1 Lloyd's Rep. 183 (noted (1967) 83 L.Q.R. 494)

Deductibility of disablement pension from award for lost earnings

The plaintiff policeman was on point duty when the defendant motorist carelessly ran into him. He consequently had to leave the police force at age 36, with an invalid pension for life. He took a civilian job, but not only were the civilian wages less than his police wages but the civilian retirement pension was smaller than his police pension would have been, and payable from age 65, not age 48.

The question was whether the invalid pension he was receiving was to be set off against his loss as regards wages as well as against his loss as regards retirement pension. The trial judge held not, but the Court of Appeal reversed ([1968] 1 Q.B. 195). The House of Lords, by a majority, held that the invalid pension should be set off against the eventual pension loss but not against the current loss of wages.

Lord Pearce: My Lords, the appellant was discharged from the police force as a result of his injuries. He took civilian employment at a lower wage. There is no dispute that the respondent must recompense him for the difference between the wages he would have earned and the wages which he did in fact earn for the period until he would in any event have retired from the police force. But from that time onwards he will no longer be losing any wages as a result of the accident since he would, in any event, have ceased to earn them. But owing to his having had to leave the force early his pension will be lower than it would have been if he had continued in the force until his proper retiring age of 48. There is no dispute that he is entitled to recompense from the age of 48 for the difference between the pension which he would have got but for the accident and the pension which he will in fact receive. That is a simple comparison of pensions. Since he is claiming for that period in respect of diminution of pension it is obvious that he must give credit for the smaller pension which he will get against the larger pension which he would have got.

The problem here is whether, during the period when he is under the age of 48 and is still claiming a loss of wages, he must give credit for the premature pension which he receives from his employers during what should have been, but for the accident, his working time on full pay in the force. The fact that he must give credit after the age of 48 for his actual pension during the period when he is claiming, as a pensioner in any event, in respect only of a diminution of pension, does not shed light on the problem.

The cases on this subject show a conflict of view, each side of which has been attractively presented to us. One may summarise the two points of view in this way. On behalf of the appellant it is said that an insurance, or a pension, are the product of a man's service or a man's thrift. Their character, like that of charitable gifts, is such that it was never intended, nor is it just, that a tortfeasor should take over the benefit of them by getting a credit for them in the account of damages that he must pay. And it is they rather than the accident which are the true source of the benefit. For the respondent it is said that damages are not to be punitive; that *Gourley's* case ([1956] A.C. 185) had laid down that only a plaintiff's actual loss to his pocket can be recovered; that since the accident caused the pension as well as the losses, both must be taken into account; and that for good or ill, the smooth with the rough, a defendant takes a plaintiff as he finds him; so that if he knocks down a pensionable plaintiff he gets the benefit of the pension.

The word "punitive" gives no help. It is simply a word used when a court thinks it unfair that a defendant should be saddled with liability for a particular item. There is nothing punitive in calling on a defendant to pay that which the law says is a just recompense for the injury the plaintiff has caused. Nor does causation, I think, really provide an answer. The pension could not have arisen had not the man by the terms of his employment earned it or by his own thrift provided for it outside his employment. That is the real source of the pension. On the other hand, the potential pension thus provided would not have come into play had not the accident occurred. Each is certainly a *causa sine qua non* and probably each is entitled to be called a *causa causans*. Strict causation seems to provide no satisfactory line of demarcation.

Again, *Gourley's* case does not, nor was it intended to, throw light on this problem. By a convention (rather than any clear principle) which the weight and idiosyncrasies of modern taxation had made obsolete, tax was disregarded in assessment of damages. *Gourley's* case corrected this and laid down that in a plaintiff's claim for damages it was his actual net loss of wages, not his theoretical gross loss which must be regarded. The real loss must be measured. But that case was not directed to considering how far adventitious payments received by a plaintiff must be introduced into the credit side of his account. In dealing with the point before them in *Gourley's* case their Lordships relied on the dominant rule that there should be *restitutio in integrum*. A man should be put financially in the position in which he would have been but for the accident. But if they were intending to say that that general rule applied strictly to all benefits from every source received by a plaintiff, then the plaintiff must clearly bring into account all benefits from public subscription or kindness of relatives or private insurance. Clearly they had no such intention. . . .

The maxim that a defendant must take a plaintiff as he finds him does not solve this problem. True, if he knocks down a high wage earner he must take the consequences; and if he knocks down a low wage earner or a man of character who will go on earning wages in spite of disabilities, a defendant gains thereby. But, if pressed to its logical conclusion, that maximum would entitle the defendant to say that he takes the plaintiff as he finds him in respect of generous relatives who will subsidise him in misfortune and thrifty private insurances which have cancelled out the losses caused by the defendant. One may cut down the maxim by saying that a defendant takes a plaintiff as he finds him in respect of all potential benefits from the [plaintiff's] employment. There is no inherent logic in this. It may provide a convenient line to draw if, but only if, the line is one which there is reason to draw at that particular point. And on which side of that line does one put gifts of a generous employer?

One must, I think, start with the firm basis that *Bradburn v Great Western Railway Co* ((1874) L.R. 10 Ex. 1) was rightly decided and that the benefits from a private insurance by the plaintiff are not to be taken into account. . . .

No help can be derived from various cases where courts have drawn a distinction between pensions where there was a discretion to withhold the pension and pensions where there was no such discretion. If pensions in general are to be taken into account, then such a discretion does not take them out of the account. It merely calls for some large or small or negligible discount in the value to be attached to the pension, according to whether the withholding of it is a real practical danger or (as in most cases) a mere theoretical danger.

Nor do I think that a dividing line can be drawn between contributory and non-contributory pensions. It would be unreal. The present case is an example of the unreality. There was no pension fund and the employers did not pay their contribution. The whole arrangement was merely a part of the wage structure, and no doubt for bargaining about wages it was useful to allocate notional contributions to employers and employed. What the employer pays actually or notionally to a pensions fund is part of the total cost which he is prepared to pay in respect of the employee's service. . . .

Throughout the whole subject . . . run equitable considerations. It seems to me possible that on those grounds there might be some difference of approach where it is the employer himself who is the defendant tortfeasor, and the pension rights in question come from an insurance arrangement which he himself has made with the plaintiff as his employee.

If one starts on the basis that *Bradburn*'s case ((1874) L.R. 10 Ex. 1), decided on fairness and justice and public policy, is correct in principle, one must see whether there is some reason to except from it pensions which are derived from a man's contract with his employer. These, whether contributory or non-contributory, flow from the work which a man has done. They are part of what the employer is prepared to pay for his services. The fact that they flow from past work equates them to rights which flow from an insurance privately effected by him. He has simply paid for them by weekly work instead of weekly premiums.

Is there anything else in the nature of these pension rights derived from work which puts them into a different class from pension rights derived from private insurance? Their "character" is the same, that is to say, they are intended by payer and payee to benefit the workman and not to be a subvention for wrongdoers who will cause him damage.

. . .

In my opinion, the character of the pension rights in this case brings them within the general principle of *Bradburn*'s case ((1874) L.R. 10 Ex. 1), and there is no adequate equitable reason to exclude them from it.

Parliament in 1959 has by implication expressed a similar view on the fairness and justice of the matter and the question of public policy inherent in it. The cases under Lord Campbell's Act had taken a different turn and, unlike the cases under the common law, had brought pensions into account in assessing damages. The Fatal Accidents Act 1959 directed that pensions should *not* be taken into account. It may have done this, regardless of what should be the fair and just principle, simply in order to bring cases under that Act into line with common law cases. If so, it would be unfortunate that the common law cases should now change direction and get out of line once more. It is, however, far more likely that Parliament excluded the taking into account of pensions because it thought that the principle of exclusion laid down in common law cases was fairer and more in accordance with public policy and that, therefore, cases under Lord Campbell's Act should be brought into line with it. If this be so, it is some confirmation of the view which I have expressed.

I would, therefore, allow the appeal. . . .

Lord Pearson (dissenting): . . . As to causation, was the pension in the present case too remote in the sense that it was caused by something remote from and wholly collateral to the accident and its direct and natural train of consequences? The accident disabled the plaintiff, and it caused his compulsory retirement, and as the employment was pensionable—had pension rights attached to it—his retirement was not a retirement with nothing to live on but a retirement on pension. By reason of the accident his salary ceased and his pension began. The pension was intended to take the place *pro tanto* of his salary. I do not see how you can reasonably separate the cessation of the employment from the commencement of the pension. Both salary and pension were payable under the same contract, both were derived from the same employment, the one being current remuneration for present services and the other being deferred remuneration for past services, but each being part of the reward for his services under that contract in that employment. The plaintiff claims that the cessation of salary was caused by the accident, and it must follow, in my opinion, that the commencement of the pension was equally caused by the accident, because the two events coincided in time and were linked together. In the circumstances it is grievously artificial to contend that the loss of salary is admissible and to be taken into account but the receipt of the pension is to be excluded and disregarded. Moreover, it is conceded that the salary earned in the new clerical employment under a different employer is to be taken into account and deducted from the lost salary in ascertaining the net loss. That clerical employment is a new employment coming into existence under a new contract made some time after the old salary had ceased. If that new salary is not too remote, how can the pension under the old contract be too remote? . . .

Lord Wilberforce and **Lord Reid** made up the majority; **Lord Morris** joined **Lord Pearson** in dissent.

Notes:

1. This marginal decision, which made P.C. Parry better off by £3.92 per week, is very regrettable. It gives a special bonus to people whose terms of employment provide for an invalidity or disablement pension, *i.e.* those, such as policemen and firemen, whose job exposes them to particular risk. Sometimes that risk results from carelessness on someone's part. When such carelessness occurs, it is idiotic to give the victim more than enough. He may not have accepted the risk, but he has been paid for it already. This consideration entirely justifies the "firemen's rule," whereby a fireman injured in a fire cannot claim damages from the person who negligently started it. The rule, adopted by the two most liberal jurisdictions in the United States, was rejected by our House of Lords in *Ogwo v Taylor* [1987] 3 All E.R. 961. The combination of *Parry* and *Ogwo* is quite unacceptable. Hopes were raised in 1988 when the House of Lords deducted from lost wages the payments received under a long term sickness benefits scheme arranged by the employer with an insurance company (*Hussain v New Taplow Paper Mills* [1988] 1 All E.R. 541), but they were dashed three years later when, despite an invitation to overrule it, the House decided to affirm *Parry v Cleaver.*

Indeed, in *Smoker v London Fire Authority* [1991] 2 All E.R. 449 the defendant employer had made the major contributions towards the disability pension, but it was still made to pay full lost wages, so fireman Smoker kept nearly £10,000 pension in addition to £13,325 for two years lost wages; as said by Lord MacDermott, quoted by Lord Lowry in *Smoker,* "It is easy to stigmatise such a result as unjust, unreasonable or contrary to public policy. But . . . it is the legal result that follows from *Parry v Cleaver* . . . " The courts are here creating an unjust enrichment of the plaintiff at the defendant's expense. Again, in *Longden v British Coal Corp.* [1998] 1 All E.R. 289 at 301 Lord Hope said: "The effect of *Parry v Cleaver* . . . is that incapacity and disability pensions fall outside the general rule that prima facie all receipts due to the accident must be set against losses claimed to have arisen because of the accident." Thus a person wholly disabled will obtain, until the retirement date, full lost wages plus full disability pension. Yet some people continue to be surprised that a very large number of policemen retire early on grounds of stress provoked by work, and then proceed—with the proceeds—to a normal active life.

2. It is not irrelevant to note that *The Times* of October 22, 1990 reported that the firemen's union had succeeded in procuring the disbandment of a Special Projects Group within the London Fire Authority which in its short existence had investigated 432 claims made by firemen, found only one of them fully justified, and saved the public some £2.2 million falsely claimed. Even so, the union boasted that it had won £5,271,473 for its members that year, £1 million more than the year before. It is hardly surprising that false claims are made when the House of Lords awards more than true claims merit.

3. Of course there are some unexceptionable claims. When Mr Champion slipped on an egg dropped in the canteen by a colleague (the only witness) who admitted negligence and the Fire Authority, in settling with him, omitted to include any sum for the loss of the joy he had had in working as a fireman, Mr Champion returned to court and obtained a supplement under this head: *Champion v London Fire Authority* [1990] Times L.R. 513.

4. *Social Security Benefits.* The mere fact of disablement entitles a person to social security benefits, and disablement resulting from a tort entitles him to damages as well. Some accommodation needs to be made between these sums because though he is entitled to both, it would be wrong if he could keep both. The state normally pays up first, simply because the fact of injury is ascertained more quickly than its cause, but as soon as the tortfeasor's liability has been admitted or imposed, the state can recoup from him what it paid to the victim during the five years since the injury. The "compensator" must first send the state the sums it certifies as disbursed, and then remit the balance, if any, to the victim.

The victim is entitled to receive all the damages agreed or awarded for pain and suffering and loss of amenity, since recoupment applies only to damages for lost earnings, cost of care and loss of mobility; from these, however, the totality of the specified social security benefits must be deducted, so the victim may be left with nothing under these heads. Even so, the tortfeasor must remit to the Compensation Recovery Unity the whole amount certified even if this exceeds the sums otherwise payable to the victim, which is quite likely if the victim is contributorily negligent to a considerable degree. For some of the problems, see *Williams v Devon C.C.* [2003] EWCA Civ 365. The Scheme does not apply to damages payable under the Fatal Accidents Act, compensation orders or sums paid by the Criminal Injuries Compensation Authority, but the Minister has not exercised his power to exempt small sums, which used not to be included.

5. *Medical Treatment.* The rules above relate to monetary benefits. The state also provides benefits in kind, in particular the medical services commonly needed by personal injury victims. Until recently tortfeasors did not have to pay for the victim's medical treatment if he used the National Health Service: the victim had no claim since he had not paid for the treatment, and the NHS had no claim since it was simply out of pocket. Hospitals which treated victims of traffic accidents could claim smallish sums from the motorist under the Road Traffic Act 1988, ss.157 and 158, regardless of whether the motorist was at fault or not, and these sums could add up—£16.64 million in 1997–98—but now the Road Traffic (NHS Charges) Act 1999 has instituted a regime analogous to that for social security payments. It applies only to treatment provided to those injured as a result of the use of a motor vehicle on a highway in respect of whom damages are payable. The charges to be met by the tortfeasor's insurer (or the MIB) were originally fixed at £354 *per* outpatient and £435 *per* day *per* in-patient, subject to a maximum of £10,000. This is expected to raise the premiums payable by motorists by between £6 and £9 *per* year.

These schemes which make money for the state make work for everyone—courts, victims, tortfeasors and civil servants—but in one respect they are more efficient than the continental schemes. In Britain the provider of the benefit has no need to sue the tortfeasor: it simply waits until the victim has done so. Continental systems use the device of subrogation, enabling the benefit provider to use the victim's claim *pro tanto*; this means, of course, that if the victim's claim is reduced by his contributory negligence, so also is that of the benefit provider.

Question
    A victim, permanently unemployed, loses his unemployment benefit on being injured, and receives in lieu a virtually equivalent injury benefit. However, the latter is recoupable, *i.e.* is deducted from his damages, whereas the former is not, so he ends up worse off, though there is no drop in actual income.
    Can the victim hold the tortfeasor liable for this loss? If so, on what basis? See *Hassall v Secretary of State* [1995] 3 All E.R. 909 and *Neal v Bingle* [1998] 2 All E.R. 58.

Section 3.—Fatal Accidents

Notes:
    1. Claims in cases of fatal accidents are statutory. Reference should be made to the text of the Fatal Accidents Act 1976, above p.113, where some of the comments are relevant to the question of the damages recoverable. The computation of damages under the Act differs from that in personal injury cases in two critical respects. First, as to the compensable harm. Whereas in personal injury cases human harm is readily compensated, the courts held that only pecuniary harm was compensable under the Act, thereby differing from the view of Mr Grewgious in *Edwin Drood* that "Death is *not* a matter of pounds, shillings and pence". In 1982, however, the legislature introduced a claim for bereavement (s.1A), a fixed sum of £7,500, reducible only if the claimant or the deceased, who must be the claimant's spouse or unmarried minor child, was contributorily negligent. In the result, the unmarried cohabitee of two years standing may claim for pecuniary loss, modified in view of the precarious nature of the relationship (s.3(4)), but has no claim for grief at the loss of her partner.
    Secondly, as to set-offs. Whereas the courts used to set off against the gross pecuniary loss any benefits accruing to the claimants from the death—including the widow's chance of remarrying an equally generous provider!—the legislature has progressively provided that benefits are not to be taken into account, culminating in s.4 of the Act which requires them all to be ignored.
    2. The two points come together when a child is orphaned. "Although damages cannot be recovered for the loss of their mother's love, they can be recovered for the loss of those services capable of being valued

in terms of money which she would have rendered to them as their mother had she survived" (per Buckley L.J. in *Hay v Hughes* [1975] 1 All E.R. 257 at 268). If those services are replaced gratuitously by a grandmother, stepmother or the father himself, the question arises whether there is no loss to the child or whether there is a loss, made good by a benefit accruing as a result of the death, which must be disregarded under s.4.

The cases are difficult to reconcile because the facts can vary so much, but in *ATH v MS* [2002] EWCA Civ 792 Kennedy L.J. felt able to say: " . . . in the light of the authorities, the position is reasonably clear. Where, as here, infant children are living with and are dependent on one parent, with no support being provided by the other parent, in circumstances where the provision of such support in the future seems unlikely, and the parent with whom they are living is killed, in circumstances giving rise to liability under the Fatal Accidents Act, after which the other parent (who is not the tortfeasor) houses and takes responsibility for the children, the support which they enjoy after the accident is a benefit which has accrued as a result of the death and, pursuant to s.4 of the 1976 Act, it must be disregarded, both in the assessment of loss and in the calculation of damages."

This seems unproblematical. In the case, however, the deceased mother's administrators, who brought the claim, hated the father, who was now looking after the children, doubtless because he had been convicted and sentenced for trying to kill her. The fact that they would certainly not let the father have any of the proceeds of the claim (and the father of course had no claim of his own as carer, and no claim under the Act, not even for bereavement, since he had suffered no loss and was already divorced), explains the next paragraph of Kennedy L.J.'s judgment: "However, such damages can only be awarded on the basis that they are used to reimburse the voluntary carer for services already rendered, and are available to pay for such services in the future. In the words used by Lord Bridge in *Hunt v Severs* damages are held on trust and if the terms of the trust seem unlikely to be fulfilled then the court awarding damages must take steps to avoid that outcome."

3. Another problem arises from the interplay of the rule that a claim lies only for a loss due to the death and the statutory provision that benefits accruing from it are to be ignored. Take the case where the deceased did not work for a living but supported his family out of the proceeds of his investments. Those investments pass to the family under his will, and continue to produce proceeds. What is their loss? The puzzle was put in amusing terms by Staughton L.J. in *Wood v Bentall Simplex* (CA, February 27, 1992), for the reference to which I am grateful to Professor Tettenborn: "Can the dependants inherit the goose and still claim that they have been deprived of eggs?" Until s.4 of the Act is repealed, the answer seems to be that they may, though in *O'Loughlin v Cape Distribution* [2001] EWCA Civ 178 the widow seemed content that she should receive the monetary value of her late husband's skills in managing his property companies, which devolved on her.

4. Do not be taken in by the draftsman's use of the word "dependants". The purpose of the Act is to make the tortfeasor liable for the loss suffered by specified relatives (called "dependants", whether they are or not) by reason of the death. It is certainly the common case that what is lost is what the deceased would have provided out of his earnings, now brought to an end by the death, but the loss need not take the form of loss of dependency at all. Consider *Davies v Whiteways Cyder* [1974] 3 All E.R. 168, noted above, p.115.

Question

The Duke of Domnium has a large rental income and would very likely have continued to provide his only child, Edmund, with £15,000 pocket money annually. The Duke, an avid but untalented gambler who would certainly have dissipated his capital had he lived for the expected forty years more, is killed on the way to the casino by a hit-and-run driver, and Edmund inherits the capital unimpaired. How much has Edmund lost by the death? How much will he get from the Motor Insurers Bureau?

Section 4.—Property Damage

OWNERS OF THE STEAMSHIP *MEDIANA* v OWNERS OF LIGHTSHIP *COMET* (THE "MEDIANA")

House of Lords [1900] A.C. 113; 69 L.J.P. 35; 82 L.T. 95; 16 T.L.R. 194; 48 W.R. 398; 9 Asp.M.L.C. 41

The Mersey Docks and Harbour Board were under a statutory duty to light four stations on the approaches to the River Mersey. For this purpose they had six lightships, one of which was kept to replace any lightship withdrawn for overhaul and one of which, the *Orion*, was kept for emergencies, at a cost of £1,000 *per* year, including interest on the capital invested in her.

The *Mediana* collided with the *Comet* and sank her. The Board towed the *Orion* out to take her place, which she occupied for 74 days, a period during which there was no other call for the *Orion's* services. The Board claimed, *inter alia*, "Loss of use of the lightship *Comet*, or hire of the services of the lightship *Orion*—74 days at £4 4s.—£310 6s."

The registrar allowed this item. Phillimore J. disallowed it. The Court of Appeal allowed it [1899] p.127, and the owners of the *Mediana* appealed without success to the House of Lords.

Earl of Halsbury L.C.: . . . Now, in the particular case before us, apart from a circumstance which I will refer to immediately, the broad proposition seems to me to be that by a wrongful act of the defendants the plaintiffs were deprived of their vessel. When I say deprived of their vessel, I will not use the phrase "the use of the vessel." What right has a wrongdoer to consider what use you are going to make of your vessel? More than one case has been put to illustrate this: for example, the owner of a horse, or of a chair. Supposing a person took away a chair out of my room and kept it for 12 months, could anybody say you had a right to diminish the damages by showing that I did not usually sit in that chair, or that there were plenty of other chairs in the room? The proposition so nakedly stated appears to me to be absurd; but a jury have very often a very difficult task to perform in ascertaining what should be the amount of damages of that sort. I know very well that as a matter of common sense what an arbitrator or a jury very often do is to take a perfectly artificial hypothesis and say, "Well, if you wanted to hire a chair, what would you have to give for it for the period"; and in that way they come to a rough sort of conclusion as to what damages ought to be paid for the unjust and unlawful withdrawal of it from the owner. Here, as I say, the broad principle seems to me to be quite independent of the particular use the plaintiffs were going to make of the thing that was taken, except—and this I think has been the fallacy running through the arguments at the Bar—when you are endeavouring to establish the specific loss of profit, or of something that you otherwise would have got which the law recognises as special damage. In that case you must show it, and by precise evidence, so much so that in the old system of pleading you could not recover damages unless you had made a specific allegation in your pleading so as to give the persons responsible for making good the loss an opportunity of inquiring into it before they came into court. But when we are speaking of general damages no such principle applies at all, and the jury might give whatever they thought would be the proper equivalent for the unlawful withdrawal of the subject-matter then in question. It seems to me that that broad principle comprehends within it many other things. There is no doubt in many cases a jury would say there really has been no damage at all: "We will give the plaintiffs a trifling amount"—not nominal damages, be it observed, but a trifling amount; in other cases it would be more serious.

It appears to me, therefore, that what the noble and learned Lords [in *The Greta Holme* [1897] A.C. 596] . . . intended to point out, and what Lord Herschell gives expression to in plain terms, was that the unlawful keeping back of what belongs to another person is of itself a ground for real damages, not nominal damages at all. Of course, I observe that it has been suggested that this was not an action for trover or detinue; but although those are different forms of action, the principle upon which damages are to be assessed does not depend upon the form of action at all. I put aside cases of trespass where a high-handed procedure or insolent behaviour has been held in law to be a subject of aggravated damages, and the jury might give what are called punitive damages. Leaving that aside, whatever be the form of action, the principle of assessing damages must be the same in all courts and for all forms of what I may call the unlawful detention of another man's property.

My Lords, that seems to me to be so plain that I confess I have been somewhat puzzled to learn that it has been decided in the Admiralty Courts that the loss of the use of a vessel under circumstances of this case had been treated (if it has really been so treated I have serio͟ about it) as something for which no moneys counted could possibly be allowed. I ͞ that I am very glad such a principle has not been affirmed by your Lordships' ͞ it seems to me to be inconsistent with principle and very unreasonable in ͞

Note:

In view of the very clear terms of this decision of the House of Lords, it is with some surprise that one finds a decision of the Court of Appeal thus represented in the headnote: " . . . since the plaintiffs had not proved that they would have used the copper during the period of detention . . . they were entitled only to nominal damages . . . " *Brandeis Goldschmidt v Western Transport* [1981] Q.B. 864. Intriguing though it is that the plaintiffs recovered only £5 from defendants who wrongly detained 42 tons of their copper for over seven months, during which period its market value fell by £3,588, the decision seems to have turned on the view that if you try to prove you have lost a specific sum and fail to prove it, you can recover nothing; it is a warning for barristers rather than a lesson for students.

In the next case, by contrast, the claimants did claim a specific sum rather than the general damages to which *The Mediana* entitled them.

LAGDEN v O'CONNOR

House of Lords [2003] UKHL 64, [2003] 3 W.L.R. 1571, [2004] 1 All E.R. 277

If your car is negligently damaged, how much can you claim for a temporary substitute?

Lord Nicholls of Birkenhead: My Lords, this appeal is a sequel to the decision of the House in *Dimond v Lovell* [2002] 1 A.C. 384. It represents a further step in clarifying the obligations of motor insurers regarding the cost of hire of a replacement car while a damaged car is undergoing repair. It is part of the long continuing contest between motor insurers and credit hire companies. The issue raised is narrow, and the amount of money involved in this case is modest. But the issue is important because it raises a principle of general application affecting many people.

When one person's car is damaged by negligent driving on the part of another motorist and the damaged car is economically repairable, the owner of the damaged car loses the use of his vehicle while it is being repaired. In the ordinary course the damages payable by the negligent driver include, in addition to the cost of repairs, damages for loss of use of the damaged car. In the ordinary course the reasonable cost of providing the innocent motorist with a suitable replacement vehicle while his own car is off the road crystallises the amount of loss suffered by him under this head of loss. In practice it is a convenient yardstick by which to measure the damages payable to the innocent driver for temporary loss of use of his own car.

In cases of this type accident hire companies, or credit hire companies, as they are variously known, provide a service additional to hiring out replacement cars. Unlike the arrangements normally made by car hire companies, credit hire companies do not require the motorist to produce an acceptable debit or credit card in advance ("up front"). Nor, in practice, is the hirer required to pay the hire charges in any other way. Instead, when a motorist seeks a replacement car for the period while his own car is off the road, the company checks whether the motorist seems to have an unanswerable claim against the other driver. Having satisfied itself on this score, the company provides the car sought and then seeks to recover its charges from the negligent driver's insurers. For these services, which go beyond simple car hire, credit hire companies charge an additional fee.

In *Dimond v Lovell* [2002] 1 A.C. 384 the majority of the House expressed the view that a car owner cannot recover this additional fee element from the negligent motorist or his insurers. The damages recoverable for loss of use are limited to the 'spot rate' quoted by hirers other than accident hire companies. In the case of a hiring from an accident hire company the equivalent spot rate will ordinarily be the net loss after allowance has been made for the additional benefits the accident hire company has provided: see Lord Browne-Wilkinson [2002] 1 A.C. 384, 390, Lord Hoffmann, at p.403, and Lord Hobhouse of Woodborough, at p.407.

Dimond v Lovell Mrs Dimond could have found the money needed to hire a replacement ~he was reimbursed by Mr Lovell or his insurers. The case proceeded on this basis. ~ enough, she preferred to take advantage of the services of an accident hire firm.

But what if the innocent motorist, like many people, is unable to afford the cost of hiring a replacement car from a car hire company? Unlike Mrs Dimond, he cannot find the necessary money. So, unless he can use the services of a credit hire company, he will be unable to obtain a replacement car. While his car is being repaired he will have to make do as best he can without a car of his own. If this happens, he will be without his own car and in practice will receive little or no recompense for the inconvenience involved.

My Lords, the law would be seriously defective if in this type of case the innocent motorist were, in practice, unable to obtain the use of a replacement car. Here, as elsewhere, a negligent driver must take his victim as he finds him. Common fairness requires that if an innocent plaintiff cannot afford to pay car hire charges, so that left to himself he would be unable to obtain a replacement car to meet the need created by the negligent driver, then the damages payable under this head of loss should include the reasonable costs of a credit hire company. Credit hire companies provide a reasonable means whereby innocent motorists may obtain use of a replacement vehicle when otherwise they would be unable to do so. Unless the recoverable damages in such a case include the reasonable costs of a credit hire company the negligent driver's insurers will be able to shuffle away from their insured's responsibility to pay the cost of providing a replacement car. A financially well-placed plaintiff will be able to hire a replacement car, and in the fullness of time obtain reimbursement from the negligent driver's insurers, but an impecunious plaintiff will not. This cannot be an acceptable result.

There remains the difficult point of what is meant by "impecunious" in the context of the present type of case. Lack of financial means is, almost always, a question of priorities. In the present context what it signifies is inability to pay car hire charges without making sacrifices the plaintiff could not reasonably be expected to make. I am fully conscious of the open-ended nature of this test. But fears that this will lead to increased litigation in small claims courts seem to me exaggerated. It is in the interests of all concerned to avoid litigation with its attendant costs and delay. Motor insurers and credit hire companies should be able to agree on standard enquiries, or some other means, which in practice can most readily give effect to this test of impecuniosity. I would dismiss this appeal.

Lord Slynn and **Lord Hope of Craighead** agreed with **Lord Nicholls; Lord Scott of Foscote** and **Lord Walker of Gestingthorpe** dissented.

Questions:
  1. What if Lagden's car had been totalled, irreparable?
  2. What if Lagden had been a company, like the claimant in *The Edison* (immediately below)?

Notes:
   1. The dissentients were uneasy at the test of "impecuniosity" or "no other choice", as likely to promote litigation rather than reduce it, as *Dimond v Lovell* had sought to do by laying down that in all cases the recoverable amount was the market rate rather than, as the Court of Appeal had held, what was foreseeable.
   2. Even the dissentients, however, were ready to depart from a famous House of Lords decision, *The Edison* [1933] A.C. 449, where the defendants negligently sank the plaintiffs' dredger, then engaged on work in Patras Harbour under a contract which provided for heavy penalties for delay. Scrutton L.J. described the litigation as follows (1934) L.T. 279, 281: "The plaintiffs, who had bought the dredger for £4,000 and had taken her out to Patras for another £2,000, making £6,000 in all, and insured her for £5,500, discovered that by her loss they had lost some £23,500, which they proceeded to claim. The claim was made up on the basis: We are very poor, consequently we cannot do what a rich man would have done, and so we have had to make a series of elaborate and expensive arrangements of finance in order to carry out our harbour contract. Langton J. gave judgment, confirming a reference on those lines for a sum of £19,000–odd, and I can quite understand the defendants' anger, as it was rather provocative to claim for an old dredger more than twice its value on the plaintiffs' own computation. The matter then came to the Court of Appeal, which took the line that it is well established that the damages one can recover for the total loss of a ship are: her value to

the owner at the time of the loss, taking into account her engagements, plus interest from the time of the loss; and we assessed the value at £9,000, being of opinion that that more than amply paid the plaintiffs for what they had lost. On appeal, the House of Lords laid down the same principle on which we thought we were acting, . . . but sent the matter to assess the damages on the principles they had laid down. The registrar gave £11,000–odd; so that the plaintiffs got £2,000 more on the judgment of the House of Lords."

3. *The Edison* was mentioned, along with along with many other famous cases, in *The Sivand* [1998] 2 Lloyd's Rep. 97. The defendant's tanker carelessly collided with the plaintiff's harbour installation, destroying three mooring dolphins and seriously damaging a berthing dolphin. The repairs proved unexpectedly expensive, for though the repair firm selected by the plaintiffs was reputable and perfectly careful and the contract effected with it was quite normal in the business, the bill submitted by the repair firm to the plaintiffs was enormous because of a totally unexpected event, the risk of which was put on the plaintiffs by the contract: the sea-bed and subsoil on which the legs of the jack-up barge employed by the repair firm proved unforeseeably unstable, despite all proper tests, and the barge capsized and was lost. The defendant tanker-operators were held liable. This was not a case where the plaintiffs had suffered further property damage because of some intervening event: it was a case, according to Hobhouse L.J., where the plaintiffs took reasonable steps to mitigate the damage by making a sensible contract for repair, and the defendants must pay what it cost them. It was suggested that it might have been otherwise if the repair firm had gone bankrupt and a substitute firm had to be employed at exorbitant expense: *sed quaere.*

4. *The Edison* does, however, illustrate the problem which arises when there is a great discrepancy between the value of property and the loss caused by its destruction: the dredger was "worth" £6,000 or so, yet the plaintiffs claimed that its destruction had cost them £23,500. It seems right as a basic principle that the person whose capital good has been destroyed should receive the cost of a replacement plus an indemnity for incidental outgoings and temporary lost profits, *i.e.* its value as a going concern. Consider also the facts of *Wimpey* (above, p.56) where the damaged crane-barge was the lynch-pin of a huge construction programme in which others than its hirer were very heavily implicated. The subsequent reassertion of the rule that only the owner or possessor of a thing may sue for loss due to its destruction may perhaps confirm *The Edison's* emphasis on the value of the thing rather than the plaintiff's loss. So, too, in cases where there is concurrent liability in tort and contract, the relatively limited quantum of recovery in contract cases may have a moderating effect on the concurrent tort claim.

5. The damages payable for business premises and chattels destroyed by fire were considered in *Dominion Mosaics v Trafalgar Trucking Co* [1990] 2 All E.R. 246. Fire in October 1983 diminished by £60,000 the value of the plaintiff's premises in Stratford, East London, where they had been installed for two years, leaving a site-value of £25,000. Rebuilding would have cost about £570,000, plus lost profits meanwhile, so in March 1984 the plaintiff took a 36-year lease of other, slightly larger premises for £390,000; there was an annual ground rent of £2,500 and rates of £70,000, compared with rates of only £10,000 on the original premises. The new premises needed and received considerable alteration, but business picked up. In 1986 the plaintiff bought the freehold of the new premises for £60,000 and then sold them the following year for £690,000, having found other premises to lease in the Mile End Road at an annual rent of £55,000.

The judge held that the defendants must pay the £390,000 cost of acquiring the lease, since that was a perfectly reasonable thing to do, that the value of the original site was balanced by the ground-rent on the new premises, and that the defendant could not invoke the favourable sale of the new premises after the acquisition of the freehold. The Court of Appeal agreed, noting that the £390,000 would not enrich the plaintiff, since his insurer, which had put up the money, would be subrogated to it.(!)

Among the chattels destroyed were 11 machines for displaying carpets which the plaintiff had got very cheap, for £13,500, shop-soiled after an exhibition at Olympia a few months previously. The plaintiff had not replaced them, as that would cost £65,000. The judge awarded £13,500, but the Court of Appeal raised this to £65,000, the defendant not having given any evidence about their condition, and there being no second-hand market in such machines.

6. Valuation of property is a complex matter with a specialist profession which practises it (and, to judge by the law reports, makes quite a few errors). It involves turning a thing into money, and the translation is unstraightforward. This is partly because things are indivisible and money is not. If your building is destroyed and on the balance of probabilities the destruction is due to my negligence, then I pay its full value (see above). But suppose by my actionable fault I cause you to lose a sale of your building (that is, I do not destroy a thing but cause you money loss), and that it is more probable than not (but of course not absolutely certain) that but for my fault the sale would have gone forward. In this case, it appears that your claim will be discounted by the chance that the purchaser might have changed his mind. So held in *Blue Circle* v *Ministry of Defence* [1998] 3 All E.R. 385.

7. Repair/replacement or market value? This was discussed in *The Maersk Colombo* [2001] 2 Lloyd's Rep. 275 where the defendant's vessel negligently collided with and demolished one of the port authority's cranes. Reinstatement would cost over over £2 million, the market value was £665,000. The trial judge's award of the latter sum was upheld by the Court of Appeal, since it would have been quite unreasonable to replace that crane, the claimants being about to take delivery of two others.

But it would be an error to suppose that these alternatives are exhaustive. In *Ruxley Electronics v Forsyth* [1996] 1 A.C. 344 where the value of the claimant's property was unaffected and replacement of the swimming pool would have been totally unreasonable in view of the very slight deviation from the contractual specifications, the claimant was awarded a sum to make up for his failure to get what he had contracted for. Again if, as is often the case, a vehicle is worth less after repair than before, there is no reason why that shortfall may not be made good in addition to the cost of the repairs, as in *Payton v Brooks* [1974] R.T.R. 169.

INDEX

[Only the first of successive page references is given.]